AF504092

30 Millennia of Painting

Authors: Victoria Charles, Klaus H. Carl, Joseph Manca, Megan McShane, Donald Wigal

© 2012 Confidential Concepts, worldwide, USA
© 2012 Parkstone Press International, New York, USA

© 2012 Joseph Albers Estate, Irish Visual Artists Rights Organisation (IVARO), Dublin,
   IR/ VG Bild-Kunst, Bonn
© 2012 Karel Appel Foundation, Irish Visual Artists Rights Organisation (IVARO), Dublin, IR
© 2012 Hans Arp Estate, Irish Visual Artists Rights Organisation (IVARO), Dublin,
   IR/ VG Bild-Kunst, Bonn
© 2012 Jean-Michel Atlan Estate, Irish Visual Artists Rights Organisation (IVARO), Dublin,
   IR/ ADAGP, Paris
© 2012 Corneliu Baba Estate, Irish Visual Artists Rights Organisation (IVARO), Dublin,
   IR/ Visarta, Bucarest
© 2012 Francis Bacon Estate, Irish Visual Artists Rights Organisation (IVARO), Dublin,
   IR/ DACS, London
© 2012 Giacomo Balla Estate, Irish Visual Artists Rights Organisation (IVARO), Dublin, IR/ SIAE, Rome
© 2012 Baltasar Balthus Estate, Irish Visual Artists Rights Organisation (IVARO), Dublin,
   IR/ ADAGP, Paris
© 2012 Georg Baselitz, Michael Werner Gallery
© 2012 Willi Baumeister Estate, Irish Visual Artists Rights Organisation (IVARO), Dublin,
   IR/ VG Bild-Kunst, Bonn
© 2012 Jean Bazaine Estate, Irish Visual Artists Rights Organisation (IVARO), Dublin, IR/ ADAGP, Paris
© 2012 Max Beckmann Estate, Irish Visual Artists Rights Organisation (IVARO), Dublin,
   IR/ VG Bild-Kunst, Bonn
Art © Thomas Hart Benton / Licensed by VAGA-DACS, New York, NY
© 2012 Roger Bissière Estate, Irish Visual Artists Rights Organisation (IVARO), Dublin,
   IR/ADAGP, Paris
© 2012 Pierre Bonnard Estate, Irish Visual Artists Rights Organisation (IVARO), Dublin, IR/ ADAGP, Paris
© Tate London 2012, David Bomberg
© 2012 Georges Braque Estate, Irish Visual Artists Rights Organisation (IVARO), Dublin,
   IR/ ADAGP, Paris
© 2012 Bernard Buffet Estate, Irish Visual Artists Rights Organisation (IVARO), Dublin, IR/ ADAGP, Paris
© 2012 Alberto Burri, Fondazione Palazzo Albizzini
© 2012 Carlo Carra Estate, Irish Visual Artists Rights Organisation (IVARO), Dublin, IR/ SIAE, Rome
© 2012 Marc Chagall Estate, Irish Visual Artists Rights Organisation (IVARO), Dublin, IR/ ADAGP, Paris
© 2012 Gaston Chaissac Estate, Irish Visual Artists Rights Organisation (IVARO), Dublin,
   IR/ ADAGP, Paris
© 2012 Whitney Museum of American Art, John Stuart Curry
© 2012 Salvador Dalí, Gala-Salvador Dalí Foundation/ Irish Visual Artists Rights Organisation (IVARO),
   Dublin, IR
Art © Stuart Davis Estate / Licensed by VAGA-DACS, New York, NY
© 2012 Georgio de Chirico Estate, Irish Visual Artists Rights Organisation (IVARO), Dublin,
   IR/ SIAE, Rome
© 2012 The Willem de Kooning Foundation, Irish Visual Artists Rights Organisation (IVARO), Dublin, IR
© L &M Services B.V. Amsterdam 20051203
© 2012 Paul Delvaux Estate, Irish Visual Artists Rights Organisation (IVARO), Dublin,
   IR/ SABAM, Brussels
© 2012 Maurice Denis Estate, Irish Visual Artists Rights Organisation (IVARO), Dublin, IR/ ADAGP, Paris
© 2012 Paul Derain Estate, Irish Visual Artists Rights Organisation (IVARO), Dublin, IR/ ADAGP, Paris
© 2012 Otto Dix Estate, Irish Visual Artists Rights Organisation (IVARO), Dublin,
   IR/ VG Bild-Kunst, Bonn
© 2012 Jean Dubuffet Estate, Irish Visual Artists Rights Organisation (IVARO), Dublin, IR/ ADAGP, Paris
© 2012 Irish Visual Artists Rights Organisation (IVARO), Dublin, IR/ ADAGP,
   Paris/Succession Marcel Duchamp
© 2012 Raoul Dufy Estate, Irish Visual Artists Rights Organisation (IVARO), Dublin, IR/ ADAGP, Paris
© 2012 Max Ernst Estate, Irish Visual Artists Rights Organisation (IVARO), Dublin, IR/ ADAGP, Paris
© 2012 Maurice Estève Estate, Irish Visual Artists Rights Organisation (IVARO), Dublin, IR/ ADAGP, Paris
© 2012 James Ensor Estate, Irish Visual Artists Rights Organisation (IVARO), Dublin,
   IR/ SABAM, Brussels
© 2012 Jean Fautrier Estate, Irish Visual Artists Rights Organisation (IVARO), Dublin,
   IR/ ADAGP, Paris
© 2012 Lyonel Feininger Estate, Irish Visual Artists Rights Organisation (IVARO), Dublin,
   IR/ VG Bild-Kunst, Bonn
© 2012 Lucio Fontana Foundation, Milan
© 2012 Samuel L. Francis Foundation, California/ Irish Visual Artists Rights Organisation (IVARO), Dublin, IR
© 2012 Helen Frankenthaler, copyright reserved
© 2012 Lucian Freud
© 2012 Whitney Museum of American Art, Mark Gertler
© 2012 Alberto Giacometti Estate, Irish Visual Artists Rights Organisation (IVARO), Dublin,
   IR/ ADAGP, Paris
© 2012 Albert Gleizes Estate, Irish Visual Artists Rights Organisation (IVARO), Dublin, IR/ ADAGP, Paris
© 2012 Natalia Goncharova Estate, Irish Visual Artists Rights Organisation (IVARO), Dublin,
   IR/ ADAGP, Paris
© 2012 Arshile Gorky Estate, Irish Visual Artists Rights Organisation (IVARO), Dublin, IR
Art © George Grosz/ Licensed by VAGA-DACS, New York, NY
© 2012 Francis Gruber Estate, Irish Visual Artists Rights Organisation (IVARO), Dublin, IR/ ADAGP, Paris
© 2012 Richard Hamilton Estate, Irish Visual Artists Rights Organisation (IVARO), Dublin,
   IR/ DACS, London
© 2012 Marsden Hartley, copyright reserved
© 2012 Hans Hartung Estate, Irish Visual Artists Rights Organisation (IVARO), Dublin,
   IR/ ADAGP, Paris
© 2012 David Hockney
© 2012 Hundertwasser Archives, Vienna
© 2012 Johannes Itten Estate, Irish Visual Artists Rights Organisation (IVARO), Dublin,
   IR/ ProLitteris Zurich
© 2012 Alexei von Jawlensky Estate, Irish Visual Artists Rights Organisation (IVARO), Dublin,
   IR/ VG Bild-Kunst, Bonn
Art © Jasper Johns/ Licensed by VAGA-DACS, New York, NY
© 2012 fam. Jorn/ Irish Visual Artists Rights Organisation (IVARO), Dublin, IR/ COPY-DAN,
   Copenhagen
© 2012 Banco de México Diego Rivera & Frida Kahlo Museums Trust. AV. Cinco de Mayo no 2, Col.
   Centro, Del. Cuauhtémoc 06059, México, D.F.
© 2012 Wasily Kandinsky Estate, Irish Visual Artists Rights Organisation (IVARO), Dublin,
   IR/ ADAGP, Paris
© 2012 Ellsworth Kelly
© 2012 Ernst Kirchner, by Indeborg and Dr Wolfgang Henz-Ketter, Wichtrach/Bern
© 2012 Paul Klee Estate, Irish Visual Artists Rights Organisation (IVARO), Dublin, IR/ VG Bild-Kunst, Bonn
© 2012 Yves Klein Estate, Irish Visual Artists Rights Organisation (IVARO), Dublin, IR/ ADAGP, Paris
© 2012 Franz Kline Estate, Irish Visual Artists Rights Organisation (IVARO), Dublin, IR
© 2012 Oskar Kokoschka Estate, Irish Visual Artists Rights Organisation (IVARO), Dublin,
   IR/ Pro Litteris, Zurich
© 2012 Frantisek Kupka Estate, Irish Visual Artists Rights Organisation (IVARO), Dublin,
   IR/ ADAGP, Paris
© 2012 Wilfredo Lam Estate, Irish Visual Artists Rights Organisation (IVARO), Dublin,
   IR/ ADAGP, Paris
© 2012 Mikhail Larionov Estate, Irish Visual Artists Rights Organisation (IVARO), Dublin,
   IR/ ADAGP, Paris
© 2012 Marie Laurencin Estate, Irish Visual Artists Rights Organisation (IVARO), Dublin,
   IR/ ADAGP, Paris
© 2012 Fernand Léger Estate, Irish Visual Artists Rights Organisation (IVARO), Dublin, IR/ ADAGP, Paris

© 2012 Imperial War Museum, London
© 2012 Tamara de Lempicka Estate, Irish Visual Artists Rights Organisation (IVARO), Dublin,
   IR/ ADAGP, Paris
© 2012 André Lhote Estate, Irish Visual Artists Rights Organisation (IVARO), Dublin,
   IR/ ADAGP, Paris
© 2012 Roy Lichtenstein Estate, Irish Visual Artists Rights Organisation (IVARO), Dublin,
   IR/ ADAGP, Paris
© 2012 Max Liebermann Estate, Irish Visual Artists Rights Organisation (IVARO), Dublin,
   IR/ VG Bild-Kunst, Bonn
© 2012 Morris Louis Estate, Garfinkle & Associates, Washington
© 2012 Alberto Magnelli Estate, Irish Visual Artists Rights Organisation (IVARO), Dublin, IR/ ADAGP, Paris
© 2012 C. Herscovici, Brussels/ Irish Visual Artists Rights Organisation (IVARO), Dublin, IR
© 2012 Alfred Manessier Estate, Irish Visual Artists Rights Organisation (IVARO), Dublin,
   IR/ ADAGP, Paris
© 2012 Albert Marquet Estate, Irish Visual Artists Rights Organisation (IVARO), Dublin,
   IR/ ADAGP, Paris
© 2012 André Masson Estate, Irish Visual Artists Rights Organisation (IVARO), Dublin, IR/ ADAGP, Paris
© 2012 Henri Matisse, Les Héritiers Matisse, Irish Visual Artists Rights Organisation (IVARO), Dublin,
   IR/ADAGP, Paris
© 2012 Sucession H. Matisse, Paris/ Irish Visual Artists Rights Organisation (IVARO), Dublin, IR
© 2012 Henri Michaux Estate, Irish Visual Artists Rights Organisation (IVARO), Dublin,
   IR/ ADAGP, Paris
© 2012 Sucesio Miró, Irish Visual Artists Rights Organisation (IVARO), Dublin, IR/ ADAGP, Paris
© 2012 Giorgio Morandi Estate, Irish Visual Artists Rights Organisation (IVARO), Dublin,
   IR/ SIAE, Rome
Art © Robert Motherwell / Licensed by VAGA-DACS, New York, NY
© 2012 Edvard Munch Estate, Irish Visual Artists Rights Organisation (IVARO), Dublin, IR/ BONO, Oslo
© Tate London 2012, Paul Nash
© 2012 Barnett Newman Estate, Irish Visual Artists Rights Organisation (IVARO), Dublin,
   IR/ ADAGP, Paris
© 2012 Benn Nicholson Estate, Irish Visual Artists Rights Organisation (IVARO), Dublin,
   IR/ DACS, London
© 2012 Emil Nolde Estate, Irish Visual Artists Rights Organisation (IVARO), Dublin,
   IR/ VG Bild-Kunst, Bonn
© 2012 The Georgia O'Keeffe Museum, Irish Visual Artists Rights Organisation (IVARO), Dublin, IR
© Roland Penrose Estate, England 2012. All rights reserved. The Penrose Collection
   www.rolandpenrose.co.uk
© 2012 Francis Picabia Estate, Irish Visual Artists Rights Organisation (IVARO), Dublin,
   IR/ ADAGP, Paris
© 2012 Estate of Pablo Picasso/ Irish Visual Artists Rights Organisation (IVARO), Dublin, IR
© 2012 Serge Poliakoff Estate, Irish Visual Artists Rights Organisation (IVARO), Dublin, IR/ ADAGP, Paris
© 2012 The Pollock-Krasner Foundation/ Irish Visual Artists Rights Organisation (IVARO), Dublin, IR
Art © Robert Rauschenberg/ Licensed by VAGA-DACS, New York, NY
© 2012 Ad Reinhardt Estate, Irish Visual Artists Rights Organisation (IVARO), Dublin, IR
© Bridget Riley, all rights reserved
© 2012 Jean-Paul Riopelle Estate, Irish Visual Artists Rights Organisation (IVARO), Dublin,
   IR/ SODRAC, Montreal
© 2012 Banco de México Diego Rivera & Frida Kahlo Museums Trust. Av. Cinco de Mayo
   no 2, Col. Centro, Del. Cuauhtémoc 06059, México, D.F.
Art © Estate of Larry Rivers / Licensed by VAGA-DACS, New York, NY
© 2012 The Norman Rockwell family Entities
© Norman Rockwell Art Collection Trust, Norman Rockwell Museum, Stockbridge, Massachussets
Art © James Rosenquist/ Licensed by VAGA-DACS, New York, NY
© 2012 Kate Rothko Prizel & Christopher Rothko/ Irish Visual Artists Rights Organisation (IVARO),
   Dublin, IR
© 2012 Georges Rouault Estate, Irish Visual Artists Rights Organisation (IVARO), Dublin,
   IR/ ADAGP, Paris
© 2012 Sucession Antonio Saura/ www.antoniosaura.org/ Irish Visual Artists Rights Organisation
   (IVARO), Dublin, IR/ Vegap, Madrid
© 2012 Oskar Schlemmer Estate, Irish Visual Artists Rights Organisation (IVARO), Dublin, IR/ ADAGP, Paris
© 2012 Karl Schmidt-Rotluff Estate, Irish Visual Artists Rights Organisation (IVARO), Dublin,
   IR/ VG Bild-Kunst, Bonn
© 2012 Kurt Schwitters Estate, Irish Visual Artists Rights Organisation (IVARO), Dublin,
   IR/ VG Bild-Kunst, Bonn
© 2012 Gino Severini Estate, Irish Visual Artists Rights Organisation (IVARO), Dublin, IR/ ADAGP, Paris
© 2012 Walter Sickert Richard Estate, Irish Visual Artists Rights Organisation (IVARO), Dublin,
   IR/ DACS, London
© 2012 Pierre Soulages Estate, Irish Visual Artists Rights Organisation (IVARO), Dublin, IR/ ADAGP, Paris
© 2012 Chaim Soutine Estate, Irish Visual Artists Rights Organisation (IVARO), Dublin, IR/ ADAGP, Paris
© 2012 Stanley Spencer Estate, Irish Visual Artists Rights Organisation (IVARO), Dublin, IR/ DACS, London
© 2012 Nicolas de Staël Estate, Irish Visual Artists Rights Organisation (IVARO), Dublin, IR/ ADAGP, Paris
© 2012 Frank Stella Estate, Irish Visual Artists Rights Organisation (IVARO), Dublin, IR
© 2012 Clyfford Still, copyrights reserved
© Tate London 2012, Graham Sutherland
D.R.© Rufino Tamayo/ Herederos/ México/2012/ Fundacion Olga y Rufino Tamayo, A.C.
© 2012 Yves Tanguy Estate, Irish Visual Artists Rights Organisation (IVARO), Dublin, IR
© 2012 Antoni Tàpies Estate, Irish Visual Artists Rights Organisation (IVARO), Dublin, IR/ VEGAP, Madrid
© 2012 Vladimir Tatlin Estate, Irish Visual Artists Rights Organisation (IVARO), Dublin, IR/ ADAGP, Paris
© 2012 Mark Tobey, copyrights reserved
© 2012 Maurice Utrillo Estate, Irish Visual Artists Rights Organisation (IVARO), Dublin, IR/ ADAGP, Paris
© 2012 Suzanne Valadon Estate, Irish Visual Artists Rights Organisation (IVARO), Dublin,
   IR/ ADAGP, Paris
© 2012 Kees van Dongen Estate, Irish Visual Artists Rights Organisation (IVARO), Dublin,
   IR/ ADAGP, Paris
© 2012 Bram van Velde Estate, Irish Visual Artists Rights Organisation (IVARO), Dublin,
   IR/ ADAGP, Paris
© 2012 Victor Vasarely Estate, Irish Visual Artists Rights Organisation (IVARO), Dublin, IR/ ADAGP, Paris
© 2012 Edouard Vuillard Estate, Irish Visual Artists Rights Organisation (IVARO), Dublin,
   IR/ ADAGP, Paris
© 2012 Maria Helena Vieira da Silva Estate, Irish Visual Artists Rights Organisation (IVARO), Dublin,
   IR/ ADAGP, Paris
© 2012 Jacques Villon Estate, Irish Visual Artists Rights Organisation (IVARO), Dublin, IR/ ADAGP, Paris
© 2012 Maurice de Vlaminck Estate, Irish Visual Artists Rights Organisation (IVARO), Dublin,
   IR/ ADAGP, Paris
© 2012 Andy Warhol Foundation for the Visual Arts/ Irish Visual Artists Rights Organisation (IVARO),
   Dublin, IR
Art © Estate of Tom Wesselmann / Licensed by VAGA-DACS, New York, NY
© 2012 Wolfgang Wols Estate, Irish Visual Artists Rights Organisation (IVARO), Dublin, IR/ ADAGP, Paris
Art © Estate of Grant Wood / Licensed by VAGA-DACS, New York, NY American Gothic, 1930 by Grant Wood
All rights reserved by the Estate of Nan Wood Graham / Licensed by VAGA-DACS, New York, NY
© Andrew Wyeth

All rights reserved.
No part of this publication may be reproduced or adapted without the permission of the copyright holder,
throughout the world. Unless otherwise specified, copyright on the works reproduced lies with the respective
photographers, artists, heirs or estates. Despite intensive research, it has not always been possible to establish
copyright ownership. Where this is the case, we would appreciate notification.

ISBN: 978-1-84484-815-7

Printed in Poland

30 Millennia of Painting

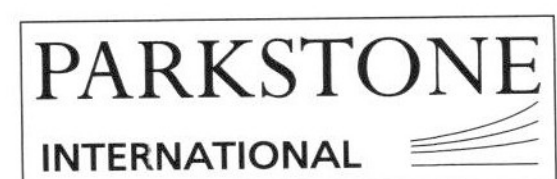

Contents

Introduction

The earliest traces of painting in the history of humanity take us back to prehistoric times. Already, during the Upper Paleolithic (35,000-10,000 BCE), man had acquired a sense of creativity and was developing his talents for painting. Soon painting became a favoured means of expression, and thus gave birth to the beginnings of art history. Prehistoric cave men decorated their grottos with coloured images, which, throughout human evolution, became increasingly complex, incorporating wild beasts, signs and parts of the human body which soon gave way to domestic animals. During the Neolithic period (9000-3300 BCE), rock art flourished and paintings became exposed to daylight, in contrast to cave paintings, which, by definition, are subterranean. At the same time, men discovered new shades of colours, using natural dyes derived from minerals such as ochre, and innovative techniques such as stump drawing. However, blue, white and green hues were still unknown. Meanwhile, the natural curves of the rock walls were cleverly used to represent animals, and the earliest forms of painting in three dimensions appeared.

Around 3000 BCE, the emergence of the first writings in Mesopotamia marked the end of prehistory. Antiquity, during which three major civilisations – Egyptian, Greek and Roman – coexisted, spanned more than three millennia. The Egyptians, with their system of hieroglyphics, were among the first to develop writing and played a pioneering role in the evolution of art. Similar to prehistoric art, Egyptian art supplies us with valuable information on the lifestyle of the era and reflects, *inter alia*, a cult devoted to veneration of the dead. Colourful paintings, abounding with details, which adorn the tombs and sarcophagi of pharaohs, reflect the importance of ceremonies dedicated to the afterlife, which was regarded as the dawn of a new life. The influence of Egypt would continue until the first century CE, when Crete and Greece asserted themselves against other civilisations. Though only painted pottery from this period has survived, its delicate and varied style offers a wonderful overview of Greek painting at the time.

From the first century BCE, Roman civilisation was dominant throughout Europe, the Balkans, and the Mediterranean region, and was largely inspired by Hellenistic Greek art. This is primarily evidenced by Roman frescos, such as those in the bourgeois villas of Pompeii and Herculaneum, which have been preserved thanks to the vagaries of nature. But after a period of hegemony, from the fourth century the Empire went into decline. However, freedom of worship established in 313 by Emperor Constantine drove the development of a strong religious imagery, which in turn gave rise to the early Christian style and simplified forms imported during the great barbarian invasions. Romanesque art, the first major art movement of the Middle Ages, grew from this foundation, and until the thirteenth century, this art reflected the strength and recent stability of Christianity. In all areas artists acted as pious illustrators of religious texts, producing works of great simplicity. Then, driven by changing mores and societies, Roman art gave way to the more elegant and complex Gothic.

Struck by the Hundred Years War (1337-1453), the fourteenth century was marked by political and religious instability, leading once more to a total renewal of art. Painting evolved toward representation and narrative, characterised by more realistic characters and the convincing treatment of space – a transformation that reflected other changes occurring in European culture, especially in Italy. Faced with a new society, in which traders, entrepreneurs and bankers were gaining in status, painters had to meet a growing demand for explicit and naturalistic art. In his *Lives of the Artists* of 1550, Vasari wrote that the naturalism of Tuscan painters like Giotto di Bondone in the early fourteenth century was a miracle, a gift to humankind to bring about an end to the stiff and formal Byzantine style that had previously held sway. Today, we recognise that it was hardly by chance or divine mercy that such a change occurred. The development in art of effective narrative, convincing spatial representation and realistic, corporeal figures with physical presence echoed other cultural changes taking place in the period, which found their most forcible expression in Italy. The monumental works of the Florentine painter Giotto and the elegant, finely wrought naturalism of the Sienese artist Duccio di Buoninsegna were just part of this larger cultural movement. Equally significant were the vernacular writings of Dante, Petrarch and Boccaccio; the vivid travel adventures of Marco Polo; the growing influence of nominalism in philosophy, which encouraged real, tangible and sensate knowledge; and the religious devotion of Saint Francis of Assisi, who found God's presence not in ideas or verbal speculation but in the chirping of birds and the glow of the sun and moon.

What had been started by the *primi lumi*, the 'first lights', in the art of painting progressed in the fifteenth century and acquired a new historical sense, causing artists to look back before the Middle Ages to the world of classical civilisation.

Italians came to admire, almost worship, the ancient Greeks and Romans for their wisdom and insight, and for their artistic and scholarly achievements. A new kind of intellectual, the humanist – a scholar of ancient letters who promoted humanist philosophy – fuelled this cultural revolution. Humanism fostered belief in the study of nature and the potential of humankind, along with a sense that secular, moral beliefs were necessary to supplement the limited tenets of Christianity. Above all, the humanists encouraged the belief that ancient civilisation was the apex of culture, and that writers and artists should be in a dialogue with those of the classical world. The result was the Renaissance – the rebirth – of Greco-Roman culture. The panels and murals of Masaccio and Piero dell Francesca captured the moral firmness of ancient Roman sculptural figures, and due to the new science of perspective portrayed them as part of our physical world. The Renaissance perspective system is based on a single vanishing point and carefully worked out transversal lines, resulting in a spatial coherence not seen since antiquity. Even more clearly indebted to antiquity were the paintings of the northern-Italian prodigy, Andrea Mantegna. His archaeological studies of antique costumes, architecture, figural poses and inscriptions resulted in the most consistent attempt by any painter to recreate Greco-Roman civilisation. Even a painter like Alessandro Botticelli, whose art evokes a dreamy spirit that had survived from the late Gothic style, created paintings with Venuses, Cupids and nymphs that responded to the subject matter of the ancients and appealed to contemporary viewers touched by humanism.

It would be better to think of 'Renaissances' rather than a single Renaissance. This is demonstrated most clearly by looking at the art of the leading painters of the High Renaissance in the fifteenth and sixteenth centuries. Giorgio Vasari saw these masters as setting out to create an art greater than nature, as idealists who improved on reality rather than imitated it, and who evoked reality thoughtfully rather than delineating it in every detail. We recognise in these painters different embodiments of the cultural aspirations of the time. Leonardo da Vinci, trained as a painter, was equally at home in his role as a scientist, and incorporated into art his research into the human body, plant forms, geology and psychology. Michelangelo Buonarroti trained as a sculptor, subsequently turning to painting to express his deep theological and philosophical beliefs, especially the idealism of Neoplatonism. His muscular, over-life-size and intense heroes could hardly differ more from the graceful, smiling, supple figures of Leonardo. Raphael of Urbino was the ultimate courtier, whose paintings embody the grace, charm and sophistication of life at Renaissance courts. Giorgione and Titian, both Venetian masters, focused on luxurious landscapes and sumptuous female nudes, using colour and free brushwork to express an Epicurean sense of life. Titian's motto *Natura Potentior Ars*, 'Art more powerful than nature', could be the philosophy of all sixteenth-century artists.

One the achievements of Italian Renaissance painters was to establish their intellectual credentials. Rather than mere craftsmen, artists – some of whom, such as Leon Battista Alberti, Leonardo da Vinci and Michelangelo, were themselves writers on this subject – made a bid to be considered on a par with other thinkers of their time, and helped raise the profession of painting in Renaissance Italy. A kind of cult sprang up around leading artists of the time, with Michelangelo, for example, called *Il Divino*, 'the divine'. Already in 1435, Alberti urged painters to associate themselves with men of letters and mathematicians, which paid off. The present-day inclusion of 'studio art' in university curricula has its origins in this new attitude to painting that arose in Italy during the Renaissance. By the sixteenth century, rather than commissioning particular works, art patrons across the Italian peninsula were happy to acquire any product of the great artists: acquiring a Raphael, Michelangelo or Titian was a goal in itself, regardless of the work in question.

While Italian Renaissance artists created highly organised spatial settings and idealised figures, northern Europeans focused on everyday reality and on the variety of life. Few painters have equalled the Netherlandish painter Jan van Eyck, for example, in his close observation of surfaces, and captured more clearly and poetically the glint of light on a pearl, the deep, resonant colours of a red cloth, or the glinting reflections that appear in glass and on metal. Scientific observation was one form of realism, while another was the intense interest in the bodies of saints and the anatomical details of the Passion of Christ. This was the age of religious theatre, when actors, dressed as biblical characters, acted out in churches and on the streets the detail of Christ's suffering and death. It is no coincidence this was also the period when masters such as the Netherlandish Rogier van der Weyden and the German Matthias Grünewald painted, sometimes with excruciating clarity, the wounds, streams of blood and pathetic countenance of the crucified Christ. The northern masters executed their painting using the skilled technique of oil, in which they excelled in Europe until the Italians adopted the medium in the later fifteenth century.

Spanning both north and south Europe during the Renaissance was Albrecht Dürer of Nuremburg. Durer followed the Italian practice of canonical measure of the human body and perspective, though he retained the emotional expressionism and sharpness of line that was widespread in German art. Though he shared the optimism of Italians, many other northern painters were pessimistic about the human condition. Giovanni Pico della Mirandola's essay on the *Dignity of Man* presaged Michelangelo's belief in the perfectibility and essential beauty of the human body and soul, but Erasmus' *Praise of Folly* and Sebastian Brant's satiric poem *Ship of Fools* belonged to the same northern European cultural milieu that produced the fantastic visions of Hieronymus Bosch's *Garden of Earthly Delights* triptych and Pieter Bruegel's raucous peasant scenes. There was hope for humankind in paradise, but little consolation on earth for beings consumed by their passions and caught in an endless cycle of desire and fruitless yearning. Northern humanists, like their Italian counterparts, called for the classical virtues of moderation, restraint and harmony – the pictures of Bruegel represented the very vices against which they warned. Unlike some of the contemporary Romanists, who had travelled from the Netherlands to Italy and been inspired by Michelangelo and other artists of the time, Bruegel travelled to Rome around 1550 but remained largely untouched by its art. Instead he turned to local inspiration and staged his scenes amidst humble settings, earning him the undeserved nickname 'Peasant Bruegel'. Brueghel was a herald of the realism and bluntness of the northern European Baroque.

The great intellectual revolt set in motion by theologians Martin Luther and John Calvin in the sixteenth century provoked the Catholic Church to respond to the challenge of the Protestants. Various church councils called for reform of the Roman Catholic Church, and participants at the Council of Trent declared that religious art should be simple and accessible to a broad public. A number of Italian painters, however, known as Mannerists, had begun developing a form of art that was complex in subject matter and style. Painters eventually responded to ecclesiastical needs as well as to the stylisations of Mannerism. We call this new era the age of the Baroque, which was ushered in initially by Caravaggio. He painted mainly religious subject matter, but in the most realistic and dramatic manner possible, and gained a following among ordinary people as well as among connoisseurs and even Church officials, who were at first sceptical of his treatment. Caravaggism swept across Italy and then the rest of Europe, as a host of painters came to adopt his chiaroscuro and suppression of vivid colouring; his earthy tones and powerful figures struck a chord with viewers across the continent who had tired of some of the artificialities of sixteenth-century art.

In addition to the Caravaggism of the early Baroque, another form of painting later called the High Baroque – the most dramatic, dynamic and painterly style yet seen – also developed, built on the foundations laid by the sixteenth-century Venetians. Peter Paul Rubens, an admirer of Titian, painted huge canvases with fleshy figures, rich landscapes, broken brushwork and flickering light and dark tones. His pictorial experiments were the starting point for the art of other northern European artists such as Jacob Jordaens and Anthony van Dyck; the latter had a large following among the European elite for his noble portrait manner. Rubens brought back the world of antiquity, painting ancient gods and goddesses, but his style was anything but classical. He found a ready market for his works among European aristocrats who liked his exuberance, and among Catholic patrons of art who found in his flamboyant sacred scenes a weapon for Counter-Reformation ideology. In Rome, Bernini was Ruben's counterpart in sculpture, providing the Catholic Church with two powerful champions for the power and majesty of the Church and Papacy. Italian Baroque painters unleashed a torrent of holy figures on the ceilings of churches in Rome and other cities, with the skies opening up to reveal Heaven itself and God's personal acceptance of the martyrs and mystics of Catholic sainthood. The Spanish painters Velásquez, Murillo and Zurburán also took up the style, using quieter movement and brushwork, but sharing with the Italians a mystical sense of light and Catholic iconography.

How different from all this were the paintings of seventeenth-century Holland! Having effectively freed themselves from Habsburg Spain by the 1580s, the Dutch practised a tolerant form of Calvinism, which eschewed religious iconography. A growing middle class and increasingly wealthy upper class acted as patrons for the delightful variety of secular paintings produced by a host of skilled painters, with individual artists specialising in moonlit landscapes, skating and tavern scenes, still-lifes, domestic interiors, ships at sea and a great variety of other subjects. From this large school of artists several individual painters stand out. Jacob van Ruisdael is the closest we have to a High Baroque landscape painter in Holland – his dark and sometimes stormy landscapes evoke the drama and movement widespread in European art of the time. Like Ruisdael, Frans Hals' painting, with its flashy, quick strokes of the brush and exaggerated colouring of skin and garments, approaches a pan-European sensibility of the High Baroque. In contrast, Jan Steen typified the realism and local character of most Dutch art of the Golden Age, and added a moral slant through the depiction of households in disarray and misbehaving peasants. Finally, the paintings of Rembrandt van Rijn stand alone, even amongst the Dutch. Raised as a Calvinist, Rembrandt shared some beliefs with the Mennonites, and was happy to depart from Calvinist strictures against representing biblical scenes. His later paintings, with their quiet introspection, make the perfect Protestant counterpart to the showy, dynamic Roman Catholic paintings of Rubens. From his early, tighter technique influenced by Dutch 'fine painters', Rembrandt developed a broad, shadowy manner derived from Caravaggio, but expressed with much greater pictorial complexity. This style later fell out of favour among the Dutch, but Rembrandt remained true to it, leaving a legacy that would be admired by nineteenth-century Romantic painters and modernists with a taste for painterly abstraction. Rembrandt was also distinctive for the universality of his art, which was steeped in knowledge of other styles and literary sources. Although he never travelled to Italy, he absorbed many of the tenets of Italian painting, and included in his works elements inspired by artists such as the late Gothic artist Antonio Pisanello and the Renaissance masters Mantegna, Raphael and Dürer. His style evolved constantly, and he had the broadest artistic mind and deepest understanding of the human condition of any painter of his age.

Clearly, just as there were many 'Renaissances' in art, there were many forms of the Baroque, and the High Baroque was challenged by the Classical Baroque, which had its philosophical roots in ancient thought and its stylistic basis in the paintings of Raphael and other High Renaissance classicists. Annibale Carracci had embraced a classical approach, and painters like Andrea Sacchi challenged the supremacy in Rome of High Baroque painters like Pietro da Cortona. However, the quintessential classicist of the seventeenth century was the Frenchman Nicolas Poussin, who developed a style perfectly suited to the growing ranks of philosophical Stoics in France, Italy and elsewhere. His solid, idealised figures, endowed with broad physical movements and firm moral purpose, acted out a range of narratives, both sacred and secular. Another Frenchman developed a different form of classicism: the Epicurean paintings of Claude Lorrain at first seem to differ sharply from those of Poussin: in Claude's pictures edges melt away, waters ripple subtly and hazy views of infinity appear in the distance. Yet both painters conveyed a sense of moderation and balance, and appealed to similar kinds of patrons. All these painters of the seventeenth century, whether or not classical in temperament, participated in the explosion of subject matter of the time; not since antiquity

had art-making seen such diversity of iconography of both sacred and profane subjects. With the exploration of new continents, contact with new and different peoples across the globe, and novel views offered by telescopes and microscopes, the world seemed to be an evolving and fractured place, and the diversity of artistic styles and pictorial subject matter reflected this dynamism.

Louis XIV (d. 1715), the self-designated Sun King who modelled himself after Apollo and Alexander the Great, favoured the classical mode of Poussin and of painters such as his court artist Charles Le Brun, who, in turn, glorified the king with a number of murky paintings celebrating his reign. There arose at the end of the seventeenth and beginning of the eighteenth century a debate over style, in which painters allied themselves with one of two camps – the Poussinists and the Rubensists. The former favoured classicism, linearity and moderation, while the latter group declared the innate primacy of free colouring, energetic movement and compositional dynamism. When Louis XIV died, the field in France was open, and the Rubensists took the lead, bringing forth a style we call Rococo, which – roughly translated – means 'pebblework Baroque', a decorative version of painterly Baroque. Rather than a continuation of the style of Rubens, the manner of Antoine Watteau, Jean-Honoré Fragonard and François Boucher conveyed a lighter mood, with more feathery strokes of the brush, a lighter palette and even a smaller size of canvas. Erotic subject matter and light genre subjects came to dominate the style, which found favour especially among the pleasure-loving aristocrats of France, as well as their peers elsewhere in continental Europe. Rococo painters thus carried forward the debate between line and colour that had emerged in practice and theory in the sixteenth century. The argument between Michelangelo and Titian, and then between Rubens and Poussin, was a struggle that would not go away, and would return in the nineteenth century and later.

Not every artist succumbed to Rococo. A focus in the eighteenth century on particular social virtues – patriotism, moderation, duty to family, the necessity to embrace reason and study the laws of nature – were themselves at odds with the subject matter and hedonistic style of Rococo painters. In the realm of art theory and criticism, the philosophers and writers Diderot and Voltaire were unhappy with the Rococo style flourishing in France, and its days were numbered. The humble naturalism of the French artist Chardin was based in the Dutch still-life artistry of the previous century, while Anglo-American and English painters such as John Singleton Copley of Boston, Joseph Wright of Derby and Thomas Hogarth painted in styles which, in different ways, embodied a kind of fundamental naturalism that reflected the spirit of the age. A number of artists, such as Elisabeth Vigée-Lebrun and Thomas Gainsborough, incorporated into their paintings some of the lightness of touch that characterised the Rococo, but they modified its excesses and avoided some of its artificial and superficial qualities, however delightful these are.

A leitmotif of Western painting has been the persistence of classicism, and here the Rococo found its fiercest opponent. The essentials of the classical style – a dynamic equilibrium, idealised naturalism, measured harmony, restraint of colour and a dominance of line, all operating under the guiding influence of ancient Greek and Roman models – reasserted themselves in the late-eighteenth century in response to Rococo. When Jacques-Louis David exhibited his *Oath of the Horatii* in 1785, it electrified the public, and was applauded by the French including the king, gaining an international audience. Thomas Jefferson happened to be in Paris at the time of the painting's exhibition and was greatly impressed. The popularity of Neoclassicism preceded the French Revolution, but once the revolution occurred, it became the official style of the virtuous new French regime. Rococo was associated with the decadent *ancien régime*, whose painters were forced to flee the country or change their styles. Neoclassicism remained in vogue in France through the Napoleonic age, and the elegant linearity style of Jean-Auguste-Dominique Ingres replaced the works of David, who had later softened his approach to create a more decorative form of classicism suitable for the less bourgeois character of the French Empire.

If the eighteenth century was the Age of Reason and the Enlightenment, developing at the same time was an intellectual trend towards interest in the irrational and emotional. A group of painters, sometimes grouped together under the term Romantics, flourished in the late-eighteenth and first half of the nineteenth century. Many of these painters co-existed chronologically with more classical artists, and a certain amount of rivalry existed between them. Some late eighteenth- and early- nineteenth century European painters were explicitly interested in the irrational, such as Henry Fuseli in his work *Nightmare*, and Francisco Goya in some of his violent paintings of death and madness. Théodore Géricault explored insanity in some of his smaller paintings, along with themes of death, cannibalism and political corruption in his massive canvas *Raft of the Medusa*. More subtle were the painters of this period who explored the emotional effects of landscape art. John Constable's flickering light and careful study of clouds and sunlight on trees in the English countryside yielded

strikingly emotive results. The German Caspar David Friedrich, on the other hand, evoked the religious mysticism of the landscape, while the American Hudson River School painters, such as Thomas Cole, represented the warm autumnal colours and desolation of a New World wilderness that was quickly disappearing. J. M. W. Turner's paintings of seascapes, landscapes and historical scenes seemed to his contemporaries to be made of 'tinted steam', and he even edged towards modernism in his abstractness. The most influential and acclaimed of the French Romantic painters was Eugene Delacroix. He turned to the High Baroque artist Rubens for artistic inspiration, painting canvas after canvas of tiger hunts, Passion of Christ imagery, and the exotic world of Arab warriors and hunters in northern Africa. Like the Baroque masters before him, Delacroix used dramatic spatial diagonals, cut-off compositional elements and bravura colourism with great effect. Delacroix gained the artistic and even personal enmity of Ingres, prompting contemporaries to recognise in their art the timeless struggle of line versus colour.

The kind of anti-Romantic realism of Flaubert's novel *Madame Bovary* found expression in the art of the Realist painting school. Gustave Courbet's unadorned representation of nature and village life attempts to show us the world without elaboration. His challenge 'show me an angel and I will paint one' is the sentiment that led to his monumental *Burial at Ornans,* a carefully composed work that he and critics of the time saw as little more than raw reality. More traditional, but also based on close observation of nature, were the paintings of Jean-François Millet and the Barbizon School painters, led by Theodore Rousseau. Among the other Realists were Honoré Daumier, who recorded contemporary urban life, the folly of civic officials and lawyers, the natural goodness of labourers and the weariness of the poor. Contemporary with the French Realists were the English Pre-Raphaelite painters, who turned their backs on the idealism and classicism they associated with the Royal Academy, finding inspiration instead in the detailed particularity and 'honesty' of painting in Italy before Raphael and the High Renaissance. Dante Gabriel Rossetti and Edward Burne-Jones found solace in exotic stories of the Middle Ages, in accounts of early British history and in all manner of moralising tales and parables. They painted with oils, but with the care of tempera paints and without the broad treatment of the brush, scumbling of colours and rapid glazing that the oil medium makes possible. However, they would not be the last painters in the West to reject the pictorial possibilities of oil paint, or to defy the conventions of the traditional academies of art.

As urbanism and industrialism advanced in nineteenth-century Europe, a new and unexpected development occurred in painting with the rise of Impressionism. Claude Monet, Auguste Renoir, Camille Pissarro and others in their circle painted with rapid strokes and with an insubstantiality never before seen in painting except in sketches. Sometimes capturing the idylls of the countryside and at other times the light, smoke, colour and movement of urban scenes, they turned their backs on the historical and concentrated instead on conveying the evanescence of appearances. Rejected at first by critics and the public because of their insouciance with academic rules, the Impressionists had a lasting impact on art and, as their style developed, the modernity of their work became even more apparent. Monet's late canvases, which he finished not in front of the visual source but in the studio, sometimes long afterwards, became almost abstract. Renoir eventually sought to recreate the firm linearity he had discovered in Italian art, and his figurative works became ever more planned in design and sugary sweet in colouring. The traditionalist painters Jean-Léon Gérôme and William Bouguereau in France and Ilya Repin in Russia achieved worldly success and acclaim with their more academic and conservative approaches, but the Impressionists had the greater impact on the development of modernism, and their artistry soon inspired new branches of painting.

The Post-Impressionists were a group of artists who understood the potentialities of the way the Impressionists used the brush. Paul Cézanne was determined to make something permanent of the art of the Impressionists, endowing his pictures with the compositional solidity he found in classicism. He was intent on 'redoing Poussin after Nature', and developed a rough kind of classicism, which at the same time obscured the edges of things, and focused on the lighting, texture and colouring of the paint surface. Vincent van Gogh also built on Impressionism, imbuing it with a mystical spirit. Paul Gauguin sought subject matter in the primitive regions of France and the South Pacific, painting with patches of sometimes barely mediated colour. Georges Seurat's art theory returned to some of the rhetoric of early Impressionism, using a technique based on the optical mixing of colours applied in small dots, while at the same time, like Cézanne, endowing his figures with an almost neoclassical calm, presence and *gravitas*.

The explosion of styles that had emerged during the later nineteenth century continued into the twentieth, when the freedom and individualism of modernism found expression in a profusion of approaches. Thinkers in a number of fields in the early-twentieth century discovered the essential instability of form and existence: atonalism in music, the theory of relativity in physics and the theories of psychoanalysis all pointed to a world of subjectivity and shifting viewpoints. For their part, the Cubists, led by Pablo Picasso and Georges Braque, systematically broke down ('analysed') reality in their Analytic Cubism, almost eliminating colour, consistent light direction and even the singularity of viewpoint, and turned completely away from narrative in favour of immobile subjects such as still-life and portraiture. In the history of styles, it can be said that the Cubists demolished the Renaissance project — a project accepted by academic painters of the nineteenth century — of constructing a spatial box in which meaningful events unfold under conditions of convincing space, colour and light. Eschewing pure, non-representational abstraction, the Cubists relied instead on creating a tension between what the viewer sees and expects to see. Picasso, who had earlier painted in an academic narrative manner as a youth, in his poetic and more representational Blue and Pink periods, later experimented almost endlessly, at times dabbling with primitivism, Neoclassicism and Surrealism. Not since Giotto had a single painter done so much to change the field of art. The works of the French painter Fernand Léger, along with Marcel Duchamp's *Nude Descending a Staircase*, were by-products of the style of Picasso and Braque — an expanded and more dynamic expression of their ideas that included figures in architectural settings.

Picasso's art was often witty and clever. Much of twentieth-century painting was more serious, and works like Picasso's *Guernica*, portraying the tragedy of war, represented a move away from the playfulness of his early Cubist styles. Surrealist art, such as the dream paintings of Salvador Dalí or the ominous atmospheres of the works of Giorgio de Chirico, capture some of the alienation and psychological intensity of modern life. The Futurists — Italian painters influenced by the Cubists — turned to dynamic, even violent, movement in their paintings, and their art presaged the unpleasant mixture of modernism, urbanism and aggression that, not by coincidence, fuelled the Fascist regime of Benito Mussolini. Quite unlike the outwardly intense Futurists, another group of artists in the late-nineteenth and early-twentieth centuries took to exploring inner subjectivity — the period of civilisation that gave us Freud and Jung was bound to include painters drawn to the theme of human psychology. Edvard Munch's expressionism and psychological insight was matched in its intensity perhaps only by that of the German painters Ludwig Kirchner and Emil Nolde. A religious sentiment, also deeply emotive, flourished at the same time in the abstracted art of the French Catholic painter Georges Rouault and the Russian-Jewish Marc Chagall.

The rise of abstraction in art has been much discussed, but it is arguable that no such thing is possible. The Dutchman Piet Mondrian saw in his abstractions various theological, gender and existential themes, and his *Broadway Boogie Woogie*, as its name suggests, expresses the frenetic jazz culture of New York. Kasimir Malevitch's abstract geometric paintings carry ontological and divine connotations, while Wassily Kandinsky's abstractions are fraught with mysticism and spiritual meaning. Jackson Pollock's Abstract Expressionist drip paintings contain a strong human presence in the kinesthetic style itself, and he labelled his works with telling titles such as *Autumn Rhythm* and *Lucifer*. The Dutch-born Willem De Kooning's canvases are filled with an explosive and frantic application of paint, often illustrating highly charged subject matter. Mark Rothko's fields of bleeding colours sprang from the artist's philosophical notions; he wanted his viewers to be deeply moved by his pictures. Colour and form had come to fill the gap left by the Virgin Mary and martyred saints, classical gods and triumphant generals of earlier art, while the older techniques of oil painting were substituted in the twentieth century with new substances: acrylic and aluminium paints, encaustic, enamel and other binding agents, with the occasional quotidian object mixed in or glued onto the surface for good measure.

A reaction to the psychological intensity of the Abstract Expressionists was inevitable, and it took two forms. One was in a new objectivity and minimalism, championed by sculptors such as Donald Judd and David Smith, but also by painters such as Ellsworth Kelly and Frank Stella, who set out to remove much of the human emotion, mysticism and moral subjectivity from painting. Another response was found in Pop Art, which vividly reinstated the represented object, often in mirthful ways. Andy Warhol's soup cans, the collages of Richard Hamilton and the comic-book style of Roy Lichtenstein, often large in scale, were serious in intent. The commercial products of modern societies come spilling on to the canvases of Pop Artists, who ask us to consider the nature of consumerism and mass production as well as issues of artistic representation.

In the end, painting has triumphed in Western art over a host of opponents. In the Renaissance, the debate raged over the *paragone*, that is, the comparison of the visual arts, with Michelangelo and his camp proclaiming that sculpture was more real, more literally tangible and less deceptive than painting. Leonardo and others fought back, with words and deeds, and one could argue that painting remained the preeminent art from the Renaissance to the twentieth century. It is telling that the average viewer can only name a few prominent sculptors of the Renaissance, but might easily name a small army of painters from that period. The same is true of the nineteenth century: in nineteenth-century France, for example, beyond Rodin and perhaps Carpeaux and Barye, sculptors were overshadowed by the many schools of painters who came forth with innovative ideas. Painting has overcome the supply of cheaper prints that flooded the markets from the fifteenth century, attempts by some Baroque artists to merge painting with other visual arts, the promise of greater verisimilitude claimed by photography in the nineteenth century and the competition offered by moving pictures in the twentieth. Digital media have threatened challenge once again in the early twenty-first century. But painting is too powerfully present, too flexible in results and too rooted in our sensibilities to give way easily to upstarts. Even in practical terms, paintings can be rolled up and shipped, or, when not in use, they can be stacked, yet they can also fill a blank wall or ceiling with great effect. You cannot turn a painting off with a switch or an easy click of the mouse. They are flat, like the pages of our books and the screens on our computers, and can be reproduced in a compatible, two-dimensional format, without necessitating the difficult decisions of lighting called for in the reproduction of sculpture, or the questions of viewpoint as in the photography of architecture. Renaissance thinkers believed a painter could exercise divine powers and, like God himself, create an entire world. Many thousands of different pictorial worlds have been created since then.

The works chosen for this book demonstrate the variety of great painting to be found in our public museums. Surely, painting continues to have a lasting appeal in a changing world. Will the field continue to produce masterpieces? That is a more difficult question to answer. The works collected here indicate that physical craftsmanship is an important component of successful painting. It is also clear that painters succeed when they 'stand on the shoulders of giants' and respond to the art of the past, be it in admiration or in rebellion. Perhaps the world is awaiting the next great painter who, like Raphael, Rembrandt and Picasso, is steeped in the history of art and has the knowledge, sincerity and technical skill to create something new and outstanding. If painters of the future produce works that are little more than sarcastic one-liners, or are by nature ephemeral in form and meaning, or disdain or ignore the whole history of art, painting has little hope of success. However, manual skill and the determination to create a novel yet savvy work of art can go a long way towards preserving the art form. The pages of this book contain, without setting out to do so, a blueprint for painting's future.

– Joseph Manca

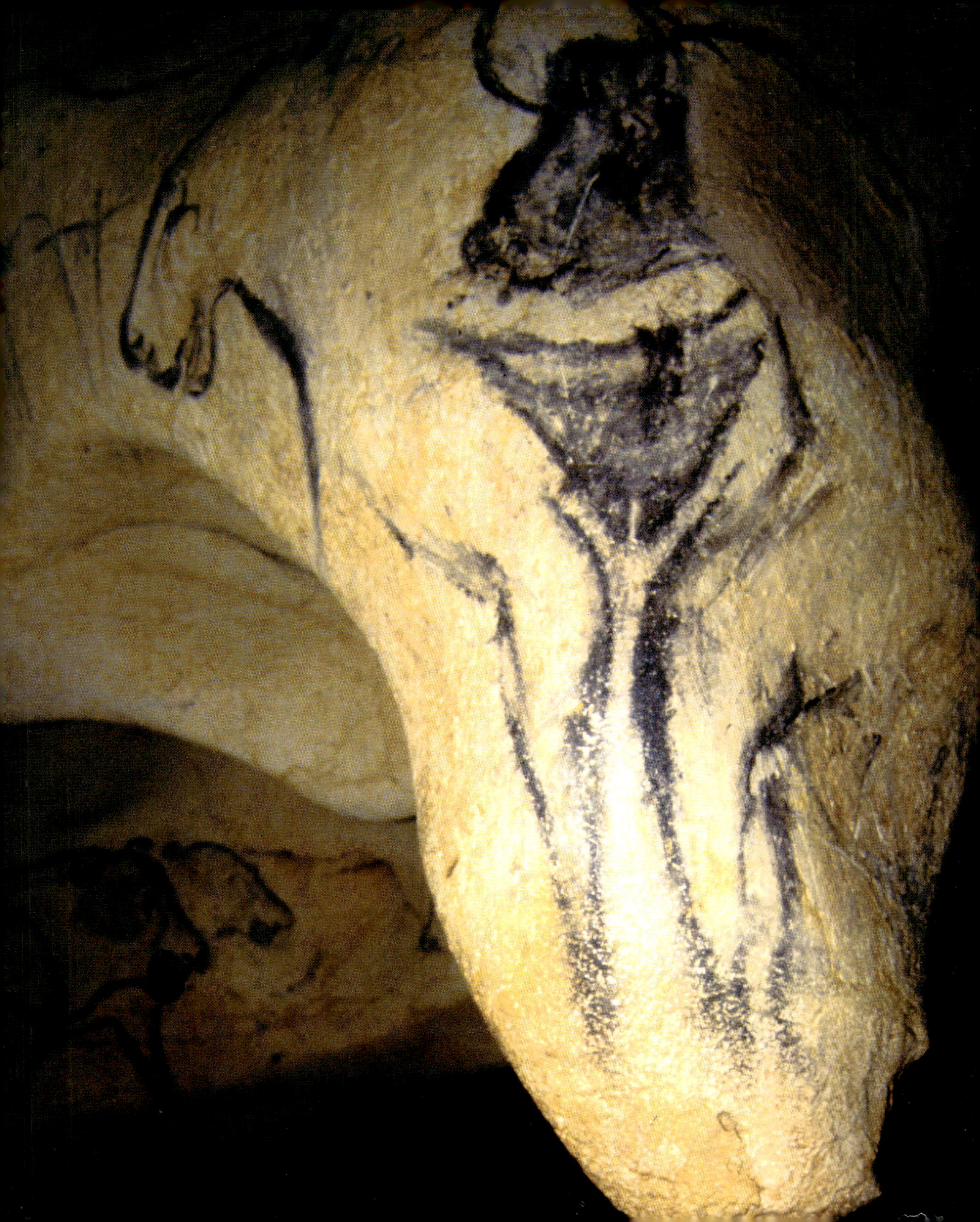

Prehistory

Defined as the period between the appearance of man (about 3 million years BCE) and the invention of writing (about 3000 BCE), prehistory, both from an artistic and historical point of view, was a period particularly rich in information, with cave art a unique source that continues to deliver valuable information on the lifestyle of prehistoric humans. In prehistoric times we can distinguish three main periods, or, more exactly, three successive ages: the Stone Age, divided between the Paleolithic period, based on hewn stone, and the Neolithic, based on polished stone and protohistoric metal, followed by the Bronze and Iron Ages.

As evidenced by their relics, each period, from an artistic point of view, has its specific characteristics. And even if some early signs of creative activity dating from the Lower Paleolithic (about 3,000,000-300,000 BCE) have been found, it is in the Upper Paleolithic (35,000-10,000 years BCE) that art really developed. At that time, favourite themes were animals (buffalo, deer, mammoths, etc.), flora and fauna endowed with anthropomorphic characteristics. These features are also frequently found in the decoration of objects of common use.

However, the figures remain very obscure and difficult to interpret. Some may represent sexual symbols, others as means to convey information. From the Neolithic period (9000-3300 BCE), the lifestyle of prehistoric humans changed significantly and became more sedentary, due to the discovery and development of agriculture and livestock farming. Hunter-gatherers became farmers and breeders. For the first time in the history of mankind, man put in place a system of production that enabled him to control his own vital resources. Cave art reflected these social changes and helped nurture a new mentality, which was reflected in the appearance of fresh figurative elements and domestic animals on cave walls.

To achieve their paintings, prehistoric men showed great ingenuity, using techniques such as finger- or smear-painting, as well as natural dyes such as yellow, red or brown ochre. They also employed coal and manganese oxide to obtain black, and exploited the natural curves of the walls to represent animals and create relief. Europe has some of the most spectacular painted caves, such as those of Lascaux, Chauvet and Cosquer, but there are also fine examples of prehistoric art in the Algerian desert, in South Africa and in Latin American countries such as Argentina and Brazil.

1. **Anonymous**, *The Minotaur of the Chauvet Pont-d'Arc Cave*,
c. 30,000-28,000 BCE, Paleolithic.
Vallon Pont d'Arc.

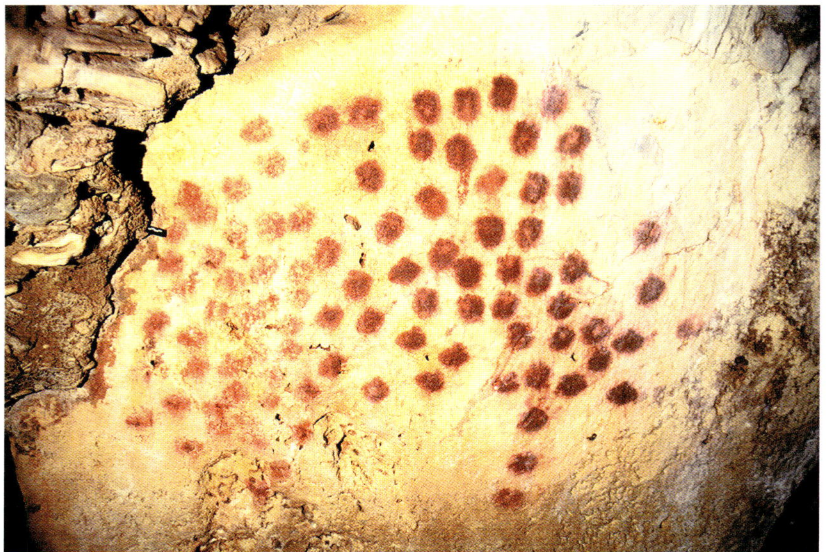

5. **Anonymous**, *Penguin*,
c. 20,000-16,000 BCE,
Cosquer Cave, Calanque de Morgiou.

The entrance to the underwater Cosquer Cave is located 37 metres below the Mediterranean Sea. Situated in the Calanque de Morgiou, near Marseille in France, the cave is named after the diver who discovered it in 1985. It is decorated with over 200 painted and carved figures, dating from the Upper Paleolithic, which correspond to two periods of occupation: an early phase (around 27,000 BCE) and a more recent phase (around 19,000 BCE). The cave is best known for its many paintings of marine animals, including a penguin. This is the first time penguins are shown in quaternary art, although the bones of the great auk Alca impennis have been reported in several Mediterranean habitats of the Upper Paleolithic (Gibraltar, southern Italy, Gulf of Genoa). The carving reproduced here seems likely to be of the great auk that died out in the 1840s.

2. **Anonymous**, Prints of Palms and Fingers,
c. 30,000-28,000 BCE, Paleolithic.
Chauvet Cave, Vallon Pont d'Arc.

The Chauvet Cave, located in Ardèche, Vallon Pont d'Arc in France, is named after the cave explorer Jean-Marie Chauvet, who discovered it in 1994, and measures 500 metres in length. Its paintings go back to the Upper Paleolithic (c. 35,000-10,000 BCE), making them among the oldest known cave paintings in the world, and are famous for their depiction of humans, especially hands, as evidenced by the prints of palms and fingers located in the Brunel chamber. What looks like a concentration of large red dots are actually prints of right-hand palms. To achieve these prints, the artist may have simply placed his hand on the wall or painted the outline by brush; or he may have used his hand as a stencil, spraying paint from the mouth or charcoal powder through a reed.

4. **Anonymous**, *Panel of the Megaceros*, c. 30,000-28,000 BCE,
Paleolithic. Megaceros gallery, Chauvet Cave, Vallon Pont d'Arc.

3. **Anonymous**, Stencil of human hands, 25,000 BCE.
Gargas Cave, Aventignan.

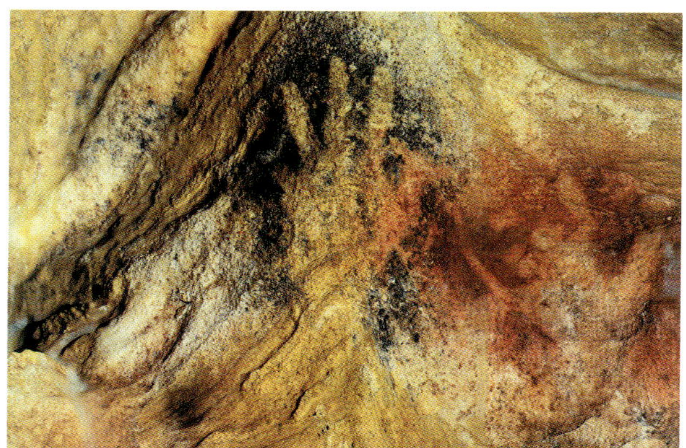

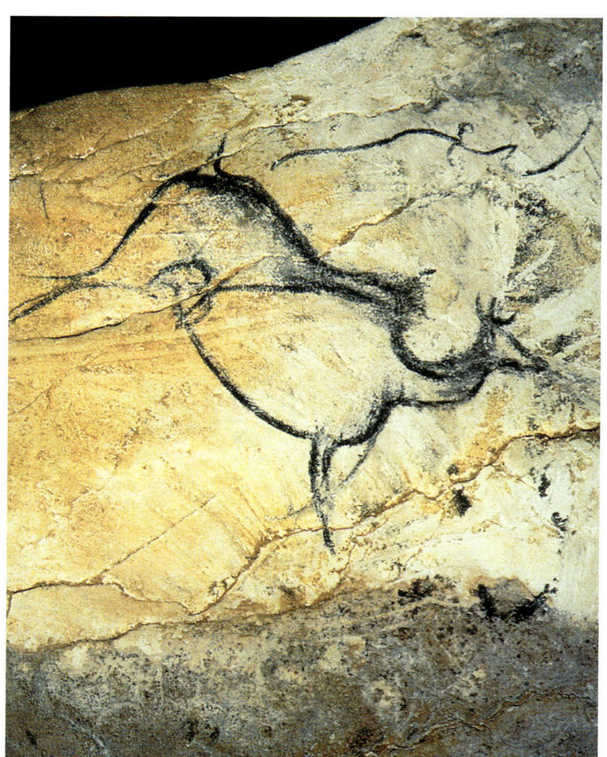

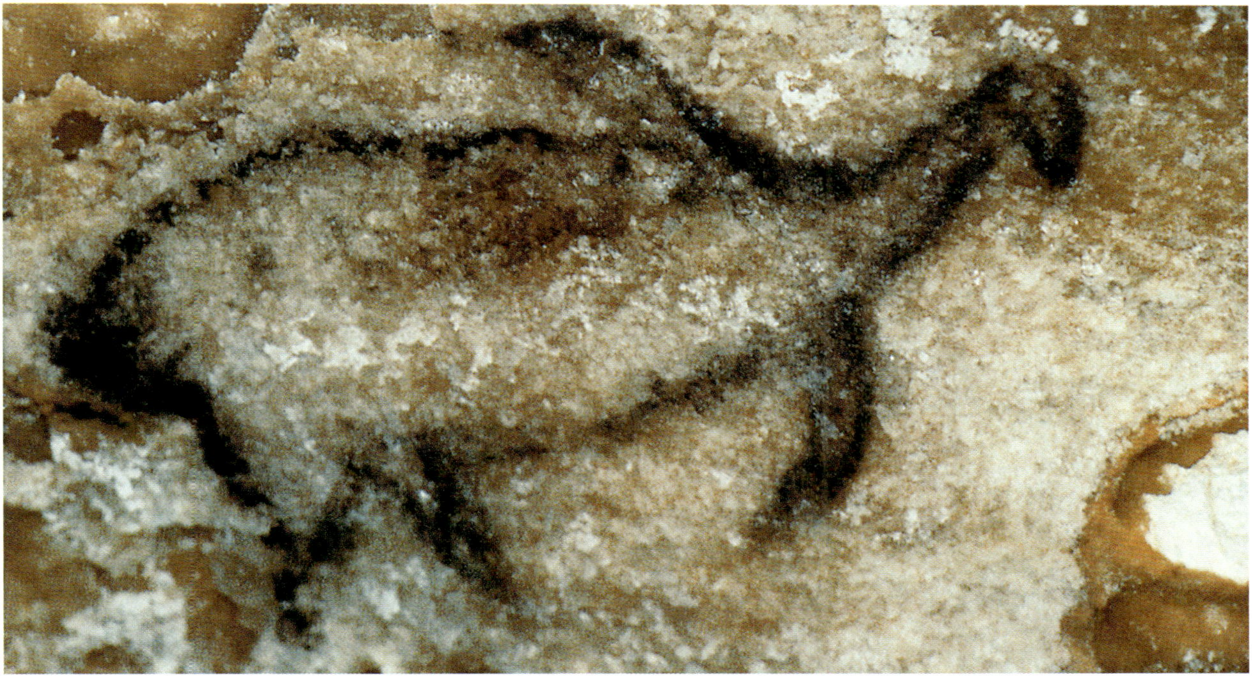

5.

6. **Anonymous**, *Kite-Man* and *The Sorcerer*,
c. 17,000-10,000 BCE, Paleolithic.
Cave of the Trois Frères, Montesquieu-Avantès.

The cave of the Trois Frères, located in the Midi-Pyrénées near Ariège, in the village of Montesquieu-Avantès, is from the Upper Paleolithic and contains numerous representations dating from the Magdalenian. It is famous, inter alia, for the representation of therianthropes (half-human, half-animal figures, such as a deer-man), which are particularly rare in cave art and their significance remains uncertain. There are various interpretations of this painting: the figure could represent a shaman in a trance, a god of animals or a sorcerer practising magic rituals. Even today, this image raises many questions.

7. **Anonymous**, *Baby Mammoth Brought back to Life*,
c. 26,000-25,000 BCE, Paleolithic.
Cave of Arcy-sur-Cure, Arcy-sur-Cure.

The cave of Arcy-sur-Cure is a major site for the study of the Middle and Upper Paleolithic in northern France, and is located at the village of Arcy-sur-Cure, Yonne, in the southern Paris basin, between Auxerre and Avallon. It consists of a set of caves formed by the river Cure in a limestone massif that emerged at the end of the Mesozoic Era (251 to 65.5 million years BCE). Eleven prehistoric caves, of which the first was explored 150 years ago, show the remains of continuous human occupation for more than 200,000 years. The cave paintings were carried out in ochre and charcoal. Most numerous are the red, which are divided into separate panels displaying more than 140 graphic units, including about 60 animals. This bestiary is largely dominated by mammoths, as evidenced by the baby mammoth in the Waves chamber.

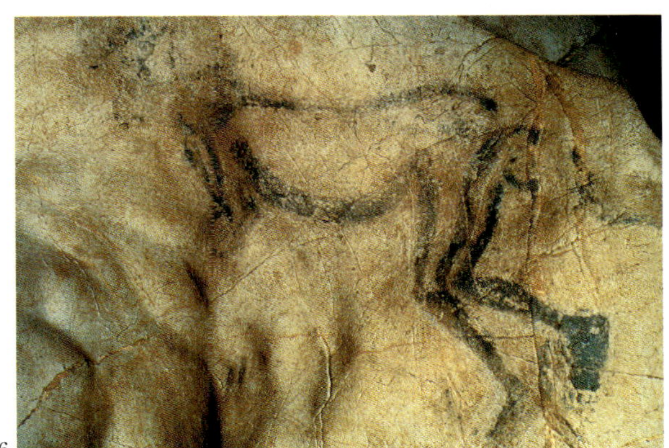

6.

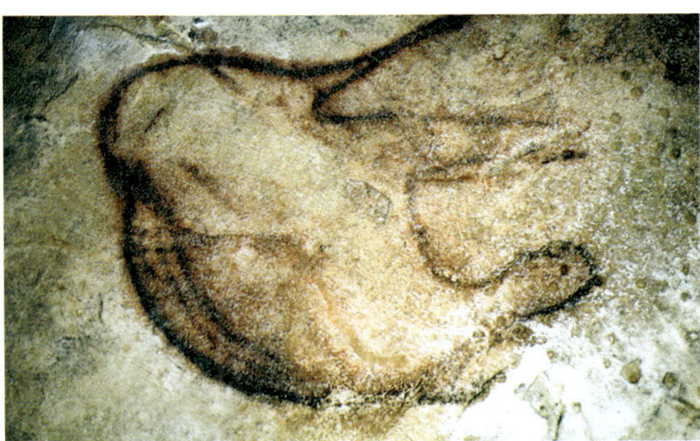

7.

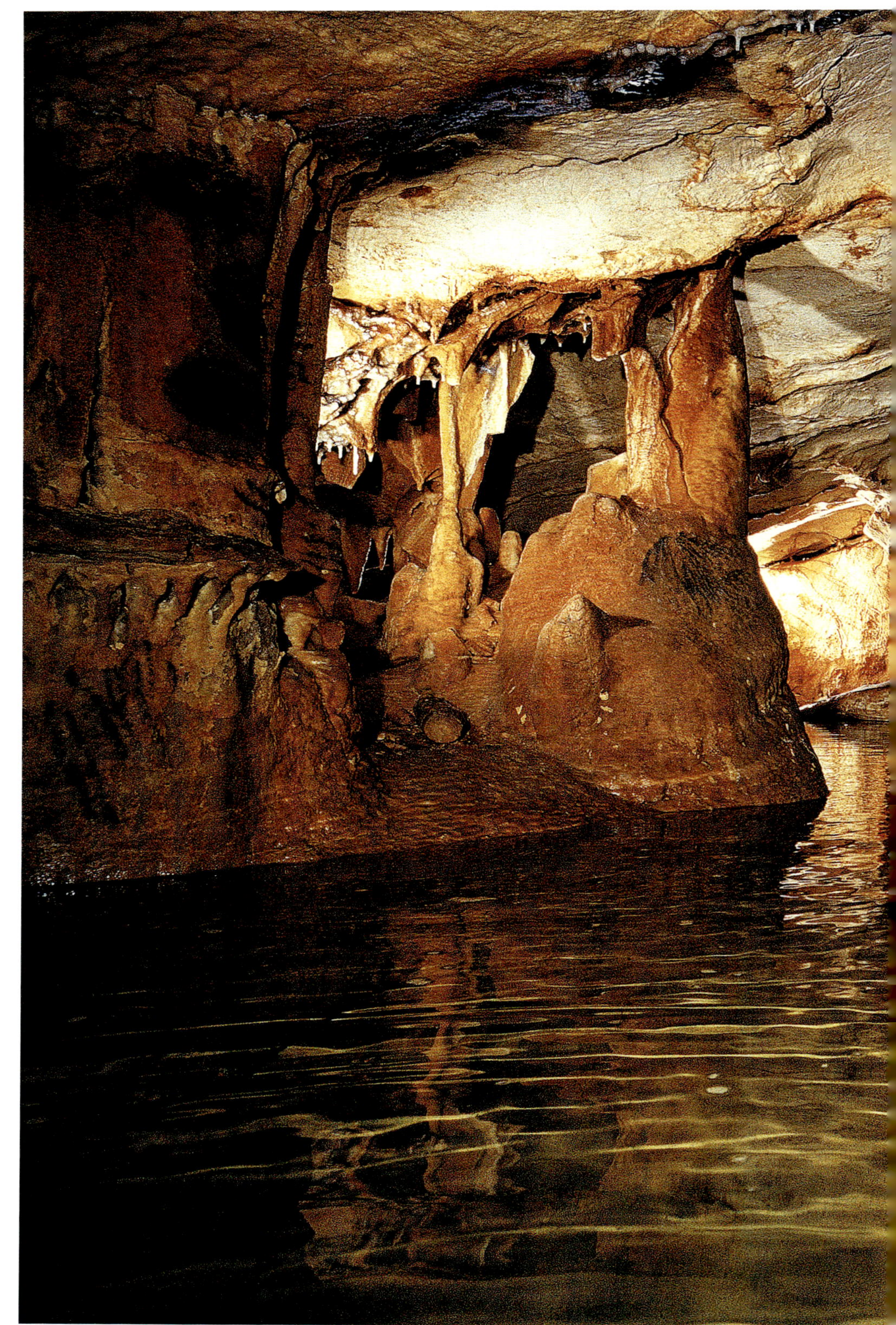

8. **Anonymous,**
   Panel of Black Horses,
   c. 20,000-16,000 BCE,
   Palaeolithic.
   Cosquer cave, Cassis.

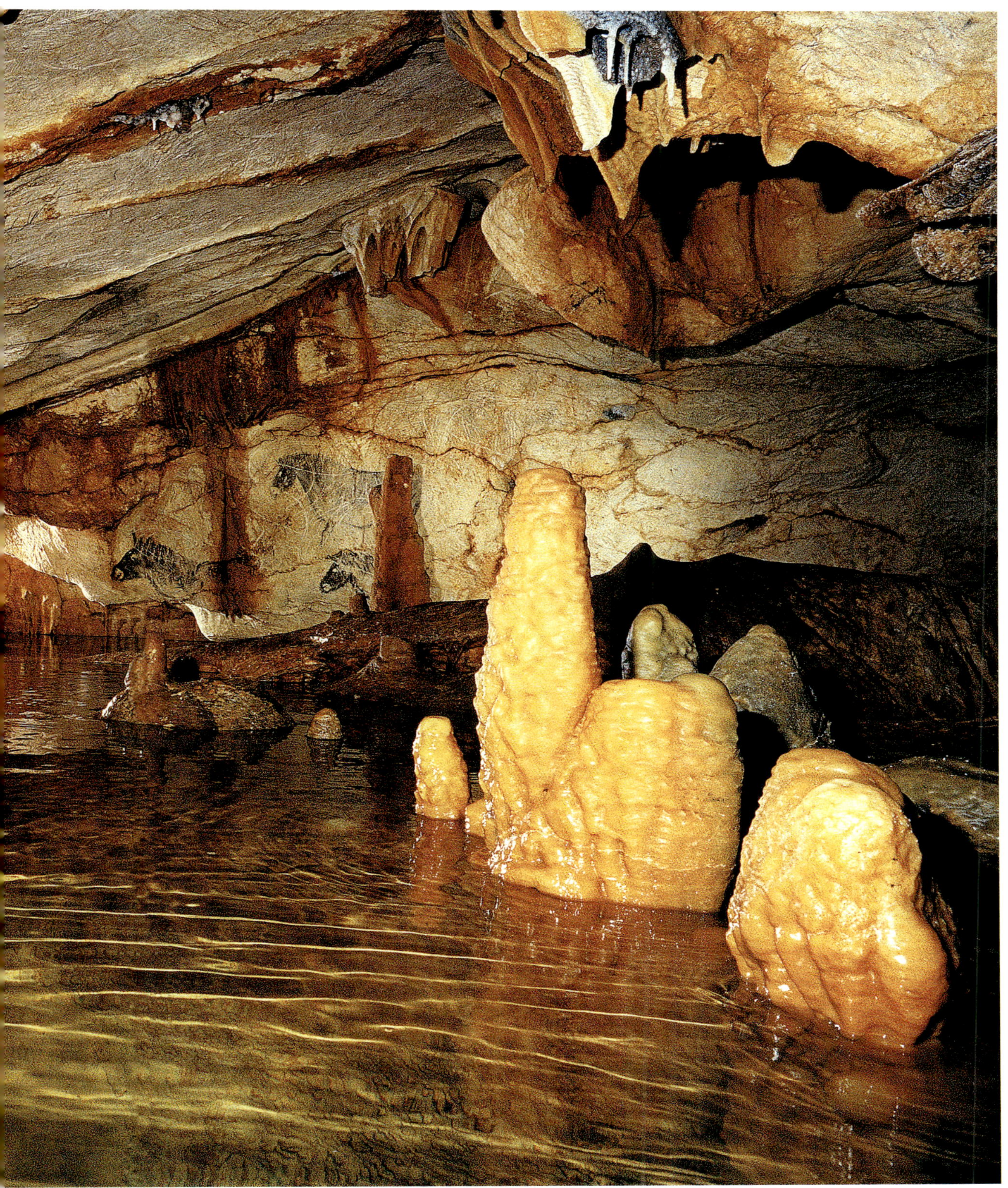

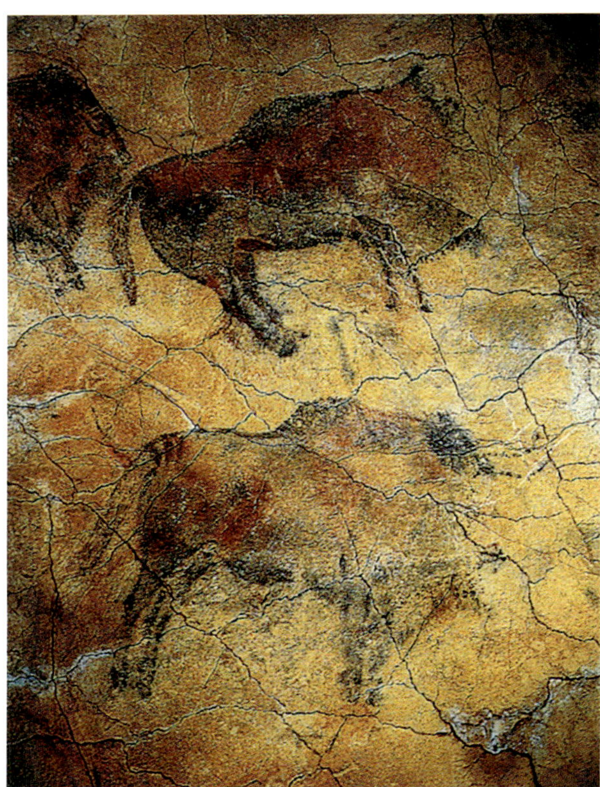

9. **Anonymous**, *Bison*, c. 15,000-10,000 BCE, Palaeolithic.
Altamira Cave, Santillana del Mar.

The cave of Altamira is located in Santillana del Mar, Spain, and measures 270 metres long. Discovered in 1879, its paintings represent the first contact between archaeologists and prehistoric art. For a long time regarded as false, they have now been authenticated as dating from the late Upper Paleolithic with carbon-14 dating. The cave consists of several chambers including the largest, called the Bison Chamber, but the most impressive feature is the polychrome ceiling showing a herd of bison in different poses. To produce the brown, yellow and red tones, the artists used charcoal, ochre or hematite.

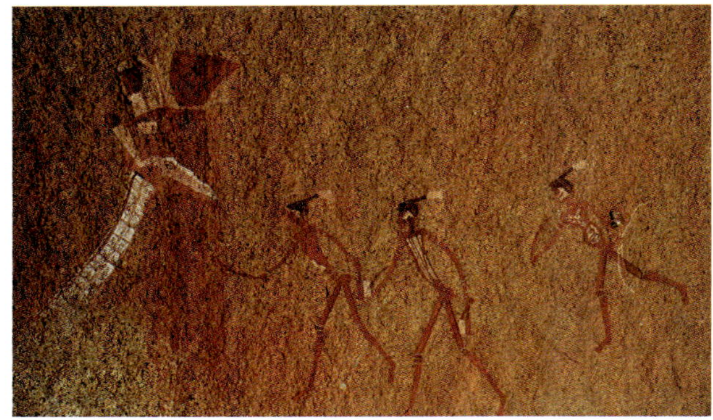

10. **Anonymous**, *The Ceremony of the Rain*, c. 16,000 BCE, Paleolithic. Length: 96 cm.
Near Brandberg Mountain, Namibia.

11. **Anonymous**, *Head of a Bison*, c. 15,000-10,000 BCE, Paleolithic.
Cave of El Castillo, Puente Viesgo.

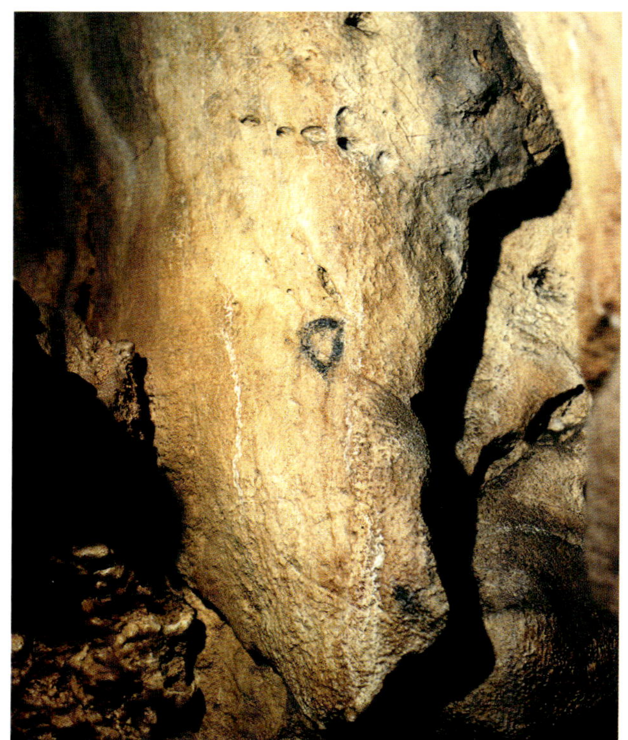

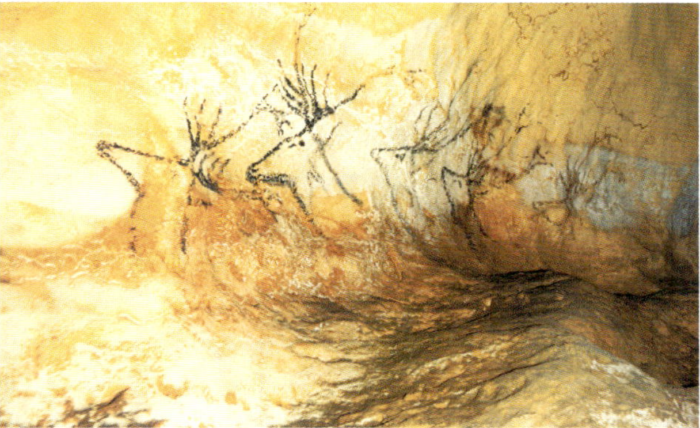

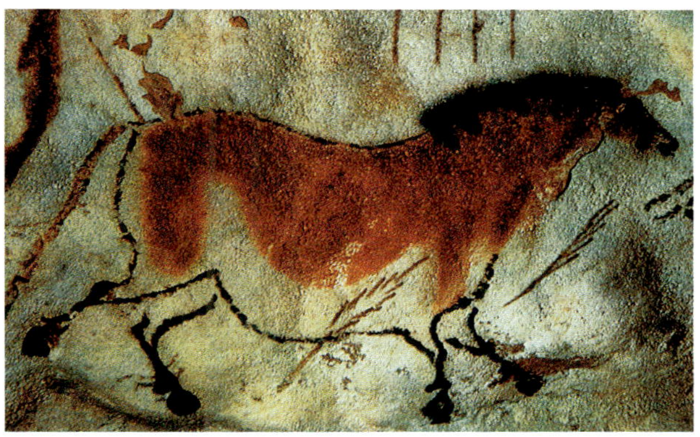

12. **Anonymous**, *Swimming Deer*, c. 18,000-12,000 BCE.
Lascaux caves, Montignac.
© National Centre for Paleolithic Prehistory, Ministry of Culture and Communication.

13. **Anonymous**, *Second Chinese Horse*, c. 15,000-10,000 BCE.
Lascaux caves, Montignac.
© National Centre for Paleolithic Prehistory, Ministry of Culture and Communication.

14. **Anonymous**, *Hall of Bulls*, c. 15,000-10,000 BCE.
Lascaux caves, Montignac.
© National Centre for Paleolithic Prehistory, Ministry of Culture and Communication.

Accidentally discovered by four teenagers in 1940, the Lascaux cave is located in France, Dordogne, in the Corrèze department and is 150 metres long. It is one of the most important and finely decorated of all Paleolithic caves, with paintings some 17,000 years old. The cave is also a historic monument, a UNESCO World Heritage Site, and has been nicknamed the 'Sistine Chapel of cave art' on account of the number and aesthetic quality of its works. It is divided into several chambers, the best known and spectacular of which is the Hall of Bulls, named after its four giant black bulls, including one which, at 5.2 metres long, is the largest cave-art animal ever found. The animals are all in motion – herds of horses, charging bulls, felines, cattle, bison and even a rhinoceros – and show an understanding of perspective that would not reappear until the Renaissance. Most of the major images have been painted onto the walls using mineral pigments, although some designs have also been carved into the stone.

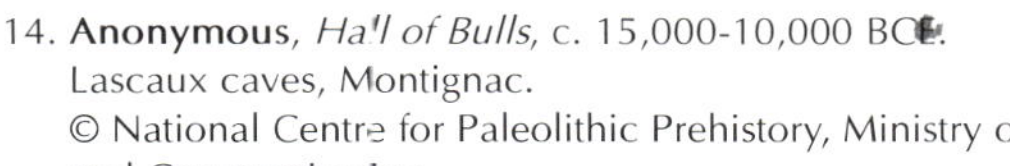

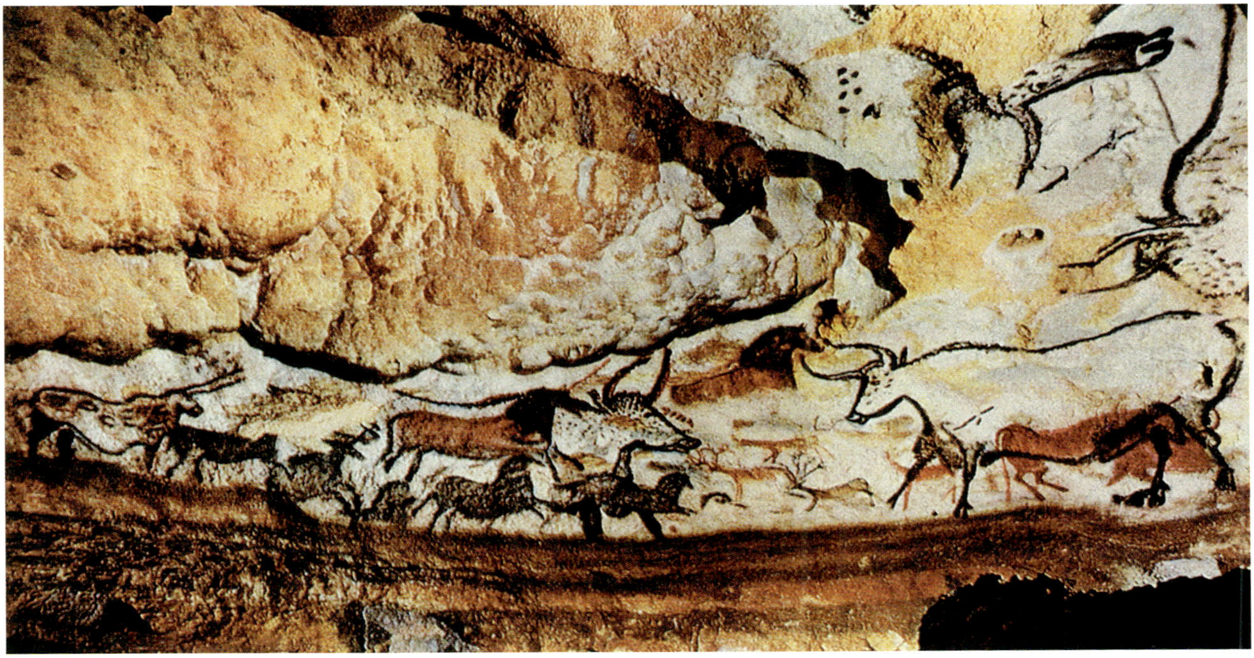

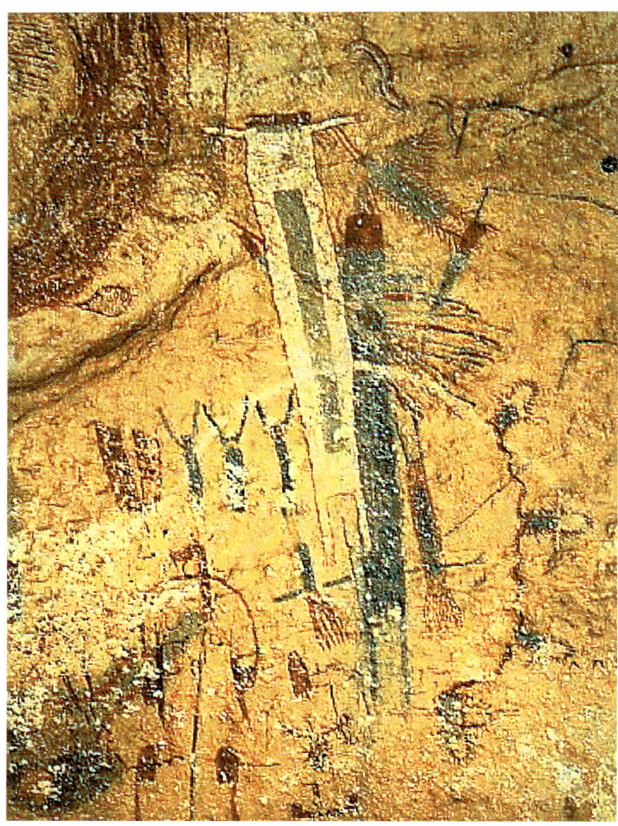

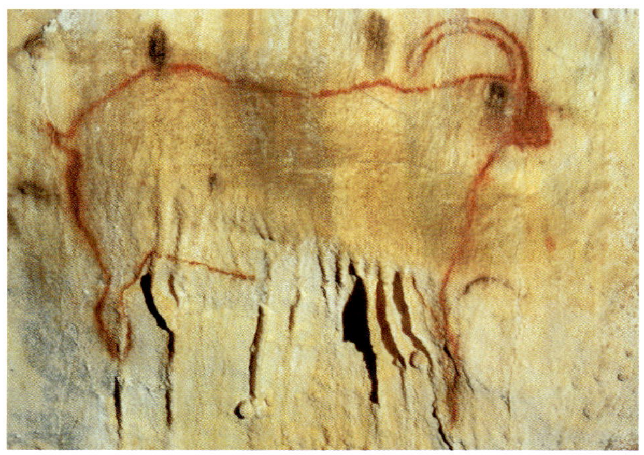

16. **Anonymous**, Ibex in Relief, to 12,000 BCE, Neolithic.
Length: 80 cm. Cougnac Cave, Payrignac.

15. **Anonymous**, Rock shelter, c. 12,000-7,000 BCE, Neolithic.
Panther Cave, Seminole Canyon.

17. **Anonymous**, A Mass of Hands, c. 9000-7000 BCE, Neolithic.
Cueva de las Manos, near Rio Pinturas.

18. **Anonymous**, Rock shelter, c. 9000-7500 BCE, Neolithic.
Cueva de las Manos, near Rio Pinturas, southern Patagonia.

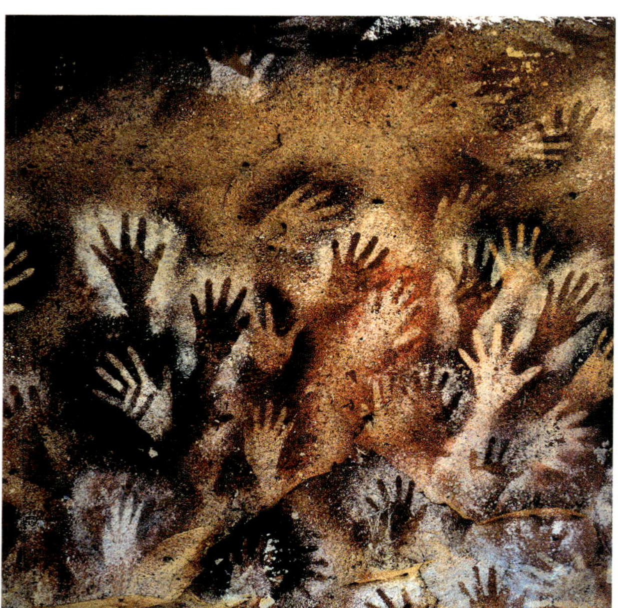

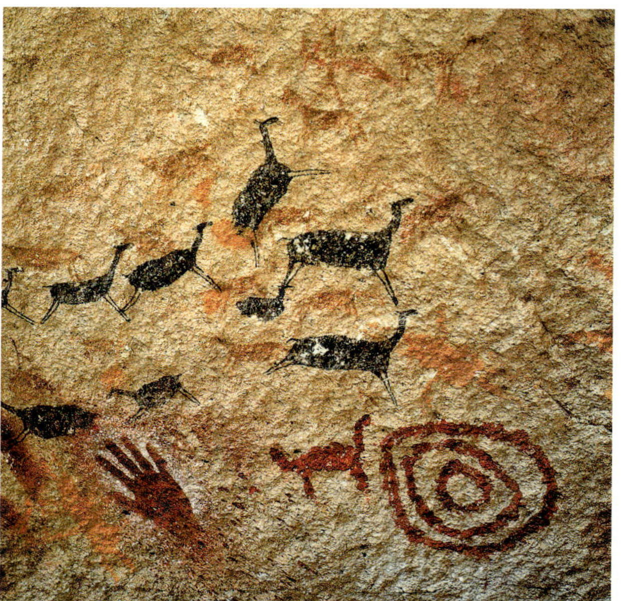

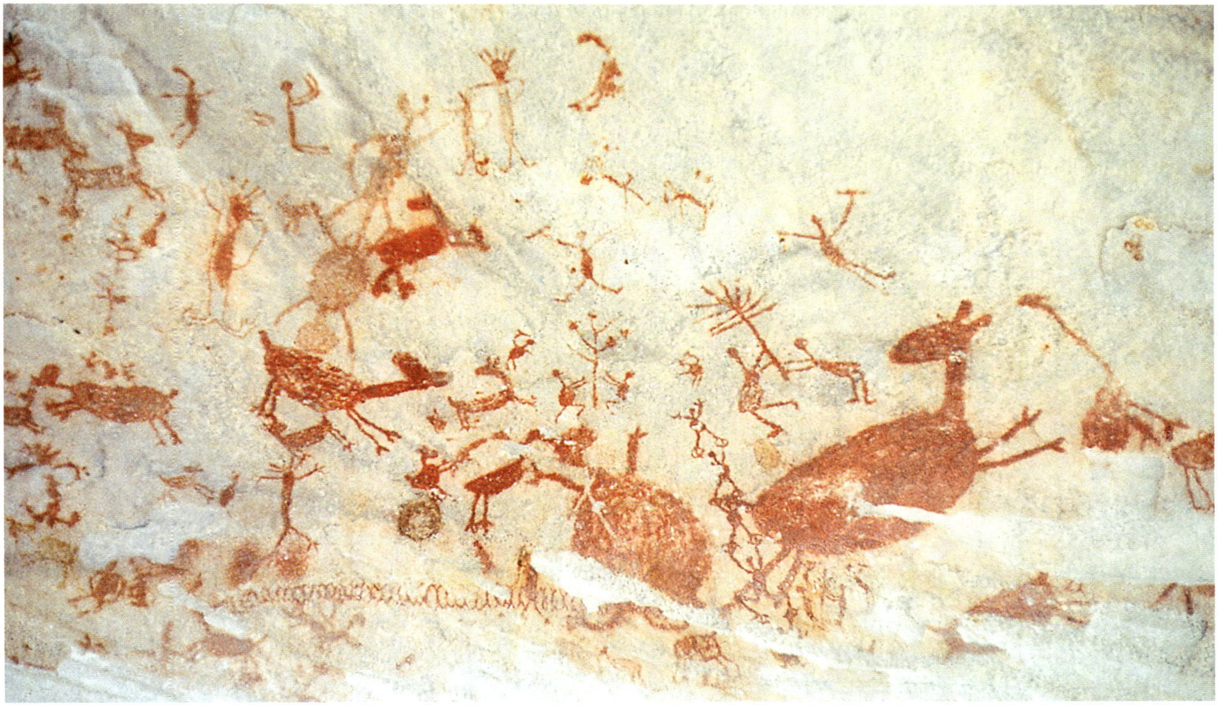

19. **Anonymous**, panel from the Entrada do Pajaú rock shelter,
c. 4000 BCE, Neolithic. Length: 150 cm.
Serra da Capivara National Park, Piauí, Brazil.

20. **Anonymous**, traditional superimposed images and signs from
the Entrada do Pajaú rock shelter, c. 4000 BCE, Neolithic.
Serra da Capivara National Park, Piauí, Brazil.

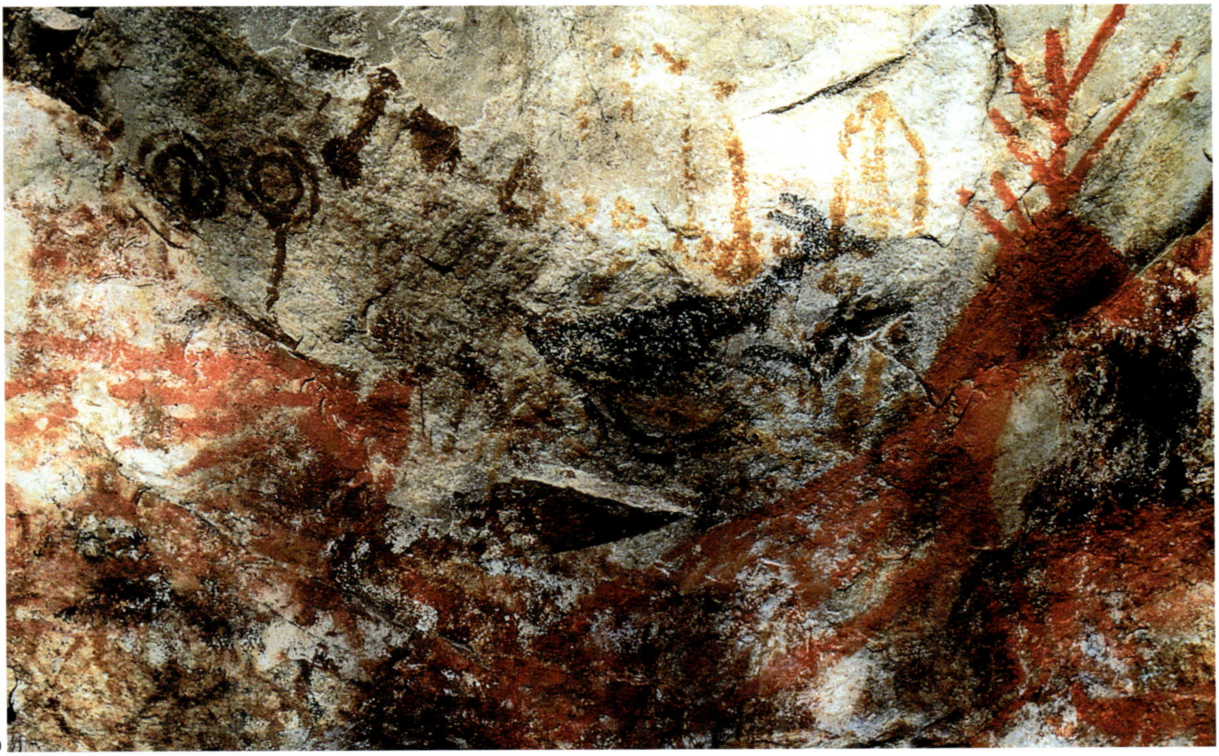

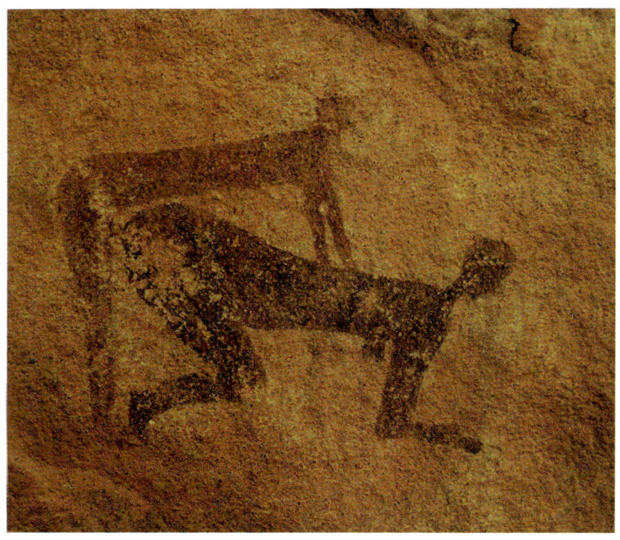

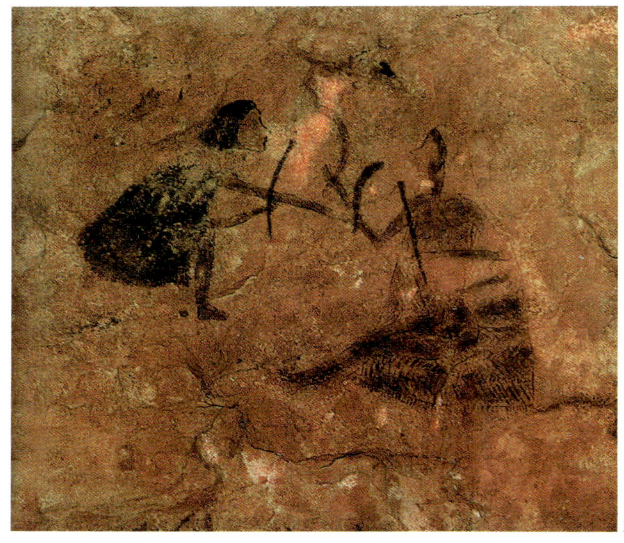

21. **Anonymous**, *The Coupling*, c. 5000-3000 BCE, Neolithic.
Aouanrhet Massif, Libya.

22. **Anonymous**, *Dialogue*, c. 3000-2000 BCE, Prehistoric.
Tadrart Acacus, Libya.

23. **Anonymous**, *Praying Bicoloured Deer*, 2000 BCE, Bronze Age.
Baja California, Mexico.

24. **Anonymous**, *The Black Archer*, Jabbaren site, c. 3000-2000 BCE,
Bronze Age. Length: 20 cm. Tassili n'Ajjer, Algiers.

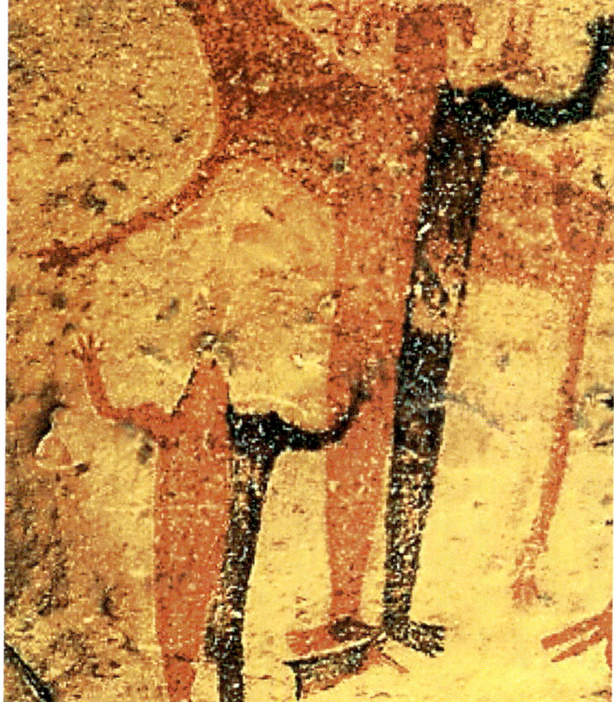

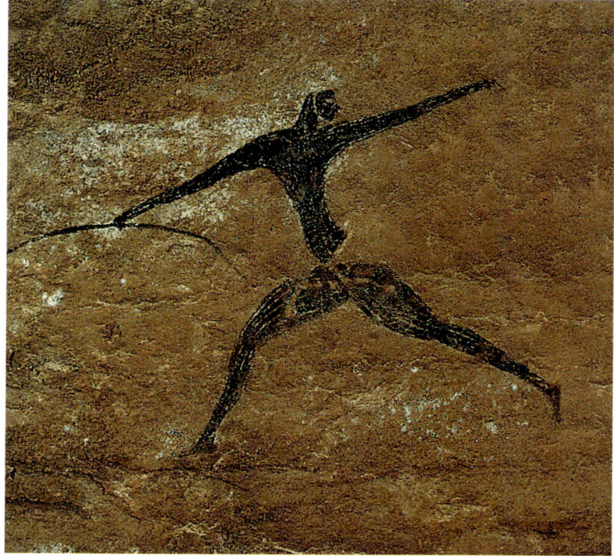

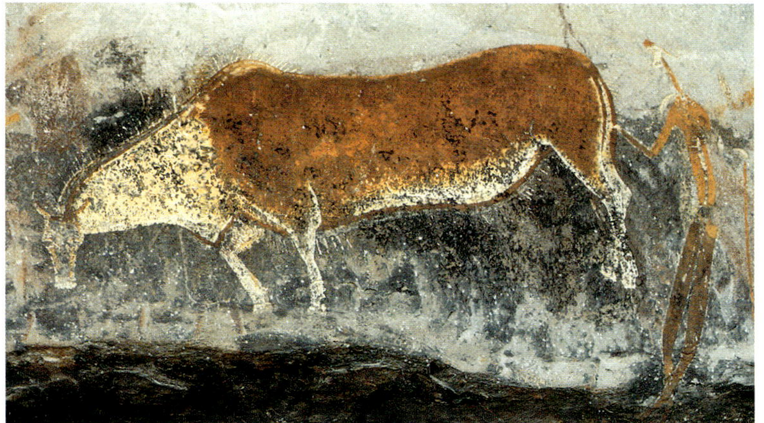

25

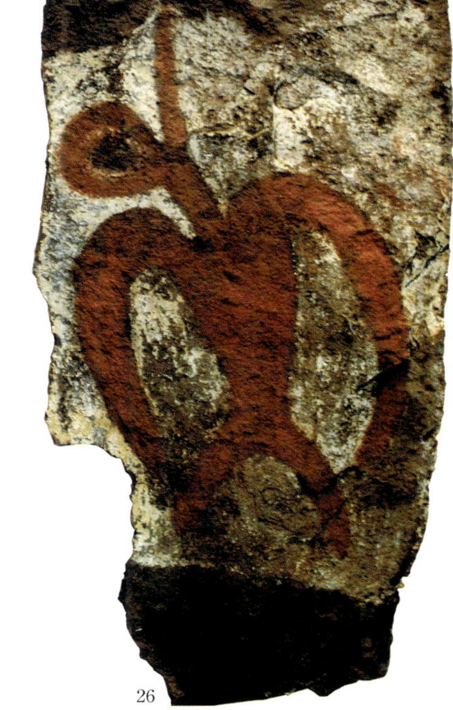

26

25. **Anonymous**, *Scene of the Agony of the Momentum*, c. 1500 BCE,
Bronze Age. Length: 68 cm.
uKhahlamba Drakensberg Park, Kamberg, South Africa.

26. **Anonymous**, *Bird Man Rock Painting*, Bronze Age.
Painted Slab from Orongo Easter Island.

27. **Anonymous**, *The Wedding*, c. 1000 BCE, Bronze Age.
Vitlycke Rock, Tanum, Sweden.

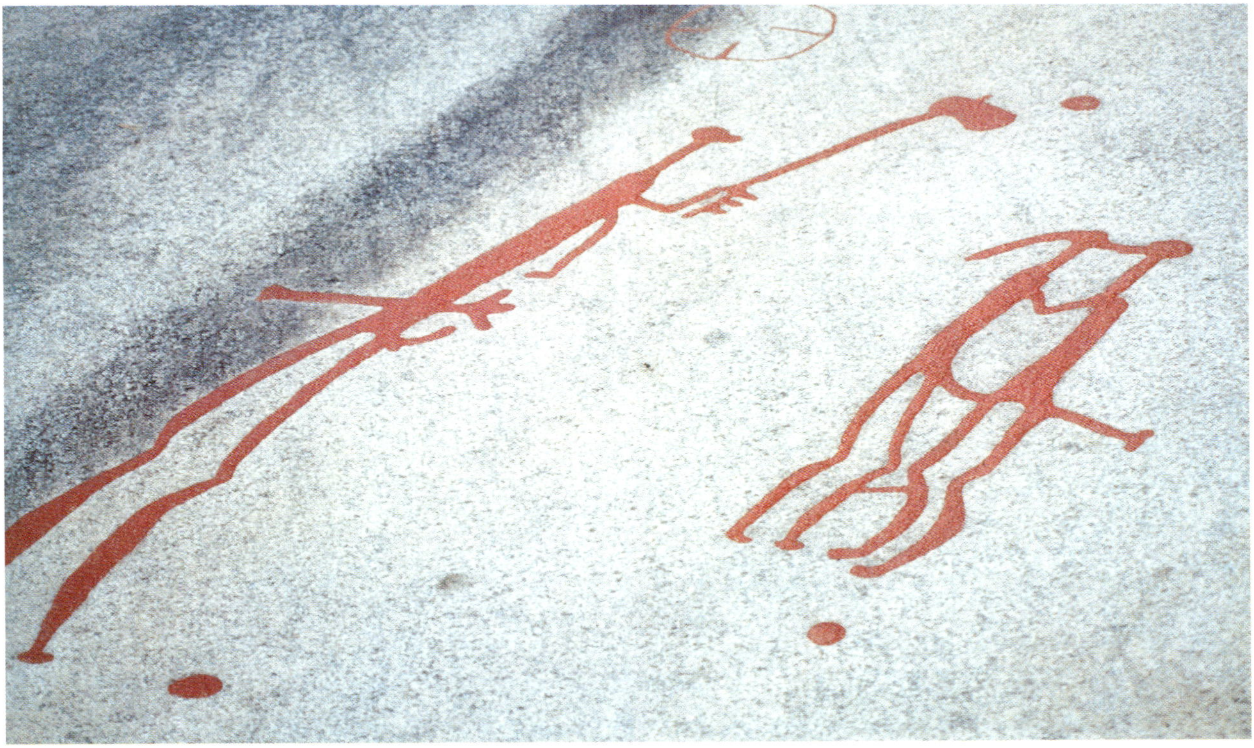

27

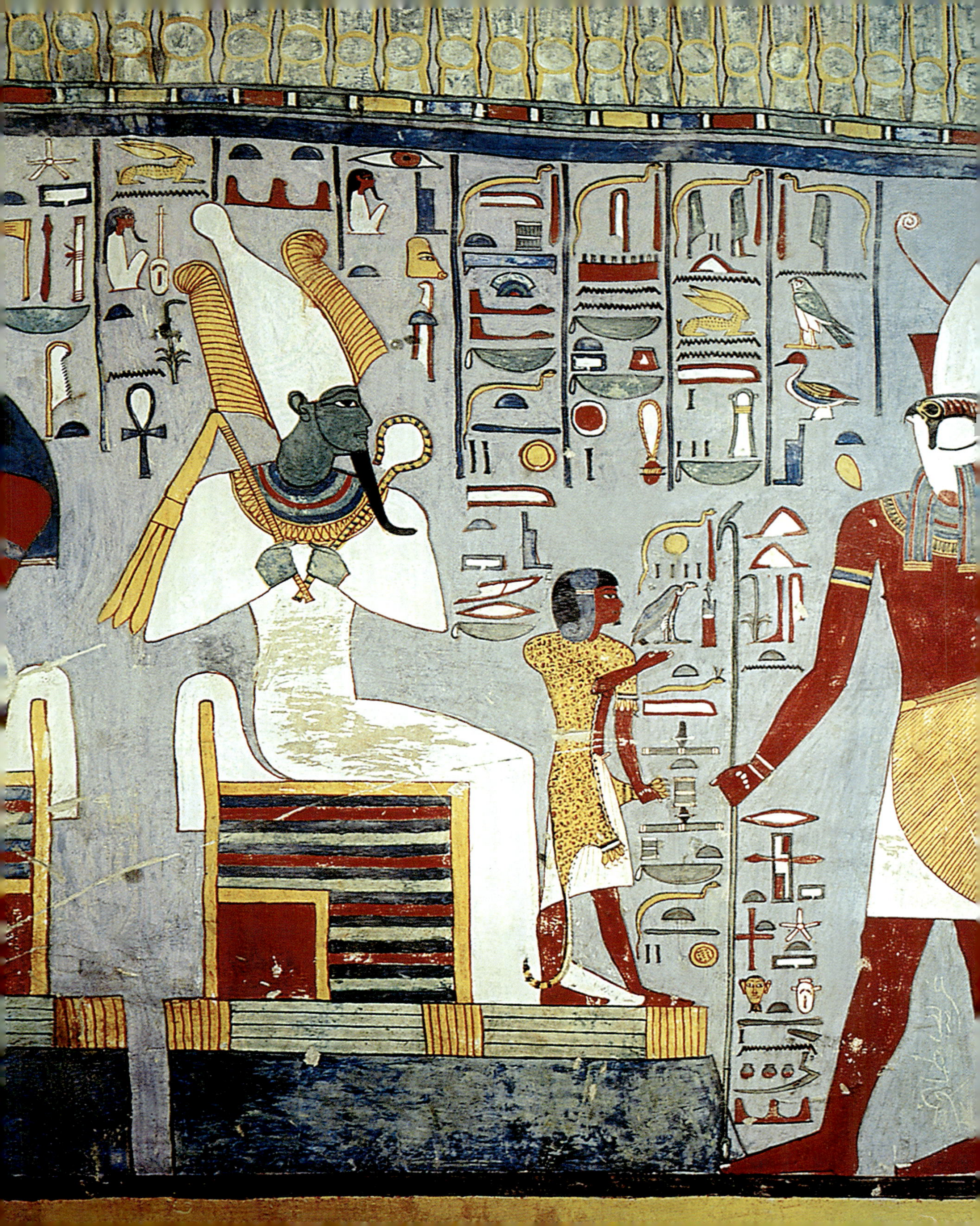

Antiquity

Antiquity, which began with the appearance of the earliest forms of writing, covered more than three millennia. It is the longest period of history experienced by humanity, and reveals the diversity of the great civilisations that evolved within it. In art, the Egyptians played a pioneering role. Indeed, they were among the first to develop a concept of idealised, well-proportioned human figures, and a narrative tradition in painting and relief sculpture. Egyptians also developed an original painting technique, which would later be called egg tempera. Still used today, this method consists of mixing coloured pigments, finely ground and dissolved in water, with a binder such as gum or egg yolk. In the tenth century BCE, despite the influence of other Mediterranean and Near Eastern civilisations – particularly the Egyptian – the ancient Greek civilisation stands out, not only for its cultural but also for its military and political importance. In the arts, there are traditionally three styles, each characteristic of a distinct period: the Archaic, Classical and Hellenistic. Like several other European cultures, the Greeks considered painting the noblest form of art. Their preferred canvas was wood, as the Pitsa panels (No. 69), detailing the scene of a sacrifice, indicate. Unfortunately, although some graves have retained remnants of polychromy, especially in Macedonia, Italy, Alexandria, Cyrene and Thessaly, few traces of Greek painting have survived to this day. Painted pottery constitutes the largest category of remains and provides an interesting insight into contemporary aesthetics. There were four major successive periods, each with an evocative name: the Geometric (900-750 BCE), Oriental (700-625 BCE), Black-figure (600-470 BCE) and Red-figure (around 530 BCE).

Like the timeless canons of Greek relief and sculpture, Greek painting was an inspiration for many people, including the Etruscans – whose paintings, such as those in the tombs of Tarquinia, were mainly ornamental – and, later, the Romans. From the first century BCE, as the result of its military and political success, Rome was on its way to becoming a great power, eventually growing to an empire that extended from Scotland to North Africa and Mesopotamia. Our knowledge of ancient Roman painting comes mainly from frescos on the walls of villas at Pompeii and Herculaneum. The four Pompeian styles define four periods of mural painting. The first, or masonry, style (140-80 BCE) was largely influenced by Hellenistic art, and imitates rich marble mansions. The second is the architectural style (80-15 BCE) and is characterised by decorative *trompe-l'oeil* effects, which transcend the flatness of the walls to create a sense of relief and depth. During the third or ornate style (15 BCE-63 CE), figurative, mythological and landscape paintings bring the walls of houses to life. Finally, the fantasy style (63-79 CE), perfectly illustrated by the Vettii house (Nos. 96, 126, 130), achieved a remarkable and complex fusion of architectural and decorative styles.

During the last few centuries of its existence the Roman Empire went into military, economic, cultural and moral decline. In 313 CE, Emperor Constantine established freedom of worship through promulgation of the Edict of Milan, as the result of which, Christians, long persecuted in the empire, became accepted. With Christianity established as the state religion, Roman art developed a strong religious imagery that led to the Early Christian style.

28. **Anonymous**, *Burial Chamber and Tomb of Ramses I*, Valley of the Kings, XIX Dynasty (1320-1200 BCE), Ancient Egyptian. Egyptian Museum, Cairo.

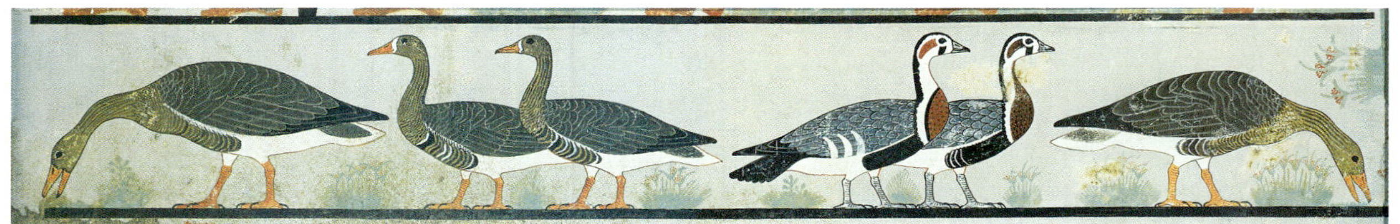

29. **Anonymous**, *Meidum Geese*, 4th Dynasty (2694-2563 BCE),
Ancient Egyptian. Painted limestone, 27 x 172 cm.
Atete grave, Meidum.

Discovered in the mastaba of the vizier and his wife Nefermaat Itet by Auguste Mariette in 1871, the famous Meidum Geese were part of a scene of birds captured with nets. Going back to the era of Snefru (4th Dynasty, 2670-2450 BCE), this frieze is one of the oldest and most distinctive of Egyptian wall paintings. The stylised design, attention to detail and application of colours in areas on a layer of stucco over a coating of earth show features of major frescos that will appear later. The goose is a symbol of vigilance and an announcement of imminent danger; accentuated by its divergent symmetry, the scene illustrates the destruction of evil forces.

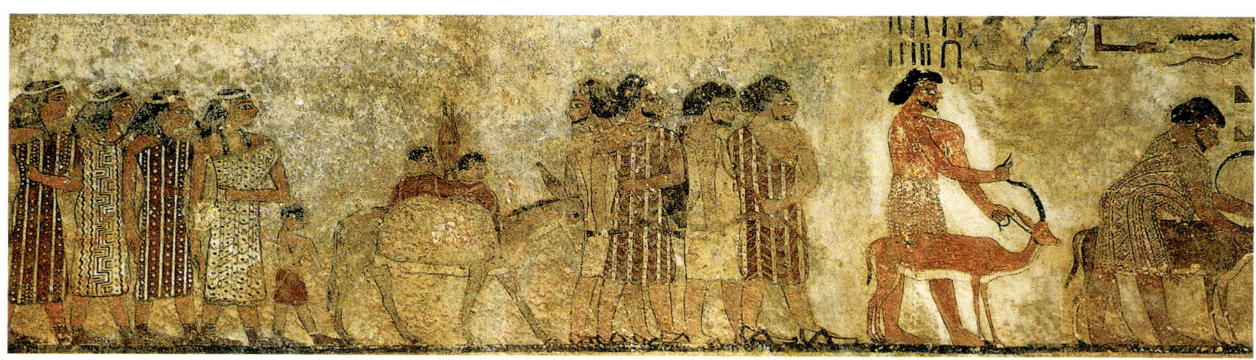

30. **Anonymous**, *Caravan of Asians*, 12th Dynasty (1991-1786 BCE).
Ancient Egyptian. Khnoumotep III grave, Beni Hasan.
Egyptian Museum, Cairo.

31. **Anonymous**, *Musicians and Dancers*, 5th Dynasty (2563-2364 BCE),
Ancient Egyptian. Saqqara.
Painted limestone, length: 154 cm.
Egyptian Museum, Cairo.

32. **Anonymous**, *The Slaughter of an Ox*, 1st Intermediate Period
(2181-2060 BCE), Ancient Egyptian.
Tomb of Iti, Gebelein. Height: 58 cm.
Museo Egizio, Turin.

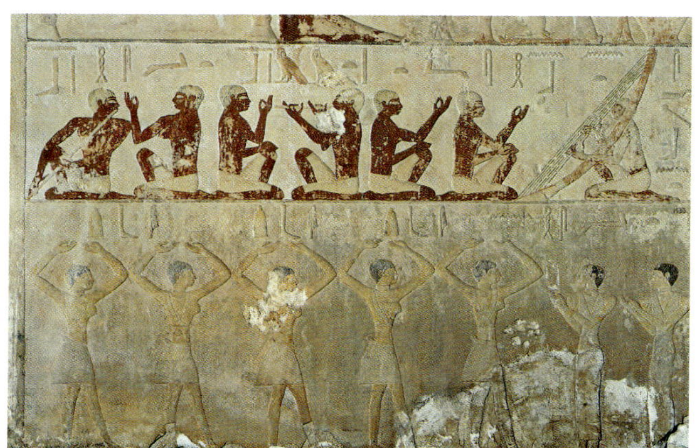

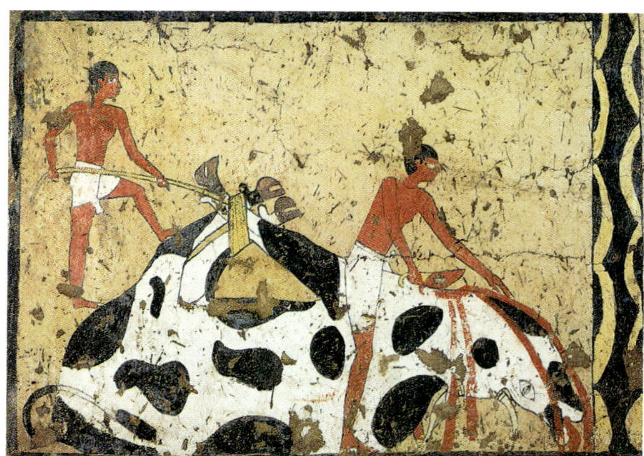

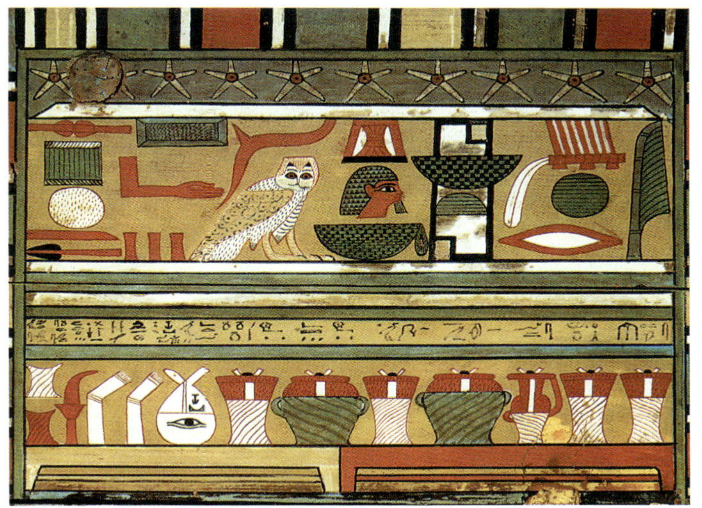

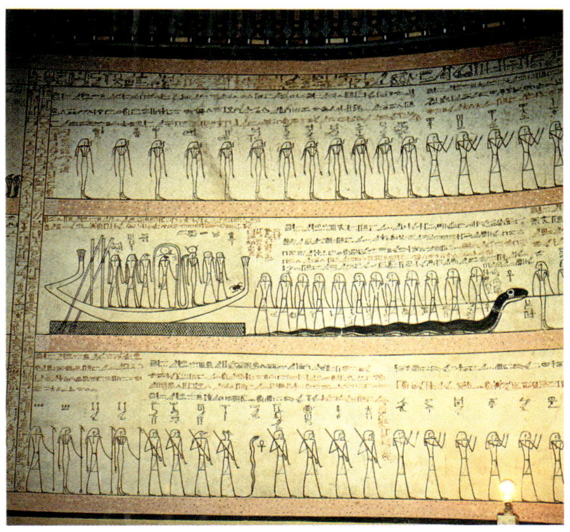

33. **Anonymous**, Detail of the decoration of a sarcophagus,
    12th Dynasty (1991-1786 BCE), Ancient Egyptian. El Bersheh.
    Sarcophagus: 70 x 233 x 65 cm. Egyptian Museum, Cairo.

34. **Anonymous**, Burial chamber,
    18th Dynasty (c. 1570-1320 BCE), Ancient Egyptian.
    Tomb of Tuthmosis III, Valley of the Kings, near Luxor.

35. **Anonymous**, Wall decoration,
    18th Dynasty (c. 1570-1320 BCE), Ancient Egyptian.
    Tomb of Tuthmosis IV, Valley of the Kings, near Luxor.

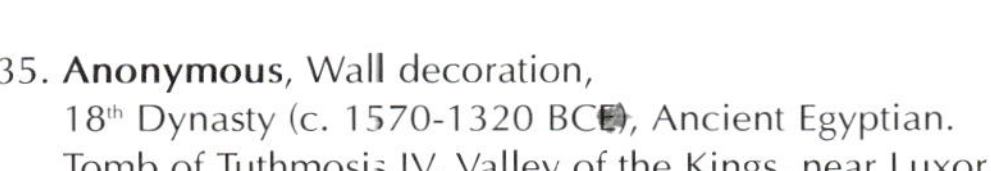

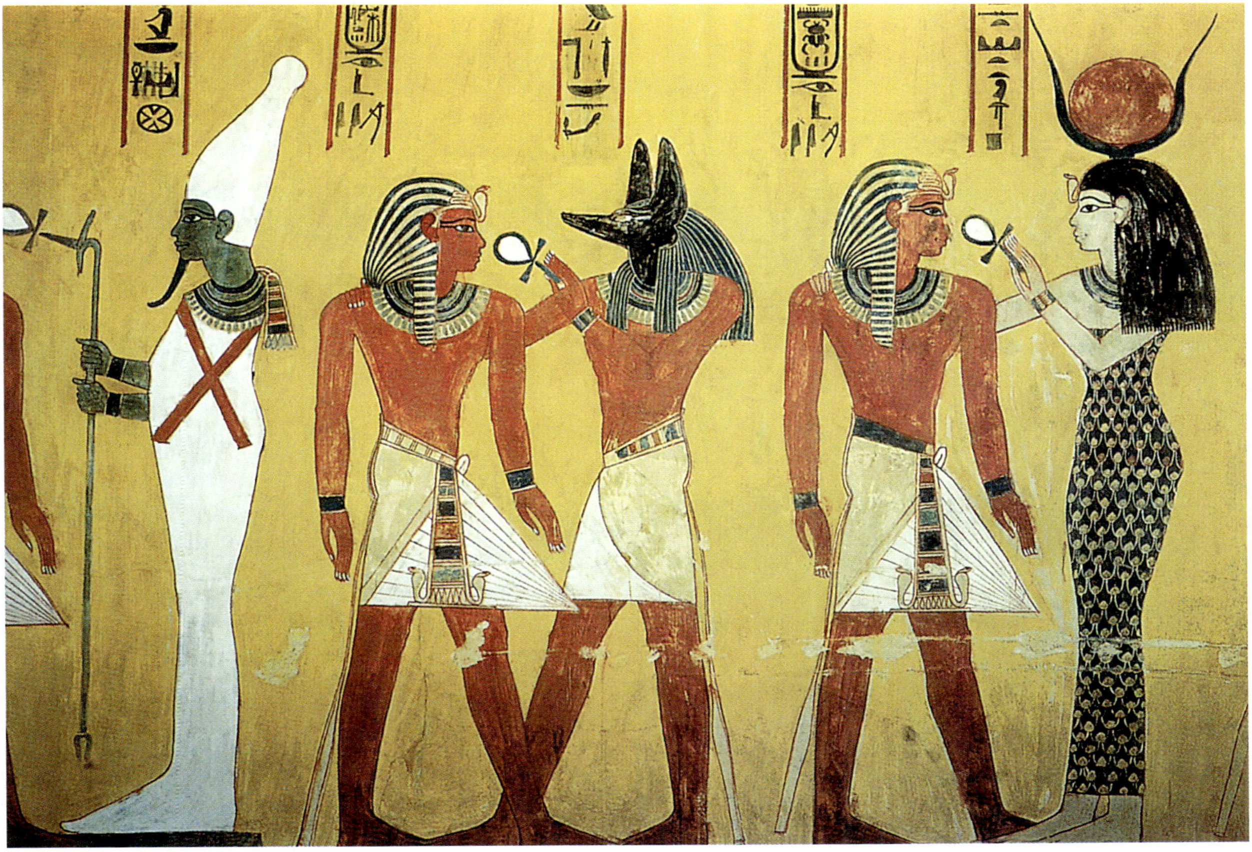

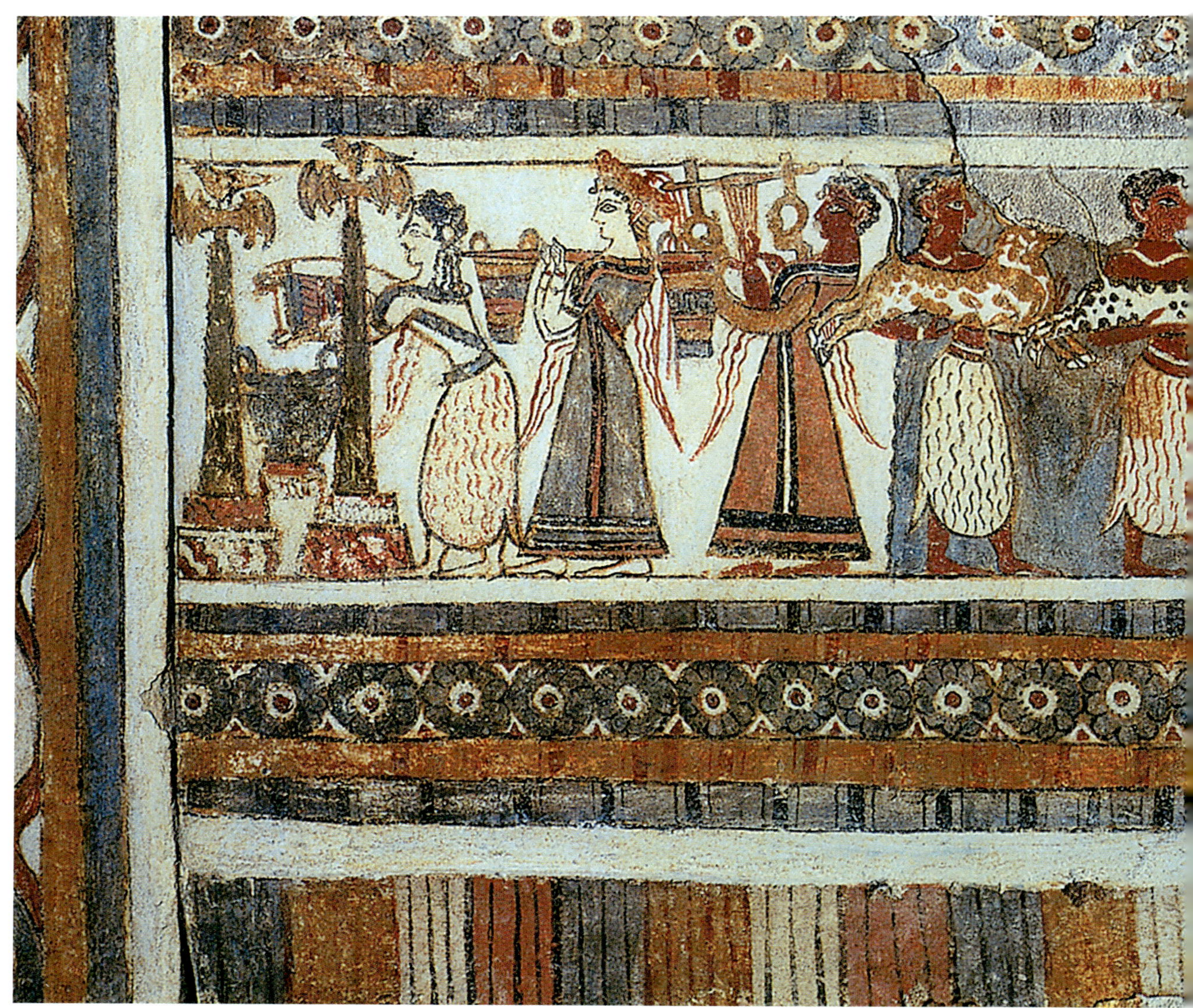

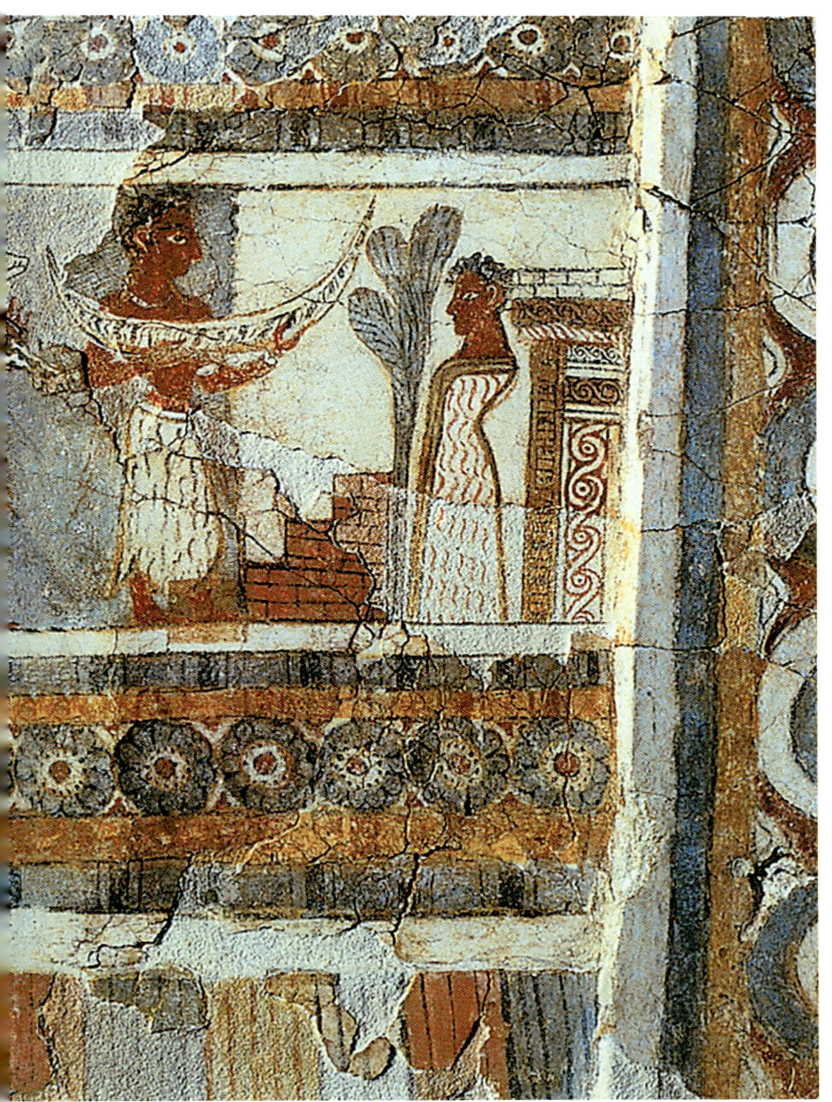

36. **Anonymous**, Religious scene,
    1450-1400 BCE, Ancient Greek.
    Hagia Triada. Terracotta.
    Archaeological Museum of Heraklion,
    Heraklion.

*Hagia Triada or Agia Triada, which means
the Holy Trinity in Greek, is a Minoan
archaeological site close to Phaistos, Crete,
which contains the remains of a complex of
buildings, including lavish homes, antique
piping, and tombs. In these villas several
fragments of fresco have been discovered,
which, when restored, provided an idea of
the decorations that once adorned the walls
of palaces and houses. This sarcophagus,
discovered in the early nineteenth century
by Italian archaeologists, is painted with
scenes of a funeral ritual and reflects, among
other things, Cretan life at the time. The
votive tablet is a rare preserved example of
Greek painting depicting an expressive
sacrificial scene. The followers, easily
identifiable by the crowns on their heads,
approach the altar to make offerings.*

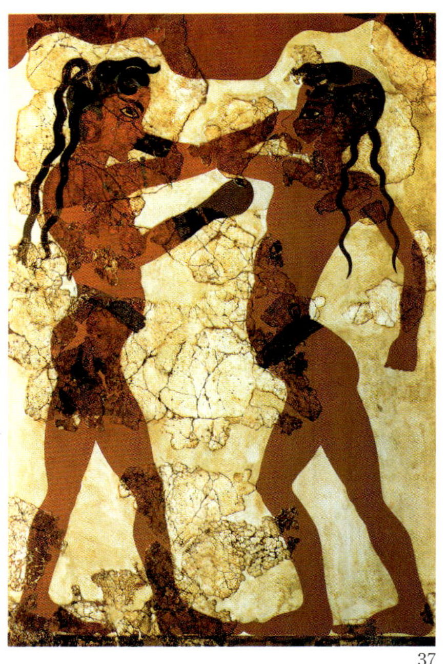
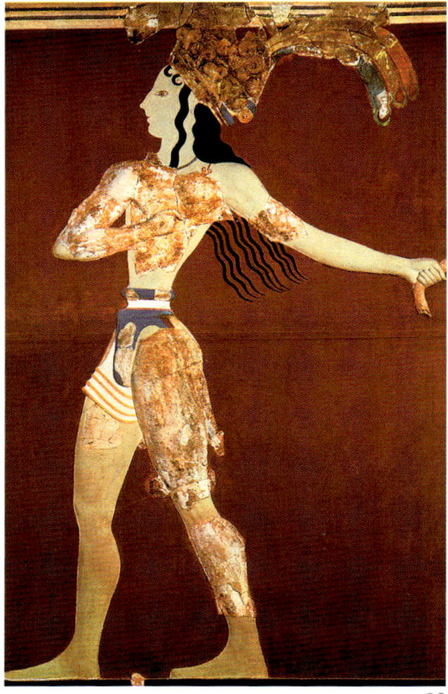
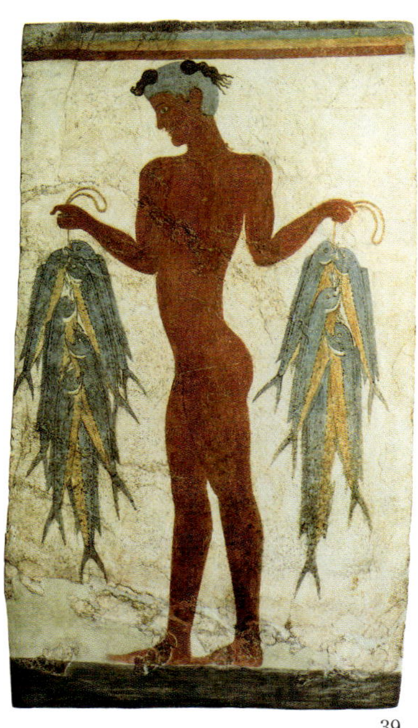

37
38
39

37. Anonymous, Fight scene between two boys, 16th century BCE,
Ancient Greek. Thera. Fresco, 275 x 94 cm.
National Museum of Athens, Athens.

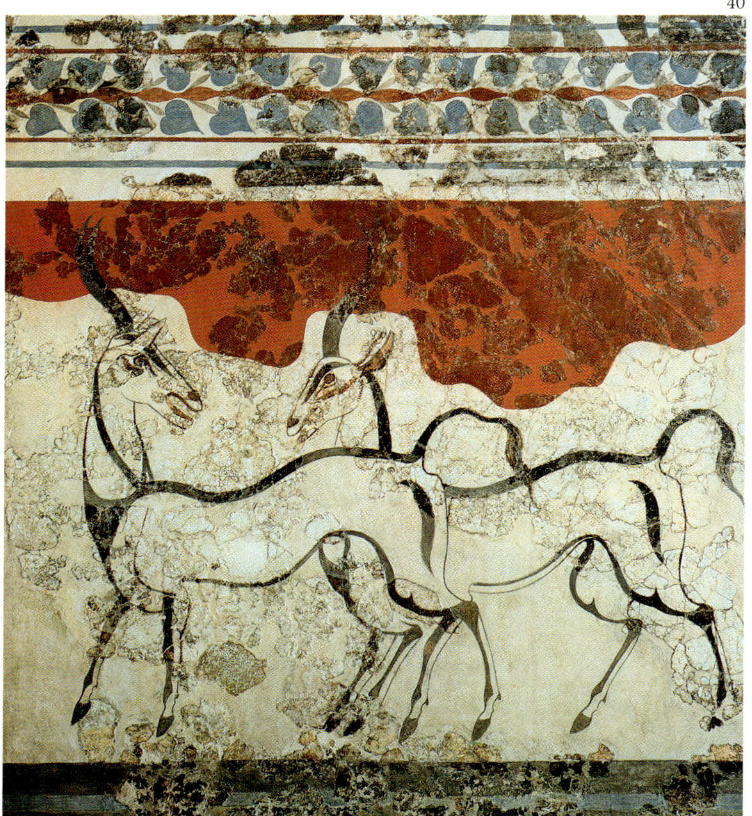

40

38. Anonymous, *Prince of the Lilies*, 1700-1400 BCE,
Ancient Greek. Palace of Knossos. Crete. Fresco.
Archaeological Museum of Heraklion, Heraklion.

39. Anonymous, *The Fisherman*, c. 1550-1500 BCE,
Ancient Greek. Thera. Fresco.
National Museum of Athens, Athens.

*The frescoes of Akrotiri were discovered in 1970
on the ancient Greek island of Santorini in the
Cyclades archipelago, and are the oldest known
wall paintings in Europe. As well as an important
source of information on human activities and
domestic environments of the time, these paintings
demonstrate great artistic freedom, as evidenced by
the fisherman. Discovered in the West House of
the Akrotiri excavation site, it shows a young naked
man, probably returning from a successful fishing
trip, presenting his catch as an offering strung on
strings by the gills. Such a young man, whose
shaved head and hat denote the religious character
of the scene, is extremely rare in Minoan art.*

40. Anonymous, *The Antelopes*, c. 1550-1500 BCE,
Ancient Greek. Thera. Fresco, 275 x 200 cm.
National Museum of Athens, Athens.

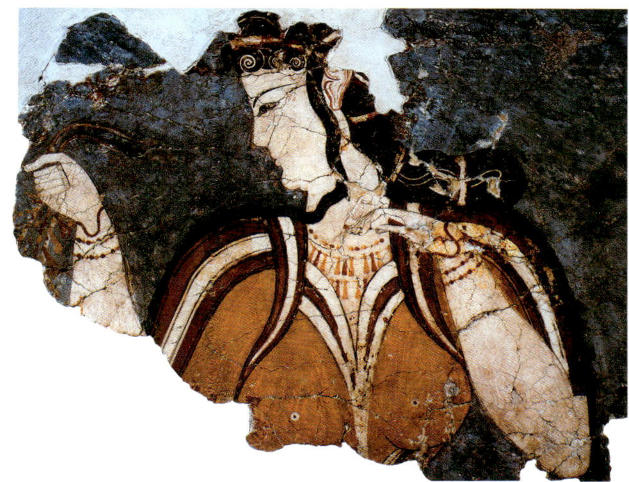

41. **Anonymous**, *The Queen of Mycenae*,
Pre-Hellenic, 12th century BCE, Ancient Greek. Mycenae. Fresco.
National Museum of Athens, Athens.

*The ancient city of Mycenae, located on a hill north east of the
plain of Argos in the Peloponnese, was surrounded by cyclopean
walls, that is to say, huge blocks assembled to form a defensive
barrier. The city was discovered during excavations in the late
nineteenth century, but it was not until the beginning of the
twentieth century that the Mycenaean civilisation was properly
identified and separated from Minoan civilisation. The Queen of
Mycenae is a fresco dating from the twelfth century BCE, and
represents the Mycenaean pantheon of goddesses. She is richly
dressed and coiffed, and accepts a necklace as a gift. The scene
is a testimony of the religious practices of the time, though the
Mycenaean cult is far from being elucidated.*

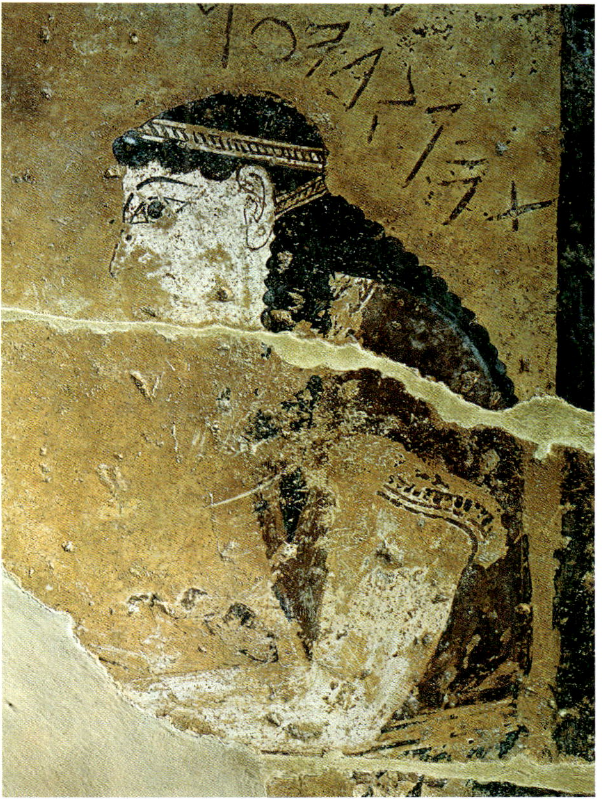

42. **Anonymous**, *Chelidon*, second half of the 7th century BCE,
Ancient Greek. Temple of Apollo, Thermos. JC clay painted,
height: 88 cm. National Museum of Athens, Athens.

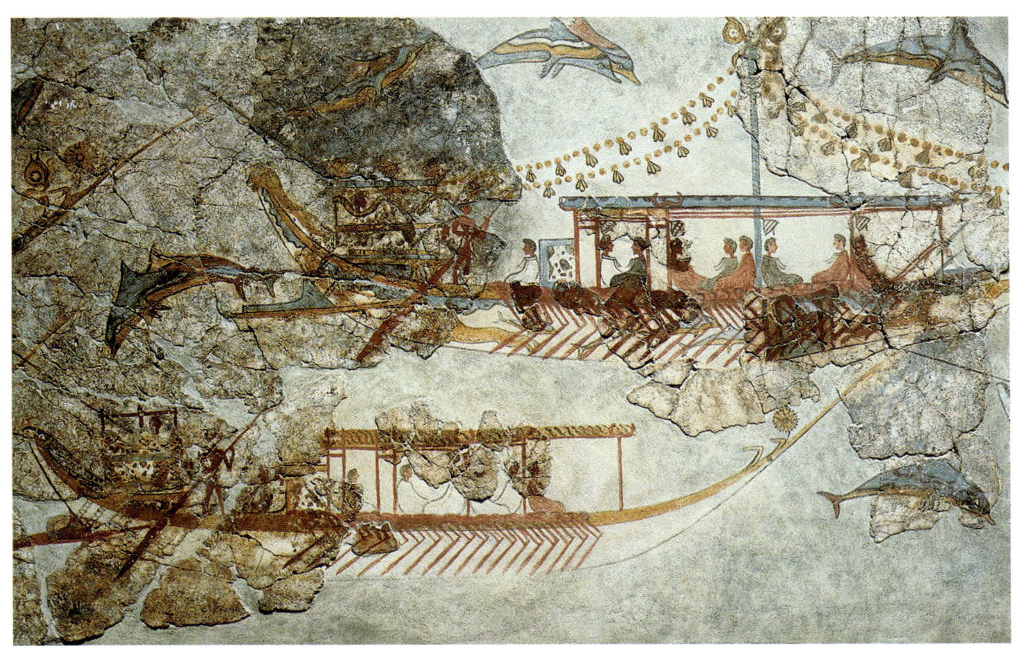

43. **Anonymous**,
Departure of Ships,
c. 1550-1500 BCE,
Ancient Greek. Thera.
Fresco, 43 x 390 cm.
National Museum of
Athens, Athens.

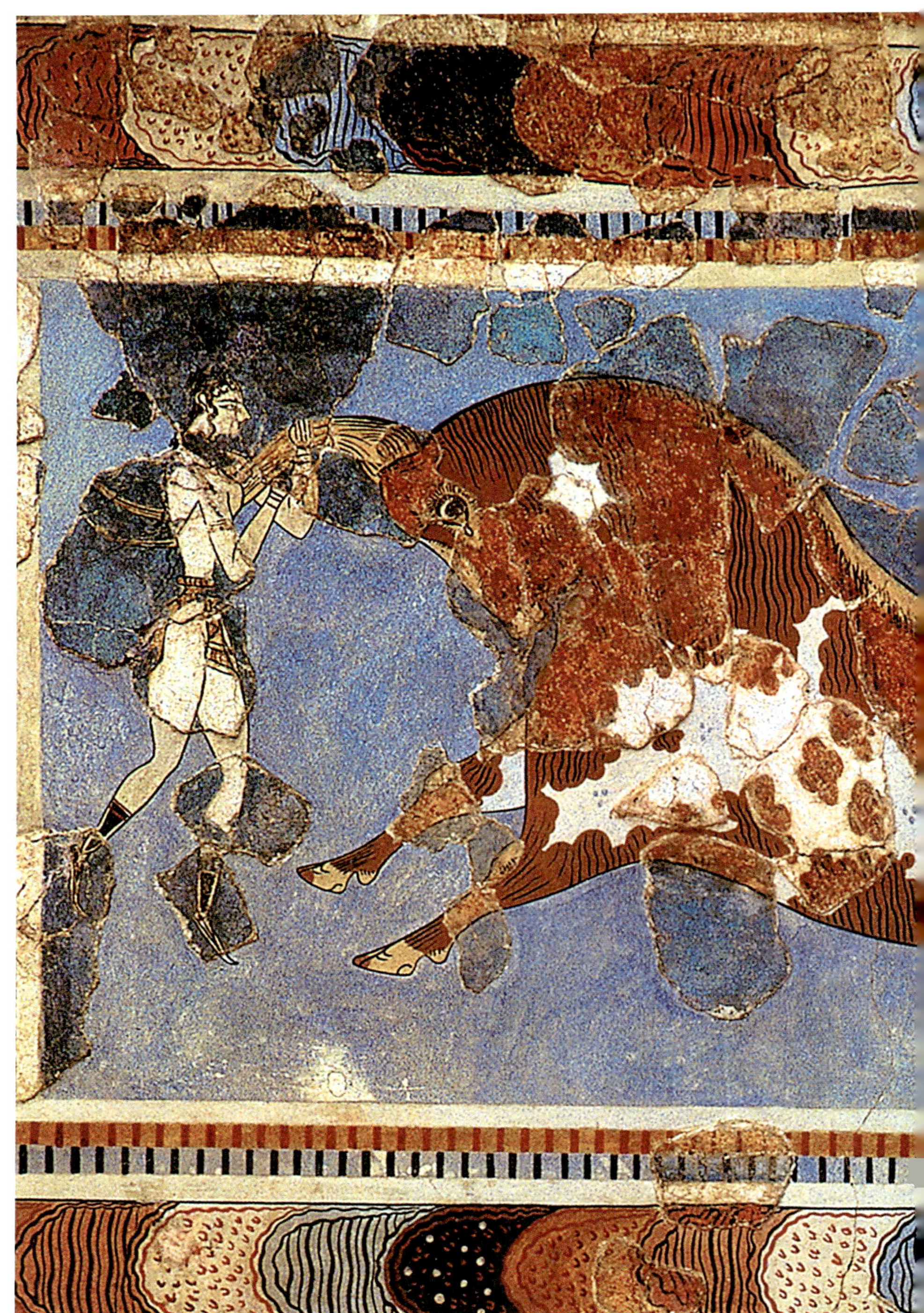

44. **Anonymous**,
Bullfighting Scene,
1700-1400 BCE,
Palace of Knossos, Crete.
Fresco, length: 62.3 cm.
Archaeological Museum of
Heraklion, Heraklion.

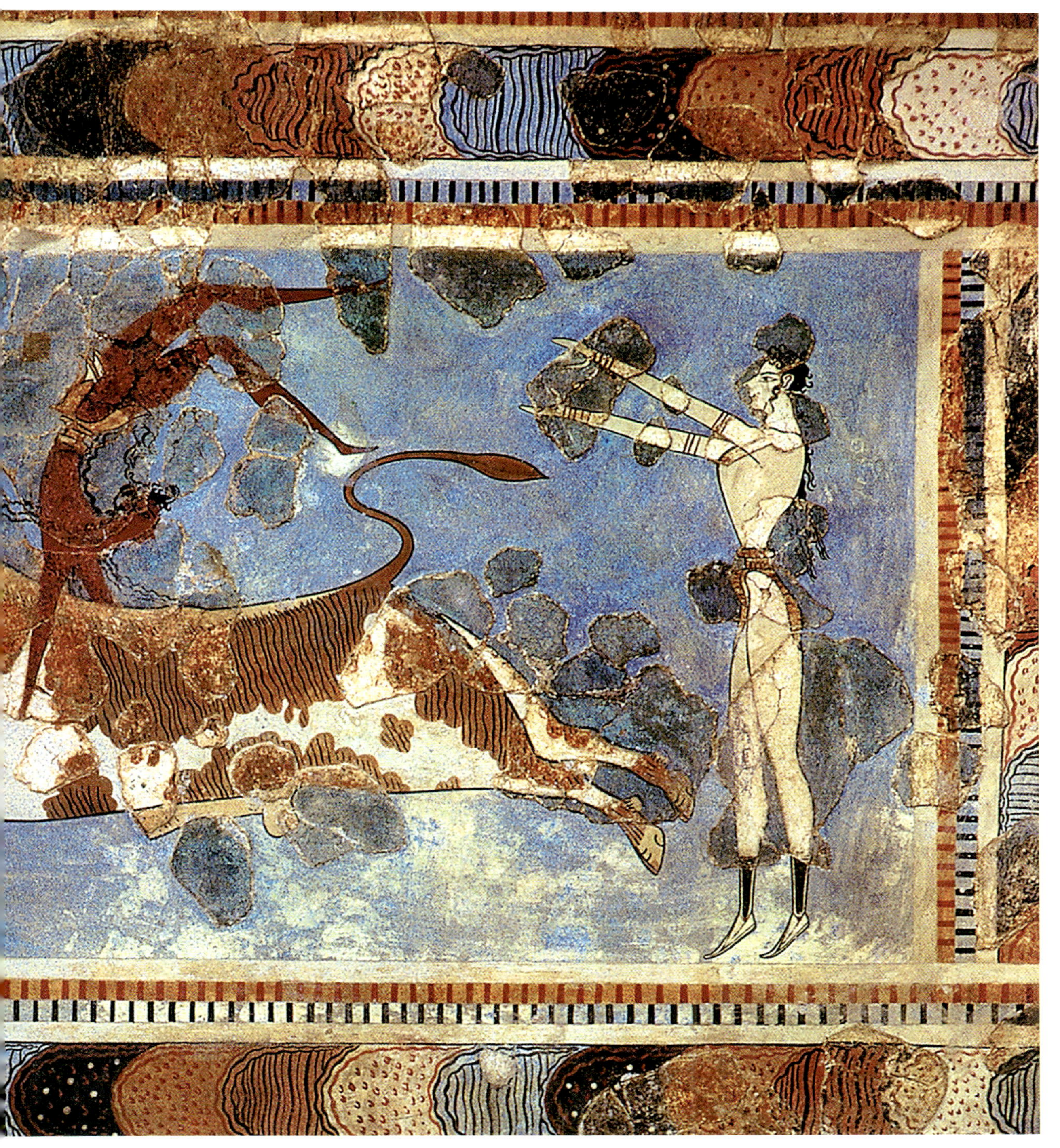

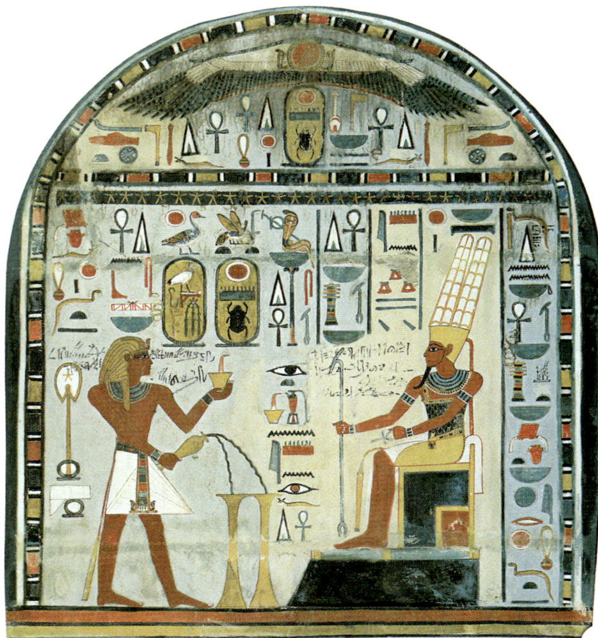

45. **Anonymous**, *The Queen of the Mountain Temples of Hatshepsut and Mentuhotep Deir el-Bahari*,
18th Dynasty (c. 1570-1320 BCE), Ancient Egyptian.
Egyptian Museum, Cairo.

46. **Anonymous**, *Nebamon Hunting in the Marshes*,
end of the 18th Dynasty (c. 1570-1320 BCE), Ancient Egyptian.
Nebamon Tomb, Thebes. The British Museum, London.

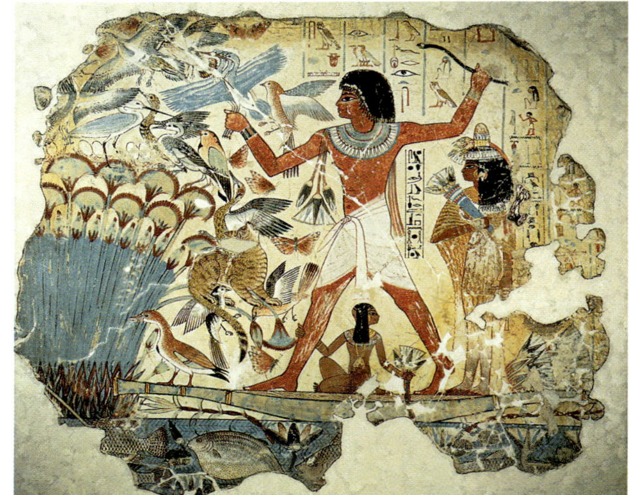

47. **Anonymous**, *The Joy of Living*,
18th Dynasty (c. 1570-1320 BCE), Ancient Egyptian.
Malgatta. Egyptian Museum, Cairo.

46

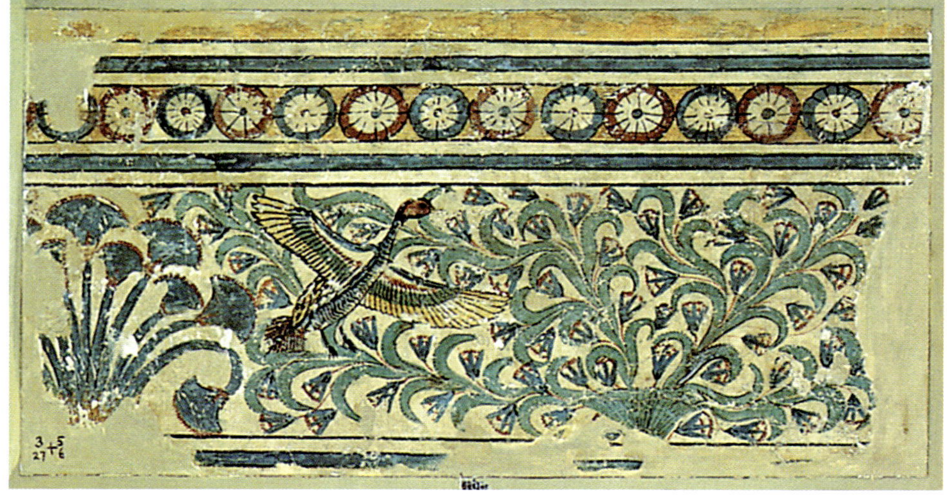

47

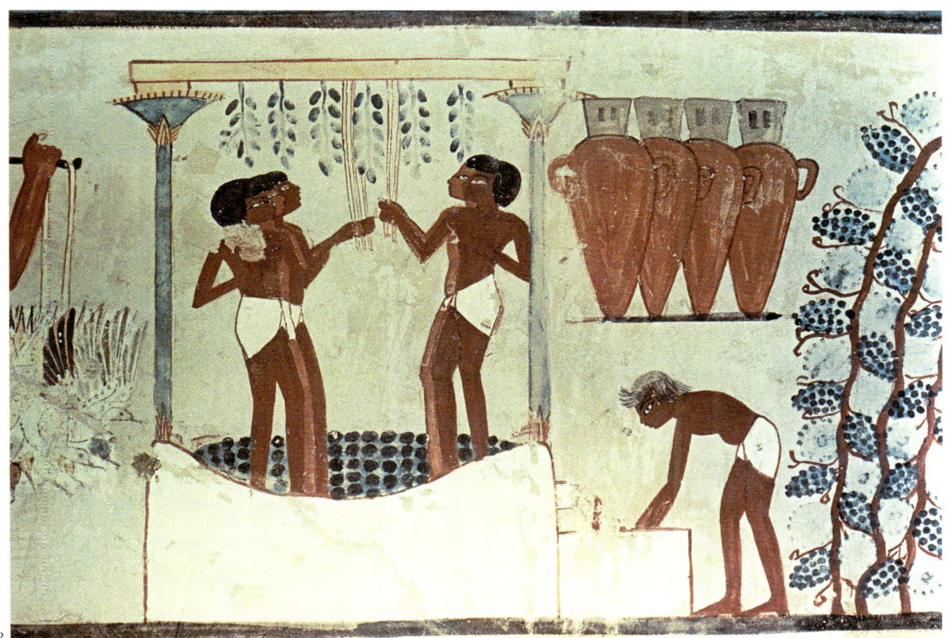

48

48. **Anonymous**, *The Pressing*, 18th Dynasty (c. 1570-1320 BCE), Ancient Egyptian. Nakht Tomb, Sheikh Abd el-Qurna, probably created during the reign of Tuthmosis IV (1425-1405 BCE), western Thebes, near Luxor.

49. **Anonymous**, *The Barbers*, 18th Dynasty (c. 1570-1320 BCE), Ancient Egyptian. Tomb of Userhat, Sheikh Abd el-Qurna, near Luxor.

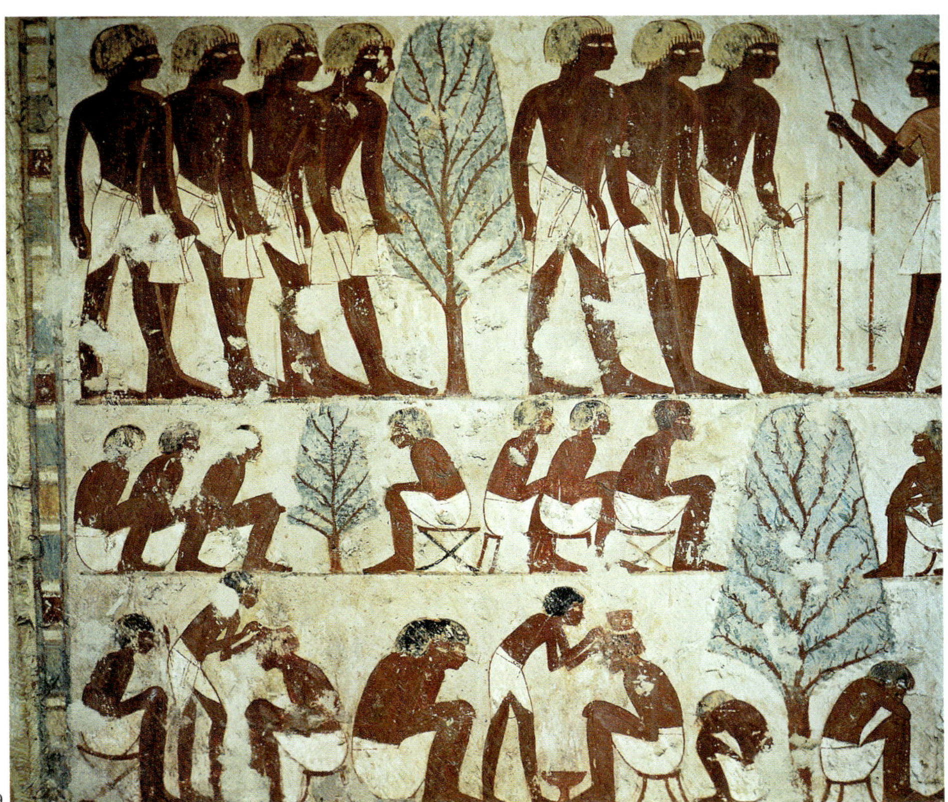

49

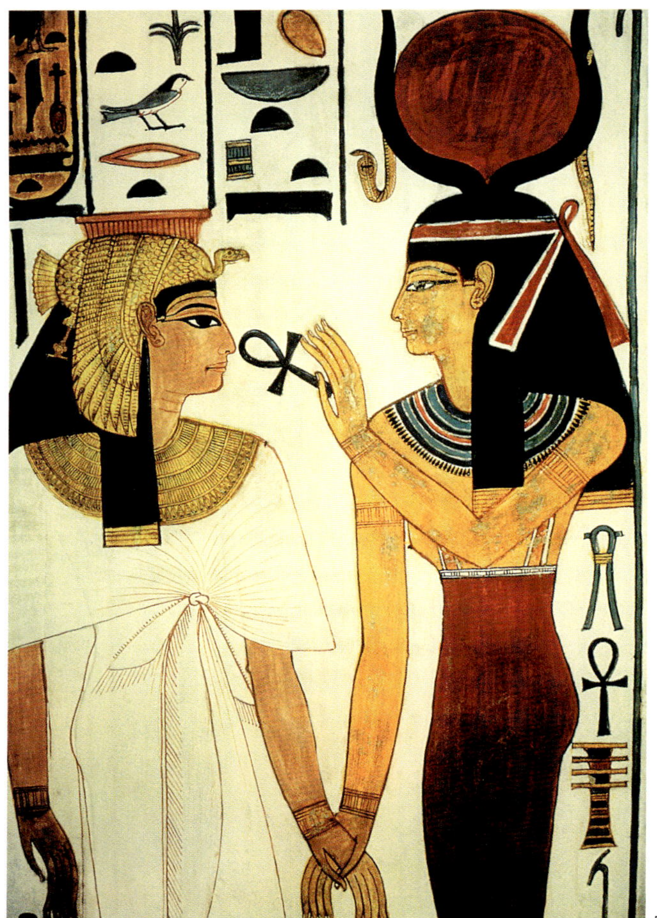

50

51. **Anonymous**, *Love of Music*, 18th Dynasty (c. 1570-1320 BCE),
Ancient Egyptian, probably reign of Tuthmosis IV (1425-1405 BCE).
Thebes, near Luxor.

52. **Anonymous**, *Anubis* (mummified), 19th Dynasty (1320-1200 BCE),
Ancient Egyptian.
The deceased's grave, Sennedjem, Deir el-Medina, near Luxor.

*This ancient Egyptian tomb, which belonged to a master craftsman
of the necropolis during the reigns of Seti I and Ramses II, was
discovered in 1886. Exceptionally, the tomb had not been plundered
and all its funerary equipment was intact. A mass grave, in which
three generations of the same family were buried, it was decorated
with colourful paintings and was surprisingly well preserved. The
inspiration was essentially religious, depicting the deceased and his
wife, together with various deities. Here, the body is lying on a
leonine patterned bed (head, tail and legs). Anubis, who is associated
with a funeral cult and protection of the deceased, prepares the latter
for his final journey.*

50. **Anonymous**, *Isis and Nefertari*, 19th Dynasty (c. 1320-1200 BCE),
Ancient Egyptian.
Nefertari Tomb, Meryenmout, Valley of the Queens, near Luxor.

*Nefertari was the first great royal wife of Ramses II. Her name
means 'the beautiful is back', and she was the most influential of
the pharaoh's wives. Discovered in 1904, the tomb created for
her is known for its magnificent murals, and is undoubtedly the
finest example of the style of that period and worthy of a
pharaoh. The tomb contains scenes, sometimes with a short
text, illustrating chapters from the Book of the Dead. In the
antechamber, Chapter 17, relating to the regeneration of the
deceased at dawn, is illustrated on the west and north walls.
Chapter 148, spread out on a large scale over several levels,
adorns the south wall of the first annexed chamber. This scene
takes place in the death chamber, which is 90 square metres in
size. Three different parts are juxtaposed for offerings. After having
performed a journey of initiation, Nefertari, who is related to the
goddess Hathor and was deified in her lifetime – an extremely
rare occurrence – finally meets Isis who offers her the ankh, the
symbol of eternal life.*

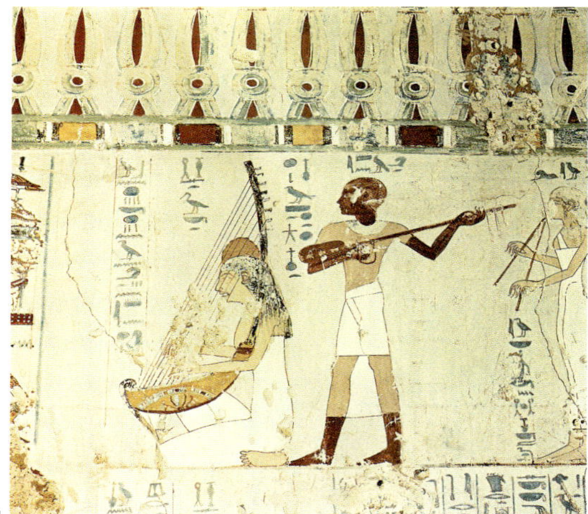

51

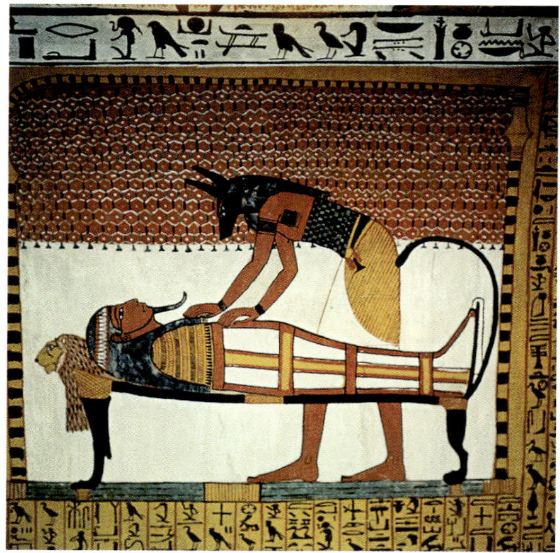

52

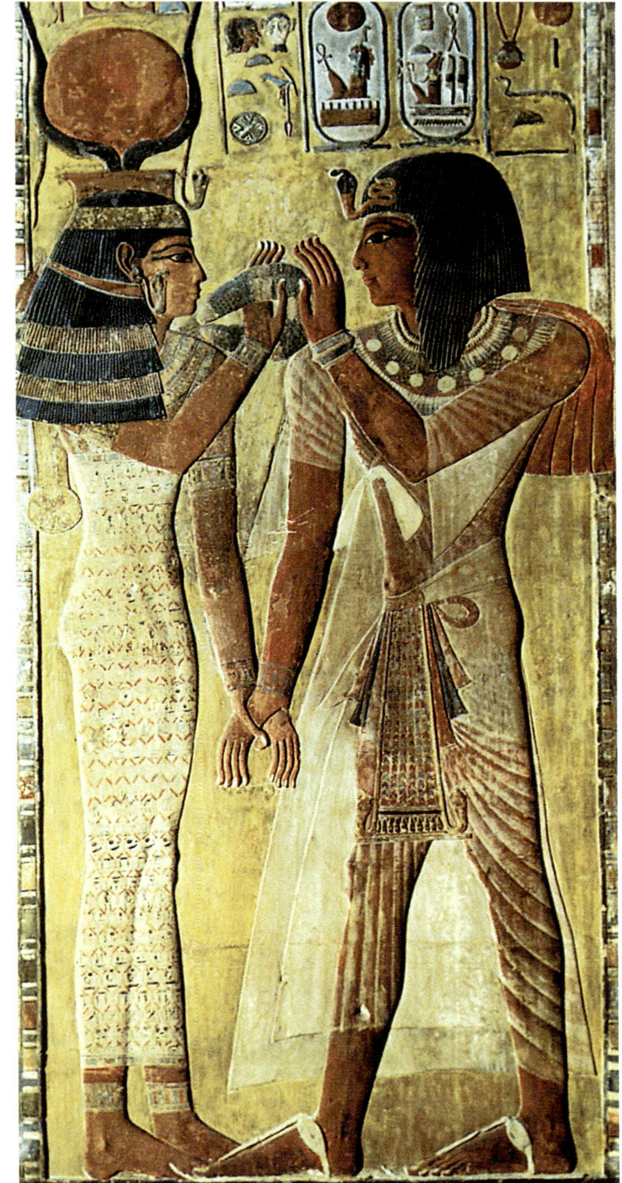

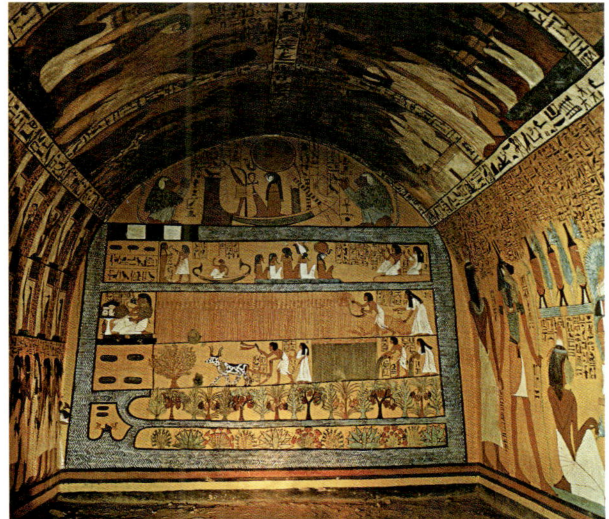

54. **Anonymous**, *The Fields of Iarou*,
19th Dynasty (c. 1320-1200 BCE), Ancient Egyptian.
Sennedjem Tomb, Deir el-Medina, near Luxor.

53. **Anonymous**, *Protection of Hathor*,
19th Dynasty (c. 1320-1200 BCE), Ancient Egyptian.
Tomb of Seti I, Valley of the Kings.
Painted limestone, 226.5 x 105 cm. Musée du Louvre, Paris.

This tomb of Seti I, built during his lifetime, was discovered in 1817. It shows a completely new design unique in its bipartite arrangement, whereby the upper and lower parts of the tomb are separated. Moreover, the decoration painted on the walls is entirely in relief. Here, Hathor, goddess of love and festivities, also considered to be the 'eye' of Re, welcomes Seti I to his new kingdom. It was also her duty to bring heavenly food to the dead of the underworld, and to touch the necklace of the deceased pharaoh. This gesture of touch is associated with milk, fertility and protection; it also aids the deceased in their passage to the afterlife and gives access to eternal life. The garments of the two characters are adorned and reflect the refinement and art of the reign of Seti I. The divine hairstyle is sophisticated and the jewels show the colours of the precious materials with which they were made (gold, silver, lapis lazuli, turquoise and carnelian). If the symmetry of the characters is typical of Egyptian art, the joined hands is quite unusual.

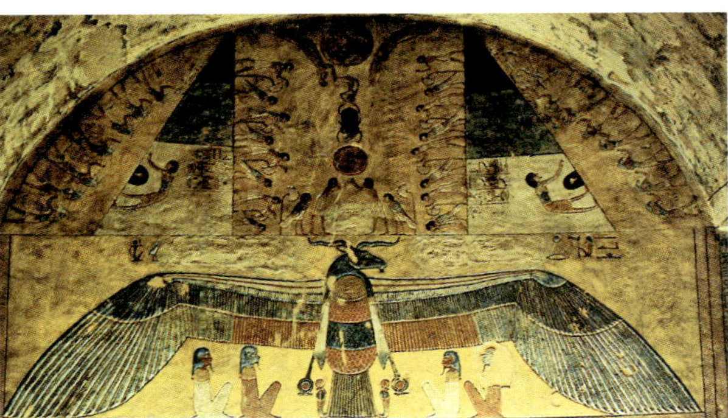

55. **Anonymous**, Room of the sarcophagus, 19th and 20th Dynasties
(c. 1320-1085 BCE), Ancient Egyptian.
Tomb of Tausert and Sethnakht, Valley of the Kings, near Luxor.

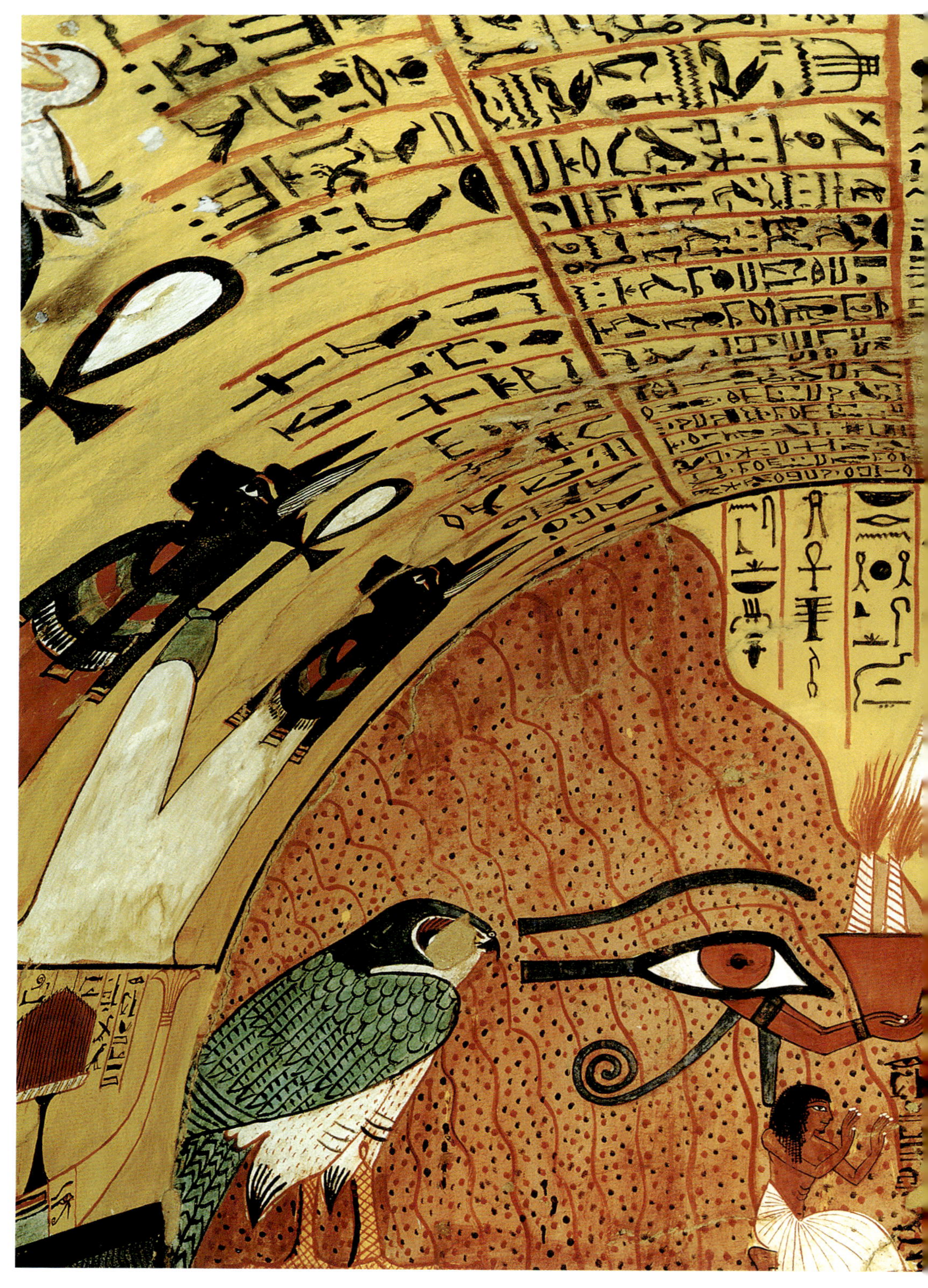

56. **Anonymous**, Mural, 19th Dynasty (c. 1320-1200 BCE), Ancient Egyptian.

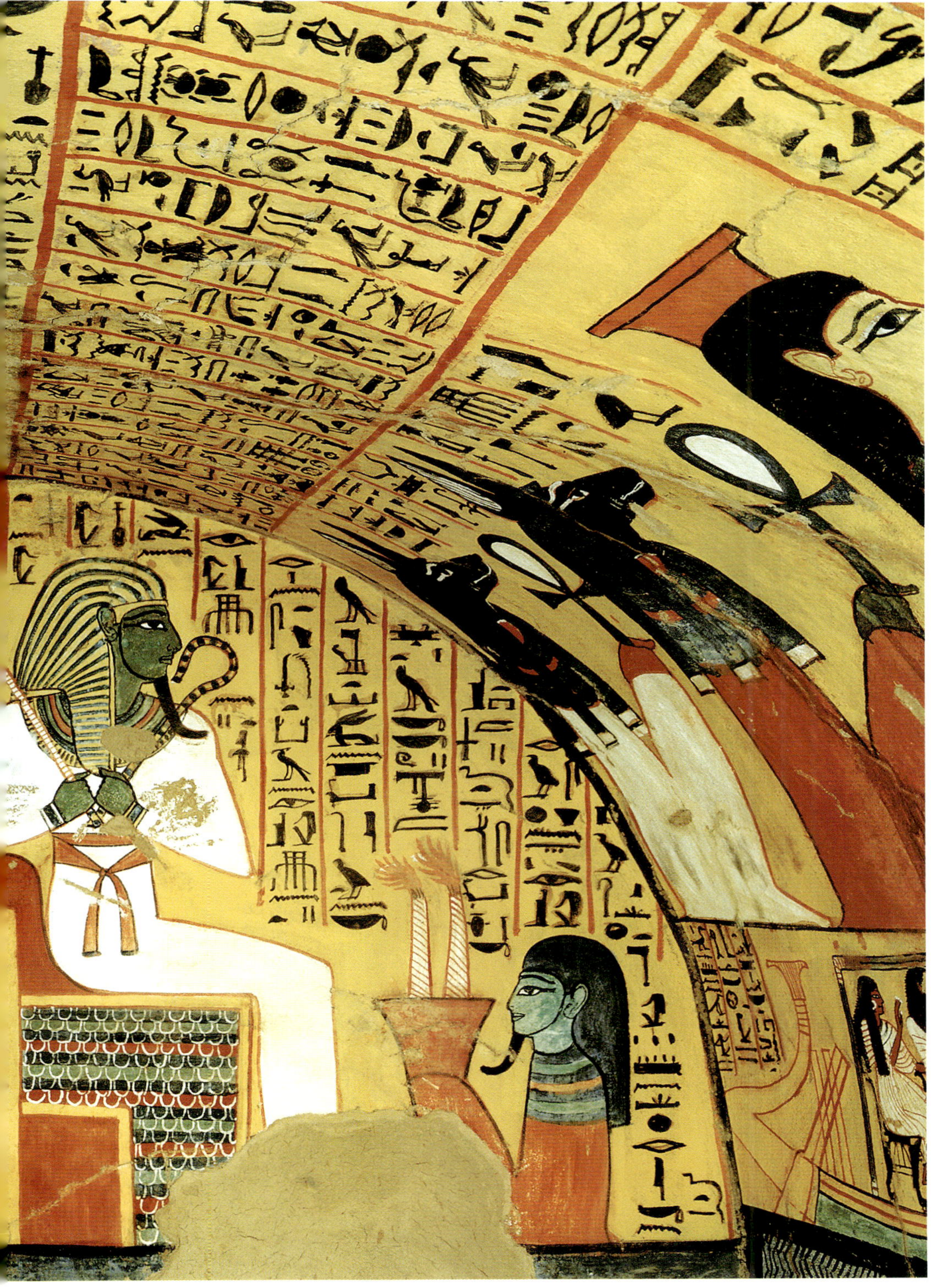

Tomb of Pached, Deir el-Medina, near Luxor.

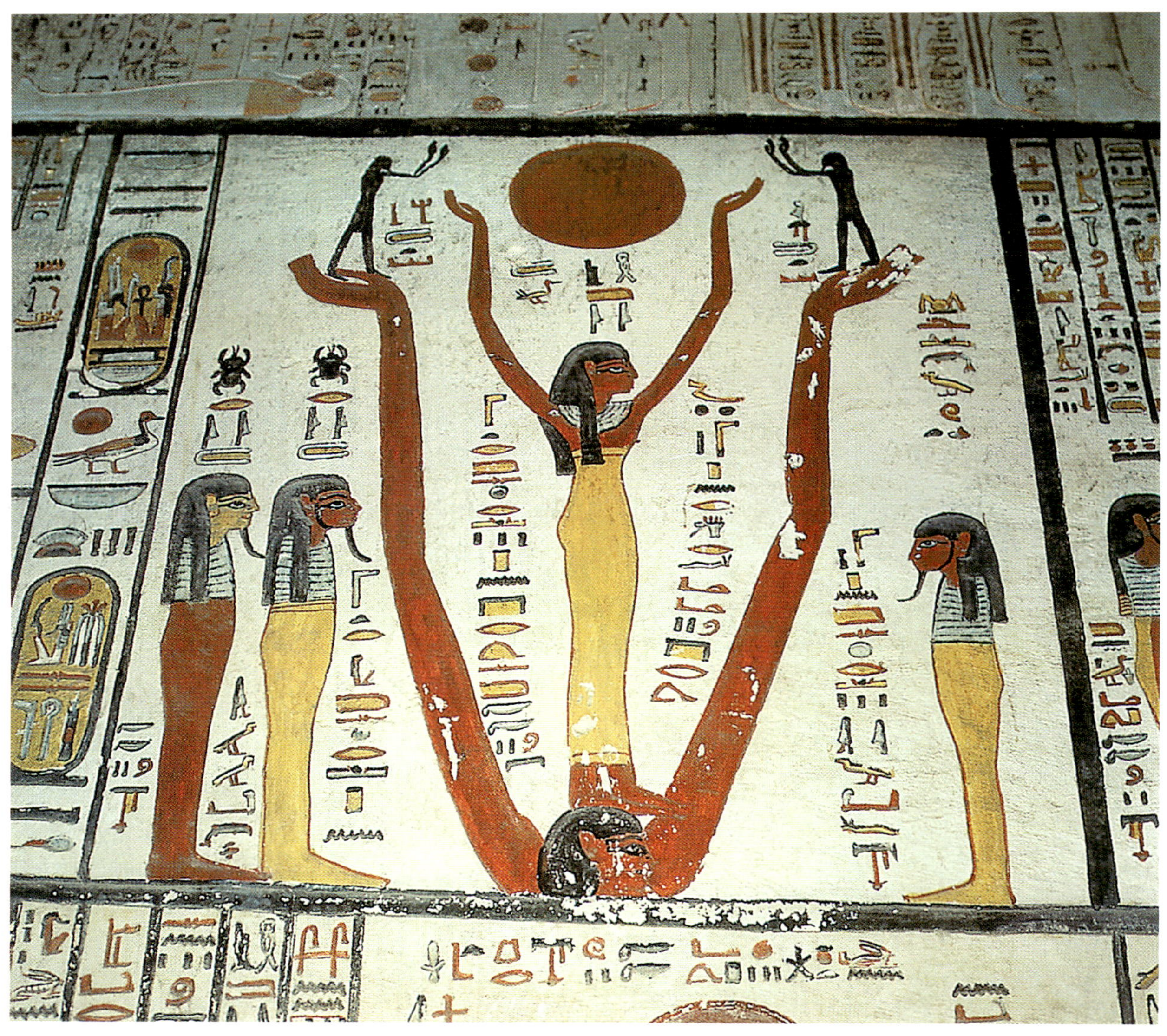

57. **Anonymous**, *The Elevation of the Solar Disc*,
20th Dynasty (c. 1200-1085 BCE), Ancient Egyptian.
Tomb of Ramses V and Ramses VI, Valley of the Kings, near Luxor.

The painted decoration of the Tomb of Ramses VI, originally designed for Ramses V, is of remarkable complexity. It shows various books of ancient Egypt, such as the Book of Doors and Caves, the Book of the Cow from Heaven and even the famous Book of the Dead. In the hall of the sarcophagus, which is decorated with wall frescos, themes from the mysterious Book of the Earth or Aker can be found. A divinity of ancestral origin, Aker was required to open the doors of the Earth so that the boat of Ra could access the lower world. On the right side of the same wall, there is a new representation of the goddess Nut. Goddess of Creation, she absorbs the solar disk every night and raises it every morning by moving up her arms from the depths of the underworld, which is the scene represented here. Her limbs, on both sides of the disc, symbolise the east and west. As a guardian of the dead, she is frequently represented on tombs.

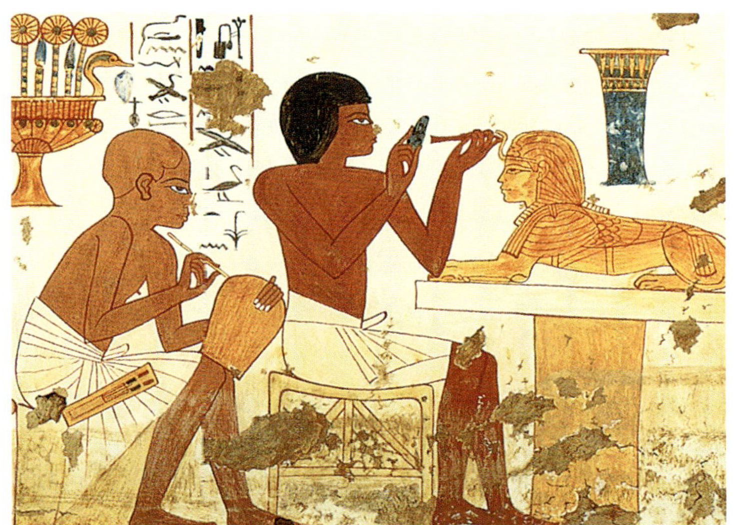

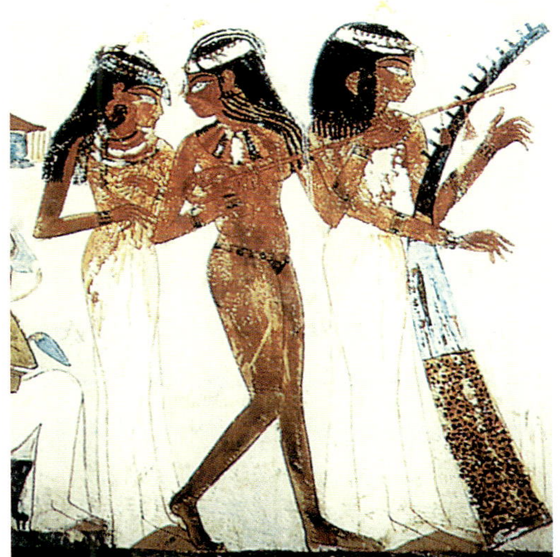

58. **Anonymous**, *Artisan Working on an Egyptian Golden Sphinx*,
c. 1380 BCE, Ancient Egyptian.
Thebes. The British Museum, London.

59. **Anonymous**, *Celebration*,
18th Dynasty (c. 1570-1320 BCE), Ancient Egyptian.
Nakht Tomb, Sheikh Abd el-Qurna, probably reign of
Tuthmosis IV (1425-1405 BCE), near Luxor.

60. **Anonymous**, *Weighing of the Heart and Trial by Osiris*, from
the Book of the Dead of Hunefer, 1275 BCE, Ancient Egyptian.
Painted papyrus, height: 39 cm. The British Museum, London.

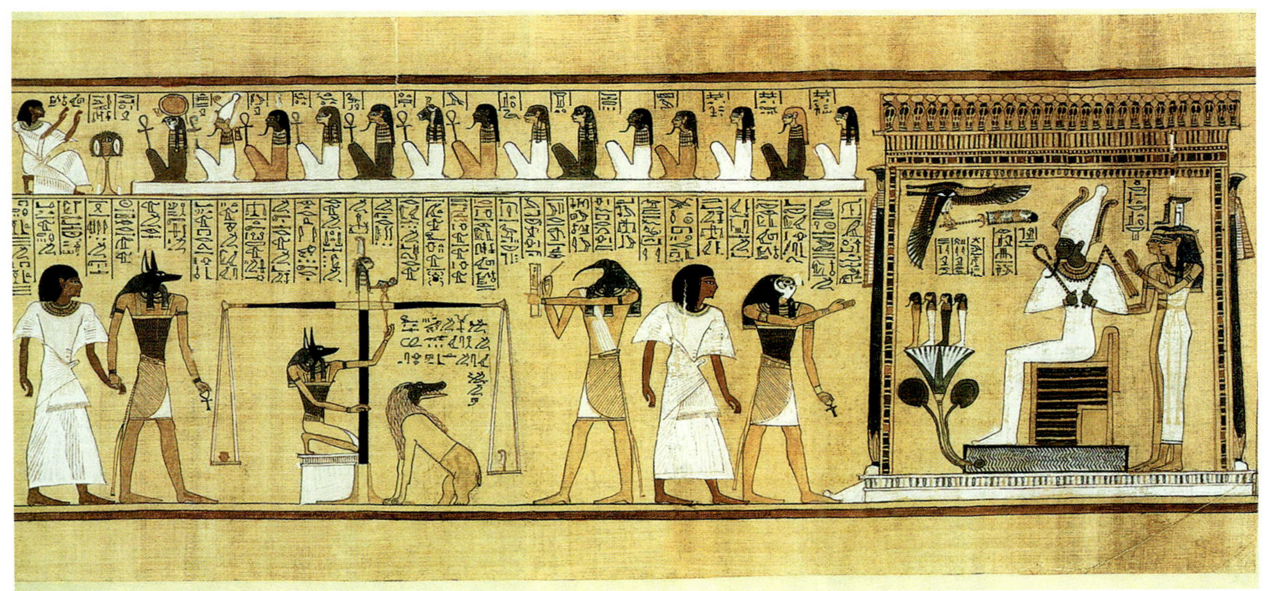

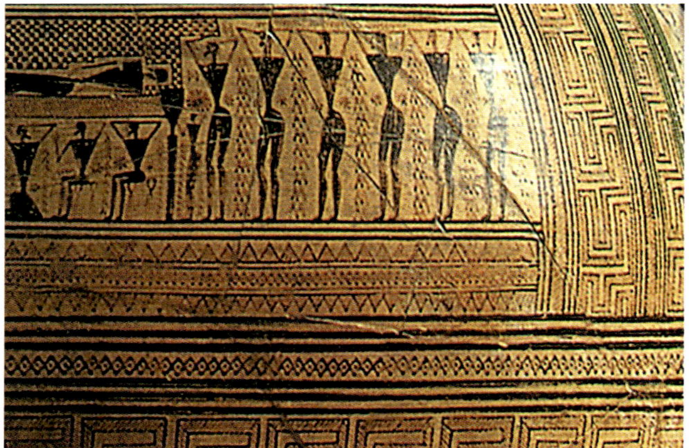

61. **Dipylon Master**, *Untitled*, detail from geometric amphora,
760-750 BCE, Ancient Greek.
Painted ceramic. Archaeological Museum of Ceramics, Athens.

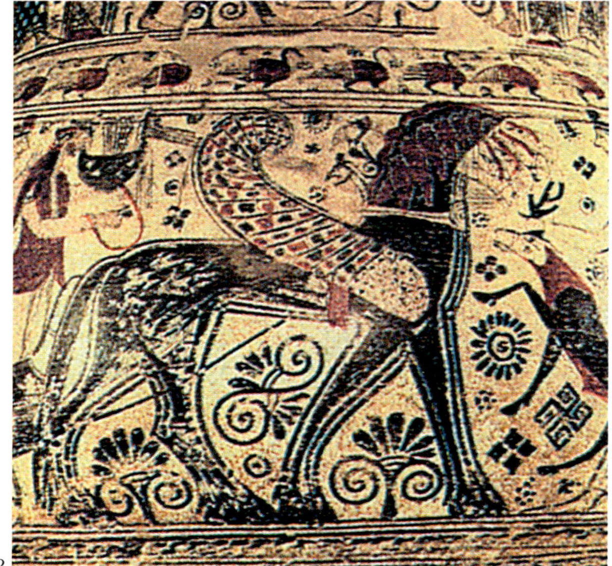

62

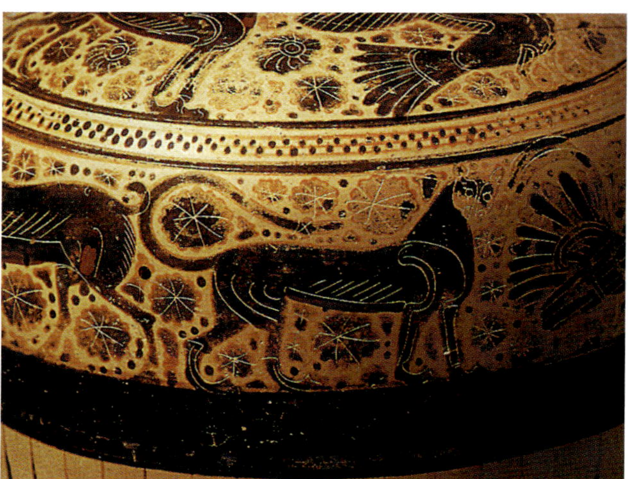

63

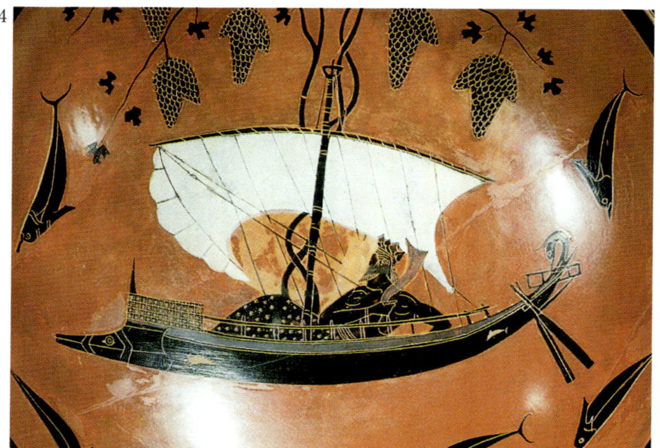

64

62. **Anonymous**, *Return of Apollo to Delos, Hosted by Artemis*,
detail from proto-attic funeral amphora, c. 640 BCE, Ancient Greek.
Painted ceramic, height of amphora: 98 cm.
National Museum of Athens, Athens.

63. **Anonymous**, *Untitled*, detail from an oenochoe,
7th century BCE, Ancient Greek. Painted ceramic.

64. **Exekias**, *Dionysus in his Boat*, detail from black-figure cup,
c. 540-530 BCE, Ancient Greek.
Painted ceramic, diameter of cup: 30 cm.
Staatliche Antikensammlungen, Munich.

65. **Euphronios**, *Ephebes in the Bath*, detail from red-figured volute
krater, c. 500 BCE, Ancient Greek. Painted ceramic.
Staatliche Museen zu Berlin, Preussischer Kulturbesitz, Berlin.

65

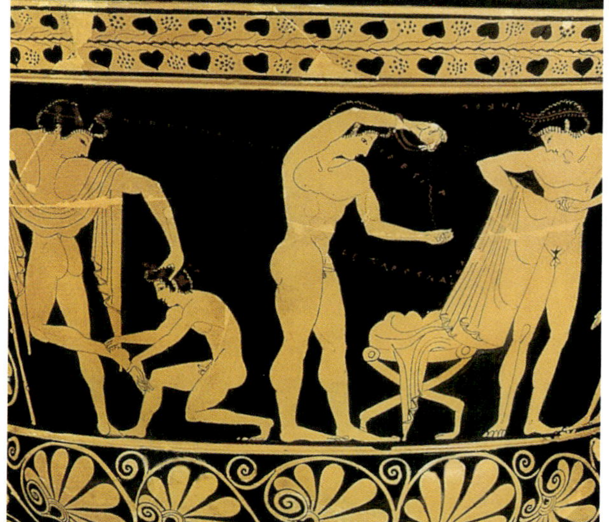

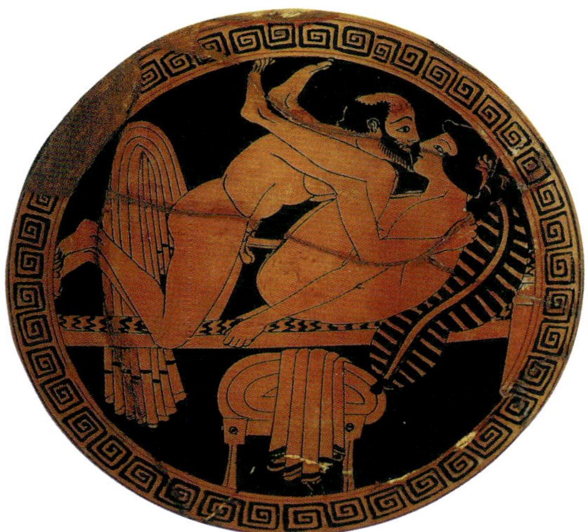

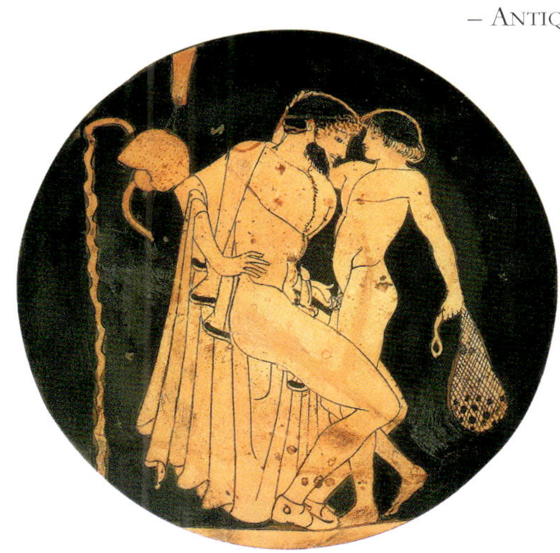

66. **Triptolemus Painter**, Erotic scene, detail from attic
   red-figured krater, 5th century BCE, Ancient Greek.
   Painted ceramic. Tarquiniese Museo Nazionale, Tarquinia.

67. **Brygos Painter**, *Erastes Seeking an Eromenos*, detail from attic
   red-figured krater, 5th century BCE, Ancient Greek.
   Painted ceramic. The Ashmolean Museum, Oxford.

68. **Andokides Painter**, *Hercules Resting in the Presence of Athena*,
   c. 510 BCE, Ancient Greek.
   Red-figured amphora. Staatliche Antikensammlungen, Munich.

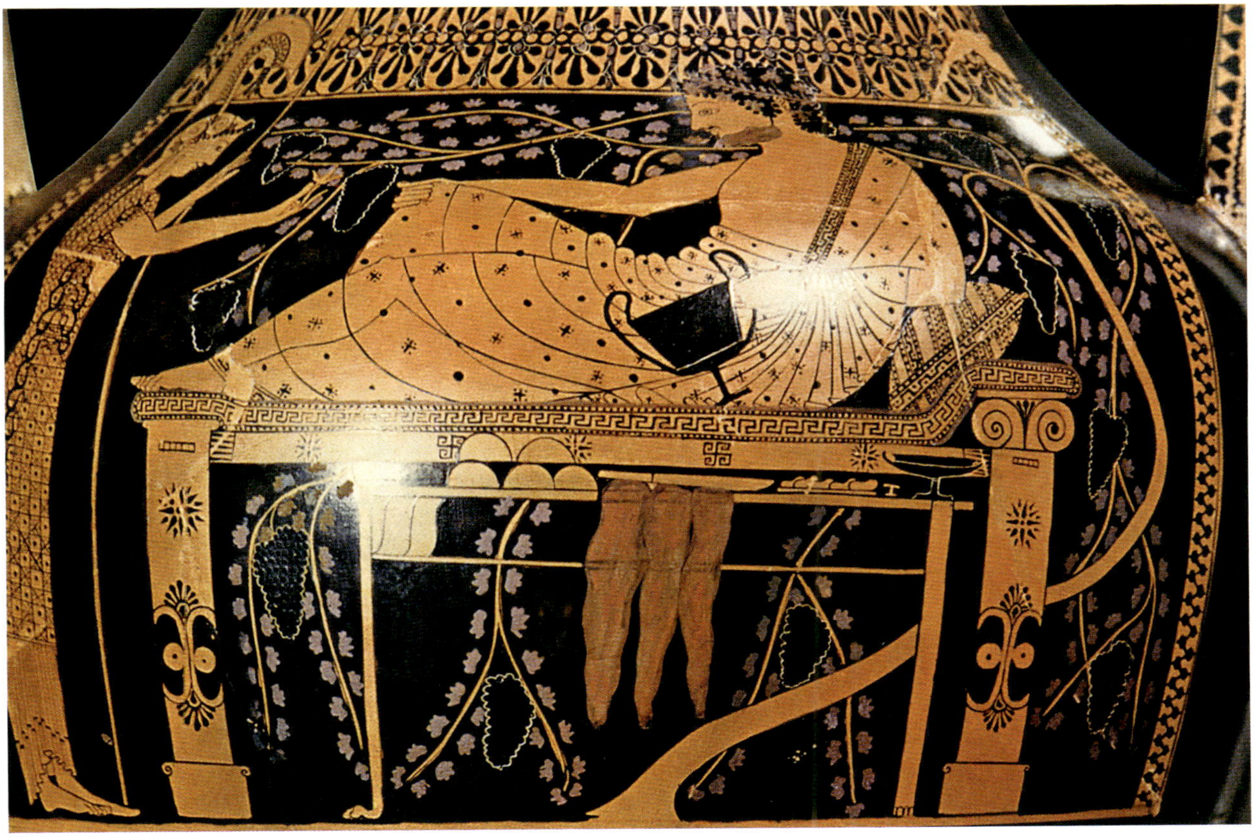

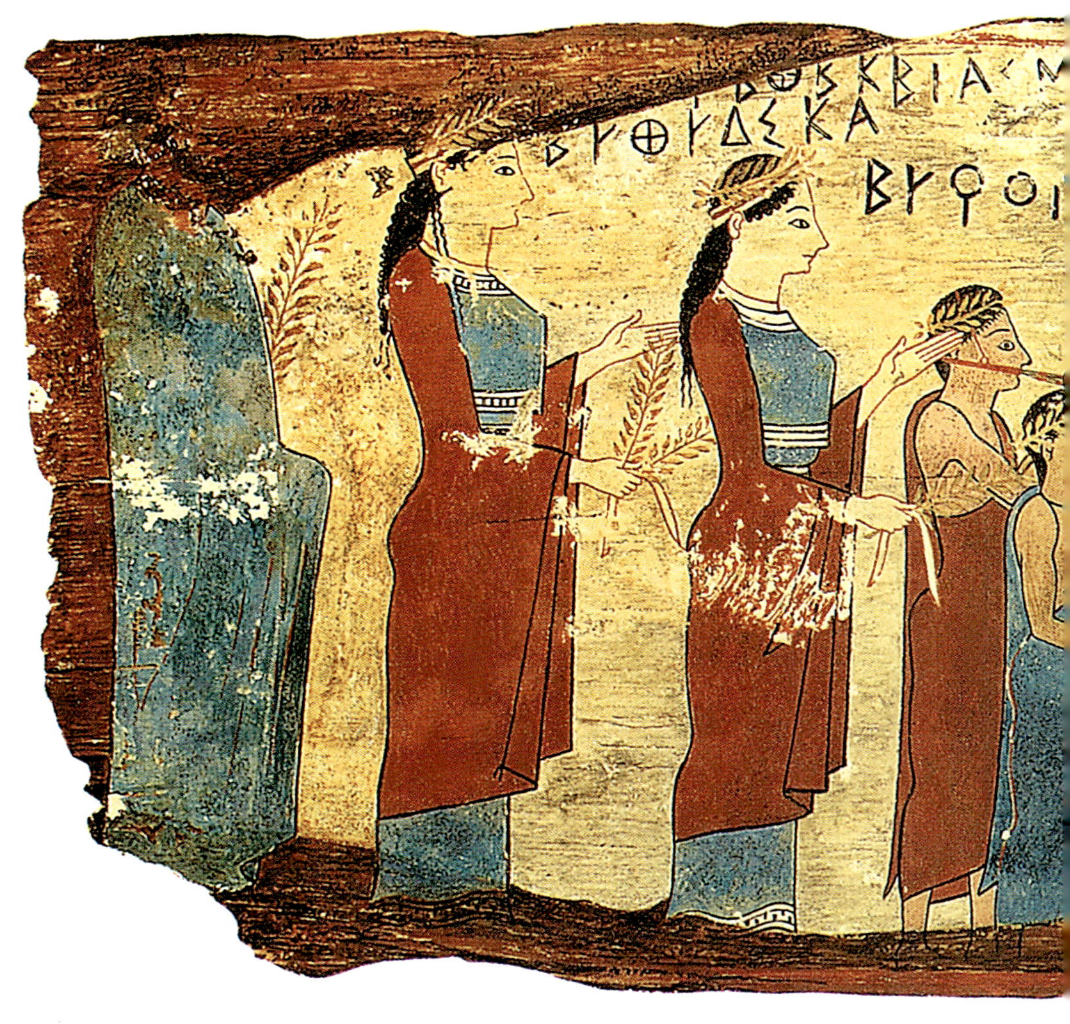

69. **Anonymous**, *Scene of Sacrifice*, 6th century BCE, Ancient Greek.
Wood painting.
Excavation site at Sicyon, Corinthia, Greece.

Discovered in the Cave of Pits in Corinth, this wooden tablet belongs to a series constituting the earliest examples of Greek painted panels. Covered with stucco, the tablet was decorated with mineral pigments of eight different colours (black, white, blue, red, green, yellow, purple and brown), with each colour broken down by shadows and gradients of all kinds. Moreover, it seems that the black outlines were drawn first and the colours were then used to

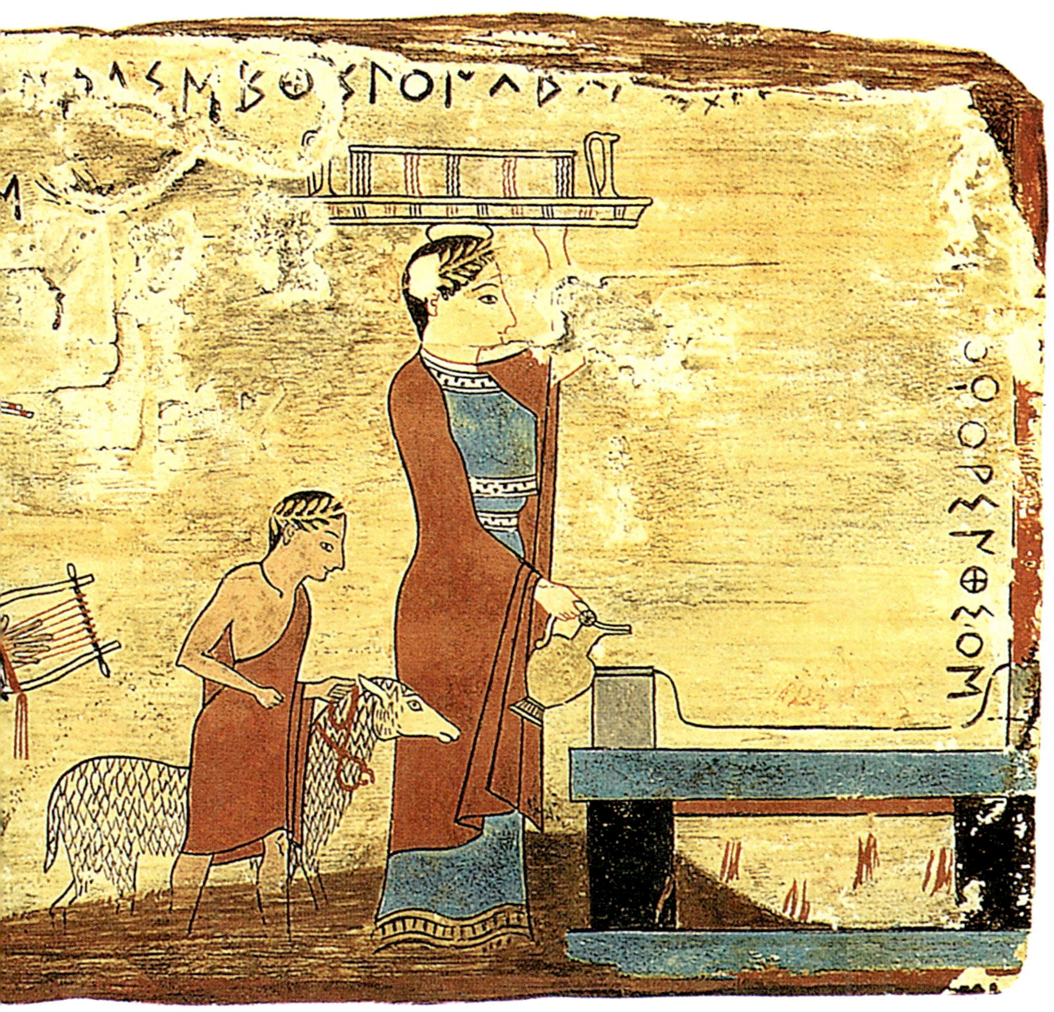

fill the gaps. Depicting a scene of sacrifice, the painting shows three
women dressed in chitons or peplos, approaching an altar. They are
accompanied by musicians playing the lyre or aulos. Near the altar,
a person makes a libation. Behind him, another small figure,
perhaps a slave, approaches the lamb, the object of the sacrifice.
On top of the tablet, an inscription in the Corinthian alphabet gives
the names of two women to whom the work is dedicated.

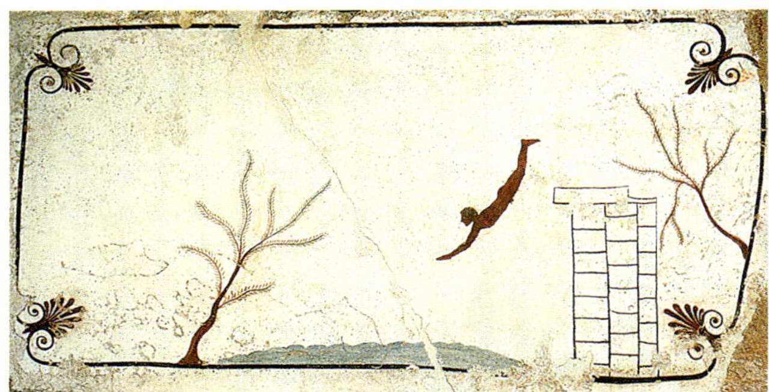

70. **Anonymous**, *The Diver*, c. 480-470 BCE, Ancient Greek.
Tomb of the Diver. Fresco, height: 50 cm.
Archaeological Museum of Paestum, Paestum.

*The Tomb of the Diver was discovered by the archaeologist
Mario Napoli in the summer of 1968, during the excavation of a
small Italian cemetery near Paestum. Its name comes from the
scene painted on the cover slab, depicting a naked athlete
plunging into the water beyond the Pillars of Hercules, which
symbolised the known world at that time. The scene may also
represent a leap into the unknown or to death. The fresco in the
tomb owes its importance to being the only example of Greek
figurative rock painting from this period yet found, and has
remained in perfect condition.*

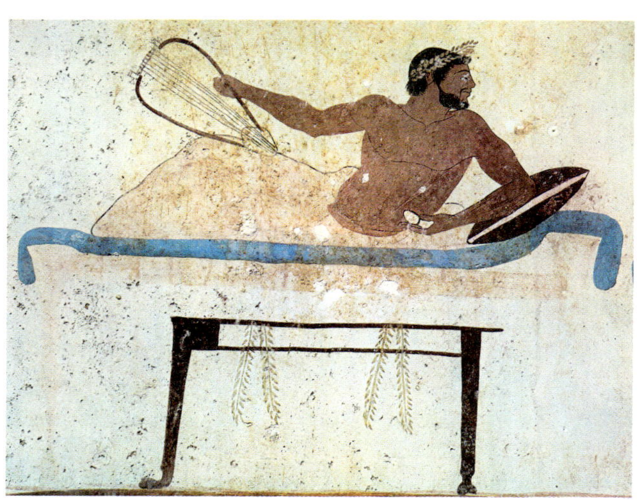

71. **Anonymous**, *Banquet Scene, Musician Lying Down*,
480-470 BCE, Ancient Greek. Tomb of the Diver. Fresco,
height: 50 cm. Archaeological Museum of Paestum, Paestum.

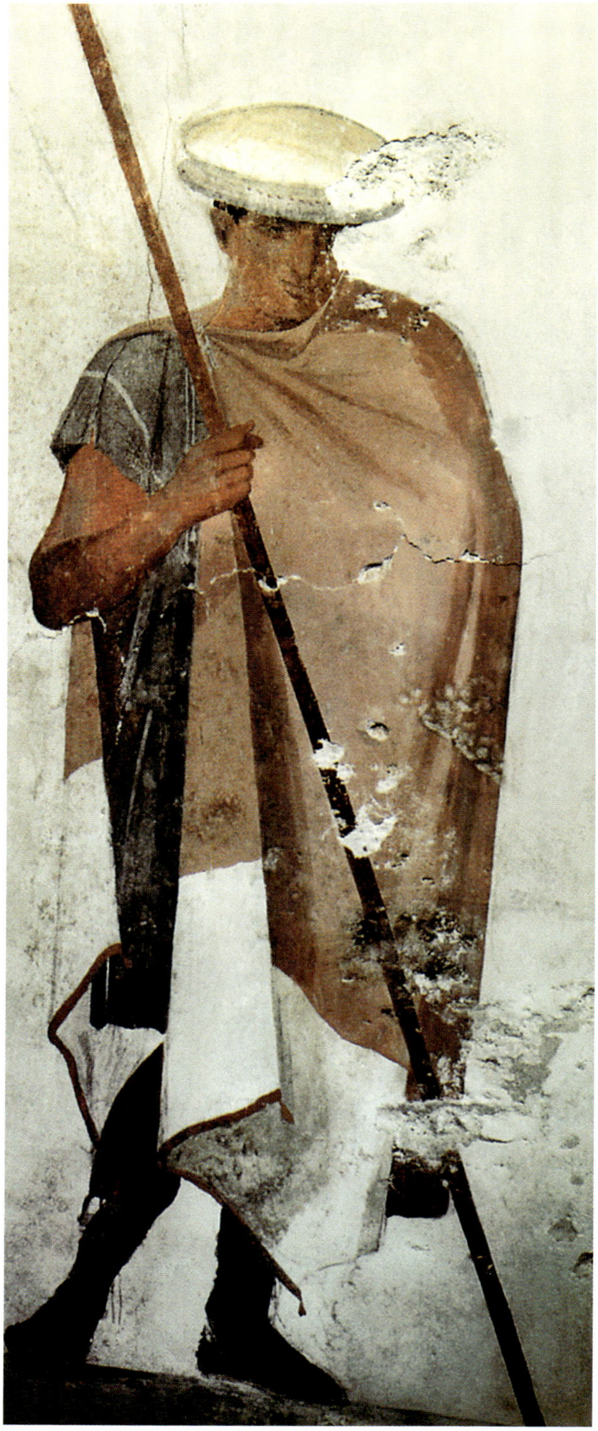

72. **Anonymous**, *The Young Sarissa Carrier, Keeper of the Tomb*,
last quarter of the 4th century BCE, Ancient Greek.
Aghios Athanassios, Thessaloniki.

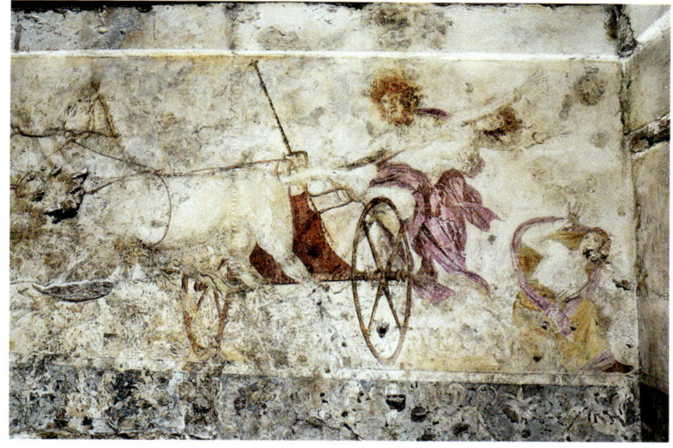

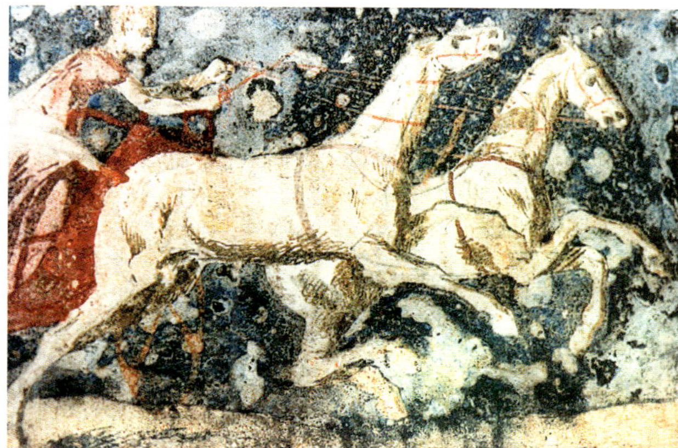

73. **Anonymous**, *Hades*, third quarter of the 4th century BCE, Ancient Greek.
Tempera. Tomb of Persephone, Vergina, Greece.

Illustrating one of the most popular Greek legends, this mural tells of the abduction of Persephone by Hades. According to ancient Greek myth, Hades, god of the underworld, captured his niece Persephone, daughter of Demeter and Zeus, to become his queen in the kingdom of the dead. Deprived of her daughter for part of the year, Demeter, due to inconsolable grief, gave birth to the different seasons. This representation also gave its name to the Tomb of Vergina, 'Tomb of Persephone', the ancient capital of the kingdom of Macedonia, in which it was discovered. In a completely different style and executed with rapid strokes and a variety of pictorial effects, another painting, showing the abduction of Persephone, adorned one of the long sides of the grave. According to Pliny, this work should be attributed to Nicomachus. Others believed it to be the work of his pupil, Philoxenos of Eretria.

74. **Anonymous**, detail of *Chariot Race*,
last quarter of the 4th century BCE, Ancient Greek.
Vergina, Greece.

75. **Anonymous**, Wall decoration, third quarter of the 4th – first quarter of the 3rd century BCE, Ancient Greek.
Tomb of Lyson and Callicles, Lefkadia. Tempera.

76. **Anonymous**, *Divine Epiphany*, third quarter of the 4th century BCE, Ancient Greek. Painting on the backrest of a throne, Tomb of Eurydice, Vergina, Greece. Tempera on marble.

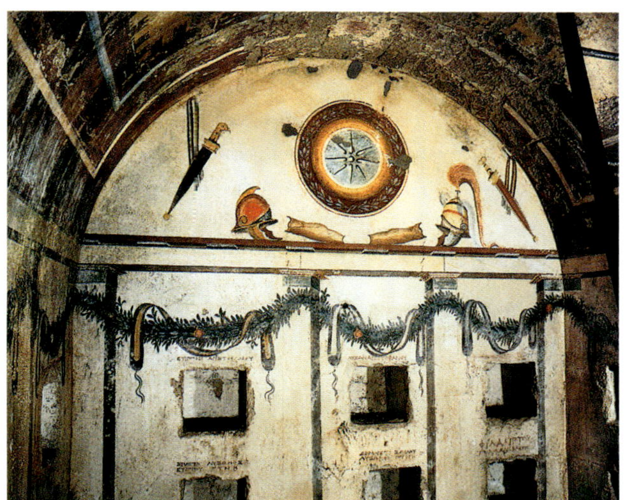

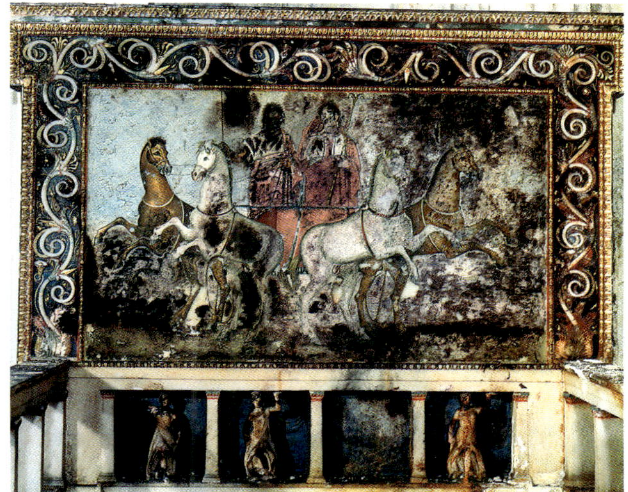

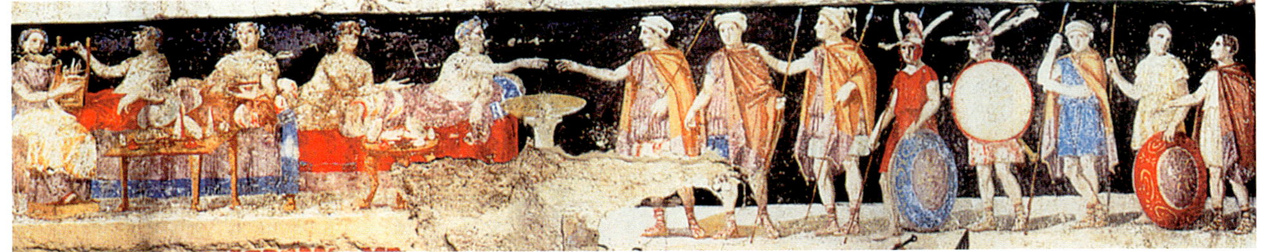

77. **Anonymous**, *Tomb at Agios Athanasios*,
    late 4th-early 3rd century BCE, Ancient Greek.
    Thessaloniki.

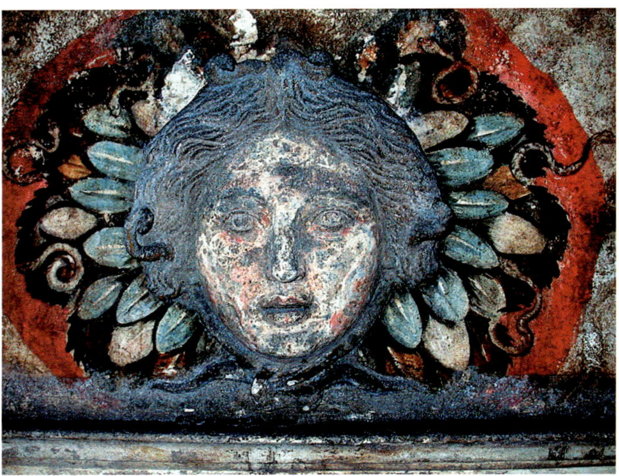

78. **Anonymous**, detail of a candelabrum,
    first half of the 3rd century BCE, Ancient Roman.
    Via dei Cristallini, Naples.

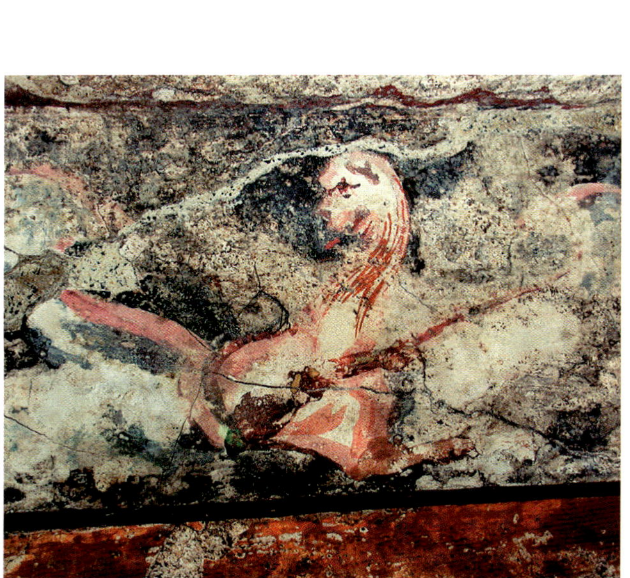

79. **Anonymous**, Female figure seated on the south side,
    c. 1st-4th century BCE, Ancient Greek.
    Cist grave, Amphipolis.

80. **Anonymous**, detail of *Griffon*,
    first half of the 3rd century BCE, Ancient Roman.
    Via dei Cristallini, Naples.

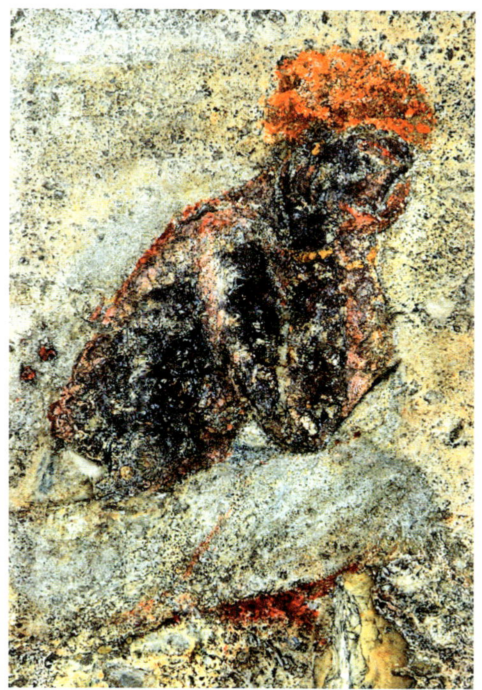

81. **Anonymous**, *Setting of a Metope*, Tomb of the Swing,
    last quarter of the 3rd-first quarter of the 2nd century BCE,
    Ancient Greek. Cyrene. Painted limestone, 34 x 28 cm.

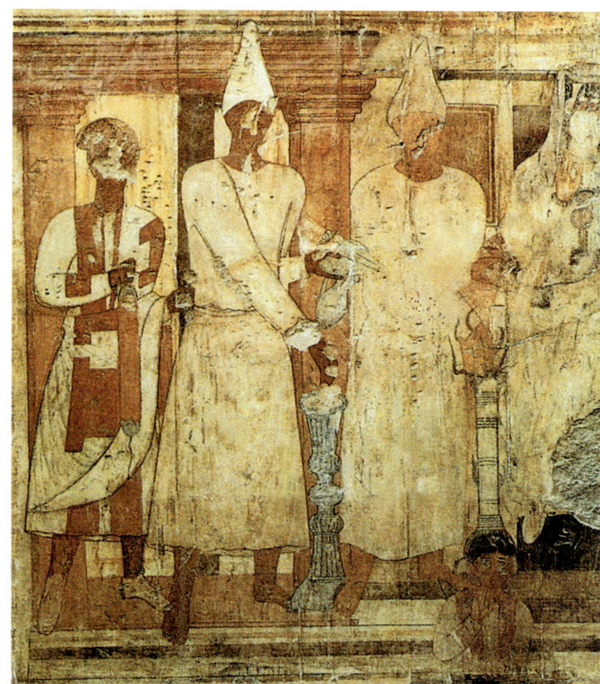

82. **Anonymous**, detail from *Scene of Sacrifice*, late 1st century CE,
    Ancient Greek. Fresco.
    Dura-Europos, near Salhiyé, Syria.

83. **Anonymous**, Le Parisienne, 1400-1350 BCE, Ancient Greek.
    Palace of Knossos, Crete.
    Fragment of the *Campstool Fresco*, height: 22 cm.
    Archaeological Museum of Heraklion, Heraklion.

84. **Anonymous**, *Warrior on Horseback*, c. 340-320 BCE,
    Ancient Greek. Fresco, height: 1.45 m.
    Museum of Paestum, Paestum.

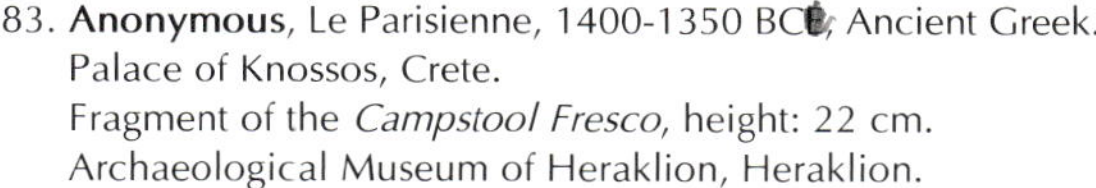

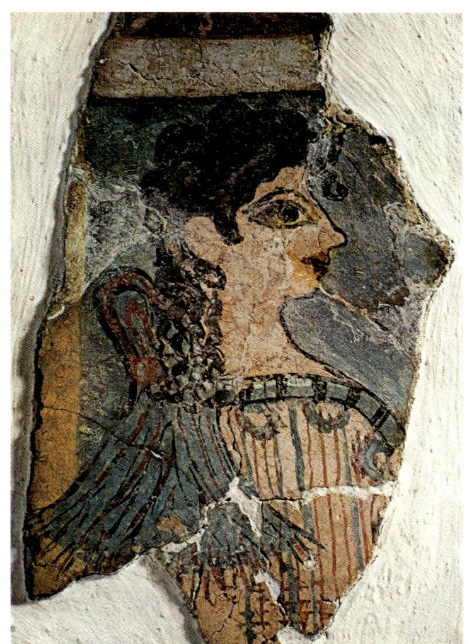

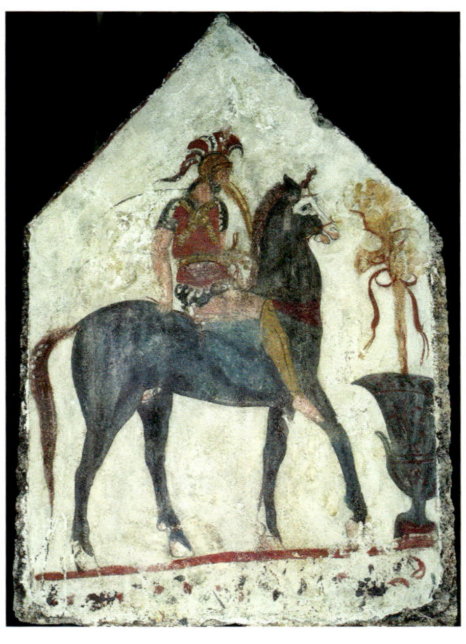

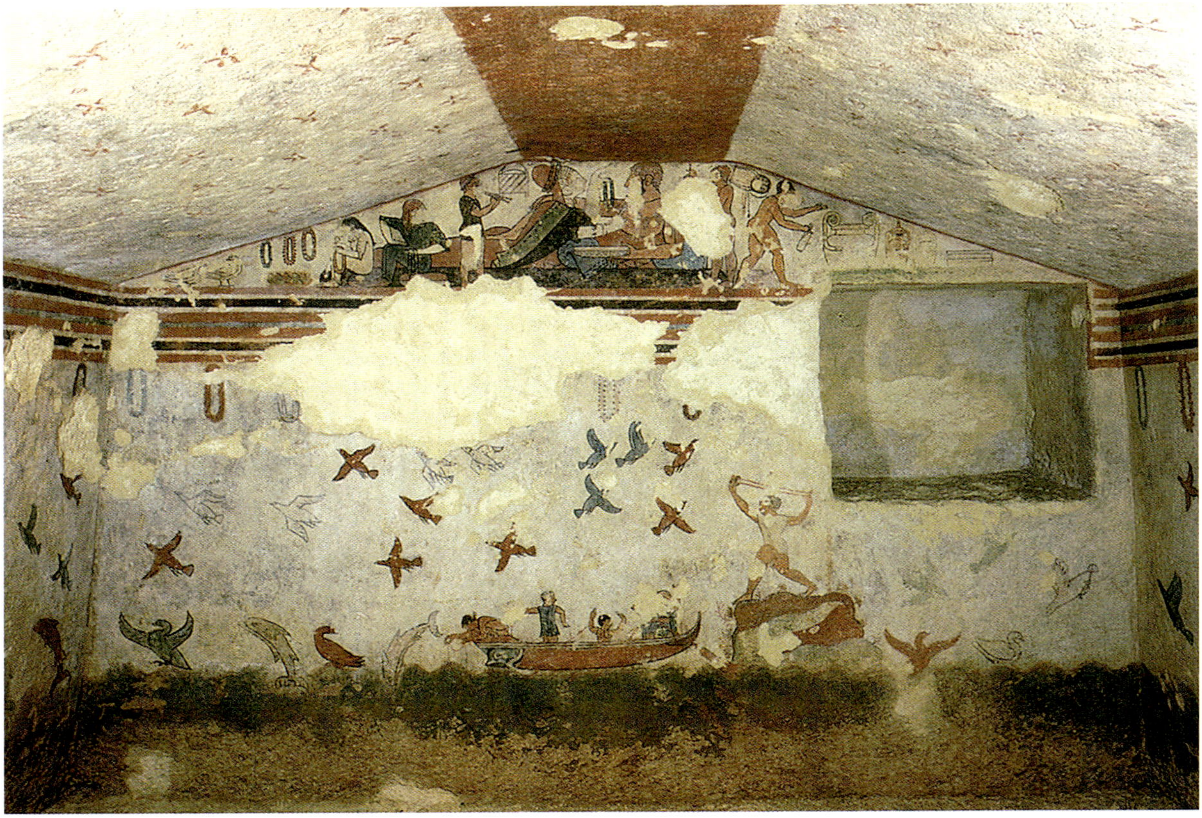

85. **Anonymous**, *Etruscan Tomb*, 600 BCE, Ancient Roman.
Tarquinia, Italy. Fresco.

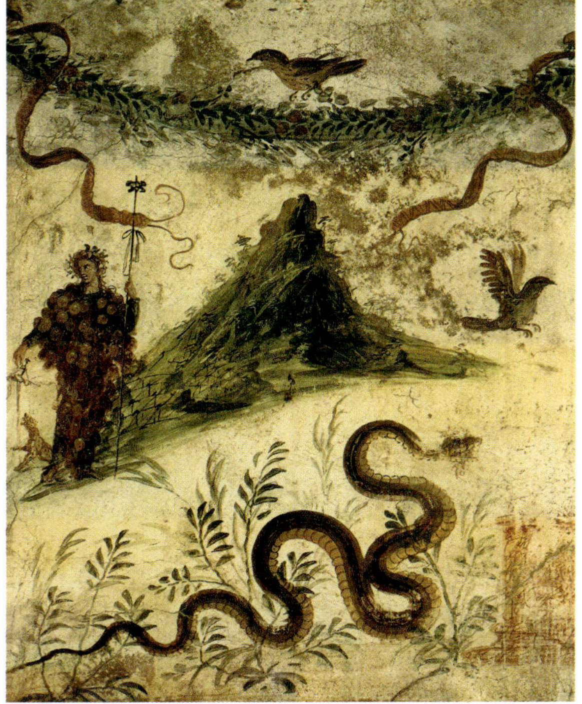

86. **Anonymous**, *Vesuvius as a Sacred Landscape*, Centennial House,
68-79 CE, Ancient Roman. Fresco.
Museo Archeologico Nazionale, Pompeii.

87. **Anonymous**, *Coupling of a Nymph and Satyr*,
first half of the 2nd century BCE, Ancient Roman.
House of the Faun, Pompeii. Fresco.

88. **Anonymous**, *Head of a Faun*, 2nd century BCE, Ancient Roman.
Herculaneum. Fresco.
Museo Archeologico Nazionale, Naples.

Herculaneum, the ancient Roman city founded by Hercules, was successively occupied by the Oscans, Etruscans, Samnites, Greeks and finally by Roman colonies. In the 1st century CE, the city had become one of the most popular resorts of rich Roman families. When, in 79 CE, the unexpected eruption of Vesuvius occurred, like Pompeii, the city was completely buried under a thick layer of volcanic material, which preserved it over the centuries that followed. The excavation, undertaken in the 18th century, recovered the city as it was after the eruption, and archaeologists were able to find many works of art, including domestic murals such as Head of a Faun.

89. **Anonymous**, detail from *The Warrior*, c. 350 BCE,
Ancient Greek. Fresco, Sarcophagus of the Amazons.
Tarquinia, Italy.

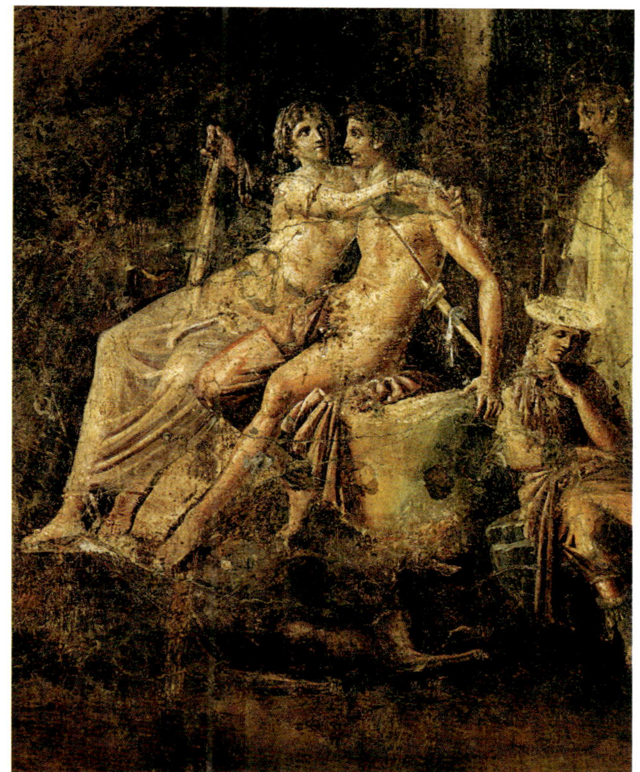
87

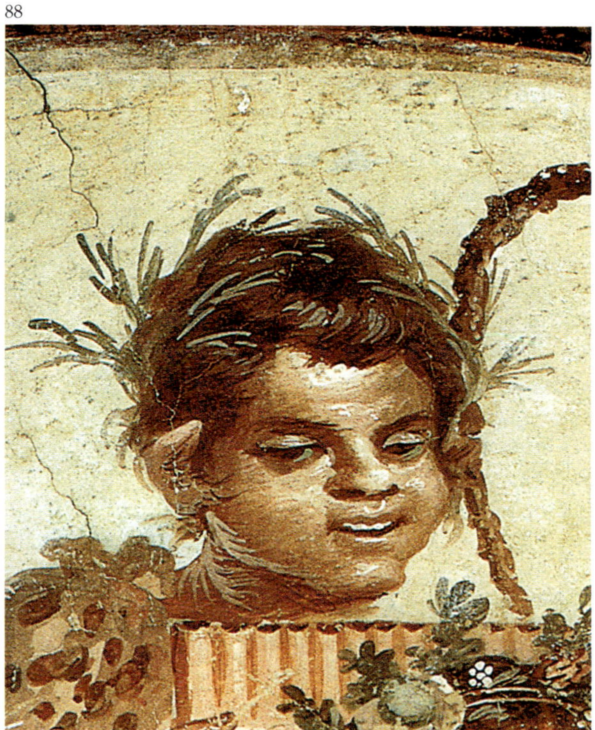
88

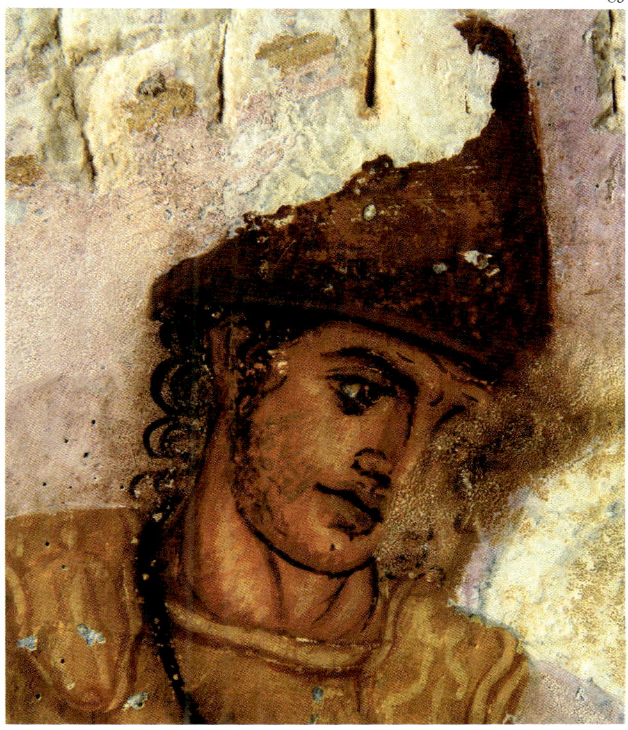
89

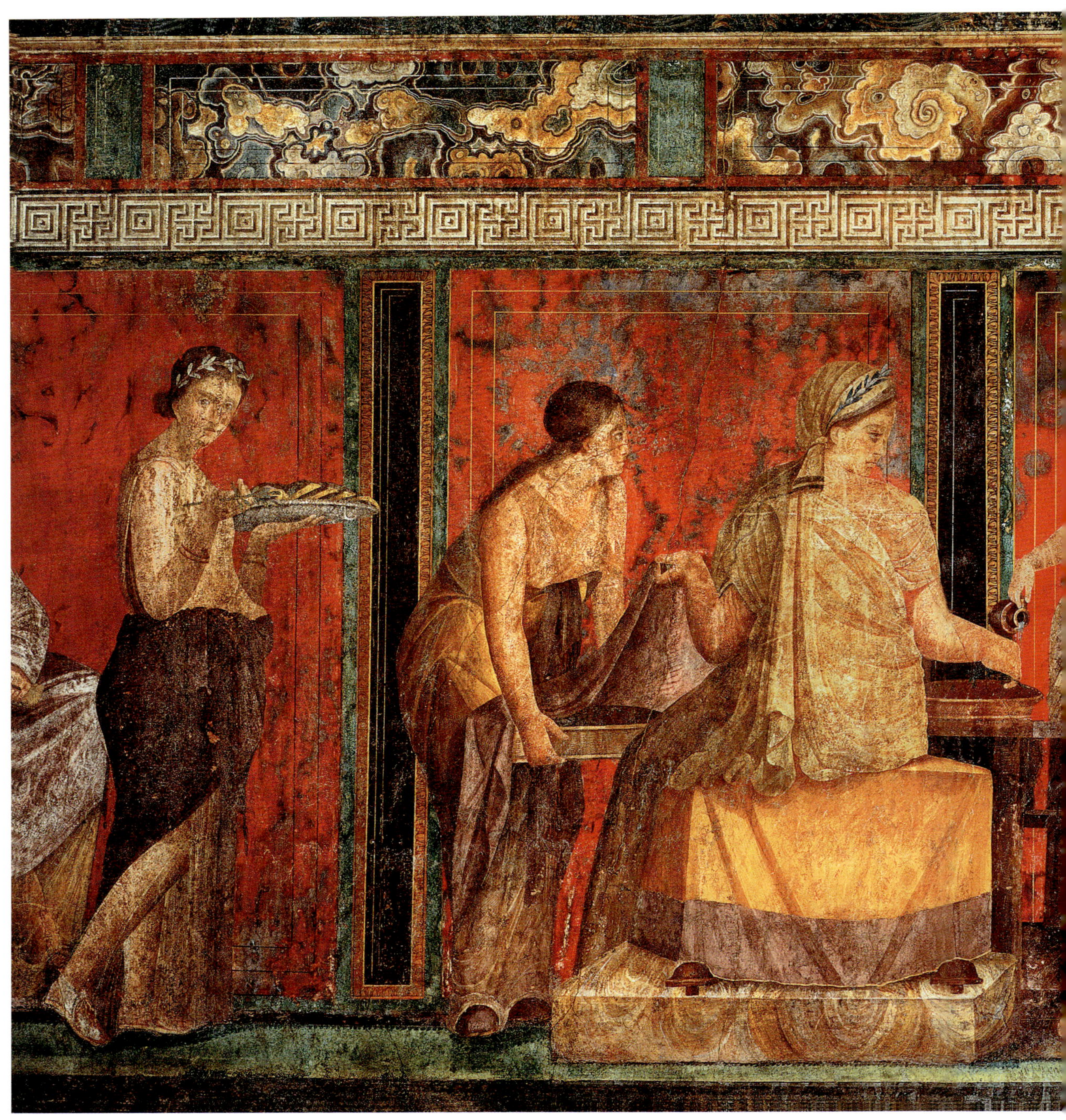

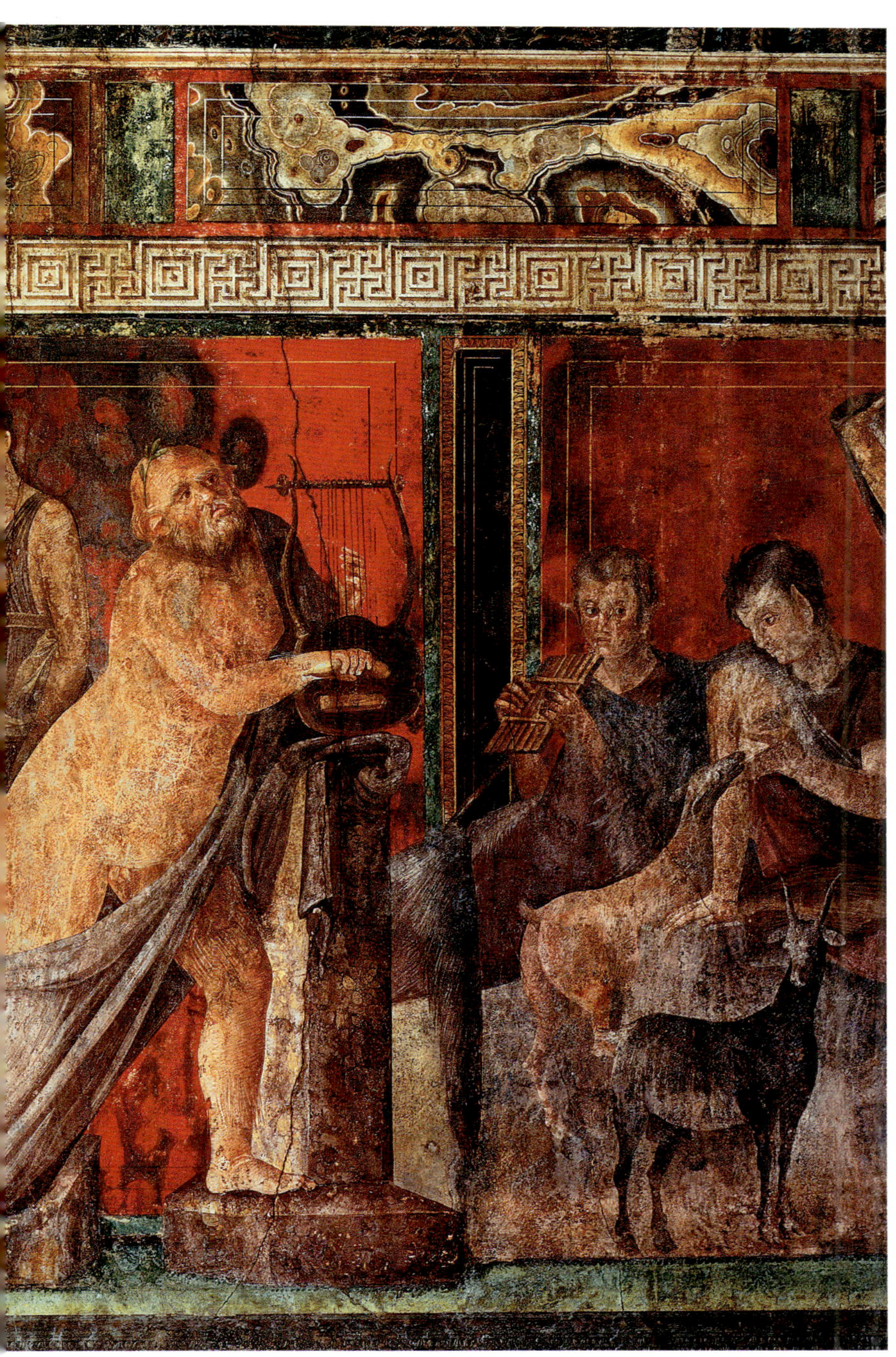

90. **Anonymous**, *Priestesses Preparing Ritual Offerings, while Silenus Plays the Lyre, Accompanied by Two Satyrs with a Pan Flute*,
2nd -1st century BC, Ancient Roman. Villa of the Mysteries, Pompeii. Fresco.

Located on the outskirts of Pompeii, outside the archaeological zone itself, the Villa of the Mysteries is a remarkable building, on account of its size and the complexity of its architecture. Built around the second century BC, the villa was renovated and embellished during the imperial era, when it acquired the glory we know today. The frescos adorning its walls excited particular enthusiasm. Aside from their extraordinary state of preservation, the paintings are exceptional for their rich colours and scenes; the subject of religious cults that existed alongside the official religion is also very unusual.

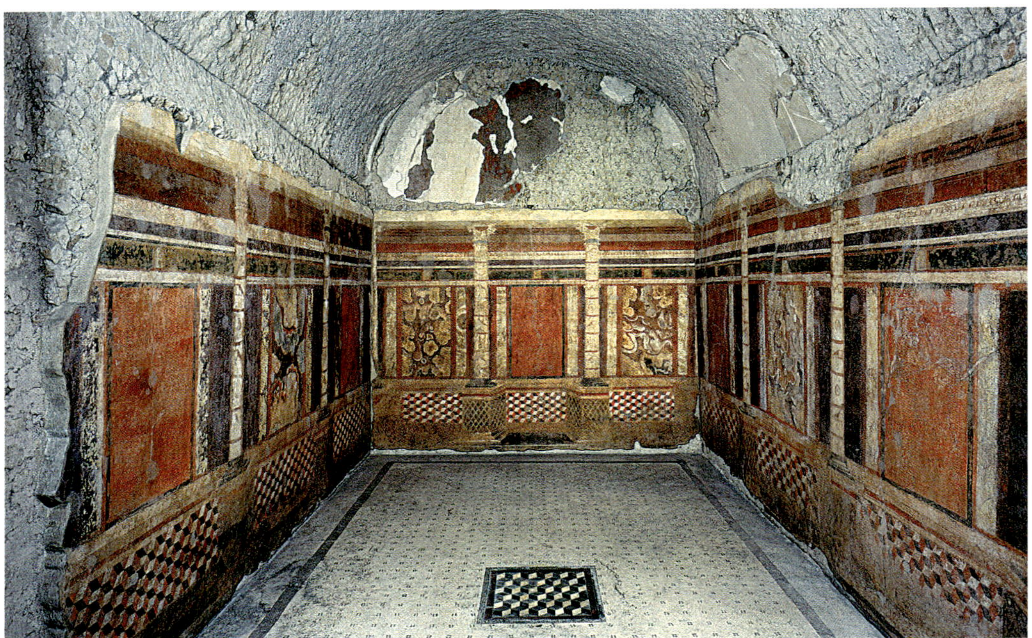

91. **Anonymous**, decorated room in the Home of the Griffins, Palatine Hill, late 2nd or early 1st century BCE, Ancient Roman. Rome. Fresco.

92. **Anonymous**, Pictorial decoration of a room, mid 1st century BCE, Ancient Roman. Villa of Poppea, Oplontis, Fresco. Torre Annunziata, Campania.

Located in Oplontis, one of the suburbs of Roman Pompeii, the Villa of Poppea dates from the first century BCE. Having belonged to Poppea Augusta, a wealthy aristocrat who was also the mistress of the emperor Nero, this villa was still in construction at the time of the eruption of Vesuvius. Consisting of sumptuous, richly coloured frescos, the decor of this house is typical of the second and fourth Pompeian styles. The sequenced frescos follow one another from room to room. And, due to the art of perspective, they form an architectural trompe l'oeil, creating dramatic effects of depth.

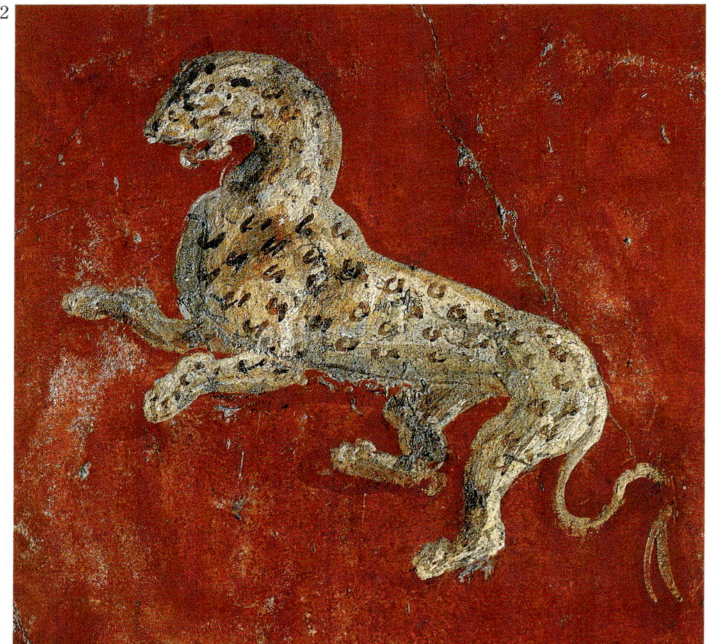

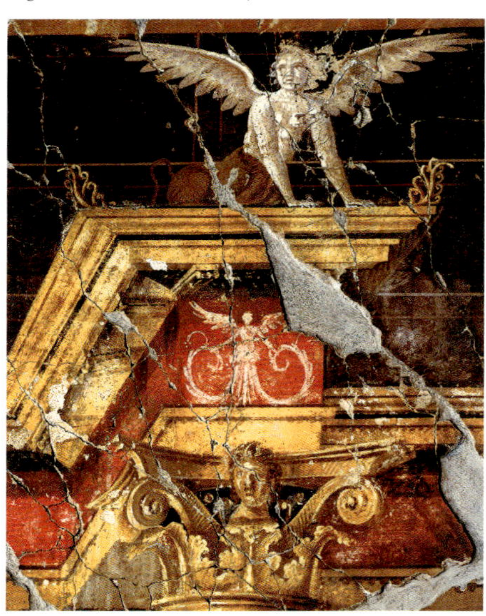

93. **Anonymous**, west wall of the triclinium with the Temple of Hera, mid 1st century BCE, Ancient Roman. Villa of Poppea, Oplontis, Fresco. Torre Annunziata, Campania.

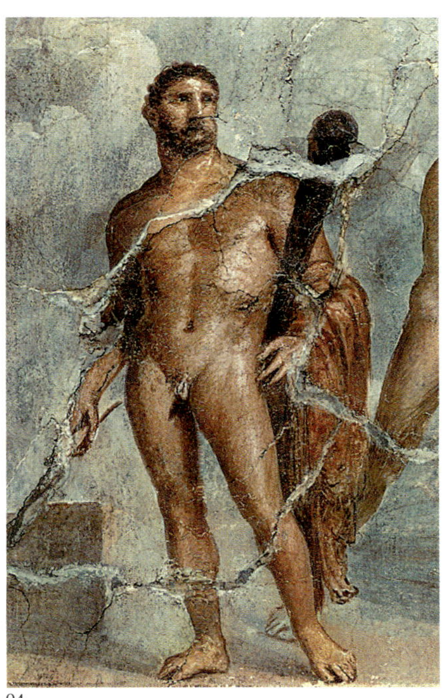

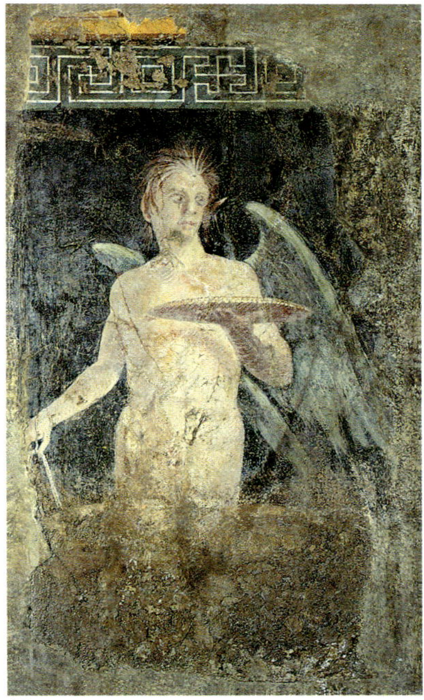

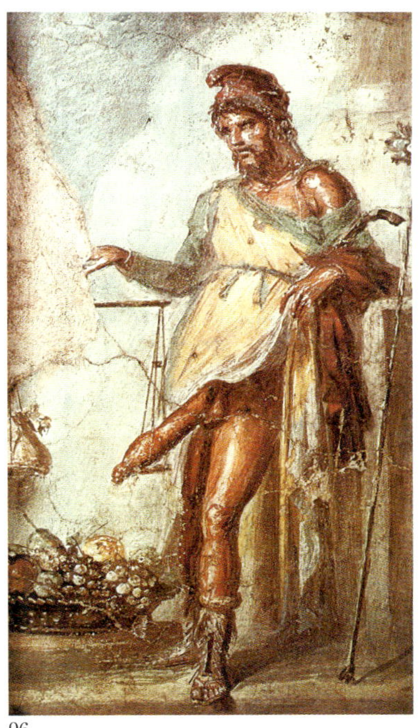

94

95

96

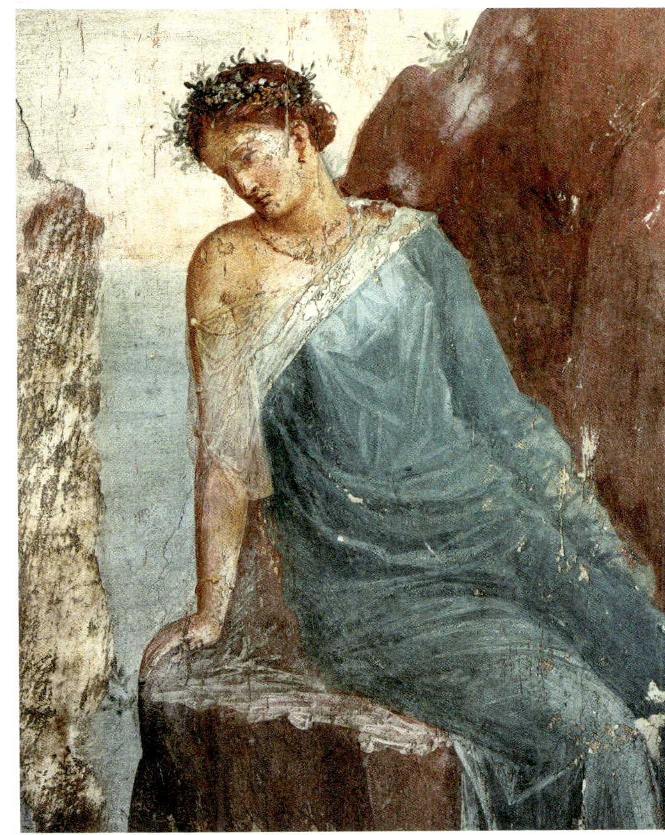

97

94. **Anonymous**, *Herakles*, 2nd-1st century BCE, Ancient Roman.
College of Augustales, Herculaneum. Fresco. Near Naples.

*The founder of Herculaneum, Hercules (the Latin form of
the Greek Herakles) is one of the most popular heroes of
antiquity. Demigod, son of Zeus and Alcmene (a mere
mortal, the wife of King Amphitryon), he personified
strength and courage. According to legend, at birth, his aunt
Hera sent two serpents to devour him in his crib, but the
infant strangled them with his own hands. After various
exploits, he went to Argos where he married Megara,
daughter of Creon, king of Thebes. But made mad by the
evil machinations of his aunt, Hercules killed his wife and
children. To expiate this crime he was sentenced to obey
one of his most ardent enemies, King Eurystheus. The latter
imposed a series of tests upon him, known as the Labours of
Hercules. Aside from these famous 12 labours, Hercules
travelled throughout the world, carrying arms, as seen here
with his club, that only he could handle and with which he
exterminated tyrants, bandits and monsters.*

95. **Anonymous**, *Winged Genius*, third quarter of the 1st century
BCE, Ancient Roman. Villa of Publius Fannius Sinistor,
Pompeii. Fresco, 126 x 71 cm.

96. **Anonymous**, *Priapus*, 1st century BCE, Ancient Roman.
House of Vettii, Pompeii. Fresco.

97. **Anonymous**, detail from *Daedalus and Icarus*,
last decade of the 1st century BCE, Ancient Roman.
Imperial Villa, Pompeii. Fresco.

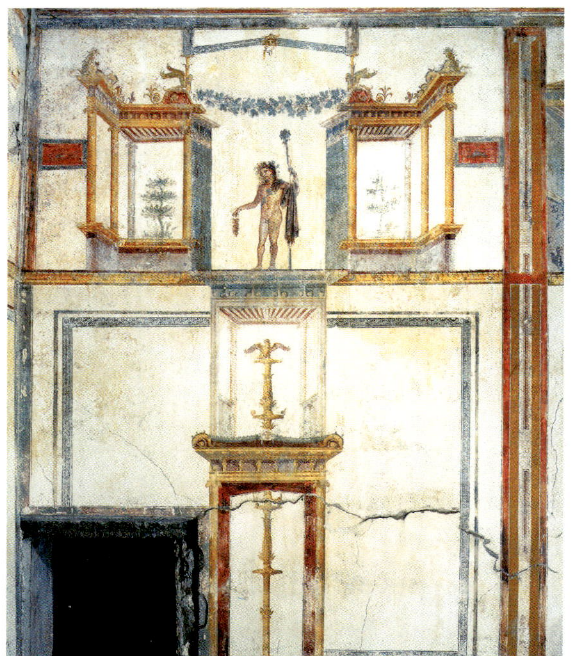

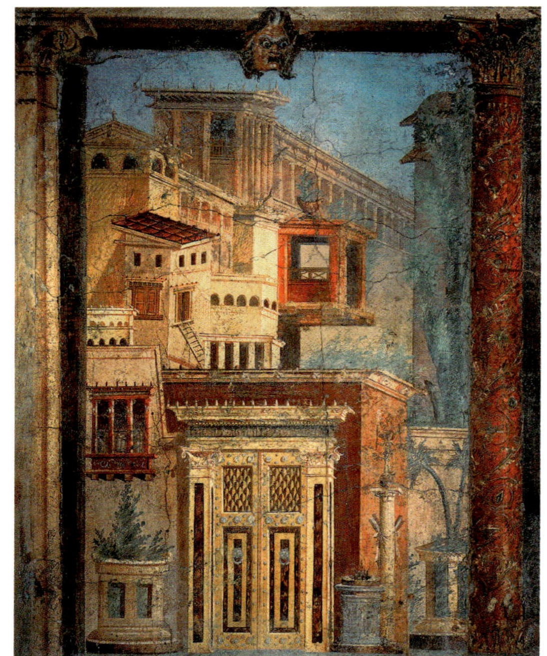

98. **Anonymous**, Pictorial decoration,
    late 1st century BCE-1st century CE, Ancient Roman.
    Home of Julius Polybius, Pompeii. Fresco.

99. **Anonymous**, *Cubiculum*, 50-40 BCE.
    Publius Fannius Synistor Villa, Boscoreale, Ancient Rome.
    Fresco. The Metropolitan Museum of Art, New York.

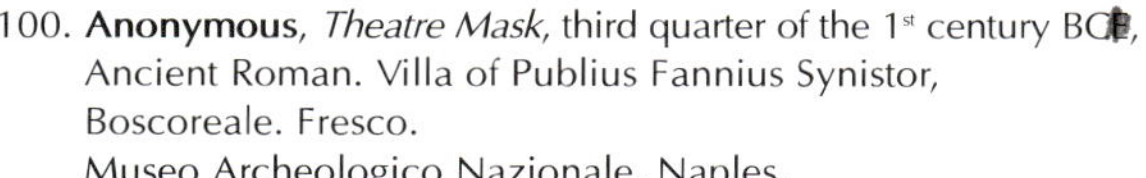

100. **Anonymous**, *Theatre Mask*, third quarter of the 1st century BCE,
    Ancient Roman. Villa of Publius Fannius Synistor,
    Boscoreale. Fresco.
    Museo Archeologico Nazionale, Naples.

101. **Anonymous**, *Ducks and Antelopes*,
    1st century BCE, Ancient Roman.
    Villa of the Papyri, Herculaneum. Fresco.
    Museo Archeologico Nazionale, Naples.

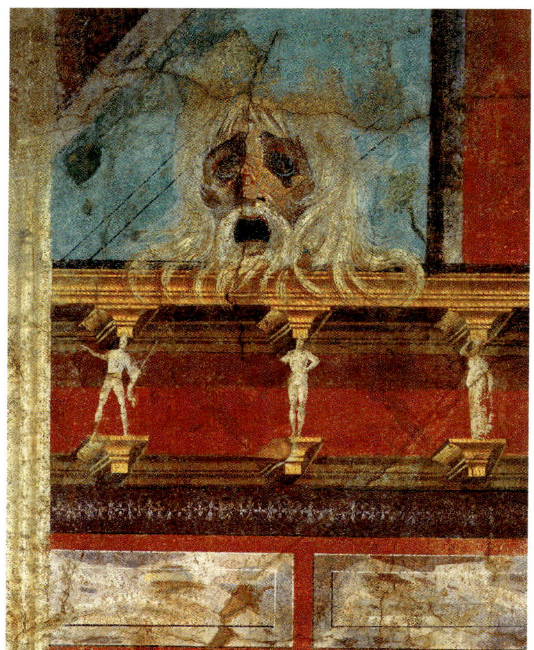

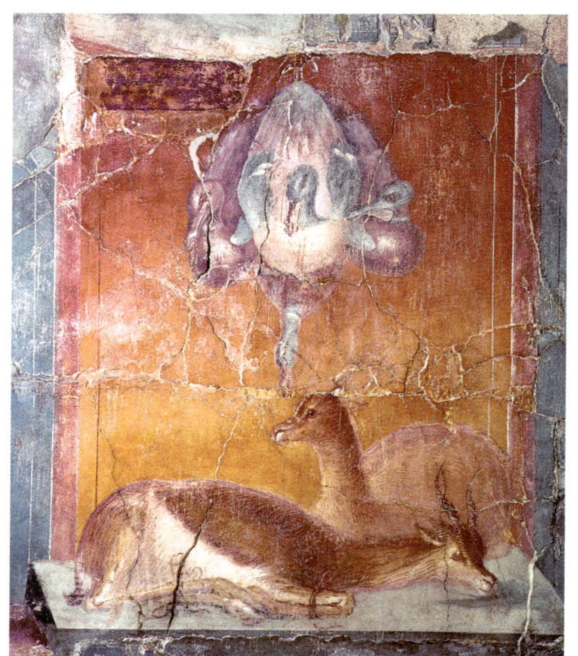

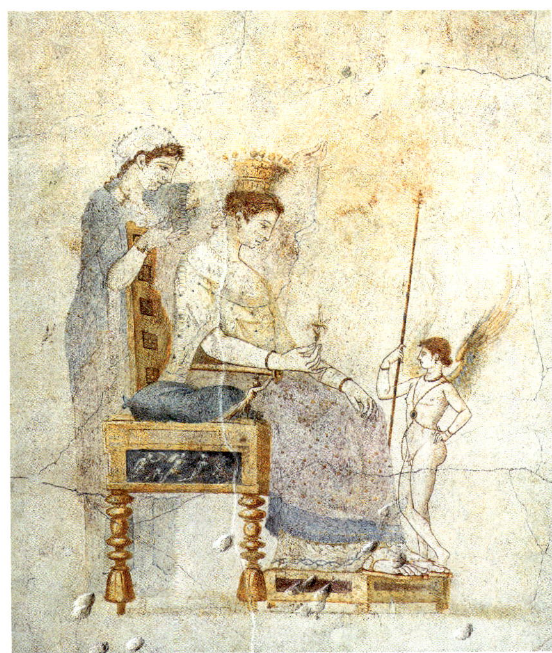

102. **Anonymous**, *The Toilet of Venus*, 1ˢᵗ century BCE,
Ancient Roman. Fresco.
Museo Nazionale Romano, Palazzo Massimo alle Terme, Rome.

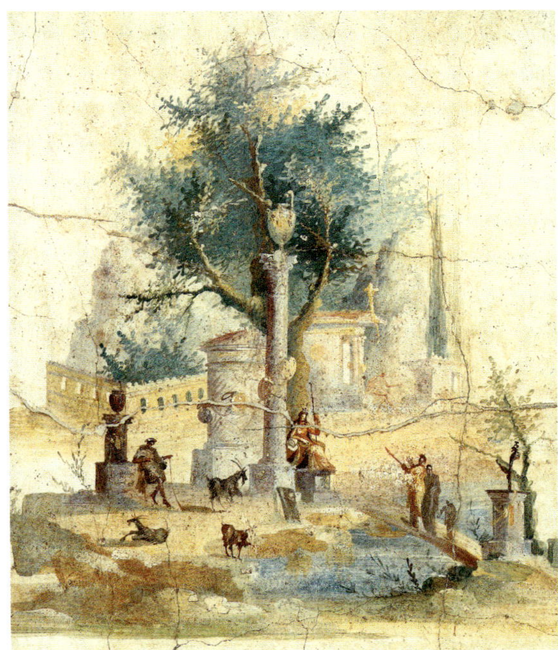

103. **Anonymous**, *Landscape with Rustic Sanctuary*, c. 10 BCE,
Ancient Roman. Villa Agripa Postumus, Boscotrecase. Fresco.
Museo Archeologico Nazionale, Naples.

104. **Anonymous**, *Grenadier, Bird and Cage Leaning against the
Railing*, 1ˢᵗ century BCE, Ancient Roman.
Villa of Livia, Prima Porta. Fresco.
Museo Nazionale Romano, Palazzo Massimo alle Terme, Rome.

105. **Anonymous**, detail of pictorial decoration with *trompe l'oeil*
garden and fountain with birds, 25-50 CE, Ancient Roman.
House of the Golden Bracelets, Pompeii. Fresco.

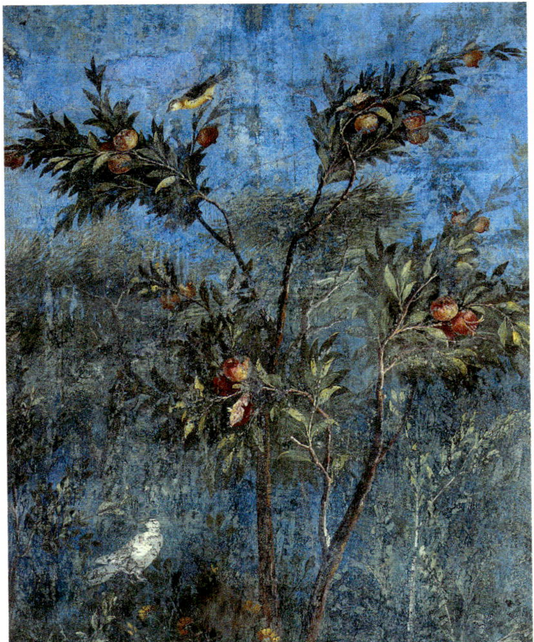

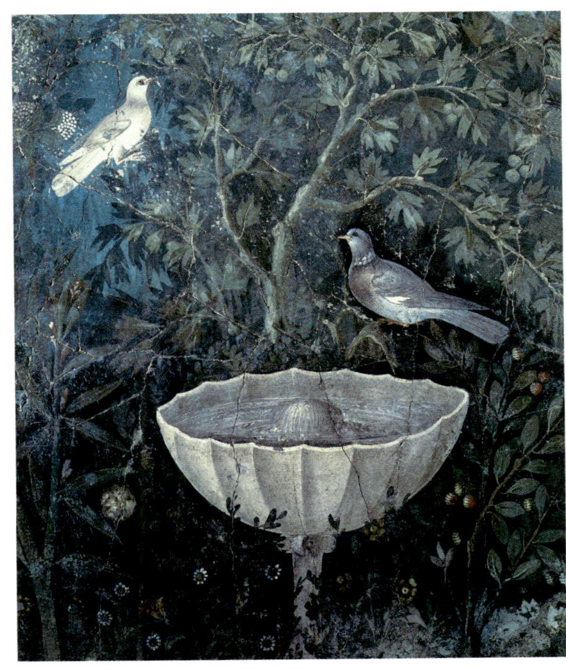

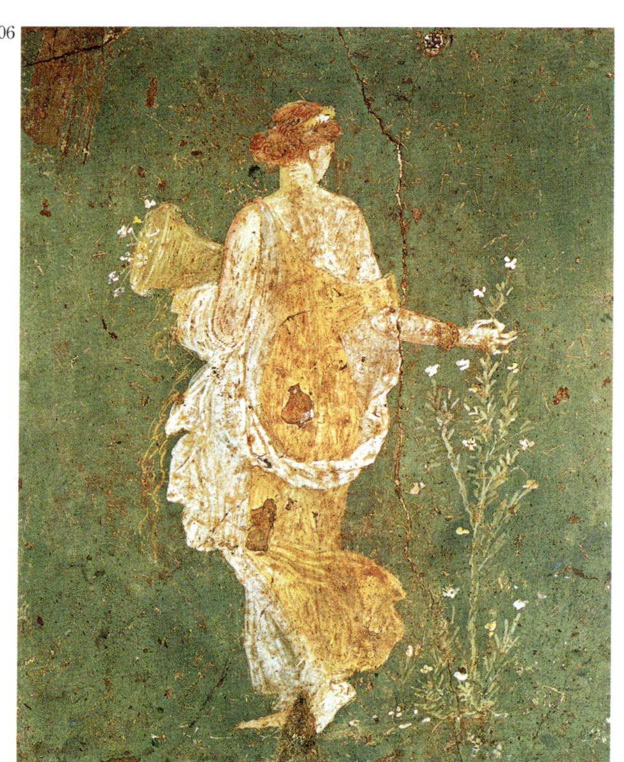

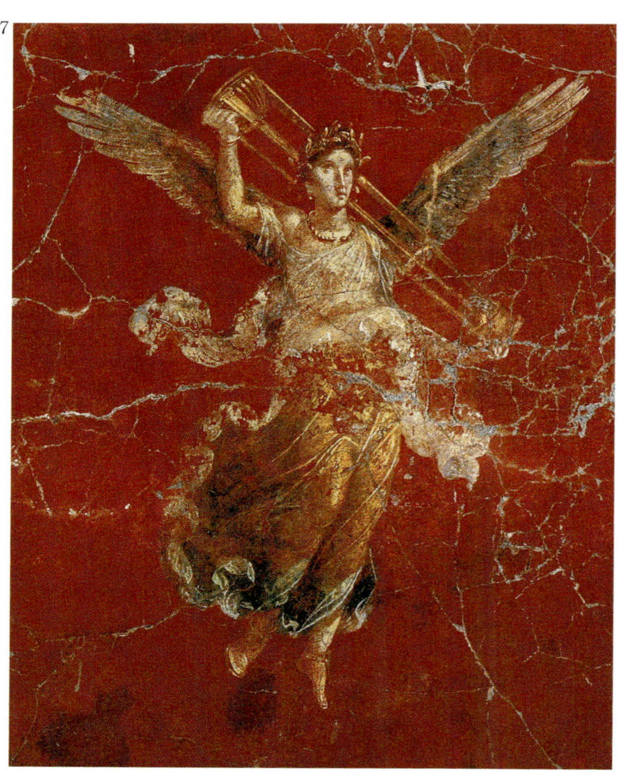

106. **Anonymous**, *Girl Picking Flowers*, 1ˢᵗ century CE,
Ancient Roman. Stabiae. Fresco.
Museo Archeologico Nazionale, Naples.

107. **Anonymous**, *Victory and Delphic Tripod*, 1ˢᵗ century CE,
Ancient Roman. Murecine, Pompeii. Fresco.

108

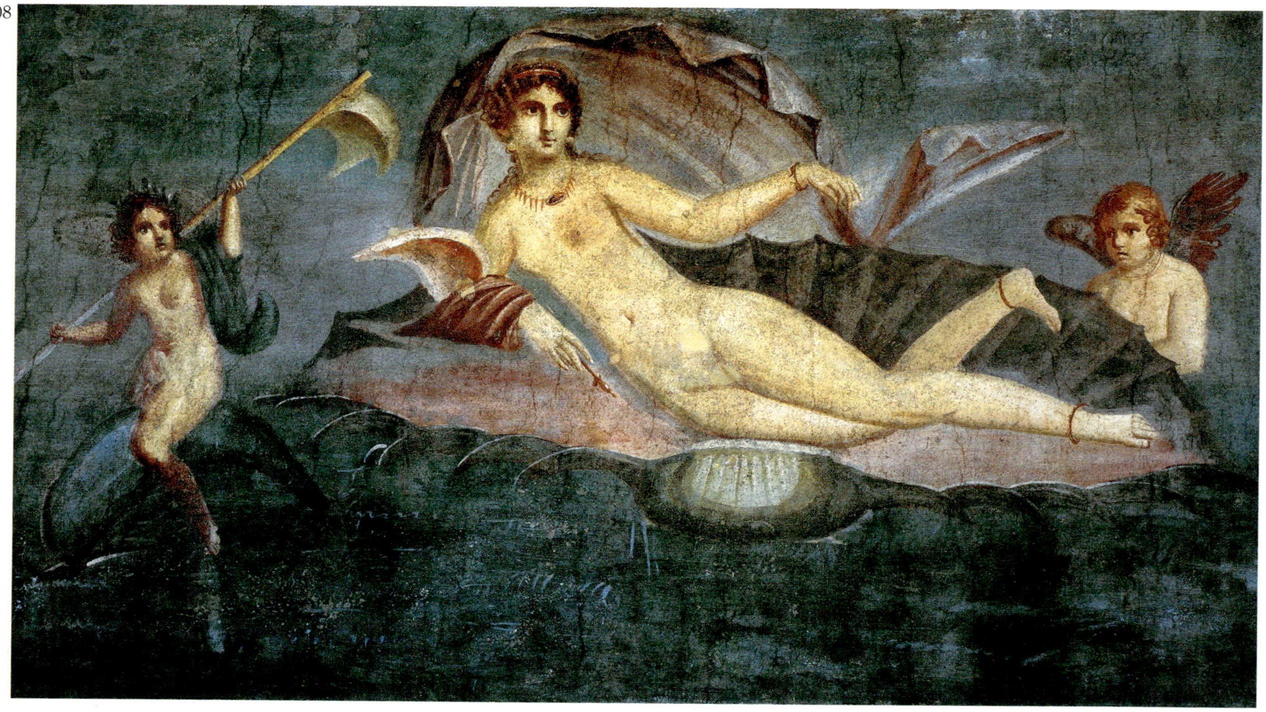

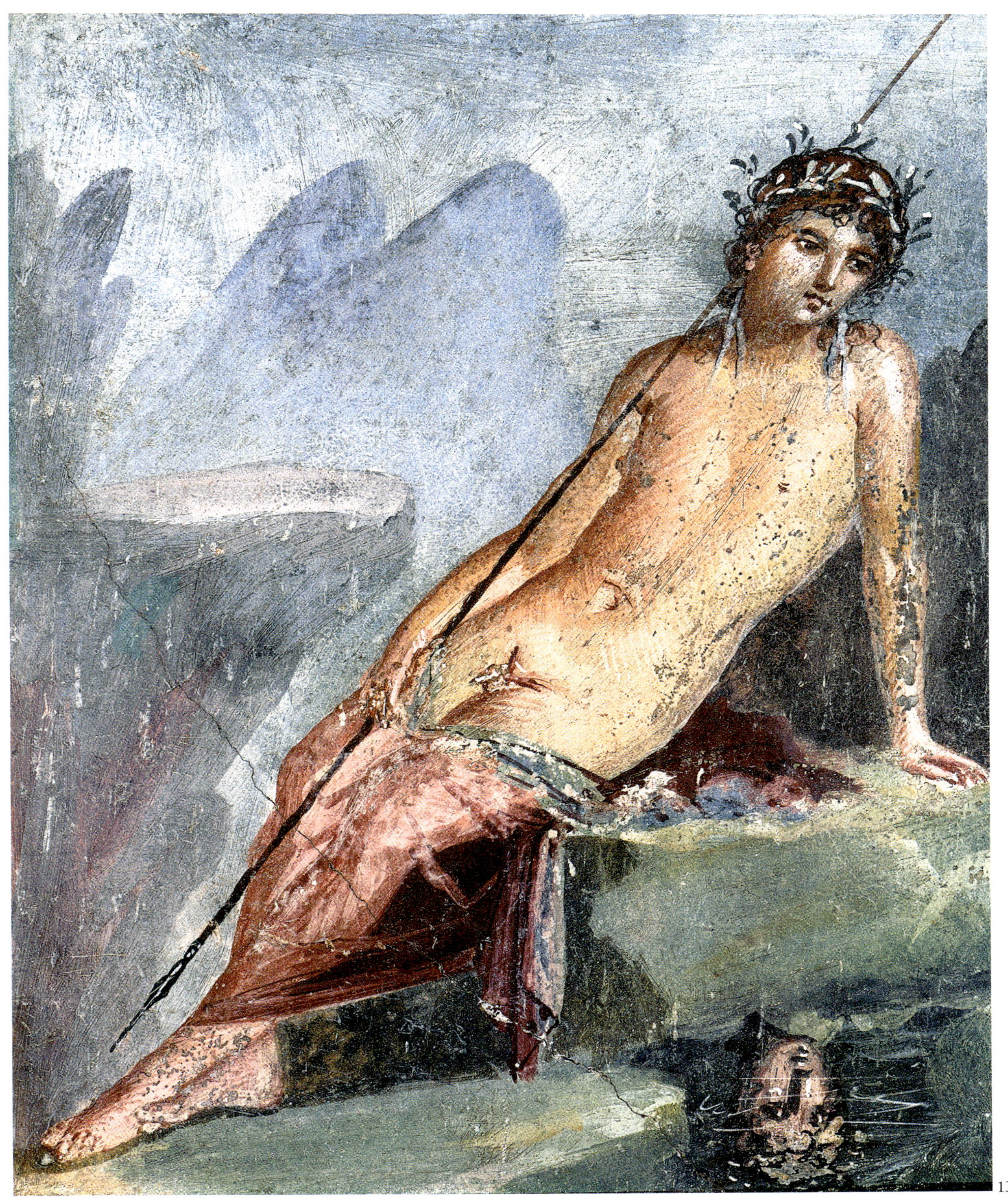

108. **Anonymous**, detail from *The Birth of Venus from a Shell*, 1st century CE, Ancient Roman. Home of the Venus in the Shell, Pompeii. Fresco.

109. **Anonymous**, *Narcissus Admiring Himself in the Water of a Stream*, 1st century CE, Ancient Roman. Marcus Lucretius Fronto house, Pompeii. Fresco.

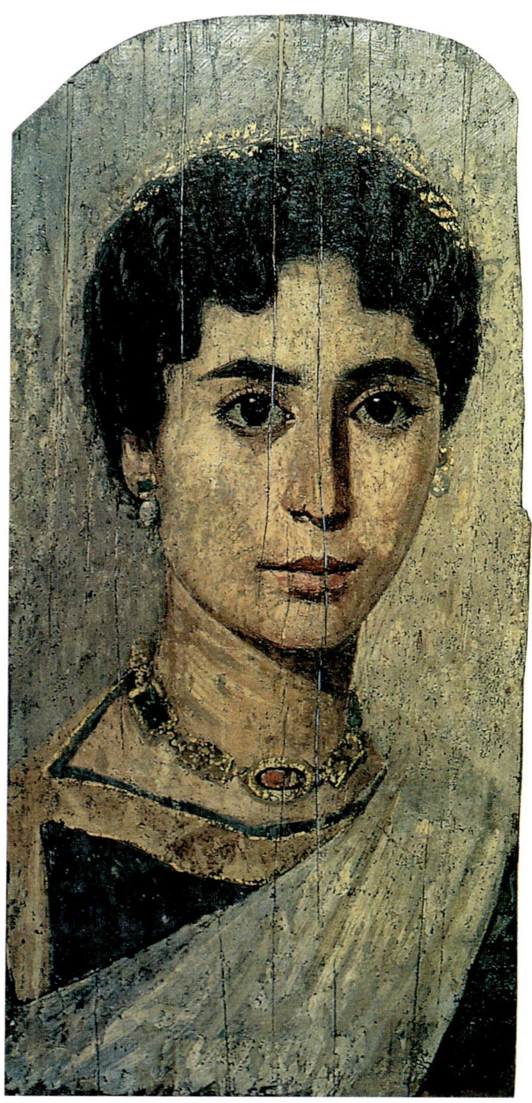

110. **Anonymous**, *Young Aristocrat*, c. 160-170 CE,
Ancient Egyptian. Er-Rubayat, Fayoum.
Encaustic on wood, 44.2 x 20 cm.
The British Museum, London.

Discovered in 1888 by Flinders Petrie in Egypt, the Fayum portraits are a series of figures from the 1ˢᵗ-4ᵗʰ centuries CE. They represent the people who crossed the Fayoum and are therefore an essential source of information on the civilisations of the time. This portrait of the cemetery from Er-Rubayat is distinguished by its style, materials and techniques. Here, lime and polish were preferred to the oak and tempera usually employed in these portraits. The woman, whose hairstyle reflects the fashion of the time, wears a crown of gold leaves, a purple robe with gold bands and a white coat. The quality of the portrait, the rich jewellery of precious stones and the beauty of her dress tells us that the woman belonged to high society.

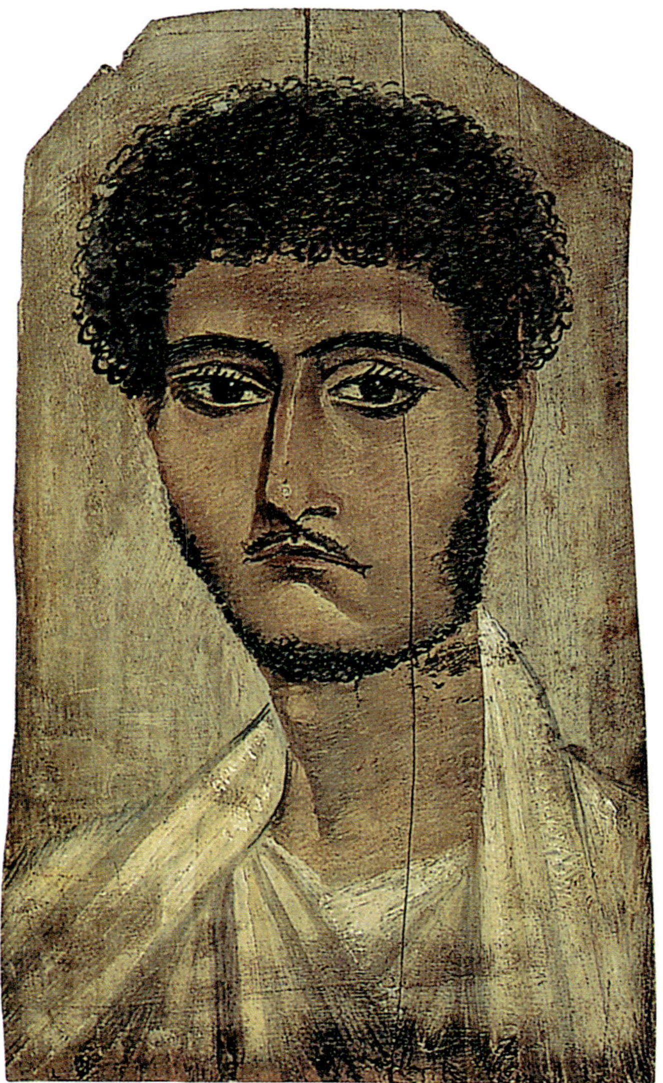

111. **Anonymous**, *Portrait of a Young Man*, c. 70-120 CE, Ancient Egyptian.
Hawara. Encaustic on cedar wood, 38.3 x 22.8 cm.
The British Museum, London.

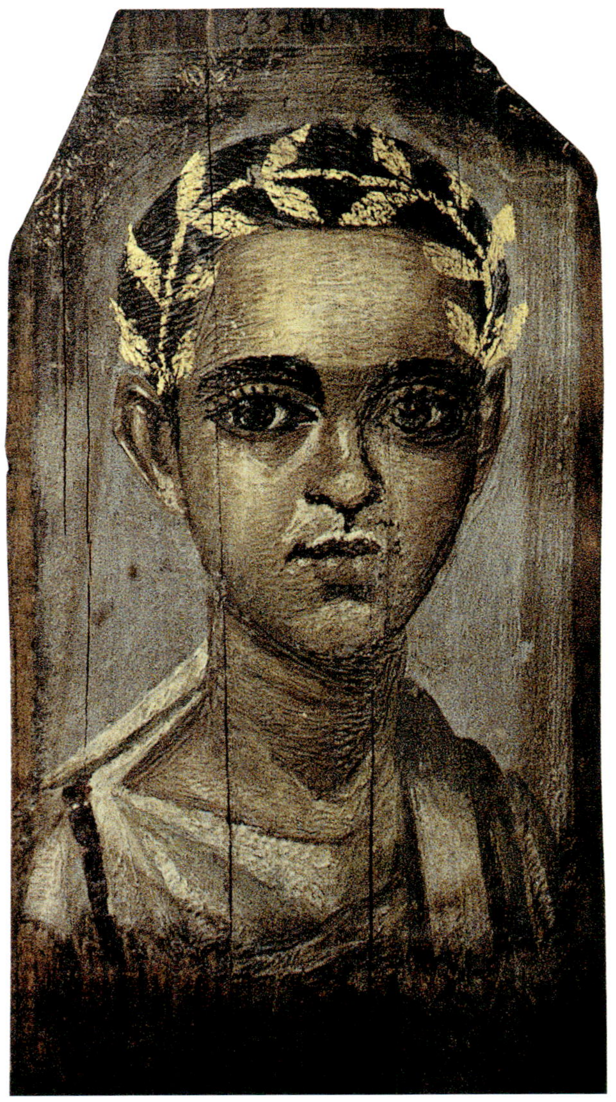

112. **Anonymous**, *The Child*, late 1st-early 2nd century CE, Ancient Egyptian. Fayoum. Encaustic on wood, 35.5 x 16.5 cm. Egyptian Museum, Cairo.

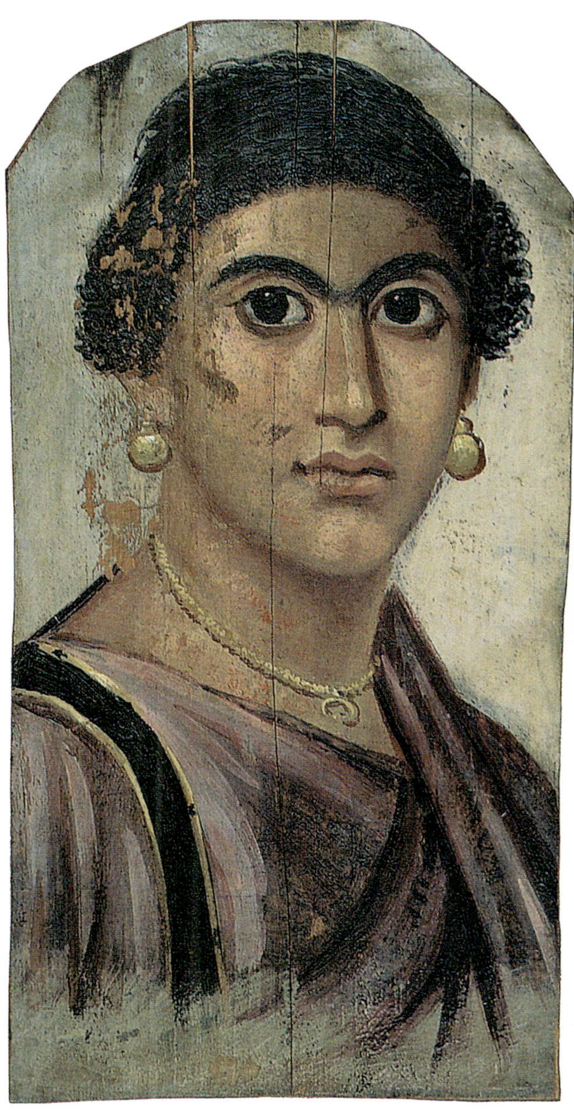

113. **Anonymous**, *Portrait of a Lady*, c. 50-70 CE, Ancient Egyptian. Hawara. Encaustic on cedar wood, 21.5 x 41.6 cm. The British Museum, London.

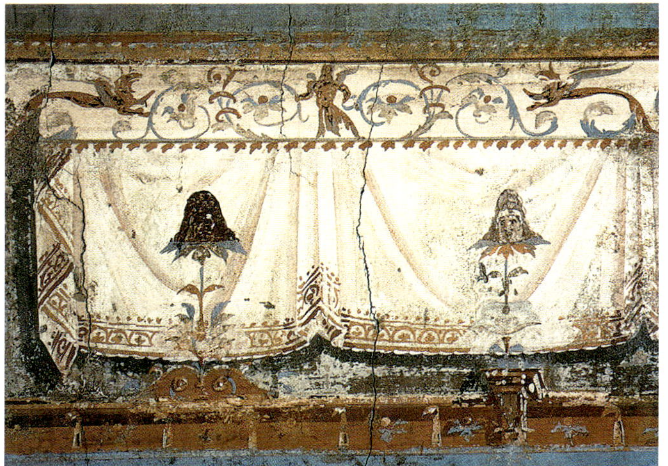

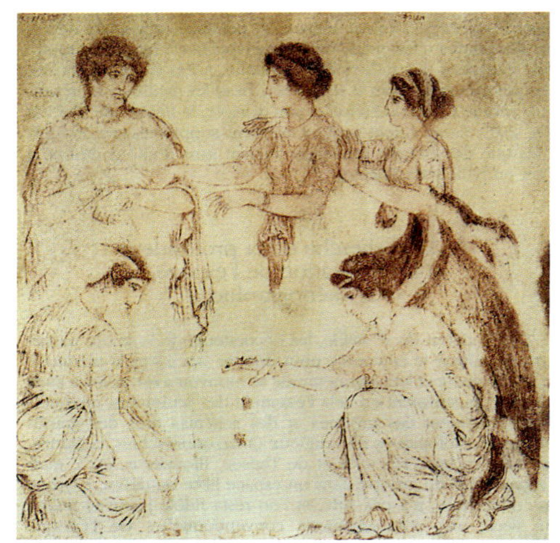

114. **Anonymous**, *Curtain and Theatre Mask*,
1st century BCE-4th century CE, Ancient Roman.
House of the Grand Portal, Herculaneum. Fresco.

115. **Alexandros of Athens**, *Women Playing Jacks*,
1st century BCE-4th century CE, Ancient Roman.
Herculaneum. Painting on marble.
Museo Archeologico Nazionale, Naples.

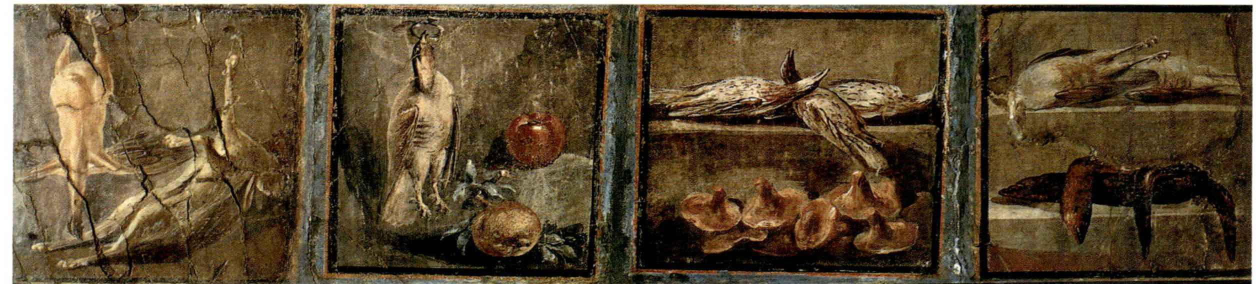

117. **Anonymous**, Wall decoration, c. 77 CE, Ancient Roman.
House of Marcus Fabius Rufus, Pompeii. Fresco.

116. **Anonymous**, *Chicken and Rabbit, Partridge and Pomegranate,
Thrushes and Mushrooms*, 1st century BCE-4th century CE,
Ancient Roman. Deer House, Herculaneum. Fresco.
Museo Archeologico Nazionale, Naples.

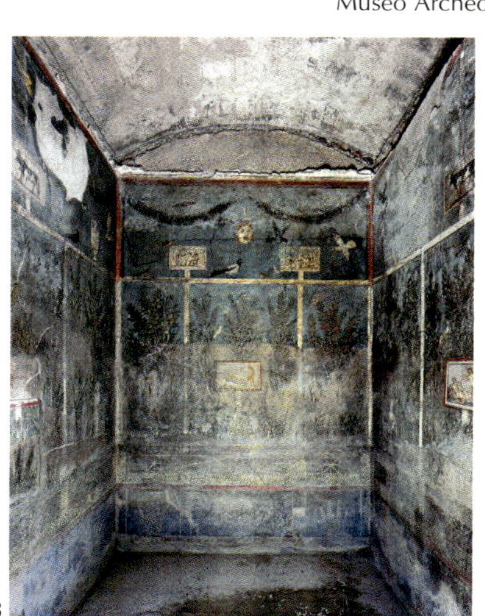

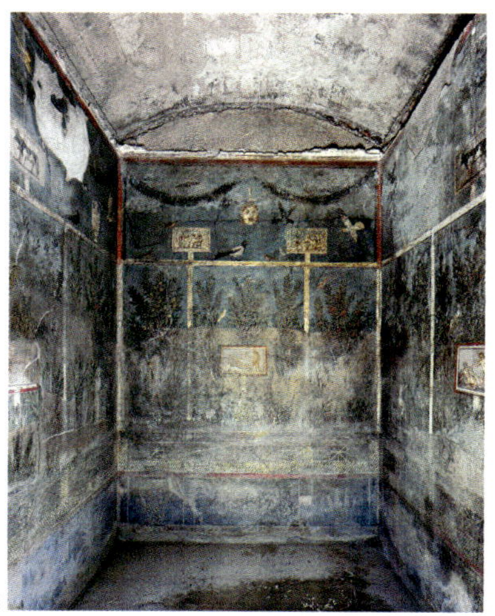

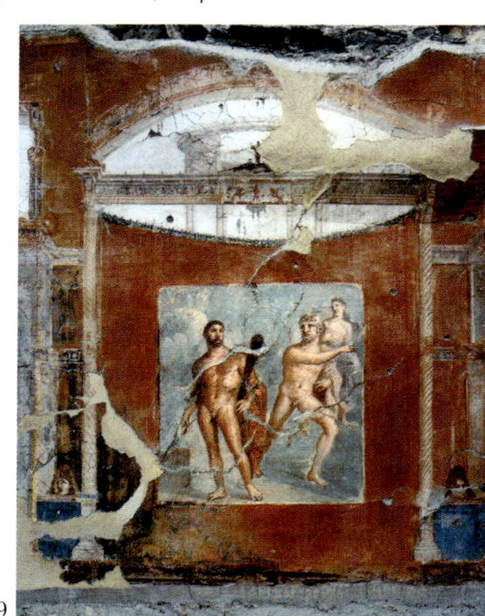

117   118   119

118. **Anonymous**, Representation of a garden, 1st century BCE,
Ancient Roman. Orchard house. Pompeii. Fresco.

119. **Anonymous**, *Hercules and Achelous*,
1st century BCE-4th century CE, Ancient Roman.
College of Augustales, Herculaneum. Fresco.

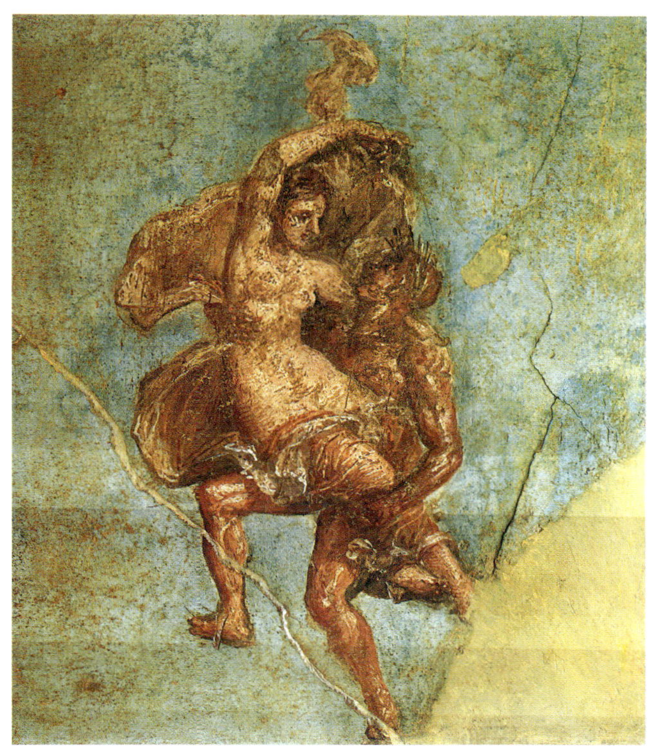

120. **Anonymous**, Erotic scene, 1st century BCE, Ancient Roman.
Pompeii. Fresco.

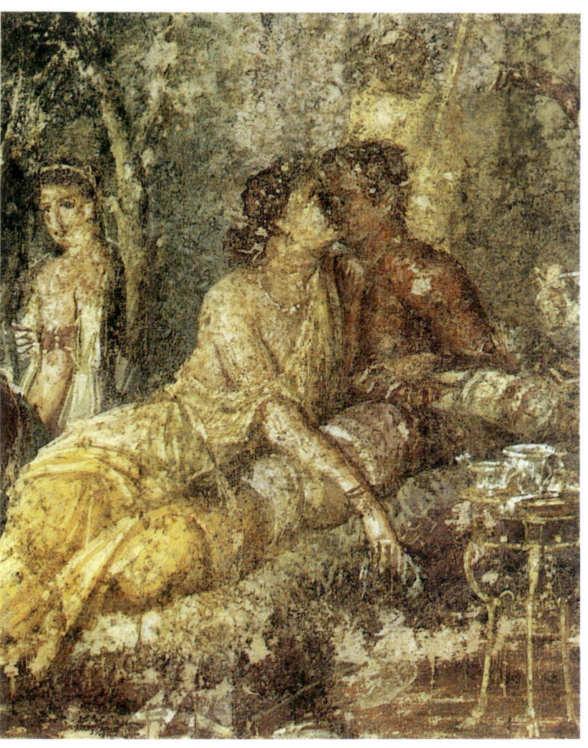

121. **Anonymous**, *Banquet Scene in the Open*, 1st century CE,
Ancient Roman. Pompeii. Fresco.
Museo Archeologico Nazionale, Naples.

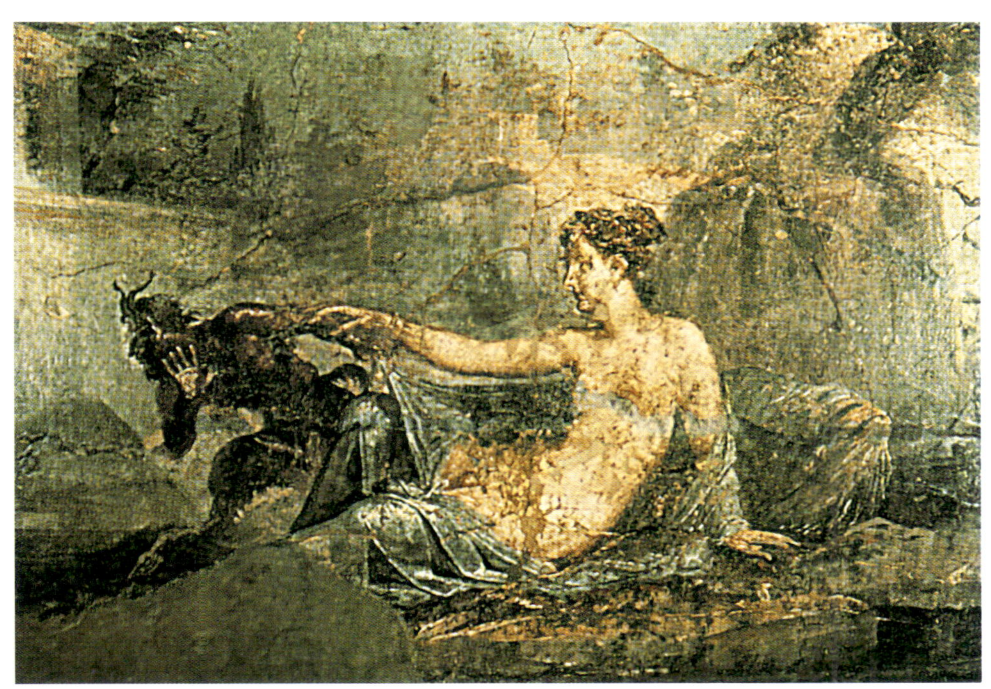

122. **Anonymous**,
*Hermaphrodite with
Pan*, 54-68 CE, Ancient
Roman. House of
Dioscuri, Pompeii.
Fresco.
Museo Archeologico
Nazionale, Naples.

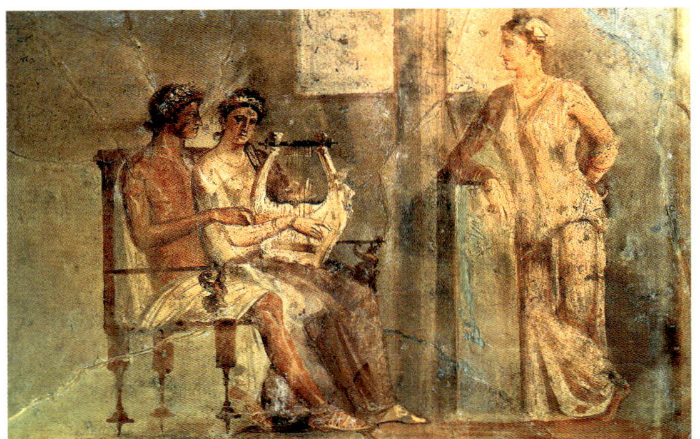

123. **Anonymous**, *Young Woman Learning the Sitar under the Supervision of her Mother*, first century CE, Ancient Roman. Fresco. Museo Archeologico Nazionale, Naples.

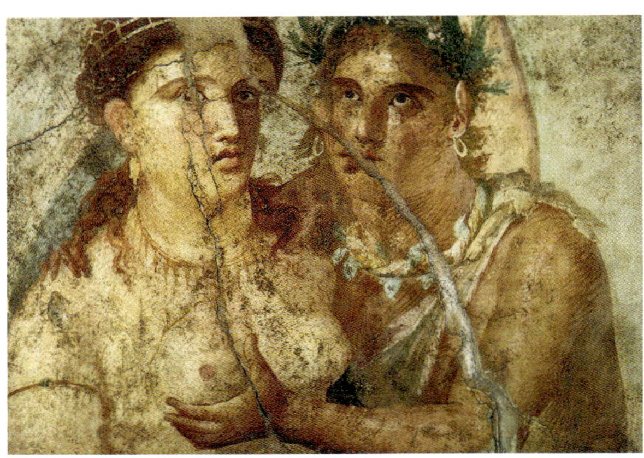

124. **Anonymous**, *Satyr and Maenad*, 1ˢᵗ century BCE, Ancient Roman. House of L. Jucundus Caecilius, Pompeii. Fresco. Museo Archeologico Nazionale, Naples.

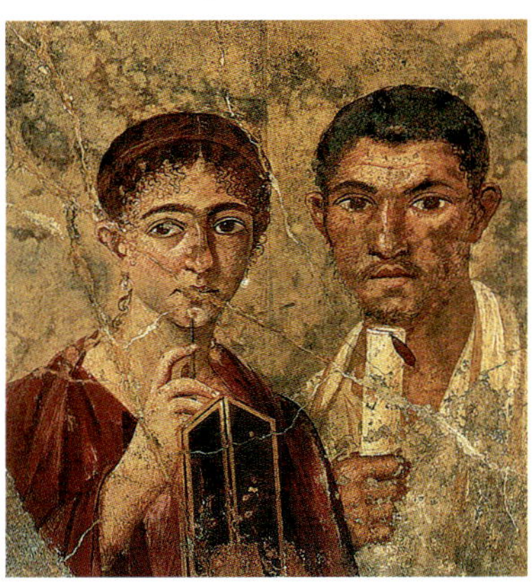

125. **Anonymous**, *The Baker and his Wife*, 1ˢᵗ century CE, Ancient Roman. Pompeii. Fresco, 48.9 x 41 cm. Museo Archeologico Nazionale, Naples.

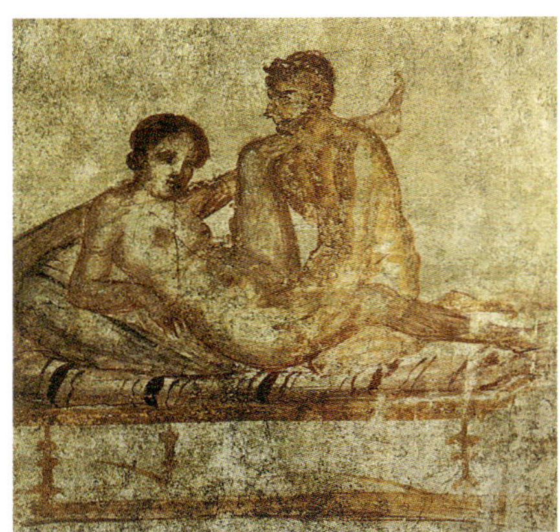

126. **Anonymous**, Erotic scene, 1ˢᵗ century CE, Ancient Roman. House Vettii, Pompeii. Fresco.

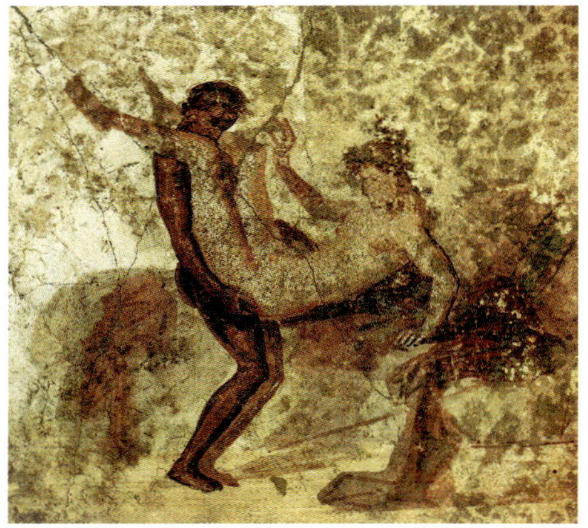

127. **Anonymous**, *Man Standing with Legs of a Reclining Woman around his Neck*, 1ˢᵗ century CE, Ancient Roman. House of Punished Love, Pompeii. Fresco.

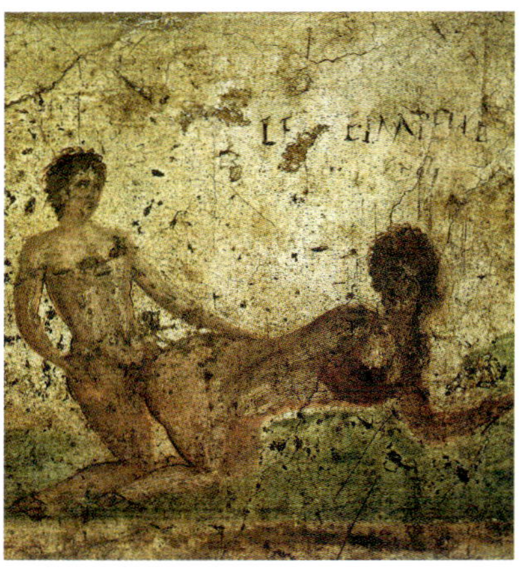

128. **Anonymous**, *Coitus a Tergo*, 1ˢᵗ century CE, Ancient Roman. Pompeii. Fresco.

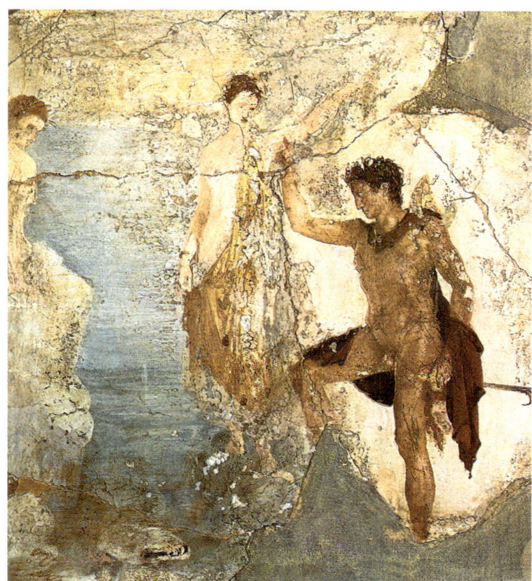

129. **Anonymous**, *Andromeda Freed by Perseus*, 60-79 CE,
Ancient Roman Herculaneum. Fresco.
Museo Archeologico Nazionale, Naples.

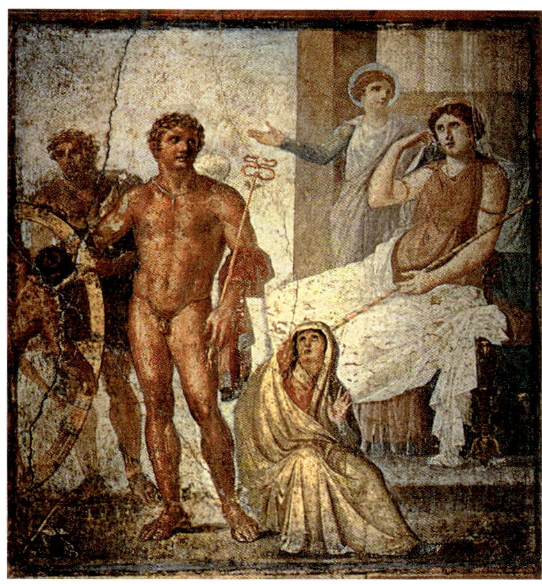

130. **Anonymous**, *The Punishment of Ixion*, late 1ˢᵗ century CE,
Ancient Roman.
Vettii house, Pompeii. Fresco.

131. **Anonymous**, *Three Christians in the Furnace*, 3ʳᵈ-4ᵗʰ century CE,
Early Christian. Catacomb of Priscilla, Rome. Fresco.

Located on the Via Salaria in Rome, the catacomb of Priscilla is in an old quarry from the Roman era, used from the late second to the fourth century for the burial of Christians. It is one of the largest and oldest of Roman catacombs and is named after Priscilla, wife of the consul Acilius, a martyr who converted to Christianity and was killed on the orders of Emperor Domitian. On some walls and ceilings you can see decorations depicting biblical scenes.

Among these, there are frescos of the Old and New Testaments, and three Christians thrown into the furnace. The painting illustrates a biblical story from the book of Daniel. Shadrach, Meshach and Abednego, three Jewish friends, who refused to worship the golden statue of Nebuchadnezzar, king of Babylon, were thrown into the furnace but miraculously saved by God. Here, they can be seen amid the flames singing a hymn.

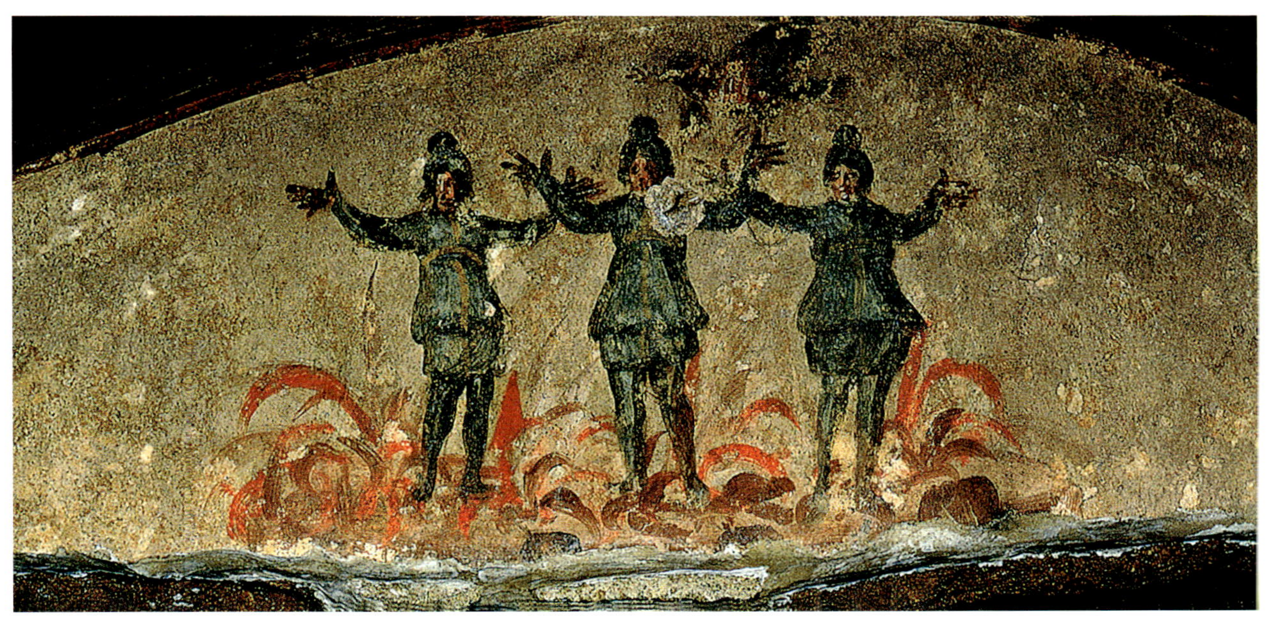

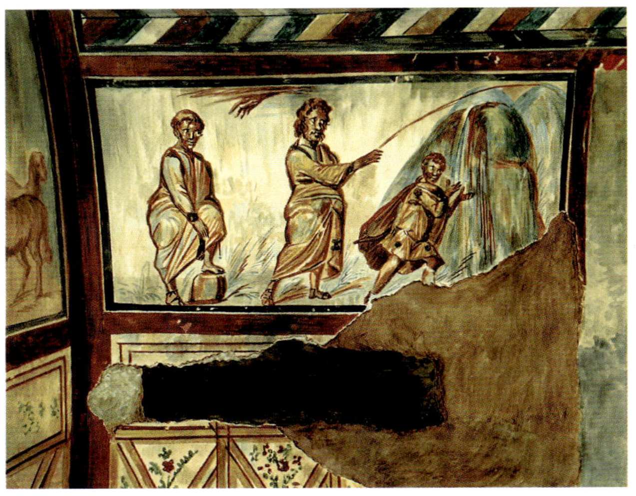

132. **Anonymous**, *Moses and Peter*, 3rd-4th century CE, Early Christian. Catacomb of St Callistus, Rome. Fresco.

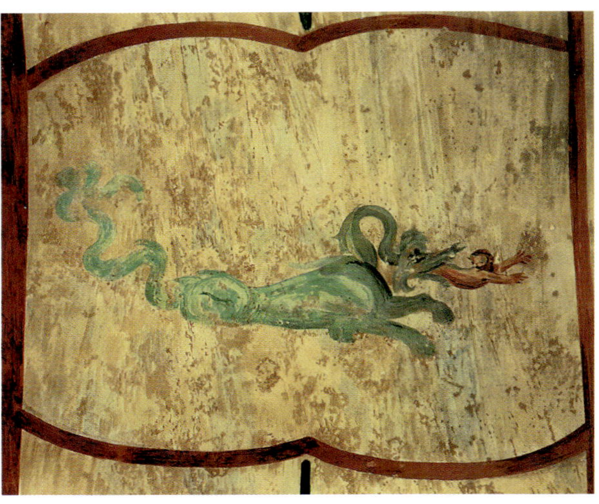

133. **Anonymous**, *Jonah in the Belly of the Whale*, 3rd-4th century CE, Early Christian. Catacomb of Priscilla, Rome. Fresco.

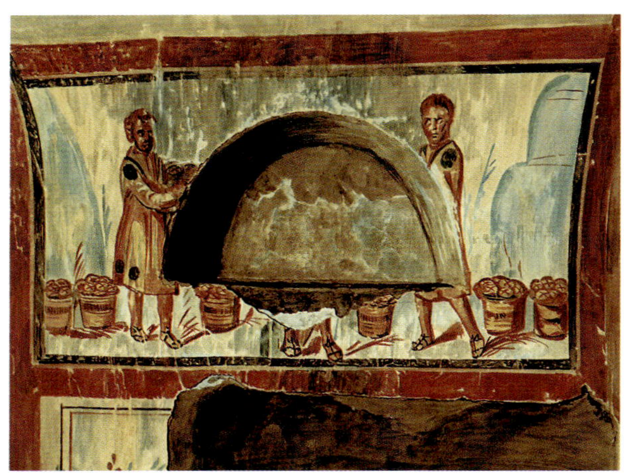

134. **Anonymous**, *The Multiplication of the Loaves and Fishes*, 3rd-4th century CE, Early Christian. Catacomb of St Callistus, Rome. Fresco.

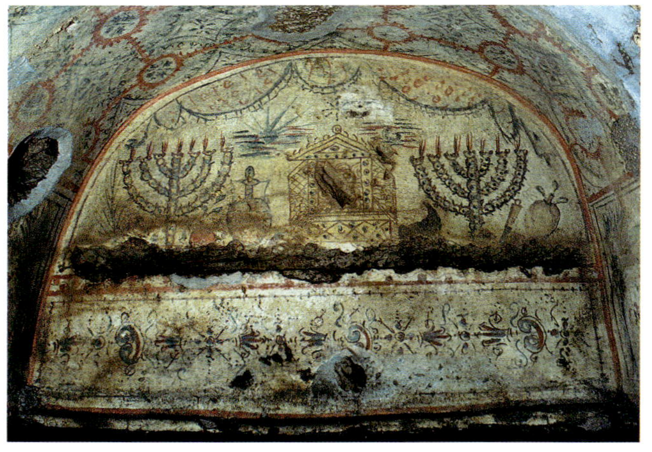

135. **Anonymous**, *Candlestick from the Torah*, 4th century CE, Early Christian. Torlonia catacomb, Rome. Fresco.

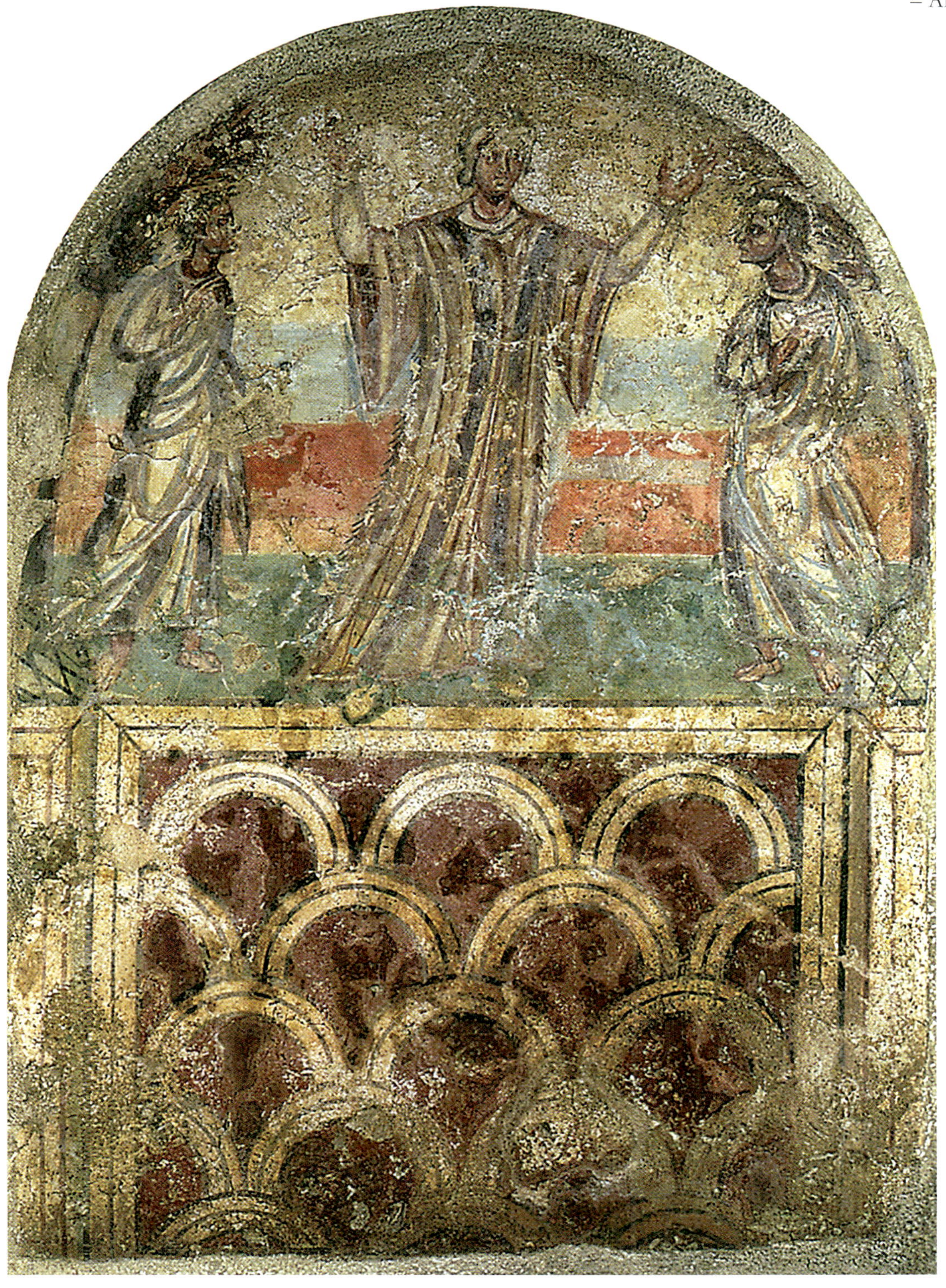

136. **Anonymous**, *Susanna and the Elders*, 5th century CE, Early Christian. Fresco.
Museum of Byzantine Culture, Thessaloniki.

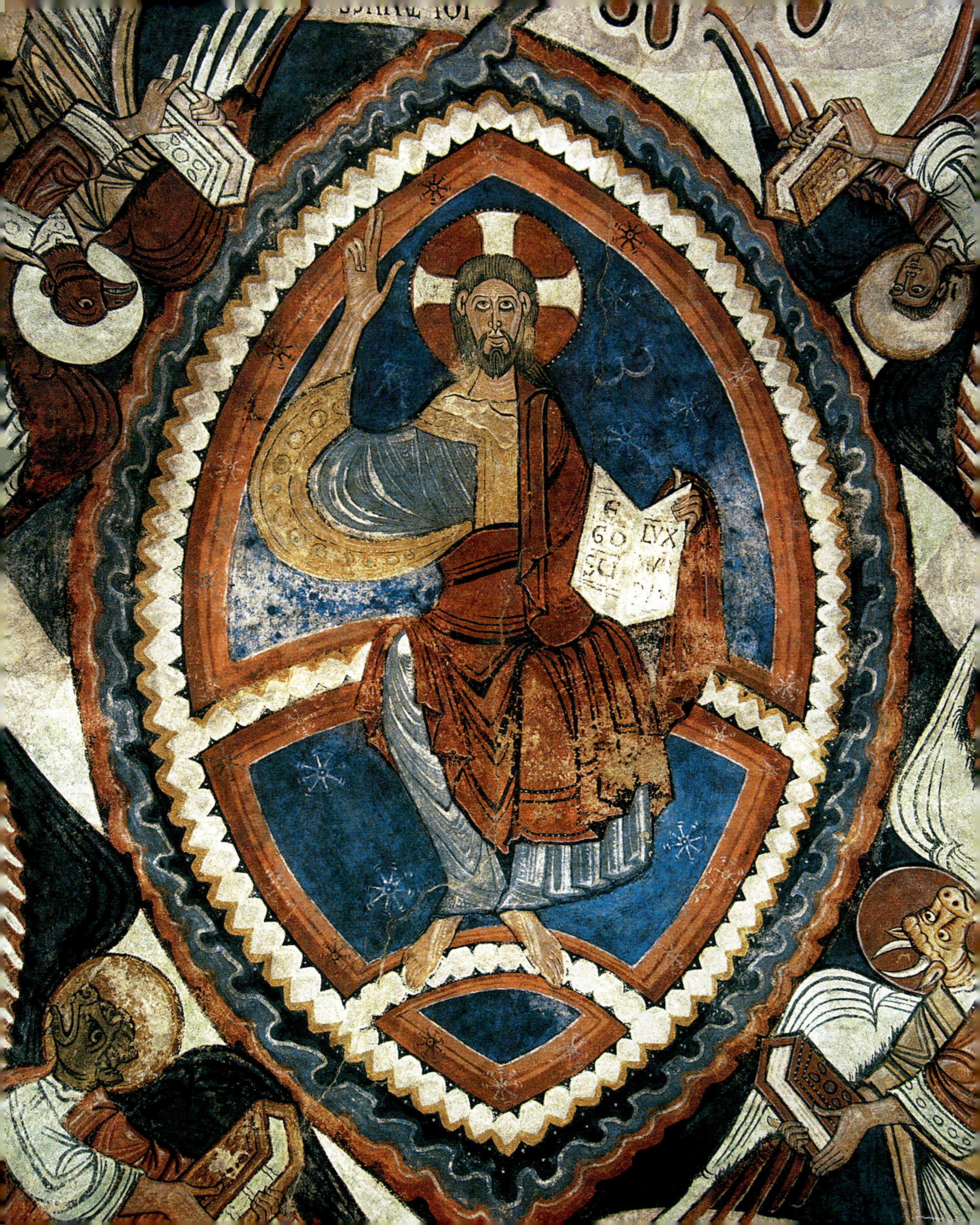

EGO
SU
LVX

The Middle Ages

Historically, the Middle Ages are defined as the period between the fall of the western Roman Empire, which in 476 marked the end of antiquity, and the collapse of Constantinople in 1453. For a long time wrongly regarded as a 'sterile' period, the millennium was, in fact, an epoch rich in art, when the canons of the classical era were harmonised with the customs and morals of the time. As early as the second century, the dominance of Christianity and the restrictions demanded from its followers had given birth to early Christian art, which drew its origins from Rome. Until the thirteenth century, this new society was characterised mainly by sobriety. In architecture and sculpture, forms remained simple and massive, superficiality was banned and art became a powerful symbol of the strength and stability of Christianity. But over the centuries, despite prevailing through such features as ogive ribs, the Romanesque style gradually gave way to the more refined art of Gothic. Religious and intellectual centres abandoned their rural environments and moved to towns such as Paris, which, under Philip II, grew into the capital of Gothic Europe, becoming renowned for its university and manuscript illumination as well as for its architecture. In the *Divine Comedy*, Dante describes the city as the 'capital of the art of illumination'. The rest of Europe tried to reproduce Gothic, but German and English architects showed less interest in the elevation displayed by France's great Reims and Amiens cathedrals. England's achievements were more political in nature: the Magna Carta of 1215 and the creation of parliament during the reign of Edward I. The fourteenth century was a less prosperous period, when the Catholic Church was marked by the schism between the Orthodox Church in the East and the Roman Catholics in the West, which in turn contributed to the social chaos caused by the Hundred Years War (1337-1453). At the same time, Italy, the birthplace of painters such as Giotto and Simone Martini, was governed by an aristocratic elite, which controlled international trade through a sophisticated economic system. The prosperity this brought was interrupted at the end of 1340 by the Black Death, the bubonic plague that in five years decimated Europe's population.

While Europe was experiencing economic and social upheaval, the Ottoman Empire and Islamic states rose to power. The Great Schism that occurred after the election of 1378, and which produced two rival popes, one based in Avignon, the other in Rome, worsened the situation considerably. Meanwhile, the secular sphere experienced a significant shift with the arrival in Italy of vernacular literature. Although Latin was still the official language of Church and State documents, the intellectual and philosophical ideas expressed in this language became more accessible. Dante, Petrarch and Boccaccio were all involved in the establishment of Italian as a common language, which gave the *Divine Comedy* and the *Decameron* a wider audience. Petrarch, for his part, developed ideas of individualism and humanism. Much more than just a philosophical system, humanism was a code of civil conduct that contained ideas about education and encompassed a range of issues based not on faith or religious scholarship but on reason. Classical Latin literature from Greco-Roman antiquity permitted the development of ethical rules governing civil society, such as participation in the civil service and government, defence of the state and contribution to the general good. The humanists translated not only Greek and Roman texts that had been previously neglected, but also composed new writings consecrated to the humanistic cult of glory. As if to illustrate the final moments of this extraordinary time, there was a burgeoning of illuminated manuscripts, of which the *Très Riches Heures du Duc de Berry* (*The Very Rich Hours of the Duke of Berry*, p. 93) is the most sumptuous and beautiful example.

137. **Anonymous**, *Christ in Glory*, c. 1100-1120, Romanesque. Basilica de San Isidoro, Leon. Fresco.

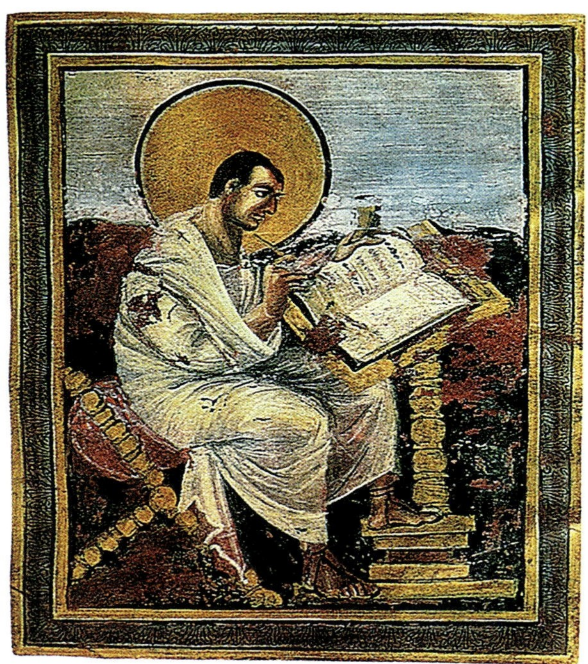

138. **Anonymous**, *St Matthew*, c. 800, Romanesque.
Parchment. Graphische Sammlung Albertina, Vienna.

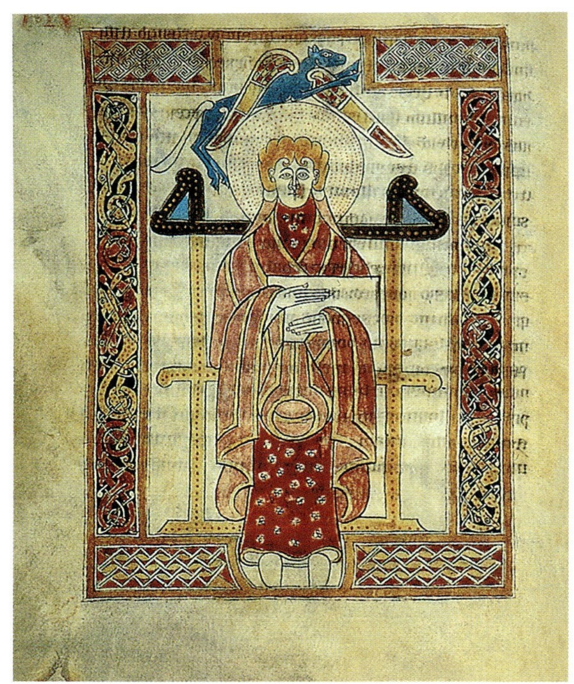

139. **Anonymous**, *St Luke*, c. 750, Romanesque.
Parchment, 29.5 x 22.5 cm. Abbey Library, St Gallen.

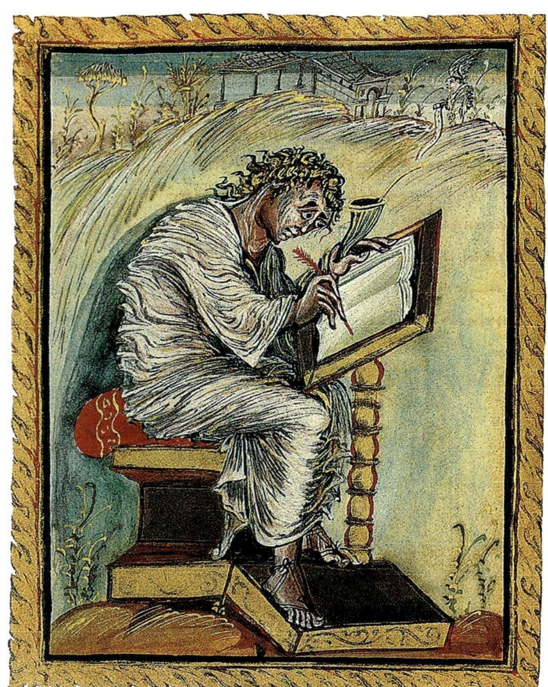

140. **Anonymous**, *Gospel of Ebbo. St Matthew*, c. 830,
Romanesque. Parchment.
Médiathèque d'Epernay, Epernay.

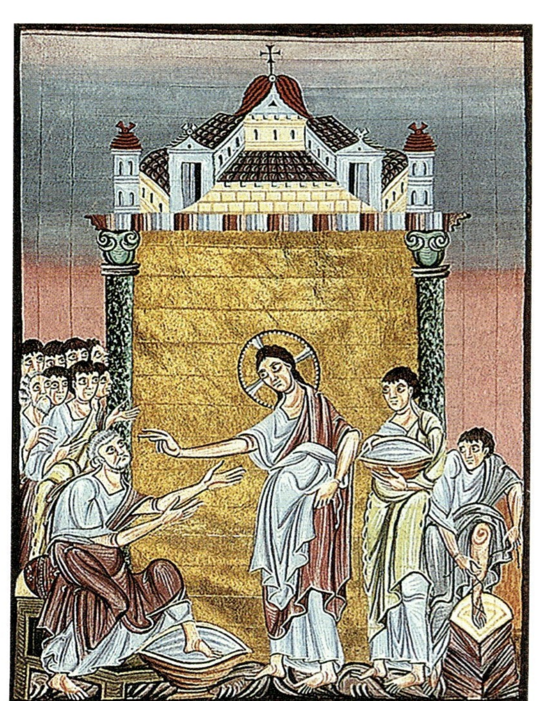

141. **Anonymous**, *Christ Washing the Apostles' Feet – Otto III
Gospels*, c. 1000, Romanesque.
Parchment. Bayerische Staatsbibliothek, Munich.

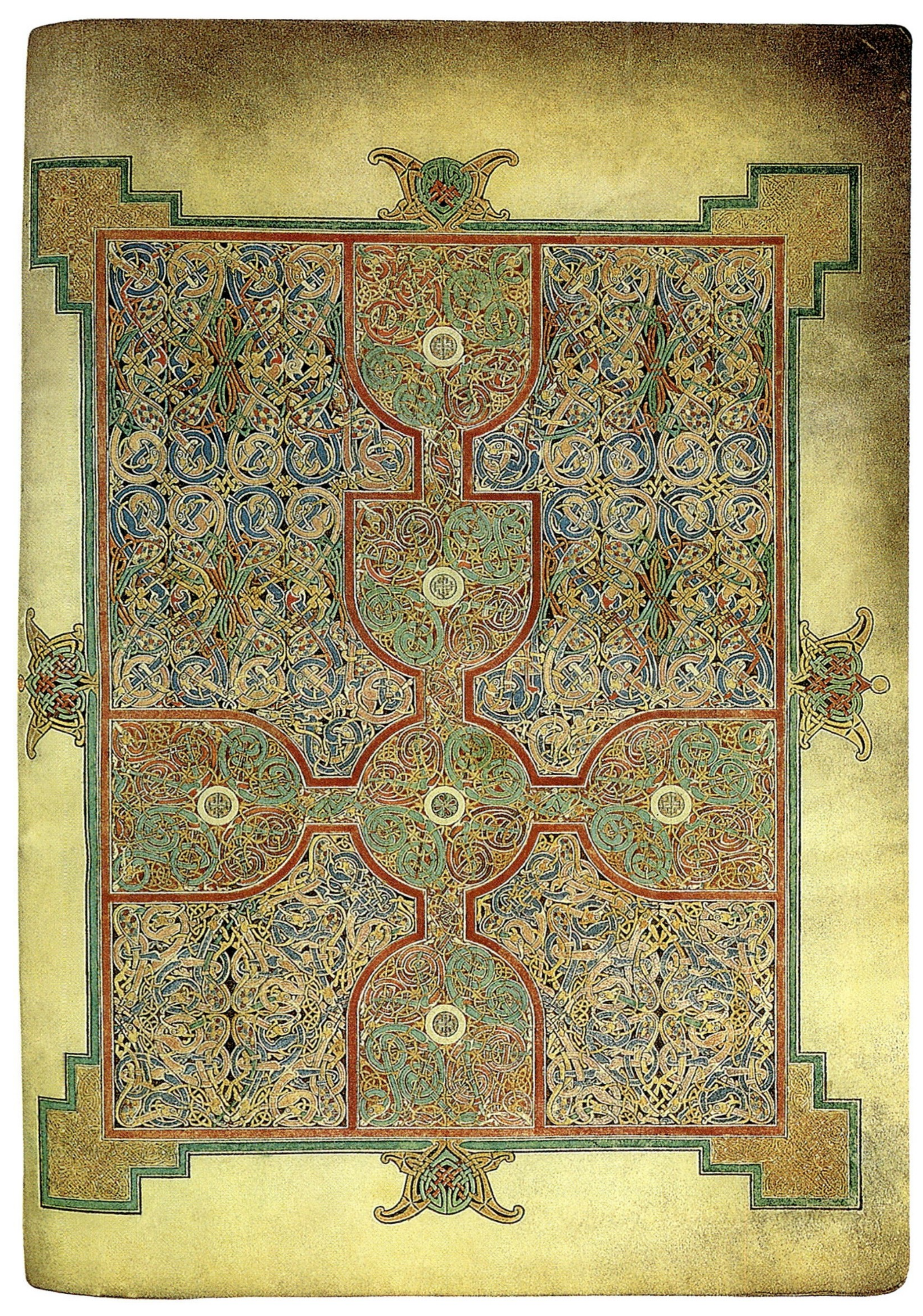

142. **Anonymous**, *Page from the Lindisfarne Gospels*, c. 698, Romanesque. Parchment.
The British Museum, London.

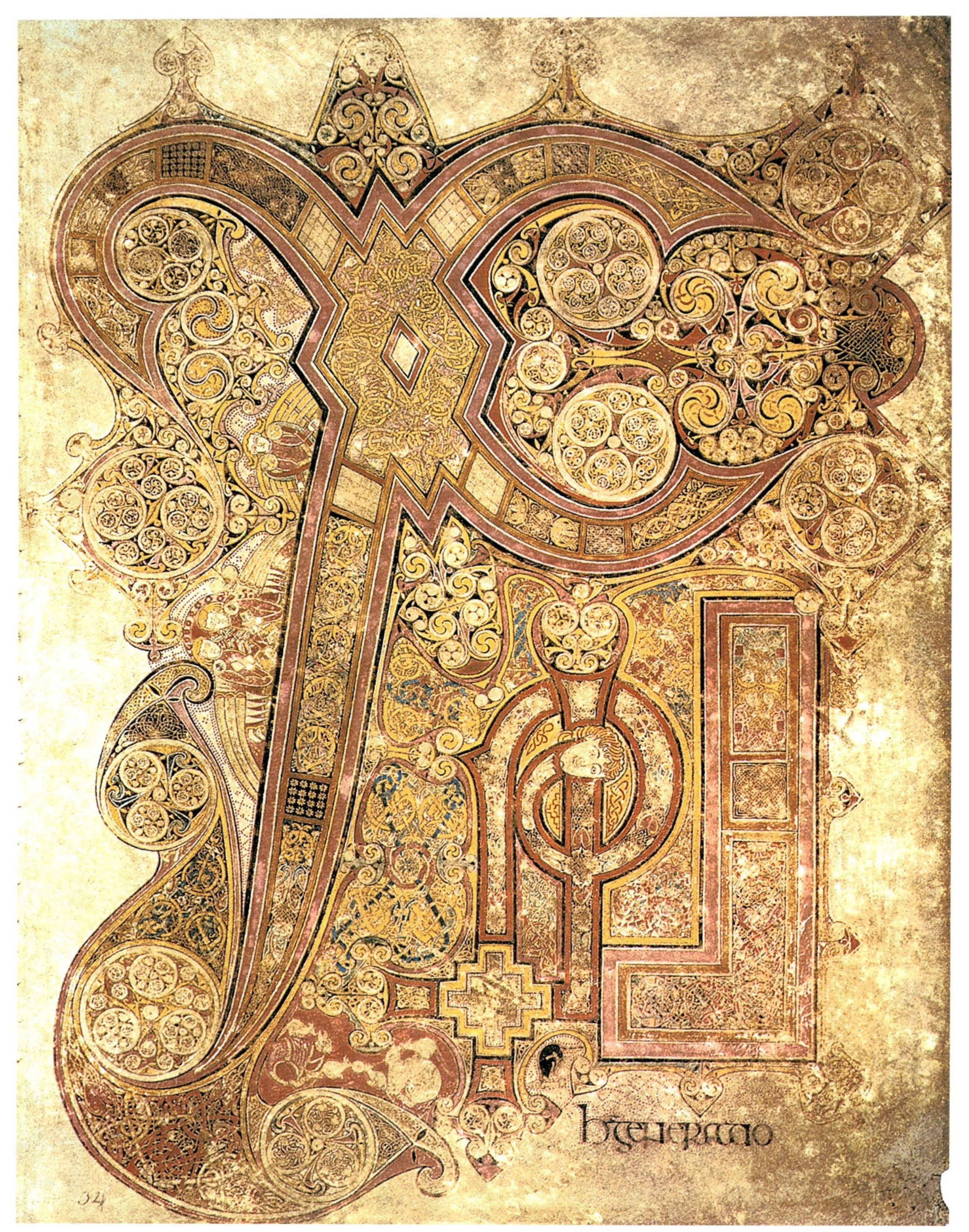

143. **Anonymous**, *Book of Kells. Monogram of the Incarnation*, early 9th century, Romanesque. Parchment, 33 x 25 cm.
Trinity College Library, Dublin.

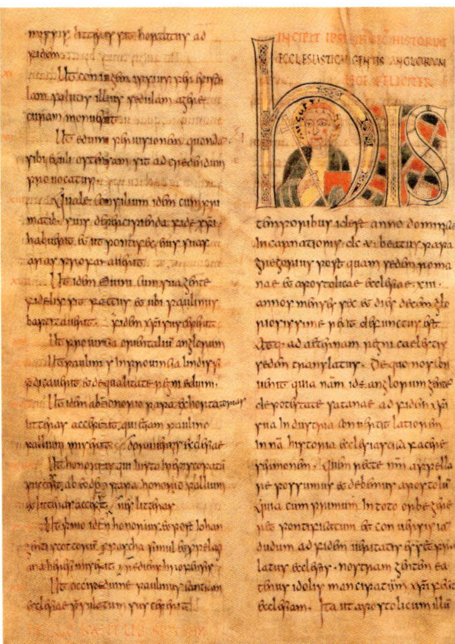

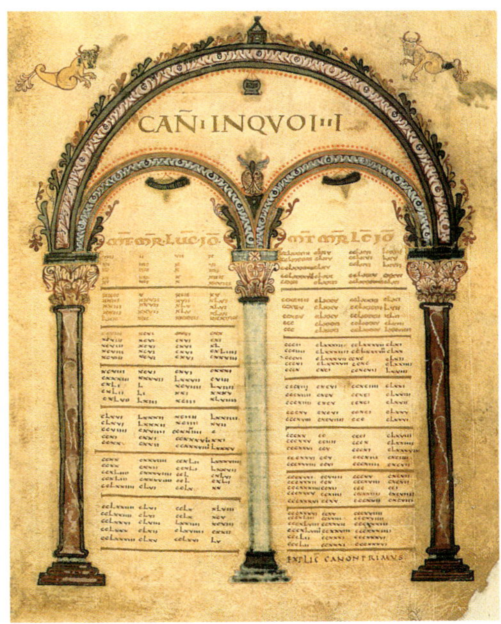

144. Anonymous, *Tetraevangelium. First Table of Canons*, 10th century, Romanesque. Parchment, 29.7 x 22.5 cm. Library, Tours.

145. Anonymous, *Historia Ecclesiastica Anglorum Gentis*, introductory leaflet with illuminated original, c. 731, Romanesque. Parchment, 27 x 19 cm. Northumbria.

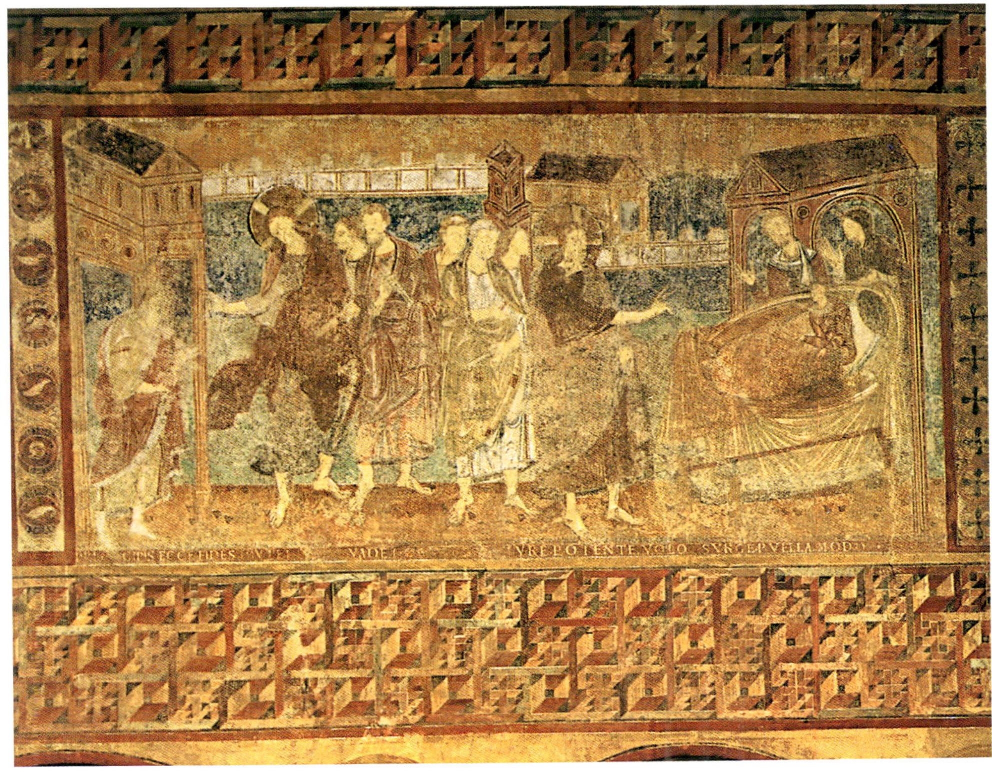

146. Anonymous, *Healing of a Woman*, c. 980, Romanesque. Mural. Oberzell Church, Reichenau.

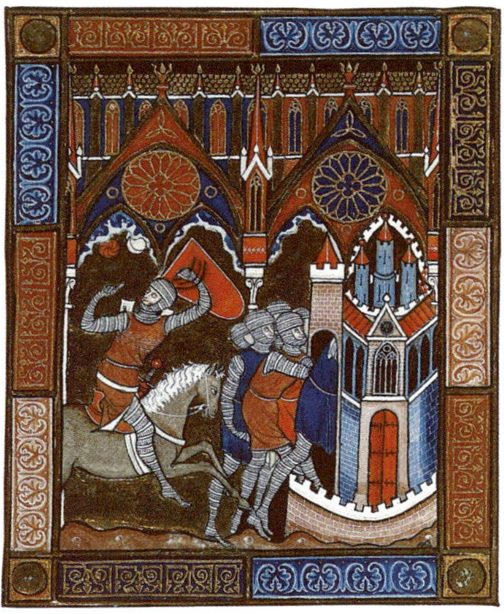

147

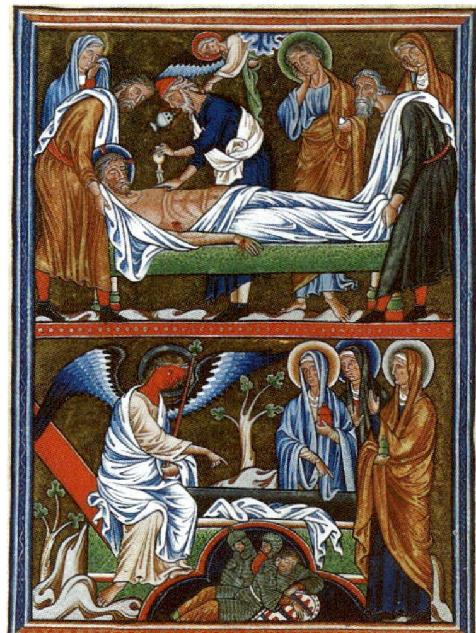

148

147. **Workshop of Louis IX**,
Early Renaissance, France, Danish,
Joshua Stops the Sun and Moon,
From the Psalter of Louis IX of
France, c. 1258-1270.
Manuscript illumination, 21 x 14.5 cm.
Bibliothèque Nationale, Paris.

148. **Workshop of the Ingeborg**,
Early Renaissance, Danish,
*Embalming of the Body of Christ and
the Three Marys at the Empty Tomb*,
From the Psalter of Queen Ingeborg of
Denmark, c. 1213.
Manuscript illumination, 30.4 x 20.4 cm.
Musée Condé, Chantilly.

149. **Giotto di Bondone**, 1267-1337, Early Renaissance, Florentine School, Italian,
The Demons are Cast out of Arezzo (detail), 1296-1297. Fresco.
Upper Church of San Francesco, Assisi.

150. **Giotto di Bondone**, 1267-1337, Medieval, Florentine School, Italian,
Flight into Egypt, 200 x 185 cm, 1303-1305. Fresco.
Cappella Scrovegni (Arena Chapel), Padua.

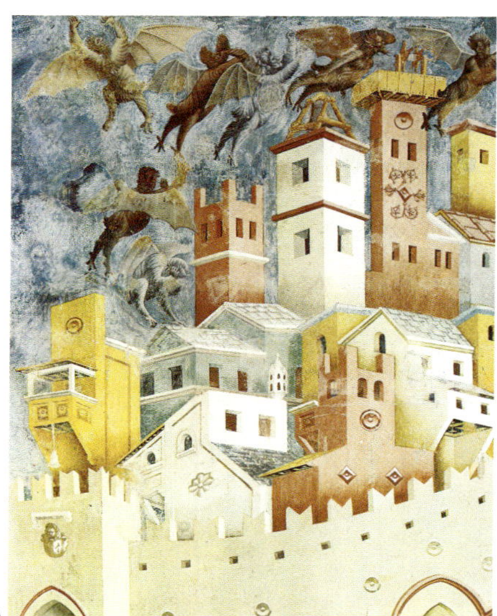

149

150

GIOTTO DI BONDONE
(1267 VESPIGNANO – 1337 FLORENCE)

His full name was Ambrogiotto di Bondone, but he is known today, as he was in his own time, by the contraction, Giotto, a word which has come to stand for almost all the great things that art has accomplished. In his own day Giotto's fame as a painter was supreme; he had numerous followers, and these *Giotteschi*, as they were styled, perpetuated his methods for nearly a hundred years. In 1334, he designed the beautiful *Campanile* (bell tower), which stands beside the cathedral in Florence, and represents a perfect union of strength and elegance, and was partly erected in his lifetime. Moreover, the sculptured reliefs which decorate its lower part were all from his designs, though he lived to execute only two of them. Inspired by French Gothic sculpture, he abandoned the stiff presentations of the subjects as in Byzantine styles and advanced art towards more realistic presentation of contemporary figures and scenes so as to be more narrative. His breakthrough influenced subsequent development in Italian art. His significant departure from past presentations of the Maestà, starting around 1308 (in *Madonna di Ognissanti*), brought to it his knowledge of architecture and its perspectives. However, the disproportion of subjects in the presentation is a device intended to rank the subjects by their importance, as was done in Byzantine icons.

Thus, architect, sculptor, painter, friend of Dante and of other great men of his day, Giotto was the worthy forerunner of that galaxy of brilliant men who populated the later days of the Italian Renaissance.

MASO DI BANCO
(ACTIVE 1320 – 1350)

Florentine painter, Maso di Banco is undoubtedly the greatest pupil of Giotto but as he was not mentioned by Vasari we don't know much of his career. His greatest works are the frescoes illustrating the legend of St Sylvester in the Bardi Chapel of Santa Croce in Florence, where one can appreciate the clarity of his work and the harmonies of colours. As he was a follower of Ghiberti, his work also shows architectural settings and massive figures that anticipate the monumental style of Piero della Francesca and Masaccio.

151. **Duccio di Buoninsegna**, 1255-1319,
Early Renaissance, Sienese School, Italian,
Christ Entering Jerusalem, 1308-1311.
Tempera on panel, 100 x 57 cm.
Museo dell'Opera del Duomo, Siena.

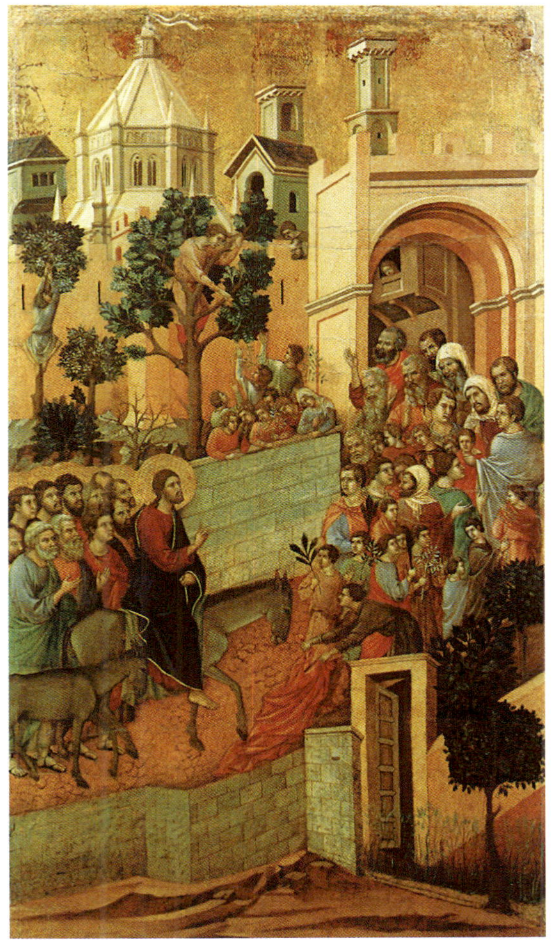

152. **Maso di Banco**,
active 1320-1350,
Early Renaissance,
Florentine School,
Italian, *Pope St Sylvester's
Miracle*, c. 1340. Fresco.
Cappella di Bardi di
Vernio, Santa Croce,
Florence.

*Here Maso di Banco
represents the scene of
the "dragon miracle": on
the left the Pope chains
the dragon, then he brings
the dead Magi back to
life. On the right side,
Emperor Constantine and
his suite look at the scene
in astonishment.*

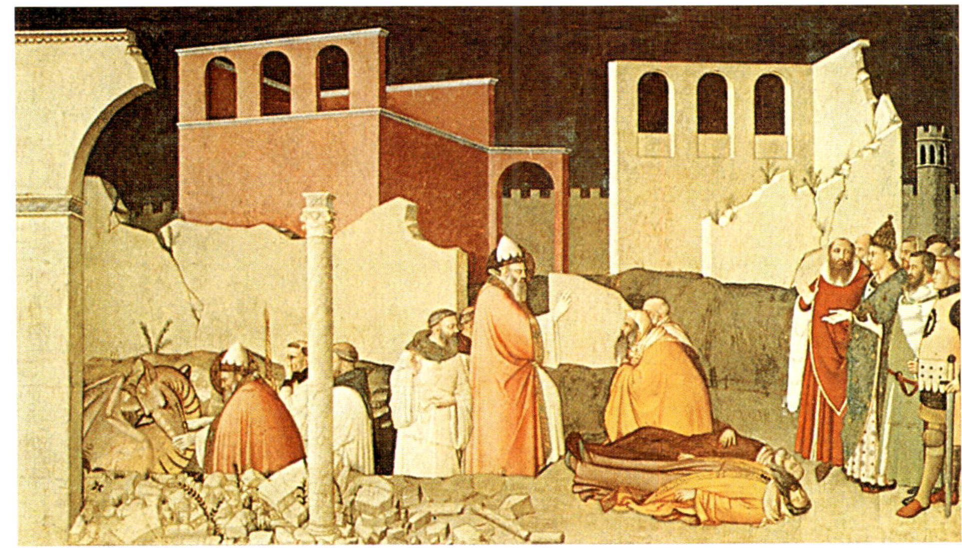

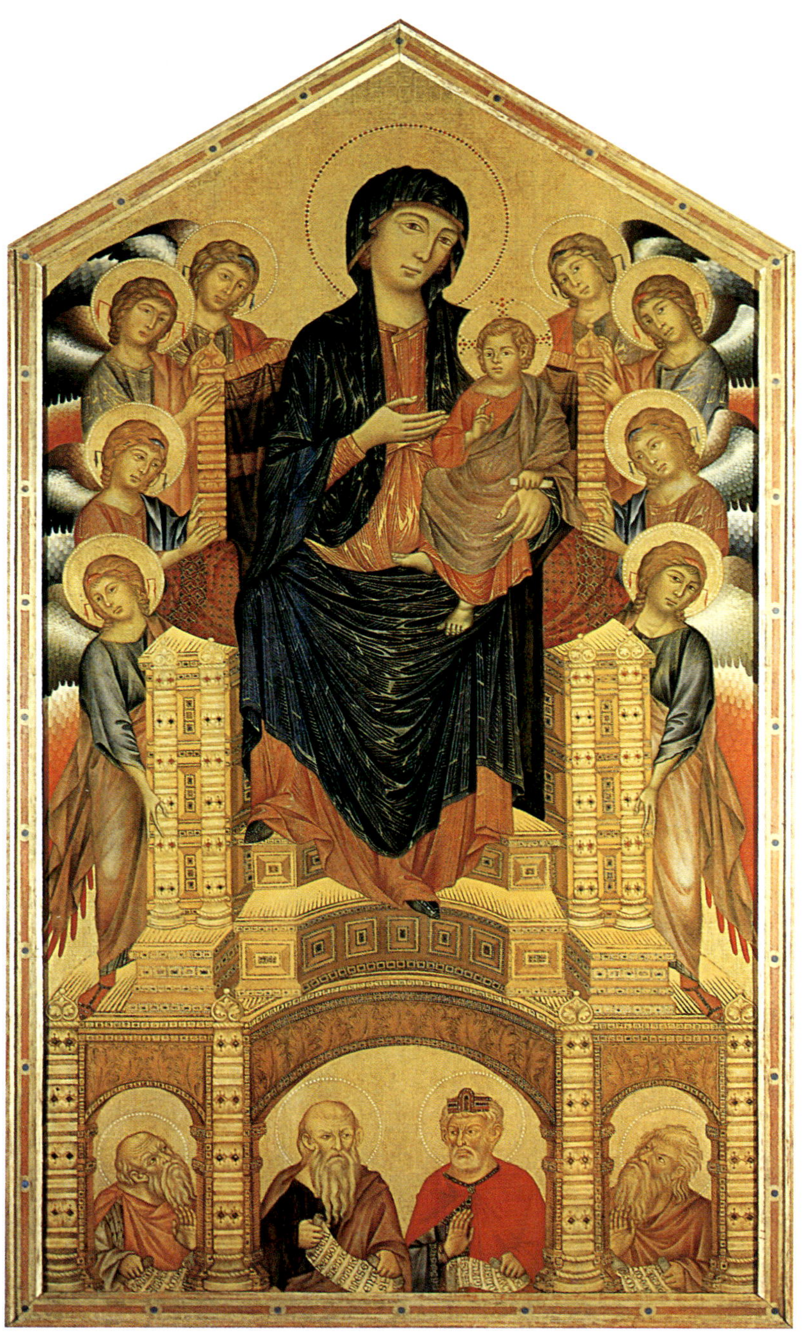

Cimabue painted this altarpiece for the Holy Trinity church in Florence, which is unprecedented, albeit at first it appears very similar to his works of the previous decade. It is smaller than his Maestà (1260), to which it can be contrasted on several key points. The differences are important as the artist moves himself and the art world beyond the rigid poses of the Byzantine icons to more three-dimensionality. While there remains a strict symmetry of figures, the intentional distortion of figures as in his earlier art is abandoned for more natural animation. It is seen in each of the fourteen figures, including the prophets (left to right) Jeremiah, Abraham, David and Isaiah, as they apparently find apposite scriptural references.

CIMABUE
(CENNI DI PEPO)
(C. 1240 FLORENCE – 1302 PISA)

After learning the art of making mosaics in Florence, Cimabue developed in the medieval Byzantine style, advancing towards more realism. He became the first Florentine master. Some of his works were monumental. His most famous student was Giotto. He painted several versions of the Maestà, "majesty, enthroned in glory", traditionally referring to Mary in setting, that show some human emotions, such as *Madonna and Child Enthroned with Angels and Prophets.*

154. **Duccio di Buoninsegna**, 1255-1319, Sienese School, Florence, Italian, *Madonna and Child Enthroned with Six Angels (Rucellai Madonna)*, 1285. Tempera on panel, 450 x 290 cm. Galleria degli Uffizi, Florence.

Duccio's Madonna is seated on an elaborate throne. Although Our Lady and her child appear to be three-dimensional and realistic, the surrounding environment is stylised, disregarding the principles of perspective. Hierarchic scale, often used in medieval times, is featured, depicting the most important subject, Mary, as the largest. The symmetrical distribution of the six angels, three on each side of the Madonna, may be symbolic of the order that Mary, as Mother Church, imposes on her subjects. Yet above all she remains the loving mother.

DUCCIO DI BUONINSEGNA
(1255 – 1319 SIENA)

Duccio di Buoninsegna, originally a carpenter and manuscript illuminator, was influenced by Cimabue and the Sienese school of painting. With Giotto, he was one of the transitional artists between the Gothic and the Renaissance ages, showing Byzantine elements throughout. Also a profound innovator, he painted his figures with greater weight and solidity, and more characterisation than had been seen previously in Siena. He is considered as one of the seminal artists in the development of the Sienese school.

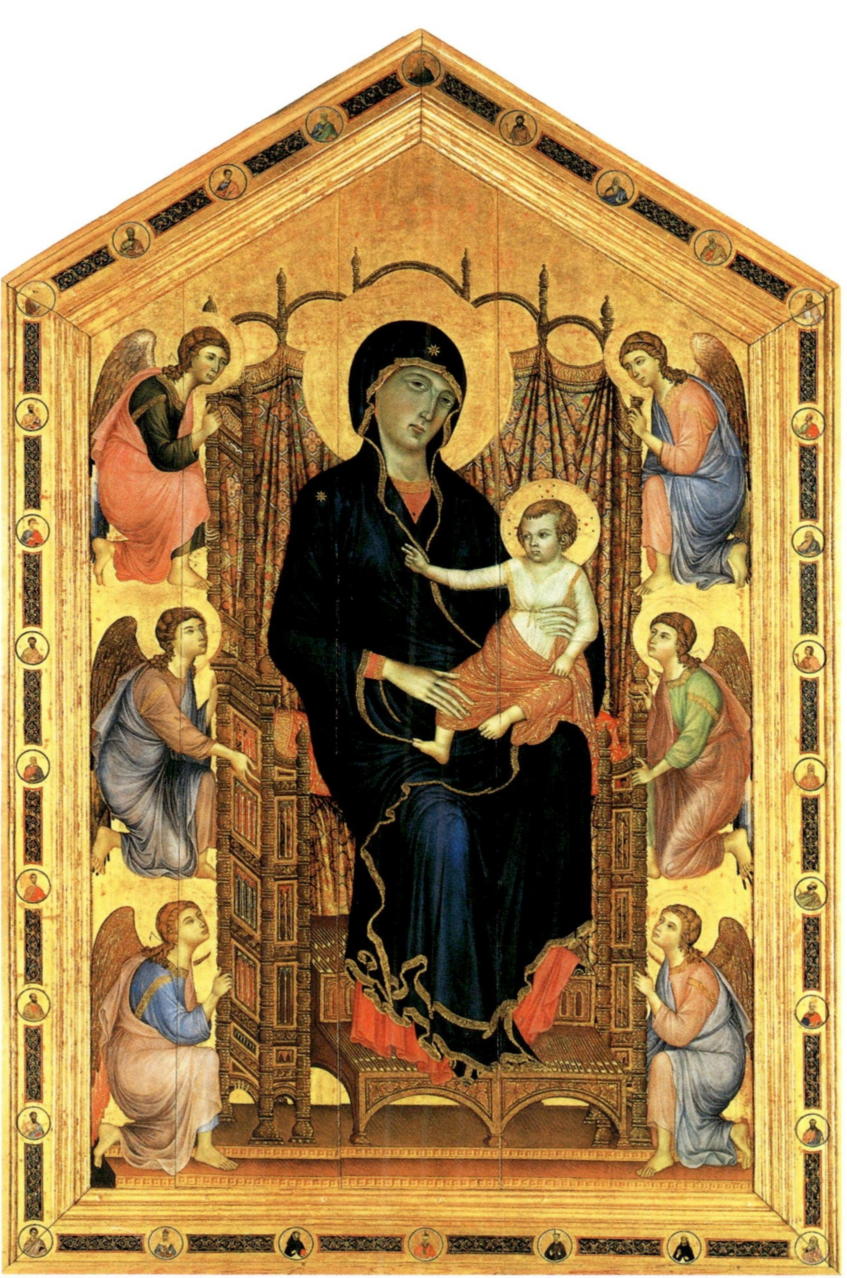

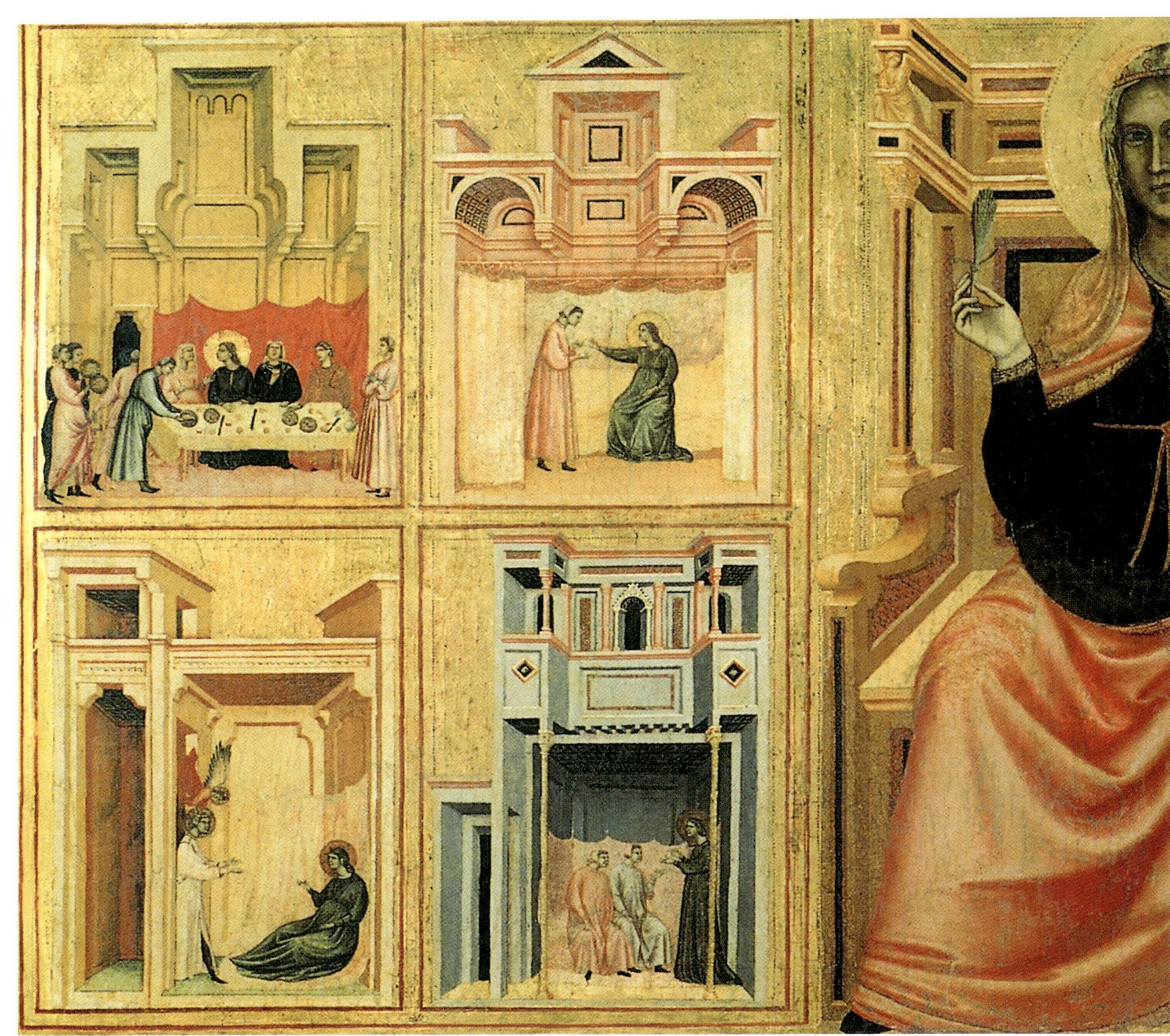

155. **Master of St Cecilia**, Early Renaissance, Italian,
Saint Cecilia Altarpiece, after 1304.
Tempera on panel, 85 x 181 cm.
Galleria degli Uffizi, Florence.

80

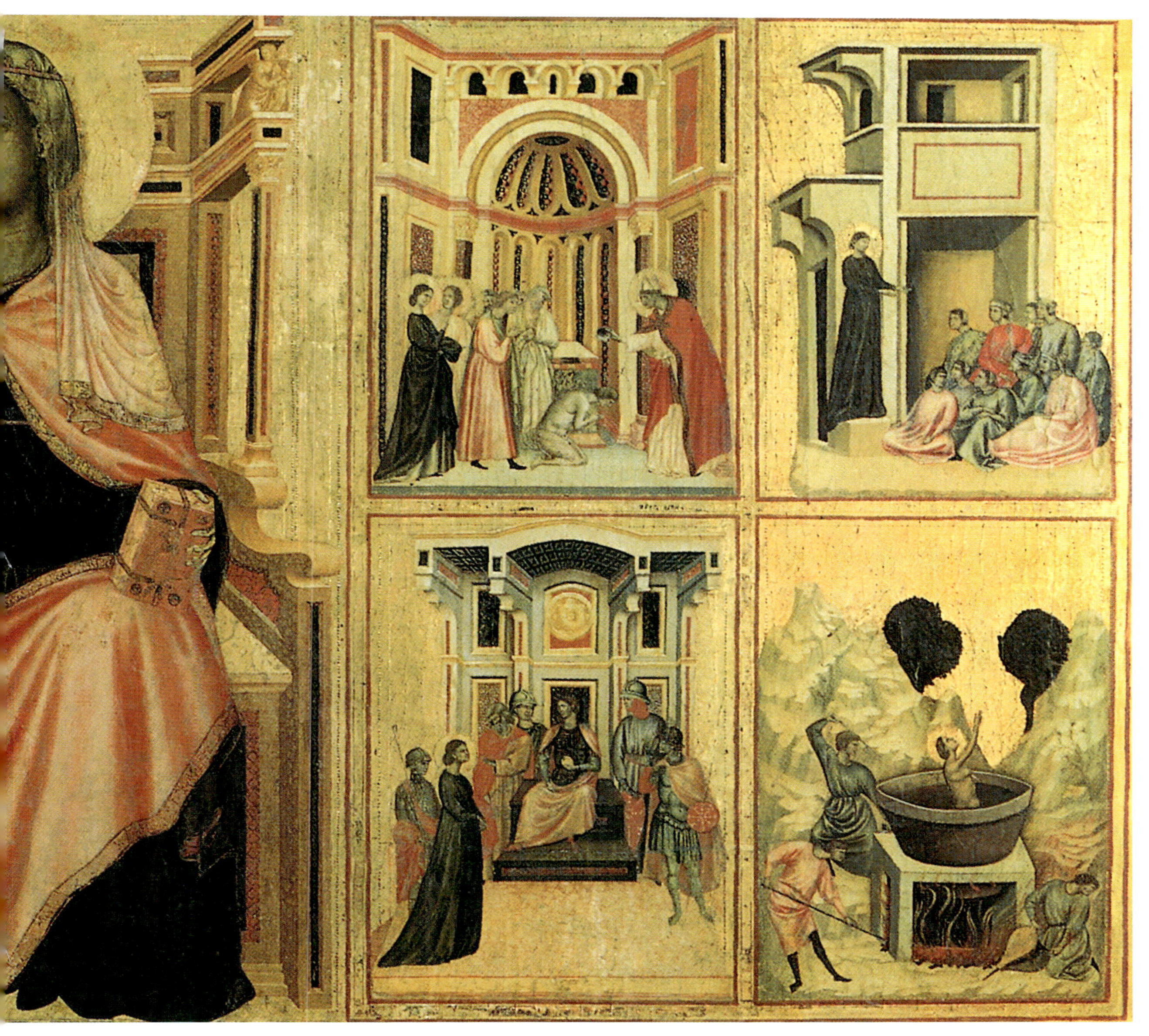

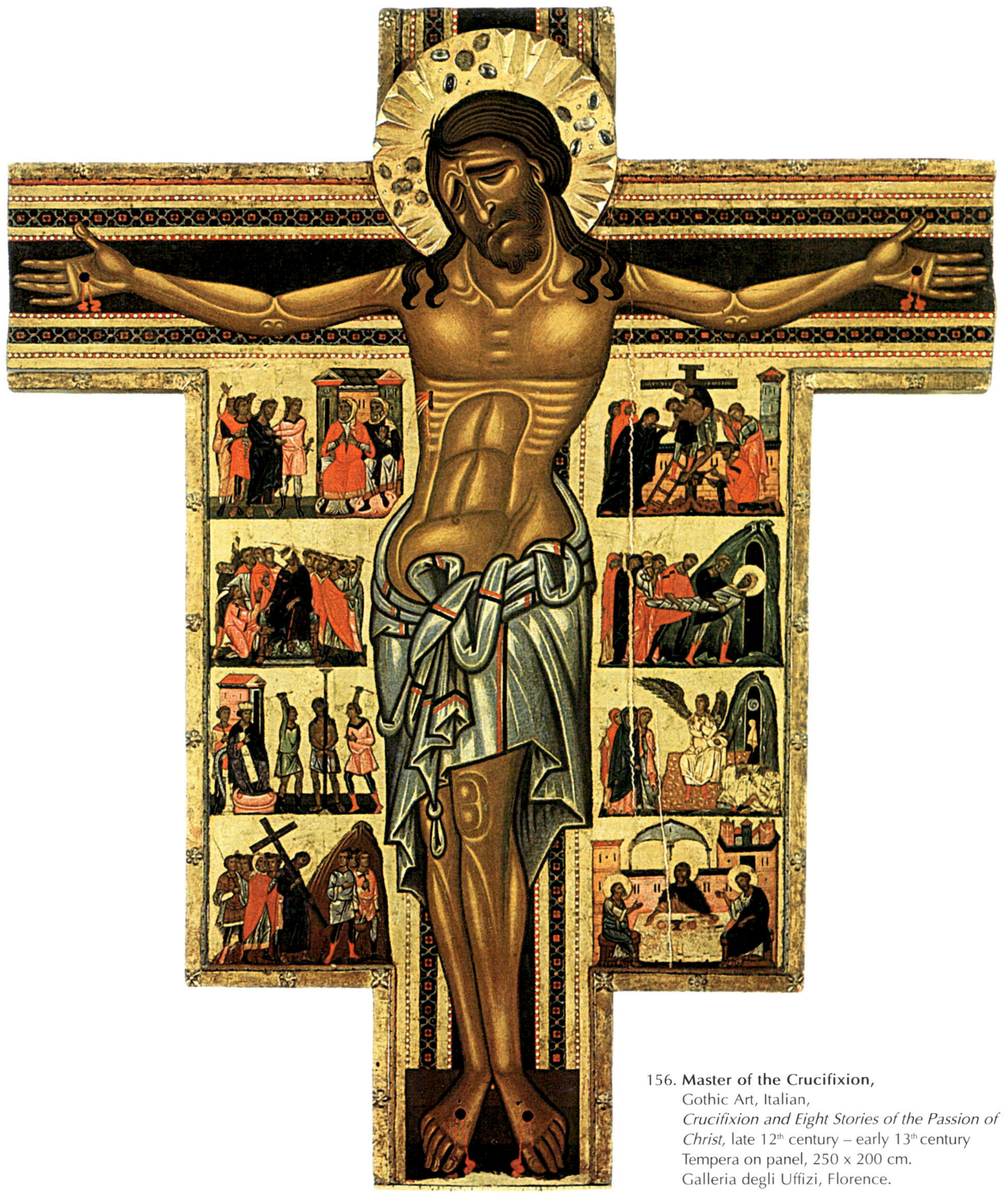

156. **Master of the Crucifixion,**
Gothic Art, Italian,
Crucifixion and Eight Stories of the Passion of Christ, late 12th century – early 13th century
Tempera on panel, 250 x 200 cm.
Galleria degli Uffizi, Florence.

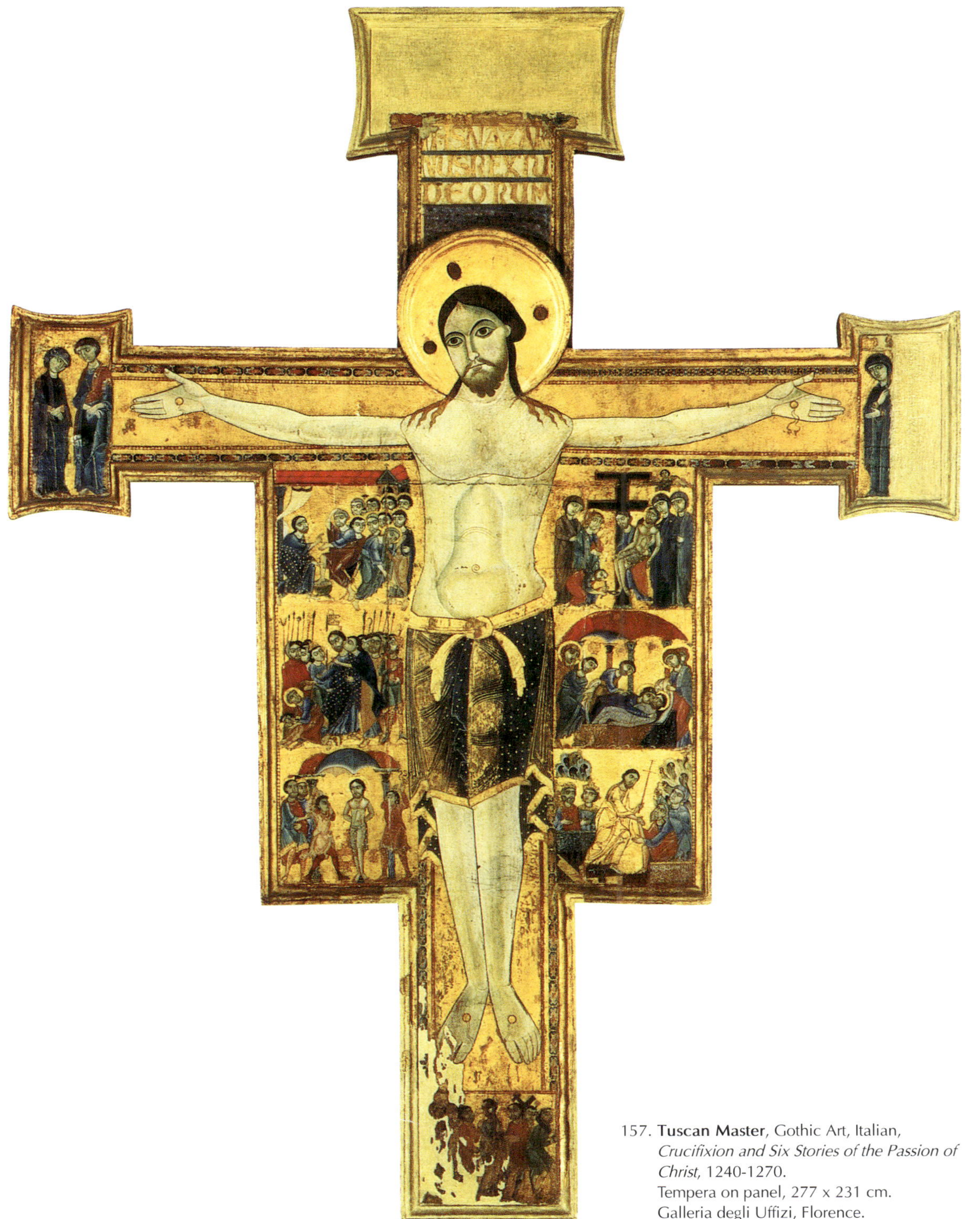

157. **Tuscan Master**, Gothic Art, Italian,
*Crucifixion and Six Stories of the Passion of
Christ*, 1240-1270.
Tempera on panel, 277 x 231 cm.
Galleria degli Uffizi, Florence.

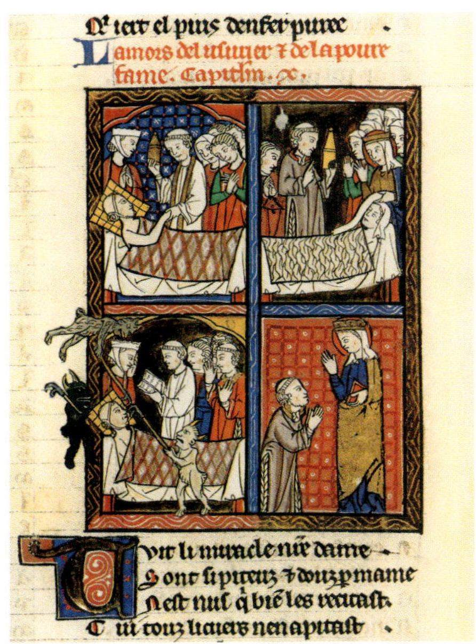

158. **Gautier de Coinci**, 1177-1236, French, *Life and Miracles of the Virgin*, late 13th century. Manuscript illumination. Stolen from the Library St Petersburg, St Petersburg.

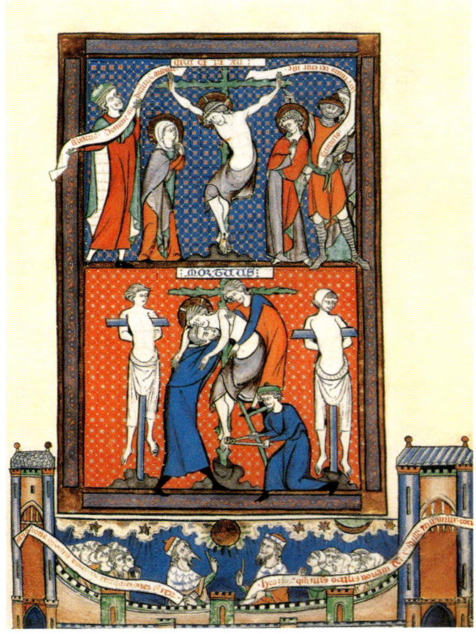

159. **Anonymous**, *Crucifixion* (top) and *Deposition* (bottom), Reims Missal, 1285-1297. Gothic. Parchment, 23.3 x 16.2 cm.

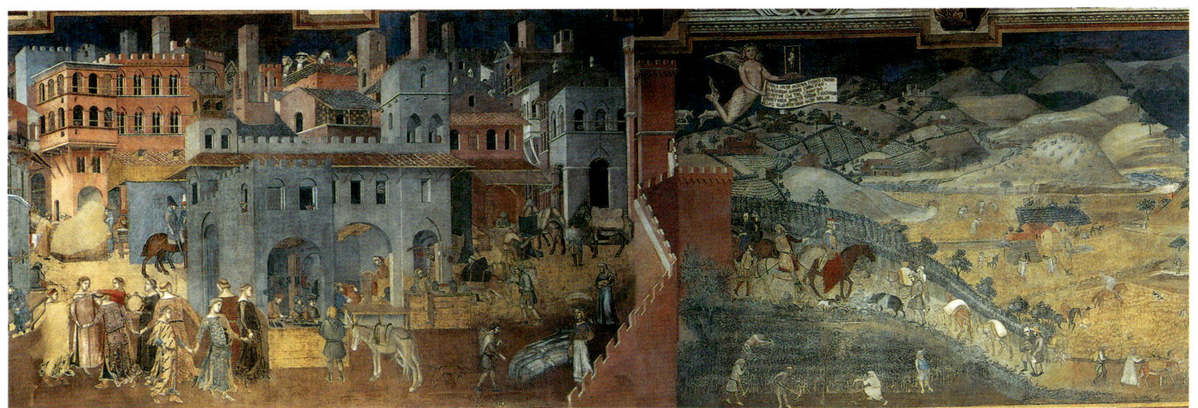

160. **Ambrogio Lorenzetti**, *Effects of Good and Bad Government*, 1290-1348, 1339, Early Renaissance. Palazzo Pubblico, Siena. Fresco.

AMBROGIO LORENZETTI
(C. 1290 – 1348 SIENNA)

Ambrogio Lorenzetti, like his brother Pietro, belonged to the Sienese School dominated by the Byzantine tradition. They were the first Sienese to adopt the naturalistic approach of Giotto. There is also evidence that the brothers borrowed tools from each other. They were both major masters of naturalism. With the three-dimensional, Ambrogio foreshadowed the art of the Renaissance. He is well known for the fresco cycle *Allegory of the Good and Bad Government*, remarkable for its depiction of characters and of Sienese scenes. The frescos on the wall of the Hall of Nine (Sala della Pace) in the Palazzo Pubblico are one of the masterworks of their secular programs. Ghiberti regarded Ambrogio as the greatest of Sienese fourteenth-century painters.

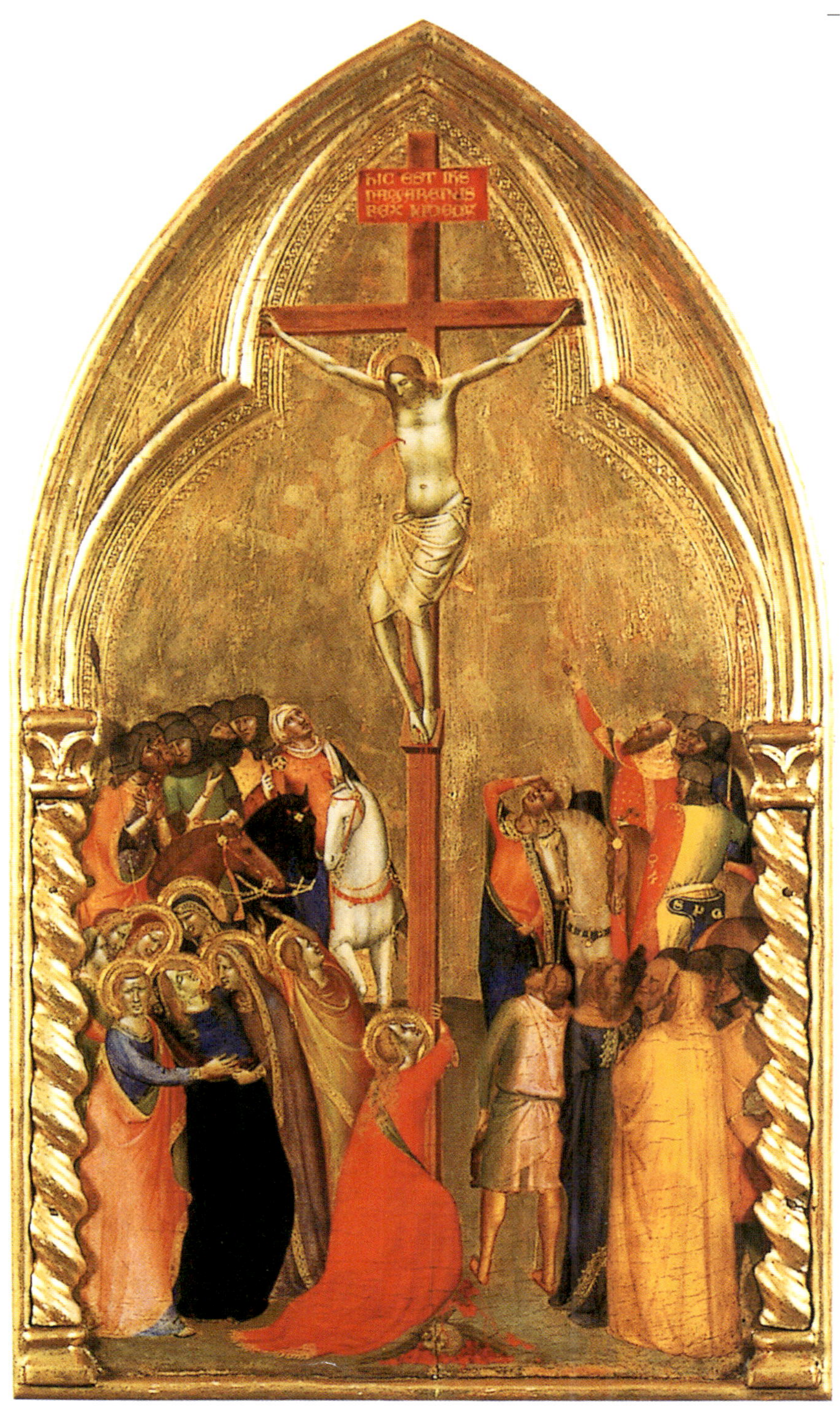

161. **Bernardo Daddi** (Attributed to), c. 1290-1350, Early Renaissance, Florentine School, Italian, *Crucifixion*, c. 1335. Tempera on panel, 36 x 23.5 cm. The National Gallery of Art, Washington, D.C.

Daddi is believed to have been Giotto's student and his work strongly shows his influence. Daddi, on his side, influenced Florentine art until the second half of the century.

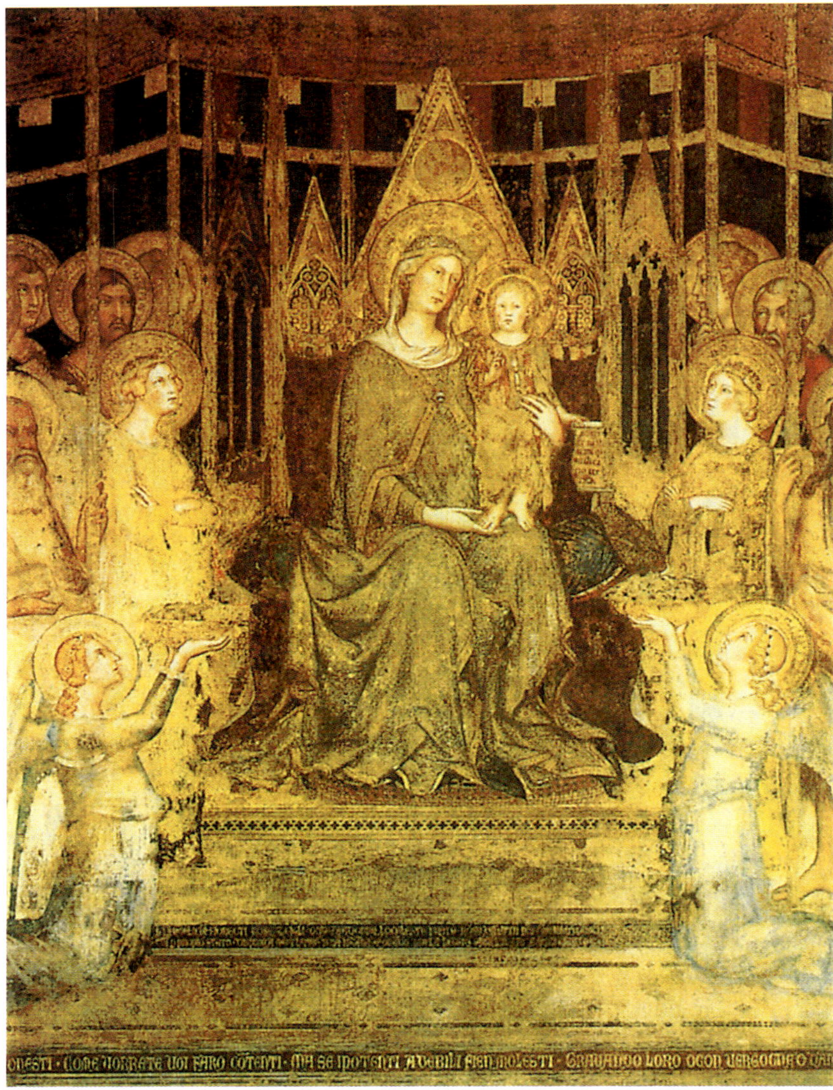

162. **Simone Martini**, 1284-1344,
Gothic Art, Sienese School, Italian,
Maestà (detail), 1317. Fresco.
Palazzo Pubblico, San Gimignano.

*In this painting, the traces of Byzantine
influence remain such as in the style of
throne and stacking of figures as if on
tiers. But overall the influence of the
Gothic painters Duccio and Giotto are
in greater evidence. Several of the saints
carry symbols of themselves, often the
instruments of their martyrdom. Each
pole supporting the canopy is held by
one of the saints. While the size of
each figure is somewhat uniform, the
Byzantine tradition of sizing figures in
proportion to their importance still
remains. This piece is the artist's earliest
known work. The transparency of the
angelic gowns is not an accidental
effect from top layers fading over the
years, but rather the effect is the result
of a clever technique. Only seven years
after its competition it had to be restored
because of water damage. The fresco is
surrounded by a frame decorated with
twenty medallions depicting the Blessing
Christ, the Prophets and the Evangelists
and with smaller shields containing the
coat-of-arms of Siena.*

SIMONE MARTINI
(1284 SIENA – 1344 AVIGNON)

A Sienese painter, he was a student of Duccio. Influenced by his master and by the sculptures
of Giovanni Pisano, he was even more influenced by French gothic art. First painting in Sienna,
he worked as a court painter for the French Kingdom in Naples where he started to incorporate
non-religious characters in his paintings. Then he worked in Assisi and Florence where he painted
with his brother-in-law Lippo Memmi.

In 1340-1341 Simone Martini went to Avignon in France, where he met Petrarch, illustrating a
Virgil codex for him. His last works were created in Avignon where he died. Simone Martini gave
a great sweetness to his religious compositions while, at the same time, he was the first who dared
to employ his art for purposes not wholly religious.

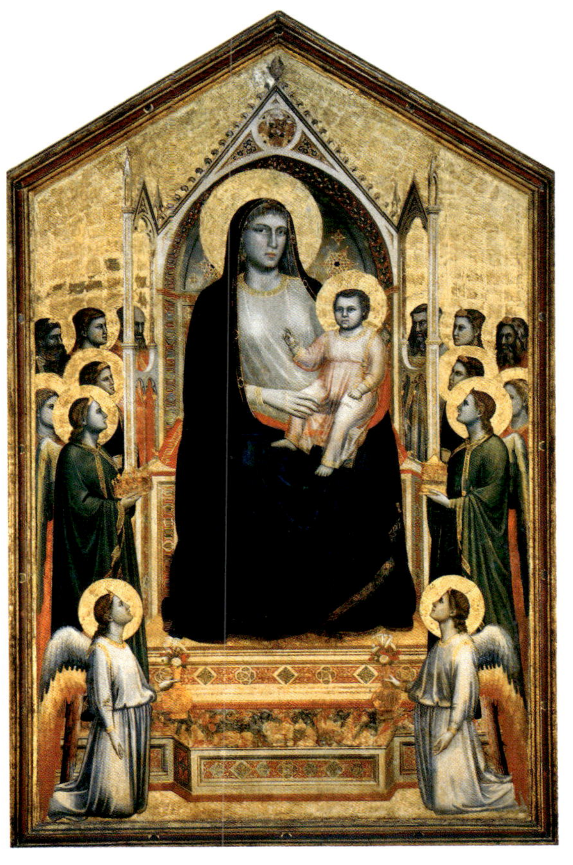

163. Giotto di Bondone,
c. 1267-1337, Early Renaissance, Florentine School, Italian,
Ognissanti Madonna (Madonna in Maestà), 1305-1310.
Tempera on panel, 325 x 204 cm.
Galleria degli Uffizi, Florence.

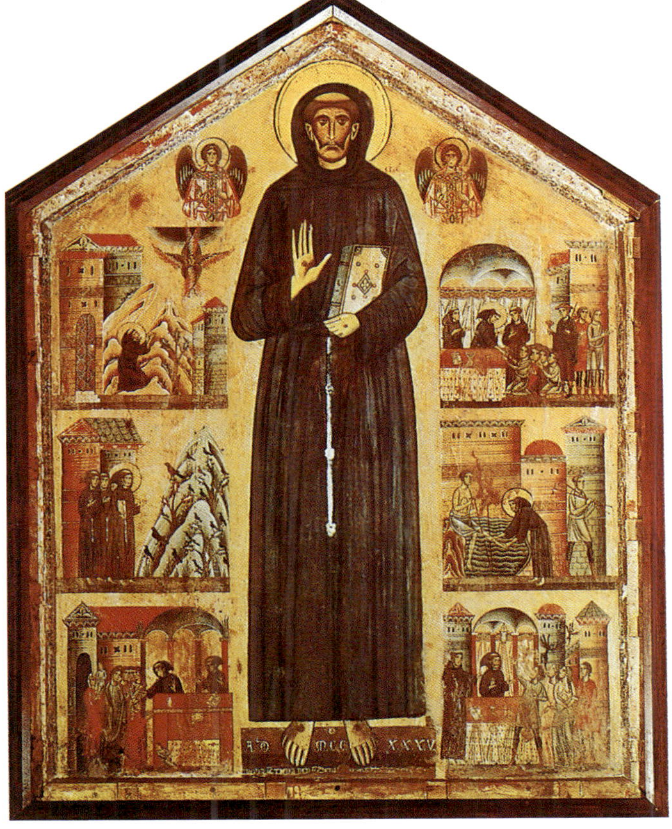

164. Bonaventura Berlinghieri,
1205/1210-c. 1274, Gothic Art, Italian,
St Francis and Scenes From his Life, 1235.
Tempera on wood, 160 x 123 cm.
San Francesco, Pescia.

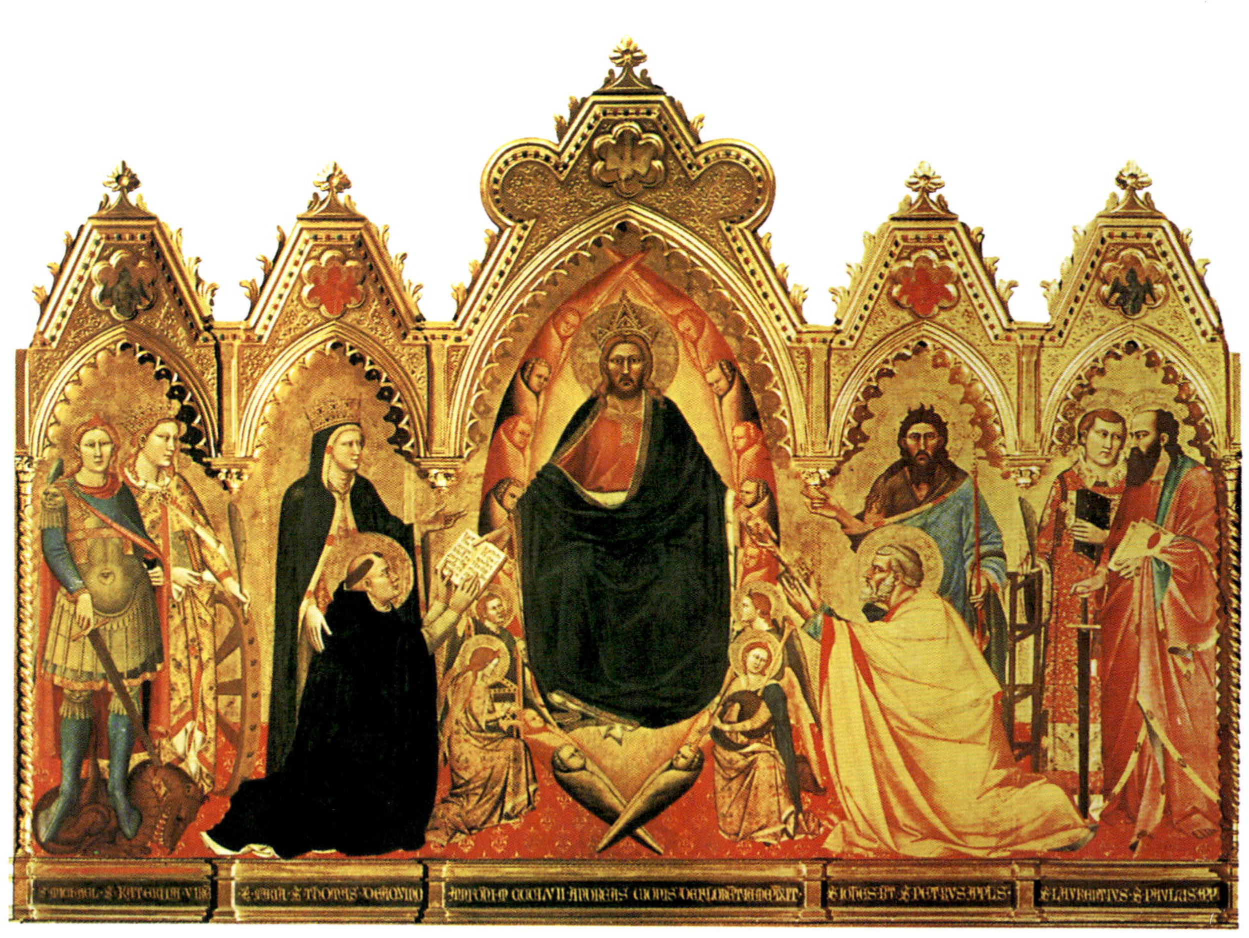

165. **Andrea di Cione Orcagna**, c. 1320-1368,
Gothic Art, Florentine School, Italian,
The Redeemer with the Madonna and Saints, 1354-1357.
Tempera on panel. Strozzi Chapel, Santa Maria Novella, Florence.

*It was originally the altarpiece of the Strozzi Chapel of Santa Maria
Novella, Florence. In this painting Orcagna reverted from a more
naturalistic style to the Byzantine remote and monumental figural
type with resplendent colours and lavish use of gold.*

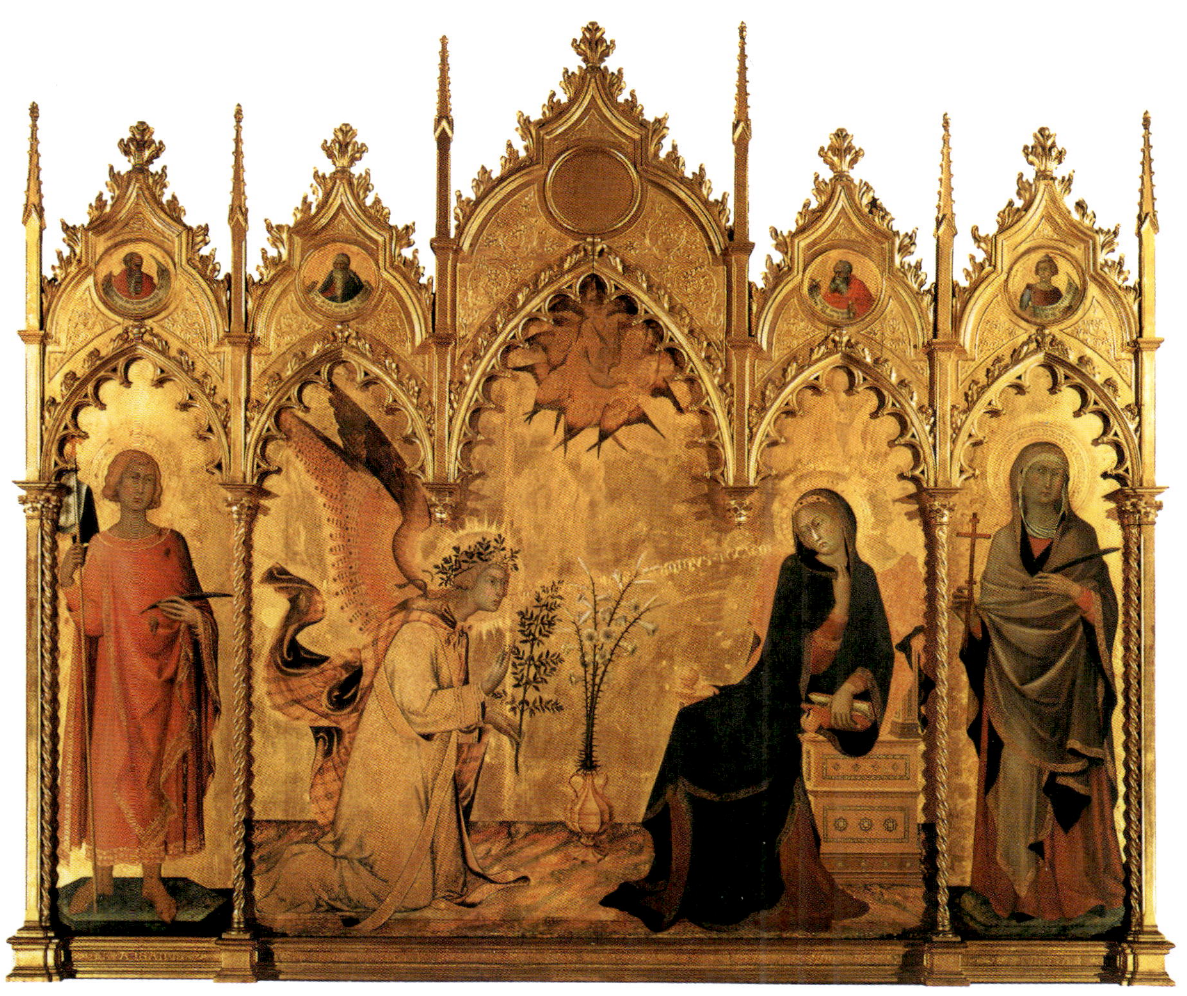

166. **Simone Martini** and **Lippo Memmi**, 1284-1344 and 1317-1347,
Early Renaissance, Sienese School, Italian,
Altar of *The Annunciation*, 1333.
Tempera on panel, 184 x 210 cm. Galleria degli Uffizi, Florence.

Simone Martini came from the same school as Duccio. He followed the Pope to Avignon, in 1344, during the Schism. The frame of this painting was added in the nineteenth century. The Virgin is represented without volume; she is more spirit than substance and can be compared on that point to Duccio's virgins. Looking for beauty and the depiction of details, the painter moves away from the works by Giotto. Simone Martini uses a much nuanced game of colours (gold, browns and pinks). He introduces depth in the foreground, using an edge that gives emphasis to the distance and that obliges the viewer to step back. His study of perspective from nature is made obvious on the depiction of the vase in the centre.

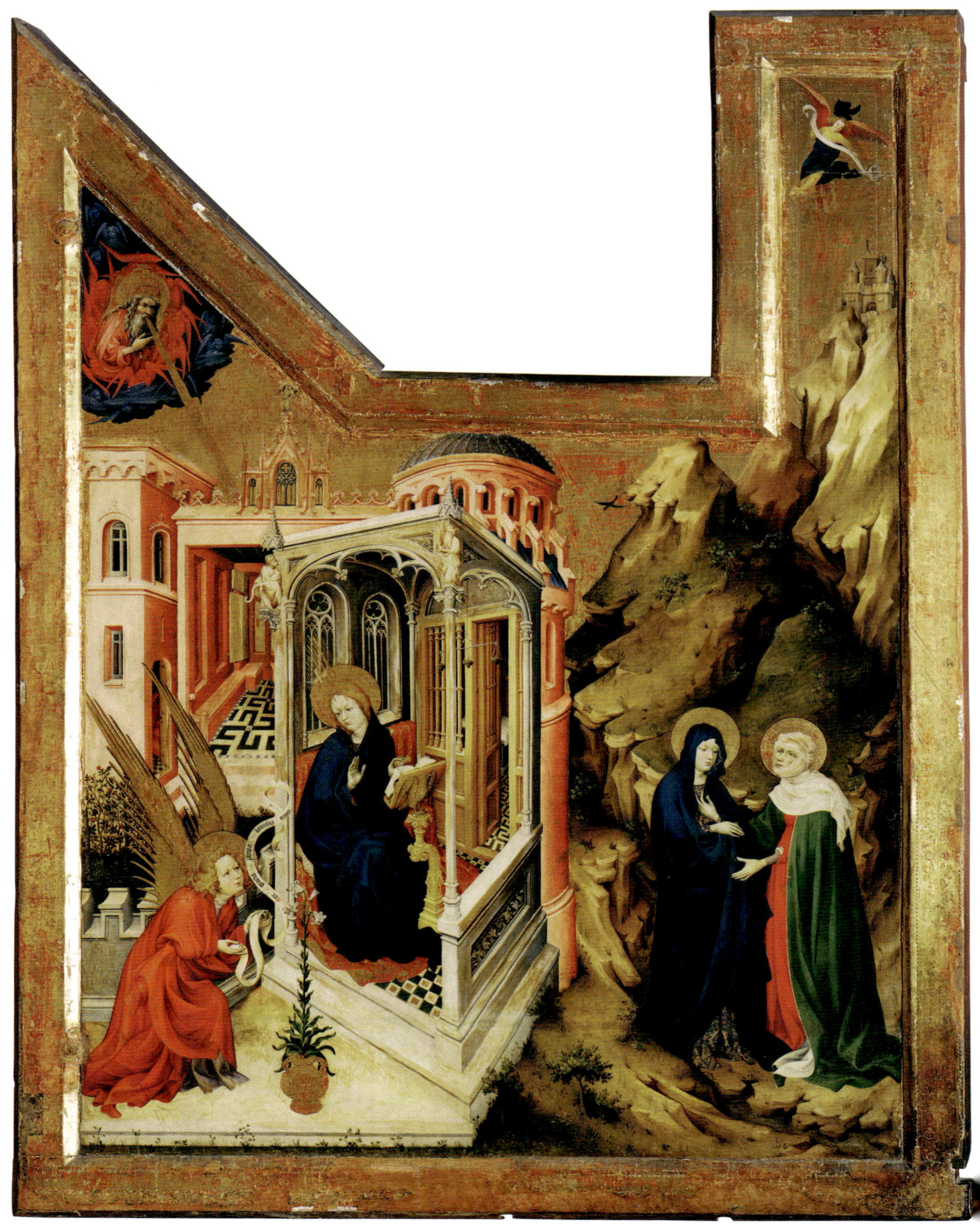

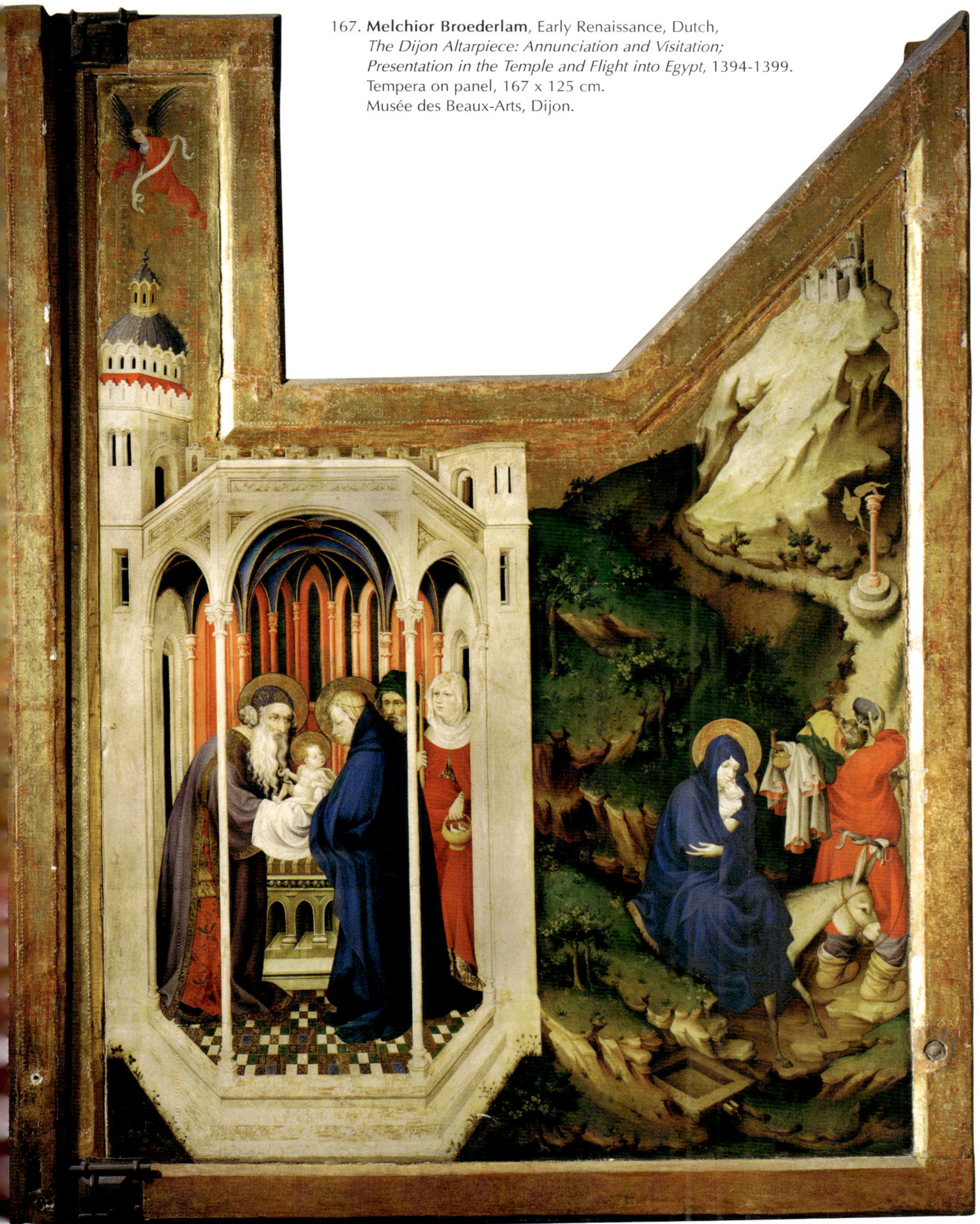

167. **Melchior Broederlam**, Early Renaissance, Dutch,
The Dijon Altarpiece: Annunciation and Visitation;
Presentation in the Temple and Flight into Egypt, 1394-1399.
Tempera on panel, 167 x 125 cm.
Musée des Beaux-Arts, Dijon.

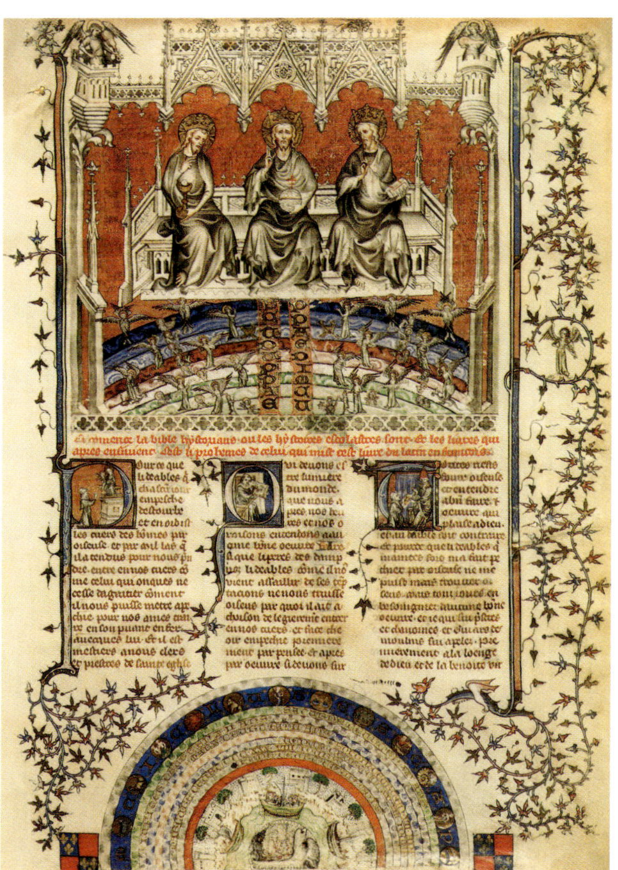 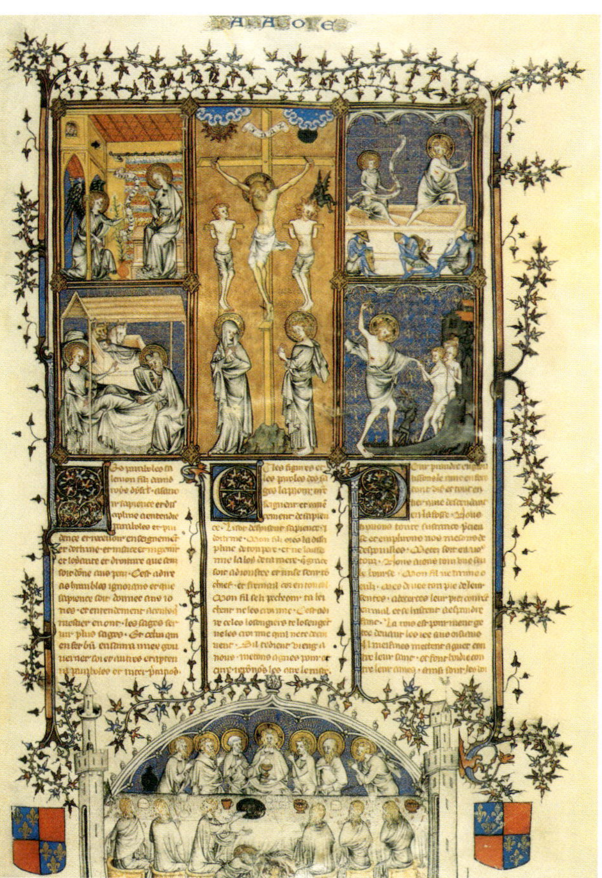

168. **Guyart des Moulins**, Early Renaissance, French,
La Bible Historiale, Third quarter of the 14th century.
Illuminated manuscript.
Stolen from the Library St Petersburg, St Petersburg.

169. **Guyart des Moulins**, *New Testament* (frontispiece), *La Bible Historiale*, third quarter of the 14th century, Early Renaissance.
Parchment, 30.5 x 20.3 cm.
Musée Condé, Chantilly.

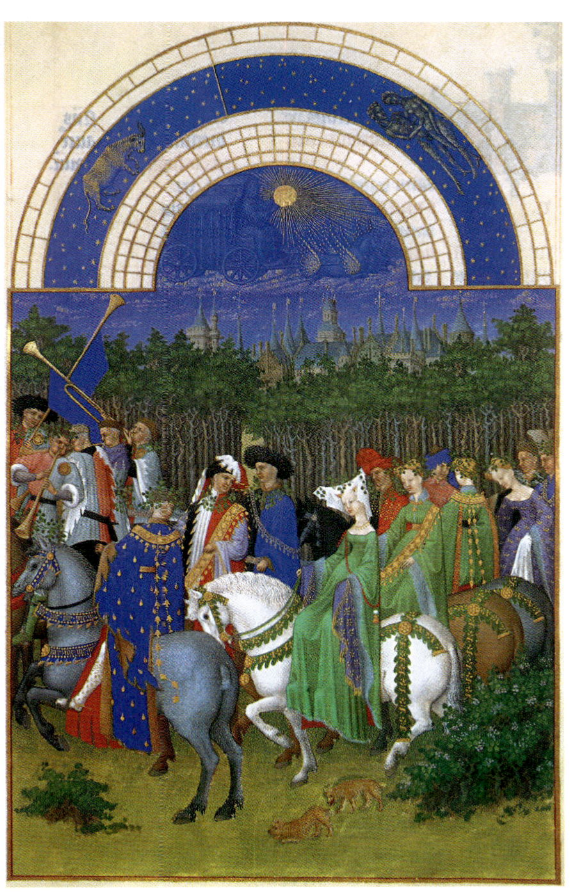

170. **Limbourg Brothers**, *The Very Rich Hours of the Duke of Berry: May*, 1412-1416, Early Renaissance.
Illuminated manuscript, 29 x 21 cm.
Musée Condé, Chantilly.

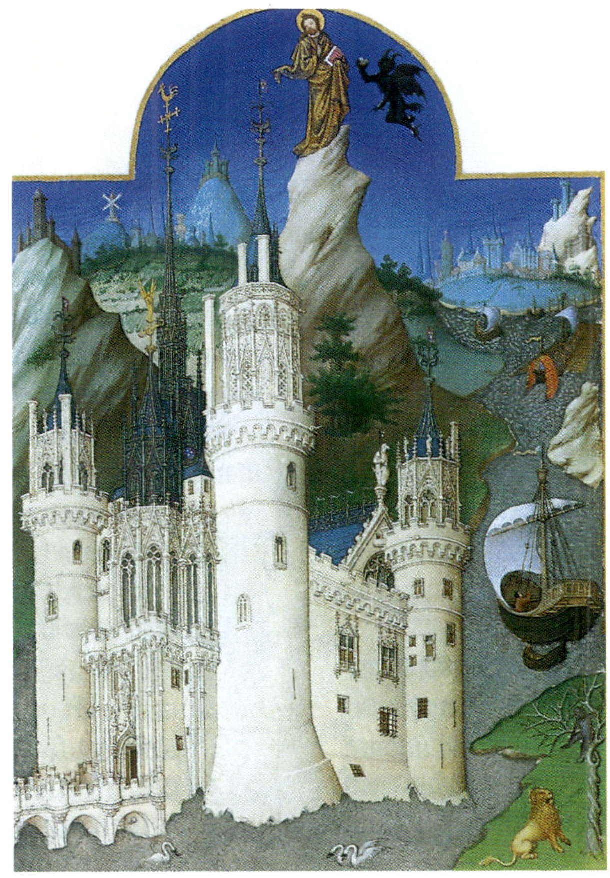

171. **Limbourg Brothers**, *The Very Rich Hours of the Duke of Berry: The Temptation of Christ*, 1412-1416, Early Renaissance.
Illuminated manuscript, 29 x 21 cm.
Musée Condé, Chantilly.

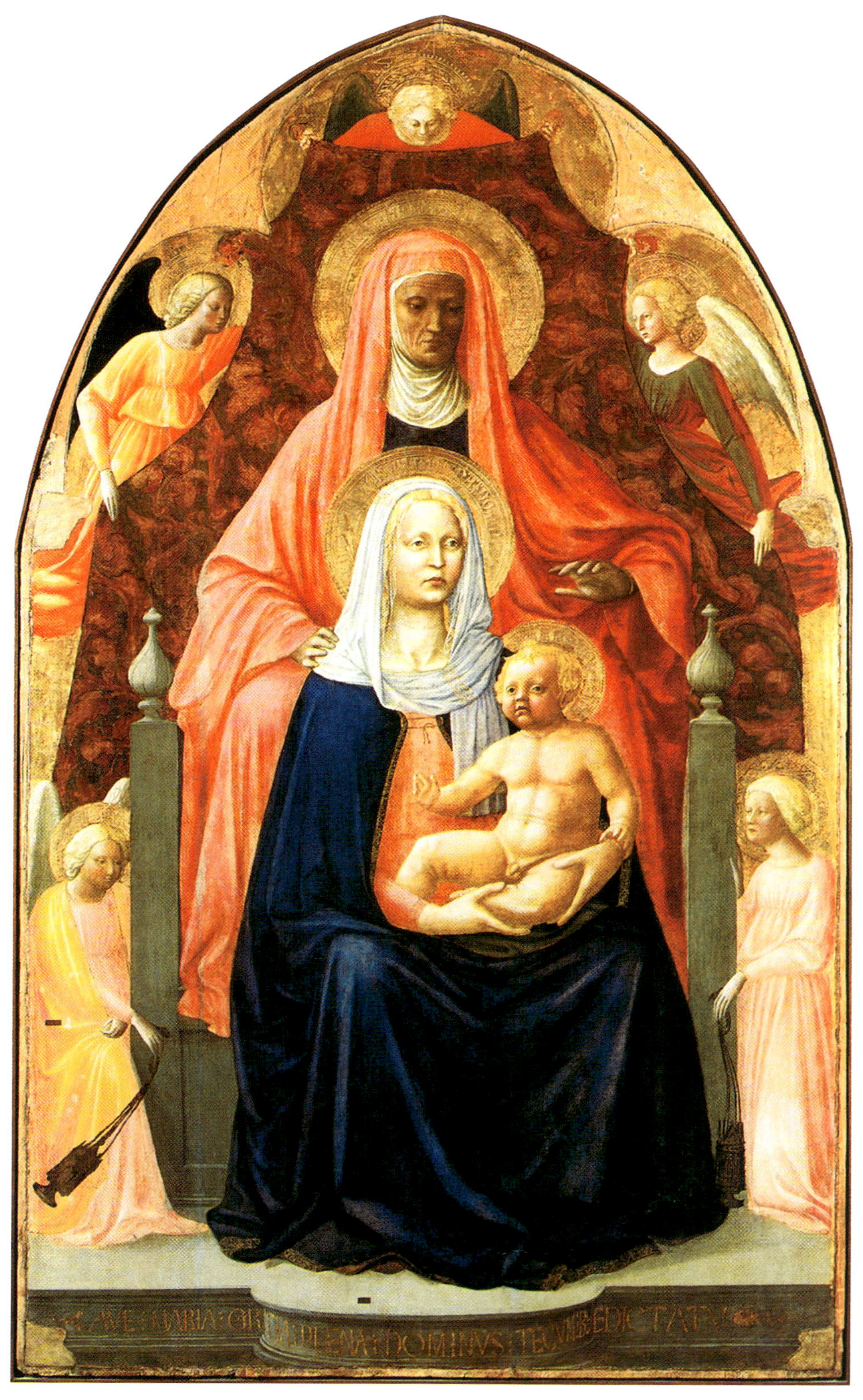

The Renaissance

For the European economy, the Renaissance was a fundamental time. In the fifteenth century the great families of Europe, such as the Medici in Florence, were actively involved in international business development. Together with increased wealth from trade, art began to display a new opulence, thanks to innovative techniques and materials.

In the 1440s, Johann Gutenberg developed letterpress printing in northern Europe, a printing system that was more efficient and cheaper than woodcut and that helped to make the Bible more accessible. At the same time, artists all over Europe were turning away from tempera painting, done with egg, in favour of oil painting. Filippo Brunelleschi discovered the principles of perspective, a revolutionary method of simulating three-dimensional space that overcame the lack of depth in medieval paintings. In 1452, the Renaissance man, humanist, scientist and artist of genius, Leonardo da Vinci, was born. This period also marked the beginnings of the great explorations. In 1492, Christopher Columbus crossed the Atlantic Ocean and discovered the Americas. Soon after, in 1497, the Portuguese explorer Vasco da Gama sailed to India and around the Cape of Good Hope. Through international trade, these routes played a major part in increasing the wealth and power of Europe.

The sixteenth century marked the apogee of the Renaissance. The age began with the Protestant Reformation when Martin Luther published his 85 theses in 1517, and John Calvin tried to officially reform the Catholic Church. These movements led to the founding of Protestantism, which emphasised personal faith rather than church doctrine. At the same time, during the 1530s the English Reformation, supported by Henry VIII, led to the formation of the Church of England. In these tumultuous times, the Catholic Church responded by taking extreme measures to control faith through the Holy Office and the Inquisition, and through the Council of Trent (1545-1563), which established the Counter Reformation. In art, this religious upheaval eventually put an end to Mannerism. Northern countries embraced Protestantism one after the other, producing significant changes in systems of artistic patronage. With the growth of world trade, a new class of merchants arose who commissioned secular works of art, such as still-lifes and paintings of landscapes, while the formation of guilds and municipal militia created a new market for group portraits. In the north many patrons were individuals, but in Italy the Catholic Church remained the principal source of art patronage. In France, on the other hand, patronage was the prerogative of the king. Francis I (1494-1547) was widely regarded as the embodiment of the Renaissance patron and had a taste for refined style and a humanist love of knowledge.

172. **Tommaso Masaccio**, 1401-1428, Renaissance, Florentine School, Italian, *Madonna and Child with St Anne Metterza*, c. 1424. Tempera on panel, 175 x 103 cm. Galleria degli Uffizi, Florence.

Masaccio was deeply influenced by Giotto's work. This work doesn't show superfluous decoration. Its bare aspect, and the treatment of perspective, prove how Masaccio changed drastically the traditional pictorial expression.

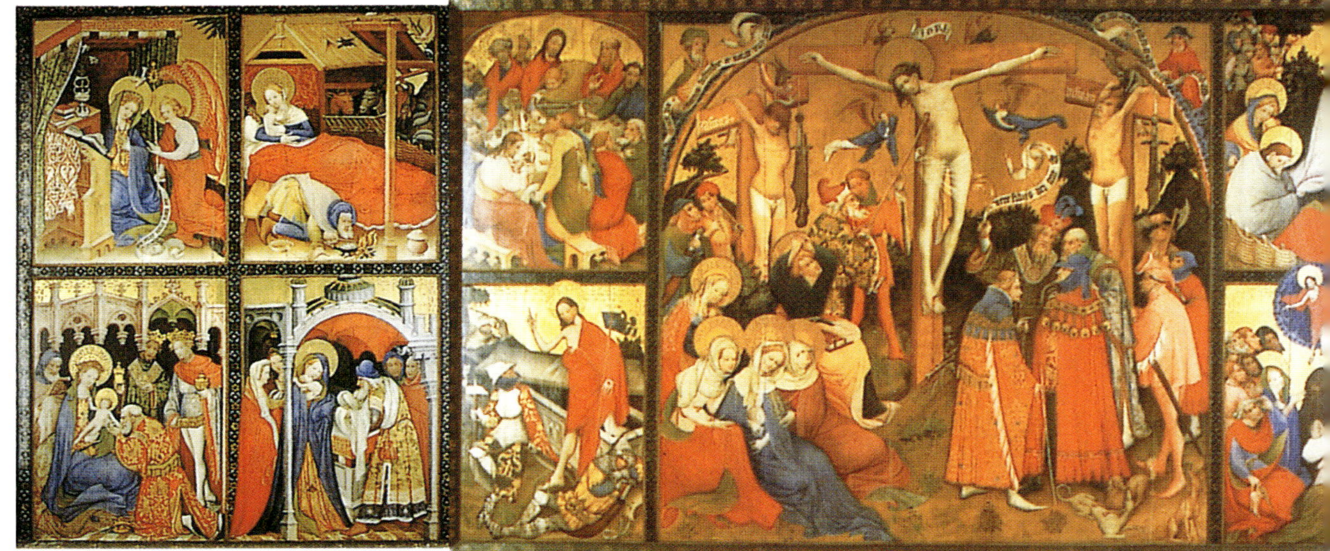

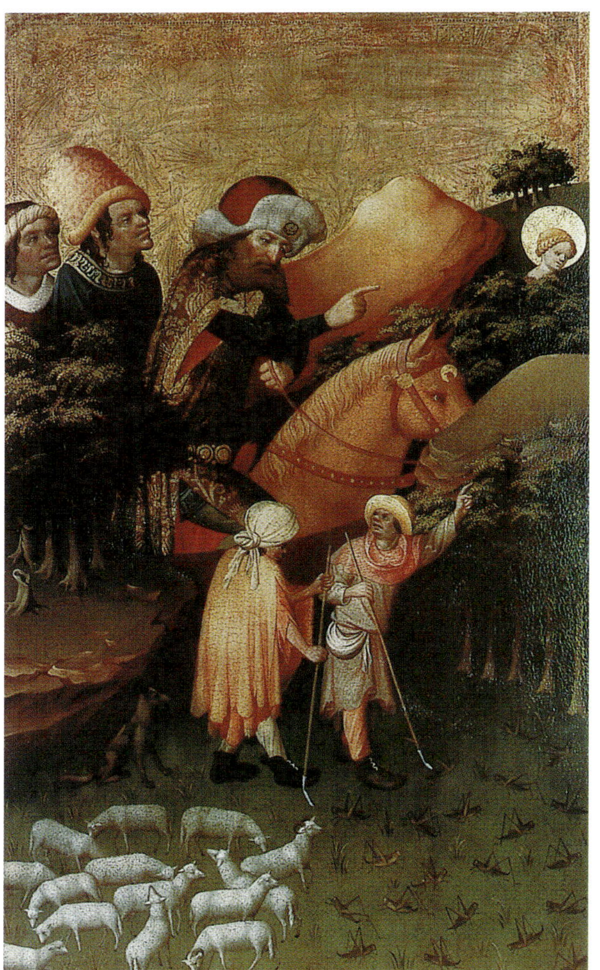

174

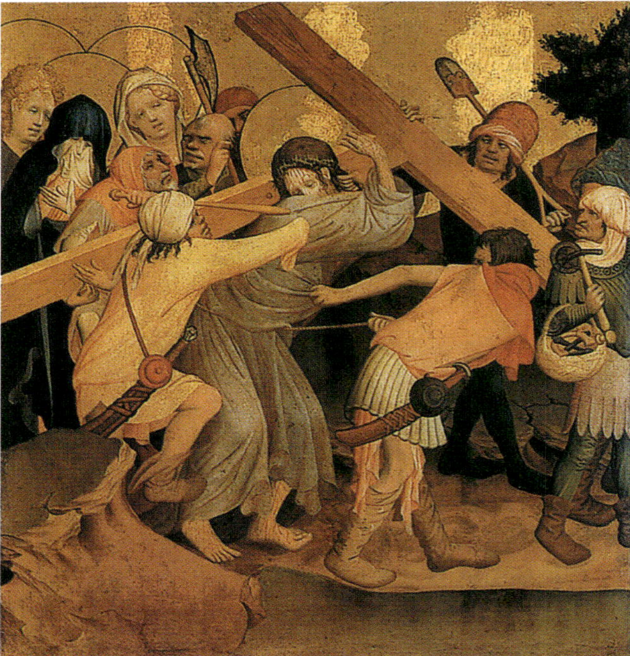

175

175. **Frater Francke**, 1380-c. 1430, International Gothic, German,
Christ Carrying the Cross, 1424.
Tempera on panel, 99 x 88.9 cm. Kunsthalle, Hamburg.

174. **Frater Francke**, 1380-c. 1430, International Gothic, German,
Pursuit of St Barbe, 1410-1415. Tempera on panel.
National Museum, Helsinki.

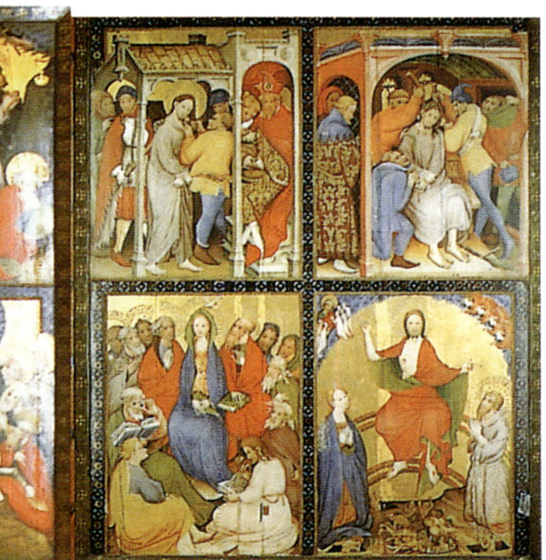

173

173. **Konrad von Soest**, active 1394-1422,
Northern Renaissance, German,
The Wildunger Altarpiece, c. 1403.
Oil on panel. 158 x 267 cm.
Church of Bad Wildungen, Bad Wildungen.

176. **Tommaso Masaccio**, 1401-1428, Renaissance, Florentine
School, Italian,
The Expulsion of Adam and Eve from the Garden, 1425.
Fresco, 208 x 88 cm. Brancacci Chapel of Santa Maria
della Carmine, Florence.

*This scene represents the expulsion of Adam and Eve
following the Original Sin. Rays coming from the gate of
Paradise represent the Voice of the Creator. The source of
light, however, is to the right, as can be seen from the
shadows. The Archangel Gabriel with his symbolic sword
hovers above. The breakthrough element in the fresco is the
depiction of human emotion by way of the body language
and facial expressions of the couple. The important
comparison to be made here is between this work and that
of Michelangelo's treatment of the same biblical moment
in his larger* The Expulsion of Adam and Eve from the
Garden *on the Sistine Chapel ceiling. The latter was done
only seventy-five years after the Masaccio, yet there is a leap
ahead towards realistic, albeit monumental, rendering of the
human forms of the couple. The figure of the angel in the
Michelangelo expresses more depth and aggression.
However, a few months before the Michelangelo, Dürer's
Adam and Eve (1509) gives the couple even more realistic
shape, yet the infamous fig leaves are used and the poses are
rather lifeless, compared even to the Masaccio.*

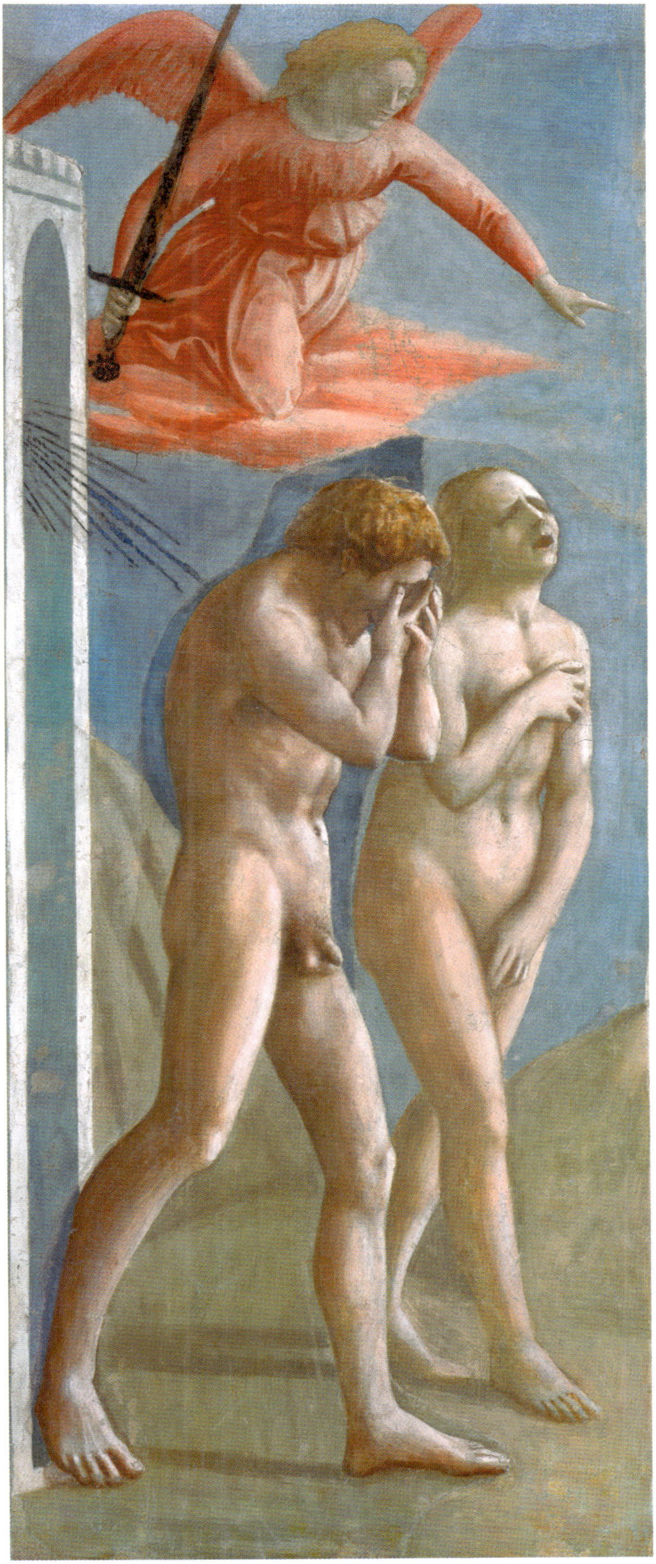

176

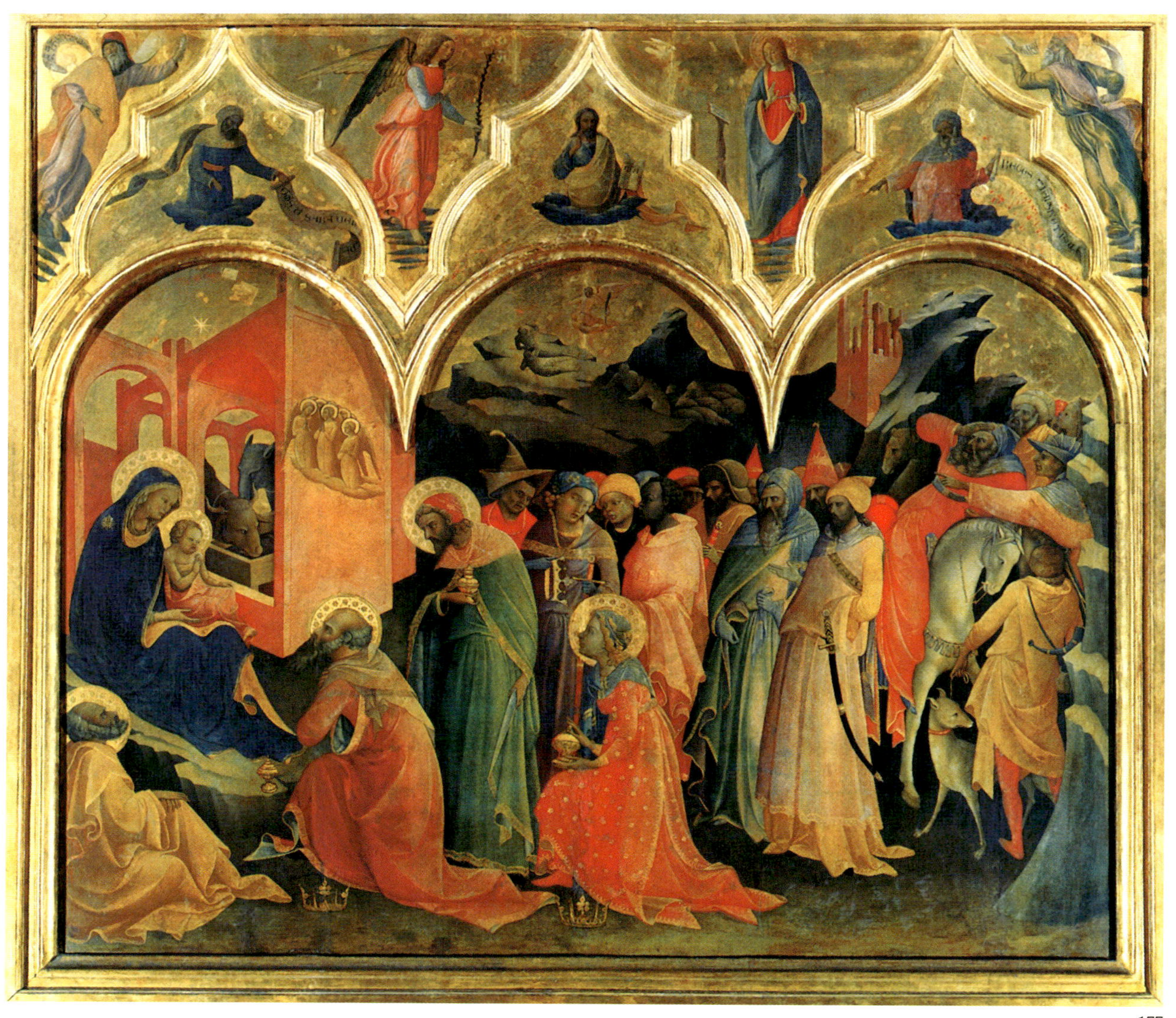

177. **Lorenzo Monaco**, c. 1370-1424,
International Gothic, Italian, *Adoration of the Magi*, 1421-1422.
Tempera on panel, 115 x 170 cm.
Galleria degli Uffizi, Florence.

178. **Gentile da Fabriano,** 1370-1427, International Gothic, Italian,
Adoration of the Magi, 1423. Tempera on panel, 303 x 282 cm.
Galleria degli Uffizi, Florence.

*The large, beautifully gilded altarpiece for the Strozzi Chapel of
The Holy Trinity in Florence presents the Epiphany event. In its
three lower panels, with details like that of Dutch miniatures, it
also shows three other related events from the New Testament:
The Nativity, the Flight into Egypt, and the Presentation of Jesus in
the Temple. The elegantly dressed three kings and their large
entourages, with horses and a large dog nearly dominate the
scene. Gentile's subjects in subsequent paintings, such as Golden
Alms of St Nicholas (1423), become more natural as if anticipating
the masters of Italian Renaissance painting.*

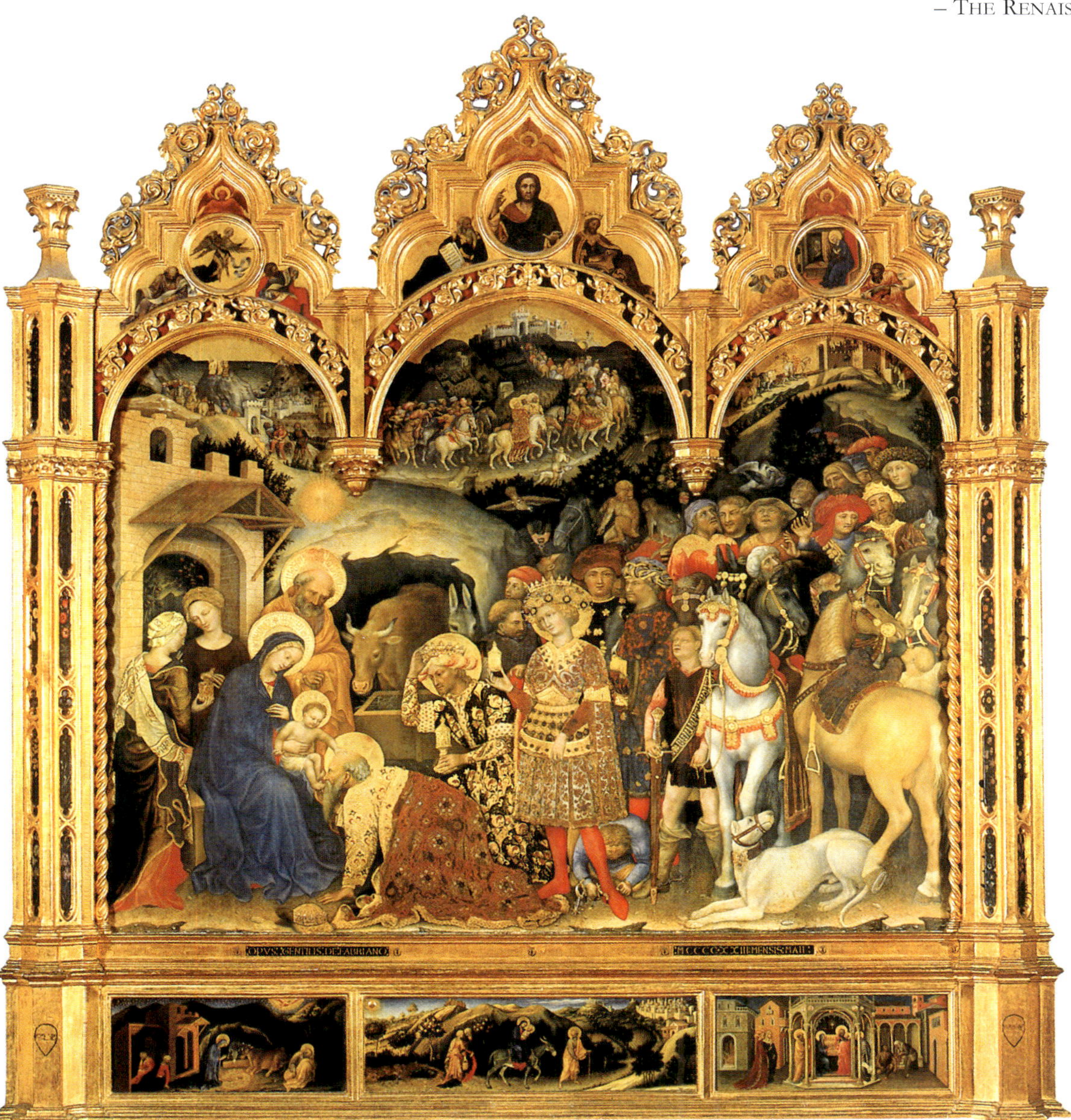

178

GENTILE DA FABRIANO
(1370 FABRIANO – 1427 ROME)

Fabriano was a leader of Italian late Gothic. His works were religious, characterised with elegant gold gilding. His masterpiece is the altarpiece, *Adoration of the Magi* (1423). Shortly afterwards he showed new insight into perspective with foreshortening of his subjects as in *Golden Alms of St Nicholas* (1425).

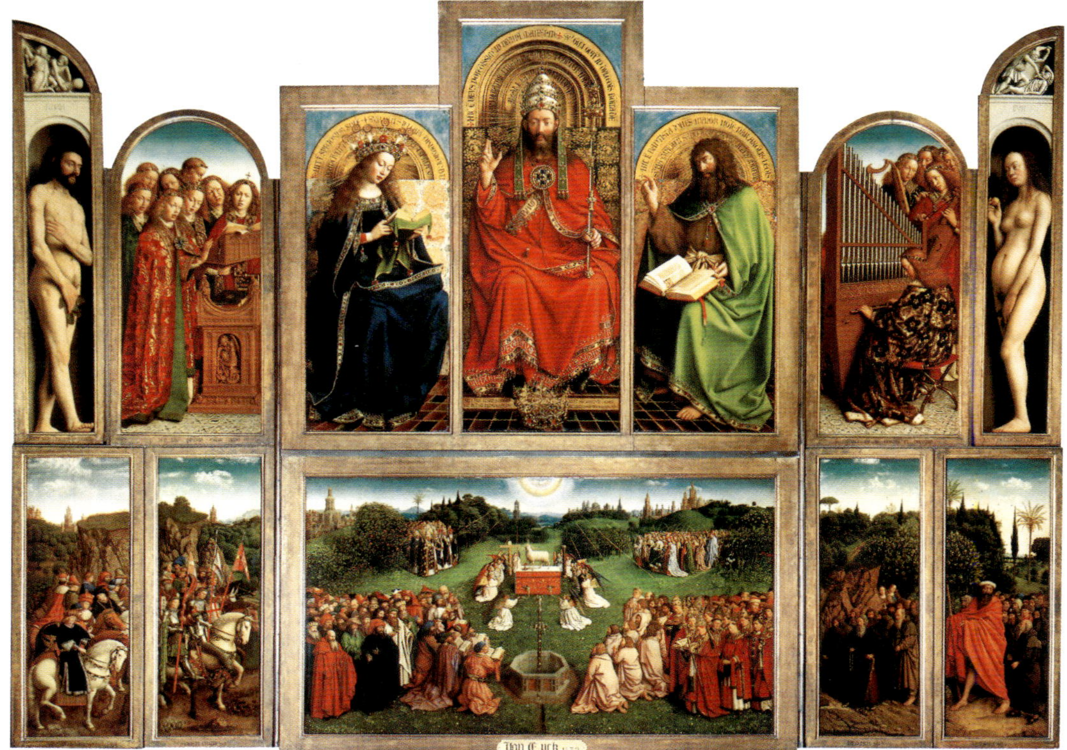

179. **Jan van Eyck**, c. 1390-1441, Northern Renaissance, Flemish, *The Adoration of the Lamb* (Ghent Altarpiece, *central panel*), 1432. Oil on panel, 350 x 461 cm (wings open); 350 x 223 cm (wings closed). Cathedral of St Bavo, Ghent.

Jan van Eyck was the first popular oil painter. Being the most famous work of Jan van Eyck, the Ghent Altarpiece brings together twelve panels initially realised for St John's Church in Ghent. The central panel shows a life-sized Christ and a great deal of attention is given to the depiction of precious brocade (in the tradition of international style) and in the rendering of light. The three central panels show a triple portrait: of Mary-Sophia, of God the Father/Jesus, and of John the Baptist. Mary-Sophia is depicted enthroned, wearing the gem-encrusted golden crown of the divine Queen of Heaven, her dark blue robes adorned with a golden trim. The book she reads bears the symbolism of the Madonna as Holy Wisdom (Hagia Sophia). The blending of Mary with Sophia, the feminine aspect of God, was still acceptable in art during the early Renaissance, even as the patristic Church began to strongly discourage this line of thinking.

JAN AND HUBERT VAN EYCK
(C. 1390 NEAR MAASTRICHT – 1441 BRUGES)
(C. 1366 MAESEYCK – 1426 BRUGES)

Little is known of these two brothers; even the dates of their births being uncertain. Their most famous work, begun by Hubert and finished by Jan, is the altarpiece, *The Adoration of the Lamb*. Jan, as perhaps also Hubert, was for a time in the service of Philip the Good, Duke of Burgundy. He was entered in the household as "varlet and painter", but acted at the same time as a confidential friend, and for his services received an annual salary of two horses for his use, and a "varlet in livery" to attend on him. The greater part of his life was spent in Bruges.

Their wonderful use of colour is another reason of the fame of the Van Eycks. Artists came from Italy to study their pictures, to discover what they themselves must do in order to paint so well, with such brilliance, such full and firm effect, as these two brothers. For the latter had found out the secret of working successfully with oil colours. Before their time, attempts had been made to mix colours in the medium of oil, but the oil was slow in drying, and the varnish added to remedy this had blackened the colours. The Van Eycks, however, had hit upon a transparent varnish which dried quickly and without injury to the tints. Though they guarded the secret jealously, it was discovered by the Italian Antonello da Messina, who was working in Bruges, and through him published to the world. The invention made possible the enormous development in the art of painting which ensued.

In these two brothers the grand art of Flanders was born. Like "the sudden flowering of the aloe, after sleeping through a century of suns," this art, rooted in the native soil, nurtured by the smaller arts of craftsmanship, reached its full ripeness and expanded into blossom. Such further development as it experienced came from Italian influence; but the distinctly Flemish art, born out of local conditions in Flanders, was already fully-grown.

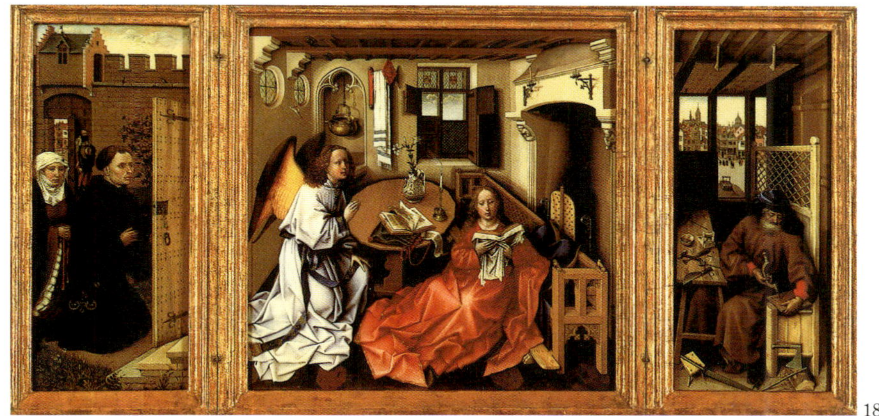
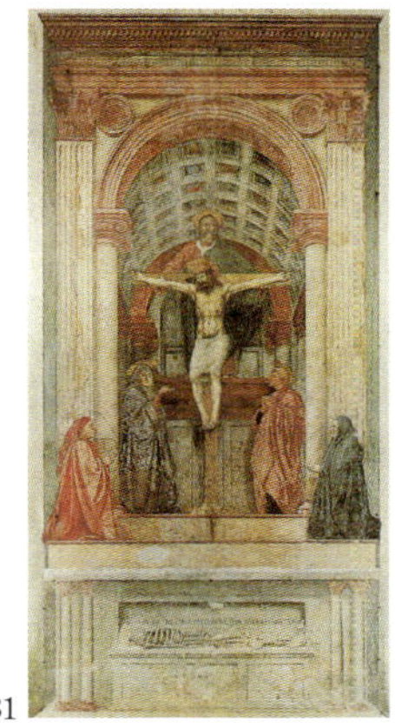

180   181

180. Robert Campin (Master of Flémalle), c. 1375-1444, Northern Renaissance, Flemish, *Annunciation: The Merode Altarpiece*, 1425-1430. Oil on panel, 64.3 x 62.9 cm (central panel); 64.5 x 27.4 cm (side panels). The Metropolitan Museum of Art, New York.

Three names have been suggested to identify the master: Jacquest Daret, Rogier van der Weyden and Robert Campin. The work shows his taste for anecdotal details.

181. Tommaso Masaccio, 1401-1428, Renaissance, Florentine School, Italian, *Holy Trinity*, c. 1428. Fresco, 667 x 317 cm. Santa Maria Novella, Florence.

TOMMASO MASACCIO
(1401 SAN GIOVANNI VALDARNO – 1427 ROME)

He was the first great painter of the Italian Renaissance, innovating with the use of scientific perspective. Masaccio, originally named Tommaso Cassai, was born in San Giovanni Valdarno, near Florence. He joined the painters' guild in Florence in 1422.

His influences came from the work of his contemporaries, the architect Brunelleschi and sculptor Donatello, from whom he acquired the knowledge of mathematical proportion he used for scientific perspective, and the knowledge of classical art that led him away from the prevailing Gothic style.

He inaugurated a new naturalistic approach to painting that was concerned less with details and ornamentation than with simplicity and unity, less with flat surfaces than with the illusion of three-dimensionality.

Together with Brunelleschi and Donatello, he was a founder of the Renaissance. Masaccio's work exerted a strong influence on the course of later Florentine art and particularly on the work of Michelangelo.

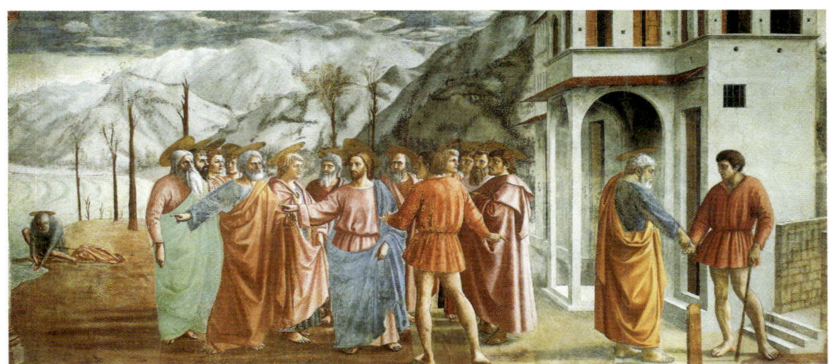

182. Tommaso Masaccio, 1401-1428, Renaissance, Florentine School, Italian, *The Tribute Money*, c. 1428. Fresco, 255 x 598 cm. Brancacci Chapel of Santa Maria della Carmine, Florence.

Before they were written down as gospels, the oral tradition of the early church passed along fascinating stories about the life of Jesus, including miracles, miraculous healings, and other spectacular events. One such miraculous moment in the life of St Peter, the most dominant of the apostles of Jesus, recalls when The Master told Peter, formerly a fisherman, to pay a tax collector with a coin that Peter would find in the mouth of a fish. This fresco shows Peter on the left catching the fish. On the right he gives the coin to the tax collector. In the middle of the work, Jesus is discussing matters with his apostles and the same tax collector. Jesus is mid-way in the vertical and slightly to the left of the horizontal mid-point. Masaccio shows a great master of perspective in this work. The characters are put in circle (not in the disposition of a frieze) and the grounds are depicted behind each other, terracing each other. The character in the foreground is all in volumes, with a strong modelling of his legs. His back to the viewer, he closes the composition and inserts depth into the painting.

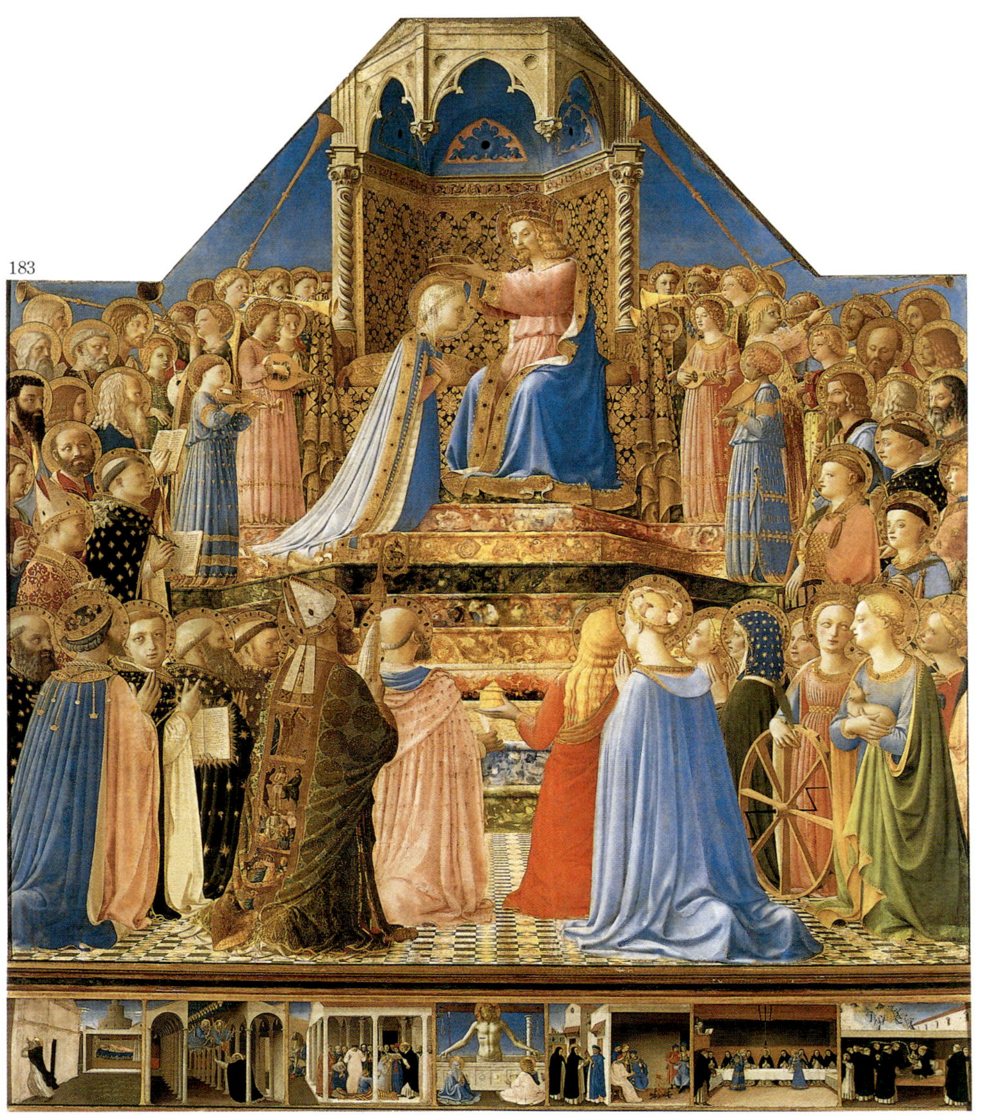

183. **Fra Giovanni Angelico**, 1387-1455, Early Renaissance, Florentine School, Italian, *The Coronation of the Virgin*, 1430-1432. Oil on wood, 213 x 211 cm. Musée du Louvre, Paris.

Painted for the convent church of San Domenico, Fiesole, the theme of The Coronation of the Virgin *is taken from apocryphal texts largely spread during the thirteenth century by Jacobus de Voragine's* Golden Legend.

184. **Fra Giovanni Angelico**, 1387-1455, Early Renaissance, Florentine School, Italian, *Annunciation*, 1433-1434. Tempera on panel, 176 x 185 cm. Museo Diocesano, Cortona.

The pious Dominican monk, Fra Angelico, formerly the young painter Guido di Pietro, brings a wealth of oral tradition and Christian doctrine to the picture. As the Old Adam is expelled from Paradise (upper left corner) by an angel, another angel announces good news to the world: the New Adam wishes to come to the world to save it from the Original Sin. Mary is asked to assist in this divine plan and she replies to God through the messenger, "Fiat voluntas tua" ("Thy will be done"). Dialogue between the Virgin and Archangel Gabriel, the heavenly messenger, are texts in Latin from the Gospel according to Luke. Mary's reply is painted upside down, as if literally reflecting God's will. As if the wings and halo weren't enough, the artist surrounds Gabriel with golden rays of light. Mary's halo is even more radiant. Various spring flowers, symbols of Mary's purity, surround the structure. Three groups of details frame the principle subjects, with the little flowers in the lower left, the patterned stars design in the ceiling, and the gold-leaf chair of the Virgin. A relief representing God the Father is in the circle between the archways, while a glowing dove symbolising the Holy Spirit hovers nearby.

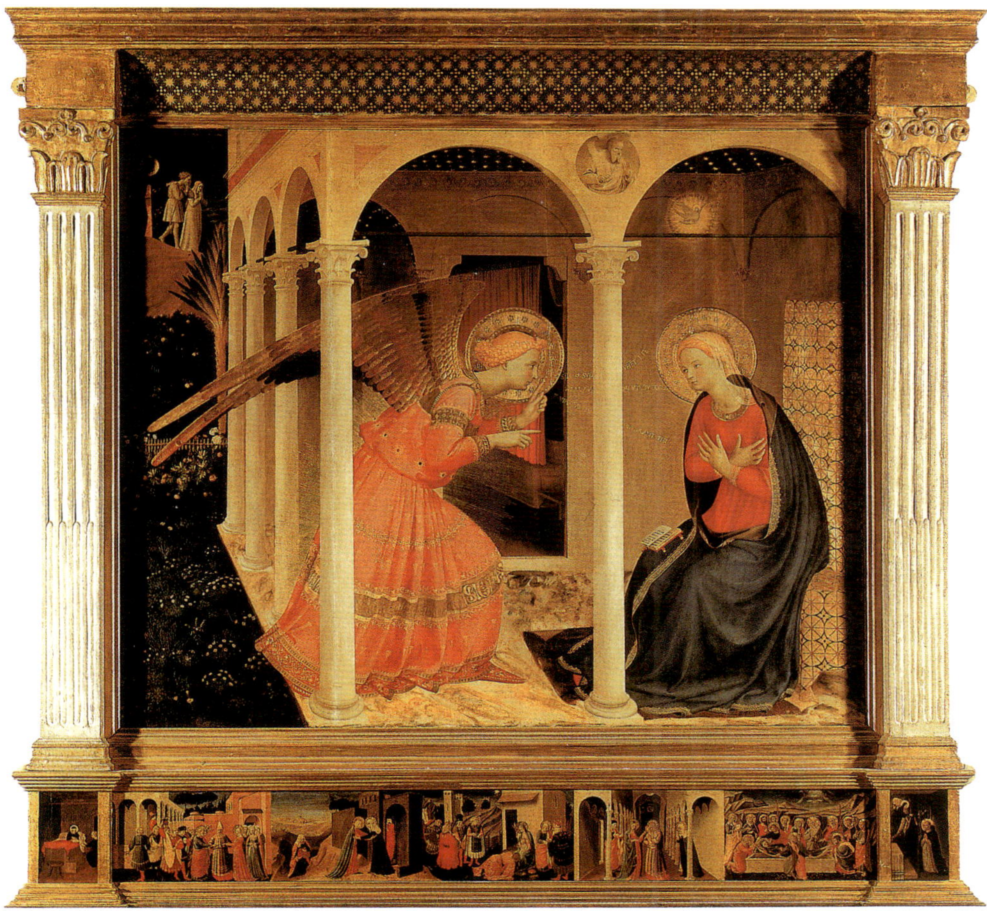

184

FRA GIOVANNI ANGELICO
(1387 VICCHIO – 1455 ROME)

Secluded within cloister walls, a painter and a monk, and brother of the order of the Dominicans, Angelico devoted his life to religious paintings.

Little is known of his early life except that he was born at Vicchio, in the broad fertile valley of the Mugello, not far from Florence, that his name was Guido de Pietro, and that he passed his youth in Florence, probably in some *bottegha*, for at twenty he was recognised as a painter. In 1418 he entered in a Dominican convent in Fiesole with his brother. They were welcomed by the monks and, after a year's novitiate, admitted to the brotherhood, Guido taking the name by which he was known for the rest of his life, Fra Giovanni da Fiesole; for the title of *Angelico*, the "Angel," or *Il Beato*, "The Blessed," was conferred on him after his death.

Henceforth he became an example of two personalities in one man: he was all in all a painter, but also a devout monk; his subjects were always religious ones and represented in a deeply religious spirit, yet his devotion as a monk was no greater than his absorpt on as an artist. Consequently, though his life was secluded within the walls of the monastery, he kept in touch with the art movements of his time and continually developed as a painter. His early work shows that he had learned of the illuminators who inherited the Byzantine traditions, and had been affected by the simple religious feeling of Giotto's work. Also influenced by Lorenzo Monaco and the Sienese School, he painted under the patronage of Cosimo de Medici. Then he began to learn of that brilliant band of sculptors and architects who were enriching Florence by their genius. Ghiberti was executing his pictures in bronze upon the doors of the Baptistery; Donatello, his famous statue of *St George* and the dancing children around the organ-gallery in the Cathedral; and Luca della Robbia was at work upon his frieze of children, singing, dancing and playing upon instruments. Moreover, Masaccio had revealed the dignity of form in painting. Through these artists the beauty of the human form and of its life and movement was being manifested to the Florentines and to the other cities. Angelico caught the enthusiasm and gave increasing reality of life and movement to his figures.

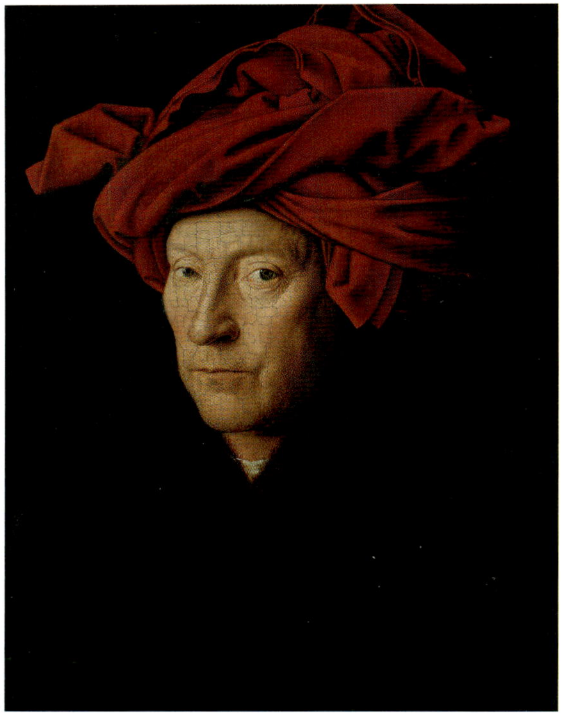

185

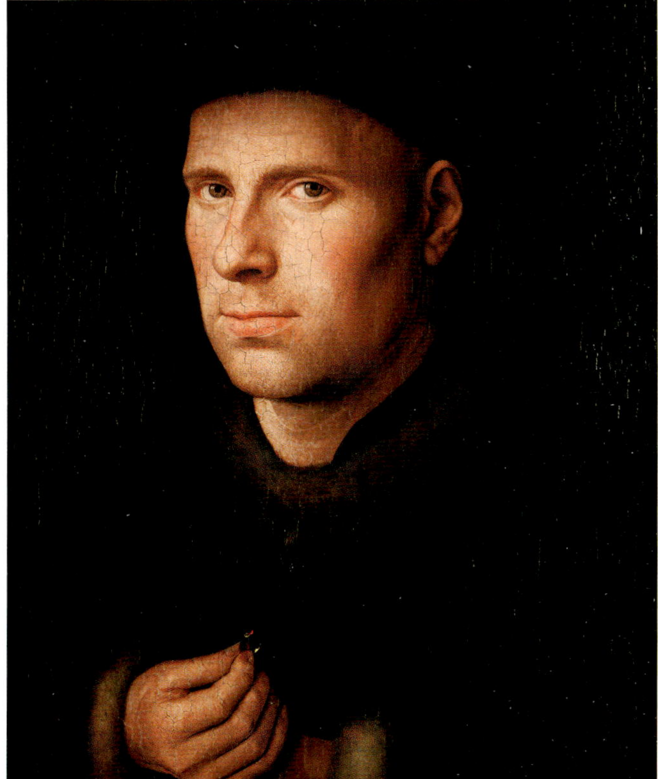

186

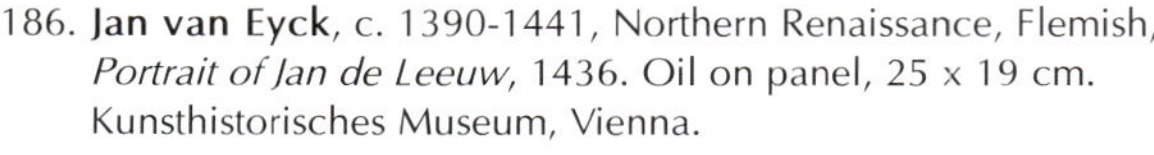

185. **Jan van Eyck**, c. 1390-1441, Northern Renaissance, Flemish,
Man in Red Turban (Self-Portrait?), 1433. Oil on panel, 26 x 19 cm.
National Gallery, London.

186. **Jan van Eyck**, c. 1390-1441, Northern Renaissance, Flemish,
Portrait of Jan de Leeuw, 1436. Oil on panel, 25 x 19 cm.
Kunsthistorisches Museum, Vienna.

*Considered the founder of western portraiture, Van Eyck depicts here
Jan de Leeuw, member of the Goldsmith Guild in Bruges.*

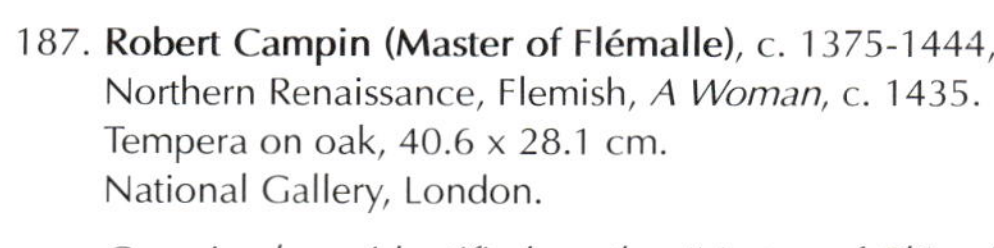

187. **Robert Campin (Master of Flémalle)**, c. 1375-1444,
Northern Renaissance, Flemish, *A Woman*, c. 1435.
Tempera on oak, 40.6 x 28.1 cm.
National Gallery, London.

*Campin, long identified as the 'Master of Flémalle', painted three-
dimensional figures with details of the face made clearly visible. This
portrait was a pendant to a Portrait of a Man (London, National
Gallery), presumably the husband of the woman represented.*

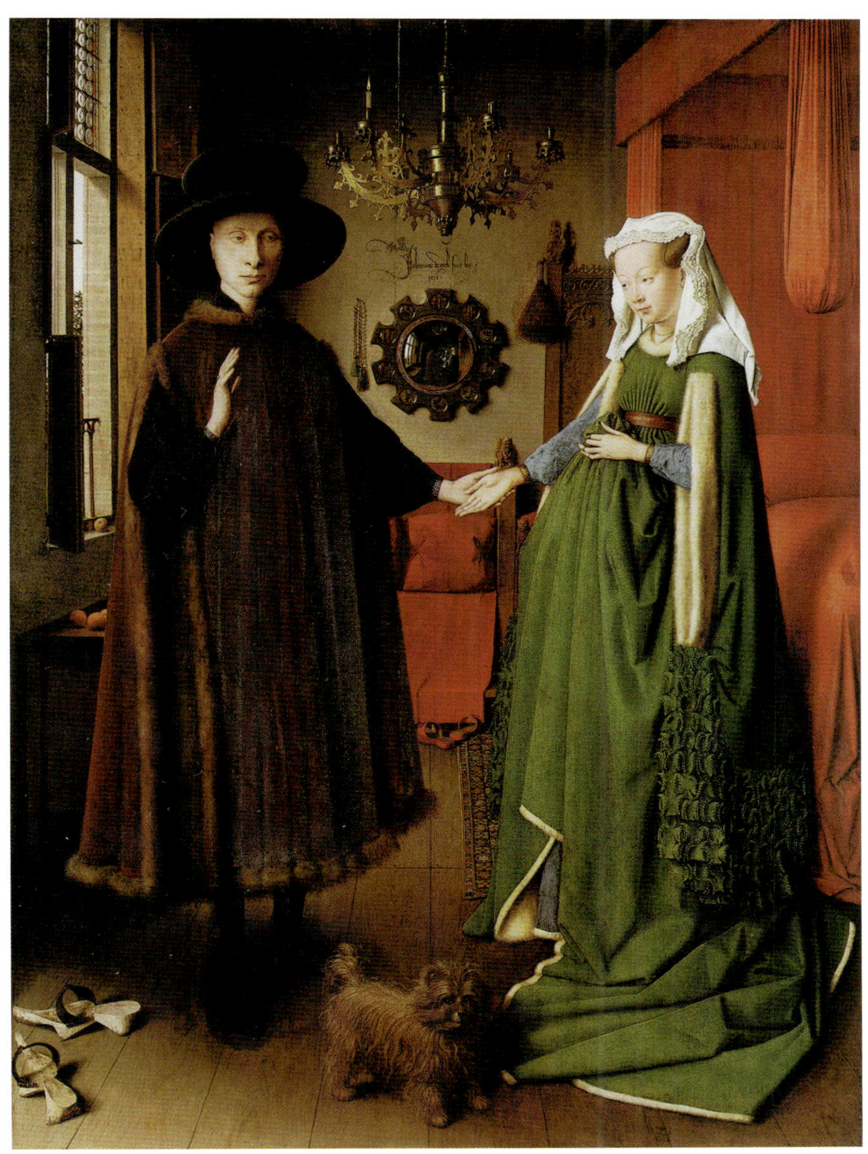

188. **Jan van Eyck**, c. 1390-1441, Northern Renaissance, Flemish,
The Arnolfini Portrait, 1434. Oil on oak panel, 82.2 x 60 cm.
National Gallery, London.

One of the most discussed of all paintings, Van Eyck's masterpiece of natural symbolism presents objects which have been given special meaning apposite to this couple's marriage, yet the same objects are appropriate to the scene in themselves. The work is, in effect, a visual in how one can find synchronicity and deeper meaning in everyday circumstances. The lines between the neatly groomed dog and the pairs of discarded shoes create a triangle. The dog (symbolising loyalty) complements the shoes (also symbolising domesticity). The man's feet are firmly in the middle of the lower triangle, indicating his vow of stability. The faces of the married couple and their clasped hands form the same size-and-shape triangle. The couple stands hand-in-hand as their other hands wear wedding rings, as if their love is authentic and complemented by, rather than caused by, their wedding vows. In the middle of that triangle is a mirror in a circular shape recalling eternity. Ten of the 'Stations of the Cross' are symbolised around the frame of the mirror. Prayer beads hang on the wall to the left of the stations-mirror. The reflection of the mirror shows the couple from the mirror's point of view, as if creating a circle of time and space. A statue of a saint on the bedpost is crushing a dragon (symbolising evil). The elaborate signature of the artist is on the wall below the mirror. The chandelier holds a single, lit candle. A superstition at the time suggested that a single, lit candle near the wedding bed would assure fertility.

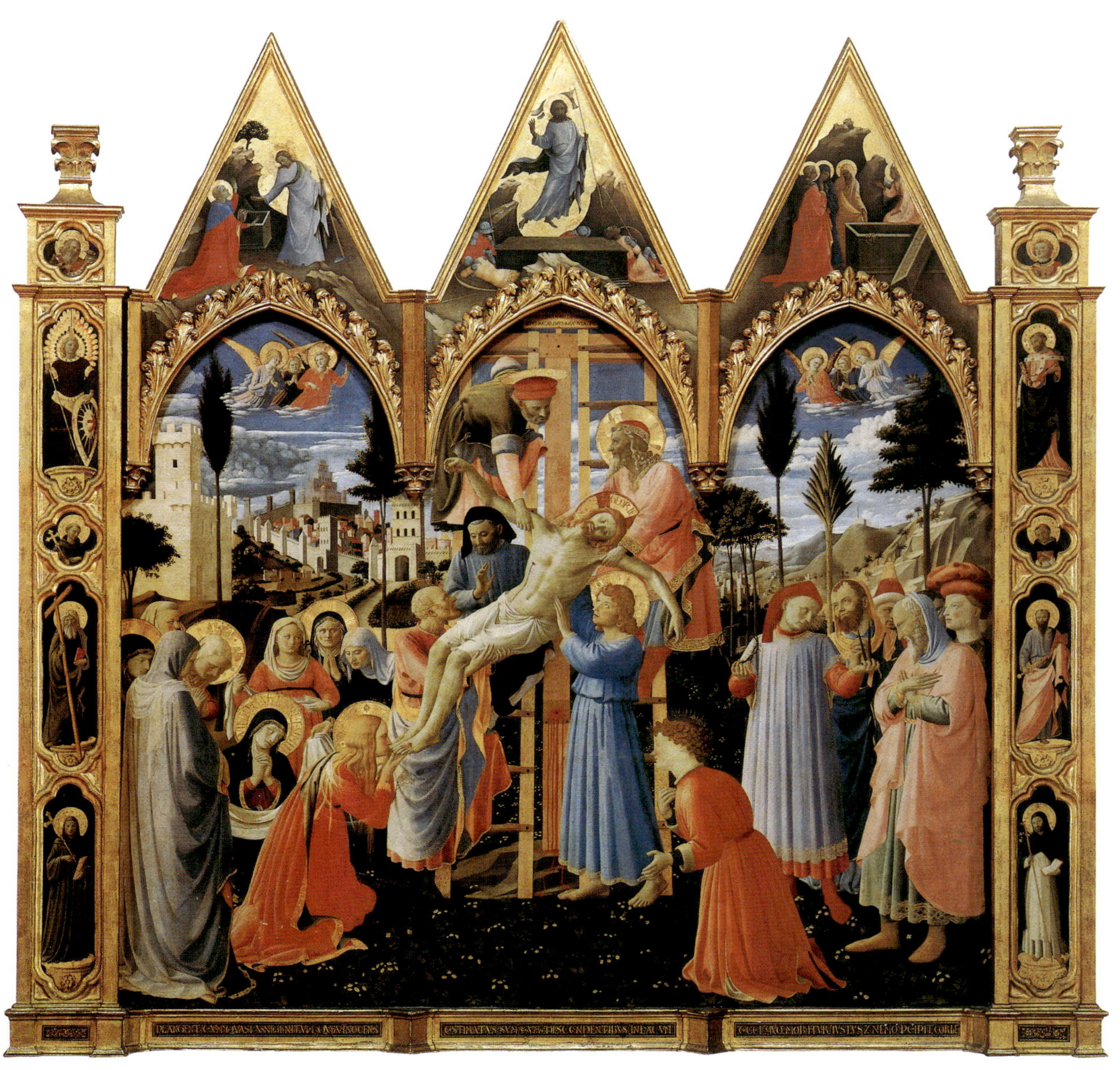

189. **Fra Giovanni Angelico,** 1387-1455, Early Renaissance, Florentine School, Italian, *The Deposition (Pala di Santa Trinita)*, 1437-1440. Tempera on panel, 176 x 185 cm. Museo di San Marco, Florence.

This painting was originally an altarpiece in the sacristy of the church Santa Trinita in Florence. The main panel figures the Deposition and the pilasters on each side represent different saints. Fra Angelico was officially beatified by the Vatican in 1984 but he has long been called Beato Angelico (The Blessed Angelico).

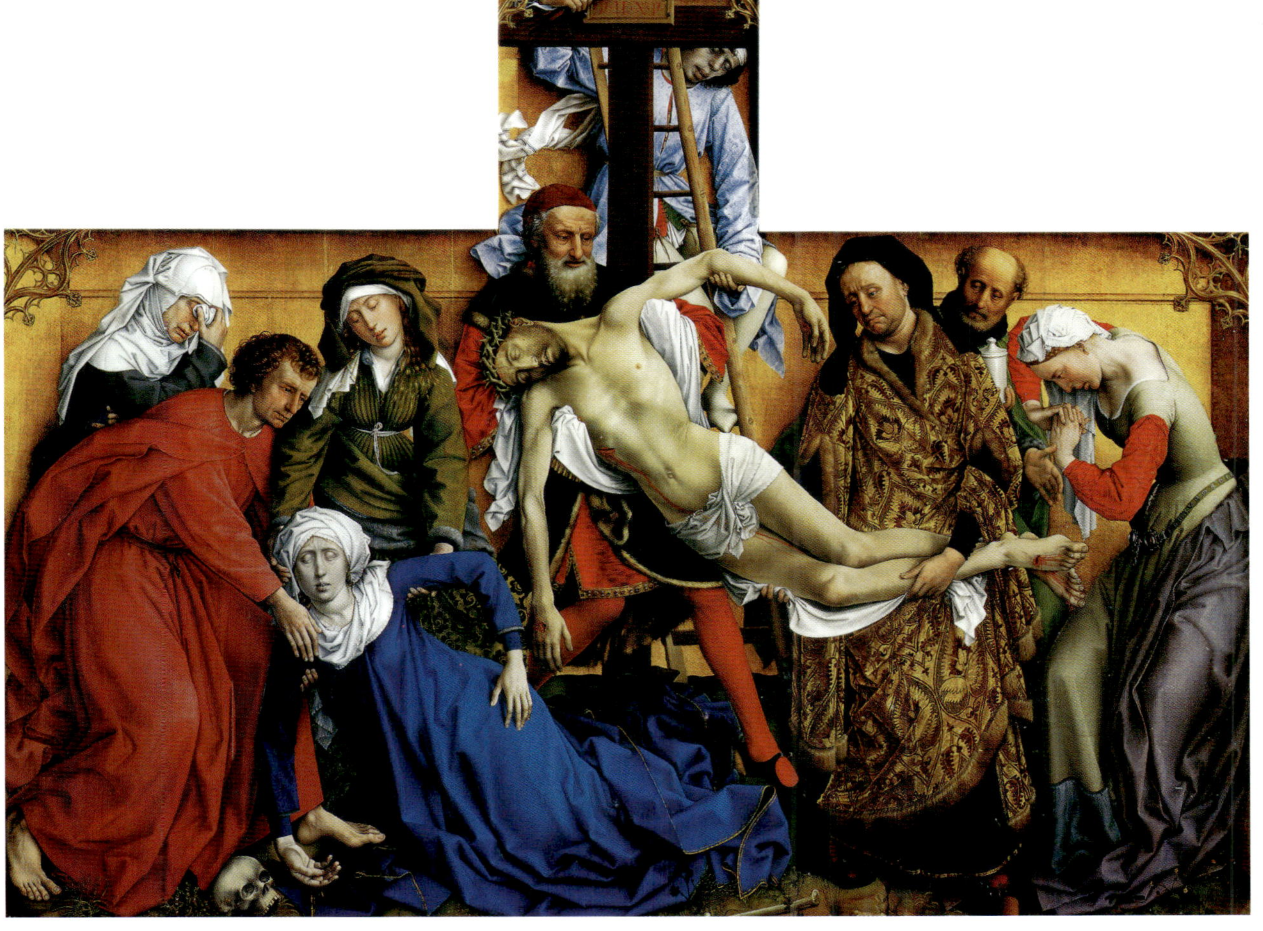

190. **Rogier van der Weyden**, 1399-1464, Northern Renaissance, Flemish, *Deposition*, c. 1435. Oil on panel, 220 x 262 cm. Museo Nacional del Prado, Madrid.

The life-sized figures and the gold background recall the influence of Campin on Van der Weyden as the composition imitates the low-reliefs from Tournai (where the artist came from).

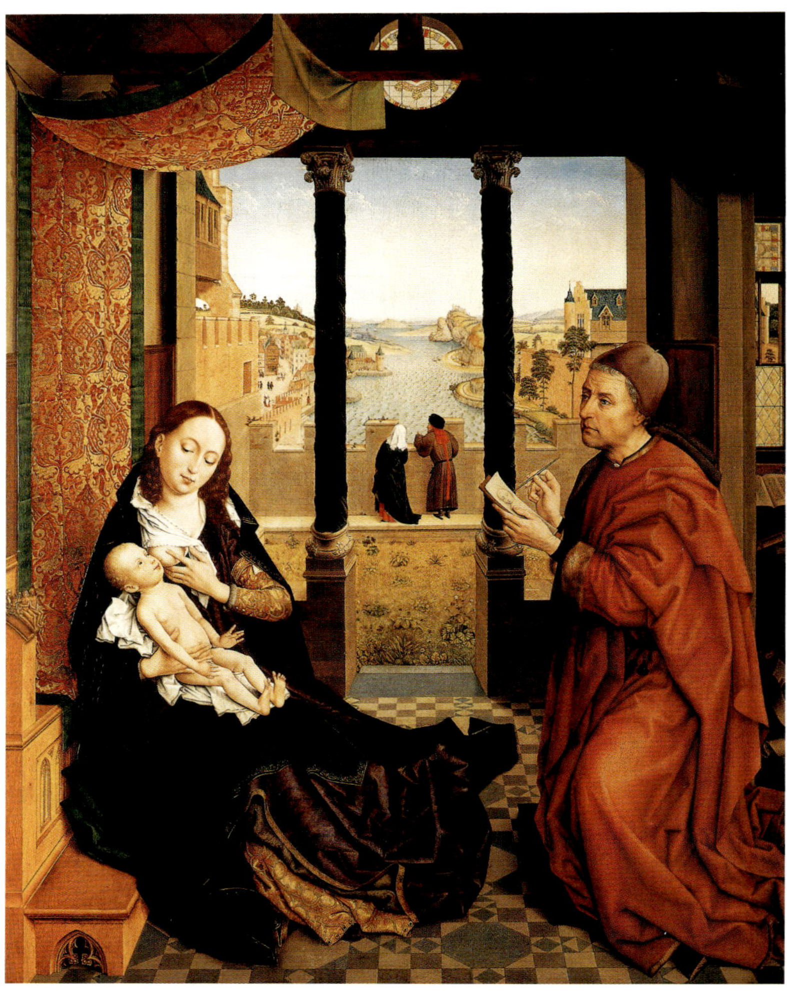

ROGIER VAN DER WEYDEN
(1399 TOURNAI, FLANDERS – 1464 BRUSSELS)

He lived in Brussels where he was the city's official painter (from 1436), but his influence was felt throughout Europe. One sponsor was Philip the Good, an avid collector. Van der Weyden is the only Fleming who truly carried on Van Eyck's great conception of art. He added to it a pathos of which there is no other example in his country except, though with less power and nobility, that of Hugo van der Goes towards the end of the century. He had a considerable influence on the art of Flanders and Germany. Hans Memling was his most renowned pupil. Van der Weyden was the last inheritor of the Giottesque tradition and the last of the painters whose work is thoroughly religious.

St Luke the Apostle, who is the accredited author of one of the four accepted versions of the New Testament Gospel, is also by tradition the first painter of the Virgin's portrait. Rogier van der Weyden kept up this tradition in his own picture of St Luke Drawing the Virgin. *This meticulously detailed work, typical of the Flemish tradition, shows Mary seated under a canopy as she attempts to nurse her infant, and Luke in front of her, drawing her face. A panoramic view can be seen between the columns in the background. Nursing-Madonna images had been part of the Marian tradition and lore since the Middle Ages. "Mary's milk" had, indeed, been a source of veneration in the form of a miracle-working substance regarded as one among many holy relics during medieval times, and reverence for it lasted well into Renaissance times. The origins of such a tradition and symbolism go back several thousands of years into antiquity, when Creator Goddesses like Isis were celebrated as symbolic milk-givers in their roles as compassionate and nurturing Universal Mothers. The milky ribbon of stars called the Milky Way was believed to symbolise the Goddess, and Marian lore inherited that popular tradition.*

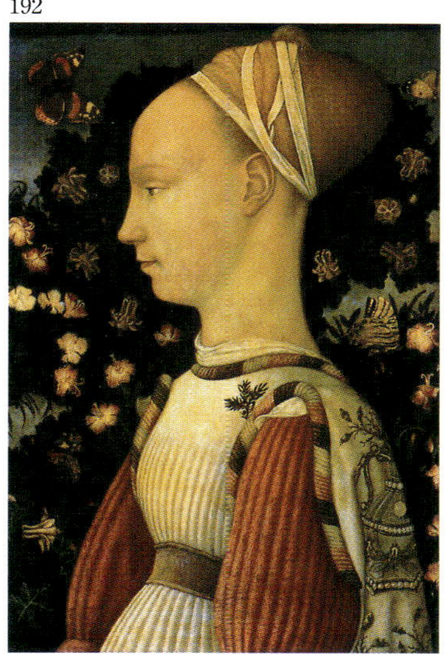

192

192. Antonio Puccio Pisanello, 1395-1455,
International Gothic, Italian,
Portrait of a Princess of the House of Este, c. 1435-1440.
Oil on panel, 43 x 30 cm. Musée du Louvre, Paris.

Pisanello is regarded as the preeminent master of the International Gothic style in Italian painting, but most of his major works have perished. This portrait of a young woman (assumed to be Ginevra d'Este) is flat – due to the use of medieval patterns in a 'modern' way, and its flowers and butterflies, though drawn from nature, seem like ornamental patterns from French or Flemish tapestries.

193. Stefano di Giovanni di Console Sassetta,
1392-c. 1450, Early Renaissance, Sienese School,
Italian, *The Mystic Marriage of Saint Francis with Chastity*,
1437-1444. Tempera on panel, 95 x 58 cm.
Musée Condé, Chantilly.

Sassetta's work shows certain conservatism, especially in the architectural structures of International Gothic design. However, his figures are set in the unity of Renaissance pictorial space.

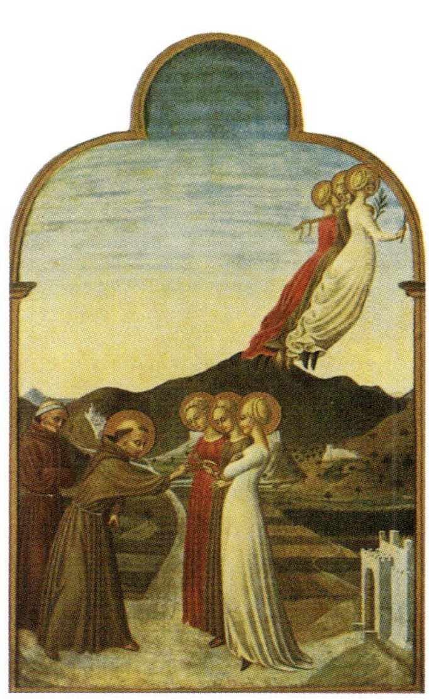

193

194. Robert Campin (Master of Flémalle), c. 1375-1444,
Northern Renaissance, Flemish, *Virgin and Child before a Firescreen*, c. 1440. Tempera on oak, 63.4 x 48.5 cm.
National Gallery, London

Robert Campin of Tournai is also called the 'Master of Flémalle', because three paintings now in the Städelsches Kunstinstitut were wrongly supposed to have come from Flémalle. Together with Van Eyck, he may be considered the founder of the Netherlandish painting of the Early Renaissance. The Virgin seems somehow clumsy, almost plebeian. The halo is replaced by the fire screen, which testifies of the homely detail and down-to-earth realism of the artist.

195. Giovanni di Paolo, 1403-1482, Early Renaissance,
Sienese School, Italian, *Madonna of Humility*, c. 1442.
Tempera on panel, 62 x 48.8 cm.
Courtesy of Museum of Fine Arts,
Marie Antoinette Evans Fund, Boston.

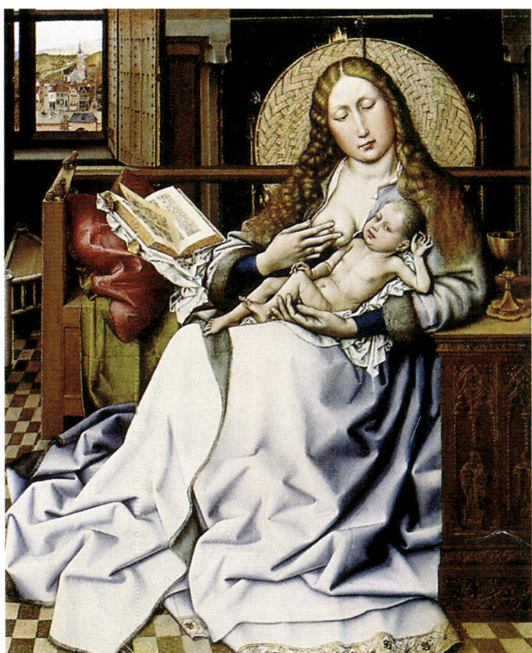

194

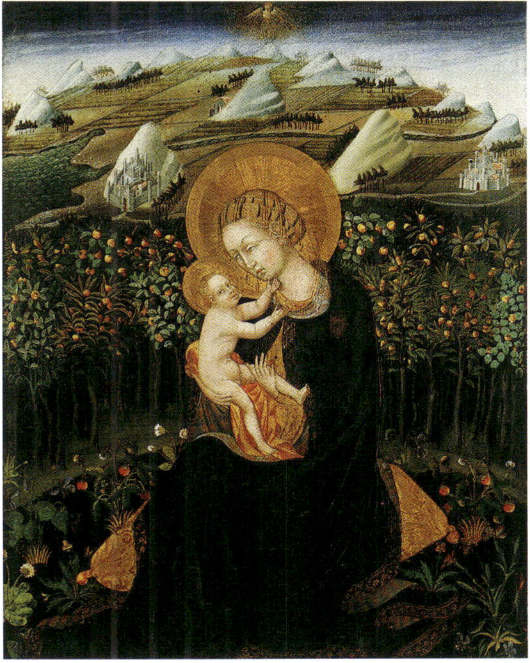

195

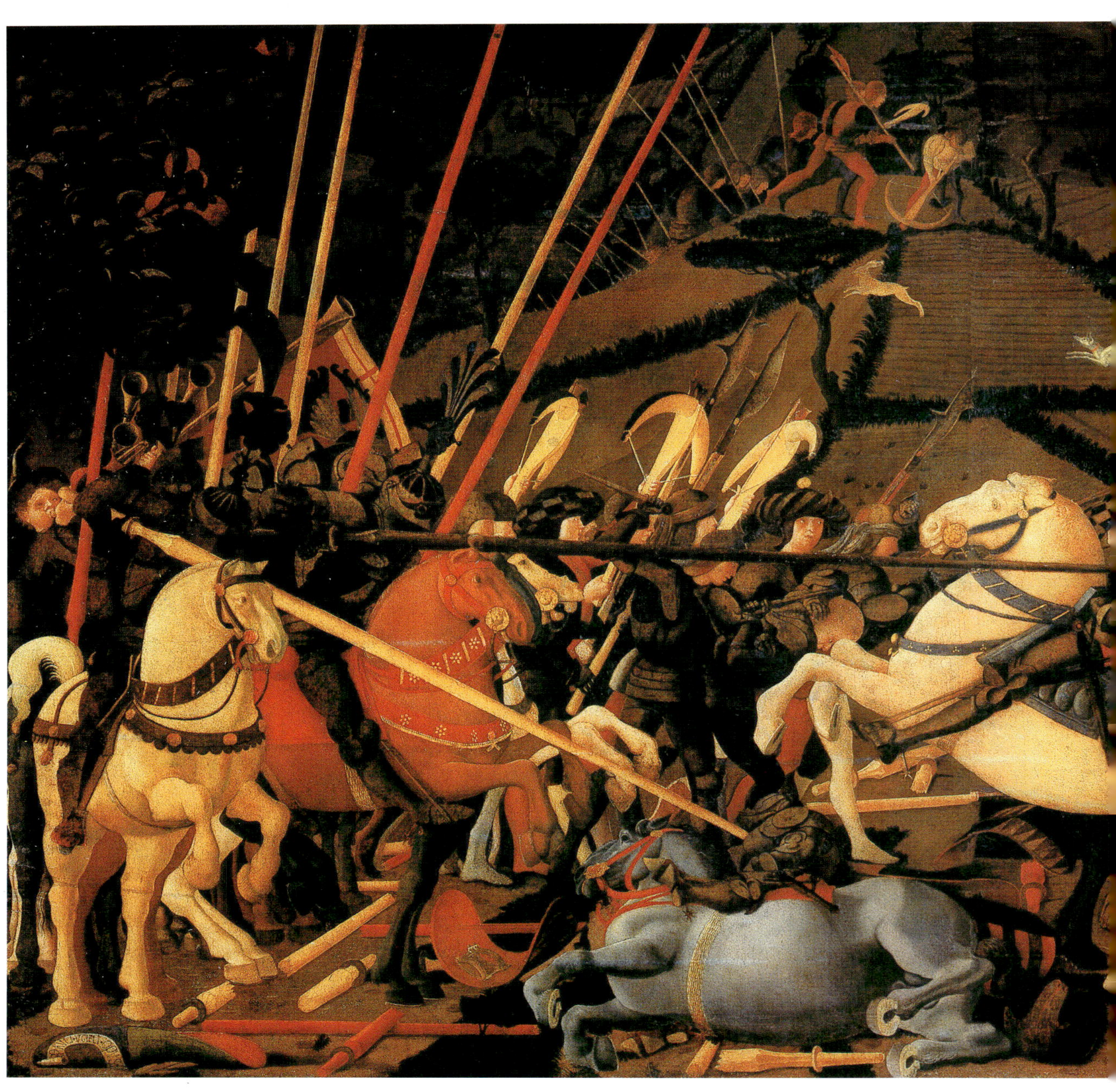

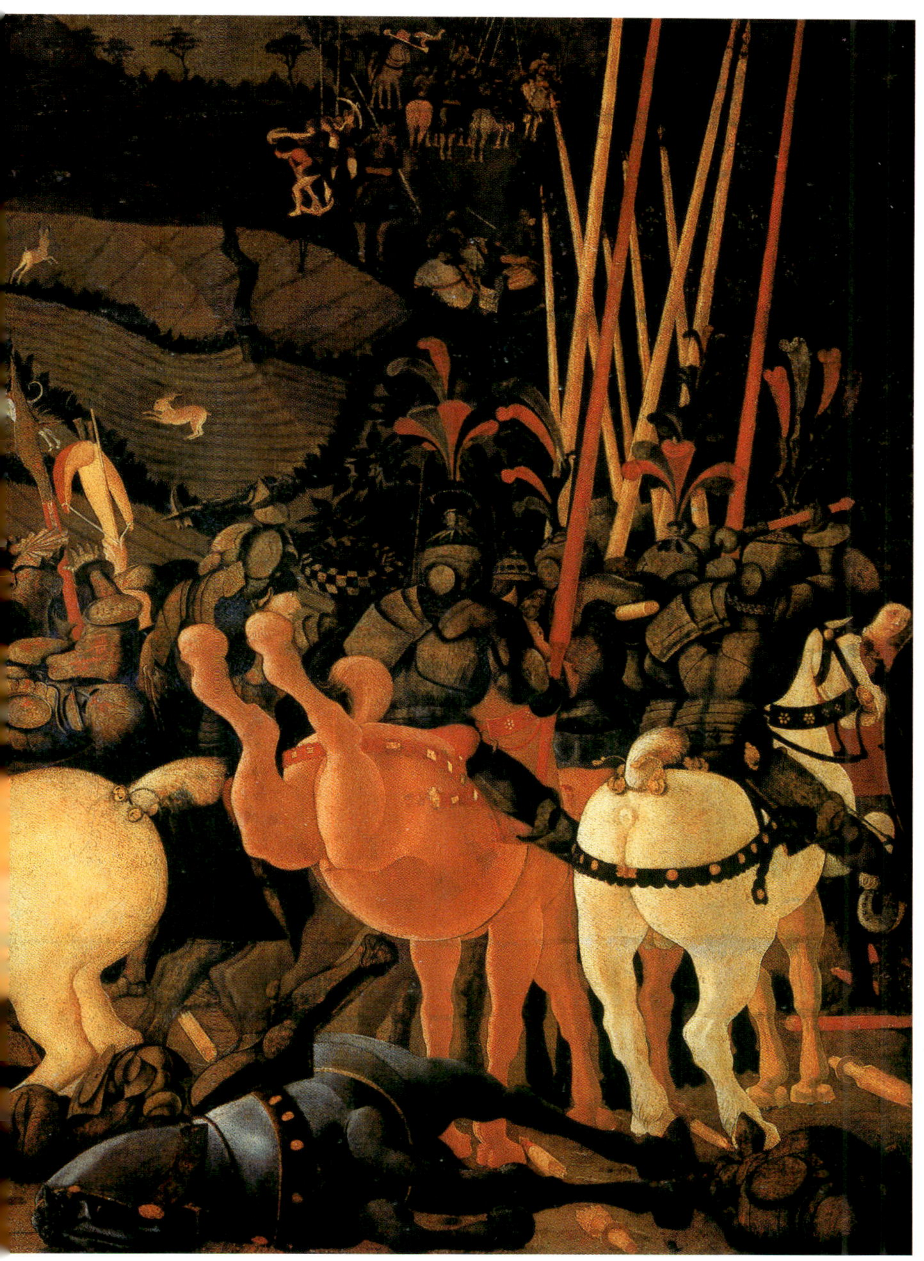

PAOLO UCCELLO
(1397 – 1475 FLORENCE)

Paolo di Dono was called 'Uccello' because he loved birds and the Italian word for bird is *uccello*. As well as painting on panel and in fresco, he was also a master of mosaics, especially in Venice, and produced designs for stained glass. We can feel the influence of Donatello especially in a fresco representing the *Flood and the Recession*, whereas the figures in this work is reminiscent of Masaccio's frescos of Brancacci chapel. His perspectives studies are very sophisticated, recalling the Renaissance art treatises of Piero della Francesca, da Vinci or Dürer. He was a major proponent of the Renaissance style. However, if his masterwork *The Battle of San Romano* (1438-1440) has Renaissance elements, Uccello's gold decorations on the surface of his masterpieces are indebted to the Gothic style.

196. **Paolo Uccello**, 1397-1475, Early Renaissance, Florentine School, Italian,
The Battle of San Romano (Full title *'Niccolò Mauruzi da Tolentino at the Battle of San Romano'*), 1438-1440.
Egg tempera with walnut oil and linseed oil on poplar,
181.6 x 320 cm.
Galleria degli Uffizi, Florence.

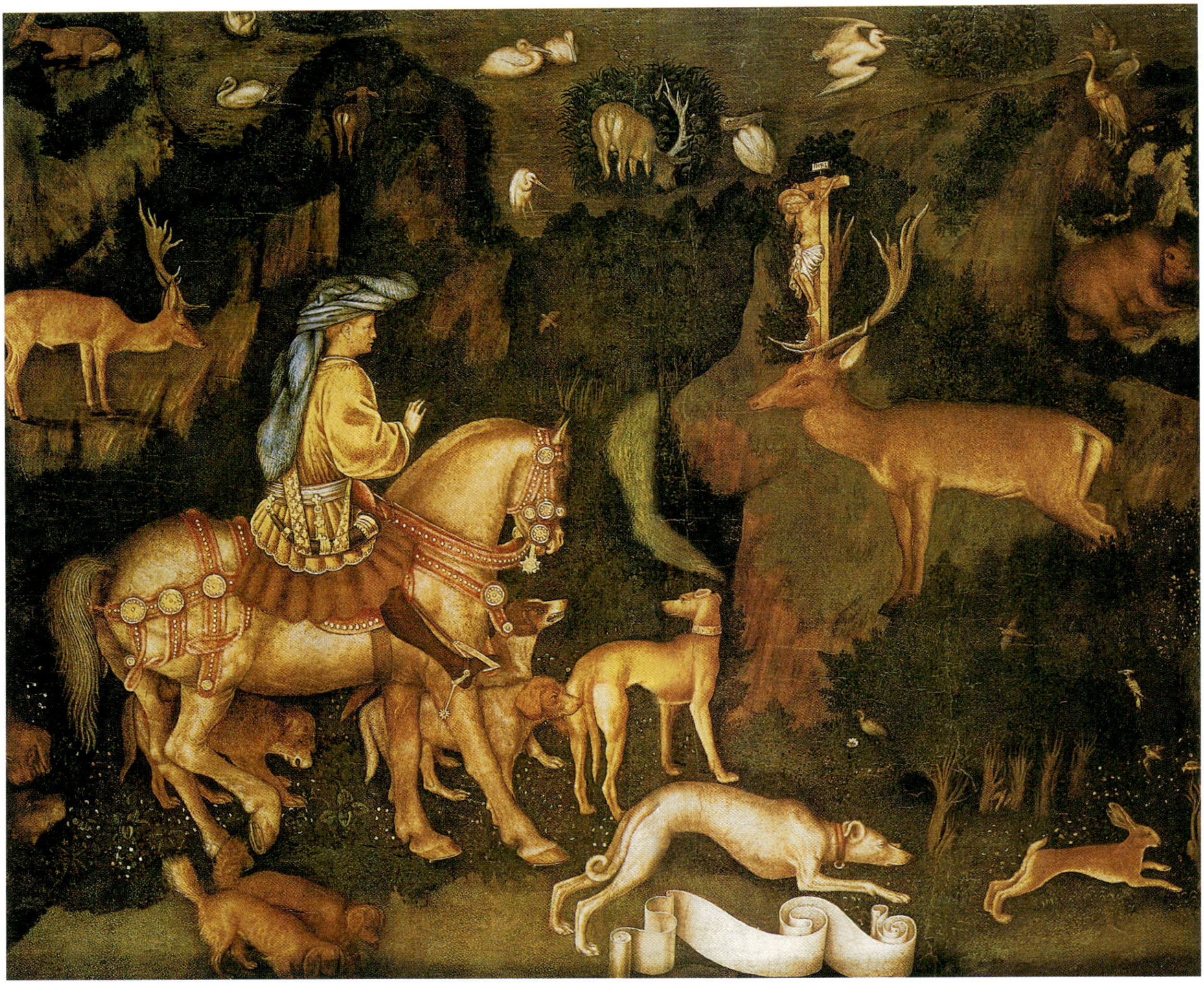

197. **Antonio Puccio Pisanello**, 1395-1455,
International Gothic, Italian,
The Vision of Saint Eustace, 1438-1442. Tempera on panel,
54.8 x 65.5 cm. National Gallery, London.

*Pisanello has carefully studied the animals in this painting,
using both drawings from pattern books as well as studies
from life.*

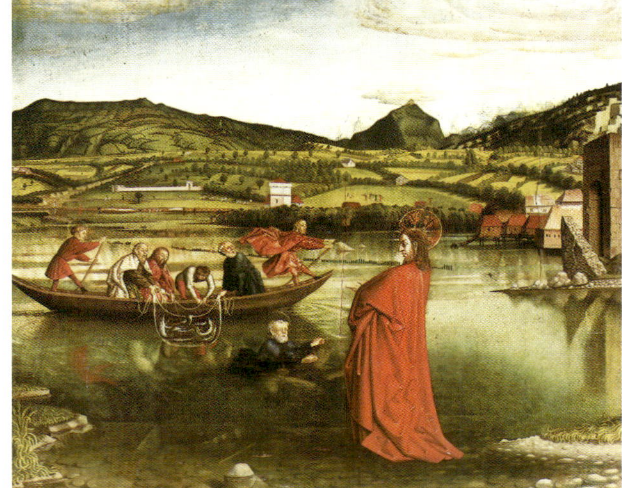

198. **Konrad Witz**, c. 1400-1445, International Gothic, Swiss,
The Miraculous Draught of Fishes, 1444.
Oil on panel, 129 x 155 cm.
Museum of Art and History, Geneva.

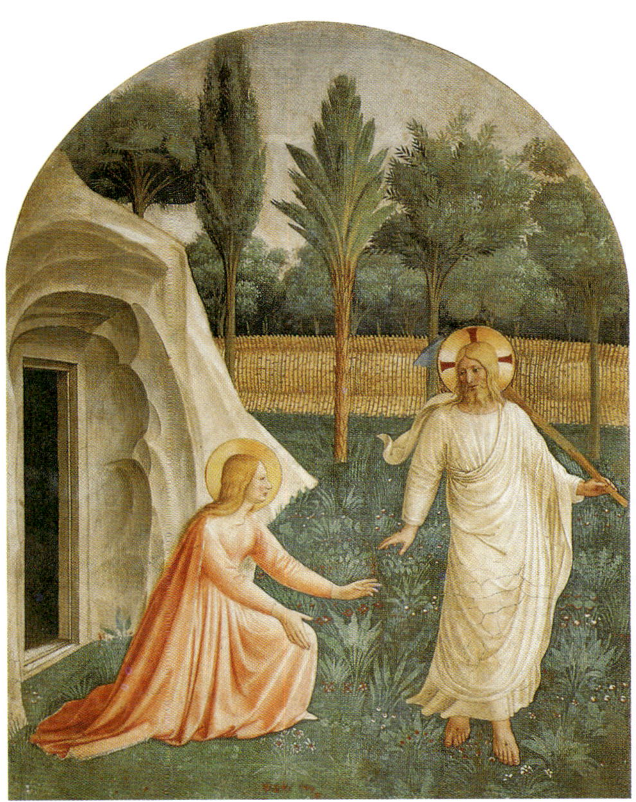

199. **Fra Giovanni Angelico**, 1378-1445, Early Renaissance,
Florentine School, Italian, *Noli Me Tangere,* 1440-1441.
Fresco, 180 x 146 cm.
Convento di San Marco, Florence.

200. **Piero della Francesca**, c. 1416-1492,
Early Renaissance, Italian, *The Baptism of Christ*, 1445.
Tempera on panel, 167 x 116 cm. National Gallery, London.

*The suspended dove symbolising the Holy Spirit is at the exact
middle point of the circle implied in the upper part of the
painting, while the navel of Jesus is the mid-point of the
rectangle implied at the bottom portion of the painting. The
upper mid-point alludes to the divinity of Jesus, while the
lower mid-point relates to his humanity. The God-man is at
geometric centre of the scene. The vertical balance is likewise
between the heavenly angels on the left and the earthly
community on the right. The latter includes a follower of the
Baptist who is either getting dressed after his own baptism or
preparing to be baptised. The group watching probably
represents the sceptics or the undecided. Sansepolero, in
northern Italy, was the hometown of the artist and the sponsor
of most of the artist's mature works. In the tradition of such
commissions, the sponsor appears in the painting. The town is
pictured in the distance between Jesus and the left vertical
third of the painting. Young plants in the foreground indicate
new life, as the rebirth offered by baptism would symbolise
thereafter for Christians. The Hebrew bible had predicted that
the ones who prepared the way for the Lord would make the
crooked straight, symbolised here as the river and roads in the
landscape. All the roads and rivers lead to the feet of The Way,
the name the seminal Christian community gave their religion
as well as a descriptive title for their Messiah.*

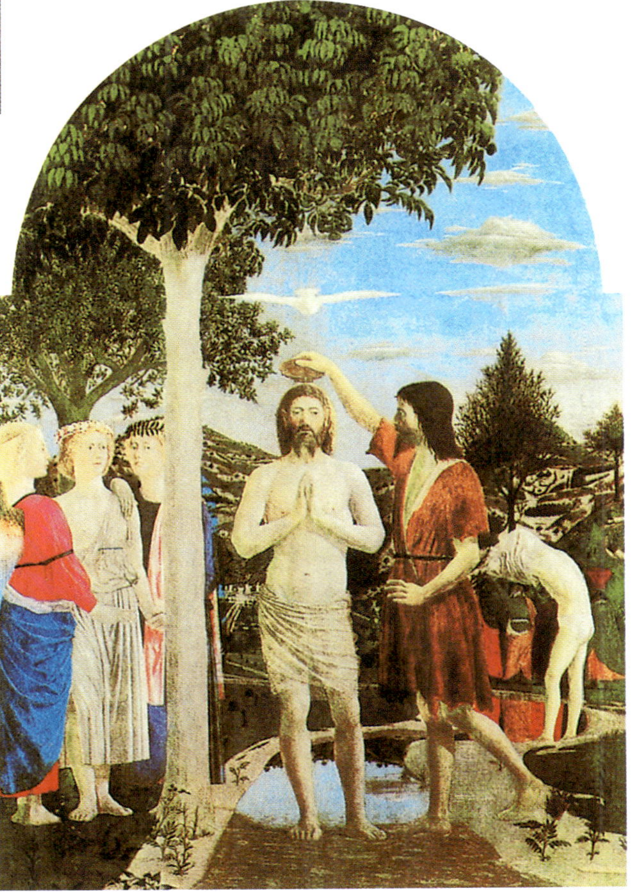

200

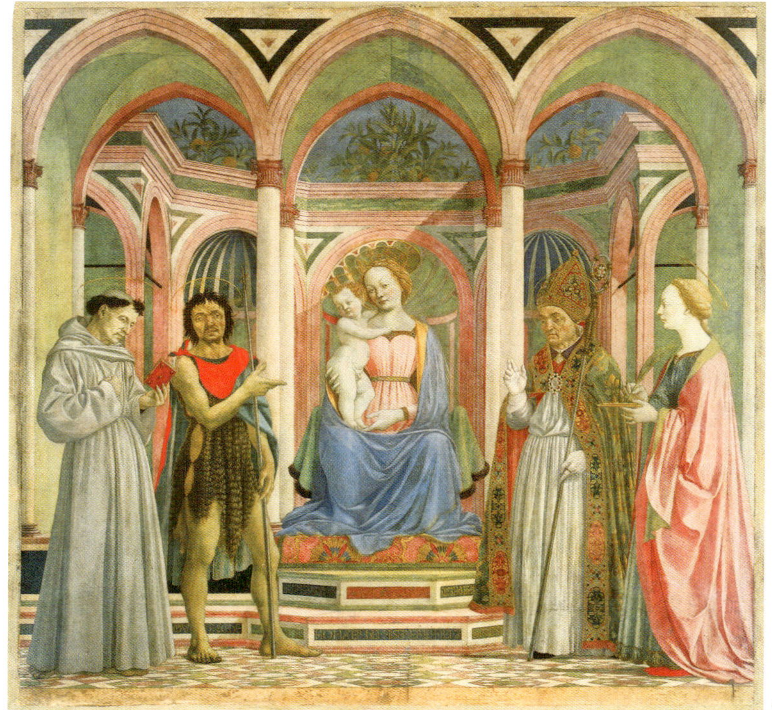

201

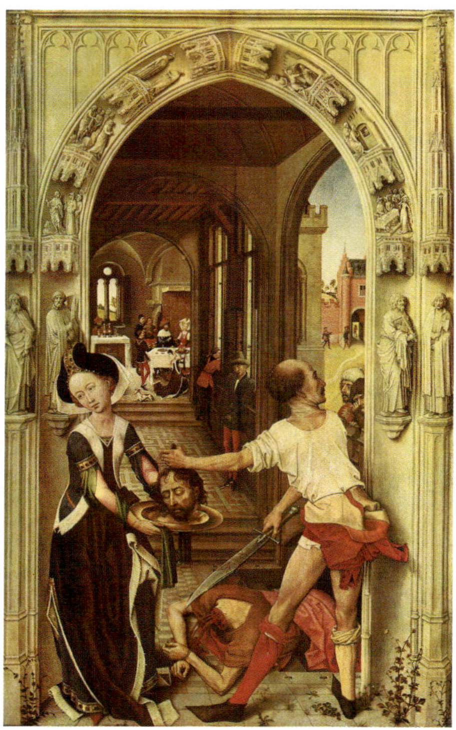

202

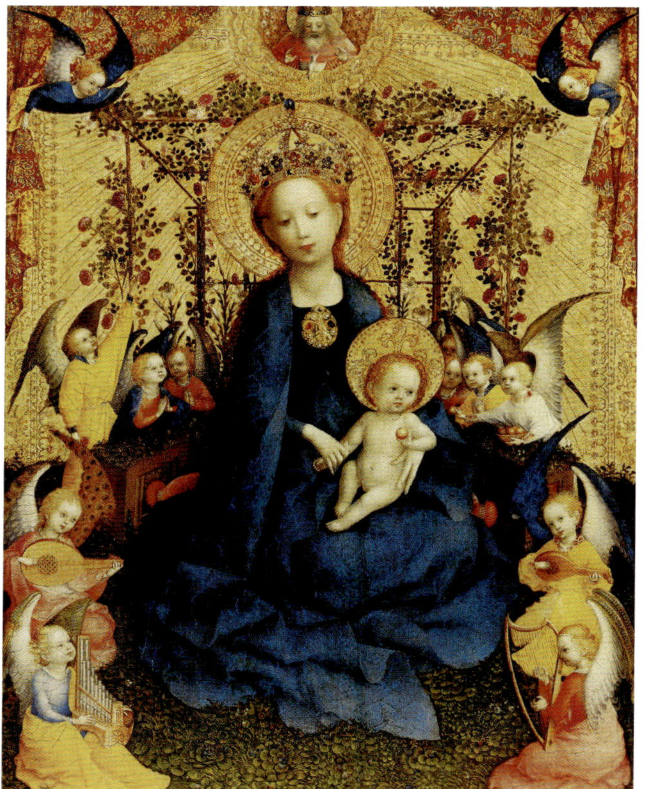

201. Domenico Veneziano, 1400-1461, Early Renaissance,
Florentine School, Italian,
The Madonna with Child and Saints, 1445.
Tempera on wood, 209 x 216 cm.
Galleria degli Uffizi, Florence.

*Painted for the high altar of the Uzzano in Santa Lucia dei
Magnoli, this is perhaps Veneziano's greatest achievement.
Veneziano, renowned for his use of perspective and colour,
depicts the "sacra conversazione" within a harmonious
architectural structure rendered more delicate by pastel
shades of rose and green.*

202. Rogier van der Weyden, 1399-1464,
Northern Renaissance, Flemish,
Triptych: St John Altarpiece (right panel), c. 1446-1453.
Oil on oak panel, 77 x 48 cm (each panel).
Gemäldegalerie, Alte Meister, Berlin.

*Van der Weyden gives a particularly strong effect of depth in
the side panels of this altarpiece, with the succession of
rooms in the background.*

203. Stephan Lochner, c. 1410-1451,
Northern Renaissance, German,
Madonna of the Rose Bush, c. 1448.
Mixed technique on panel, 51 x 40 cm.
Wallraf-Richartz-Museum, Cologne.

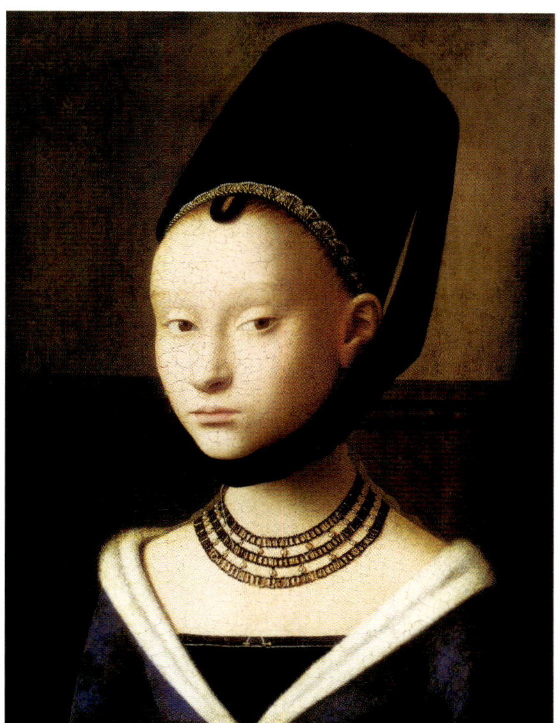

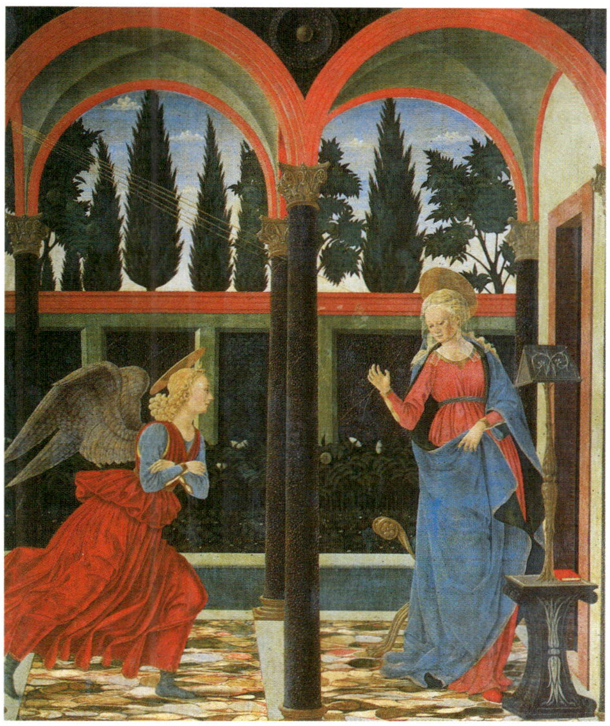

204. **Petrus Christus**, c. 1410-1473, Northern Renaissance, Flemish,
Portrait of a Young Girl, after 1446.
Oil on panel, 29 x 22.5 cm. Gemäldegalerie, Alte Meister, Berlin.

The most popular painting by Christus, this portrait is composed of simple volumes. The painter places the sitter in a defined setting, new to Flemish painting, which was traditionally depicted with a neutral, dark background (such as in Van Eyck's and Van der Weyden's portraits).

205. **Alesso Baldovinetti**, c. 1425-1499, Early Renaissance,
Florentine School, Italian, *Annunciation*, c. 1447.
Tempera on panel, 167 x 137 cm.
Galleria degli Uffizi, Florence.

JEAN FOUQUET
(1420 – 1481 TOURS)

A painter and illuminator, Jean Fouquet is regarded as the most important French painter of the fifteenth century. Little is known about his life but it is quite sure that he executed, in Italy, the portrait of Pope Eugenius IV. Upon his return to France, he introduced Italian Renaissance elements into French painting. He was the court painter to Louis XI. Whether he worked on miniatures rendering the finest detail, or on larger scale in panel paintings, Fouquet's art had the same monumental character. His figures are modelled in broad planes defined by lines of magnificent purity.

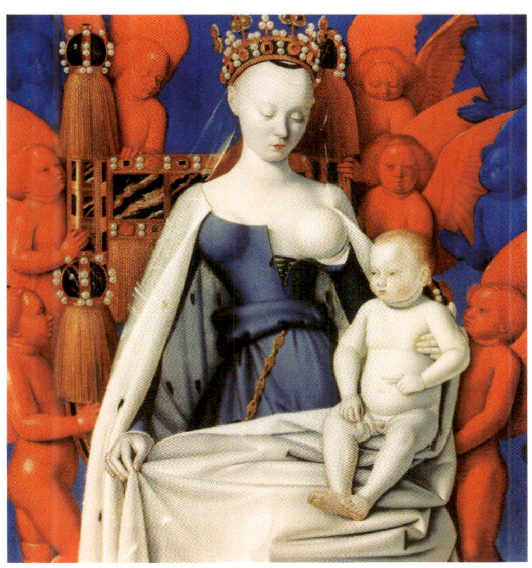

206. **Jean Fouquet**, c. 1420-1481, Early Renaissance, French,
Virgin and Child Surrounded by Angels (right panel of *Meulun's diptych*), c. 1450.
Oil on panel, 91 x 81 cm. Royal Museum of Fine Arts, Antwerp.

The particularity of this painting is due to its geometric composition, set in a convex pentagon often used by Fouquet. The volume given accentuates the sculptural aspect of this Virgin whose face was inspired by Agnes Sorel (the mistress of Charles VII). The diptych assembles the portrait of a Virgin with the one of the patrons in prayer in front of his protector saint.

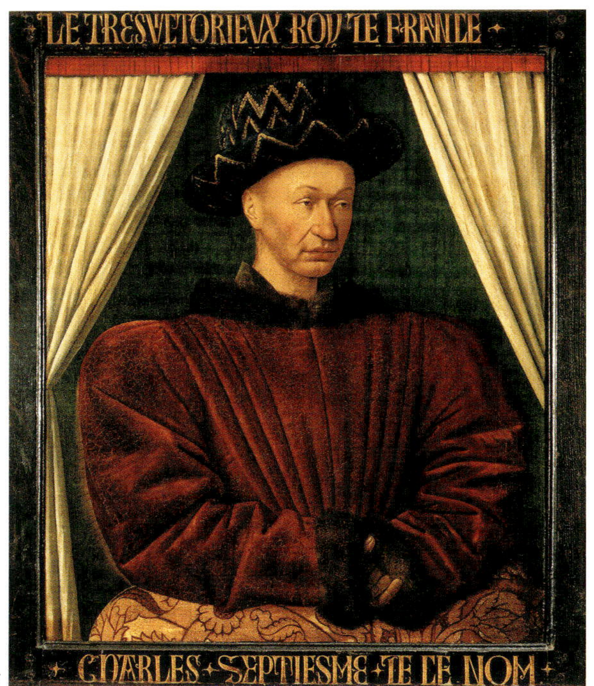

207

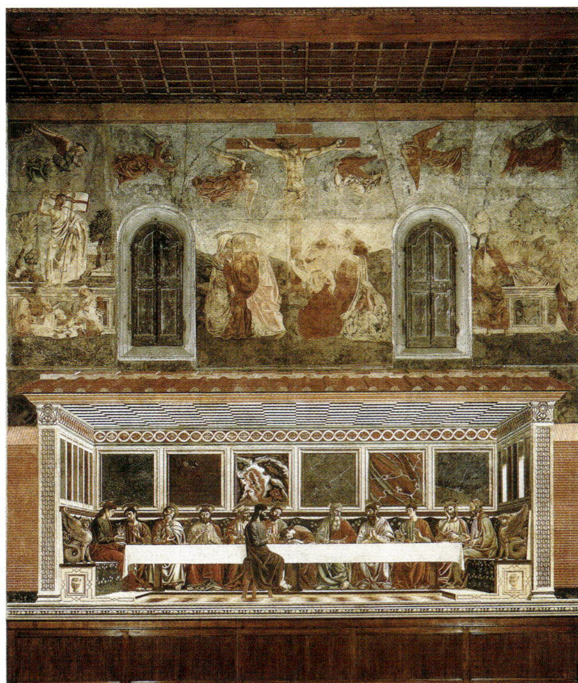

208

207. Jean Fouquet, c. 1420-1481, Early Renaissance, French,
Portrait of Charles VII of France, c. 1450-1455.
Oil on oak panel, 86 x 71 cm.
Musée du Louvre, Paris.

The particularity of this painting is due to its squared shape, nearly full-scale, exceptional at the time. The frontal representation is characteristic of the official portraits of monarchs in the West. The two white curtains stand as symbols of majesty. From the years 1420 to 1430 the upper-body intimate portrait was a new fashion spread by Flemish masters. Here Fouquet carries out a synthesis between the traditional full-length representation and the upper-body representation. He enlarges the king's stature, exploiting the fashion of padded shoulders. This work was painted in a precise political context: at the time, the victories of French royalty were being celebrated. This portrait will have a great influence on Jean Clouet and Holbein, who both travelled through the city of Bourges.

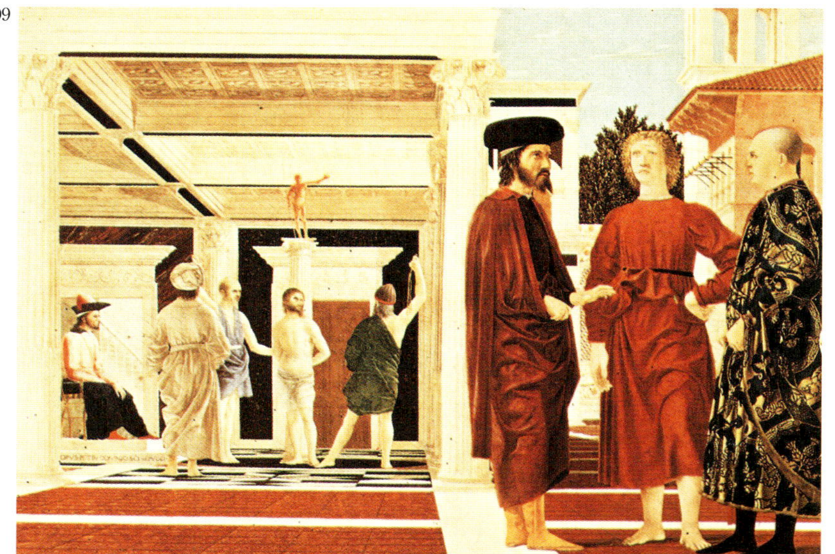

209

208. Andrea del Castagno, 1446-1497,
Early Renaissance,
Florentine School, Italian, *Last Supper*
and above *Resurrection, Crucifixion and Entombment*, c. 1445-1450.
Fresco, 980 x 1025 cm.
Convent of Sant'Apollonia, Florence.

209. Piero della Francesca, c. 1416-1492,
Early Renaissance, Italian,
The Flagellation of Jesus, c. 1450.
Oil and tempera on panel,
58.4 x 51.5 cm.
Galleria Nazionale delle Marche, Urbino.

Through the scientific use of perspective in a measured, symmetrical manner and its symbolic contents, The Flagellation *contributes to the humanistic rendition of figures in painting and characterises the painter's interests in mathematics. The architecture is a predominant part of the scene, which is divided by the column supporting the temple.*

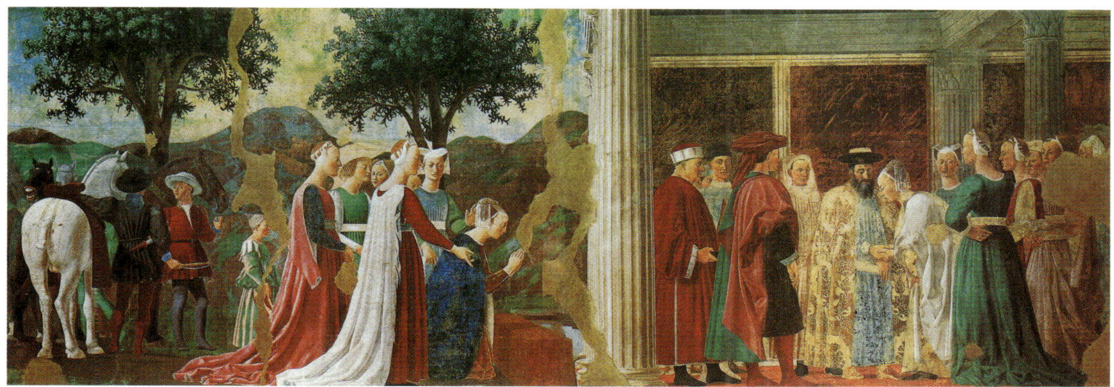

210. **Piero della Francesca**,
c. 1416-1492, Early
Renaissance, Italian, *Adoration
of the Holy Wood and the
Meeting of Solomon and the
Queen of Sheba*, 1450-1465.
Fresco. Choir of the Church of
San Francesco, Arezzo.

*The cycle of frescos was
commissioned by the richest
family in Arrezo, the Bacci. The
theme of the cycle is taken from
the* Golden Legend *by Jacobus
de Voragine.*

211. **Petrus Christus**, c. 1410-1473,
Northern Renaissance, Flemish,
The Lamentation, c. 1455.
Oil on panel, 101 x 192 cm.
Musées Royaux des Beaux-Arts,
Brussels.

PIERO DELLA FRANCESCA
(1416 – 1492, BORGO SAN SEPULCRO)

Forgotten for centuries after his death, Francesca has been regarded, since his rediscovery in the early twentieth century, as one of the supreme artists of the *Quattrocento*. Born in Borgo San Sepolcro (now Sansepolcro) in Umbria he spent much of his life there. His major work is a series of frescos on the *Legend of the True Cross* in the choir of San Francesco at Arezzo (c. 1452-c. 1465).

While influenced at the beginning of his life by all the great masters of the generation before, his work represents a synthesis of all the discoveries these artists had made in the previous twenty years. He created a style in which monumental, meditative grandeur and almost mathematical lucidity are combined with limpid beauty of colour and light. He was a slow and thoughtful worker and often applied wet cloths to the plaster at night so that - contrary to normal fresco practice – he could work for more than one day on the same section. Piero's later career was spent working at the humanist court of Federico da Montefeltro at Urbino. Vasari said Piero was blind when he died, and failing eyesight may have been his reason for giving up painting. He had considerable influence, notably on Signorelli (in the weighty solemnity of his figures) and Perugino (in the spatial clarity of his compositions). Both are said to have been Piero's pupils.

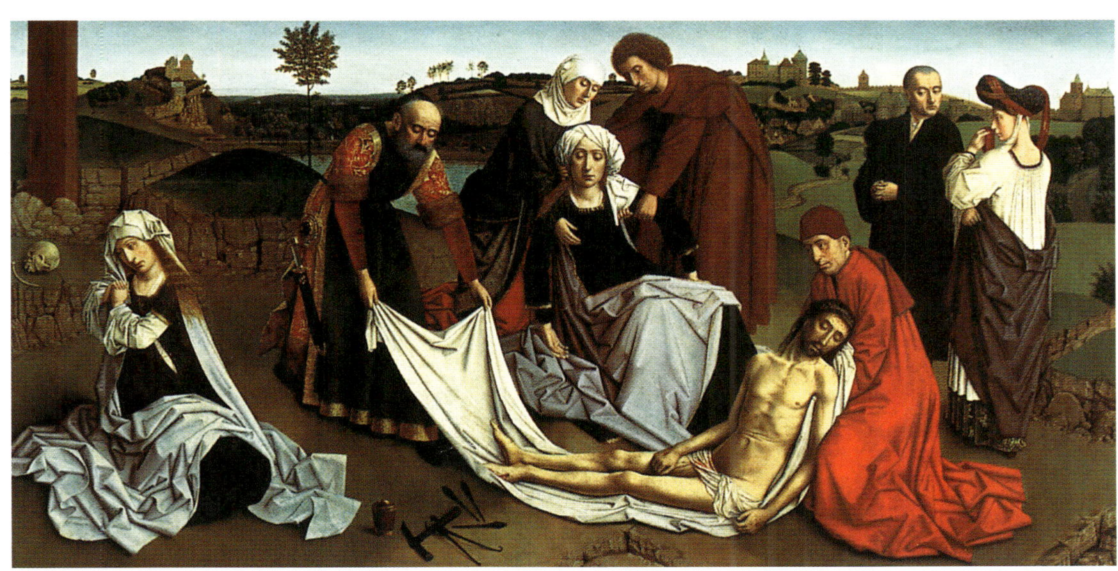

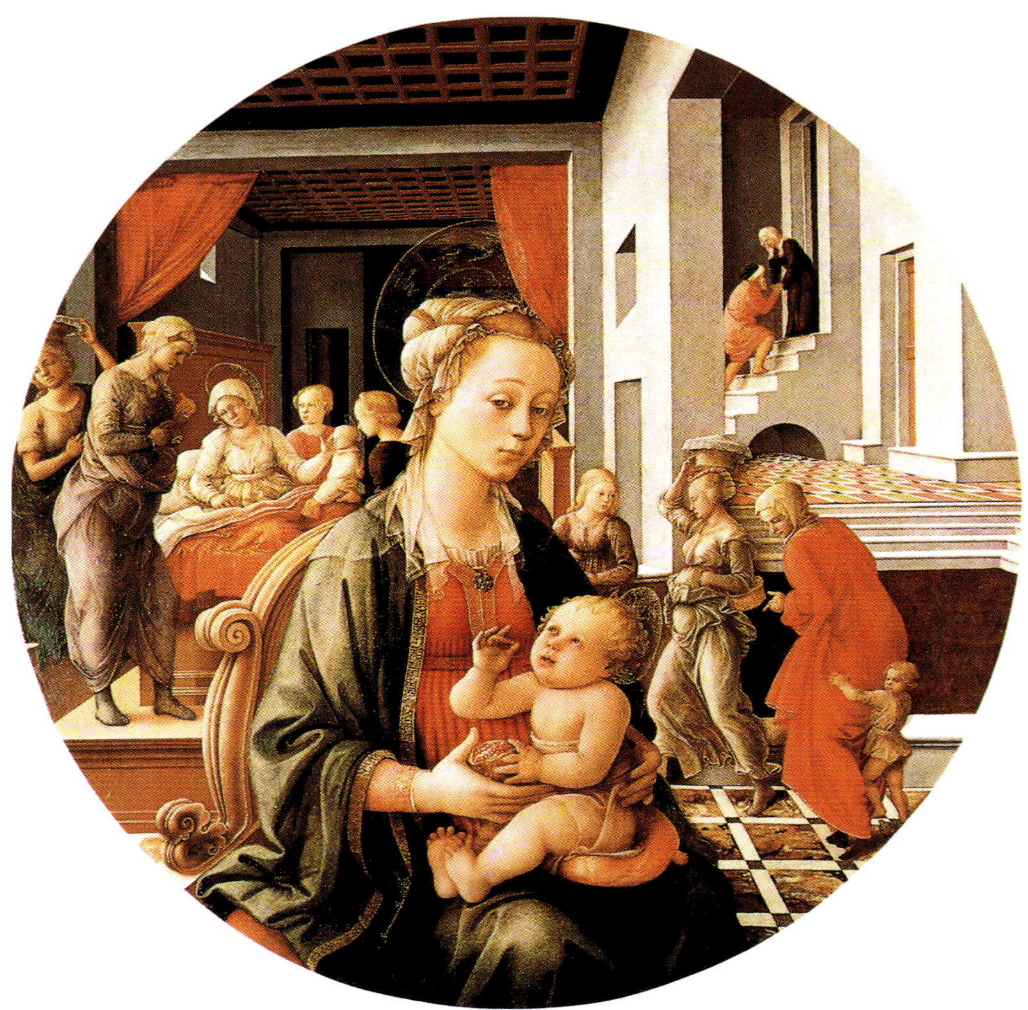

212. Fra Filippo Lippi, c. 1406-1469,
Early Renaissance, Florentine School, Italian.
Virgin with the Child and Scenes from the Life of St Anne, c. 1452.
Tempera on wooden panel, Tondo, diameter: 135 cm. Palazzo Pitti, Florence.

Oral tradition, later encouraged by art such as this, names Anna and Joachim as Mary's parents, but there is no scriptural basis for the notion. In this masterpiece, often called The Bartolini Tondo, *three highlights in the life of Anna are presented. The background scenes are dedicated to the Virgin's mother, St Anne (or Anna), and include the first meeting of Anne and her husband-to-be Joachim, and a scene of the subsequent birth of Mary. In the foreground, is the Madonna with her child. Like Persephone, the Greek goddess of natural cycle, she is holding a pomegranate, a symbol of rebirth, fertility and abundance in nature. The infant Jesus is also holding the fruit, and with his raised right hand, he is bringing its seed toward his mouth. The pensive expression of Mary in many paintings of her with the child Jesus is often interpreted as reflecting her prophetic awareness of the future sufferings that will befall her only son. But in this case the Virgin might be recalling her mother's life. The surrounding scenes might be intended to show her recollection of her mother. The artist's mastery of detail as in the transparency of Mary's veil and her fine features were inspirations for the later masterpieces of his most famous pupil, Botticelli.*

FRA FILIPPO LIPPI
(1406 FLORENCE – 1469 SPOLETO)

A Carmelite monk, he lived in a monastery in Florence at the same time as Masolino and Masaccio were painting frescos in Florence. He was ordained a priest in Padua in 1434.

His works show the aesthetic interest of his time through sophisticated drawing and his ability to obtain transparent effects on opaque colours. After his death, his workshop members completed his unfinished frescos. Botticelli was one of his students, as was his son Filippino Lippi. The works of the two former Fra Lippi students link the Early and High Renaissance periods. Works include major fresco cycles for Santa Maria Novella in Florence and for Santa Maria sopra Minerva in Rome.

213. **Rogier van der Weyden**, 1399-1464,
Northern Renaissance, Flemish,
Adoration of the Magi (triptych, central panel), c. 1455.
Tempera on wood, 138 x 153 cm.
Alte Pinakothek, Munich.

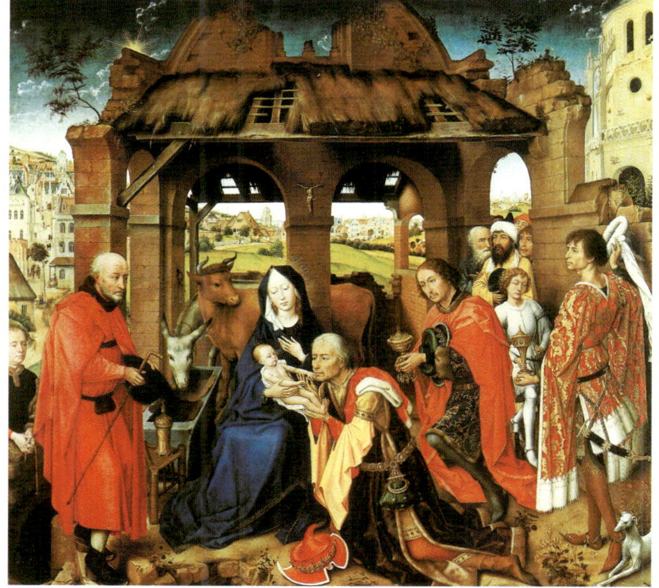

214. **Benozzo Gozzoli**, 1420-1497, Early Renaissance,
Florentine School, Italian, *The Procession of the Magi,
Procession of the Youngest King* (detail), 1459-1463.
Fresco. Palazzo Medici Riccardi, Florence.

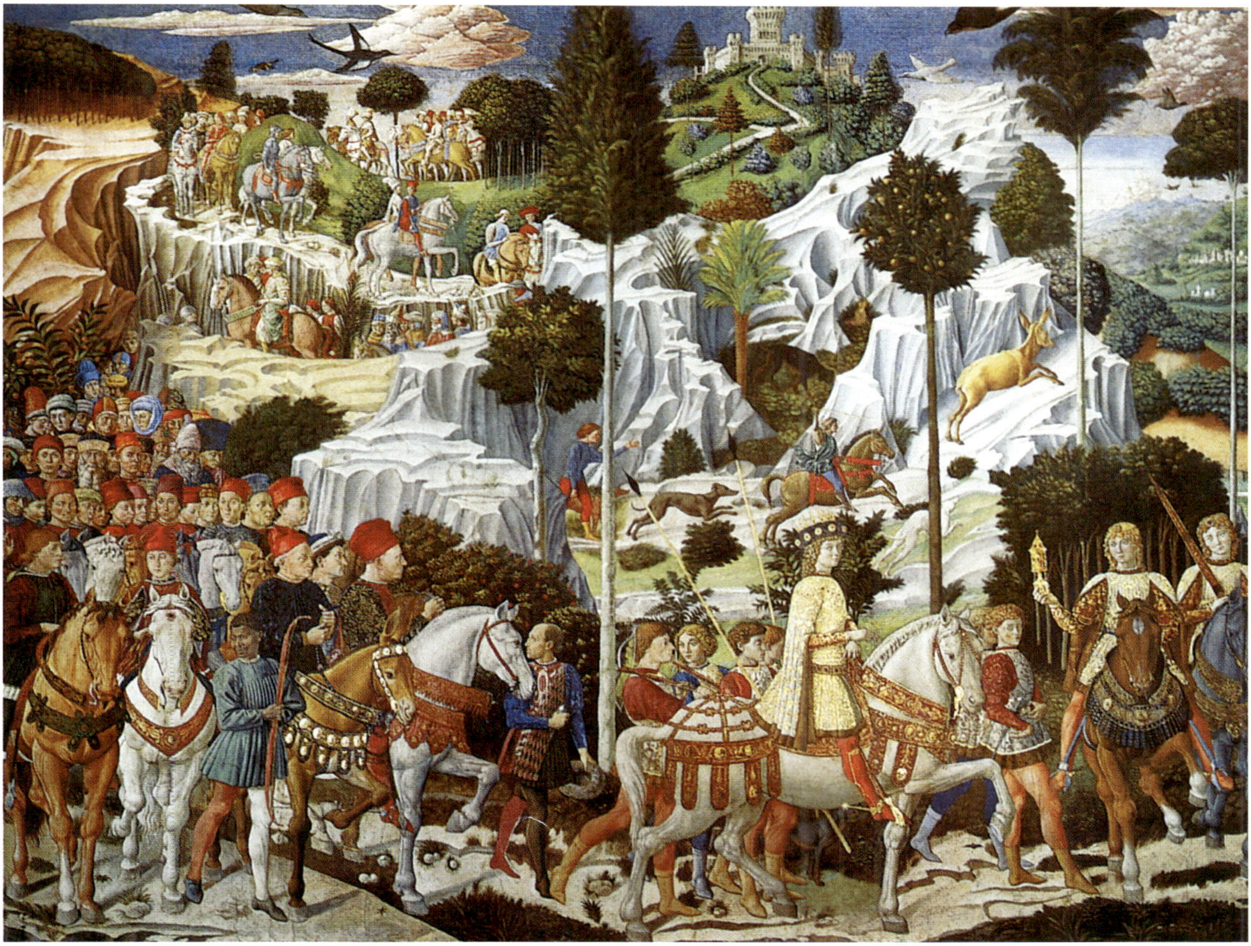

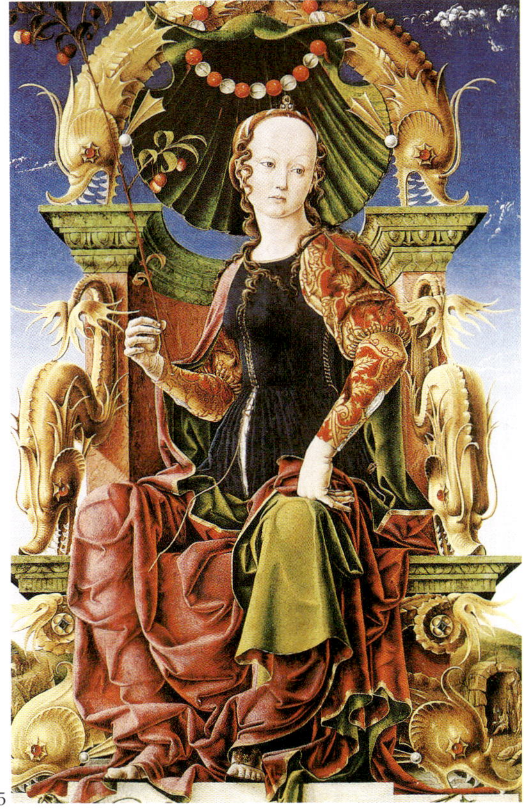

215

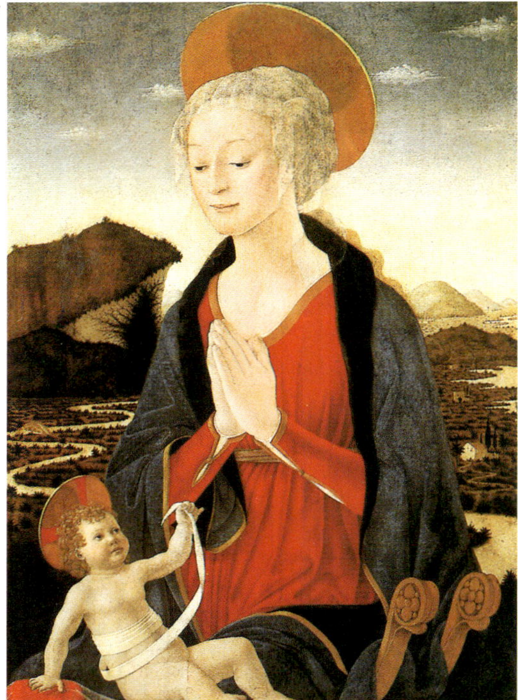

217

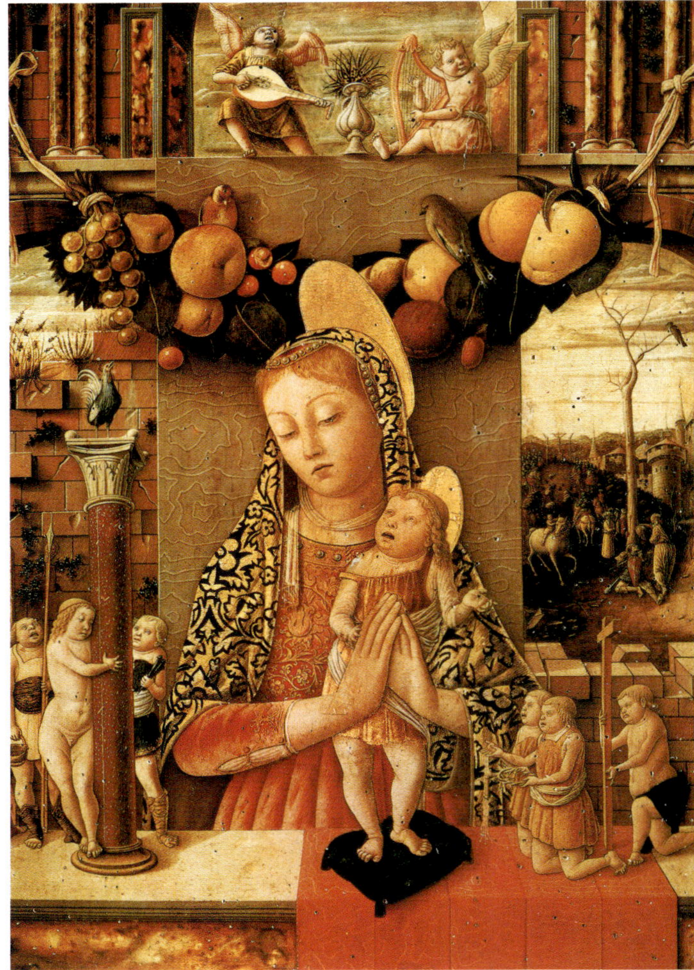

216

215. **Cosimo di Domenico di Bonaventura Tura**, c. 1431-1495,
Early Renaissance, Ferrarese School, Italian, *The Spring*, c. 1455-1460.
Oil with egg tempera, 116.2 x 71.1 cm. National Gallery, London.

*Favoured court artist of the Este family, Tura depicted a series of Muses for
the commissioner's studiolo.*

216. **Carlo Crivelli**, c. 1430/1435-1495, Late Gothic Style, Venetian school,
Italian, *Madonna of the Passion*, c. 1460. Tempera on panel, 71 x 48 cm.
Museo di Castelvecchio, Verona.

*All of religious subjects, Crivelli's compositions remain within the late
Gothic style and the constant use of a golden background is part of the
painter's archaism. However, the depth given to the characters is a sign
of modernity.*

217. **Alesso Baldovinetti**, c. 1425-1499, Early Renaissance, Florentine School,
Italian, *Madonna and Child*, c. 1460. Tempera on panel, 104 x 76 cm.
Musée du Louvre, Paris.

*Alesso Baldovinetti was a Florentine painter as well as a mosaic- and
stained-glass-maker. His paintings show the influence of Domenico
Veneziano and Fra Angelico.*

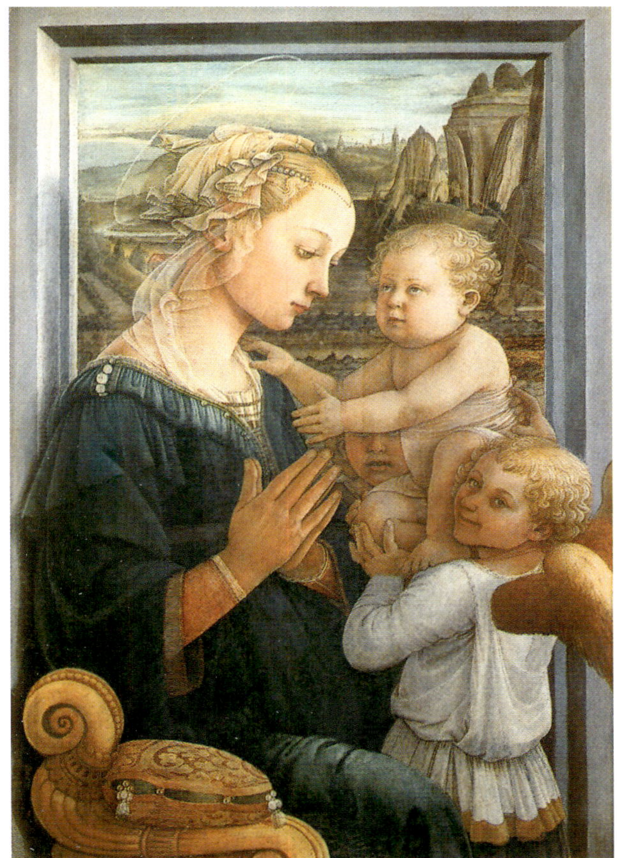

218. **Fra Filippo Lippi**, c. 1406-1469, Early Renaissance,
Florentine School, *Madonna with the Child and Two Angels*, 1465.
Tempera on wood, 95 x 62 cm.
Galleria degli Uffizi, Florence.

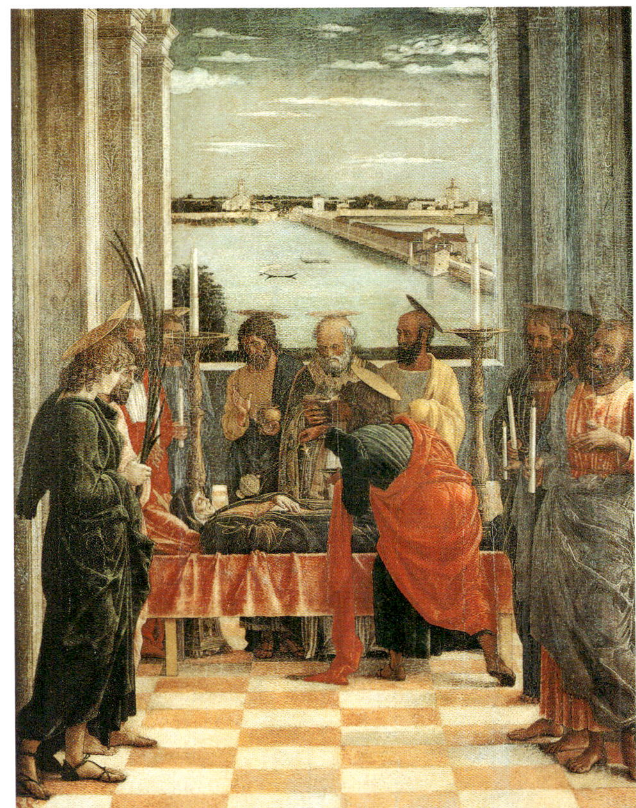

219. **Andrea Mantegna**, 1431-1506, Early Renaissance,
Florentine School, Italian, *Death of the Virgin*, c. 1461.
Oil on panel, 54 x 42 cm.
Museo Nacional del Prado, Madrid.

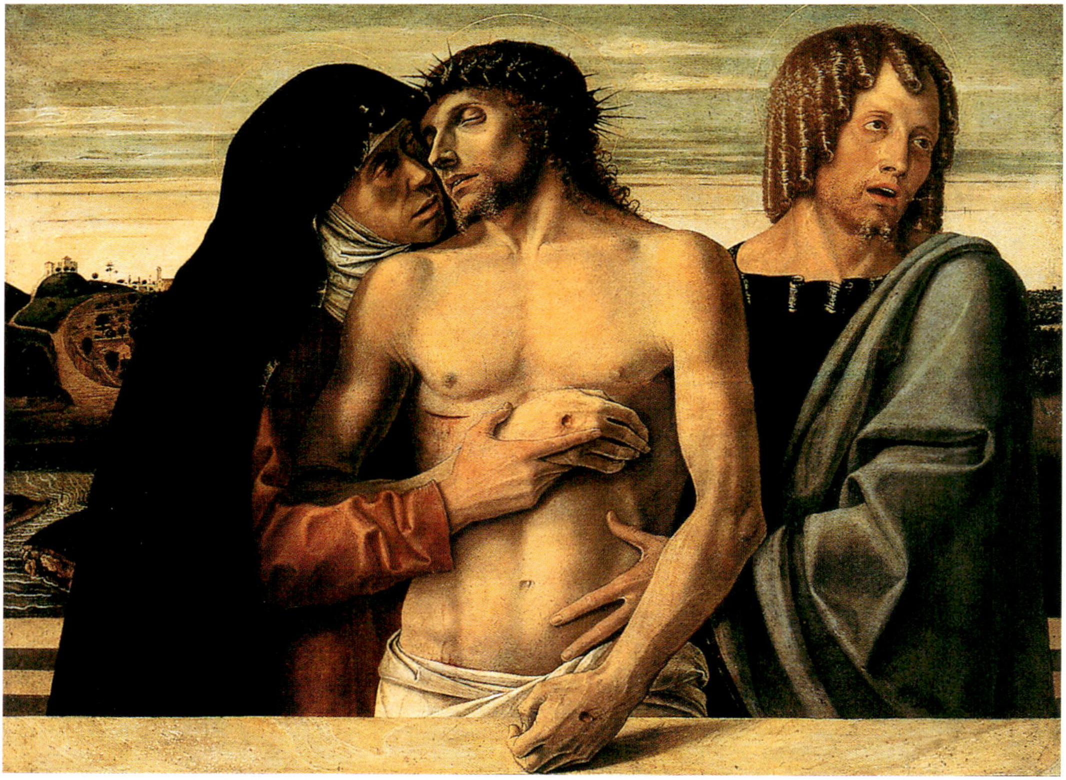

220

221

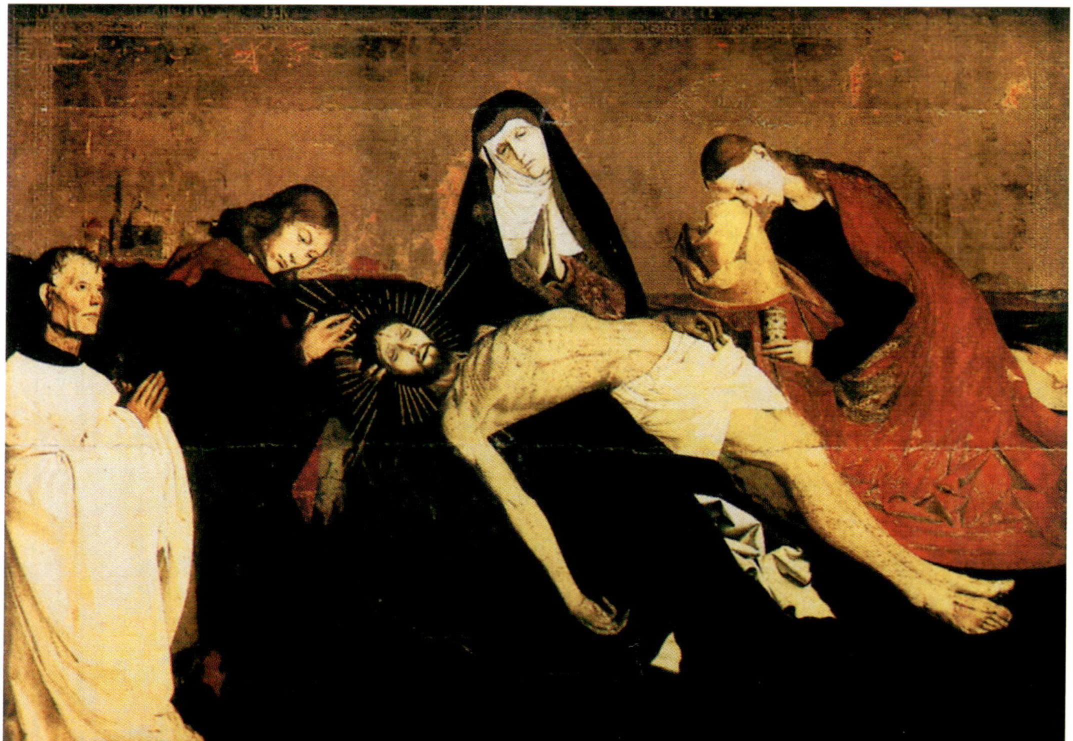

220. **Giovanni Bellini,**
c. 1430-1516, Early Renaissance, Venetian School, Italian,
Dead Christ Supported by the Madonna and St John (Pietà), c. 1460.
Oil on panel, 60 x 107 cm. Pinacoteca di Brera, Milan.

Bellini knows the Florentine pictorial researches (a lot of Florentine artists travelled to Venice at the time) and he introduced oil painting in Venice. Traditionally, the Virgin was holding the dead Christ on her knees. In this painting Bellini proposes a new iconography and a new-size landscape format. In the foreground, a stone pedestal evokes the tomb of Christ. The search for volume and geometry is characteristic of the artist's work.

221. **Enguerrand Quarton**, active 1444-1466, Early Renaissance,
Provence School, French, *Pietà of Villeneuve-les-Avignon*, c. 1460.
Oil on panel, 160 x 218 cm.
Musée du Louvre, Paris.

Masterpiece of the art from Provence, this painting, with its gilded background, still betrays the influence of Byzantine art. On the left, the donor is portrayed. He is represented as an intercessor between the divine group and the viewer.

223. **Hans Pleydenwurff**, *Crucifixion*, Hof Altarpiece, c. 1465.
Mixed media on pine wood, 177 x 112 cm.
Alte Pinakothek, Munich.

Here Hans Pleydenwurff uses patterns inspired by Rogier van der Weyden's Deposition (Alte Pinakothek, Munich). Flemish painting also influenced the artist's use of warm rich colours.

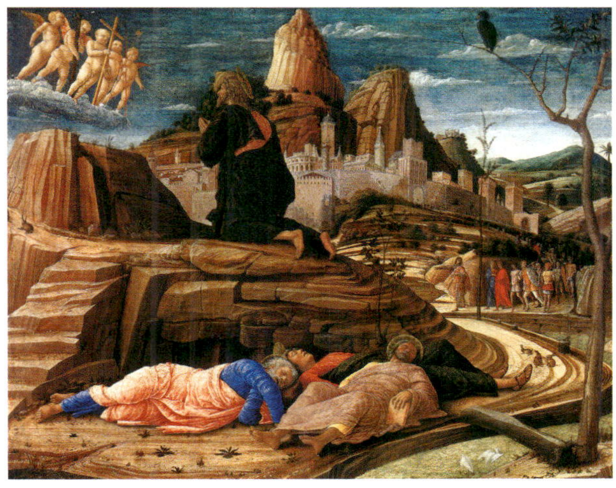

222. **Andrea Mantegna**, 1431-1506, Early Renaissance,
Florentine School, Italian, *The Agony in the Garden*, c. 1460.
Egg tempera on wood, 62.9 x 80 cm.
National Gallery, London.

Mantegna took his inspiration from the drawing of his brother-in-law, Jacopo Bellini, in this painting.

224. **Piero della Francesca**, c. 1416-1492, Early Renaissance,
Italian, *Resurrection*, 1463.
Mural in fresco and tempera, 225 x 200 cm.
Museo Civico, Sansepolcro.

223 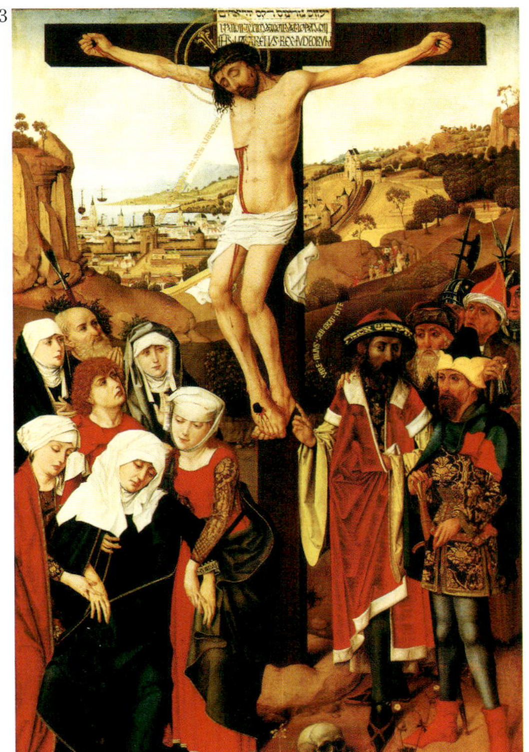

224 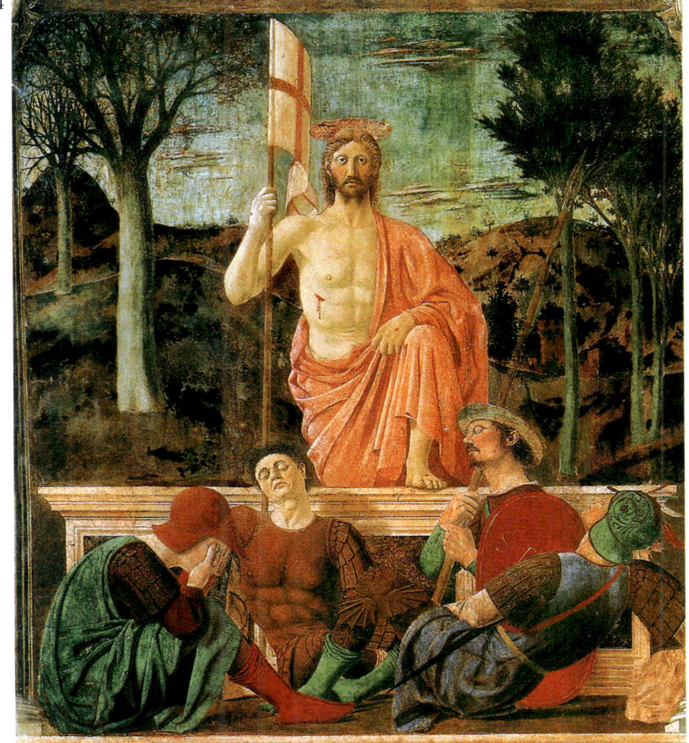

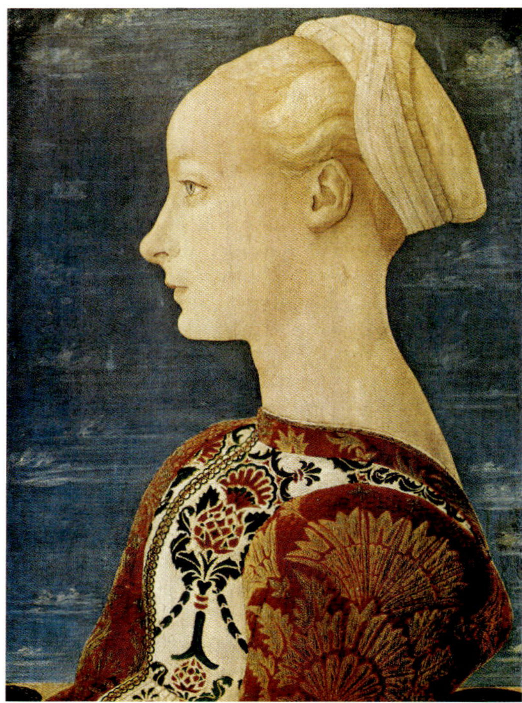

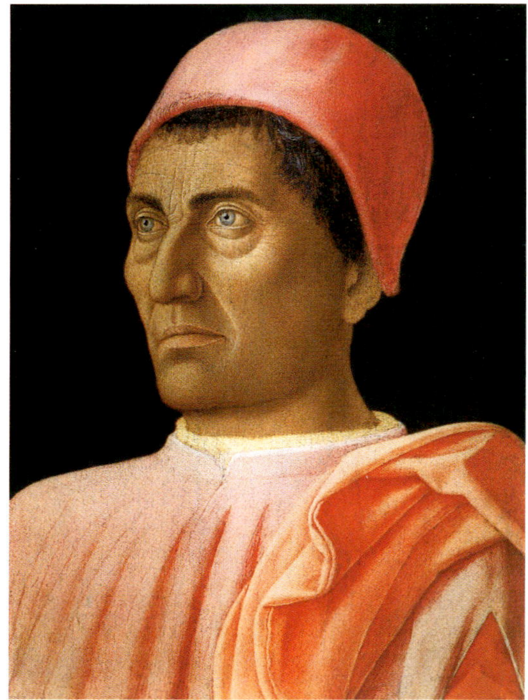

225. **Domenico Veneziano**, 1410-1461, Early Renaissance,
Florentine School, Italian, *Portrait of a Young Woman*, c. 1465.
Oil on panel, 51 x 35 cm.
Gemäldegalerie, Alte Meister, Berlin.

226. **Andrea Mantegna**, 1431-1506, Early Renaissance, Florentine
School, Italian, *Portrait of Carlo de Medici*, 1467.
Oil on panel, 40.6 x 29.5 cm.
Galleria degli Uffizi, Florence.

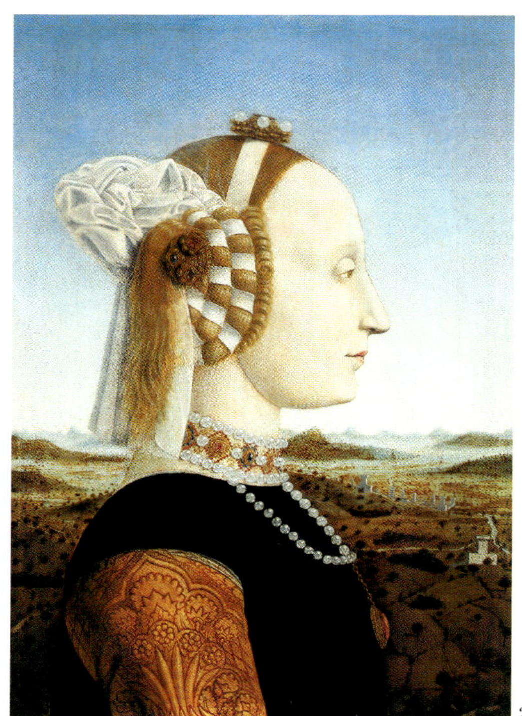

227

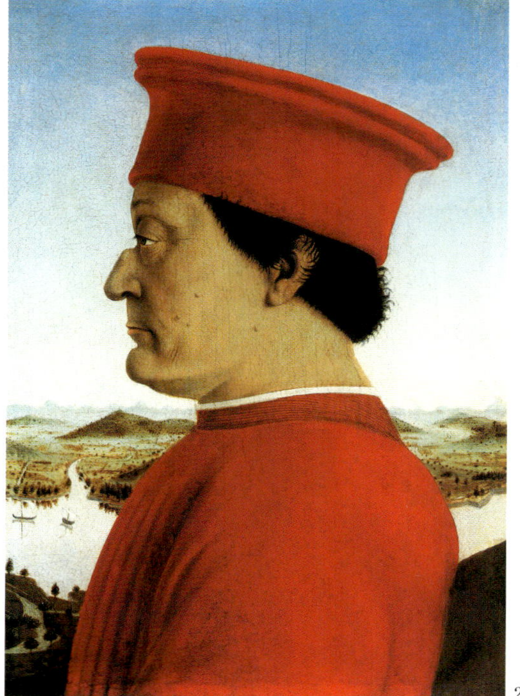

228

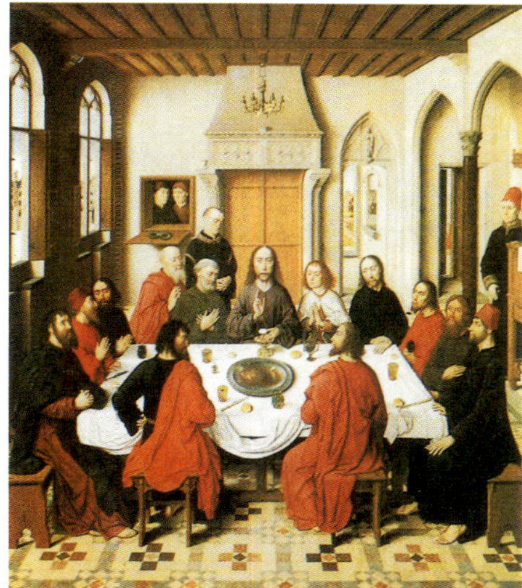

229

229. **Dirk Bouts**, c. 1410-1475, Northern Renaissance, Flemish,
The Last Supper, c. 1467.
Oil on panel, Altarpiece, 180 x 150 cm.
Collégiale Saint-Pierre, Louvain.

A major work by Bouts, The Last Supper *was commissioned by
the Confraternity of the Holy Sacrament in Louvain. The painter
received the mission to conform to the advice of two theologians
in the depiction of the scene. This is the first time that the consecration
of bread is the moment chosen in the Last Supper's representation,
rather than the prediction of the betrayal.*

230. **Dirk Bouts**, c. 1415-1475, Northern Renaissance, Flemish,
The Ordeal by Fire, 1470-1475.
Oil on panel. Musées Royaux des Beaux-Arts, Brussels.

*Characteristic of the revival of a Gothic tendency in the fifteenth-
century bourgeoisie, this painting, belonging to the genre of justice
scenes, emphasises the figures' verticality and their lack of volume.*

227. **Piero della Francesca**, c. 1416-1492, Early Renaissance, Italian,
*Diptych: Portrait of Duke Federico da Montefeltro and Battista
Sforza (left panel)*, c. 1465.
Oil and tempera on panel, 47 x 33 cm.
Galleria degli Uffizi, Florence.

228. **Piero della Francesca**, c. 1416-1492, Early Renaissance, Italian,
*Diptych: Portrait of Duke Federico da Montefello and Battista
Sforza (right panel)*, c. 1465.
Oil and tempera on panel, 47 x 33 cm.
Galleria degli Uffizi, Florence.

*As it was painted from the funeral mask of the chief warrior
Montefeltro, the face of the sitter remains hieratic. The profile
portrait takes its inspiration from the ancient medals and testifies
to a certain will to preserve conventional aspects: Federico is
blind in one eye and this representation enables not to offend.
Nevertheless, he is depicted with great realism (bent nose and
wart are shown). The elegance of the portrait rejoins the precepts
of Alberti (enounced in De Pictura). The recent discovering of oil
painting enables more realism and subtlety, especially in the
illusionism one can see in the background landscape.*

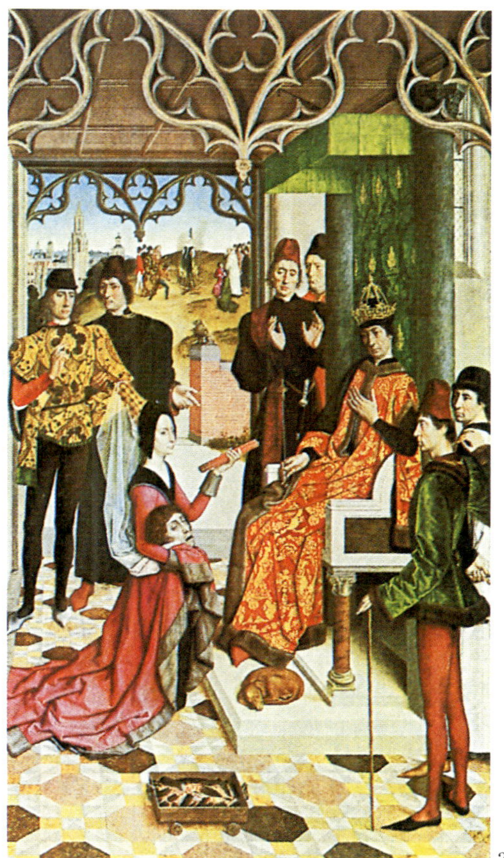

230

ANDREA MANTEGNA
(1431 ISOLA DI CARTURO – 1506 MANTOVA)

Mantegna; humanist, geometrist, archaeologist, of great
scholastic and imaginative intelligence, dominated the whole
of northern Italy by virtue of his imperious personality.
Aiming at optical illusion, he mastered perspective. He
trained in painting at the Padua School where Donatello and
Paolo Uccello had previously attended. Even at a young age
commissions for Andrea's work flooded in, for example the
frescos of the Ovetari Chapel of Padua.

In a short space of time Mantegna found his niche as a
modernist due to his highly original ideas and the use of
perspective in his works. His marriage with Nicolosia
Bellini, the sister of Giovanni, paved the way for his *entree*
into Venice.

Mantegna reached an artistic maturity with his *Pala San
Zeno*. He remained in Mantova and became the artist for one
of the most prestigious courts in Italy – the Court of Gonzaga.
Classical art was born.

Despite his links with Bellini and Leonardo da Vinci,
Mantegna refused to adopt their innovative use of colour or
leave behind his own technique of engraving.

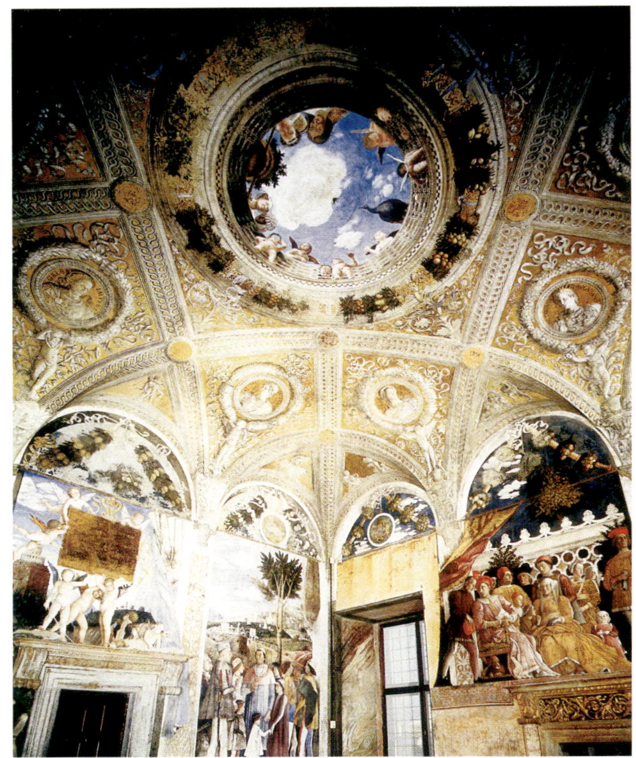

231

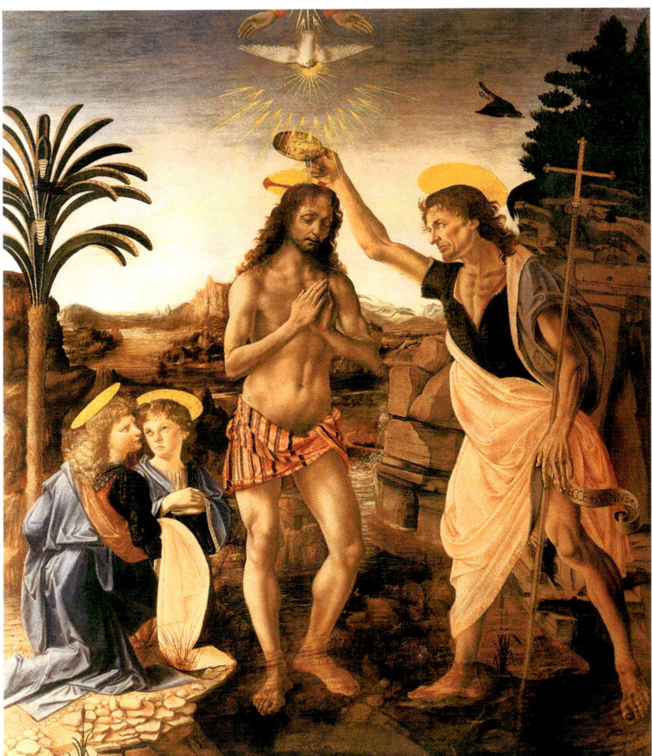

232

233

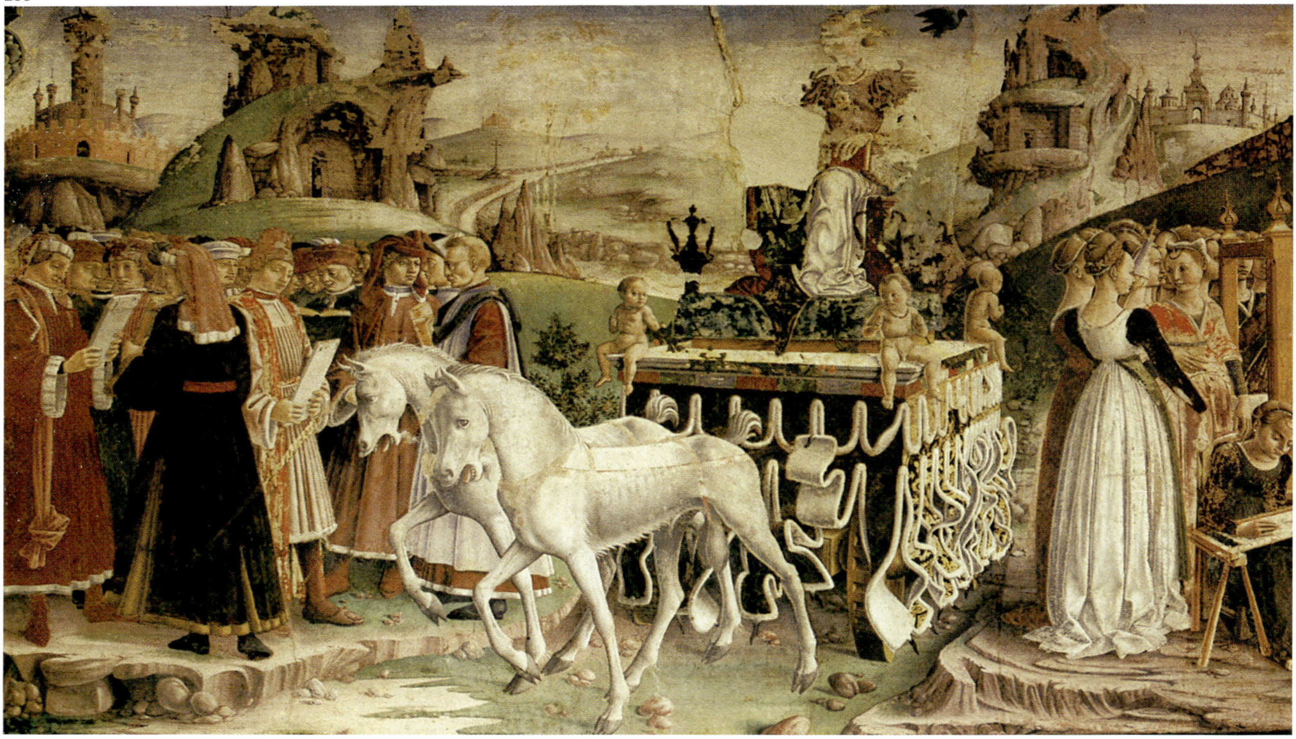

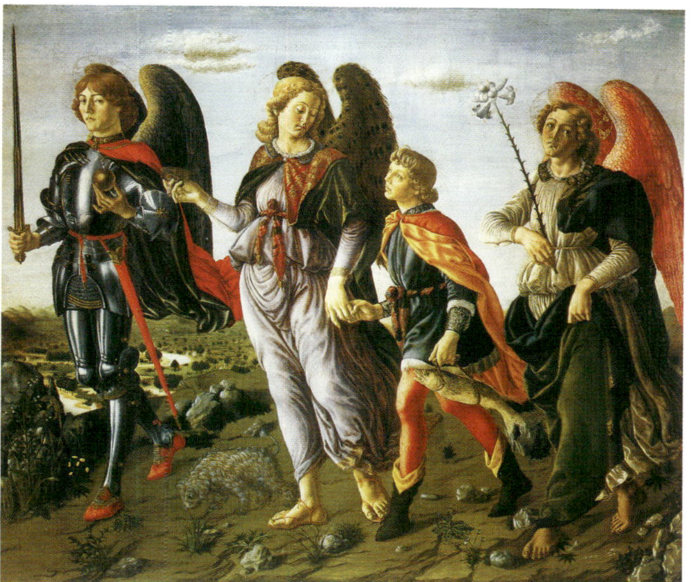

234

234. Francesco Botticini, c. 1446-1498, Early Renaissance, Florentine School, Italian, *Tobias and the Three Archangels*, c. 1470.
Tempera on panel, 135 x 154 cm.
Galleria degli Uffizi, Florence.

235. Hugo van der Goes, c. 1440-1482, Northern Renaissance, Flemish, *Diptych: The Fall of Man and the Lamentation* (left panel), c. 1470-1475.
Tempera on wood, 32.3 x 21.9 cm.
Kunsthistorisches Museum, Vienna.

Contemporary of Piero della Francesca, Van der Goes is resolute to depict reality while using refined colours. His painting is more and more illusionist here and betrays the artist's like for details and depiction of light.

235

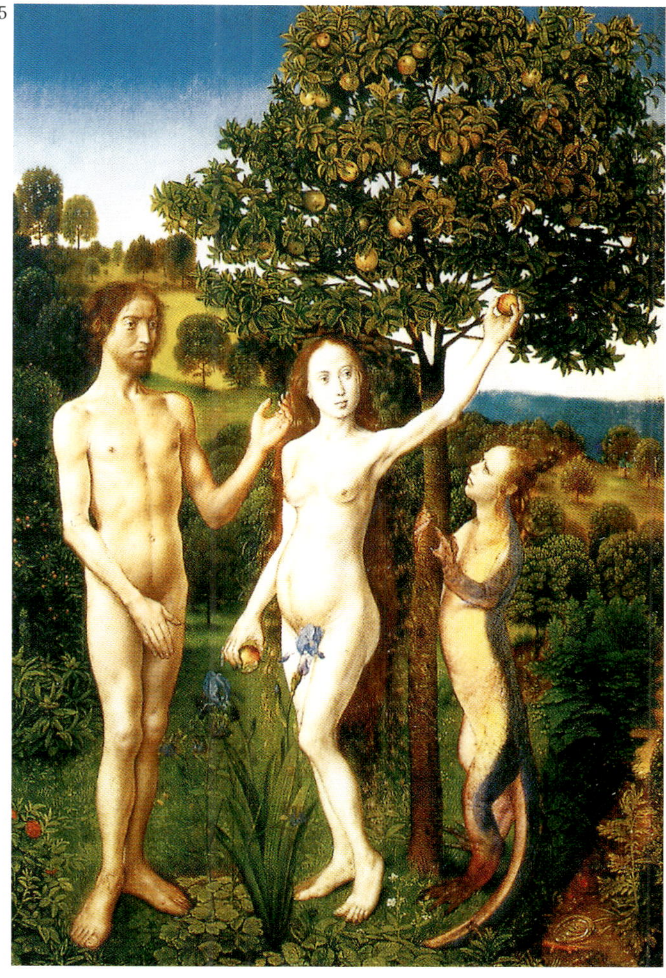

231. Andrea Mantegna, 1431-1506, Early Renaissance, Florentine School, Italian, *Camera Picta, Ducal Palace*, 1465-1474. Fresco. Palazzo Ducale, Mantova.

Mantegna's originality comes to the foremost obviously in the central part of the ceiling, which breaks from the seriousness and formality of the rest of the room. It is perhaps Mantegna's most delightful and creative invention: the centre of the vault seems to open up, the first painting of the Renaissance to apply the notion of illusionism not just to an easel picture or wall but to a ceiling as well. This view upwards completes the trompe-l'œil vision Mantegna created in the Camera Picta, which is the first illusionistic room of the Renaissance; the ideal of the flat picture space as an extension of the real world is here given a spectacular expression, as a viewer in the middle of the room can see clouds overhead, fictive curtained walls, and classical architectural framework.

232. Andrea del Verrocchio, c. 1435-1488, Early Renaissance, Florentine School, Italian, *The Baptism of Christ*, c. 1470.
Oil on panel, 177 x 151 cm.
Galleria degli Uffizi, Florence.

233. Francesco del Cossa, 1436-1477, Early Renaissance, Ferrarese School, Italian, *The Triumph of Minerva: March, from the Room of the Months*, 1467-1470.
Fresco. Palazzo Schifanoia, Ferrara.

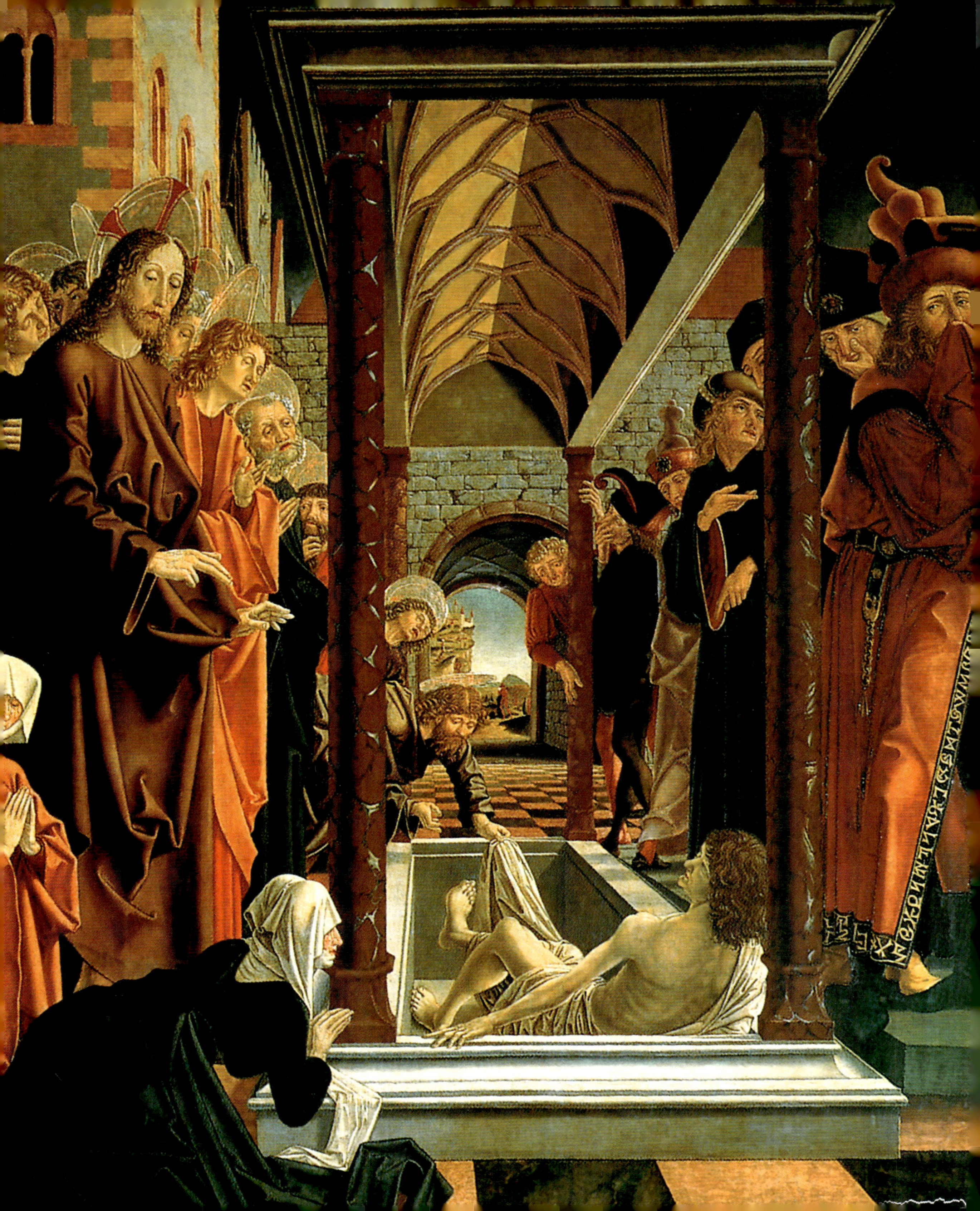

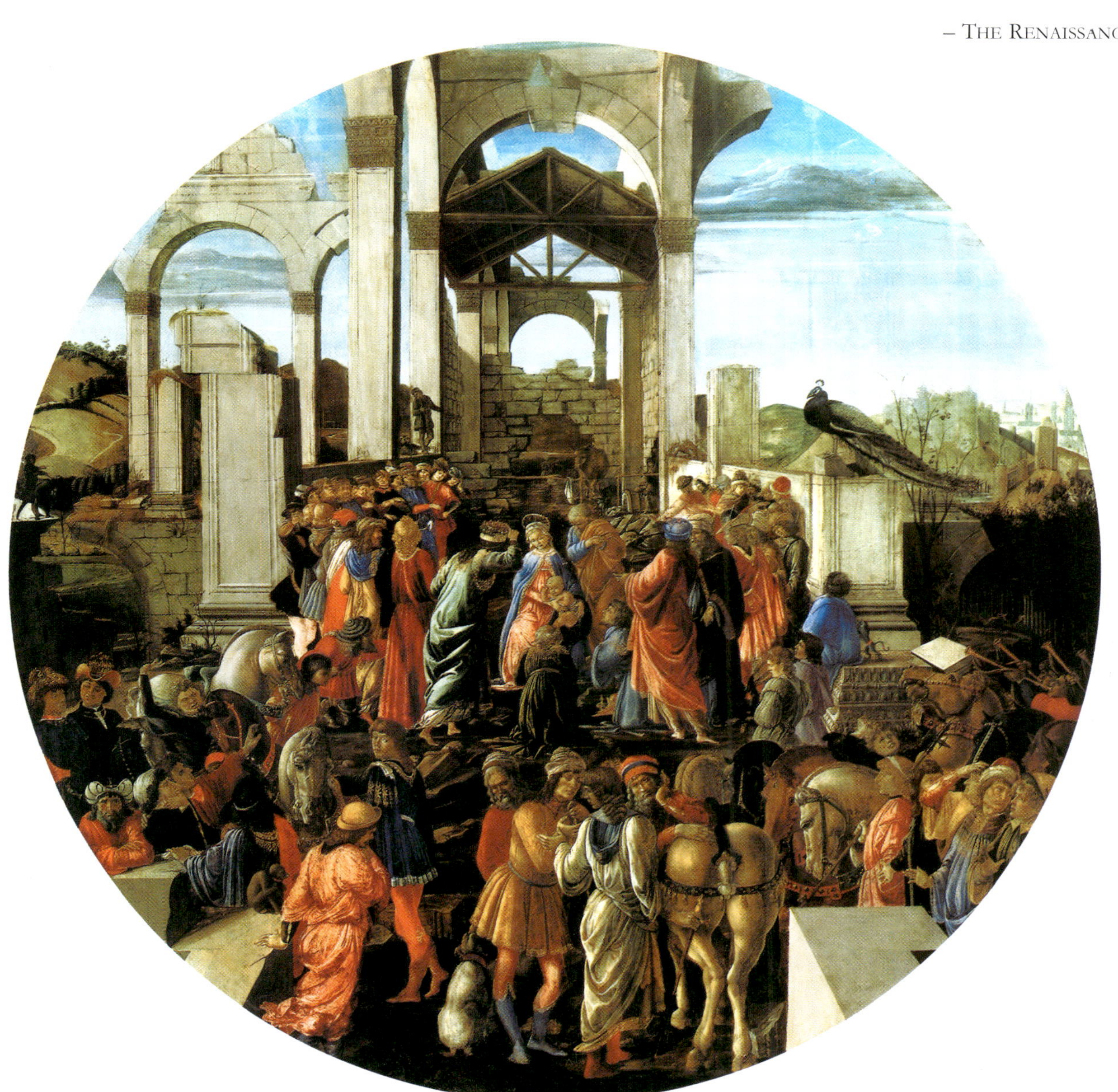

236. Michael Pacher, c. 1430-1498, Northern Renaissance, Austrian,
St Wolfgang Altarpiece: Resurrection of Lazarus, 1471-1481.
Tempera on wood, 175 x 130 cm.
Parish Church, St Wolfgang.

237. Sandro Botticelli (Alessandro di Mariano Filipepi), 1445-1510,
Early Renaissance, Florentine School, Italian,
Adoration of the Kings, c. 1470-1475.
Tempera on poplar, Tondo, diameter: 130.8 cm.
National Gallery, London.

*This painting, in which the artist also depicted himself, shows
the Magi but in reality it is the Medici family, his patrons and
rulers of Florence. The Magi kneeling in front of Jesus Christ
represents Cosimo the Elder, the founder of the dynasty.
Cosimo's son Piero can be seen from the back in red in the
centre and Lorenzo the Magnificent is the young man on his
right, wearing a black and red mantle.*

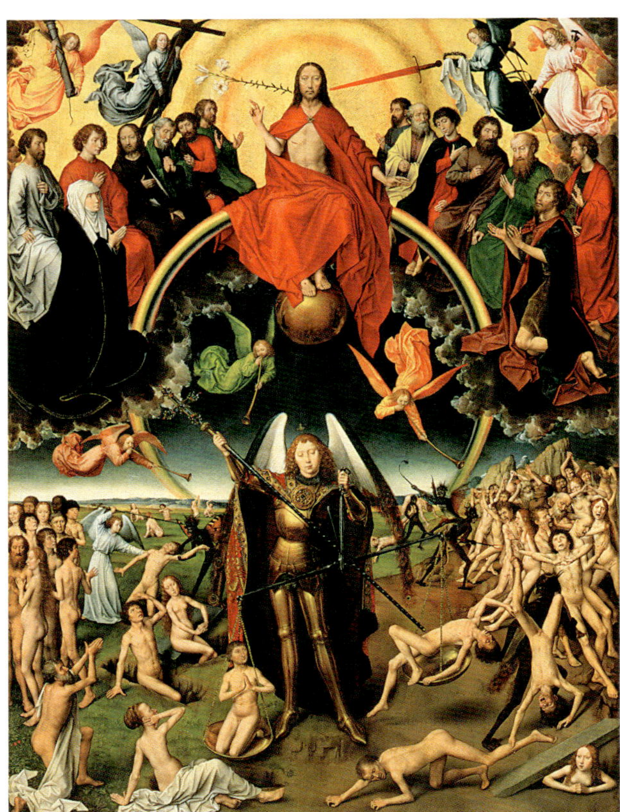

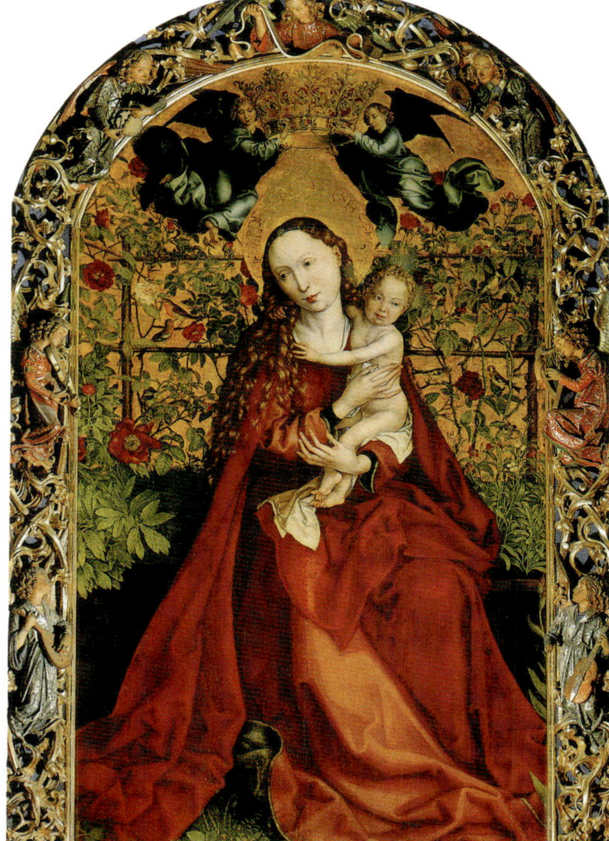

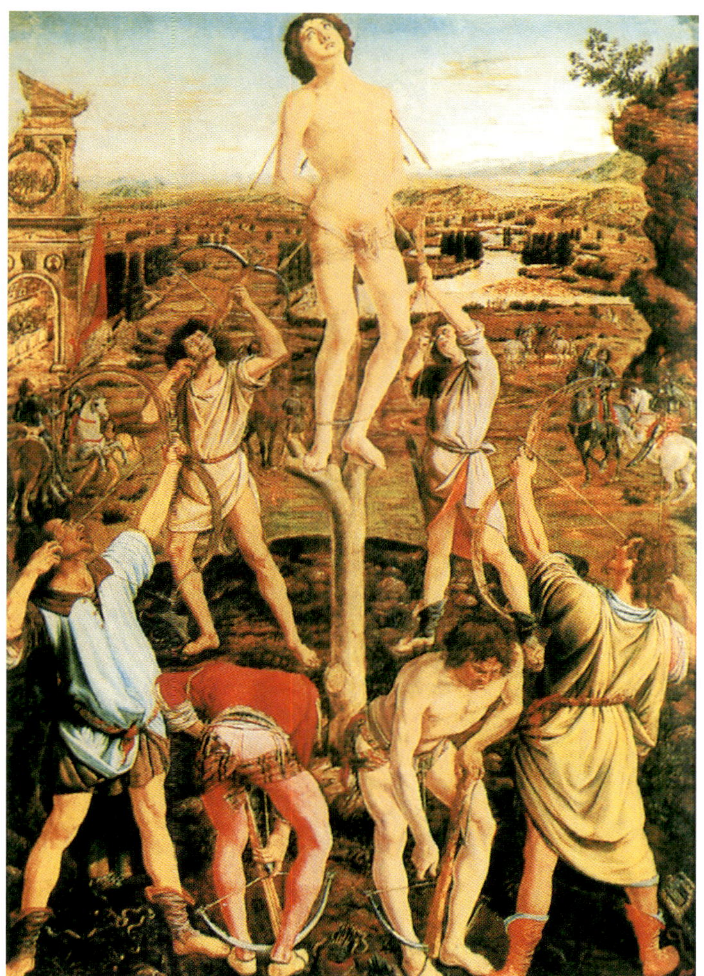

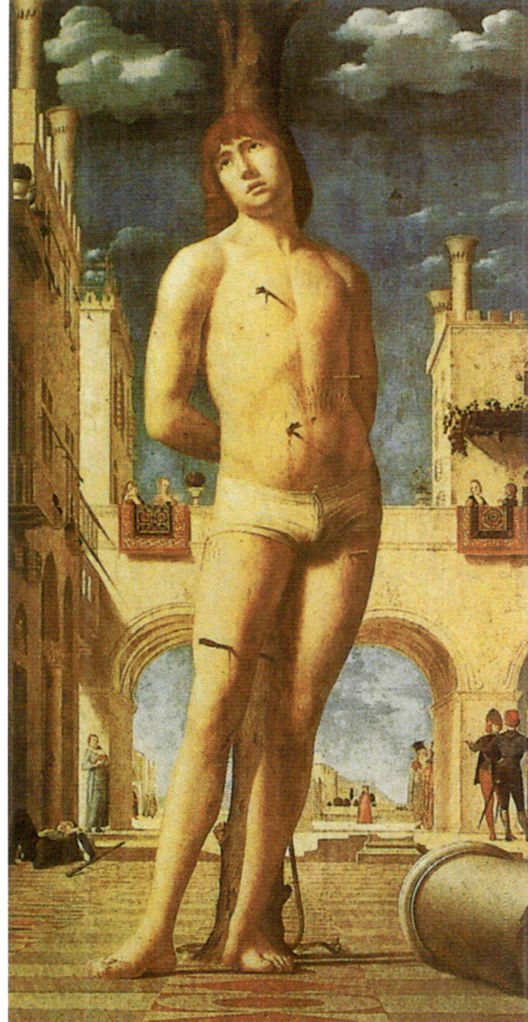

240. **Antonio del Pollaiuolo**, 1432-1498,
Renaissance, Florentine School, Italian,
Martyrdom of Saint Sebastian, 1475.
Oil on poplar, 291.5 x 202.6 cm.
National Gallery, London.

The pyramidal composition and the attention paid to the quality of the drawing are characteristic of the Florentine researches at the time.

241. **Antonello da Messina**, 1430-1479, Early Renaissance, Southern
Italian School, Italian, *St Sebastian*, c. 1476.
Panel transposed on canvas, 171 x 85 cm.
Gemäldegalerie Alte Meister, Dresden.

Antonello da Messina had a fundamental influence on Venetian painting (especially on Bellini) because of his knowledge of oil painting (that he learnt from the Flemish artists). He also used a lot of this knowledge for his portraits. This painting was a pendant to St Christopher. The perspective has a very low vanishing point and the frame is narrowed so that the saint is monumentalised.

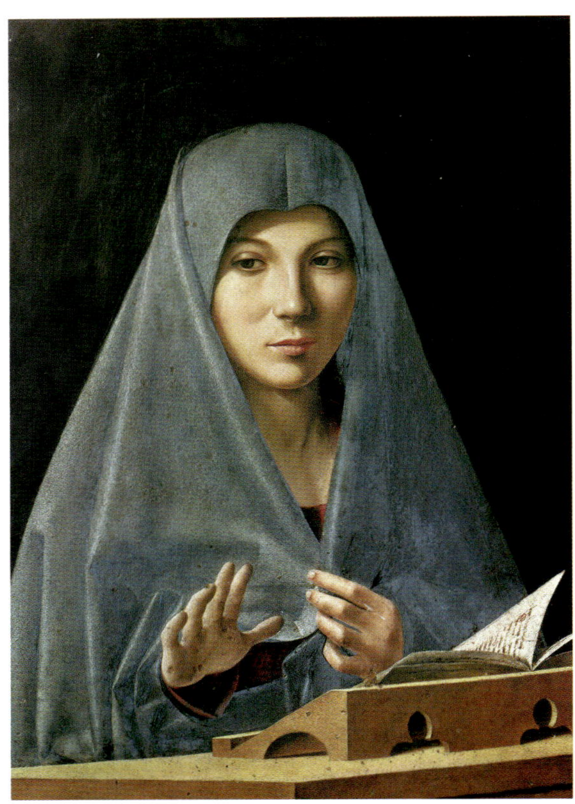

242. **Antonello da Messina**, 1430-1479, Early Renaissance,
Southern Italian School, Italian, *Virgin Annunciate*, 1475.
Oil on panel, 45 x 35 cm.
Museo Nazionale, Palermo.

*The half-length representation of Mary and the absence of the
Archangel Gabriel make an exceptional iconography out of this
painting of the Annunciation.*

243. **Leonardo da Vinci**, 1452-1519, Early Renaissance, Florentine
School, Italian, *The Annunciation*, c. 1472.
Oil and Tempera on panel, 98 x 217 cm.
Galleria degli Uffizi, Florence.

Leonardo da Vinci's The Annunciation *is one of the most
popular versions of this subject. The angel, carrying white lilies,
kneels to the Madonna, who is seated next to a building and has
raised her left hand in a gesture of surprise. They both represent
the ideal beauty and exuberance of youth. The Virgin's right
hand is resting on the page of a book, symbolic of her knowledge
as Mary-Sophia, the personification both of Wisdom and of the
Logos, the Word of God. Below her hand, the shell that adorns
the furniture represents the connection between Mary and the
ancient Roman goddess of love, Venus.*

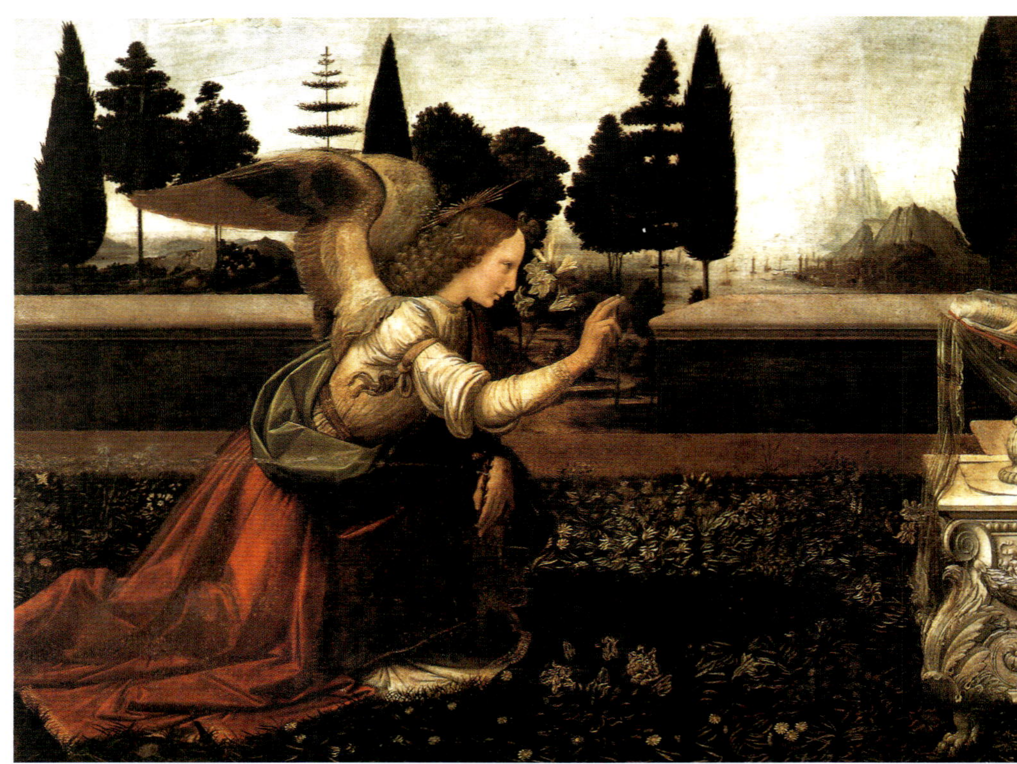

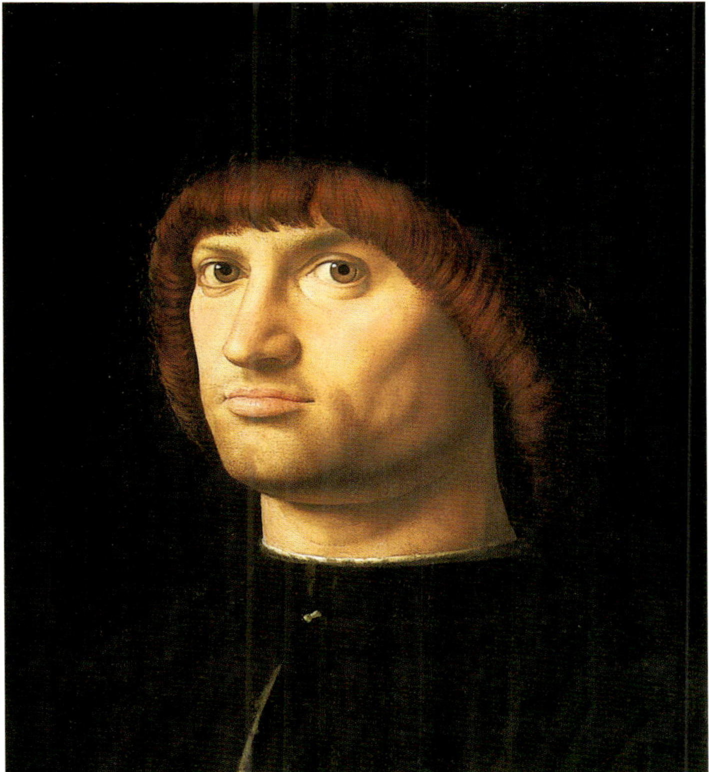

244. **Antonello da Messina**, 1430-1479, Early
Renaissance, Southern Italian School, Italian,
Portrait of a Man (Le Condottiere), 1475.
Oil on panel, 36 x 30 cm.
Musée du Louvre, Paris.

This three-quarters view portrait on a dark
background moves away from the profiles from
the Early Renaissance. The face of the man is
deeply individualised and betrays the influence of
Flemish painters such as Van Eyck or Campin.

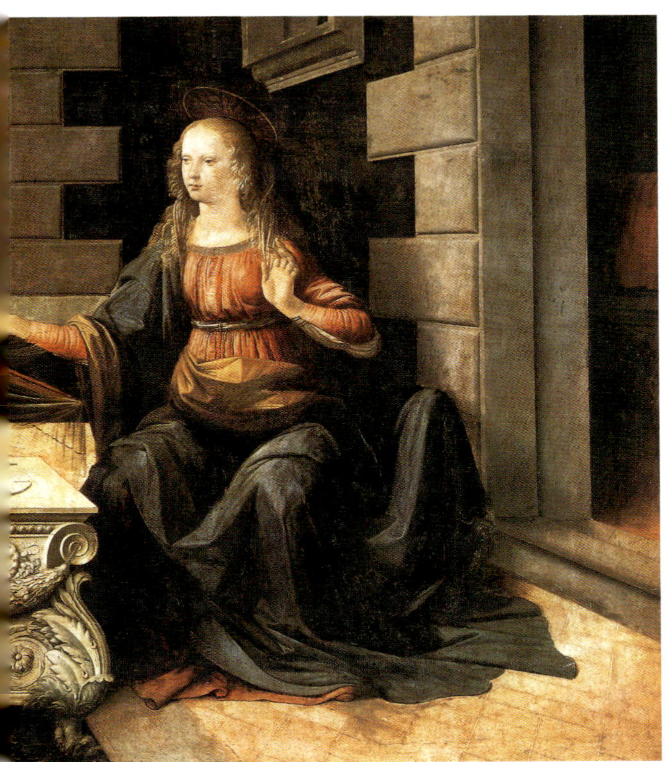

ANTONELLO DA MESSINA
(1430 – 1479 MESSINA)

If little is known about his life, the name of Antonello da
Messina corresponds to the arrival of a new technique in
Italian painting; oils. He used them especially in his
portraits where they were very popular in his day, such
as *Portrait of a Man* (1475).

Now, if this appears to be not exactly true, still his work
influenced Venetian painters. His work was a combination
of Flemish technique and realism with typically Italian
modelling of forms and clarity of spatial arrangement.
Also, his practice of building form with colour, rather
than line and shade, greatly influenced the subsequent
development of Venetian painting.

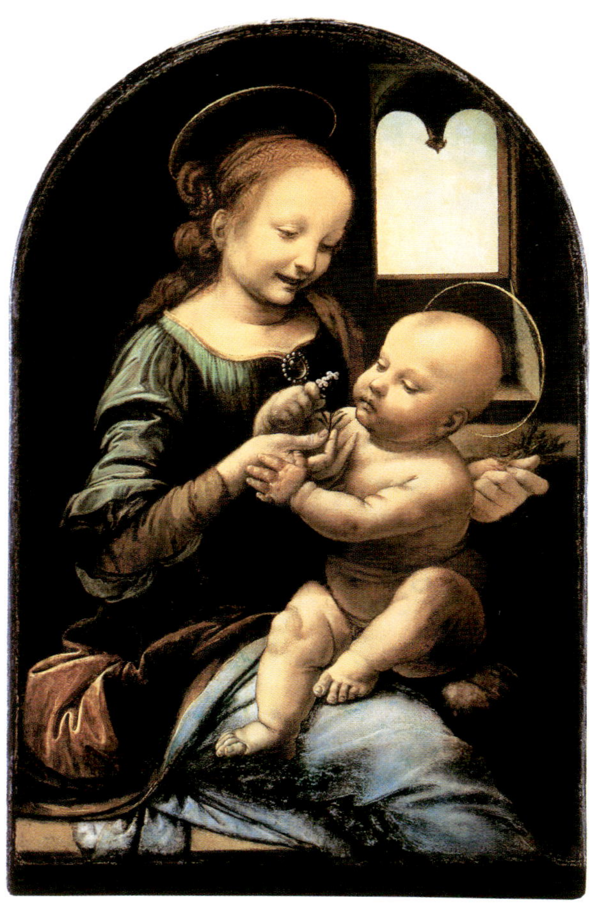

245. **Leonardo da Vinci**, 1452-1519, Early Renaissance,
Florentine School, Italian,
Madonna with a Flower (Madonna Benois), 1478.
Oil on canvas, 49.5 x 33 cm.
The State Hermitage Museum, St Petersburg.

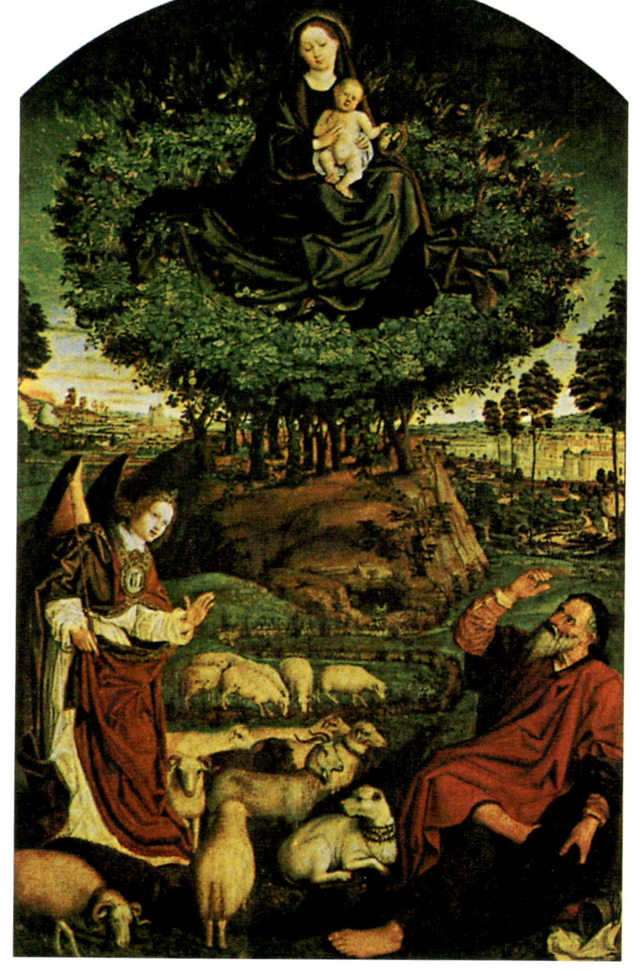

246. **Nicolas Froment**, 1430-1485, Early Renaissance, French,
The Burning Bush, c. 1475.
Tempera on panel, 410 x 305 cm.
Cathédrale St Sauveur, Aix-en-Provence.

Central panel of Froment's triptych commissioned by King René of Provence, this is the most important work of the Provençal artist. The kneeling figures on the wing portray the donor and his wife.

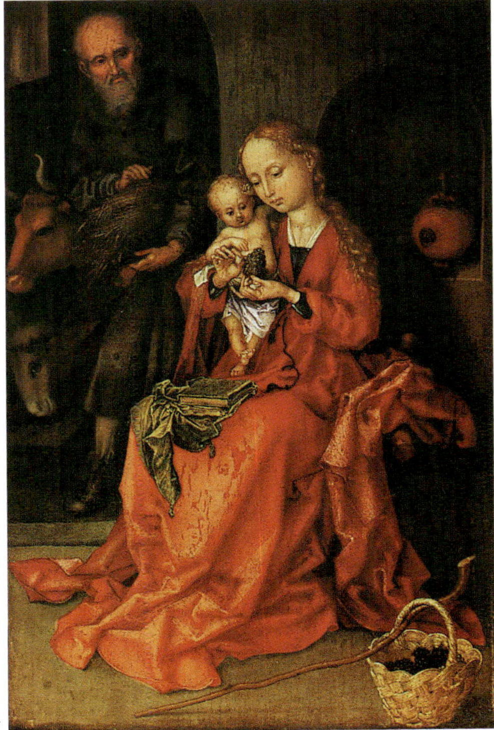

247

247. **Martin Schongauer**, 1450-1491,
Northern Renaissance, German,
The Holy Family, 1475-1480. Oil on panel, 26 x 17 cm.
Kunsthistorisches Museum, Vienna.

248. **Hans Memling**, 1433-1494, Northern Renaissance,
Flemish, *Madonna Enthroned with Child and Two Angels*,
late 15th century. Oil on panel, 57 x 42 cm.
Galleria degli Uffizi, Florence.

Hans Memling painted his Madonna Enthroned with Child
and Two Angels *during the second half of the fifteenth
century. The Virgin and her child are seated on a throne amid
lavish surroundings. Golden rays emanate from the Queen of
Heaven's head, and the two musical angels are eager to
entertain her son Above, an arch is adorned with cherubim
who carry beautiful garlands of fruit and flowers, an allusion
to abundance in nature, a gift which Mary, like female deities
of the past, was believed to bestow on her followers.*

249. **Hugo van der Goes**, c. 1440-1482, Northern
Renaissance, Flemish, *Adoration of the Shepherds,*
(central panel of the *Portinari Altar*), 1476-1478.
Oil on wood, 250 x 310 cm.
Galleria degli Uffizi, Florence.

*This big triptych, commissioned by the Florentine merchant,
Tommaso Portinari, for the Church of S. Egidio in Florence,
is Van der Goes' masterpiece. It shows a great emotional
intensity, rarely gained by other artists. The Child is isolated,
in the core of a devotional circle as the Virgin meditates on
his destiny. The sudden irruption of the shepherds contrasts
with the solemnity of the other characters.*

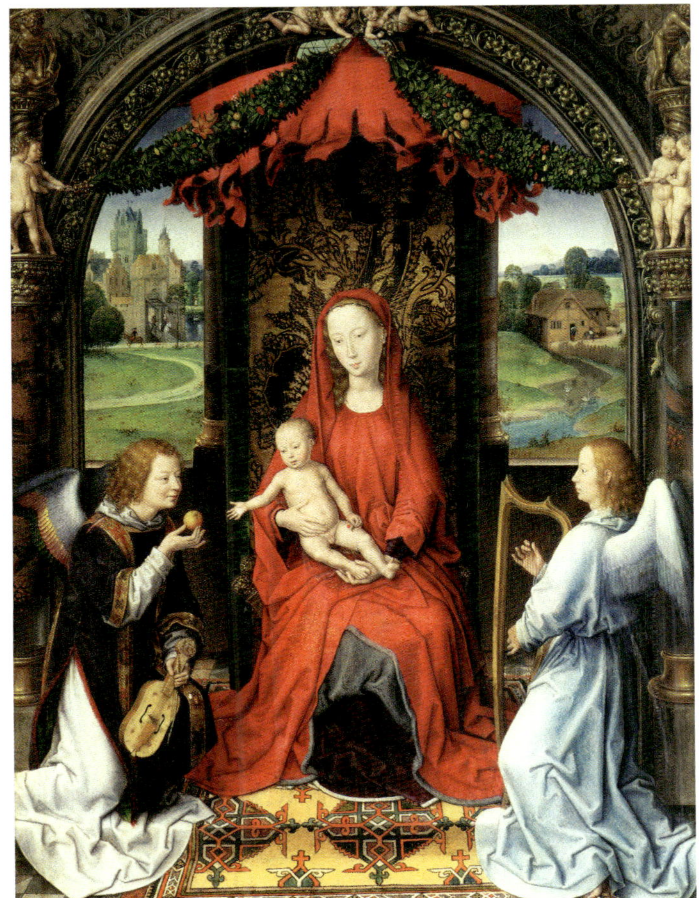

248

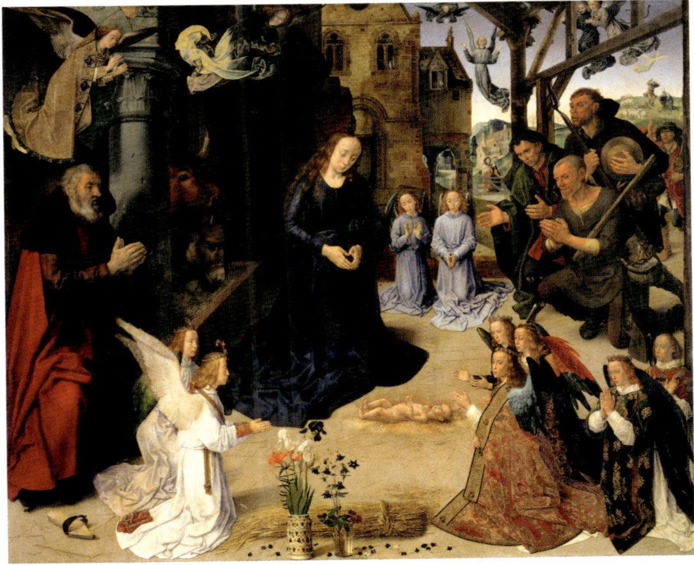

249

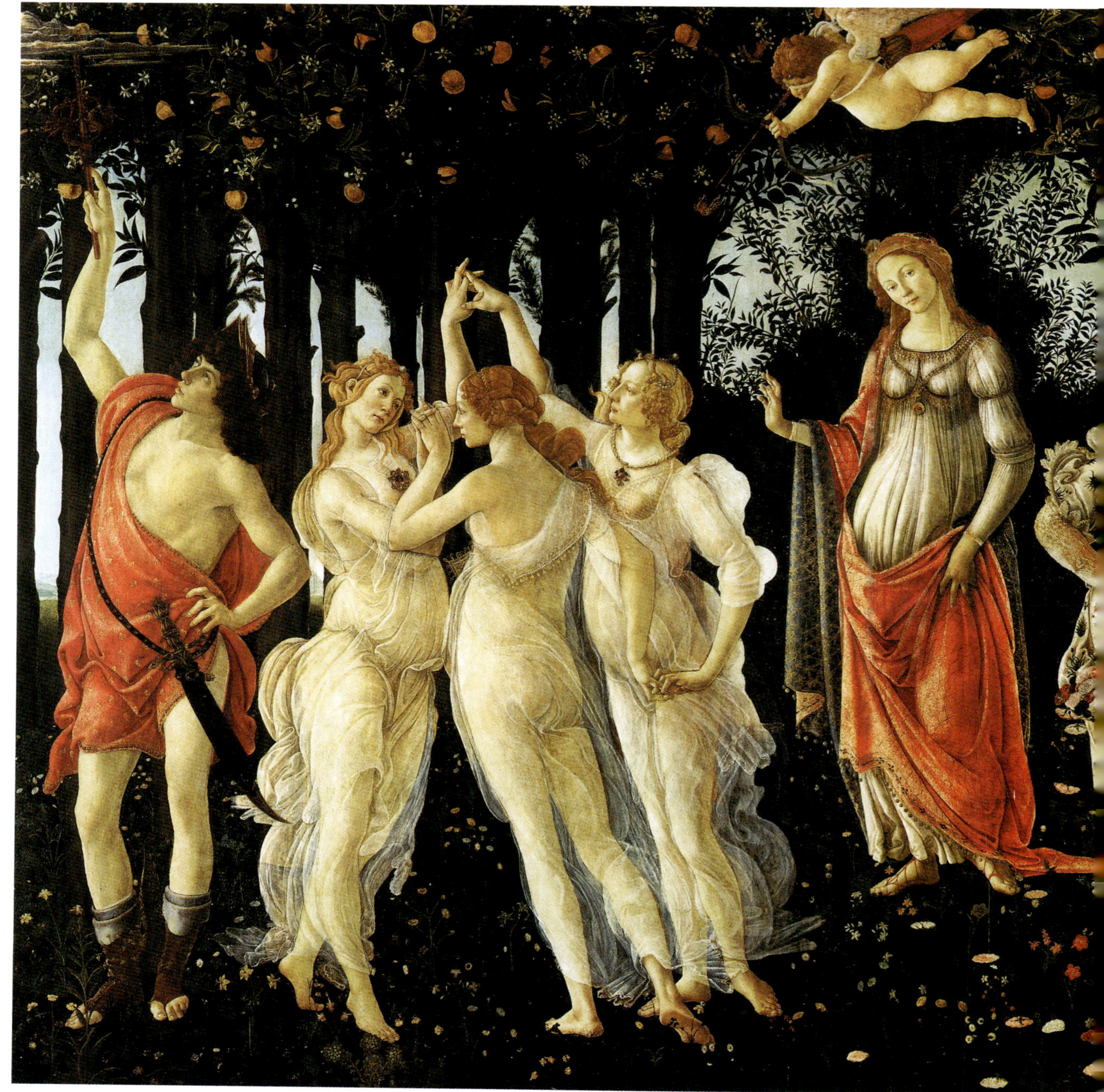

250. Sandro Botticelli (Alessandro di Mariano Filipepi),
1445-1510, Early Renaissance, Florentine School, Italian,
Primavera, c. 1478.
Tempera on panel, 203 x 314 cm. Galleria degli Uffizi, Florence.

The painting, sometimes called Primavera, *but now and again also*
Realm of Venus, *is Botticelli's most celebrated masterpiece. This*
work is one in a series of paintings depicting heathen myths and

legends in the form of antique gods and heroes. Just as
convincingly and naively, and with the same enthusiasm, Botticelli
makes the beauty of the naked human body his task. In the large
presentation of Primavera *he does indeed describe an antique*
subject, stipulated by his clients and advisers, but he penetrates it
with his mind, his imagination and his artistic sense. The
composition is built up in nine, almost life-size figures in the

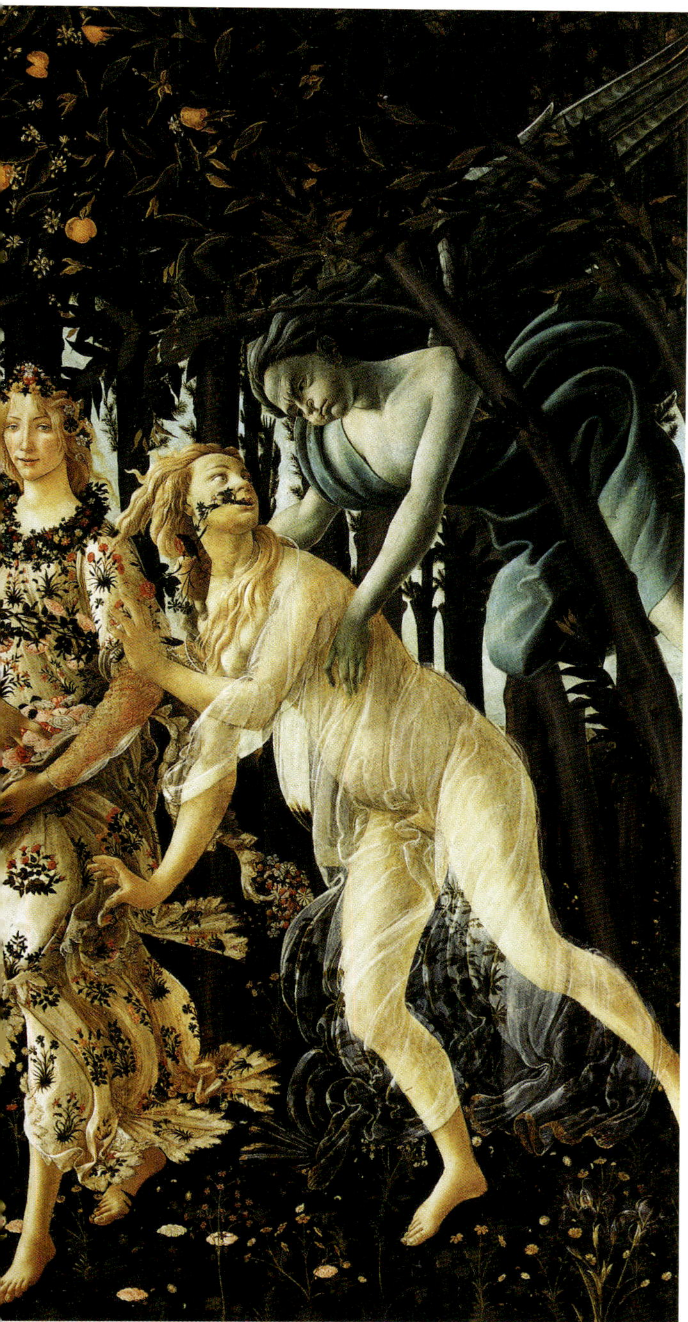

SANDRO BOTTICELLI
(ALESSANDRO DI MARIANO FILIPEPI)
(1445 – 1510 FLORENCE)

He was the son of a citizen in comfortable circumstances, and had been, in Vasari's words, "instructed in all such things as children are usually taught before they choose a calling." However, he refused to give his attention to reading, writing and accounts, so that his father, despairing of his ever becoming a scholar, apprenticed him to the goldsmith Botticello: whence came the name by which the world remembers him. However, Sandro, a stubborn-featured youth with large, quietly searching eyes and a shock of yellow hair – he has left a portrait of himself on the right-hand side of his picture of the *Adoration of the Magi* – would also become a painter, and to that end was placed with the Carmelite monk Fra Filippo Lippi. But he was a realist, as the artists of his day had become, satisfied with the joy and skill of painting, and with the study of the beauty and character of the human subject instead of religious themes.

Botticelli is a painter not of facts, but of ideas, and his pictures are not so much a representation of certain objects as a pattern of forms. Nor is his colouring rich and lifelike; it is subordinated to form, and often rather a tinting than actual colour. In fact, he was more interested in the abstract possibilities of his art rather than in the concrete. His figures do not attract us by their suggestion of bulk, but as shapes of form, suggesting rather a flat pattern of decoration. Accordingly, the lines which enclose the figures are chosen with the primary intention of being decorative.

It has been said that Botticelli, "though one of the worst anatomists, was one of the greatest draughtsmen of the Renaissance." As an example of false anatomy we may notice the impossible way in which the Madonna's head is attached to the neck, and other instances of faulty articulation and incorrect form of limbs may be found in Botticelli's pictures. Yet he is recognised as one of the greatest draughtsmen: he gave to 'line' not only intrinsic beauty, but also significance. In mathematical language, he resolved the movement of the figure into its factors, its simplest forms of expression, and then combined these various forms into a pattern which, by its rhythmical and harmonious lines, produces an effect upon our imagination, corresponding to the sentiments of grave and tender poetry that filled the artist himself.

This power of making every line count in both significance and beauty distinguishes the great master-draughtsmen from the vast majority of artists who used line mainly as a necessary means of representing concrete objects.

foreground of an orange grove. The individual figures are borrowed from Poliziano's poem about the great tournament in the spring of 1475, the Giostra, in which Giuliano was declared the winner. The artistic appearance of Primavera *which, apart from the dull old layer of varnish, is well preserved, deviates from most of Botticelli's paintings in so far as that the local colours are rather secondary. This is how the artist tried to bring out the full beauty of*

the figures' bodies, which, apart from Venus and Primavera, are more or less naked. He enhances this with the deep green background, covered with flowers and fruit. There, where local colours occur to a greater extent as, for example, in the short red robe of Mercury, the pale blue decoration of the god of wind or the blue dress and red cloak of Venus in the middle, the colours have been strongly tinted with gold ornaments and glaze.

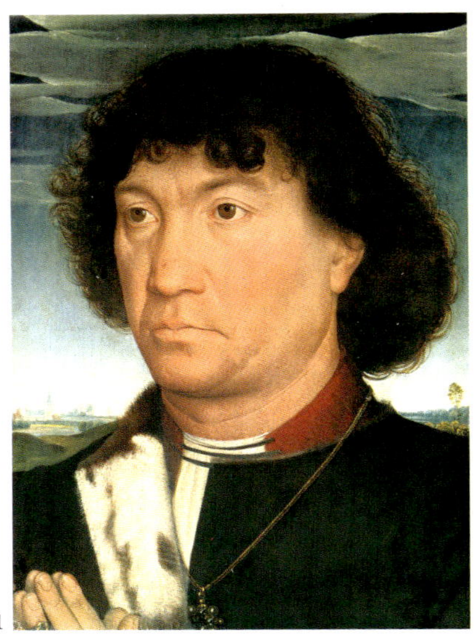

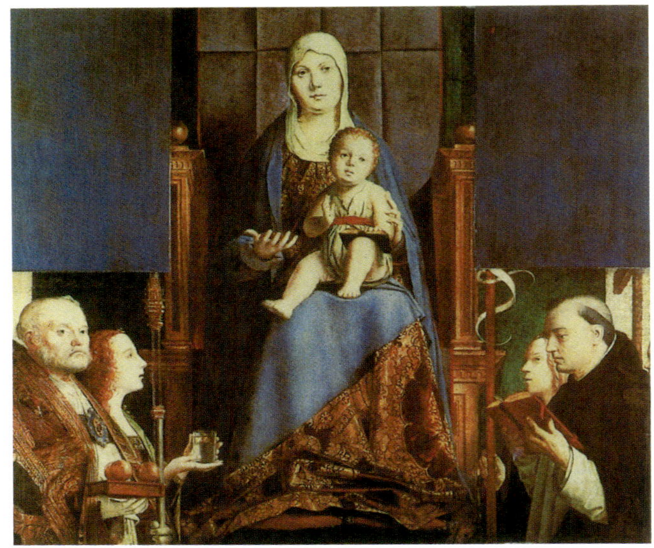

251

252

251. Hans Memling, 1433-1494, Northern Renaissance, Flemish,
Portrait of a Man at Prayer before a Landscape, c. 1480.
Oil on panel, 30 x 22 cm.
Koninklijk Kabinet van Schilderijen Mauritshuis, The Hague.

*Memling's portraits show a lot of attention paid to the position of the head
and hands. The man's devotion is made obvious here in the representation
of his hands in prayer and the church in the distance. The tightly framed
composition gives a strong sensation of intimacy to this portrait.*

252. Antonello da Messina, 1430-1479, Early Renaissance, Southern
Italian School, Italian, *San Cassiano Altar,* 1475-1476. Oil on panel,
115 x 65 cm (central panel); 56 x 35 cm (left panel); 56.8 x 35.6 cm
(right panel). Kunsthistorisches Museum, Vienna.

*This painting was a model for painters such as Bellini, with his San
Giobbe Altarpiece or Giorgione, the painter of the Castelfranco altar.*

HANS MEMLING
(1433 SELIGENSTADT, GERMANY – 1494 BRUGES)

Little is known of Memling's life. It is surmised that he
was a German by descent but the definite fact of his
life is that he painted at Bruges, sharing with the Van
Eycks, who had also worked in that city, the honour of
being the leading artists of the so-called 'School of
Bruges'. He carried on their method of painting, and
added to it a quality of gentle sentiment. In his case, as
in theirs, Flemish art, founded upon local conditions and
embodying purely local ideals, reached its fullest
expression.

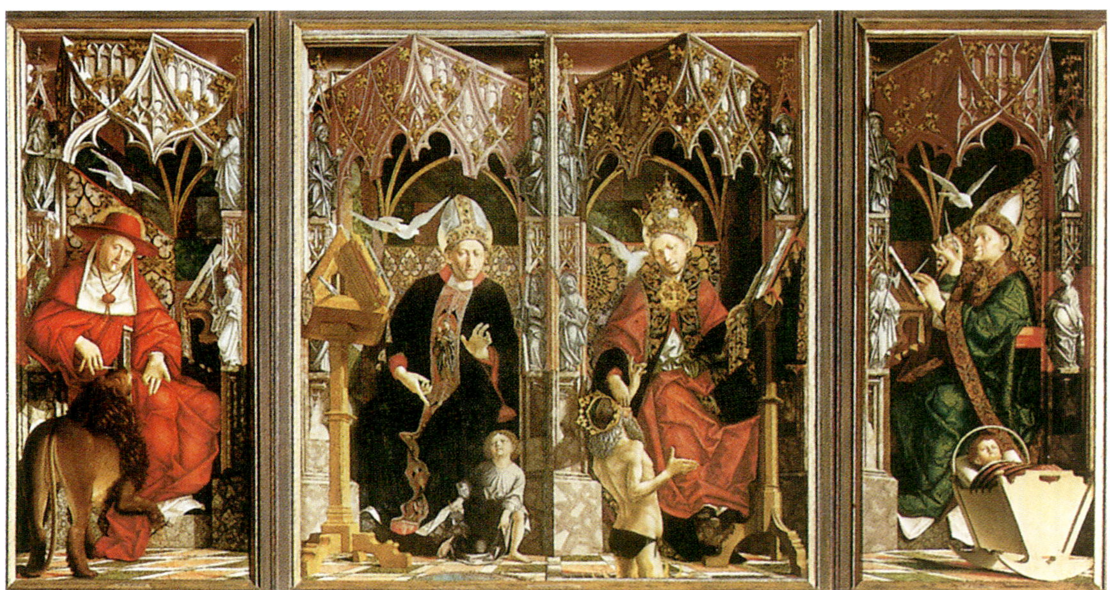

253

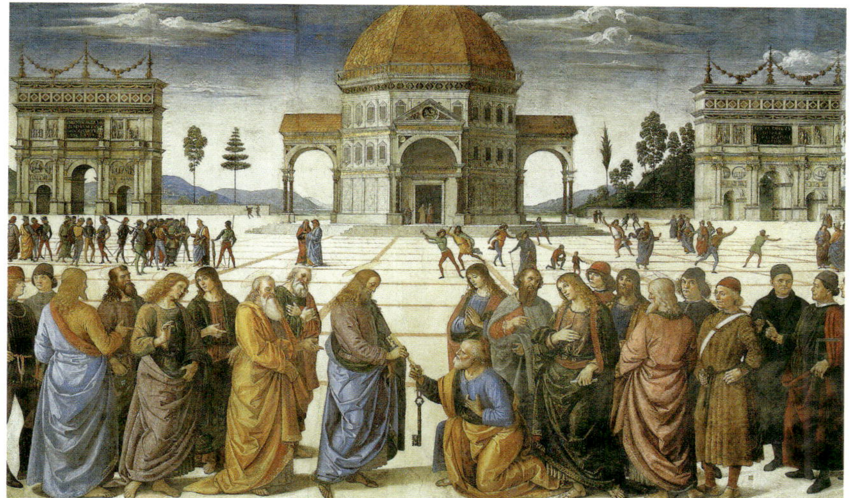

254

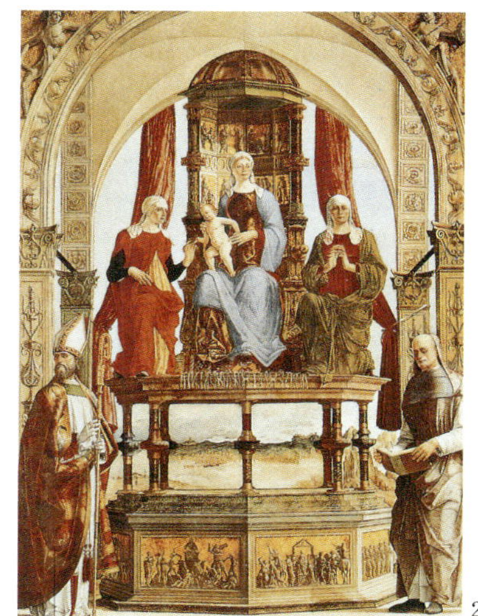

255

254. Pietro Perugino, 1450-1523,
High Renaissance, Florentine School, Italian,
Christ Giving the Keys to St Peter, 1481-1482.
Oil on wood. Vatican Museums, Rome.

*The fresco is from the cycle of the life of Christ in the Sistine Chapel.
The principal group, showing Christ handing the keys to the kneeling
St Peter, is surrounded by the other Apostles.* Christ Giving the Keys
to St Peter *shows the search for a classical rhythm. The artist begins
to emancipate from the teaching of Piero della Francesca realising a
frieze of characters placed on different grounds.*

256. Leonardo da Vinci, 1452-1519, Early Renaissance,
Florentine School, Italian, *Adoration of the Magi*,
c. 1481. Tempera, oil, varnish and white lead on
panel, 246 x 243 cm.
Galleria degli Uffizi, Florence.

*The Adoration of the Magi is an unrivalled work
exclusively in brown cameos. The drawing matters
less than its special organisation. The central
characters (the Virgin and the Magi) draw a pyramidal
shape. This kind of shape is unifying the composition
and will influence Raphael. Taking his inspiration in
the traditional representation of the Magi, Leonardo
proposes a new iconography: all the characters are
depicted in action; each of them is individualised by
a particular facial expression or movement. The
central position of the Virgin and Child is enhanced
by the gyratory movement surrounding them.*

253. Michael Pacher, c. 1430-1498, Northern
Renaissance, Austrian,
Altarpiece of the Early Church Fathers, c. 1480.
Oil on panel, 216 x 380 cm.
Alte Pinakothek, Munich.

*Gothic in the canopies, the characters' poses and
the contorted hands, the altar of the Austrian painter
is also strongly influenced by Italian art in the use of
perspective, low viewpoint and figures close to the
picture plane recalling Mantegna's works.*

255. Ercole de'Roberti, 1450-1496, Early Renaissance,
Ferrarese School, Italian, *Madonna with Child and Saints*, 1480.
Oil on panel, 323 x 240 cm.
Pinacoteca di Brera, Milan.

*Ercole de'Roberti inherited the tradition of Tura and Cossa
with their precise line and metallic colours against elaborately
fanciful ornamentation. But he developed a very personal and
expressive style in his works. In this altarpiece, which is his
first documented work, his style is independent although it
shows the influence of his Ferrarese antecedents. The altarpiece
reveals a familiarity with Venetian art and the work of Giovanni
Bellini and Antonello da Messina in particular.*

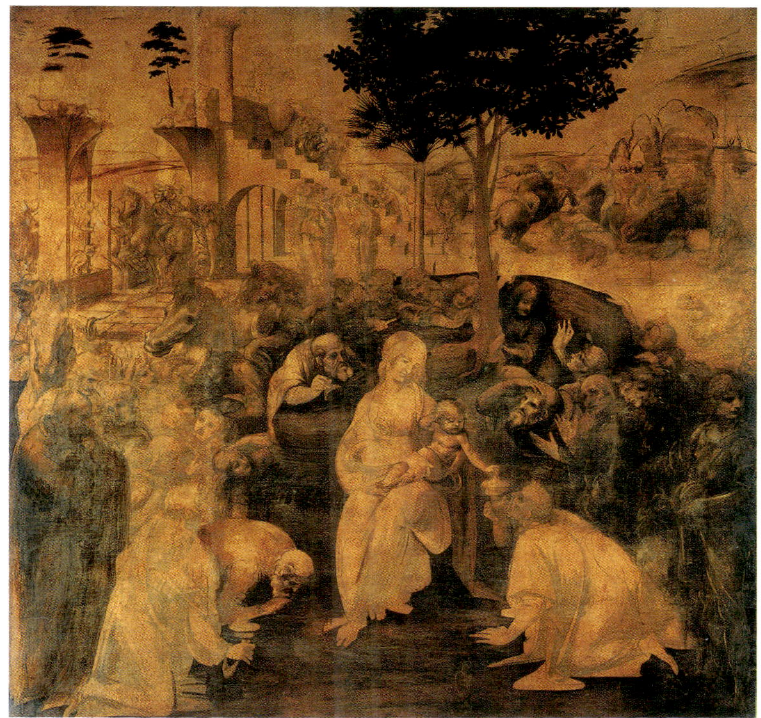

256

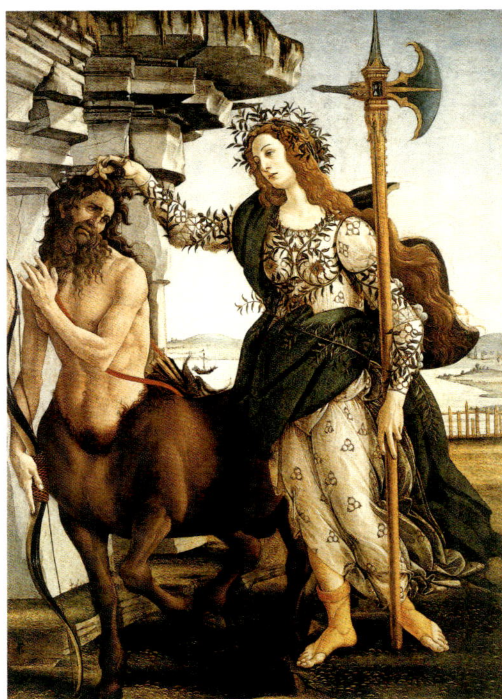

257

257. **Sandro Botticelli (Alessandro di Mariano Filipepi)**, 1445-1510, Early Renaissance, Florentine School, Italian, *Pallas and the Centaur*, c. 1482. Tempera on canvas, 205 x 147.5 cm. Galleria degli Uffizi, Florence.

258. **Sandro Botticelli (Alessandro di Mariano Filipepi)**, 1445-1510, Early Renaissance, Florentine School, Italian, *The Birth of Venus*, c. 1482. Tempera on canvas, 173 x 279 cm. Galleria degli Uffizi, Florence.

The title announces the influence here of the Roman classics, as it selects the Roman name, rather than the Greek name for the goddess of love – Aphrodite. The geometric centre of the work is the gesture of modesty near the left hand of Venus, the central figure, although the triangular arrangement of the overall work leads our eye to accept her upper torso as central. Her long tresses and flowing garments throughout make the overall geometric arrangement soft and dynamic. The sides of an equilateral triangle are formed by the bodies of the figures on either side of Venus; the base of the triangle extends beyond the sides of the work, making the painting seem larger than it is (Piet Mondrian will exploit that technique in a minimalist way centuries later). The mature goddess has just been born from the sea, blown ashore by Zephyr (The West Wind), and his abducted nymph Chloris. The stylised waves of the sea bring the shell-boat forward and counter-clockwise to The Hour waiting on the shore. The sea has somehow already provided a ribbon for her hair. Her introspective expression is typical of the central figures in the painter's work (See Portrait of a Man *(1417)). The Hour, symbolising Spring and rebirth, begins to clothe the naked, new-born goddess with an elegant, high fashion robe covered in flowers, similar to her own gown on which there are corn flowers. Several spring flowers are sprinkled throughout the scene: orange blossoms in the upper right; evergreen myrtle around The Hour's neck and waist; a single blue anemone between The Hour's feet; over two dozen pink roses accompany Zephyr and Chloris. Cattails in the lower left balance the strong verticals of the orange trees. Each of the figures is outlined in thin black lines, characteristic of the artist. Sometimes the artist doesn't follow his outline, but doesn't cover it up either; as we see along the right arm of Venus, the outline has become visible over the years.*

258

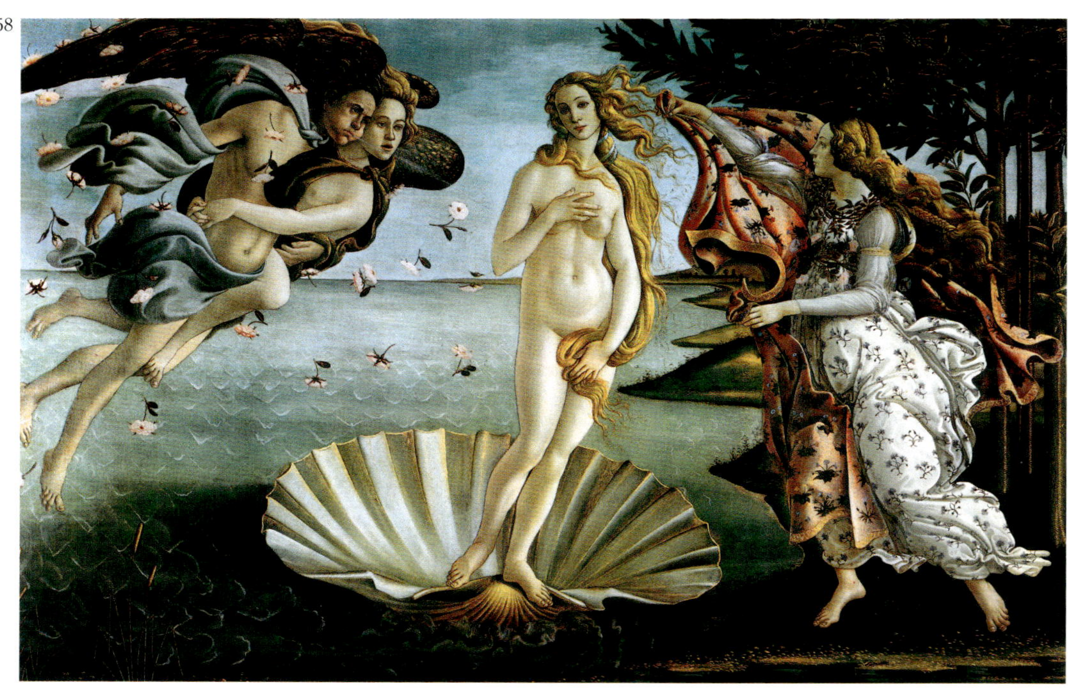

259. **Sandro Botticelli (Alessandro di Mariano Filipepi)**, 1445-1510, Early Renaissance, Florentine School, Italian,
Madonna of the Magnificat, c. 1483.
Tempera on wood, Tondo, diameter: 118 cm.
Galleria degl Uffizi, Florence.

The paintings of the Virgin by Botticelli dated between 1481 and 1485 may embody the purest essence of the physical ideal, in relation to both the Madonna and the baby Jesus, developed during the Renaissance. At the same time, a deep sense of spirituality pervades the scene, Madonna and Child with Angels, *also known as the* Madonna of the Magnificat. *Mary is represented seated, her child on her lap. The angels hold an elaborate crown above her head, reminding the viewer that she is the Queen of Heaven, while mother and child gaze in rapture at each other. The child has his hand on the page of a book, pointing at the word "Magnificat", a reference to Mary's consent to bear him, and her declaration to the archangel of the Annunciation that "my soul magnifies the Lord" (in Latin, "Magnificat anima mea Dominum").*

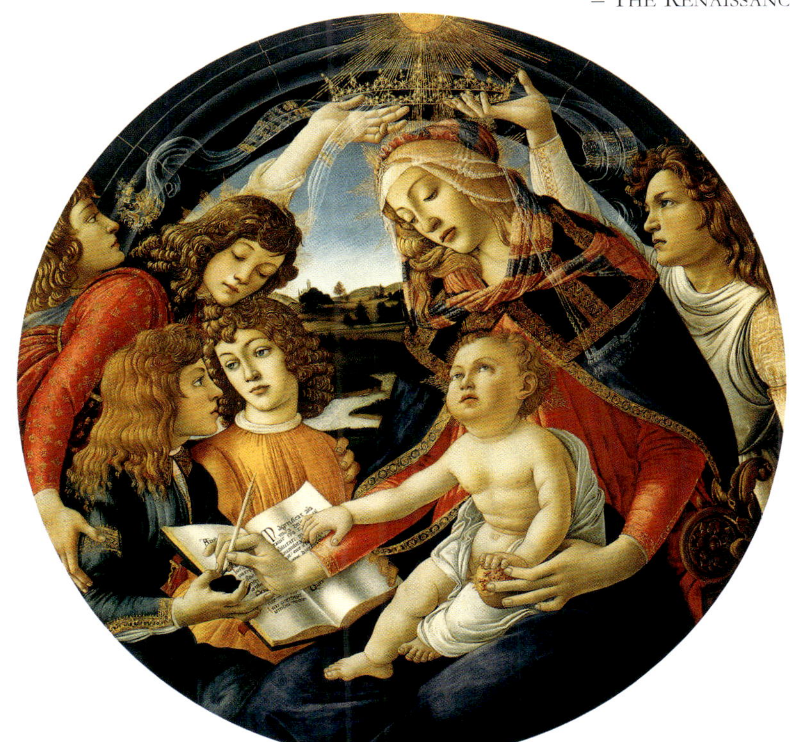

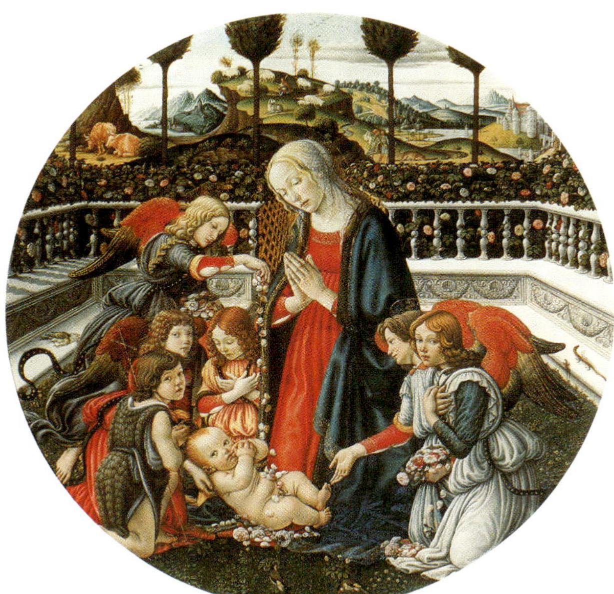

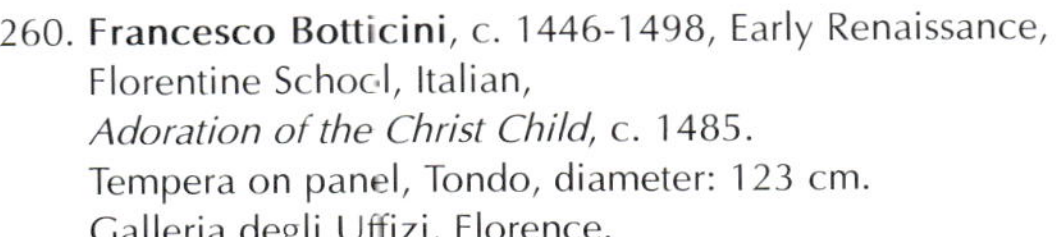

260. **Francesco Botticini**, c. 1446-1498, Early Renaissance, Florentine School, Italian,
Adoration of the Christ Child, c. 1485.
Tempera on panel, Tondo, diameter: 123 cm.
Galleria degli Uffizi, Florence.

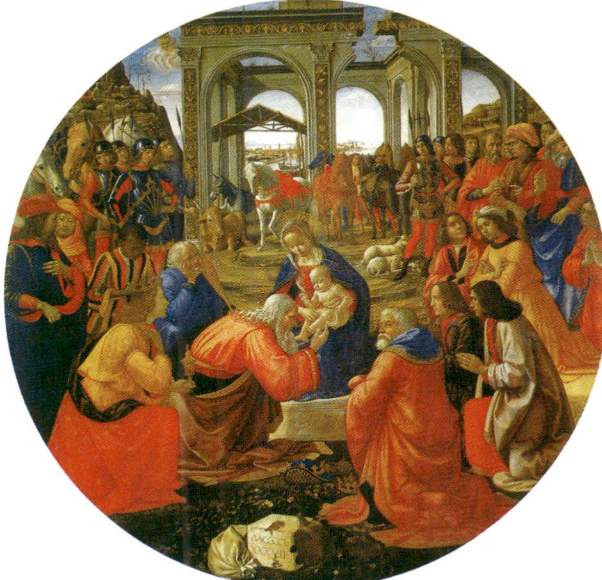

261. **Domenico Ghirlandaio**, 1449-1494, Early Renaissance, Florentine School, Italian, *Adoration of the Magi*, 1488.
Tempera on panel, Tondo, diameter: 171 cm.
Galleria degli Uffizi, Florence.

This pyramidal composition with Mary at the top was influenced by Leonardo's uncompleted Adoration of the Magi *(1481, Uffizi).*

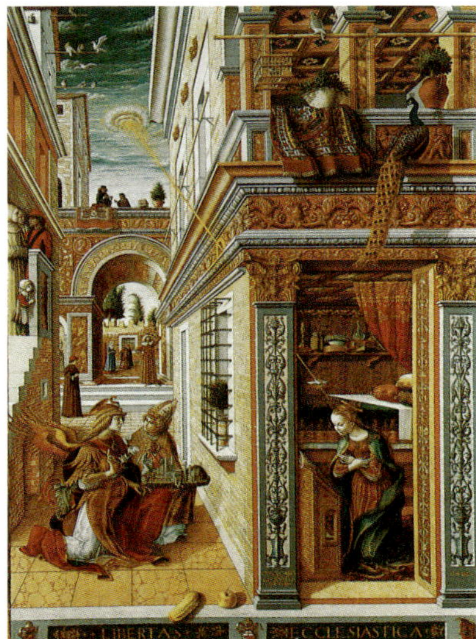

262. **Carlo Crivelli**, 1430-1495, Early Renaissance, Venetian School, Italian, *Annunciation with St Endimius*, 1486. Oil on canvas transferred to wood, 207 x 147 cm. National Gallery, London.

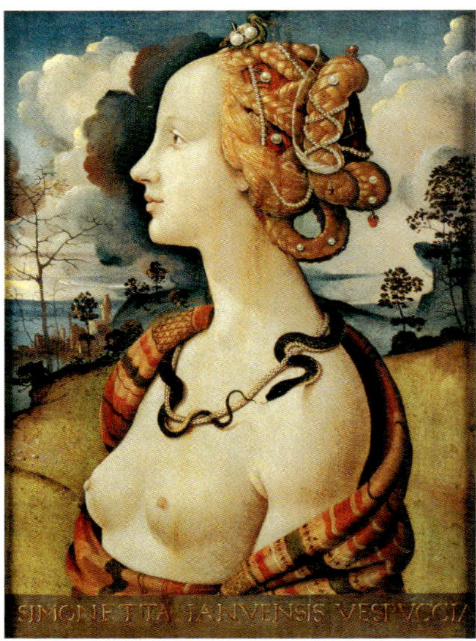

263. **Piero di Cosimo**, 1462-1521, Early Renaissance, Florentine School, Italian, *Portrait of Simonetta Vespucci*, c. 1485. Oil on panel, 57 x 42 cm. Musée Condé, Chantilly.

Here is one of the artist's finest portraits. Simonetta Vespucci is depicted as Cleopatra with the asp around her neck. The snake, also being a symbol of immortality, reinforces the strange atmosphere of this work.

264. **Domenico Ghirlandaio**, 1449-1494, Early Renaissance, Florentine School, Italian, *An Old Man with his Grandson*, 1488. Tempera on panel, 62 x 46 cm. Musée du Louvre, Paris.

This is the first time that a character is portrayed with such realism showing clearly disfiguring details. This portrait conveys the deep affection between the man and the boy. The motif of the open window on a landscape in the background was borrowed from the Flemish Renaissance and brought to Italy in the mid-fifteenth century by artists such as Filippo Lippi.

265. **Leonardo da Vinci**, 1452-1519, Renaissance, Florentine School, Italian, *Lady with an Ermine (Portrait of Cecilia Gallerani)*, 1483-1490. Oil on panel, 54 x 39 cm. Czartoryski Museum, Cracow.

Favourite portrait of the Duke of Milan, the Lady with an Ermine *is part of a series of animated portraits painted by Leonardo in Milan: dynamism is given by the bust facing the left side of the panel and the head turned toward the right.*

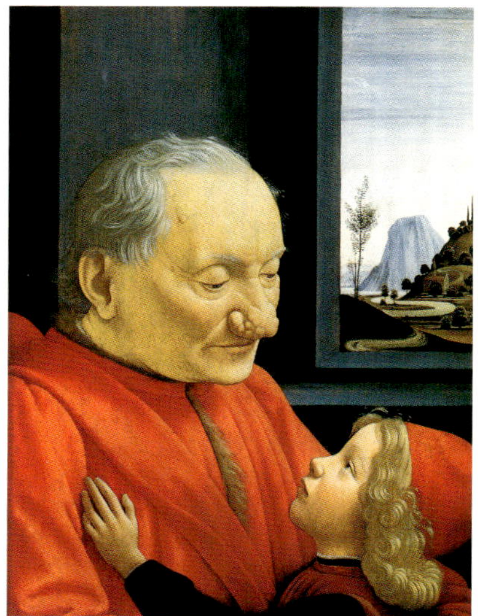

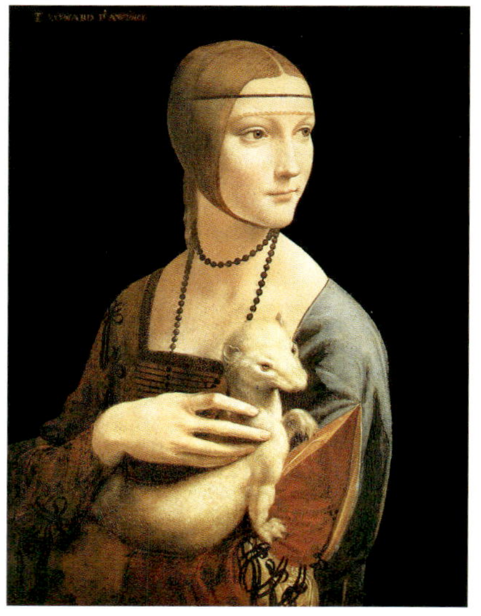

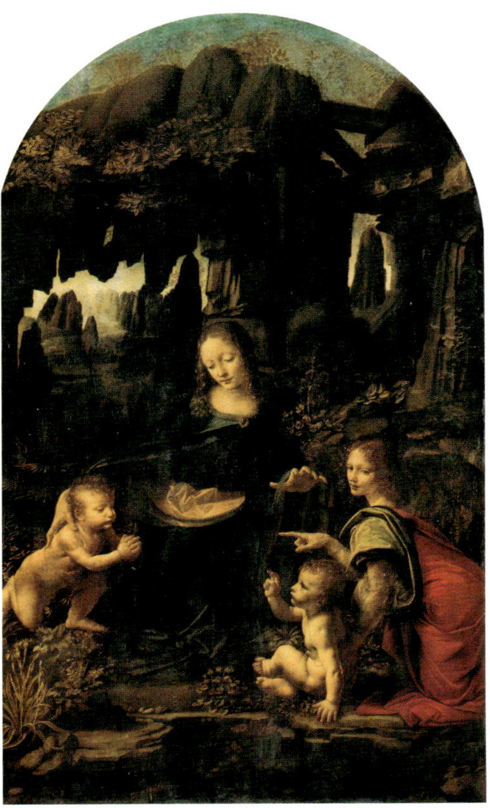

266

266. **Leonardo da Vinci**, 1452-1519, High Renaissance, Florentine School, Italian,
The Virgin of the Rocks (The Virgin with the Infant Saint John Adoring the Infant Christ Accompanied by an Angel), 1483-1486.
Oil on panel, 199 x 122 cm. Musée du Louvre, Paris.

The Virgin of the Rocks, *also by Leonardo da Vinci, is probably the most well-known painting of the Virgin and Child within the Western world. Now located in the Louvre, this work is one of the best examples of the use of atmospheric perspective and the correct foreshortening of the human figure. The cavern and the group of figures are all seen as through a veil of shadowy mist. Leonardo believed that his destiny was to recreate the beauty of nature on his canvas. The figure of the Madonna occupies the apex of the pyramid-based composition of this painting – the most important location – due to her high ranking within contemporary Christian belief. She is accompanied by the infants Jesus and St John, and an angel. All four reflect the Renaissance ideal of the human form. Leonardo altogether eliminated the use of the halo effects to further humanise the group. The Virgin is depicted as the perfect woman, yet she also projects her tender Earth Mother qualities reminiscent of those seen in ancient renderings of the Great Goddess Isis.*

267. **Fra Filippo Lippi**, c. 1406-1469, Early Renaissance, Florentine School, Italian,
Madonna and the Child Enthroned with Saint John the Baptist, Victor, Bernard and Zenobius (Altarpiece of the Otto di Pratica), 1486.
Tempera on panel, 355 x 255 cm. Galleria degli Uffizi, Florence.

268. **Sandro Botticelli (Alessandro di Mariano Filipepi)**,
1445-1510, Early Renaissance, Florentine School, Italian,
The Coronation of the Virgin, c. 1490.
Tempera on panel, 378 x 258 cm. Galleria degli Uffizi, Florence.

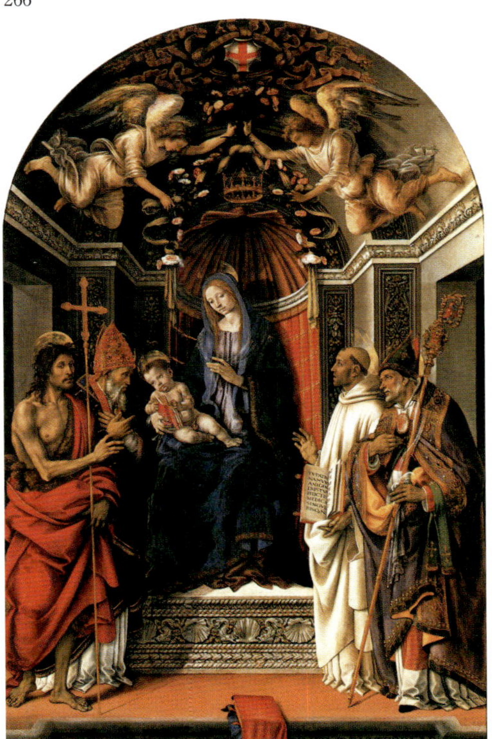

267

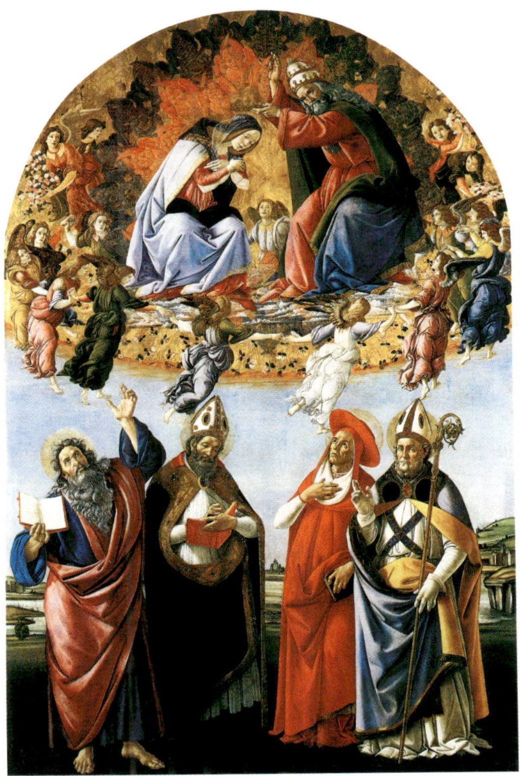

268

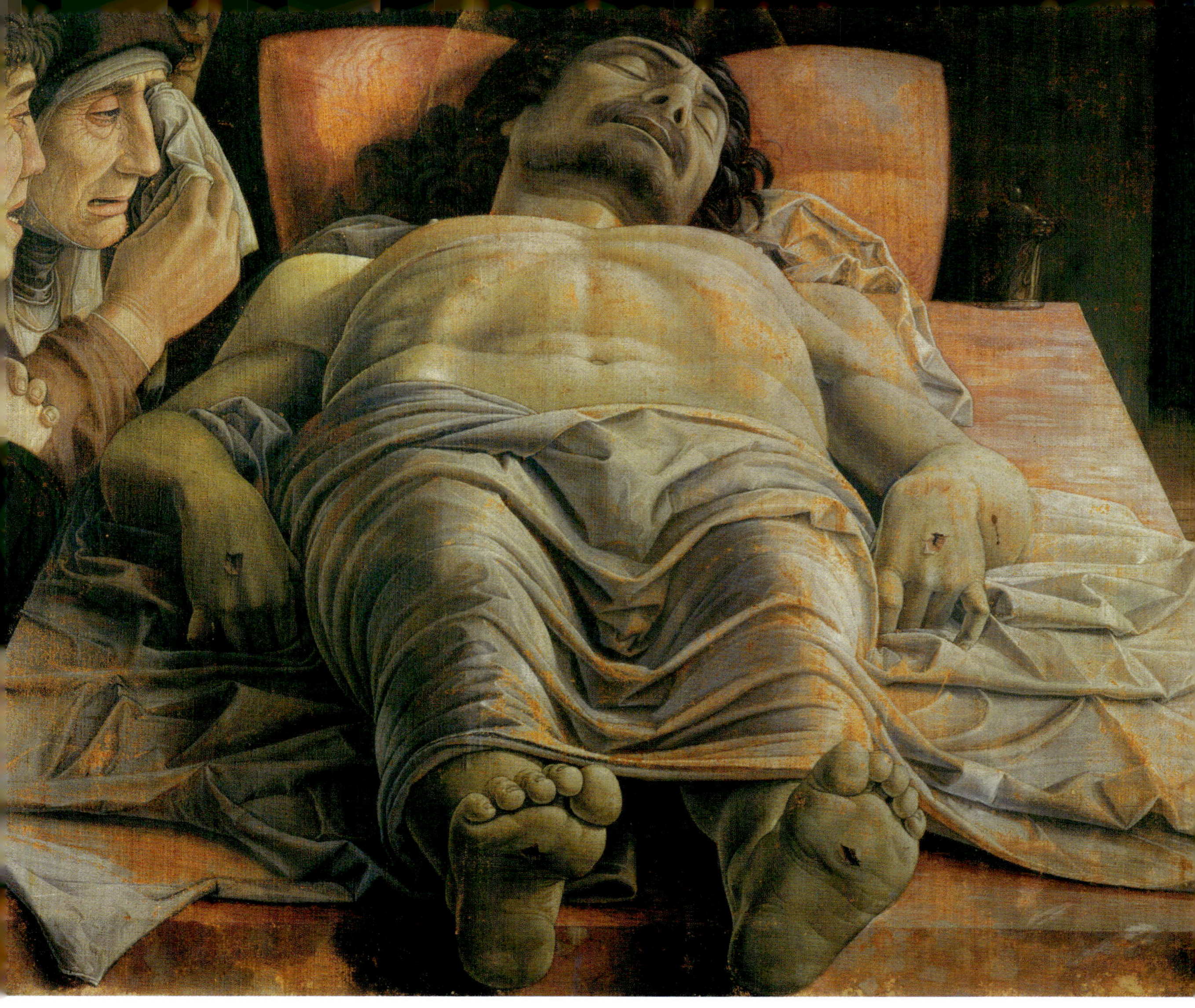

269. **Andrea Mantegna**, 1431-1506, Early Renaissance, Florentine
School, Italian, *The Lamentation over the Dead Christ*, c. 1490.
Tempera on canvas, 68 x 81 cm. Pinacoteca di Brera, Milan.

*A nearly monochromatic vision of Jesus mourned by three figures
was in Mantegna's collection at the time of his death; this Dead
Christ includes Saint John, Mary, and Mary Magdalene. His
inventory of 1506 referred to a work fitting this description,
presumably the very same picture, and it ended up in Gonzaga
collections later in the century. This is a searing image of Christ
laid out on his funeral slab, an intense vision of Christ's suffering
and death. The wounds in his hands are like torn paper, as is the
spear gash in his side. Mantegna has played with the rules of
perspective here, making the head large; it should be much
smaller than the feet because the figure is strongly foreshortened.
To make the work in proper perspective would have made the
face of Christ too small to elicit strong empathy from the viewer.
The monochromatic, golden-brown colouring helps to move this
painting to another realm of passion and religious fervour. The
viewers would sympathise with the sorrowful Mary, John, and
Mary Magdalene who appear in truncated form on the left,
pouring out their grief in open mourning.*

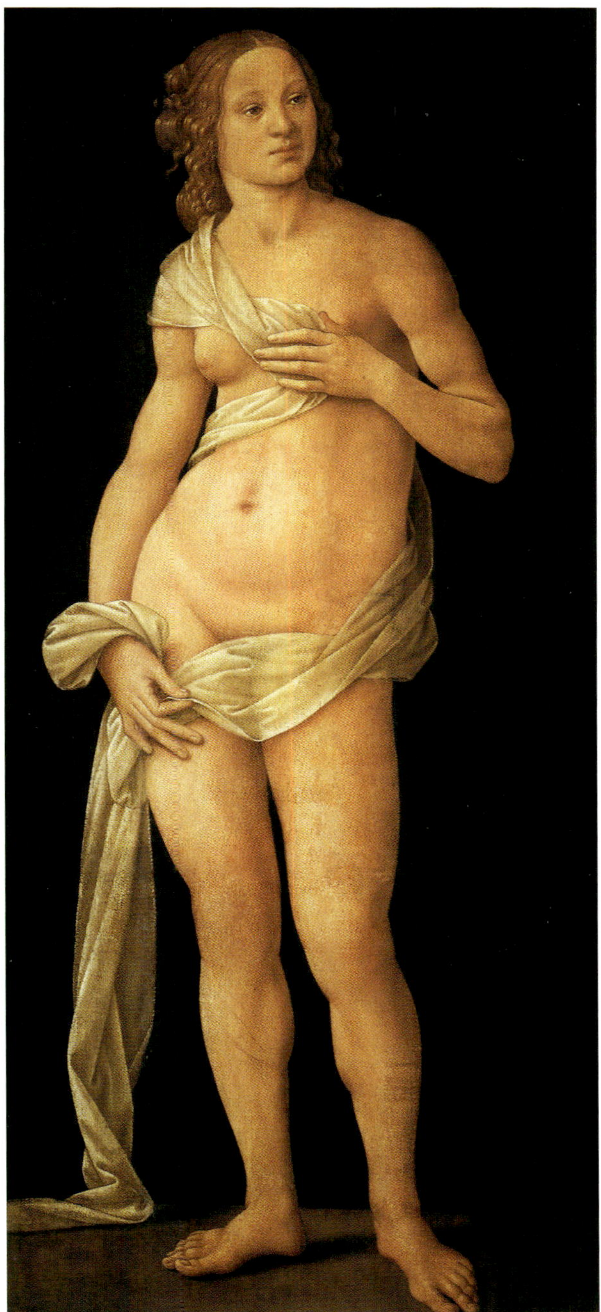

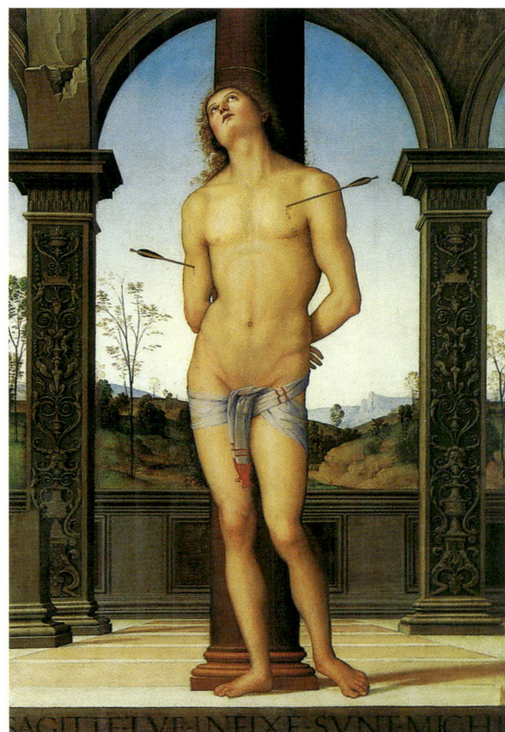

271

270. **Lorenzo di Credi**, c. 1458-1537, High Renaissance,
Florentine School, Italian, *Venus*, c. 1493.
Oil on canvas, 151 x 69 cm. Galleria degli Uffizi, Florence.

271. **Pietro Perugino**, 1450-1523, High Renaissance,
Florentine School, Italian, *St Sebastian*, c. 1490-1500.
Oil on wood, 176 x 116 cm. Musée du Louvre, Paris.

PIETRO PERUGINO
(1450 CITTA DELLA PIEVE – 1523 PERUGIA)

Perugino's art, like Fra Angelico's, had its roots in the old Byzantine tradition of painting. The latter had departed further and further from any representation of the human form, until it became merely a symbol of religious ideas. Perugino, working under the influence of his time, restored body and substance to the figures, but still made them, as of old, primarily the symbols of an ideal. It was not until the seventeenth century that artists began to paint landscape for its own sake.

However, the union of landscape and figures counts very much for Perugino, because one of the secrets of composition is the balancing of what artists call the full and empty spaces. A composition crowded with figures is apt to produce a sensation of stuffiness and fatigue; whereas the combination of a few figures with ample open spaces gives one a sense of exhilaration and repose. It is in the degree to which an artist stimulates our imagination through our physical experiences that he seizes and holds our interest. When Perugino left Perugia to complete his education in Florence he was a fellow-pupil of Leonardo da Vinci in the sculptor's *bottegha*. If he gained from the master something of the calm of sculpture, he certainly gained nothing of its force. It is as the painter of sentiment that he excelled; though this beautiful quality is confined mainly to his earlier works. For with popularity he became avaricious, turning out repetitions of his favourite themes until they became more and more affected in sentiment.

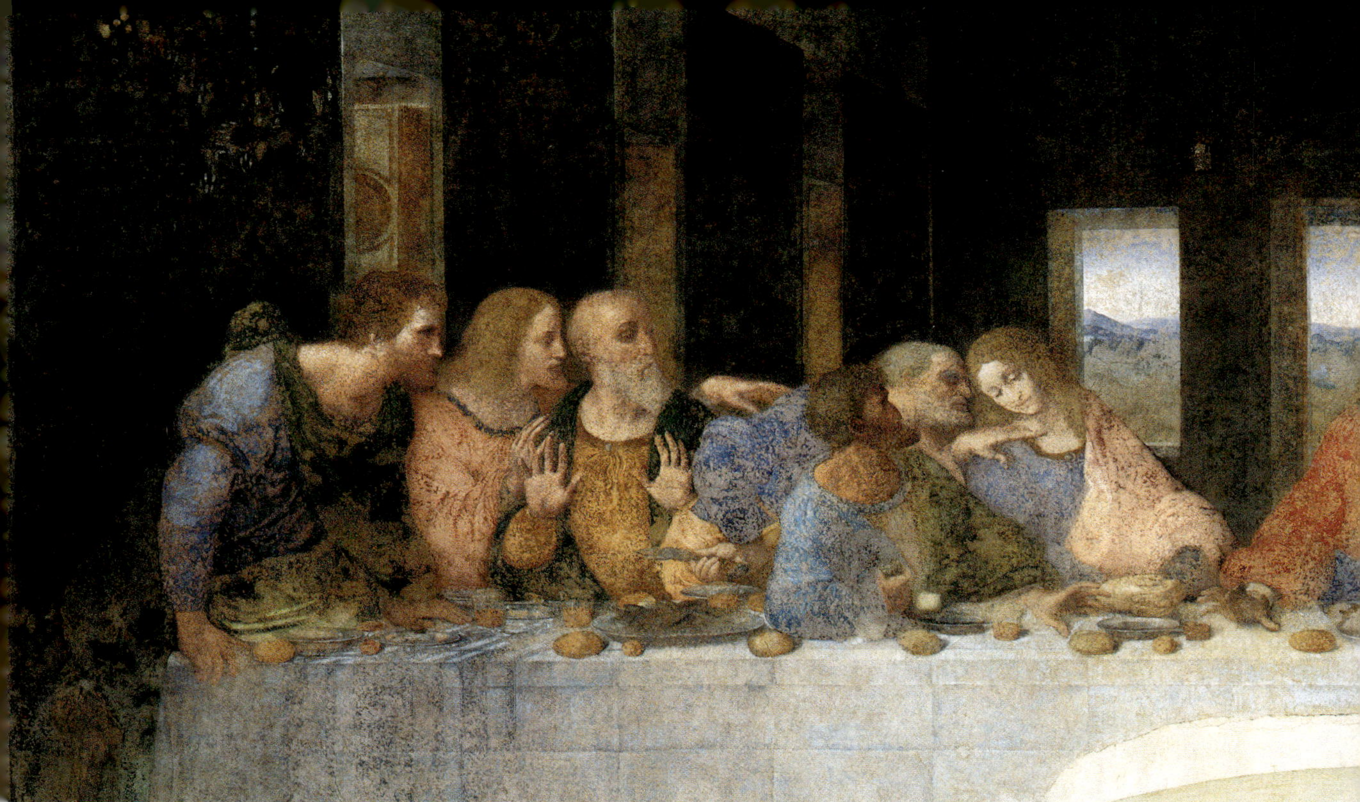

272. **Leonardo da Vinci**, 1452-1519, Renaissance, Florentine School, Italian,
The Last Supper, 1495-1498.
Oil and tempera on stone, 460 x 880 cm.
Convent of Santa Maria delle Grazie, Refectori, Milan.

The perfection of grouping achieved in The Last Supper *would of itself be sufficient to mark an epoch in the annals of painting. Its ease and rhythm are sublime. The figures, placed on two planes in perspective, are further arranged in groups of three, with the exception of Christ, who, isolated in the centre, dominates the action. If we turn to expression and gesture, we must again do homage to the master's extraordinary perception of dramatic effect. The Saviour has just uttered the fateful words: "One of you shall betray me," with sublime resignation. In a moment, as by an electric shock, he has excited the most diverse emotions among the disciples, according to the character of each. Sadly, Leonardo painted in oil and tempera on a dry wall, such a defective process that three-quarters of the work may be said to have been destroyed by the middle of the sixteenth century. The skill and the knowledge necessary in order not to destroy their balance, to vary the lines without detracting from their harmony, and finally to connect the various groups, were so tremendous that neither reasoning nor calculation could have solved a problem so intricate; but for a sort of divine inspiration, the most gifted artist would have failed.*

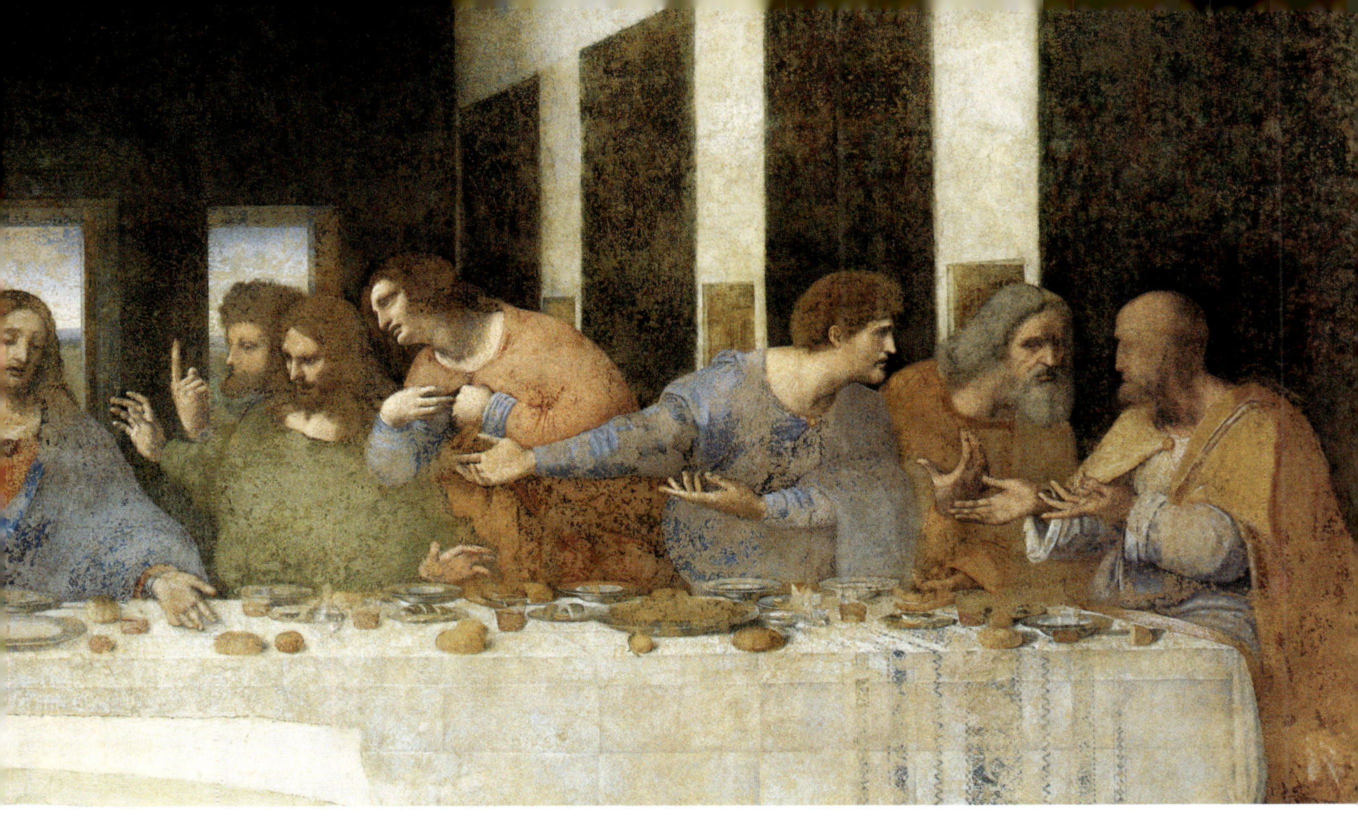

LEONARDO DA VINCI
(1452 VINCI – 1519 LE CLOS-LUCÉ)

Leonardo's early life was spent in Florence, his maturity in Milan, and the last three years of his life in France. Leonardo's teacher was Verrocchio. First he was a goldsmith, then a painter and sculptor: as a painter, representative of the very scientific school of draughtsmanship; more famous as a sculptor, being the creator of the Colleoni statue at Venice, Leonardo was a man of striking physical attractiveness, great charm of manner and conversation, and mental accomplishment. He was well grounded in the sciences and mathematics of the day, as well as a gifted musician. His skill in draughtsmanship was extraordinary; shown by his numerous drawings as well as by his comparatively few paintings. His skill of hand is at the service of most minute observation and analytical research into the character and structure of form.

Leonardo is the first in date of the great men who had the desire to create in a picture a kind of mystic unity brought about by the fusion of matter and spirit. Now that the Primitives had concluded their experiments, ceaselessly pursued during two centuries, by the conquest of the methods of painting, he was able to pronounce the words which served as a password to all later artists worthy of the name: painting is a spiritual thing, *cosa mentale*.

He completed Florentine draughtsmanship in applying to modelling by light and shade, a sharp subtlety which his predecessors had used only to give greater precision to their contours. This marvellous draughtsmanship, this modelling and chiaroscuro he used not solely to paint the exterior appearance of the body but, as no one before him had done, to cast over it a reflection of the mystery of the inner life. In the *Mona Lisa* and his other masterpieces he even used landscape not merely as a more or less picturesque decoration, but as a sort of echo of that interior life and an element of a perfect harmony.

Relying on the still quite novel laws of perspective this doctor of scholastic wisdom, who was at the same time an initiator of modern thought, substituted for the discursive manner of the Primitives the principle of concentration which is the basis of classical art. The picture is no longer presented to us as an almost fortuitous aggregate of details and episodes. It is an organism in which all the elements, lines and colours, shadows and lights, compose a subtle tracery converging on a spiritual, a sensuous centre. It was not with the external significance of objects, but with their inward and spiritual significance, that Leonardo was occupied.

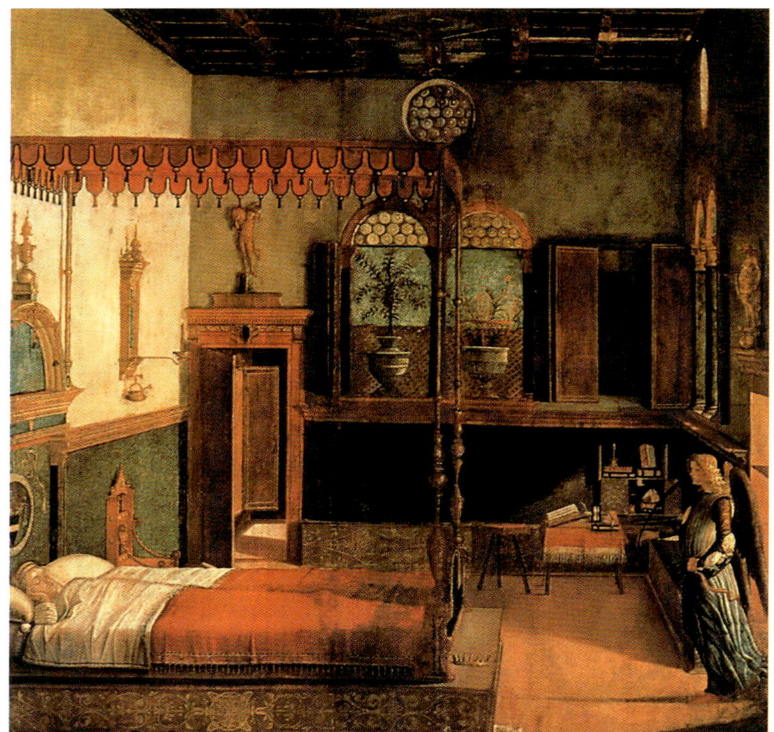
273

VITTORE CARPACCIO
(C. 1465 VENICE – C. 1525 CAPODISTRIA)

Carpaccio was a Venetian painter strongly influenced by Gentile Bellini. The distinguishing characteristics of his work are his taste for fantasy and anecdote and his eye for minutely-observed crowd details. After completing the cycles of Scenes from the Lives of St Ursula, St George and St Jerome, his career declined and he remained forgotten until the nineteenth century. He is now seen as one of the outstanding Venetian painters of his generation.

273. **Vittore Carpaccio,** c. 1465-c. 1525,
High Renaissance, Venetian School, Italian,
The Dream of St Ursula, 1495.
Tempera on canvas, 274 x 267 cm.
Galleria dell'Accademia, Venice.

274. **Giovanni Bellini**, c. 1430-1516,
Early Renaissance, Venetian School, Italian,
Sacred Allegory, c. 1490.
Oil on panel, 73 x 119 cm.
Galleria degli Uffizi, Florence.

274

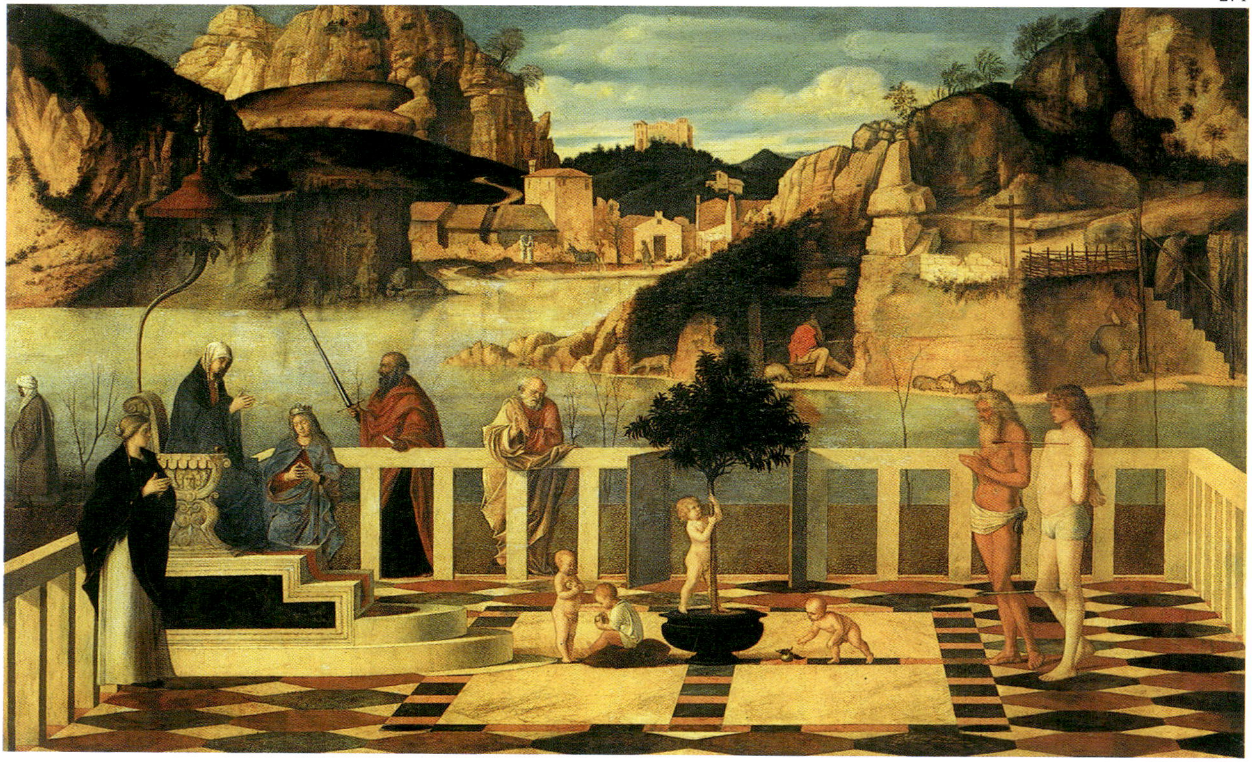

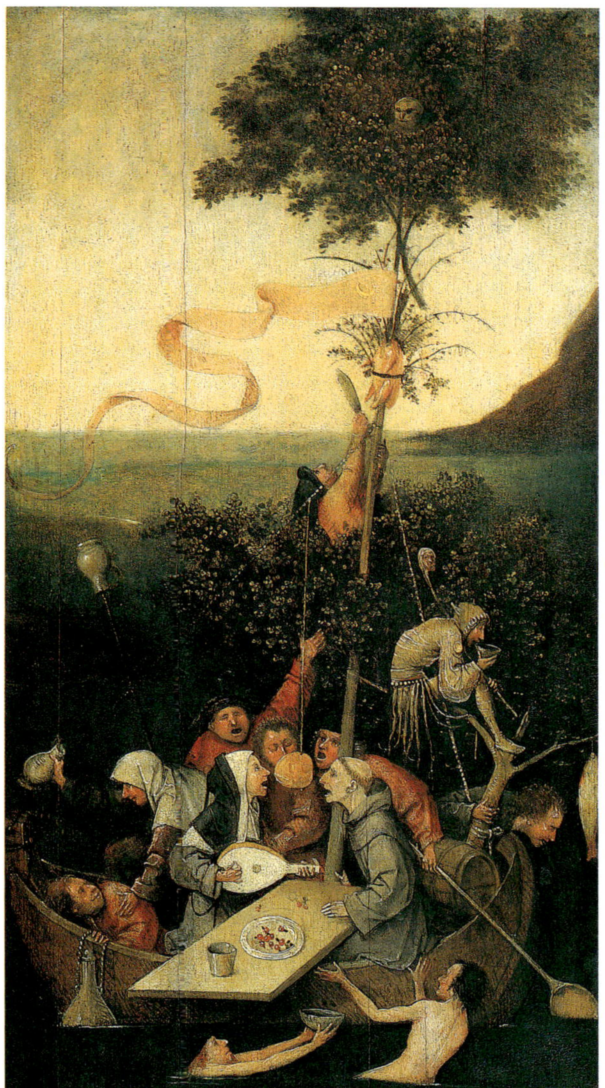

275

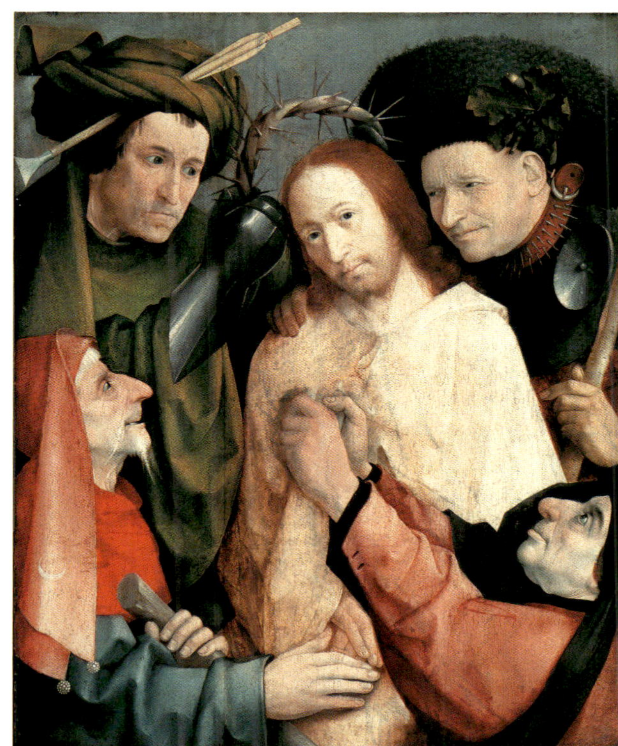

276

277

275. **Hieronymus Bosch,** c. 1450-1516, Northern Renaissance, Dutch, *The Ship of Fools,* after 1491. Oil on panel, 58 x 33 cm. Musée du Louvre, Paris.

276. **Hieronymus Bosch,** c. 1450-1516, Northern Renaissance, Dutch, *Christ Mocked (The Crowning with Thorns),* 1490-1500. Oil on oak panel, 73.8 x 59 cm. National Gallery, London.

277. **Fra Bartolomeo,** 1473-1517, High Renaissance, Florentine School, Italian, *Portrait of Girolamo Savonarola,* c. 1498. Oil on panel, 47 x 31 cm. Museo di San Marco, Florence.

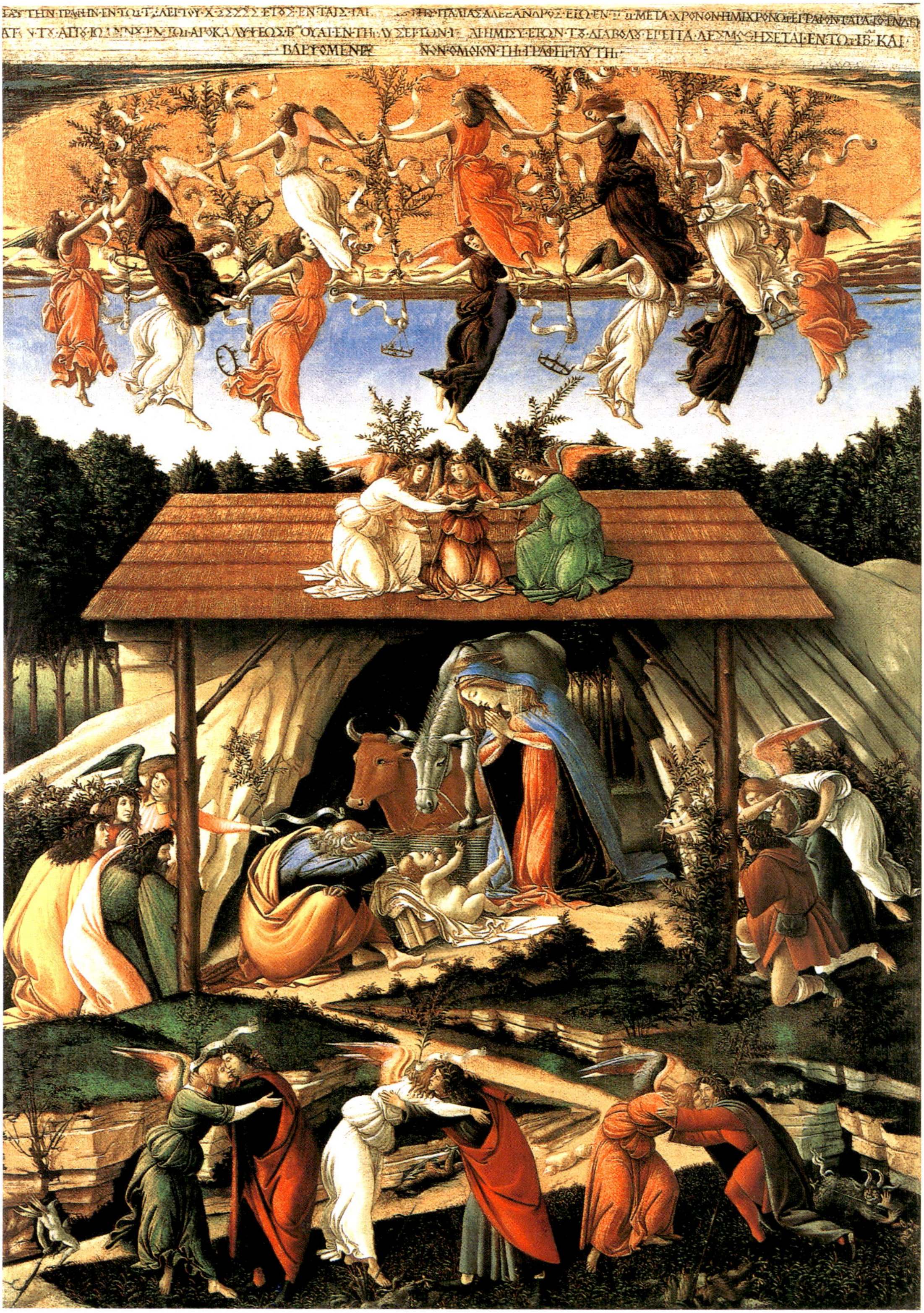

278

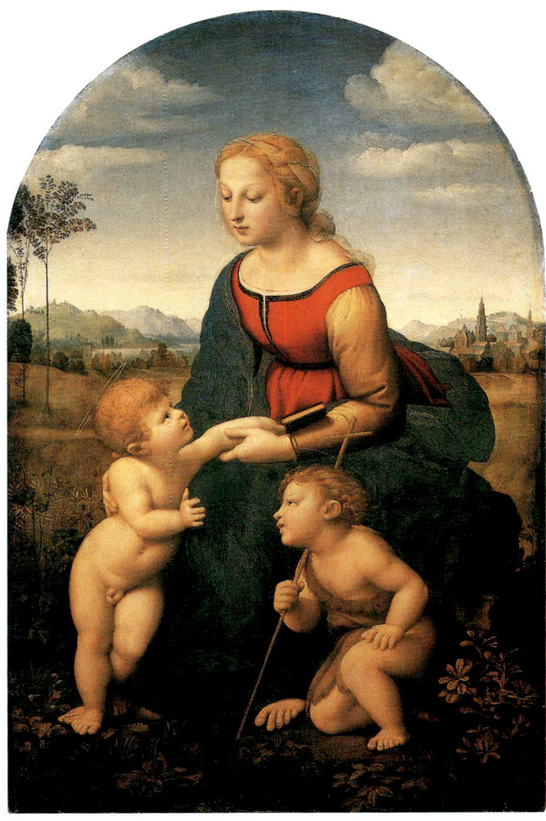

279

279. Raphael (Raffaello Sanzio), 1483-1520,
High Renaissance, Florentine School, Italian,
*The Virgin and Child with the Infant Saint John the
Baptist (La Belle Jardinière),* 1507-1508.
Oil on wood, 122 x 80 cm. Musée du Louvre, Paris.

*La Belle Jardinière, or The Virgin and Child with the Infant
St John the Baptist, completed in 1507, shows the trio
surrounded by a pleasant rural environment. The similarity
between the Madonna of the Goldfinch and this depiction
of the Madonna is more than coincidental: it represents
the ideal of female beauty according to Raphael. Perhaps
the same model was used in both paintings.*

278. Sandro Botticelli (Alessandro di Mariano Filipepi),
1445-1510, Early Renaissance, Florentine School,
Italian, *Mystic Nativity,* c. 1500.
Oil on canvas, 108.6 x 74.9 cm.
National Gallery, London.

*Inscribed in Greek at the top: "This picture, at the end
of the year 1500, in the troubles of Italy, I Alessandro, in
the half-time after the time, painted, according to the
eleventh [chapter] of Saint John, in the second woe of
the Apocalypse, during the release of the devil for three-
and-a-half years; then he shall be bound in the twelfth
[chapter] and we shall see [him buried] as in this
picture." Botticelli's picture has been called the Mystic
Nativity because of its mysterious symbolism.*

280. Piero di Cosimo, 1462-1521, High Renaissance, Florentine School,
Italian, *Immaculate Conception and Six Saints,* c. 1505.
Oil on panel, 206 x 173 cm.
Galleria degli Uffizi, Florence.

280

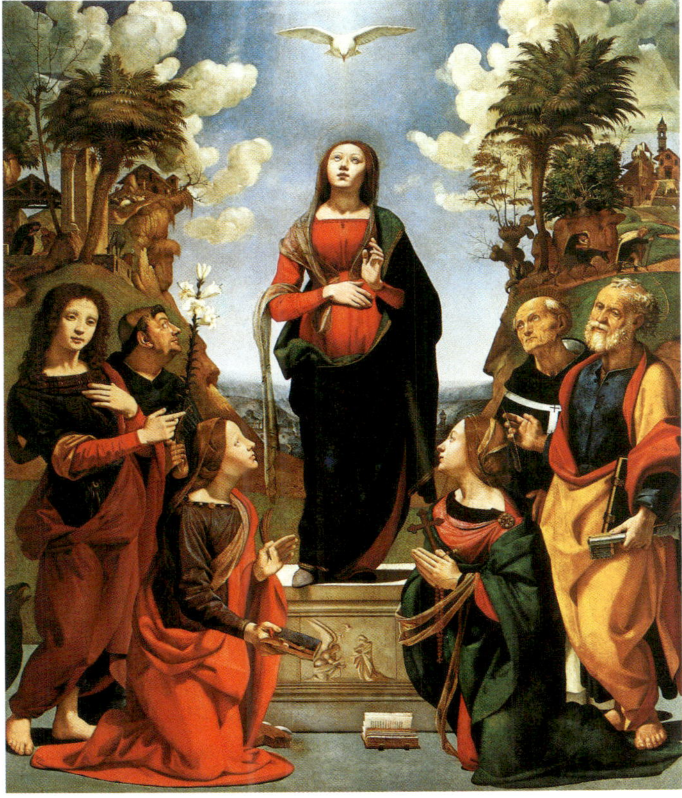

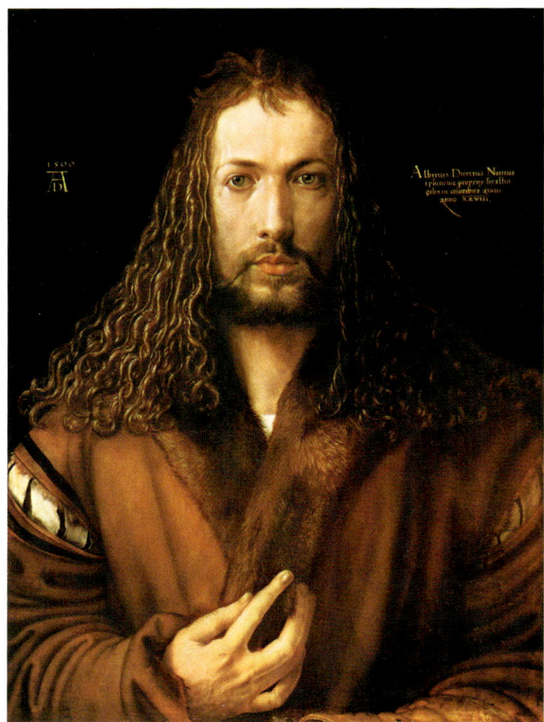

281. **Albrecht Dürer,** 1471-1528, Northern Renaissance, German, *Self-portrait in a Fur-Collared Robe,* 1500. Oil on limewood panel, 67.1 x 48.9 cm. Alte Pinakothek, Munich.

This flattering, Christ-like portrait is also innovative as the artist represented himself frontally. The painting bears the inscription: "Thus I, Albrecht Dürer from Nuremberg, painted myself with indelible colours at the age of 28 years."

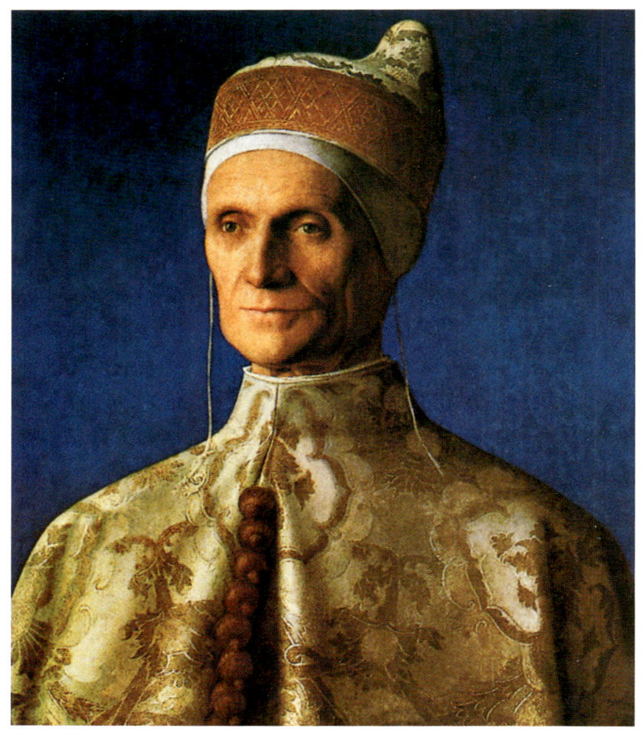

282. **Giovanni Bellini**, c. 1426-1516, Early Renaissance, Venetian School, Italian, *The Doge Leonardo Loredan,* c. 1501-1505. Oil on poplar, 61 x 45 cm. National Gallery, London.

Bellini was an exquisite portrait painter. His Doge Leonardo Loredan, *the elected ruler of Venice, is painted in a completely revolutionary way and had some beautiful effects. Rather than using gold-leaf to show the richness of the material of the Doge's robe, he painted the surface in a rough way, thus catching the light and rendering a metallic look.*

ALBRECHT DÜRER
(1471 – 1528 NUREMBERG)

Dürer is the greatest of German artists and most representative of the German mind. He, like Leonardo, was a man of striking physical attractiveness, great charm of manner and conversation, and mental accomplishment, being well grounded in the sciences and mathematics of the day. His skill in draughtsmanship was extraordinary; Dürer is even more celebrated for his engravings on wood and copper than for his paintings. With both, the skill of his hand was at the service of the most minute observation and analytical research into the character and structure of form. Dürer, however, had not the feeling for abstract beauty and ideal grace that Leonardo possessed; but instead, a profound earnestness, a closer interest in humanity, and a more dramatic invention. Dürer was a great admirer of Luther; and in his own work is the equivalent of what was mighty in the Reformer. It is very serious and sincere; very human, and addressed the hearts and understanding of the masses. Nuremberg, his hometown, had become a great centre of printing and the chief distributor of books throughout Europe.

Consequently, the art of engraving upon wood and copper, which may be called the pictorial branch of printing, was much encouraged. Of this opportunity Dürer took full advantage.

The Renaissance in Germany was more a moral and intellectual than an artistic movement, partly due to northern conditions. The feeling for ideal grace and beauty is fostered by the study of the human form, and this had been flourishing predominantly in southern Europe. But Albrecht Dürer had a genius too powerful to be conquered. He remained profoundly Germanic in his stormy penchant for drama, as was his contemporary Mathias Grünewald, a fantastic visionary and rebel against all Italian seductions. Dürer, in spite of all his tense energy, dominated conflicting passions by a sovereign and speculative intelligence comparable with that of Leonardo. He, too, was on the border of two worlds, that of the Gothic age and that of the modern age, and on the border of two arts, being an engraver and draughtsman rather than a painter.

283. **Leonardo da Vinci**, 1452-1519,
Renaissance, Florentine School, Italian,
Mona Lisa (La Gioconda), c. 1503-1506.
Oil on poplar panel, 77 x 53 cm.
Musée du Louvre, Paris.

Everybody knows this portrait: oval face with broad, high forehead; dreamy eyes beneath drooping lids; a smile very sweet and a little sad, with a suggestion of conscious superiority. This small painting, one of only thirty extant works by Leonardo, ended up in the collection of the French King, Francis I, and was displayed in the castle of Fontainebleau until the reign of Louis XIV. It is the most famous portrait, one of the first easel paintings, the most often reproduced and satirised, and one of the most influential works of the Italian Renaissance, if not of all European art. The model was probably the wife of the Marquis Francesco del Giocondo, a Florentine merchant. The work is the perfection of Leonardo's pioneering technique of "sfumato," creating atmospheric scenery, or the layering of glazes in a way that blends one colour seamlessly to another. The work also demonstrates his mastery of anatomy, perspective, landscape and portrait painting. The disposition of the sitter, in three-quarter view and the background landscape is characteristic of Florentine painting at the time. But this picture is no longer presented to us as an almost fortuitous aggregate of details and episodes. It is an organism in which all the elements, lines and colours, shadows and light compose a subtle tracery converging on a spiritual, sensuous centre. On this small panel, Leonardo depicted an epitome of the universe, creation and created: woman, the eternal enigma, the eternal ideal of man and the sign of the perfect beauty to which he aspires, evoked by a magician in all its mystery and power. Mona Lisa represents a vast revelation of the eternal feminine.

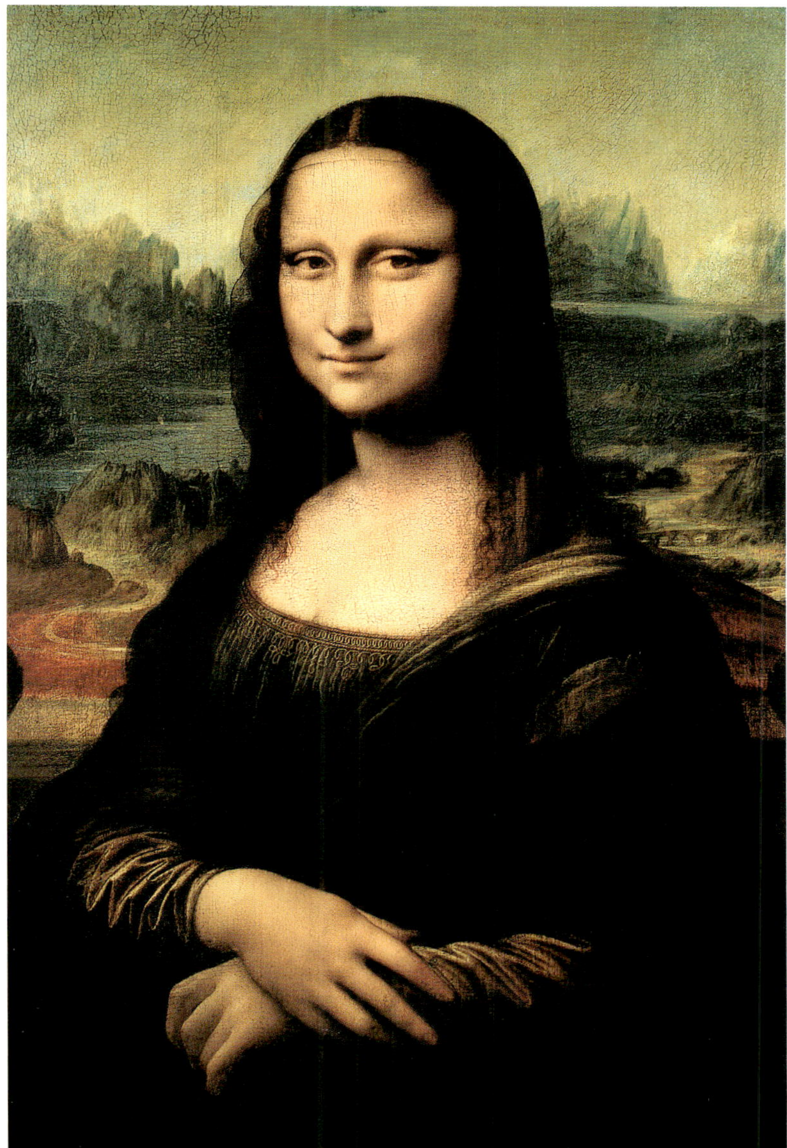

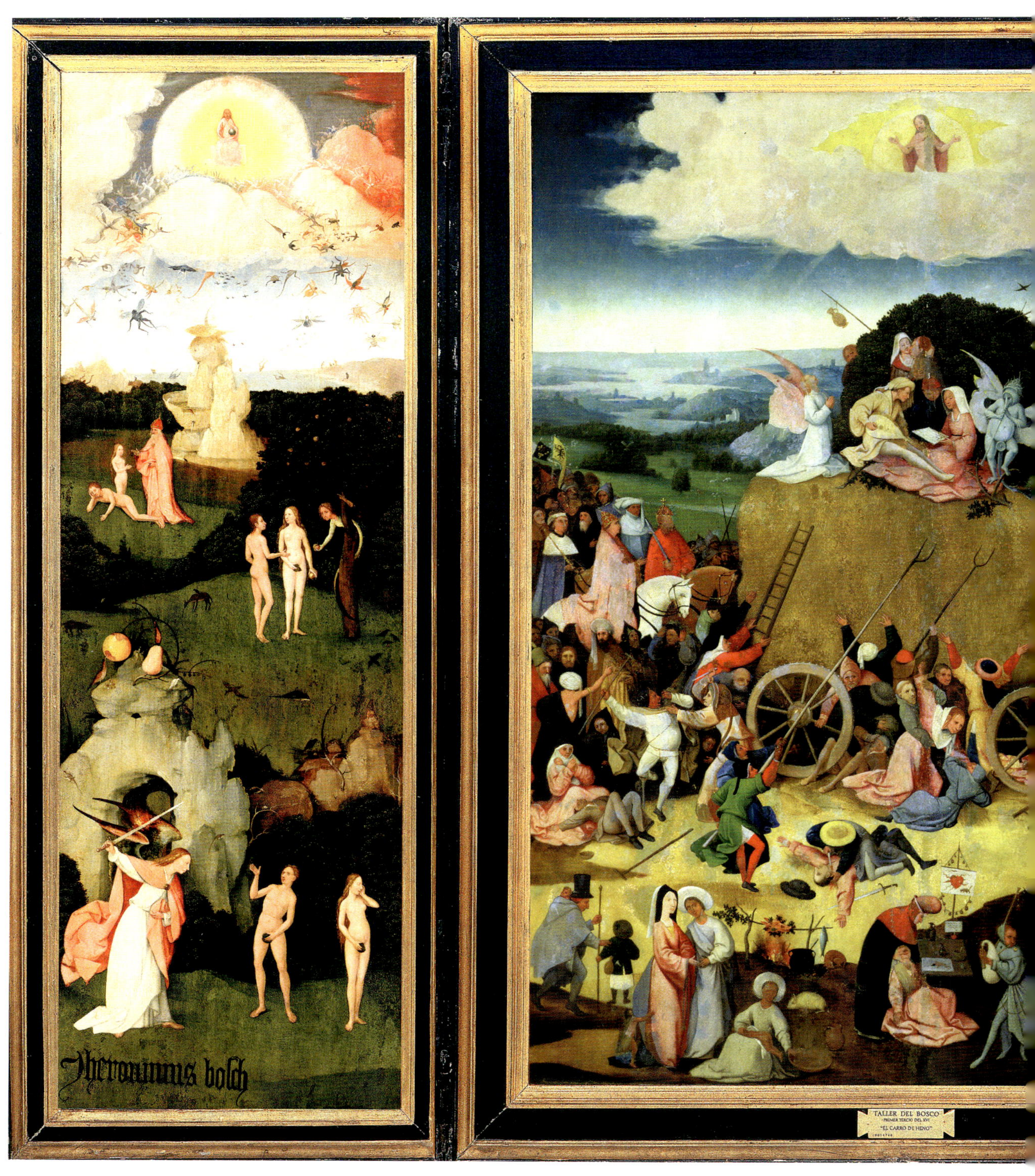
Jheronimus bosch
TALLER DEL BOSCO
PRIMER TERCIO DEL XVI
"EL CARRO DE HENO"

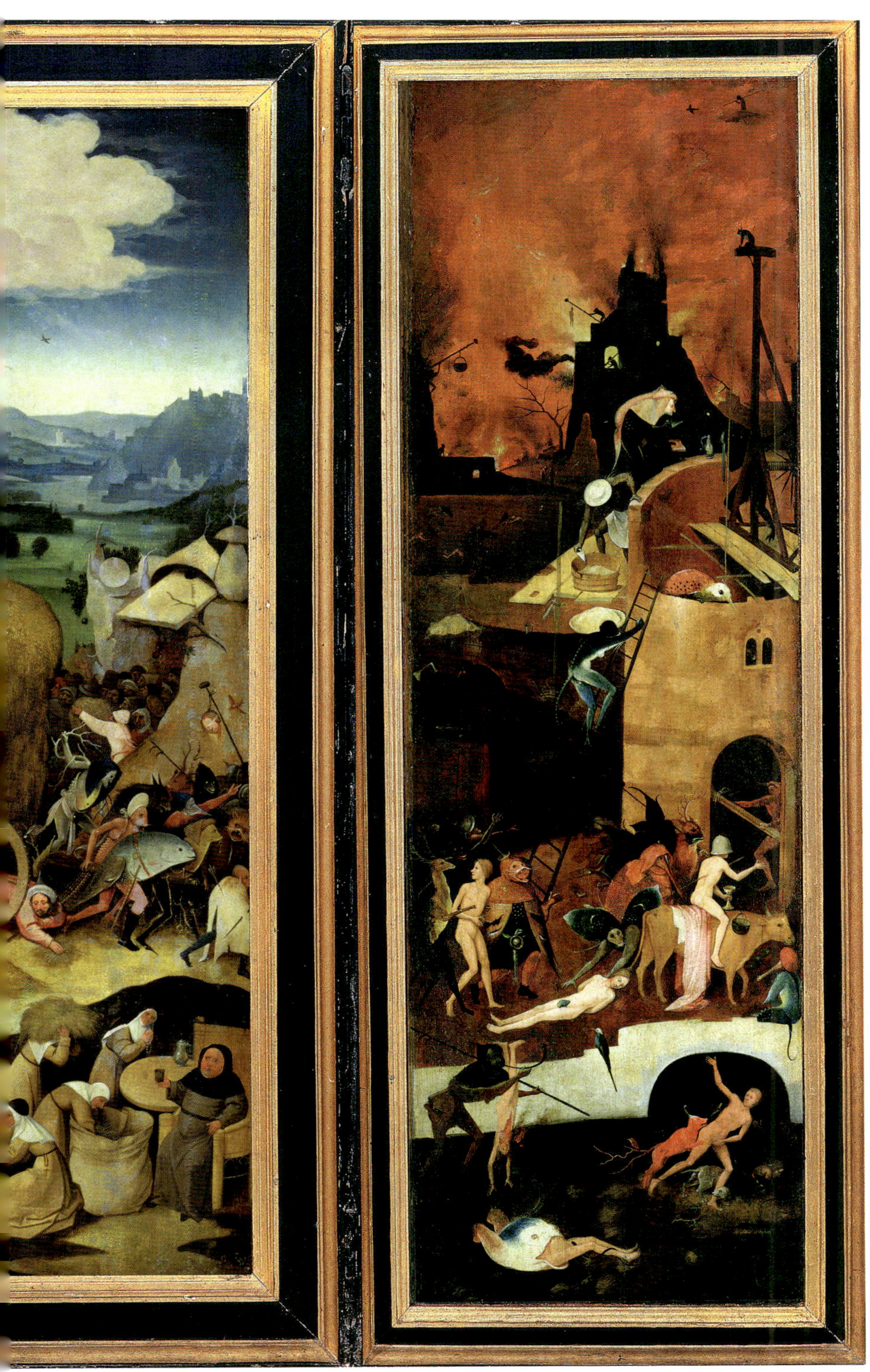

284. Hieronymus Bosch,
c. 1450-1516, Northern Renaissance, Dutch,
The Haywain (triptych), c. 1500.
Oil on panel, 135 x 100 cm.
Museo Nacional del Prado, Madrid.

The central painting, now supposed to be an illustration of the Flemish proverb, "The world is a haystack; everyone takes what he can grab thereof," is dominated by a gigantic hay wagon which, according to Jacques Combe, "evok[es] at the same time the late Gothic motif of the procession of pageant, and the Renaissance Triumph… drawn by semi-human, semi-animal monsters and headed straight for hell, followed by a cavalcade of ecclesiastical and lay dignitaries. From all sides of the wagon men scrabble over one another to pull hay from the giant stack. The only heed they take of their fellows is to thrust them out of their way or to raise hands against them. One sticks a knife into the throat of the unfortunate competitor whom he has pinned to the ground."

Many among the greedy mob wear ecclesiastical garb, indicating Bosch's attitude that the holy as well as profane are involved in this scavenging. A fat monk sits in a large chair and lazily sips a drink while several nuns do service for him, packing bundles of hay into the bag at his feet. One of his nuns turns to the lure of sexual enticement, symbolised by the fool playing a bagpipe, to whom she offers a handful of hay in hopes of winning his favours.

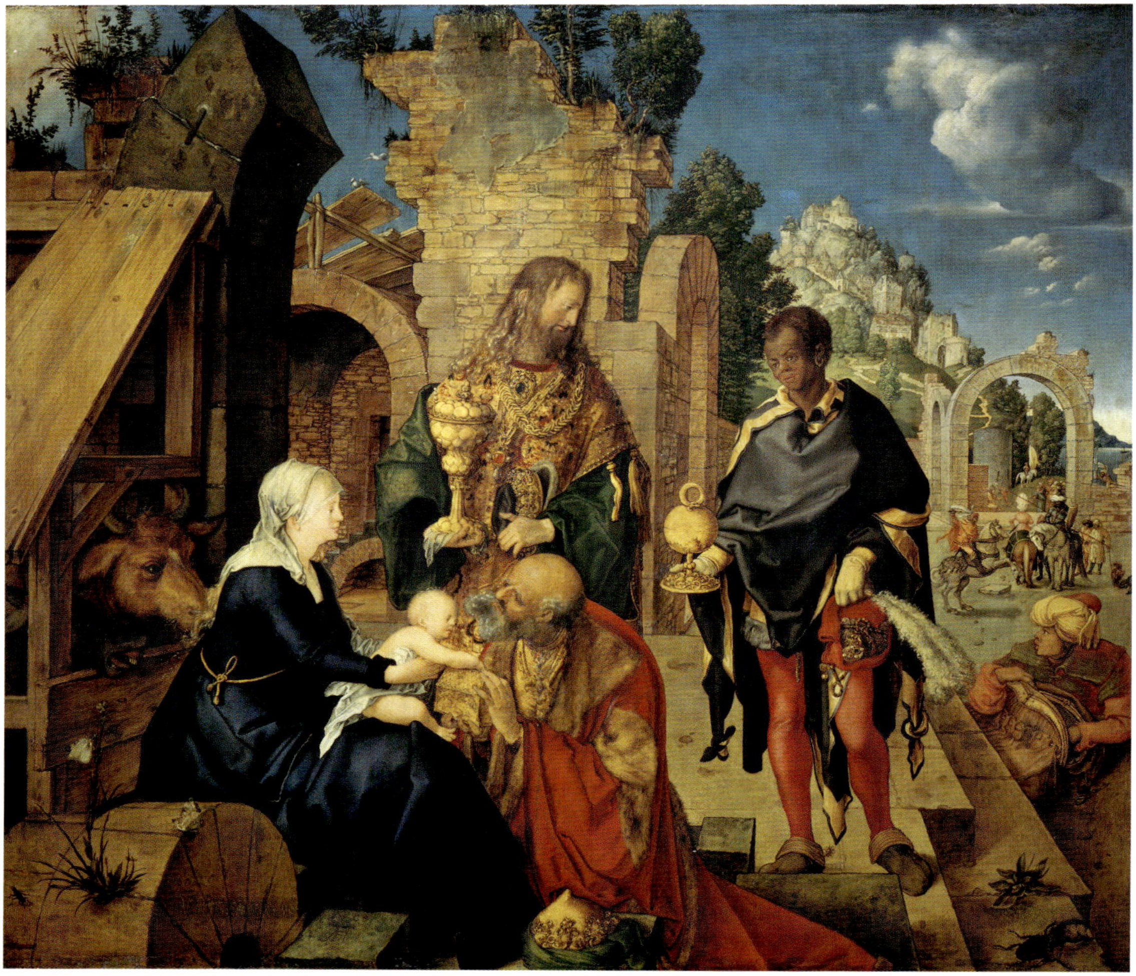

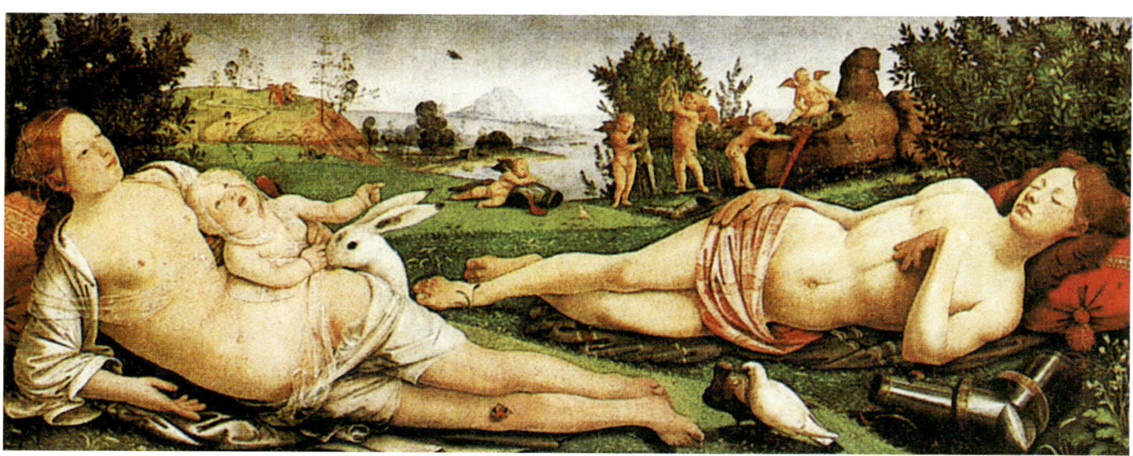

285. **Albrecht Dürer,** 1471-1528, Northern Renaissance, German,
Adoration of the Magi, 1504.
Oil on panel, 98 x 112 cm.
Galleria degli Uffizi, Florence.

286. **Piero di Cosimo**, 1462-1521, High Renaissance, Florentine
School, Italian, *Venus, Mars and Cupid*, c. 1500.
Oil on panel, 72 x 182 cm.
Stiftung Staatliche Museen, Gemäldegalerie, Berlin.

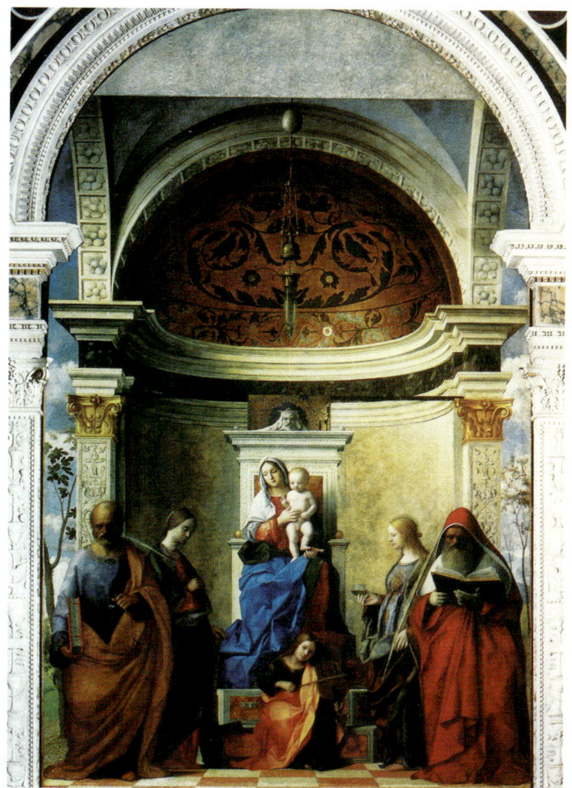

287. **Giovanni Bellini**, c. 1430-1516, Early Renaissance,
Venetian School, Italian,
St Zaccaria Altarpiece, 1505.
Oil on wood, transferred to canvas, 402 x 273 cm.
Church of San Zaccaria, Venice.

*This altarpiece is often considered as the most perfect painting
of sacra conversazione. Bellini brings to life the traditional
figure of the Virgin and saints. Here, the composition of the
painting (an apse surrounding the Madonna and the saints)
becomes the continuation of the altar.*

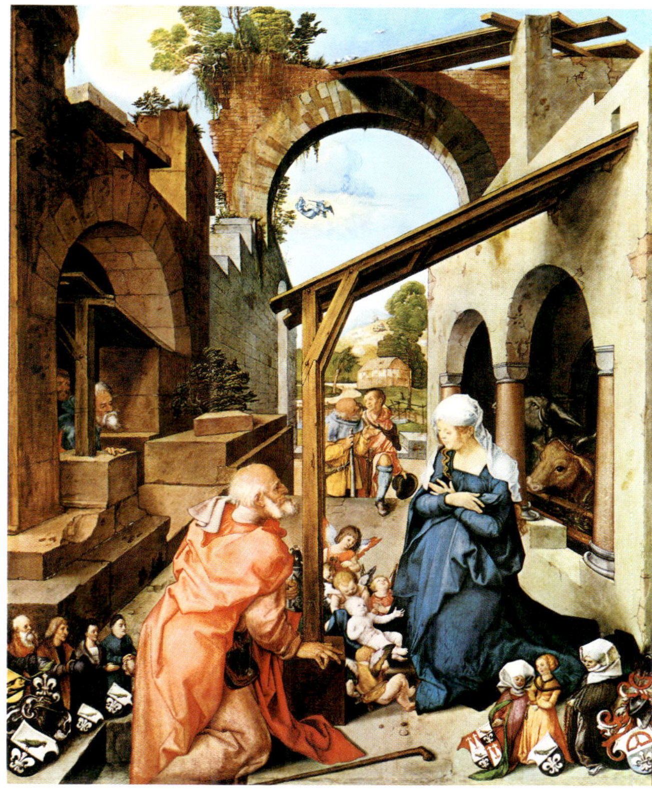

288. **Albrecht Dürer,** 1471-1528, Northern Renaissance, German,
Paumgartner Altar (Middle panel), 1502-1504.
Oil on lime panel, 155 x 126 cm.
Alte Pinakothek, Munich.

*The central panel is conceived in the traditional Gothic style but Dürer
uses perspective with extreme rigour. It depicts a Nativity, set in an
architectural ruin of a palatial building.*

GIOVANNI BELLINI
(1430 – 1516 VENICE)

Giovanni Bellini was the son of Jacopo Bellini, a Venetian painter who was settled in Padua at the
time Giovanni and his elder brother, Gentile, were in their period of studentship. Here, they came
under the influence of Mantegna, who was also bound to them by the ties of relationship, since
he married their sister. To his brother-in-law, Bellini owed much of his knowledge of classical
architecture and perspective, and his broad and sculptural treatment of draperies. Sculpture and the
love of the antique played a large part in Giovanni's early impressions, and left their mark in the
stately dignity of his later style. This developed slowly during his long life. Bellini died of old age,
indeed in his eighty-eighth year, and was buried near his brother, Gentile, in the Church of Ss.
Giovanni e Paulo. Outside, under the spacious vault of heaven, stands the Bartolommeo Colleoni,
Verrocchio's monumental statue, which had been among the elevating influences of Bellini's life
and art. After filling the whole of the north of Italy with his influence, he prepared the way for the
giant colourists of the Venetian School, Giorgione, Titian, and Veronese.

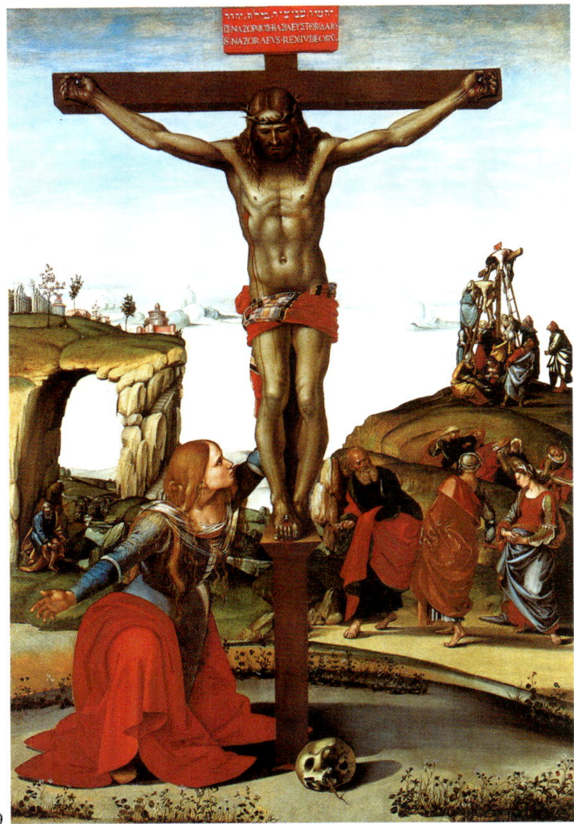
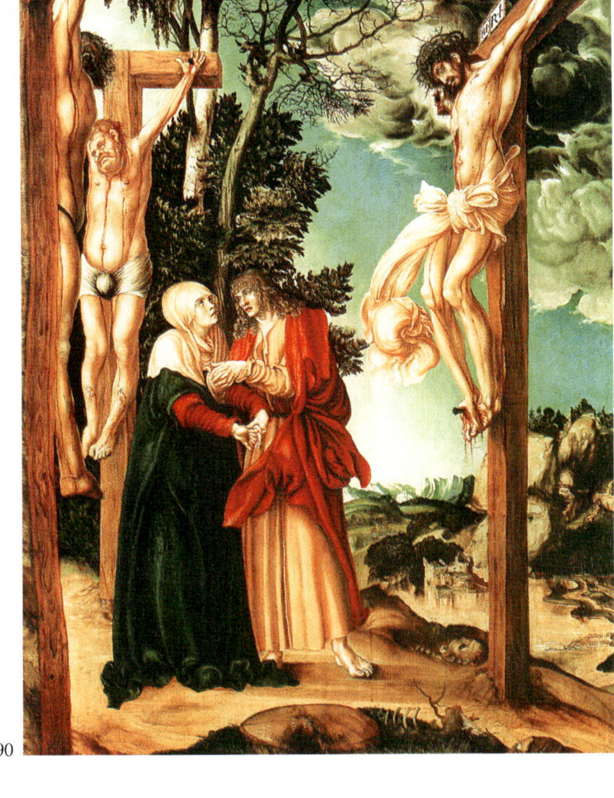

289. **Luca Signorelli,** c. 1445-1523, High Renaissance, Tuscan
School, Italian, *Crucifixion,* c. 1500. Oil on canvas, 247 x 117.5 cm.
Galleria degli Uffizi, Florence.

290. **Lucas Cranach the Elder,** 1472-1553, Northern Renaissance,
German, *The Crucifixion,* 1503.
Oil on pine panel, 138 x 99 cm. Alte Pinakothek, Munich.

The Crucifixion *is a subject derived from an incident described
only by St John. When Christ was hanging on the Cross, he
saw John and Mary standing near, "He said to his mother,
'Woman, behold your son!' Then he said to the disciple,
'Behold, your mother!'" (John 19: 26f). The compositional scheme
of the crucifixion, which was established some 500 years before
Cranach, was symmetrical: Christ on the Cross in the centre,
Mary to the right of him and John to the left, both turned to face
the viewer. This arrangement began to strike Cranach's
contemporaries as too stylised. Cranach moved the Cross from
the centre, presented it side-on, and has the two looking up to
Christ in such a way that the faces of all the figures are visible.
The first hesitant attempt of this kind was made by Albrecht Dürer
in a Crucifixion painted in Nuremberg in 1496 for the chapel of
the Wittenberg castle. It is believed that Cranach adopted the
device from that work.*

LUCA SIGNORELLI
(C. 1445 – 1523 CORTONA)

Signorelli was a painter from Cortona but was active in various cities of central Italy like Florence, Orvieto and Rome. Probably a
pupil of Piero della Francesca, he added solidity to his figures and a unique use of light, as well as having an interest in the
representation of actions like contemporary artists, the Pollaiuolo brothers.

In 1483, he was called to complete the cycle of frescos in the Sistine Chapel in Rome, which means he must have had a solid
reputation at that time. He painted a magnificent series of six frescos illustrating the end of the world and *The Last Judgment* for the
Orvieto Cathedral. There can be seen a wide variety of nudes displayed in multiple poses, which were surpassed at that time only
by Michelangelo, who knew of them. By the end of his career, he had a large workshop in Cortona where he produced conservative
paintings, including numerous altarpieces.

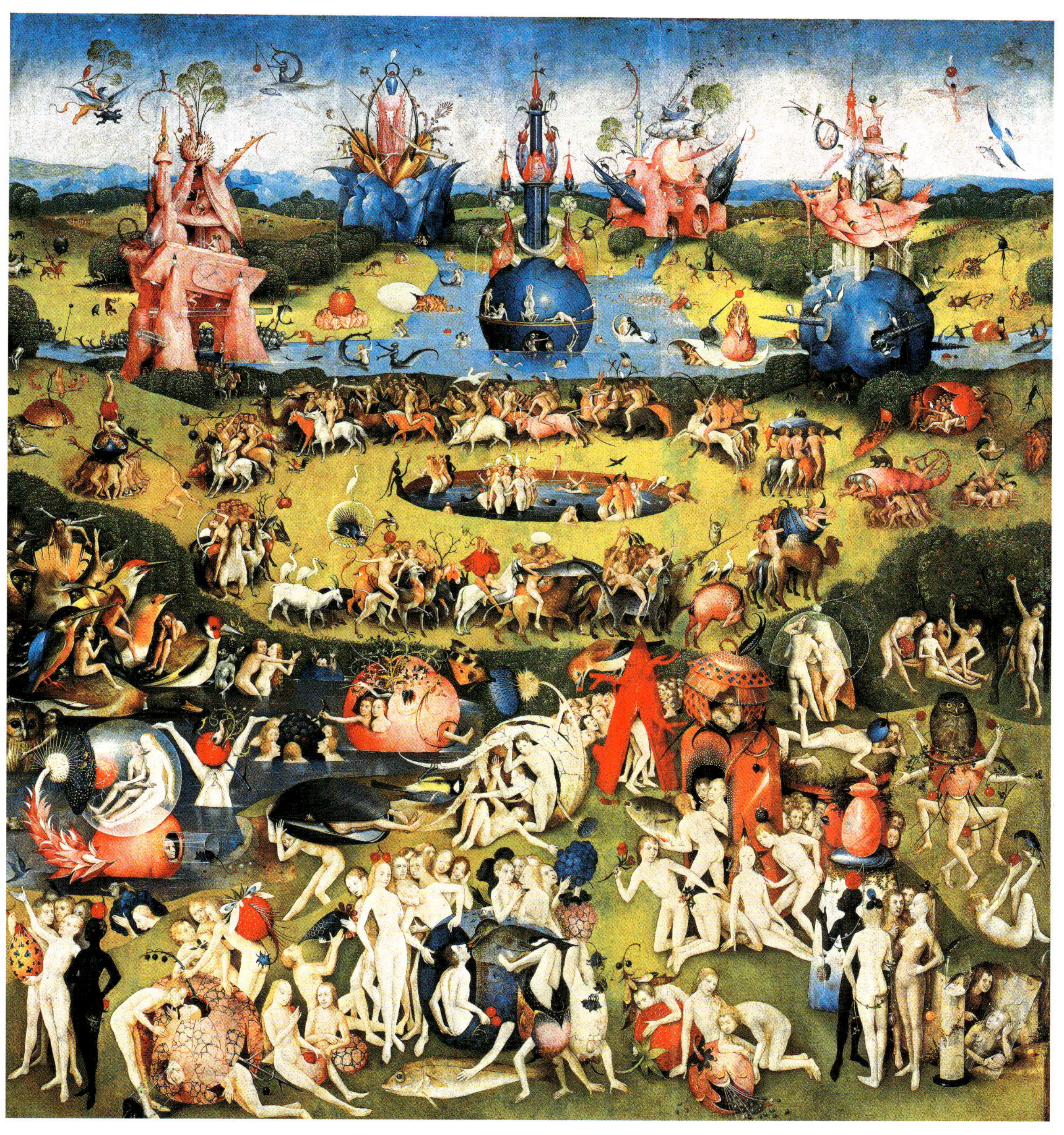

291. **Hieronymus Bosch,** c. 1450-1516, Northern Renaissance, Dutch,
The Garden of Earthly Delights (central panel of the triptych), c. 1504. Oil on panel, 220 x 195 cm. Museo Nacional del Prado, Madrid.

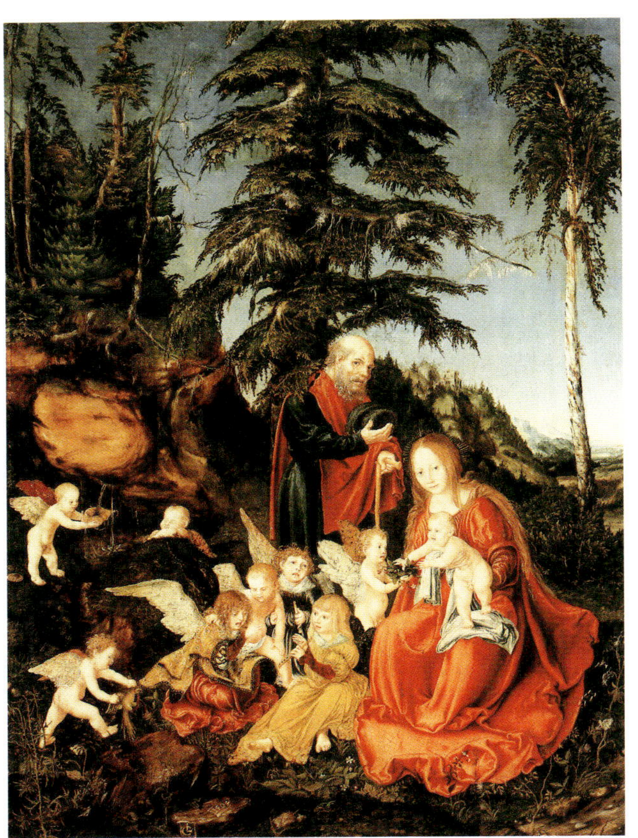

292. **Lucas Cranach the Elder,** 1472-1553,
Northern Renaissance, German,
Rest on the Flight into Egypt, 1504.
Tempera on panel, 69 x 51 cm.
Stiftung Staatliche Museen, Gemäldegalerie, Berlin.

The charming little scene is inscribed in a circle, at the centre of which is the offering of the strawberry. But this cosy little circle is not at all the centre of the painting. Above, on the left and below, it is surrounded by wild nature, and nature in its own way is involved in the concerns of the Holy Family. The clear sky greets them with the smile of the new day. The rising sun imparts a silvery hue to the clumps of grey moss on the branches of a mighty fir-tree which extends protectively towards a melancholy birch that waves its springy branches. The hills, repeating one another, draw the gaze in to the sunny distance, telling Joseph, "Egypt lies there." The earth is glad to offer Mary a soft carpet of grass sprinkled with flowers. The clear stream bending around the meadow becomes a boundary to protect the fugitives from their pursuers. Nobody before Cranach had painted nature so straightforwardly, as if directly from life. Nobody before him had been able to form such an intimate link between nature and scriptural figures. Nobody managed to animate every little detail so that all of them together breathe in unison. It was not pantheistic rationalisation that expressed itself here, but the primitive instinct aroused in Lucas' spirit through contact with his native land.

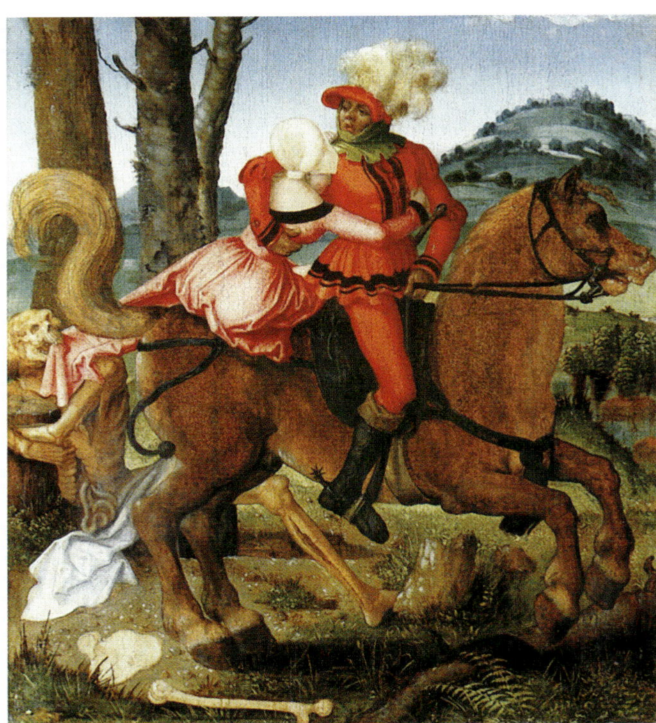

293. **Hans Baldung Grien,** c. 1484-1545,
Northern Renaissance, German,
The Knight, the Young Girl and Death, c. 1505.
Oil on panel, 355 x 296 cm.
Musée du Louvre, Paris.

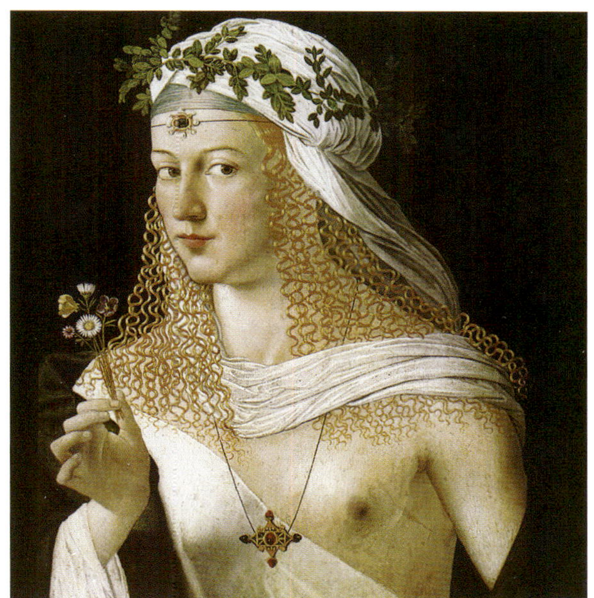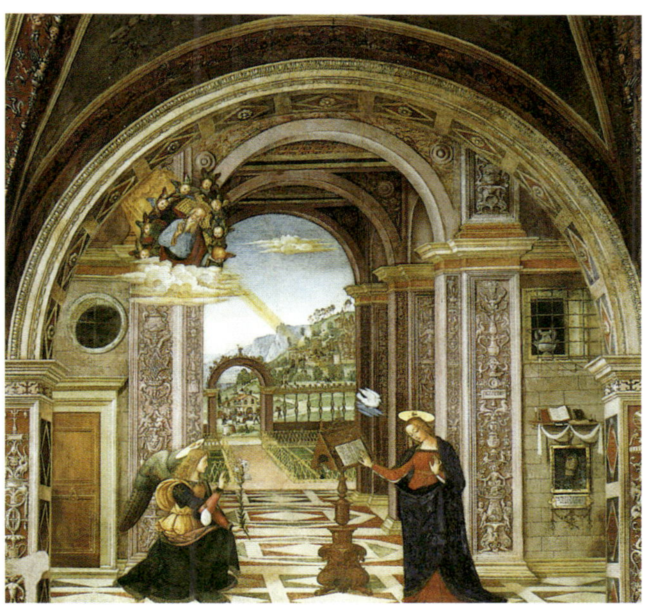

294. **Bartolomeo Veneto,** c. 1502-1555, High Renaissance, Venetian School, Italian, *Portrait of a Woman.* Oil on panel, 43.5 x 34.3 cm. Städelsches Kunstinstitut, Frankfurt.

295. **Bernardino Pinturicchio,** 1454-1513, Early Renaissance, Italian, *Annunciation,* 1501. Fresco. Santa Maria Maggiore, Spello.

296. **Master of the Saint Bartholomew Altar,** active c. 1475-1510, Northern Renaissance, German, *St Bartholomew Altarpiece,* 1505. Oil on panel, 129 x 161 cm (central panel), 129 x 74 cm (side panels). Alte Pinakothek, Munich.

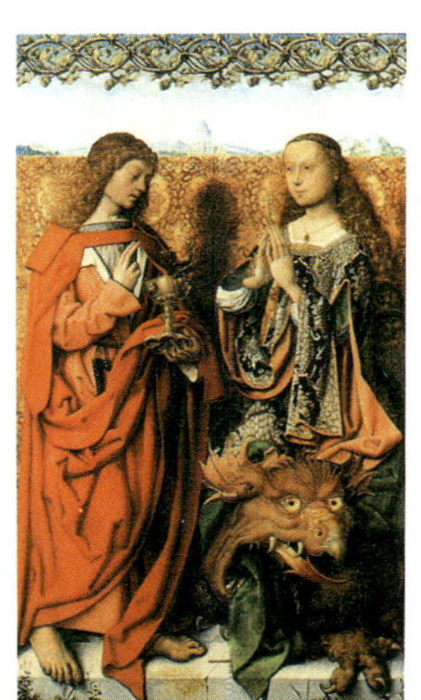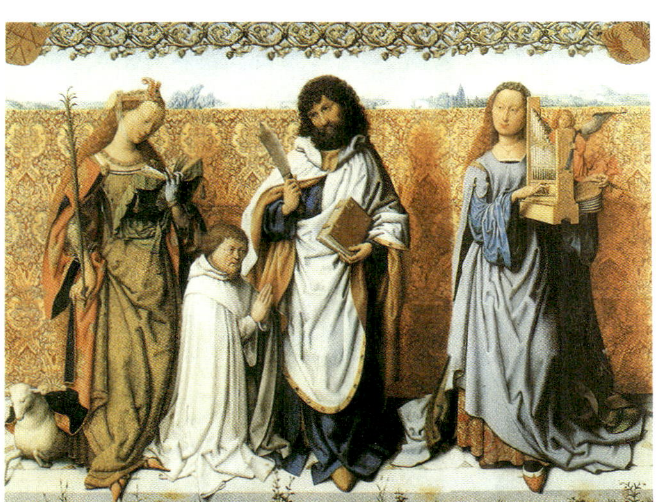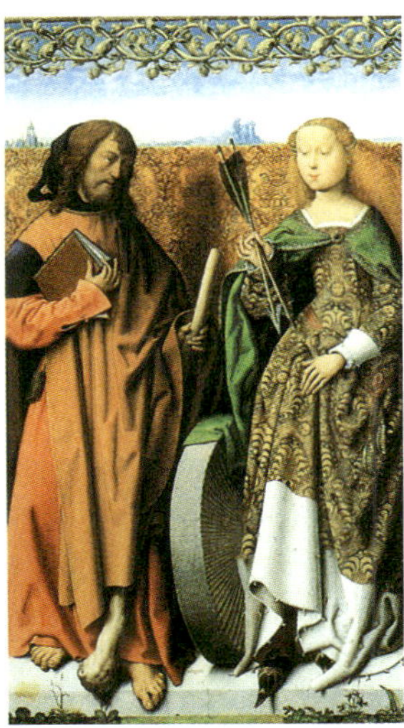

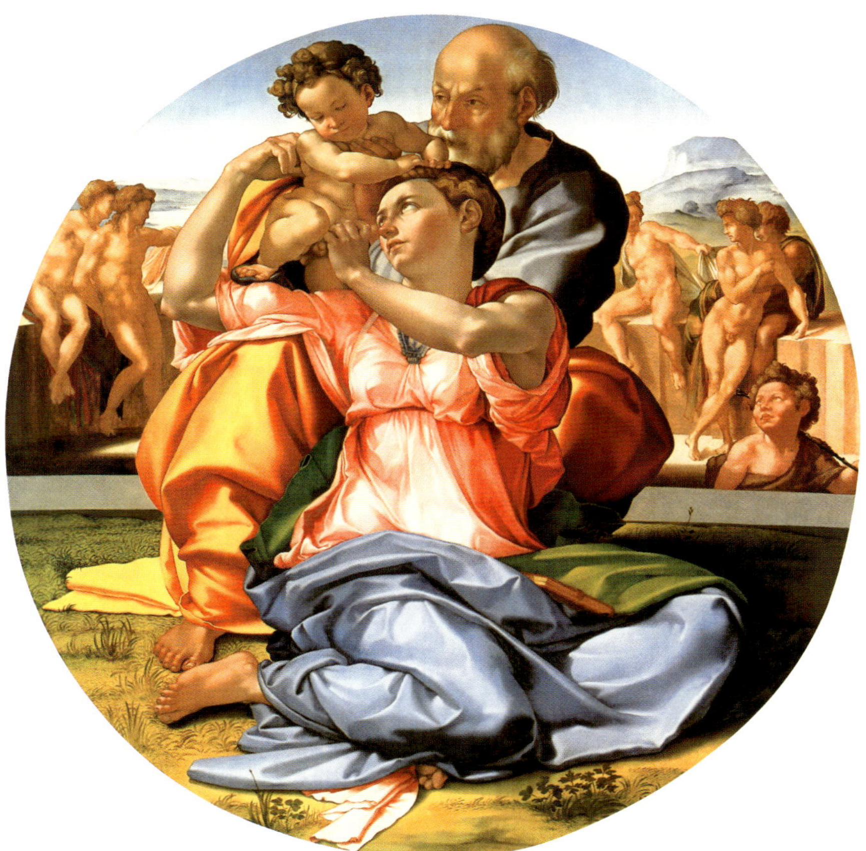

The Holy Family with the Young St John the Baptist, *also called the* Tondo Doni, *was painted by Michelangelo, a commission to celebrate the marriage of Agnolo Doni and Maddalena Strozzi. The fact that this work was not created for a church might explain Michelangelo's apparent freedom to place several young male nudes in the background, behind the little figure of St John. The young, strong and elegantly poised figure of Mary, holding her infant up on her shoulder, is contrasted with the figure of Joseph, who is depicted – as was also customary during medieval times in order to de-emphasise his importance as a father – subject to the ravages of old age. The child, like the mother, is active and full of life. This is another work in which Mary and Jesus appear to be fully human.*

MICHELANGELO BUONARROTI
(1475 CAPRESE – 1564 ROME)

Michelangelo, like Leonardo, was a man of many talents; sculptor, architect, painter and poet, he made the apotheosis of muscular movement, which to him was the physical manifestation of passion. He moulded his draughtsmanship, bent it, twisted it, and stretched it to the extreme limits of possibility. There are not any landscapes in Michelangelo's painting. All the emotions, all the passions, all the thoughts of humanity were personified in his eyes in the naked bodies of men and women. He rarely conceived his human forms in attitudes of immobility or repose.

Michelangelo became a painter so that he could express in a more malleable material what his titanesque soul felt, what his sculptor's imagination saw, but what sculpture refused him. Thus this admirable sculptor became the creator, at the Vatican, of the most lyrical and epic decoration ever seen: the Sistine Chapel. The profusion of his invention is spread over this vast area of over 900 square metres. There are 343 principal figures of prodigious variety of expression, many of colossal size, and in addition a great number of subsidiary ones introduced for decorative effect. The creator of this vast scheme was only thirty-four when he began his work.

Michelangelo compels us to enlarge our conception of what is beautiful. To the Greeks it was physical perfection; but Michelangelo cared little for physical beauty, except in a few instances, such as his painting of *Adam* on the Sistine ceiling, and his sculptures of the Pietà. Though a master of anatomy and of the laws of composition, he dared to disregard both if it were necessary to express his concept: to exaggerate the muscles of his figures, and even put them in positions the human body could not naturally assume. In his later painting, *The Last Judgment* on the end wall of the Sistine, he poured out his soul like a torrent.

Michelangelo was the first to make the human form express a variety of emotions. In his hands emotion became an instrument upon which he played, extracting themes and harmonies of infinite variety. His figures carry our imagination far beyond the personal meaning of the names attached to them.

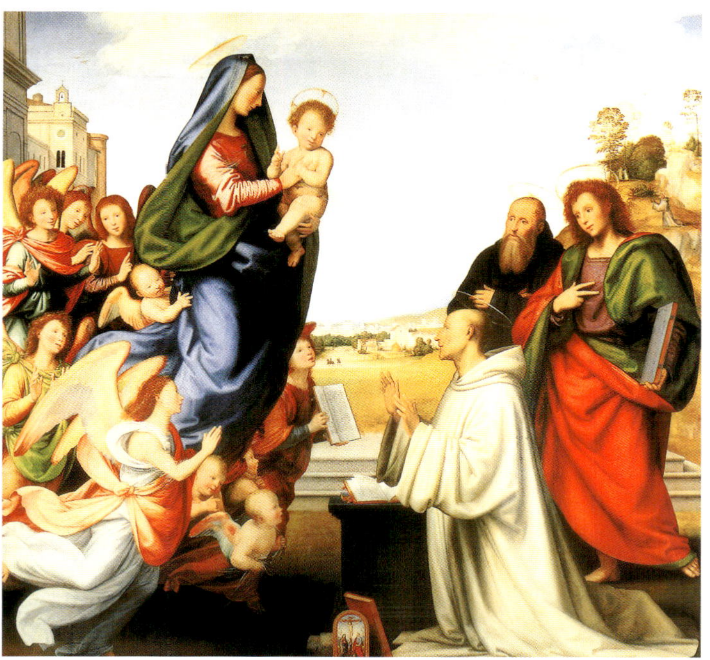

298

298. **Fra Bartolomeo,** 1473-1517, High Renaissance,
Florentine School, Italian, *Vision of St Bernard*, c. 1505.
Oil on panel, 220 x 213 cm.
Galleria dell'Accademia, Florence.

*Key figure of the cinquecento, Bartolomeo sums up in his
works the contradictions existing in Florence between
Raphael's style and the early Mannerism.*

299. **Raphael (Raffaello Sanzio),** 1483-1520,
High Renaissance, Florentine School, Italian,
The Madonna of the Goldfinch, 1506.
Oil on panel, 107 x 77.2 cm.
Galleria degli Uffizi, Florence.

The patron who commissioned the Madonna of the
Goldfinch *– a man called Lorenzo Nasi – was a wealthy
merchant, and the painting commemorated his wedding
to Sandra Canigiani. Raphael painted the figure of the
Madonna in the centre, using the standard pyramidal
design for the composition. In her left hand Mary holds
a book, while her right arm encloses the child Jesus,
whose small hands enfold the goldfinch. The infant St John
endeavours to caress the bird. The figures are idealised,
and both Mary and Jesus have barely visible haloes over
their heads, rendered in perspective, in order not to disturb
the realism of the style employed. A panoramic landscape
opens up the background to a considerable depth.*

299

RAPHAEL (RAFFAELLO SANZIO)
(1483 URBINO – 1520 ROME)

Raphael was the artist who most closely resembled
Pheidias. The Greeks said that the latter invented
nothing; rather, he carried every kind of art invented by
his forerunners to such a pitch of perfection that he
achieved pure and perfect harmony. Those words, "pure
and perfect harmony," express, in fact, better than any
others what Raphael brought to Italian art. From
Perugino, he gathered all the weak grace and gentility of
the Umbrian School, he acquired strength and certainty
in Florence, and he created a style based on the fusion
of Leonardo's and Michelangelo's lessons under the light
of his own noble spirit.

His compositions on the traditional theme of the Virgin
and Child seemed intensely novel to his contemporaries,
and only their time-honoured glory prevents us now
from perceiving their originality. He has an even more
magnificent claim in the composition and realisation of
those frescos with which, from 1509, he adorned the
Stanze and the Loggia at the Vatican. The sublime, which
Michelangelo attained by his ardour and passion, Raphael
attained by the sovereign balance of intelligence and
sensibility. One of his masterpieces, *The School of Athens*,
(fig. 308), was created by genius: the multiple detail, the
portrait heads, the suppleness of gesture, the ease of
composition, the life circulating everywhere within the
light are his most admirable and identifiable traits.

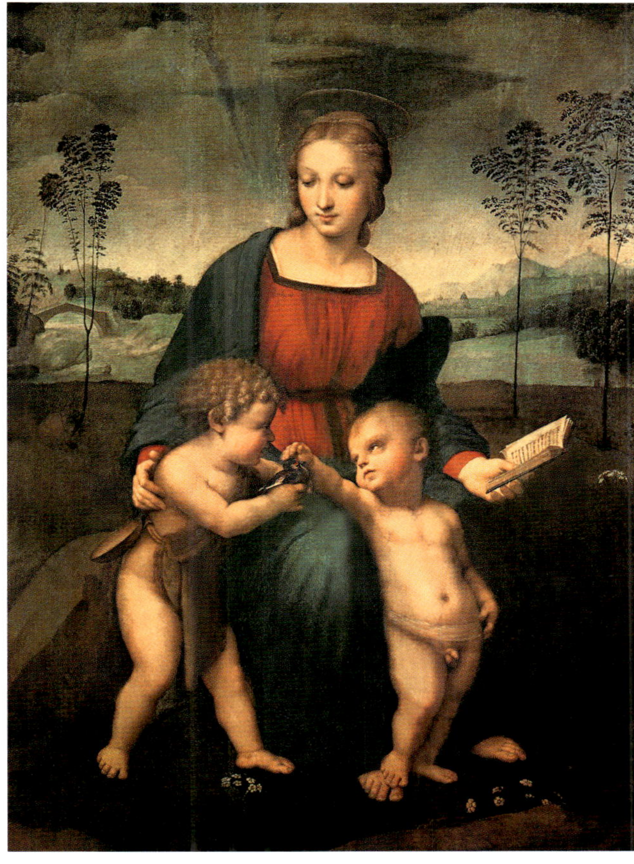

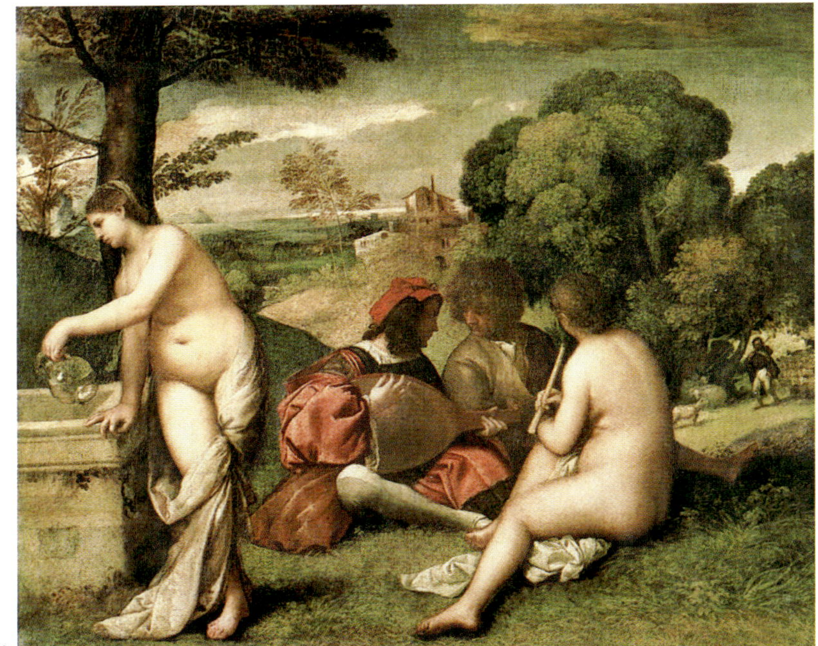

300

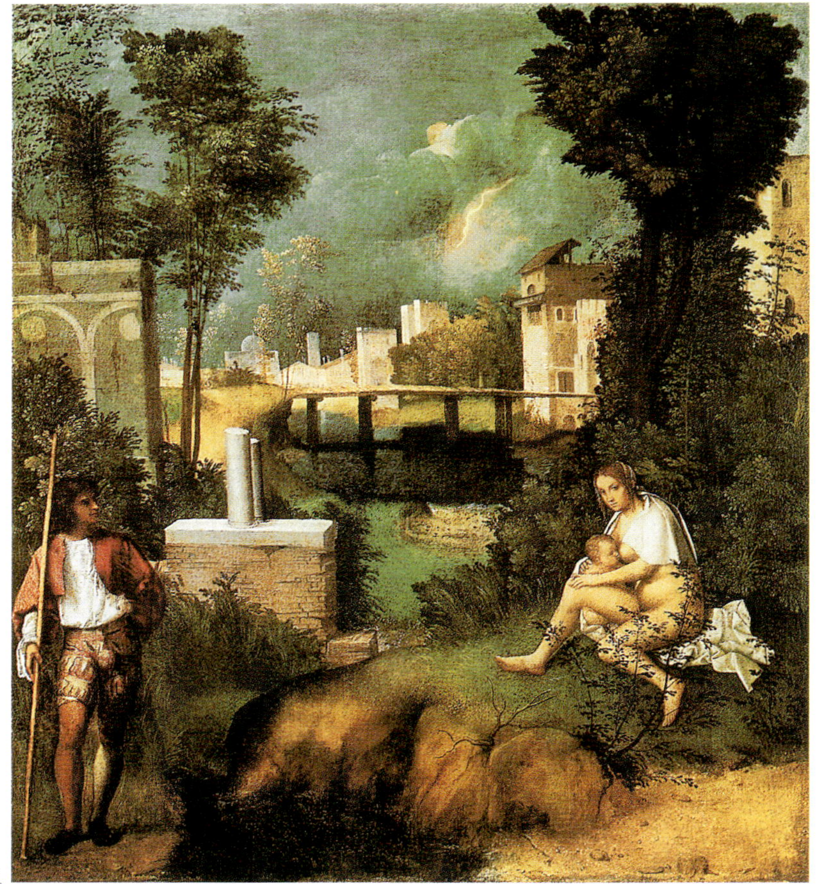

301

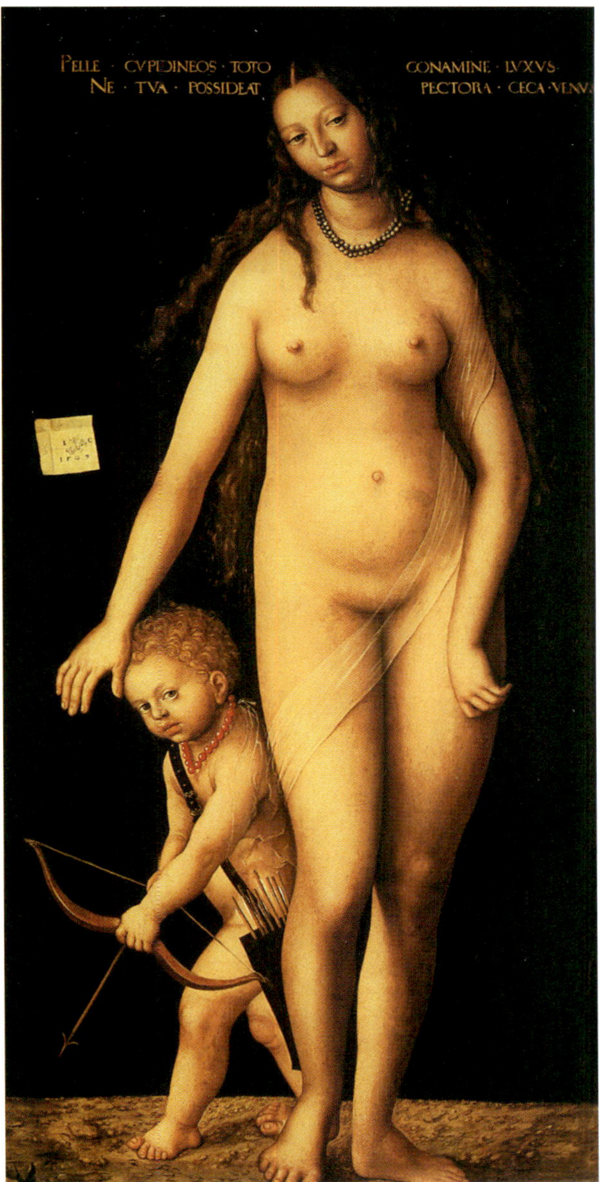

302

302. **Lucas Cranach the Elder,** 1472-1553, Northern Renaissance, German, *Venus and Cupid*, 1509.
Oil on canvas transferred from wood, 213 x 102 cm.
The State Hermitage Museum, St Petersburg.

This is the earliest depiction of Venus in northern Europe and Cranach's first work on a theme taken from classical mythology.

303. **Albrecht Dürer,** 1471-1528, Northern Renaissance, German, *Adam and Eve*, 1507.
Oil on panel, 209 x 81 cm and 209 x 83 cm.
Museo Nacional del Prado, Madrid.

The rules of proportion concerning the human body were a persistent theme in Dürer's oeuvre. His early efforts produced stiff postures, but he found how to keep the overall appearance beautiful and graceful. He hangs a plaque with an inscription and his unique logo signature on the tree, as he did in a similar signature statement on the wall in his 1498 self-portrait (fig. 281). Eve's disposition seems coquettish, which would be appropriate for the traditional interpretation of the Genesis story. Adam's expression might reflect his confused interest.

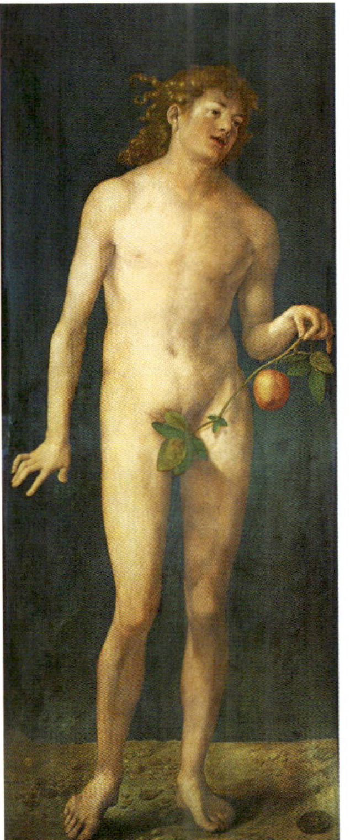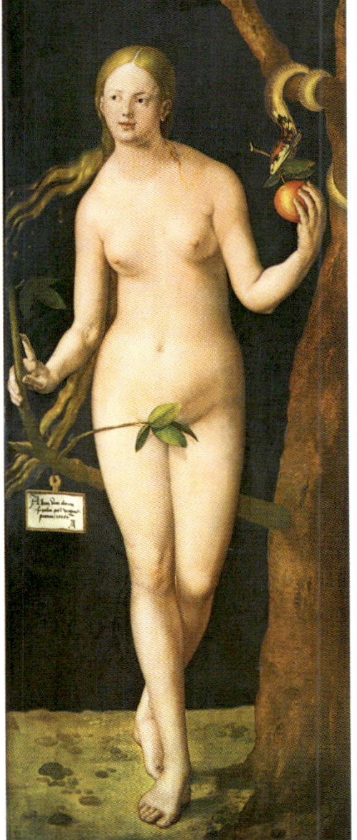

303

300. **Giorgione (Giorgio Barbarelli da Castelfranco),** 1477-1510, Early Renaissance, Venetian School, Italian,
The Pastoral Concert, c. 1508.
Oil on canvas, 109 x 137 cm.
Musée du Louvre, Paris.

301. **Giorgione (Giorgio Barbarelli da Castelfranco),** 1477-1510, Early Renaissance, Venetian School, Italian,
The Tempest, c. 1507,
Oil on canvas, 82 x 73 cm.
Galleria dell'Accademia, Venice.

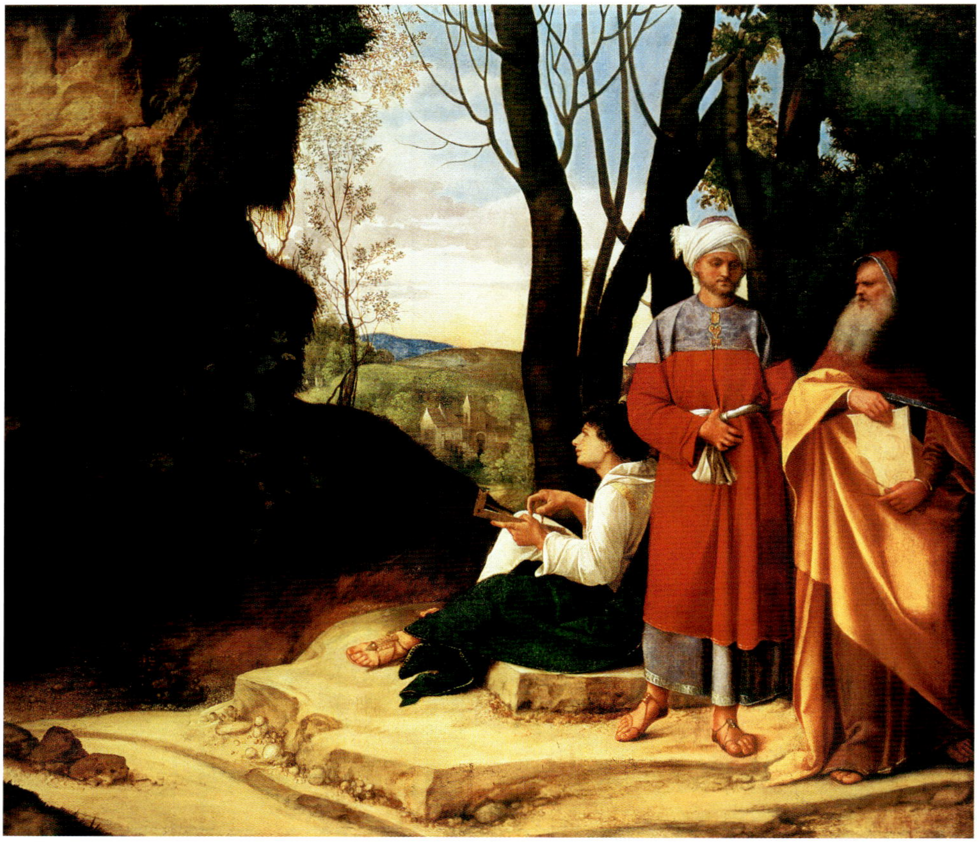

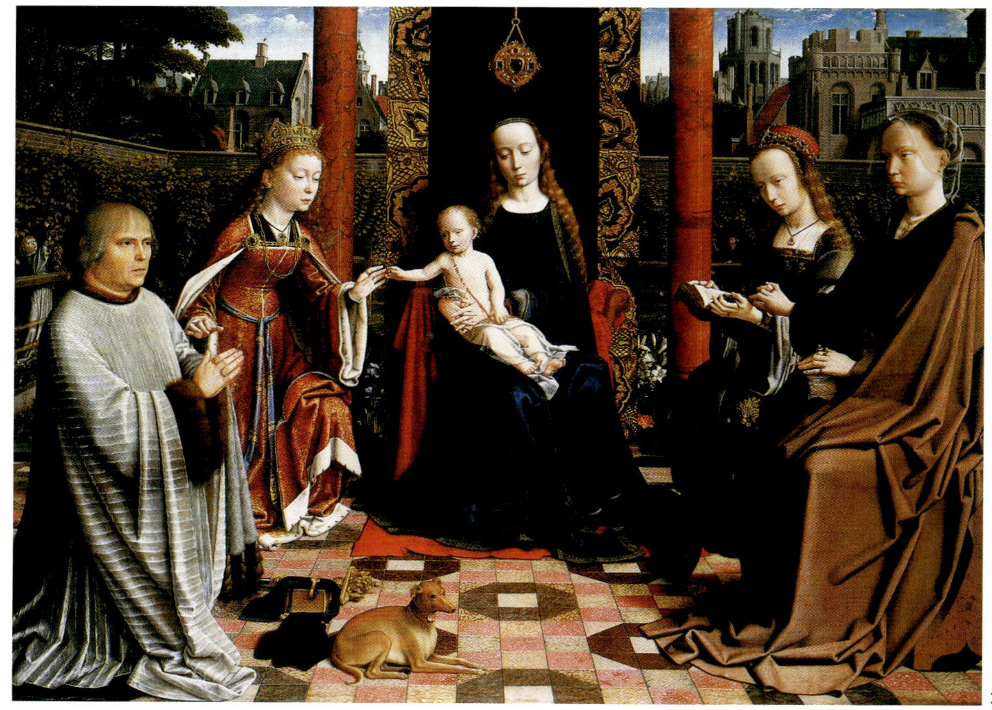

304

305

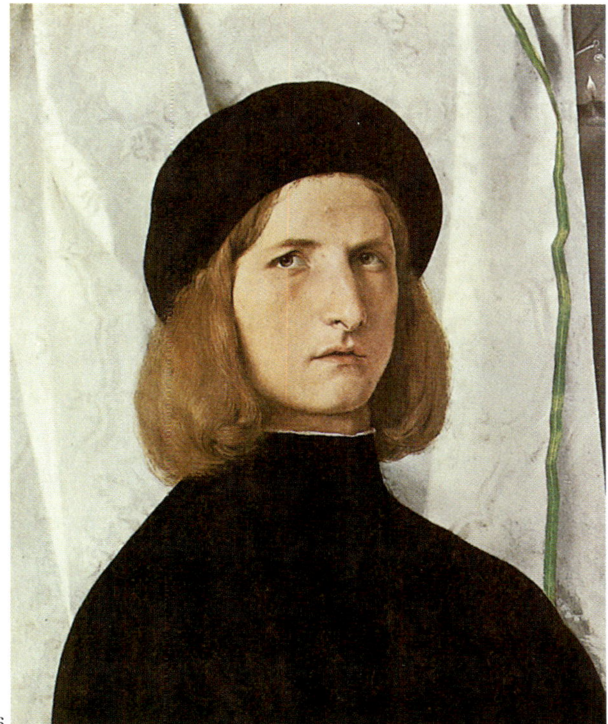

306

LORENZO LOTTO
(1480 VENICE – 1556 LORETO)

Lotto trained in the studio of Giovanni Bellini with Giorgione and Titian. He worked in many cities apart from Venice, and ended his life blind in a monastery. Known for his portraits, he actually worked mainly as a religious painter. His work, extremely erratic, shows a variety of influences from Italy as well as northern Europe, but also an acute sense of observation and freshness that is atypical of central Venetian tradition.

304. **Giorgione (Giorgio Barbarelli da Castelfranco),** 1477-1510, Early Renaissance, Venetian School, Italian, *The Three Philosophers,* 1508-1509. Oil on canvas, 123.5 x 144.5 cm. Kunsthistorisches Museum, Vienna.

Characteristic in its style of Giorgione's use of light to create mood, The Three Philosophers *illustrates the "figure in landscape" painting initiated by the artist.*

305. **Gérard David,** 1460-1523, Northern Renaissance, Flemish, *The Virgin and Child with Saints and Donor,* 1505-1510. Oil on oak panel, 105.8 x 144.4 cm. National Gallery, London.

Gérard David was a pupil of Vien, who considered him the reformer of the French School. In this painting, the Virgin is surrounded by Saint Barbara, Mary Magdalene and Saint Catherine. The kneeling figure is Richard de Visch van der Capelle, the commissioner of the painting.

306. **Lorenzo Lotto,** 1480-1556, High Renaissance, Venetian School, Italian, *Portrait of a Youth Against a White Curtain,* c. 1508. Oil on panel, 42.3 x 35.5 cm. Kunsthistorisches Museum, Vienna.

One of Lotto's early paintings, it is still influenced by the artist's teacher, Giovanni Bellini, especially in the use of light. Lotto painted this portrait with a great realism, capturing the individual character of the sitter.

307. **Michelangelo Buonarroti,** 1475-1564, High Renaissance, Florence, Italian, *Delphic Sibyl,* 1508-1512. Fresco, 350 x 380 cm. Musei Vaticani, Sistine Chapel, Vatican.

Art historian Germain Bazin compared the face of Michelangelo's Delphic Sibyl *(1511) to the face of Carlo Crivelli's* Madonna della Candeletta *(1488), and Raphael's* Madonna del Granduca *(1505). He demonstrated the breakthrough importance of this detailed figure from the Sistine Chapel ceiling. While the three works might be less than two decades apart, as Bazin points out, "The clear-cut draughtsmanship of the fifteenth century seeks precision of structure; whereas the sixteenth century painter smoothes out all the outlines of his modelling by gentle transitions. Raphael sacrifices expression to harmony, while Michelangelo achieves a synthesis of conflicting elements." (Germain Bazin,* History of Art from Prehistoric Times to the Present, *Houghton Mifflin, 1959, p. 243).*

307

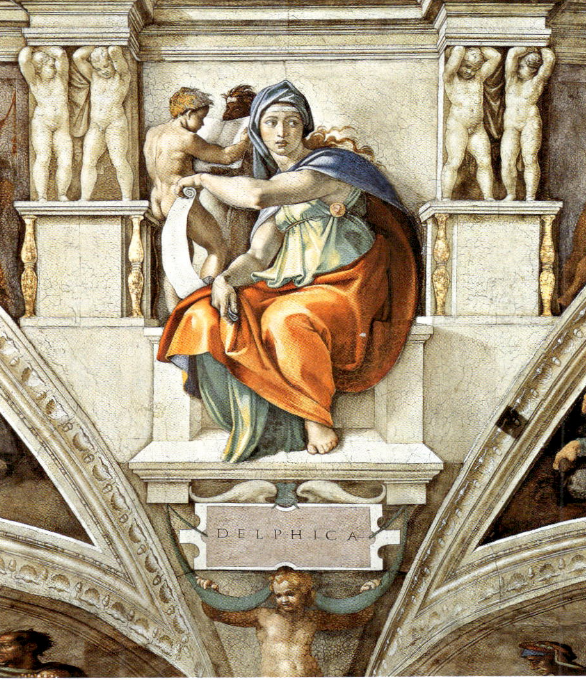

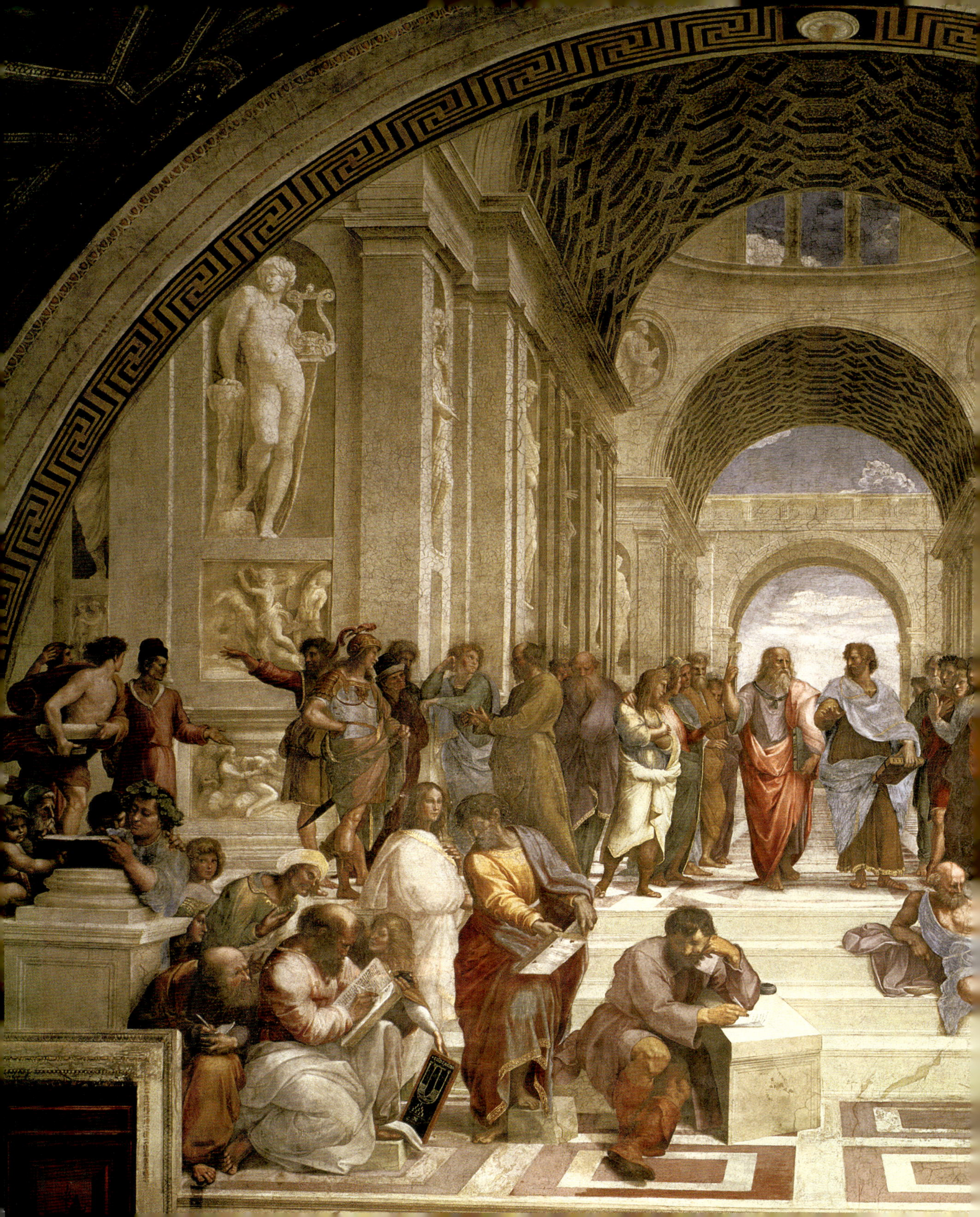

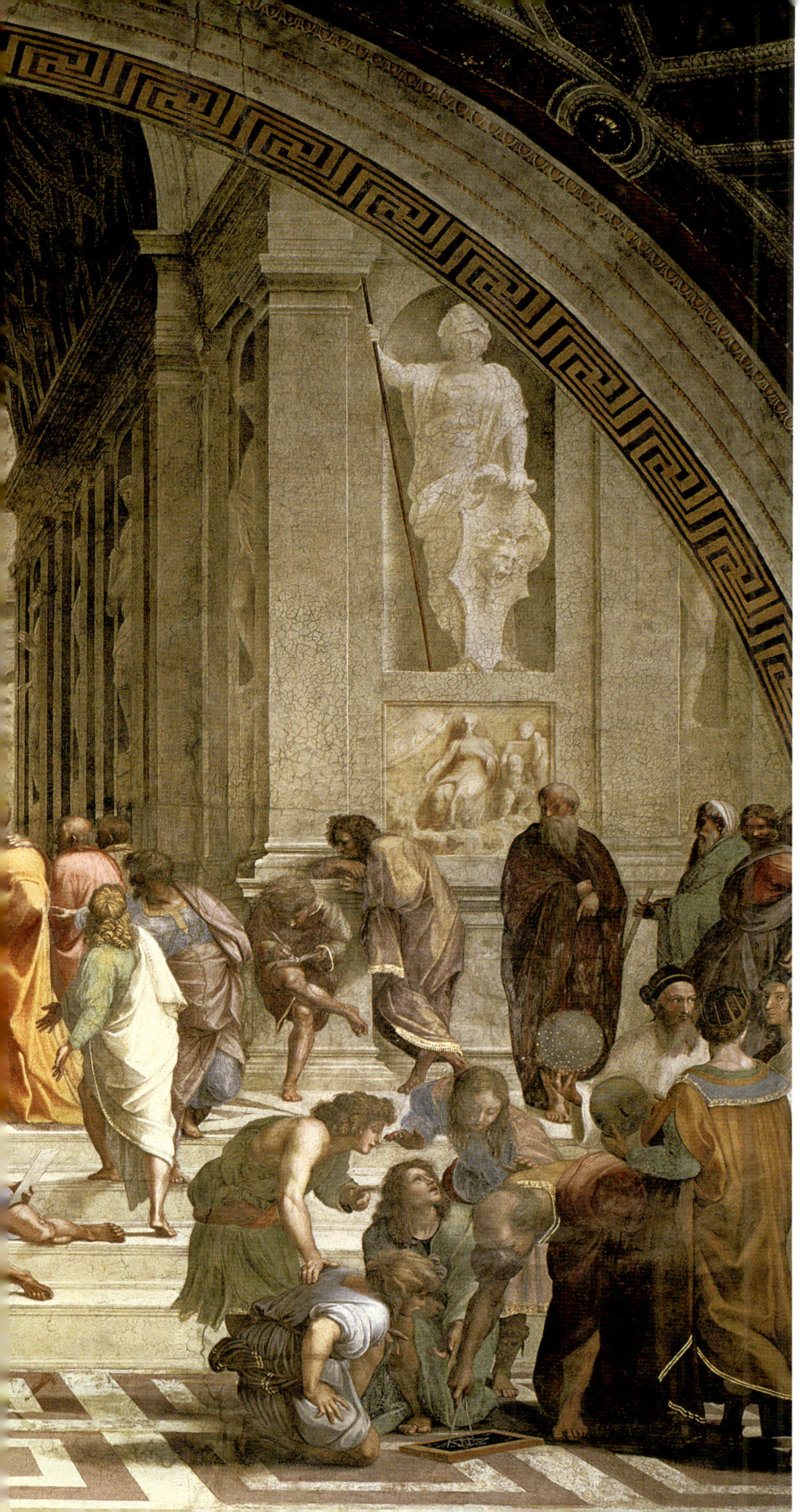

308. Raphael (Raffaello Sanzio),
1483-1520, High Renaissance,
Florentine School, Italian,
The School of Athens, 1509-1510,
Fresco width at the base 770 cm.
Stanza della Segnatura, Vatican.

Alleged pupil of Perugino, Raphael worked in Florence from 1504 to 1508, until he was called to Rome by Julius II. The Pope encircled himself with artists and wanted to raise Rome as the capital city of the Christian world: Bramante constructed a basilica, Michelangelo was working on the ceiling of the Sistine Chapel and Raphael worked on the decoration of the Vatican rooms until his death in 1520.

In The School of Athens, *Raphael used painted architecture to share out the groups of characters in space and distribute the light. He used construction motifs from the end the Roman Empire that also inspired Bramante in the construction of St Peter's Basilica. In the iconography, he included the idea of the "Temple of Philosophy" launched by the Tuscan humanist, Marsile Ficin. The light is depicted in a very realistic way, the colours are bright and the white is dominant: in* The School of Athens, *this is the light that brings knowledge. The composition is set around two central characters: Plato, holding the Time in one hand and pointing to the sky with the other hand, and Aristotle, holding the Ethic and a hand turned toward the earth. Raphael gives great importance to the groups of characters, each group a pretext depicting expressive, theatrical attitudes characteristic of Raphael's works.*

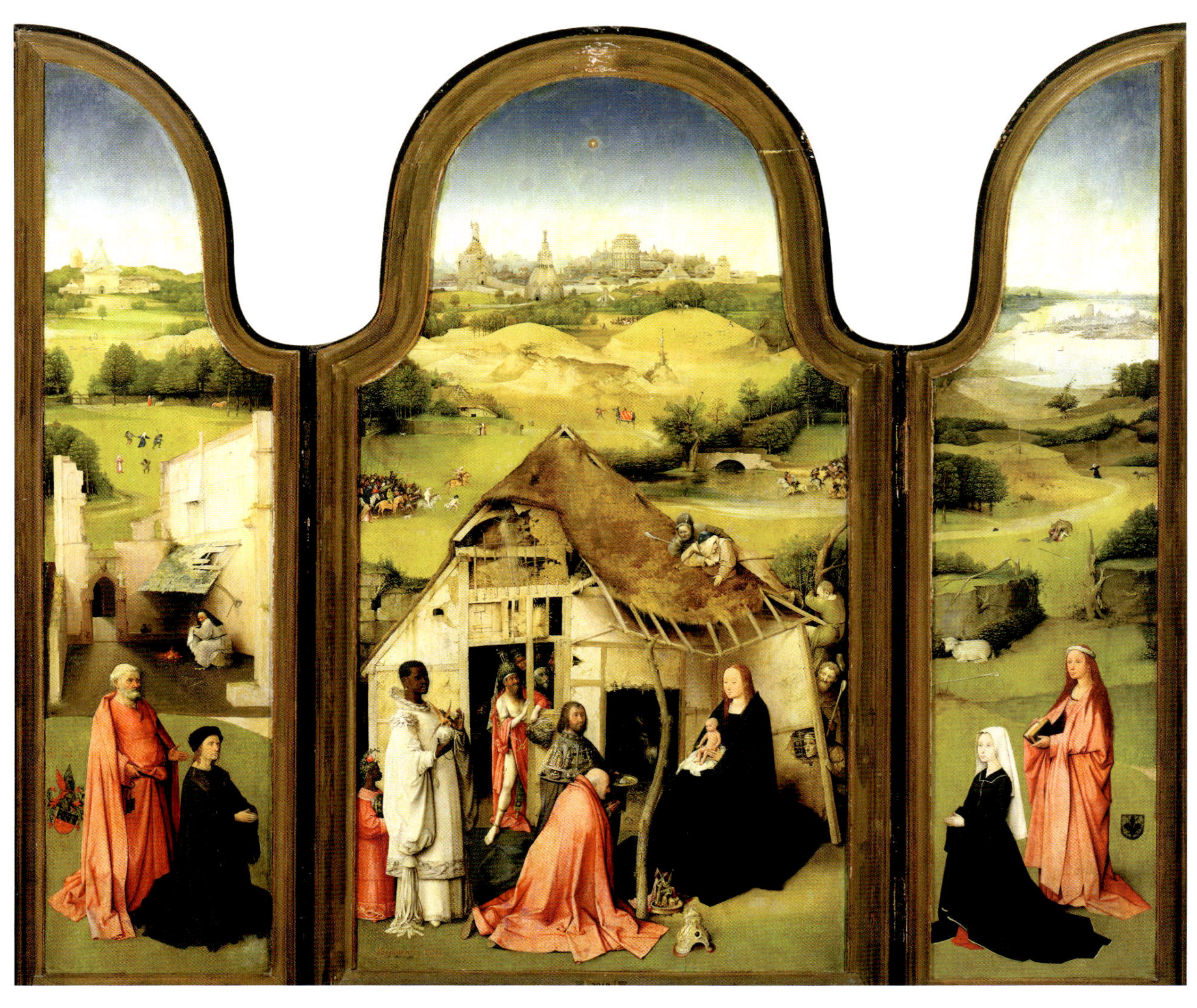

309. **Hieronymus Bosch**, *Adoration of the Magi*, c. 1510.
Oil on wood, 138 x 138 cm.
Museo Nacional del Prado, Madrid.

HIERONYMUS BOSCH
(C. 1450 – 1516 'S-HERTOGENBOSCH)

Born in the middle of the century, Bosch experienced the drama of the highly charged Renaissance and its wars of religion. Medieval traditions and values were crumbling, paving the way to thrust humankind into a new universe where faith lost some of its power and much of its magic. His favourite allegories were hell, heaven and lust. He believed that everyone had to choose between one of two options: heaven or hell. Bosch brilliantly exploited the symbolism of a wide range of fruit and plants to lend sexual overtones to his themes.

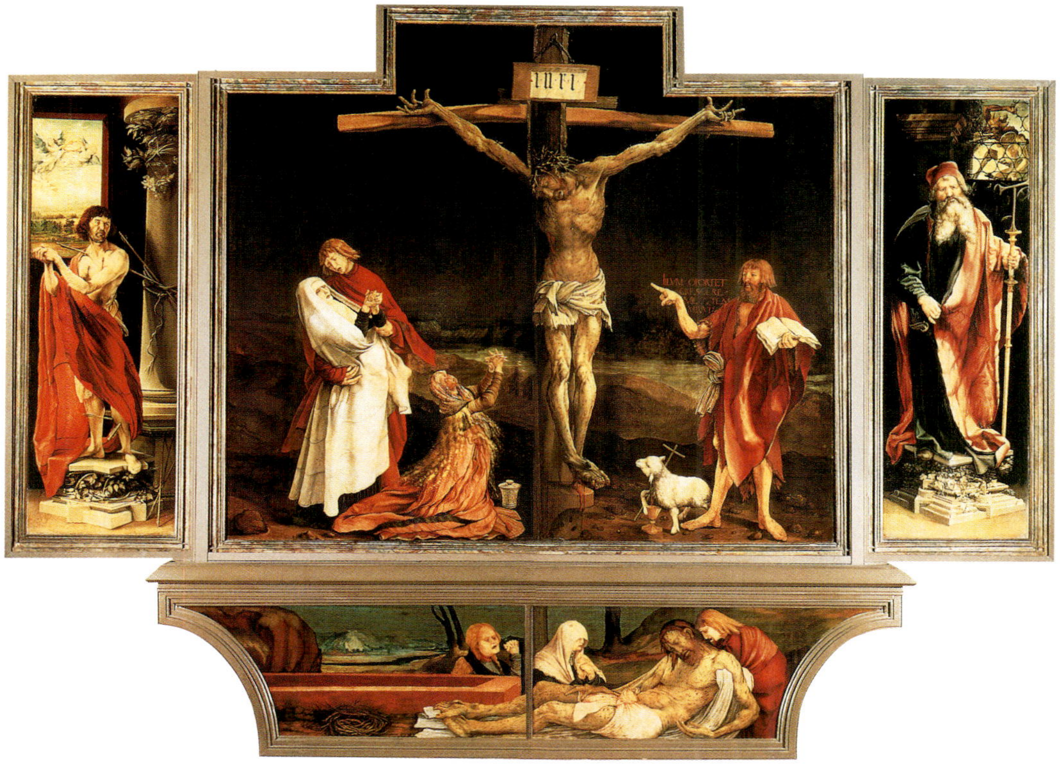

310. **Matthias Grünewald,** c. 1475-1528, Northern Renaissance,
German, *Isenheim Altarpiece,* closed: *Crucifixion,* 1515.
Oil on wood, 269 x 307 cm. Musée d'Unterlinden, Colmar.

Realism is expressed in the mutilated body of Jesus, but the work is symbolic, thematically expressed in the words of John the Baptist displayed next to his figure, "He must increase; I must decrease." As in many Byzantine icons, the size of each person in the scene is relative to the person's importance, from Jesus down to the smallest, Mary Magdalene, who kneels at the base of the cross. The expressive hands of each subject point toward realism. However, the work might be the last of the famous medieval altarpieces to

retain characteristic Gothic elements. In the foreground, the Agnus Dei pours its blood into the chalice of life-giving salvation.

The characters' dramatic expressions and the colours (black and red) arouse devotion; borrowings from Masaccio and Gossaert. Mary is shown as a co-redemptor: she seems as vivid as her son, and wears, like him, white robes.

Saint Anthony, attacked by a monster and Saint Sebastian, pierced with arrows, stand on each side of the Crucifixion.

MATTHIAS GRÜNEWALD
(C. 1475 WÜRZBURG – 1528 HALLE AN DER SAALE)

Grünewald and Dürer were the most prominent artists of their era. Painter, draughtsman, hydraulic engineer and architect, he is considered the greatest colourist of the German Renaissance. But, unlike Dürer, he did not make prints and his works were not numerous: ten or so paintings (some of which are composed of several panels) and approximately thirty-five drawings. His masterpiece is the *Isenheim Altarpiece,* commissioned in 1515.

His works show a dedication to medieval principles, to which he brought expressions of emotion not typical of his contemporaries.

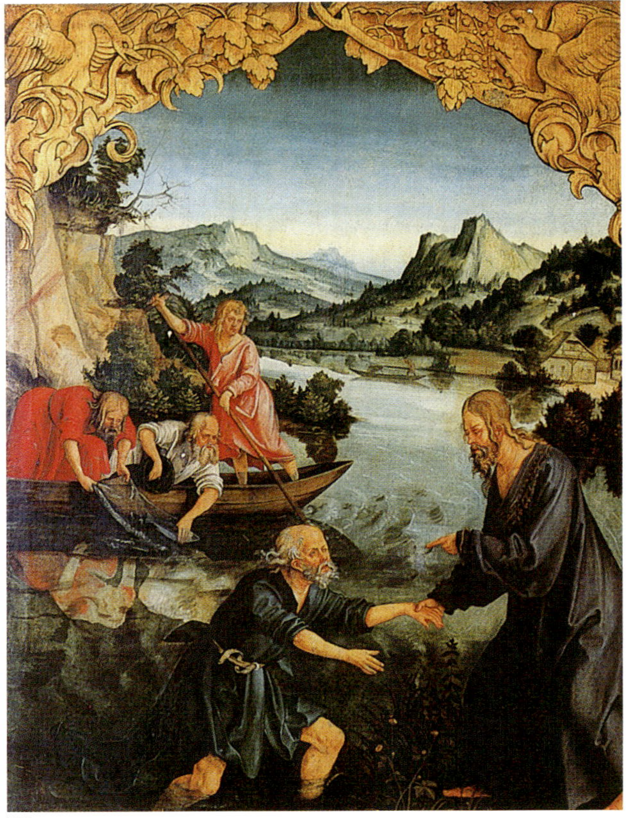

311

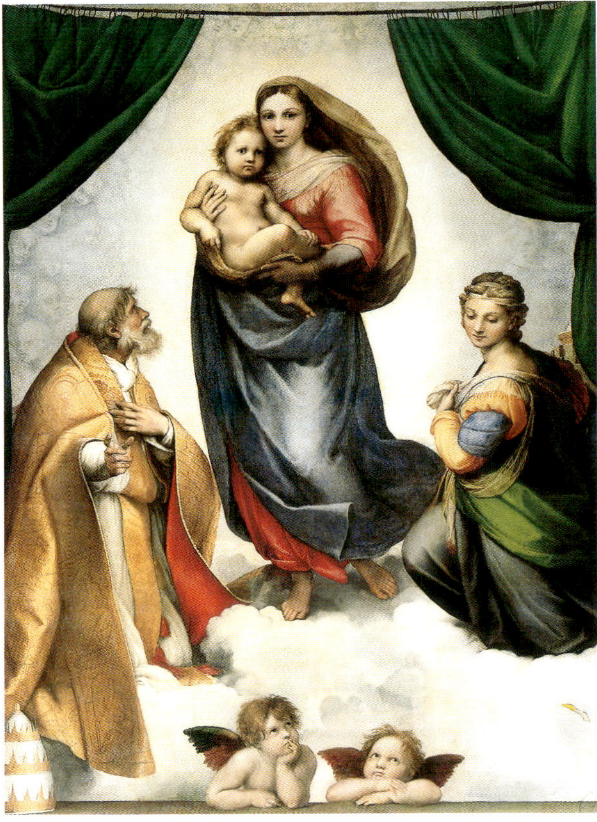

312

313

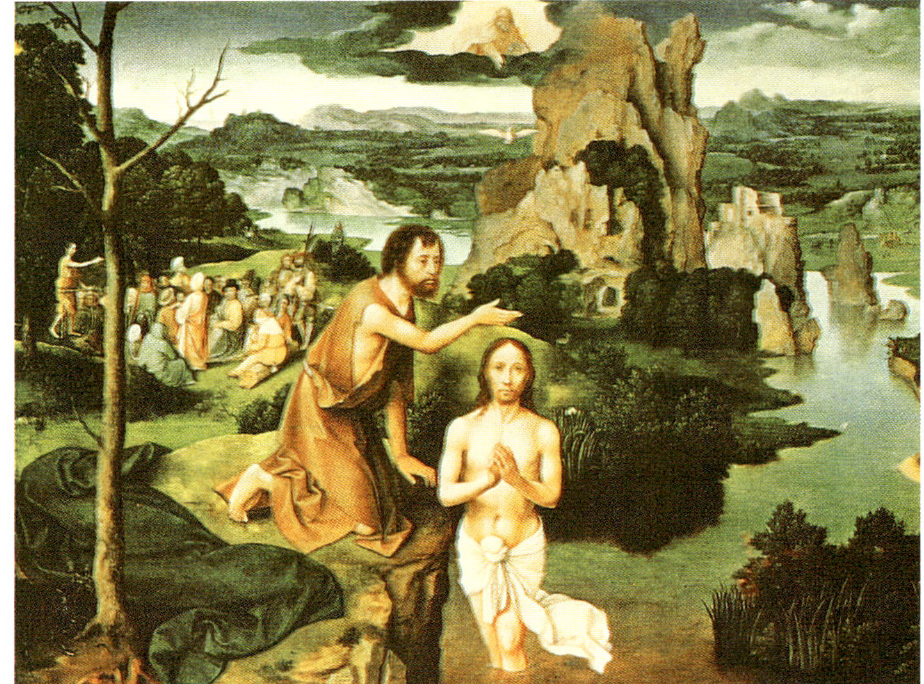

311. **Hans Süss von Kulmbach,** 1480-1522, Northern Renaissance, German, *The Calling of St Peter,* c. 1514-1516, Oil on panel, 130 x 100 cm. Galleria degli Uffizi, Florence.

312. **Raphael (Raffaello Sanzio),** 1483-1520, High Renaissance, Florentine School, Italian, *Sistine Madonna,* 1512-1513. Oil on canvas, 269 x 201 cm. Gemäldegalerie Alte Meister, Dresden.

313. **Joachim Patinir**, c. 1480-1524, Northern Renaissance, Flemish, *The Baptism of Christ,* c. 1515, Oil on oak, 59.7 x 76.3 cm, Kunsthistorisches Museum, Vienna.

Patinir is one of the greatest landscape painters. He sets the scene in this imaginary landscape. Two scenes are represented here: in the foreground, the baptism, and in the background, the Baptist preaches in a wood before a great congregation.

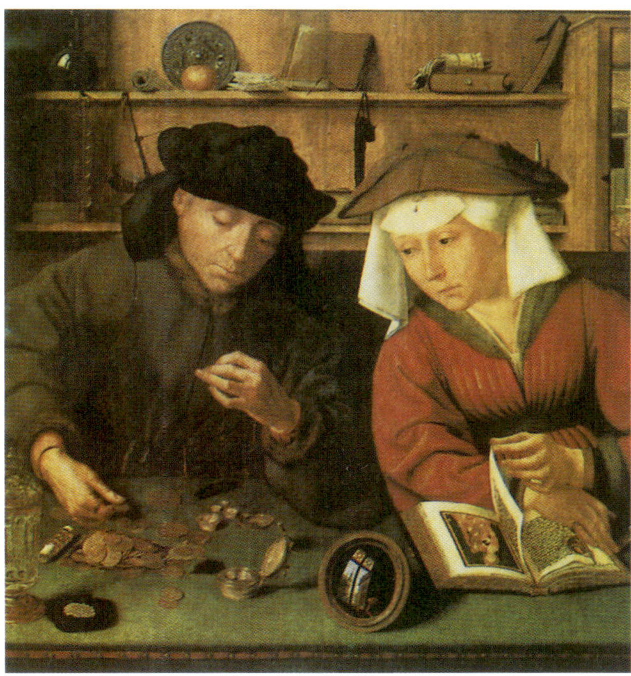

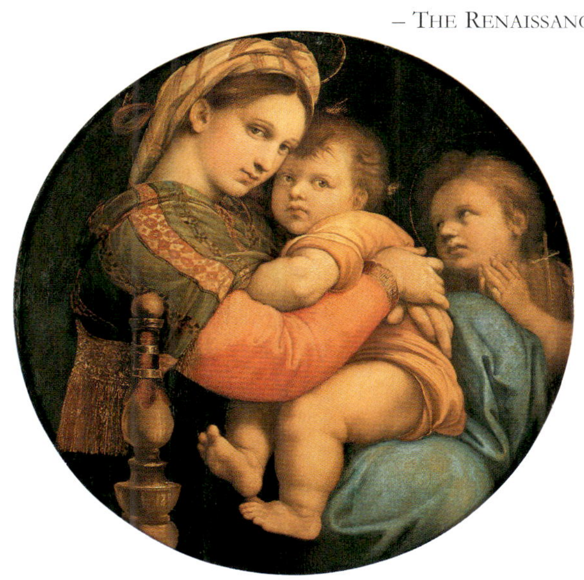

314. **Quentin Massys,** 1465-1530, Northern Renaissance, Flemish,
The Moneylender and His Wife, 1514.
Oil on panel, 71 x 68 cm. Musée du Louvre, Paris.

The Moneylender and His Wife *announces the development of
genre painting in Flanders during the sixteenth century. The
influence of Van Eyck is noticeable in the representation of the
painter himself in the convex mirror in the foreground.*

315. **Raphael (Raffaello Sanzio),** 1483-1520, High Renaissance,
Florentine School, Italian, *Madonna della Seggiola (Madonna
of the Chair),* 1514-1515. Oil on panel, Tondo, diameter: 71 cm.
Palazzo Pitti, Florence.

316. **Titian (Tiziano Vecellio),** 1490-1576, High Renaissance,
Venetian School, Italian, *Sacred and Profane Love,* c. 1514.
Oil on canvas, 118 x 279 cm. Galleria Borghese, Rome.

*Originally, this painting intended to depict earthly and heavenly
loves. The title, giving a moralistic meaning to the figures, is the
result of an eighteenth-century interpretation. The beauty and
serenity coming out of this picture characterise the new
researches of the painter at this time. The figure with the vase of
jewels symbolises the ephemeral happiness on earth, whereas
the one bearing the burning flame symbolises God's love and
perpetual joy in paradise.*

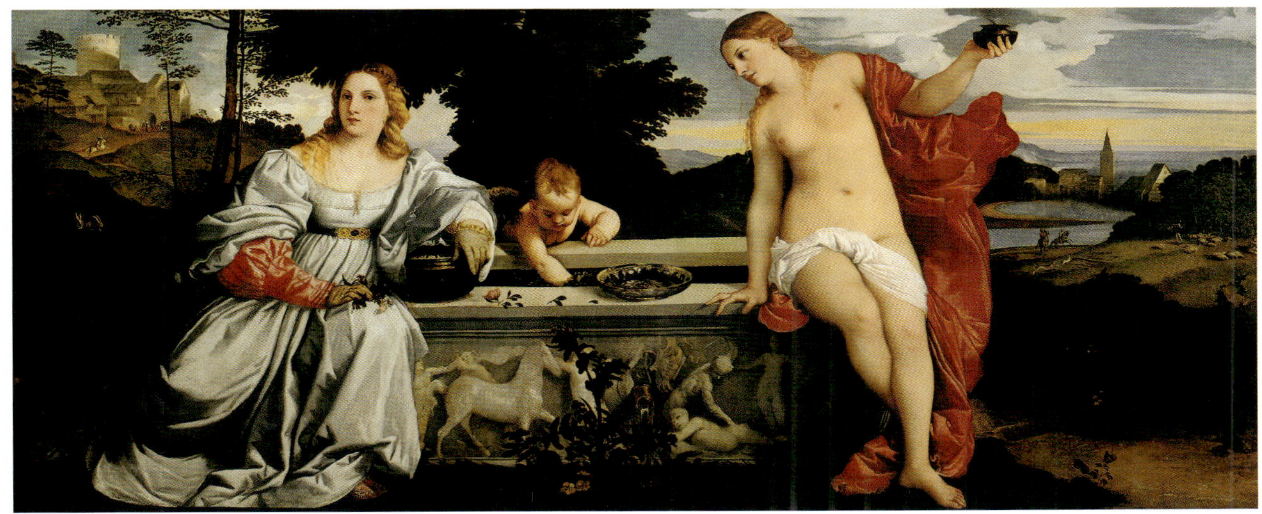

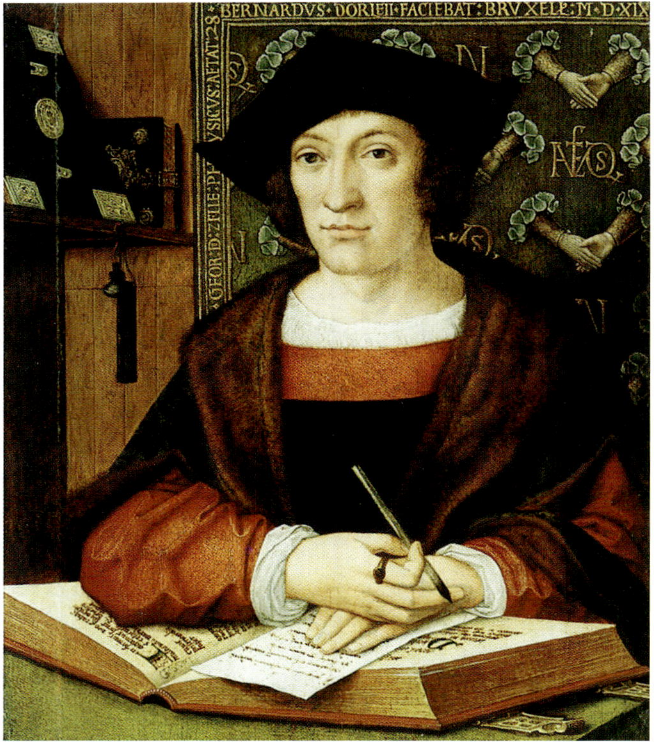

317

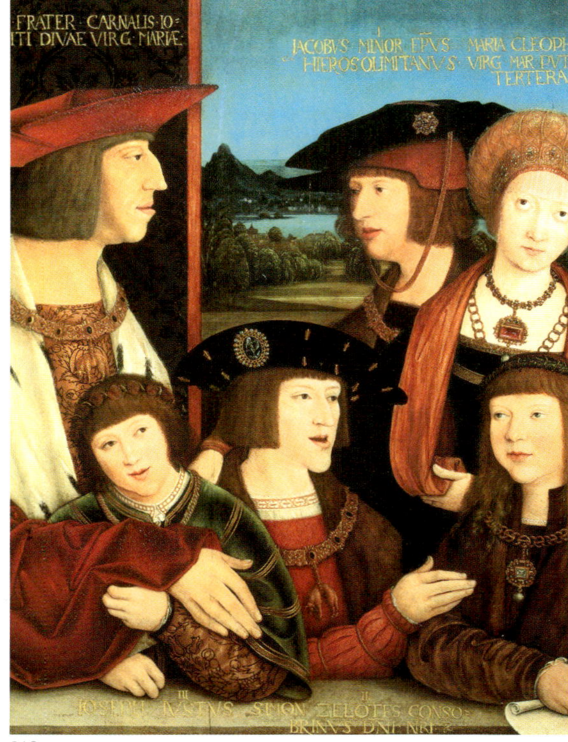

318

319

317. Bernaert van Orley, 1491/1492-1542,
Northern Renaissance, Flemish,
Joris van Zelle, 1519. Oil on oak, 39 x 32 cm.
Musées Royaux des Beaux-Arts, Brussels.

318. Bernhard Strigel, c. 1460-1528,
Northern Renaissance, German,
Emperor Maximilian I with His Family, 1516.
Oil on panel, 72.8 x 60.4 cm.
Kunsthistorisches Museum, Vienna.

319. Andrea del Sarto, 1486-1530,
High Renaissance, Florentine School, Italian,
Portrait of a Young Man, c. 1517.
Oil on linen, 72.4 x 57.2 cm. National Gallery, London.

*One of the major artists of Florentine Classicism, del Sarto
shows in his portraits the first components of Mannerism.*

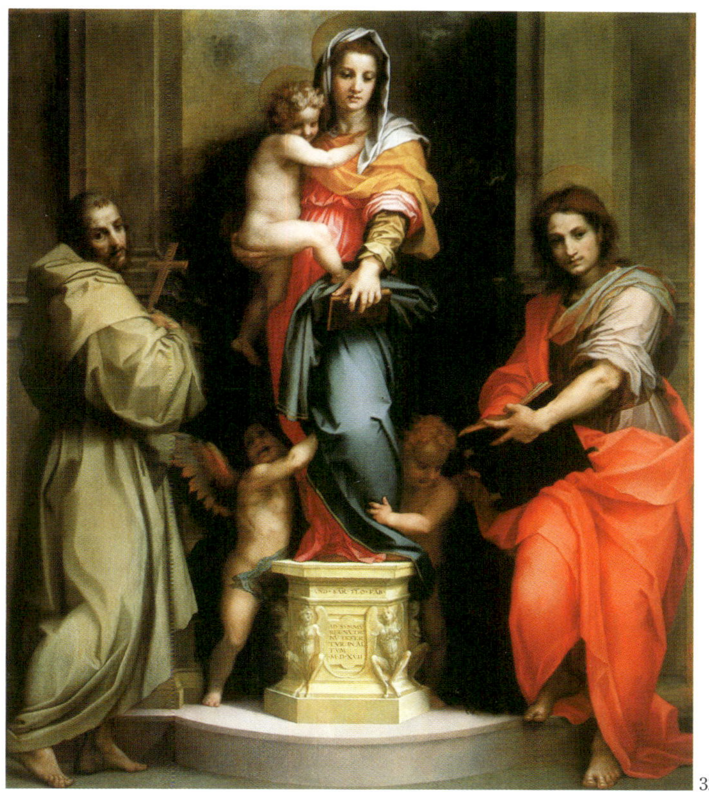

320

ANDREA DEL SARTO
(1486 – 1530 FLORENCE)

The epithet 'del sarto' (of the tailor) is derived from his father's profession. Apart from a visit to Fontainebleau in 1518-1519 to work for Francis I, Andrea was based in Florence all his life. A pioneer of Mannerism and a leading fresco painter of the High Renaissance, Andrea selected subjects that were nearly always covered in bright solidly coloured robes without adornment. Major works include the John the Baptist series at the Chiostro dello Scalzo (1511-1526) and his *Madonna of the Harpies* (1517). Andrea suffered from being the contemporary of such giants as Michelangelo and Raphael, but he undoubtedly ranks as one of the greatest masters of his time.

321

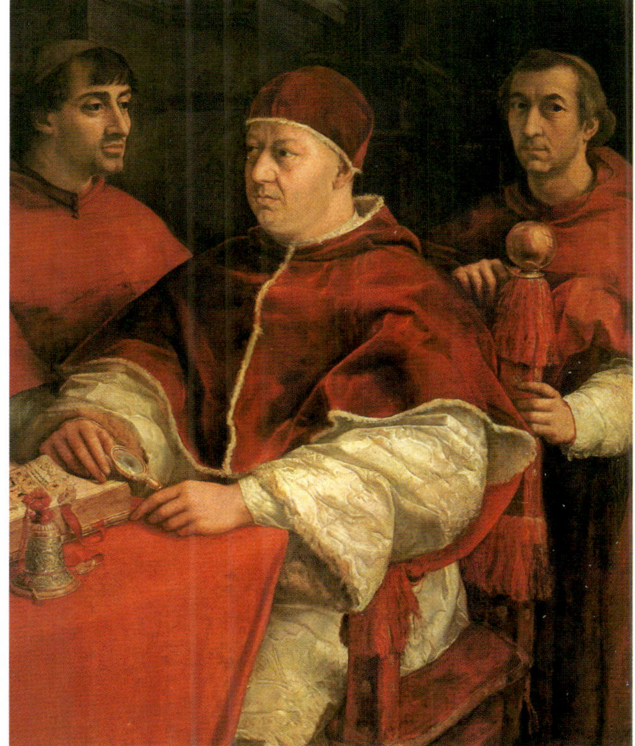

320. **Andrea del Sarto,** 1486-1530, High Renaissance, Florentine School, Italian, *Madonna of the Harpies,* 1517. Oil on panel, 208 x 178 cm. Galleria degli Uffizi, Florence.

The work is oddly named, not for herself or her child, Jesus. Not even for St Francis in his monkish robe on her right, or St John the Evangelist, holding a book. Rather, it is named for the images of bird-like creatures representing demons shown on the pedestal on which the Virgin Mary stands, symbolising the her power and that of her son over evil: The Italian word for evil female demons appearing in the form of birds is harpie. As the most recent interpretation, this unusual presentation of Virgin is a depiction of the Book of Revelations. The Madonna of the Harpies *bears witness to the elegant and solemn manner of artists of the early sixteenth century.*

321. **Raphael (Raffaello Sanzio),** 1483-1520, High Renaissance, Florentine School, Italian, *Portrait of Pope Leo X with Cardinals Guilio de 'Medici and Luigi de' Rossi,* 1518-1519. Oil on panel, 155.2 x 118.6 cm. Galleria degli Uffizi, Florence.

Leo X was elected Pope after Julius II and gathered around him many of Rome's leading writers, philosophers and artists. This portrait displays the painter's virtuosity in the rendering of texture in harmonious nuances of colour.

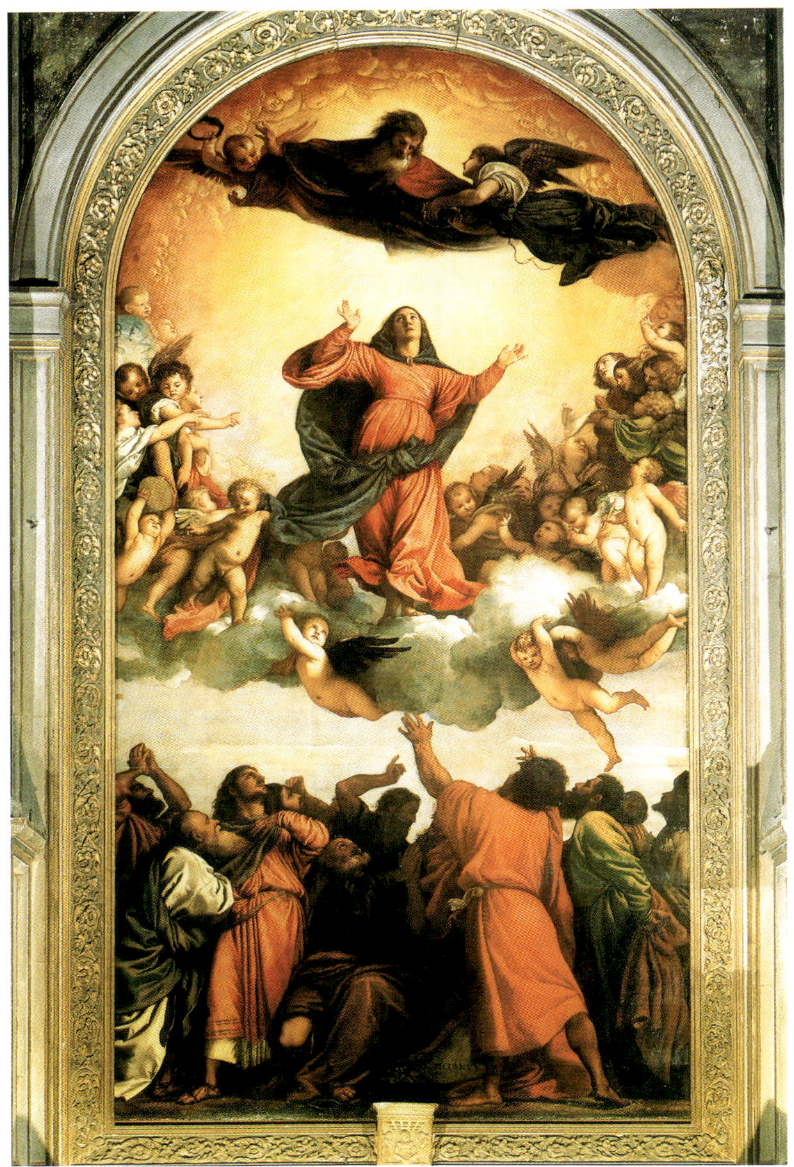

322. Titian (Tiziano Vecellio), 1490-1576, High Renaissance, Venetian School, Italian, *Assumption of the Virgin,* 1516-1518. Oil on panel, 690 x 360 cm. Santa Maria Gloriosa dei Frari, Venice.

Classicism and naturalism are associated here, and emotions are depicted with a dramatic intensity breaking with Venetian painting, revealing Michelangelo's and Raphael's influence. The picture is composed of three orders: the Apostles (embodiment of humankind), the Virgin (in the centre) and above the Eternal Father.

323. Correggio (Antonio Allegri), 1489-1534, High Renaissance, Parma School, Italian, *Vision of St John the Evangelist on Patmos,* 1520. Fresco. San Giovanni Evangelista, Parma.

Contemporary with Raphael and Titian, Correggio was essentially influenced by Mantegna in his murals. He refused to submit this composition to pre-existing architectural norms and created his own extraordinary, illusionist architecture. The general composition is conceived around a fitting of concentric circles, creating dynamism. Correggio refers to Michelangelo in the representation of the nude and its muscle structure but the outline remains more blurred and integrates variations of light and shadow inspired by Leonardo. The innovative use of coloured shadows is especially notable.

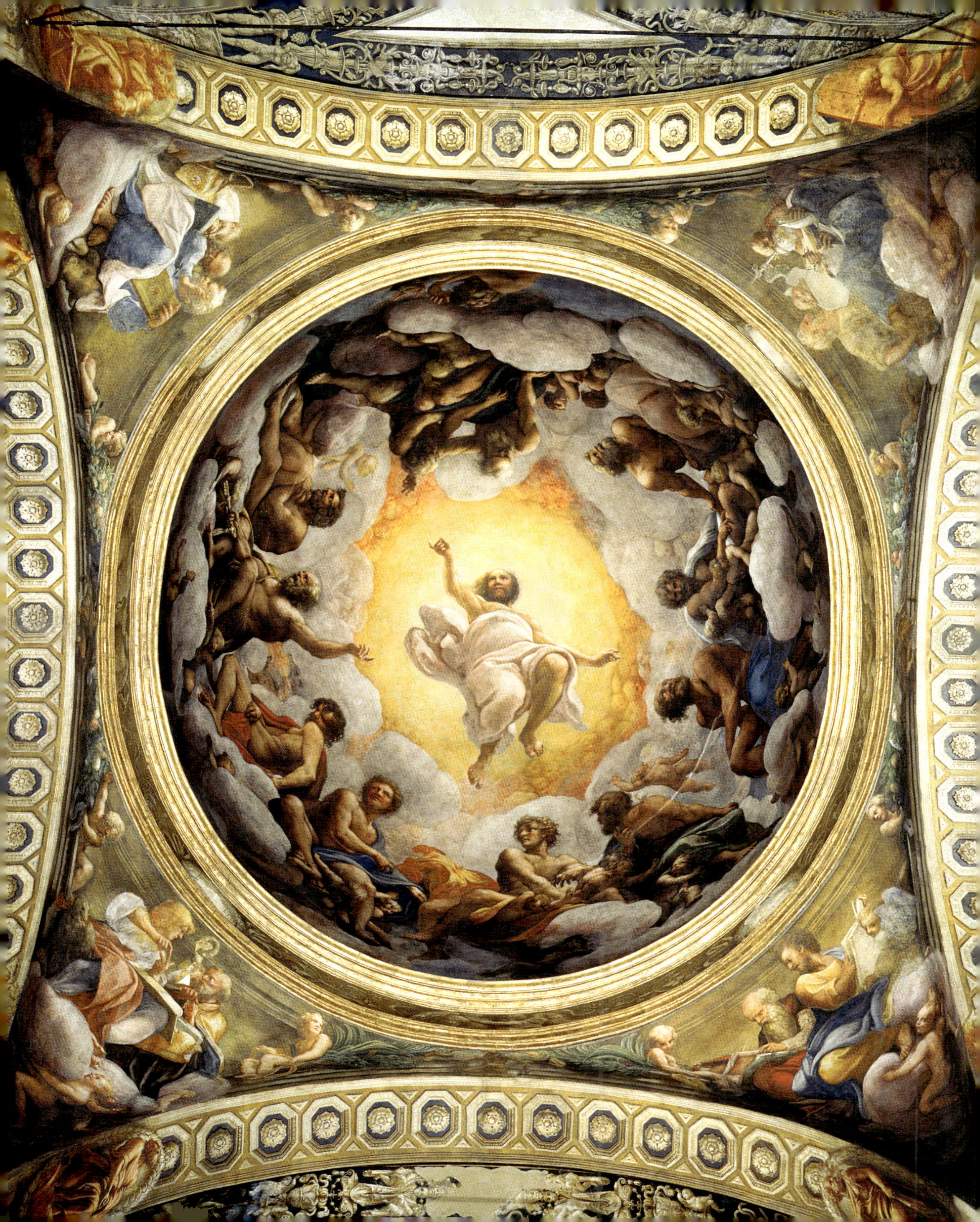

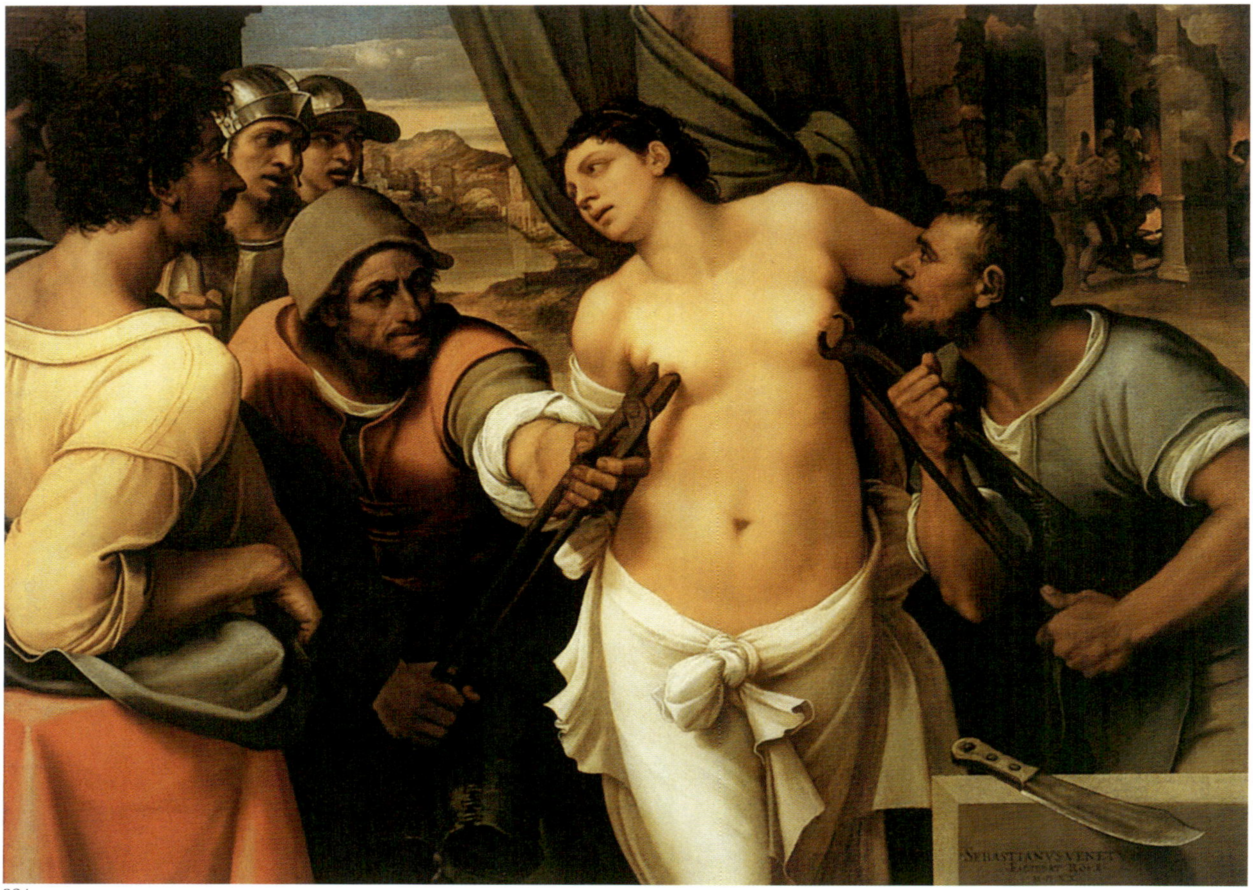

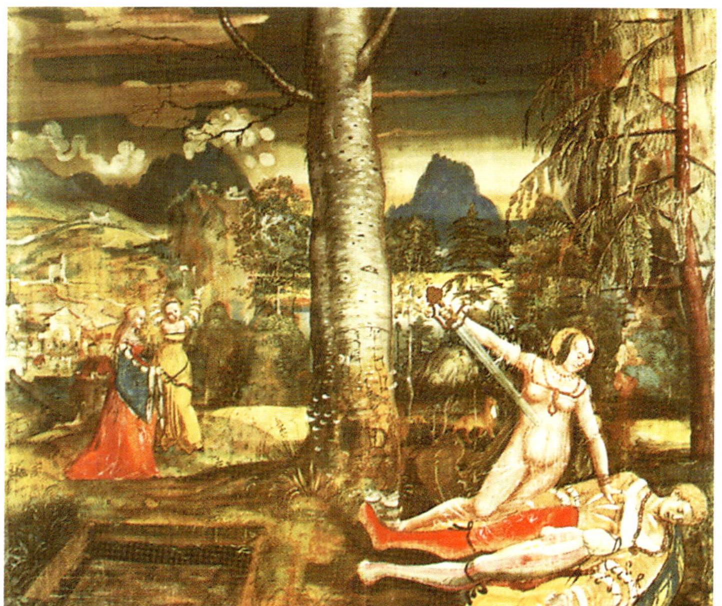

324

325

324. **Sebastiano del Piombo,** 1485-1547,
High Renaissance, Venetian School, Italian,
The Martyrdom of St Agatha, 1520.
Oil on panel, 127 x 178 cm. Palazzo Pitti, Florence.

*Michelangelo had a great influence on Sabastiano del
Piombo's muscular figures and the masculine shape of
his female character.*

325. **Niklaus Deutsch,** 1484-1530, Northern Renaissance,
German, *Pyramus and Thisbe,* c. 1520. Tempera on
canvas, 152 x 161 cm. Kunstmuseum, Basle.

*Deutsch's paintings are related to the ones of Baldung
Grien and Grünewald. This painting is among his
later ones.*

326. **Correggio (Antonio Allegri),** 1489-1534, High
Renaissance, Parma School, Italian, *Rest on the
Flight to Egypt with Saint Francis,* c. 1517.
Oil on canvas, 123.5 x 106.5 cm.
Galleria degli Uffizi, Florence.

328. **Palma il Vecchio,** 1480-1528, High Renaissance,
Venetian School, Italian, *The Holy Family with Mary
Magdalene and the Infant Saint John*, c. 1520.
Oil on wood, 87 x 117 cm.
Galleria degli Uffizi, Florence.

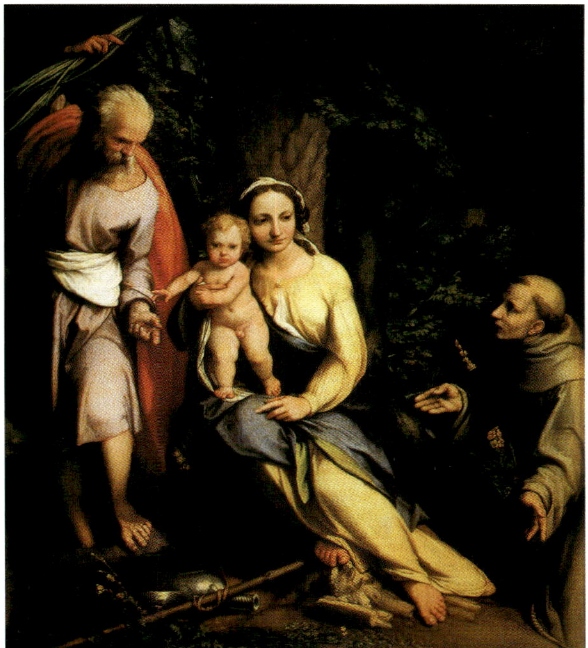

326

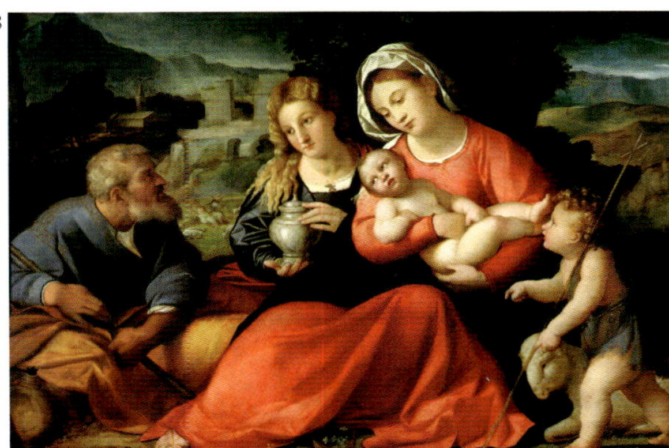

328

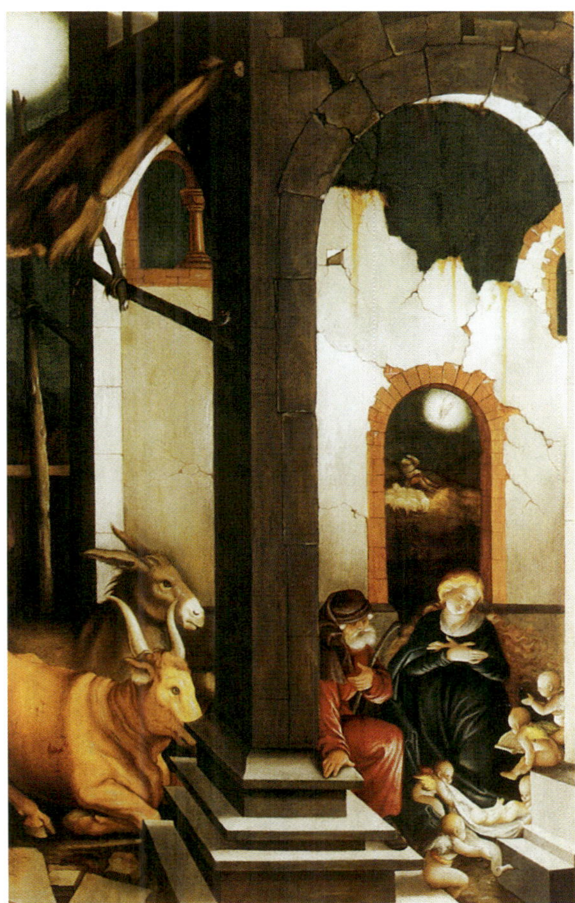

327. **Hans Baldung Grien,** c. 1484-1545,
Northern Renaissance, German, *Nativity*, 1520.
Oil on panel, 105.5 x 70.4 cm. Alte Pinakothek, Munich.

*Hans Baldung signed with his monogram 'G' which stands for
'Grien', his nickname. He was probably dubbed with this name
because of his liking for the colour green.*

CORREGGIO (ANTONIO ALLEGRI)
(C. 1489 – 1534 CORREGGIO)

Correggio founded the Renaissance school in Parma, but little
is known of h s life. He was born in the little town of Correggio
near Parma. There he was educated, but in his seventeenth
year an outbreak of the plague drove his family to Mantova,
where the young painter had an opportunity of studying the
pictures of Mantegna and the collection of works of art
accumulated originally by the Gonzaga family and later by
Isabella d'Est₌. In 1514 he went back to Parma, where his
talents found ample recognition; and for some years the story
of his life is the record of his work, culminating in his
wonderful re-creation of light and shade.

It was not, however, a record of undisturbed quiet, for the
decoration which he made for the dome of the cathedral was
severely criticised. Choosing the subject of the Resurrection, he
projected upon the ceiling a great number of ascending figures,
which, viewed from below, necessarily involved a multitude of
legs, giving rise to the apt description that the painting
resembled a "fry of frogs". It may have been the trouble which
later ensued with the chapter of the cathedral, or depression
caused by the death of his young wife, but at the age of thirty-
six, indifferent to fame and fortune, he retired to the
comparative obscurity of his birth place, where for four years he
devoted himself to the painting of mythological subjects: scenes
of fabled beings removed from the real world and set in a
golden arcadia of dreams. His work prefigures mannerism and
baroque style.

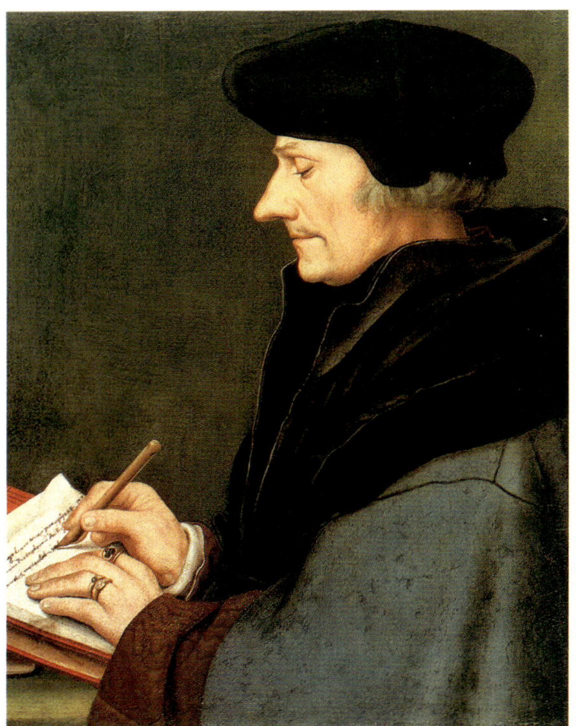 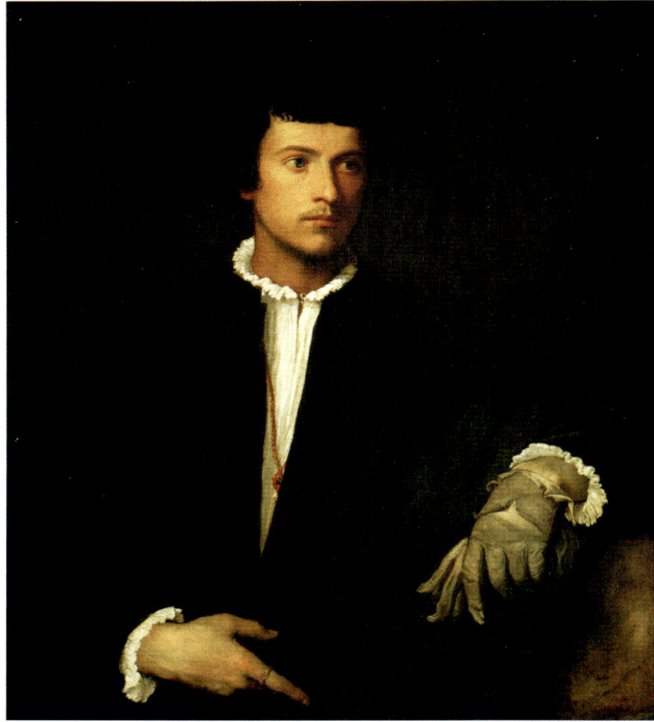

329   330

329. Hans Holbein the Younger, 1497-1543,
Northern Renaissance, German,
Portrait of Erasmus of Rotterdam Writing, c. 1523.
Oil on wood, 36.8 x 30.5 cm.
Kunstmuseum, Öffentliche Kunstsammlung, Basle.

Three portraits of Erasmus by Holbein are known. The
painter encountered the humanist in Basle. When
Holbein went to London, he was received there by a
friend of Erasmus, Thomas Moore, who would later write
about the painter, "Such a man, according to Erasmus,
that since centuries, the sun has never seen more loyal
and frank, more devoted and wiser."

330. Titian (Tiziano Vecellio), 1490-1576,
High Renaissance, Venetian School, Italian,
Man with a Glove, c. 1525.
Oil on canvas, 100 x 89 cm. Musée du Louvre, Paris.

Titian invented a kind of expressive and natural portrait
on a dark background that inspired pre-romantic
painters from the end of the eighteenth century.

331. Giovanni Francesco Caroto, 1480-1555,
High Renaissance, Veronese School, Italian,
Red-Headed Youth Holding a Drawing.
Oil on canvas, 37 x 29 cm.
Museo di Castelvecchio, Verona.

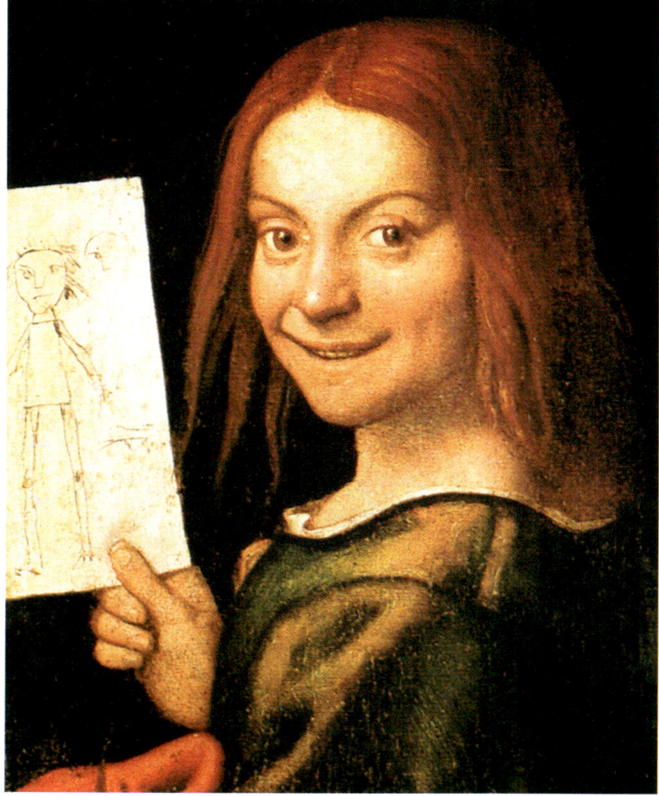

331

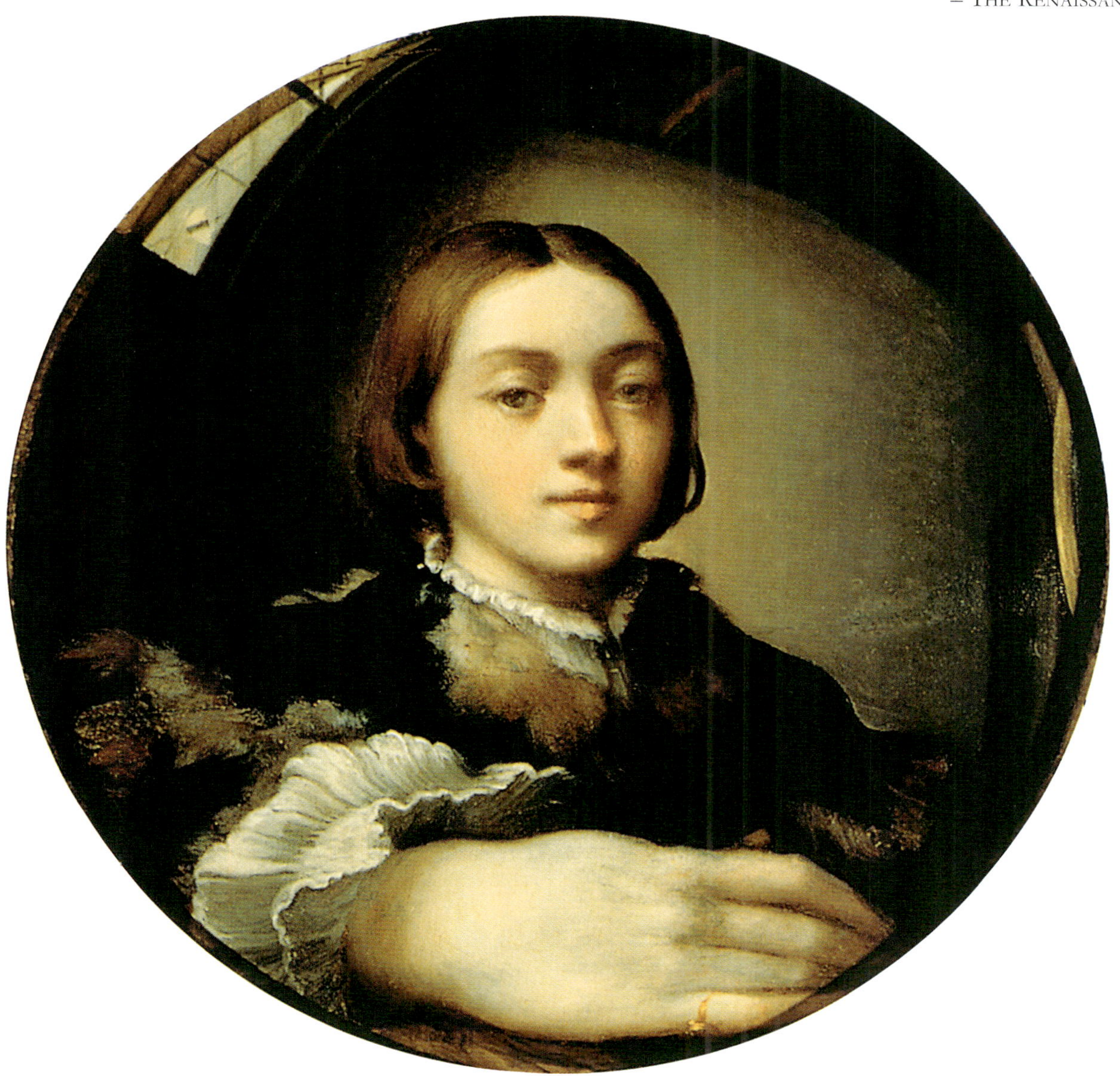

332. Parmigianino (Girolamo Francesco Mazzola), 1503-1540,
Mannerism, Parma School, Italian,
Self-portrait in a Convex Mirror, c. 1523-1524.
Oil on wood, Tondo, diameter: 24.4 cm.
Kunsthistorisches Museum, Vienna.

Vasari celebrated in Vite de' più eccellenti architetti, pittori, et scultori Italiani *Parmigianino's unusual special-effects, "Inquiring one day into the subtleties of art, he began to draw himself as he appeared in a barber's convex glass. He had a ball of wood made at a turner's and divided it in half, and on this he set himself to paint all that he saw in the glass, and because the mirror enlarged everything that was near and diminished what was distant, he painted the hand a little large."*

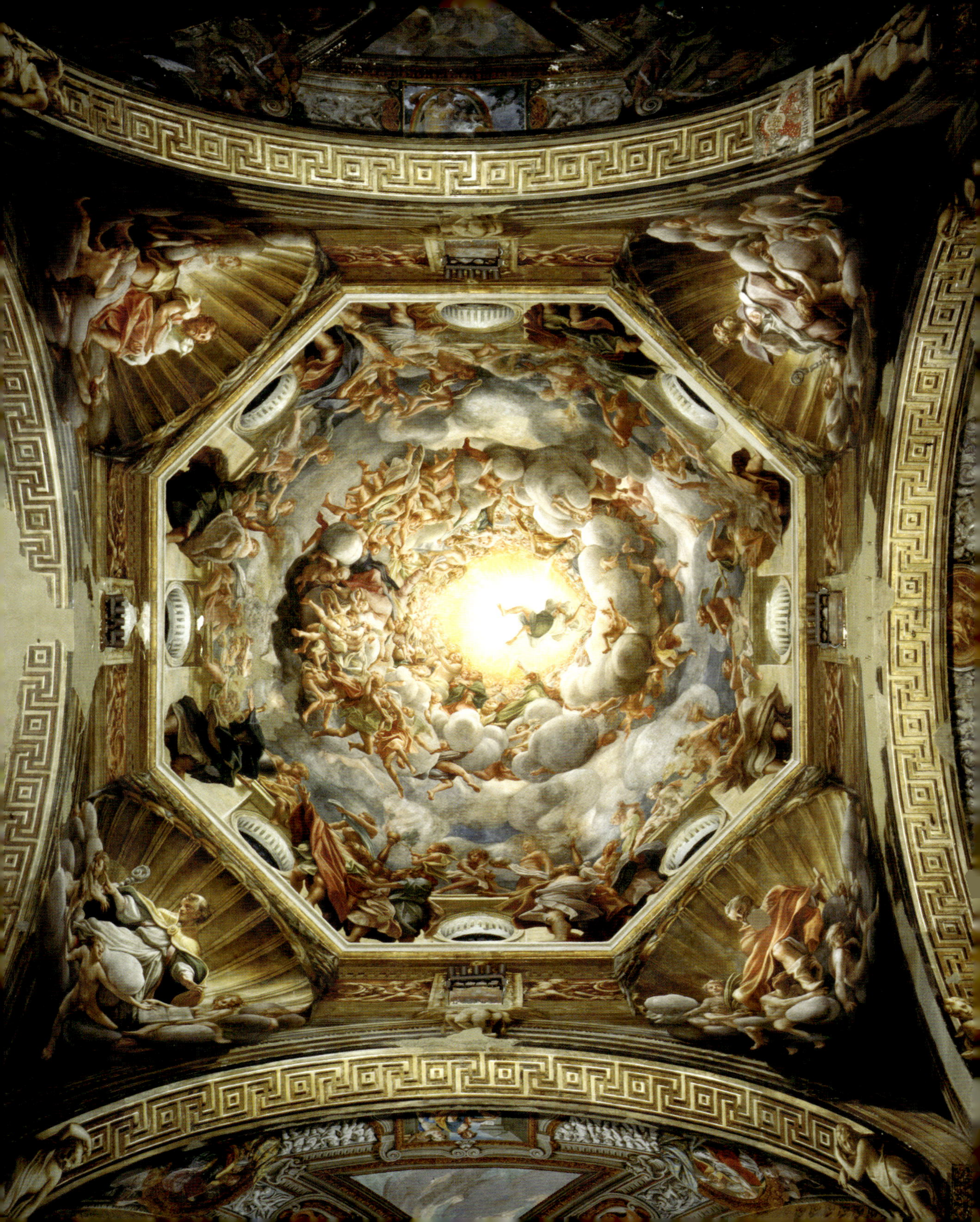

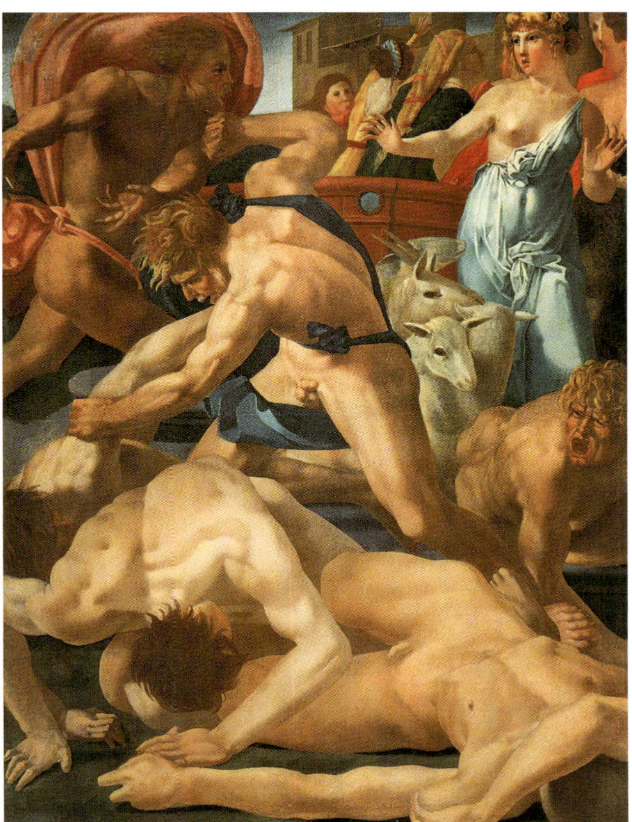

334

334. Rosso Fiorentino, 1494-1540, Mannerism, Florentine School, Italian, *Moses Defending the Daughters of Jethro*, 1523. Oil on canvas, 160 x 117 cm. Galleria degli Uffizi, Florence.

This is the most abstract of Rosso's compositions. The artist was inspired by Michelangelo's Battle of Cascina, *which remained in the state of a cartoon.*

333. Correggio (Antonio Allegri), 1489-1534, High Renaissance, Parma School, Italian, *Assumption of the Virgin*, 1526-1530. Fresco, 1093 x 1195 cm. Duomo, Parma.

The artist received the order to paint frescos for Parma's cathedral in 1520. The domes indicate the artist's skills in depicting anatomy and perspective.

335. Jacopo Pontormo, 1494-1557, Mannerism, Florentine School, Italian, *Deposition*, 1525-1528. Oil on panel, 313 x 192 cm. Cappella Capponi, Santa Felicità, Florence.

335

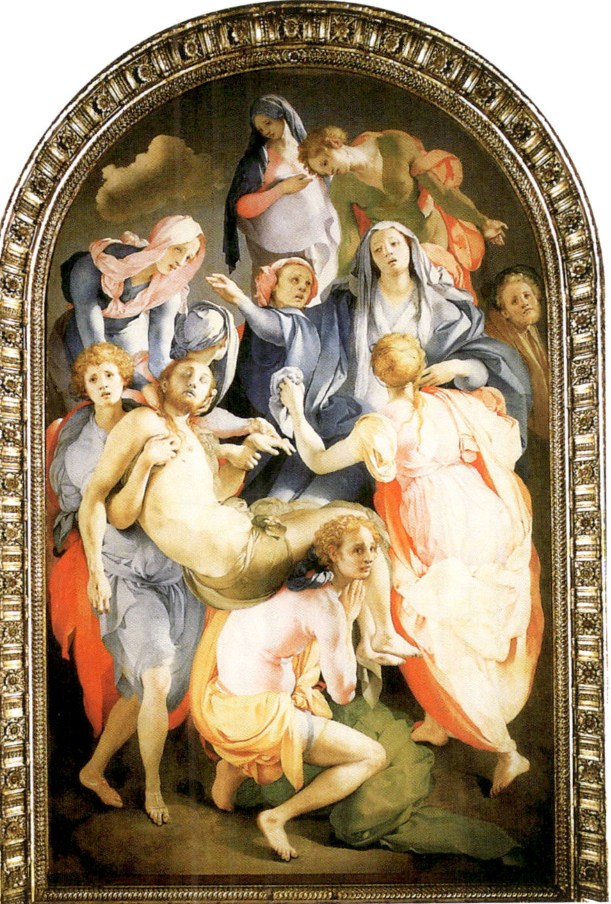

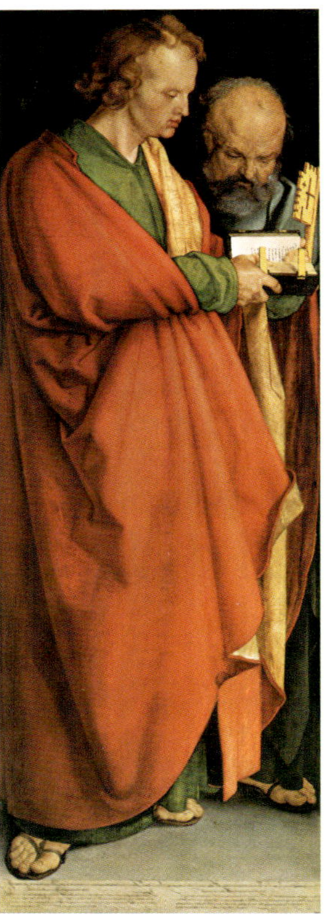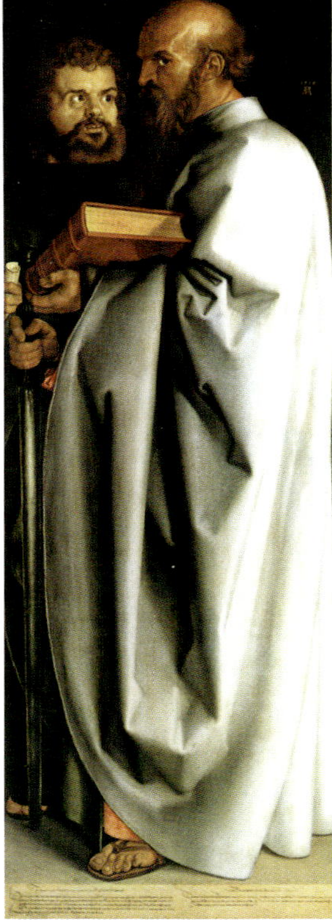

336

338. **Hans Baldung Grien,** c. 1484-1545, Northern Renaissance, German, *Virgin and Child with Parrots,* c. 1527.
Oil on panel, 91 x 63.2 cm.
Germanisches Nationalmuseum, Nuremberg.

339. **Hans Holbein the Younger,** 1497-1543, Northern Renaissance, German, *Portrait of Nikolaus Kratzer, Astronomer,* 1528.
Tempera on oak, 83 x 67 cm.
Musée du Louvre, Paris.

337

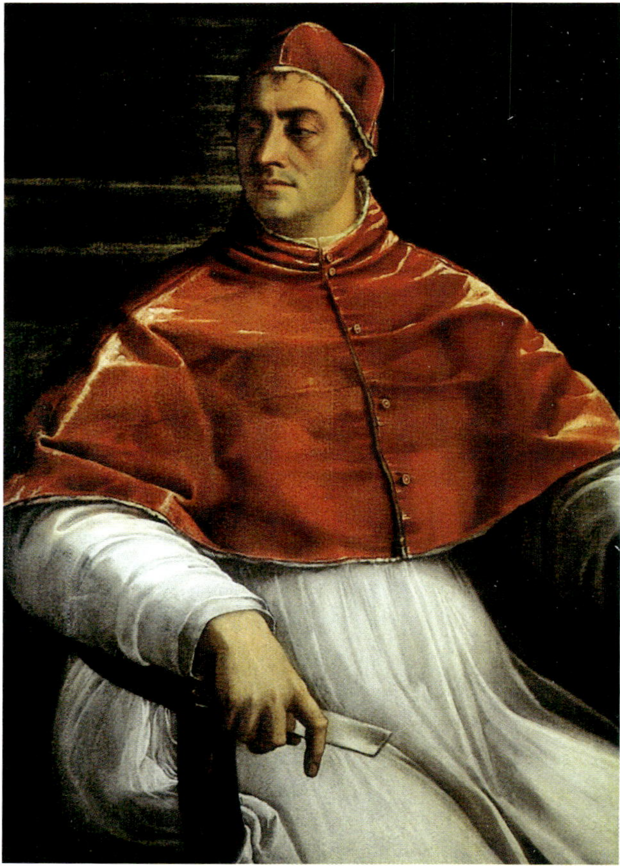

336. **Albrecht Dürer,** 1471-1528, Northern Renaissance, German, *The Four Holy Men,* 1526.
Oil on lindenwood panels, 215 x 76 cm.
Alte Pinakothek, Munich.

The artist gave this masterpiece, painted during the last years of his life, to his hometown of Nuremberg. In the work we see less of how the artist imagines four of the apostles might have looked, than we see which character traits in each subject the artist wanted to present. Saints John and Peter are depicted on the left and Mark with Paul on the right. Peter holds a large key, as a reminder that Jesus gave him the "keys of the kingdom". Peter and his proverbial keys are seen also in El Greco's The Burial of Count Orgaz (1586). The evangelist John seems to be pointing out something from scripture to the first head of the Church, as if books existed in that format in the times of these first century men. Paul holds a formidable volume, possibly one of his own many epistles, in contrast to the little scroll held by Mark, the writer of the shortest gospel. Each pair seems to be caught in an informal moment. The use of colours is judicious here; the contrasts between complementary colours (red, green, blue, yellow) enhance the plasticity of the characters.

337. **Sebastiano del Piombo,** 1485-1547, High Renaissance, Venetian School, Italian, *Portrait of Pope Clement VII,* 1526.
Oil on panel. Museo Nazionale di Capodimonte, Naples.

In 1531, Pope Clement VII gave Sebastiano the position of "Piombo" (Italian for lead), keeping the papal seals that were made of lead.

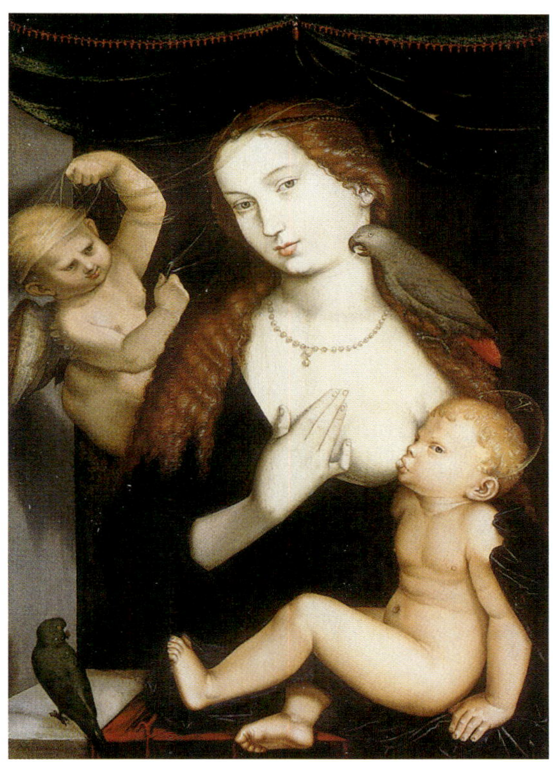

338

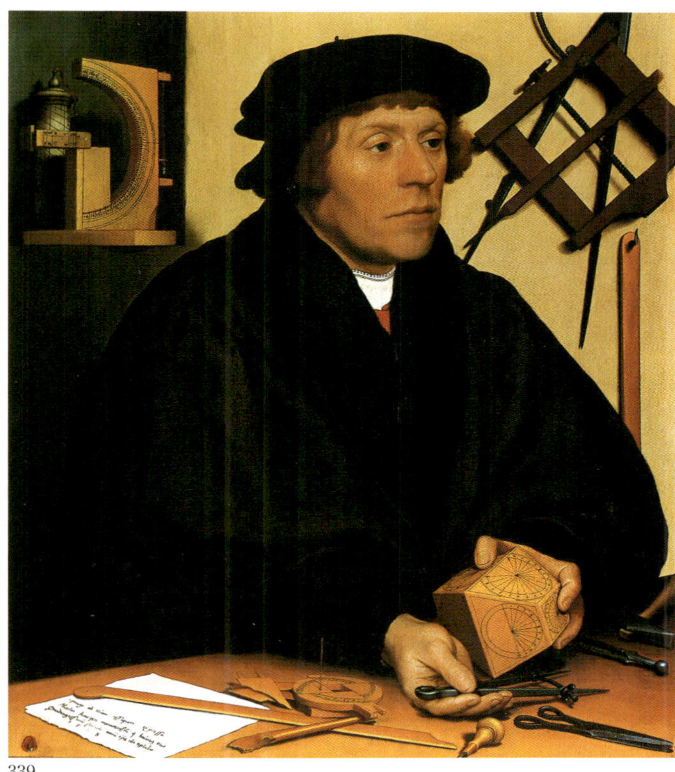

339

340. **Lucas van Leyden,** 1494-1533, Northern Renaissance, Dutch,
The Engagement, 1527.
Oil on panel, 30 x 32 cm.
Koninklijk Museum voor Schone Kunsten, Antwerp.

341. **Lorenzo Lotto,** 1480-1556, High Renaissance,
Venetian School, Italian, *Lucretia,* 1530-1532.
Oil on canvas, 96.5 x 110.6 cm. National Gallery, London.

*The portrait proclaims the virtues of the character with the
Latin inscription on the paper on the table, taken from the
Roman historian, Livy: "After Lucretia's example, let no
violated woman live."*

340

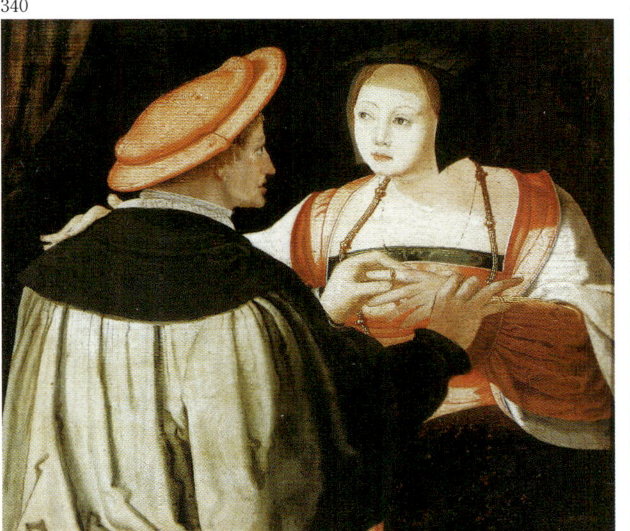

341

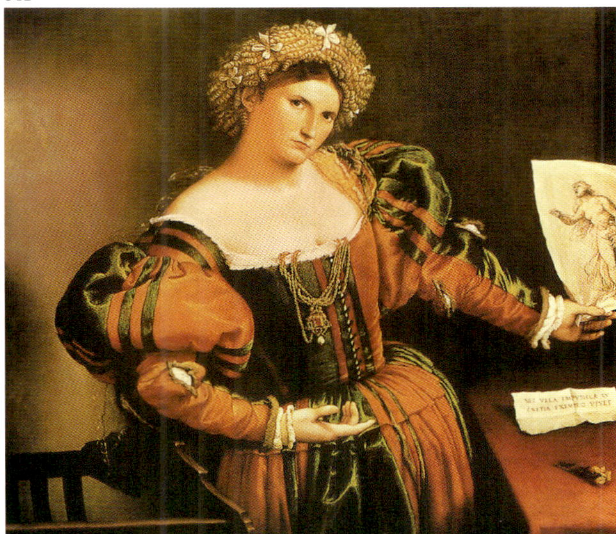

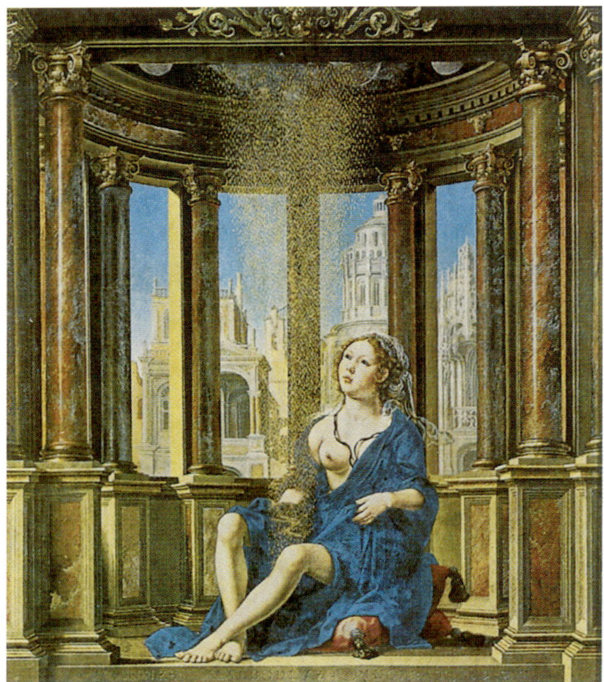

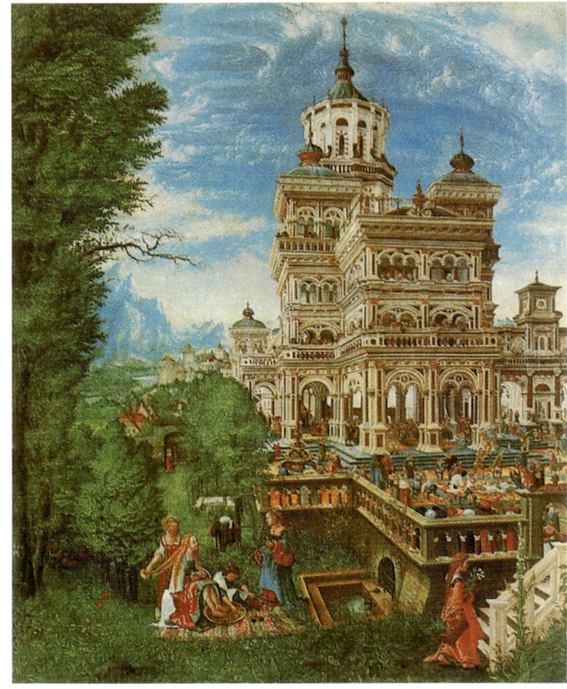

342. **Jan Gossaert (Mabuse),** 1478-1532, Northern Renaissance, Flemish, *Danaë,* 1527. Oil on panel, 114.2 x 95.4 cm. Alte Pinakothek, Munich.

Danaë is one of Gossaert's later works and testifies to the artist's meticulous manner at the end of his career.

343. **Albrecht Altdorfer,** 1480-1538, Northern Renaissance, German, *Susanna in the Bath,* 1526. Oil on panel, 74.8 x 61.2 cm. Alte Pinakothek, Munich.

345. **Alejo Fernández,** 1475-1545, High Renaissance, Spanish, *The Virgin of the Navigators,* 1530-1540. Oil on panel, Alcázar, Seville.

344

345

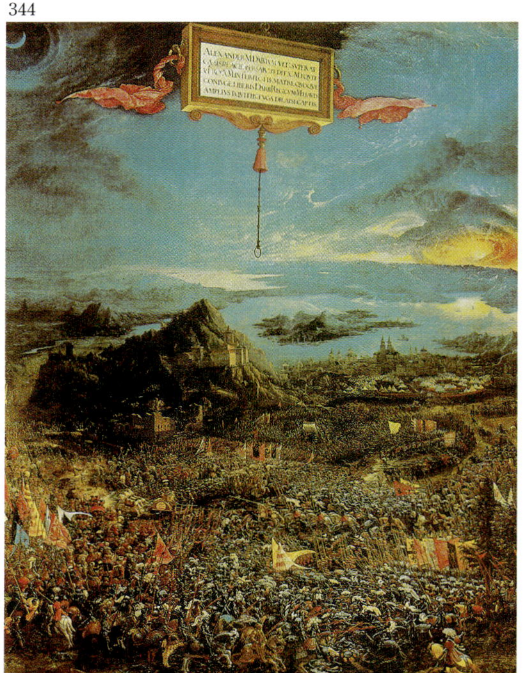

344. **Albrecht Altdorfer,** 1480-1538, Northern Renaissance, German, *The Battle at the Issus (Alexander's Victory),* 1529. Oil on panel, 158.4 x 120.3 cm. Alte Pinakothek, Munich.

Even though the majority of his works are based on religious themes, Altdorfer was one of the first artists of his time to paint landscapes as an independent genre. The Battle at the Issus is an incredible example of the use of colour in the artist's work. The landscape seen from above recalls the works of Patinir and the mountains' shapes those of Leonardo.

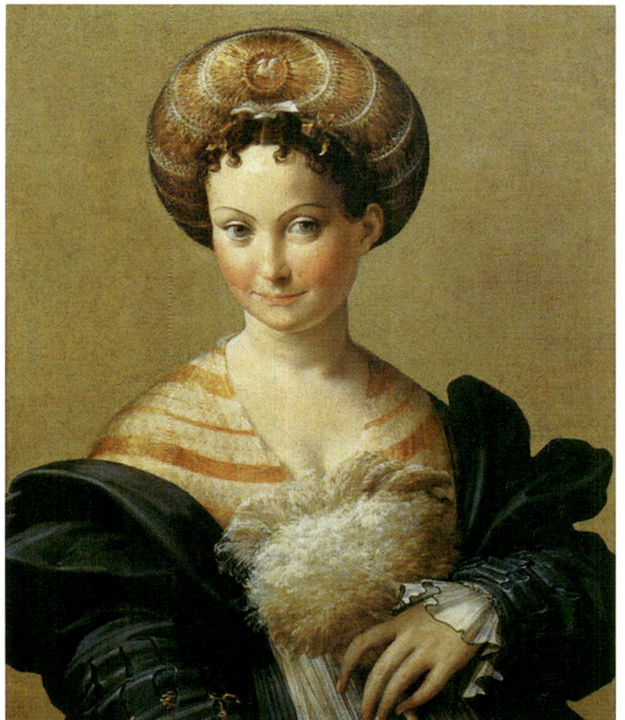

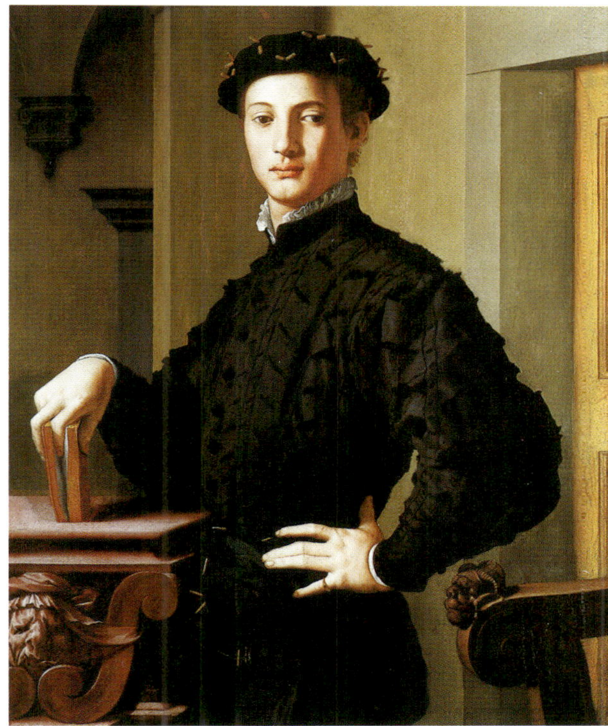

346   347

346. **Parmigianino (Girolamo Francesco Mazzola),** 1503-1540,
Mannerism, Parma School, Italian, *Turkish Slave,* 1530-1531.
Oil on wood, 67 x 53 cm.
Galleria Nazionale, Parma.

347. **Agnolo Bronzino**, 1503-1572, Mannerism, Florentine School,
Italian, *Portrait of a Young Man,* c. 1530.
Oil on wood, 95.6 x 74.9 cm.
The Metropolitan Museum of Art, New York.

*Bronzino was engaged in court portraiture. He introduces here
witty motifs such as the grotesque head on the table, appreciated
in literary circles.*

348. **Jean Clouet,** c. 1485-1541, Mannerism, French,
Francis I, King of France, c. 1530.
Oil on panel, 96 x 74 cm.
Musée du Louvre, Paris.

*This portrait attributed to Jean Clouet reveals the influence of the
School of Fontainebleau and of the realism of the Flemish
school. The painter paid particular attention to the depiction of
the costume and golden chain of the sitter, sumptuously dressed
in Italian fashion.*

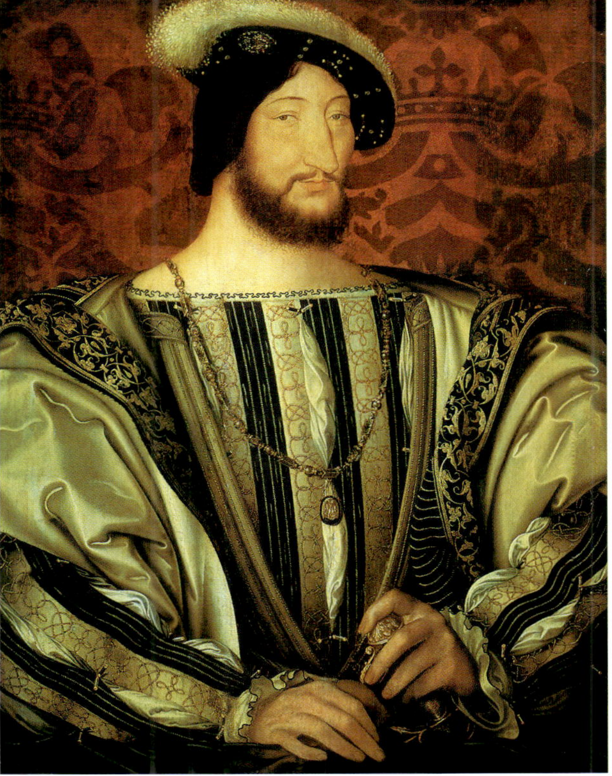

348

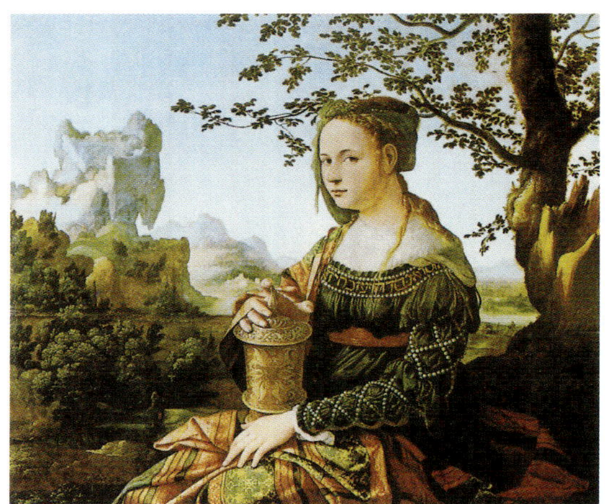

349. **Jan van Scorel,** 1495-1562, Northern Renaissance, Dutch,
Mary Magdalene, c. 1530. Oil on panel, 67 x 76.5 cm.
Rijksmuseum, Amsterdam.

*Influenced by Raphael and his travel to Italy, Van Scorel
makes his composition dynamic by depicting the sitter
slightly to the right of the middle axis, her shoulder turned in
the opposite direction to her head.*

351. **Hans Holbein the Younger,** 1497-1543,
Northern Renaissance, German, *The Ambassadors
(Jean de Dinteville and Georges de Selve),* 1533.
Oil on oak, 207 x 209.5 cm. National Gallery, London.

The perspective in The Ambassadors *presents three different
viewpoints, passing virtually seamlessly from a distant point of
view to close-up and diagonal views. The pictorial reality alone
makes it possible for these mutually exclusive perspectives to
co-exist. The overall effect of the picture is dominated by the
imposing life-sized appearance of the two men, whose posture
and gaze confront the viewer en face. The rich details of the
still-life elements and the crucifix above Jean de Dinteville in*

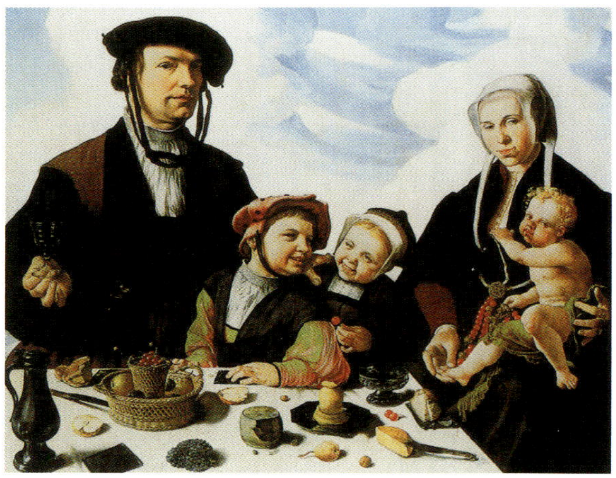

350. **Maarten van Heemskerck,** 1498-1574,
Northern Renaissance, Dutch, *Family Portrait,* 1532.
Oil on panel, 118 x 140 cm. Staatliche Museen, Kassel.

*This painting well represents the combination of Early
Netherlandish painting and Italian painting: the composition and
plasticity given to the characters derives from the Italian
experience, whereas the abundance of details in the foreground
characterises Netherlandish painting.*

*the upper left-hand corner need to be viewed close up. The
anamorphosis, on the other hand, straightens out when the viewer
relinquishes a head-on position and stands next to the picture at
an angle, to the right of Georges de Selve as it were, his head at
the level of the crucifix. Thus, the viewer becomes, in a manner
of speaking, the third protagonist. The vantage point from which
the viewer regards the skull is in the extension of a diagonal axis
generated by the anamorphosis, to the right of the picture.*

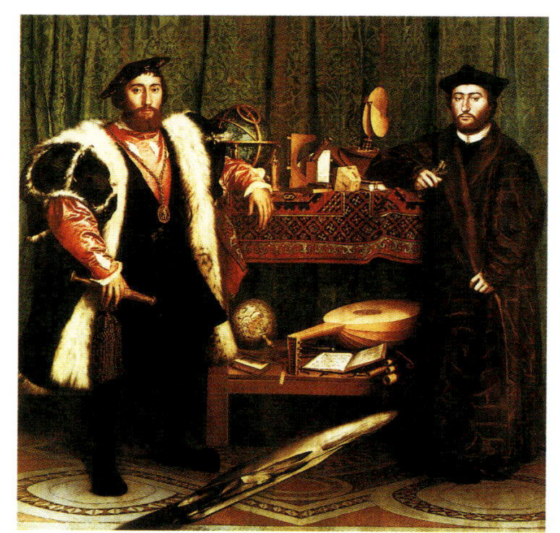

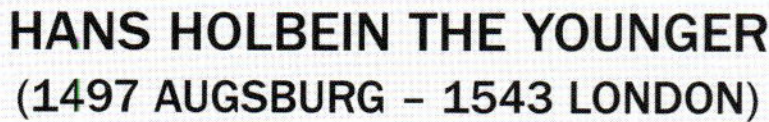

HANS HOLBEIN THE YOUNGER
(1497 AUGSBURG – 1543 LONDON)

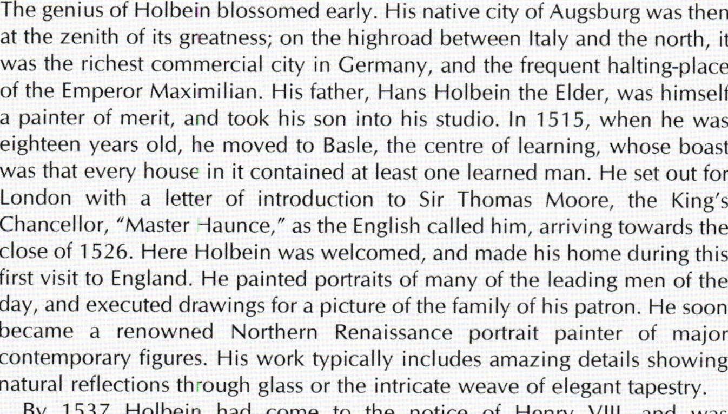

The genius of Holbein blossomed early. His native city of Augsburg was then
at the zenith of its greatness; on the highroad between Italy and the north, it
was the richest commercial city in Germany, and the frequent halting-place
of the Emperor Maximilian. His father, Hans Holbein the Elder, was himself
a painter of merit, and took his son into his studio. In 1515, when he was
eighteen years old, he moved to Basle, the centre of learning, whose boast
was that every house in it contained at least one learned man. He set out for
London with a letter of introduction to Sir Thomas Moore, the King's
Chancellor, "Master Haunce," as the English called him, arriving towards the
close of 1526. Here Holbein was welcomed, and made his home during this
first visit to England. He painted portraits of many of the leading men of the
day, and executed drawings for a picture of the family of his patron. He soon
became a renowned Northern Renaissance portrait painter of major
contemporary figures. His work typically includes amazing details showing
natural reflections through glass or the intricate weave of elegant tapestry.

By 1537 Holbein had come to the notice of Henry VIII, and was
established as court painter, a position he held until his death.

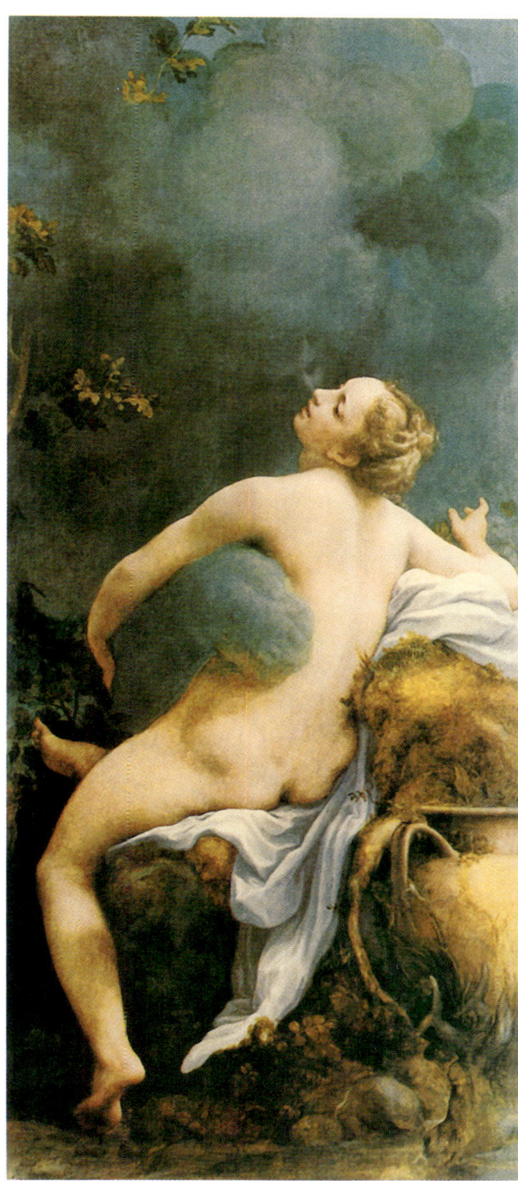

352. **Correggio (Antonio Allegri),** c. 1490-1534,
High Renaissance, Parma School, Italian, *Jupiter and Io*,
1531. Oil on canvas, 163.5 x 70 cm.
Kuntshistorisches Museum, Vienna.

This is one of four works inspired by Ovid's Metamorphoses.
These works were commissioned by Ludovico de Gonzaga
who wished to offer them to Charles V for his consecration,
but finally kept them for his studiolo. The choice of the
theme is rather a pretext to the representation of nudity. The
sensuality and voluptuous bodies, characterising Correggio's
style, are pushed to their extreme. At the same time, Titian
was painting Venus of Urbino (fig. 357). Therefore, the
mythological painting evolves toward a more erotic and
monumental representation of the human form.

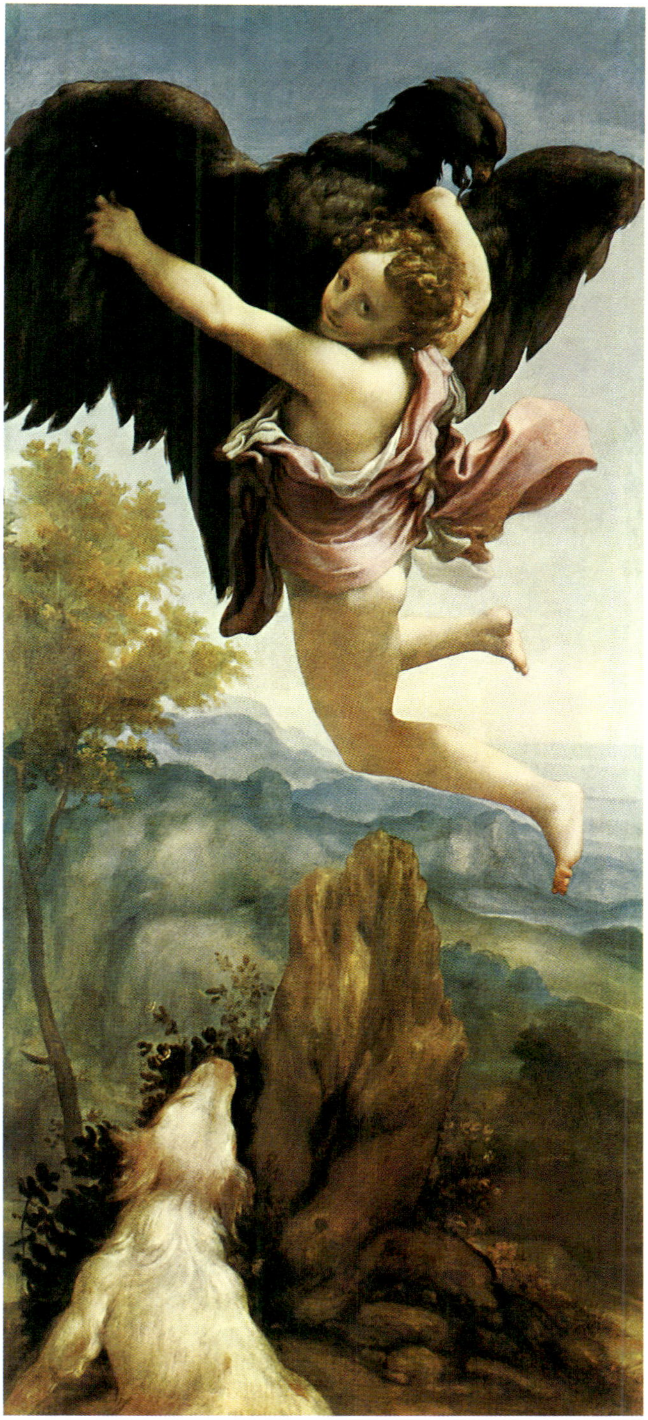

353. **Correggio (Antonio Allegri),** c. 1489-1534, High Renaissance,
Parma School, Italian, *Abduction of Ganymede*, 1531.
Oil on canvas, 163 x 71 cm. Kunsthistorisches Museum, Vienna.

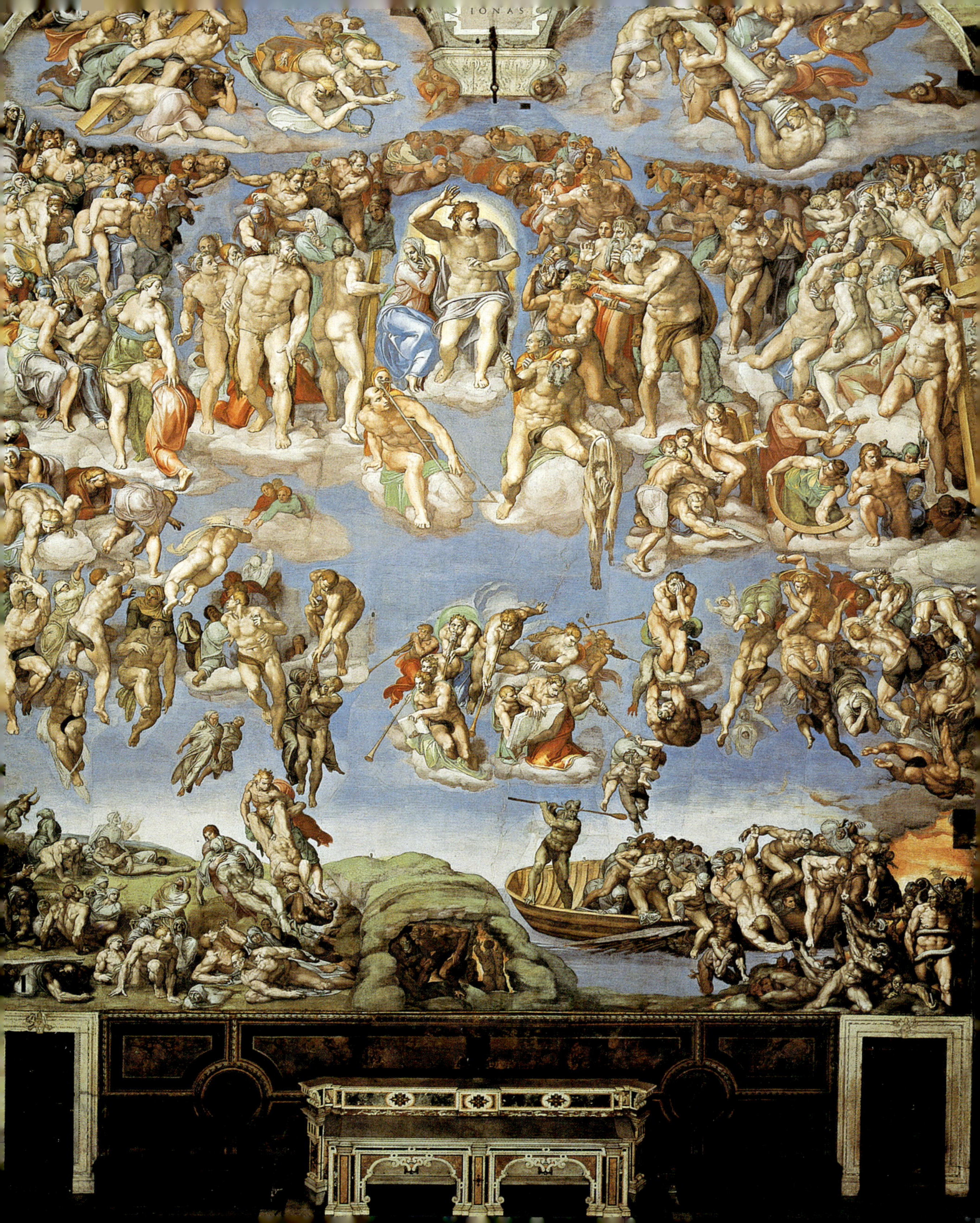

IONAS

354. **Michelangelo Buonarroti,** 1475-1564, High Renaissance, Florence, Italian,
The Last Judgment, 1536-1541. Fresco, 12.2 x 13.7 m.
Musei Vaticani Capella Sistina, Vatican.

Started before the death of Clement VII, The Last Judgment *took until 1541 to complete, all of eight years.*

Overall, The Last Judgment *consists of twelve major groups. In the two uppermost lunettes, angels on one side are carrying a column, while others bring along a crucifix from the other end. Circled in angels and prophets to bear witness further down, Christ presides. Next, comes the group of the Elect. Still further down, we see the Elect rising toward heaven, with a group of angels blowing trumpets in the middle as the Damned on the right are being offloaded into hell. At the very bottom, the waking dead rise from their tombs while Charon's ark stands right of centre.*

Religious inspiration seems most wanting in the depiction of the wingless angels holding the instruments of Passion. Like some of Correggio's works, Michelangelo resorted to mass-scale foreshortenings: the figures are arranged with no rendering of depth, using ready-made, over-confident foreshortenings that make them look like two-dimensional cut-outs, cloned one after the other with no attempt at individualisation.

Towering in anger from above the clouds with his right arm raised as if to throw a curse, Christ looks thoroughly agitated, very far removed from the grandeur and majesty that Michelangelo awarded his Jehovah for the ceiling frescos. Next to Christ, the Virgin backs down by turning her head away. Around them, the Just and the Elect are troubled and worried for fear that this divine, merciless anger will strike them down too. St Peter also appears insecure as he enters the scene, with an anxious, hesitant look on his face as he produces the keys, these now suddenly useless symbols of his authority. Slinging a frame from his shoulder, a terrified St Lawrence looks furtively at Christ. Flayed skin in hand, the brilliantly executed St Bartholomew holds up the skinning knife to Christ's view. Throughout the work, there is only anguish and terror, not a whit of serenity.

Once dear to Michelangelo, the realism that replaced lofty spiritual doctrine in The Last Judgment *transpires principally in the lower left scene depicting the resurrection of the dead. Looking strong and healthy except for a few skeletons, the dead rise up with more or less difficulty; some arch their backs to throw off the soil, others cross the divide one step at a time, still others throw their hands behind them for leverage to stand up.*

The most poignant and famous episode is that of Charon's ark, best approached through the enigmatic little scene in the lower middle. There we see a cavern befitting Cyclops, packed with demons watching for the Damned as their beastly appearances aggravate the horrors of hell, a theme ill-suited to painting.

To the right, the River Styx unfurls its rolling muddy waters as an overcrowded skiff ferries the Damned to their fate on the other bank. Upright at one end of the teetering vessel, Charon, with horned forehead and claw-tipped feet whom Dante describes as "the fiery-eyed demon whose oars strike the hesitant", raises his oar to press the grim masses onward.

355. **Paris Bordone,** 1500-1571, High Renaissance, Venetian School, Italian,
The Fisherman Presenting the Ring to the Doge Gradenigo, 1534.
Oil on canvas, 370 x 300 cm. Galleria dell'Accademia, Venice.

356. **Giulio Romano,** c. 1499-1546, Mannerism, *The Fall of the Giants* (detail),
1526-1534. Fresco. Palazzo del Tè, Mantova.

Romano's frescos in the Palazzo del Te testify to his classical learning and, later, had a great impact on Mannerist painters.

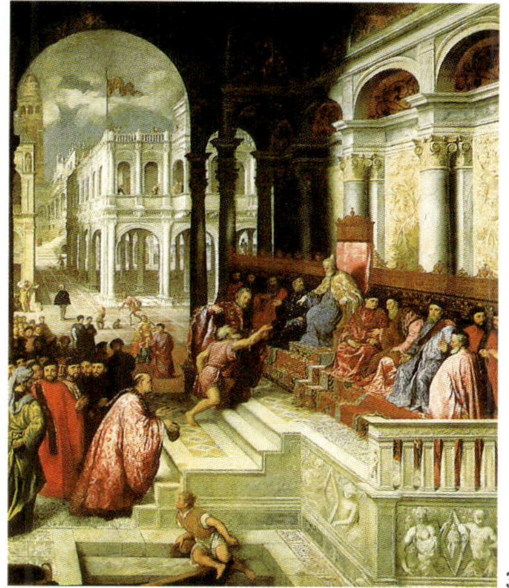

355

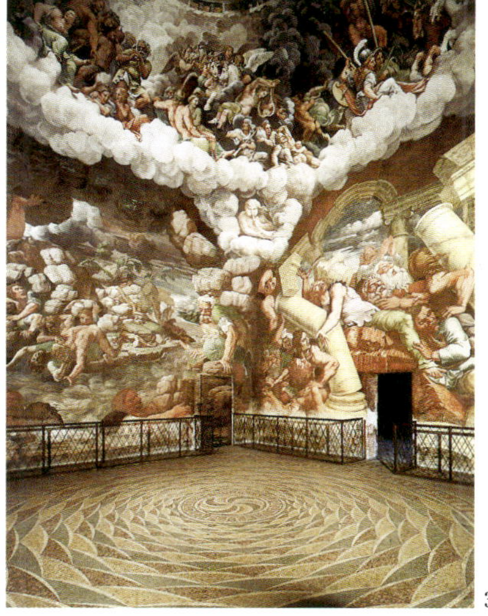

356

PARIS BORDONE
(1500 TREVISO – 1571 VENICE)

Bordone was born in Treviso but he settled in Venice where he soon became Titian's pupil and was strongly influenced not only by him, but also by Giorgione.

His work was appreciated by the elite all across Europe thanks to his beautiful depictions of women, his giorgionesque pastoral scenes and mythologies, and the monumental architectural settings in which he excelled. Although his art is now eclipsed by that of other Venetian painters like Titian, Veronese or Tintoretto, Bordone was considered during his lifetime as an accomplished artist.

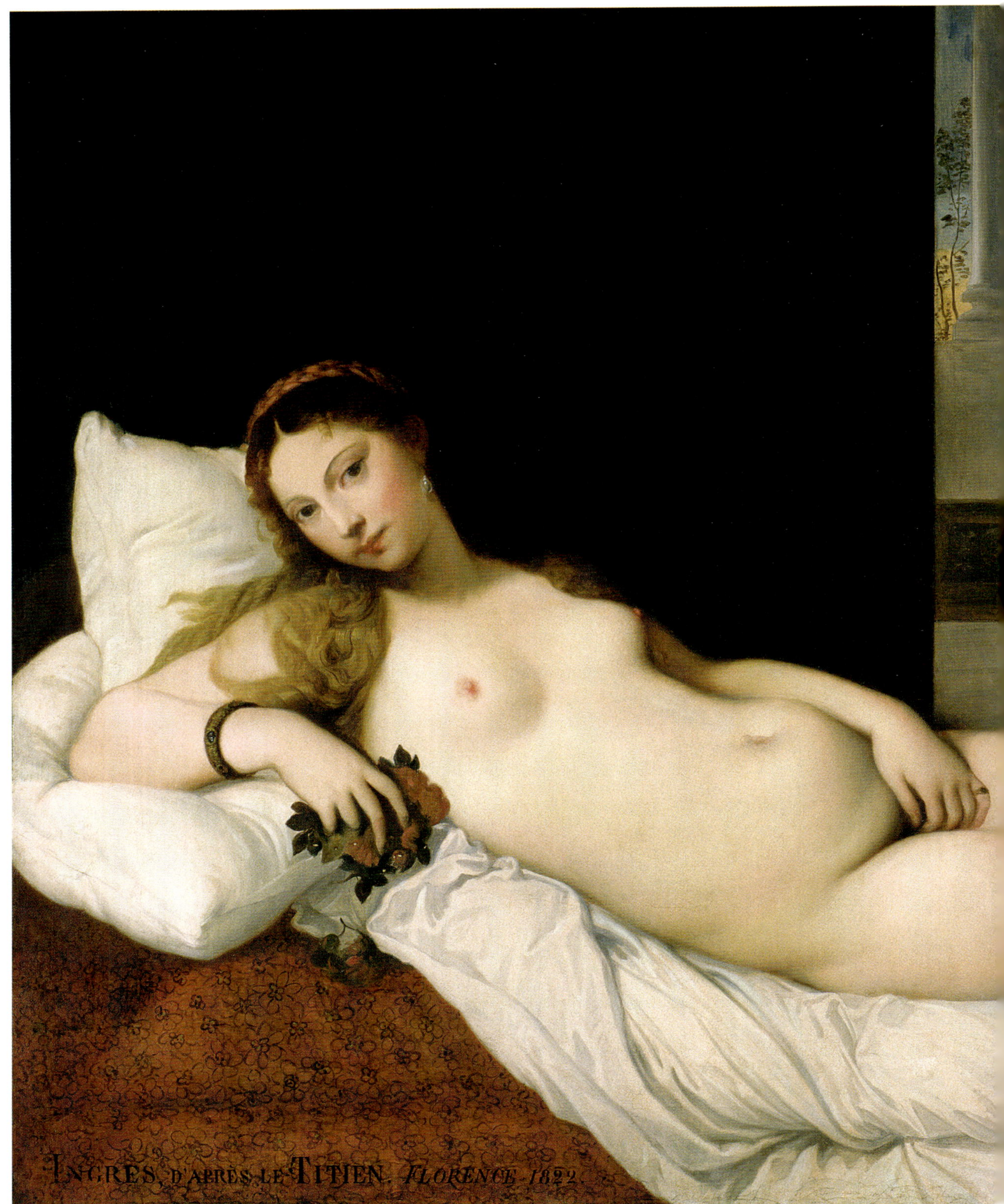
INGRES D'APRÈS LE TITIEN. FLORENCE 1822.

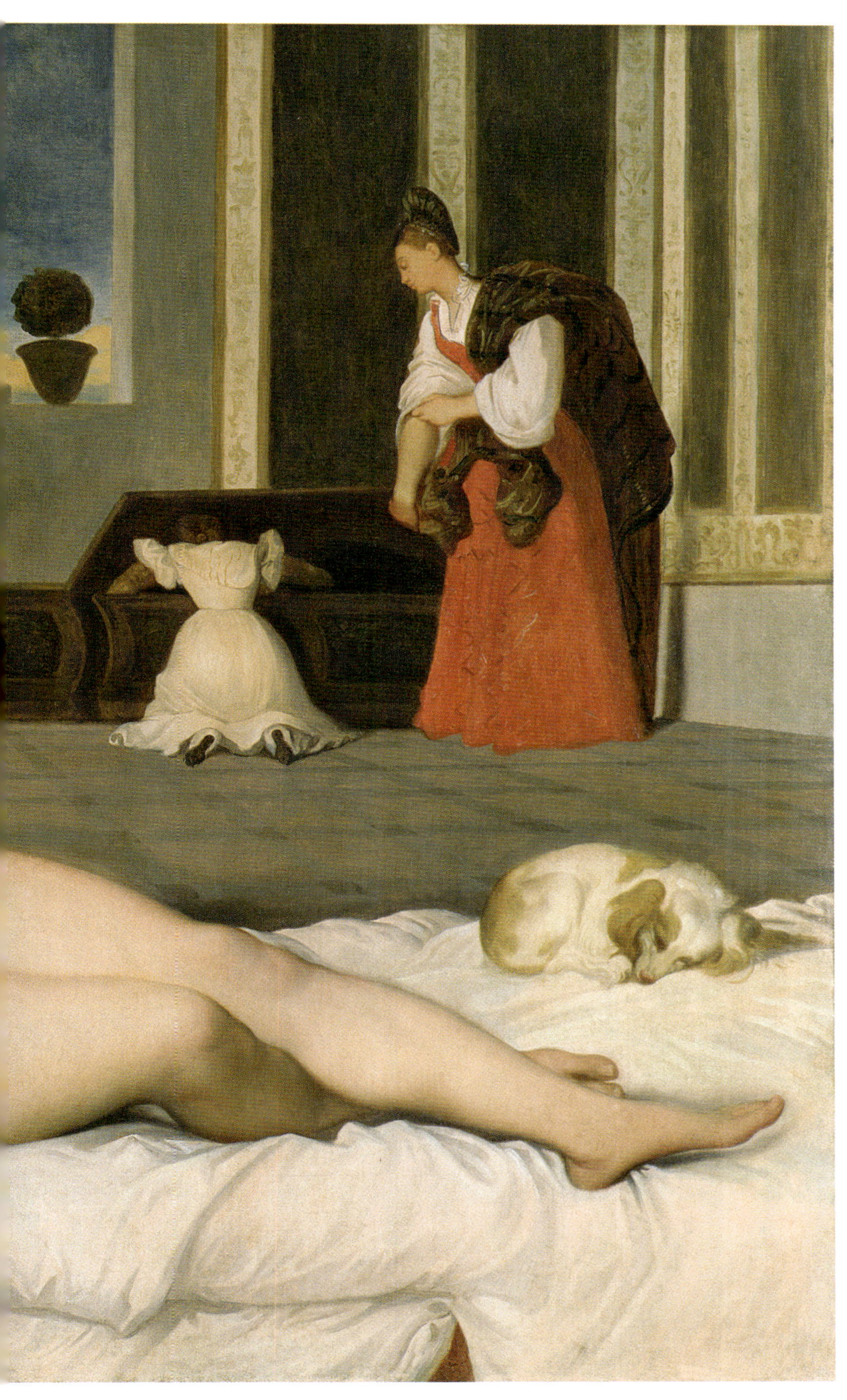

357. **Titian (Tiziano Vecellio),**
1490-1576,
High Renaissance, Venetian
School, Italian,
Venus of Urbino, 1538.
Oil on canvas, 119 x 165 cm.
Galleria degli Uffizi, Florence.

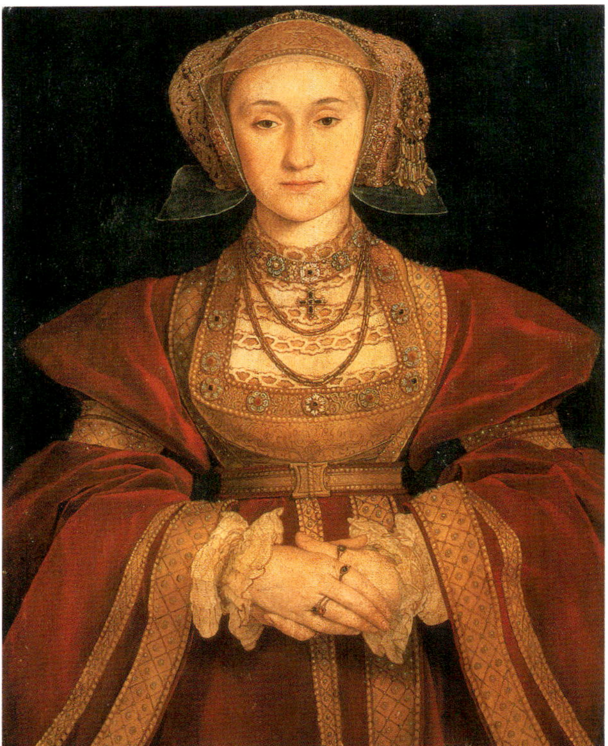

358. **Hans Holbein the Younger,** 1497-1543, Northern
Renaissance, German, *Portrait of Anne of Cleves,
Queen of England,* 1539.
Tempera on paper mounted on canvas, 65 x 48 cm.
Musée du Louvre, Paris.

360. **Marinus van Reymerswaele,** 1493-1567, Northern
Renaissance, Flemish, *Money-Changer and his Wife,* 1539.
Oil on panel, 83 x 97 cm.
Museo Nacional del Prado, Madrid.

*This painting is closely related to Quentin Massys' picture of
the same subject (fig. 314).*

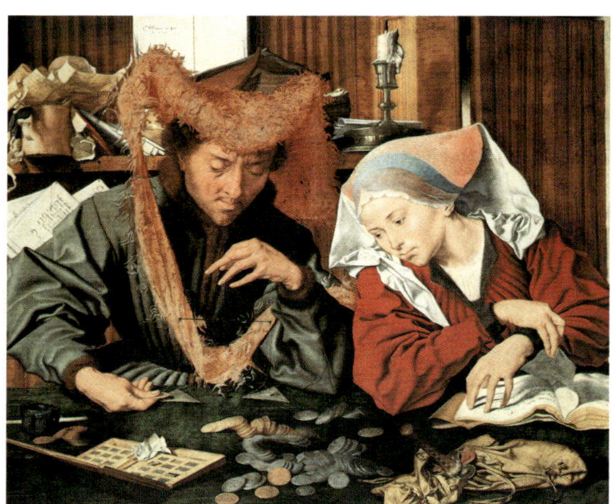

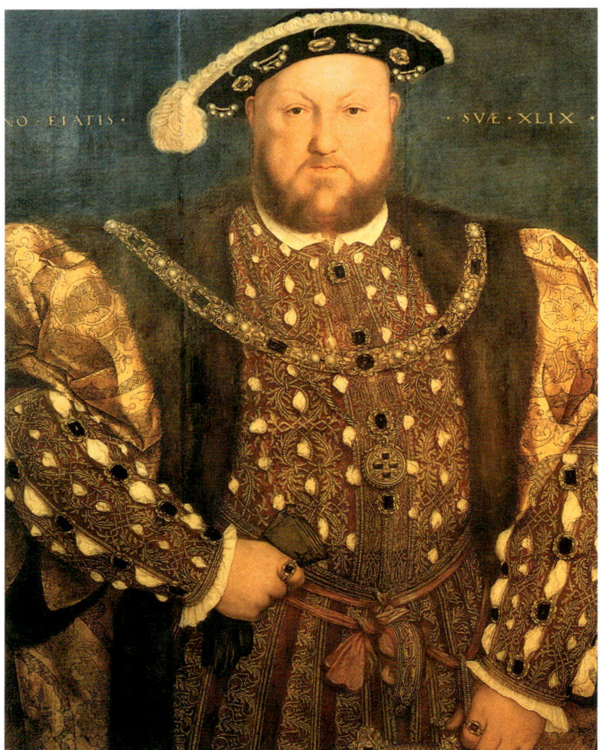

359. **Hans Holbein the Younger,** 1497-1543,
Northern Renaissance, German, *Portrait of Henry VIII,* c. 1539.
Tempera on panel, 89 x 75 cm.
Galleria Nazionale d'Arte Antica, Rome.

FRANCESCO PRIMATICCIO
(1504 BOLOGNA – 1570 PARIS)

Primaticcio's master was Guilio Romano, the most famous heir
of Raphael. He started working with him in 1526 in Mantova
then in 1532 was sent by his master to the court of France in the
castle of Fontainebleau to work for Francis I. There he met
another Italian painter, Rosso Fiorentino, who had arrived in
1530. The two Italians are known as the painters who brought
High Renaissance art to France and their work is known as the
Ecole de Fontainebleau. When Rosso died in 1540, Primaticcio
became the master of the numerous artists working on the
decoration of the castle.

Painter of the King, he was also an architect and a sculptor. He
organised his workshop like those of his old masters Romano and
Raphael, drawing and conceiving but leaving the work to his
talented assistants. His most famous works in the castle are the
gallery of Francis I and the ceiling of the ballroom.

Virtuoso and ambitious artist, Primaticcio developed a
scholastic art mixed with sensual delight and epic heroism. He
directed a world of gods and heroes. His gracious and seducing
formulae, that were creative and poetic without precedent,
created a primatician style that spread throughout Europe.

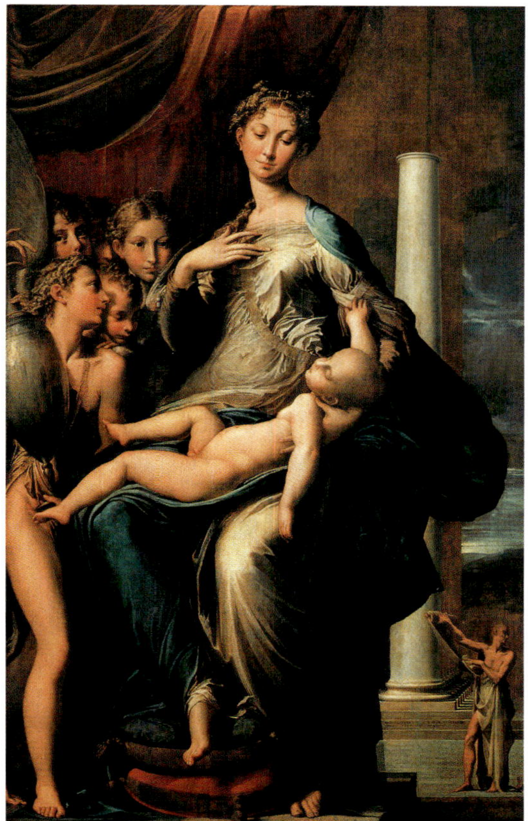

361. **Parmigianino (Girolamo Francesco Mazzola),**
1503-1540, Mannerism, Parma School, Italian,
Madonna with Long Neck, c. 1535.
Oil on wood, 216 x 132 cm.
Galleria degli Uffizi, Florence.

*A somewhat mysterious image of the Madonna
and her son was created by the Mannerist artist
Parmigianino. This work features the large, centrally-
located figure of the Virgin. Her elongated, seated
body holds the nude child Jesus on her lap. A
group of angels keeps her company, while the
viewer is offered a glimpse of a freestanding
column surrounded by a considerable depth of open
space. A disproportionately small male figure is
next to the column. The Madonna has the look of
an aristocratic lady of nobility or a queen, her
divinity overshadowed by her humanity.*

363. **Jacopo Bassano**, c. 1510-1592, High Renaissance,
Venetian School, Italian, *The Adoration of the
Shepherds,* 1544-1545.
Oil on canvas, 140 x 219 cm.
National Gallery of Scotland, Edinburgh.

*Son of Francesco Bassano the Elder, Jacopo
adopted some of his father's style as he created
religious paintings.*

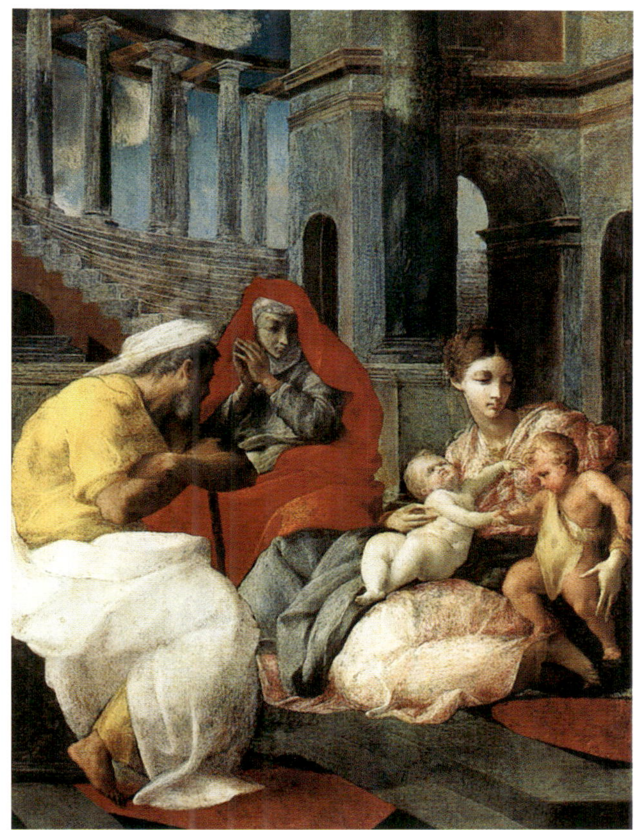

362. **Francesco Primaticcio,**
1504-1570, Mannerism, School of Fontainebleau, Italian,
The Holy Family with St Elisabeth and St John the Baptist, 1541-1543.
Oil on slate, 43.5 x 31 cm.
The State Hermitage Museum, St Petersburg.

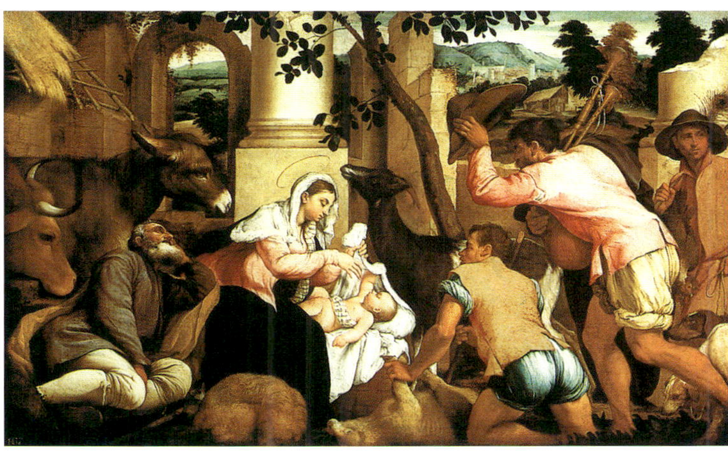

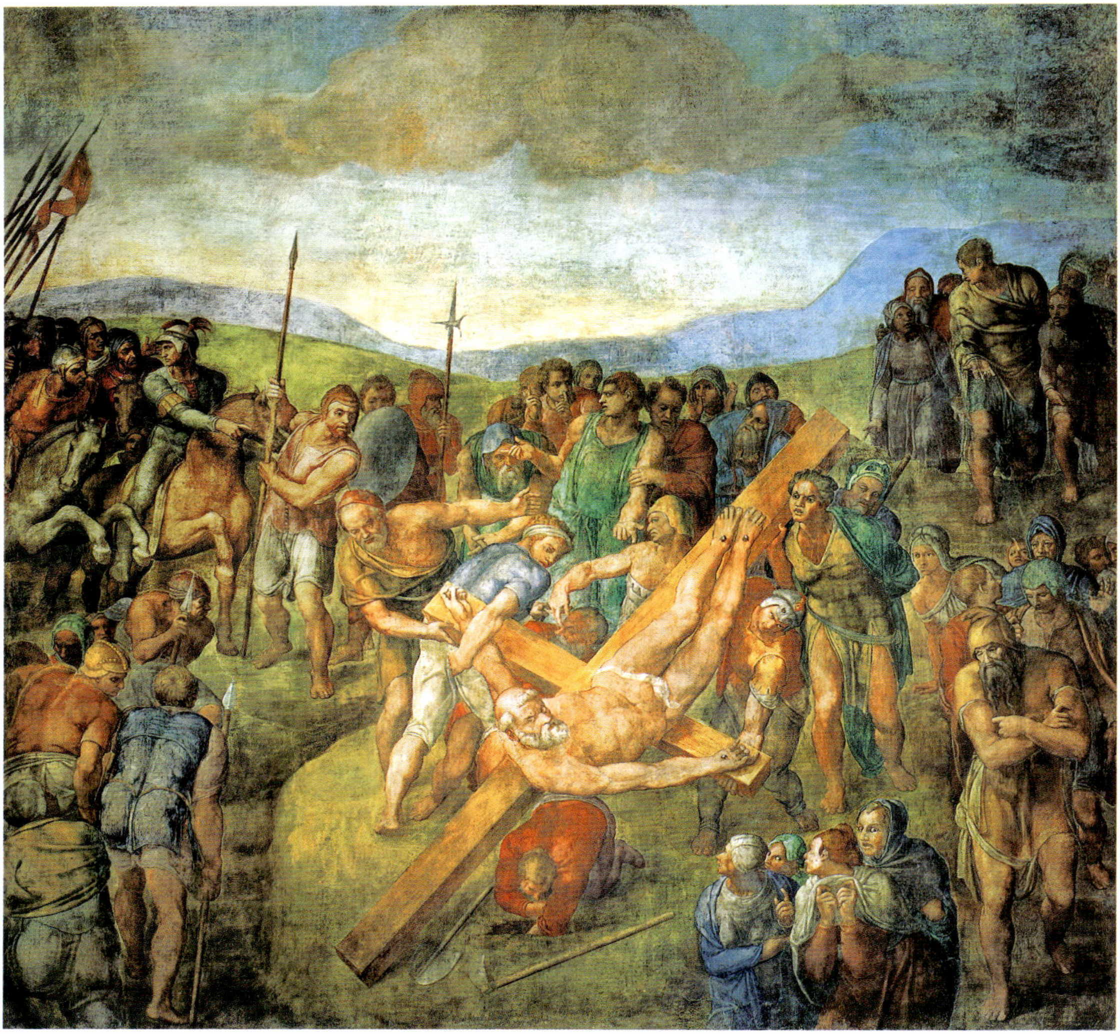

364. **Michelangelo Buonarroti,** 1475-1564,
High Renaissance, Florence, Italian,
Martyrdom of St Peter, 1546-1550.
Fresco, 625 x 662 cm.
Cappella Paolina, Palazzi Pontifici, Vatican.

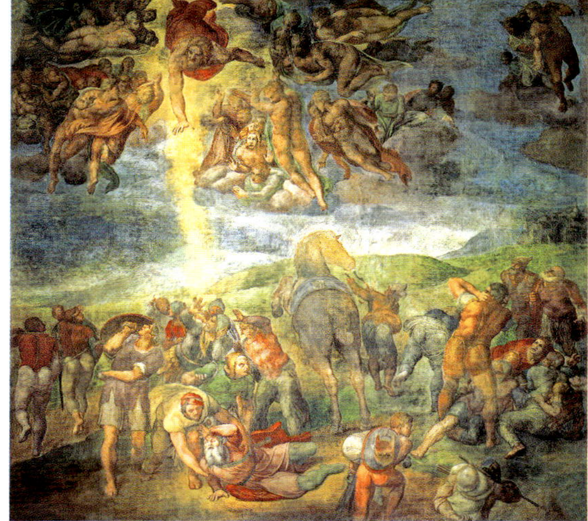

365. **Michelangelo Buonarroti,** 1475-1564,
High Renaissance, Florence, Italian,
Conversion of St Paul, 1542-1545.
Fresco, 625 x 661 cm.
Cappella Paolina, Palazzi Pontifici, Vatican.

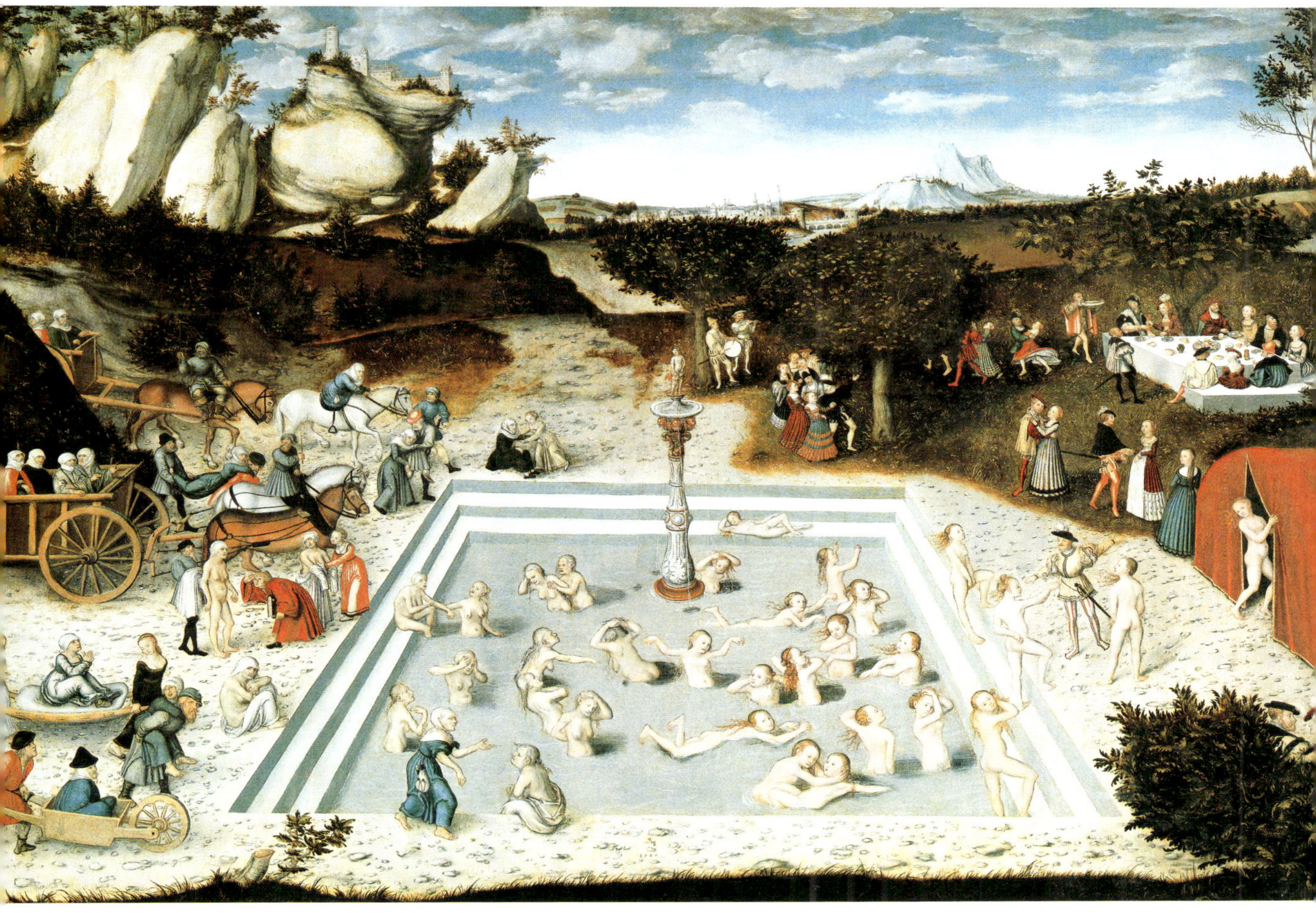

366. **Lucas Cranach the Elder,** 1472-1553, Northern Renaissance,
German, *Fountain of Youth*, 1546.
Oil on lime panel, 122.5 x 186.5 cm. Staatliche Museen, Berlin.

*The fountain, crowned by a statue of Venus and Cupid, is a sort of
"font of love" accessible only to women. It is not enough to say that
its waters restore lost youth – they affect a resurrection because the
magical bath transforms old women whose vital energy is already
exhausted. Venus' spring is the boundary between death and life.*

*The women step onto the bank of life, as if into the next world, as
happy captives of the goddess of love. This really is another world:
the garden of love on the right bank and the ugly conglomeration
of rocks on the left form a contrast as sharp as that between youth
and old age.*

LUCAS CRANACH THE ELDER
(1472 KRONACH – 1553 WEIMAR)

Lucas Cranach was one of the greatest artists of the Renaissance, as shown by the diversity of his artistic interests as
well as his awareness of the social and political events of his time. He developed a number of painting techniques
which were afterwards used by several generations of artists. His somewhat mannered style and splendid palette are
easily recognised in numerous portraits of monarchs, cardinals, courtiers and their ladies, religious reformers,
humanists and philosophers. He also painted altarpieces, mythological scenes and allegories, and he is well-known
for his hunting scenes. As a gifted draughtsman, he executed numerous engravings on both religious and secular
subjects, and as court painter, he was involved in tournaments and masked balls. As a result, he completed a great
number of costume designs, armorials, furniture, and parade-ground arms. The high point of the German
Renaissance is reflected in his achievements.

367. **Titian (Tiziano Vecellio),** 1490-1576,
High Renaissance, Venetian School, Italian, *Pope Paul III and his Cousins Alessandro and Ottavio Farnese,* c. 1546.
Oil on canvas, 200 x 127 cm.
Museo Nazionale di Capodimonte, Naples.

This triple portrait catches the nature of the sitters. The free movements of the characters and the restrained and emaciated face of Paul III contribute to the extraordinary qualities of this group.

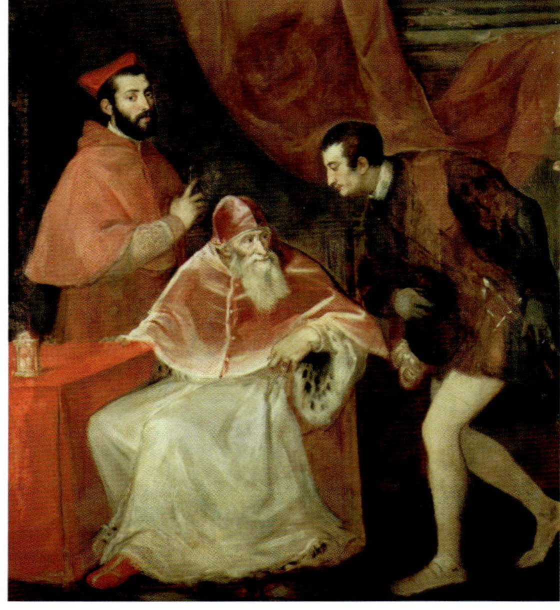

367

368. **Agnolo Bronzino,** 1503-1572,
Mannerism, Florentine School, Italian, *Portrait of Eleonora da Toledo with her Son Giovanni de' Medici,* 1545.
Oil on panel, 115 x 96 cm. Galleria degli Uffizi, Florence.

368

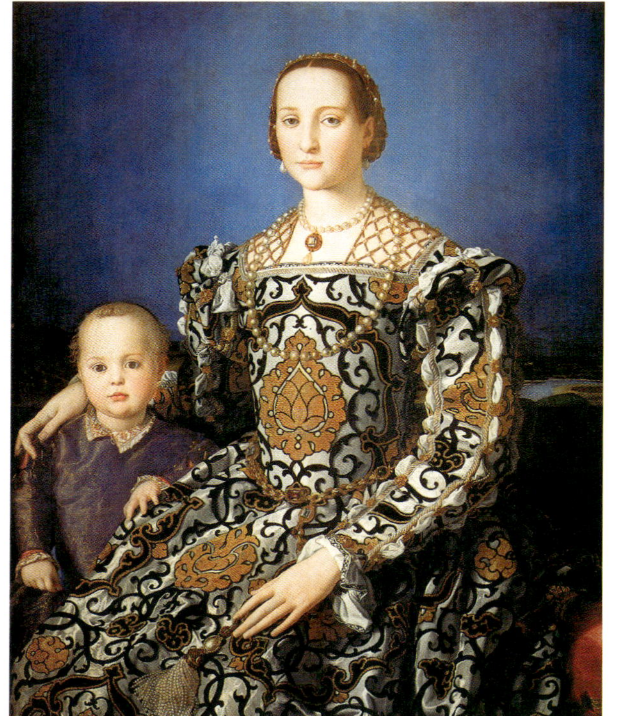

AGNOLO BRONZINO (AGNOLO DI COSIMO)
(1503 – 1572 FLORENCE)

Florentine Mannerist painter Bronzino, (originally Agnolo di Cosimo), whose nickname may be derived from his dark complexion, was the pupil and adopted son of Pontormo. If he kept his master's manners for maniacal insistence on accurate drawing, he added a very personal use of colour, applied in a clear and compact fashion giving the aspect of varnish.

He excelled as a portraitist in the court of Duke Cosimo I de Medici, where he was a court painter for most of his career, but was less successful as a religious painter. Actually, he painted the type of religious work that gave a bad reputation to Mannerism. However, he was skilled in the nude as in *Allegory with Venus and Cupid* (fig. 371). His work influenced the evolution of European court portraiture for a century thanks to his cold and unemotional representation that conveyed an almost insolent assurance.

369. **Titian (Tiziano Vecellio),** 1490-1576, High Renaissance,
Venetian School, Italian, *Emperor Charles V at Mühlberg,* 1548.
Oil on canvas, 332 x 279 cm.
Museo Nacional del Prado, Madrid.

Talented portraitist Titian became the accredited painter of Charles V, who considered him the most prestigious portrait painter of the time. He later had a great influence on Rubens in this field. The originality of this painting is in the scenery. Charles V is represented entirely and in action, in a triumphant and noble attitude, celebrating the victory of Charles V over the Protestants in 1547. Titian makes out of this subject a realist portrait, depicting the wilted face of the king in his old age.

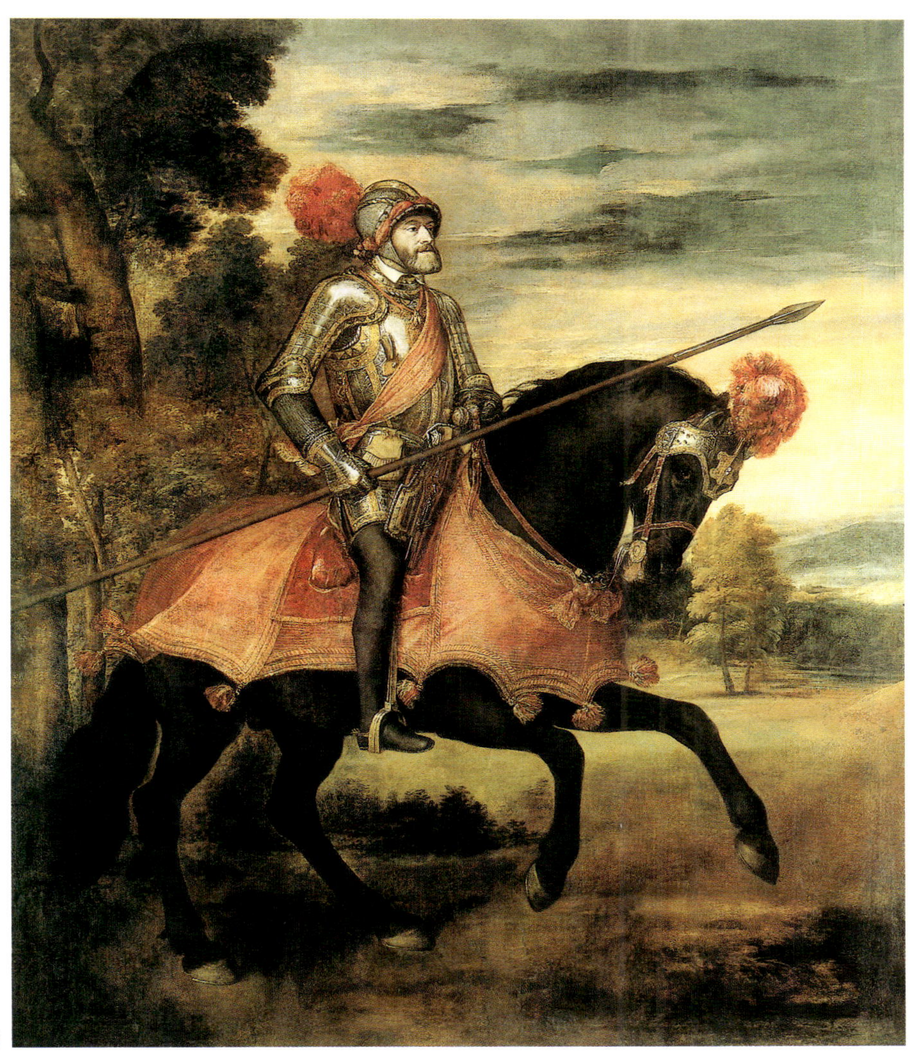

369

TITIAN (TIZIANO VECELLIO)
(1490 PIEVE DI CADORE – 1576 VENICE)

Titian was at once a genius and a favourite of fortune; he moved through his long life of pomp and splendour serene and self-contained. The details of his early life are not certain. He was of an old family, born at Pieve in the mountain district of Cadore. By the time that he was eleven years old he was sent to Venice, where he became the pupil, first of Gentile Bellini, and later of Gentile's brother, Giovanni. Then he worked with the great artist Giorgione. He worked on major frescos in Venice and Padua, as well as commissions in France for Francis I (1494-1547), in Spain for Charles V (1500-1558). His equestrian portrait of Charles V (1549) symbolises a military victory over Protestant princes in 1547. Titian then went to Rome for commissions by Pope Paul III (1534-1549), then in Spain to work exclusively for Philip II (1527-1598).

No artist's life was so completely and consistently superb; and such, too, is the character of his work. He was great in portraiture, in landscape, in the painting of religious and mythological subjects. In any one of these departments others have rivalled him, but his glory is that he attained an eminence in all; he was an artist of universal gifts – an all-embracing genius; equable, serene, majestic. Titian's beautiful reclining women, whether called Venus or any other name, are among the most original of the creations of the Venetian school and particularly of its great masters, to which he and Giorgione belonged. His works differ greatly from the Florentine nude, which is generally standing, resembling sometimes, in the fine precision of its contours, the precious work of a goldsmith and sometimes the great marble of a sculptor.

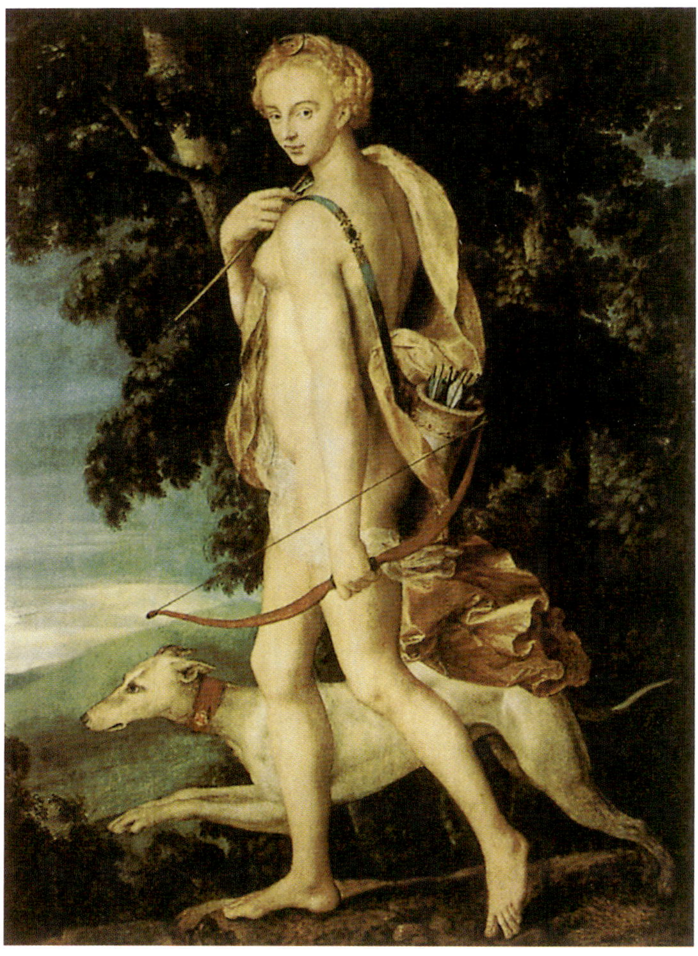

370

370. **Master of the Fontainebleau School,** 1525-1575, Second School of Fontainebleau, French, *Diana Huntress*, c. 1555. Oil on canvas, 191 x 132 cm. Musée du Louvre, Paris.

The proportions of the sitter recall the Mannerism of the First School of Fontainebleau founded by Rosso Fiorentino and Primaticcio. However, the landscape in the background characterises the manner of the Second School of Fontainebleau, announcing the French landscape painting of the seventeenth century. This anonymous work is nonetheless very characteristic of the Second School of Fontainebleau referring to both Flemish and Italian art.

371. **Agnolo Bronzino**, 1503-1572, Mannerism, Florentine School, Italian, *An Allegory with Venus and Cupid,* 1540-1550. Oil on wood, 146.5 x 116.8 cm. National Gallery, London.

This picture was sent to the King of France in 1568, its erotic and erudite character suiting the taste of the ruler. This painting shows eroticism under the pretext of a moralising allegory.

372. **Cecchino del Salviati (Francesco de' Rossi),** 1510-1563, Mannerism, Florentine School, Italian, *Charity,* c. 1556. Oil on panel, 156 x 122 cm. Galleria degli Uffizi, Florence.

373. **Tintoretto (Jacopo Robusti),** 1518-1594, Mannerism, Venetian School, Italian, *The Bathing Susanna*, 1560-1562. Oil on canvas, 146.6 x 193.6 cm. Kunsthistorisches Museum, Vienna.

Tintoretto managed to preserve the colours and light from Venetian tradition and even stated that he aspired to combine the colours of Titian and the drawing of Michelangelo. The painting describes the scene of the Old Testament of how Susanna is surprised at the bath by two intruders.

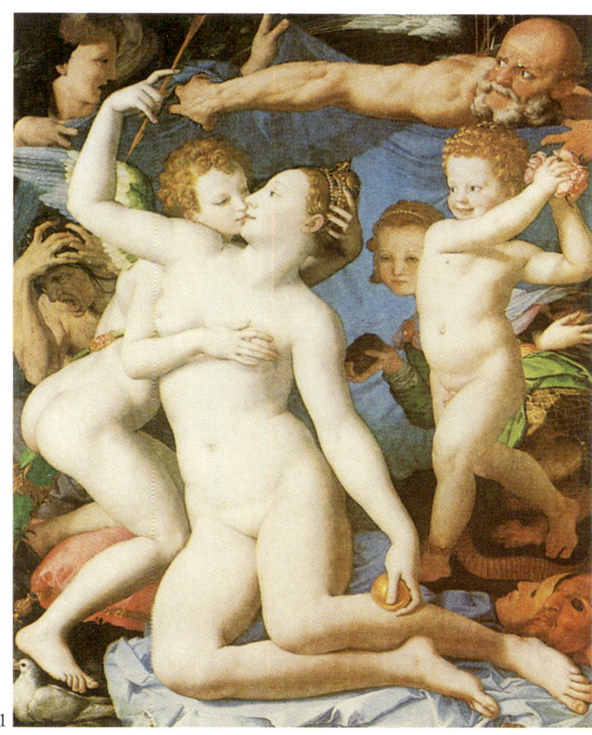

371

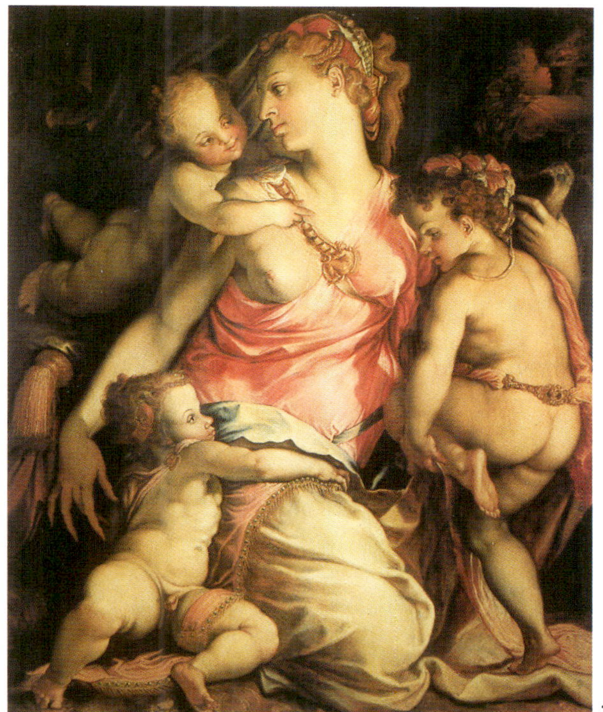

372

373

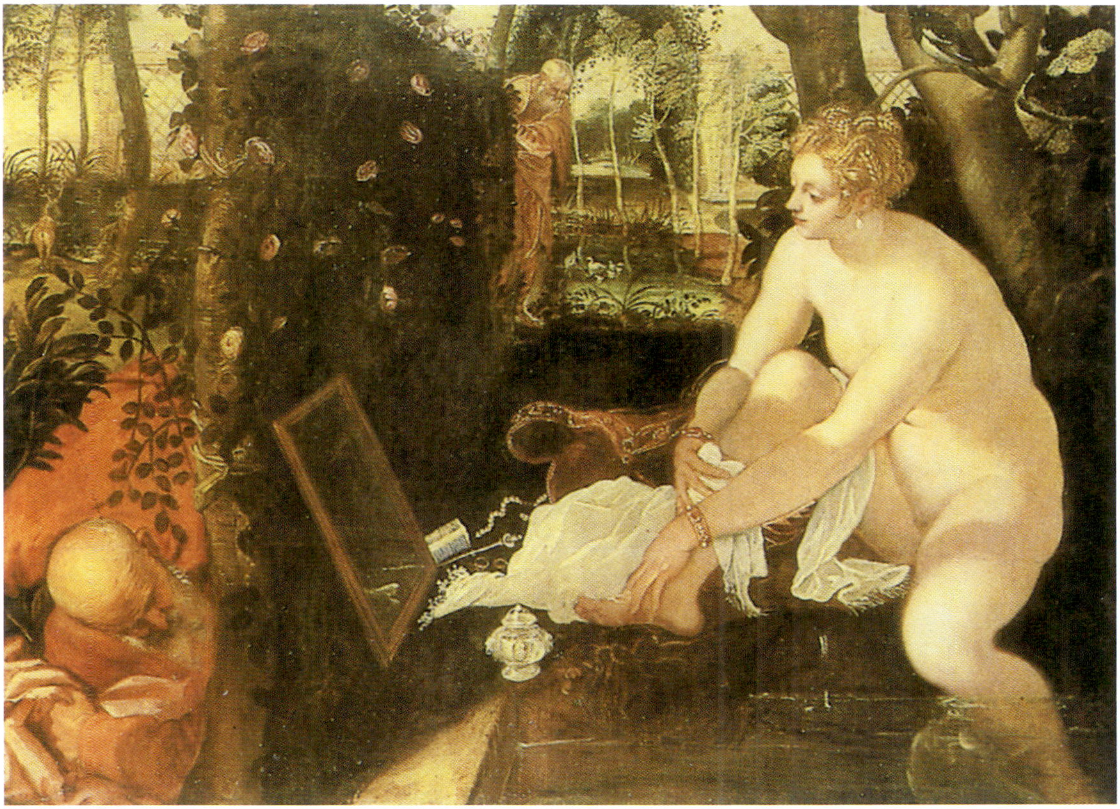

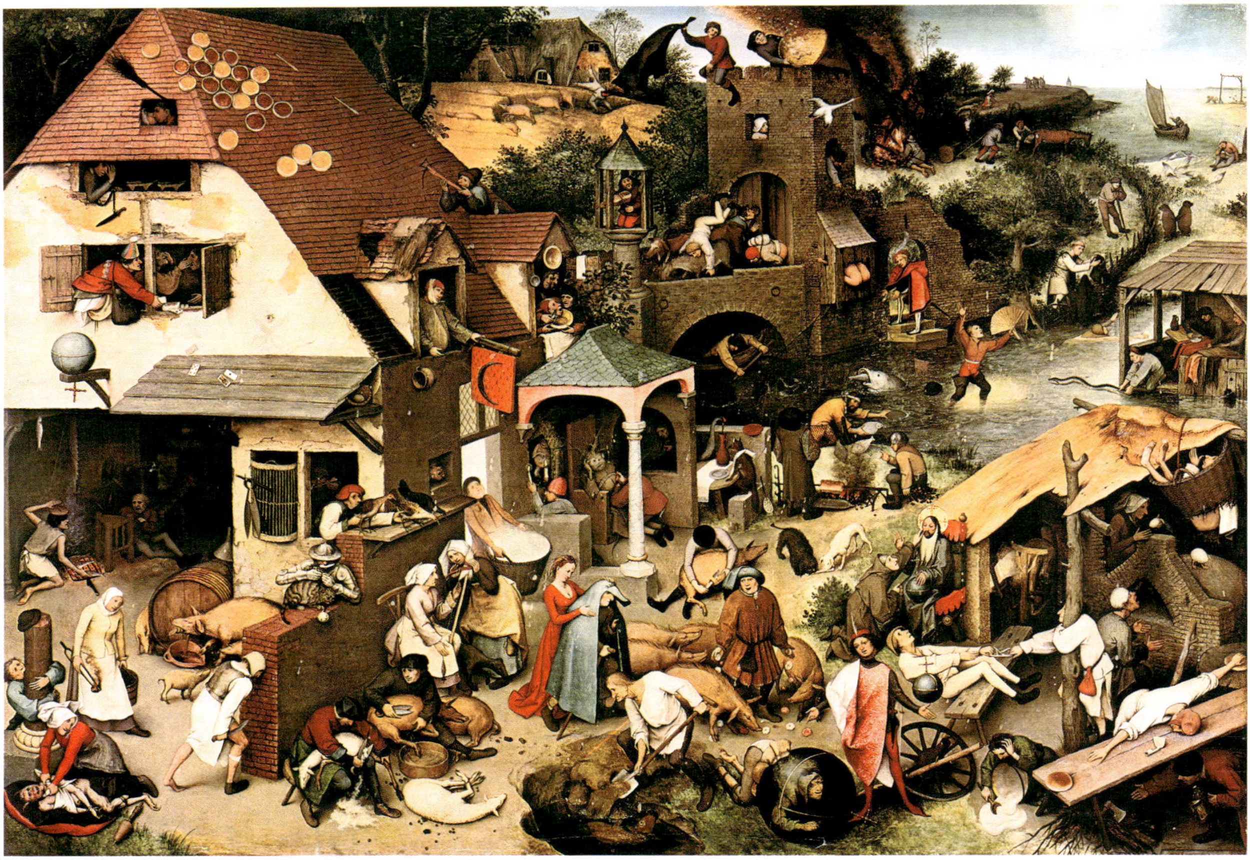

374. **Pieter Bruegel the Elder**, c. 1525-1569, Northern Renaissance,
Flemish, *Netherlandish Proverbs,* 1559.
Oil on oak panel, 117 x 163 cm.
Stiftung Staatliche Museen, Gemäldegalerie, Berlin.

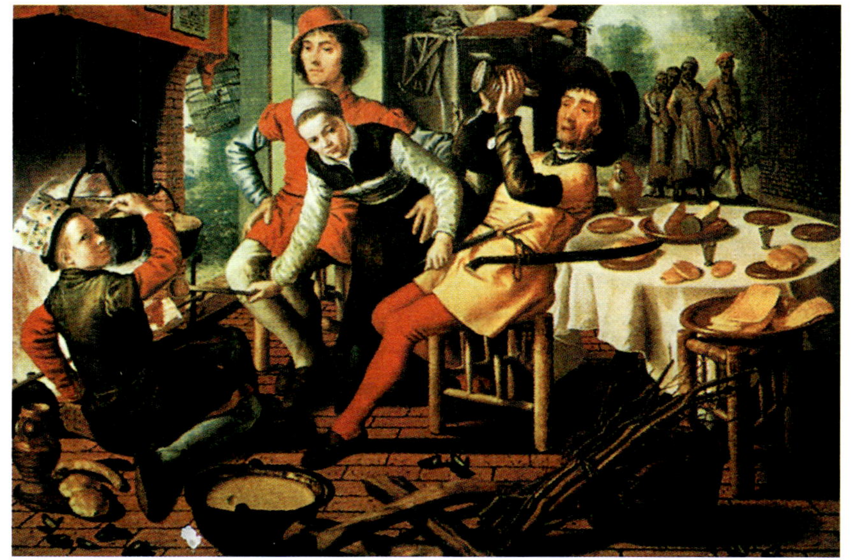

375. **Pieter Aertsen,** 1508-1575,
Northern Renaissance, Dutch,
Peasants by the Hearth, 1556.
Oil on panel, 142.3 x 198 cm.
Museum Mayer van den Bergh,
Antwerp.

*Just as Bruegel, Aersten is interested in
a national and rustic realism.*

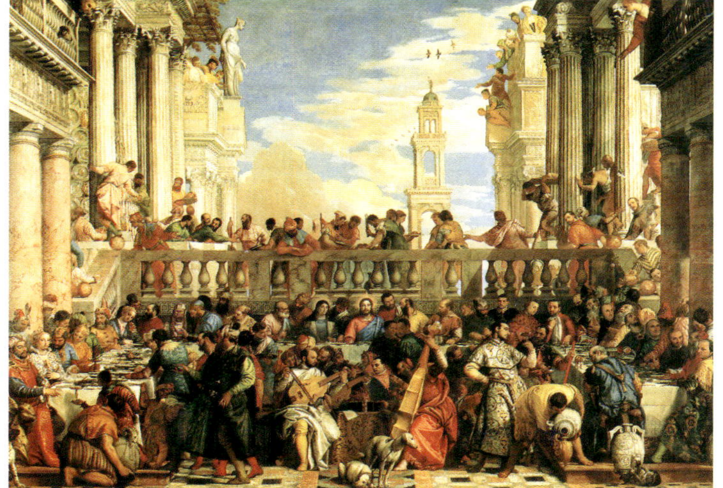

376

376. **Veronese (Paolo Caliari)**, 1528-1588, Mannerism,
Venetian School, Italian,
The Wedding Feast at Cana, c. 1562-1563.
Oil on canvas, 677 x 994 cm. Musée du Louvre, Paris.

*Born in Verona, a city open to the development of
Mannerism, Veronese remains nevertheless independent
in style. In contrast to Titian and his dramatic and realist
paintings, Veronese's works represent the joyful
contemplation of beauty. Influenced by Mantegna, he
also takes his inspiration in the hue of colours from the
Gothic period. His sojourn in Mantova led him to
discover Michelangelo and Raphael and he also met
Correggio.* Wedding Feast at Cana – *commissioned as
part of the reconstruction of the Benedictine convent of
San Giorgio Maggiore in Venice – decorated the
refectory. At the time Veronese had already set his
reputation in the city as he had already depicted the
decorations of the church San Sebastiano and of the
Doge Palace. The scene represents the first miracle of
Christ but transposed here within a Venetian feast.
Dramatised by the architecture, Veronese takes his
inspiration in Palladio's contemporary constructions for
the architecture and multiplies the vanishing points. The
columns show the three architectural orders: Doric,
Corinthian and Composite. The painter uses precious
pigments, imported from the East. The richness of the
colours is an important point in Venetian painting. This
work, restored between 1990 and 1992 has found once
again its original colours.*

VERONESE (PAOLO CALIARI)
(1528 VERONA – 1588 VENICE)

Paolo Veronese was one of the great masters of
the late Renaissance in Venice with Titian and
Tintoretto, the three of them seen as a triumvirate.
Originally named Paolo Caliari, he was called
Veronese from his native city of Verona. He is
known for his works of supreme colouring and
for his illusionistic decorations in both fresco
and oil. His large paintings of biblical feasts
executed for the refectories of monasteries in
Venice and Verona are especially celebrated
(like *The Marriage of Cana*). He also painted
many portraits, altarpieces and historical and
mythological paintings. He headed a family
workshop that remained active after his death.
Although highly successful, he had little
immediate influence. To the Flemish baroque
master Peter Paul Rubens and to the eighteenth-
century Venetian painters, especially Giovanni
Battista Tiepolo, however, Veronese's handling of
colour and perspective supplied an indispensable
point of departure.

The quality of his paintings is of sober
restraint. Veronese is simply what he was – a
painter. The purpose of his pictures is immediately
self-evident. Some people will say that this
self-evidence is the proper scope of painting; that
"art for art's sake" should be the sole object of the
painter; that the representation of anything else
but what is apparent to the eye is going outside
the province of the art. The best answer to this
is that not solely laymen, but artists in all
periods – artists of such personality that they
cannot be ignored – have tried to reinforce the
grandeur of mere appearances with something
that shall appeal to the mind and soul of all.

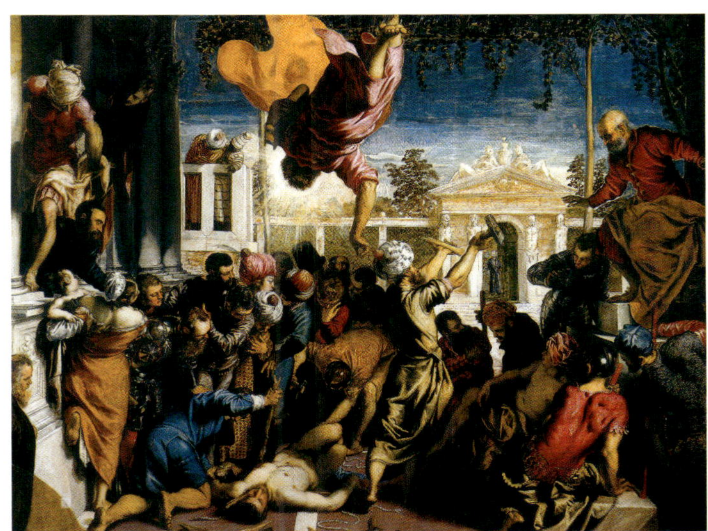

377

377. **Tintoretto (Jacopo Robusti)**, 1518-1594,
Mannerism, Venetian School, Italian, Flemish,
The Miracle of St Mark Freeing the Slave, c. 1565.
Oil on canvas, 415 x 541 cm.
Galleria dell'Accademia, Venice.

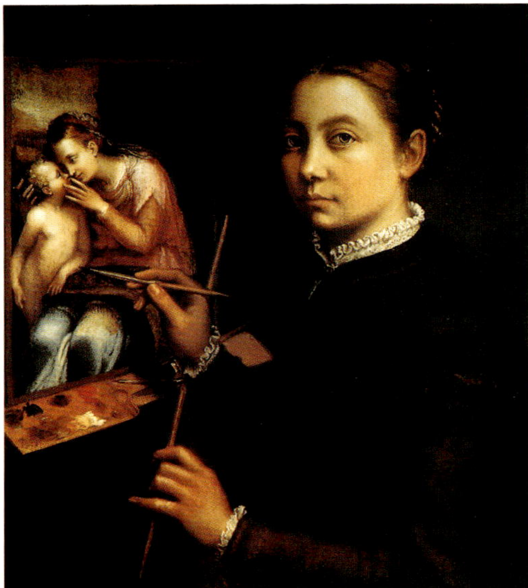

378. **Sofonisba Anguissola,** c. 1532-1625, Mannerism,
Italian, *Self-portrait at the Easel*, 1556.
Oil on panel, 66 x 57 cm.
Museum Zamek, Lancut (Poland).

*Anguissola (also spelt Anguisciola), inspired by the
legend of St Luke as artist, depicted herself standing
in front of her easel and painting the Madonna and
Child. Her round face is turned towards the invisible
Mary and the viewer. The painting on her easel (some
art historians assume that the painting within the
painting actually existed) shows a seated Madonna
leaning towards her child, who is standing next to
her. The Virgin is tenderly kissing her beloved Son.
Anguissola was using the popular theme of the
kissing Madonna to convey her message of the
supreme and profound love that the Mother of the
Church has for her child and, by inference, for all her
human children.*

379. **Veronese (Paolo Caliari),** 1528-1588,
Mannerism, Venetian School, Italian, *The Mystical
Marriage of Saint Catherine of Alexandria*, 1562.
Oil on canvas, 130.5 x 130 cm.
Musée Fabre, Montpellier.

*This painting well illustrates Venetian painting.
Here, Veronese works as well on the colours as on
the quality of drawing.*

TINTORETTO (JACOPO ROBUSTI)
(1518 – 1594 VENICE)

His father being a dyer of silk (tintore), Tintoretto was given this
nickname in his youth, "The Little Dyer", "Il Tintoretto".

Tintoretto became the most important Italian Mannerist painter of
the Venetian school. St Mark, the patron saint of Venice, is thematic in
two of his most important works. Most of his major works were on
religious themes.

About his career, a story tells us that the Brothers of the Confraternity
of San Rocco gave Tintoretto a commission for two pictures in their
church, and then invited him to enter a competition with Veronese and
others for the decoration of the ceiling in the hall of their school. When
the day arrived, the other painters presented their sketches, but
Tintoretto, being asked for his, removed a screen from the ceiling and
showed it already painted. "We asked for sketches", they said. "That is
the way", he replied, "I make my sketches." They still demurred, so he
made them a present of the picture, and by the rules of their order they
could not refuse a gift. In the end they promised him the painting of all
the pictures they required, and during his lifetime he covered their walls
with sixty large compositions.

Yet it is his phenomenal energy and the impetuous force of his work
which are particularly characteristic of Tintoretto and earned for him the
sobriquet among his contemporaries, *Il Furioso*. He painted so many
pictures, and on so vast a scale, that some show the effects of over-haste
and extravagance, which caused Annibale Carracci to say that, "while
Tintoretto was the equal of Titian, he was often inferior to Tintoretto."

The main interest of his work is his love for foreshortening and it is
said that to help him with the complex poses he favoured, Tintoretto
used to make small wax models which he arranged on a stage and
experimented on with spotlights for effects of light and shade and
composition. This method of composing explains the frequent repetition
in his works of the same figures seen from different angles.

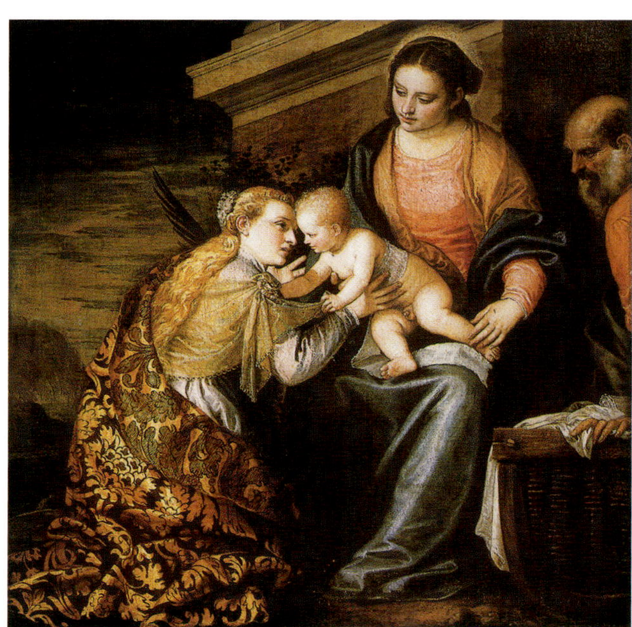

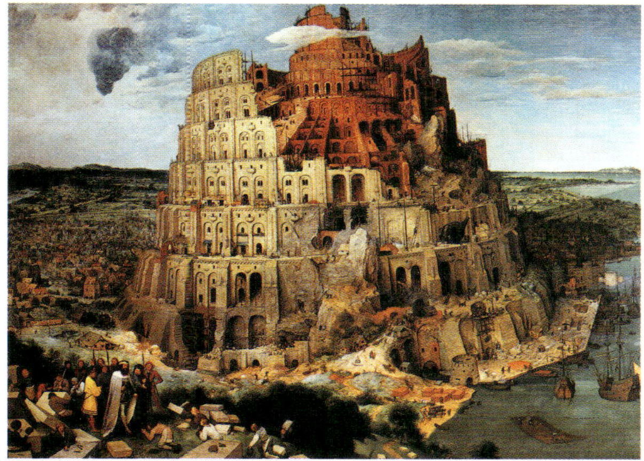

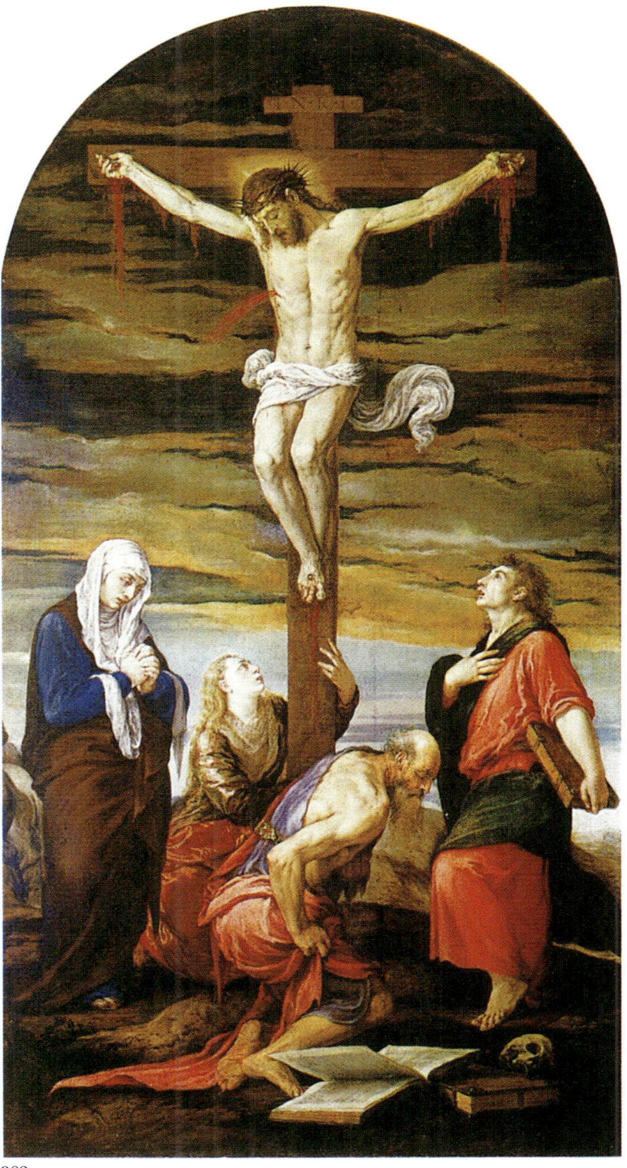

380. **Pieter Bruegel the Elder**, c. 1525-1569, Northern Renaissance, Flemish, *The Tower of Babel,* 1563. Oil on oak panel, 114 x 155 cm. Kunsthistorisches Museum, Vienna.

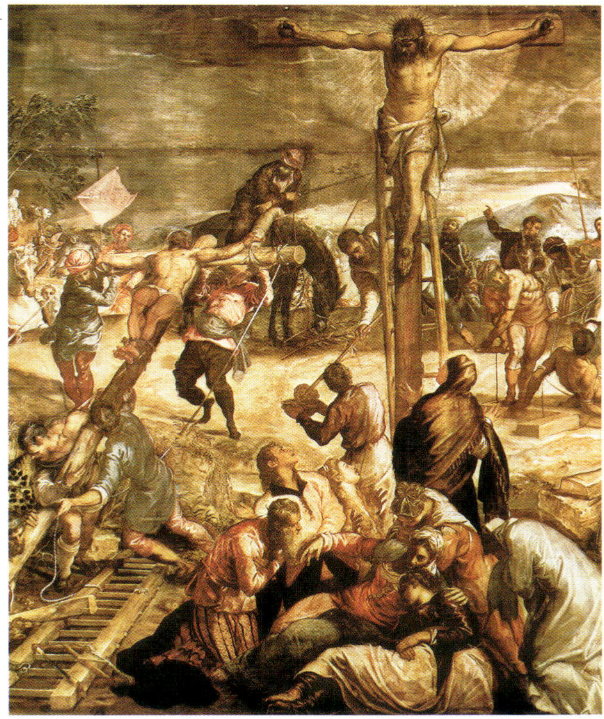

381. **Tintoretto (Jacopo Robusti),** 1518-1594, Mannerism, Venetian School, Italian, *Crucifixion* (detail), 1565. Oil on canvas, 536 x 1224 cm. Scuola di San Rocco, Venice.

Tintoretto proposes here a new representation of the Crucifixion: although Christ is on the Cross, life doesn't seem to stop. While Mary faints and followers are mourning, other people are depicted working away at other tasks.

382. **Jacopo Bassano**, c. 1510-1592, Mannerism, Venetian School, Italian, *The Crucifixion*, 1562. Oil on panel, 315 x 177 cm. Museo Civico, Treviso.

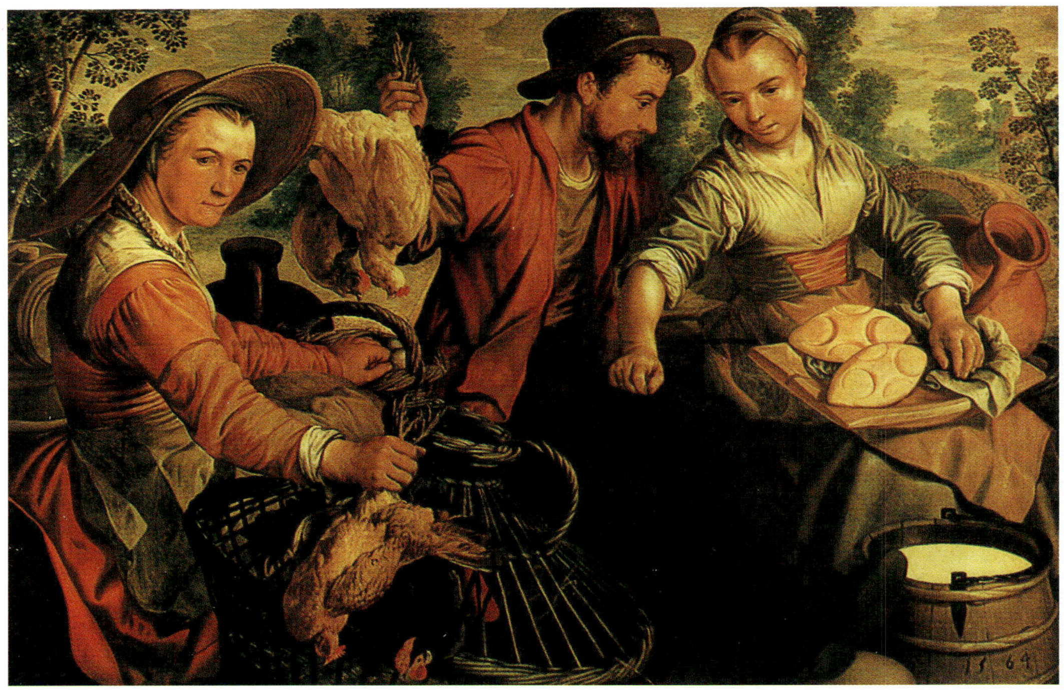

383. **Joachim Beuckelaer**, c. 1530-1573, Mannerism, Flemish, *At the Market*, 1564.
Oil on panel, 128 x 166 cm.
Pushkin Museum of Fine Arts, Moscow.

384. **Pieter Bruegel the Elder**, c. 1525-1569, Northern Renaissance, Flemish, *Peasant Wedding*, 1568.
Oil on panel, 114 x 164 cm.
Kunsthistorisches Museum, Vienna.

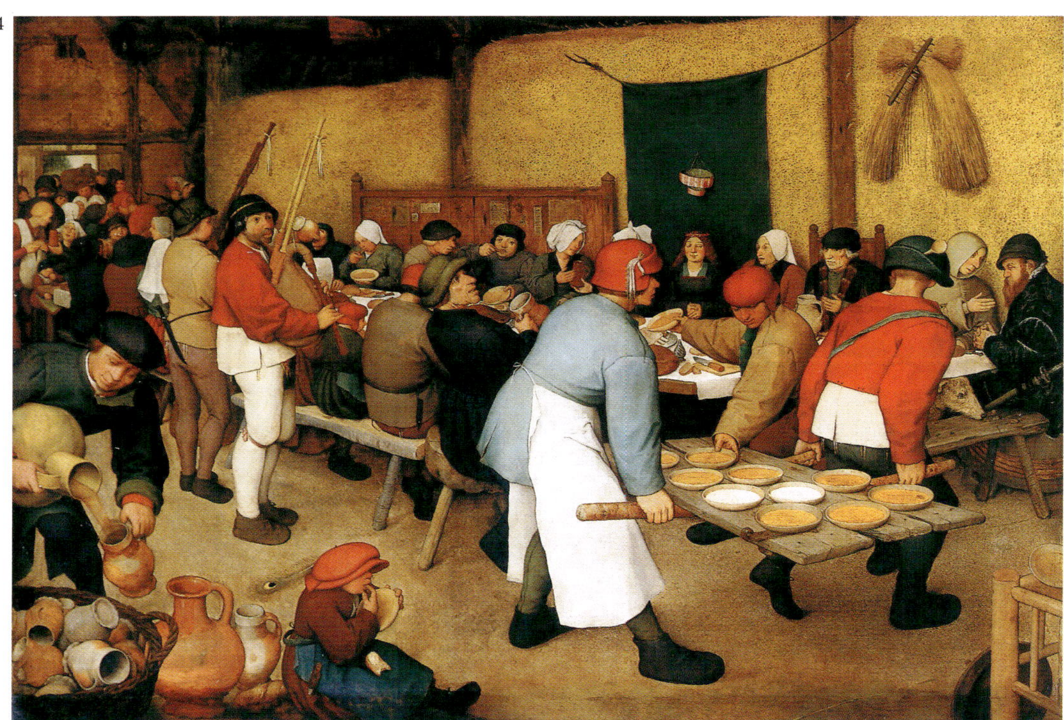

385

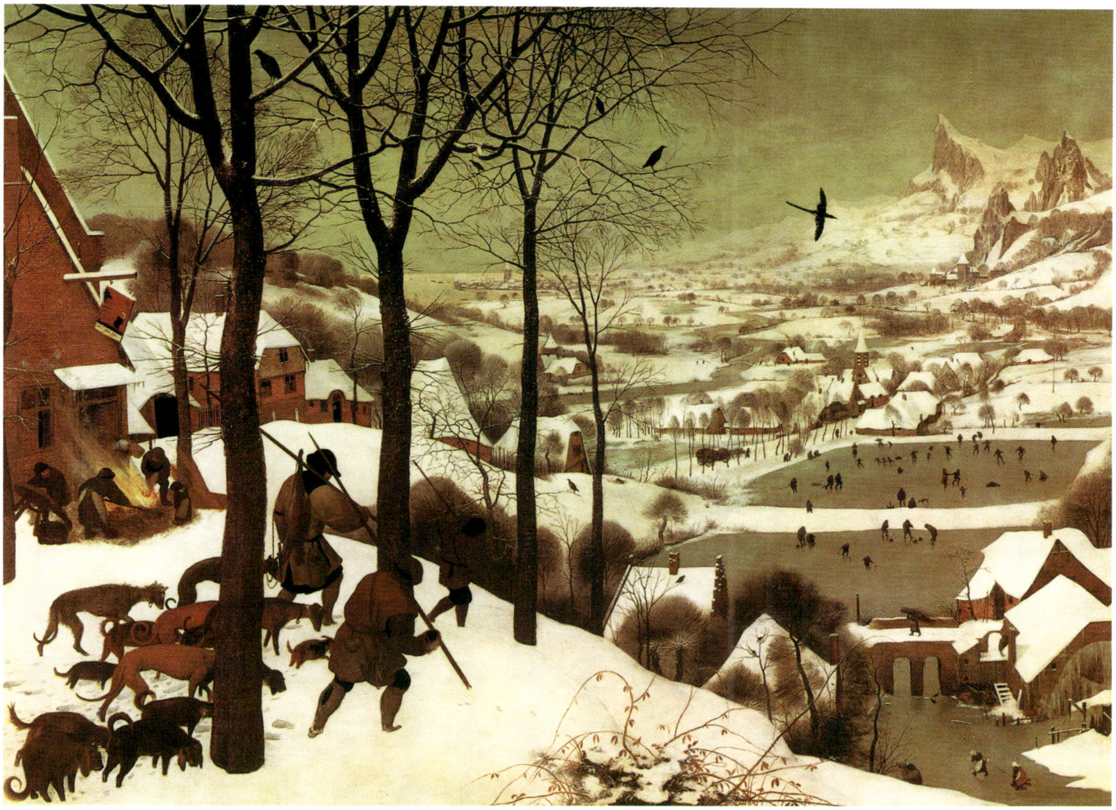

PIETER BRUEGEL THE ELDER
(1525 NEAR BREDA – 1569 BRUSSELS)

Pieter Bruegel was the first important member of a family of artists who were active for four generations. Firstly a drawer before becoming a painter, he painted religious themes, such as Babel Tower, with very bright colours. Influenced by Hieronymus Bosch, he painted large, complex scenes of peasant life and scripture or spiritual allegories, often with crowds of subjects performing a variety of acts, yet his scenes are unified with an informal integrity and often with wit. In his work, he brought a new humanising spirit. Befriending the Humanists, Bruegel composed true philosophical landscapes in the heart of which man accepts passively his fate, caught in the track of time.

385. **Pieter Bruegel the Elder**, c. 1525-1569, Northern Renaissance, Flemish, *The Hunters in the Snow*, 1565. Oil on panel, 117 x 162 cm. Kunsthistorisches Museum, Vienna.

386. **Pieter Bruegel the Elder**, c. 1525-1569, Northern Renaissance, Flemish, *The Land of Cockayne*, 1567. Oil on panel, 52 x 78 cm. Alte Pinakothek, Munich.

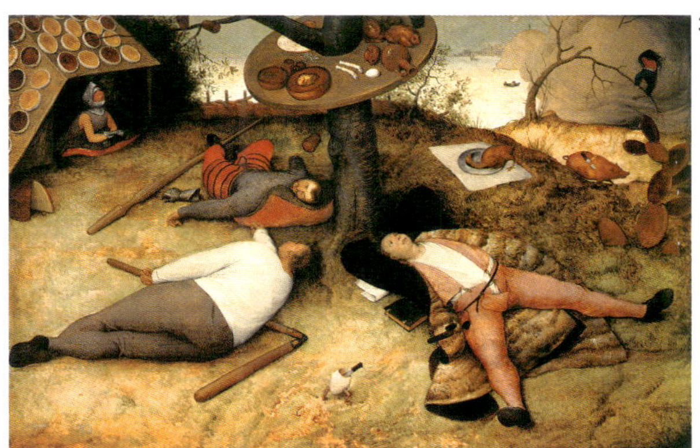
386

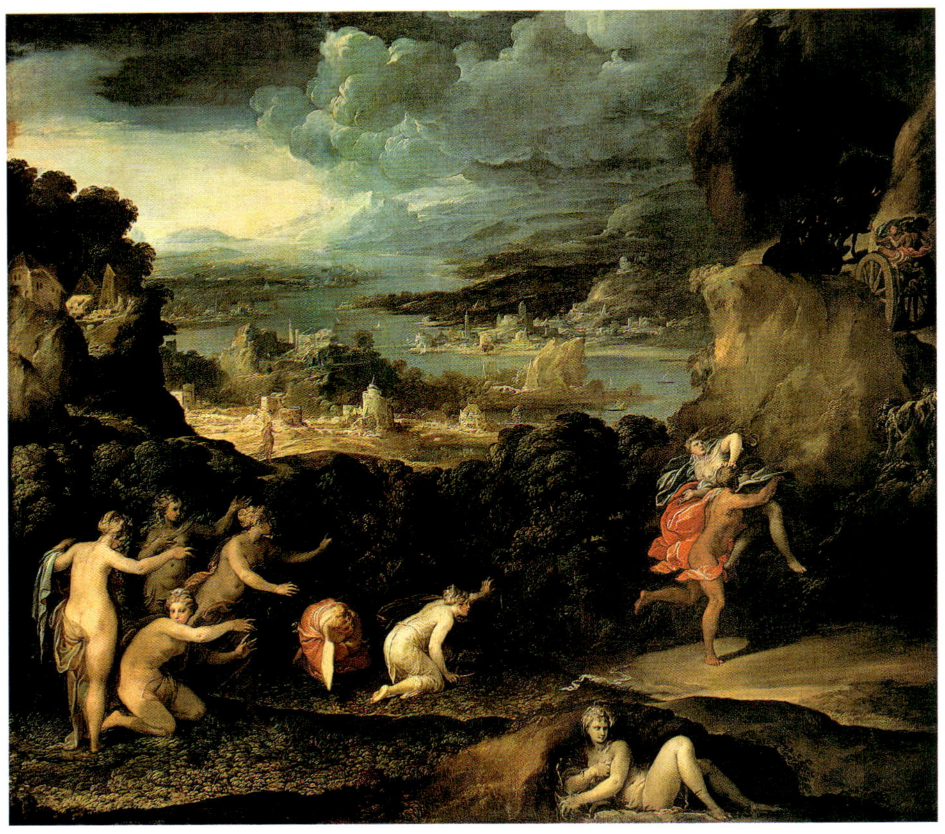

387. **Nicolò dell' Abbate,** 1510-1571, Mannerism, Italian,
The Rape of Proserpine, 1552-1570.
Oil on canvas, 196 x 216 cm. Musée du Louvre, Paris.

388. **Veronese (Paolo Caliari),** 1528-1588, Mannerism, Venetian School,
Italian, *The Adoration of the Magi,* after 1571.
Oil on canvas, 206 x 455 cm. Gemäldegalerie Alte Meister, Dresden.

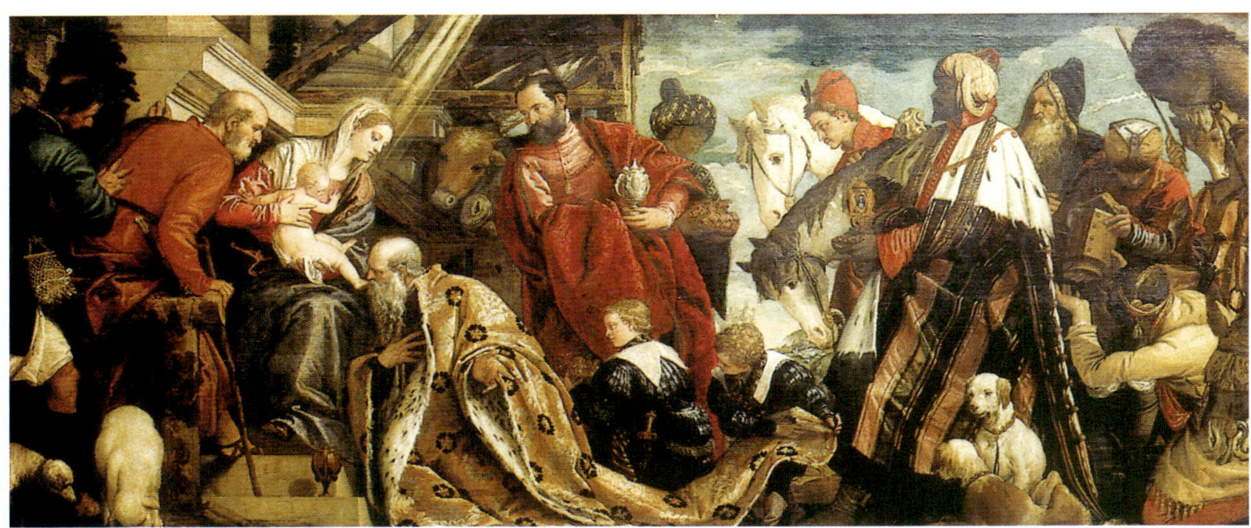

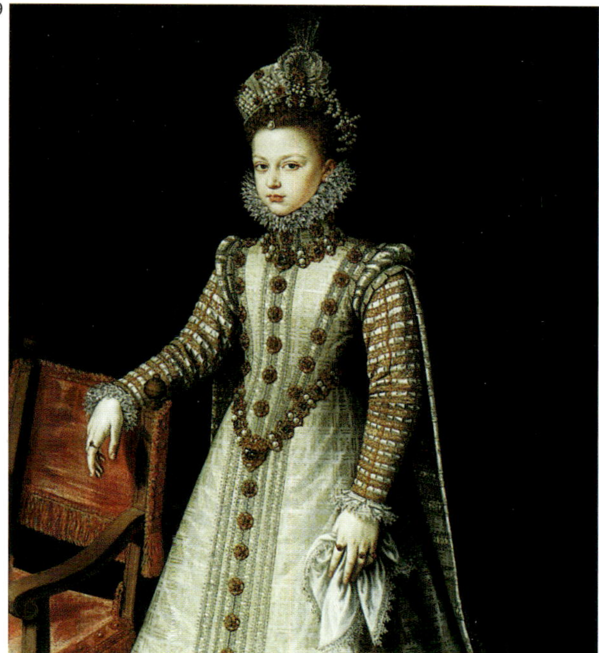

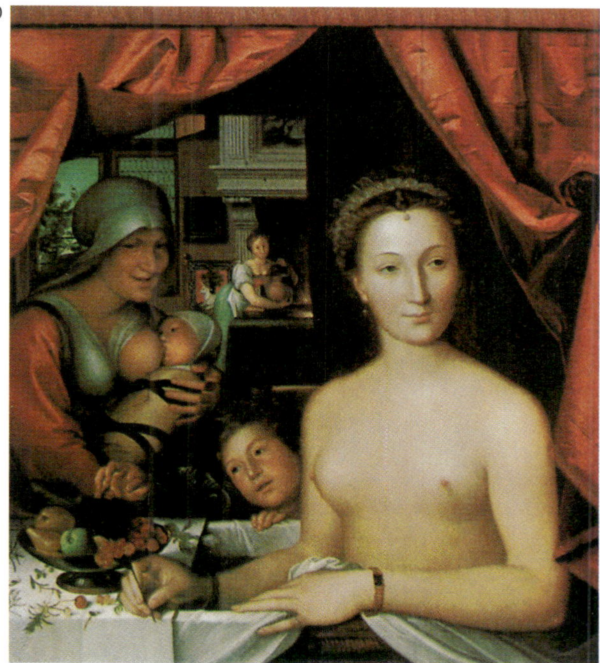

389. **Alonzo Sánchez Coello,** 1531-1588, Mannerism, Spanish,
The Infanta Isabella Clara Eugenia, after 1570.
Oil on canvas, 116 x 102 cm.
Museo Nacional del Prado, Madrid.

390. **François Clouet,** c. 1505-1572, Mannerism, French,
A Lady in Her Bath, c. 1571.
Oil on panel, 92.1 x 81.3 cm.
The National Gallery of Art, Washington D.C.

A midwife nurses a baby, as the nude lady seems to reflect on what to write next with the instrument in her right hand. A mischievous child is about to grab a piece of fruit from the centrepiece on the board spread across the lady's bathtub. Domestic activity goes on elsewhere as the drapes are parted briefly for an intimate peek into a moment in the lady's life. The work includes several symbols of hope for the future; the open window, the nursing child, spring flowers, and the cheerful mid-wife. A balance and interplay of the many circles and ovals throughout the work is achieved by a few strong horizontal lines.

391. **Annibale Carracci,** 1560-1609, Baroque, Italian,
The Fishing, c. 1585-1588.
Oil on canvas, 136 x 255 cm. Musée du Louvre, Paris.

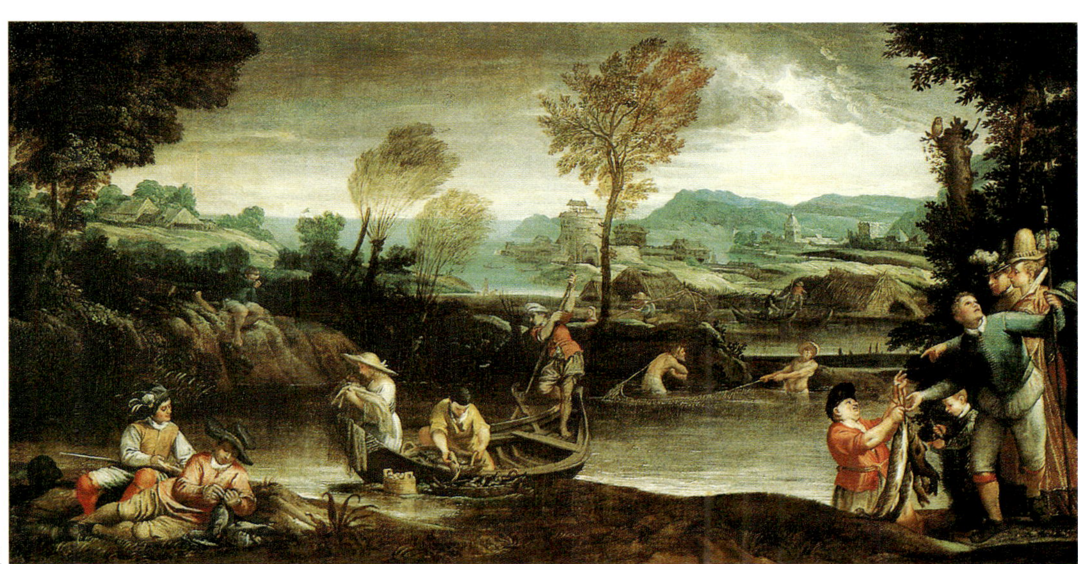

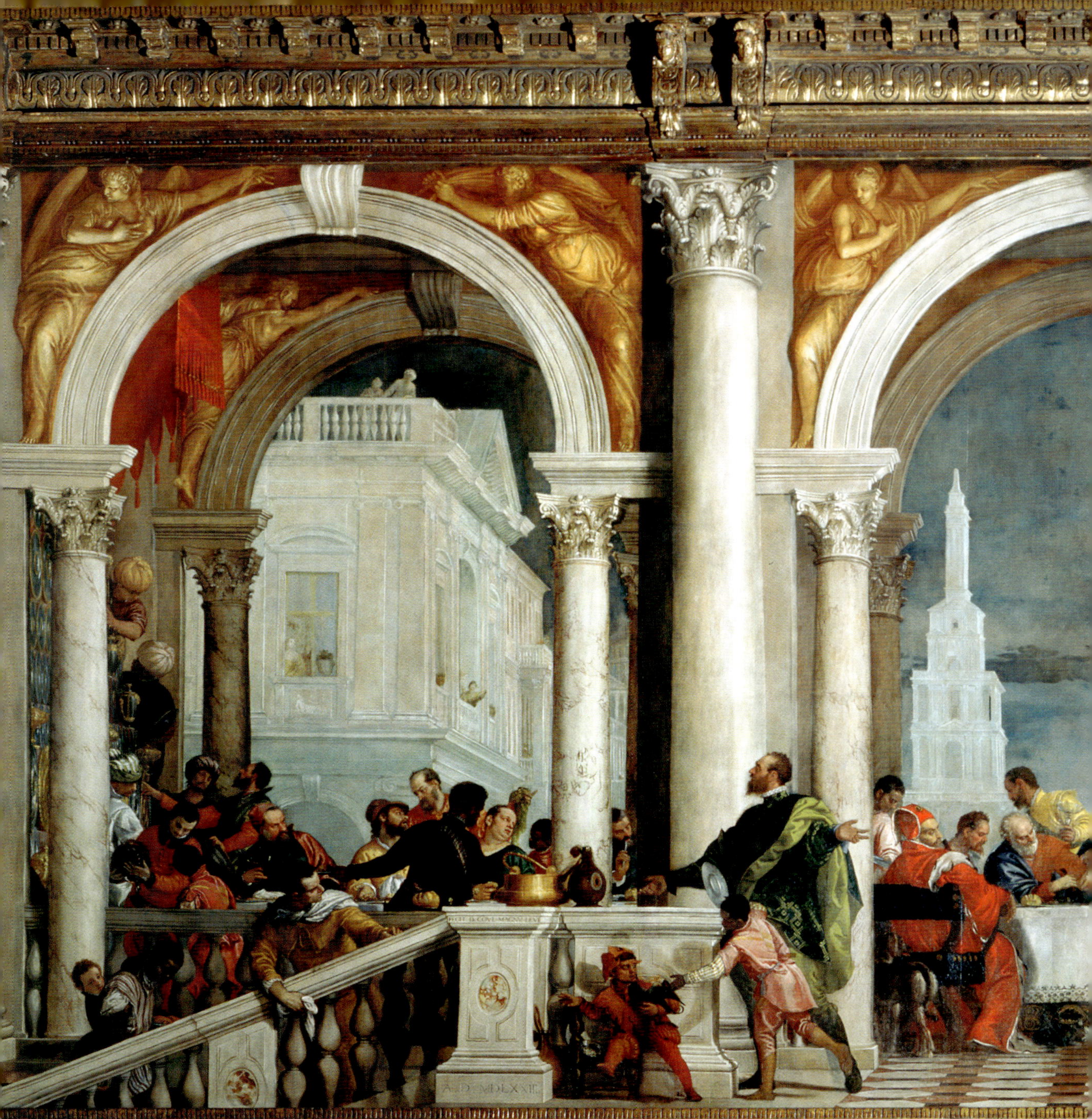

392. **Veronese (Paolo Caliari),** 1528-1588, Mannerism, Venetian School, Italian, *Feast in the House of Levi,* 1573. Oil on canvas, 555 x 1280 cm. Galleria dell'Accademia, Venice.

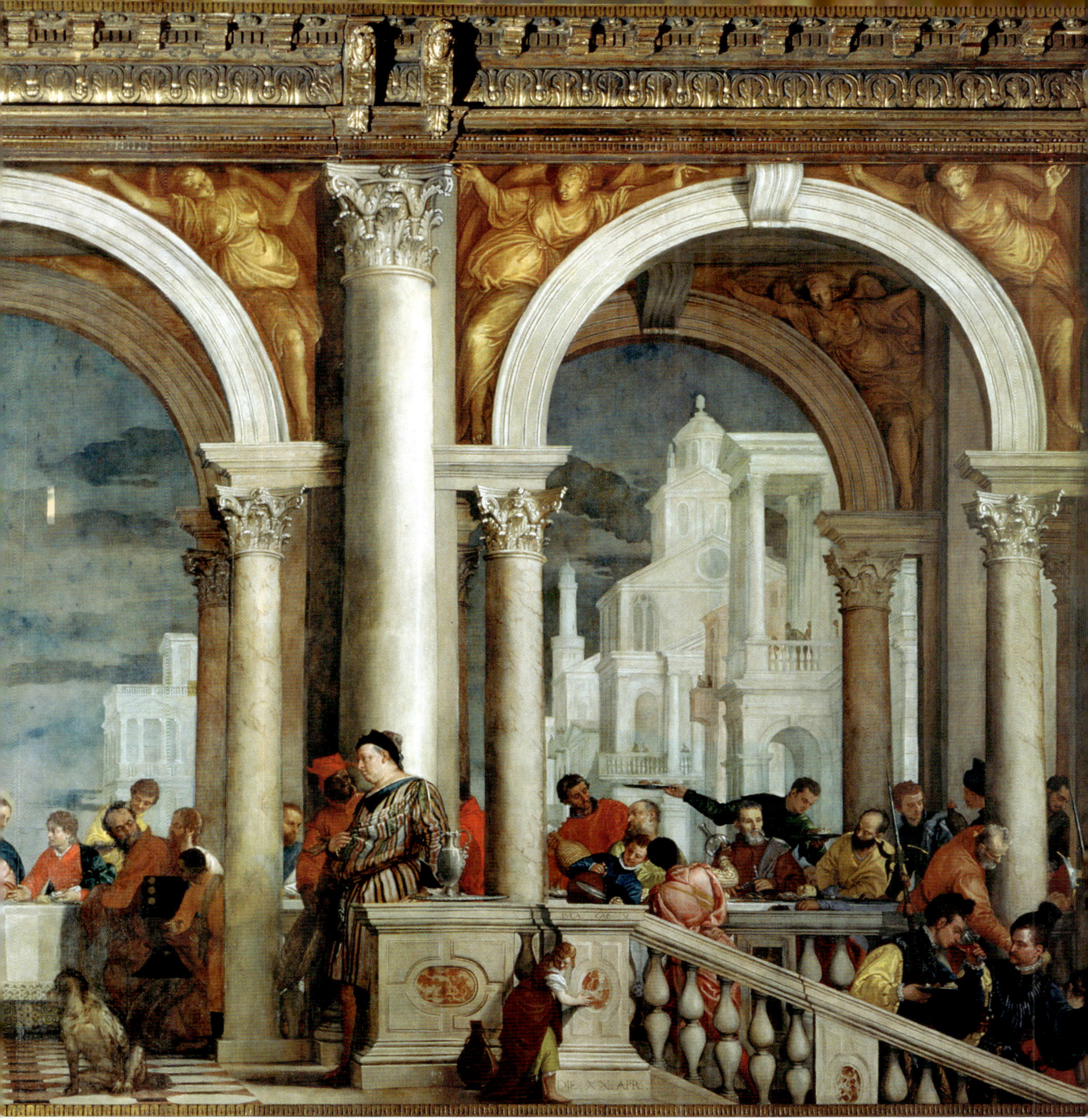

Painted for the convent refectory, this work was initially called The Last Supper *and renamed* Feast in the House of Levi *after the Inquisition objected to Veronese's festive version.*

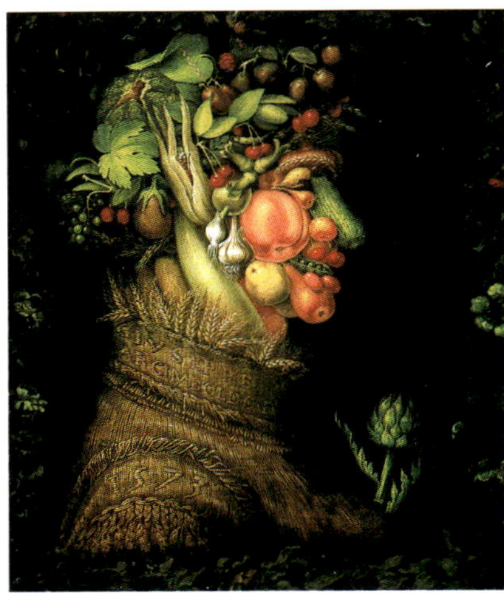

393. **Giuseppe Arcimboldo,** 1530-1593, Mannerism,
Italian, *Summer,* 1573.
Oil on canvas, 76 x 64 cm.
Musée du Louvre, Paris.

395. **Tintoretto (Jacopo Robusti),** 1518-1594,
Mannerism, Venetian School, Italian,
Christ in the House of Mary and Martha, c. 1580.
Oil on canvas, 197.5 x 131 cm.
Alte Pinakothek, Munich.

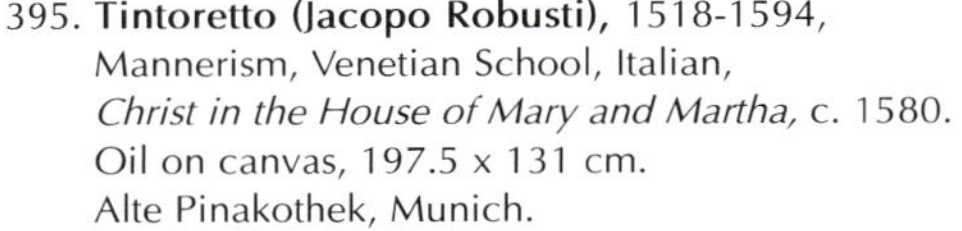

395

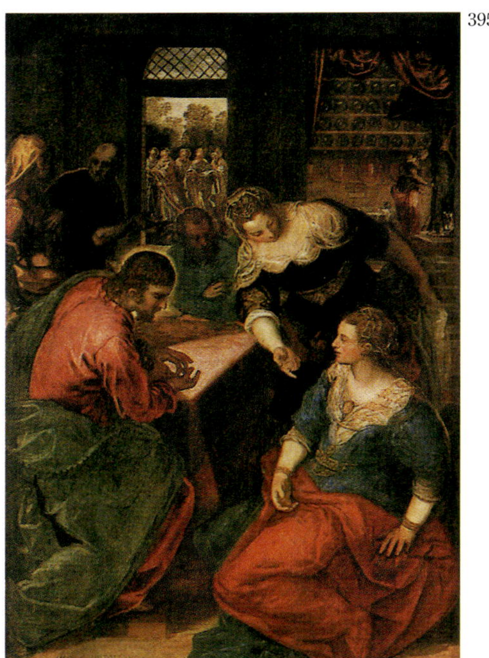

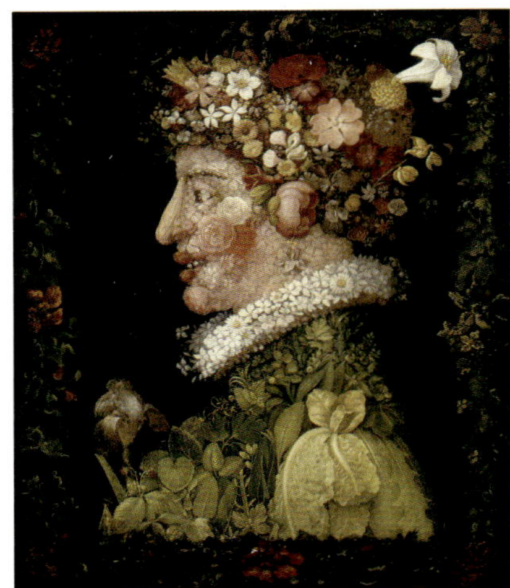

394. **Giuseppe Arcimboldo,** 1530-1593, Mannerism, Italian,
Spring, 1573. Oil on canvas, 76 x 64 cm. Musée du Louvre, Paris.

Arcimboldo produced his first series of the Seasons under the patronage
of Maximilian II, at the Habsburg court in Vienna, creating portraits
made of fruit, flowers, fish or other inanimate objects.

396. **El Greco (Domenikos Theotokópoulos),** 1541-1614, Mannerism,
Native from Crete but considered a Spanish painter,
Burial of Count Orgaz, 1586-1588. Oil on canvas, 480 x 360 cm.
Church of Santo Tomé, Toledo.

In the geometric centre of the painting, the dead benefactor's guardian
angel escorts the count's soul towards Mary as John the Baptist pleads
on behalf of the count to the Resurrected Jesus. Observing it all is St
Peter, who has the keys to heaven loosely in hand indicating they are
merely symbols. Somewhere in the heavenly crowd of saints (upper
right), probably easily located by his contemporaries, is King Philip II of
Spain. Below, the count's body is in the arms of St Augustine in bishop's
vestment assisted by St Stephen, the first martyr. Stephen appropriately
wears his deacon's vestment on which is a scene of his own fatal
stoning. The artist's torch-bearing son is shown in the lower left. His
birth date is seen on the handkerchief stuck in his pocket. The artist
depicts himself (directly above St Stephen) as the only face looking
directly at the viewer. Over all, the heavenly half of the work is dynamic,
but sombre; the earthy half is static and introspective.

GIUSEPPE ARCIMBOLDO
(C. 1530 – 1593 MILAN)

At his debut, Arcimboldo's contemporaries could not have imagined he
would become what he is now famous for. His youthful works were
normally made for cathedrals in Milan or Monza, but it is from 1562,
when he was summoned to the Imperial court in Prague, that his style and
subjects changed.

For the court he imagined original and grotesque fantasies made of
flowers, fruit, animals and objects composed to form a human portrait. Some
were satiric portraits, and others were allegorical personifications. If his work
is now regarded as a curiosity of the sixteenth century, it actually finds its
roots in the context of the end of the Renaissance. At that time, collectors
and scientists started to pay more attention to nature, looking for natural
curiosities to exhibit in their curio cabinets.

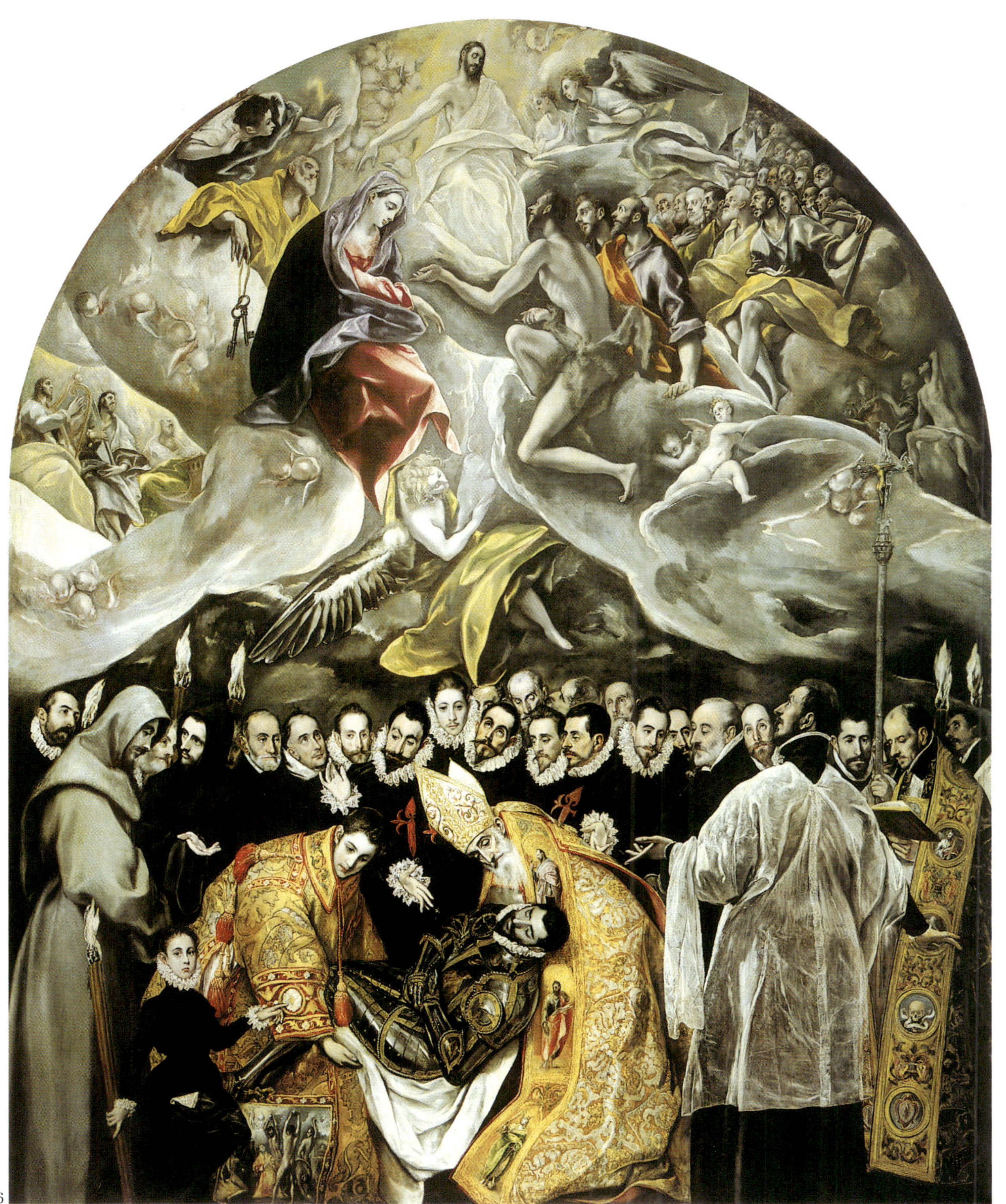

397.

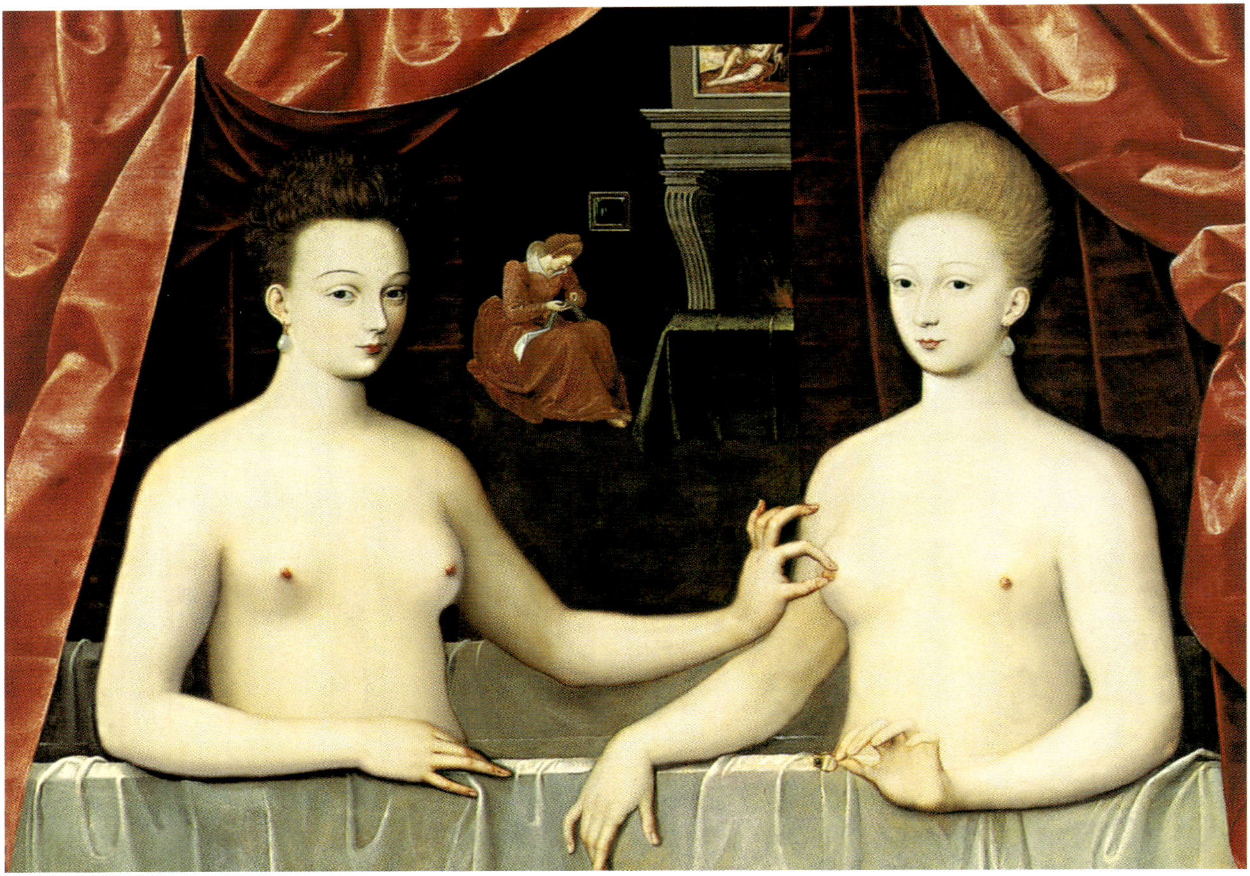

397. Master of the Fontainebleau School, 1525-1575, Second
School of Fontainebleau, French,
Gabrielle d'Estrée and the Duchesse de Villars, 1594.
Oil on panel, 96 x 125 cm. Musée du Louvre, Paris.

*The ostentatious gesture is thought to insinuate the maternity of
Gabrielle d'Estrée, who gave birth to Henri IV's bastard, César de
Vendôme in 1594. She holds a ring, symbol of her love for the king
and tne marriage he promised her.*

398.

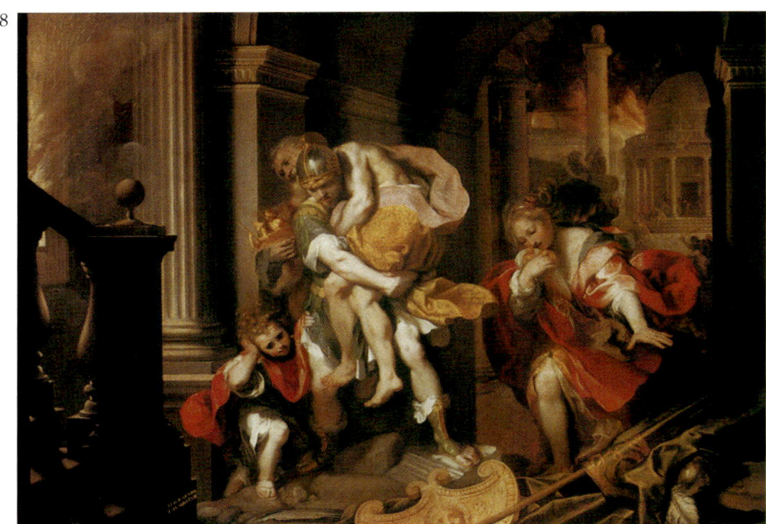

399.

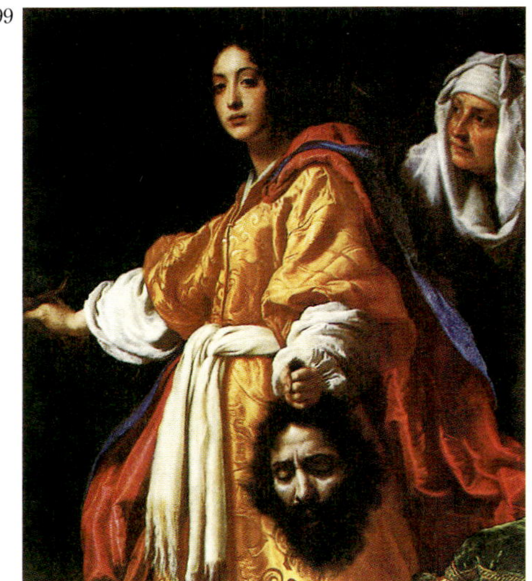

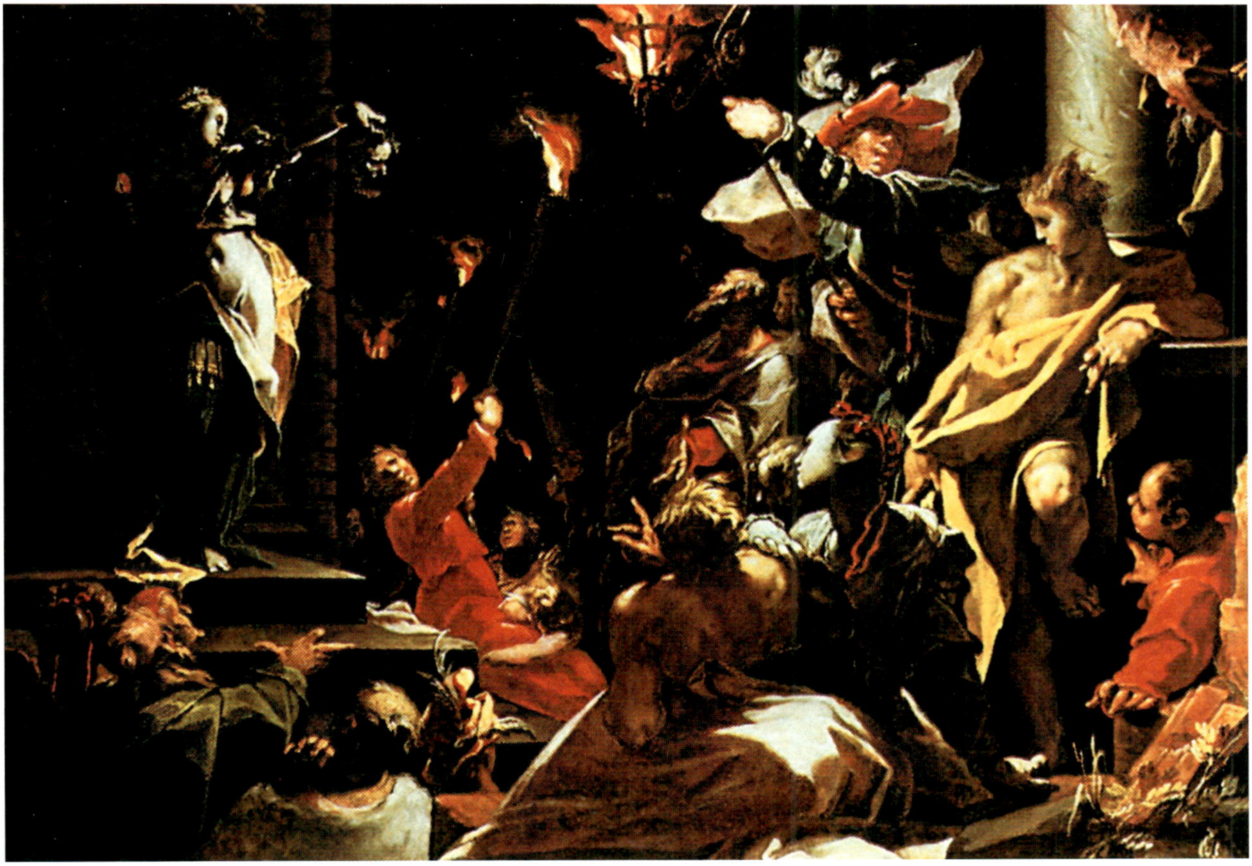

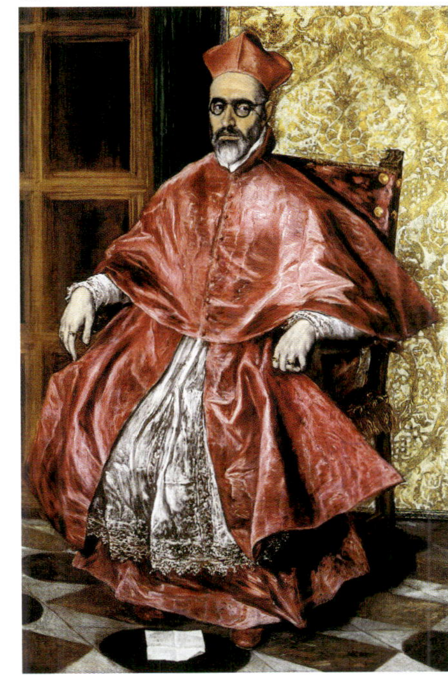

398. Federico Barocci(o), 1526-1612, Mannerism, Italian, *The Flight of Aeneas from Troy (2nd version),* 1598. Oil on canvas, 184 x 258 cm. Galleria Borghese, Rome.

The greatest painter between Correggio and Caravaggio, Barocci has also been influenced by Raphael. The flight from Troy is his only known classical subject.

399. Cristofano Allori, 1577-1621, High Renaissance, Florentine School, Italian, *Judith with the Head of Holofernes,* c. 1613.
Oil on canvas, 120.4 x 100.3 cm. Palazzo Pitti, Florence.

One of the most famous paintings in the eighteenth and nineteenth centuries in Italy, Judith with the Head of Holofernes is increased in its dramatic effects through the intensified contrasts between the dark face of Holofernes and the depiction of Judith with warm and light colours.

400. Abraham Bloemaert, 1566-1651, Baroque, Dutch, *Judith with the Head of Holofernes,* 1593. Oil on panel, 44 x 34 cm. Kunsthistorisches Museum, Vienna.

Bloemaert inscribes himself in the Mannerist movement and was particularly influenced by the Dutch painter Frans Floris. The dramatic effect in this painting also shows the influence of Caravaggio's chiaroscuro.

401. El Greco (Domenikos Theotokópoulos), 1541-1614, Mannerism, Native from Crete but considered a Spanish painter, *Portrait of a Cardinal,* probably Cardinal Don Fernando Niño de Guevara, 1600.
Oil on canvas, 170.8 x 108 cm. The Metropolitan Museum of Art, New York.

El Greco's portraits retain the psychological insight of the sitter. This painting is one of the most startling portrayals of the cleric.

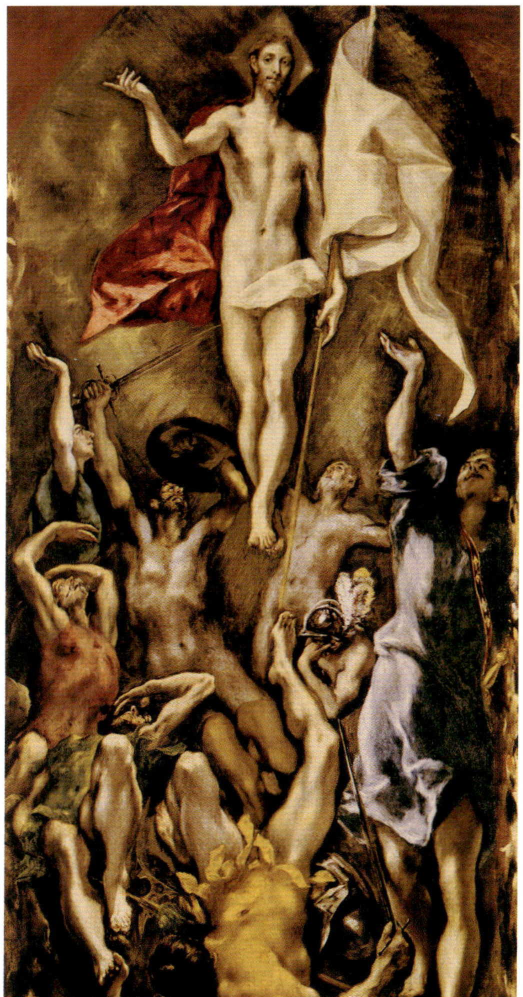

402. **El Greco (Domenikos Theotokópoulos)**, 1541-1614,
Mannerism, Native from Crete but considered a Spanish painter,
The Resurrection, c. 1590. Oil on canvas, 275 x 127 cm.
Museo Nacional del Prado, Madrid.

*This great interpretation of the subject was painted for the
Colegio de Doña Maria in Madrid and probably formed a pair
with a painting of the Pentecost of the same size.*

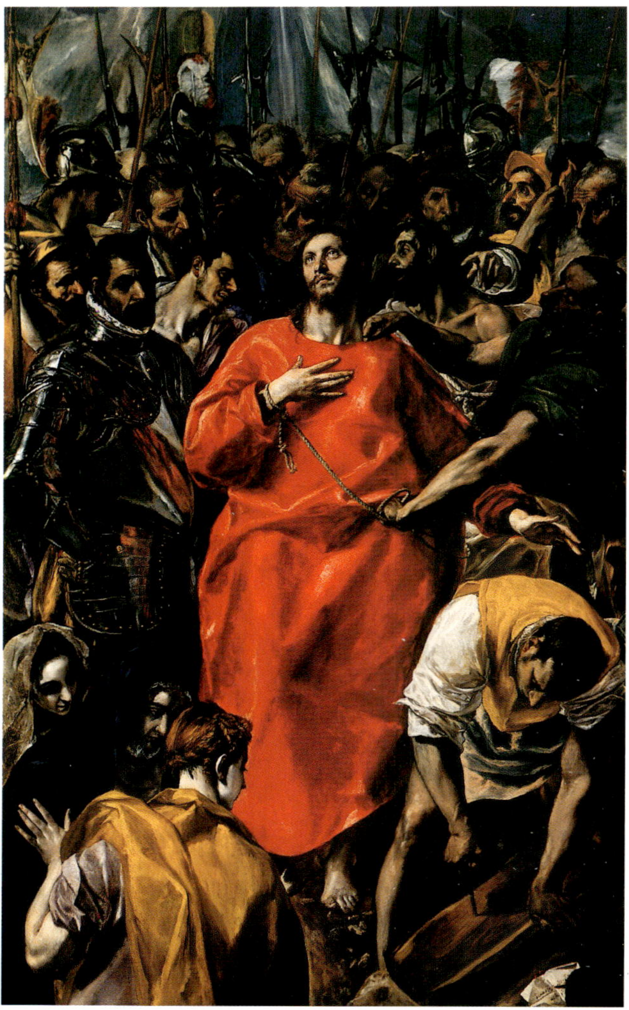

403. **El Greco (Domenikos Theotokópoulos)**, 1541-1614, Mannerism,
Native from Crete but considered a Spanish painter, *El Espolio
(Christ Stripped of his Garments),* c. 1608.
Oil on canvas, 285 x 173 cm.
Sacristy of the Cathedral of Toledo, Toledo.

*The powerful effect of the painting is due to its size, bigger than
nature, on the strictly centralised composition as well as on the
forceful use of colour, recalling Venetian painting and, particularly,
the works of Titian.*

EL GRECO (DOMENIKOS THEOTOKÓPOULOS)
(1541 CRETE – 1614 TOLEDO)

"The Greek" was an icon painter who immigrated to Venice. There he began his blending of Byzantine influences
with that of the Italian High Renaissance masters. He studied under Titian and was influenced by Tintoretto. Some
years on, he lived in Rome for about two years, then travelled to Madrid and later found his permanent home in
Toledo, where he died. It was mainly in Spain where he focused on distinctively Catholic subjects. The elongated
bodies and unusual colour arrangements became distinctive.

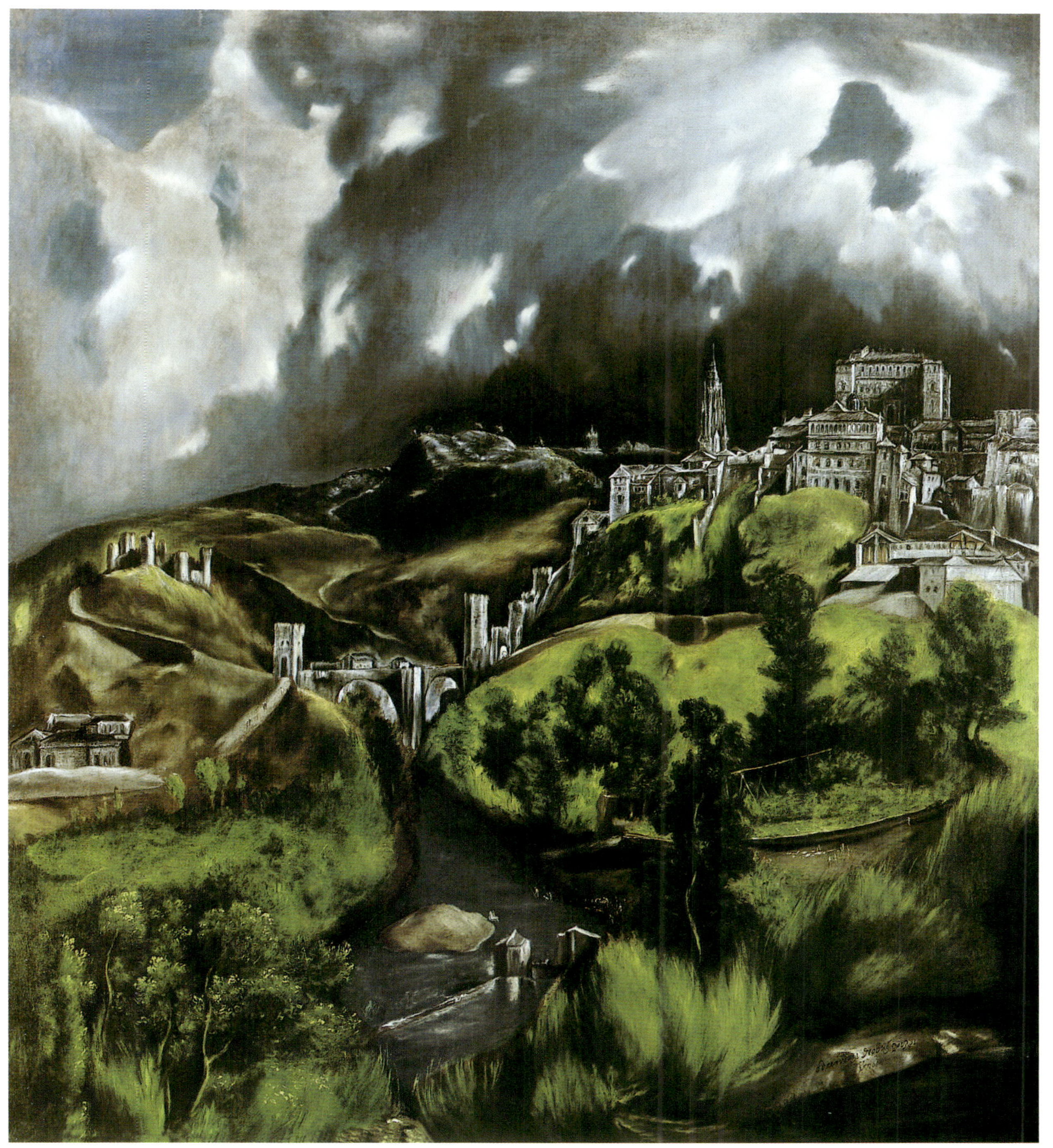

404. **El Greco (Domenikos Theotokópoulos),** 1541-1614, Mannerism, Native from Crete but considered a Spanish painter, *View of Toledo,*
c. 1610. Oil on canvas, 121.3 x 108.6 cm. The Metropolitan Museum of Art, New York.

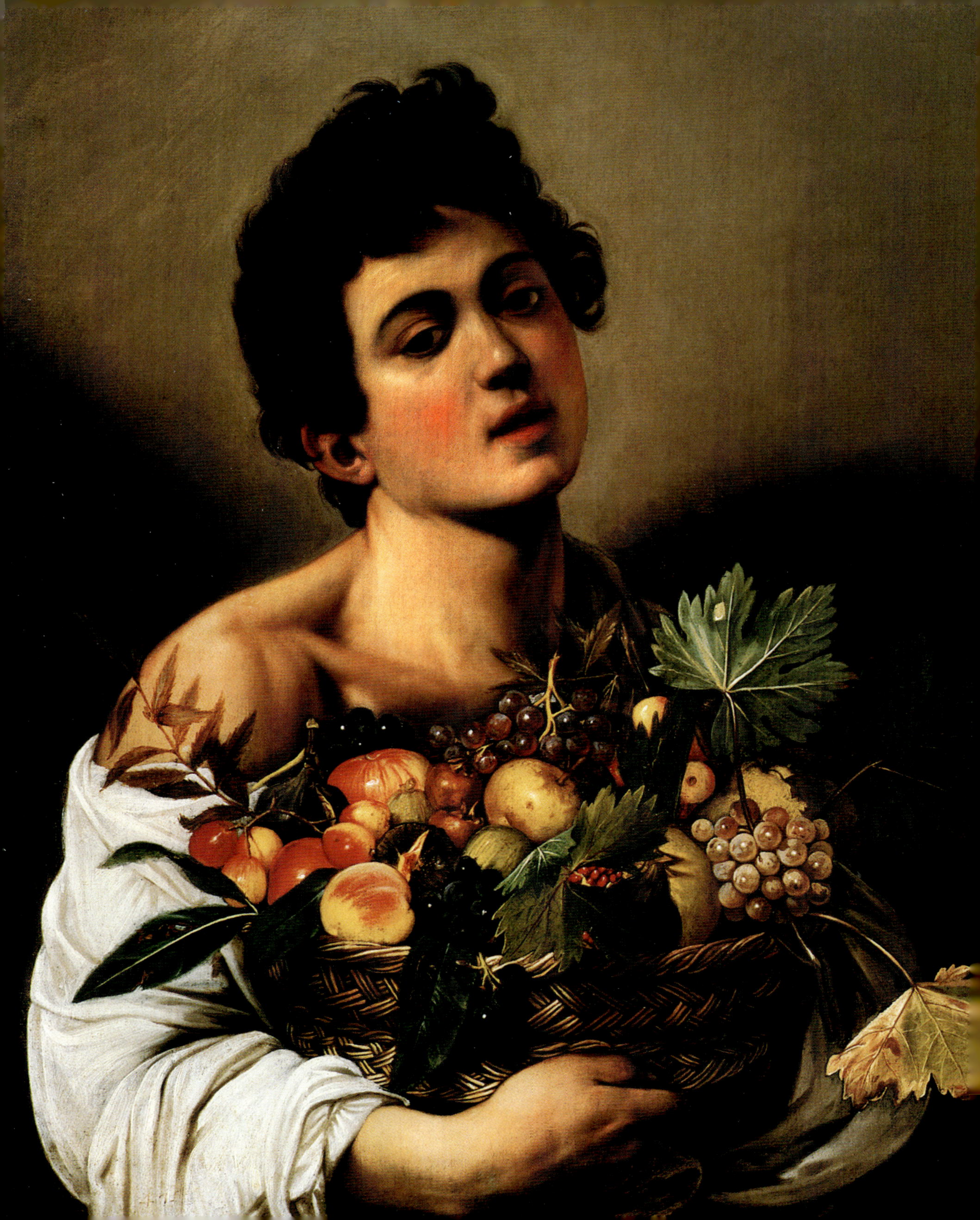

Baroque

In Europe, the early Baroque era was marked by the Thirty Years War (1618-1648), caused partly by the religious conflicts between Catholics and Protestants in the previous century. But this war, which ended with the Treaty of Westphalia, introduced greater freedom of religion to much of Europe and led to the creation of nation-states. With increasing prosperity and the growth of European markets, a wealthy new class that favoured the arts and luxury goods was born.

Though the seventeenth century is universally known as the age of Baroque art, national traits can be distinguished. In Italy, the Baroque period was shaped by the Counter-Reformation, which was triggered by the Catholic clergy and the edicts promulgated at the Council of Trent. Due to the popularity of St Ignatius of Loyola, founder of the Jesuit order who was canonised in 1622, the Jesuits had a powerful influence on the arts. The Church had lost much of its power following the Reformation, so tried to regain the hearts of the faithful by campaigning for the expansion of church aisles to accommodate more people, as in Saint-Pierre or the mother church of the Jesuits, Il Gesù, in Rome.

The Dutch Republic, founded after the official recognition of the United Provinces of the Netherlands by the Treaty of Westphalia (1648), was essentially Protestant. Thus, while the country was experiencing unprecedented economic success, religious art was still undergoing censorship, and Baroque art, with its exaltation of drama, sensuality and movement, had little impact. In France, a stimulating environment for French classicism was created by the patronage of Louis XIV, manifested by the construction of Versailles and the foundation in 1648 of the Académie des Beaux Arts (Academy of Fine Arts). At the same time, French philosophers contributed to the dissemination of ideas based on reason. In an attempt to systematically record existing knowledge, Denis Diderot produced the first encyclopedia (35 volumes, 1751-1780), and became one of the first art critics when he published his comments on the Paris Salon, an exhibition of paintings and sculptures organised by the Academy. Meanwhile, Voltaire protested against royal despotism and the hegemony of the Church, and Descartes, in 1637, published his philosophical and mathematical treatise, *Discours de la méthode* (Discourse on Method). Scientifically, the period was marked by the invention in Italy in 1609 of Galileo's telescope, which helped Johannes Kepler understand the laws governing planetary motion.

The eighteenth century, then, was marked by the Enlightenment. Thanks to learned ladies of the Rococo period, salons were growing in the courts of France, Austria and Germany. These helped to encourage the spread of the arts and sciences, such as Sir Isaac Newton's law of universal gravitation, as well as important Enlightenment ideas such as John Locke's views on liberalism. Amid this intellectual tumult, the foundations of the modern era were laid. Indeed, the American founding fathers, Benjamin Franklin and Thomas Jefferson, emphasised their commitment to the principles of the Enlightenment. In the 1740s, the Industrial Revolution began in England, driven by technological advances such as steam power and the first use of steel in the construction (1776). Meanwhile, fuelled by the excavations of Herculaneum (1738) and Pompeii (1748), interest in classical antiquity resurfaced. Neoclassicism, characterised by moral content and powerfully structured compositions, exalted patriotic values, and in France Napoleon Bonaparte, who was crowned emperor in 1804, used the paintings of David and a system of symbols referencing the Roman Empire to assert his authority.

405. **Caravaggio (Michelangelo Merisi)**, 1571-1610, Baroque, Italian, *Boy with a Basket of Fruit*, c. 1595.
Oil on canvas, 70 x 67 cm, Galleria Borghese, Rome.

The subject of the painting is definitely the basket of fruit. The sitter and the basket of fruit receive the diagonal cellar light characteristic of the artist's style.

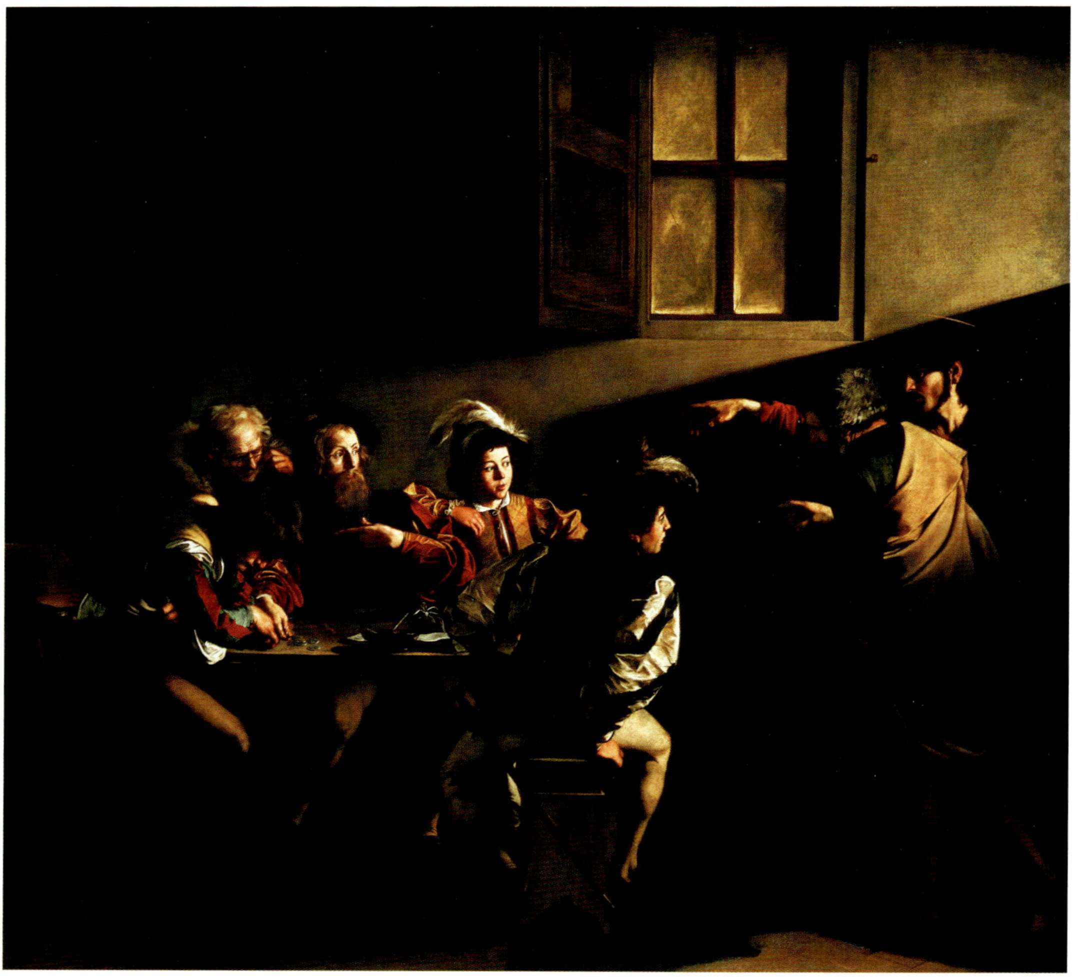

406. **Caravaggio (Michelangelo Merisi)**,
The Calling of Saint Matthew, 1599-1600.
Oil on canvas, 322 x 340 cm.
San Luigi dei Francese, Rome.

MICHELANGELO MERISI DA CARAVAGGIO
(1571 CARAVAGGIO – 1610 PORT'ERCOLE)

After staying in Milan for his apprenticeship, Michelangelo da Caravaggio arrived in Rome in 1592. There he started to paint with both realism and psychological analysis of the sitters. Caravaggio was as temperamental in his painting as in his wild life. As he also responded to prestigious Church commissions, his dramatic style and his realism were seen as unacceptable. Chiaroscuro had existed well before he came on the scene, but it was Caravaggio who made the technique definitive, darkening the shadows and transfixing the subject in a blinding shaft of light. His influence was immense, firstly through those who were more or less directly his disciples. Famous during his lifetime, Caravaggio had a great influence upon Baroque art. The Genoese and Neapolitan Schools derived lessons from him, and the great movement of Spanish painting in the seventeenth century was connected with these schools. In the following generations the best endowed painters oscillated between the lessons of Caravaggio and the Carracci.

407. Caravaggio (Michelangelo Merisi), 1571-1610,
Baroque, Italian, *The Fortune-Teller,* c. 1594.
Oil on canvas, 99 x 131 cm.
Musée du Louvre, Paris.

In the first period of his career, Caravaggio often depicted humble characters, anti-heroic, in non-historical paintings. The artist focused on the sensuality of the characters in this new representation of the theme.

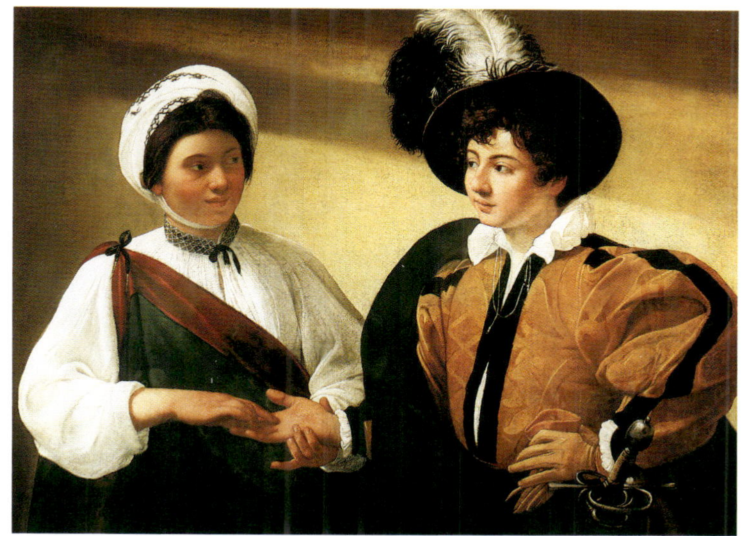

407

408. Caravaggio (Michelangelo Merisi), 1571-1610, Baroque,
Italian, *Bacchus,* c. 1596.
Oil on canvas, 95 x 85 cm. Galleria degli Uffizi, Florence.

This is the first time in the history of painting that the theme of Bacchus is used as a pretext to gather objects such as fruit or a glass of wine. This is an early work of Caravaggio but it already shows the elements of the artist's style such as the tenebrism (tenebroso) of the dark background, the androgynous face of the lute player or the still-life in the foreground.

409. Guido Reni, 1575-1642, Classicism, Italian,
David with the Head of Goliath, c. 1605.
Oil on canvas, 237 x 137 cm.
Musée du Louvre, Paris.

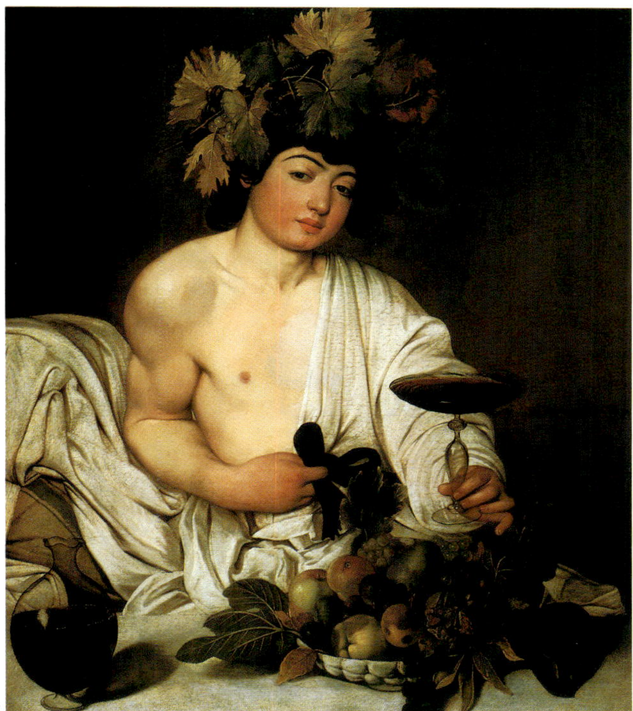

408

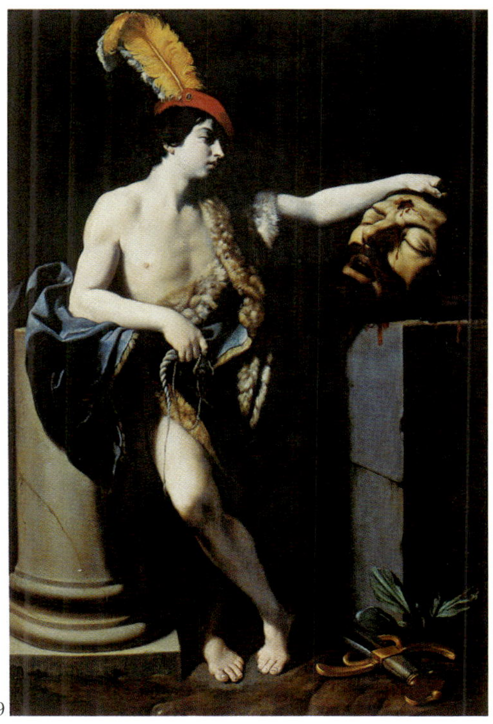

409

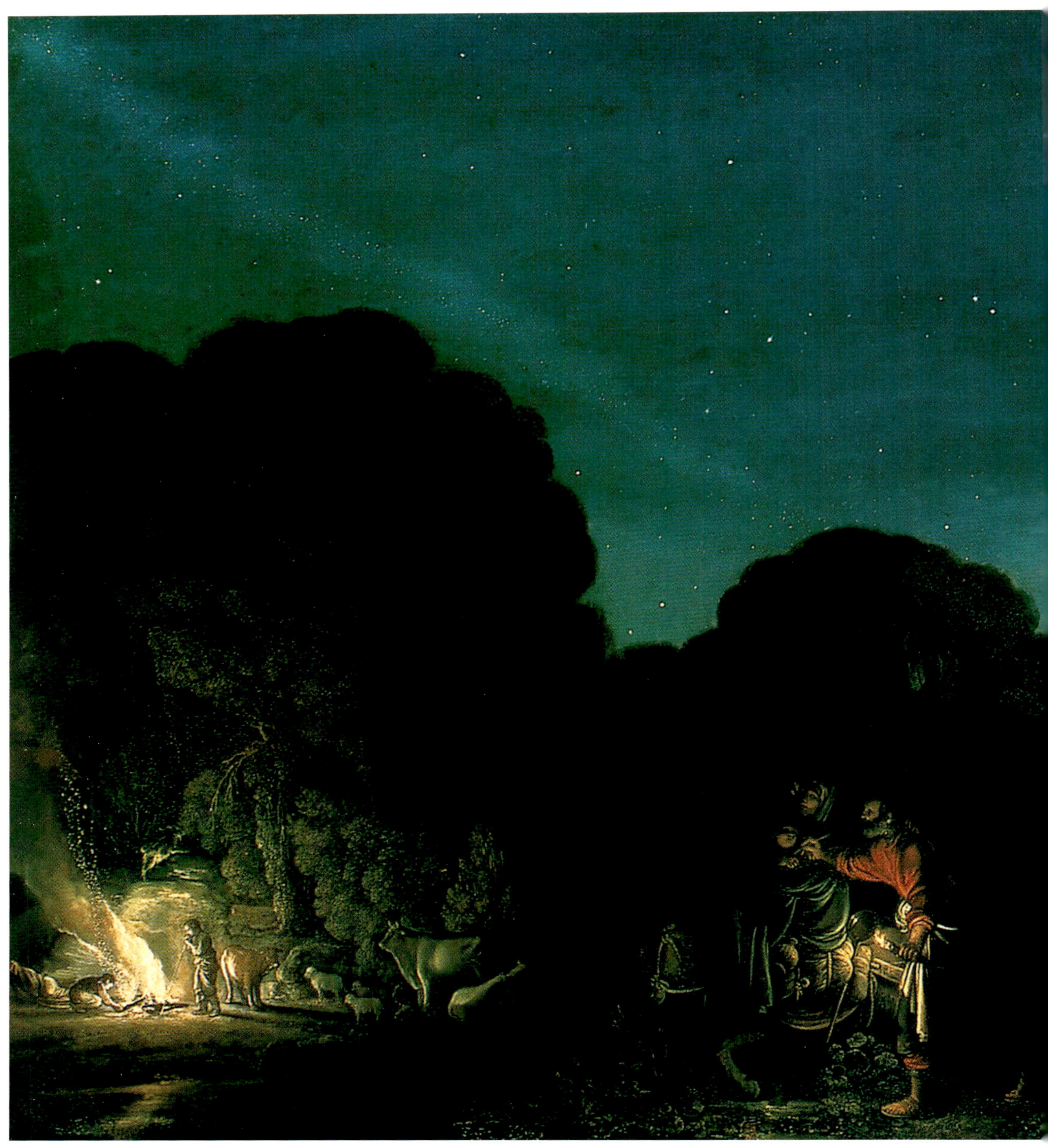

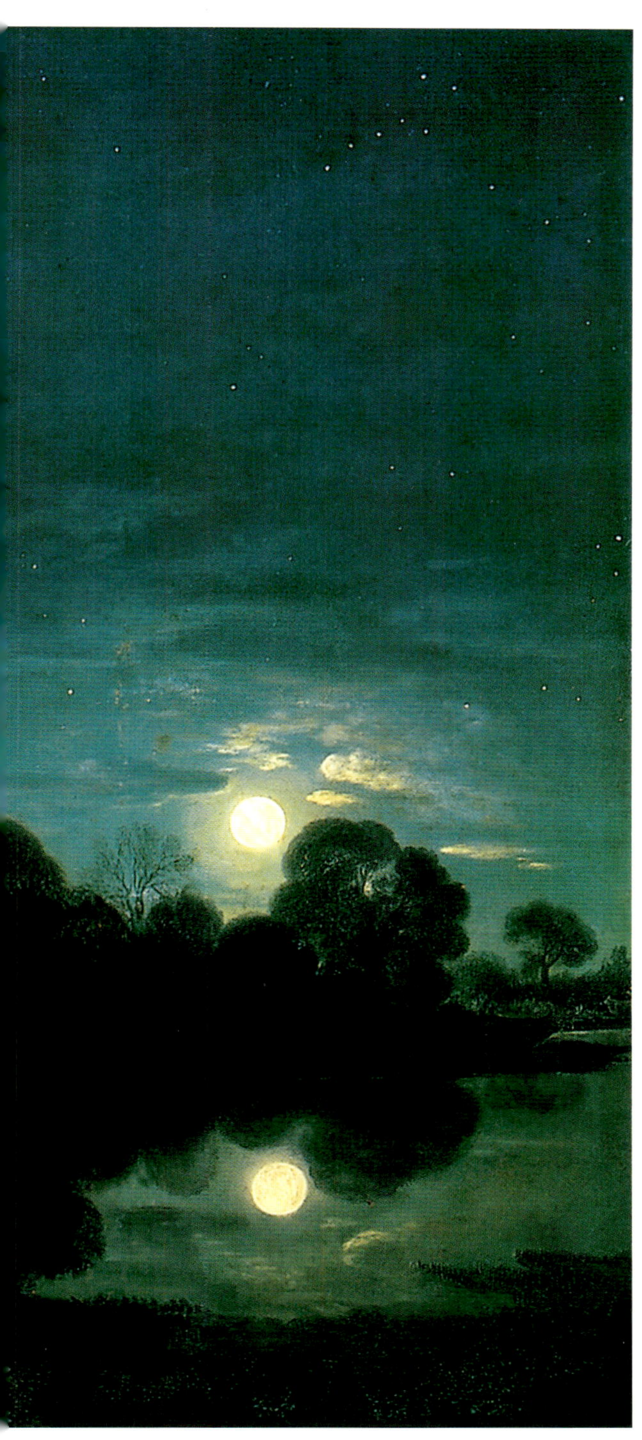

410. **Adam Elsheimer,** 1578-1610, Mannerism/Baroque, German,
Flight into Egypt, 1609. Oil on copper, 31 x 41 cm.
Alte Pinakothek, Munich.

*Famous for his night scenes, Elsheimer shows a great sensitivity
to the effects of light. This miniature-like painting shows a new
type of landscape, romantic and encircling the characters with
chiaroscuro effects.*

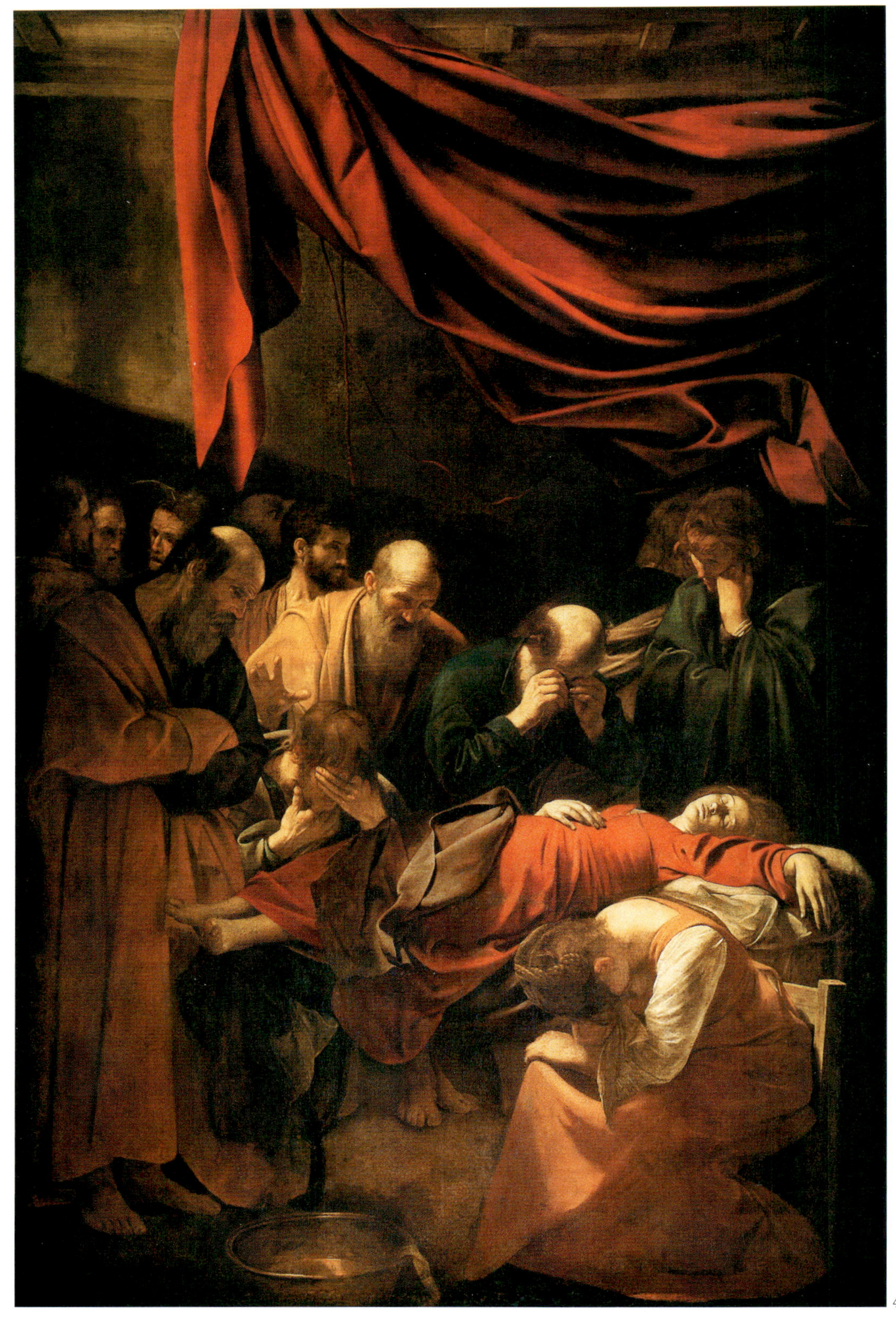

411

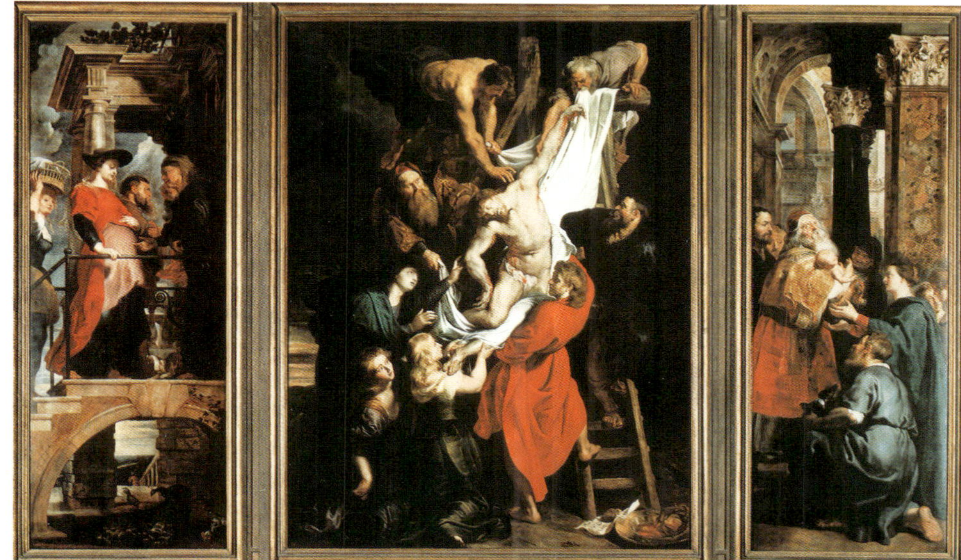

412. **Peter Paul Rubens,**
1577-1640, Baroque,
Flemish, *Descent from
the Cross,* 1612-1614.
Oil on panel, 421 x 311 cm
(central panel),
460 x 150 cm (wings).
O.-L. Vrouwekathedraal,
Antwerp.

412

411. **Caravaggio (Michelangelo Merisi),** 1571-1610, Baroque, Italian,
The Death of the Virgin, 1601-1605/1606.
Oil on canvas, 369 x 245 cm.
Musée du Louvre, Paris.

*This painting, much admired by Rubens, was rejected by its
commissioner because of its lack of conformism; the Madonna was
suspected to be modelled on a prostitute, her legs were exposed, and
her swollen body was too realistic.*

PETER PAUL RUBENS
(1577 SIEGEN – 1640 ANTWERP)

The eclectic art of which the Carracci family dreamed was realised
by Rubens with the ease of genius. However, the problem was
much more complicated for a man of the north, who wished to add
to it a fusion of the Flemish and Latin spirits, of which the rather
pedantic attempts of Romanism had illustrated the difficulties. He
achieved it without losing anything of his overflowing personality,
his questing imagination, and the enchanting discoveries of the
greatest colourist known to painting.

Rubens, the greatest master of Baroque painting's exuberance,
took from the Italian Renaissance what could be of use to him,
and then built upon it a style of his own. It is distinguished by a
wonderful mastery of the human form and an amazing wealth of
splendidly lighted colour. He was a man of much intellectual
poise and was accustomed to court life, travelling from court to
court, with pomp, as a trusted envoy.

Rubens was one of those rare mortals who do real honour to
humanity. He was handsome, good and generous, and he loved
virtue. His laborious life was well ordered. The creator of so many
delightful pagan feasts went each morning to mass before
proceeding to his studio. He was the most illustrious type of
happy and perfectly balanced genius, and combined in his
personage passion and science, ardour and reflection. Rubens
expressed drama as well as joy, since nothing human was foreign
to him, and he could command at will the pathos of colour and
expression which he required in his religious masterpieces.

413. **Frans Pourbus the Younger,** 1569-1622, Baroque,
Dutch, *Louis XIII as a Child,* 1611. Oil on canvas,
165 x 100 cm. Galleria degli Uffizi, Florence.

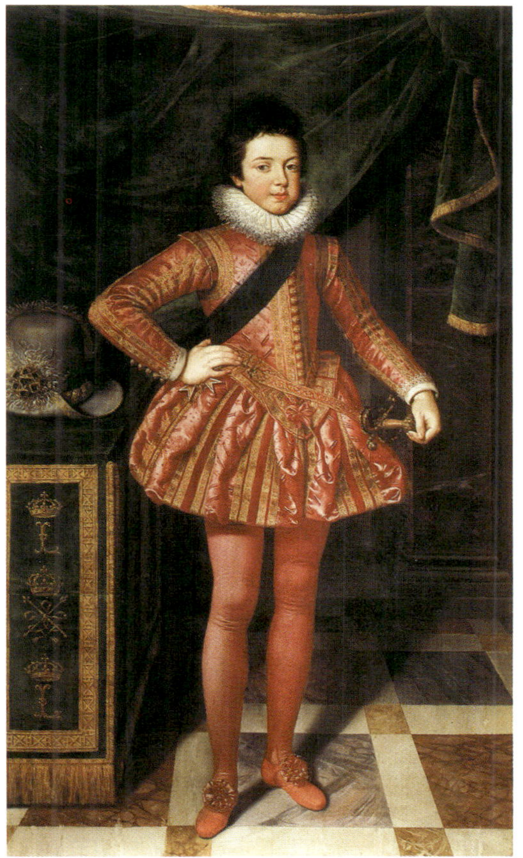

413

225

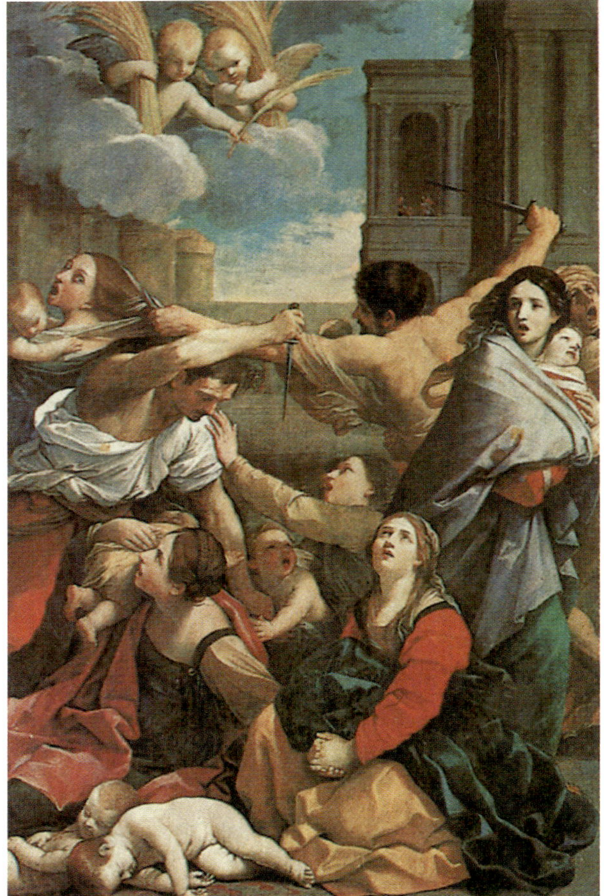

414

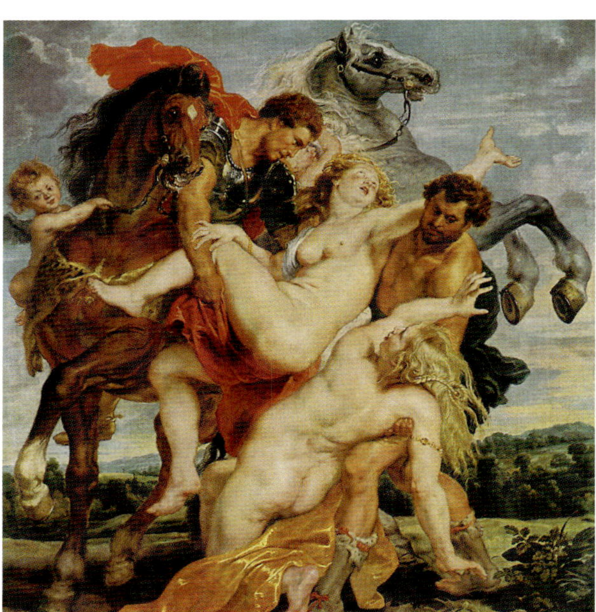

416

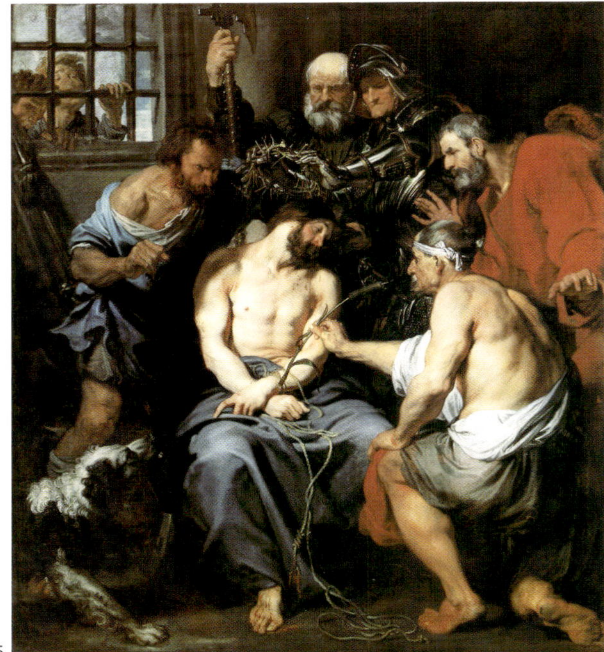

415

414. **Guido Reni**, 1575-1642, Classicism, Italian,
The Massacre of the Innocents, c. 1611.
Oil on canvas, 268 x 170 cm. Pinacoteca Nazionale, Bologna.

Guido Reni's early works betray the influence of the Caravaggesque manner and Baroque painting, but Raphael and the antique remained the main inspiration for his classical style.

415. **Anthony van Dyck**, 1599-1641, Baroque, Flemish,
Crowning with Thorns, c. 1620.
Oil on canvas, 223 x 196 cm.
Museo Nacional del Prado, Madrid.

The composition, based on Titian's works, is also influenced by Rubens and the Baroque style.

416. **Peter Paul Rubens**, 1577-1640, Baroque, Flemish,
The Rape of the Daughters of Leucippus, 1617-1618.
Oil on canvas, 222 x 209 cm. Alte Pinakothek, Munich.

GUIDO RENI
(1575 – 1642 BOLOGNA)

Guido Reni was a painter, a draughtsman and an etcher. He joined the naturalistic Carracci School when he was twenty, after having studied under Denis Calvaert. Deeply influenced by Greco-Roman art and Raphael, whom he greatly admired, by Parmigianino and by Veronese, his work was celebrated for its compositional and figural grace. He depicted the light, the perfection of the body, and shining colours. He was greatly noted and distinguished during the pontificate of Paul V.

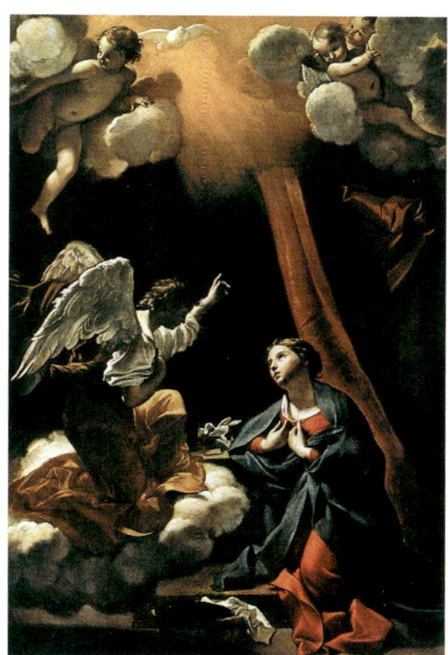

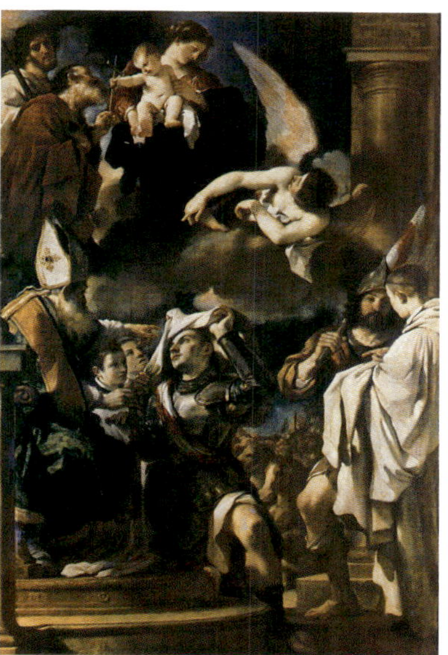

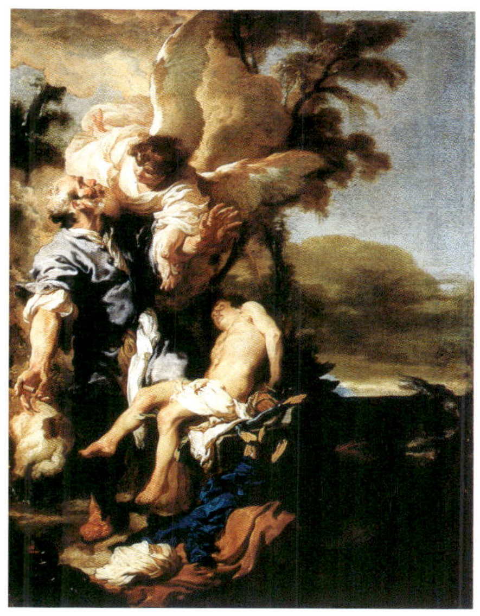

417. **Giovanni Lanfranco,** 1582-1647,
Baroque, Italian,
Annunciation, c. 1616.
Oil on canvas, 296 x 183 cm.
San Carlo Catinari, Rome.

418. **Guercino (Giovanni Francesco Barbieri),** 1591-1666, Baroque,
Bolognese School, Italian,
William of Aquitaine Receives the Crown of St Bishop Felix, 1620.
Oil on canvas, 345 x 231 cm.
Pinacoteca Nazionale, Bologna.

419. **Johann Liss,** 1597-1631, Baroque,
German, *Sacrifice of Abraham,* c. 1624.
Oil on canvas, 88 x 70 cm.
Galleria degli Uffizi, Florence.

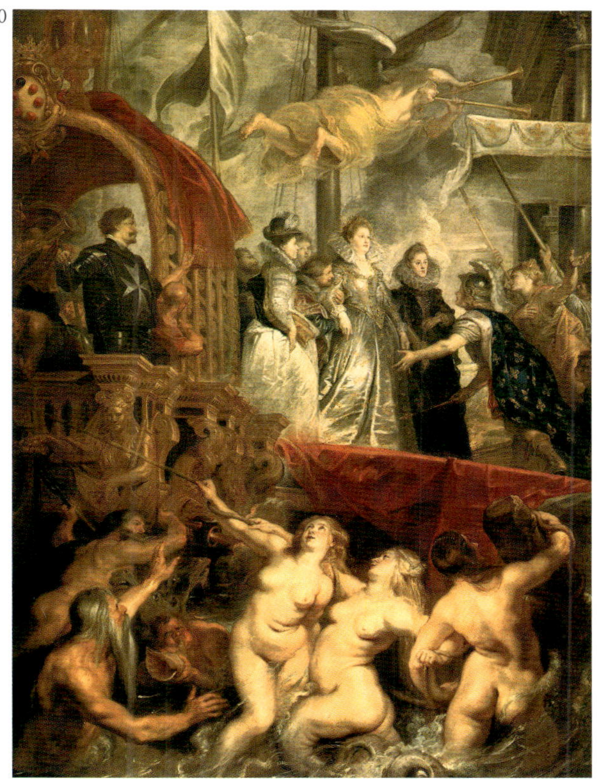

420

420. **Peter Paul Rubens,** 1577-1640, Baroque, Flemish,
The Landing of Marie de' Médici at Marseille, c. 1623.
Oil on canvas, 394 x 295 cm. Musée du Louvre, Paris.

This large painting is one of sixteen in a cycle on the life of Queen Marie de'Medici (1573-1642). The series, the most important in his prolific life, was completed in four years for the Palais du Luxembourg in Paris. The historical event being dramatically presented actually took place a month or so after the October wedding of Marie to Henry IV. In the scene, the queen's ship is in the Marseilles harbour shortly after her marriage. Both heaven and earth welcome her. The city welcomes her in the personage of allegorical figures from the legendary history of the city. Fama, the goddess from whom the word 'fame' comes, hovers above and with her double bugle announces the arrival of the Queen. Representing all of the earth, the god Neptune and three Rubenesque sirens and tritons add even more beauty and festivity to the event. In 1610, ten years after the Queen's landing, she would take charge of Paris, just one day before the King's death.

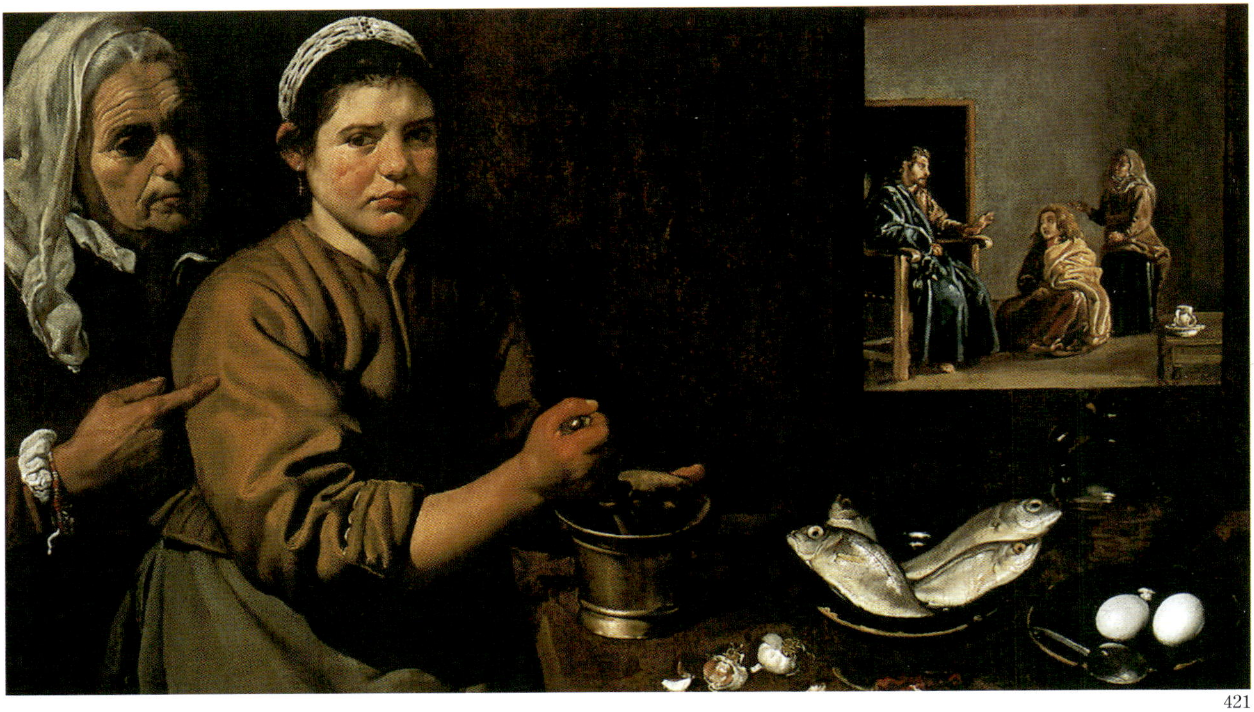

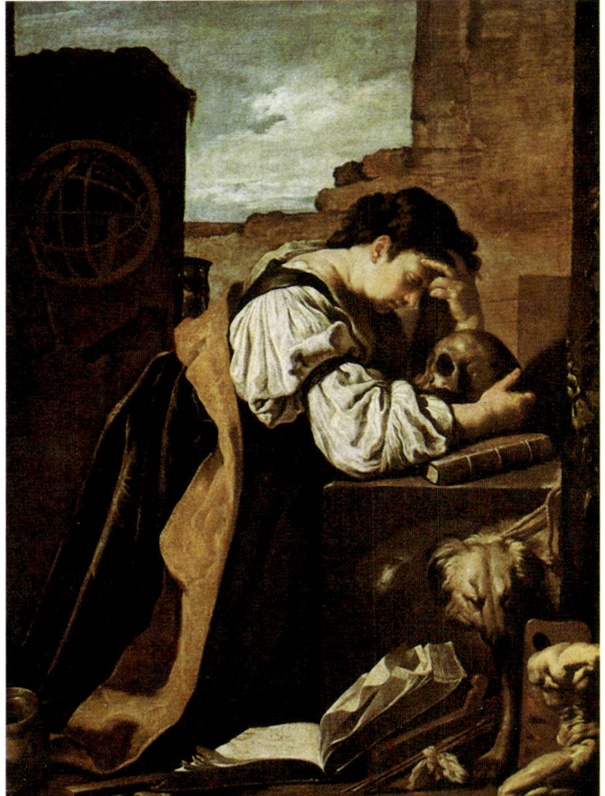

421

421. **Diego Velázquez,** 1599-1660, Baroque, Spanish,
Christ in the House of Mary and Marthe, 1618.
Oil on canvas, 60 x 103.5 cm.
National Gallery, London.

422. **Bernardo Strozzi,** 1581-1644, Baroque, Italian,
The Cook, c. 1620.
Oil on canvas, 177 x 241 cm. Galleria di Palazzo, Genoa.

423. **Domenico Fetti,** 1589-1623, Baroque, Venetian School,
Italian, *Melancholy,* c. 1620.
Oil on canvas, 171 x 128 cm. Musée du Louvre, Paris.

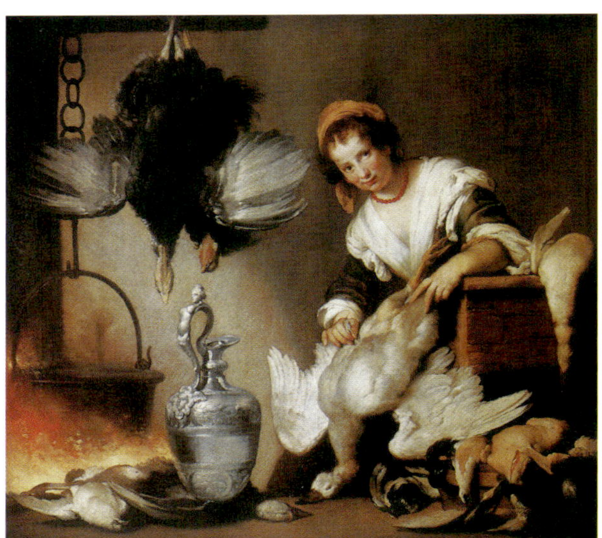

422

423

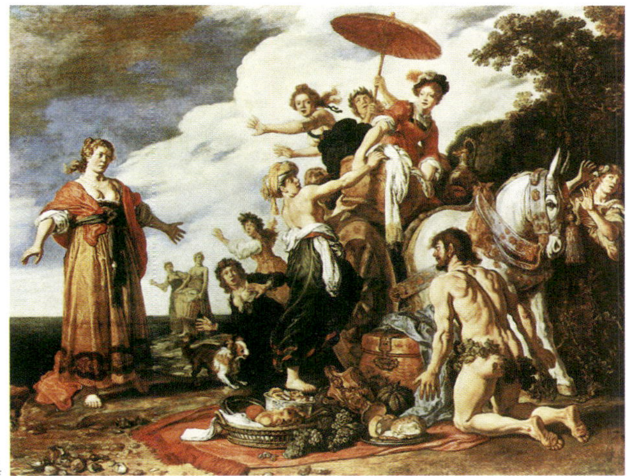

424

424. **Pieter Lastman,** 1583-1633, Baroque, Dutch,
Odysseus and Nausicaa, 1619.
Oil on panel, 91.5 x 117.2 cm. Alte Pinakothek, Munich.

425. **Anthony van Dyck,** 1599-1641, Baroque, Flemish, *Marchesa
Elena Grimaldi, Wife of Marchese Nicola Cattaneo,* c. 1623.
Oil on canvas, 242.9 x 138.5 cm.
The National Gallery of Art, Washington D.C.

426. **Orazio Gentileschi,** 1563-1639, Baroque, Italian,
The Lute Player, c. 1626. Oil on canvas, 144 x 130 cm.
The National Gallery of Art, Washington D.C.

427. **Frans Hals,** c. 1582-1666, Baroque, Dutch, *Gypsy Girl,* c. 1626.
Oil on panel, 58 x 52 cm. Musée du Louvre, Paris.

*The title of this painting was given by the donator but doesn't match
with what should rather be considered as the portrait of a courtesan.*

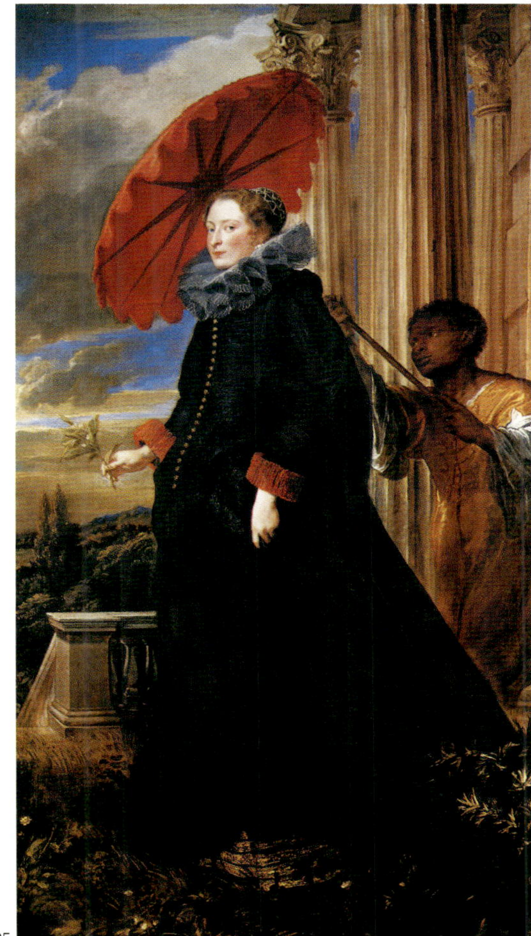

425

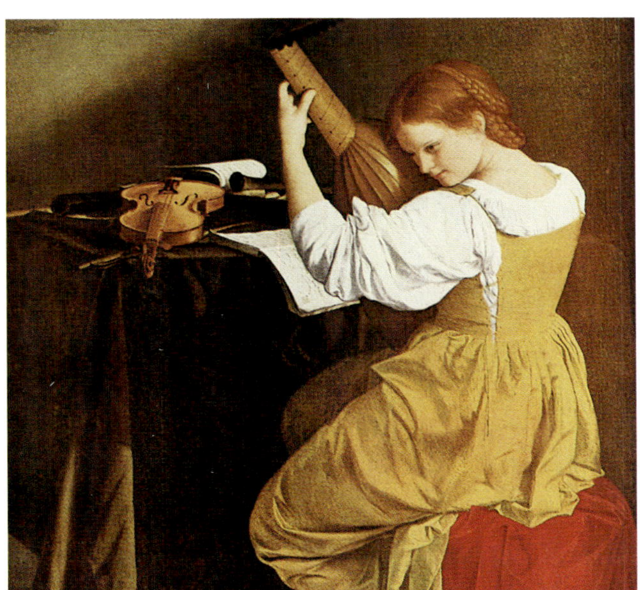

426

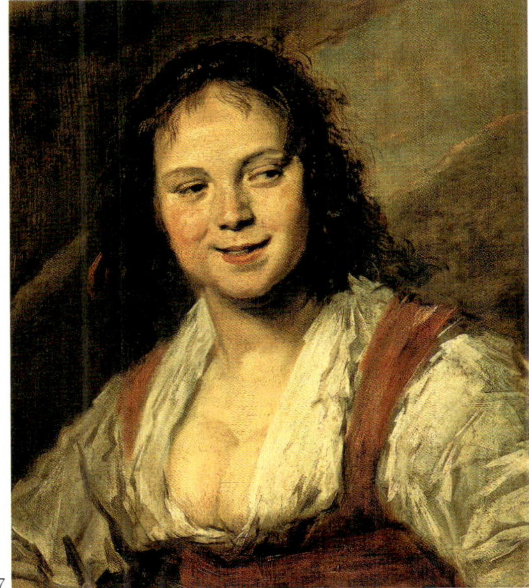

427

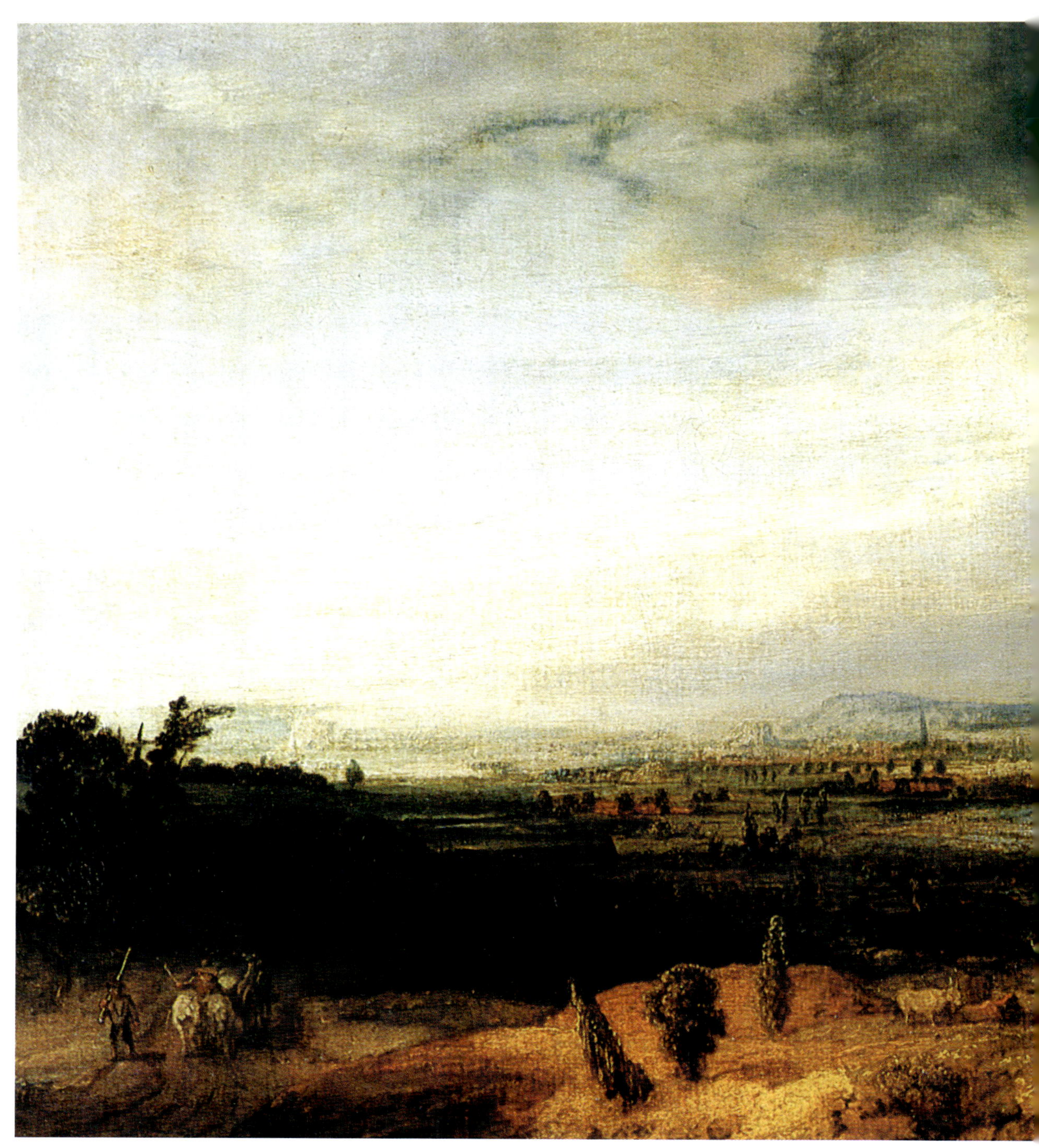

428. **Hercules Seghers,** 1589-1638, Baroque, Dutch, *Broad Valley Landscape with Rocks,* c. 1625.

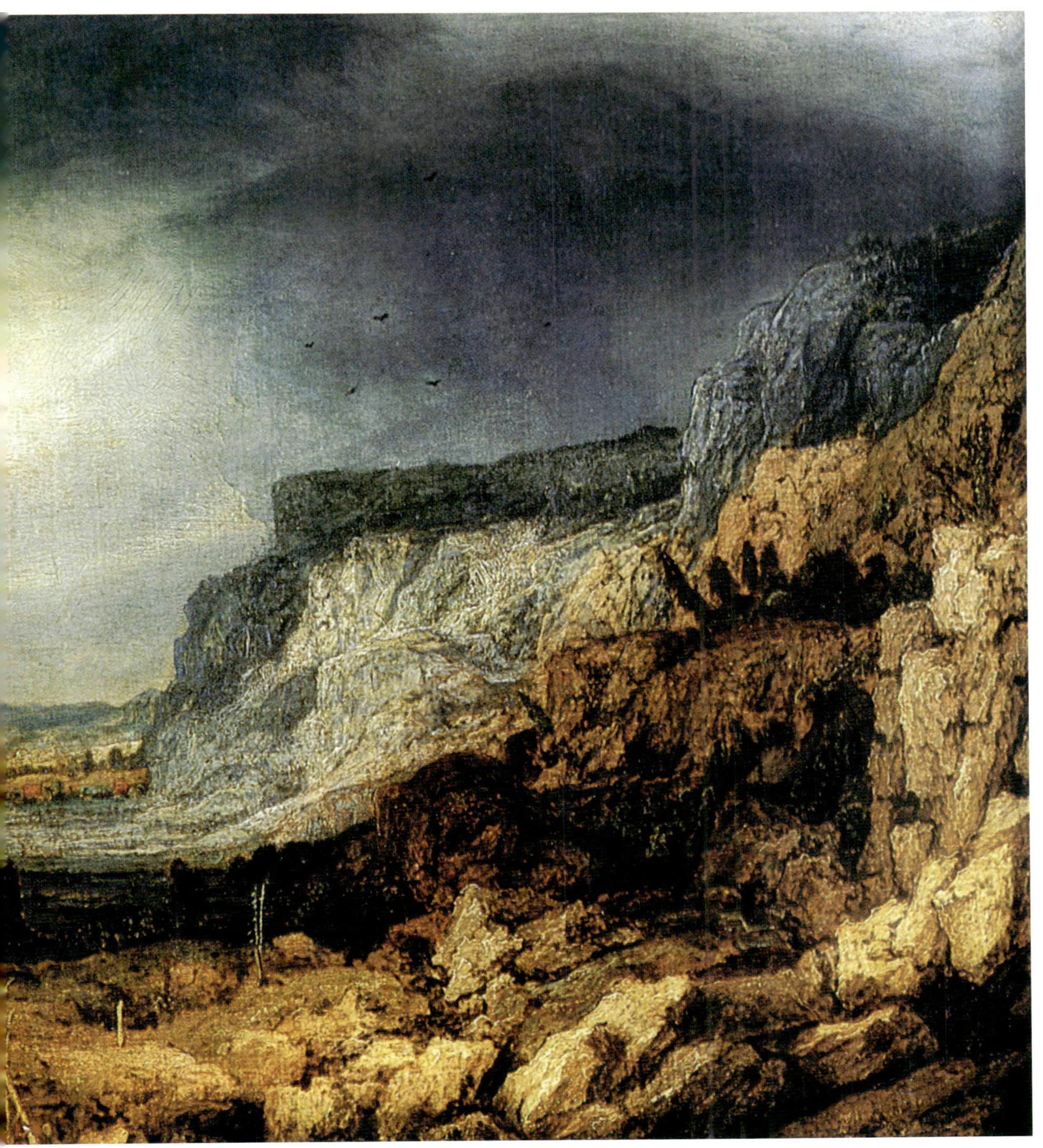

Oil on canvas transferred to panel, 55 x 99 cm. Galleria degli Uffizi, Florence.

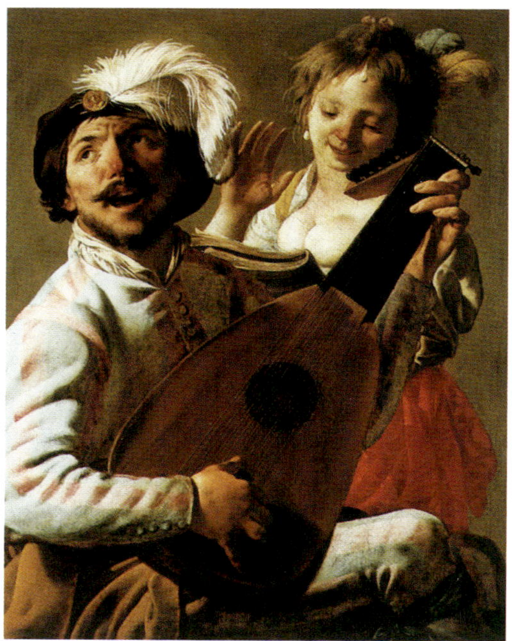

429. **Hendrick Jansz ter Brugghen,** 1588-1629, Baroque, Dutch,
Duet, 1628. Oil on canvas, 106 x 82 cm.
Musée du Louvre, Paris.

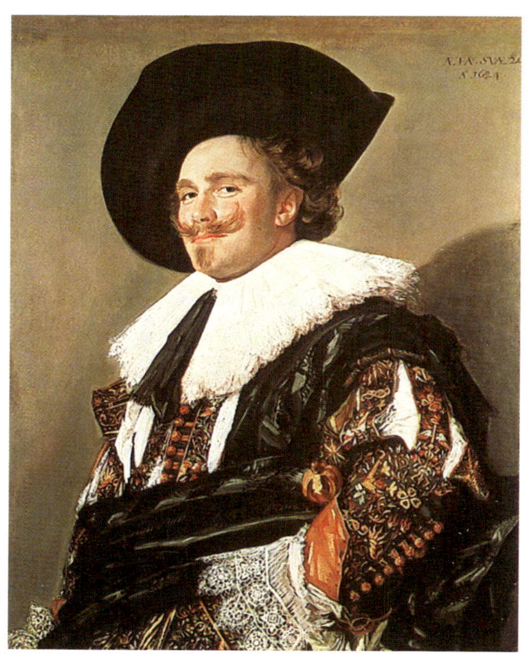

430. **Frans Hals,** c. 1582-1666, Baroque, Dutch,
The Laughing Cavalier, 1624.
Oil on canvas, 83 x 67 cm. The Wallace Collection, London.

432. **Judith Leyster,** 1609-1660, Baroque, Dutch, *Carousing Couple,* 1630.
Oil on panel, 68 x 57 cm. Musée du Louvre, Paris.

*Judith Leyster is one of the very few women to have been accepted as a member of
the Haarlem Guild of Painters. Although a contemporary historian described her as
a leading light in art, she remained unknown for a long time, and her works were
either believed lost or were attributed to Frans Hals.*

431. **Francisco de Zurbarán,** 1598-1664,
Baroque, Spanish, *St Agatha,* c. 1634.
Oil on canvas, 129 x 61 cm.
Musée Fabre, Montpellier.

*St Agatha, a third-century virgin martyred by
the Roman emperor Decius, was also painted
later by Tiepolo (1756) and Cassatt (1891).
St Agatha is the patron saint of bell makers
and is also invoked against the outbreak of
fire. This portrait is from the beginning of
the peak years of the artist's output, at the
start of his role as city painter in Seville. This
masterpiece demonstrates the Spanish artist's
ability to capture warm, realistic expressions
and intense, ascetic sobriety, a quality he
shared with his contemporary and fellow
countryman, Velázquez. Zurbarán also focused
on the rendering of sculptural volumes,
particularly noticeable in the depiction of
the draperies.*

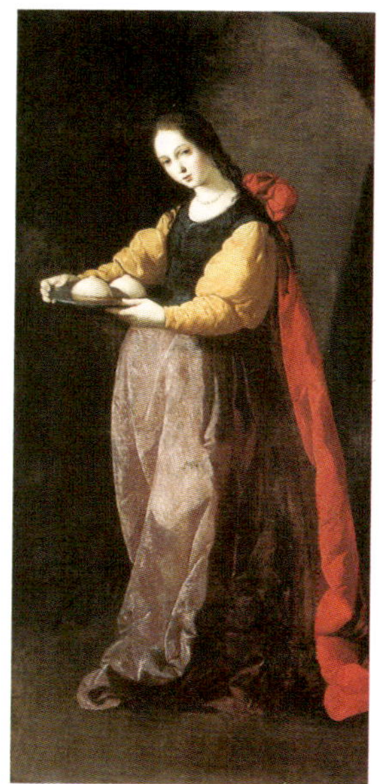

431

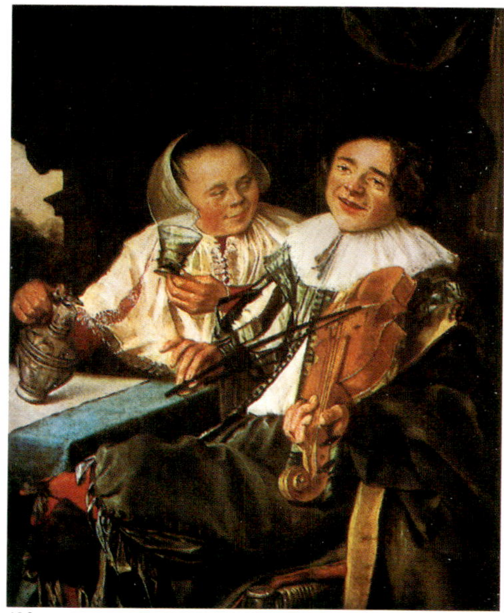

432

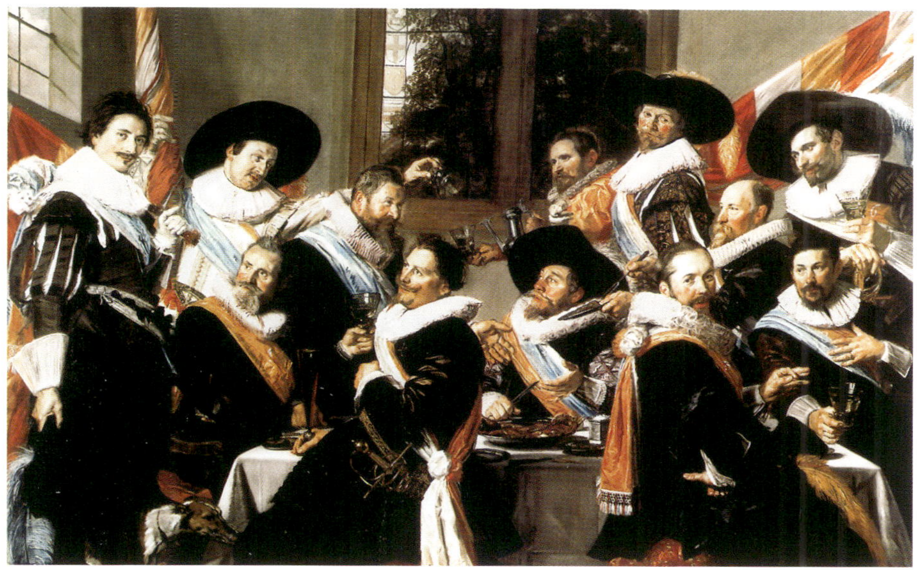

433. **Frans Hals,** c. 1582-1666, Baroque, Dutch, *Banquet of the Officers of the Civic Guard of St Adrian (the Cluveniers),* 1627. Oil on canvas, 183 x 266.5 cm. Frans-Hals-Museum, Haarlem.

This portrait is the first major group portrait by Hals, and the first monumental civic guard painting in the new era of Dutch painting. Hals revolutionised this type of painting; instead of merely painting a row of portraits, he places them in a specific context by creating a banquet scene.

FRANS HALS
(C. 1582 ANTWERP – 1666 HAARLEM)

Hals must have had fine qualities of mind; how else could he have seen things so simply and completely, and rendered them with such force and expression, inventing for the purpose a method of his own? His method was distinguished by placing his subject in clear light and by working largely in flat tones, to get at the essential facts of a subject, and to set them down rapidly and precisely, so that all may understand them and be impressed. He was, however, so shiftless that in his old age he was dependent upon the city government for support. That he received it, however, and that his creditors were lenient with him, seems to show that his contemporaries recognised greatness behind his intemperance and improvidence; and, when in his eighty-second year he died, he was buried beneath the choir of the Church of St Bavon in Haarlem.

For a long time after his death, Hals was thought little of, even in Holland, where artists forsook the traditions of their own school and went in search of other mentors – to wit, those of the Italian "grand style". It was not until well into the nineteenth century that artists returning to the truth of nature, discovered that Hals had been one of the greatest seers of the truth and one of its most virile interpreters. Today he is honoured for these qualities, and of all the much-admired Dutch pictures of the seventeenth century, his are the most characteristic of the Dutch race and of the art which it produced.

434. **Anthony van Dyck,** 1599-1641, Baroque, Flemish, *Self-Portrait,* c. 1622. Oil on canvas, 117 x 94 cm. The State Hermitage Museum, St Petersburg.

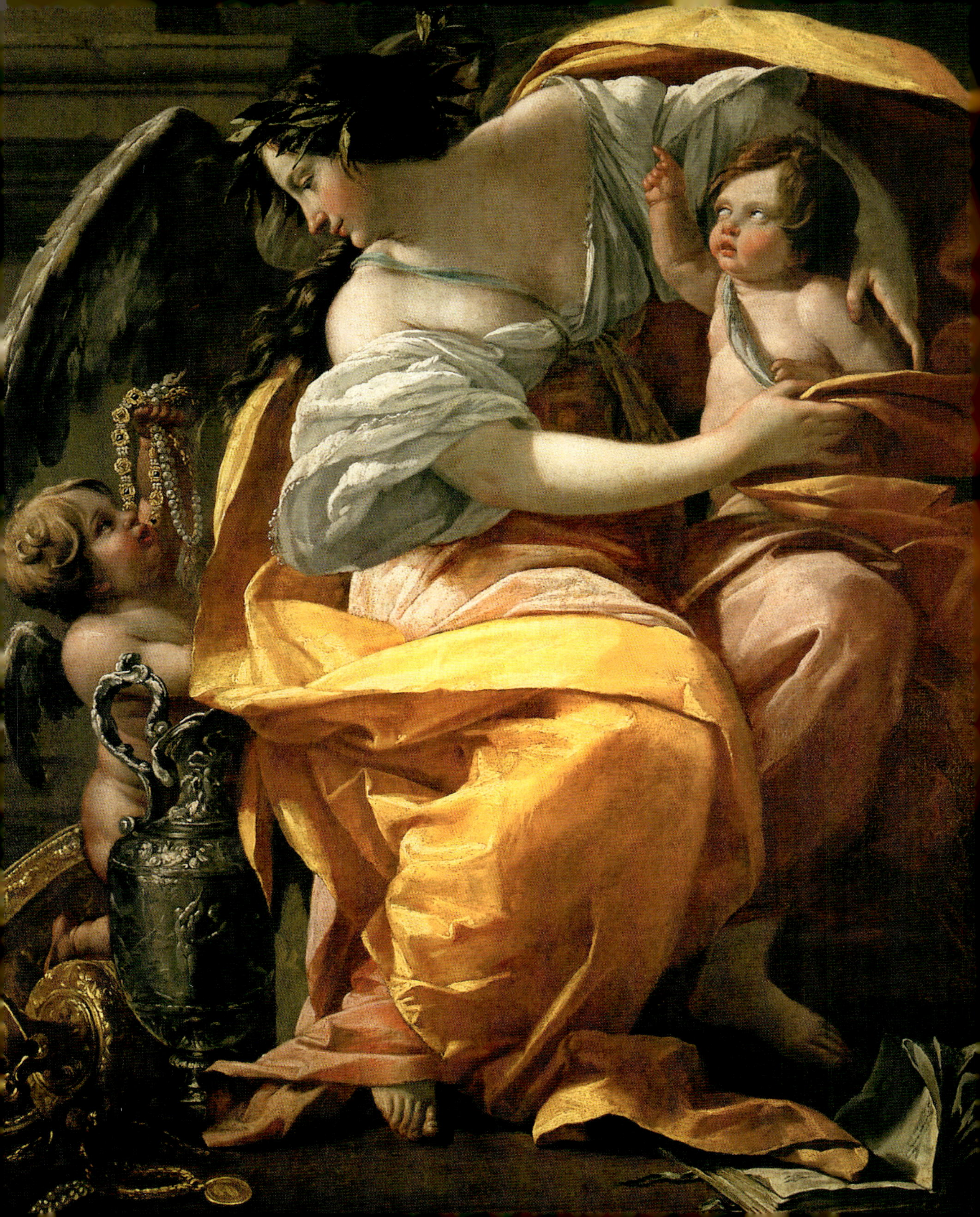

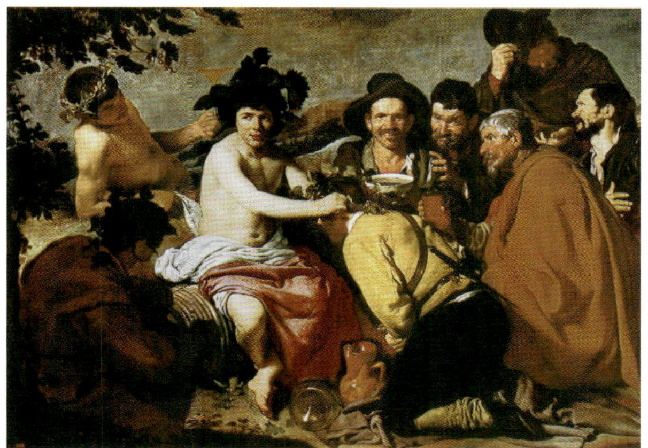

436. **Diego Velázquez,** 1599-1660, Baroque, Spanish,
The Feast of Bacchus or *The Drunkards,* 1629.
Oil on canvas, 165 x 227 cm.
Museo Nacional del Prado, Madrid.

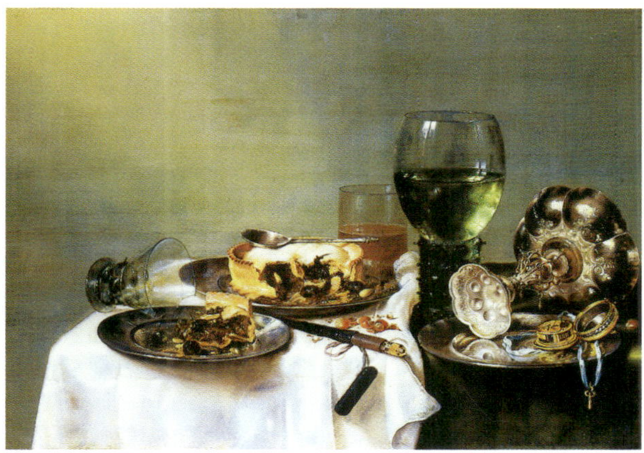

437. **Willem Claesz Heda,** 1594-1680, Baroque, Dutch,
Breakfast Table with Blackberry Pie, 1631.
Oil on panel, 54 x 82 cm.
Gemäldegalerie Alte Meister, Dresden.

*Heda is, with Pieter Claesz, the most important representative
of breakfast-piece painting in the Netherlands.*

438. **Simon Vouet,** 1590-1649, Baroque, French,
Time Overcome by Hope and Beauty, 1627.
Oil on canvas, 107 x 142 cm.
Museo Nacional del Prado, Madrid.

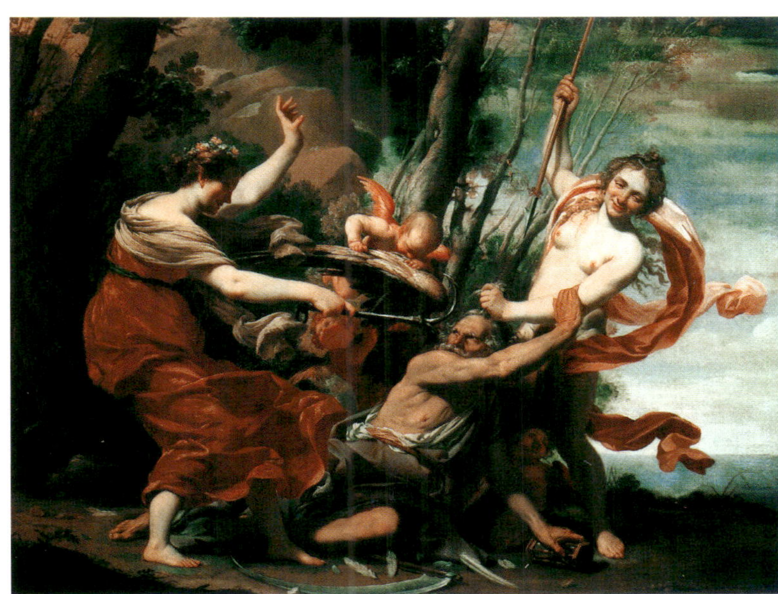

435. **Simon Vouet,** 1590-1649, Baroque,
Wealth, c. 1640.
Oil on canvas, 170 x 124 cm.
Musée du Louvre, Paris.

SIMON VOUET
(1590 – 1649 PARIS)

Vouet was exceedingly precocious. At fourteen he already enjoyed such a reputation as a portrait painter that he was invited to visit England in order to paint the portrait of a lady of quality. He was honoured also in Constantinople by Louis XIII in 1628, and for twenty years held sovereign sway over the arts. It is obvious that he was a little carried away by his enormous talent, but his clear colour and sense of decoration played a part in the evolution of French painting. He had more influence than Poussin had on Le Sueur, Le Brun, and Mignard and through them on the great work of Louis XIV's reign; the decoration of Versailles. From him derives Boucher, and hence a substantial part of eighteenth-century art.

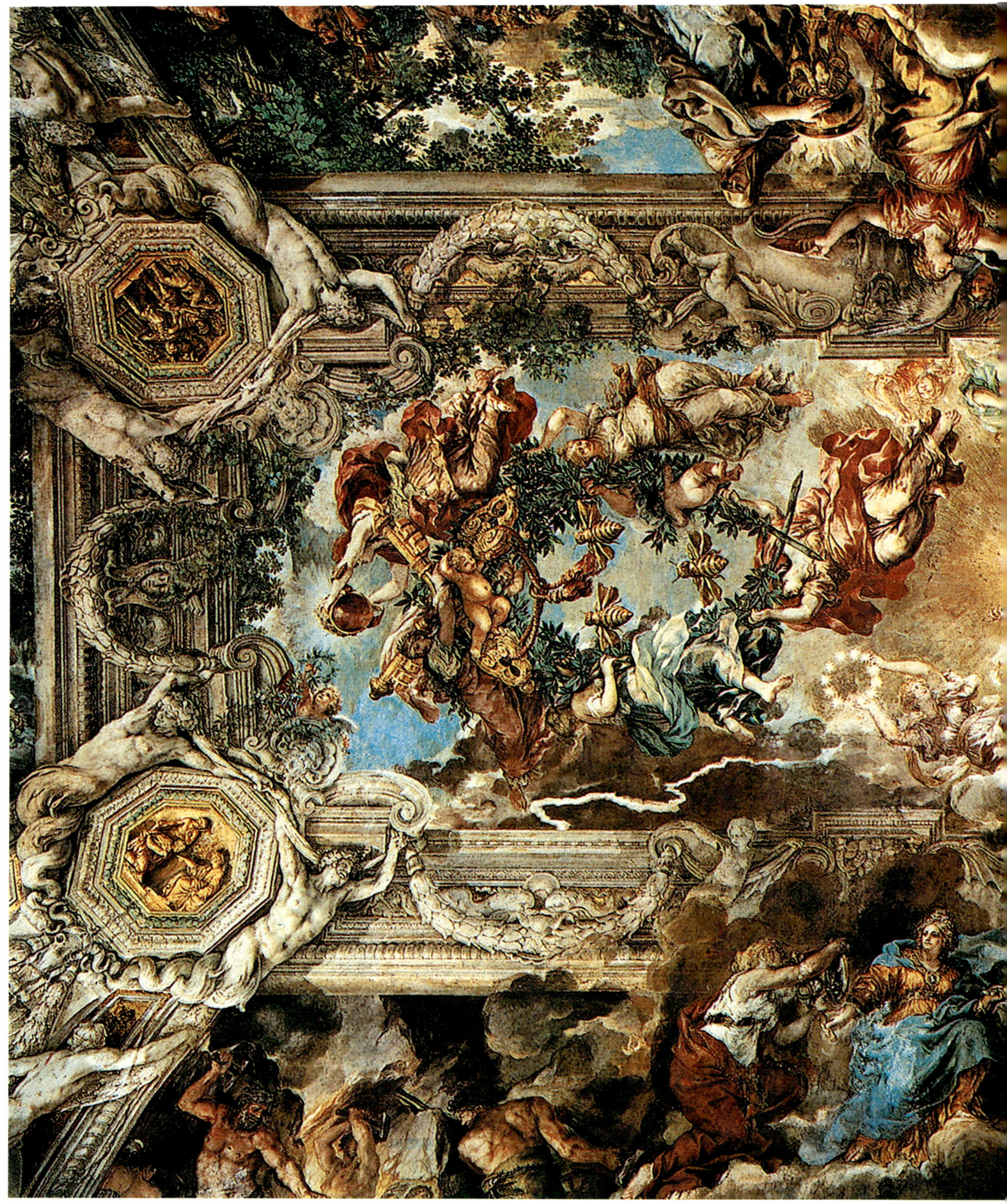

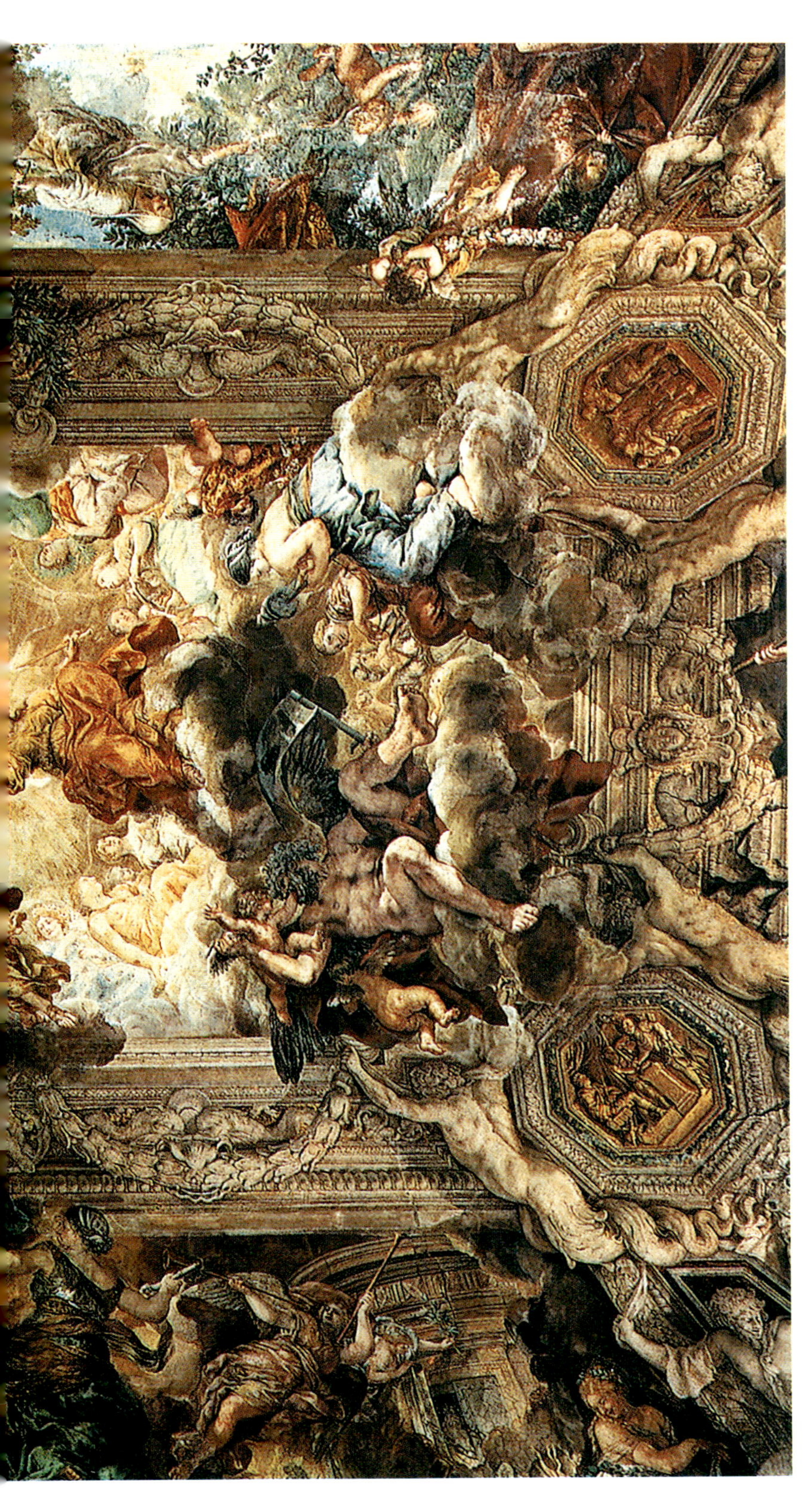

439. Pietro da Cortona (Pietro Berrettini), 1596-1669, Baroque, Italian, *Allegory of Divine Providence and Barberini Power*, 1633-1639. Fresco. Palazzo Barberini, Rome.

This fresco is one of the key works in the development of Baroque painting. It is a triumph of illusionism: the centre of the ceiling appears open to the sky and the figures seen from below (sotto insù) appear to come down into the room as well as soar out of it.

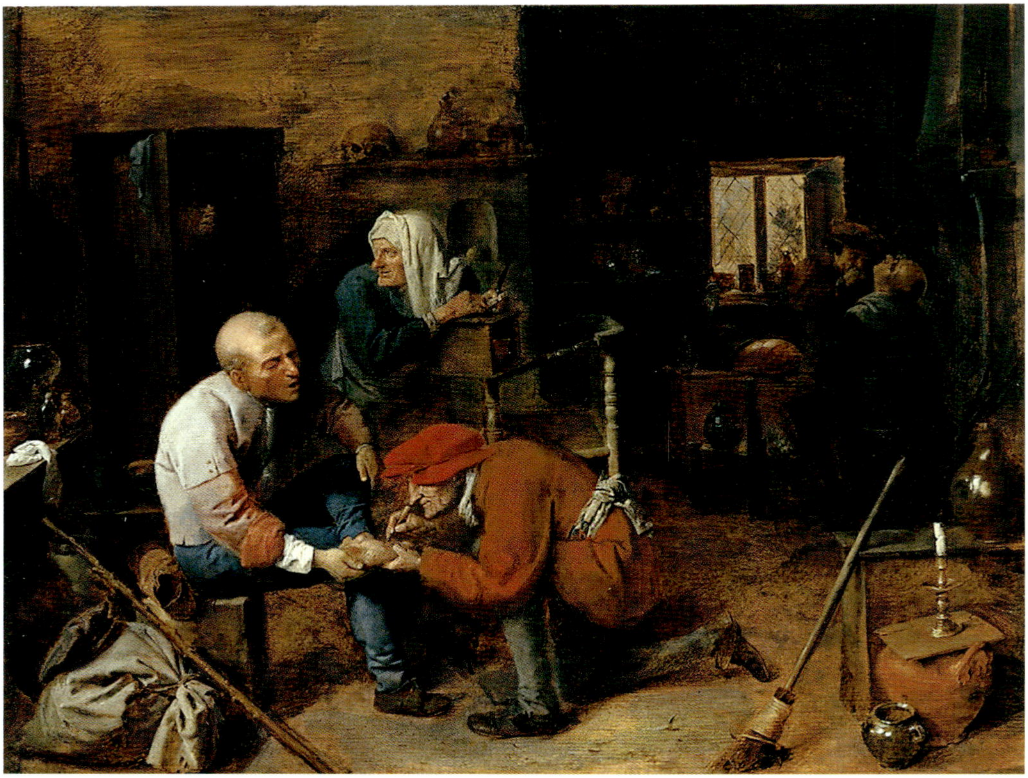

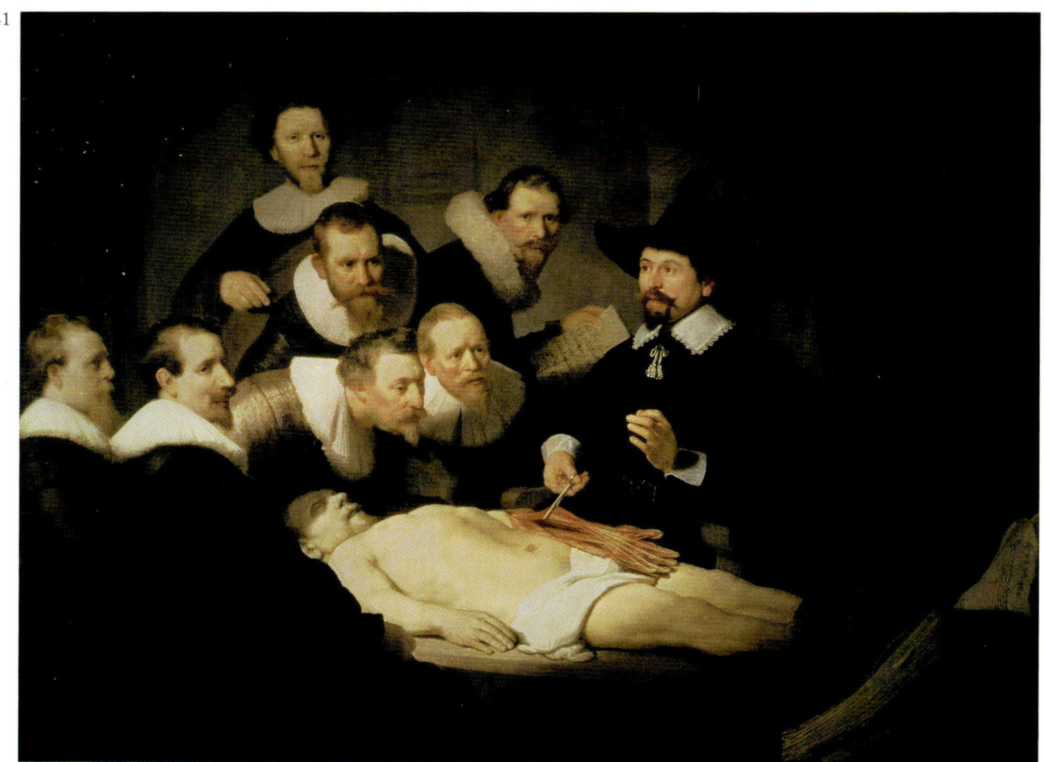

440

441

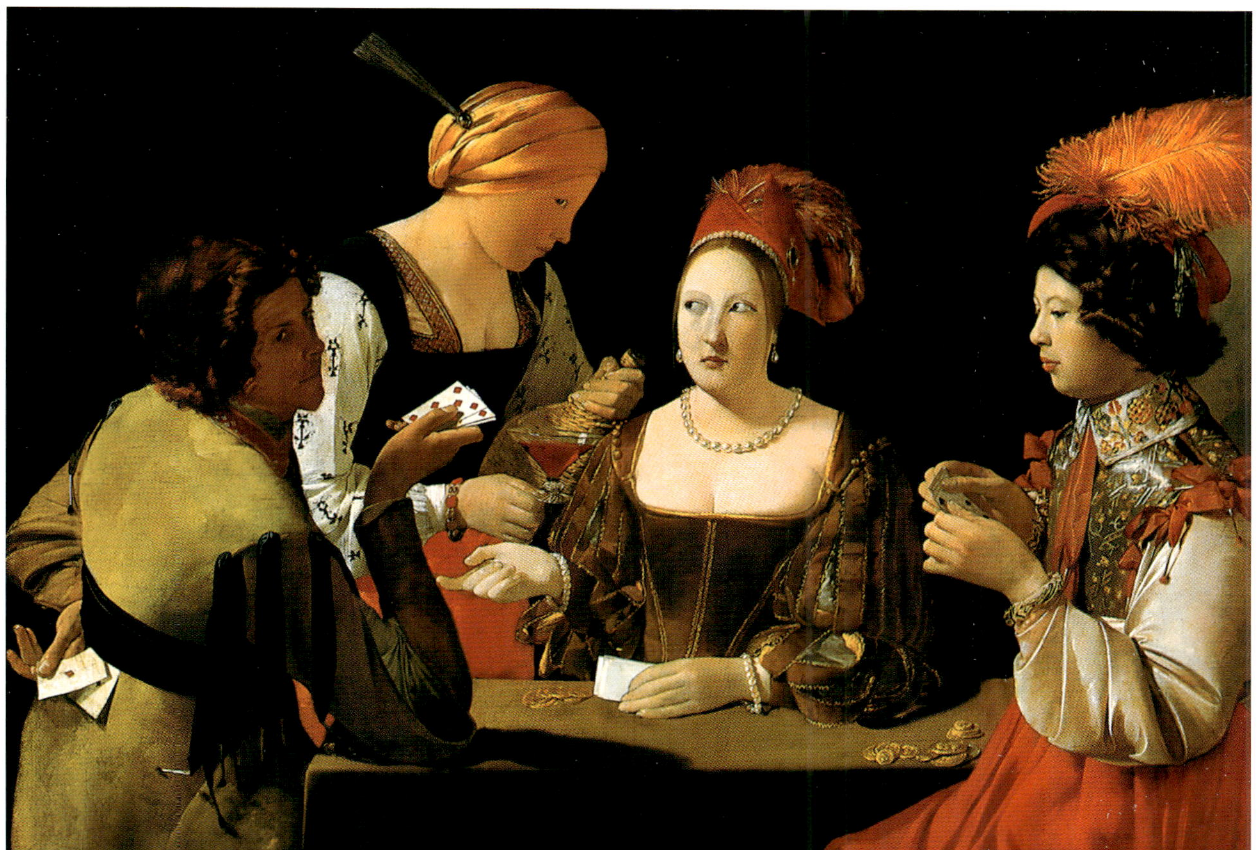

440. **Adriaen Brouwer,** 1605-1638, Baroque, Flemish,
The Operation. 1631. Oil on panel, 31.4 x 39.6 cm.
Alte Pinakothek, Munich.

441. **Rembrandt Harmensz. van Rijn,** 1606-1669, Baroque, Dutch,
The Anatomy Lesson of Dr Tulp, 1632.
Oil on canvas, 169.5 x 216.5 cm.
Koninklijk Kabinet van Schilderijen Mauritshuis, The Hague.

442. **Georges de La Tour,** 1593-1652, Baroque, French,
The Card-Sharp with the Ace of Diamonds, 1635.
Oil on canvas, 106 x 146 cm.
Musée du Louvre, Paris.

Georges de La Tour's workshop was in Lorraine, where the troops of King Louis XIII were wreaking massive destruction. But Lorraine is also a region from which numerous travels to Italy were taking place. Whether La Tour went to Italy or not is still a mystery but the painter was influenced by Caravaggio's style.

GEORGES DE LA TOUR
(1593 VIC SUR VILLE – 1652 LUNÉVILLE)

Georges de La Tour was well known in his own time but then forgotten until the twentieth century. His painting depicted genre and religious subjects, seen often in candlelight, such as his interior scenes. The influence of Caravaggio is evident in his painting, especially in the use of chiaroscuro. Simplification of form and rigour of composition in his work underlined the ideas of the Counter-Reformation.

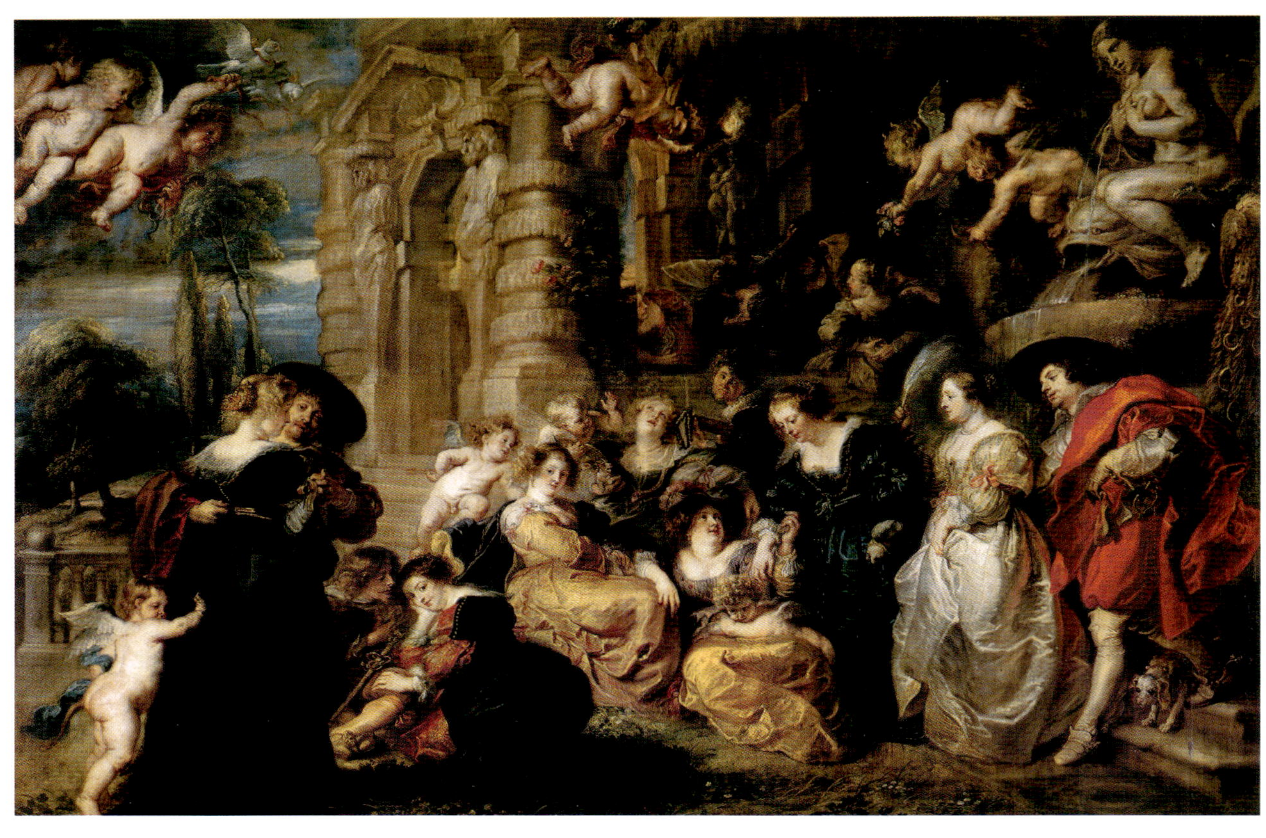

443. **Peter Paul Rubens,** 1577-1640, Baroque, Flemish, *The Garden of Love,* c. 1633. Oil on canvas, 198 x 283 cm. Museo Nacional del Prado, Madrid.

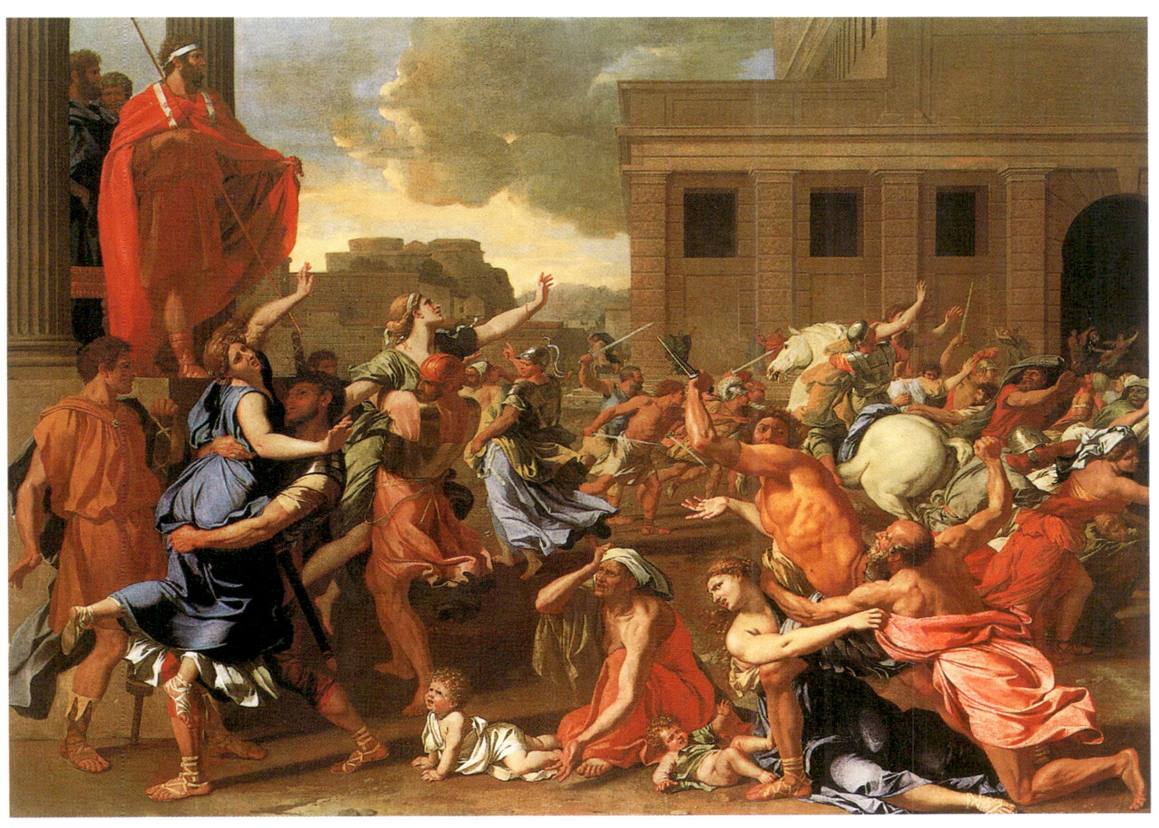

444. **Nicolas Poussin,** 1594-1665, Classicism, French,
The Abduction of the Sabine Women, 1633-1634.
Oil on canvas, 154.6 x 209.9 cm.
The Metropolitan Museum of Art, New York.

Poussin was undoubtedly a highly significant master of the historical genre. He shaped its aesthetics which, regrettably, subsequently became regarded as a set of hard-and-fast rules (a trap which the Russian followers of the founder of Classicism also fell into). We know that Poussin attributed prime significance to the actual choice of matter for depiction, giving preference to subjects which provided food for profound thought. Creatively reworking the aesthetic legacy of the Ancients, he introduced into the realm of painting the concept of the "modus" (mood of depiction), which established the functional unity of three components: the idea, the structure of the depiction, and its perception by the viewer. Composition assumed a predominant significance in his artistic system.

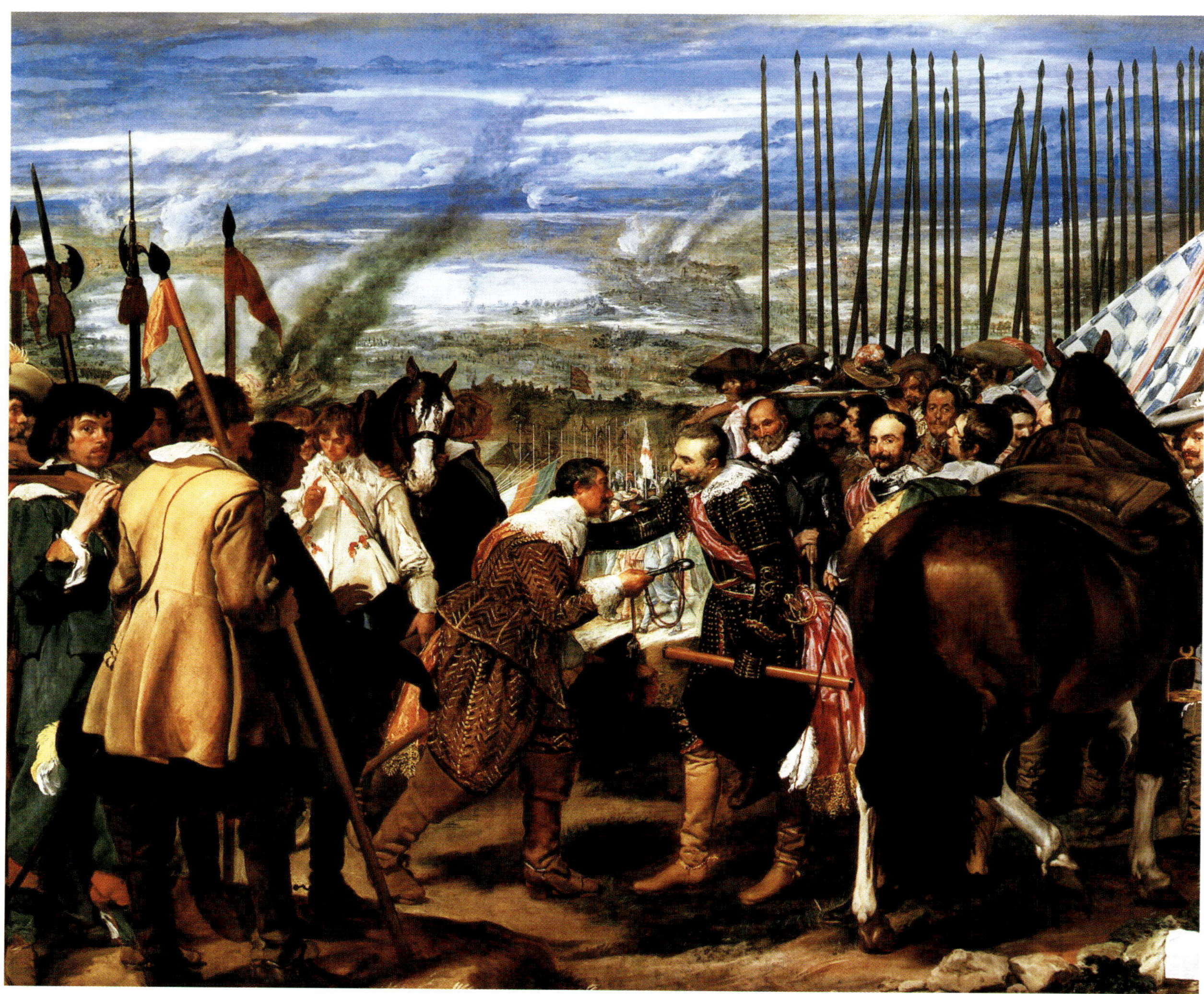

445. **Diego Velázquez,**
1599-1660,
Baroque, Spanish,
*The Surrender of
Breda,* c. 1634.
Oil on canvas,
307 x 367 cm.
Museo Nacional del
Prado, Madrid.

DIEGO VELÁZQUEZ
(1599 SEVILLA – 1660 MADRID)

Diego Velázquez was an individualistic artist of the contemporary Baroque period. At age twenty-four, Velázquez made his first trip to Madrid with his teacher, Francisco Pacheco. King Philip IV noticed his genius and appointed him court painter in 1627. Shortly afterward the artist befriended Rubens in Madrid. He developed a more realistic approach to religious art in which figures are naturalistic portraits rather than depicted in an idealistic style. The use of chiaroscuro is reminiscent of Caravaggio's works. Velázquez made at least two trips to Rome to buy Renaissance and neoclassical art for the King. In Rome, he joined the Academy of St Luke in 1650 and was knighted into the order of Santiago in 1658. His large commissioned work, *Surrender of Breda* (c. 1634), shows the defeat of the Dutch at the hands of the Spanish, and glorified the military triumph of Philip's reign. The artist painted *Pope Innocent X* (1650) during his second trip to Rome, most likely recalling similar works by Raphael and Titian. He mastered the art of portraiture because he looked beyond external trappings into the human mystery beneath his subjects, as evidenced in his remarkable series of dwarfs, who were present in many royal courts at that time. He depicted their humanity instead of doing caricatures. His later works were more spontaneous, but still disciplined. The culmination of his career is his masterwork, *Las Meninas* (fig. 489). It is indeed one of the most complex essays in portraiture. Velázquez is acknowledged to be the most important Spanish painter of his century, influencing major painters such as Goya and Manet.

ANTHONY VAN DYCK
(1599 ANTWERP – 1641 LONDON)

Van Dyck was accustomed early to Rubens' sumptuous lifestyle; and, when he visited Italy with letters of introduction from his master, lived in the palaces of his patrons, himself adopting such an elegant ostentation that he was spoken of as 'the Cavalier Painter'. After his return to Antwerp his patrons belonged to the rich and noble class, and his own style of living was modelled on theirs; so that, when in 1632 he received the appointment of court painter to Charles I of England, he maintained an almost princely establishment, and his house at Blackfriars was a resort of fashion. The last two years of his life were spent travelling on the Continent with his young wife, the daughter of Lord Gowry. His health, however, had been broken by the excesses of work, and he returned to London to die. He was buried at St Paul's Cathedral.

Van Dyck tried to amalgamate the influences of Italy (Titian, Veronese, Bellini) and Flanders and he succeeded in some paintings, which have a touching grace, notably in his *Madonnas and Holy Families*, his *Crucifixions* and *Depositions from the Cross*, and also in some of his mythological compositions. In his younger days he painted many altarpieces full of sensitive religious feeling and enthusiasm. However, his main glory was as a portraitist, the most elegant and aristocratic ever known. The great *Portrait of Charles I* in the Louvre is a work unique for its sovereign elegance. In his portraits, he invented a style of elegance and refinement which became a model for the artists of the seventeenth and eighteenth centuries, corresponding as it did to the genteel luxury of the court life of the period. He is also considered one of the greatest colourists in the history of art.

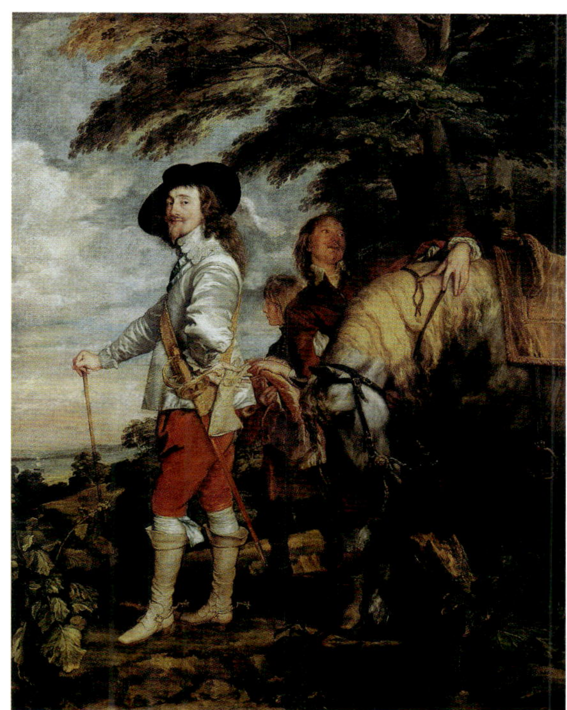

446. **Anthony van Dyck,** 1599-1641, Baroque, Flemish, *Charles I: King of England at the Hunt,* 1635. Oil on canvas, 266 x 207 cm. Musée du Louvre, Paris.

447. **Frans Hals,** c. 1582-1666, Baroque, Dutch, *Company of Captain Reinier Reael,* also known as the *'Meagre Company',* 1637. Oil on canvas, 209 x 429 cm. Rijksmuseum, Amsterdam.

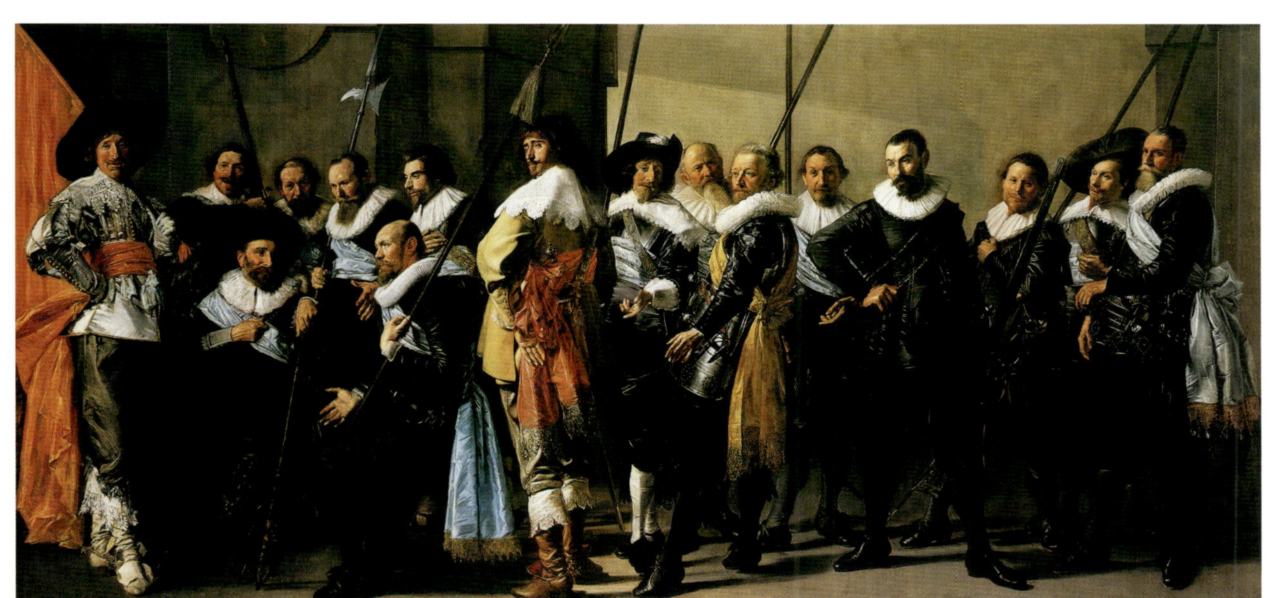

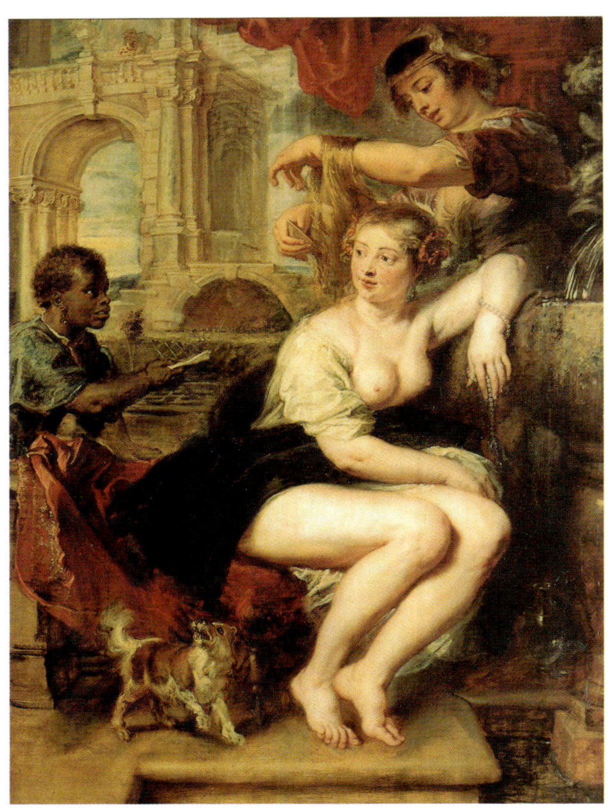

448. **Peter Paul Rubens,** 1577-1640, Baroque, Flemish, *Bathsheba at the Fountain*, 1635. Oil on oak panel, 175 x 126 cm. Gemäldegalerie Alte Meister, Dresden.

449. **Francesco Albani,** 1578-1660, Classicism, Italian, *The Rape of Europa,* 1639. Oil on canvas, 76.3 x 97 cm. Galleria degli Uffizi, Florence.

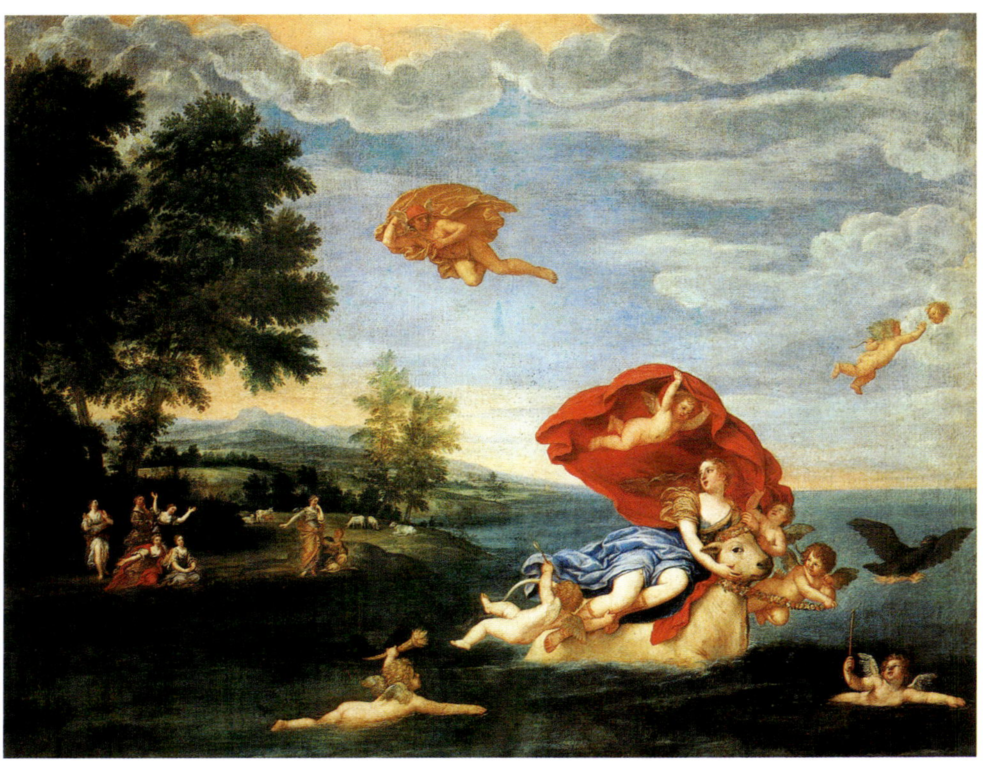

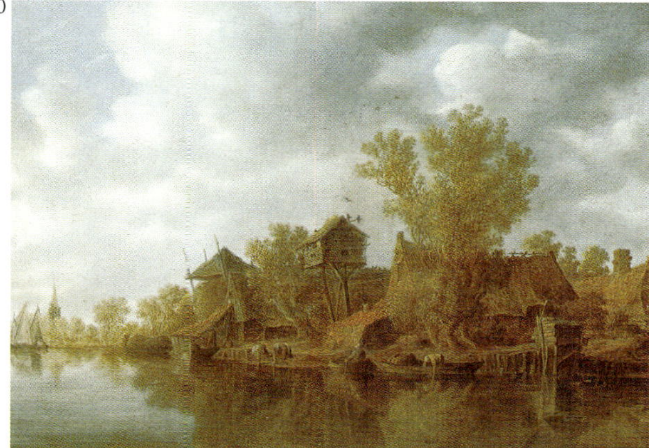

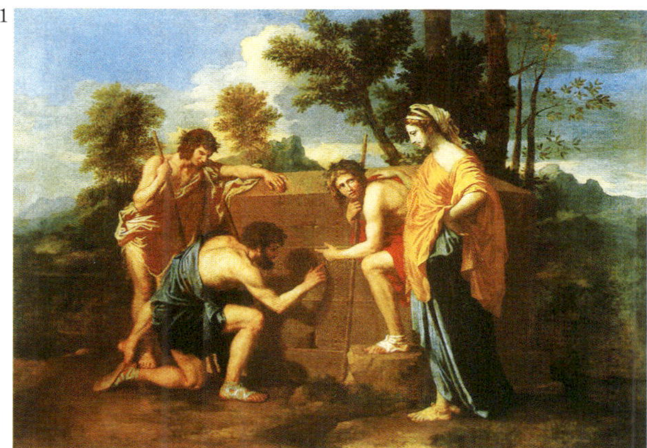

450. **Jan van Goyen,** 1596-1656, Baroque, Dutch,
River Landscape, 1636.
Oil on panel, 39.5 x 60 cm. Alte Pinakothek, Munich.

451. **Nicolas Poussin,** 1594-1665, Classicism, French,
'Et in Arcadia Ego', 1638-1639.
Oil on canvas, 85 x 121 cm. Musée du Louvre, Paris.

452. **Sébastien Bourdon,** 1616-1671, Atticism, French,
The Death of Dido, 1637-1640. Oil on canvas, 158.5 x 136.5 cm.
The State Hermitage Museum, St Petersburg.

*This painting is comparable to one on the same theme by Simon
Vouet for the lyrical style in which both are depicted. Also,
Bourdon enhanced the dramatic effects using arabesques and
rejecting strong colours, as he remained under the influence of
Venetian painting.*

NICOLAS POUSSIN
(1594 VILLERS – 1665 ROME)

Although Nicolas Poussin was only four years younger than
Vouet, his influence made itself felt in France much later. He
was not precocious like Vouet, but may be numbered amongst
those great men who have need of reflection and meditation,
whose inspiration comes only with maturity.

None of his early works has been preserved. His career begins,
historically speaking, in 1624 with his arrival in Rome at the age
of thirty. He came to Italy in quest of Raphael, whose genius he
had discerned from the engravings of Marc-Antoine while still in
Paris. The master of the Farnesine and of the Vatican Stanze and
Loggia did not disappoint him. However, Titian was a profound
surprise to him, and from that time onwards his constant
preoccupation was to reconcile the spirit of these two great
men. At times he seemed to prefer a method hovering between
these magnetic poles, and vacillated between the linear element
derived from Raphael and the warm and coloured atmosphere
which he admired in Titian. This clear-sighted and impassioned
study which Poussin devoted to Raphael and Titian appears
perfectly natural today, but this was not so in 1624, when foreign
artists in Rome had no eyes except for the Academic art derived
from the Bolognese or from the brutal naturalism of the disciples
of Caravaggio. Poussin equally detested both, and with his robust,
philosophical frankness, condemned both unsparingly. The finest
aspect of Poussin's genius is to have put into his masterpieces
more thought than it was ever given to any other painter to
express, and to have found for that poetic and philosophical
thought an original and plastic interpretation.

Poussin is one of the greatest landscape painters. His sketches
are comparable only to those of Lorrain, and are perhaps yet
finer, while some recall Turner's most dazzling watercolours.
Poussin is inferior to Titian in richness of colour as well as
fullness and purity of form; but his poet philosopher's genius
added a lofty spirituality and an indefinable touch of the heroic
to the symphony of man and nature. Poussin, who from the age
of thirty spent most of his life in Rome, remains the most French
of the great painters, and always kept in view that wise and noble
balance between reason and feeling, which was the ideal of the
Ancients and has been that of artists and writers alike in France.

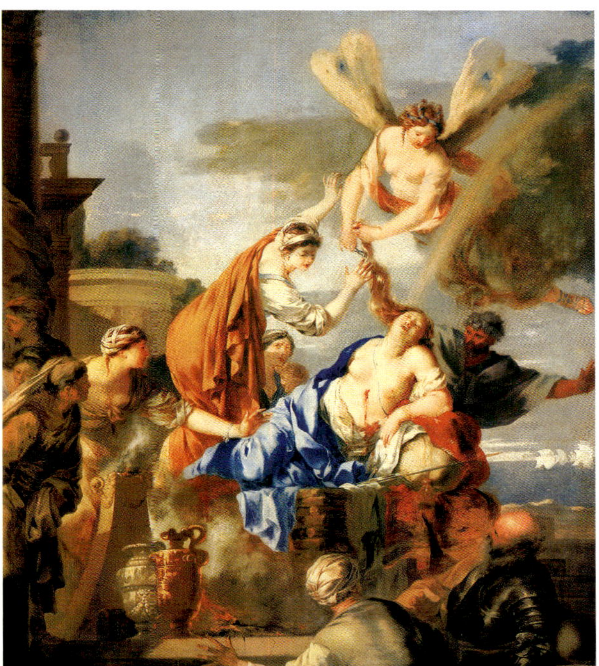

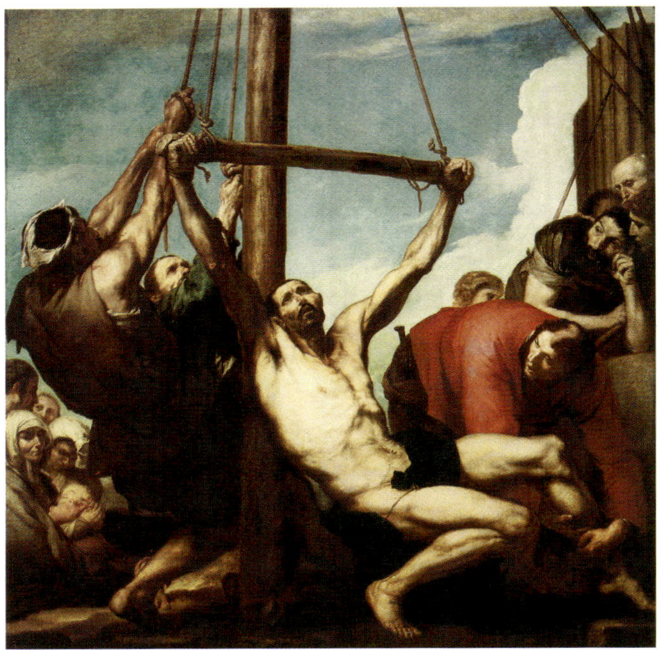

453. **José de Ribera,** 1591-1652, Baroque, Spanish,
Martyrdom of St Philip, 1639.
Oil on canvas, 234 x 234 cm.
Museo Nacional del Prado, Madrid.

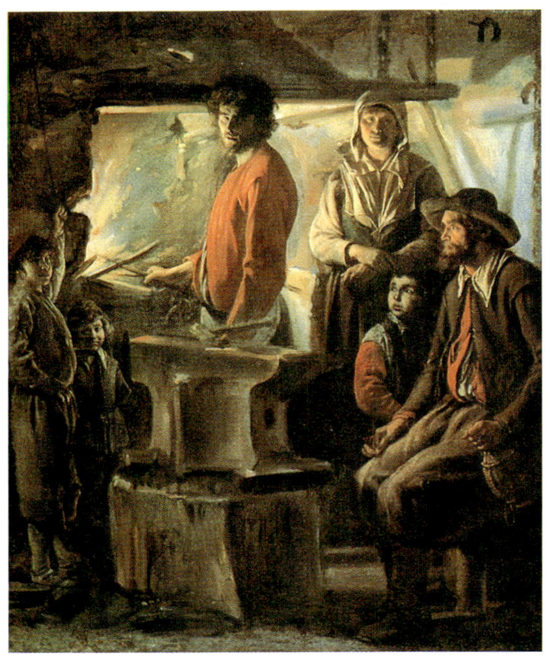

454. **Antoine Le Nain,** c. 1600-1648, Baroque, French,
Blacksmith at his Forge, c. 1640.
Oil on canvas, 69 x 57 cm.
Musée du Louvre, Paris.

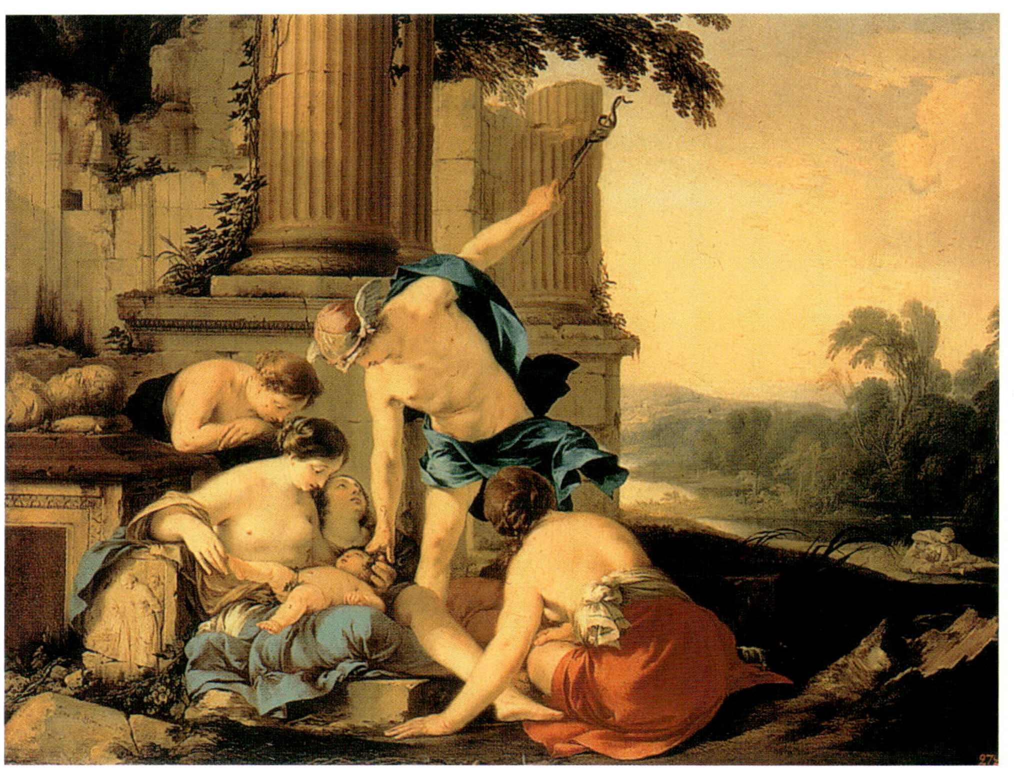

455. **Laurent de La Hyre,**
1606-1656, Atticism,
French, *Mercury Takes
Bacchus to be Brought
Up by Nymphs,* 1638.
Oil on canvas,
112.5 x 135 cm.
The State Hermitage
Museum, St Petersburg.

*Although La Hyre had
never been to Italy, he
took his inspiration from
Raphael as well as from
painters from the School
of Fontainebleau.*

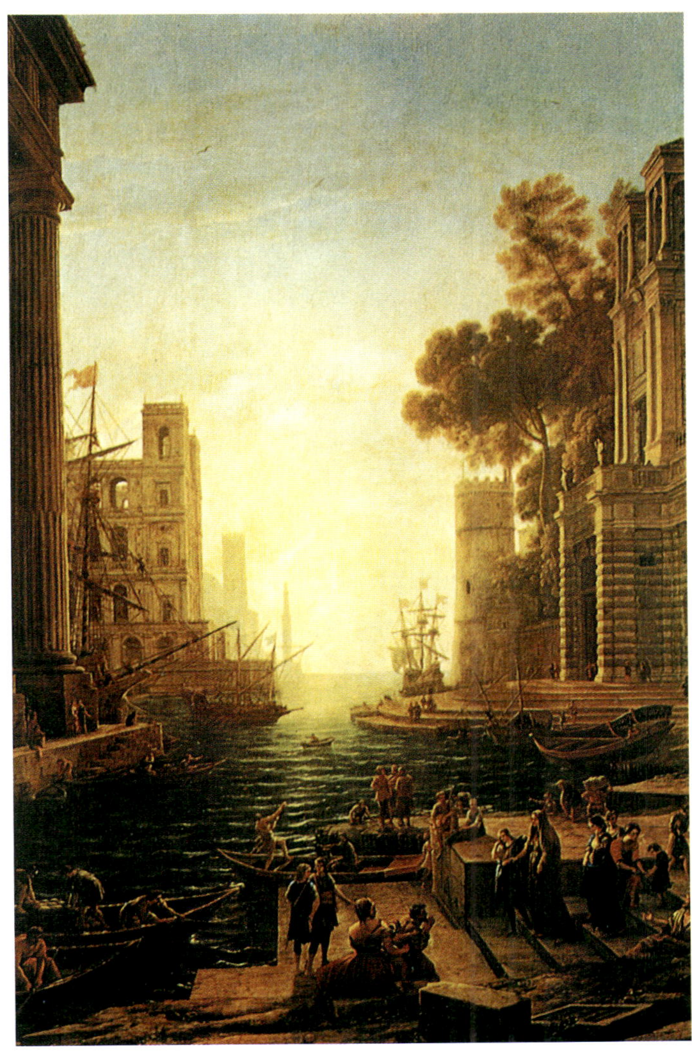

456. Claude Lorrain (Gellée), c. 1604-1682, Classicism, French, *Embarkation of St Paula Romana at Ostia*, 1639. Oil on canvas, 211 x 145 cm. Museo Nacional del Prado, Madrid.

CLAUDE LORRAIN (CLAUDE GELLÉE)
(1604 CHAMAGNE – 1682 ROME)

Claude Gellée, called Claude Lorrain was neither a great man nor a lofty spirit like Poussin. His genius cannot, however, be denied and he was, like Poussin, a profoundly original inventor within the limitations of a classical ideal. He too spent most of his life in Rome though the art he created was not specifically Italian, but French. For more than two centuries afterwards everyone in France who felt called upon to depict the beauties of nature would think of Lorrain and study his works, whether it be Joseph Vernet in the eighteenth century or Corot in the nineteenth. Outside France it was the same; Lorrain was nowhere more admired than in England. There is an element of mystery in the vocation of this humble and almost illiterate peasant whose knowledge of French and Italian was equally poor, and who used to inscribe on his drawings notes in a strange broken Franco-Italian. This mystery is in some way symbolic of that with which he imbued his pictures, *le mystère dans la lumière*. This admirable landscapist drew from within himself the greatest number of extraordinary pictures, in which all is beauty, poetry and truth. He sometimes made from nature drawings so beautiful that several have been attributed to Poussin, but in his paintings his imagination dominates, growing in magnitude as he realised his genius. He understood by listening to Poussin and watching him paint that a sort of intellectual background would be an invaluable addition to his own imagination, visions, dreams and reveries.

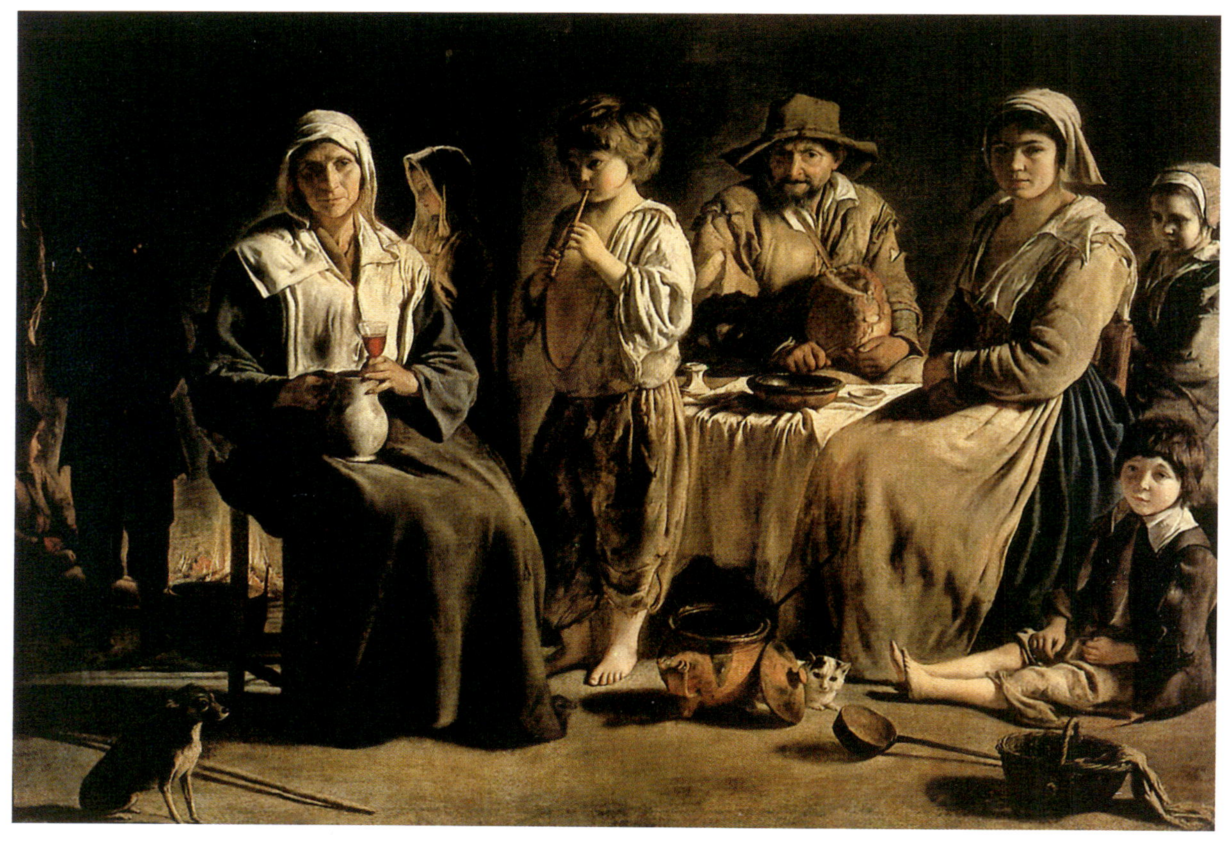

LE NAIN BROTHERS
(ANTOINE C. 1600-1648, LOUIS C. 1598-1648 AND MATHIEU C. 1607-1677 (BORN IN LAON, DIED IN PARIS))

For a long time it appeared impossible to discriminate amongst the three Le Nain brothers' individual works, which have survived under their common signature. Antoine Le Nain, who studied at Laon under a 'foreign painter' (probably from Flanders), painted in a manner and with a colouring more or less derived from Flemish models; little panels where people are assembled in modest interiors, but of the town rather than of the country. His style was still slightly archaic, but it is already possible to discern in him that love of humble truth. It was from his style the inspiration for the most original works bearing the signature derived: those of Louis, the man of genius and the breaker of new ground. It was he who produced the gatherings of peasants, which are painted with such freedom, and filled with such dignity, sobriety and humanity. Contrast these with the very different treatments of similar subjects by contemporary Spanish and Italian followers of Caravaggio on one hand, and the Flemish and Dutch on the other. Mathieu, the youngest of the brothers, survived the others by almost thirty years. His works generally possess less depth, but he painted family gatherings in which he showed himself almost as good a judge of human physiognomy and expression as his brother Louis.

457. **Louis Le Nain,** c. 1598-1648, Baroque, French, *Family of Country People,* 1640.
Oil on canvas, 113 x 159 cm.
Musée du Louvre, Paris.

The golden brown tone of the work helps create a simple and quiet moment, except for the crackling of the fire in the back and the playing of the musical instrument by the central figure. The artist has revealed the closeness of the family by drawing the viewer into their intimate circle. The circular bowl on the circular table and the circle of people around them echo the chain of six or more circles from the lower right corner, from the basket, its shadow, the ladle, its shadow, and lid, more shadows, and to the pot. In the lower right, the ladle, the child's legs and the legs of the seated lady on the right draw our attention to the group. The legs of the other seated lady do likewise from the left. The gaze of the family dog also draws our attention into the painting. It is in the lower left corner, the area where pets in group portraits are so often placed. The painter preserves the peasants' dignity, yet this is a realist painting. This aspect is emphasised by the fact that this genre scene is the size of a history painting.

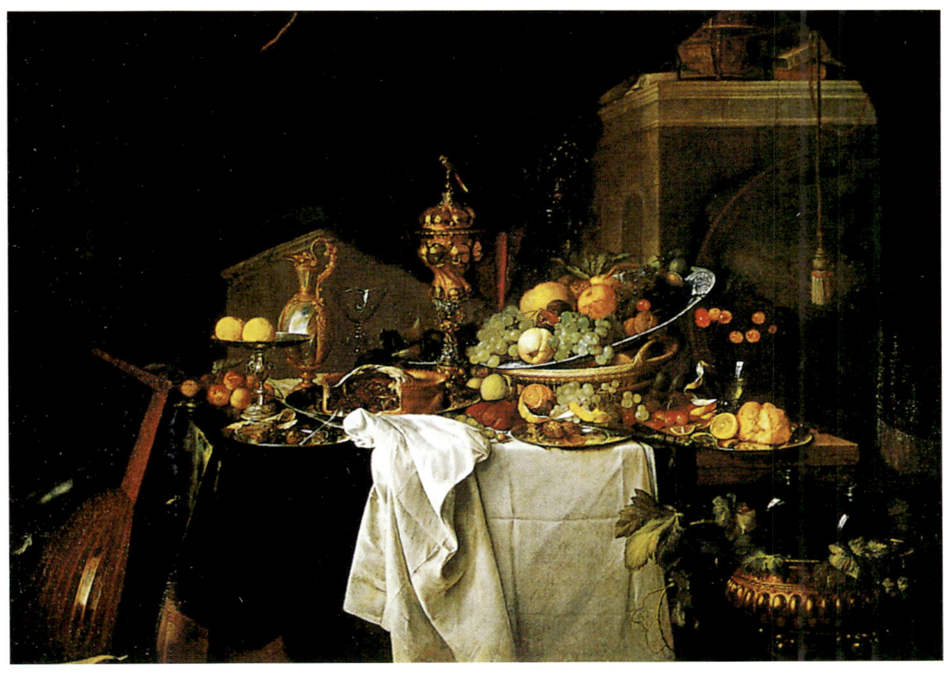

458. Jan Davidsz. de Heem,
1606-1684, Baroque, Dutch,
Still-Life with Dessert, c. 1640.
Oil on canvas, 149 x 203 cm.
Musée du Louvre, Paris.

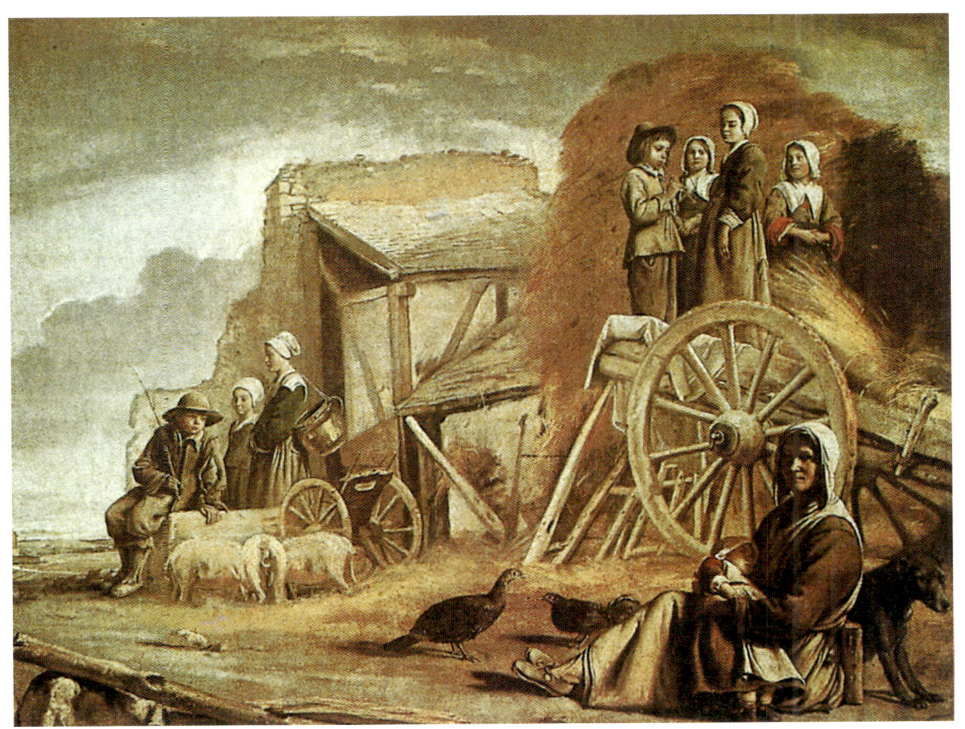

459. Louis Le Nain,
c. 1598-1648, Baroque,
French, *The Cart* or *Return
from Haymaking,* 1641.
Oil on wood, 56 x 72 cm.
Musée du Louvre, Paris.

*Usually said to have been
painted by Louis Le Nain,
the attribution of this
painting to one of the three
brothers is still uncertain.
The depiction of simple life
with delicate nuances of
colour is characteristic of
their style.*

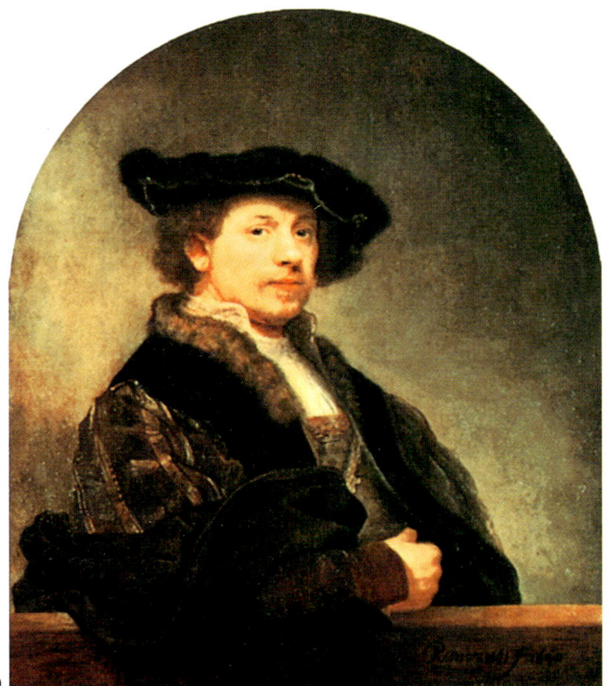

460

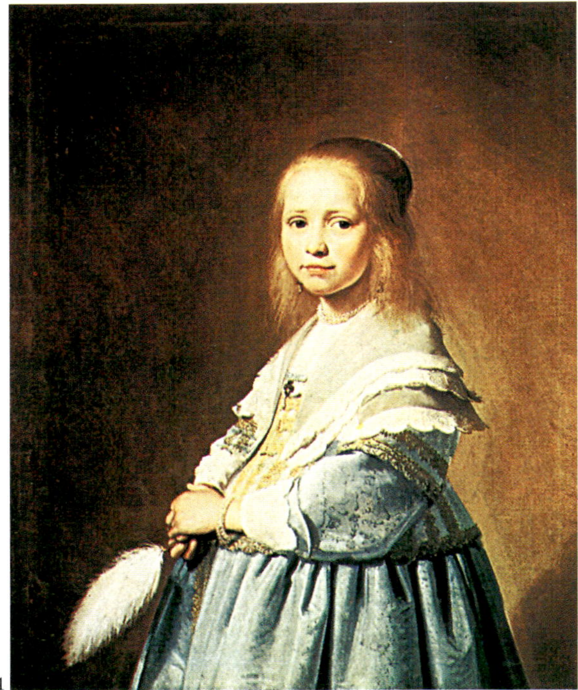

461

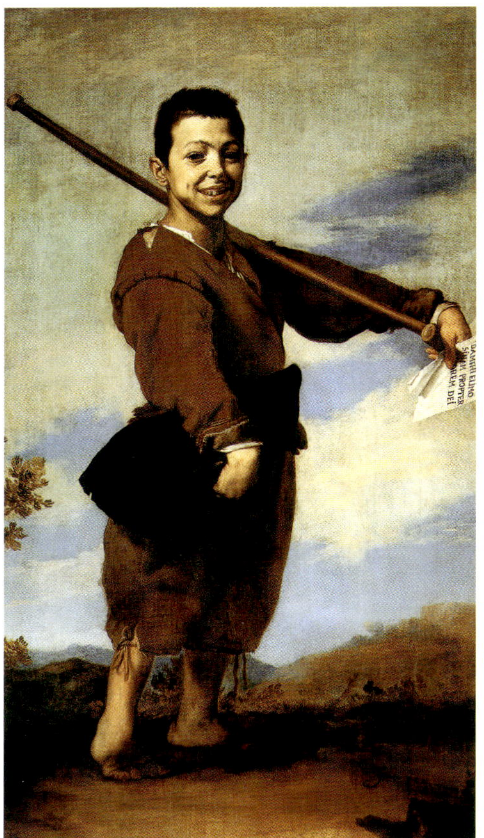

462

460. **Rembrandt Harmensz. van Rijn,** 1606-1669, Baroque, Dutch,
Self-Portrait at the Age of Thirty-Four, 1639-1640.
Oil on canvas, 102 x 80 cm. National Gallery, London.

Inspired by the Portrait of Castiglione *by Raphael (1514-1516), Rembrandt instituted a dialogue with the great Italian masters. The artist, overwhelmed by commissions, had not travelled in Italy but he knew Italian painting through other artists, who imported pieces to the Dutch provinces. Amsterdam, crossroad of exchanges, received Raphael's* Portrait of Castiglione *in a sale at Alfonso Alvarez's shop, an art broker working for Cardinal Richelieu. Rembrandt also took his inspiration from Dürer's self-portraits for the guardrail and the arm leaning in the foreground. His work remains original for the anachronistic costume setting (not being of the period) and therefore preventing us knowing his social rank.*

461. **Johannes Verspronck,** 1606-1662, Baroque, Dutch,
Portrait of a Girl Dressed in Blue, 1641.
Oil on canvas, 82 x 66.5 cm.
Rijksmuseum, Amsterdam.

Verspronck's oeuvre is one of the best representations of Haarlem's school of portraiture.

462. **José de Ribera,** 1591-1652, Baroque, Spanish,
Boy With a Club Foot, 1642. Oil on canvas, 164 x 94 cm.
Musée du Louvre, Paris.

This portrait is often called simply Clubfoot. *The charming smile of the boy is disarming and makes his request for alms (stated in Latin) on the paper he holds all the more touching. The artist also appeals to the viewer's sensitivity elsewhere, as in his earlier* The Martyrdom of St Bartholomew *(1639-1640). Influenced by Caravaggio, José de Ribera used that master's chiaroscuro technique aggressively. The technique was appropriate as he sought out his models from the unfortunate poor or handicapped. He was sometimes criticised in his day for exploiting these unfortunate people.*

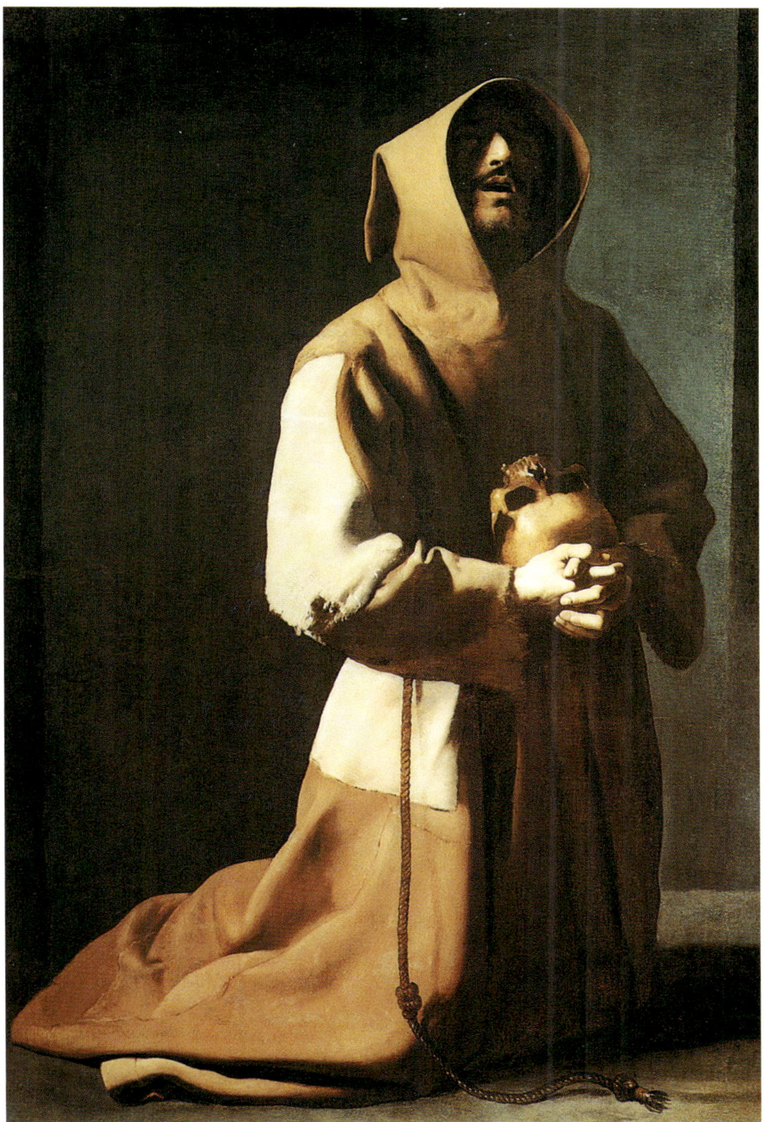

463. **Francisco de Zurbarán**, 1598-1664, Baroque, Spanish, *St Francis in Meditation*, 1639.
Oil on canvas, 152 x 99 cm. National Gallery, London.

FRANCISCO DE ZURBARÁN
(1598 FUENTE DE CANTOS – 1664 MADRID)

Contemporary and friend of Velázquez, Zurbarán distinguished himself in his religious paintings. There, his works reveal great force and mysticism. The emblematic artist of the Counter-Reformation, he was first influenced by Caravaggio and acquired an austere and dark style before getting closer to the Italian Mannerists. Later, his compositions moved away from Velázquez's realism and became lighter. He was commissioned by Franciscan and Carthusian monasteries to produce religious works, including several versions on the theme of Mary's Immaculate Conception. He also painted still-lifes, and mythological themes.

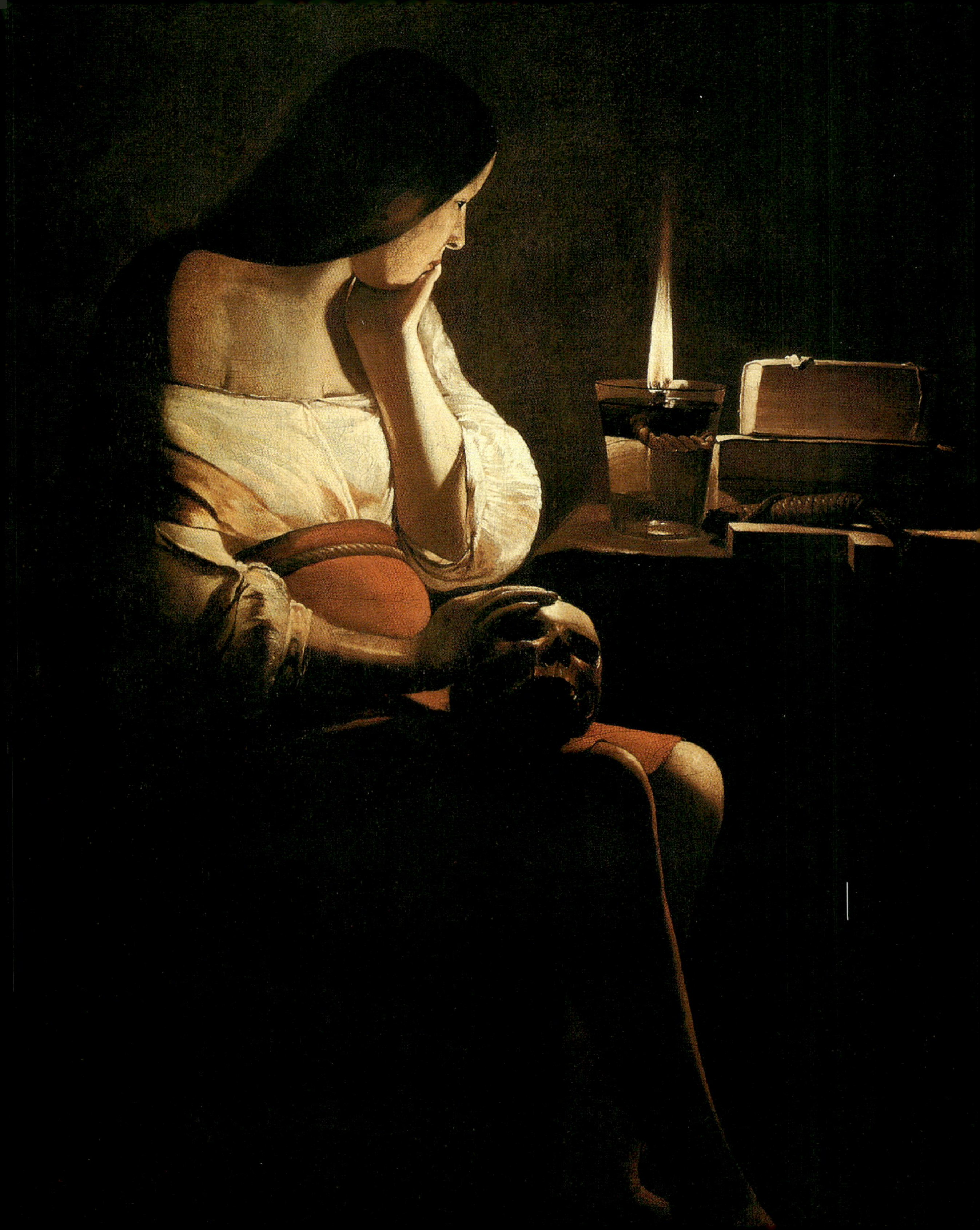

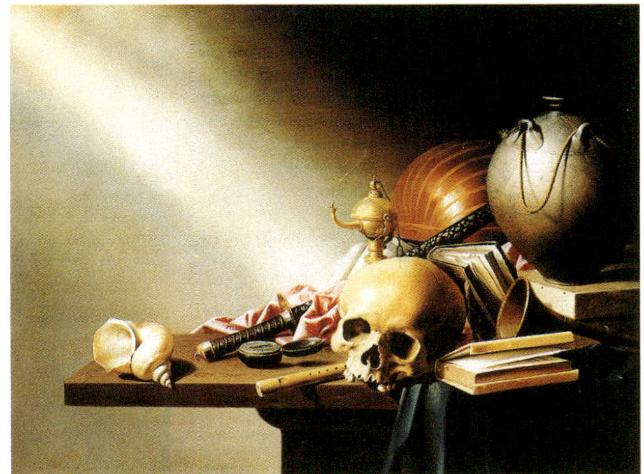

465

465. **Harmen Steenwijck,** 1612-after 1656, Baroque, Dutch,
An Allegory of the Vanities of Human Life, 1645.
Oil on oak, 39.2 x 50.7 cm.
National Gallery, London.

*Steenwijck's allegorical paintings are simple and intimate. Gold
and grey are the dominant colours and bring this painting closer
to Claesz's and Heda's works in the years 1620-1630. They are
typical of the refined manner existing in Leyde.*

466. **Georges de La Tour,** 1593-1652, Baroque, French,
Young Christ with St Joseph in the Carpenter's Shop, c. 1642.
Oil on canvas, 137 x 101 cm.
Musée du Louvre, Paris.

467. **Gerrit Dou,** 1613-1675, Baroque, Dutch,
The Mousetrap, 1645-1650.
Oil on panel, 47 x 36 cm.
Musée Fabre, Montpellier.

464. **Georges de La Tour,** 1593-1652, Baroque, French,
Magdalene of the Night Light, 1642-1644.
Oil on canvas, 128 x 94 cm.
Musée du Louvre, Paris.

*Several of the artist's masterpieces show his fascination with
candlelight and shadows, or what later came to be known as 'night'
paintings. This theme has been depicted three times by Georges de
La Tour. The Louvre painting has the most rigorous structure. Seen
here also is his skill in still-life painting as well as in portraiture. The
painter showed a great virtuosity in the depiction of light and
objects: note the magnifying effect of the glass produced by the oil
in the lamp. The viewer can bring what he knows and believes
about Mary Magdalene to the moment. She is portrayed in an
introspective mood. So often in medieval art the human skull is
symbolic of death and the inevitable fate of each human. Here that
powerful symbol is coupled with a cross as a reminder that God
incarnate chooses not to escape death.*

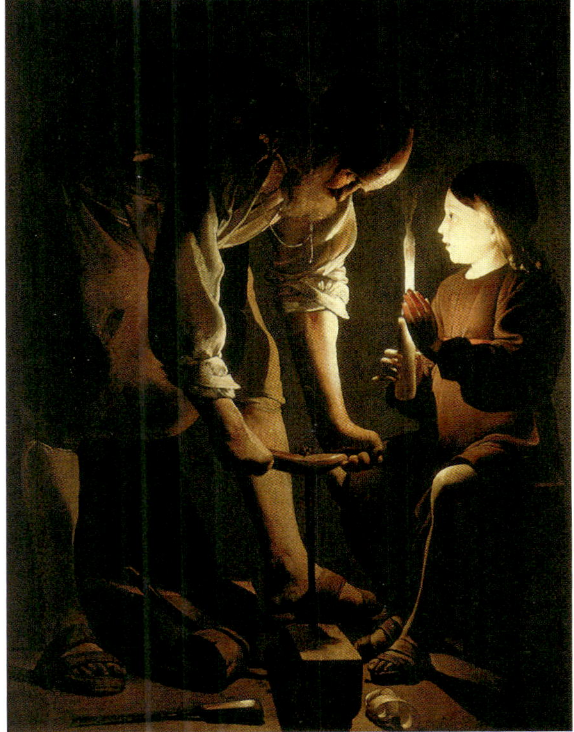

466

467

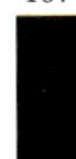

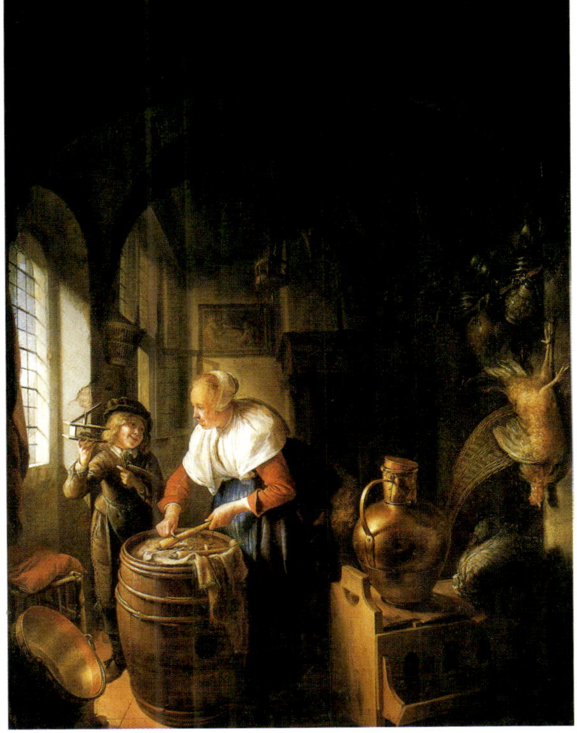

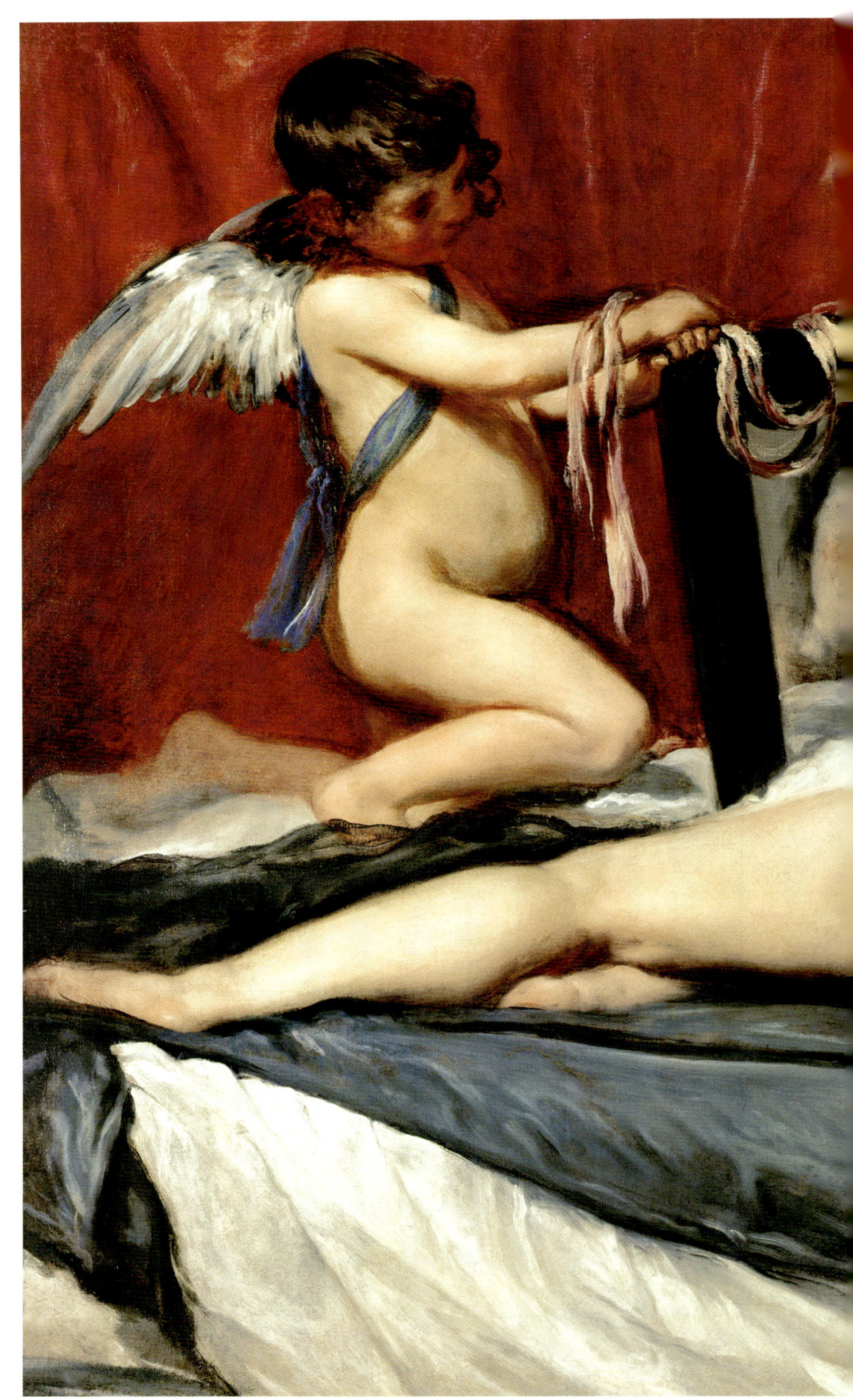

468. **Diego Velázquez,**
1599-1660, Baroque, Spanish,
The Toilet of Venus
(The Rokeby Venus), 1647-1651.
Oil on canvas, 122.5 x 177 cm.
National Gallery, London.

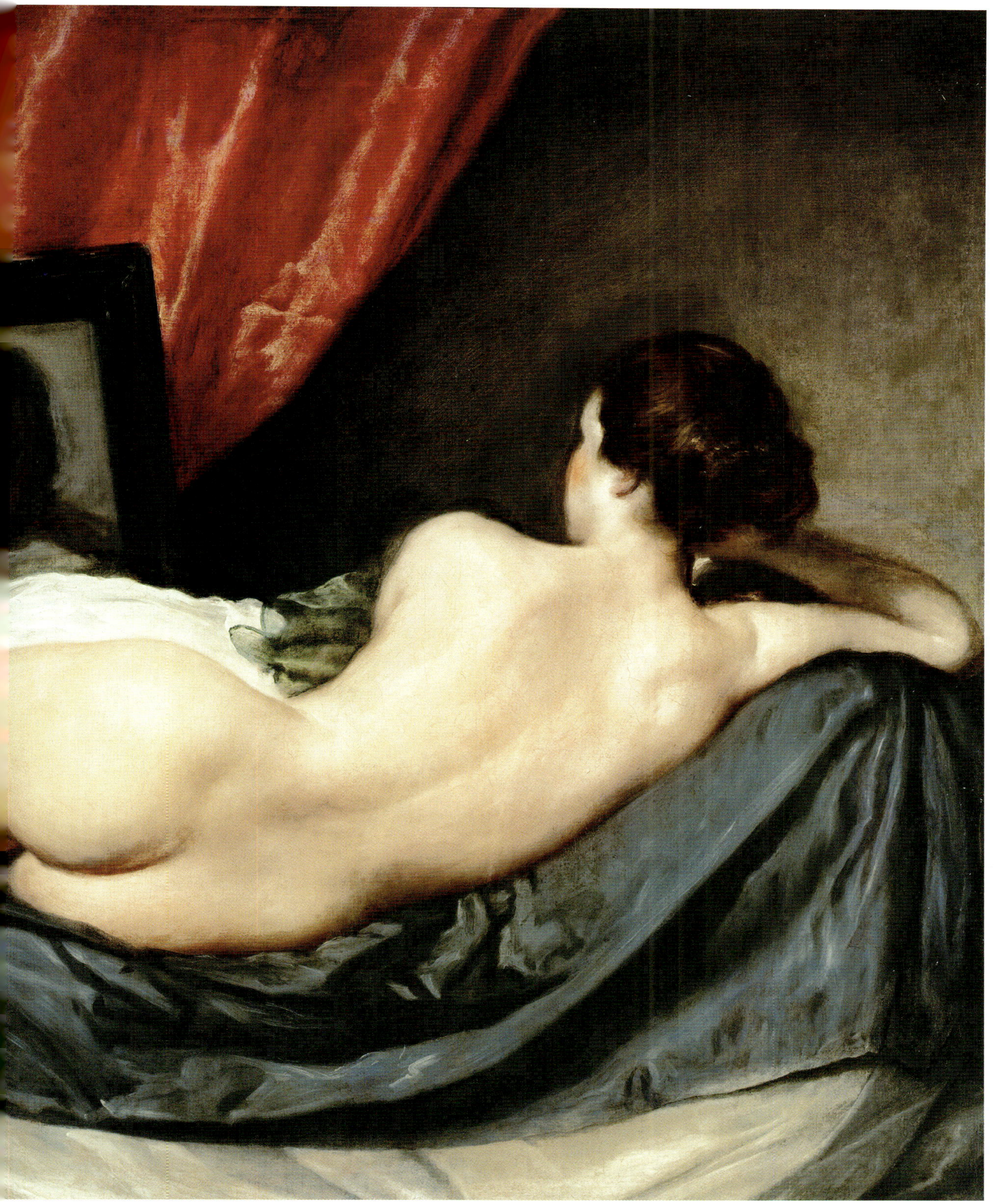

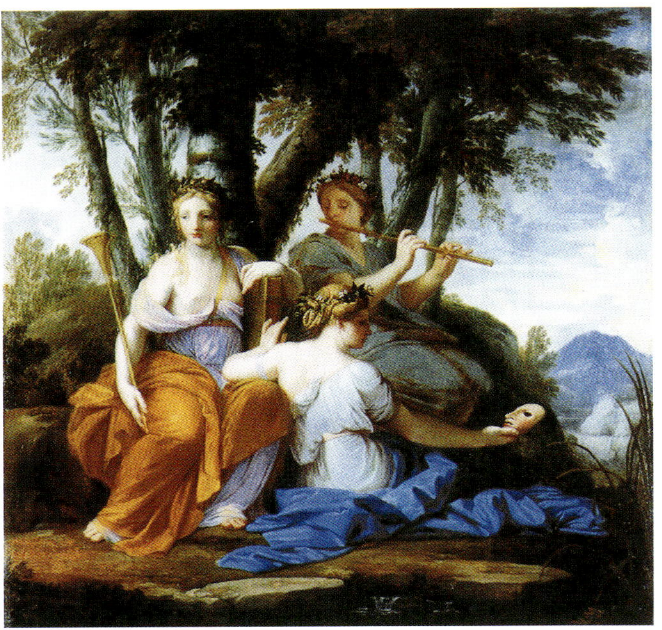

469. **Eustache Le Sueur,** 1616-1655, Atticism, French,
The Muses: Clio, Euterpe and Thalia, c. 1643.
Oil on wood, 130 x 130 cm. Musée du Louvre, Paris.

*Atticist painter (a movement gathering Le Sueur, La Hyre and Bourdon
and set in reaction against Vouet and Vignon aesthetics) Le Sueur
worked on the precision of his drawing. His works reflect the influence
of Poussin, Raphael and Carracci. In this work the artist gave homage
to Italian Mannerist painting. Made with rich and elegant colours, it
decorated the room of the Muses (Clio, muse of History, Euterpe, muse
of Music, and Thalia, muse of Comedy) in the Mansion of Lambert de
Thorigny, built by Le Vau.*

471. **Nicolas Poussin,** 1594-1665, Classicism, French,
Landscape with the Funeral of Phocion, 1648.
Oil on canvas, 114 x 115 cm. National Museum of Wales, Cardiff.

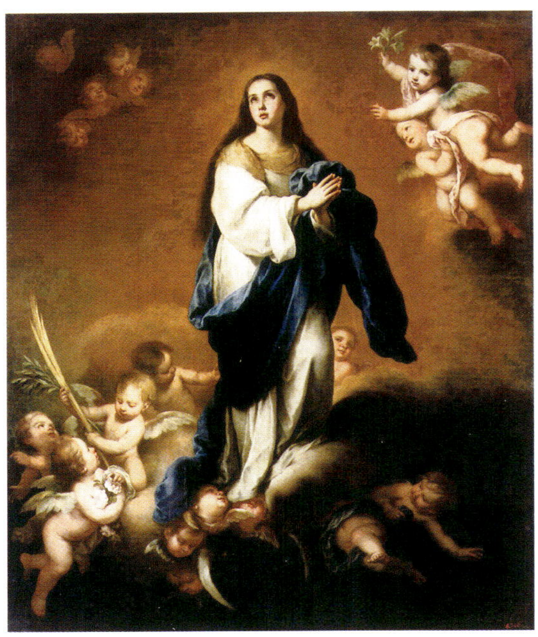

470. **Bartolomé Esteban Perez Murillo,** 1618-1682,
Baroque, Spanish,
Our Lady of the Immaculate Conception, c. 1645-1650.
Oil on canvas, 235 x 196 cm.
The State Hermitage Museum, St Petersburg.

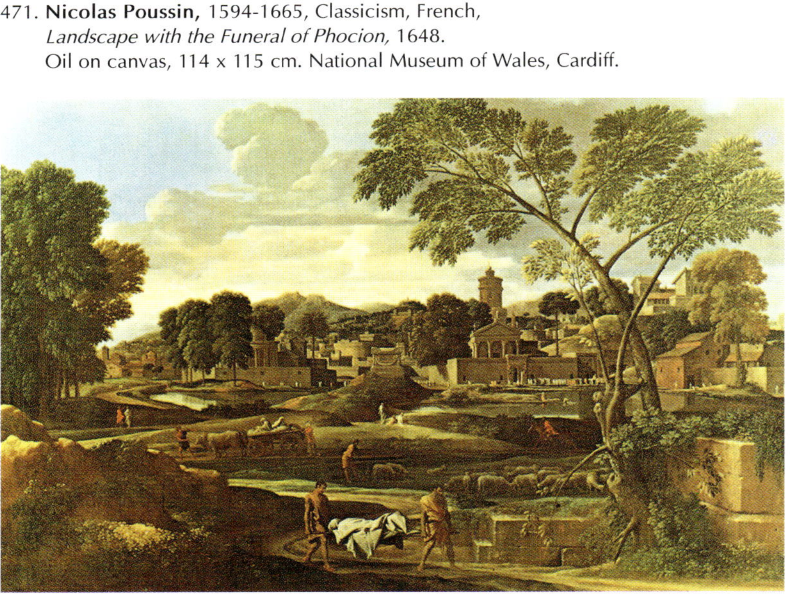

HARMEN STEENWIJCK
(1612 DELFT – 1655 LEYDE)

Harmen Steenwijck was the leading
expert of the 'Leiden vanitas painters'.
Their pictorial arrangements of books,
writing materials, rare and precious
objects, instruments, pipes and, above
all, a skull are readily interpreted as
symbols of transience and the vanity
of all earthly endeavours. They are
known as 'vanitas still-lifes'. One of
his few extant works is the
masterpiece, *The Vanities of Human
Life* (fig. 465), a visual sermon on
Calvinist interpretations of passages
from the Book of Ecclesiastes.

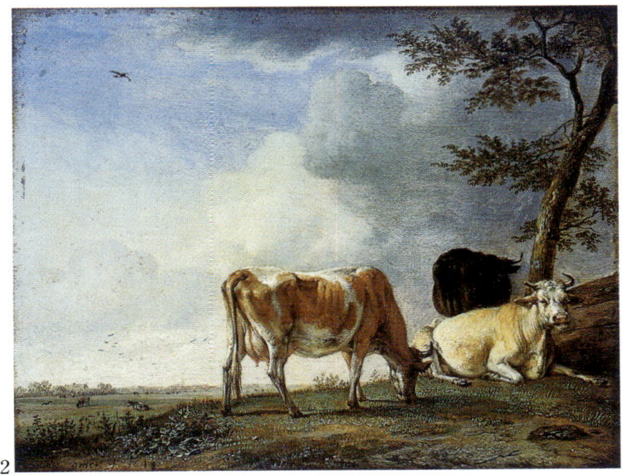

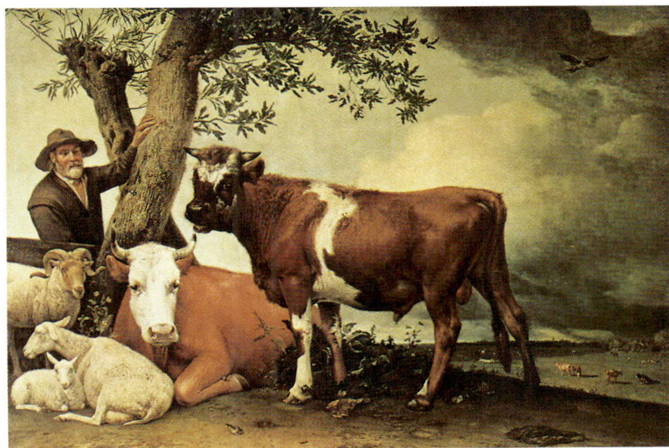
473

472. **Paulus Potter,** 1625-1654, Baroque, Dutch,
Three Cows in a Pasture, 1648.
Oil on canvas, 23.2 x 29.5 cm.
Musée Fabre, Montpellier.

*This painting, which belonged to Talleyrand, is one of Potter's
masterworks, illustrating both Italian and Dutch influences.*

473. **Paulus Potter,** 1625-1654, Baroque, Dutch,
Young Bull, 1647.
Oil on canvas, 236 x 339 cm.
Koninklijk Kabinet van Schilderijen Mauritshuis,
The Hague.

PAULUS POTTER
(1625 ENKHUIZEN – 1654 AMSTERDAM)

Dutch painter and etcher, Paulus overshadowed his father, Pieter
Potter, who signed his works 'P. Potter' whereas Paulus signed
typically with his full name, 'Paulus Potter'. Influenced by Claes
Moeyaert, he painted historic subjects such as *Abraham returning
from Canaan* (1642). However, he is mostly known for his detailed
images of cattle, horses and other farm animals in landscapes that
depict a naturalistic vision of Dutch rural scenes. He always
searched for a way to integrate his figures into landscape,
suggesting space by the positioning of the figures. Animals appear
mostly in small groups silhouetted against the sky, or in greater
numbers with peasant figures and rustic buildings.

474

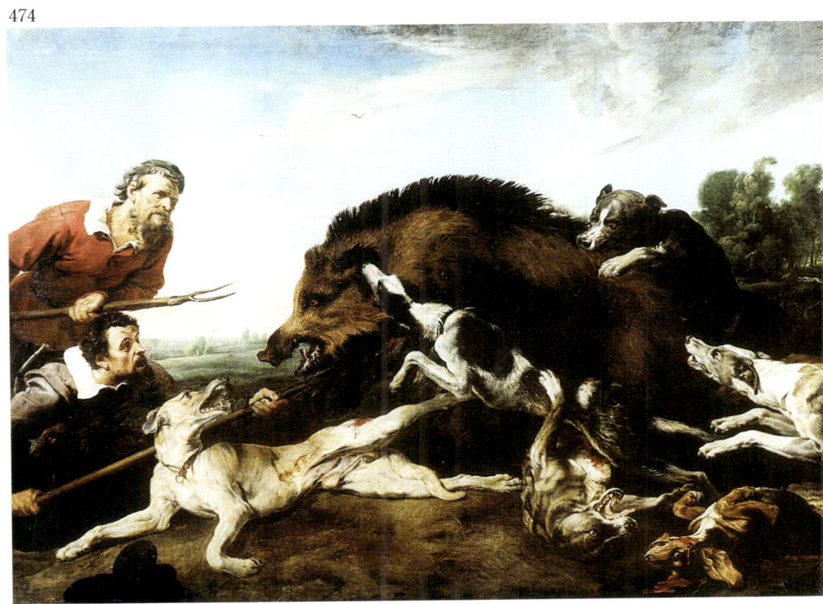

474. **Frans Snyders,** 1579-1657, Baroque,
Flemish, *Wild Boar Hunt,* 1649.
Oil on canvas, 214 x 311.
Galleria degli Uffizi, Florence.

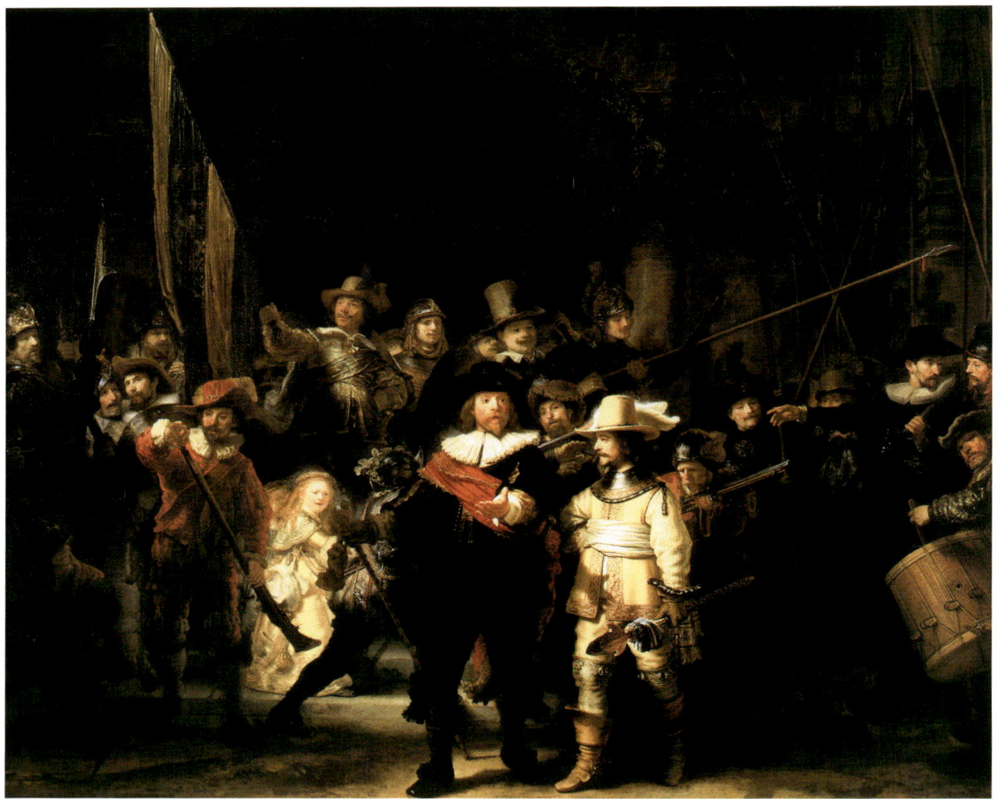

475. **Rembrandt Harmensz. van Rijn,** 1606-1669, Baroque, Dutch,
The Company of Frans Banning Cocq and Willem van Ruytenburch, also known as the *'Night Watch'*, 1642.
Oil on canvas, 363 x 437 cm.
Rijksmuseum, Amsterdam.

The theme is the one of the defence of the city by the bourgeois militia. The painting dates from the period of maturity in the artist's career. Rembrandt chose to represent the most intense moment of the scene, introducing drama and action in the work. He represented the departure of the captain towards the gates of the city. Each group is in movement and the light is spread in order to unify space.

REMBRANDT (REMBRANDT HARMENSZ. VAN RIJN)
(1606 LEYDE – 1669 AMSTERDAM)

Rembrandt is completely mysterious in his spirit, his character, his life, his work and his method of painting. What we can divine of his essential nature comes through his painting and the trivial or tragic incidents of his unfortunate life; his penchant for ostentatious living forced him to declare bankruptcy. His misfortunes are not entirely explicable, and his oeuvre reflects disturbing notions and contradictory impulses emerging from the depths of his being, like the light and shade of his pictures. In spite of this, nothing perhaps in the history of art gives a more profound impression of unity than his paintings, composed though they are of such different elements, full of complex significations. One feels as if his intellect, that genial, great, free mind, bold and ignorant of all servitude and which led him to the loftiest meditations and the most sublime reveries, derived from the same source as his emotions. From this comes the tragic element he imprinted on everything he painted, irrespective of subject; there was inequality in his work as well as the sublime, which may be seen as the inevitable consequence of such a tumultuous existence.

From the time of his tenuous beginnings and his grand successes, however, lighting played a major part in his conception of painting and he made it the principal instrument of his investigations into the arcana of interior life. It already revealed to him the poetry of human physiognomy when he painted *The Philosopher in Meditation* or the *Holy Family*, so deliciously absorbed in its modest intimacy, or, for example, in *The Angel Raphael leaving Tobias*. Soon he asked for something more. He thought of the great Venetians, borrowing their subjects and making of them an art out of the inner life of profound emotion. Mythological and religious subjects were treated as he treated his portraits. For all that he took from reality and even from the works of others, he transmuted it instantly into his own substance.

JACOB JORDAENS
(1593 – 1678 ANTWERP)

Jordaens was the pupil and son-in-law of Adam van Noort. Because he often assisted Rubens, his huge influence is very apparent. Jordaens also used the warmth of colour and the truth of nature, and mastered chiaroscuro, but he is inferior in his choice of forms. His work is characterised by great stylistic versatility. He also employed his pencil in biblical, mythological, historical and allegorical subjects, and is well-known as a portrait painter. He was also a tapestry designer and an etcher.

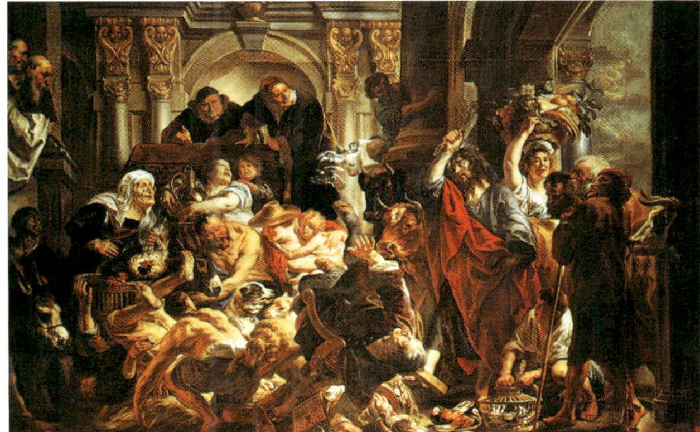

476

476. **Jacob Jordaens,** 1593-1678, Baroque, Dutch,
Jesus Driving the Merchants from the Temple, 1645-1650.
Oil on canvas, 288 x 436 cm.
Musée du Louvre, Paris.

This exceptionally lively scene testifies to the artist's ease with Baroque art. Although the scene is filled with characters and animals, it follows a strict compositional arrangement with the architecture in the background and the light bringing dynamism to the foreground.

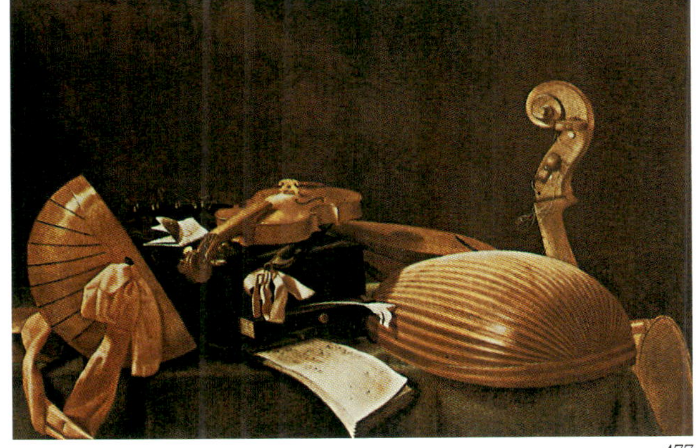

477

477. **Evaristo Baschenis,** 1617-1677, Baroque, Italian,
Still-life with Musical Instruments, c. 1650.
Oil on canvas, 115 x 160 cm.
Accademia Carrara, Bergamo.

Most of Baschenis' works depict arrangements of musical instruments, reflecting the European reverence of stringed-instrument makers in the sixteenth and seventeenth centuries.

478. **Pier Francesco Mola,** 1612-1666, Baroque, Italian,
Self-portrait, 1650-1666. Pastel on paper, 34.7 x 24.9 cm.
Galleria degli Uffizi, Florence.

Dominant figure of the neo-Venetian manner in Rome, Mola combines the aesthetics of Bolognese school with the colours of the Venetian painters.

479. **David Teniers the Younger,** 1610-1690, Baroque, Dutch,
Archduke Leopold William in his Gallery at Brussels, c. 1651.
Oil on canvas, 123 x 163 cm.
Kunsthistorisches Museum, Vienna.

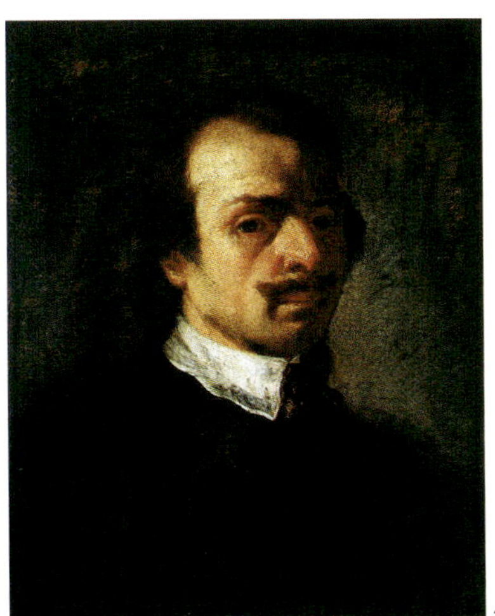

478

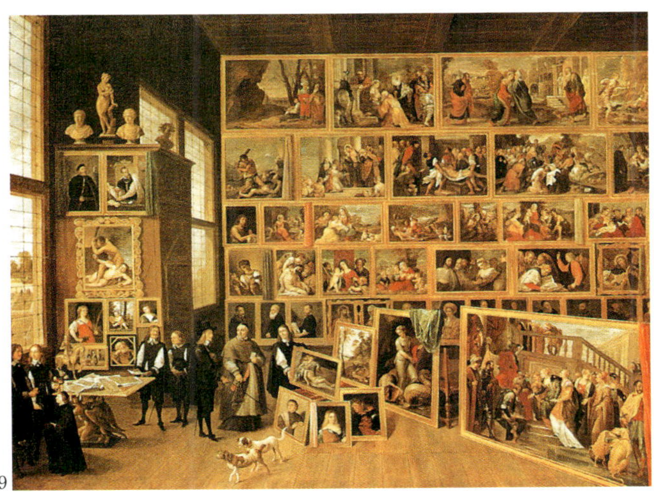

479

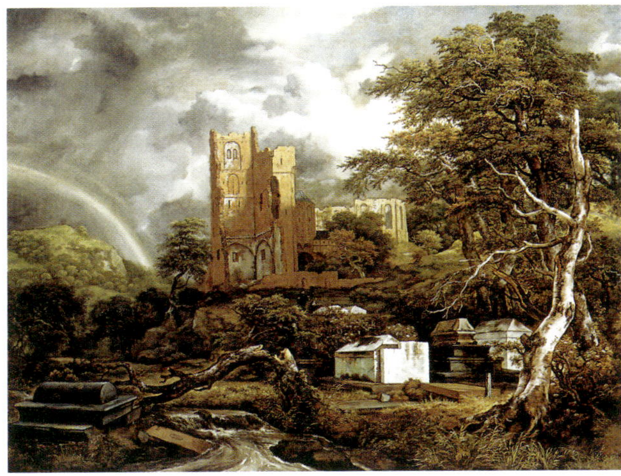

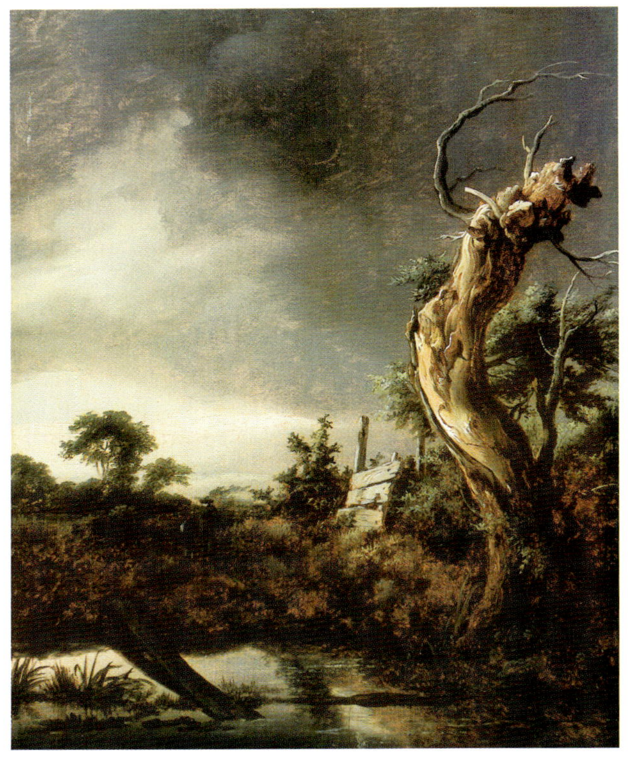

480. **Jacob van Ruisdael,** 1628-1682, Baroque, Dutch,
The Jewish Cemetery at Ouderkerk, 1653-1655.
Oil on canvas, 84 x 95 cm.
Gemäldegalerie Alte Meister, Dresden.

481. **Jacob van Ruisdael,** 1628-1682, Baroque, Dutch,
Landscape during a Storm, 1649.
Oil on canvas, 25.5 x 21.5 cm.
Musée Fabre, Montpellier.

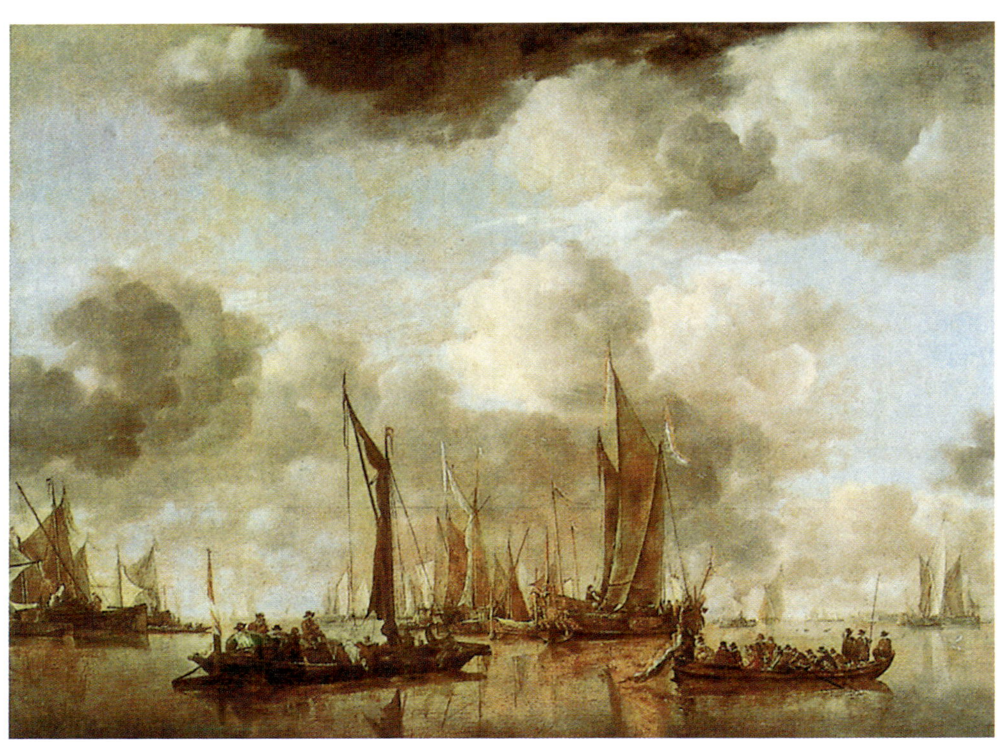

482. **Jan van de Cappelle,**
1626-1679, Baroque,
Dutch, *A Shipping
Scene with a Dutch
Yacht,* 1650.
Oil on oak panel,
85 x 115 cm.
National Gallery,
London.

*Van de Cappelle often
painted seascapes,
inventing patterns of
clouds, bringing
dynamism and drama
to the composition.*

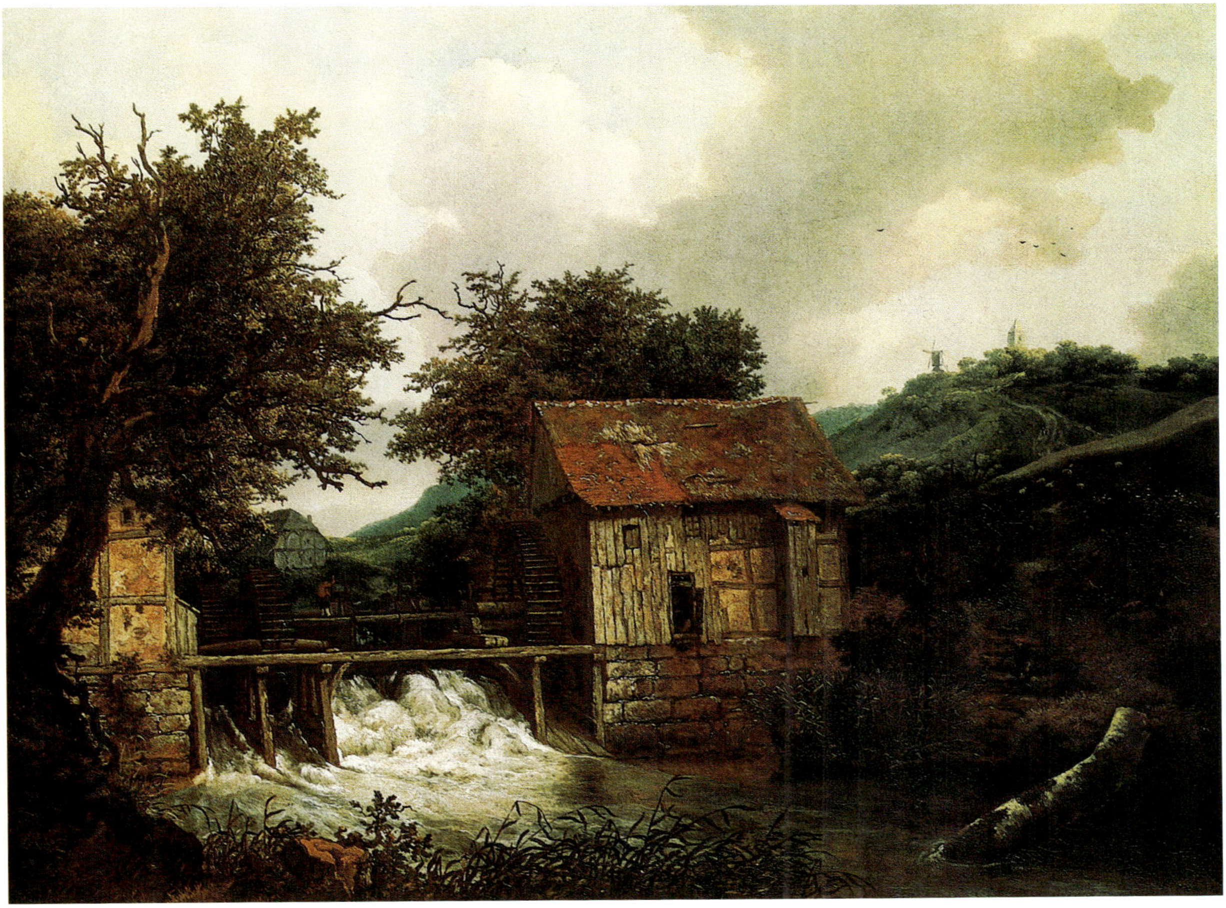

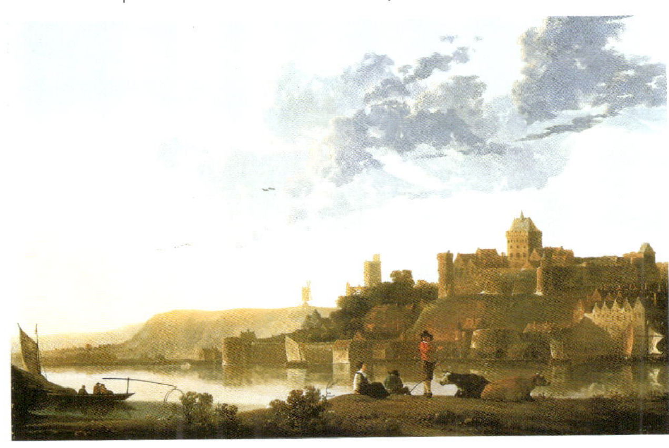

483. Jacob van Ruisdael, 1628-1682, Baroque, Dutch,
Two Watermills and an Open Sluice near Singraven, c. 1650-1652.
Oil on canvas, 87.3 x 111.5 cm.
National Gallery, London.

JACOB VAN RUISDAEL
(1628 HAARLEM – 1682 AMSTERDAM)

Ruisdael received his early training from his father, the painter and picture framer Isaack van Ruisdael and his uncle Salomon van Ruysdael (sic). He moved to Amsterdam around 1656, where he lived for the rest of his life, and where he became one of the most important Dutch landscape artists of his day. Trees became the main subject of his paintings and he imbues them with personality. His pencil is meticulous and impasto adds depth and character to the foliage and trunks. While dark clouds hovered over many of his scenes, his most sombre meditation on mortality is *The Jewish Cemetery at Ouderkerk* (fig. 480). His paintings inspired many artists such as Gainsborough, Constable and the Barbizon School. He also produced several fine etchings.

484. Aelbert Cuyp, 1620-1691, Baroque, Dutch,
View of the Valkhof at Nijmegen, c. 1655-1665.
Oil on panel, 48.9 x 73.7 cm.
Indianapolis Museum of Art, Indianapolis.

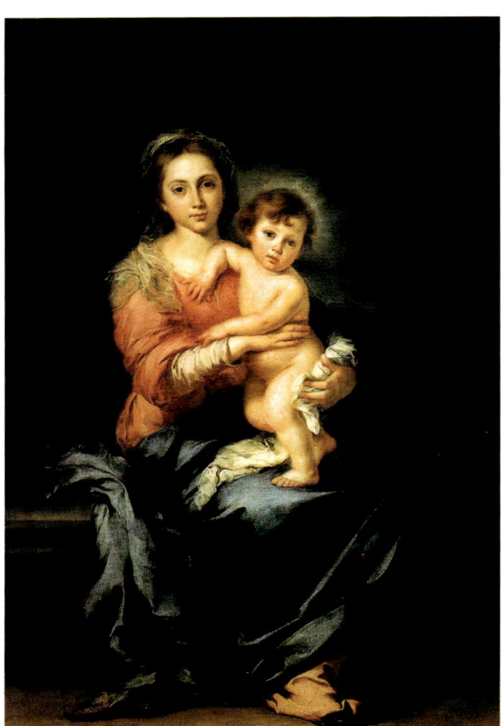

485.

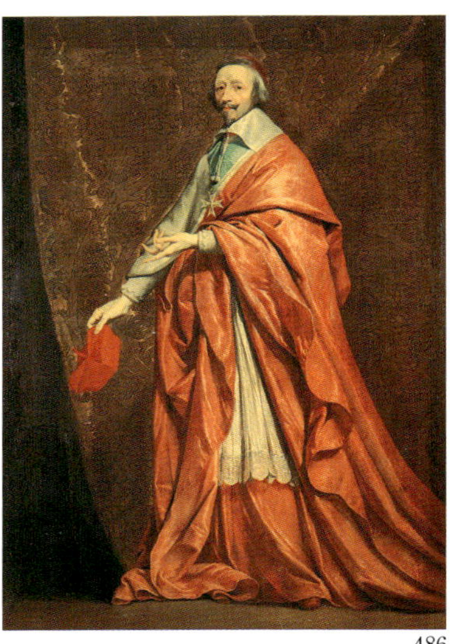

485. Bartolomé Esteban Perez Murillo, 1618-1682, Baroque, Spanish, *Madonna and Child,* c. 1655. Oil on canvas, 155 x 105 cm. Palazzo Pitti, Florence.

486. Philippe de Champaigne, 1602-1674, Classicism, French, *Cardinal Richelieu,* 1650. Oil on canvas, 222 x 155 cm. Musée du Louvre, Paris.

In such a portrait, bigger than nature, Philippe de Champaigne shows his will to get as close as possible to the physical reality of the sitter.

486

488. Nicolas Poussin, 1594-1665, Classicism, French, *The Holy Family in Egypt,* 1655-1657. Oil on canvas, 105 x 145 cm. The State Hermitage Museum, St Petersburg.

The late masterpiece The Holy Family in Egypt *is frequently underestimated, chiefly because its rhythmic structure is reduced to a somewhat abstracted combination of local colours. In point of fact it is a genuine masterpiece of integrity and compositional unity; and pure painterly taste can afford to make sacrifices for the sake of a visual value of a higher order. Calm and majesty – that is the overall atmosphere of the scene that Poussin depicted. Mary and Joseph have taken refuge in the shadow of a temple to slake their thirst and hunger. The silhouettes of these figures seem to have come down off some ancient fresco. The prime significance of the Holy Family is indicated by the placement of the group in the centre and also by the dominant vertical element, the distant temple and obelisk, which combine with the horizontally extended procession (in the same distant plane) to produce something like a system of geometrical axes. There is not a single line that is not reconciled with the others. Their rhythm is entirely devoted to harmony. The philosophical message of the "Egyptian Virgin" (Poussin's own expression) is indicated with a clarity which makes detailed commentary superfluous. In essence, what is presented is one of the key moments in the spiritual development of mankind: old superstitions are passing away into the depths of time, while advancing to the front stage of history are the Christian heroes who are destined to change the world.*

487. Emmanuel de Witte, 1616-1691, Baroque, Dutch, *Interior of the Nieuwe Kerk (New Church), Delft with the Tomb of William I of Orange, so-called William the Silent,* 1656. Oil on canvas, 97 x 85 cm. Musée des Beaux-Arts, Lille.

Once he settled in Amsterdam, de Witte concentrated on architectural paintings, primarily church interiors, both real and imaginary.

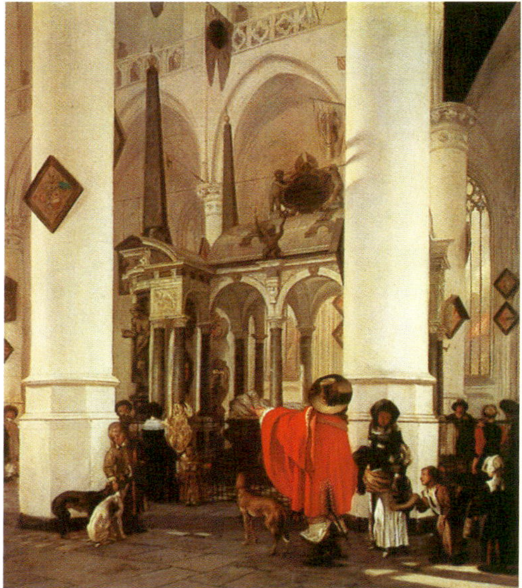

487

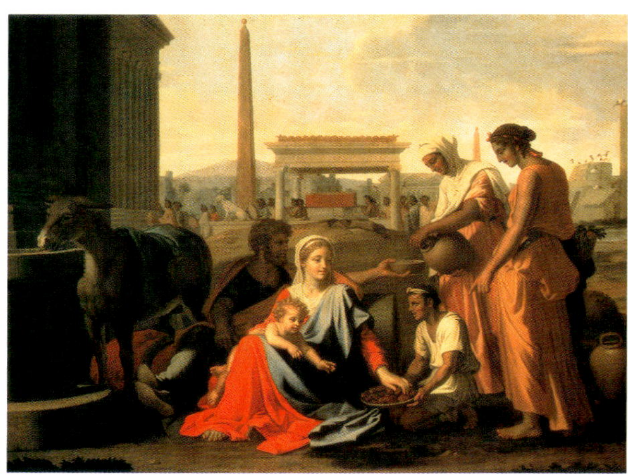

488

489. **Diego Velázquez,** 1599-1660, Baroque, Spanish,
Las Meninas, 1656.
Oil on canvas, 318 x 276 cm.
Museo Nacional del Prado, Madrid.

It is sometimes titled The Family of Philip IV *or* The Maids of
Honour. *While the adorably dressed five-year-old Infanta
Margherita is the central focus of the work, the painter (a self-
portrait) is studying the couple, who are located outside the
painting in the viewer's place, but reflected in the mirror at the
rear of the studio. Velázquez was appointed court painter to
the King. At the time of this work he had already been Lord
Chamberlain for four years. Members of the royal household
seem to be present to attend to the Infanta more than to the
royal couple. Also in attendance is a dwarf, one of the
favourite subjects of the painter, as in his* Portrait of a Dwarf at
Court *(c. 1644). In the mirror, one can see the reflection of
King Philip IV and of the Queen Marie Anne of Austria. Also
present are a nun, a man (possibly a monk or priest), and a
man waiting outside the studio, who might be eager to have
the King get back to more important matters.*

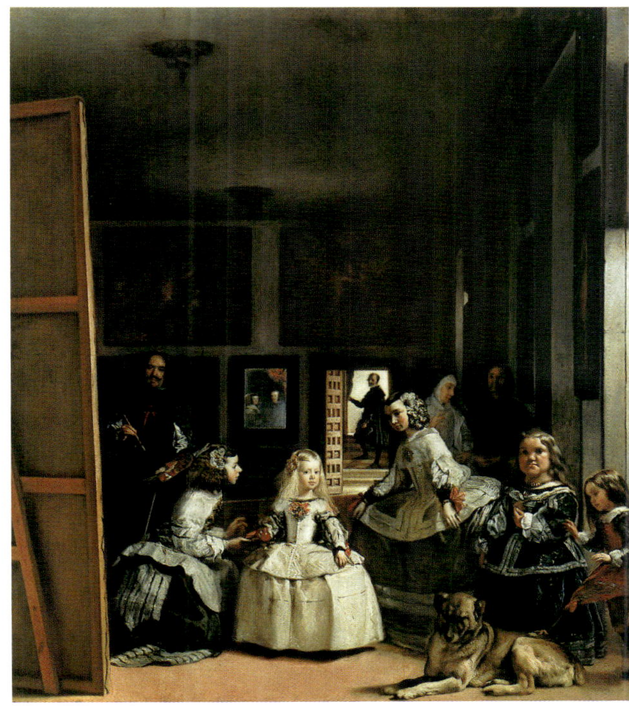

490. **Charles Le Brun,** 1619-1690, Classicism, French, *Chancellor
Séguier at the Entry of Louis XIV into Paris in 1660,* 1655-1661.
Oil on canvas, 295 x 357 cm.
Musée du Louvre, Paris.

*Pierre Séguier, French Chancellor, was Le Brun's first important
patron. Le Brun made this monumental portrait when he came
back from a trip to Italy. This official portrait displays the pomp
and dignity of the chancellor showing all the talent of Le Brun
in depicting scenery.*

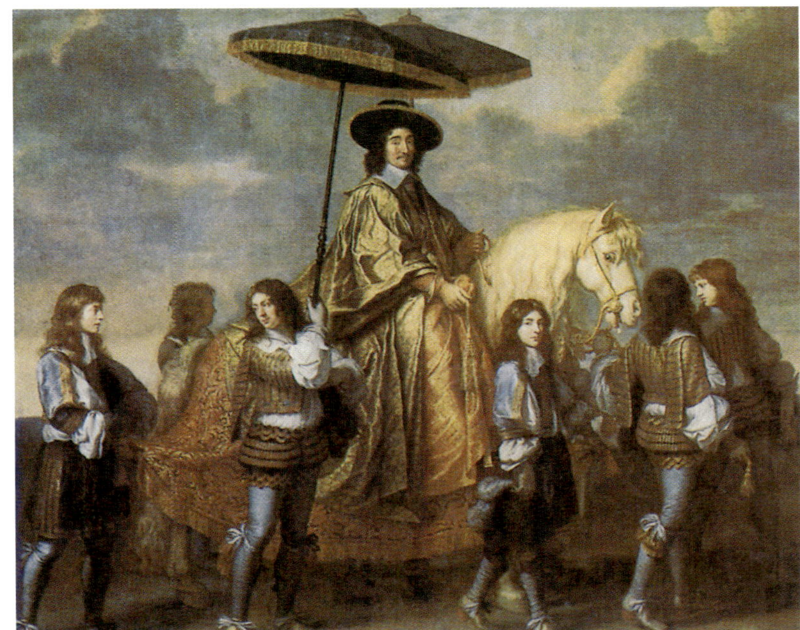

CHARLES LE BRUN
(1619 – 1690 PARIS)

Son of a sculptor, Le Brun was protected
in his youth by Chancellor Séguier. A
prodigy, he studied with grand masters
including Simon Vouet (1590-1649) and
became the court painter of Louis XIII.
He also studied later with the widely
praised Nicolas Poussin, and both had
early success as accomplished painters.
He spent four years in Italy with
Poussin, whose classical influence took
him away from Vouet's Baroque. Back
in France, Vouet advanced to be the
King's favourite painter and a pioneer in
French Neoclassicism, virtually founded
by Poussin. In 1648, Le Brun together
with Colbert, founded the Academy
of Painting and Sculpture and the
Academy of France in Rome. He worked
several years to realise the decoration
of *Château de Versailles*, especially
Escaliers des Ambassadeurs (1674-1678),
Galerie des Glaces and *Salons de la
Guerre et de la Paix* (1684-1687). He
was also in charge of *Manufacture des
Gobelins* and royal collections. At his
end of his life, he mainly painted
religious themes.

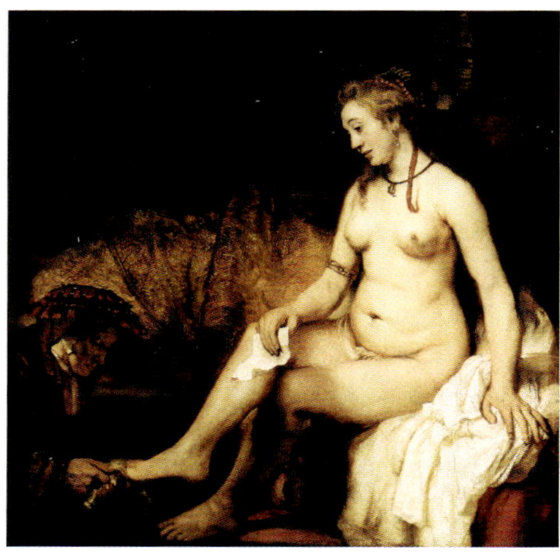

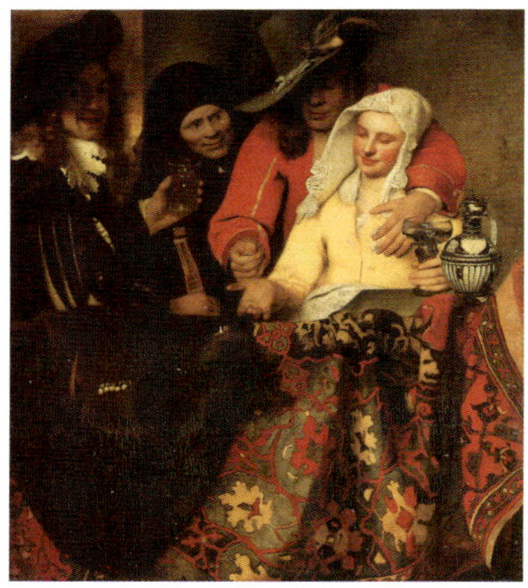

491. **Rembrandt Harmensz. van Rijn,** 1606-1669, Baroque, Dutch,
Bathsheba Bathing with King David's Letter, 1654.
Oil on canvas, 142 x 142 cm. Musée du Louvre, Paris.

*With Bathsheba, Rembrandt establishes a dialogue with the Venetians
and, especially with Veronese, seen in the feminine canon, and in the
peace and the balance of the composition. Besides, this work was
made with a free technique influenced by Titian, avoiding the
constriction of precise drawing. The tint, gold and ochre, applied with
thick touches of painting is characteristic of the late works of
Rembrandt. The painter interprets the theme in a special way, bringing
to the fore the internalisation of feelings more than the anecdotal
aspect of the story.*

493. **Pieter de Hooch,** 1629-1684, Baroque, Dutch,
The Courtyard of a House in Delft, 1658.
Oil on canvas, 74 x 60 cm.
National Gallery, London.

The Courtyard of a House in Delft *shows all the originality of the
artist and the hidden meaning often displayed in Dutch genre
painting. The stone tablet over the doorway, originally over the
entrance of the Hieronymusdale Cloister in Delft, reads, "This is in
Saint Jerome's vale, if you wish to repair to patience and meekness.
For we must first descend if we wish to be raised."*

492. **Johannes Vermeer van Delft,** 1632-1675, Baroque, Dutch,
The Procuress, 1656. Oil on canvas, 143 x 130 cm.
Gemäldegalerie Alte Meister, Dresden.

494. **Johannes Vermeer van Delft,** 1632-1675, Baroque, Dutch,
Girl Reading a Letter at an Open Window, c. 1658.
Oil on canvas, 83 x 65 cm.
Gemäldegalerie Alte Meister, Dresden.

*This painting shows the painter's range of colour tended to get
clearer at this time in his career and the white background takes
more and more space. The materials depicted are treated in a
very subtle way in an illusionist aspect (note the precious
texture of the sumptuous carpet in the foreground). A curtain
deepens and closes the composition like a jewel box. The
window, the source of light, and the reflection of the sitter in the
glass recall that the epoch is marked by scientific research on
optic radiance.*

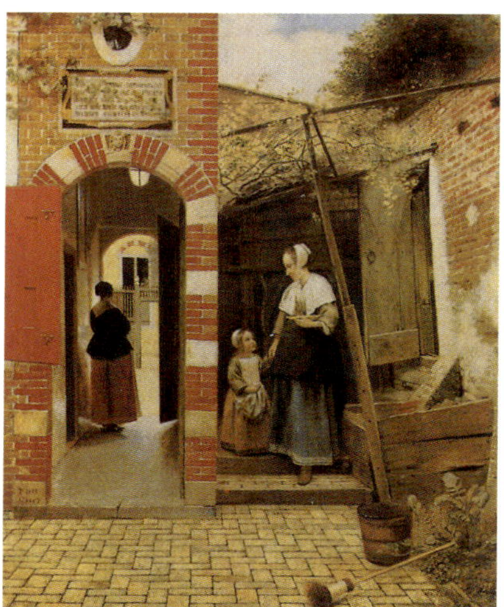

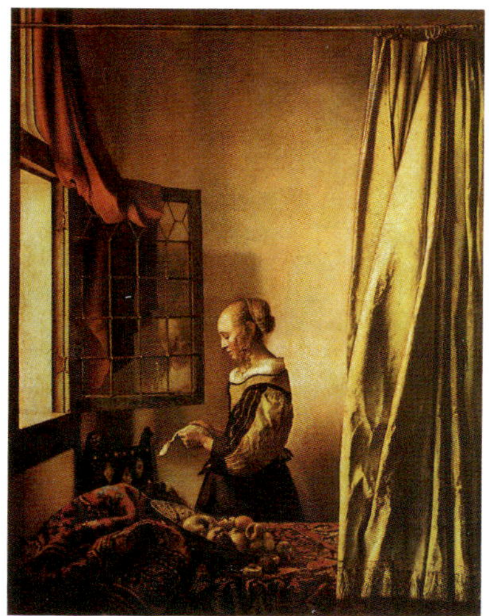

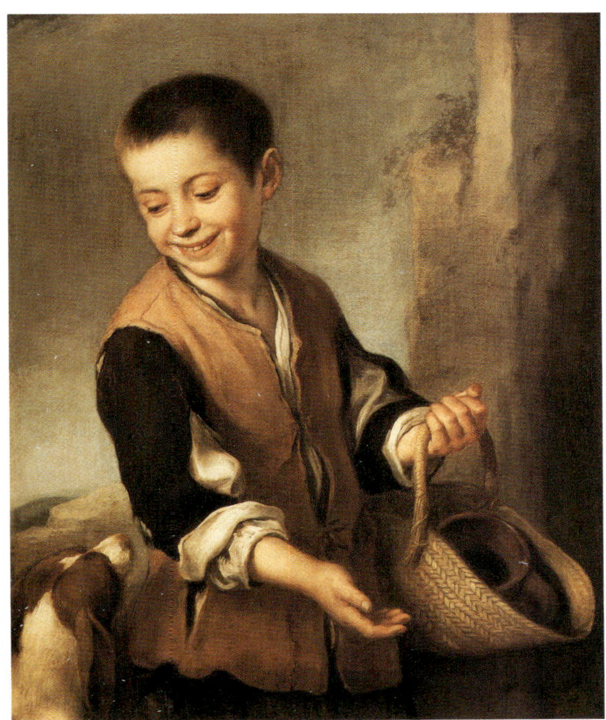

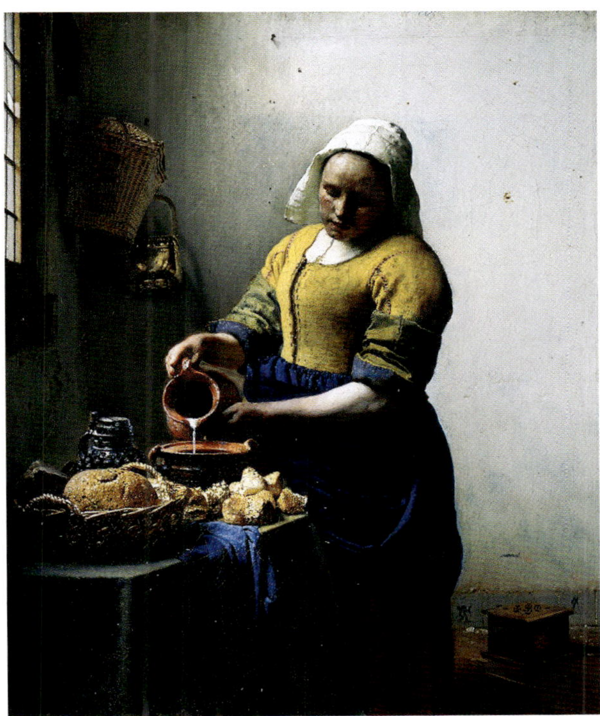

495. **Bartolomé Esteban Perez Murillo,** 1618-1682, Baroque, Spanish, *Boy with a Dog,* 1655-1660.
Oil on canvas, 70 x 60 cm.
The State Hermitage Museum, St Petersburg.

Brown noted that Murillo's genre paintings have a concealed meaning (J. Brown, "Murillo, pintor de temas eroticos. Una faceta inadvertida de su obra", Goya, 1982, Nos. 169-171, p. 35-43). He compared them with the bambocciata genre paintings executed by the Italian, Dutch and Flemish artists living in Rome in the mid-seventeenth century; such themes were very popular among the same allegories in his works. Although Brown did not mention Boy with a Dog *and* Girl with Fruit and Flowers, *thanks to his analysis their hidden symbolism can be easily revealed; the girl smiling shyly holds a basket with fruit, a symbol of maturity while the laughing boy shows the dog a basket that contains a jar, an object associated with women in the iconography of seventeenth-century art.*

496. **Johannes Vermeer van Delft,** 1632-1675, Baroque, Dutch, *The Milkmaid,* c. 1659.
Oil on canvas, 46 x 41 cm.
Rijksmuseum, Amsterdam.

Vermeer grants a plastic reality to each object depicted, and amplifies this with thickenings. The daub catches the light, which is introduced in a natural way thanks to the open window, a recurrent theme in the painter's works. The composition is minimal and stable, made around horizontals and verticals and the angle of the room keeps it steady. The sitter, concentrating on her action confers nobility to the task she does. The geometry of the character, her slow gestures and the subtle nuances of colours characterise the work of the painter.

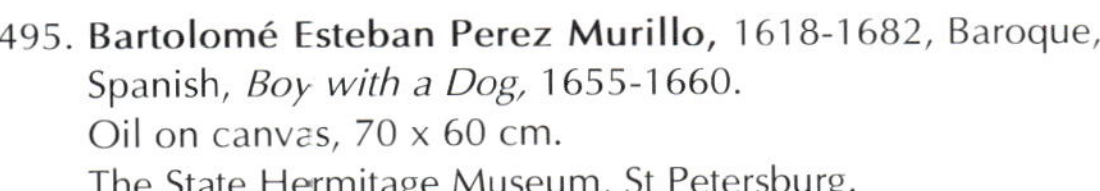

BARTOLOMÉ ESTEBAN PEREZ MURILLO
(1618 – 1682 SEVILLE)

Painter and draughtsman, Murillo began his art studies under Juan del Castillo, with some influence from Zurbarán. He painted in Seville, especially religious themes such as the Immaculate Conception, illustrating the doctrines of the Counter-Reformation. He was also one of the greatest portrait painters of his time. However his fame was established by painting genre scenes of beggar children. He founded the Seville Academy with Valdés Leal and Francisco Herrera the Younger, and became its first president. He excelled in the painting of clouds, flowers, water and drapery, and in the use of colour. His painting served as an example to such artists as Gainsborough, Reynolds and Greuze.

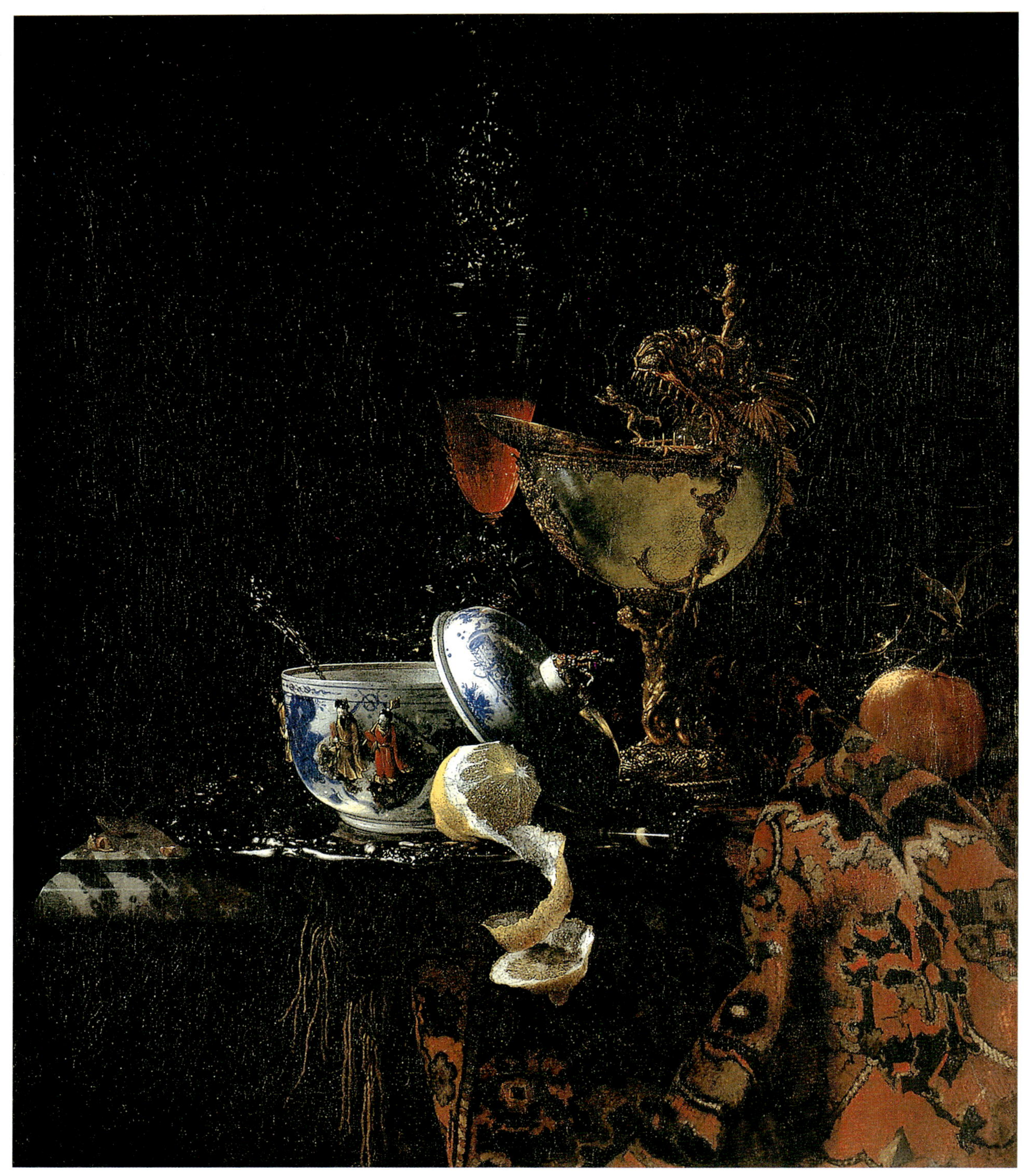

497. **Willem Kalf,** 1619-1693, Baroque, Dutch, *Still Life with Chinese Porcelain Jar,* 1662.
Oil on canvas, 64 x 53 cm. Gemäldegalerie, Alte Meister, Berlin.

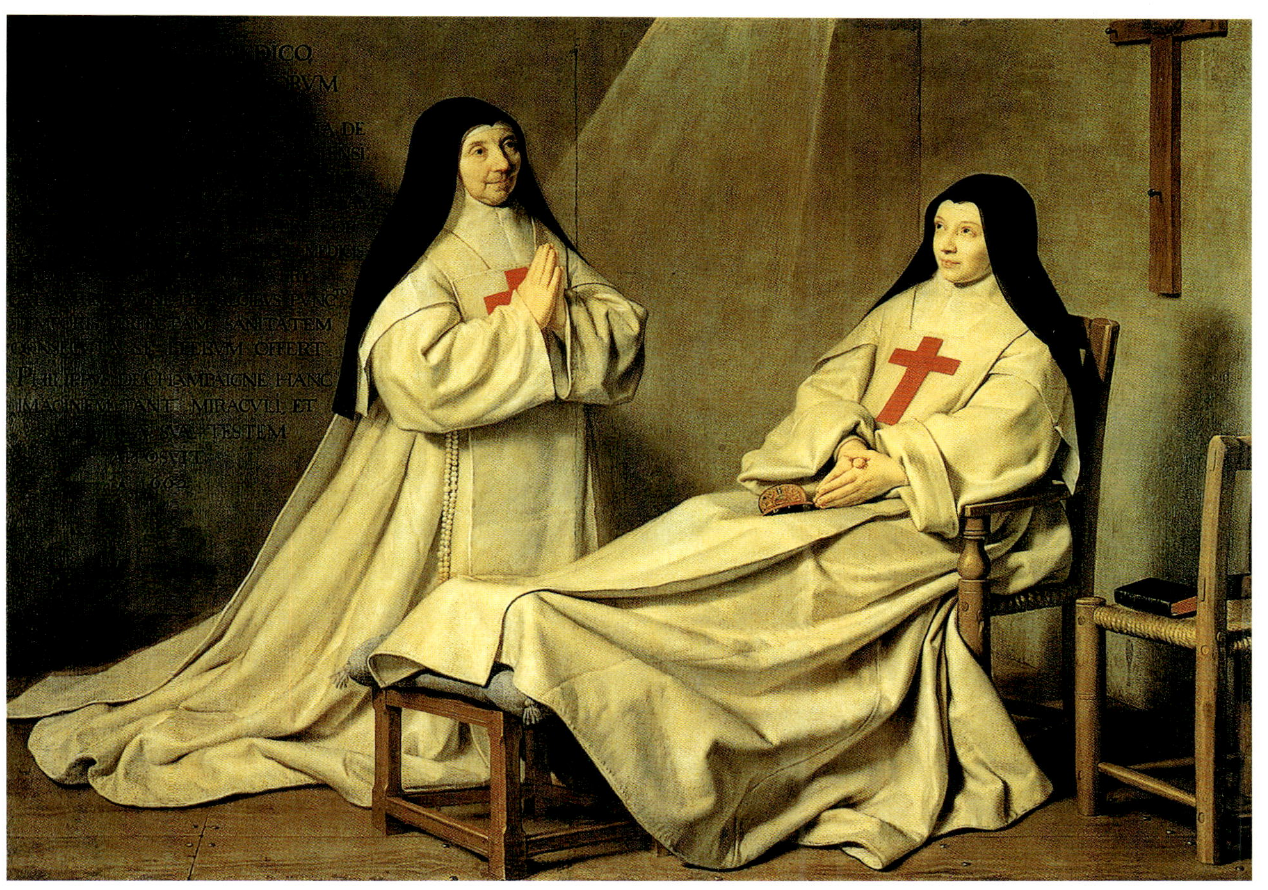

498. **Philippe de Champaigne,** 1602-1674, Classicism, French,
Ex-Voto 1662. Oil on canvas, 165 x 229 cm.
Musée du Louvre, Paris.

*The inscription in the background tells the story that inspired this
painting: the younger daughter of the painter suffered from paralysis,
but she miraculously recovered after nine days of prayers.*

PHILIPPE DE CHAMPAIGNE
(1602 BRUSSELS – 1674 PARIS)

Philippe's link to Rubens is through his teacher, Jacques Fouquières, who was an
assistant to that important Flemish painter of the Baroque. After first painting landscapes,
Philippe went to Paris in 1621 where he met Poussin. His decoration of churches won
the attention of King Louis XIII (1601-1643), as well as Cardinal Richelieu (1595-1642),
the powerful statesman who built France into a great power. The artist's portrait of the
Cardinal (1635) is among his masterworks, showing the influences of Van Dyck in his
full-length portrait style (fig. 486). He in turn introduced Flemish forms to French art.
After several personal difficulties and after his daughter, a nun, overcame a serious
illness, he painted his most devotional work, *Ex Voto 1662* or *Abbess Catherine – Agnes
Arnauld and Sister Catherine de Saint-Susanne.*

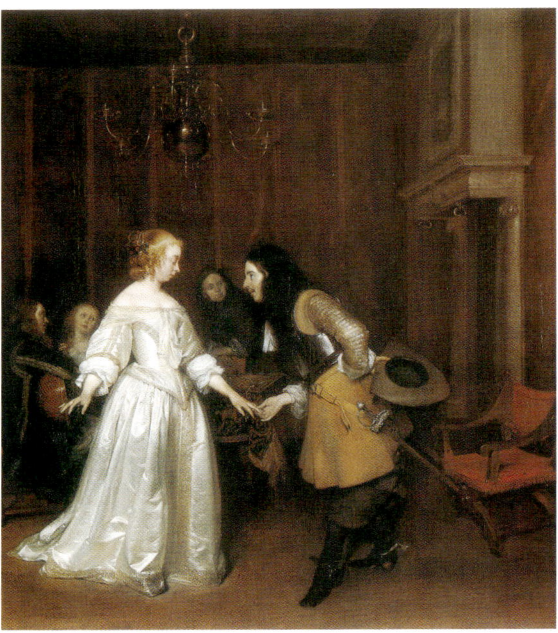

499. **Gerard ter Borch the Younger,** 1617-1681, Baroque, Dutch,
Dancing Couple, 1660.
Oil on canvas, 76 x 68 cm. Polesden Lacey, Dorking.

501. **Jan Steen,** 1626-1679, Baroque, Dutch,
As the Old Sing, so Twitter the Young, 1663-1665.
Oil on canvas, 94.5 x 81 cm. Musée Fabre, Montpellier.

*Steen is a painter of lively, popular and comic scenes. His
illustration of proverbs, such as this painting, recalls the tradition
of Bruegel.*

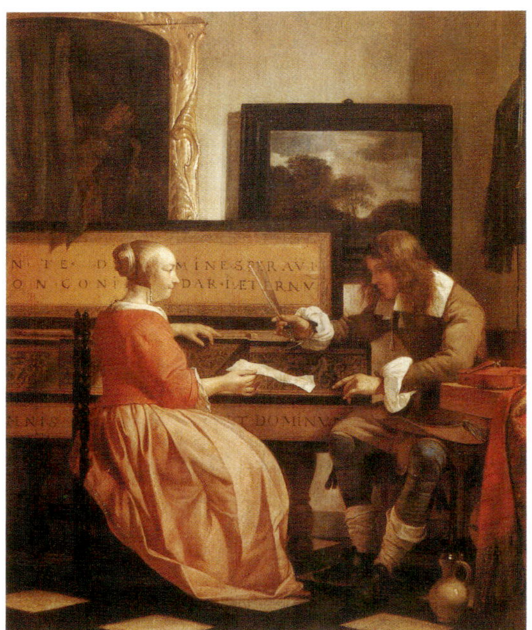

500. **Gabriel Metsu,** 1629-1667, Baroque, Dutch,
A Man and a Woman Seated by a Virginal, c. 1665.
Oil on canvas, 38.4 x 32.2 cm.
National Gallery, London.

502. **Gerrit Dou,** 1613-1675, Baroque, Dutch,
The Dropsical Lady, c. 1663.
Oil on panel, 87 x 67 cm.
Musée du Louvre, Paris.

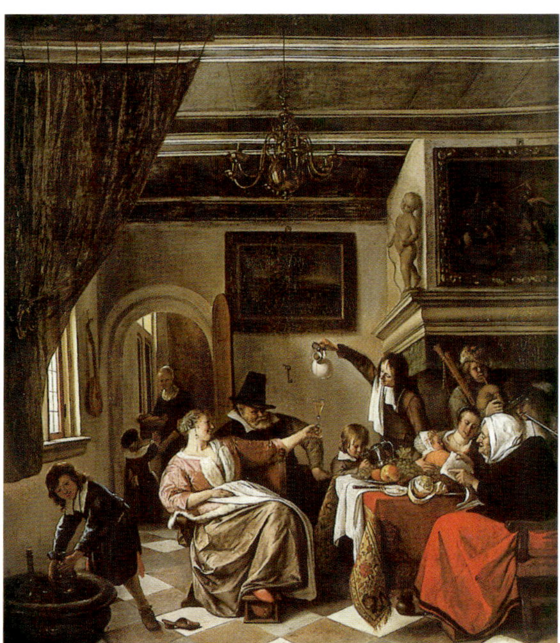

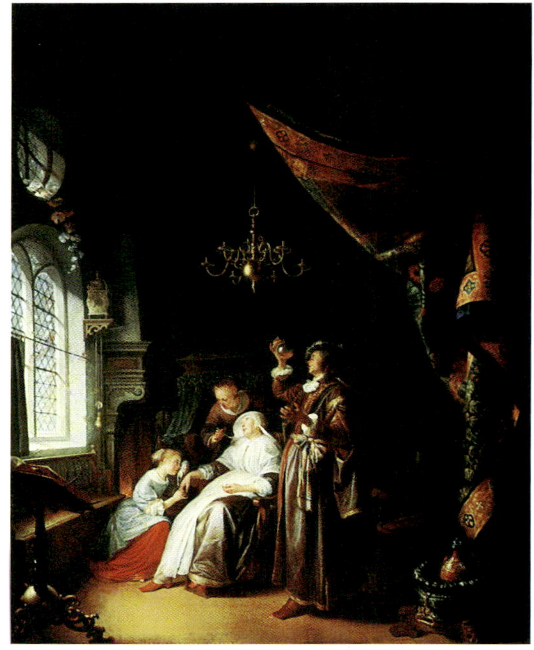

503. **Johannes Vermeer van Delft,** 1632-1675, Baroque, Dutch,
The Artist's Studio, c. 1665.
Oil on canvas, 120 x 100 cm.
Kunsthistorisches Museum, Vienna.

*The plaster death mask on the table to the artist's left in the
painting seems to be an ominous sign for the painting's future.
Between the viewer and the mask is a chair inviting the viewer
to enter and become involved in the painting. It also invites
the viewer to look at the painting from every angle. The lively
line of the tiles on the floor directs the eye to the model, while
the presence of several horizontal lines (from the ceiling
beams to the bottom edges of the easel and stool) create a
secure air of tranquillity. This work is representative of
Vermeer's interest in interior scenes and quiet atmospheres.
The drapes on the left seem to be pulled back by the viewer
so as to peek in on the artist at work. Vermeer's signature is on
the lower left corner of the map tapestry, as if forming a line
between the artist and model, perhaps implying a personal
relationship between the model and the artist. The wall map
is a picture-in-the-picture as it too has pictures-in-the-picture,
giving the picture depth of meaning as well as visual
perspective. The model's headpiece, book, and slide bugle
point to her representing Clio, the muse of history. In a
continuation of Dutch painting from the fifteenth century, the
depth is created by sweet slanting light from the window on
the left.*

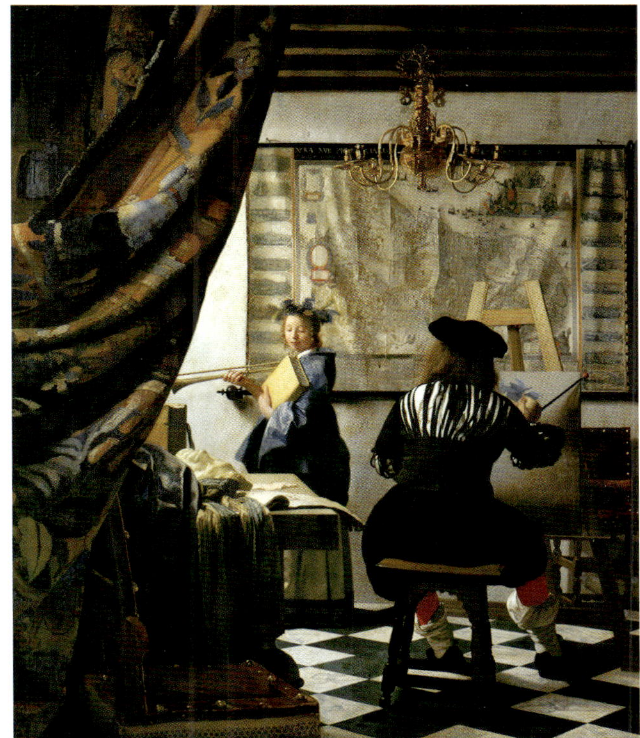

504. **Johann Heinrich Schönfeld,** 1609-1684, Baroque, German,
The Oath of Hannibal, c. 1660.
Oil on canvas, 98 x 184.5 cm.
Germanisches National-Museum, Nuremberg.

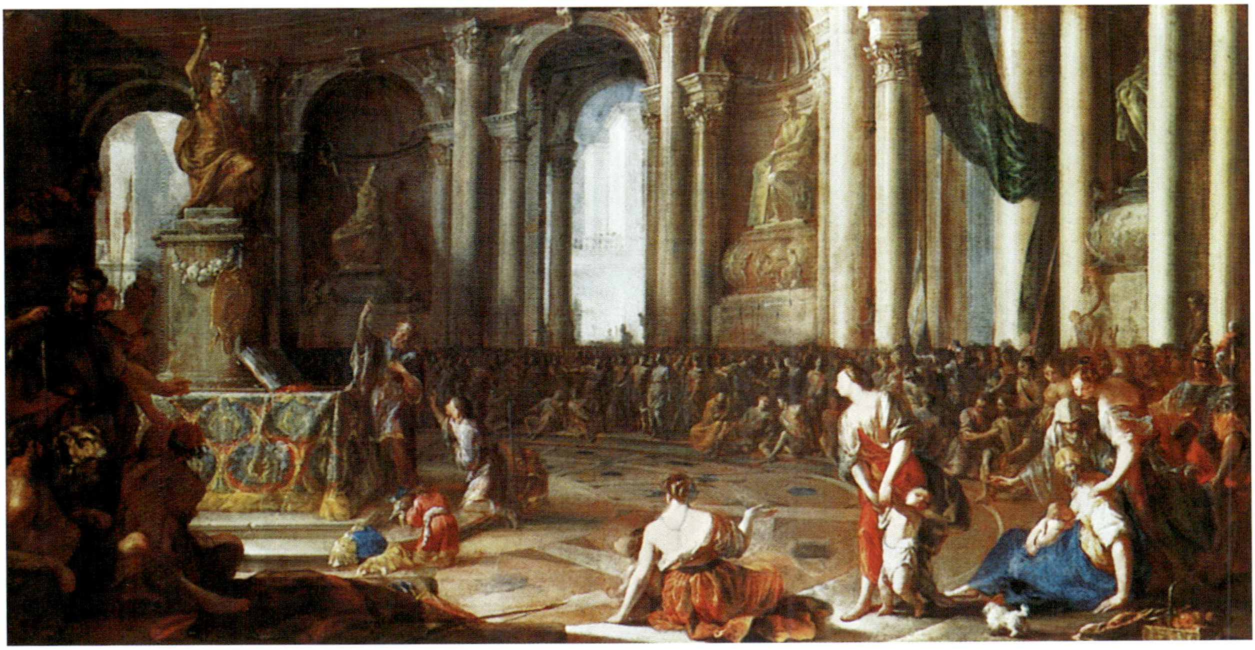

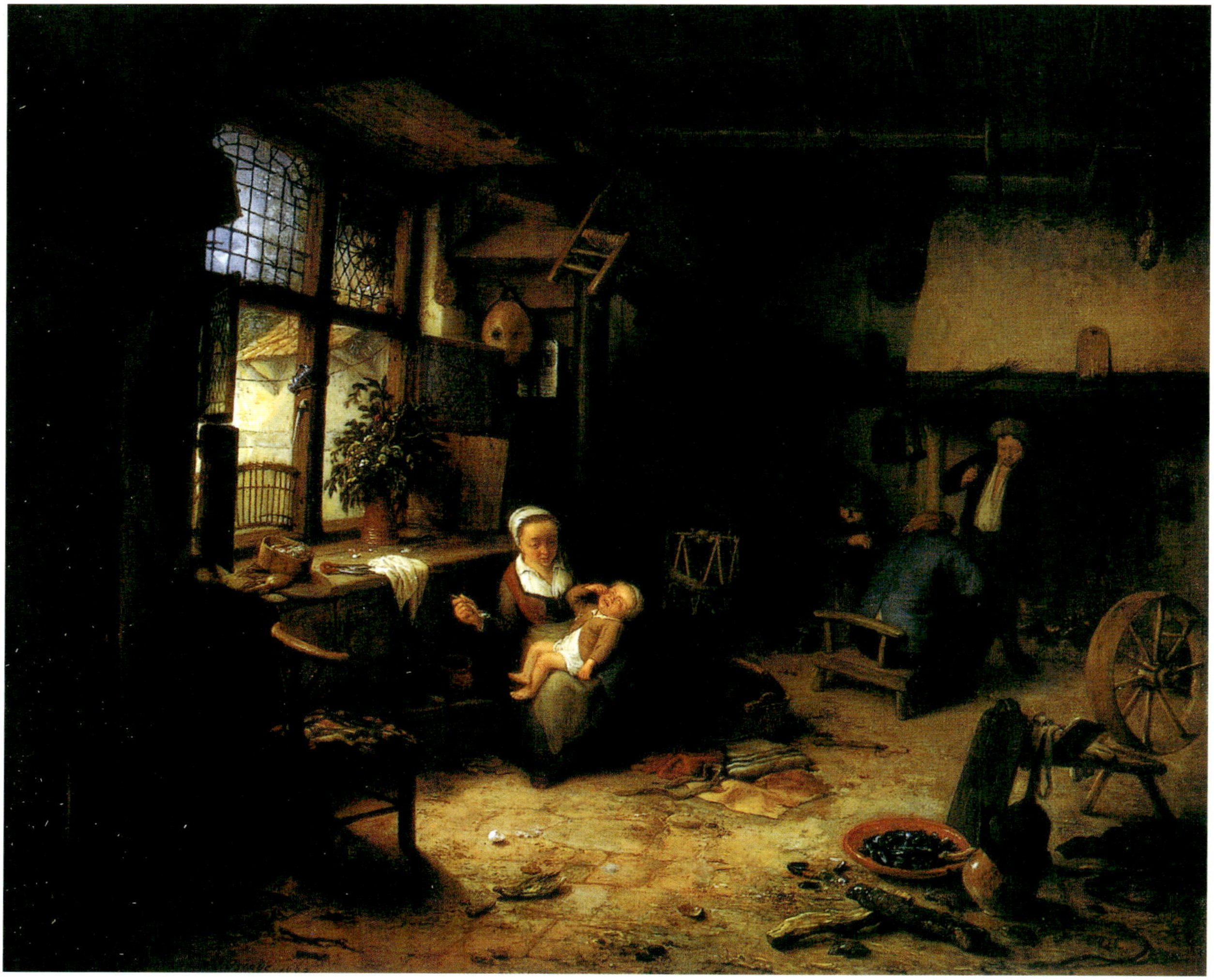

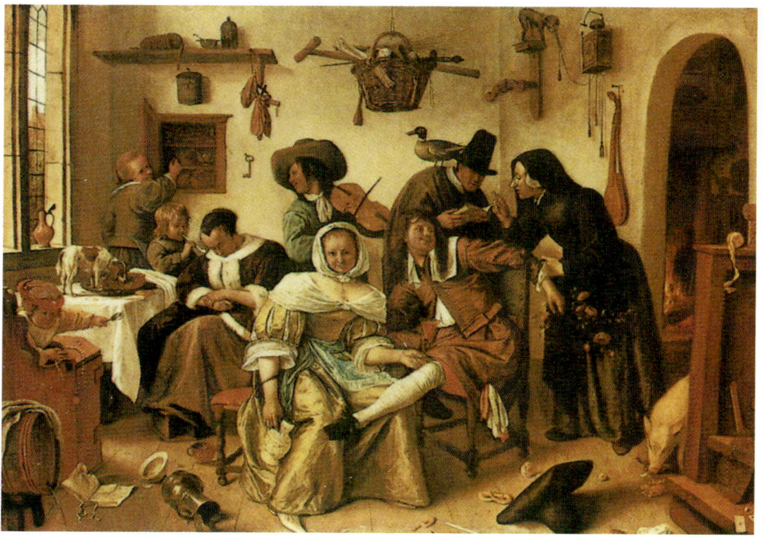

505. **Adriaen van Ostade,** 1610-1685, Baroque,
Dutch, *Interior with Peasants,* 1663.
Oil on panel, 34 x 40 cm.
The Wallace Collection, London.

506. **Jan Steen,** 1626-1679, Baroque, Dutch,
Beware of Luxury, 1663.
Oil on canvas, 105 x 145 cm.
Kunsthistorisches Museum, Vienna.

*Jan Steen depicted his historical scenes on the
grounds of genre painting. In seventeenth-century
Holland, brothel scenes were common and often
depicted without ambiguity or moral judgment.*

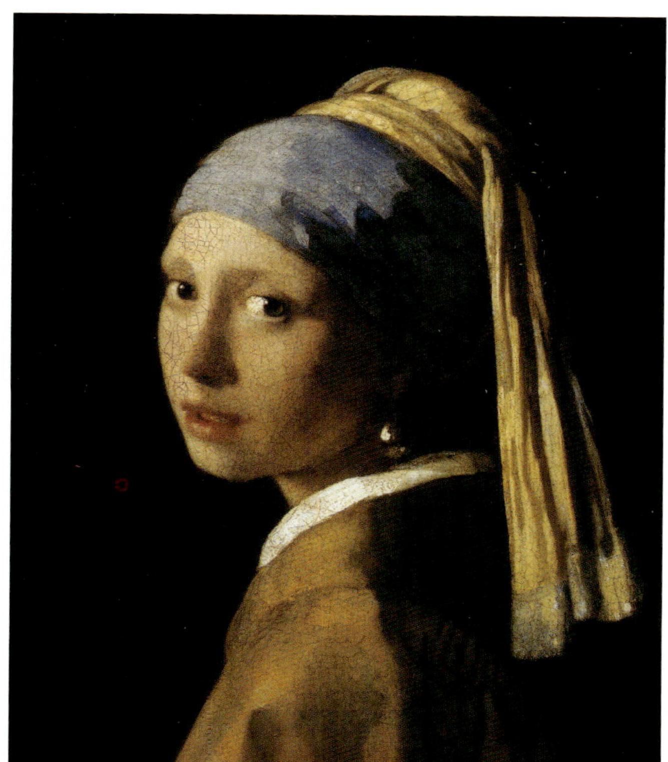

JOHANNES VERMEER VAN DELFT
(1632 – 1675 DELFT)

Vermeer is perhaps the heroic type of placid, for in none of his pictures is there the least breath of disquietude. We have the impression that he laid the strokes on slowly, but with faultless certainty, and that he was as interested in a reflection in a bottle, or a curtain on a wall, in the stuff of a carpet or a dress, as in the faces of his men and women. No apparent virtuosity, no prowess of the brush, no superfluities; all leads simply to perfection and to the maximum effect expressible through simple precision. His exactness of composition, of draughtsmanship, and of colouration in its clear and rather cold range under a silvery light, is a rare and original creation. Unlike his predecessors, he used a camera obscura to help in his meticulous rendering of perspective. He revolutionised how paint was made and used. His technique of applying paint anticipated some of the methods of the impressionists over two centuries later.

507. **Johannes Vermeer van Delft,** 1632-1675,
Baroque, Dutch, *Girl with a Pearl Earring,* c. 1665-1666,
Oil on canvas, 44.5 x 39 cm.
Koninklijk Kabinet van Schilderijen Mauritshuis,
The Hague.

508. **Bartolomé Esteban Perez Murillo,** 1618-1882,
Baroque, Spanish,
Rest on the Flight into Egypt,
c. 1665. Oil on canvas,
136.5 x 179.5 cm.
The State Hermitage
Museum, St Petersburg.

The subject of the Rest on the Flight into Egypt is related to the Flight into Egypt, the primary literary source of the New Testament (Matthew 2: 13-51). The Gospels, however, tell only about the flight of the Holy Family. The scenes of the rest on the flight are based on apocryphal literature The Seville painters who treated this subject took their guidance from Francisco Pacheco's book, Art of Painting, in which he tells in detail how the Virgin and Joseph had to hurry and could not take with them enough food and clothes, and how difficult their journey was in the wilderness.

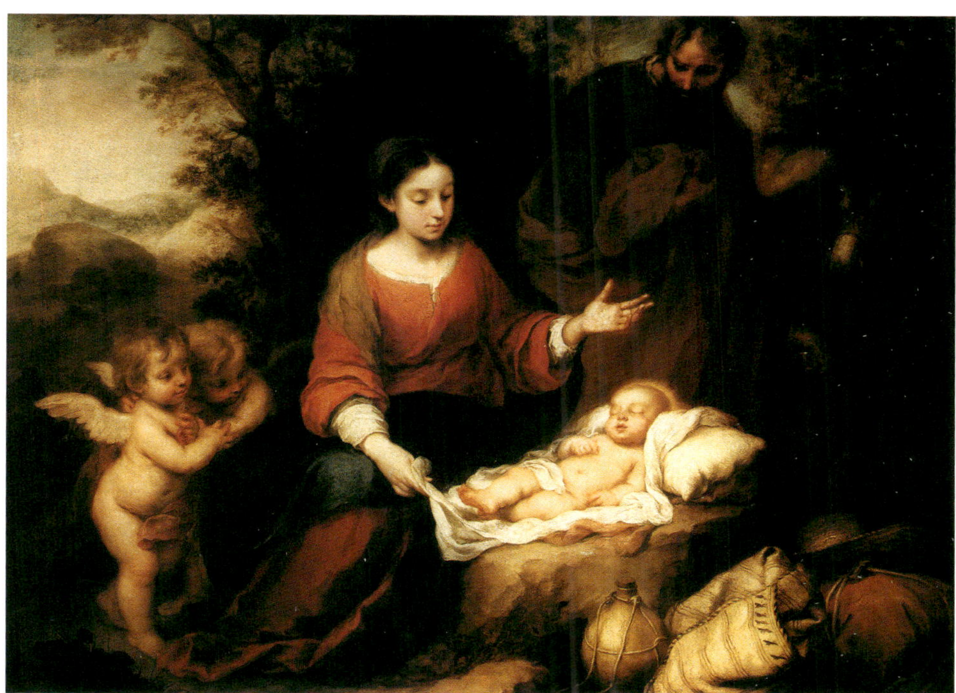

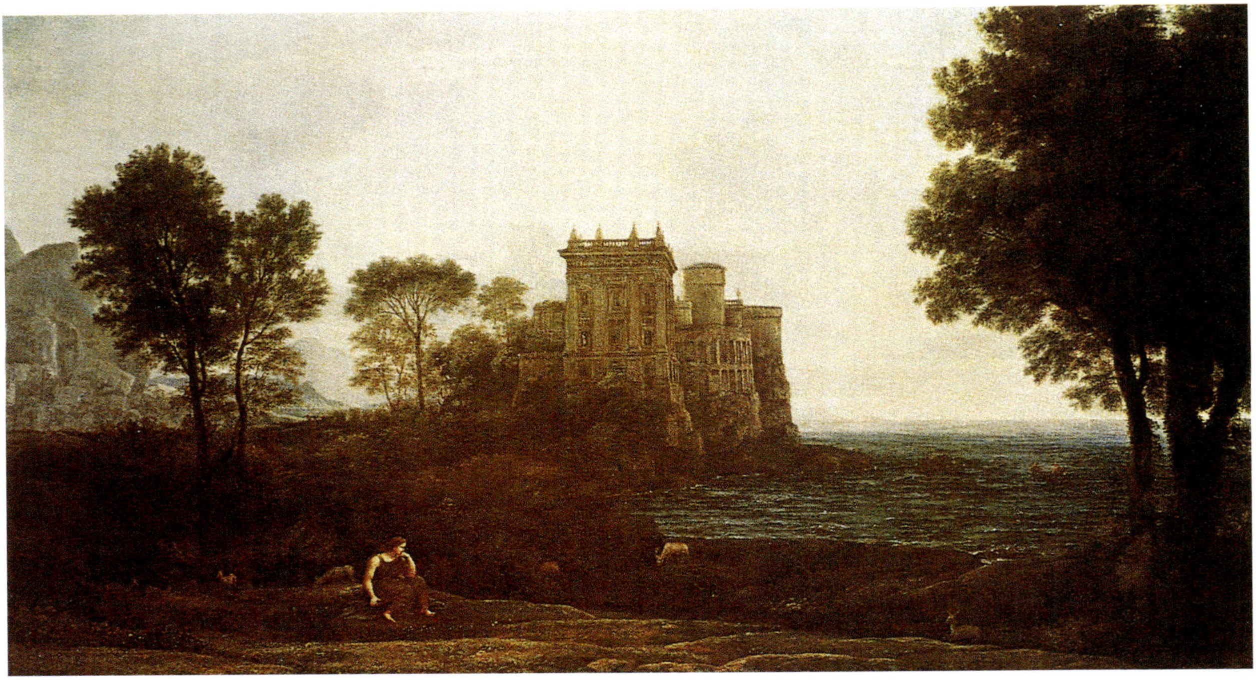

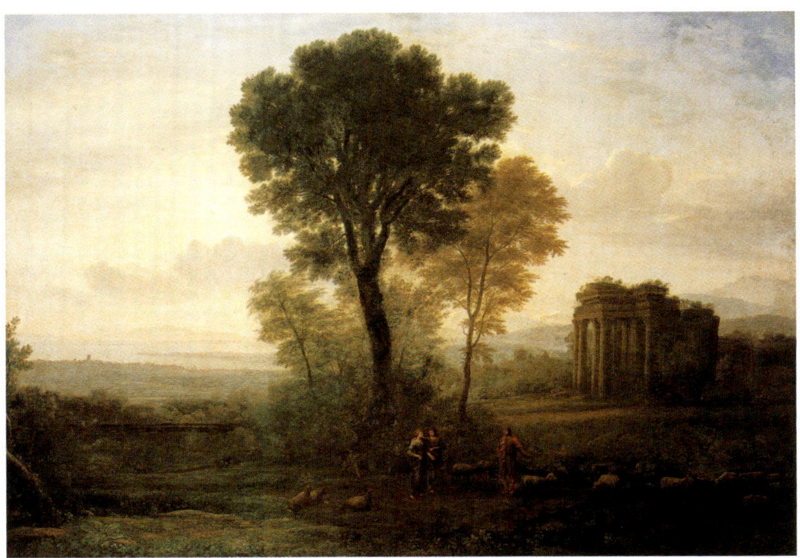

509. Claude Lorrain (Gellée), c. 1604-1682, Classicism, French,
Landscape with Psyche outside the Palace of Cupid
('The Enchanted Castle'), 1664.
Oil on canvas, 87.1 x 151.3 cm. National Gallery, London.

510. **Claude Lorrain (Gellée),** c. 1604-1682,
Classicism, French, *Landscape with Jacob,*
Rachel and Leah at the Well (Morning), 1666.
Oil on canvas, 113 x 157 cm.
The State Hermitage Museum, St Petersburg.

Landscape with Jacob, Rachel and Leah at
the Well (Morning) *is one of Lorrain's most
fascinating lyrical pieces. He recreated the
beauty of the nascent day with the same
thrill of love, the same fervour of feeling that
filled his hero's heart at young Rachel's
first appearance. In the group of people,
however, this feeling is only hinted at; its full
force is brought out by the emotional impact
of the landscape as a whole. The dominance
of the lyrical mood is due to the artist's
complete identification of the subject and
object in the process of creating art. Nature
is animated and endowed, as it were, with a
soul capable of experiencing the subtlest
gradations of feeling. Using his favourite
device of contre jour painting, he suggests
a flow of light in the direction of the
spectator, and this gives the impression of
the day dawning. The faintly outlined
crowns of trees, enveloped in the morning
mist, are echoed by the shapes of the
clouds lightly gilded by the rising sun. The
pictorial structure of the painting is based on
finely nuanced colours with prevailing
silvery tones. The colouring, clear and soft,
harmonises with the emotions aroused by
the picture.*

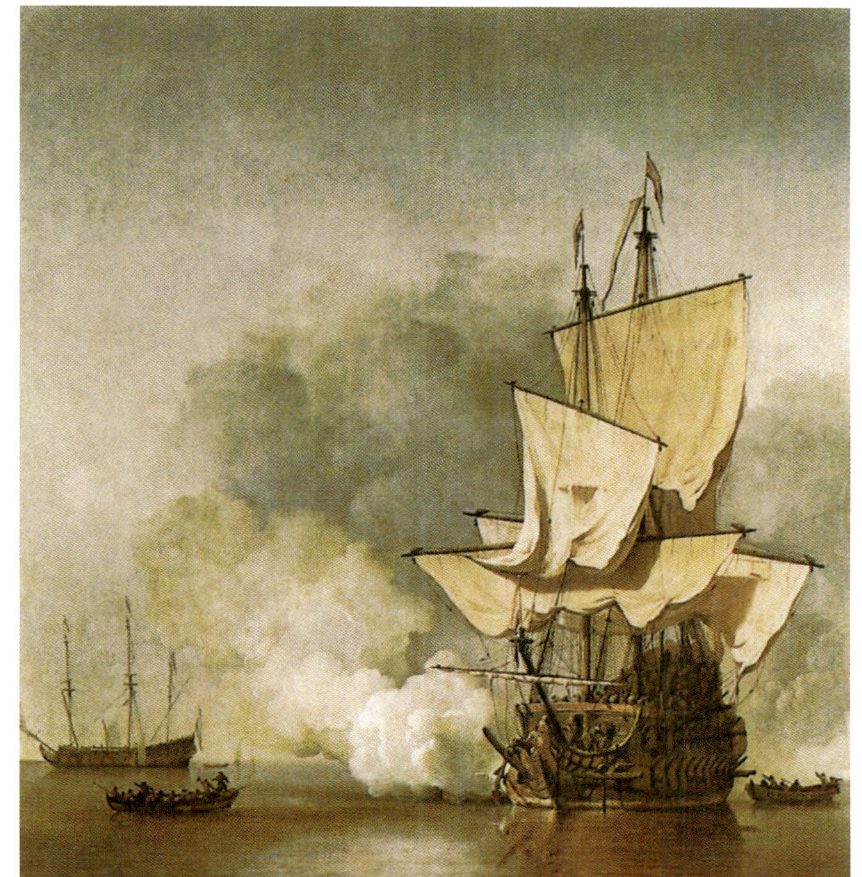

511. Willem van de Velde the Younger,
1633-1707, Baroque, Dutch,
The Cannon Shot, c. 1670.
Oil on canvas, 78.5 x 67 cm.
Rijksmuseum, Amsterdam.

A painter from Haarlem, one of the two most prestigious Dutch schools of painting, Van de Velde belonged to a family of engravers; an important activity for painters as it enabled them to broadcast and promote their works. He painted numerous panoramic views, depicting simple daily life from Haarlem. His works contrast with those of Seghers who intended to give a more dramatic representation to his landscapes.

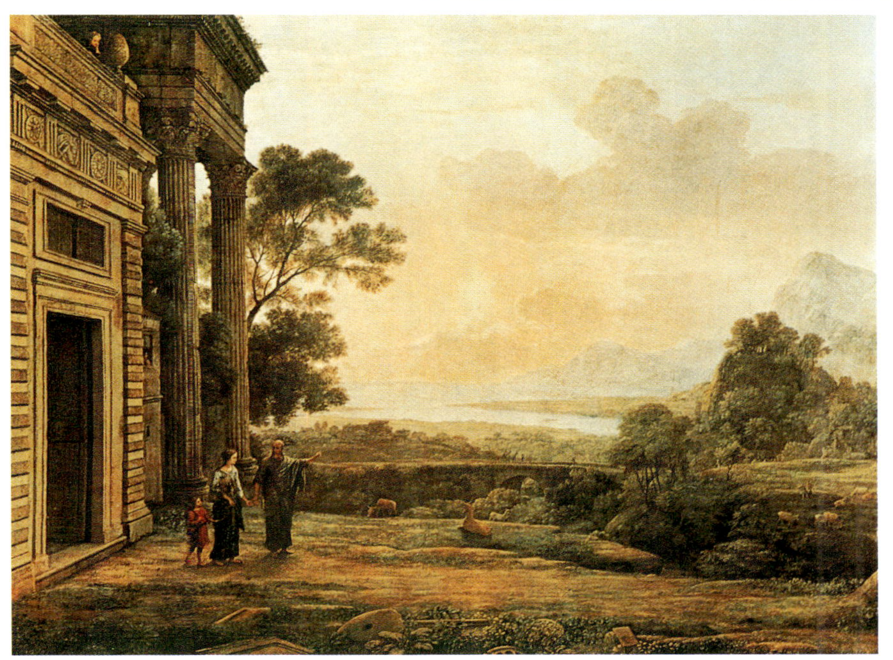

512. Claude Lorrain (Gellée),
c. 1604-1682, Classicism, French,
The Expulsion of Hagar, 1668.
Oil on canvas, 106.4 x 140 cm.
Alte Pinakothek, Munich.

At his maturity, the artist painted with a more monumental style, severe compositions and subjects often taken from the Old Testament.

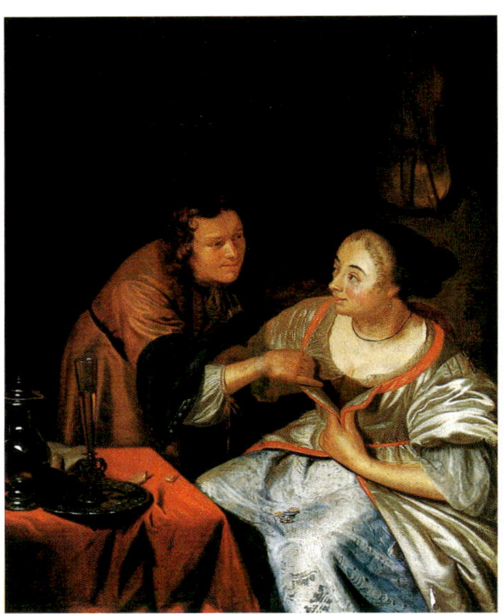

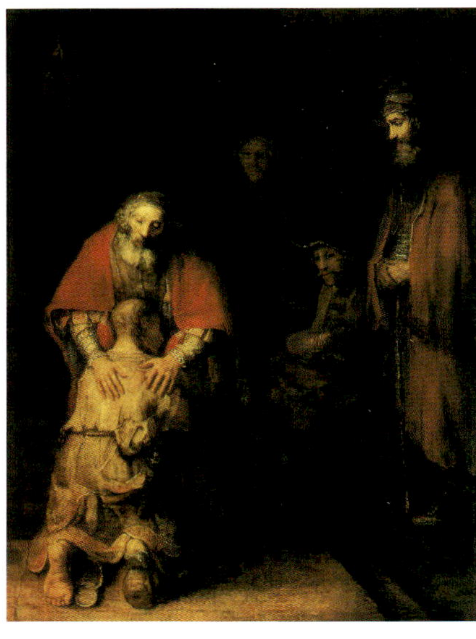

517. **Pierre Mignard**, 1612-1695, Baroque, French, *The Virgin of the Grapes*, 1640-1650. Oil on canvas, 121x 94 cm. Musée du Louvre, Paris.

Pierre Mignard studied with Vouet. He reproduced the features of his wife in his Madonna subjects.

513. **Frans van Mieris,** 1635-1681, Baroque, Dutch, *Carousing Couple,* undated. Oil on panel, Private collection.

514. **Rembrandt Harmensz. van Rijn,** 1606-1669, Baroque, Dutch, *The Return of the Prodigal Son,* 1668. Oil on canvas, 262 x 205 cm. The State Hermitage Museum, St Petersburg.

The story of the prodigal son is told here in an expressive and laconic way, about one year before the painter's death: the strict verticals of the solemn and majestic figures stand as the dominant aspect of the painting. The father's clothes and the line of his face find an extension in his son's face, underlining the union between the two men and granting a certain monumentality to the grouping. The figures seem to come out of the shadow to reach a blaze of colour. The manner is characteristic of Rembrandt's later works.

515. **Gerard ter Borch The Younger,** 1617-1681, Baroque, Dutch, *A Concert,* c. 1675. Oil on panel, 58.1 x 47.3 cm. Cincinnati Art Museum, Cincinnati.

516. **Rembrandt Harmensz. van Rijn,** 1606-1669, Baroque, Dutch, *Portrait of Two Figures from the Old Testament,* also known as *'The Jewish Bride',* 1667. Oil on canvas, 121.5 x 166.5 cm. Rijksmuseum, Amsterdam.

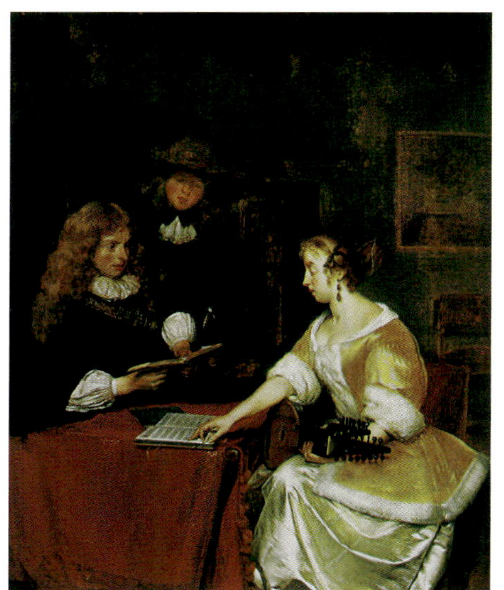

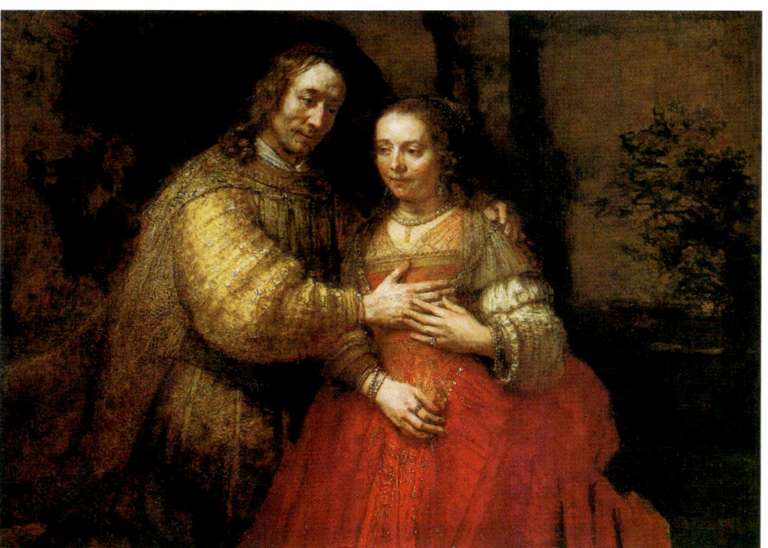

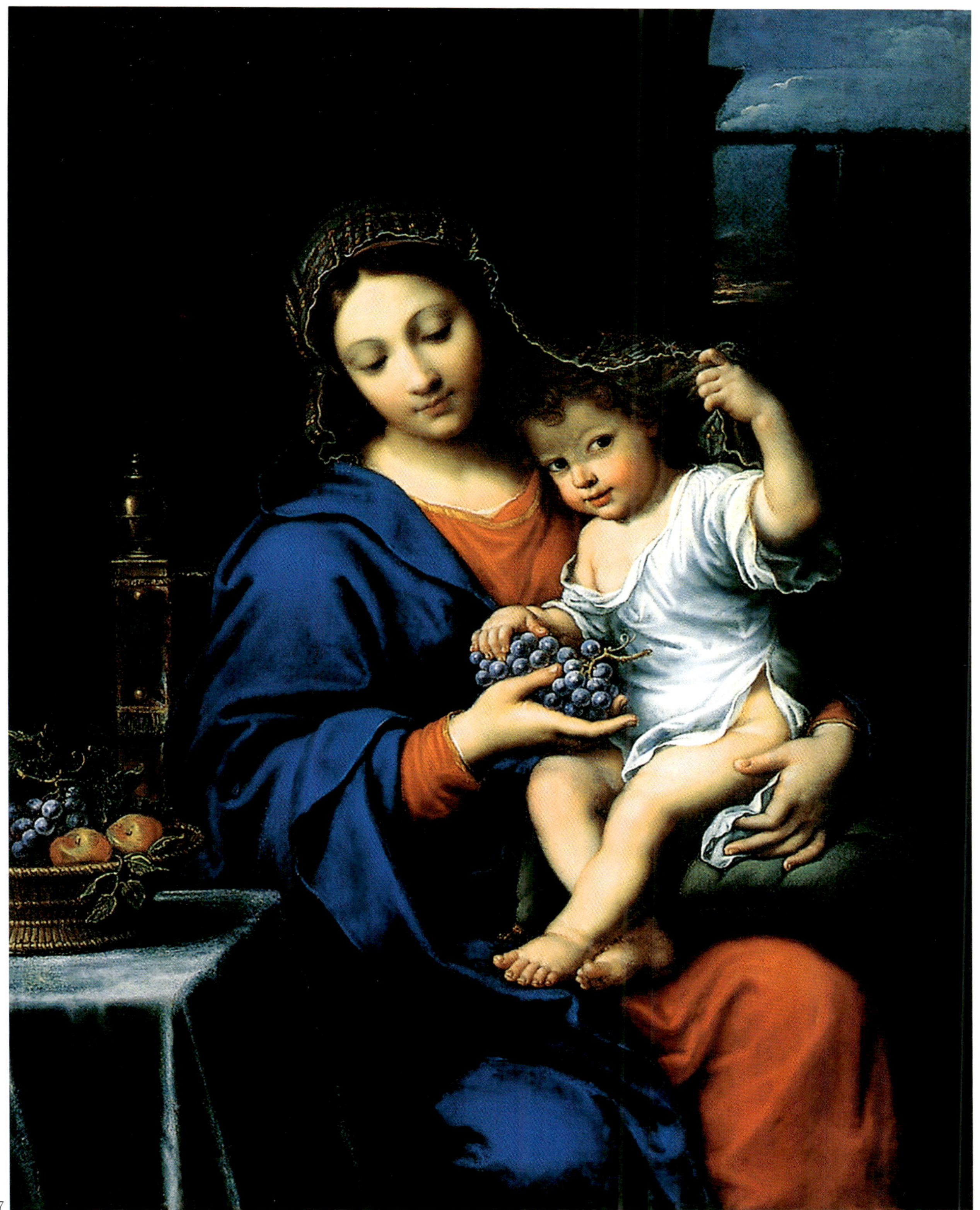

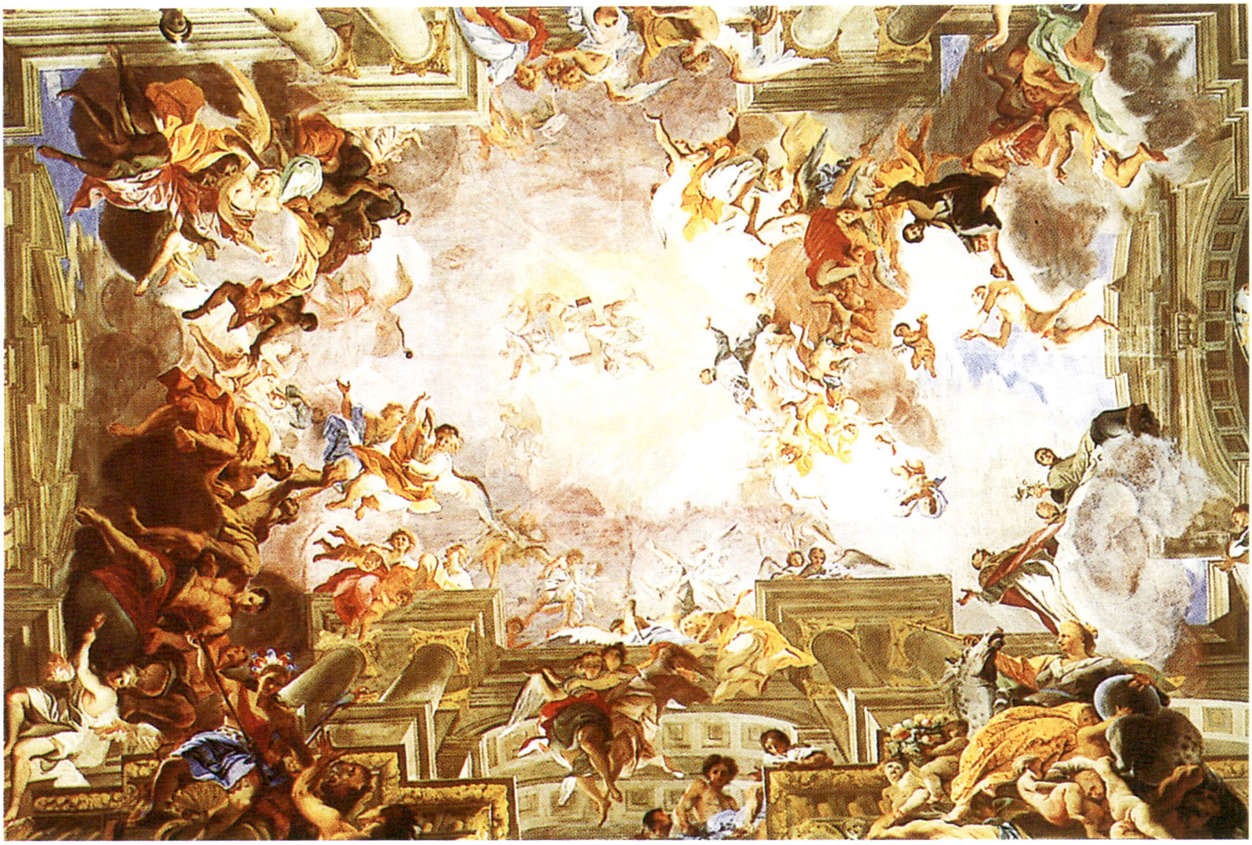

519. **Baciccio (Giovanni Battista Gaulli),** 1639-1709, High Baroque,
Italian, *Adoration of the Name of Jesus,* 1674-1679. Fresco.
Sant'Ignazio, Rome.

*Masterpiece of High Baroque illusionism, this theatrical fresco is
the result of the prestigious commission for decorating the
interior of the Jesuit church of Il Gesù in Rome.*

518. **Andrea Pozzo,** 1642-1709, High Baroque, Italian,
Allegory of the Missionary Work of the Jesuits, 1685-1694.
Fresco. Sant' Ignazio, Rome.

520. **Frans Snyders,** 1579-1657, Baroque, Flemish,
A Game Stall, c. 1675.
Oil on canvas, 177 x 274 cm. York City Art Gallery, York.

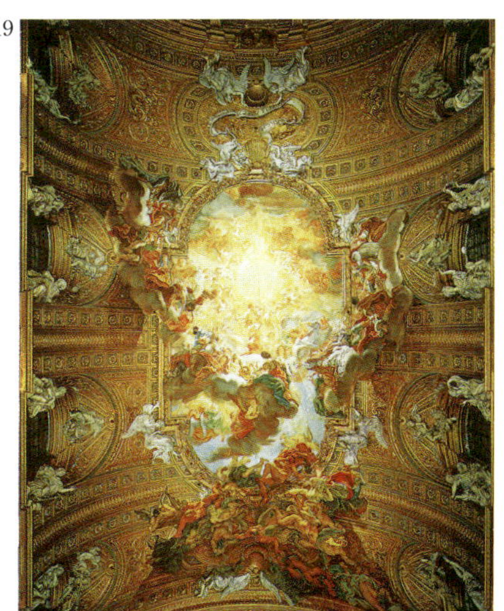

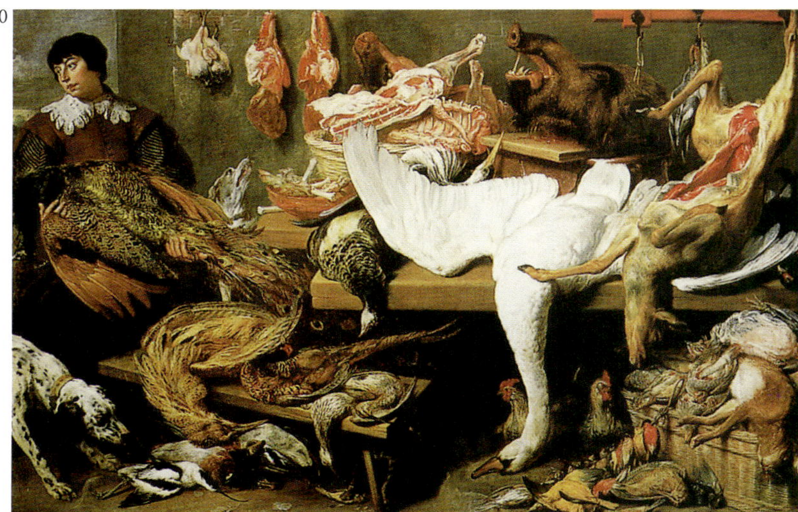

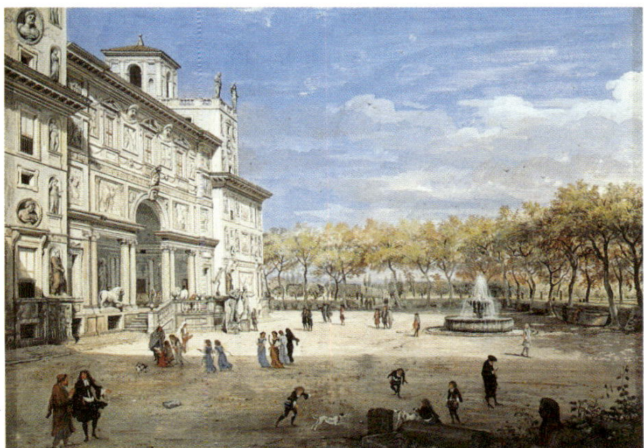

521. **Gaspar van Wittel,** c. 1653-1736, Baroque, Dutch,
The Villa Medici in Rome, 1685.
Tempera on parchment, 29 x 41 cm. Palazzo Pitti, Florence.

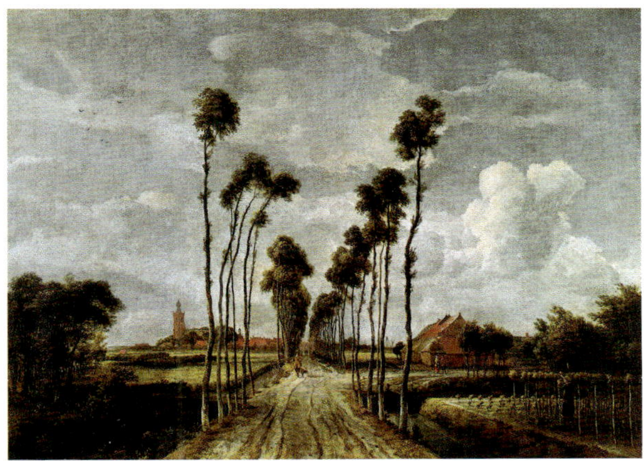

522. **Meindert Hobbema,** 1638-1709, Baroque, Dutch,
The Avenue at Middleharnis, 1689.
Oil on canvas, 103.5 x 141 cm. National Gallery, London.

This is one of the later vedute *(a painting depicting a panoramic view of a place) painted by Hobbema. Having been a pupil of Ruisdael, his landscapes were influenced by the master's manner but tended to be more simplified, all the accessory details being removed while the expanse of sky was emphasised.*

523. **Jacques Stella,** 1596-1657, Baroque, French,
Christ Served by Angels, before 1653.
Oil on canvas, 111 x 158 cm.
Galleria degli Uffizi, Florence.

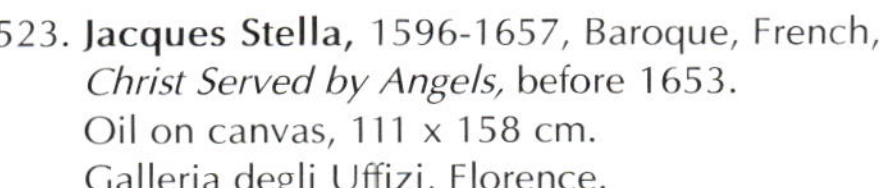

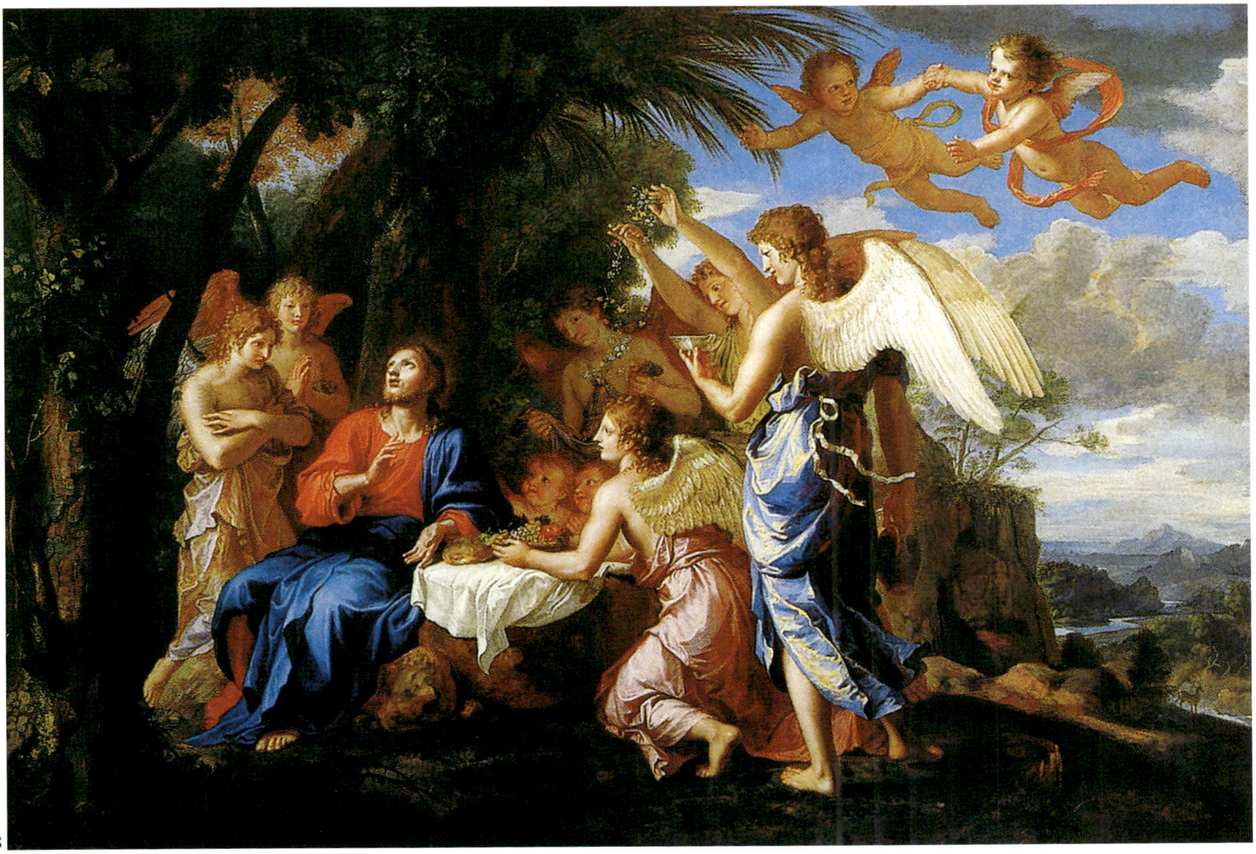

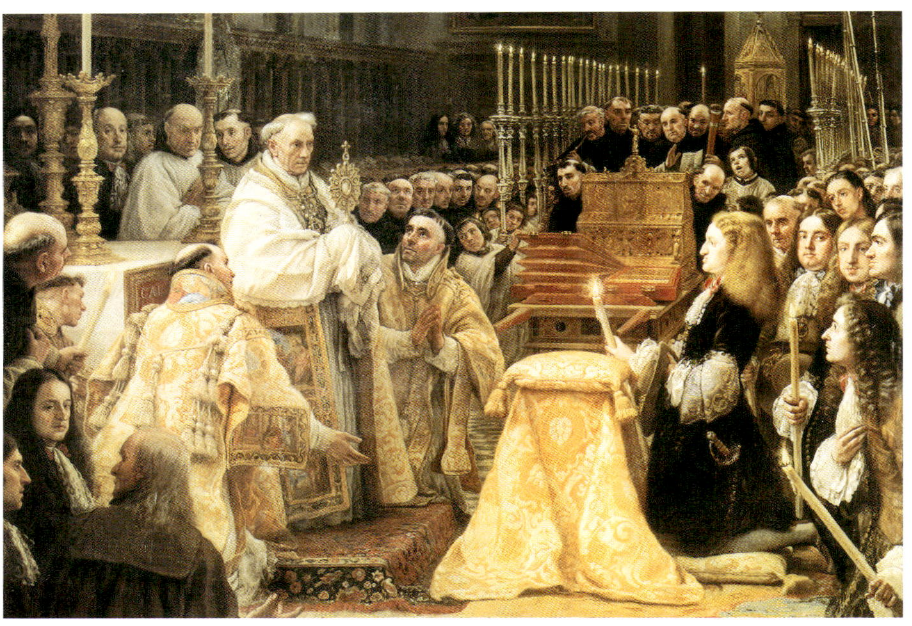

525. **Nicolas de Largillière,** 1656-1746, Rococo, French,
*The Provost and Municipal Magistrates of Paris Discussing the Celebration of Louis XIV's Dinner at the Hotel de Ville
after his Recovery in 1687,* 1689.
Oil on canvas, 68 x 101 cm. The State Hermitage Museum, St Petersburg.

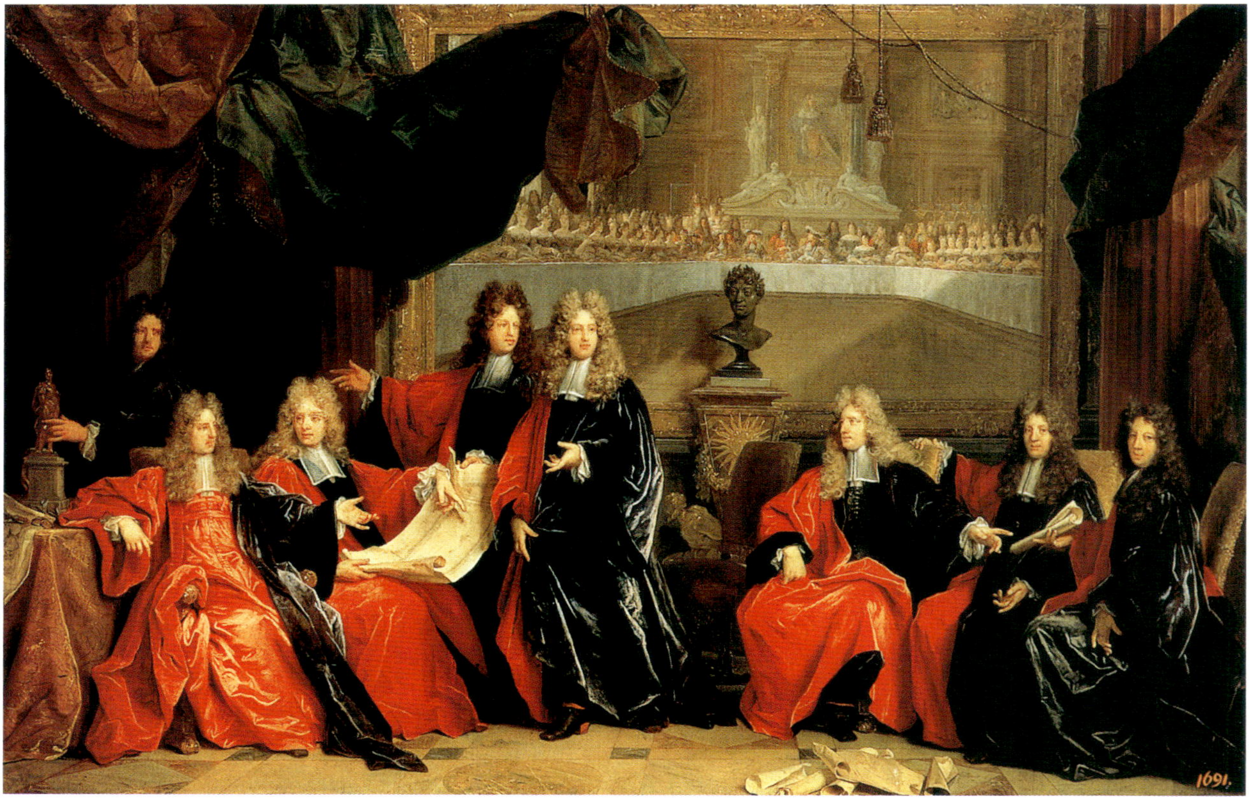

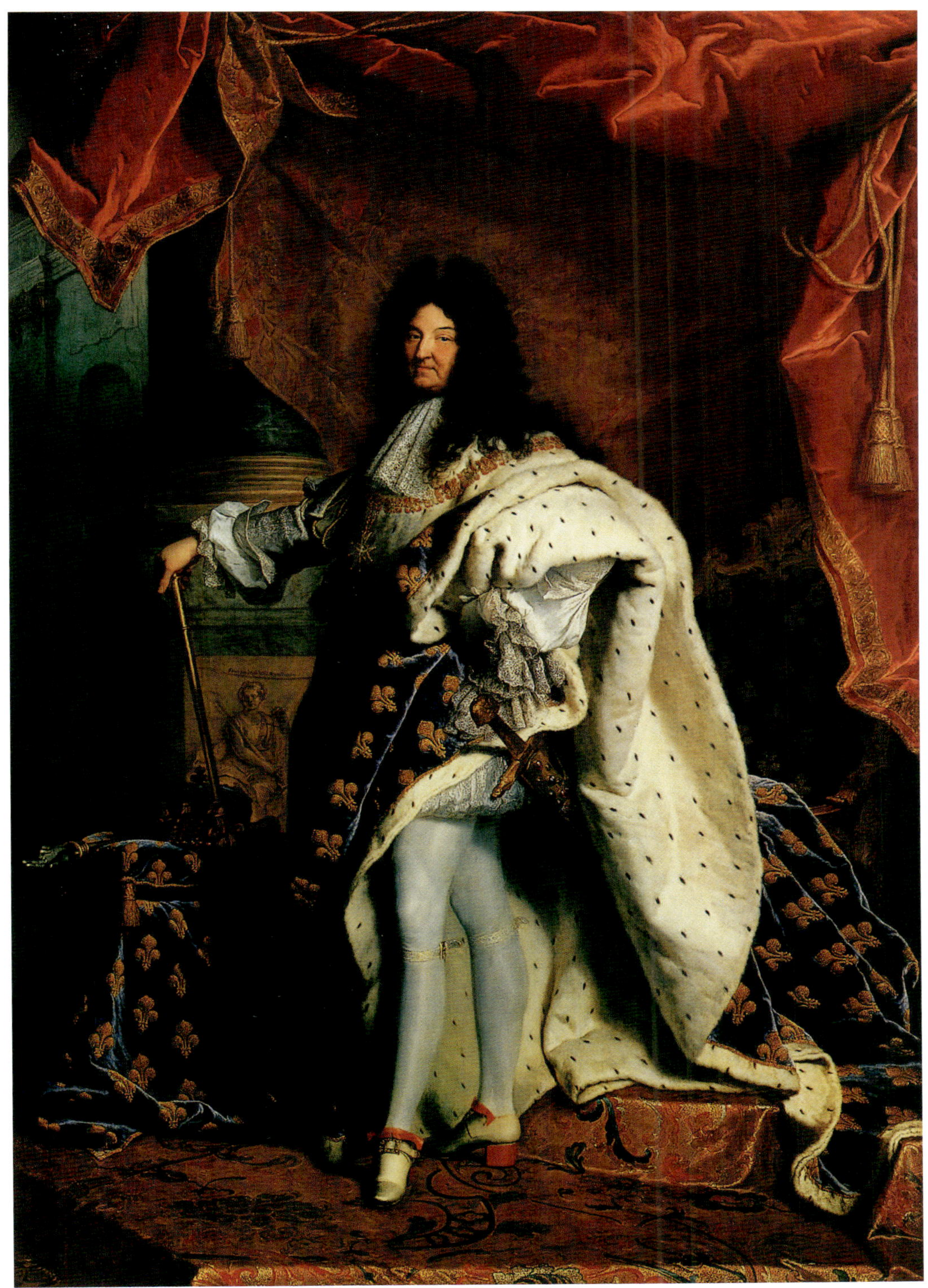

526. **Hyacinthe Rigaud**, 1659-1743, Rococo, French, *Louis XIV,* 1701. Oil on canvas, 277 x 194 cm. Musée du Louvre, Paris.

Ordered to be given to the King of Spain, this portrait was such a success at the French court that it remained in the country. It represented 'the power, pomp and circumstance' of the absolutist ruler.

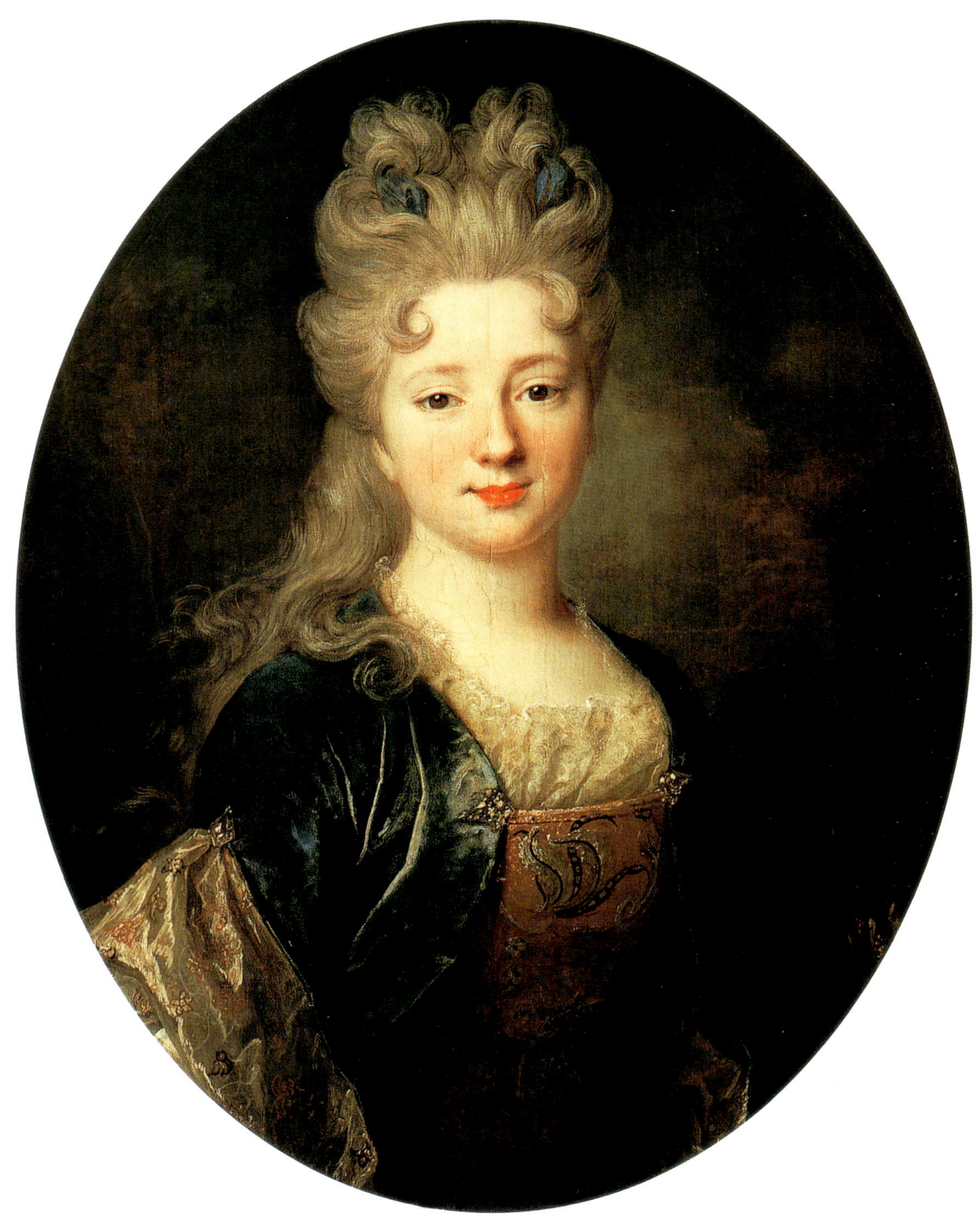

527. **Nicolas de Largillière**, 1656-1746, Rococo, French, *Portrait of a Lady,* c. 1710.
Oil on canvas, 80 x 64 cm. Pushkin Museum of Fine Arts, Moscow.

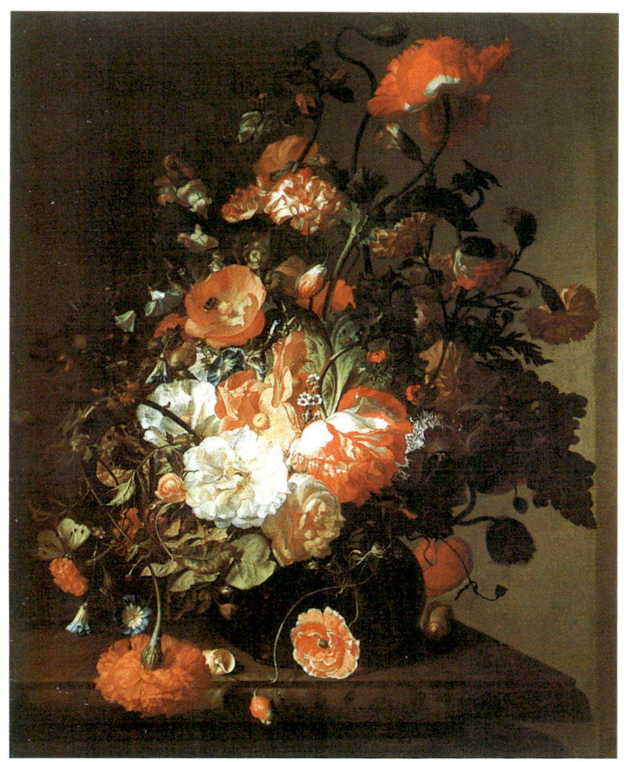

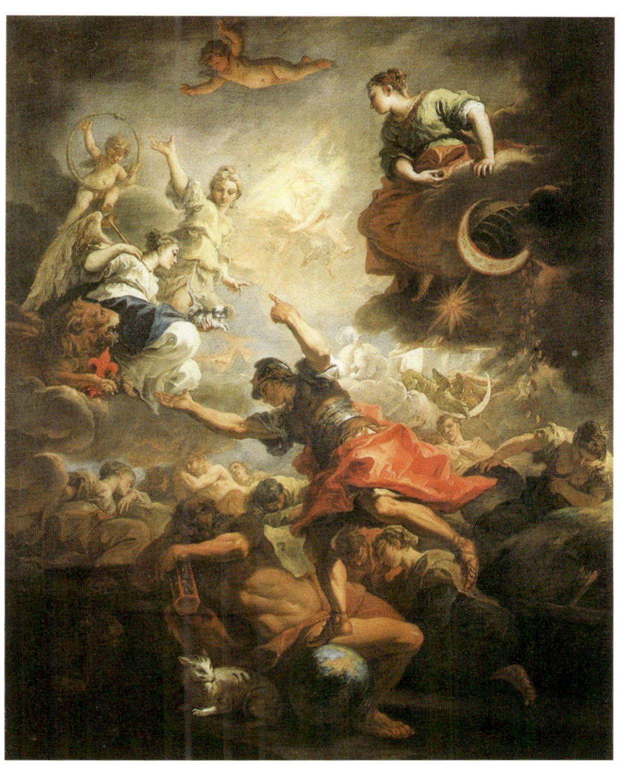

528. Rachel Ruysch, 1664-1750, Baroque, Dutch, *Flower Still-Life,* after 1700. Oil on canvas, 75.5 x 60.7 cm. The Toledo Museum of Art, Toledo.

529. Sebastiano Ricci, 1659-1734, Rococo, Italian, *Allegory of Tuscany,* 1706. Oil on canvas, 90 x 70.5 cm. Galleria degli Uffizi, Florence.

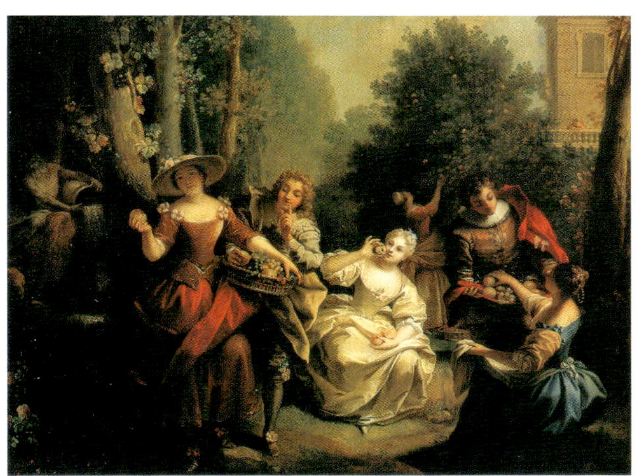

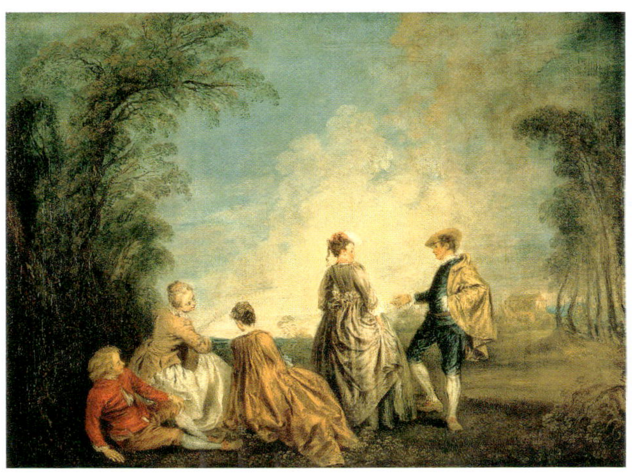

530. Jean Raoux, 1677-1734, Rococo, French, *Taste* (From the *Five Senses* series), c. 1715-1734. Oil on canvas, 56.5 x 72 cm. Pushkin Museum of Fine Arts, Moscow.

531. Antoine Watteau, 1684-1721, Rococo, French, *An Embarrassing Proposal,* c. 1716. Oil on canvas, 65 x 85 cm. The State Hermitage Museum, St Petersburg.

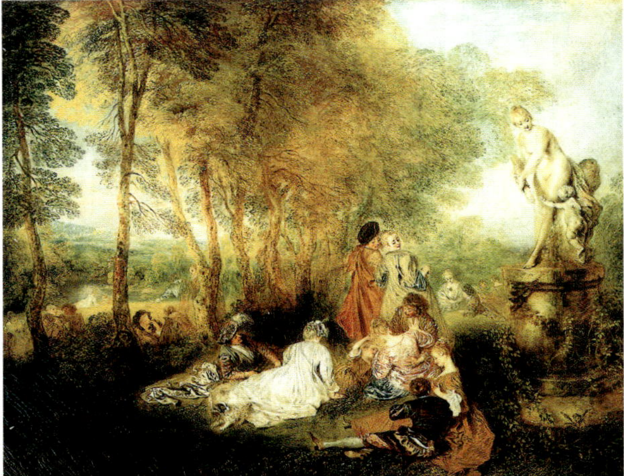

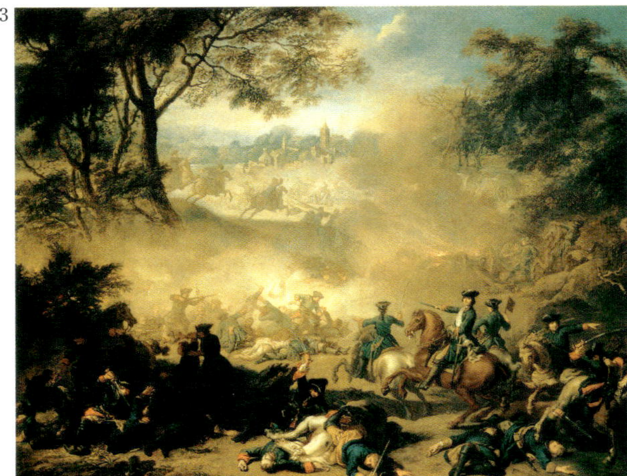

532. Antoine Watteau, 1684-1721, Rococo, French,
A Love Festival, 1717. Oil on canvas, 61 x 75 cm.
Gemäldegalerie Alte Meister, Dresden.

533. Jean-Marc Nattier, 1685-1766, Rococo, French,
The Battle of Lesnaya, 1717. Oil on canvas, 90 x 112 cm.
Pushkin Museum of Fine Arts, Moscow.

535. Antoine Watteau, 1684-1721, Rococo, French,
Gilles, 1717-1719. Oil on canvas, 185 x 150 cm.
Musée du Louvre, Paris.

This painting, either called Gilles *or* Pierrot *still has an undefined
subject. The sitter taking over the foreground is exceptionally
monumental for a work by Watteau. In the background are
the four traditional characters from the Commedia dell'arte,
accompanying Pierrot but contrasting in their attitude.*

534. Canaletto (Giovanni Antonio Canal), 1697-1768, Rococo,
Italian, *Venice: Campo S. Vidal and Santa Maria della Carità
(The Stonemason's Yard),* 1727-1728.
Oil on panel, 123.8 x 162.9 cm. National Gallery, London.

*The bold composition, the densely applied paint and the careful
execution of the figures are characteristic of Canaletto's works of
the mid to late 1720s. This unusual view across the Grand Canal
shows the campanile (bell-tower) of Santa Maria della Carita that
collapsed after the painting was made and was never rebuilt.*

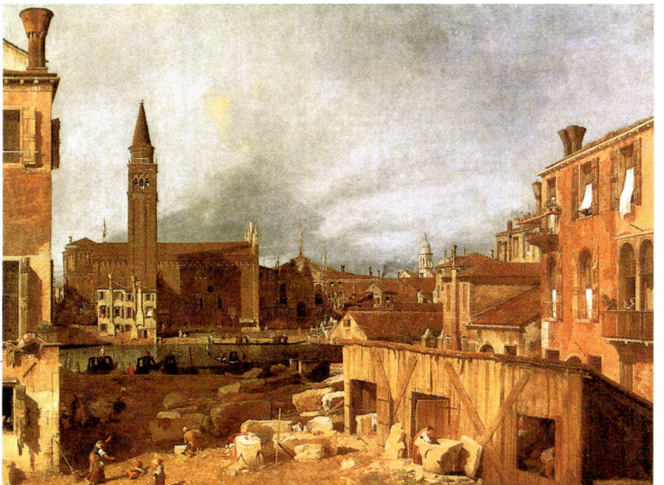

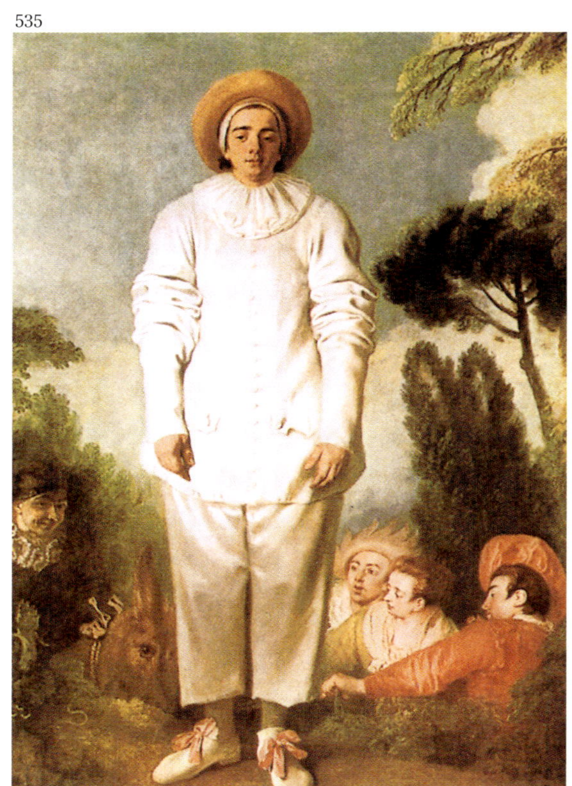

536. Jean-Baptiste Oudry, 1686-1755, Baroque, French, *Still Life with Fruit,* 1721.
Oil on Canvas, 74 x 92 cm.
The State Hermitage Museum, St Petersburg.

537. Antoine Watteau, 1684-1721, Rococo, French, *The Pilgrimage to the Island of Cythera,* 1718. Oil on canvas, 129 x 194 cm.
Schloss Charlottenburg, Berlin.

This painting caused Watteau to be dubbed with the official title of peintre de fêtes galantes. *The scene is set on the Isle of Cythera, the island of love itself; a statue of Aphrodite stands at the edge of the woods and cupids accompany their new acquaintances, hovering above the cavaliers and their female companions. There is no emotional crescendo despite the assumption implied by the artist's choice of subject. The story of Watteau's* The Pilgrimage to the Island of Cythera *is also noteworthy. The minutes of the Royal Academy of Painting and Sculpture of 30 June, 1712, stated that the painter would be given a subject by the Academy's director. Then these words were crossed out and replaced by the following statement: "The subject for his acceptance work has been left to his discretion." Watteau's choice of subject matter was undoubtedly determined by his own ideas and by his opposition not only to the official hierarchy of genres, but also to the practice of the times whereby distinguished patrons imposed their own choice of subject on painters. Watteau's* The Pilgrimage to the Island of Cythera *was probably another example of his own imaginary "theatre". In such paintings, the landscape is bathed in a soft golden hue reminiscent of Venetian painting. The gradual change of this tone, which becomes increasingly light and translucent in the distance, brilliantly conveys the atmosphere and demonstrates the golden, warm range of tones used by the artist in his prime.*

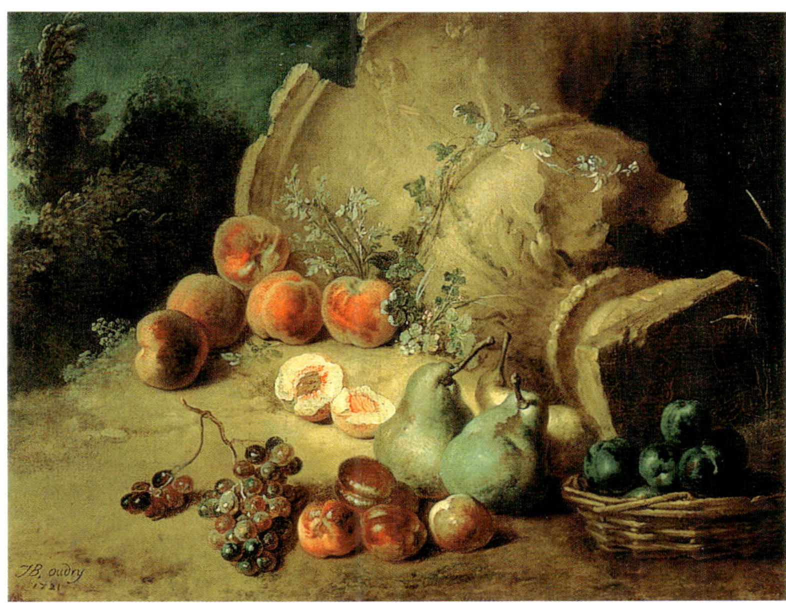

536

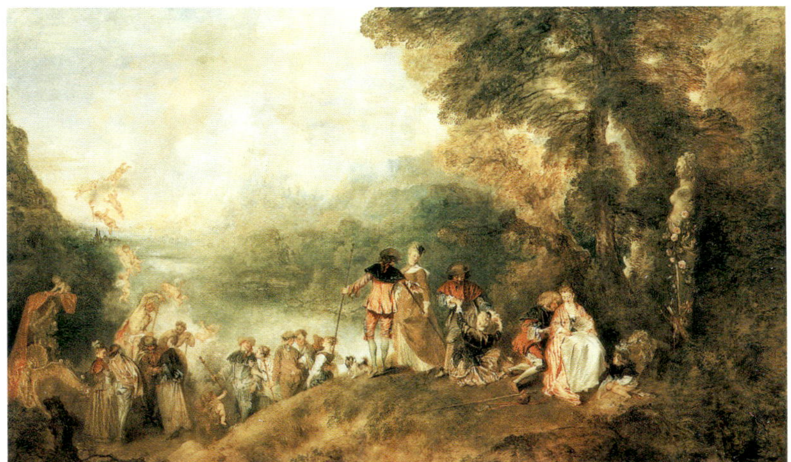

537

ANTOINE WATTEAU
(1684 VALENCIENNES – 1721 NOGENT-SUR-MARNE)

Watteau incarnates all the grace, all the intelligence, all the poetry of the eighteenth century, when French tastes were triumphant throughout the whole of Europe. He is well known as one of the key figures of Rococo art. He arrived in Paris around 1702, where he worked with Gillot, who gave him the interest in scenes of everyday life and theatrical costumes. There he also had access to the gallery of the Luxembourg palace painted by Rubens, who had a great influence on him, more by the subject he painted than by his style, meaning the idea of the *fetes galantes*. Watteau's paintings being of such a new type, he acquired in 1717, a new title given to him by the Academy, *peintre de fêtes galantes*, created expressly for him. Surprisingly, had he not existed, things would doubtless have been no different in the realm of painting.

We would, no doubt, have seen the development of the same decorative taste, the same bright, clear painting with amorous nudes and agreeable mythological subjects.

His world is indeed highly artificial, depicting some melancholy under apparent frivolity, reflecting the deep sense of love beyond the pleasure of the flesh, the enigmatic atmosphere brooding over his landscapes – tall trees in parks and glades with marble fountains and statues – and the drooping glance of lovers' eyes. He alone possessed that genius for colour which conveys a sense of softness and mystery even in brilliant light, a sense of music everywhere; that vigorous draughtsmanship which proclaims him equal to the greatest; that natural poetry arising from the dreams.

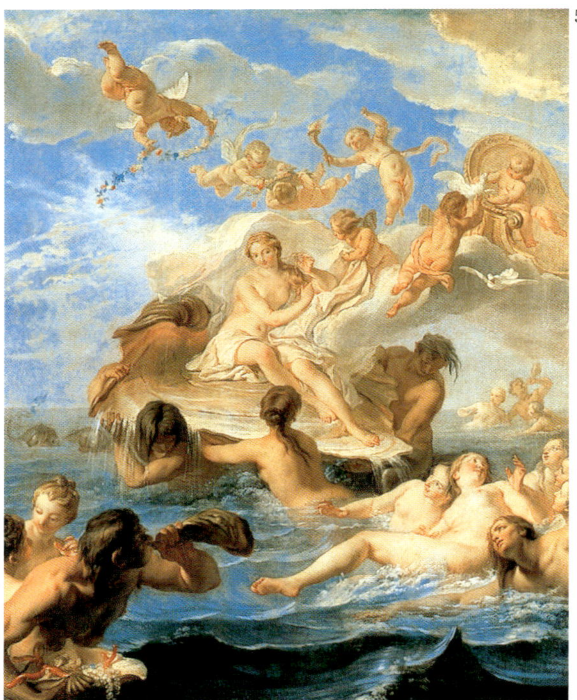

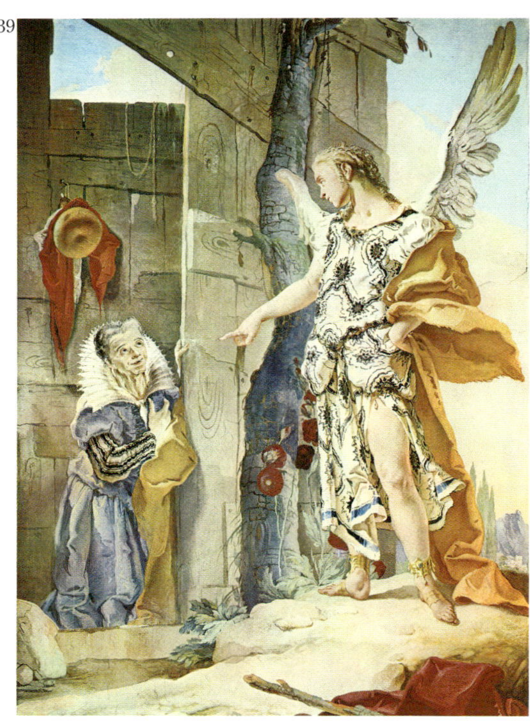

538. **Noël-Nicolas Coypel**, 1690-1734, Rococo, French,
The Birth of Venus, 1732. Oil on canvas, 81 x 65 cm.
The State Hermitage Museum, St Petersburg.

539. **Giovanni Battista Tiepolo**, 1696-1770, Rococo, Italian,
Sarah and the Archangel, 1726-1728. Fresco, c. 400 x 200 cm.
Palazzo Arcivescovile, Udine.

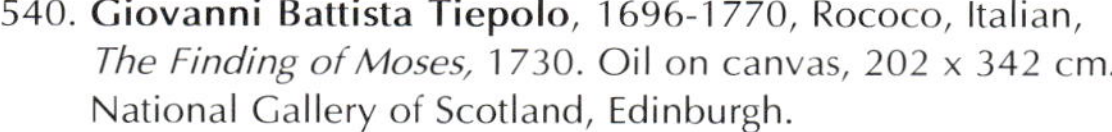

540. **Giovanni Battista Tiepolo**, 1696-1770, Rococo, Italian,
The Finding of Moses, 1730. Oil on canvas, 202 x 342 cm.
National Gallery of Scotland, Edinburgh.

*The dramatic impact of the painting is heightened by its impressive size
(the painting was originally even larger but a section has been cut, probably
in the nineteenth century), the colouring and the theatrical character.*

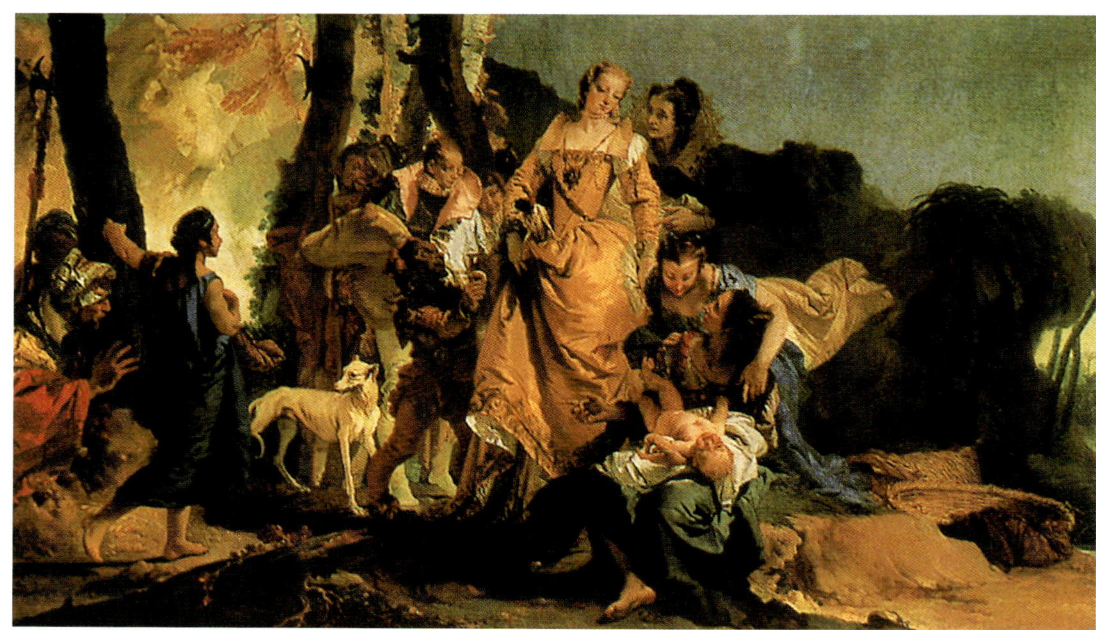

540

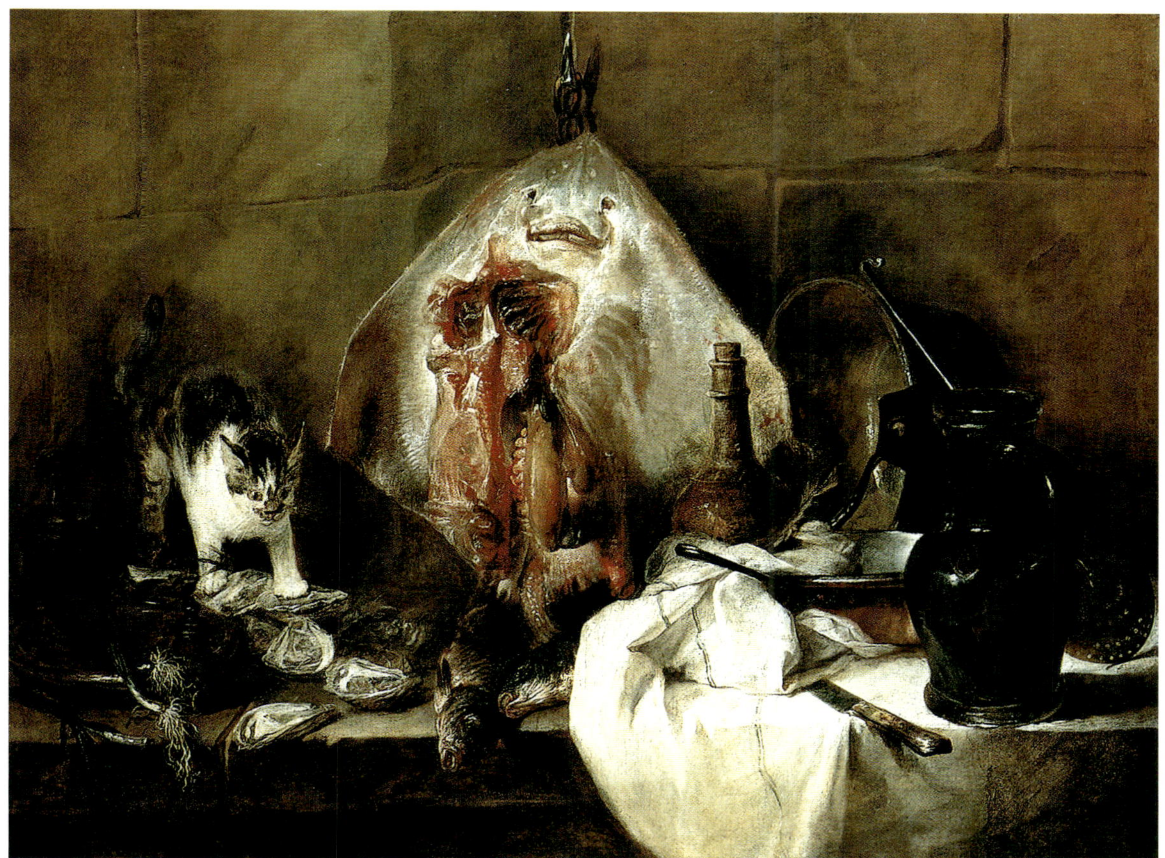

541. **Jean-Baptiste Chardin**, 1699-1779, Rococo, French,
The Ray, 1725-1726. Oil on canvas, 114 x 146 cm.
Musée du Louvre, Paris.

Nearly all the artist's works are small, thirty centimetres square or even less, but this one is a notable exception. They were made to be affordable for middle-class customers or sponsors. This work was the still-life with which Chardin was accepted at the Royal Academy of Painting and Sculpture.

The artist selected common objects for the common person. Chardin painted ordinary scenes with respect for both the hard-working middle class and their objects. Kitchen scenes were a favourite, this one dominated by a ray, a flat fish that has no bones but noted for its broad, wing-like pectoral fins.

JEAN-BAPTISTE SIMÉON CHARDIN
(1699 – 1779 PARIS)

Chardin in 1728 gained admittance to the Academy with two large canvases which were merely still-lifes: *The Ray* and *The Buffet*. Their technical merit is immediately striking: in these pieces, handled with extraordinary tact and felicity, are all the riches and subtlety of oil painting. But there also appears, even this early, the sense of intimacy and poetry of humble things which gives Chardin a place apart from even the best still-life and genre painters. Chardin is purely French; he is far nearer to the feeling of meditative quiet which animates the rustic scenes of Louis Le Nain a century earlier than to the spirit of light and superficial brilliance surrounding him, even

in the so-called realism of his time. He did not, like his predecessors, seek his models among the peasantry; he painted the petty bourgeoisie of Paris. But manners have been softened; the petty bourgeoisie were far removed from Le Nain's austere peasants. The housewives of Chardin are simply but neatly dressed and the same cleanliness is visible in the houses where they dwell. Everywhere a sort of refinement and good-fellowship constitute the charm of these little pictures of domestic life, unique in their way and superior, both in feeling and subject, to the masterpieces of some of the Dutch masters.

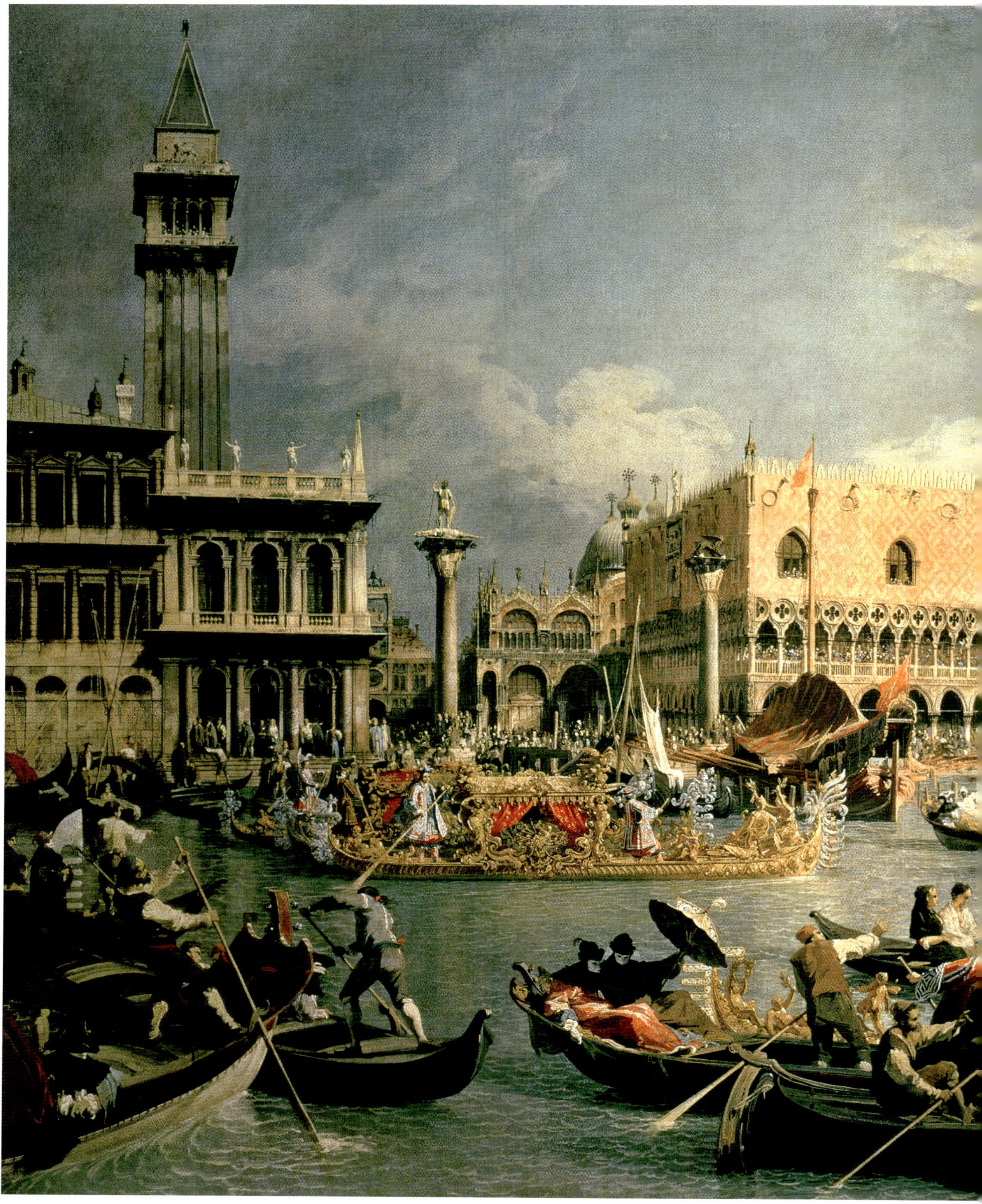

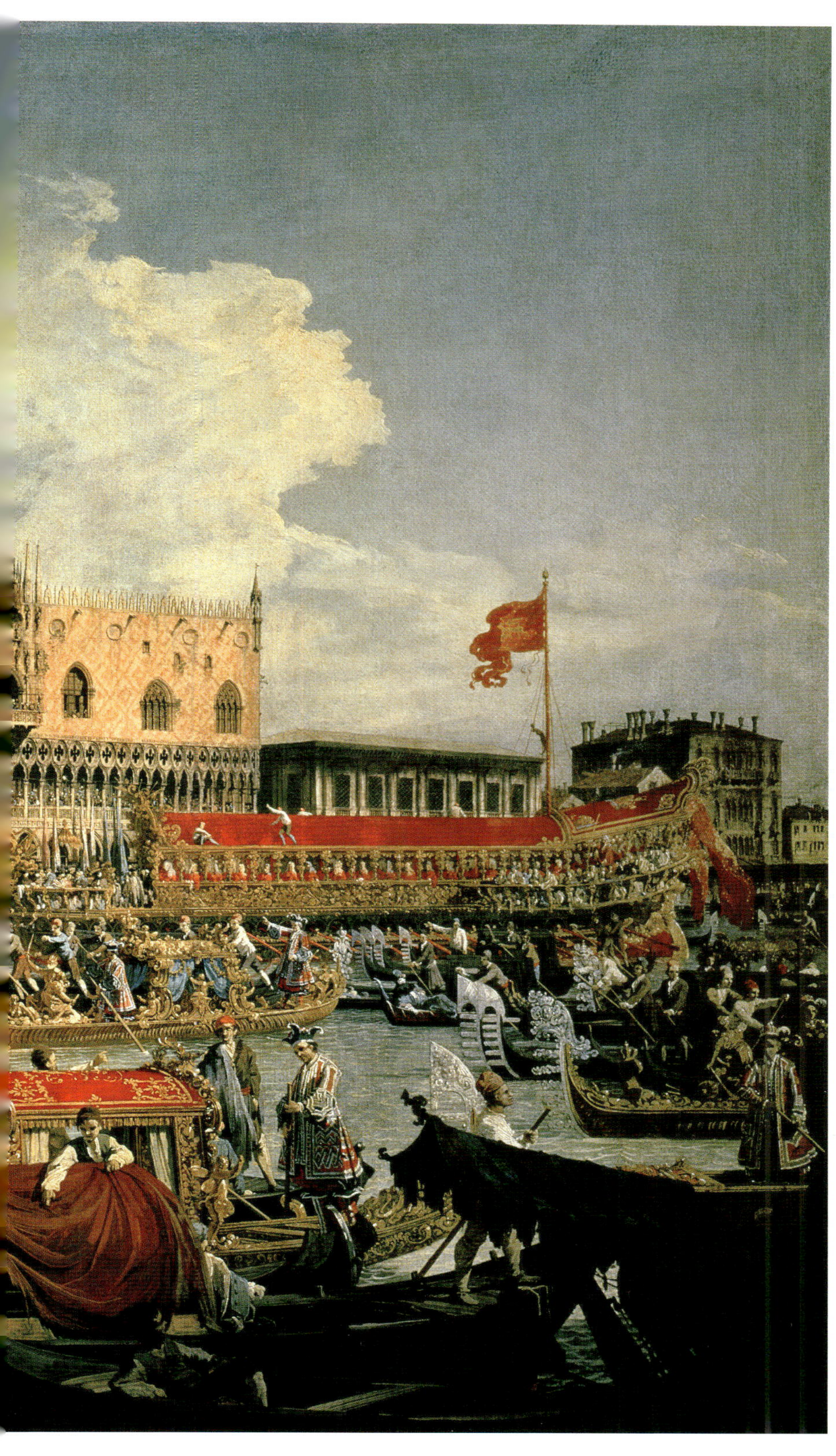

542. **Canaletto (Giovanni Antonio Canal)**, 1697-1768, Rococo, Italian, *The Bucintoro at the Molo on Ascension Day,* 1732. Oil on canvas, 182 x 259 cm. Aldo Crespi Collection, Milan.

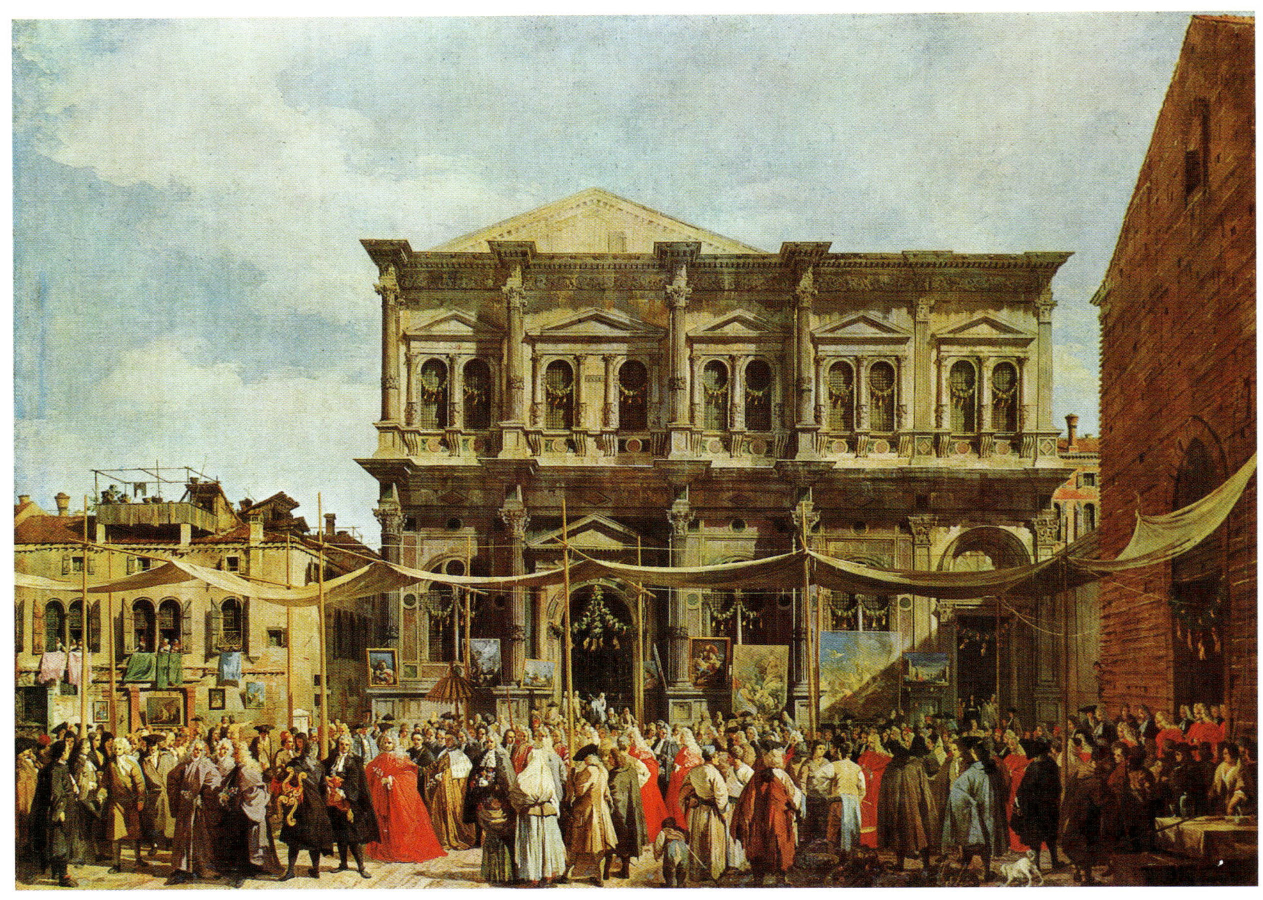

543. **Canaletto (Giovanni Antonio Canal)**, 1697-1768, Rococo, Italian,
Venice: The Feast Day of St Roch, c. 1735.
Oil on canvas, 147 x 199 cm.
National Gallery, London.

CANALETTO (GIOVANNI ANTONIO CANAL)
(1697 – 1768 VENICE)

Canaletto began his career as a theatrical scene painter, like his father, in the Baroque tradition. Influenced by Giovanni Panini, he is specialised in vedute (views) of Venice, his birth place. Strong contrast between light and shadow is typical of this artist. Furthermore, if some of those views are purely topographical, others include festivals or ceremonial subjects. He also published, thanks to John Smith, his agent, a series of etchings of Cappricci. His main purchasers were British aristocracy because his views reminded them of their Grand Tour. In his paintings geometrical perspective and colours are structuring. Canaletto spent ten years in England. John Smith sold Canaletto's works to George III, creating the major part of the Royal Canaletto Collection. His greatest works influenced landscape painting in the nineteenth century.

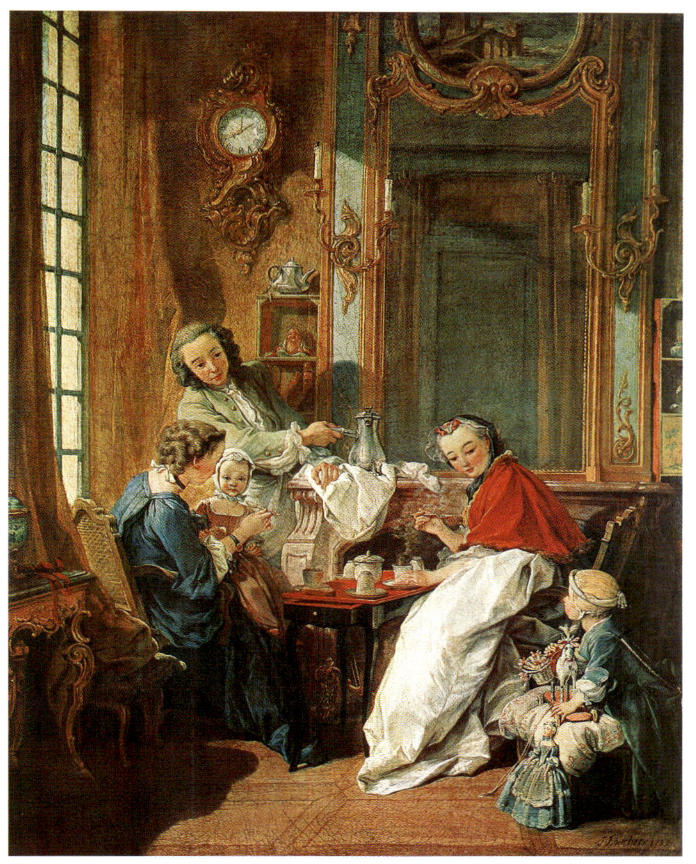

WILLIAM HOGARTH
(1697 – 1764 LONDON)

Hogarth's case is a strange one. The famous series of paintings, *The Harlot's Progress*, *The Rake's Progress*, and *Marriage à la Mode*, are pictorial moralities of a kind which seems completely outside the domain of art; for Hogarth's considerations of morality counted infinitely more than those of art and beauty. He is known to have said that he created "painted comedy" and considered it as a work "of public utility". His morality was founded on good, sturdy, practical truths and was not stirred by any breath of heroism, but he imbued it all with such verve, such powerful vitality, he paraded and set in motion such a gallery of types, of characters whose blatant truthfulness hits us in the eye, that all criticism is silenced and reservations of the fastidious melt away.

This auto-didactic personage, disdainful of all culture, this Englishman who desired to be nothing more, was not without influence on the most cultured, refined, intelligent, learned and cosmopolitan of the great English painters, the instigator and first president of the Royal Academy, a great amateur and collector and perfect gentleman, and author of remarkable writings on art.

544. **François Boucher**, 1703-1770, Rococo, French, *An Afternoon Meal*, 1739. Oil on canvas, 81 x 65 cm. Musée du Louvre, Paris.

545. **William Hogarth**, 1697-1764, Rococo, English, *A Rake's Progress, Tavern Scene*, c. 1735. Oil on canvas, 62.2 x 75 cm. Courtesy of the Trustees of Sir John Soane's Museum, London.

This work is also called The Orgy. It is scene III of the series about the exploits of a rake, a debouched or corrupt man. The location of the scene is a brothel that was popular in London at the time. Novelists describing the period have described how entertaining young ladies, shockingly without stockings, would dance while using a mirror (the silver plate on the left in the painting) and candle to display themselves provocatively. But that is merely one of several visual references in the scene of the story this art is illustrating. Viewers can see Hogarth's engraving of the work at the Metropolitan Museum of Art in New York City.

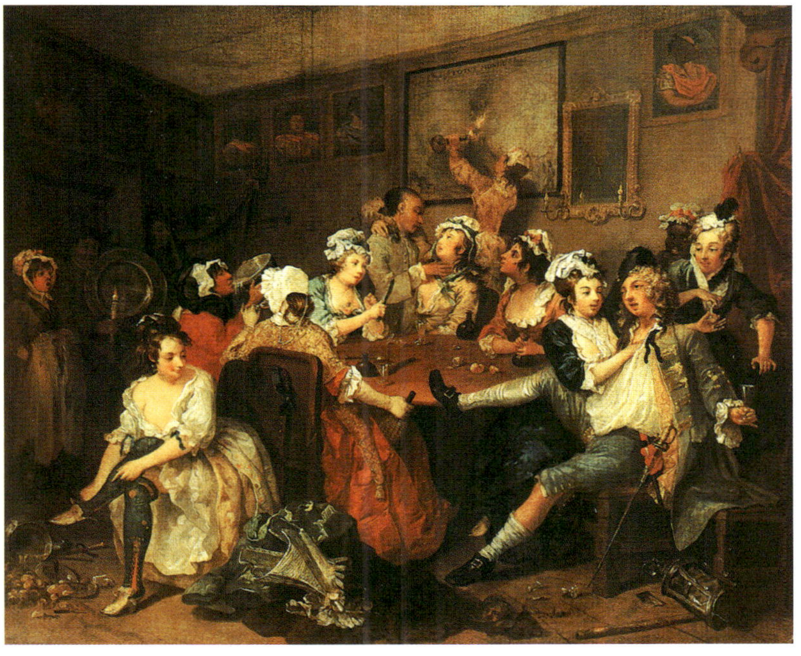

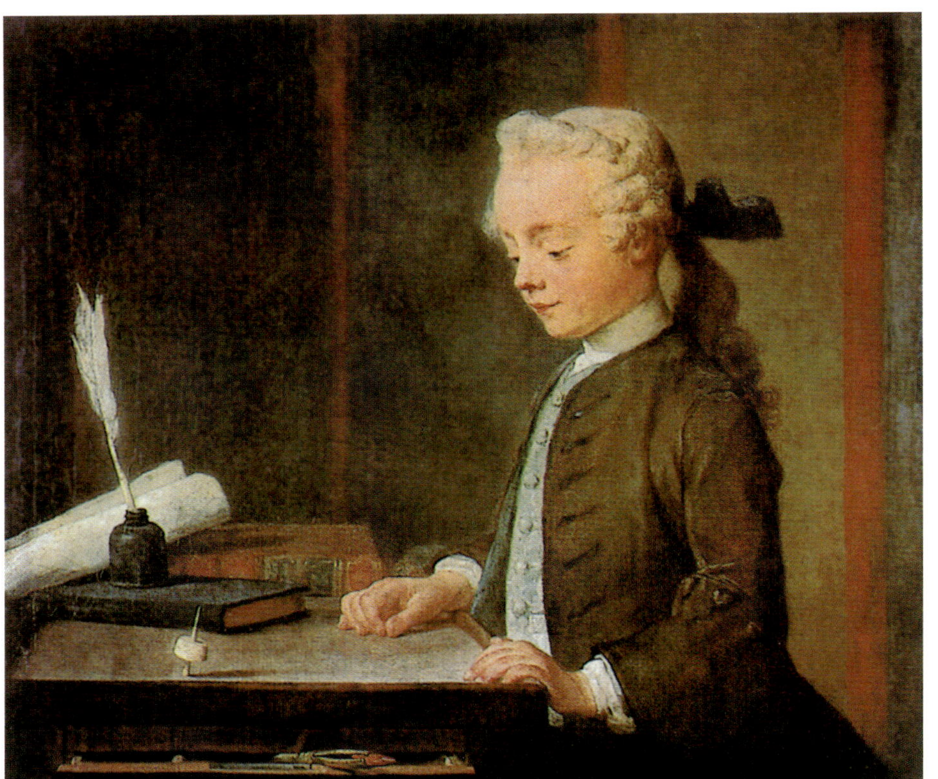

546

546. **Jean-Baptiste Chardin**,
1699-1779, Rococo, French,
Child with Top, c. 1738.
Oil on canvas, 68 x 76 cm.
Musée du Louvre, Paris.

547. **Jean-Baptiste Chardin**,
1699-1779, Rococo, French,
The Governess, 1739.
Oil on canvas, 46.7 x 37.5 cm.
National Gallery of Canada,
Ottawa.

548. **Pietro Longhi**, 1702-1785,
Rococo, Italian,
The Introduction, 1740.
Oil on canvas, 66 x 55 cm.
Musée du Louvre, Paris.

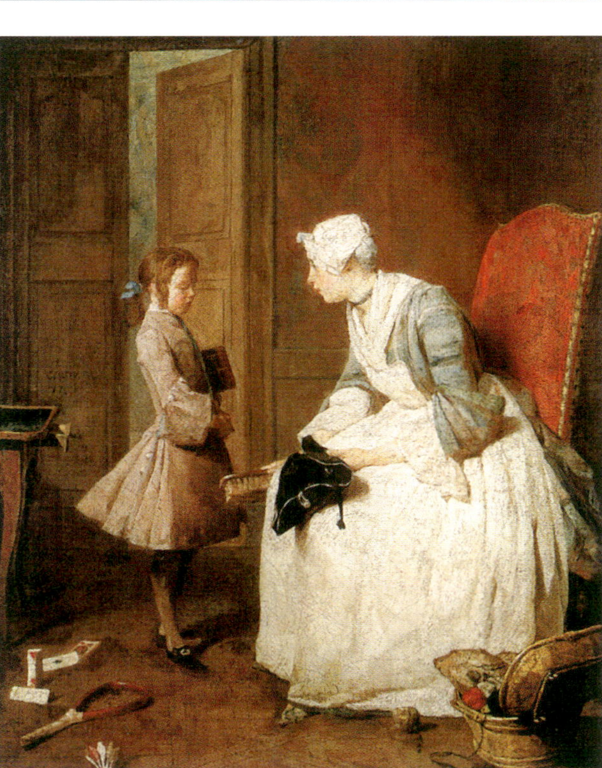

547

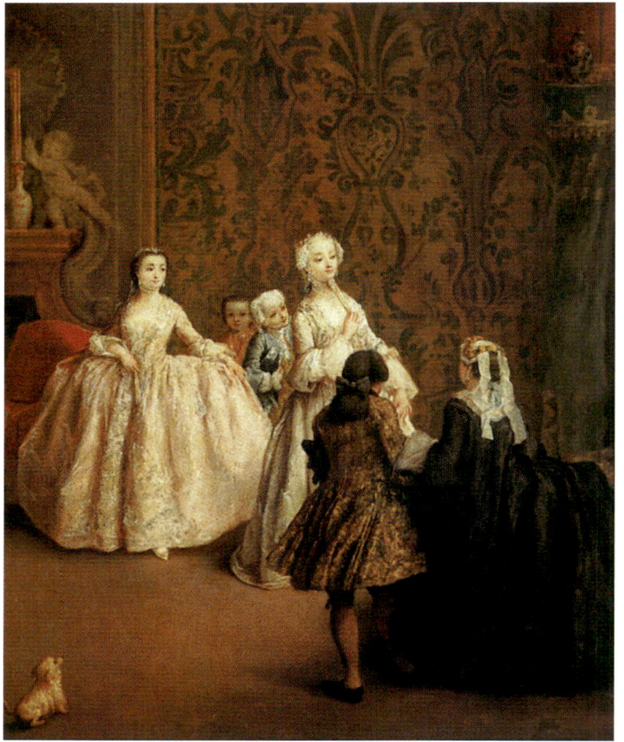

548

549. **William Hogarth**, 1697-1764, Rococo,
English, *The Shrimp Girl,* 1740-1750.
Oil on canvas, 64 x 53 cm.
National Gallery, London.

550. **Giovanni Battista Piazzetta**, 1683-1754,
Rococo, Italian, *Susanna and the Elders,* 1740.
Oil on canvas, 100 x 135 cm.
Galleria degli Uffizi, Florence.

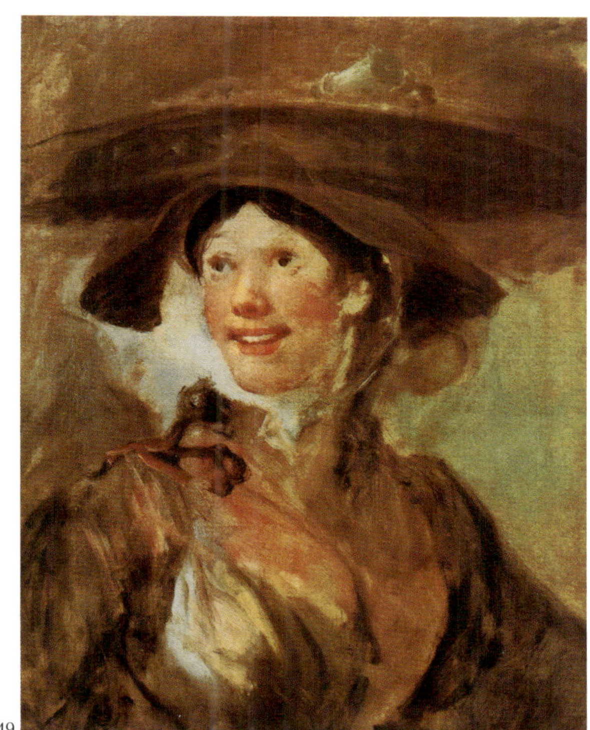

549

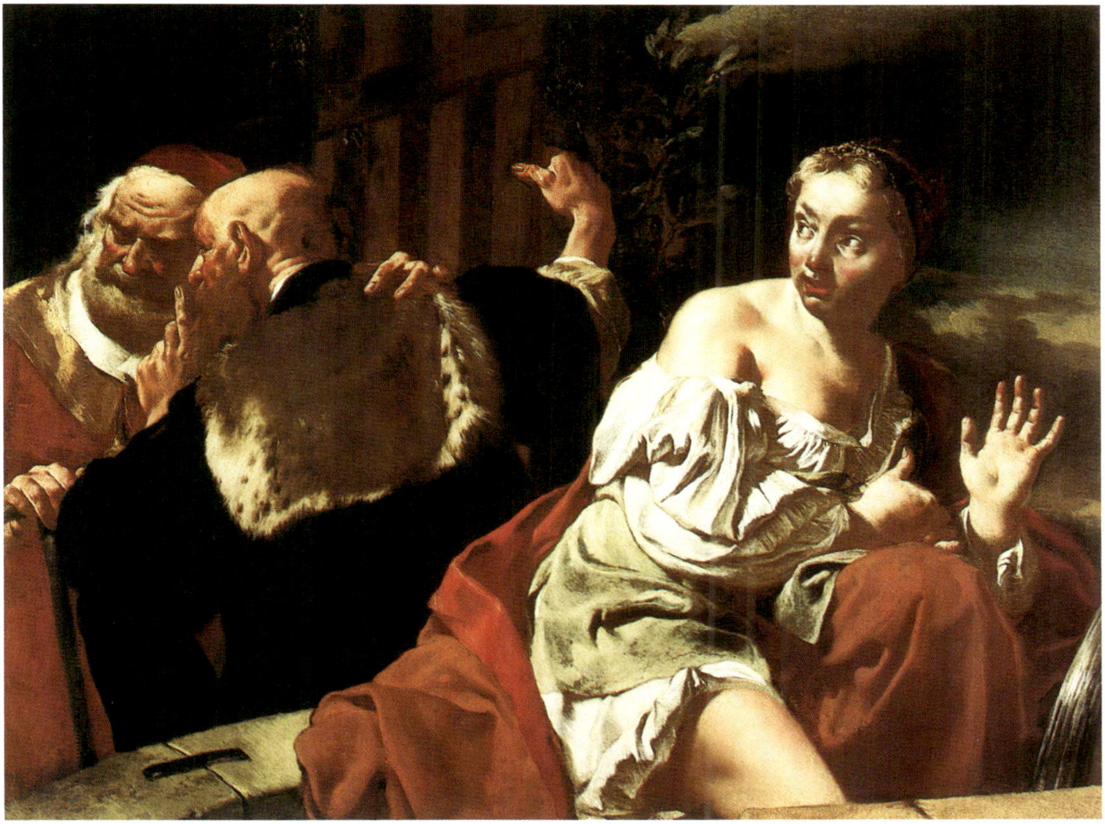

550

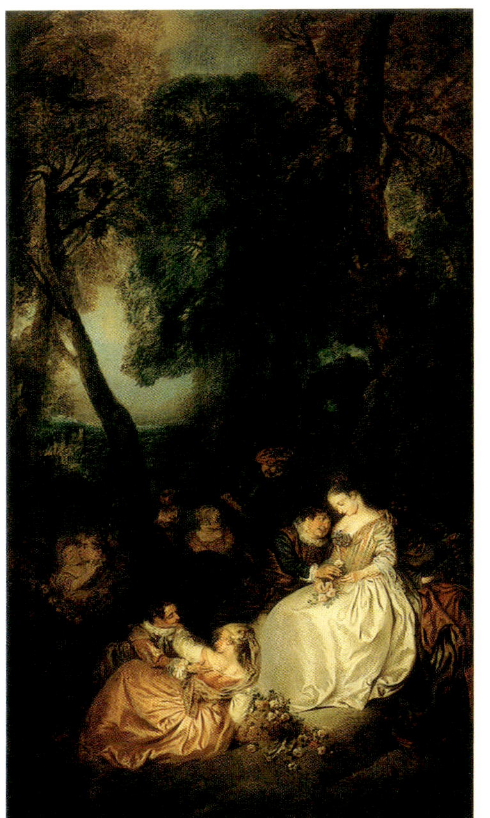

551

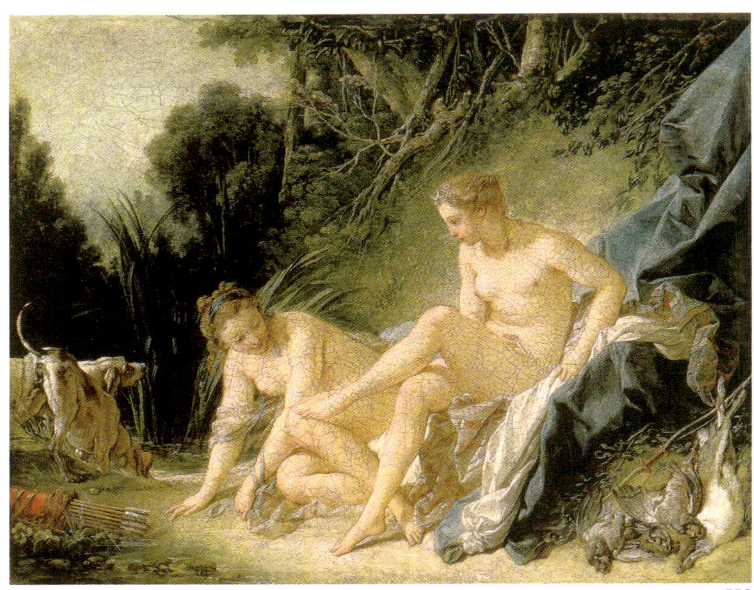

552

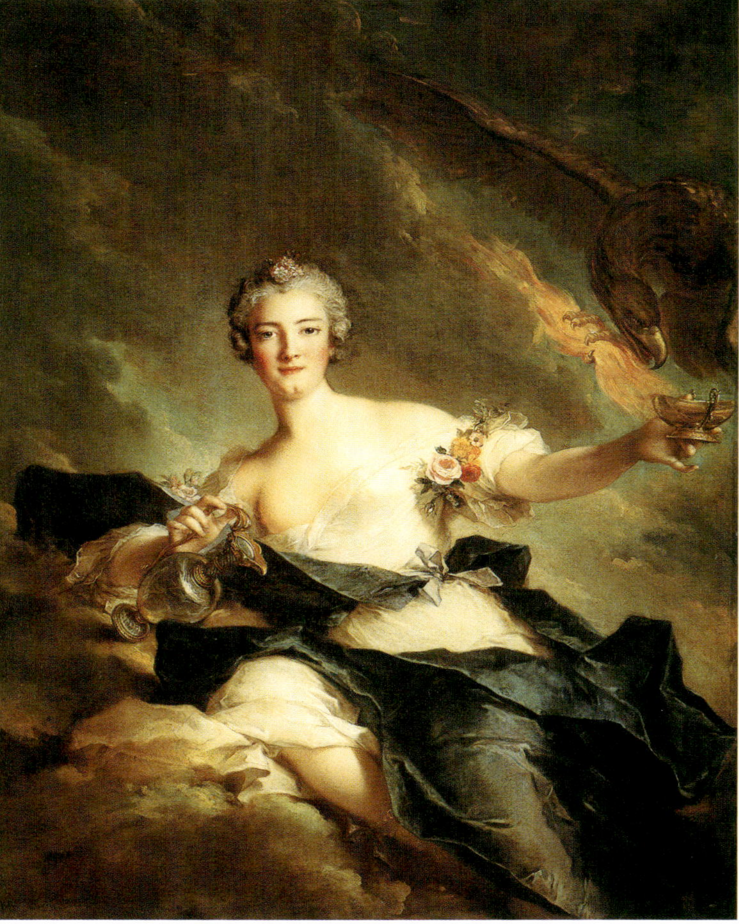

553

551. Jean-Baptiste Pater, 1695-1736, Rococo,
French, *Scene in a Park*,
first half of the 18th century.
Oil on canvas, 149 x 84 cm.
The State Hermitage Museum, St Petersburg.

552. François Boucher, 1703-1770, Rococo,
French, *Diana Resting after her Bath*, 1742.
Oil on canvas, 57 x 73 cm.
Musée du Louvre, Paris.

*This painting shows the interest that Boucher took
in the representation of women in nature. Both
are matching in a subtle combination of colours.
The sensuality of the women is enhanced by the
light coming from the left of the painting and
the modelling of their bodies. Here Diana is
accompanied by her traditional symbols: the
moon crescent, the bow and quiver.*

553. Jean-Marc Nattier, 1685-1766, Rococo,
French, *The Duchesse d'Orléans, as Hebe*, 1744.
Oil on canvas, 144 x 110 cm.
Musée du Louvre, Paris.

*Noticed by Louis XIV, Nattier specialised in
court portraiture and realised a series of
allegorical portraits marked with the soft
modelling of the faces.*

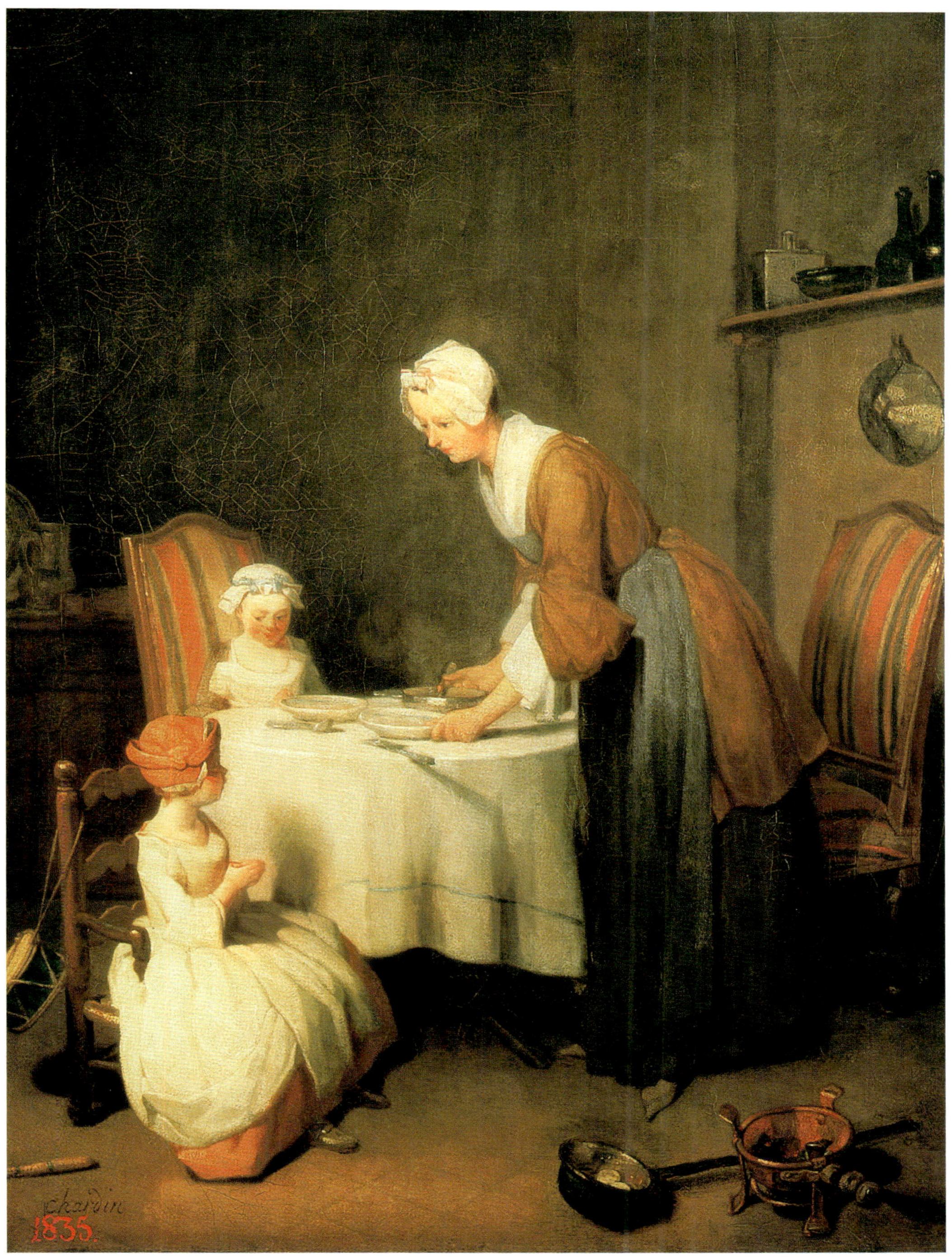

554. **Jean-Baptiste Chardin**, 1699-1779, Rococo, French, *Saying Grace (Le Benedicité),* 1744.
Oil on Canvas, 49.5 x 38.4 cm. The State Hermitage Museum, St Petersburg.

Chardin chooses here a theme often depicted by the Dutch masters of the seventeenth century. In contrast with the thick layer of painting he was using in his former works, Chardin uses here a smoother touch.

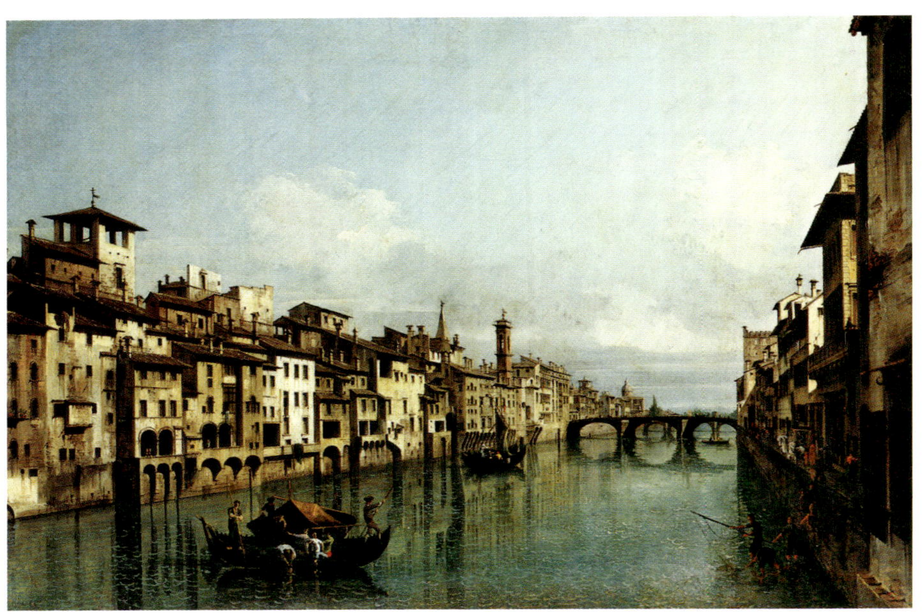

555. **Giovanni Paolo Panini**, 1691-1765, Rococo, Italian, *The River Arno with Ponte Santa Trinita*, 1742. Oil on canvas, 62 x 90 cm. Szépmüvészeti Múzeum, Budapest.

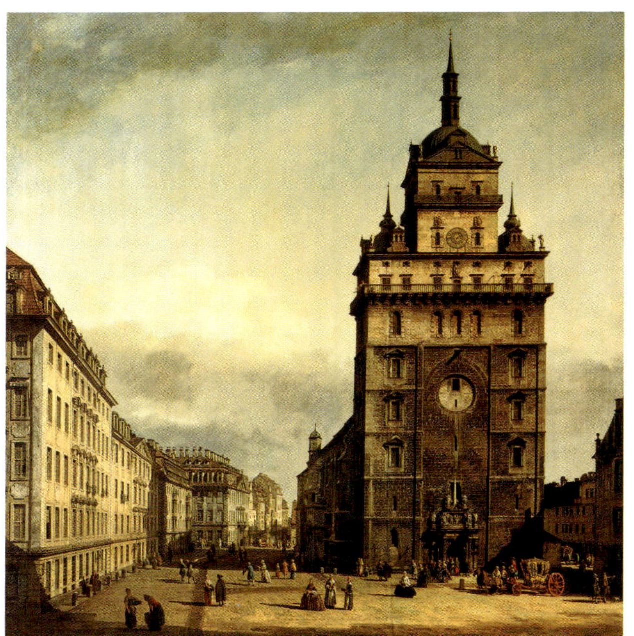

556. **Bernardo Bellotto**, 1720-1780, Rococo, Italian, *Square with the Kreuzkirche in Dresden*, 1751. Oil on canvas, 197 x 187 cm. The State Hermitage Museum, St Petersburg.

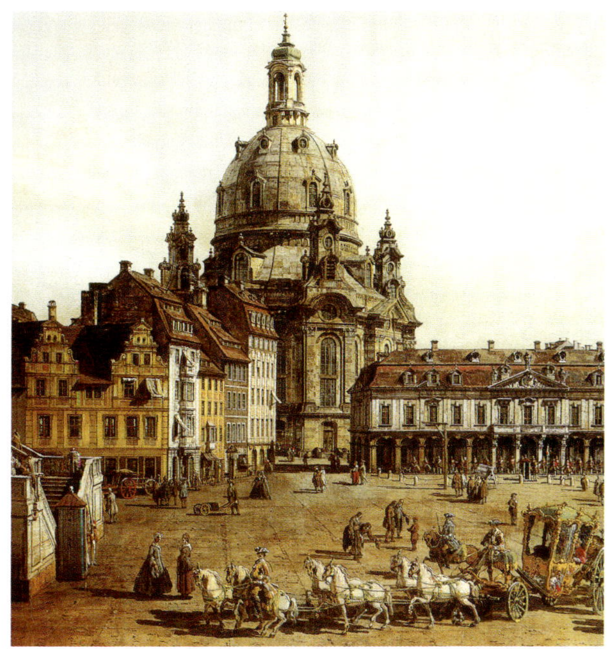

557. **Canaletto (Giovanni Antonio Canal)**, 1697-1768, Rococo, Italian, *Dresden, View from the Right Bank of the Elbe*, 1747. Oil on canvas, 133 x 237 cm. Gemäldegalerie Alte Meister, Dresden.

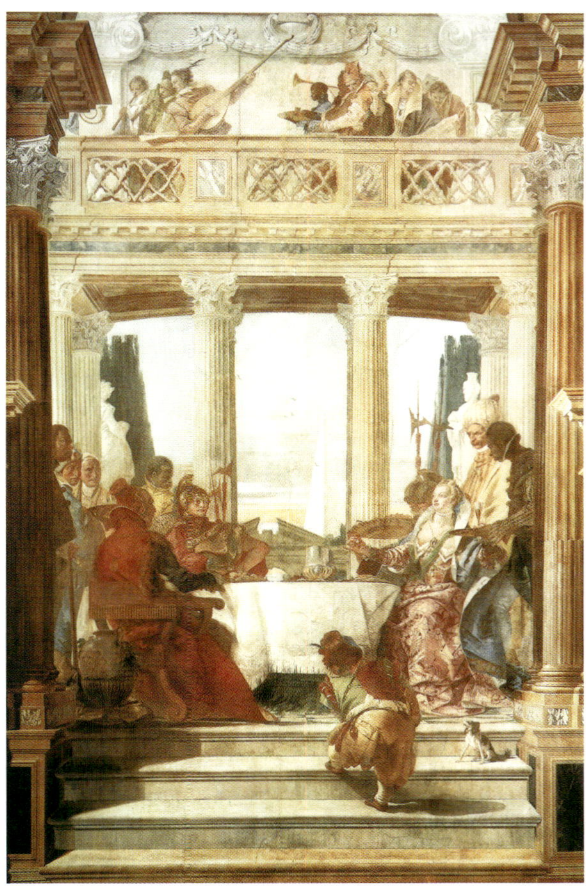

558. **Giovanni Battista Tiepolo**, 1696-1770, Rococo, Italian, *The Banquet of Cleopatra*, 1746. Fresco, 650 x 300 cm. Pallazzo Labia, Venice.

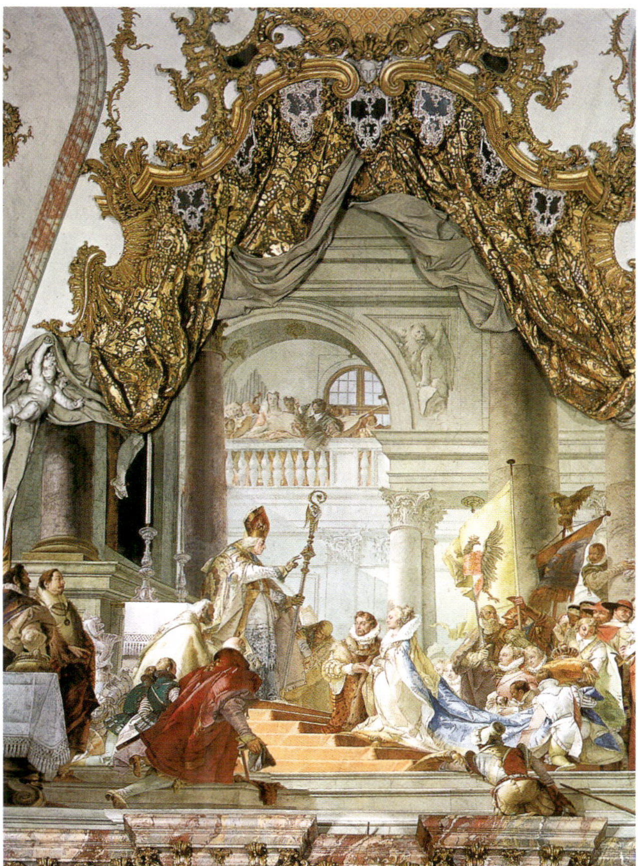

559. **Giovanni Battista Tiepolo**, 1696-1770, Rococo, Italian, *The Ceiling of the Kaisersaal: The Marriage of The Emperor Frederick Barbarosa and Beatrice of Burgundy*, 1750-1753. Fresco, 400 x 500 cm. Residence of the prince-bishop of Würzburg, Kaisersaal, Würzburg Residenz.

Asked to provide a work that would fill the space where a window once was, Tiepolo produced a dramatic recollection of the marriage of Beatrice of Burgundy and Frederick Barbarossa. Although the event took place 500 years earlier, the artist placed it in a contemporary setting. An elaborate guilt-stucco drape is drawn back by a carved putto. The steps of the bishop's platform seem to progress from the architecture of the wall. As an acknowledgment of the historical context of the event, and to give it the dignity it demanded, elements from classical periods (the architecture in the background) are atypically included. After achieving these works at the peak of mastering his technique, Tiepolo was invited to Madrid where he experienced the end of the influence of Rococo in himself. He also got caught up there in the energy of the Neoclassical as followed by the German painter Anton Raphael Mengs (1728-1779).

GIOVANNI BATTISTA TIEPOLO
(1696 VENICE – 1770 MADRID)

Giovanni Battista (Giambattista) Tiepolo was the last of the great Venetian decorators and the purest master of the Italian Rococo. He was a prodigy, a pupil of Gregorio Lazzarini, but already by age twenty-one he was established as a painter in Venice. He was an Italian artist of large-scale frescos, such as for the Residence in Würzburg and the Palacio Real in Madrid, both of which he did with his sons, Giovanni Dominico and Lorenzo, when he was in his fifties. In 1755, after his return from Würzburg, he was elected the first President of the Venetian Academy, before leaving for Spain where he died.

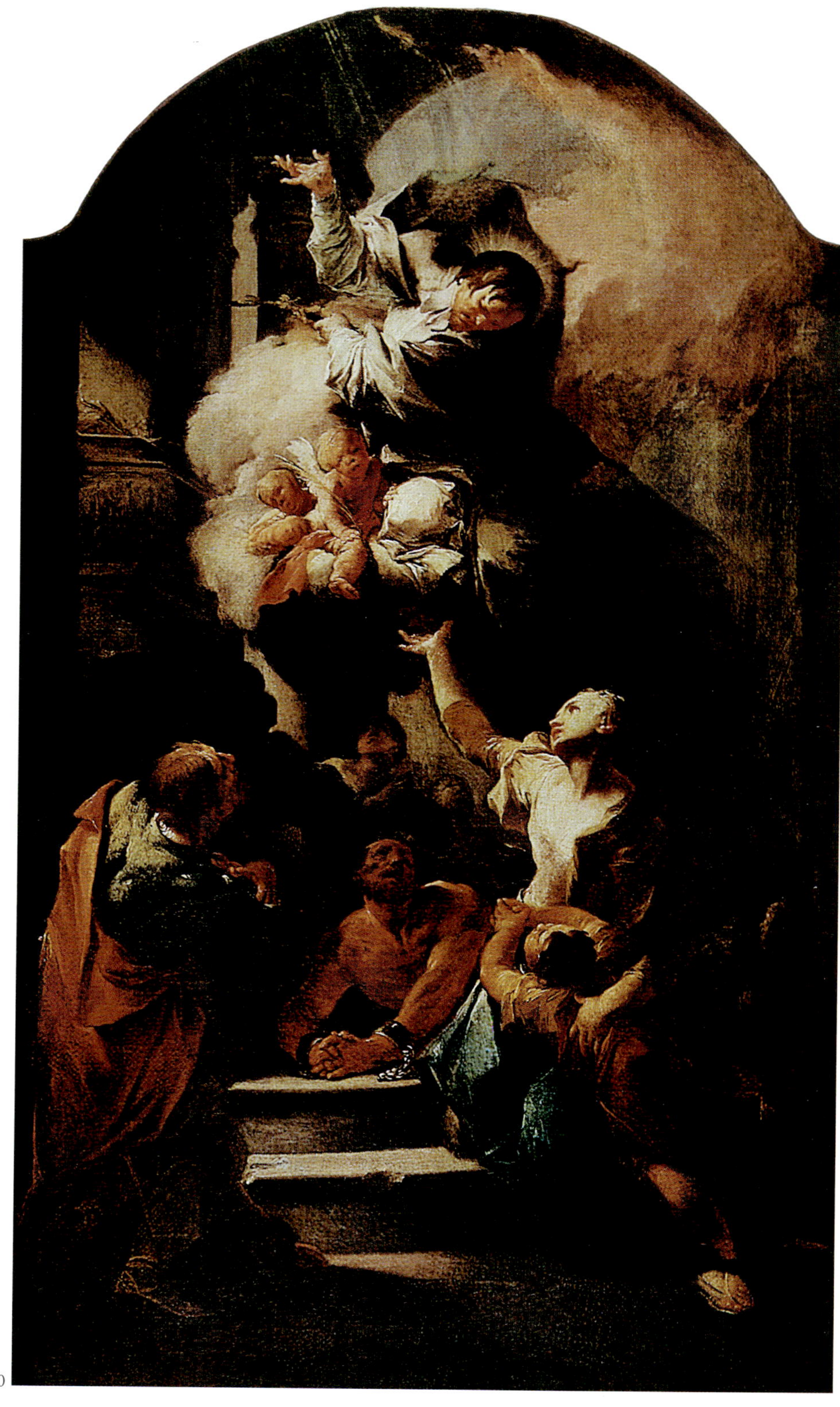

560

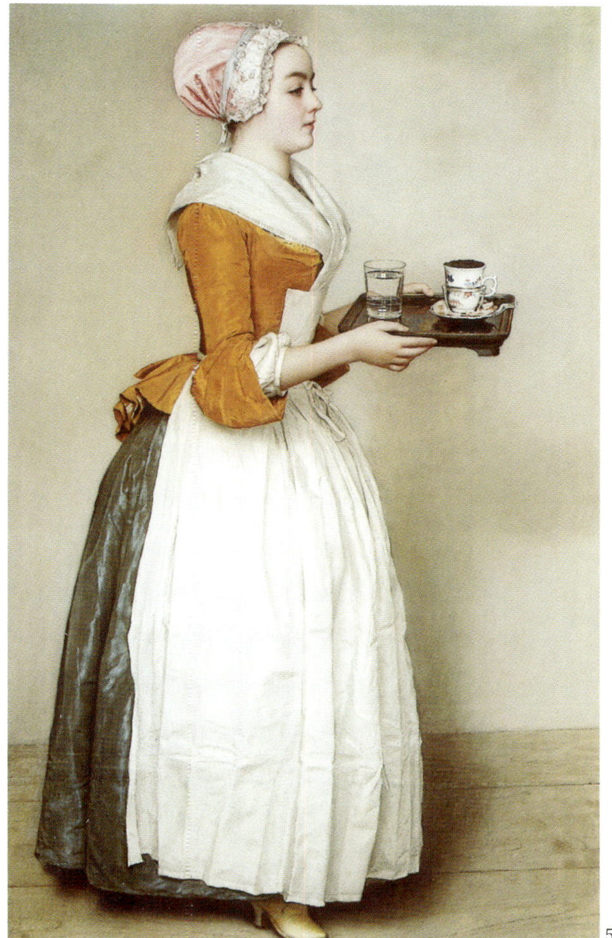

561

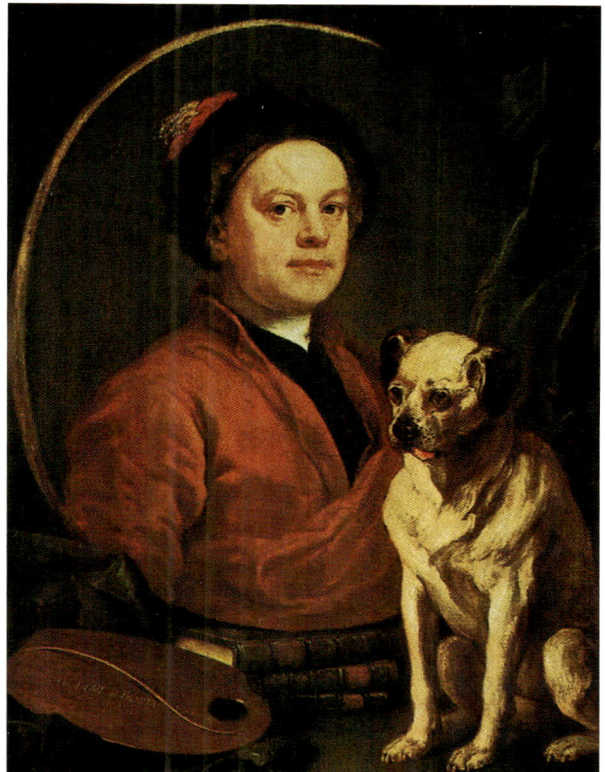

562

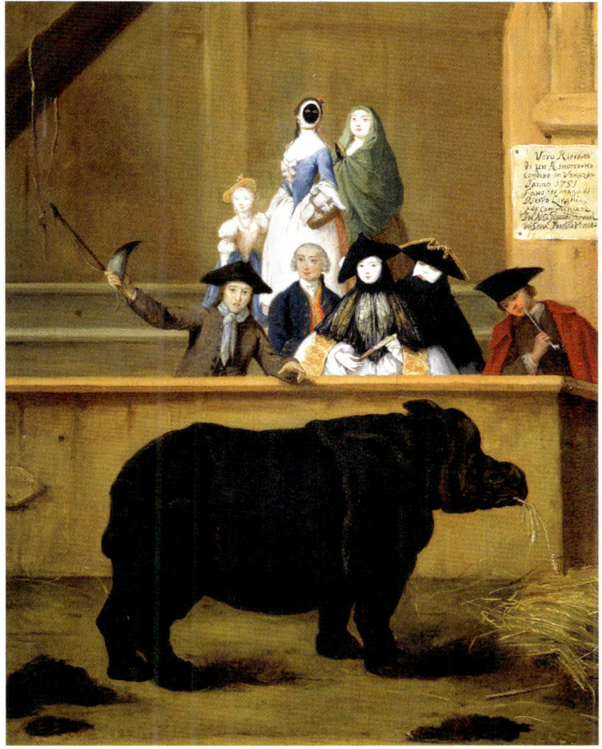

563

561. **Jean-Étienne Liotard**, 1702-1789, Baroque, Swiss,
The Chocolate-Girl, 1744-1745.
Pastel on paper. 82.5 x 52.5 cm.
Gemäldegalerie Alte Meister, Dresden.

562. **William Hogarth**, 1697-1764, Rococo, English,
The Painter and his Pug, 1745.
Oil on canvas, 90 x 70 cm. Tate Gallery, London.

563. **Pietro Longhi**, 1701-1785, Rococo, Italian,
The Rhinoceros, 1751.
Oil on canvas, 62 x 50 cm.
Ca' Rezzonico, Venice.

*Coming from exotic territories, the rhinoceros was displayed in
popular shows. Longhi depicts this Venetian scene during the
period of carnival and pays great attention to the depiction of
the characters and the atmosphere of excitement.*

560. **Paul Troger**, *Saint Sebastian Tended by Irene*, 1746.
Oil on canvas, 60 x 37 cm.
Österreichische Galerie, Vienna.

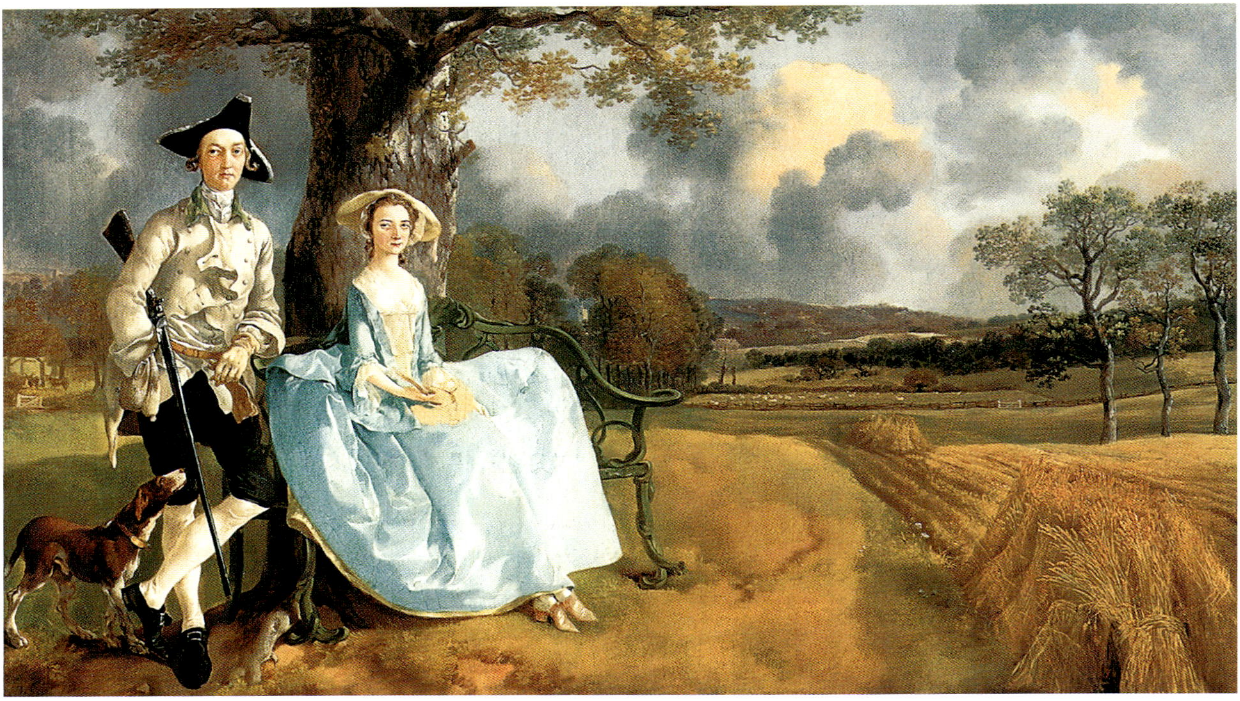

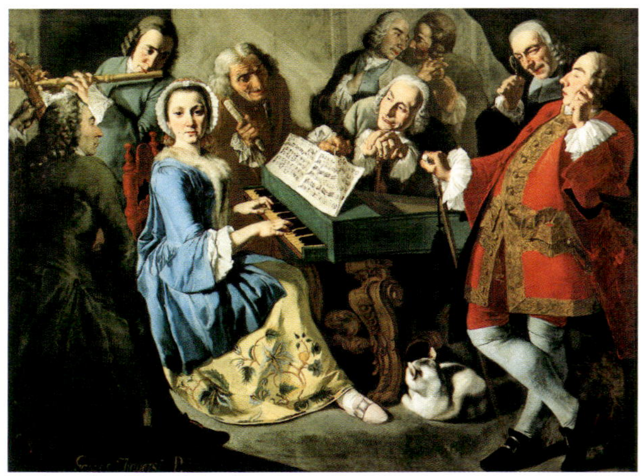

564

THOMAS GAINSBOROUGH
(1727 SUDBURY, SUFFOLK – 1788 LONDON)

Thomas Gainsborough was four years younger than Reynolds, but rivalled him in fame. He had nothing of the theorist, the teacher, the leader of a school, and he never thought of combining in his art skilful borrowings from the greatest artists of various foreign schools. Unlike Reynolds he never left England and, after several years of apprenticeship in London, spent the greater part of his life successively at Sudbury, Ipswich and Bath. Gainsborough is not an impeccable draughtsman, his compositions are not skilfully balanced like those of Reynolds, and his figures often seem disposed haphazardly on the canvas. But he has charm. He is a poet, and a poet by instinct, quivering with sensility, capricious and fantastic but always natural. Although he painted some good portraits of men he is, par excellence, the painter of women and children. A profound admirer of Van Dyck – he took him for a model – this admiration does not detract from his originality, which has a unique quality of seductiveness. On Van Dyck's themes, such as that of the boy clad in costly satin, a woman's face, long and delicate in its aristocratic grace, he composed entirely new variations.

564. **Thomas Gainsborough**, 1727-1788, Rococo, English,
Mr and Mrs Andrews, c. 1750. Oil on canvas, 70 x 119 cm.
National Gallery, London.

This portrait is the masterpiece of Gainsborough's early years. The landscape, the gun and the dog evoke Robert Andrews' estate and suggest the idea of an important landlord. His wife sits on an elaborate wooden bench; the painting of her lap is actually unfinished. The outdoor scene and informal postures of the couple follow the fashionable convention of the conversation piece.

565. **Gaspare Traversi**, c. 1722-1770, Rococo, Italian,
The Music Lesson, c. 1750.
Oil on canvas, 152 x 204.6 cm.
Nelson-Atkins Museum of Art, Kansas City.

565

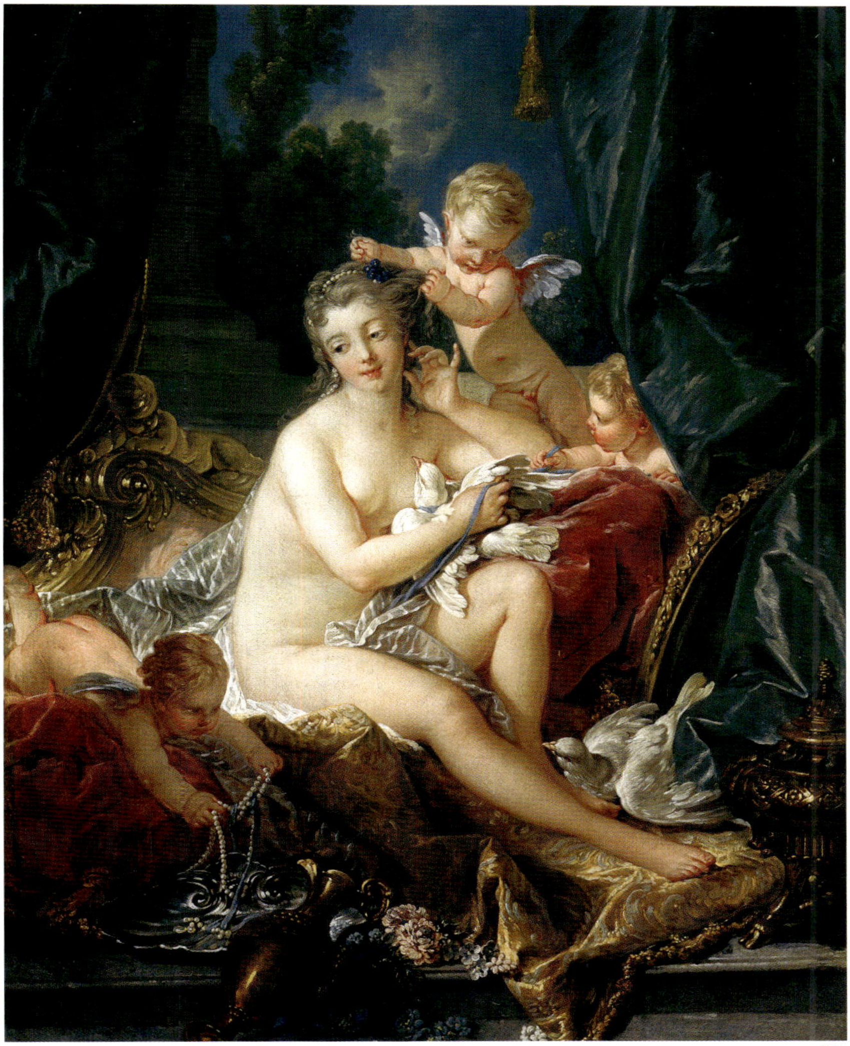

FRANÇOIS BOUCHER
(1703 – 1770 PARIS)

Boucher is typical of the artist whose ambitions are clearly defined and exactly proportioned to his capacity: he desired to please his contemporaries, to decorate walls and ceilings for them, and, in his better moments, realised perfectly what he set out to do. Thus it is he who best sums up the taste of the century. He played, *mutatis mutandis*, and with all the differences implied by the very names of the two sovereigns, Louis XIV – *le roi soleil* and Louis XV – *le bien aimé*, a role similar to that of Le Brun. He had decorative genius and the gift of composition; facile, elegant, and always perfectly balanced. He bore the weight of an immense output, illustrating a book, or finishing off a fan as aptly as he rumpled the draperies of complaisant goddesses or peopled sky and wave with rosy and golden nudes. As a decorator he had gifts in no way inferior to those of his fascinating contemporary Tiepolo; he could also paint excellent portraits, or render intimate scenes with brilliance and deftness.

566

566. **François Boucher**, 1703-1770, Rococo, French,
The Toilet of Venus, 1751.
Oil on canvas, 108.3 x 85.1 cm.
The Metropolitan Museum of Art, New York.

Commissioned by Mme de Pompadour, mistress of Louis XV, for her Château de Bellevue, this work shows Boucher's contribution to Rococo painting and to the repertoire of mythology.

567. **Gaspare Traversi**, c. 1722-1770, Rococo, Italian,
The Drawing Lesson, c. 1750.
Oil on canvas, 161.7 x 204 cm.
Nelson-Atkins Museum of Art, Kansas City.

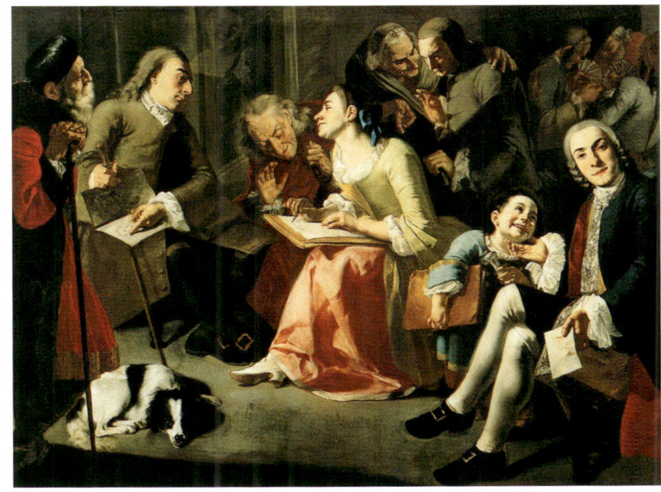

567

568

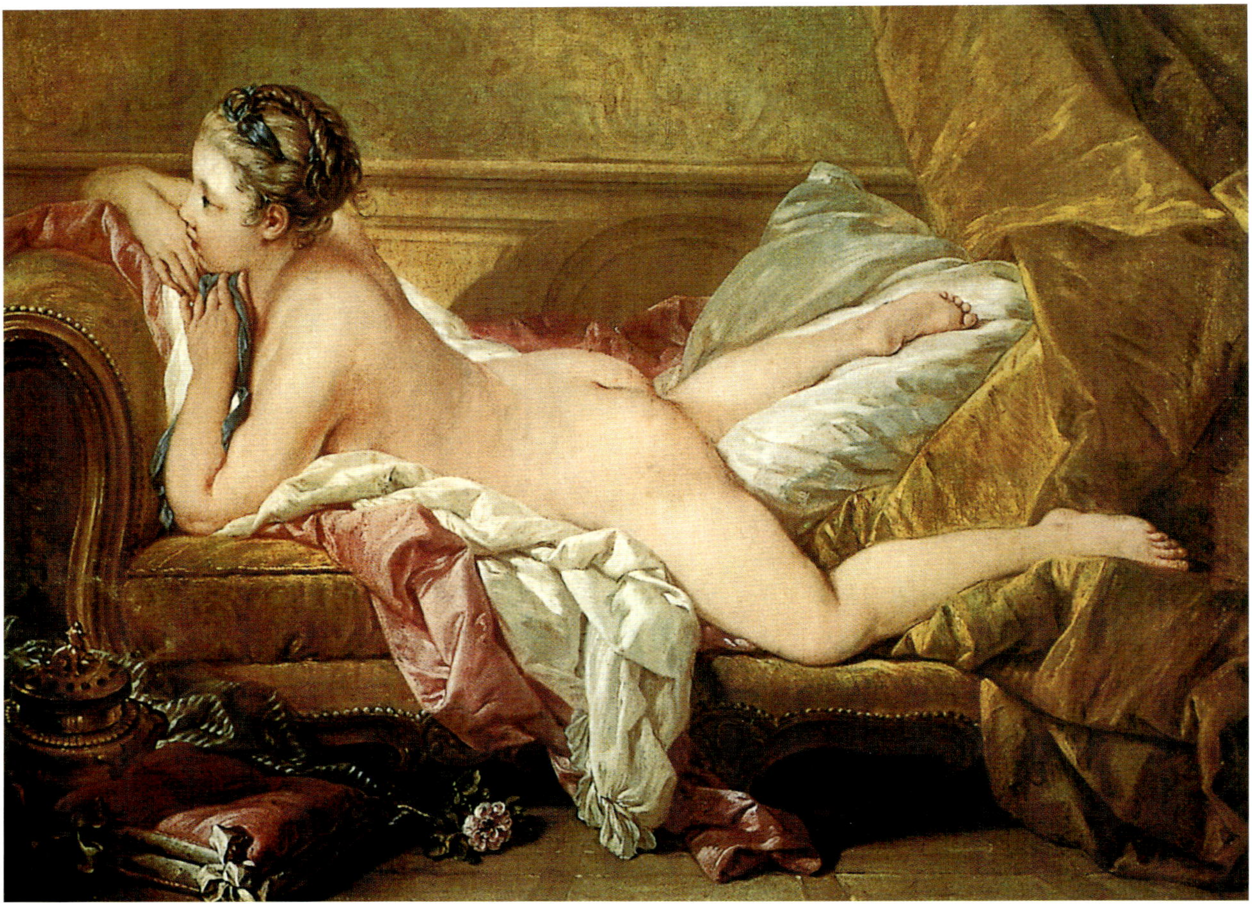

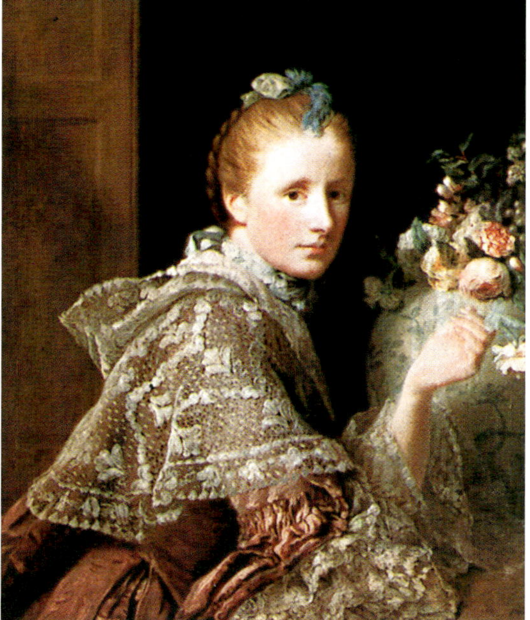

569

568. **François Boucher**, 1703-1770, Rococo, French,
Reclining Girl, 1752.
Oil on canvas, 59 x 73 cm.
Alte Pinakothek, Munich.

*At the peak of Madame de Pompadour's influence on her commissioned
artists, and as mistress of Louis XV, she called on Boucher to paint works for
her personal quarters. Like the coquettish nudes painted for her, this young
woman brings to mind scented silk, sensual touches, and other pleasures of
the flesh. She looks away, maybe into her own life, ignoring but not
resisting a voyeur's gaze. The bedding in the upper right helps push the
wall into the background, as do the hues of brown used on both the wall
and bedding. The rose and white of the sheets extend the soft flesh tones of
the relaxed but pensive maiden. Every curve in the work is soft and flowing,
as lines are only implied. Smoke circling from the incense burner in the
lower left is carried off in the direction of the maiden's daydream. The
artist's more classic and familiar work is* The Toilet of Venus *(1751).*

569. **Allan Ramsey**, 1713-1784, Rococo, Scottish,
The Artist's Wife: Margaret Lindsay of Evelick, 1758.
Oil on canvas, 74.3 x 61.9 cm.
National Gallery of Scotland, Edinburgh.

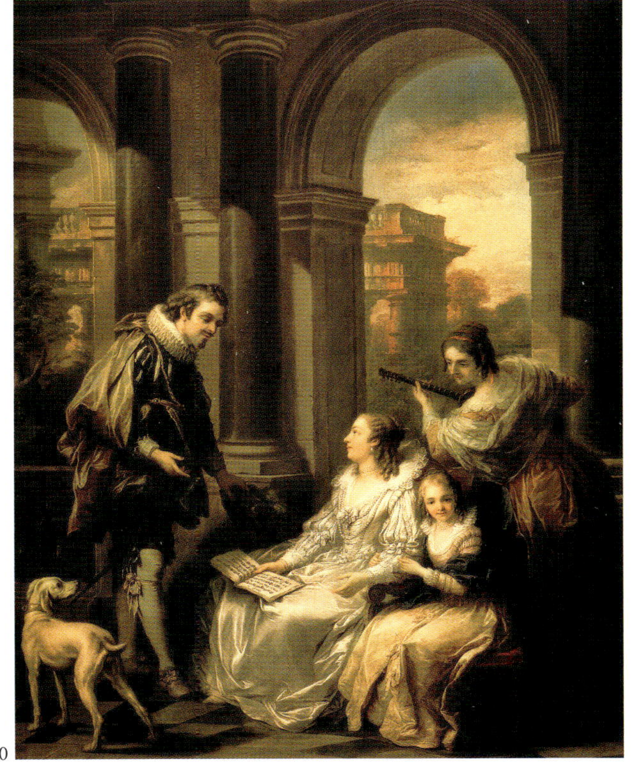

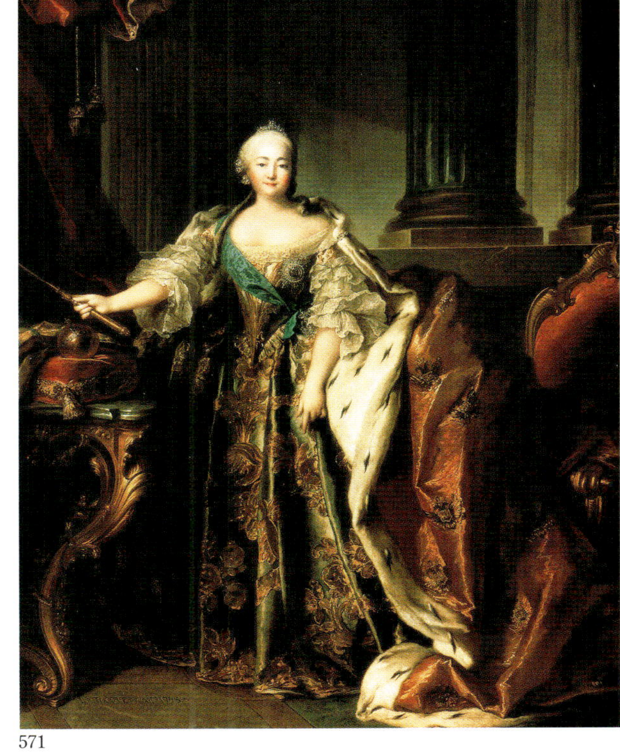

571

570. **Charles-André van Loo**, 1705-1765, Neoclassicism, French,
The Concert, 1754.
Oil on canvas, 164 x 129 cm.
The State Hermitage Museum, St Petersburg.

571. **Louis Tocque**, 1696-1772, Rococo, French,
Portrait of Empress Elizabeth Petrovna, 1758.
Oil on canvas, 262 x 204 cm.
The State Hermitage Museum, St Petersburg.

572. **Charles-André van Loo**, 1705-1765, Neoclassicism, French,
Reading from a Spanish Book, 1754.
Oil on canvas, 164 x 128 cm.
The State Herm tage Museum, St Petersburg.

573. **Joseph Vernet**, *Second View of the Port of Bordeaux Taken
from the Chateau Trompette,* 1759.
Oil on canvas, 165 x 263 cm.
Maritime Museum, Paris.

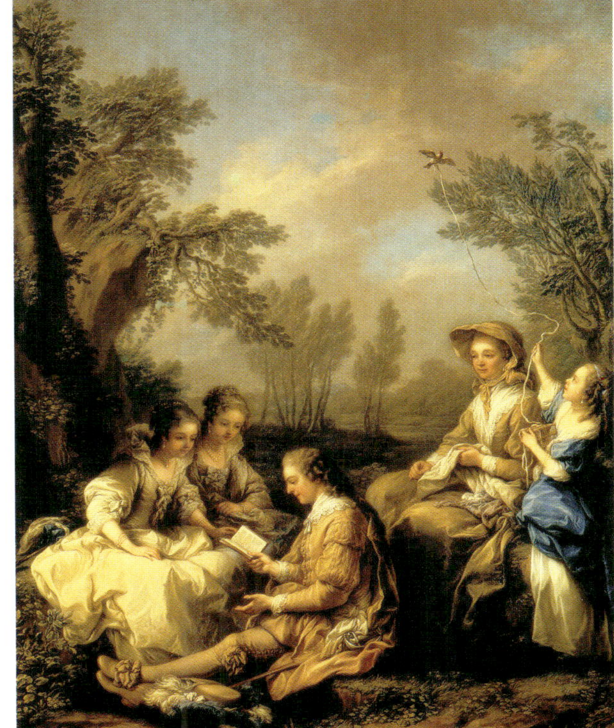

572

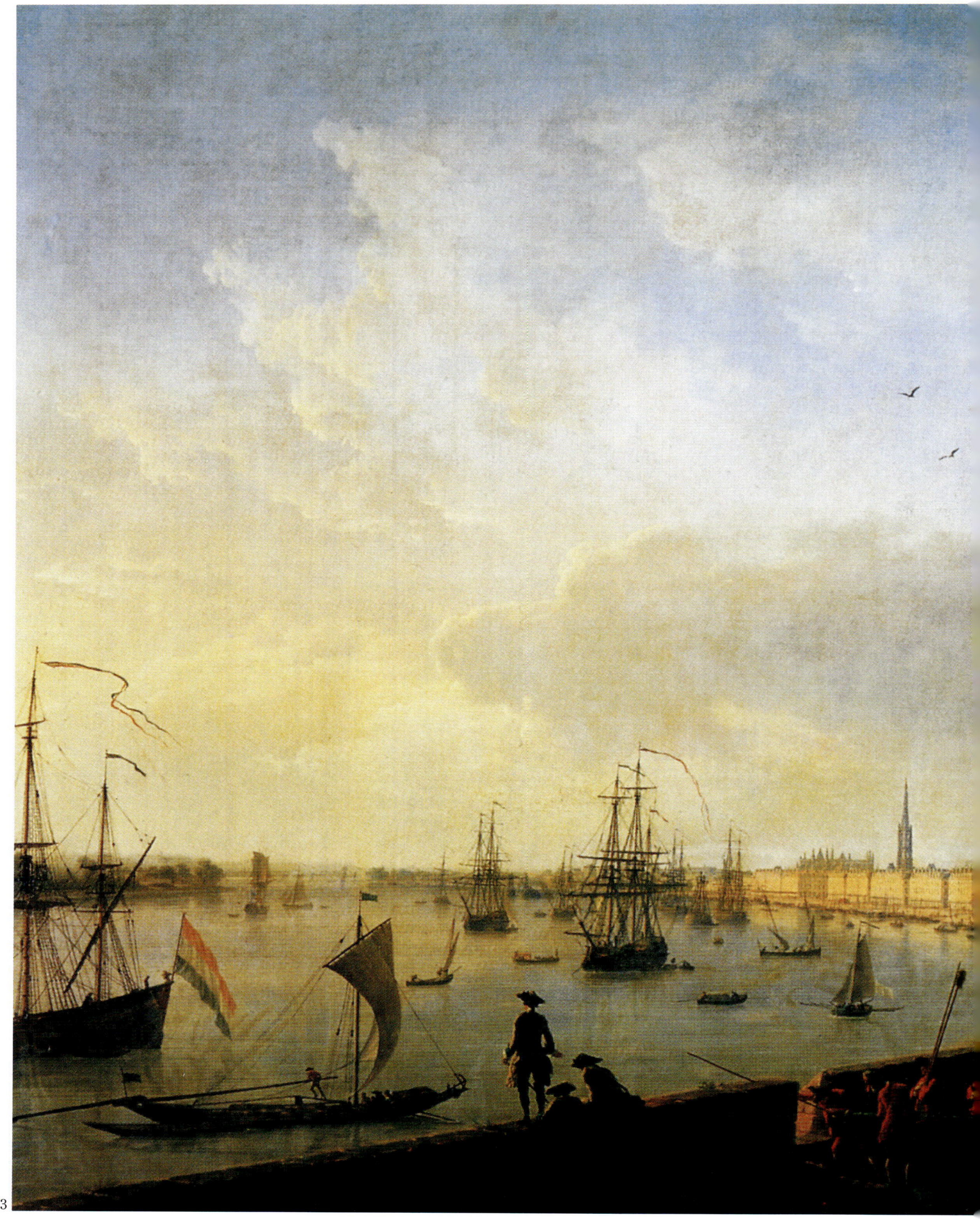

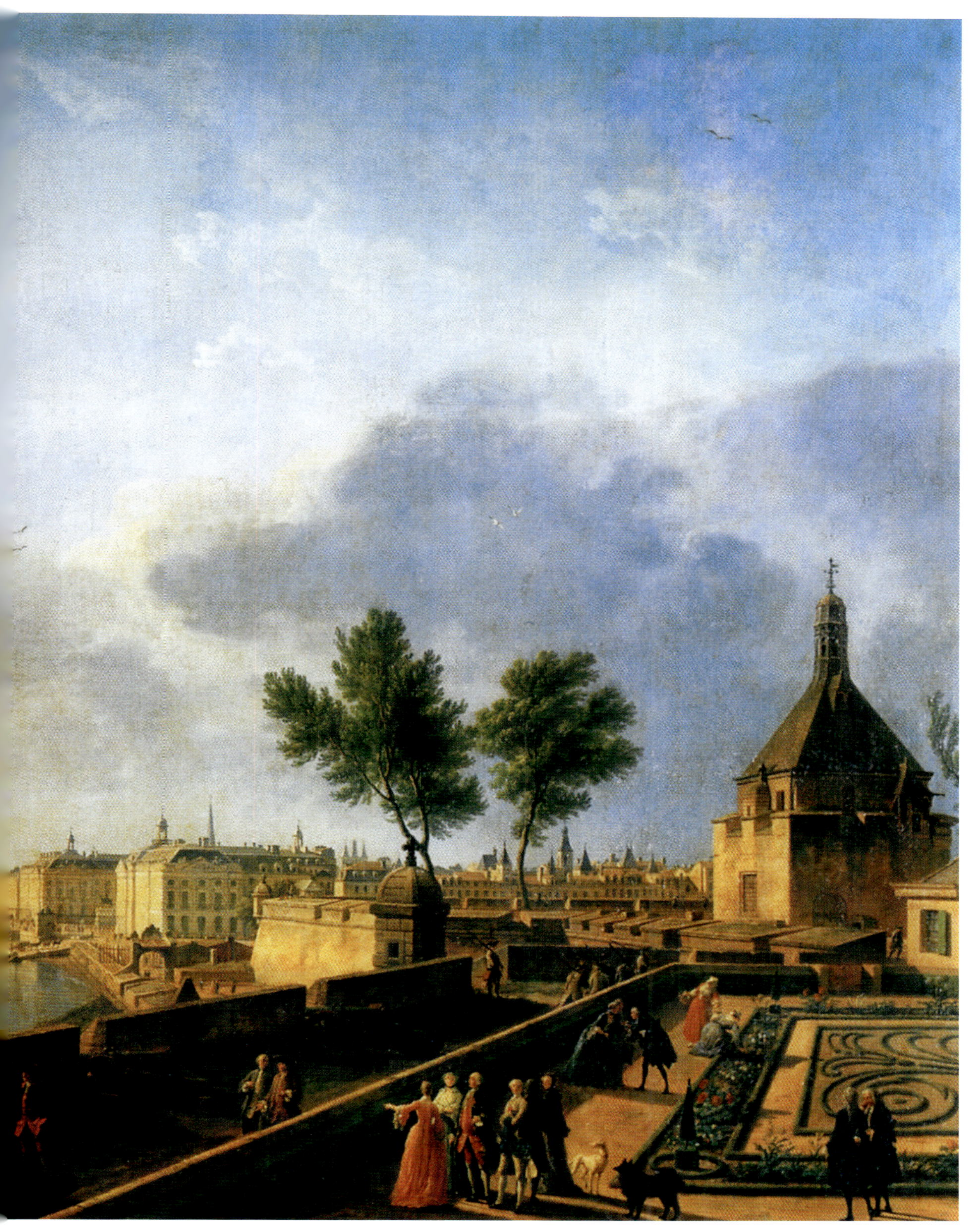

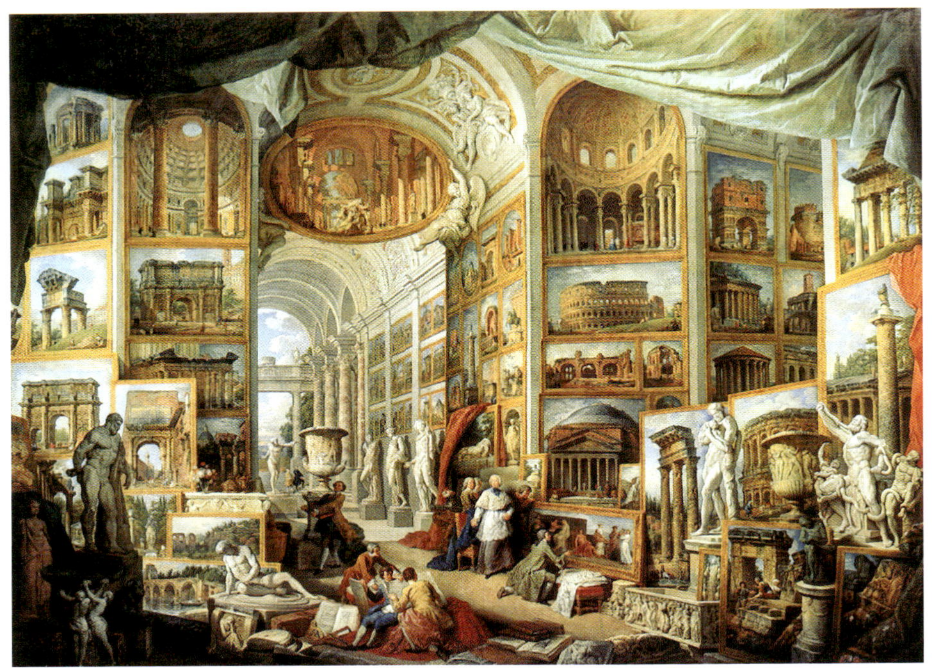

574. **Giovanni Paolo Panini**, 1691-1765, Baroque, Italian, *Roma Antica*, 1758.
Oil on canvas, 231 x 303 cm. Musée du Louvre, Paris.

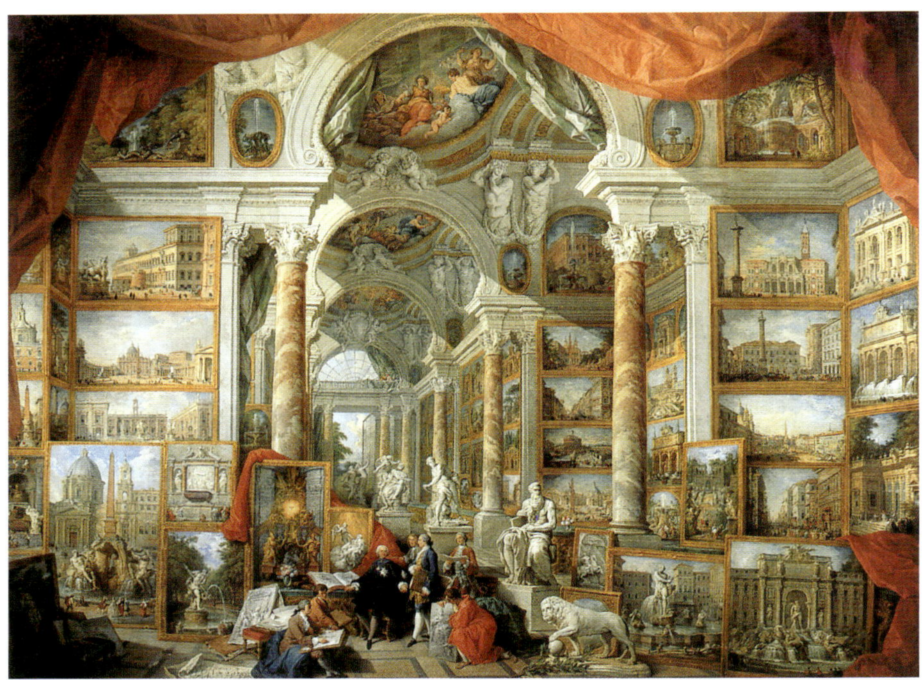

575. **Giovanni Paolo Panini**, 1691-1765, Baroque, Italian, *Picture Gallery with Views of Modern Rome*, 1759. Oil on canvas, 231 x 303 cm. Musée du Louvre, Paris.

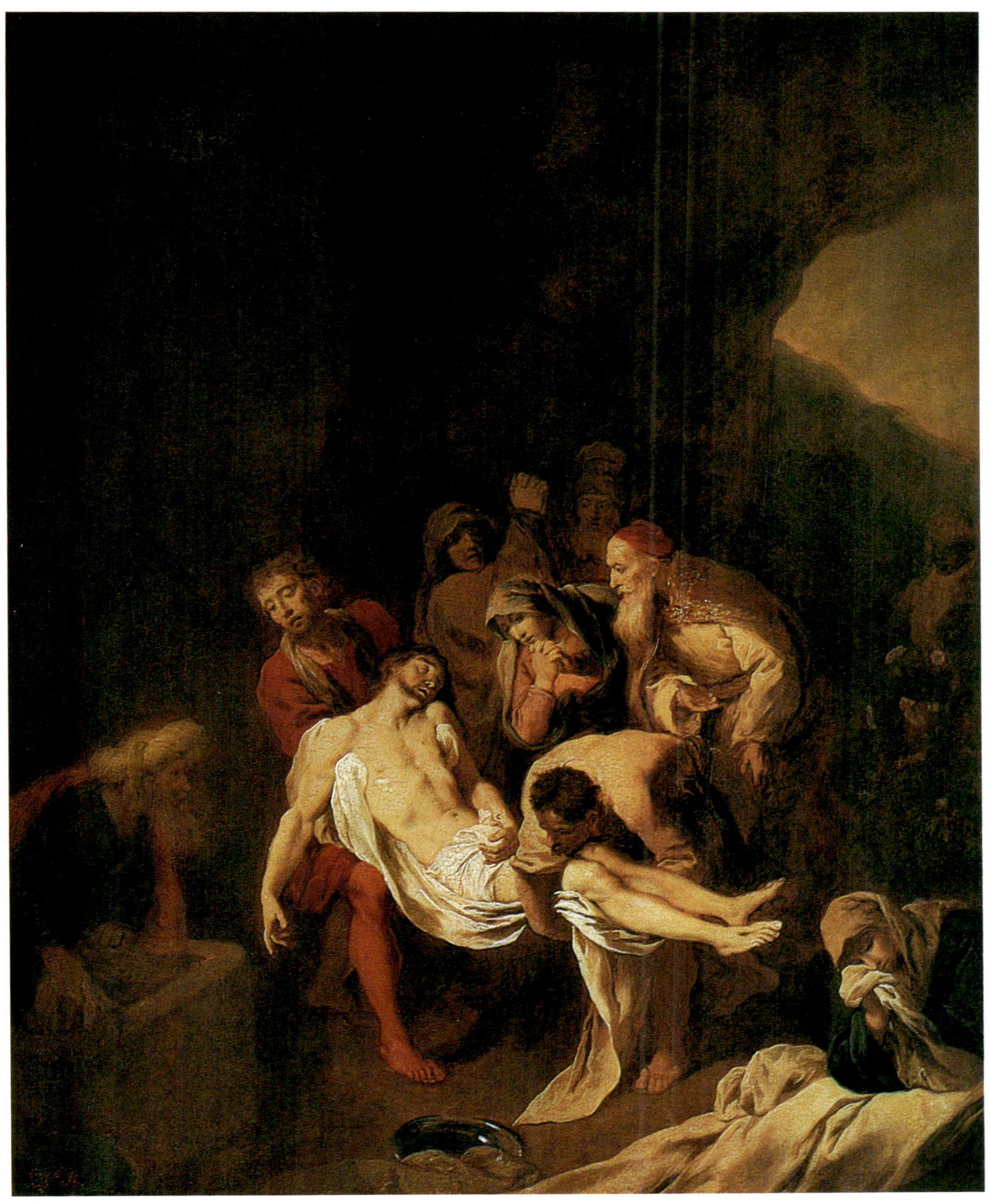

576. **Christian Wilhelm Ernst Dietrich**, 1712-1774, Rococo, German, *The Entombment*, 1759.
Oil on panel, 35 x 28 cm. The State Hermitage Museum, St Petersburg.

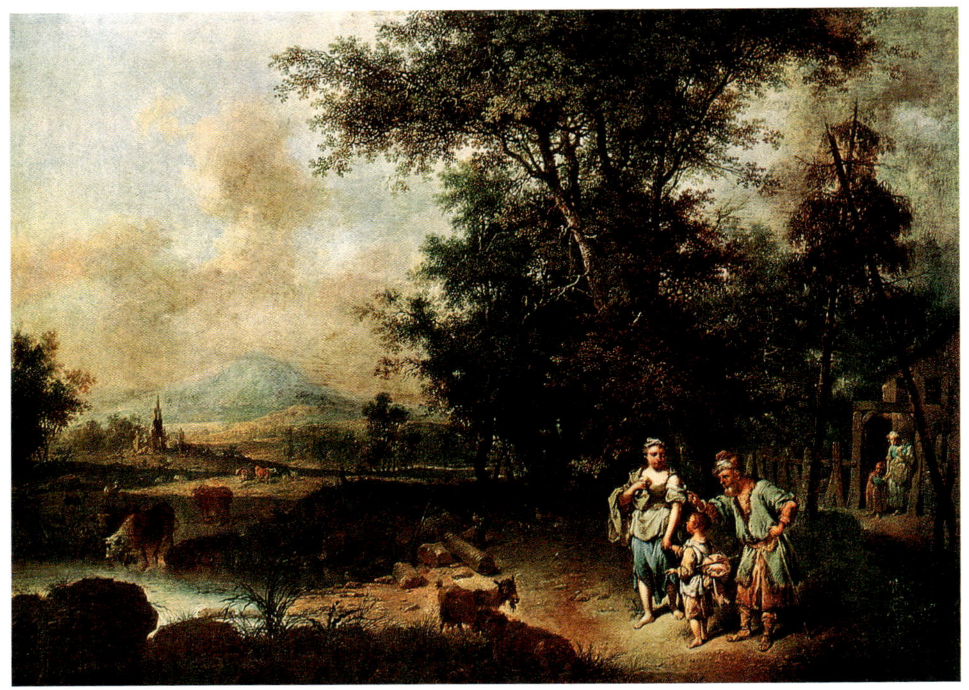

577. Johann Conrad Seekatz, 1719-1768, Rococo, German, *The Repudiation of Hagar*, 1760-1765.
Oil on canvas, 37.5 x 50.5 cm. The State Hermitage Museum, St Petersburg.

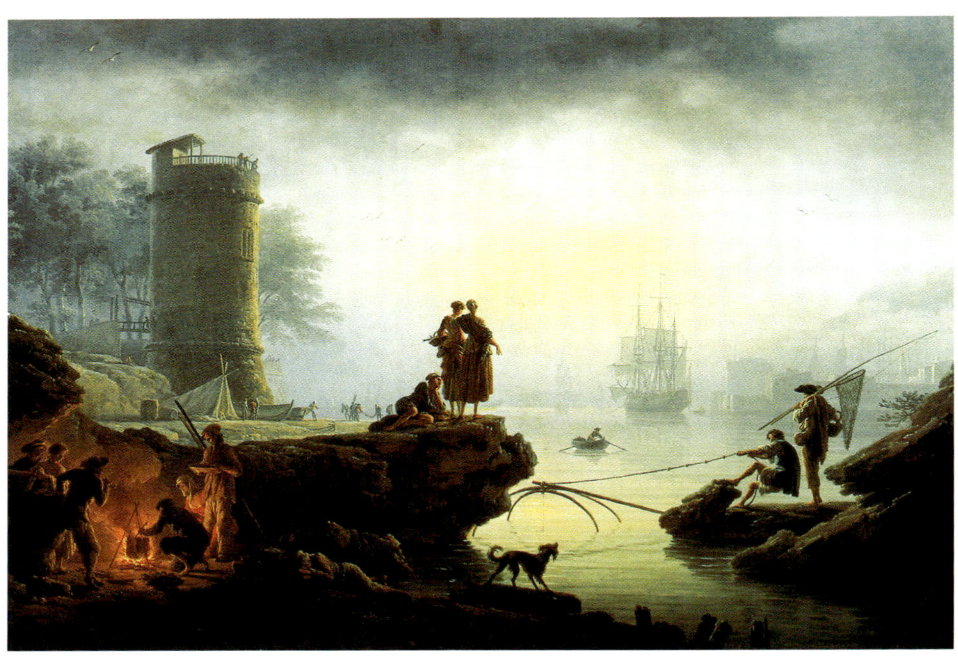

578. Joseph Vernet, 1714-1789, Neoclassicism, French, *Morning*, 1760.
Oil on canvas, 65.5 x 98.5 cm. The Art Institute of Chicago, Chicago.

579. **Jean-Honoré Fragonard**, 1732-1806, Rococo, French,
Blind-Man's Bluff, c. 1760.
Oil on canvas, 114 x 90 cm.
Toledo Museum of Art, Toledo.

580. **George Stubbs**. 1724-1806, Romanticism, English,
Mares and Foals in a River Landscape, 1763-1768.
Oil on canvas, 99 x 159 cm.
Tate Gallery, London.

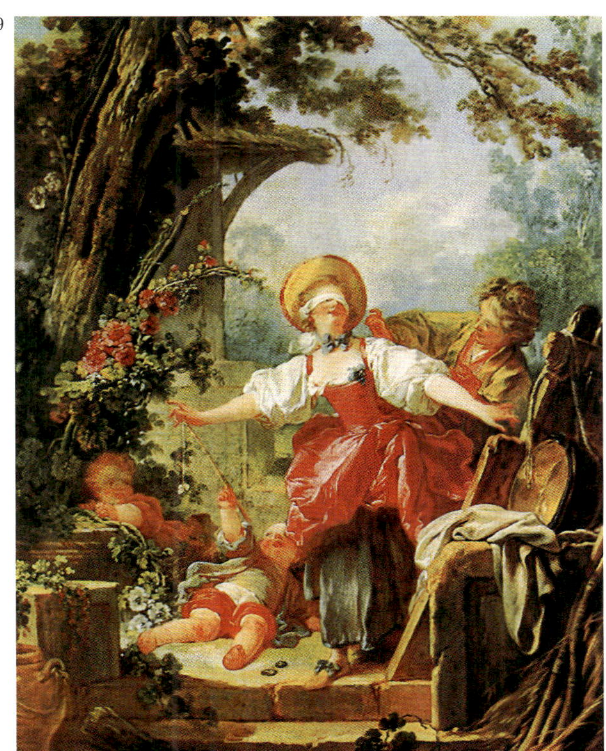

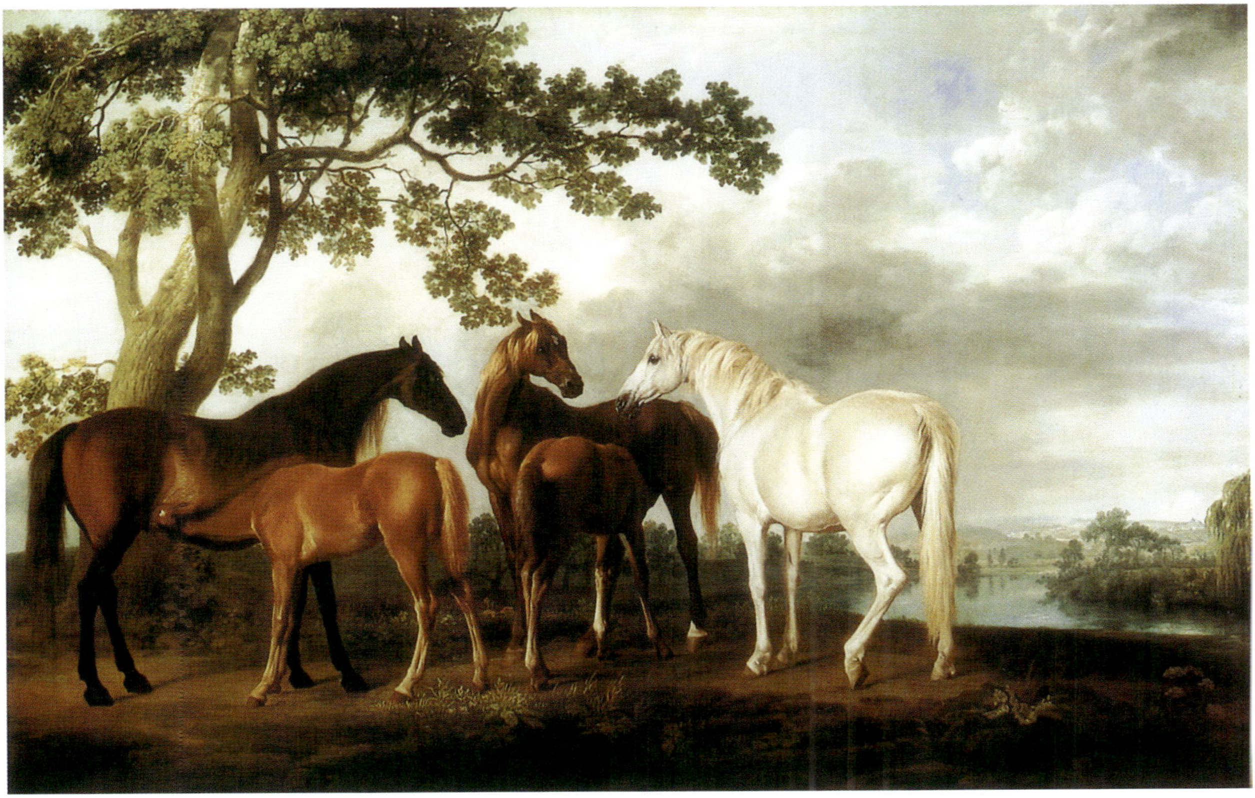

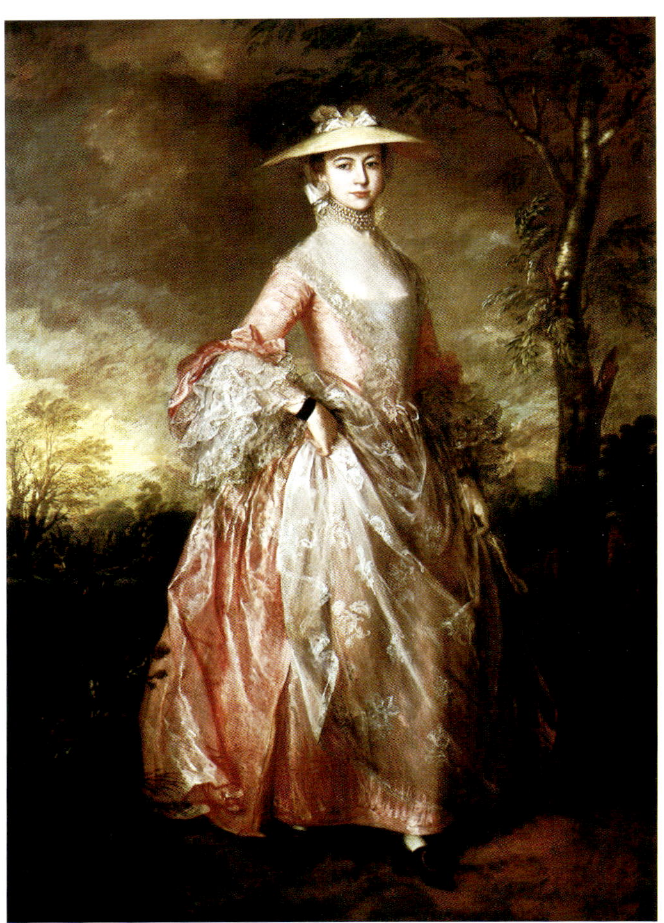

581. **Thomas Gainsborough**, 1727-1788, Rococo, English,
Mary, Countess Howe, 1760.
Oil on canvas, 244 x 152.4 cm.
Kenwood House, London.

582. **George Romney**, 1734-1802, Rococo, English,
The Leigh Family, 1767-1769.
Oil on canvas, 185.5 x 202 cm.
National Gallery of Victoria, Melbourne.

583. **Joshua Reynolds**, 1723-1792, Rococo, English,
The Countess Spencer with her Daughter Georgiana, 1760.
Oil on canvas, 122 x 115 cm.
Collection of Earl Spencer, Althorp.

581

582

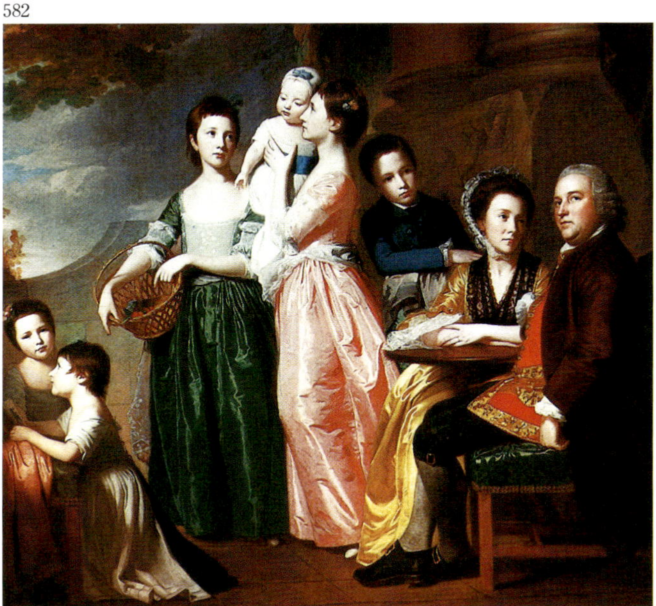

583

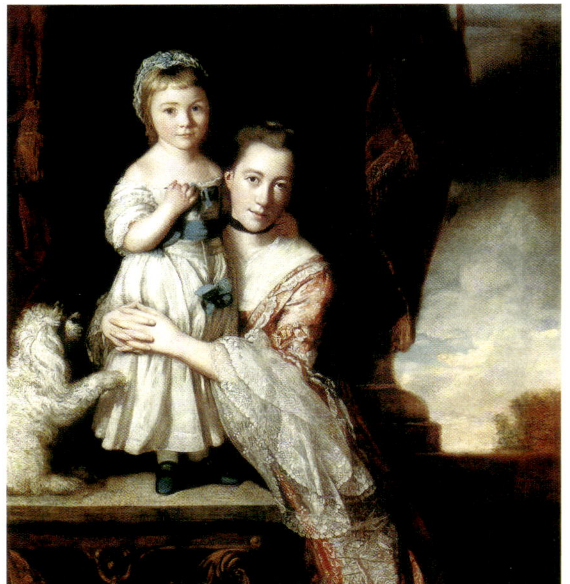

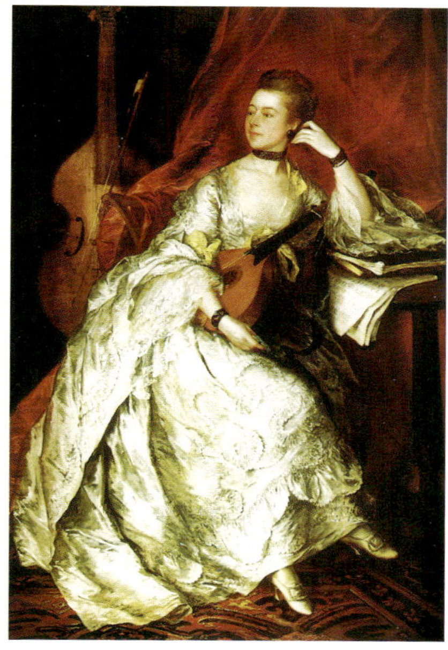

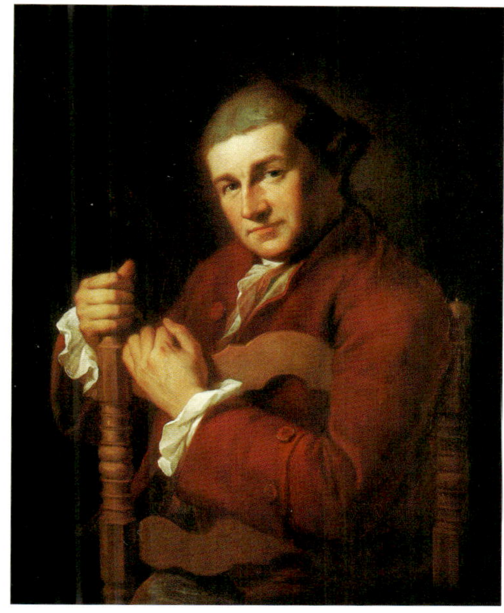

584. **Thomas Gainsborough**, 1727-1788, Rococo, English,
Miss Ann Ford, 1760. Oil on canvas, 192 x 135 cm.
Cincinnati Museum of Art, Cincinnati.

585. **Angelica Kauffmann**, 1741-1807, Neoclassicism, Swiss,
David Garrick, 1764. Oil on canvas, 84 x 69 cm.
Burghley House, Lincolnshire.

586. **Jean-Honoré Fragonard**, 1732-1806, Rococo, French,
Inspiration, c. 1769.
Oil on canvas, 80 x 64 cm.
Musée du Louvre, Paris.

587. **Alexander Roslin**, 1718-1798, Rococo, Swedish,
Woman with a Veil: Marie Suzanne Roslin, 1768.
Oil on canvas, 65 x 54 cm.
Nationalmuseum, Stockholm.

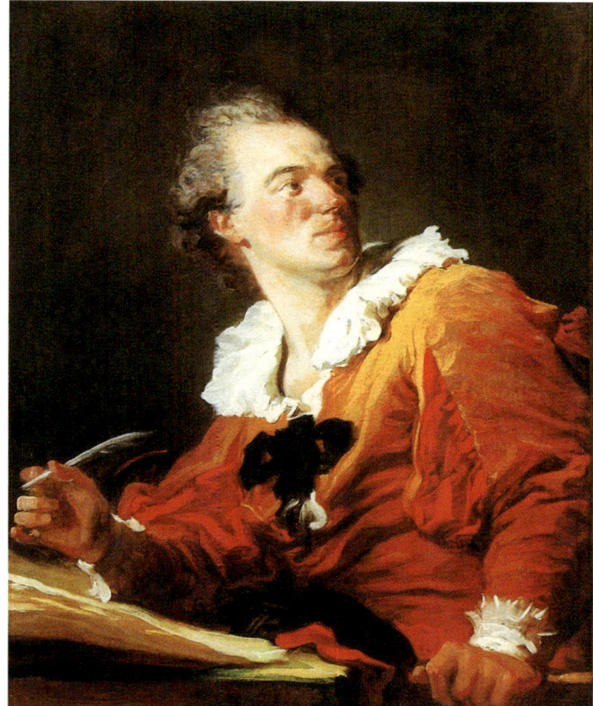

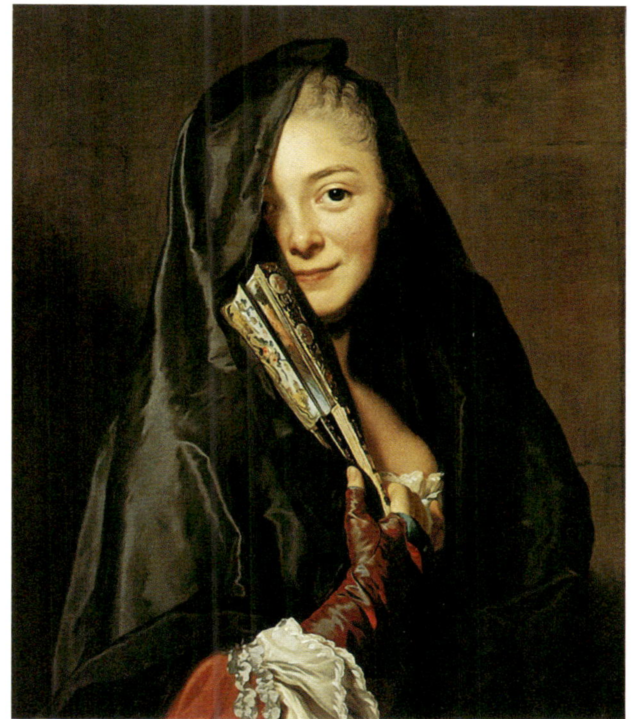

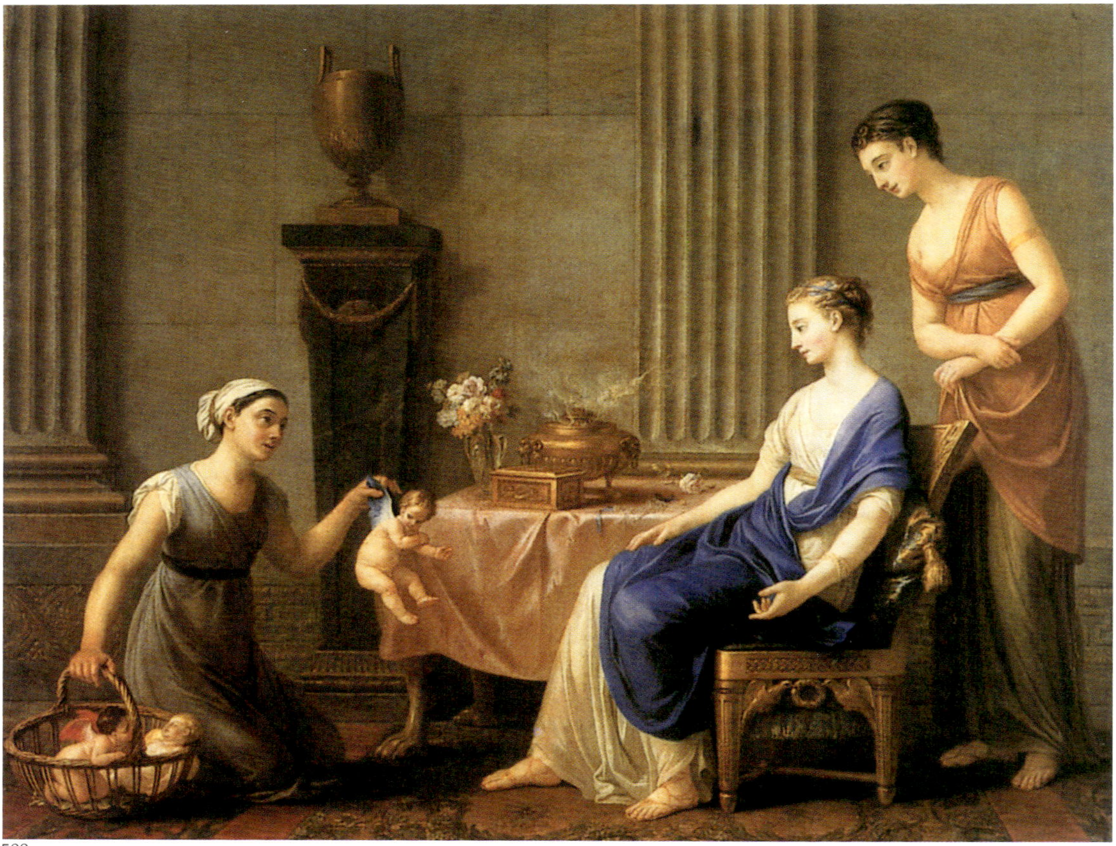

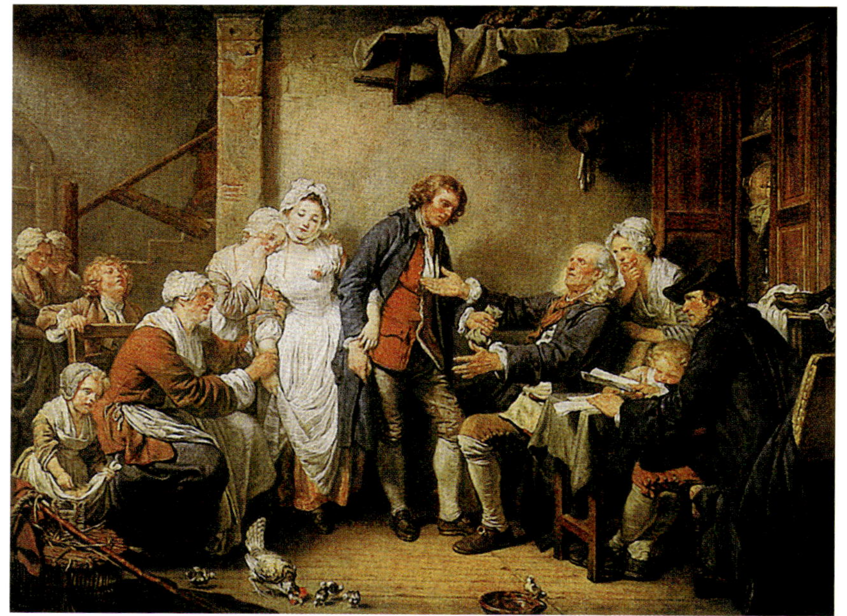

588

589

588. **Joseph-Marie Vien**, 1716-1809,
Neoclassicism, French,
The Seller of Loves, 1763.
Oil on canvas, 98 x 122 cm.
Musée National du Château,
Fontainebleau.

589. **Jean-Baptiste Greuze**, 1725-1805,
Rococo, French,
L'Accordée de village, 1761.
Oil on canvas, 92 x 117 cm.
Musée du Louvre, Paris.

L'Accordée de village *depicts a scene in
which a father is talking with his future
son-in-law, witnessed by a notary, the
crying mother and the siblings of the
future bride.*

590. **Francesco Guardi**, 1712-1793, Rococo, Italian,
An Architectural Caprice, c. 1770.
Oil on canvas, 54 x 36 cm.
National Gallery, London.

591. **Joseph Wright**, 1734-1797, Romanticism, English,
An Experiment on a Bird in the Air Pump, 1768.
Oil on canvas, 183 x 244 cm.
National Gallery, London.

Influenced by Caravaggio's realism and mystery of light, Wright was interested in the contrasts between light and shadow, as was a contemporary, Anton Raphael Mengs. Wright was specifically fascinated by the effects of candlelight, as seen in El Greco's Boy Lighting a Candle *(1573). In this work, the candle is seen as a ghostly image from the other side of the beaker in which there is a skull and cloudy liquid. Wright was also interested in drawing attention to current discoveries or advances in science. In this masterpiece of classical realism, the phenomena of vacuum, which we take for granted today, is being demonstrated. Each witness to the air pump experiment has a distinct reaction, shown mainly by facial expressions. Unfortunately, a bird will suffocate if the cruel experiment sucks too much air out of his glass container. The moon is a reference to the Lunar Society, a group of people interested in discussing science. The work might be showing the family of a member in one such group, as there is indeed a full moon.*

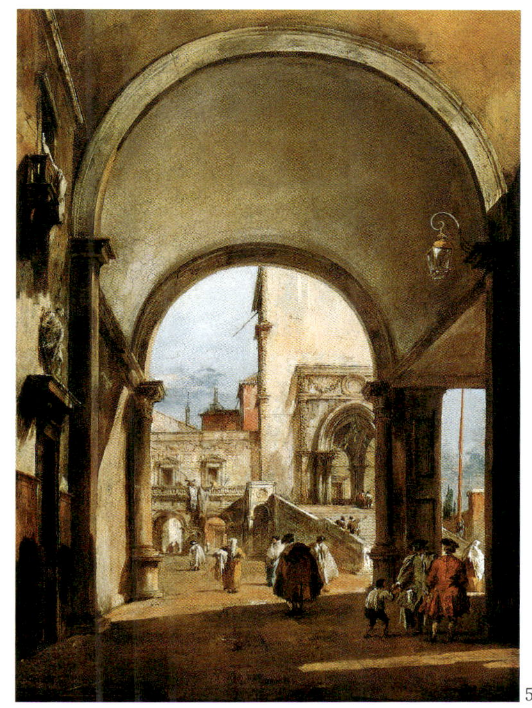

590

591

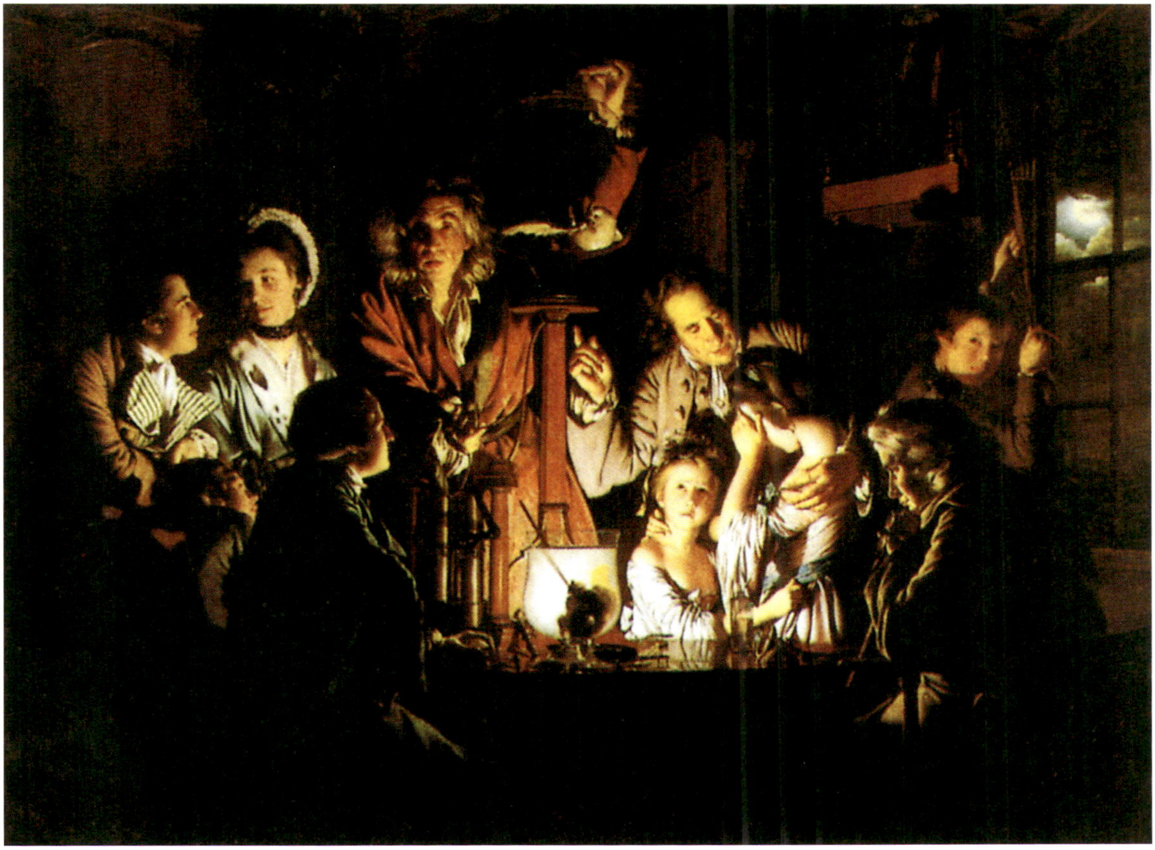

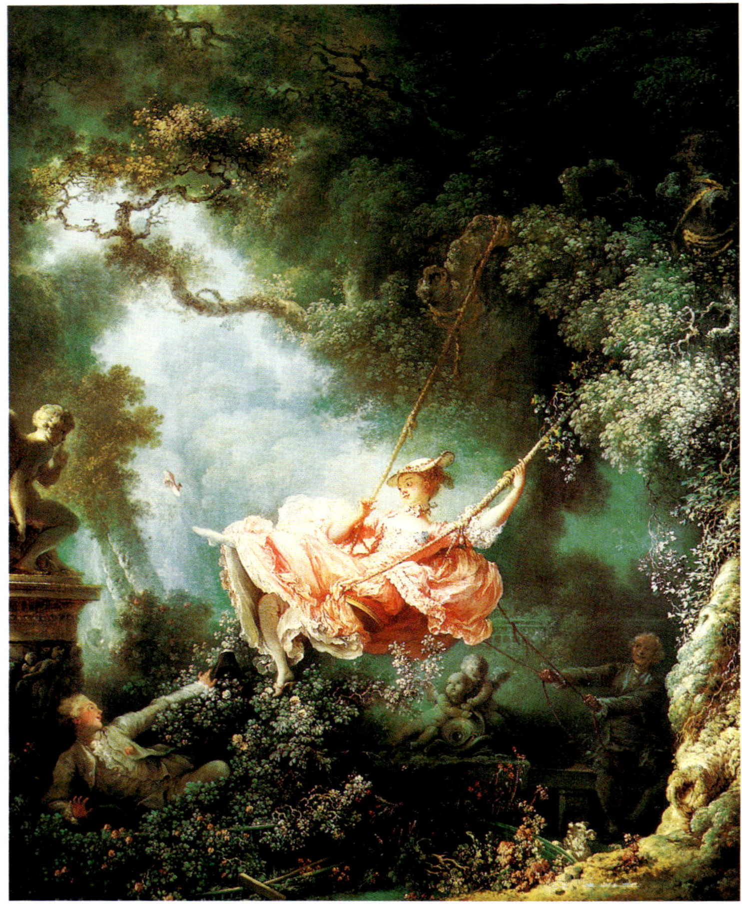

592. Jean-Honoré Fragonard, 1732-1806, Rococo, French,
The Swing, 1767.
Oil on canvas, 81 x 64.2 cm.
The Wallace Collection, London.

The Neoclassicism of the revolutionaries did not impress this genre painter. Rather, he produced fêtes-galantes (this term appears with Watteau) for patrons, such as the Rococo series of four scenes depicting the Progress of Love *(1770) intended for the boudoir of Madame du Barry's Pavilion de Louveciennes, of which* The Swing *is the most popular. Both the man's voyeurism and the lady's exhibitionism are justified by the seemingly innocent situation.*

The man 'happens' to fall at the base of a statue of cupid. He thereby 'happens' to align himself conveniently to 'accidentally' see up the young lady's petticoats. The lady's dainty left shoe is kicked into the air, again quite by accident, of course. From the shadows a servant dutifully continues to pull ropes so as to swing the teasing lady as a playful putto smiles approvingly. Fragonard's free strokes and clear palette served his gallant and fickle subjects.

JEAN-HONORÉ FRAGONARD
(1732 GRASSE – 1806 PARIS)

Fragonard closes, with a burst of fireworks, the curve of the eighteenth century opened by Watteau with his fairy poems of love and melancholy. Watteau was ethereal and profound; Fragonard was merely light. He amuses us while amusing himself; he is never moved. He painted mainly *fêtes-galantes* in Rococo style. Pupil of François Boucher, Fragonard also studied under Chardin. Always remembering Boucher's advice, he depicted romantic gardens, with their fountains, grottos, temples and terraces where one can also recognise the influence of Tiepolo. With King Louis XV as a patron he turned himself towards the depiction of the pleasure-loving and licentious court, scenes of love and voluptuousness.

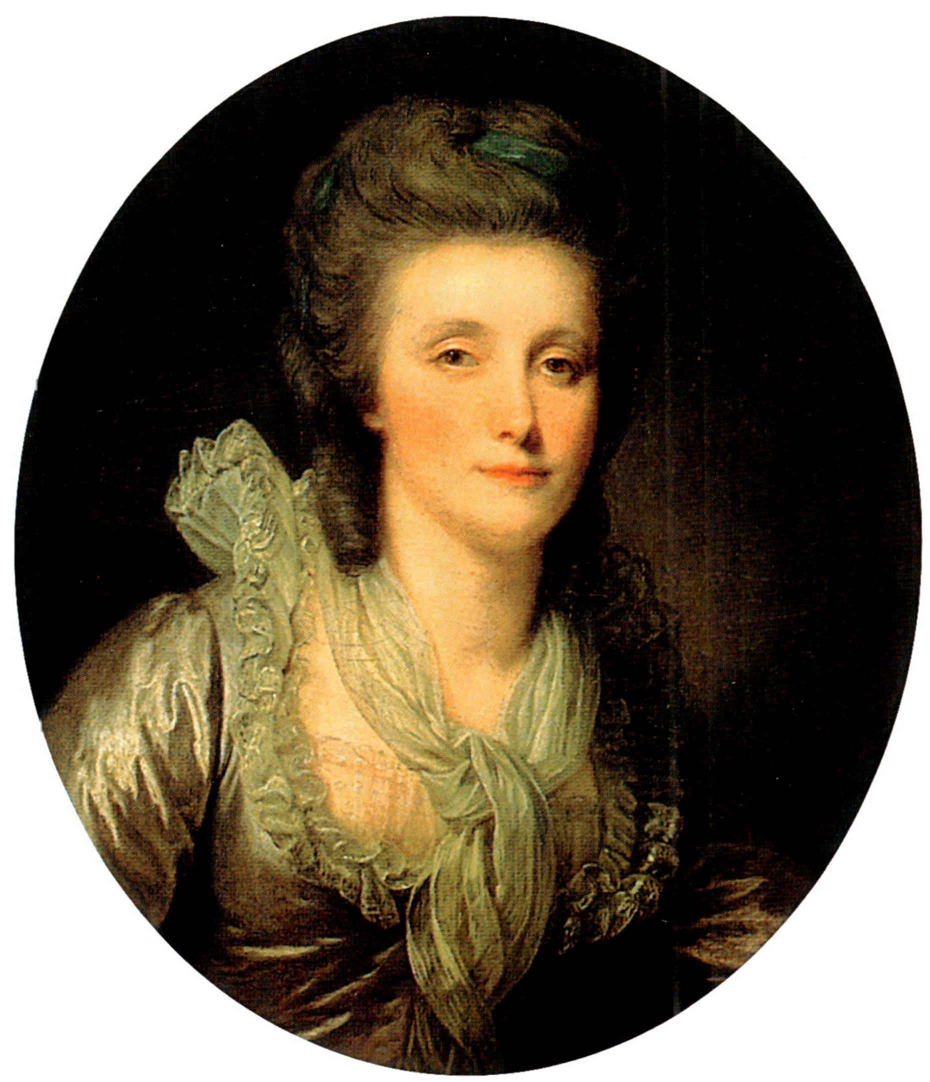

593. **Jean-Baptiste Greuze**, 1725-1805, Rococo, French, *Portrait of Countess Ekaterina Shuvalova,* c. 1770.
Oil on canvas, 60 x 50 cm. The State Hermitage Museum, St Petersburg.

JEAN-BAPTISTE GREUZE
(1725 TOURNUS – 1805 PARIS)

Greuze is without question one of the most important painters of the French school of the eighteenth century. He possessed a unique asset: he created his own style – sentimental and melodramatic genre scenes. Very early in his career his work was praised by the critics, such as Diderot who talked about "morality in paint". While *L'Accordée de village*, where every detail is like an actor playing a part, seems borrowed from some *comédie-larmoyante* or contemporary melodrama, much of Greuze's later work consisted of titillating pictures of young women, which contain thinly veiled sexual allusions under their surface appearance of mawkish innocence. The end of the century saw the end of his career as his reception piece was not accepted by the academy in 1769 and a new glorified style was appearing carried out by Jacques-Louis David: Neoclassicism.

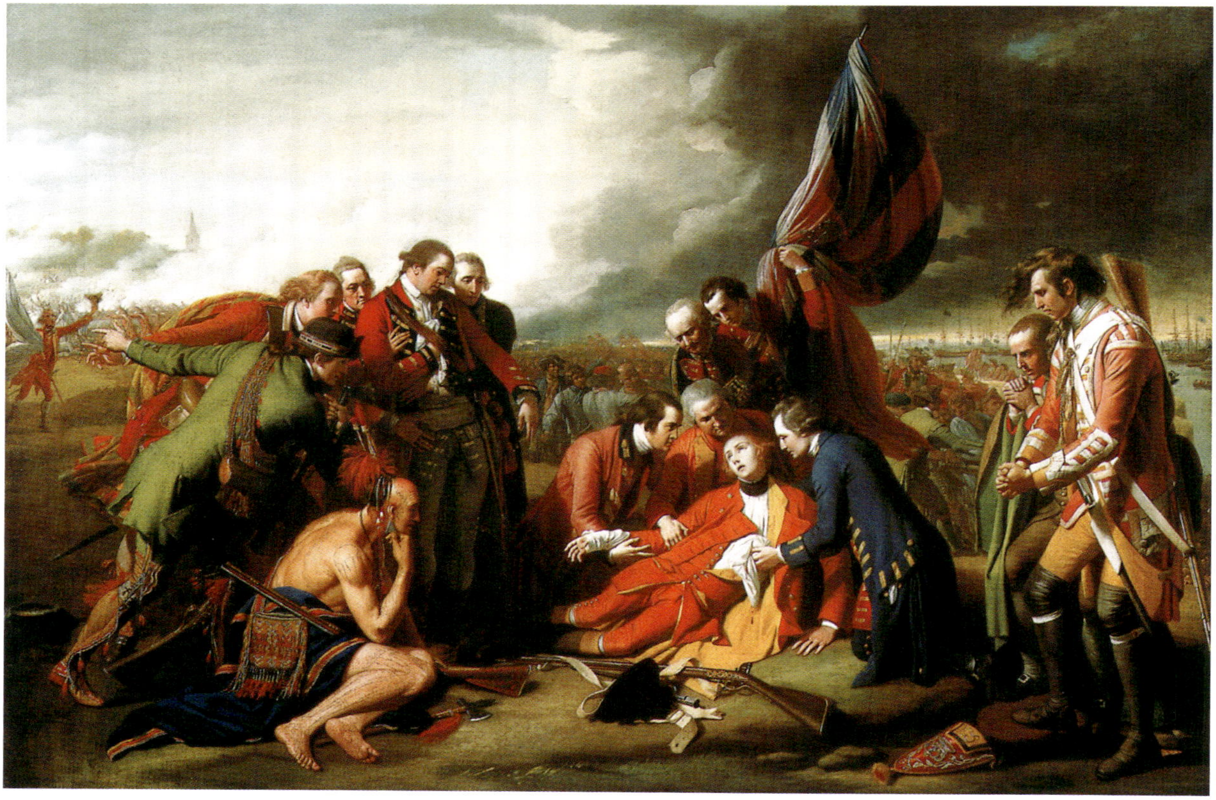

594. **Benjamin West**, 1738-1820, Neoclassicism, American,
The Death of General Wolfe, 1770.
Oil on canvas, 152 x 214 cm.
National Gallery of Canada, Ottawa.

In 1771, West upset the art world with this work, because it placed contemporary figures in a classical composition. His work was generally criticised and considered derivative, but it made a breakthrough that moved art to greater realism. He showed the expiring of the victorious British Army general, James Wolfe, on the battlefield, after the capture of Quebec, Canada from the French in 1759. Grieving officers and North American Indians surround him. His victory led to British supremacy in Canada. It was this painting that won West the appointment as painter to the King. As such he applied especially his self-taught skill of portrait painting.

595. **Benjamin West**, 1738-1820, Rococo, American,
Penn's Treaty with the Indians, 1771-1772.
Oil on canvas, 191.8 x 273.7 cm.
The Pennsylvania Academy of the Fine Arts,
Philadelphia.

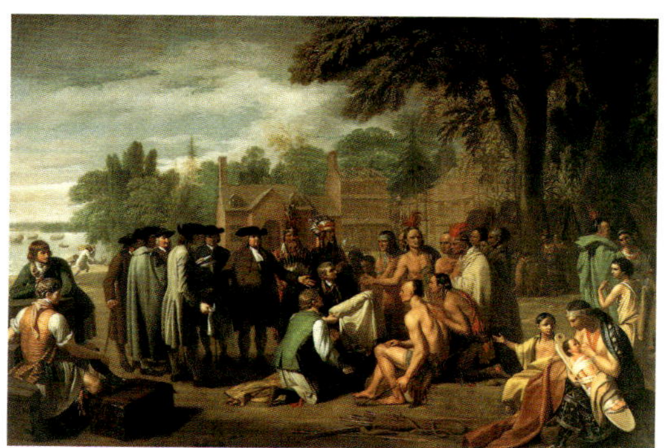

BENJAMIN WEST
(1738 SPRINGFIELD, PENNSYLVANIA – 1820 LONDON)

In 1760, West was the first American to study art in Italy. During his three years there he was influenced by Titian and Raphael, as well as the contemporary art he saw there during the advent of the Neoclassical movement. He won the attention and praise of George III, who appointed him to be a charter member of the Royal Academy. He became president of the Royal Academy in 1792. He restored and reshaped Neoclassicism in historical paintings in France over a decade before David. Yet, he also earned the title, 'Father of American Painting', not due to his paintings, but because he taught influential American painters John Singleton Copley, Charles Peale, Gilbert Stuart, and John Trumbull, as well as talented men not best known as painters, including Robert Fulton and Samuel F.B. Morse. Although he never returned to the United States, he remained true to its heritage by rejecting the offer of knighthood. He is buried in St Paul's Cathedral.

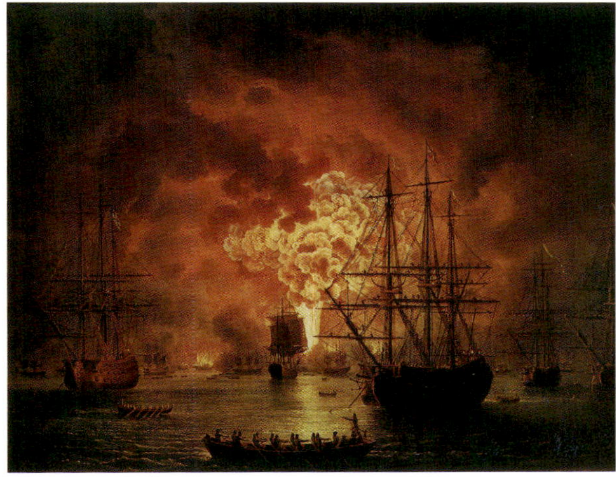

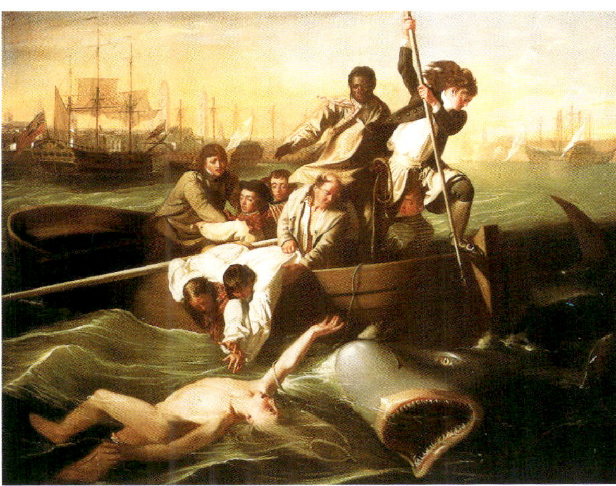

596. Jacob Philipp Hackert, 1737-1807, Neoclassicism, German,
The Destruction of the Turkish Fleet in Chesme Harbour, 1771.
Oil on panel, 162 x 220 cm.
The State Hermitage Museum, St Petersburg.

597. John Singleton Copley, 1738-1815, Realism, American,
Watson and the Shark, 1778.
Oil on canvas, 182.1 x 229.7 cm.
The National Gallery of Art, Washington D.C.

598. Francesco Guardi, 1712-1793, Rococo, Italian,
*Departure of Bucentaure towards the Lido of Venice,
on Ascension Day*, 1775-1780.
Oil on canvas, 66 x 101 cm.
Musée du Louvre, Paris.

*Around 1770, Francesco Guardi painted a series of twelve 'views' of
historical events related to the coronation of the Doge Alvise Mocenigo.
All of them work as pretext for an unusual description of some of
Venice's monuments with a great sense of space and repartition of light
and colourful details.*

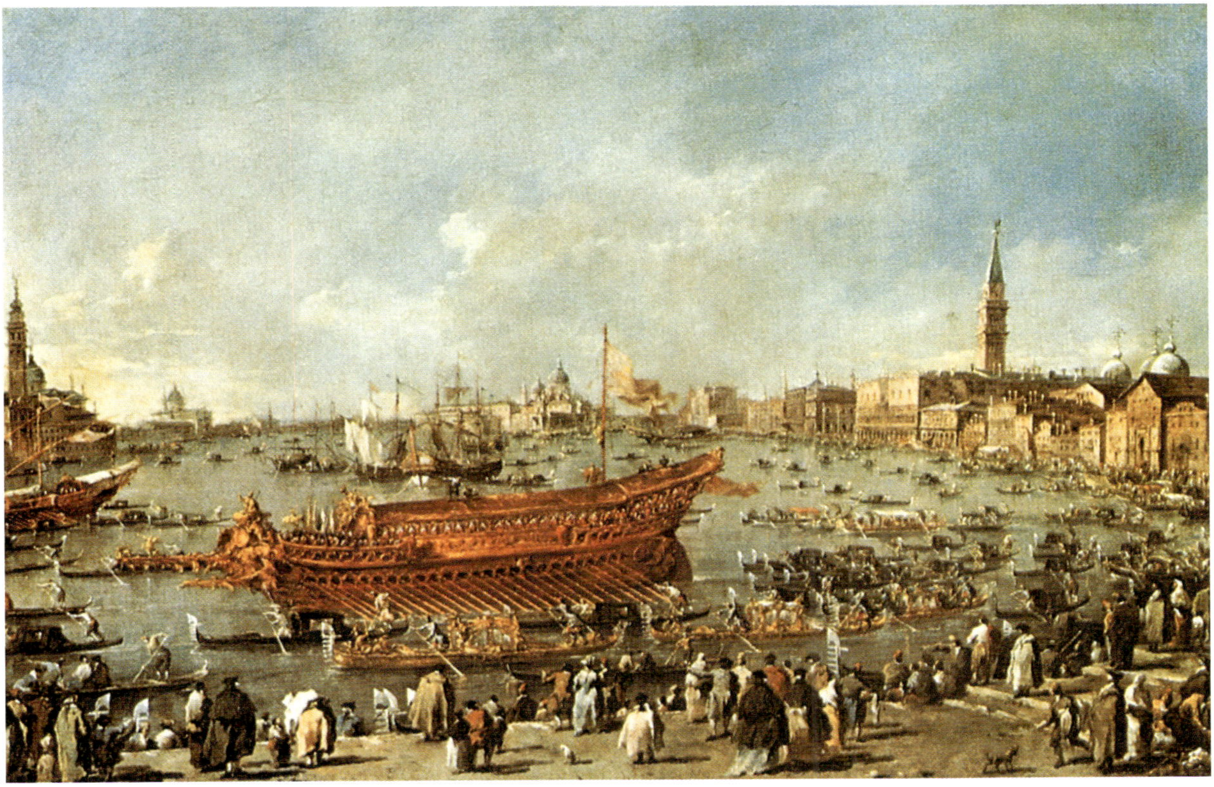

598

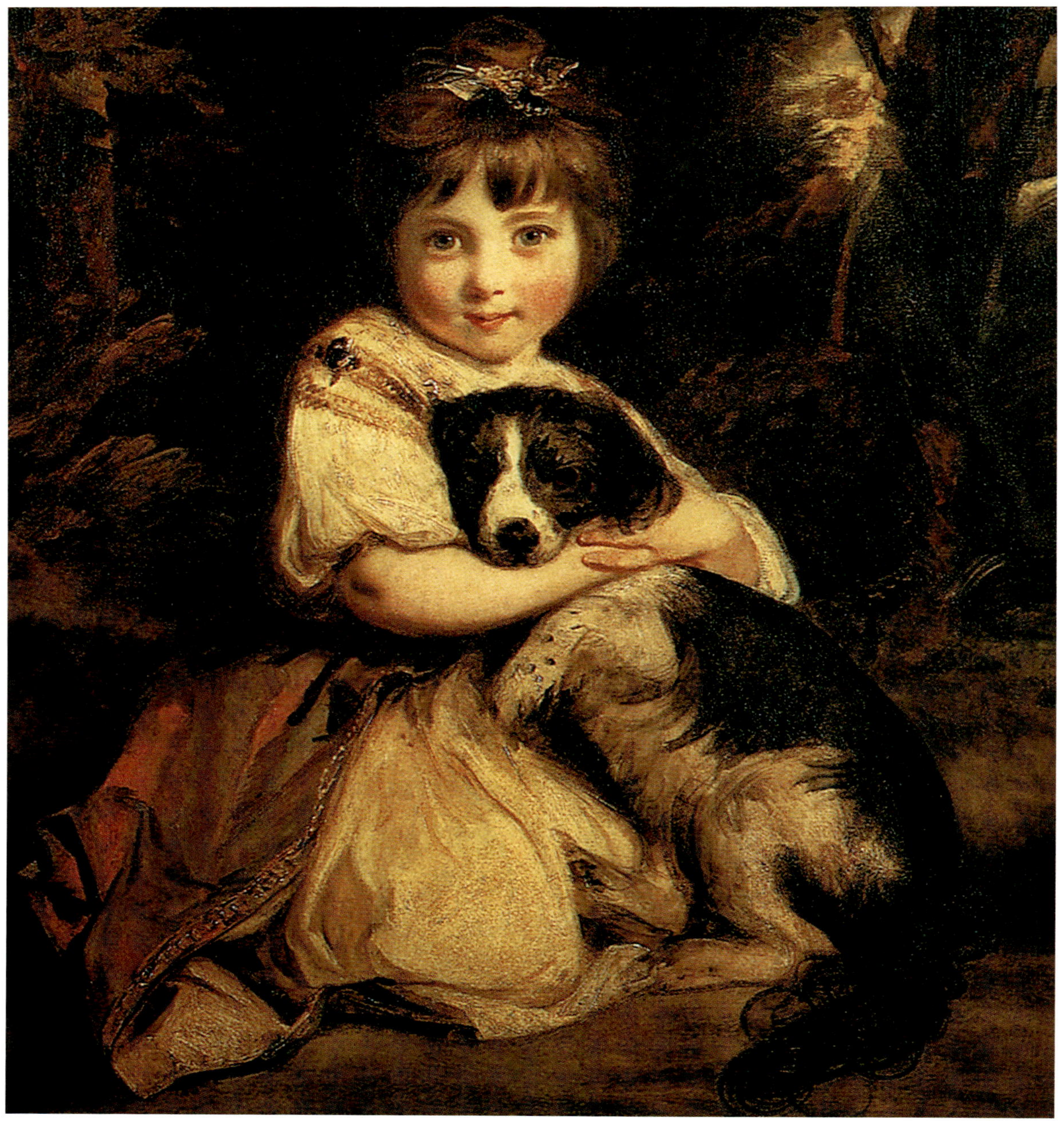

599. Joshua Reynolds, 1723-1792, Rococo, English,
Miss Bowles (and her Dog), 1775.
Oil on canvas, 91 x 71 cm.
The Wallace Collection, London.

The rosy-cheeked girl embraces her dog as if caught during a playful time together. There is a mutual affection and trust between the girl and her slightly reluctant pet, yet the formality of the pose is retained as in typical commissioned works of the period. Seen here is a simple and unpretentious example of how Reynolds, with his contemporary rival Gainsborough, followed the formal philosophies of fellow countrymen, playwright Samuel Johnson and philosopher David Hume. The artists especially respected Hume's directive that painting must respect the principles of nature as well as art. Their works ennobled their patrons and captured the sophisticated tone of the British affluent. Reynolds was very successful in retaining Old World elegance while often, such as in this work, capturing charming moments.

600. **Luis Eugenio Meléndez**,
1716-1780, Rococo, Spanish,
*Still-Life with a Box of Sweets
and Bread Twists*, c. 1770.
Oil on canvas, 49 x 37 cm.
Museo Nacional del Prado,
Madrid.

601. **Luis Eugenio Meléndez**,
1716-1780, Rococo, Spanish,
Still-Life with Melon and Pears,
c. 1770.
Oil on canvas, 64 x 85 cm.
Museum of Fine Arts, Boston.

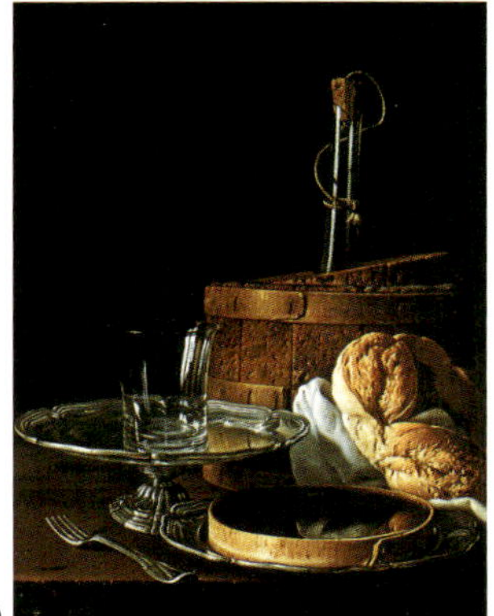

600

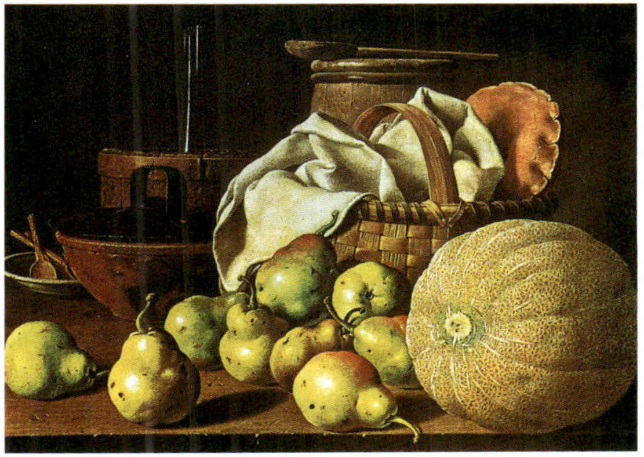

601

JOSHUA REYNOLDS
(1723 PLYMPTON – 1792 LONDON)

602. **Joshua Reynolds**, 1723-1792,
Rococo, English,
Self-portrait, 1775.
Oil on canvas, 71.5 x 58 cm.
Galleria degli Uffizi, Florence.

603. **Anton Raphael Mengs**,
1728-1779, Neoclassicism,
German, *Self-portrait*, c. 1775.
Oil on panel, 97 x 72.6 cm.
Galleria degli Uffizi, Florence.

Reynolds was a British portrait painter who dominated English artistic life in the second half of the eighteenth century. Influenced by the Italian Renaissance during a trip in Italy to Rome, Florence and Venice and later by Italian Bolognese Baroque and northern painters like Rubens and Van Dyck, he attempted to lead British painting towards continental Grand Style. In his writings, he evolved a doctrine of imitation, a fact with which he has sometimes been reproached, but wrongly so, since he succeeded in making his borrowings his own and giving to a composite creation a homogeneous, personal and national character. In 1768 he helped found the Royal Academy, was elected first president and knighted by King George III. Reynolds' discourses, delivered at the Royal Academy between 1769 and 1791, are considered the most important art criticism of that time. In them he outlined the essence of grandeur in art and suggested the means of achieving it was through rigorous academic training and study of the old masters of art.

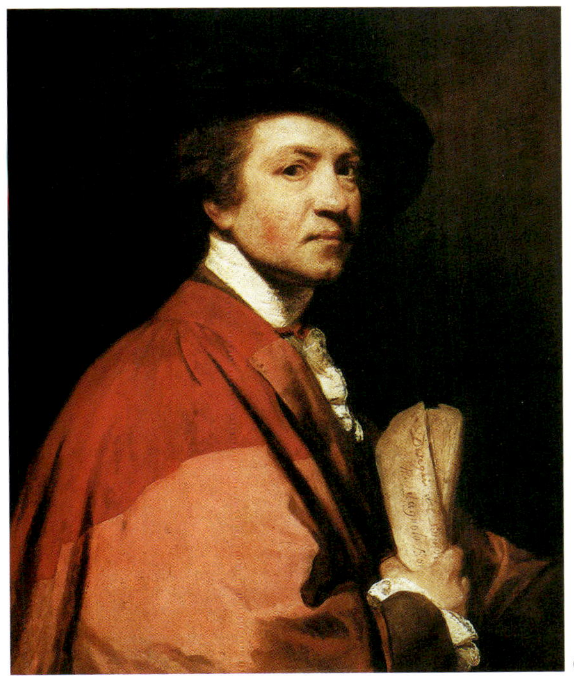

602

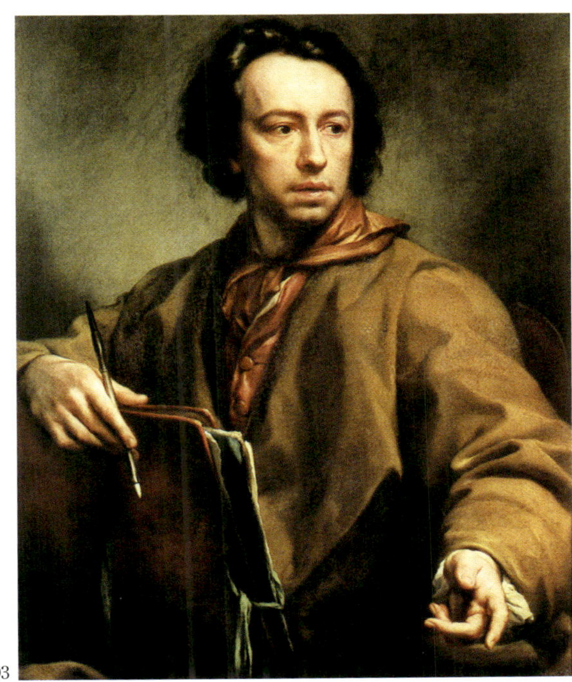

603

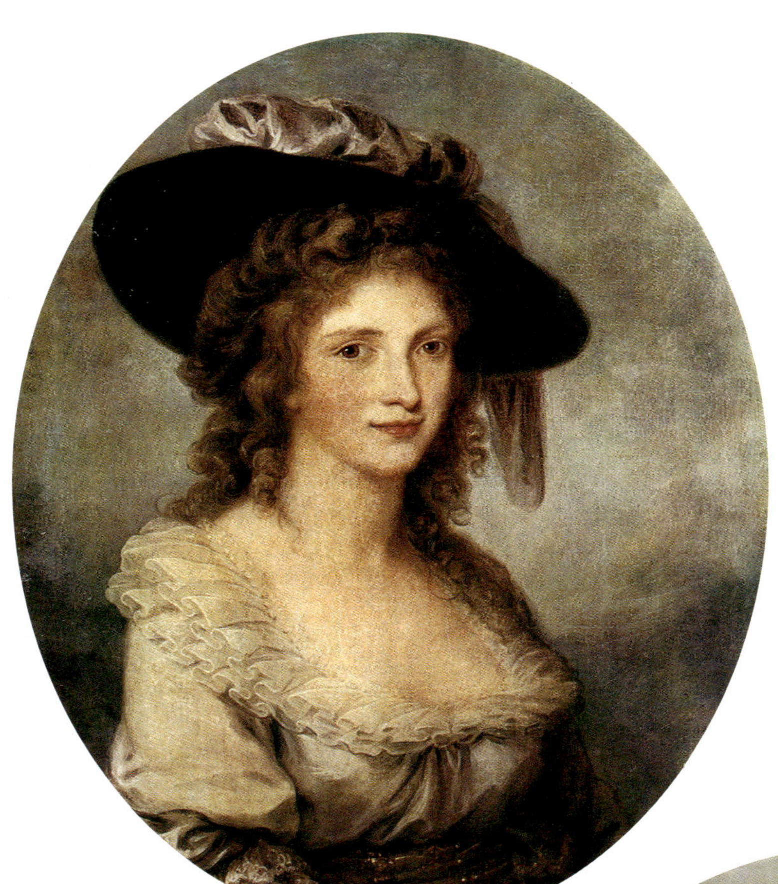

604. **Angelica Kauffmann**, 1741-1807,
Neoclassicism, Swiss,
Self-portrait, 1780-1785.
Oil on canvas, 76.5 x 63 cm.
The State Hermitage Museum, St Petersburg.

ANGELICA KAUFFMANN
(1741 CHUR – 1807 ROME)

Angelica Kauffmann was a Swiss painter,
although she was also a great musician.
Her early works were influenced by the
French Rococo whereas her later were
more influenced by the Neoclassical,
especially when she visited Italy. She was
a prolific painter of portraits, and her
portraits of female sitters are certainly her
finest works.

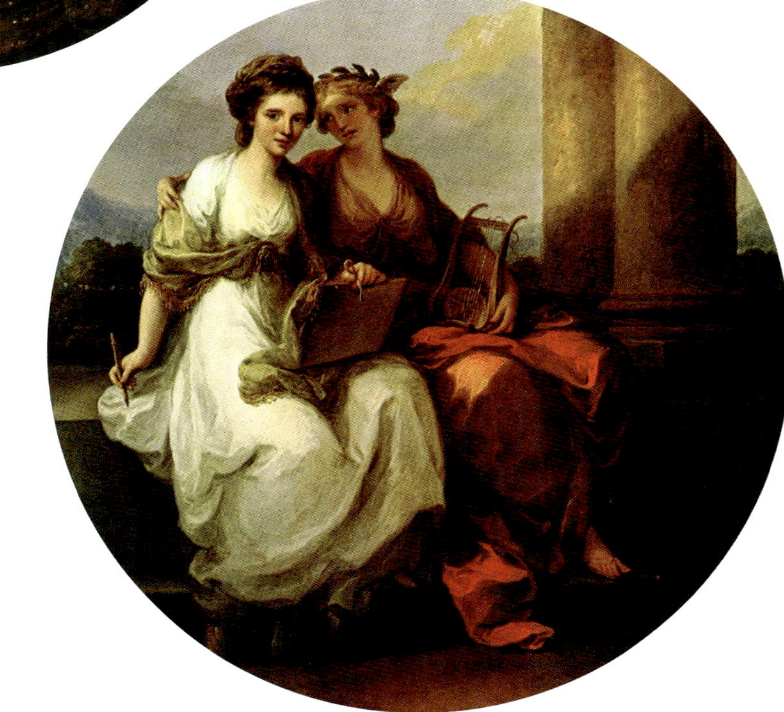

605. **Angelica Kauffmann**, 1741-1807,
Neoclassicism, Swiss, *Allegory of Poetry
and Painting,* 1782.
Oil on canvas, Tondo, diameter: 61 cm.
Private collection, London.

606. **Thomas Gainsborough**, 1727-1788,
Rococo, English. *Mr and Mrs William
Hallett ('The Morning Walk'),* 1785.
Oil on canvas, 236 x 179 cm.
National Gallery, London.

607. **Thomas Gainsborough**, 1727-1788,
Rococo, English, *Mrs Richard Brinsley
Sheridan,* 1785.
Oil on canvas, 220 x 154 cm.
The National Gallery of Art,
Washington D.C.

608. **Johann Heinrich Fuseli**, 1741-1825,
Romanticism, Swiss,
Titania and Bottom, 1780-1790.
Oil on canvas, 217 x 275 cm.
Tate Gallery, London.

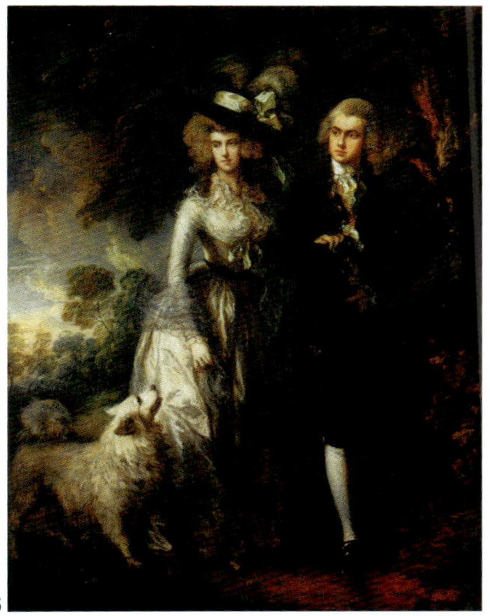

606

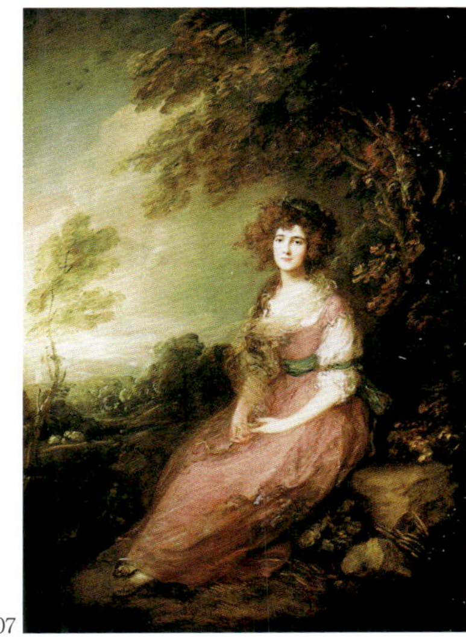

607

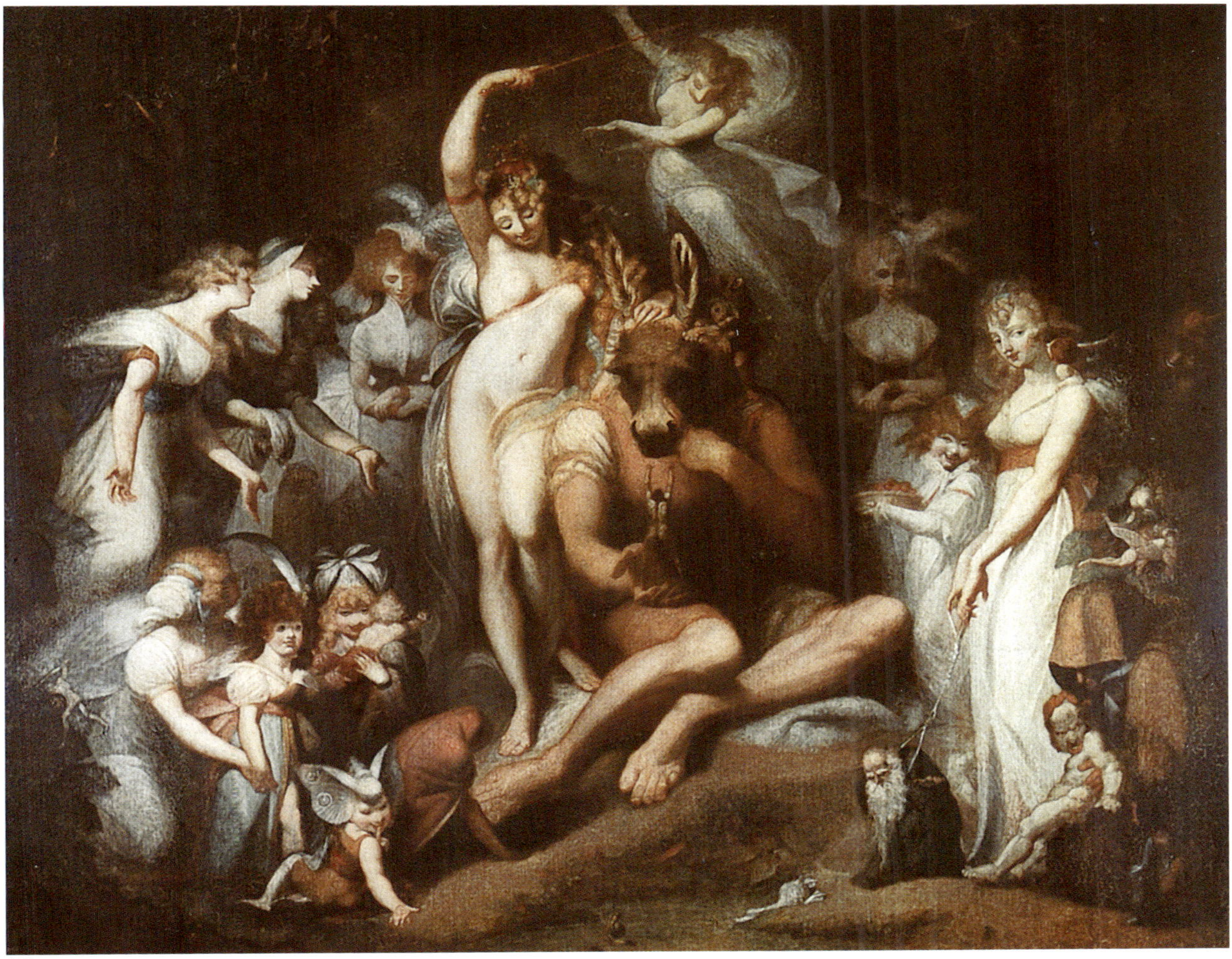

608

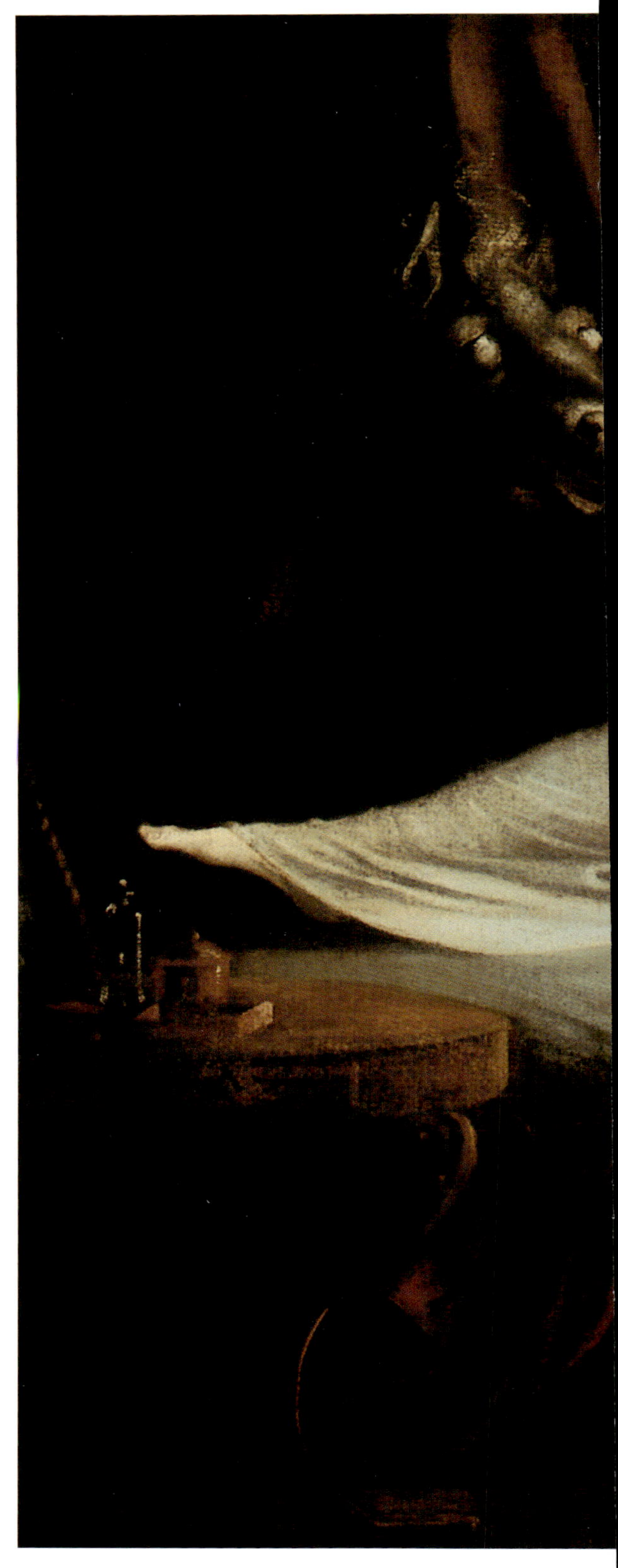

609. **Johann Heinrich Fuseli**, 1741-1825, Romanticism, Swiss,
The Nightmare, 1781.
Oil on canvas, 101.6 x 127 cm.
The Detroit Institute of Arts, Detroit.

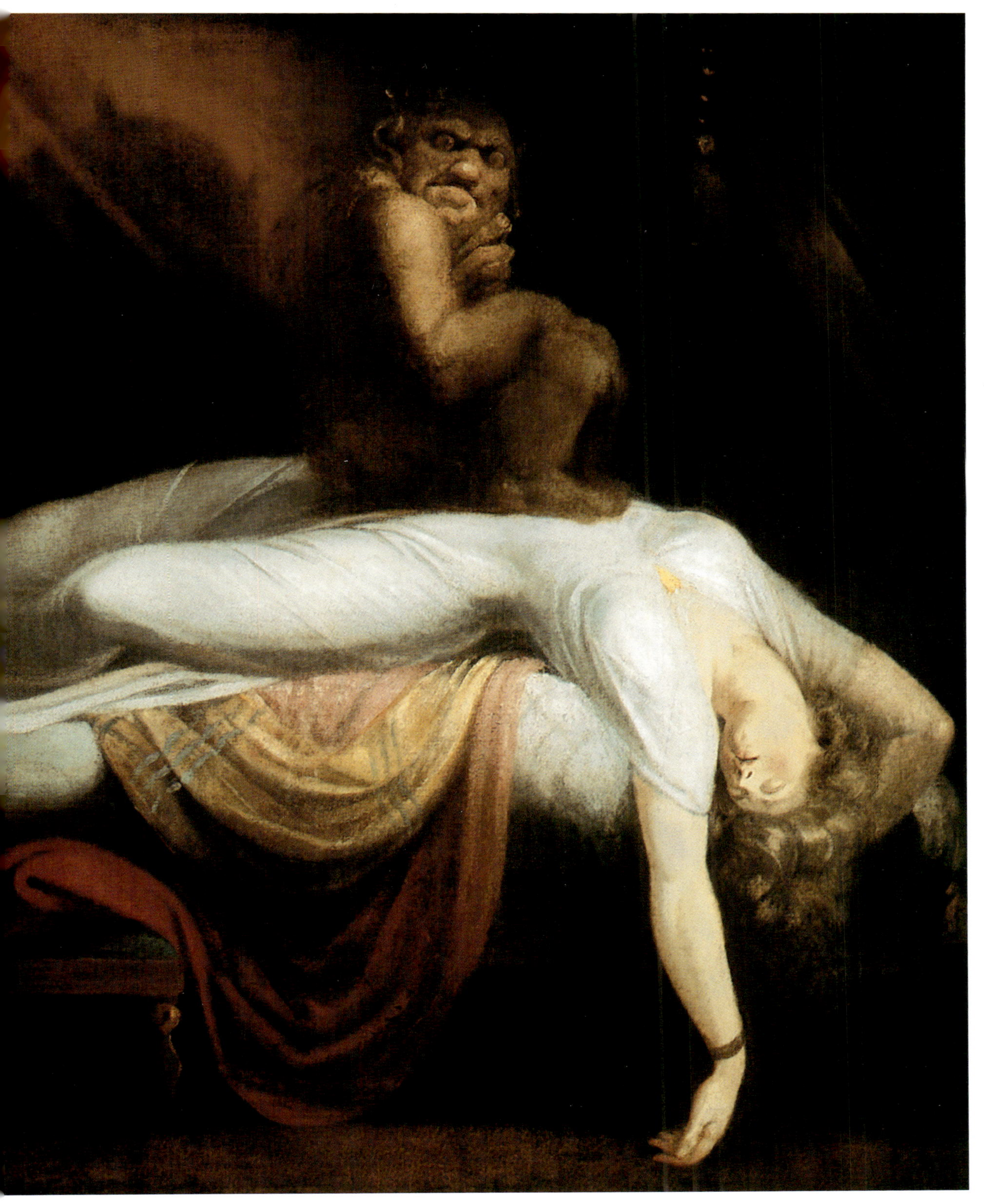

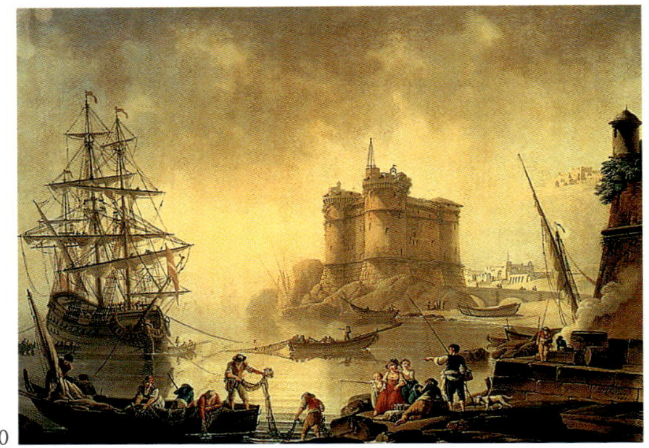

610

JOHN SINGLETON COPLEY
(1738 BOSTON – 1815 LONDON)

Copley was an American painter of portraits and historical subjects who, in 1775, studied under Benjamin West in London. Copley perfected the American Colonial style. Famous for his American portraits, he also used one of the great themes of nineteenth-century Romantic art, the struggle of man against nature, in *Watson and the Shark* (fig. 597). He was elected to the Royal Academy in 1779.

610. **Charles-François de La Croix**, 1700-1782, Romanticism, French, *Harbour with a Fortress*, 1781.
Oil on canvas, 73 x 98 cm.
The State Hermitage Museum, St Petersburg.

611. **John Singleton Copley**, 1738-1815, Realism, American, *The Death of Major Peirson, 6 January 1781*, 1783.
Oil on canvas, 251.5 x 365.8 cm.
Tate Gallery, London.

After being invaded by the French in 1781 the governor of St Helier (the capital of Jersey) surrendered. However, twenty-four year old British Major Peirson rejected the surrender. Instead, the major led a successful counter-attack, but he was killed shortly before the battle. For dramatic effect, Copley combined the moment of British victory with the death of the young commander as if it happened during the battle. In the painting, Peirson can be seen under the Union Flag. Several portraits of officers are in the painting, as is an image of Peirson's black servant. The servant is seen avenging his master's death. Peirson became a national hero, probably due, in no small part, to the popularity of this painting and the artist's convenient manipulation of history. Copley contributed to create the genre of historical painting in England, and the power of art to influence the perception of history is here demonstrated clearly.

611

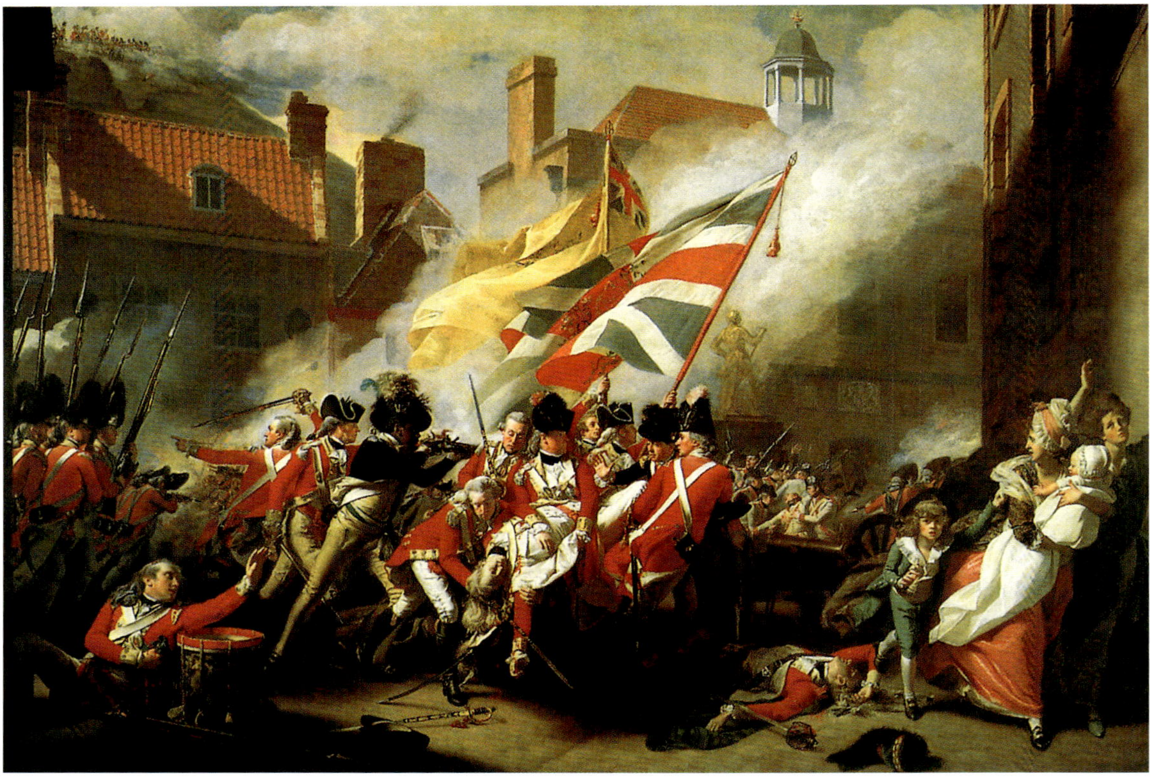

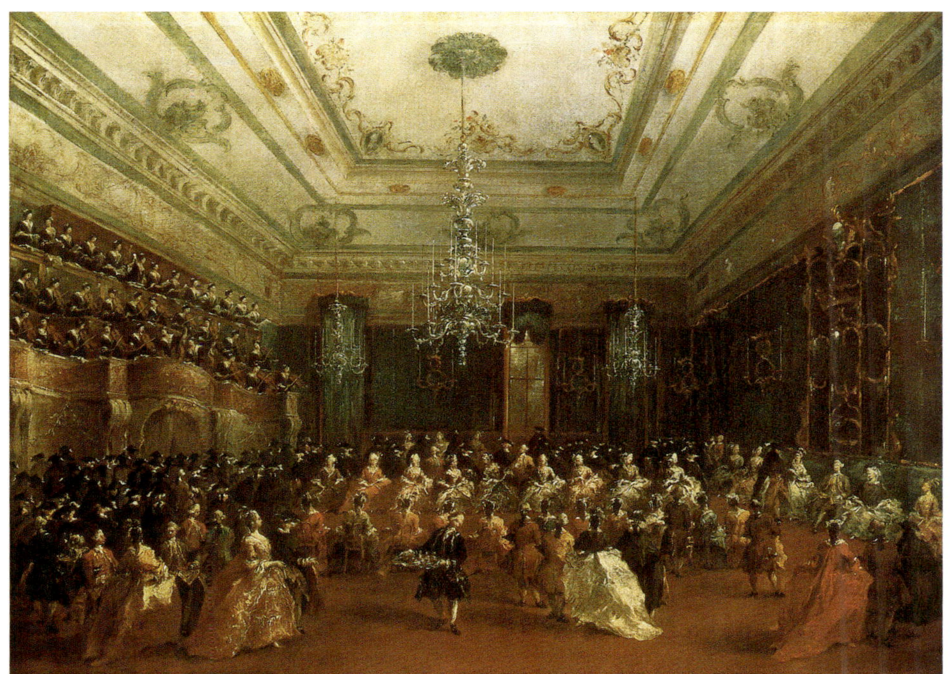

612

612. **Francesco Guardi**,
1712-1793, Rococo,
Italian, *Ladies' Concert at
the Philharmonic Hall,*
c. 1782.
Oil on canvas,
67.7 x 90.5 cm.
Alte Pinakothek, Munich.

613. **Hubert Robert**, 1733-1808,
Romanticism, French,
*Architectural Landscape
with a Canal*, 1783.
Oil on canvas,
129 x 182.5 cm.
The State Hermitage
Museum, St Petersburg.

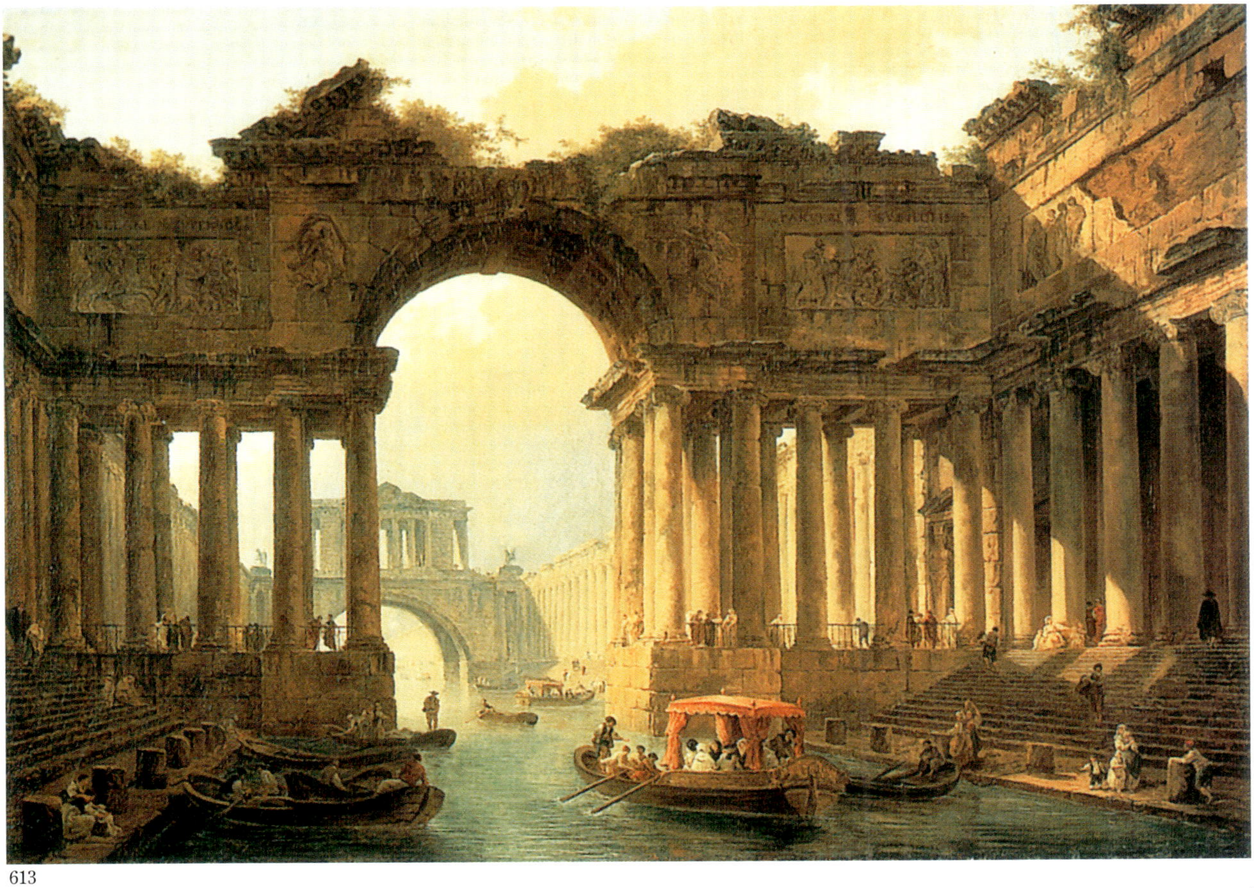

613

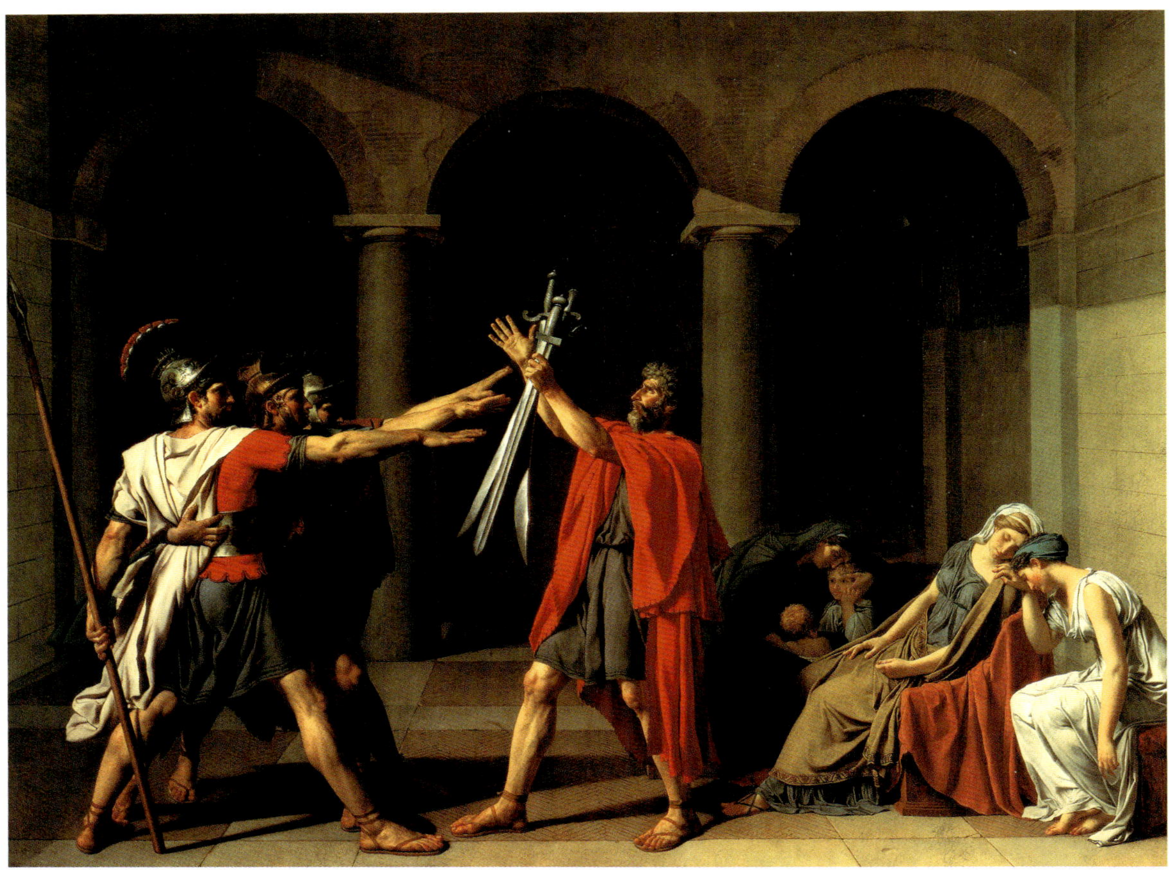

JACQUES-LOUIS DAVID
(1748 PARIS – 1825 BRUSSELS)

Celebrated nowadays as the Imperial Court Painter, David started his apprenticeship with Boucher and then with Joseph-Marie Vien, who was a famous painter renowned for his antique style. In 1774, David won the prix de Rome where he confirmed his passion for antique art. Back in Paris in 1784, he painted his *Oath of the Horatii*, a perfect example of his Neoclassical style: a return to classical painting, to the line, but with something more rigid in the choice of the subjects, influenced by Roman behaviour, love of country and individual heroism. That is why he became the official painter of the French Revolution and its Roman ideals. His *Death of Marat* (fig.623), showing Marat as a secular Christ, is a denunciation of Counter-Revolution crime. However, David stayed the official painter of the Empire, executing the monumental *Coronation of Napoleon* after 1804, the finest official picture in the world, breathing life into a huge ceremonial composition, leaving the Greeks and Romans in order to paint the doings of his contemporaries.

After the fall of the Empire, he left France for Belgium at the Restoration and finished his career there, still inspired by Antiquity but in a less didactic way.

Master of a whole generation of Academic painters like Gros, Ingres or Girodet, he thus had a great influence on the first half of nineteenth-century Academic painting.

614. **Jacques-Louis David**, 1748-1825, Neoclassicism, French, *Oath of the Horatii,* 1784.
Oil on canvas, 330 x 425 cm.
Musée du Louvre, Paris.

David recalled an important event in Roman history in which the fate of the city of Alba Longa was determined by a battle between two rival families: the Horatii from Rome and the Curiatii from Alba. One of the Curiatii's sisters was married to one of the Horatii and one of the Horatii's sisters was betrothed to one of the Curiatii. As their families resign themselves to the inevitable violence, the Horatii brothers embrace each other, strike a formal oath-taking pose in a public place and pledge loyalty to Rome. Eager to take up their swords, the brothers point their common spear beyond the approaching battle and towards the source of light and hope. David pays particular attention to the depiction of human passions, from the vigour and heroism of the Horatii brothers to the grief of the women. But, by emphasising the civic values through antic themes, The Oath of the Horatii bears the banner of Neoclassical art, which defends the priority of reason over emotion. David's painting is theatrical and highlights a precise moment at the pinnacle of the drama.

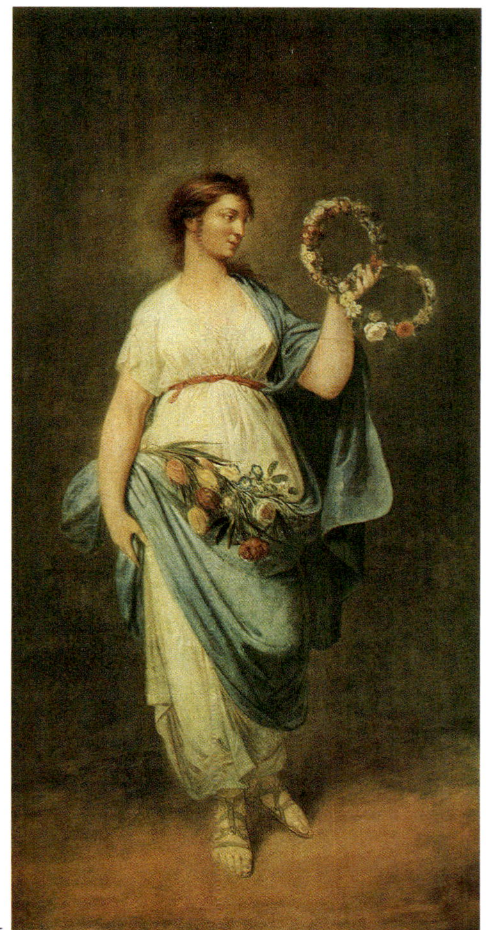

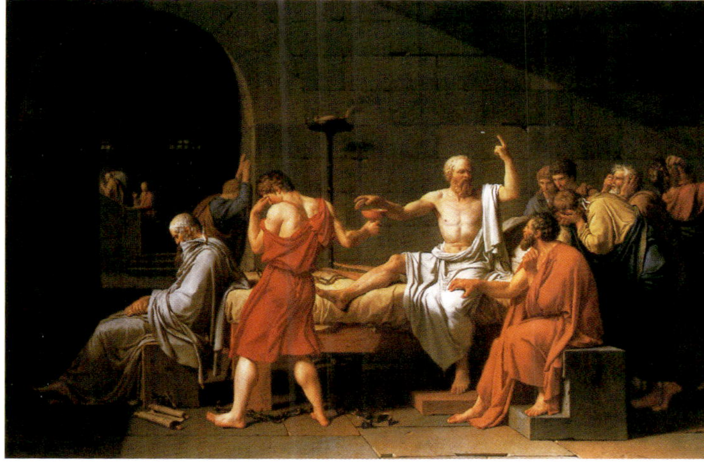

616

617

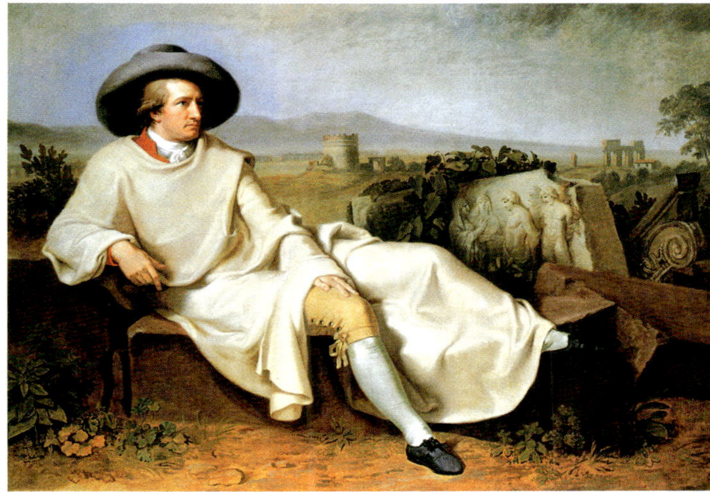

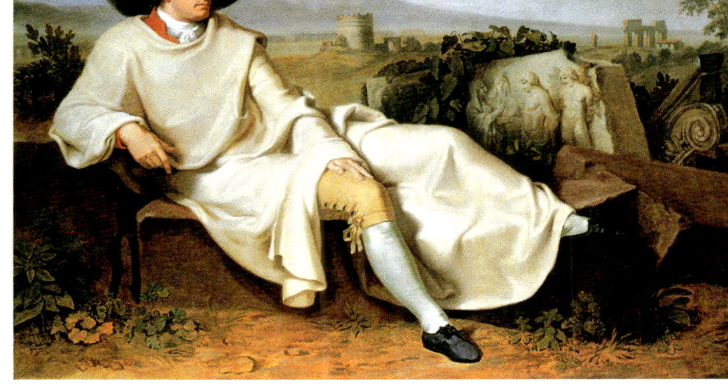

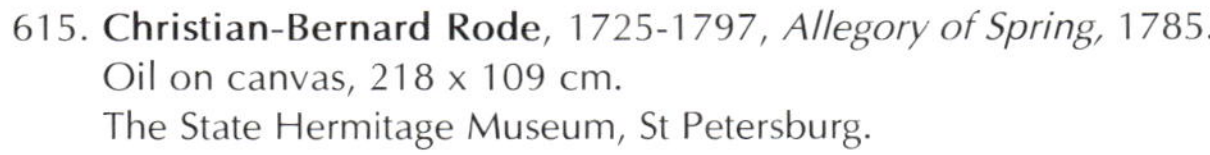

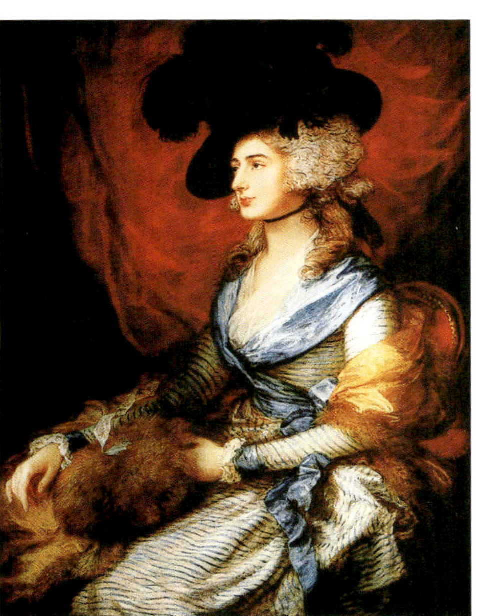

615. **Christian-Bernard Rode**, 1725-1797, *Allegory of Spring*, 1785.
Oil on canvas, 218 x 109 cm.
The State Hermitage Museum, St Petersburg.

616. **Jacques-Louis David**, 1748-1825, Neoclassicism, French,
The Death of Socrates, 1787.
Oil on canvas, 129.5 x 196.2 cm.
The Metropolitan Museum of Art, New York.

The Death of Socrates *exalts moral virtues, rejoining in this aspect the rectitude of the painting's style and composition. The printmaker and publisher John Boydell wrote to Sir Joshua Reynolds that it was "the greatest effort of art since the Sistine Chapel and the Stanze of Raphael [...]. This work would have done honour to Athens at the time of Pericles".*

617. **Johann Heinrich Wilhelm Tischbein**, 1751-1829, Romanticism, German,
Goethe in the Roman Campagna, 1786.
Oil on canvas, 164 x 206 cm. Städelsches Kunstinstitut, Frankfurt.

618. **Thomas Gainsborough**, 1727-1788, Rococo, English,
Mrs Sarah Siddons, 1785.
Oil on canvas, 126 x 99.5 cm. National Gallery, London.

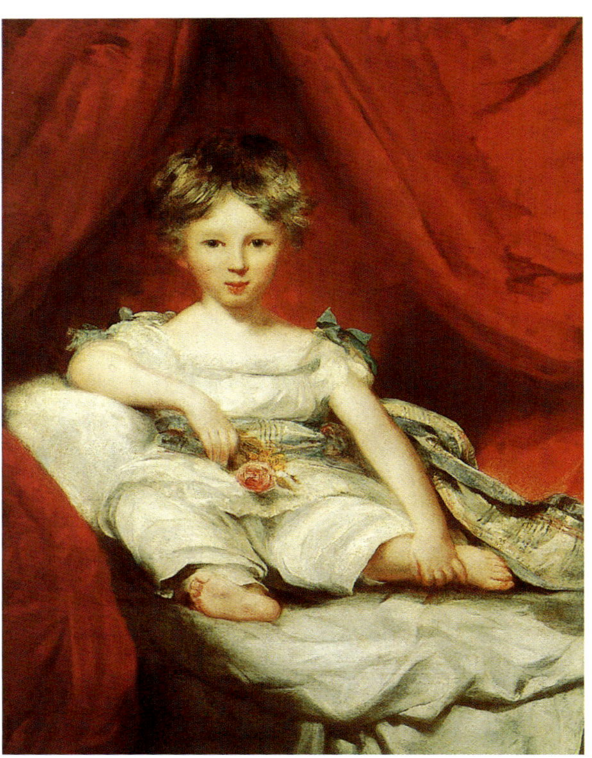

619. **Thomas Lawrence**, 1769-1830, Rococo, English,
Portrait of Master Ainslie, 1794.
Oil on canvas, 91.5 x 71.4 cm.
Fundación Lázaro Galdiano, Madrid.

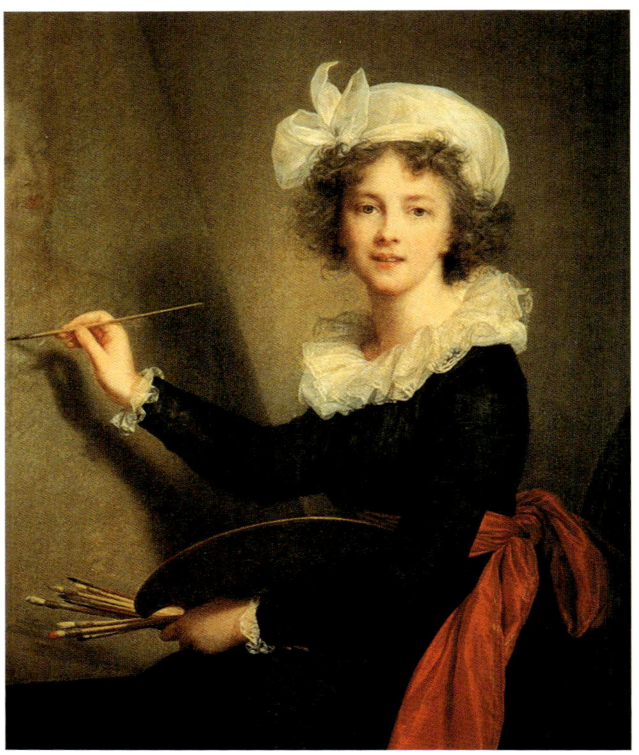

620. **Élisabeth Vigée-Le Brun**, 1755-1842, Neoclassicism, French,
Self-portrait, 1790. Oil on canvas, 100 x 81 cm.
Galleria degli Uffizi, Florence.

Élisabeth Vigée-Le Brun was very famous across Europe for the smooth and flattering style of her portraits.

ÉLISABETH VIGÉE-LE BRUN
(MARIE-LOUISE ÉLISABETH VIGÉE-LE BRUN)
(1755 – 1842 PARIS)

Élisabeth Vigée-Le Brun was her father's student but she benefited from more advice from Gabriel Francois Doyen, Jean-Baptiste Greuze and Joseph Vernet. In 1776 she married the famous painter and art dealer Jean-Baptiste-Pierre Le Brun. Before becoming a member of the Royal Academy of Painting and Sculpture in 1783, she became in 1779 the official court painter of Queen Marie-Antoinette. She made more than twenty-five portraits of her. At the beginning of the French Revolution she left France and lived in Austria and in Italy, where she was made a member of Academia di San Luca, and in Russia, where she was elected at Academy of Fine Arts of St Petersburg. She travelled also in the Netherlands, England and Switzerland before going back to Paris. Her memoirs depict a very interesting, intimate and lively vision of her times as a woman artist working in a period dominated by the royal academies. She is seen as one of the most fluent portraitists of her era and as one of the most successful female artist of all time.

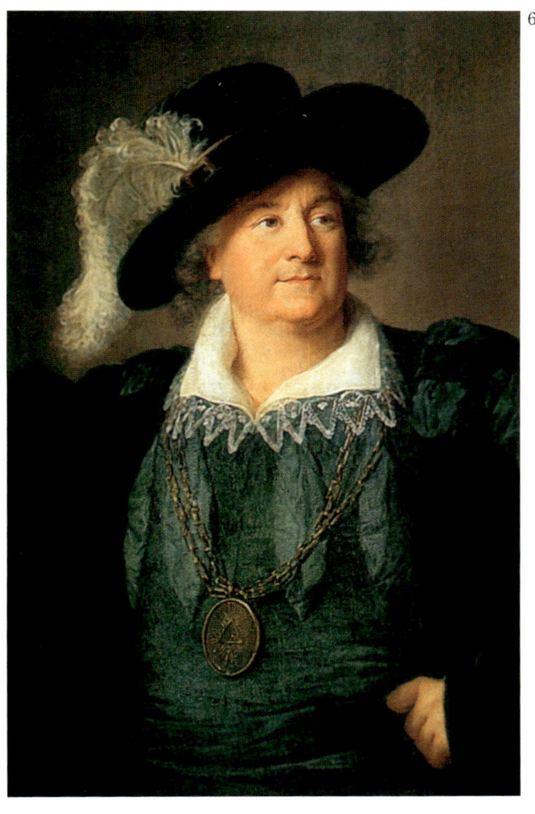

621

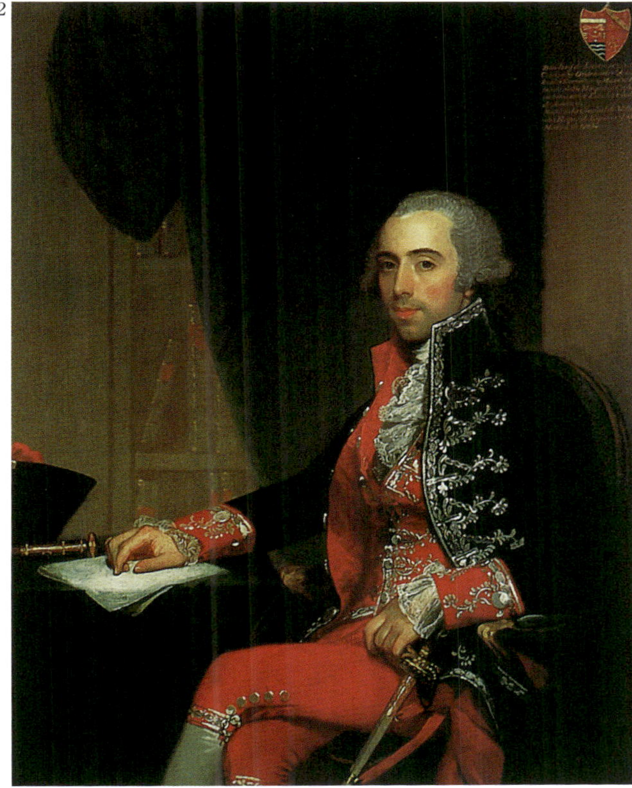

622

623

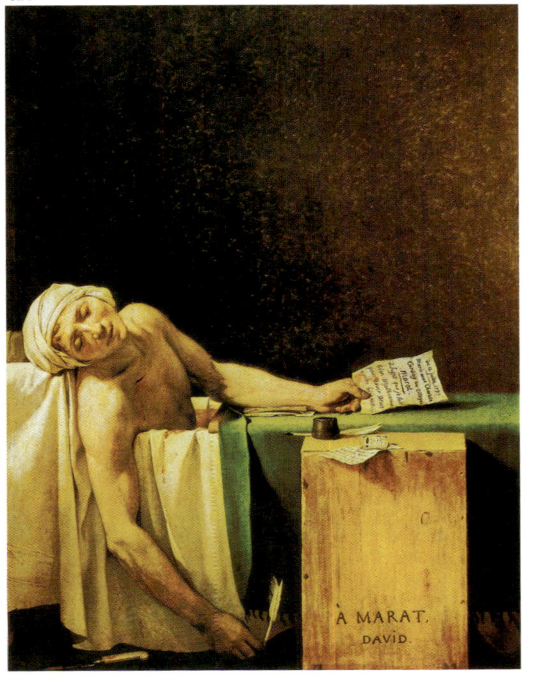

621. **Élisabeth Vigée-Le Brun**, 1755-1842, Neoclassicism, French,
Portrait of Stanislas Auguste Poniatowski, c. 1789-1796.
Oil on canvas, 101.5 x 86.5 cm. Kiev Museum of Western Art, Kiev.

622. **Gilbert Stuart**, 1755-1828, Rococo, American,
Josef de Jaudenes y Nebot, 1794. Oil on canvas, 128 x 101 cm.
The Metropolitan Museum of Art, New York.

623. **Jacques-Louis David**, 1748-1825, Neoclassicism, French,
The Death of Marat, 1793. Oil on canvas, 162 x 128 cm.
Musées Royaux des Beaux-Arts, Brussels.

*David was the greatest proponent of Neoclassicism in France during the
Napoleonic era. As a member of the National Convention (1792) he
supported the Revolution and the execution of Louis XVI. The most famous
of his major contemporary historical paintings is the one created the
following year, the same year as the assassination of his friend Jean Paul
Marat (1744-1793), by the young royalist Charlotte Corday. The man sat at
The Convention, and was a fervent spokesman of "sans-culotte". Striving to
show the victim as a political martyr of the Revolution, the artist positions
the dead victim so as to recall representations of the crucified Jesus, as in
Bronzino's* Deposition of Christ *(1549). The light from the left, which
extracts the body from the dark background, gives a dramatic intensity, not
unlike Caravaggio's manner, and a religious density. The weapon is seen on
the floor in contrast to the nearby writing quills, one of Marat's weapons for
fighting for the Revolution. His body still clutches both a quill and his final
letter, as if to show he is not giving up on his causes even in death.*

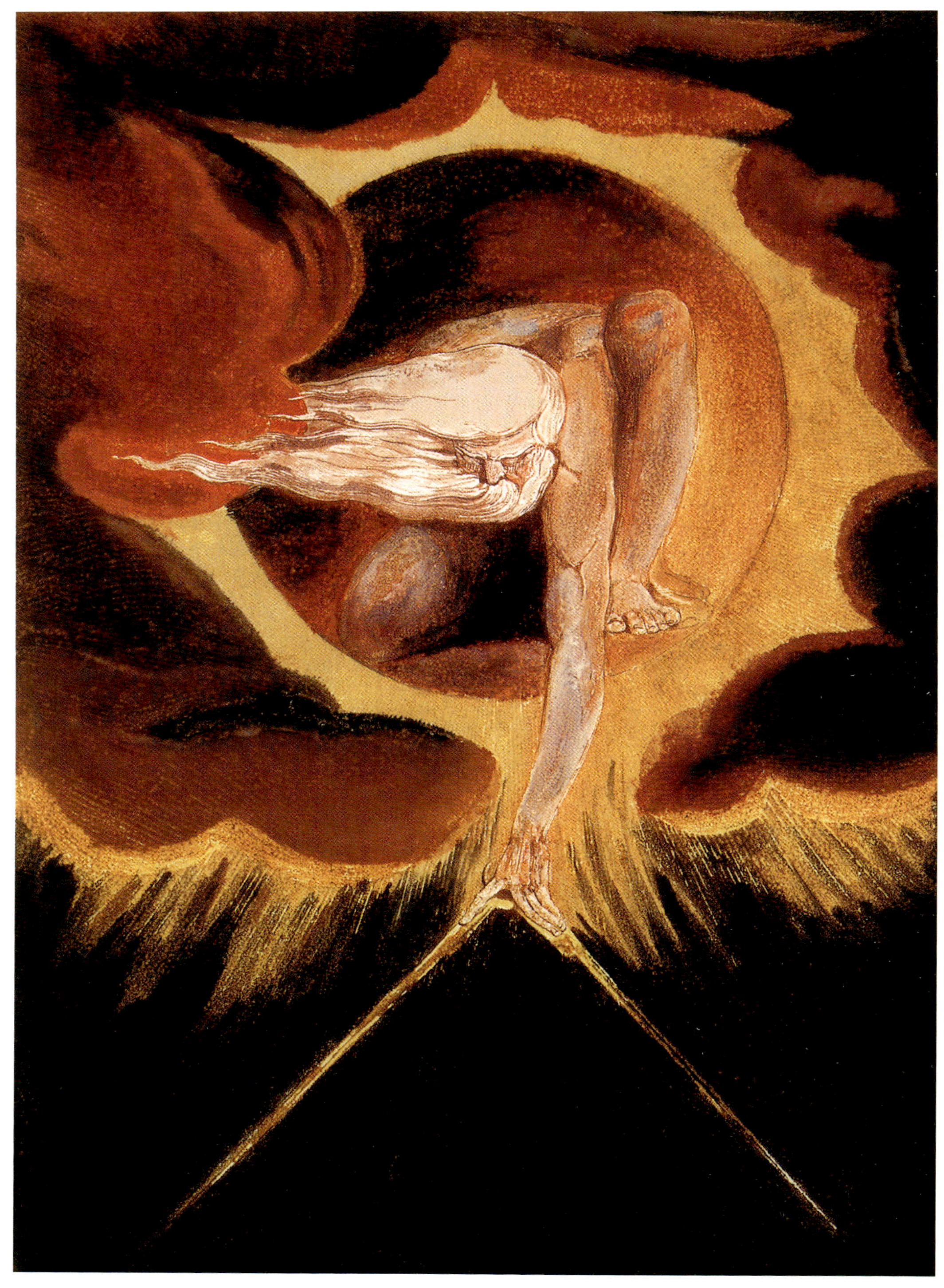

624. **William Blake**, 1757-1827, Romanticism, English,
The Ancient of Days, 1794.
Etching in relief with watercolour, 23.3 x 16.8 cm. The British Museum, London.

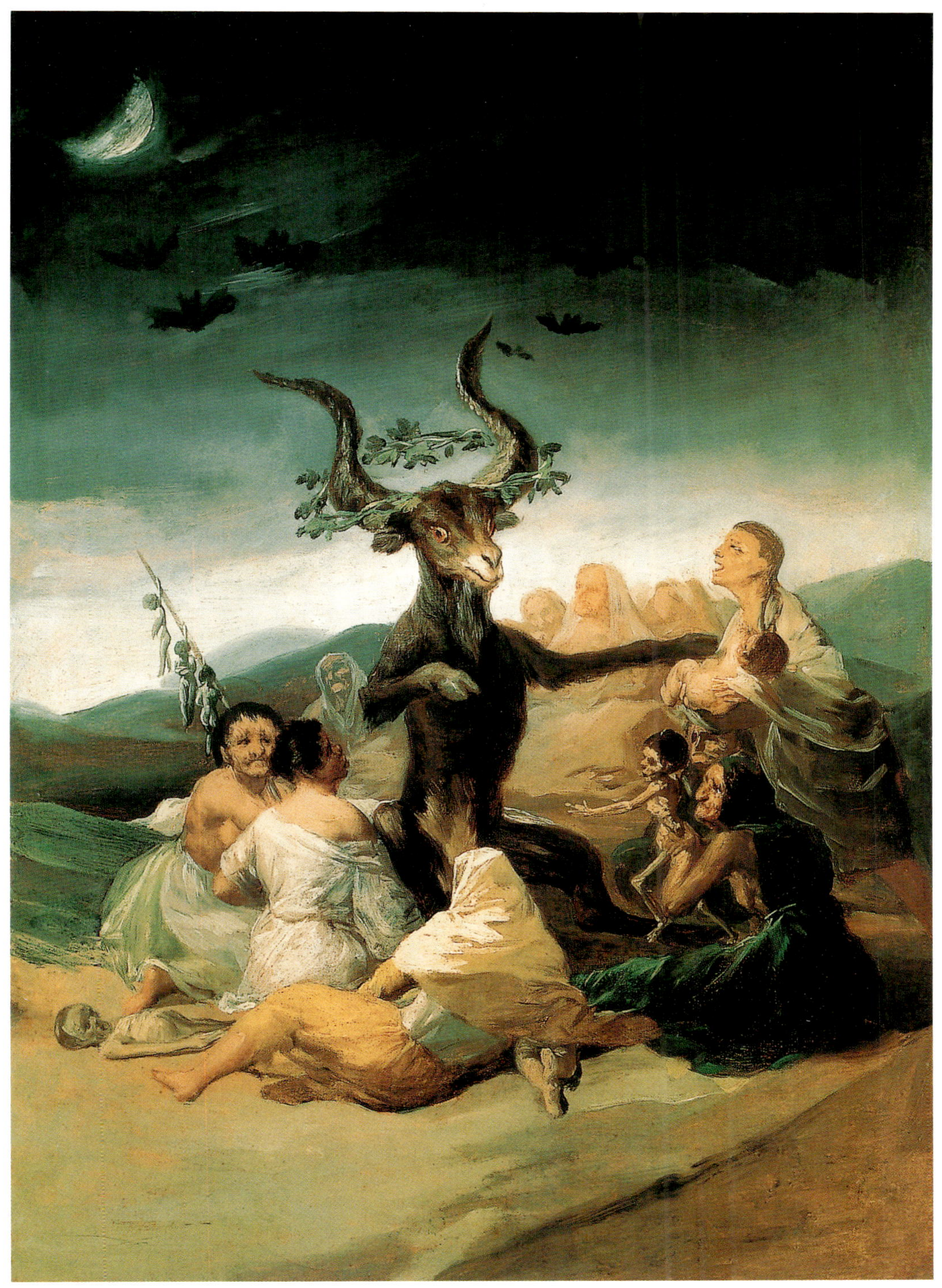

625. **Francesco de Goya y Lucientes**, 1746-1828, Romanticism, Spanish,
El Aquelarre (The Witches' Sabbath), 1797-1798.
Oil on canvas, 44 x 31 cm. Fundación Lázaro Galdiano, Madrid.

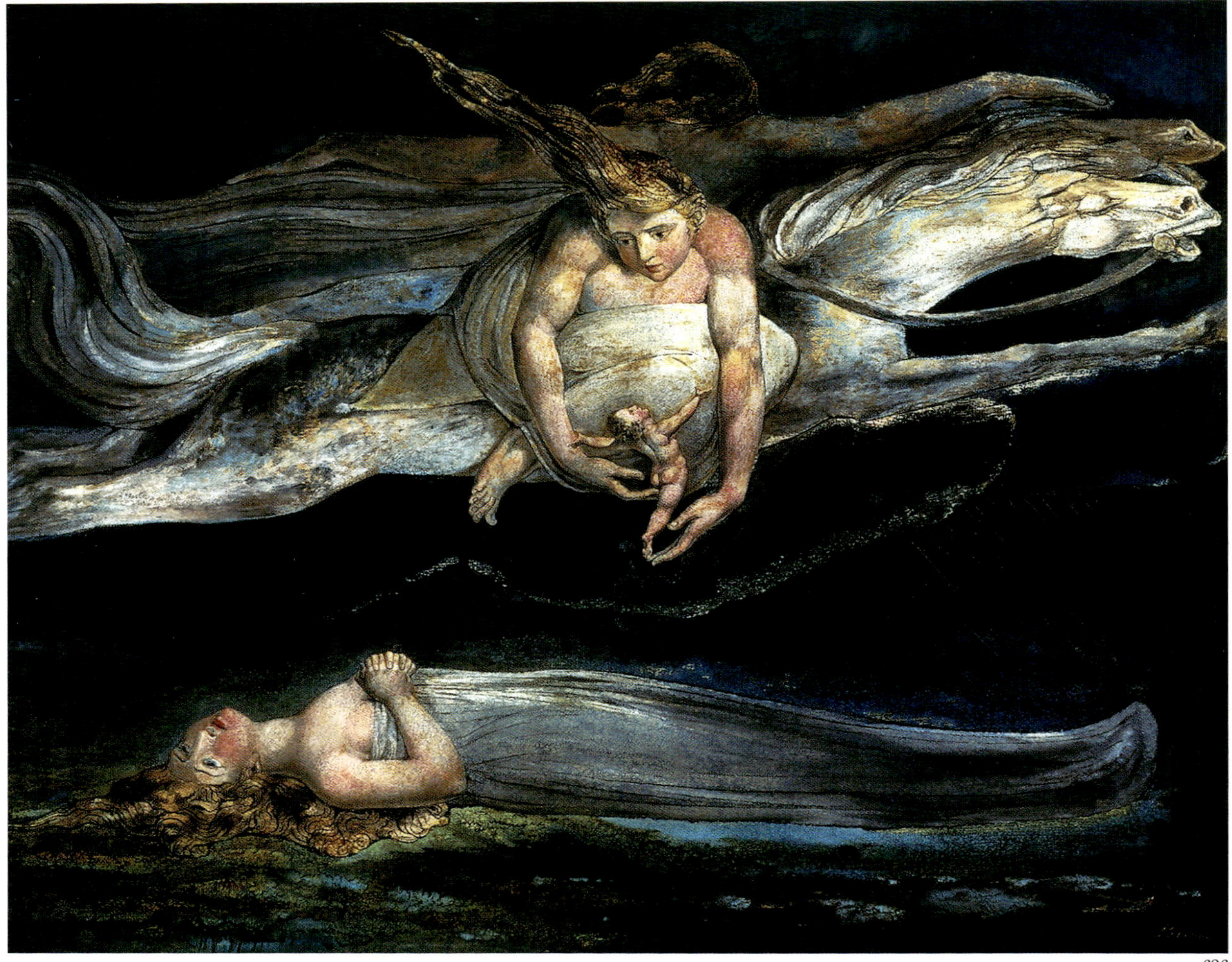

626

WILLIAM BLAKE
(1757 – 1827 LONDON)

Poet, draughtsman, engraver and painter, William Blake's work is made up of several elements – Gothic art, Germanic reverie, the Bible, Milton and Shakespeare – to which were added Dante and a certain taste for linear designs, resembling geometric diagrams, and relates him to the great classical movement inspired by Winckelmann and propagated by David. This is the sole point of contact discernible between the classicism of David and English art, though furtive and indirect. Blake is the most mystic of the English painters, perhaps the only true mystic. He was ingenious in his inner imagination, and his interpretations of ancient and modern poets reveal as true and candid a spirit as the title of his first work – poems he composed, illustrated and set to music, *Songs of Innocence* and *Songs of Experience*. Later he achieved grandeur, power and profundity, especially in certain tempera paintings. Just like others, Blake was considered an eccentric by most of his contemporaries, until his genius was recognised in the second half of the nineteenth century.

626. **William Blake**, 1757-1827, Romanticism, English, *Pity*, 1795. Watercolour heightened with ink on paper, 42 x 54 cm. Tate Gallery, London.

627. **Pierre Henri Valenciennes**, 1750-1819, Neoclassicism, French, *Storm by the Banks of a Lake*, Late 18th century. Oil on canvas, 39.8 x 52 cm. Musée du Louvre, Paris.

628. **Henry Raeburn**, 1756-1823, Romanticism, Scottish, *Reverend Robert Walker Skating on Duddingston Loch,* 1795. Oil on canvas, 76.2 x 63.5 cm. National Gallery of Scotland, Edinburgh.

This serene skater is thought to be the Reverend Robert Walker, minister of the Canongate Kirk and a member of the Edinburgh Skating Society. This small picture, showing a figure in action, is quite unlike other known portraits by Raeburn.

629. **Nicolaj Abildgaard**, 1743-1809, Romanticism, Danish, *The Spirit of Culmin Appears to his Mother*, c. 1794. Oil on canvas, 62 x 78 cm. Nationalmuseum, Stockholm.

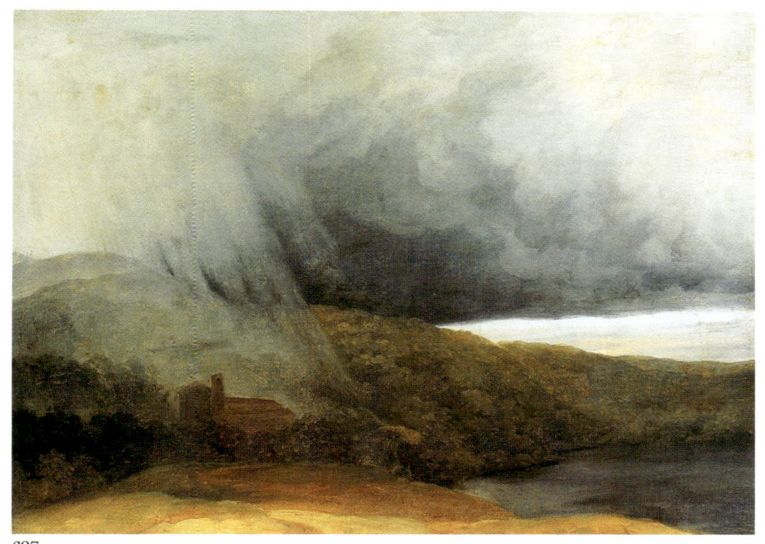

627

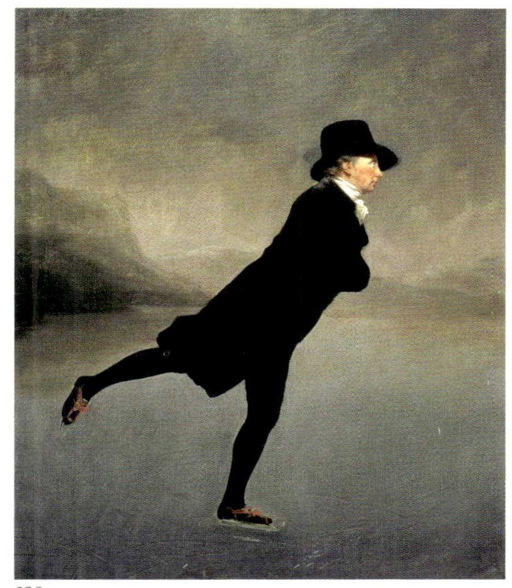

628

629

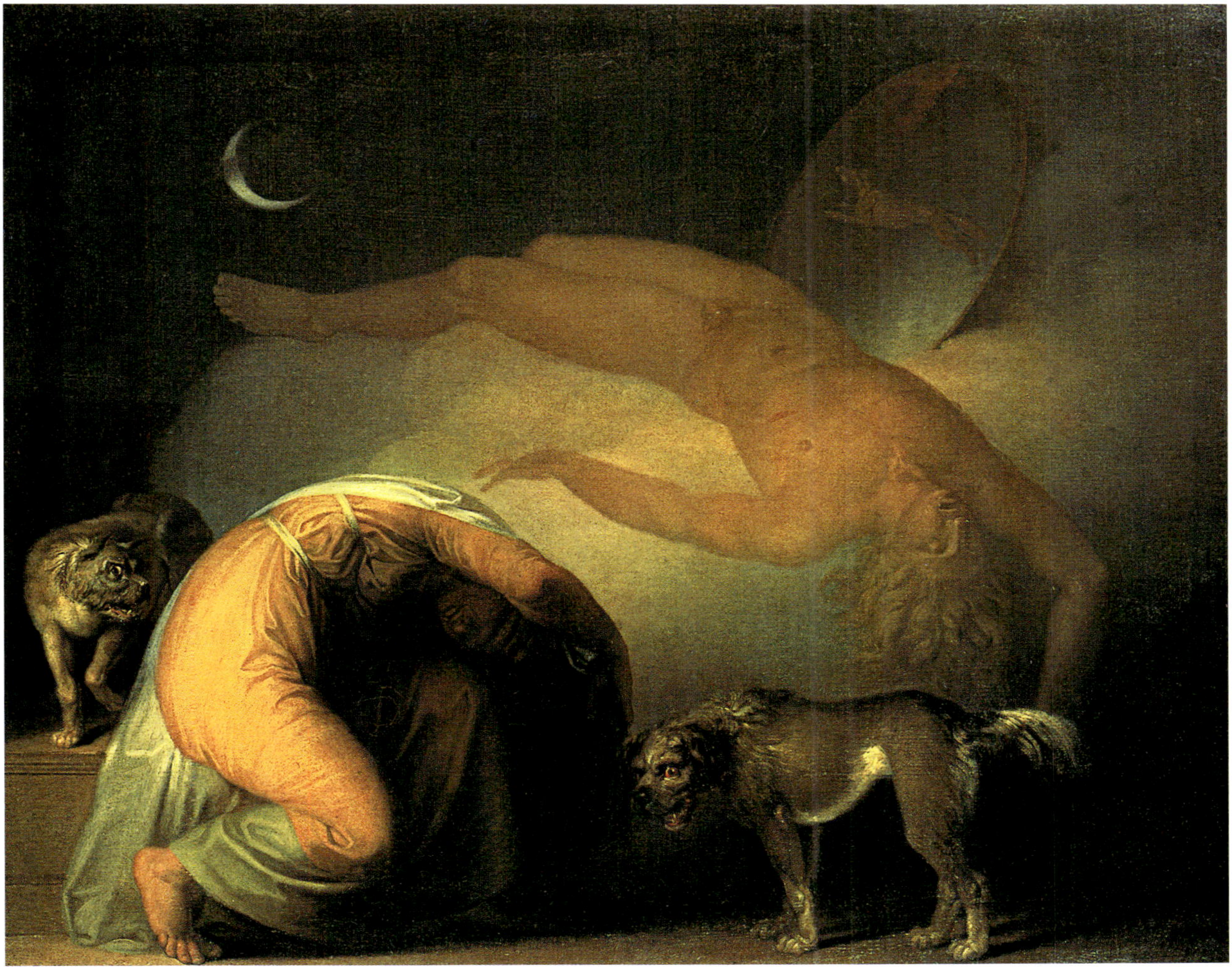

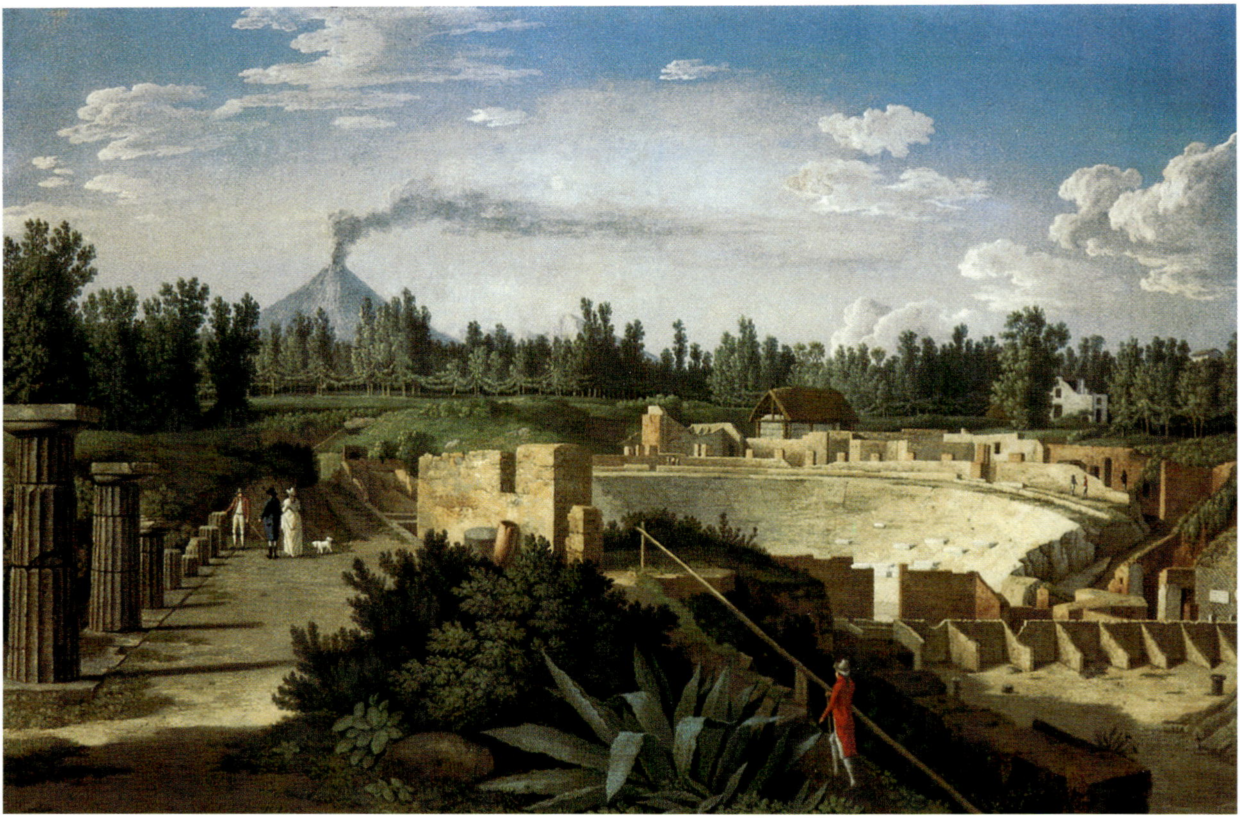

630. **Jacob Philipp Hackert**, 1737-1807, Rococo, German,
View of the Ruins of the Antique Theatre of Pompei, 1793.
Gouache on cardboard, 58.7 x 85 cm.
Goethe-Nationalmuseum, Weimar.

631. **Hubert Robert**, 1733-1808, Rococo, French,
Design for the Grande Galerie in the Louvre, 1796.
Oil on canvas, 115 x 145 cm.
Musée du Louvre, Paris.

633. **Anne-Louis Girodet**, 1767-1824, Neoclassicism, French,
Mademoiselle Lange as Danaë, 1799.
Oil on canvas, 60.3 x 48.6 cm.
Minneapolis Institue of Arts, Minneapolis.

632. **Hubert Robert**, 1733-1808, Rococo, French, *Imaginary View
of the Grande Galerie in the Louvre in Ruins,* 1796.
Oil on canvas, 115 x 145 cm.
Musée du Louvre, Paris.

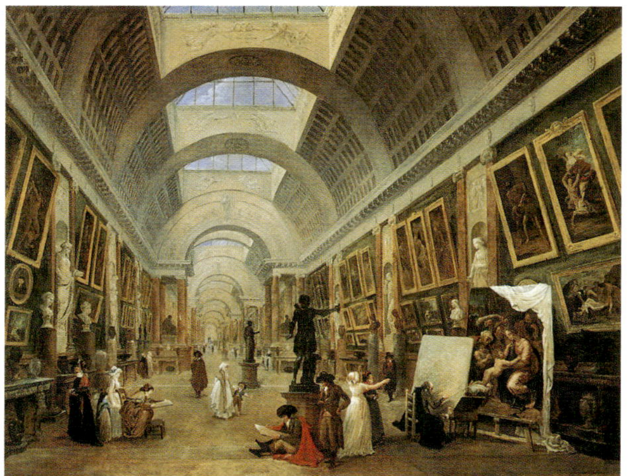

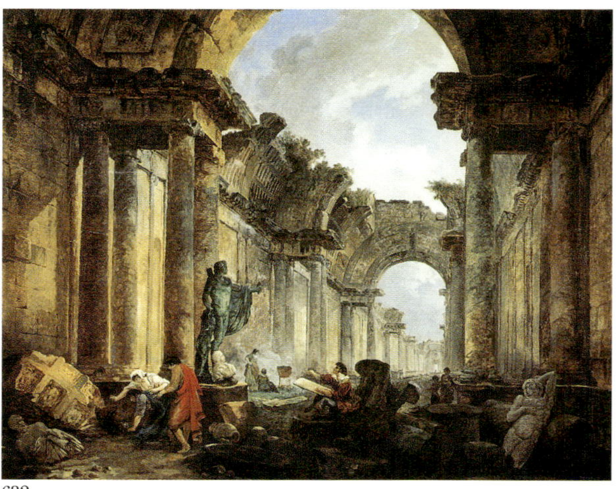

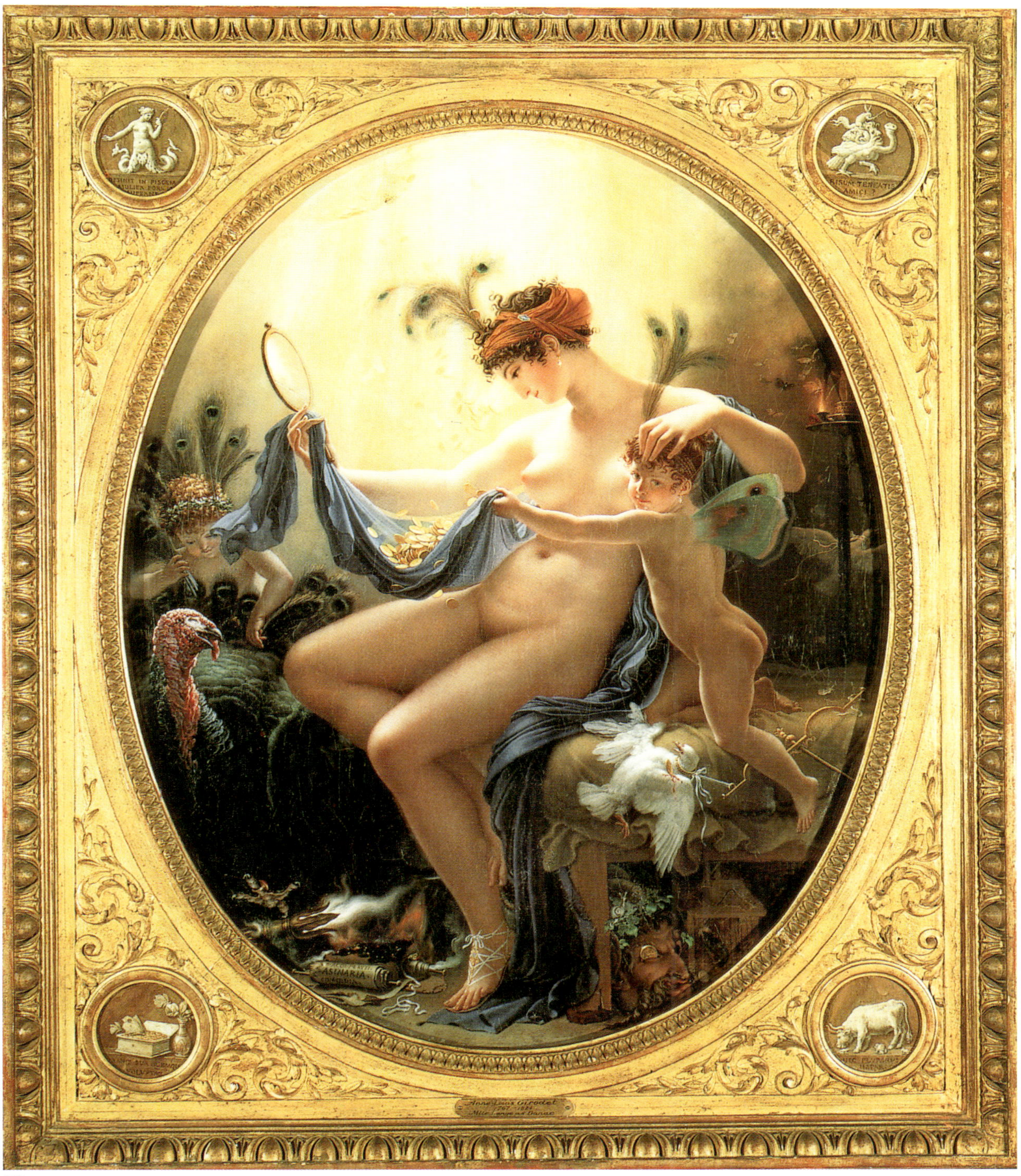

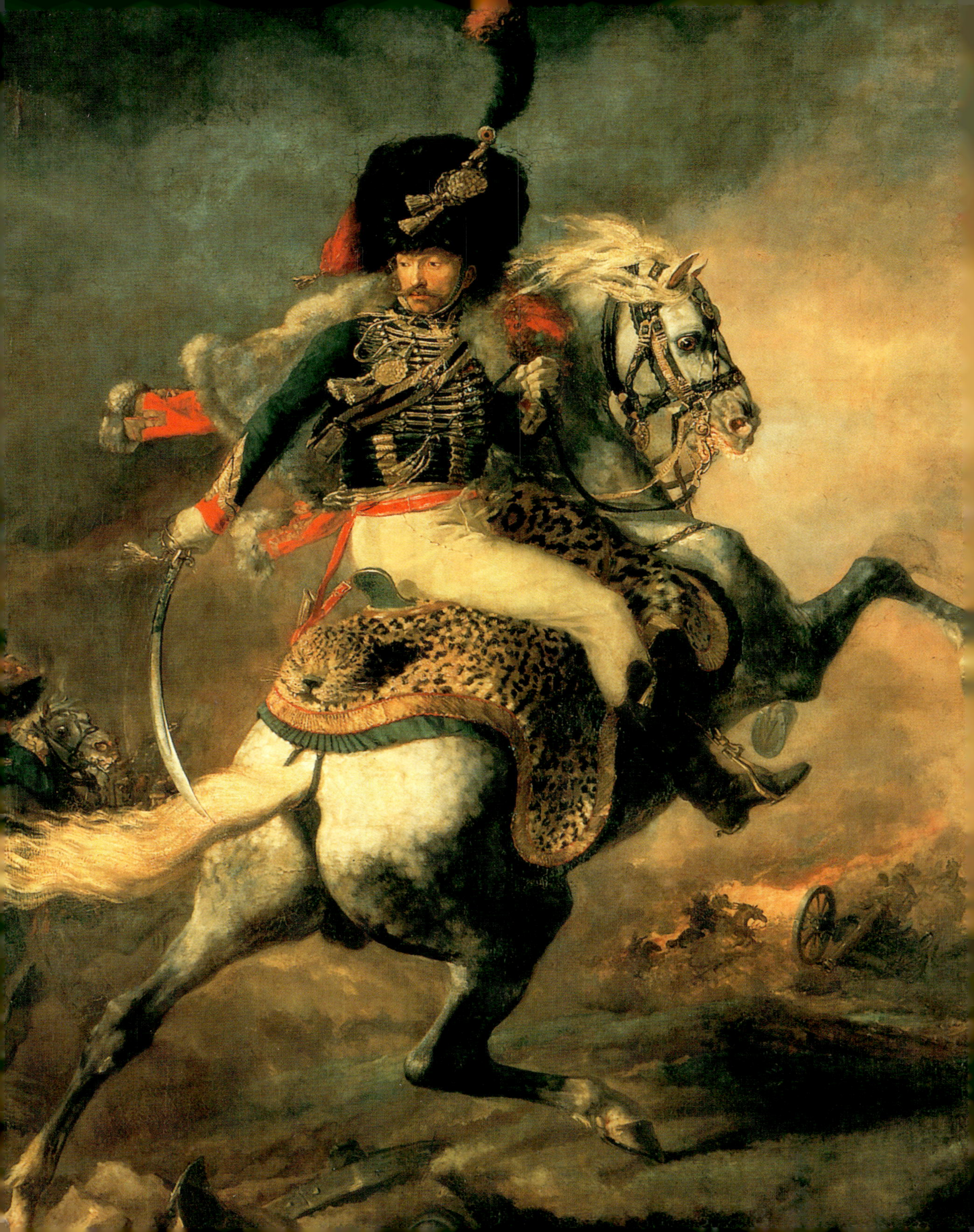

The Modern Era

At the dawn of the nineteenth century, the visual arts were dominated by Romanticism, which painters such as Delacroix took to a peak in the years 1800-1840. This heterogeneous movement focused on the individual, exalting the emotions over rationalism. The updating of older genres, including those dating from the Middle Ages, contributed to the pluralism of the Romantic style, while European colonial expansion around the world inspired a new generation of Orientalist painters.

Photography, invented in 1839, presented a challenge for Realist painting. Freed from the need to copy nature, painters began to observe the phenomenon of light as explicated in Chevreul's *The Principles of Harmony and Contrast of Colours* (1839), which led to the Impressionism of Monet and Renoir. Throughout the modern era, in response to changing societies, numerous art movements emerged. Both the Post-Impressionists such as Van Gogh and the Expressionism of artists such as Franz Marc used colour more aggressively. At the same time, Picasso freed forms from nature, and the Italian Futurists found ways to paint movement and the passing of time, helping to sow the seeds of abstraction. In the mid-nineteenth Karl Marx wrote his *Manifesto of the Communist Party* (1848) and *Das Kapital* (1867-1894), in which he outlined a new theory of the working class and the labour market in the context of social relations. Though many Realist painters, such as Courbet, wanted to represent the ordinary workers, few of them actually belonged to these classes.

Following the industrial revolution of the nineteenth century, the early twentieth century saw the emergence of an international industrial capitalism. Nationalism and imperialism also increased and in many parts of Europe there were outbreaks of protest, such as the Bolshevik Revolution of 1917 in Russia which marked the advent of communism and the end of the country's absolute monarchy. This, combined with rivalry between nations, triggered the first major event of the modern era, the First World War (1914-1918), which paved the way for the establishment of new totalitarian powers in Eastern Europe. In the midst of this chaos, Freud became interested in the workings of the unconscious, and in 1916 published his *Introduction to Psychoanalysis*. His theories would later exert a strong influence on the Surrealist movement. Then, on 24 October, 1929, the US stock market collapsed, causing widespread economic turmoil and the beginning of the Great Depression, which lasted until the outbreak of the Second World War. During these years, the economic and social conditions made many European countries vulnerable to Fascism. While Roosevelt's system of state patronage, the New Deal, infused American art with energy, in Hitler's Germany many modernist art works were labelled 'degenerate' and destroyed. For the Nazis and other totalitarian governments, art was primarily useful as a propaganda tool. The outbreak of war in 1939 plunged European nations once again into international conflict and redistributed forces across the globe.

During the postwar period, Europe gradually lost its colonies and two radically opposed superpowers, the United States built on capitalism, and the Soviet Union representing communism, emerged, giving birth to the so-called Cold War. Though armed violence broke out once again with the Vietnam War (1957-1975), hostilities between the major powers ultimately gave way to détente, leading in 1991 to the collapse of the Soviet Union. All these events led to a new geopolitical balance and required a change in mental attitudes: women became more liberated and in the US the Civil Rights movement helped bring an end to racial segregation. Faced with the violence of the modern world, artists throughout the twentieth century turned to concepts of destabilisation and the overturn of classical ideals.

634. Théodore Géricault, 1791-1824, Romanticism, French,
An Officer of the Imperial Horse Guards Charging, 1812.
Oil on canvas, 349 x 266 cm.
Musée du Louvre, Paris.

In 1812, the French Empire staggered. Géricault catches this aspect in this very realistic portrait that, rather than exalting the virtues of the war, criticises it. Géricault rejected the classical linearity and contravenes the neo-classical glacis as he painted with a thick touch. Just one character is depicted. Géricault went to the essential, and gave up the superfluous with every anecdotal element he added. The sitter, bending toward the viewer, transgresses the academic representation of cavaliers who concentrate on action.

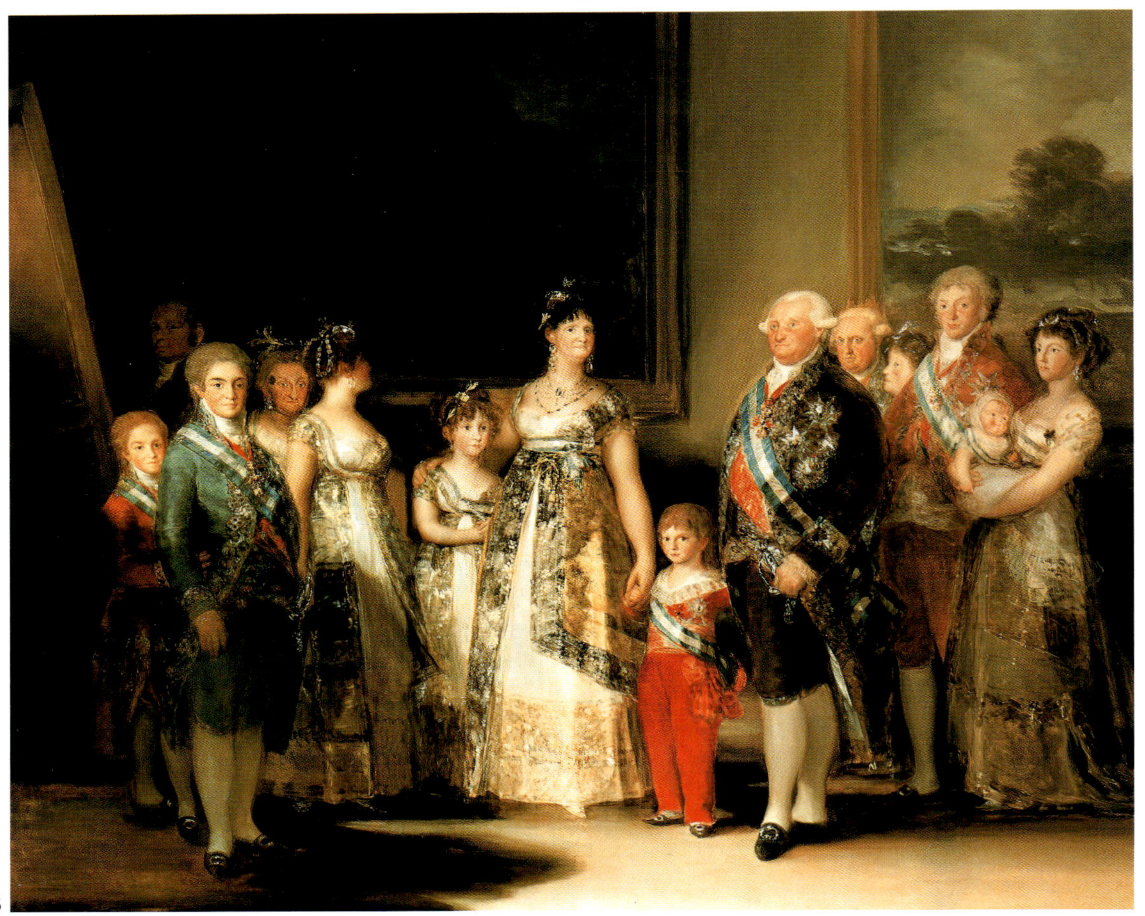

635

FRANCISCO DE GOYA Y LUCIENTES
(1746 FUENDETODOS – 1828 BORDEAUX)

Goya is perhaps the most approachable of painters. His art, like his life, is an open book. He concealed nothing from his contemporaries, and offered his art to them with the same frankness. The entrance to his world is not barricaded with technical difficulties. He proved that if a man has the capacity to live and multiply his experiences, to fight and work, he can produce great art without classical decorum and traditional respectability. He was born in 1746, in Fuendetodos, a small mountain village of a hundred inhabitants. As a child he worked in the fields with his two brothers and his sister until his talent for drawing put an end to his misery. At fourteen, supported by a wealthy patron, he went to Saragossa to study with a court painter and later, when he was nineteen, on to Madrid.

Up to his thirty-seventh year, if we leave out of account the tapestry cartoons of unheralded decorative quality and five small pictures, Goya painted nothing of any significance, but once in control of his refractory powers, he produced masterpieces with the speed of Rubens. His court appointment was followed by a decade of incessant activity – years of painting and scandal, with intervals of bad health.

Goya's etchings demonstrate a draughtsmanship of the first rank. In paint, like Velázquez, he is more or less dependent on the model, but not in the detached fashion of the expert in still-life. If a woman was ugly, he made her a despicable horror; if she was alluring, he dramatised her charm. He preferred to finish his portraits at one sitting and was a tyrant with his models. Like Velázquez, he concentrated on faces, but he drew his heads cunningly, and constructed them out of tones of transparent greys. Monstrous forms inhabit his black-and-white world: these are his most profoundly deliberated productions. His fantastic figures, as he called them, fill us with a sense of ignoble joy, aggravate our devilish instincts and delight us with the uncharitable ecstasies of destruction. His genius attained its highest point in his etchings on the horrors of war. When placed beside the work of Goya, other pictures of war pale into sentimental studies of cruelty. He avoided the scattered action of the battlefield, and confined himself to isolated scenes of butchery. Nowhere else did he display such mastery of form and movement, such dramatic gestures and appalling effects of light and darkness. In all directions Goya renewed and innovated.

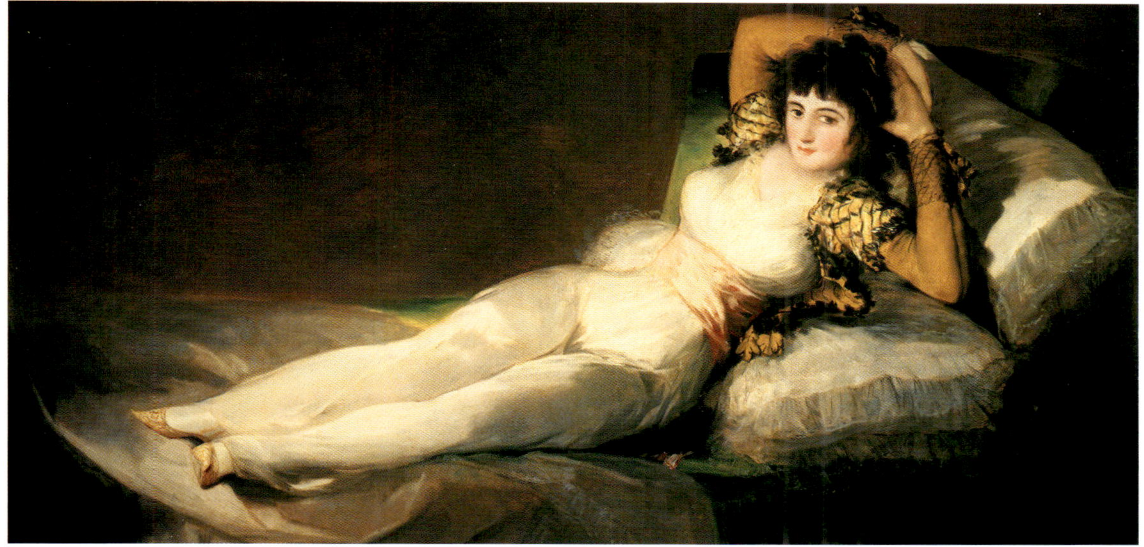

636

635. Francisco de Goya y Lucientes, 1746-1828, Romanticism, Spanish, *Family of Charles IV,* 1800-1801.
Oil on canvas, 280 x 336 cm.
Museo Nacional del Prado, Madrid.

As principal painter to Charles IV, Goya's main task was to provide numerous portraits of the king and his family. Goya's large painting of the Family of Charles IV *of 1800, places life-sized members of the royal family in an ostentatious display of costume and jewellery. Queen Maria Luisa is centre stage with her two youngest children. She wears a sleeveless dress to show off her arms, of which she was so proud that she forbade the use of gloves in court. Although the costumes sparkle, the king's and queen's expressions are so dull that they provoked the French novelist, Théophile Gautier, to compare them to "the corner baker and his wife after they have won the lottery". On the left of the painting, in blue, stands the heir to the throne, the future despot Ferdinand VII. Beside him are his brother, the Infante Don Carlos Maria Isidro, and a woman who turns towards the queen and may be Ferdinand's future wife. It is thought that her features were not included because, at the time of the painting, the engagement was not official. Peeking between the couple is Doña Maria Josefa, the king's sister, who died shortly after the completion of the painting. To the right of the king are other close relatives: his brother, the Infante Antonio Pascal; his eldest daughter, the Infanta Doña Carlota Joaquina; and, holding a child, another daughter, the Infanta Doña Maria Luisa Josefina and her husband, Don Luis de Borbón. Once again, Goya includes himself in the painting, in the shadows on the left, at work on a canvas. Without expression, he stares out of the painting as if looking at the group in a mirror. The royal family is depicted without any attempt at flattering their features, and with their decadence and pretensions clearly exposed, it is somewhat surprising that they did not object.*

636. Francisco de Goya y Lucientes, 1746-1828, Romanticism, Spanish, *The Clothed Maja,* 1800-1803.
Oil on canvas, 95 x 190 cm.
Museo Nacional del Prado, Madrid.

637. François Gérard, 1770-1837, Neoclassicism, French, *Portrait of Katarzyna Starzenska,* c. 1803.
Oil on canvas, 215 x 130.5 cm.
Picture Gallery, Lvov.

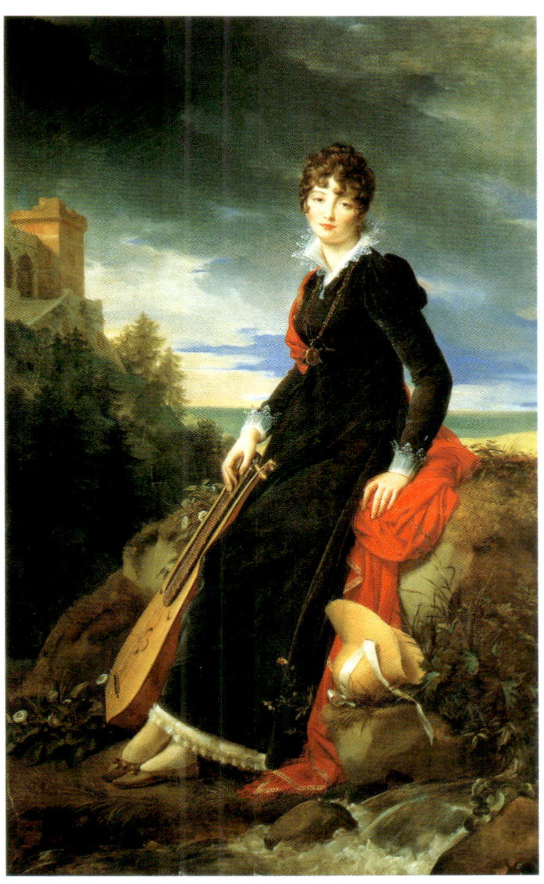

637

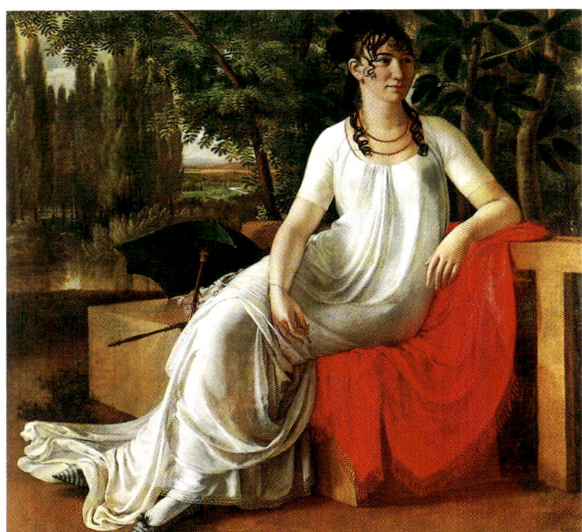

638. **Gottlieb Schick,** 1776-1812, Neoclassicism, German,
Wilhelmine von Cotta, 1802.
Oil on canvas, 133 x 140.5 cm. Staatsgalerie, Stuttgart.

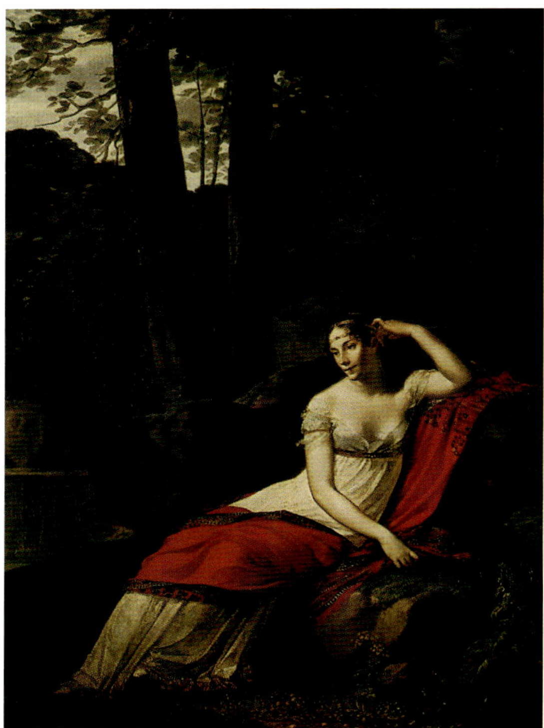

639. **Pierre-Paul Prud'hon,** 1758-1823, Neoclassicism,
French, *The Empress Joséphine,* 1805.
Oil on canvas, 244 x 179 cm. Musée du Louvre, Paris.

*His nickname was the "French Correggio". Prud'hon
represents Josephine de Beauharnais in a poetic landscape
emulating the admired English "plein-air" portraits.*

JEAN–AUGUSTE–DOMINIQUE INGRES
(1780 MONTAUBAN – 1867 PARIS)

Ingres at first seemed destined to continue brilliantly the work
of his master David both in portrait and historical painting. He
won the *Prix de Rome* in 1801. Ingres, however, soon
emancipated himself. He was only twenty-five when he painted
the Rivière portraits. These show an original talent and a taste for
composition not without some mannerism, but the mannerism is
full of charm, and the refinement of undulating lines is as far
removed as possible from the simple and slightly rough realism
which is the strength of David's portraits. His contemporary rivals
were not deceived. They attacked his "archaic" and "singular"
taste and dubbed him "Gothic" and "Chinese". During the Salon
of 1824 however, back from Italy, Ingres was promoted to leader
of the Academic style in opposition to the new romanticism led
by Delacroix.

In 1834, he was appointed director of the French School in
Rome, where he stayed for seven years. Then after his return he
was again acclaimed as master of traditional values and finished
his days in his home town in southern France. The biggest
contradiction in Ingres' career is his title of *Guardian of the
Classical Rules and Precepts,* although we still perceive
eccentricity in some of the most beautiful of his works. A pedant,
seeing the back of *La Grande Odalisque* (fig. 646) and various
exaggerations of form in *The Turkish Bath* (fig. 699) would point
to this incomparable draughtsman's faults. But are these not the
means by which a great and extremely sensitive artist interprets
his passion for the beautiful female form? When he wanted to
group a large number of people in a monumental work such as
L'Apothéose d'Homère, Ingres never attained the ease, the
suppleness, the life, or the unity which we admire in the
magnificent decorative compositions of Delacroix. On the other
hand, he had an impeccable sureness, original taste, a fertile and
appropriate invention in the pictures where only two or three
figures appear, and even more in those where he illustrates,
standing or reclining, a single effigy of the female figure, which
was the enchantment and sweet torment of his whole life.

640. **Jean-Auguste-Dominique Ingres,** 1780-1867, Neoclassicism, French,
Valpinçon Bather, 1808.
Oil on canvas, 146 x 97 cm. Musée du Louvre, Paris.

*The discovery of exotic and oriental art by the nineteeth-century artists
impacted on Ingres' depiction of women. The female nude appears
throughout the artist's body of work. His fascination with long,
immaculate backs of young women appears in several of his popular
works, including this earlier work and his Grande Odalisque (1814).
Also very late in life he carried out his theme yet again in his work The
Turkish Bath (1863) in which there are twenty such women, but the
dominant one in the foreground is displaying her beautiful back. Ingres
said he was taking Poussin as an example as the master often depicted
the same subjects several times, until he reached perfection. But Ingres
was influenced also by Tuscan mannerists such as Bronzino, and from
Raphael. In all three works, a lady wears a turban and nothing else. In
this early work, the drapery is pulled to the side to allow the voyeur an
unobstructed view, but at a respectful distance.*

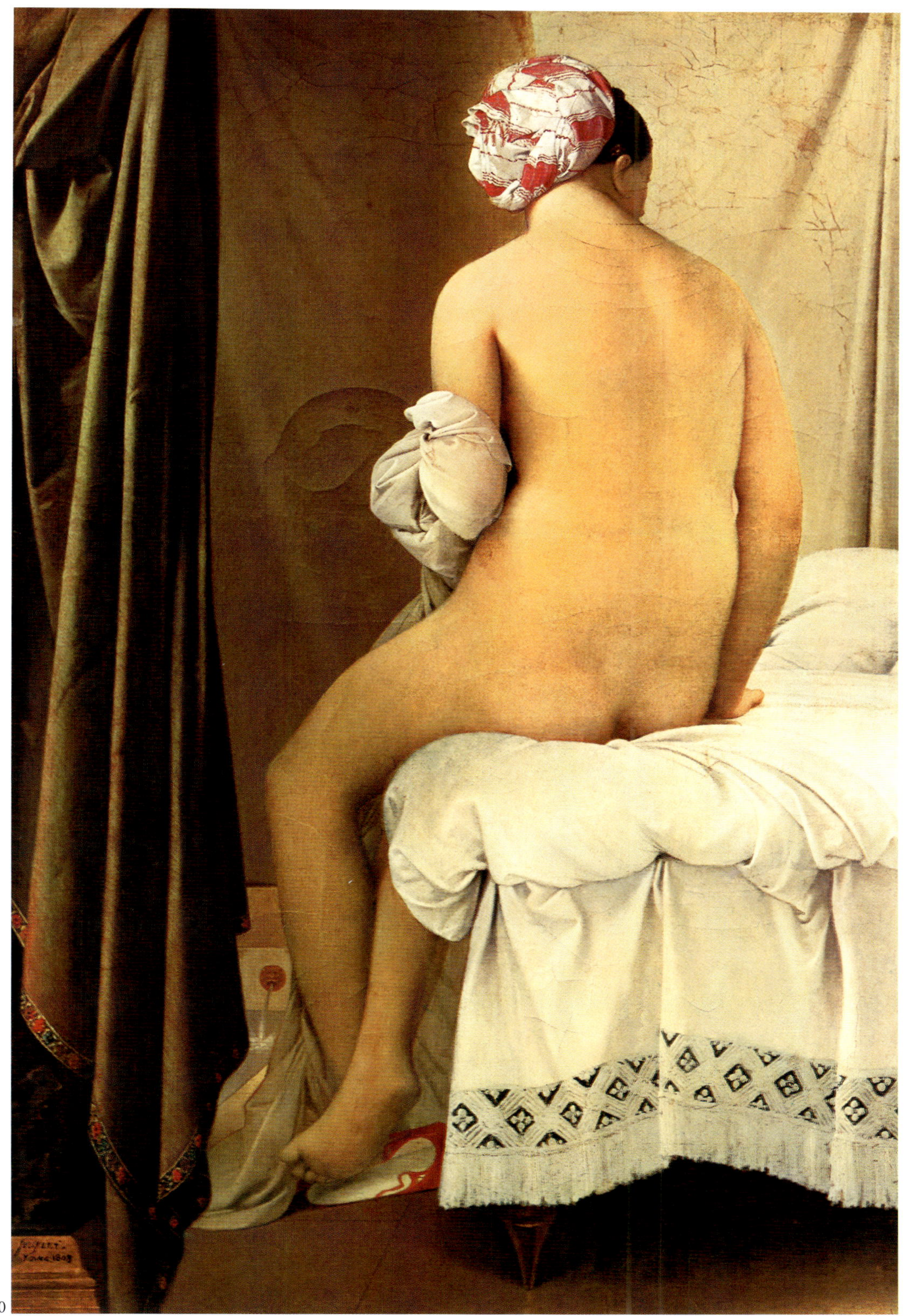

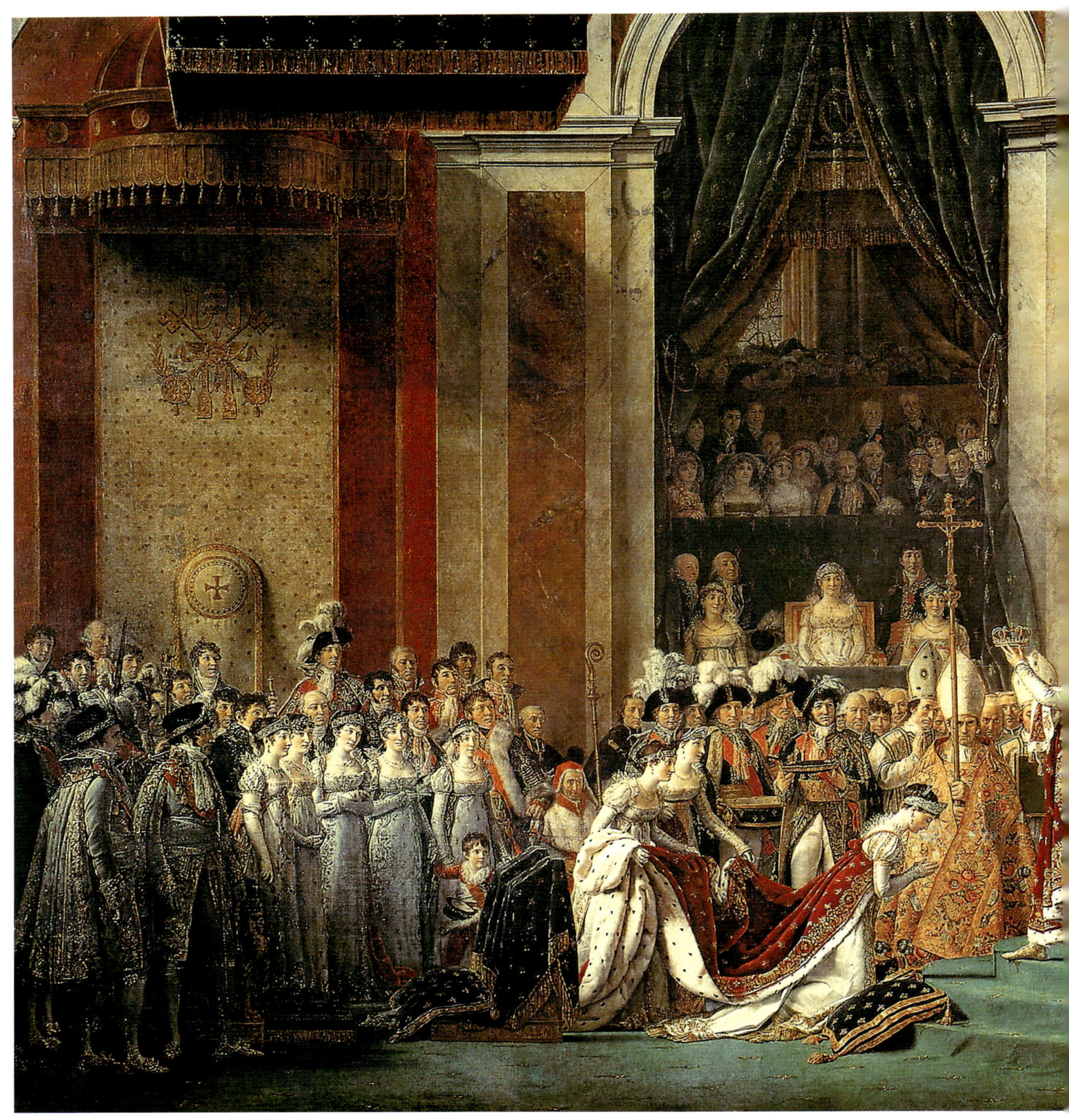

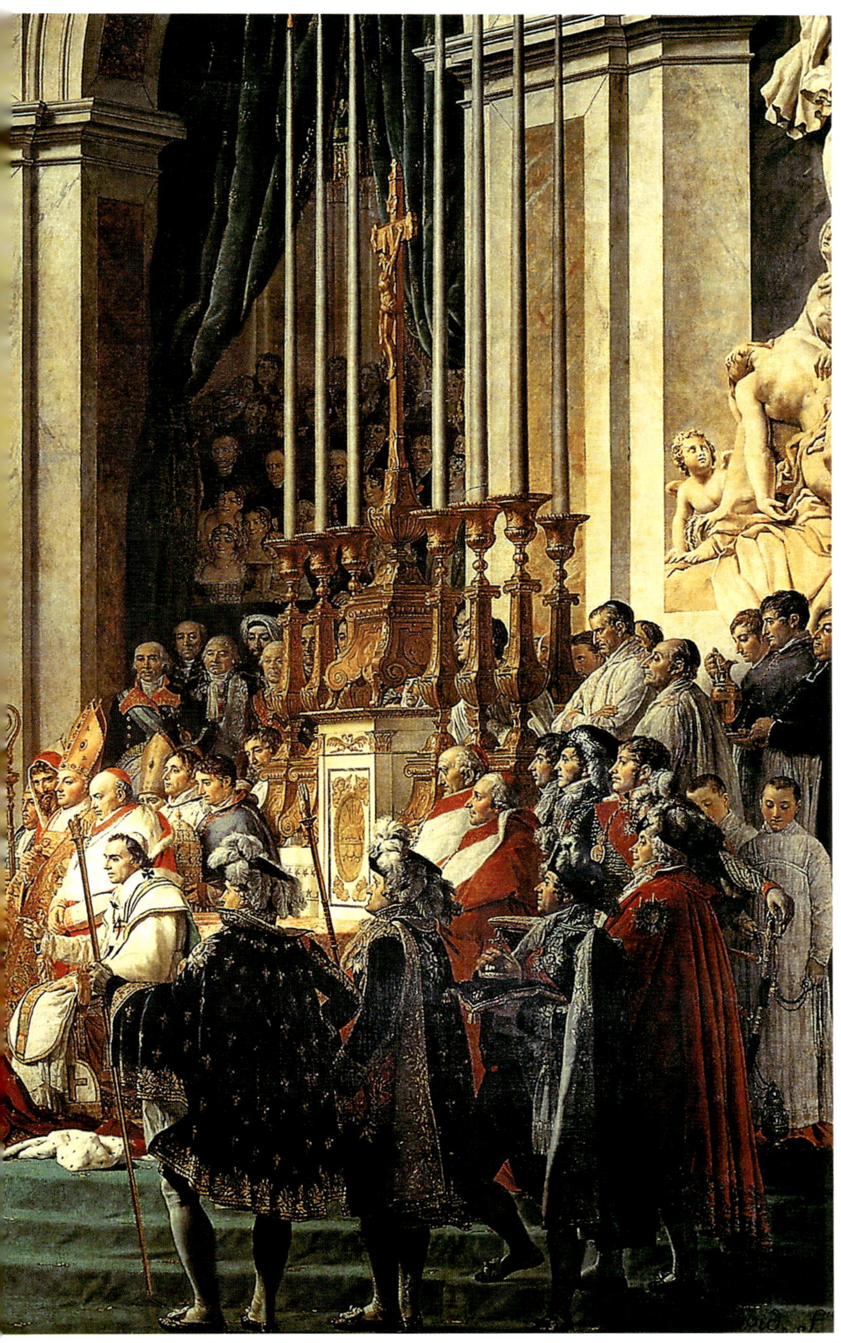

641. Jacques-Louis David, 1748-1825,
Neoclassicism, French, *Consecration of
the Emperor Napoleon I and Coronation
of the Empress Josephine*,
1806-1807.
Oil on canvas, 621 x 979 cm.
Musée du Louvre, Paris.

*There were to be three other paintings by
David in a series showing highlights in the
life of Napoleon (1769-1821), who called
the artist the country's "first painter".
However, the artist was unable to produce
the envisioned other works. The majestic
vertical columns and exceptionally tall
candles of the grand Notre Dame cathedral
in Paris, redecorated in a Neoclassical
style for the event, buttress the grandeur
of the coronation. By raising the crown as
high as he can, Napoleon is challenging
the authority of even the Church,
symbolised by the processional crucifix
held high by the Pope, Pie VII. Cardinals
and bishops witness the event with
quiet resignation. The whole imperial
court is represented: each character can
be identified. Thanks to its size, David
intended to give to this contemporising
fact an historical importance. A prominent
pietà, the altar, and even the tabernacle
are set aside so Napoleon, then the
coronation, are the centre of attention.
The problem of presenting a crowd on
tiers, as is often seen in Byzantine and
Gothic works, is partly solved here by use
of the balconies. There is an unexpected
objectivity of the artist, as a loyal follower
of the Emperor, by his nearly journalistic
or non-emotional reporting of the event
combined with the overall neo-Baroque
attention to elaborate detail. Appropriately,
this is one of the artist's very large works, if
not the largest, being nearly twice as large
as his* The Rape of the Sabine Women
*(1799), which is also displayed at the
Musée du Louvre, Paris.*

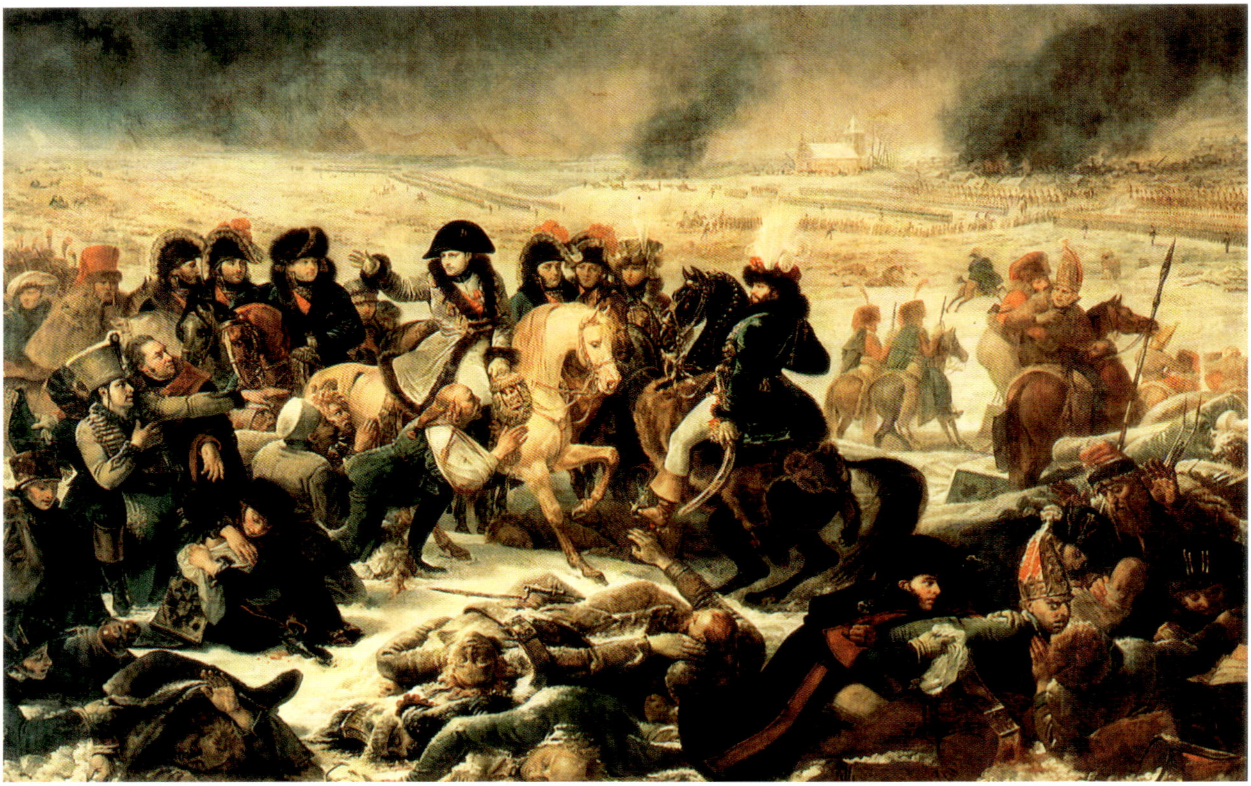

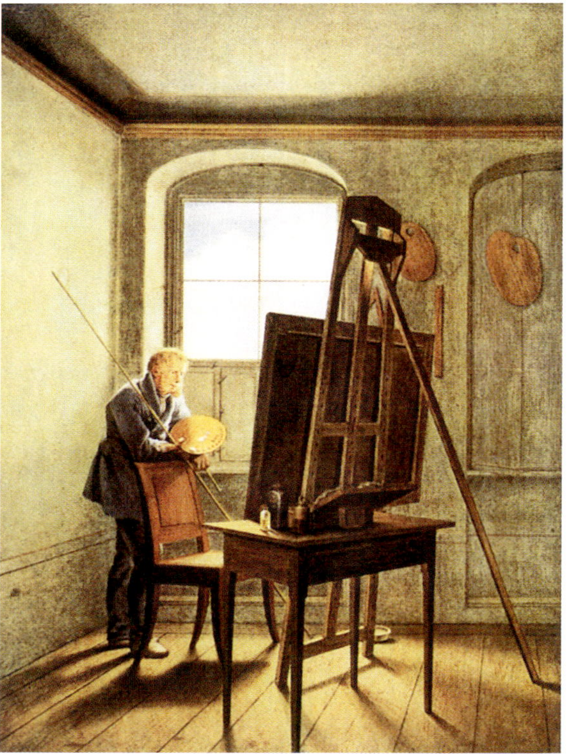

642. **Antoine-Jean Gros,** 1771-1835, Romanticism, French,
Napoléon at the Battlefield of Eylau, 1807.
Oil on canvas, 521 x 784 cm.
Musée du Louvre, Paris.

Gros respected the instructions given for the representation of Napoleon on the battle field of Eylau after the bloodbath. But he depicted the scene with an exceptional realism, new in the genre of historical painting.

643. **Georg Friedrich Kersting,** 1785-1847, Romanticism, German,
Caspar David Friedrich in his Studio, 1811.
Oil on canvas, 51 x 40 cm.
Alte Nationalegalerie, Berlin.

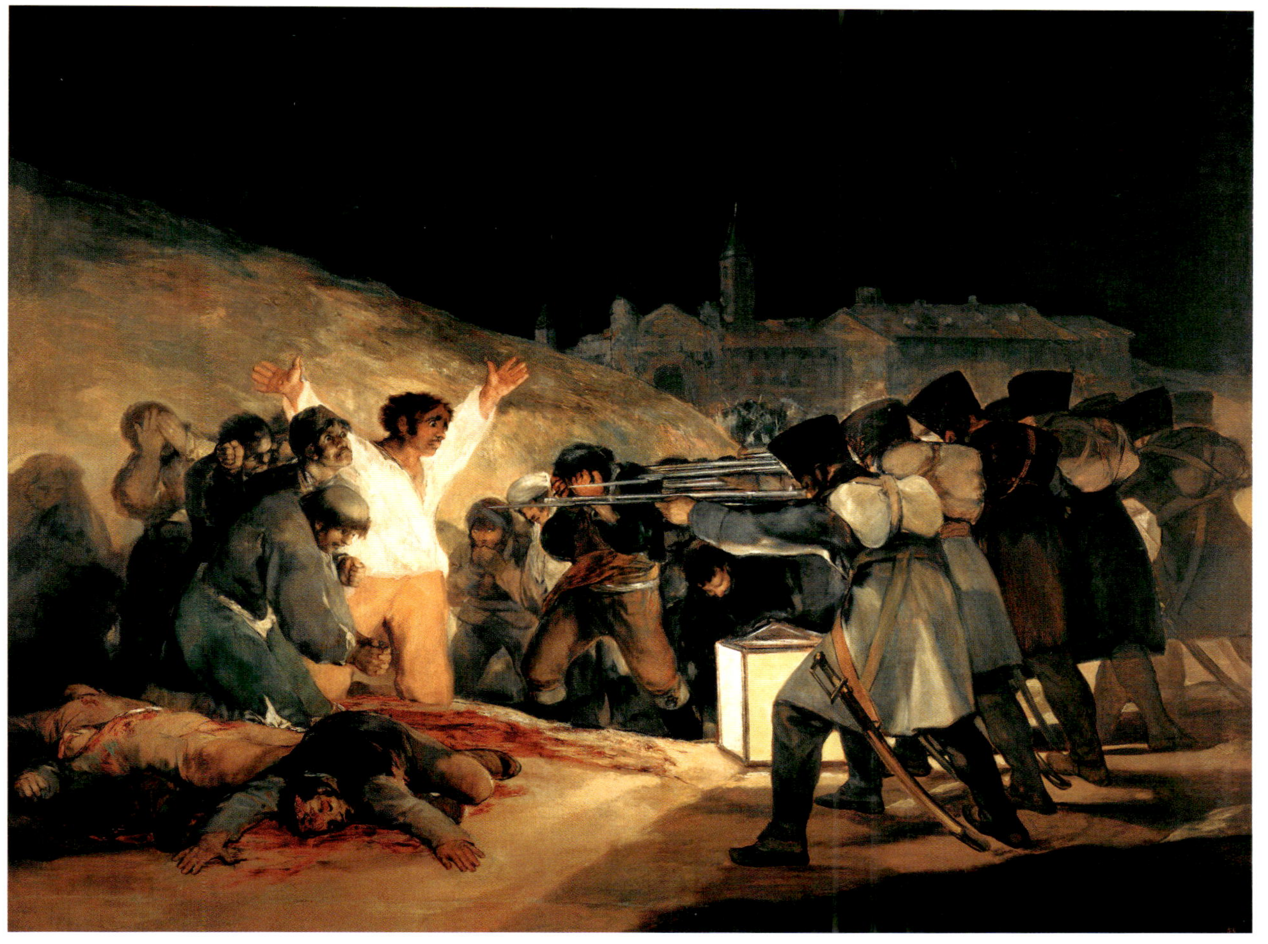

644. Francisco de Goya y Lucientes, 1746-1828,
Romanticism, Spanish, *Third of May, 1808,* 1814.
Oil on canvas, 266 x 345 cm.
Museo Nacional del Prado, Madrid.

The painting Third of May, 1808 *recalls the executions of more than forty men and women, on the hill of Principe Pio. The focal point of the painting is a man who gasps and spreads his arms in horror at his fate. His gesture suggests that he faces death with both defiance and despair. Isolated from the shadowy figures around him, the severe light of a lantern set on the ground before his executioners highlights his white shirt and yellow trousers. His innocence is implied by the brightness of his clothes, while his gesture and wounded right palm remind us of Christ crucified. Beside him, his companions give varying reactions to their hopeless situation: a Franciscan priest hangs his head in prayer while another victim tightens his fists in futile resistance. To the left, a man shields his eyes from the sight of the carnage and the gruesome pile of dead. The head of the figure in the foreground is riddled with bullets; his arms hug the ground, outstretched like those of the central figure, while his blood pours onto the barren earth. Time is frozen, but the outcome is clear. Within seconds the group will have fallen and been replaced by another that shuffles up the hill to face the firing squad. The merciless soldiers appear anonymous, their backs forming an impenetrable wall and their actions uniform as they prepare to fire, their feet set firmly apart to resist the rifles' recoil.*

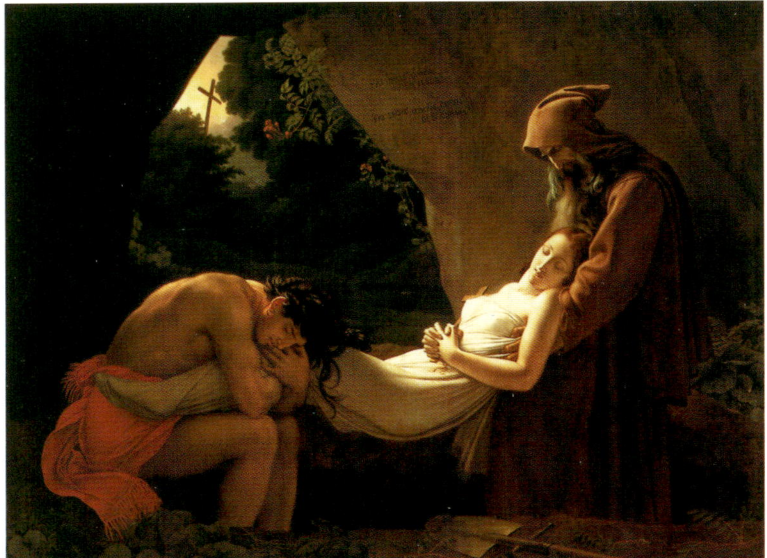

645. Anne-Louis Girodet, 1767-1824,
Romanticism, French,
The Burial of Atala, 1808.
Oil on canvas, 207 x 267 cm.
Musée du Louvre, Paris.

Pupil of David, Girodet took his inspiration from Chateaubriand's book, published in 1801. In it, Atala, in love with Chactas, who came from the enemy tribe, remembers her oath of virginity. In order not to succumb to temptation, she kills herself. The scene is represented in the tradition of the "burial of Christ". But here, passion, love, and death are mixed up. The cave opens itself on a wild and romantic landscape. The cross in the background echoes to the cross set up by the shovel and the mattock in the foreground and recalls the reason of Atala's sacrifice. This work, displayed at the Salon in 1808 in Paris, aroused much attention, and even Josephine asked for a replica.

646. Jean-Auguste-Dominique Ingres, 1780-1867, Neoclassicism,
French, *La Grande Odalisque,* 1814.
Oil on canvas, 91 x 162 cm.
Musée du Louvre, Paris.

The oriental setting is a pretext for Ingres to show his virtuosity in the depiction of materials, nacre, and silks. The proportions of the model are wrong, the body is elongated and the face flattened. Ingres got his inspiration from Italian mannerism and, for the arabesques, from the School of Fontainebleau.

646

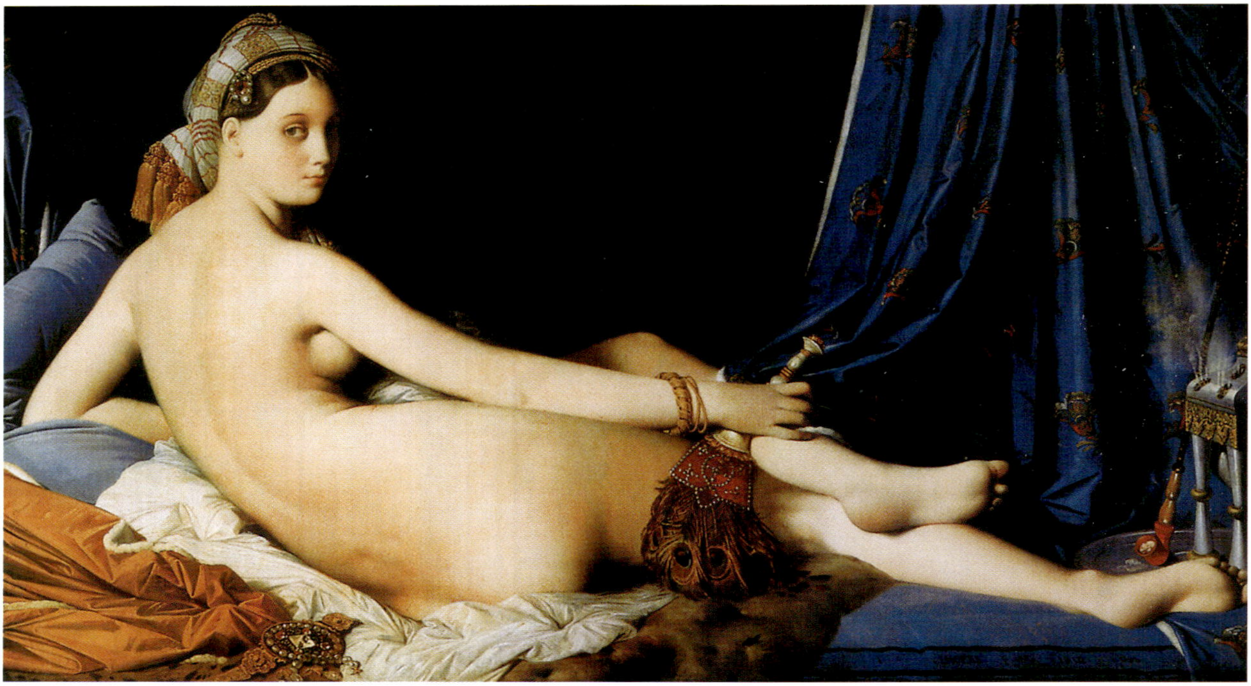

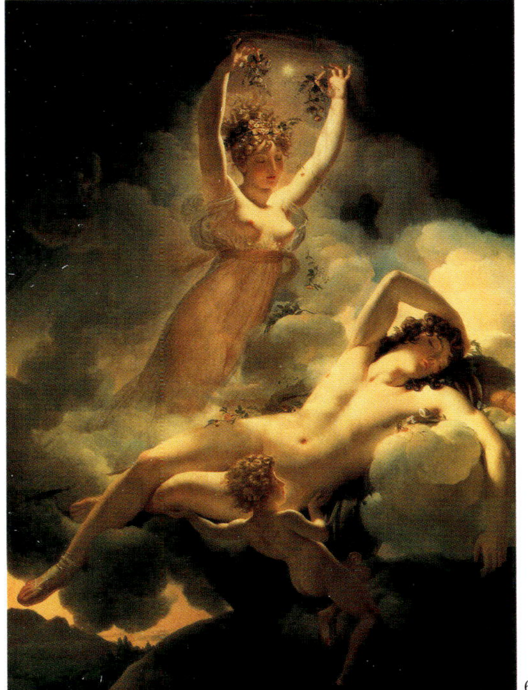

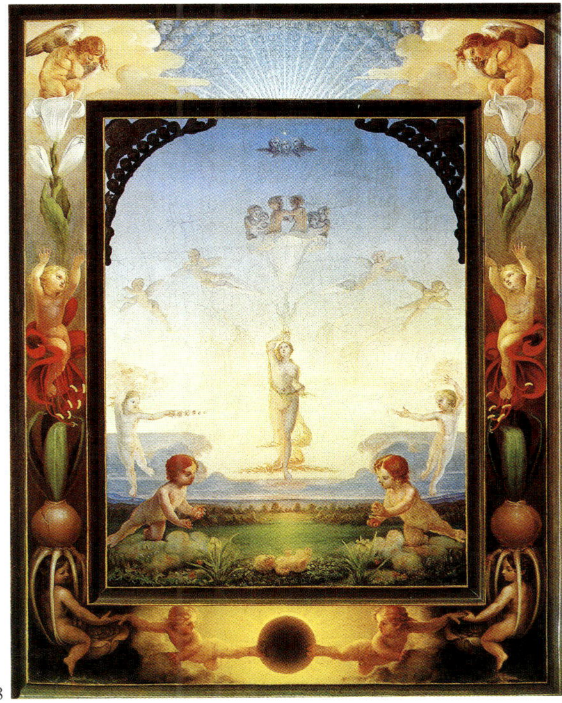

647

648

647. Pierre-Narcisse Guérin, 1774-1833, Neoclassicism, French,
Aurora and Cephalus, 1811-1814.
Oil on canvas, 257 x 178 cm.
The Pushkin Museum of Fine Arts, Moscow.

649. Caspar David Friedrich, 1774-1840, Romanticism, German,
Monk by the Sea, c. 1808.
Oil on canvas, 110 x 172 cm. Alte Nationalgalerie, Berlin.

Friedrich painted his masterpieces after a career as a theatrical scenery painter. The artist was not presenting nature realistically. Rather he was focused on the awesome quality of nature and the humbling influence nature's grandeur has on one's interior life. He especially liked the coastline, where he could witness major forces of nature interacting. The human

648. Philipp Otto Runge, 1777-1810, Neoclassicism, German,
Morning (first version), 1808-1809.
Oil on canvas, 109 x 85.5 cm.
Kunsthalle, Hamburg.

subjects in his works are always tiny relative to the largeness and the majesty of nature. In this work the figure of the monk occupies only 1/800th or so of the work area. The vastness of the sea and sky is captured. The viewer discovers little if anything about the character of the monk, standing as the only vertical line of the composition.

649

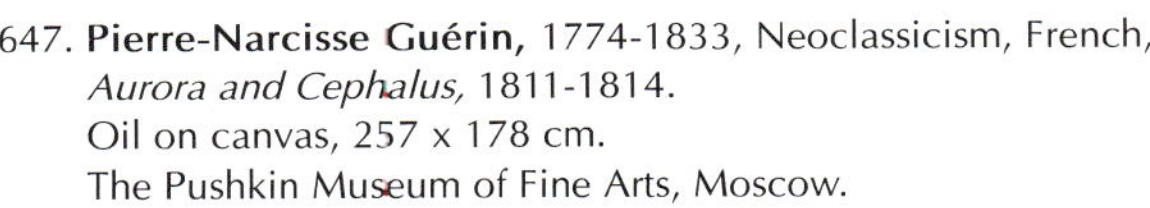

CASPAR DAVID FRIEDRICH
(1774 GEIFSWALD – 1840 DRESDEN)

Like Gainsborough, Friedrich is mostly known for his landscapes. They depict trees, hills, and misty mornings based on his strong observation of nature. Mountains symbolise an immovable faith while the trees are an allegory of hope. Therefore, his landscapes reflect his spiritual relationship with nature and his religious aspirations. His *Monk by the Sea* expresses his recurring theme of the insignificance of the individual in relation to the vastness of nature. Painter as draughtsman or printmaker, he was one of the greatest German leaders of Romanticism.

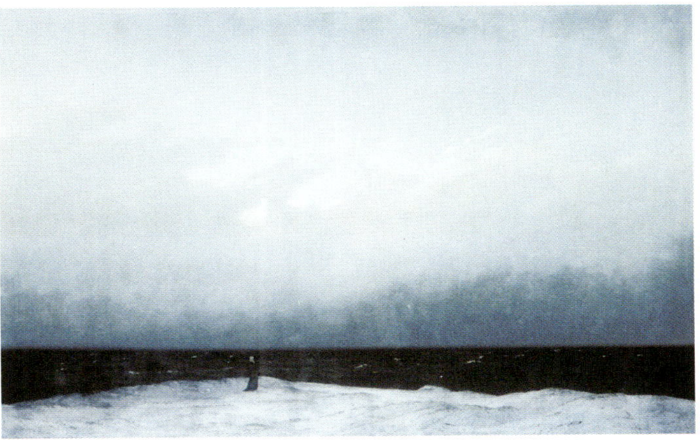

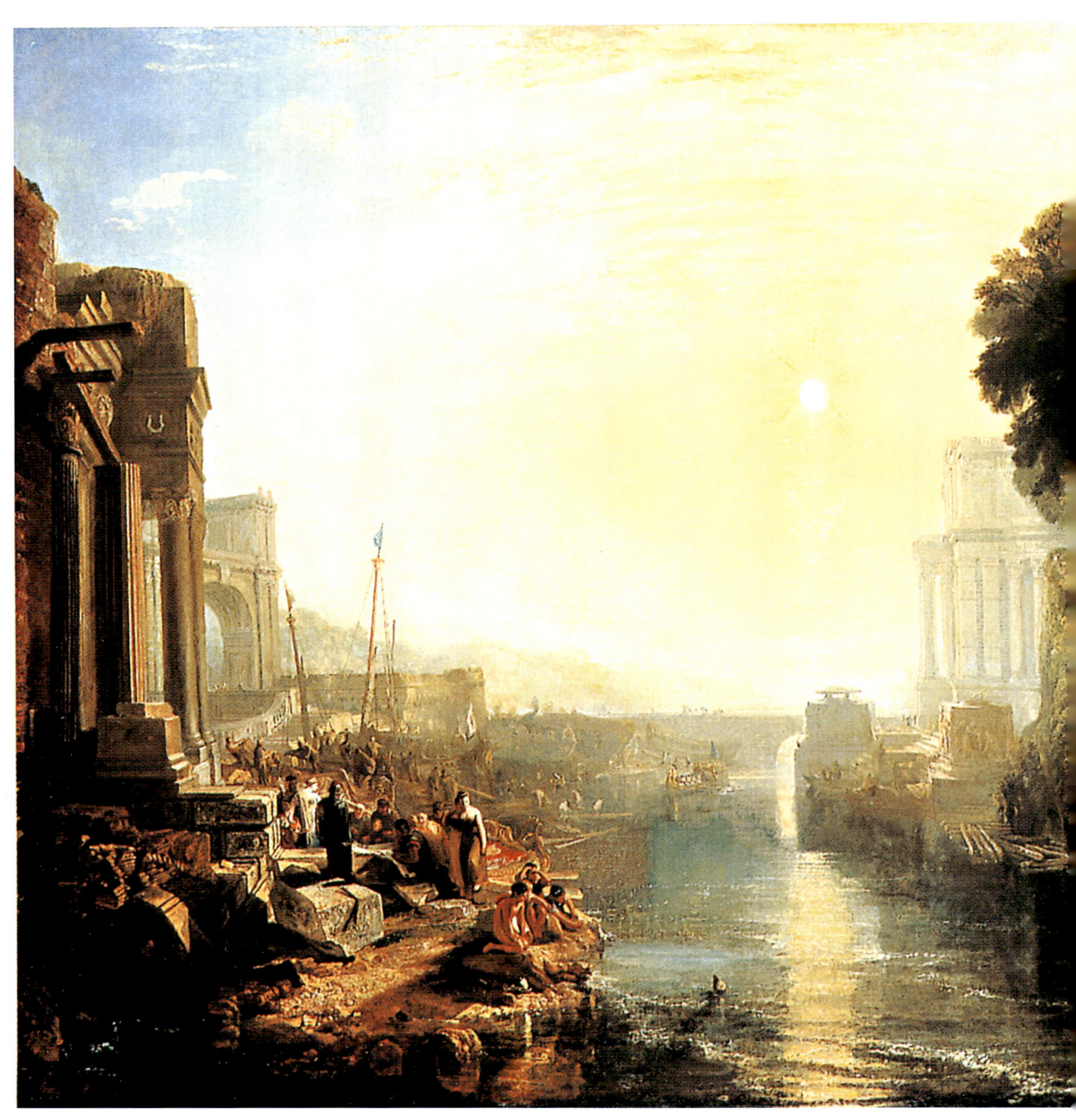

650. **J.M.W. Turner,** 1775-1851, Romanticism, English, *Dido Building Carthage,* or *The Rise of the Carthaginian Empire,* 1815.
Oil on canvas, 155.5 x 232 cm. National Gallery, London.

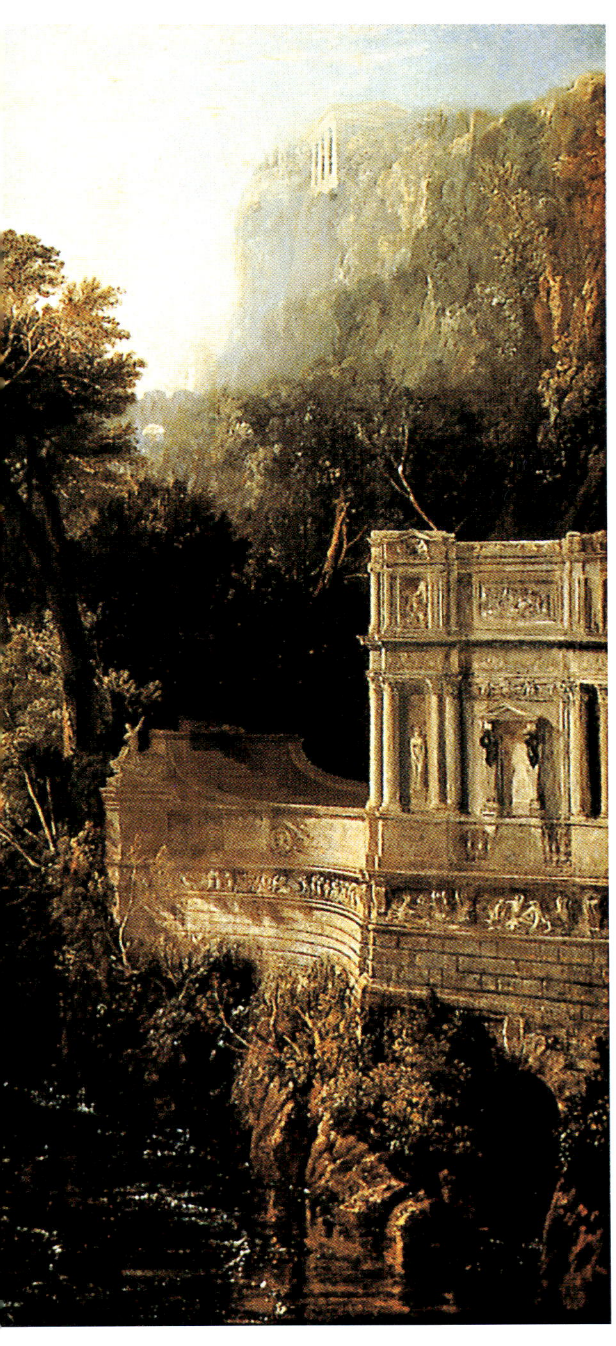

JOSEPH MALLORD WILLIAM TURNER
(1775 – 1851 LONDON)

At fifteen, Turner was already exhibiting *View of Lambeth*. He soon acquired the reputation of an immensely clever watercolourist. A disciple of Girtin and Cozens, he showed in his choice and presentation of theme a picturesque imagination which seemed to mark him out for a brilliant career as an illustrator. He travelled, first in his native land and then on several occasions in France, the Rhine Valley, Switzerland and Italy. He soon began to look beyond illustration. However, even in works in which we are tempted to see only picturesque imagination, there appears his dominant and guiding ideal of lyric landscape. His choice of a single master from the past is an eloquent witness for he studied profoundly such canvases of Claude as he could find in England, copying and imitating them with a marvellous degree of perfection. His cult for the great painter never failed. He desired his *Sun Rising through Vapour* and *Dido Building Carthage* to be placed in the National Gallery side by side with two of Claude's masterpieces. And, there, we may still see them and judge how legitimate was this proud and splendid homage.

It was only in 1819 that Turner went to Italy, to go again in 1829 and 1840. Certainly Turner experienced emotions and found subjects for reverie which he later translated in terms of his own genius into symphonies of light and colour. Ardour is tempered with melancholy, as shadow strives with light. Melancholy, even as it appears in the enigmatic and profound creation of Albrecht Dürer, finds no home in Turner's protean fairyland – what place could it have in a cosmic dream? Humanity does not appear there, except perhaps as stage characters at whom we hardly glance. Turner's pictures fascinate us and yet we think of nothing precise, nothing human, only unforgettable colours and phantoms that lay hold on our imaginations. Humanity really only inspires him when linked with the idea of death – a strange death, more a lyrical dissolution – like the finale of an opera.

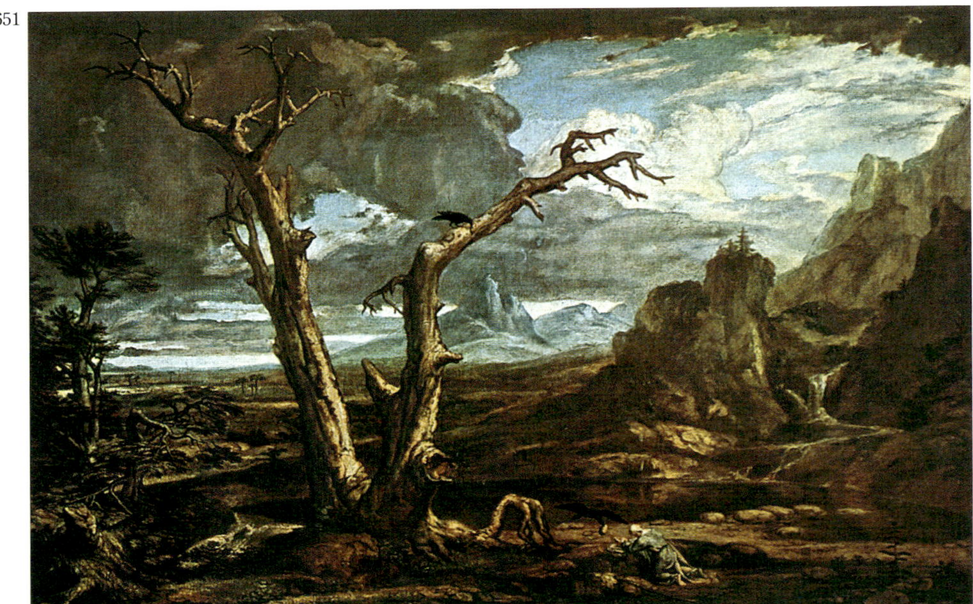

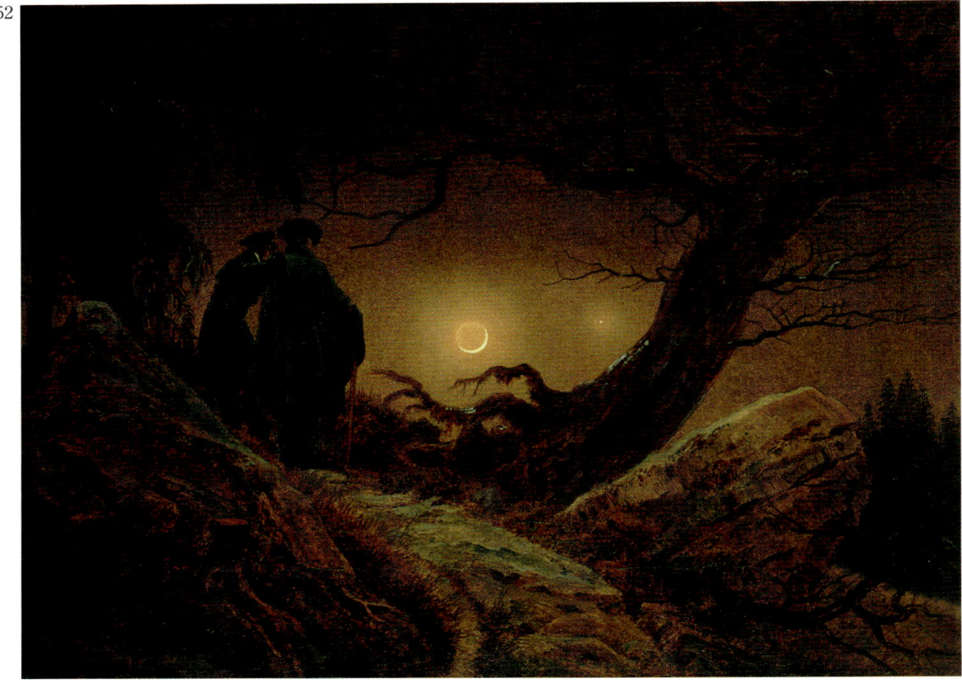

651. **Washington Allston,** 1779-1843, Romanticism, American,
Elijah in the Desert, 1818.
Oil on canvas, 125.1 x 184.8 cm.
Museum of Fine Arts, Boston.

*Samuel Taylor Coleridge said about the artist: "Washington
Allston is a man of highland rare genius, whether I contemplate
him in the character of a Poet, a Painter or a Philosophic
Analyst." Allston is known as the 'American Titian'.*

652. **Caspar David Friedrich,** 1774-1840, Romanticism, German,
Two Men Looking at the Moon, 1819.
Oil on canvas, 35 x 44 cm.
Gemäldegalerie Neue Meister, Dresden.

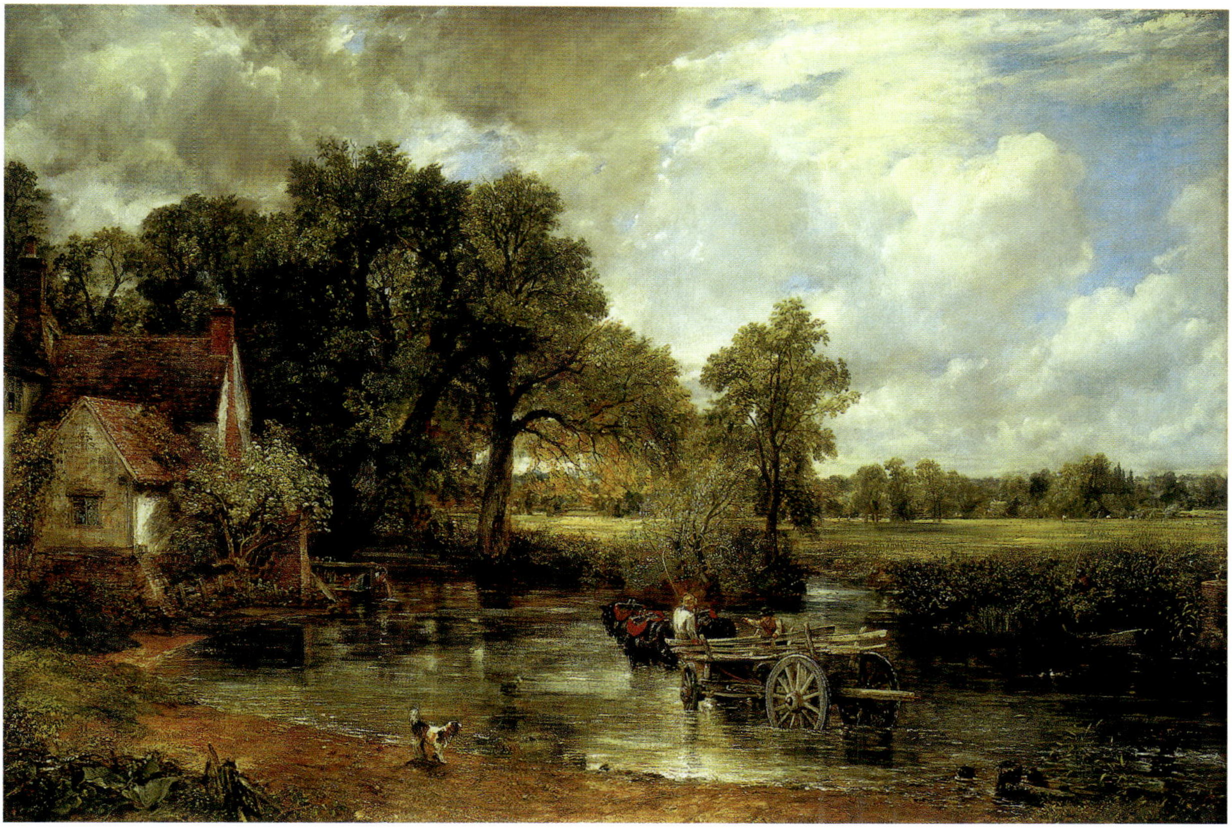

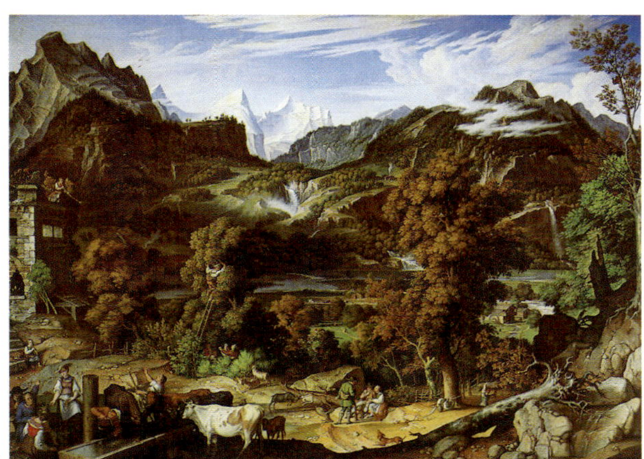

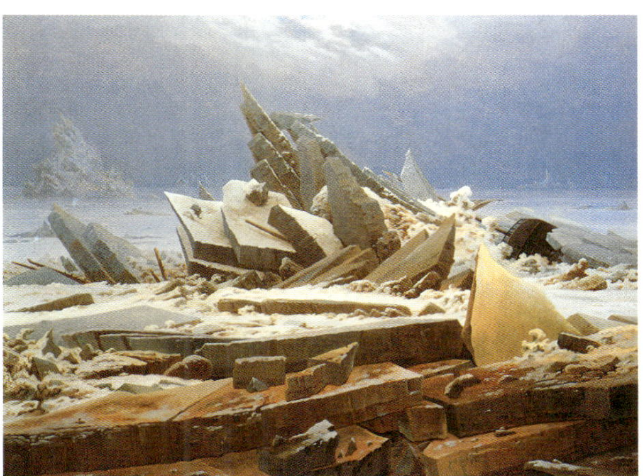

653. **John Constable,** 1776-1837, Romanticism, English (bio. p. 350),
The Hay Wain, 1821.
Oil on canvas, 130.2 x 185.4 cm.
The National Gallery, London.

654. **Joseph-Anton Koch,** 1868-1939, Neoclassicism, Austrian,
Swiss Landscape (Berner Oberland), 1817.
Oil on canvas, 101 x 134 cm.
Tiroler Landesmuseum Ferdinandeum, Innsbruck.

655. **Caspar David Friedrich,** 1774-1840, Romanticism, German,
The Sea of Ice, 1823-1824.
Oil on canvas, 96.7 x 126.9 cm. Kunsthalle, Hamburg.

Numerous sketches prove that Friedrich studied ice drifts on the River Elbe in 1821. In this work, he depicts the ice field with extreme precision, referring to both the expedition to the North Pole around 1820 by the English explorer Edward William Parry and the cold political climate in Germany in the same period.

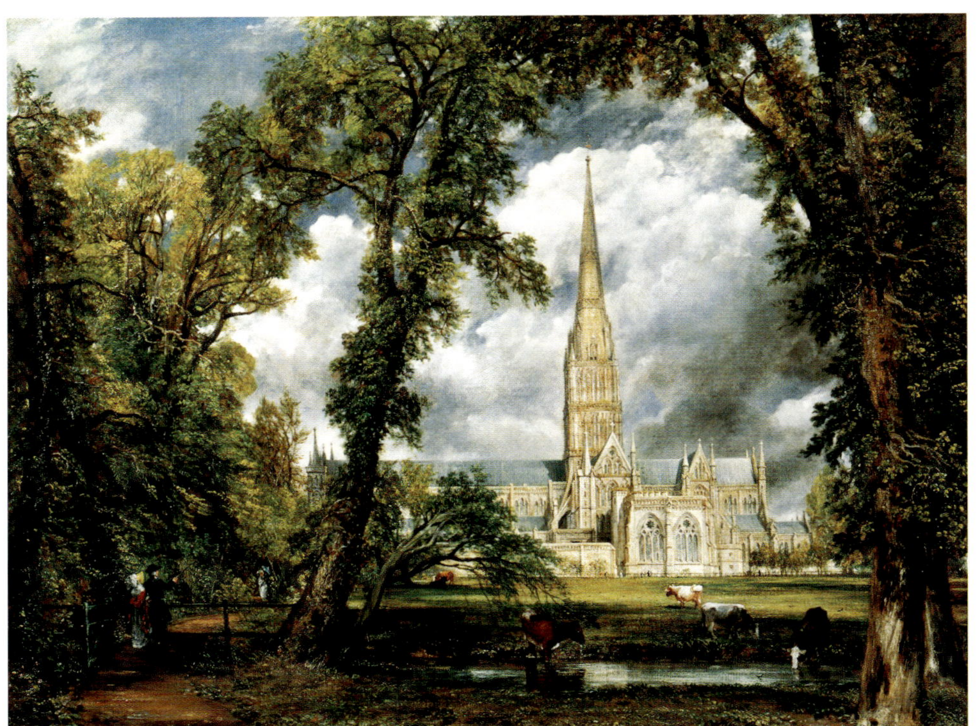

656. **John Constable,** 1776-1837, Romanticism, English,
Salisbury Cathedral from the Bishop's Grounds, 1823.
Oil on canvas, 88 x 112 cm.
Victoria and Albert Museum, London.

*In 1811, Constable was invited to stay at Salisbury,
where he was introduced to the bishop's nephew, the
Reverend John Fisher (who subsequently became
Archdeacon of the cathedral). He and Constable
enjoyed a lifelong friendship, and consequently
Salisbury and its cathedral became one of the artist's
most important subjects. This version, a south-west
view, was commissioned by Fisher's uncle for his
London house. The bishop and his wife are introduced
on the left, where they are seen apparently admiring the
church. The commission gave Constable a great deal of
trouble, for although he had sketched and drawn the
cathedral before, he then had no patron to satisfy and
could gloss over the kind of architectural detail that the
Bishop would expect to see. As he confided to John
Fisher: "It was the most difficult subject in landscape I
ever had upon my easel. I have not flinched at the work,
of the windows, buttresses, etc, etc, but I have as usual
made my escape in the evanescence of the
chiaroscuro." Unfortunately, the bishop was not as
satisfied with the chiaroscuro as the artist was; he
disliked the "dark cloud" in the painting, saying,
according to his nephew: "[If] Constable would but
leave out his black clouds! Clouds are only black when
it is going to rain. In fine weather the sky is blue." At first
Constable agreed to repaint it, but preferred in the end
to paint another, more acceptable version with the aid of
Johnny Dunthorne.*

JOHN CONSTABLE
(1776 EAST BERGHOLT – 1837 HAMPSTEAD)

John Constable was the first English landscape painter to take no lessons
from the Dutch. He is rather indebted to the landscapes of Rubens, but
his real model was Gainsborough, whose landscapes, with great trees
planted in well-balanced masses on land sloping upwards towards the
frame, have a rhythm often found in Rubens. Constable's originality
does not lie in his choice of subjects, which frequently repeated themes
beloved by Gainsborough.

Nevertheless, Constable seems to belong to a new century; he ushered
in a new era. The difference in his approach results both from technique
and feeling. Excepting the French, Constable was the first landscape painter
to consider as a primary and essential task the sketch made direct from
nature at a single sitting; an idea which contains in essence the destinies of
modern landscape, and perhaps of most modern painting. It is this
momentary impression of all things which will be the soul of the future
work. Working at leisure upon the large canvas, an artist's aim is to enrich
and complete the sketch while retaining its pristine freshness. These are the
two processes to which Constable devoted himself, while discovering the
exuberant abundance of life in the simplest of country places. He had the
palette of a creative colourist and a technique of vivid hatchings heralding
that of the French impressionists. He audaciously and frankly introduced
green into painting, the green of lush meadows, the green of summer
foliage, all the greens which, until then, painters had refused to see except
through bluish, yellow, or more often brown spectacles.

Of the great landscape painters who occupied so important a place in
nineteenth-century art, Corot was probably the only one to escape the
influence of Constable. All the others are more or less direct descendants
of the master of East Bergholt.

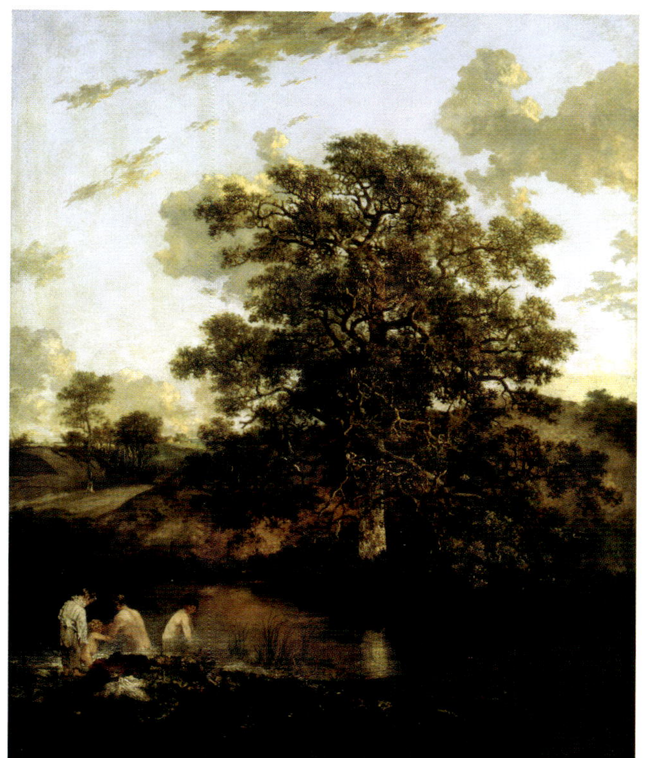

657

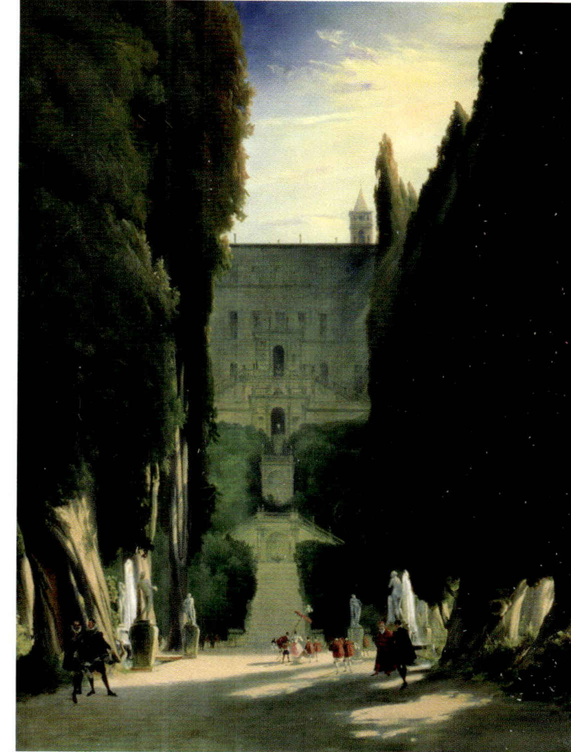

658

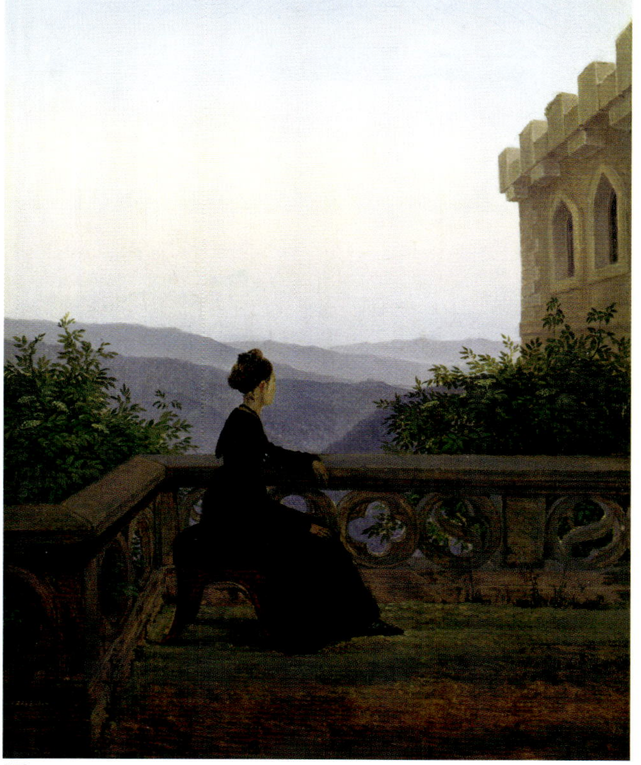

659

657. **John Crome,** 1768-1821, Romanticism, English,
The Poringland Oak, c. 1818-1820.
Oil on canvas, 125 x 100 cm. Tate Gallery, London.

*The oak was the pinnacle of tree portraiture for British
artists. It was associated with the sturdy character of the
British people, and ships constructed from it defended their
liberty. Crome's picture was exhibited in 1824 as* A Study
from Nature.

658. **Carl Blechen,** 1798-1840, Romanticism, Swiss,
The Gardens of the Villa d'Este, 1830.
Oil on canvas, 126 x 93 cm.
Alte Nationalgalerie, Berlin.

659. **Carl Gustav Carus,** 1789-1869, Romanticism, German,
Woman on a Balcony, 1824.
Oil on canvas, 42 x 33 cm.
Gemäldegalerie Neue Meister, Dresden.

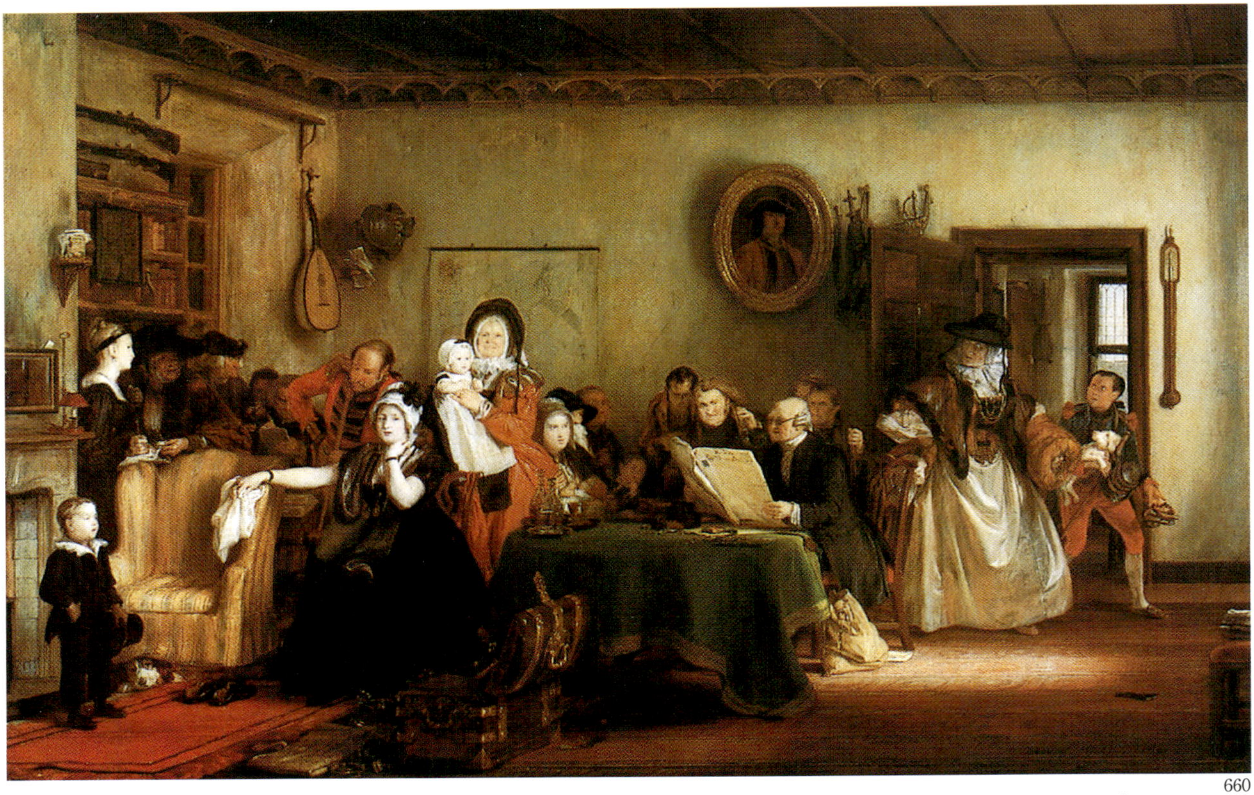

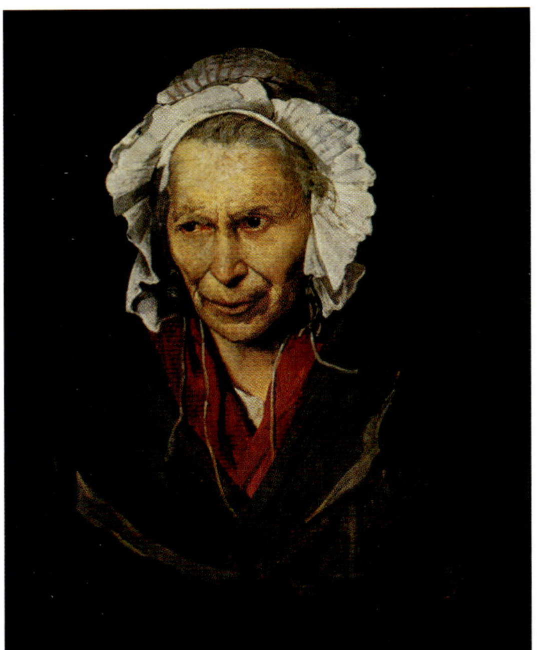

660. **David Wilkie,** 1785-1841, Genre Painter, Scottish,
Reading the Will, 1820. Oil on canvas, 76 x 115 cm.
Neue Pinakothek, Munich.

661

661. **Théodore Géricault,** 1791-1824, Romanticism, French,
The Madwoman or *The Obsession of Envy,* c. 1822.
Oil on canvas, 72 x 58 cm.
Musée des Beaux-Arts, Lyon.

*This work is part of a set of five paintings ordered by Esquiro, a reformer
of an asylum, who pleaded in favour of the recognition of monomaniacs
as normal people. Géricault reaches the psychological depth of his sitter
that he dresses conventionally in order to claim her social recognition.*

662. **Friedrich Overbeck,** 1789-1869, Nazarene, German,
Italia and Germania, 1828. Oil on canvas, 95 x 105 cm.
Gemäldegalerie Neue Meister, Dresden.

*Friedrich Overbeck was one of the founders of the Lukasbund (The
Brotherhood of St Luke), from which the Nazarenes were later to emerge.
In 1810, Overbeck went to Rome settling at the former San Isidoro cloister,
where he followed their ideals and lived as a quasi monk in seclusion.
Other artists, including Peter Cornelius and Wilhelm Schadow, soon
joined him. Their motivation was to relate art to the Church and state and
they were interested in the effect of art on the public.*

663. **Carl Anton Joseph Rottmann,** 1797-1850, Romanticism, German,
Sicyon and Corinth, c. 1836-1838.
Oil on canvas, 85.2 x 102 cm.
Neue Pinakothek, Munich.

664. **Ferdinand Victor Eugène Delacroix,** 1798-1863, Romanticism,
French, *Algerian Women in their Chamber,* 1834.
Oil on canvas, 180 x 229 cm.
Musée du Louvre, Paris.

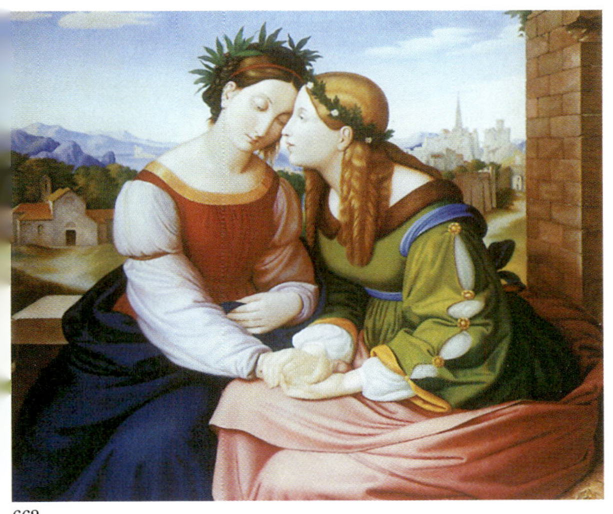

662

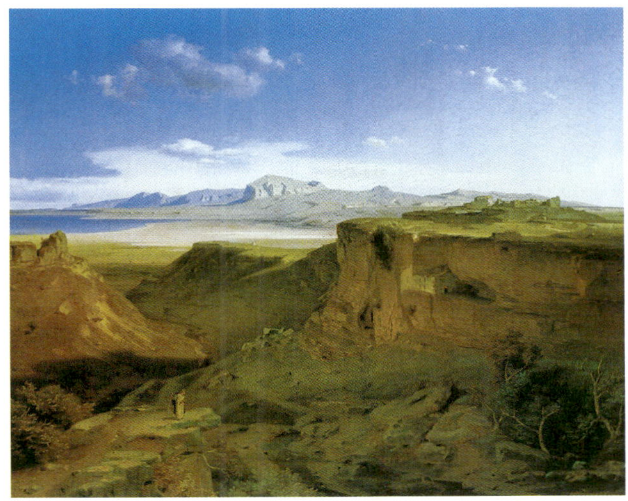

663

664

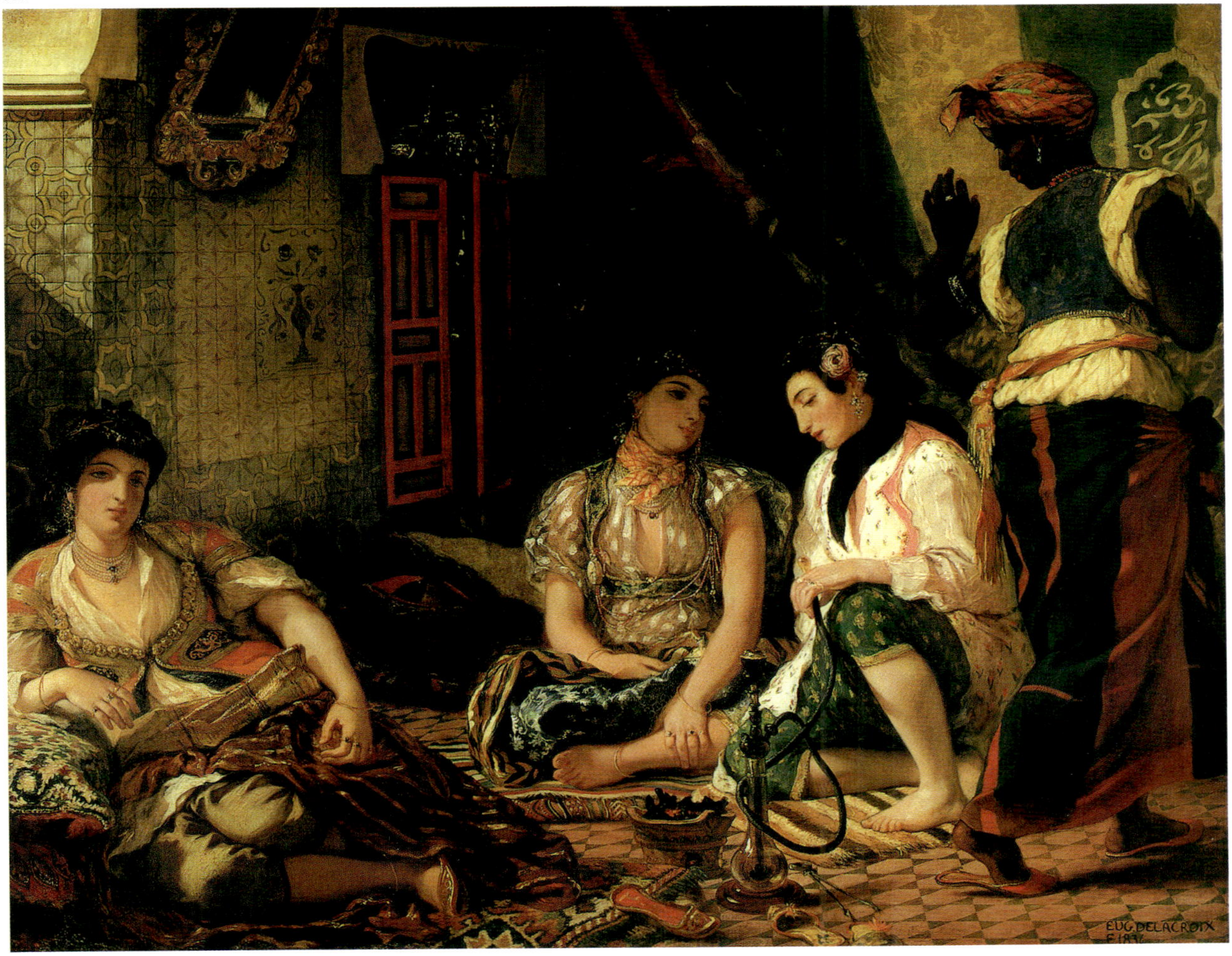

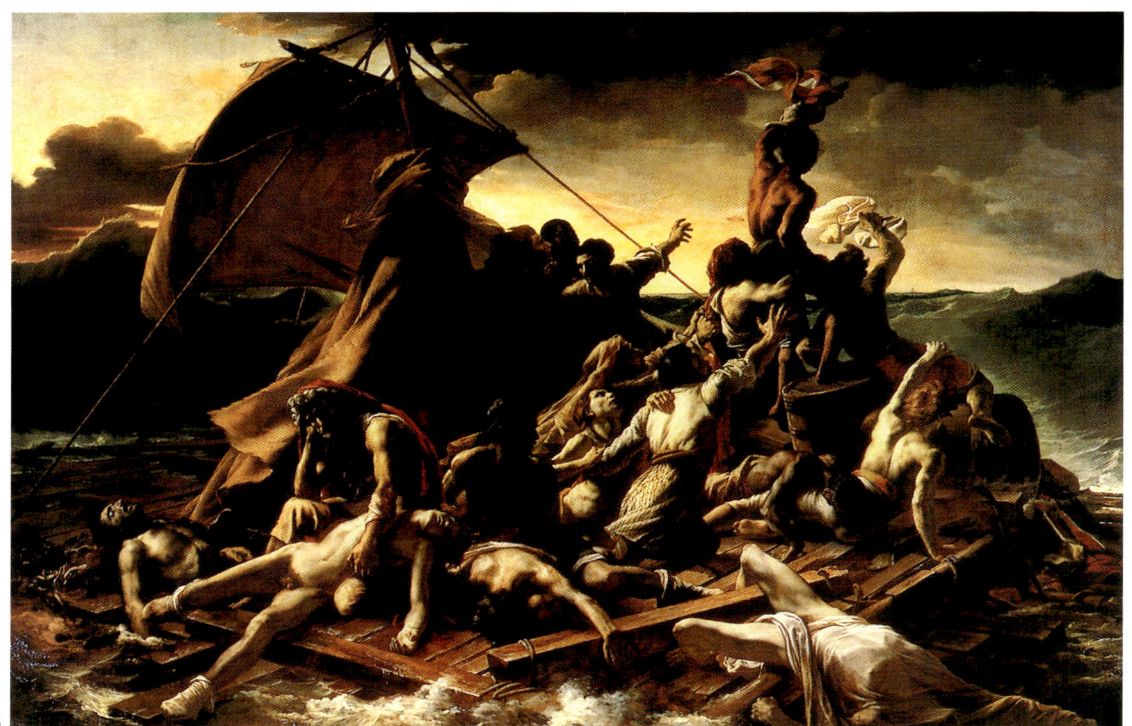

665

666

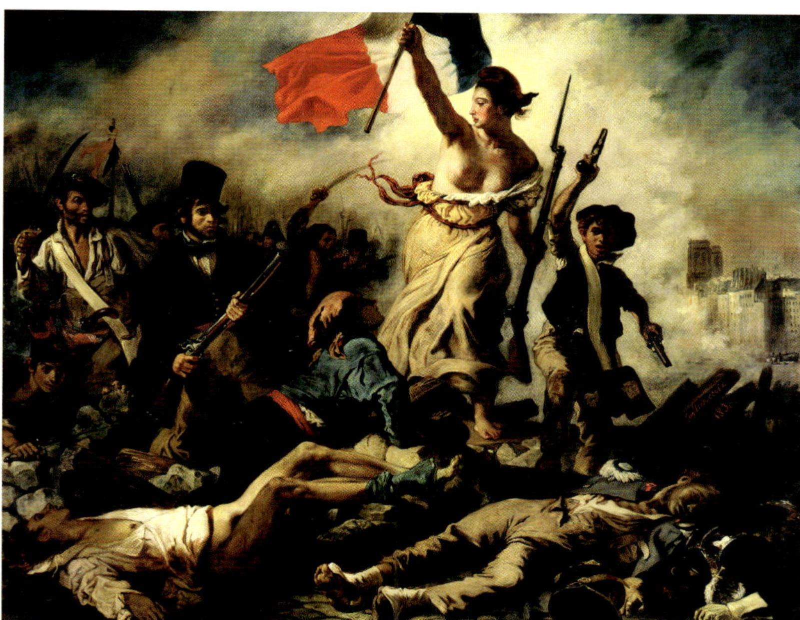

667. **Ferdinand Victor Eugène Delacroix,**
1798-1863, Romanticism, French,
Liberty Leading the People
(28 July, 1830), 1830.
Oil on canvas, 260 x 325 cm.
Musée du Louvre, Paris.

665. **Théodore Géricault,** 1791-1824, Romanticism,
French, *Raft of the Medusa,* c. 1818.
Oil on canvas, 491 x 716 cm.
Musée du Louvre, Paris.

*The work is significant in art history mainly as an
example of political controversy and protest. The
makeshift raft supports the realistic theme of the
horrific event. The geometric centre of the large work
is the dark area above the base of the mast, where
some of the most despairing survivors are. Here
Géricault applied his meticulous study of anatomy.
The dead or resigned men are collapsed along the
bottom third of the work. In the right half of the work
a pyramid of bodies builds up to its most hopeful
point, where shirts are waved as if the tiny ship on the
horizon could see their efforts. The ship in the
distance represents the Argus, the ship which rescued
the survivors. The naked and draped bodies weaken
the anecdotal aspect of the story, to reach a timeless
and also a romantic value. Géricault was influenced
by the sculptural work of Michelangelo, and by the
dramatic effects of chiaroscuro.*

666. **Ferdinand Victor Eugène Delacroix,** 1798-1863,
Romanticism, French, *The Barque of Dante,* 1822.
Oil on canvas, 189 x 241 cm.
Musée du Louvre. Paris.

*It is the first time that this theme is represented. The dark
and dramatic composition as well as the references to
Rubens and Michelangelo contribute to lead painting
toward the new orientation of Romanticism.*

FERDINAND VICTOR EUGÈNE DELACROIX
(1798 CHARENTON–SAINT–MAURICE – 1863 PARIS)

Delacroix was one of the greatest colourists of the nineteenth century,
in the sense of one who thinks and feels and expresses himself by
means of colours and sees them, in his mind's eye as a composition,
before he begins to resolve the whole into its parts, and work out the
separate details of form.

He nurtured himself upon the works of the colourists in the Louvre,
especially upon Rubens. Indirectly it came out of the heart of the
Romantic movement which had spread over Europe. Delacroix was
inspired by the writers Goethe, Scott, Byron, and Victor Hugo. His own
romantic nature flamed up through contact with theirs; he was possessed
with their souls and became the first of the Romantic painters. He took
many of his subjects from the poets of his preference, not to translate into
literal illustrations, but to make them express in his own language of
painting the most agitated emotions of the human heart.

On the other hand it is generally in the relationship of several figures, in
other words in drama, that Delacroix finds the natural and striking
expression of his ideas. His work is an immense and multiform poem, at
once lyrical and dramatic, on passions – the violent and murderous
passions which fascinate, dominate, and rend humanity. In the elaboration
and execution of the pages of this poem, Delacroix does not forego any of
his faculties as a man and an artist of vast intelligence standing on a level
with the thoughts of the greatest in history, legend and poetry. Rather, he
makes use of a feverish imagination always controlled by lucid reasoning
and cool willpower. His expressive and life-like drawing, strong and subtle
colour, sometimes composing a bitter harmony, sometimes overcast by
that "sulphurous" note already observed by contemporaries, produce an
atmosphere of storm, supplication, and anguish. Passion, movement and
drama must not be supposed to engender disorder. With Delacroix as with
Rubens, there hovers over the saddest representations, over tumults,
horrors and massacre, a kind of serenity which is the sign of art itself and
the mark of a mind master of its subject.

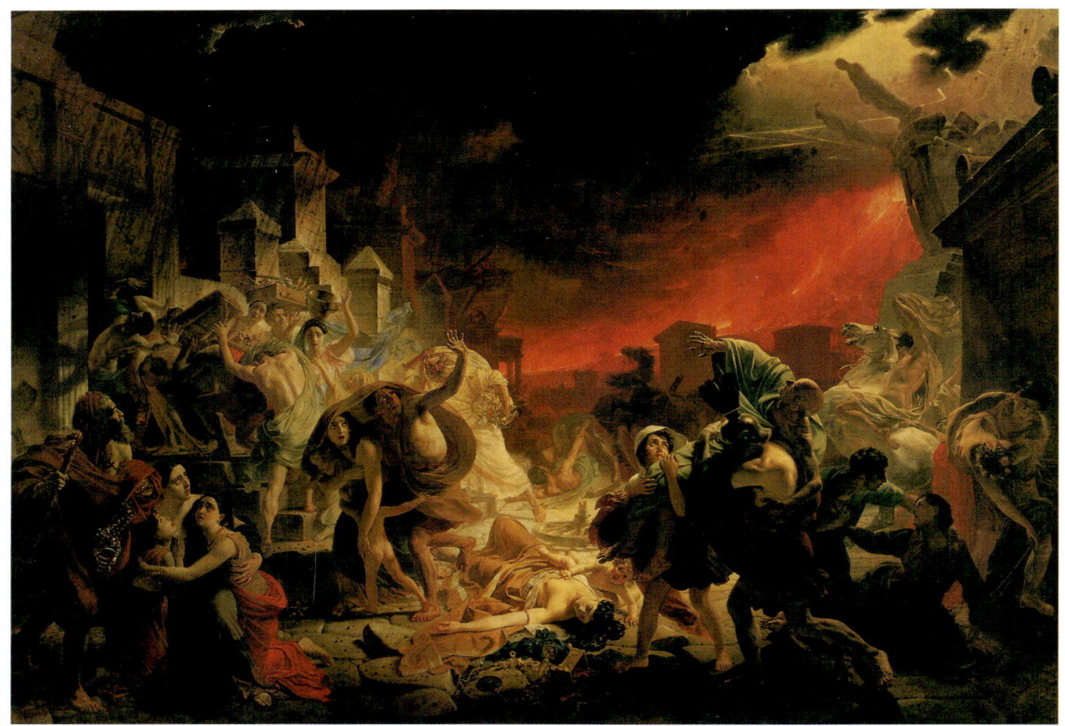

668

669

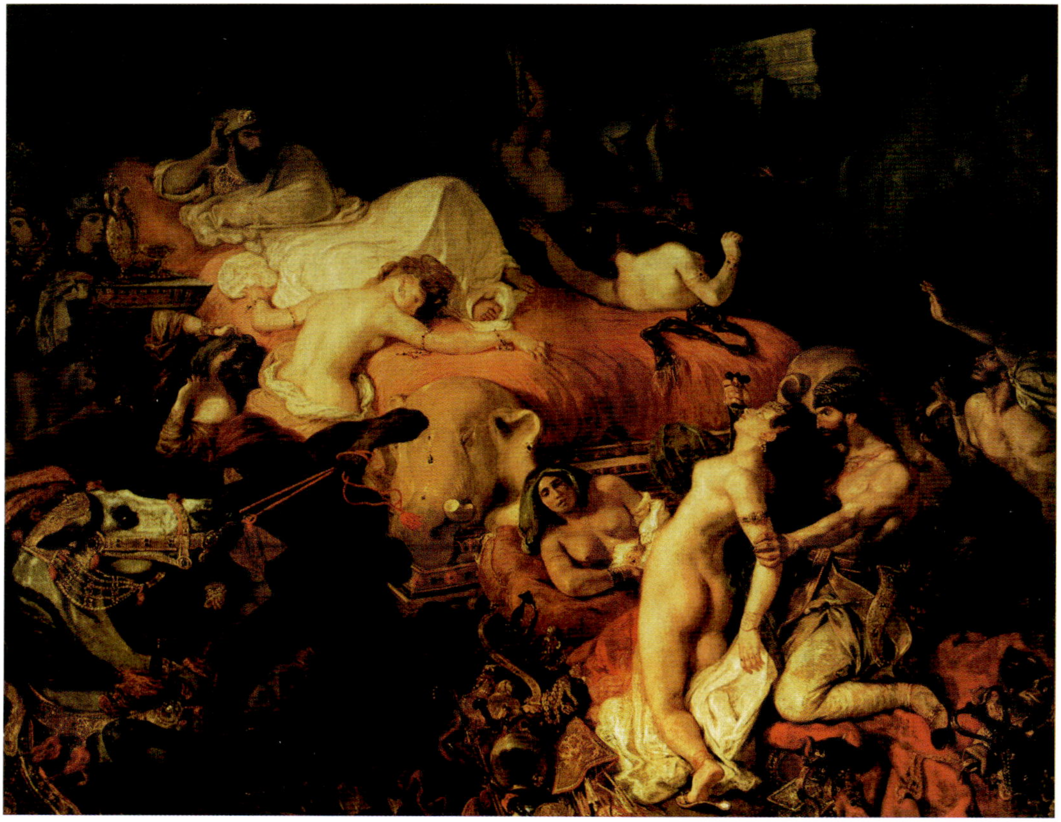

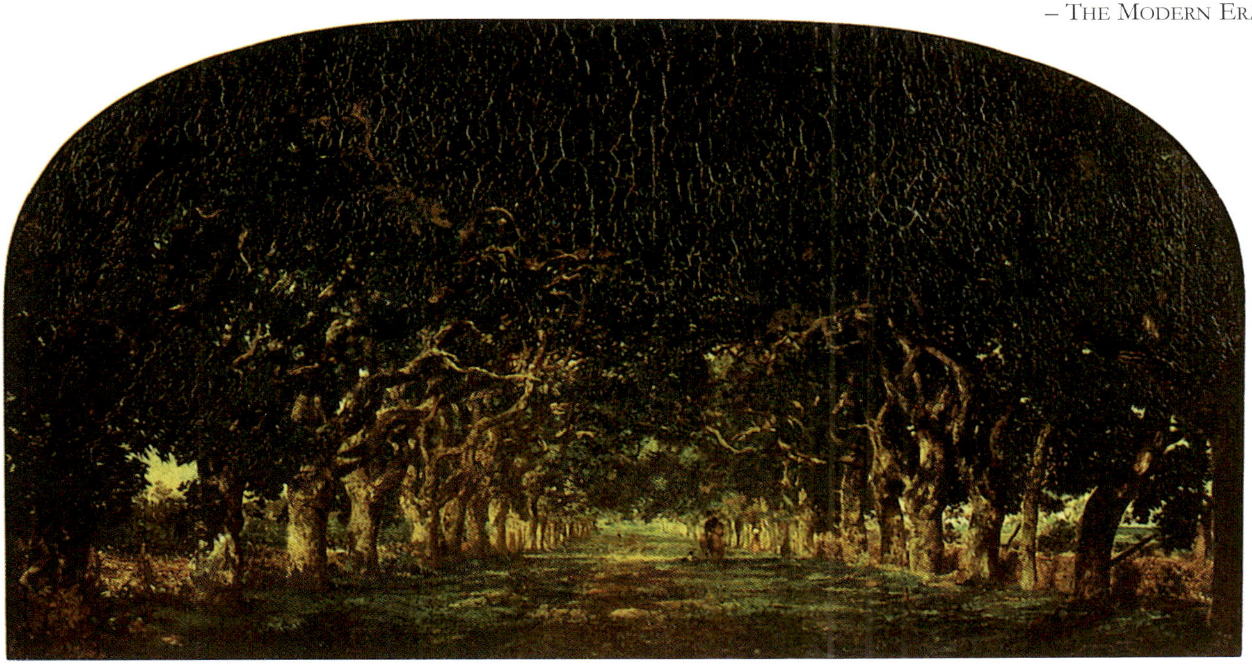

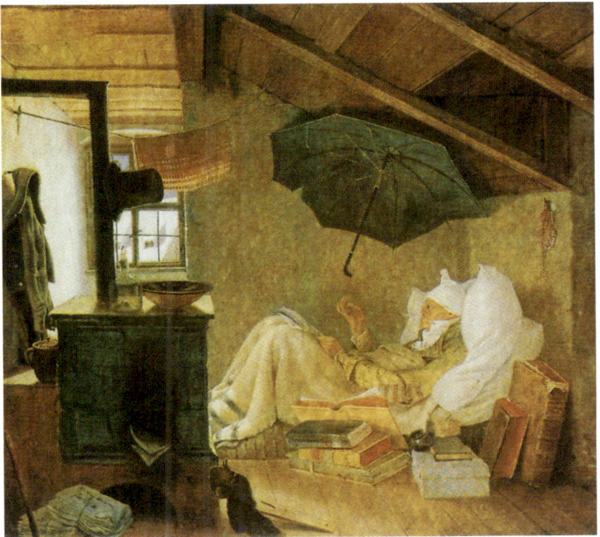

670. **Théodore Rousseau,** 1812-1867, Realism, School of
Barbizon, French. *The Avenue of Chestnut Trees,* 1841.
Oil on canvas, 79 x 144 cm.
Musée du Louvre, Paris.

668. **Karl Briullov,** 1799-1852, Romanticism, Russian,
The Last Day of Pompeii, 1830-1833.
Oil on canvas, 456 x 651 cm.
The State Russian Museum, St Petersburg.

*The ultimate manifestation of the infatuation with classical
themes was Karl Briullov's masterpiece,* The Last Day of
Pompeii. *Painted between 1830 and 1833, while he was living
in Italy, it caused a stir throughout Europe. Gogol described it
as "a feast for the eyes". It was also admired by Earl Edward
George Bulwer-Lytton, who visited Italy in 1833 and whose
almost identically entitled book was published in 1834. The
painting earned Briullov all sorts of honours, including the
prestigious Grand Prix at the Paris Salon, and was instrumental
in establishing his reputation as the greatest Russian painter of
his day.*

669. **Ferdinand Victor Eugène Delacroix,** 1798-1863,
Romanticism, French, *Death of Sardanapalus,* 1827.
Oil on canvas, 392 x 496 cm.
Musée du Louvre, Paris.

*This painting was inspired by Byron's Sardanapale. Its dynamic
and colourful composition, its arabesques, and its fierceness
mixed with sensuality led the classical painters to consider this
work subversive.*

671. **Carl Spitzweg,** 1808-1885, Romanticism, German,
The Poor Poet, 1839. Oil on canvas, 36.2 x 44.6 cm.
Neue Pinakothek, Munich.

*Spitzweg often depicted caricatures of contemporary society
with some realist effects borrowed to Dutch painting of the
seventeenth century.*

672

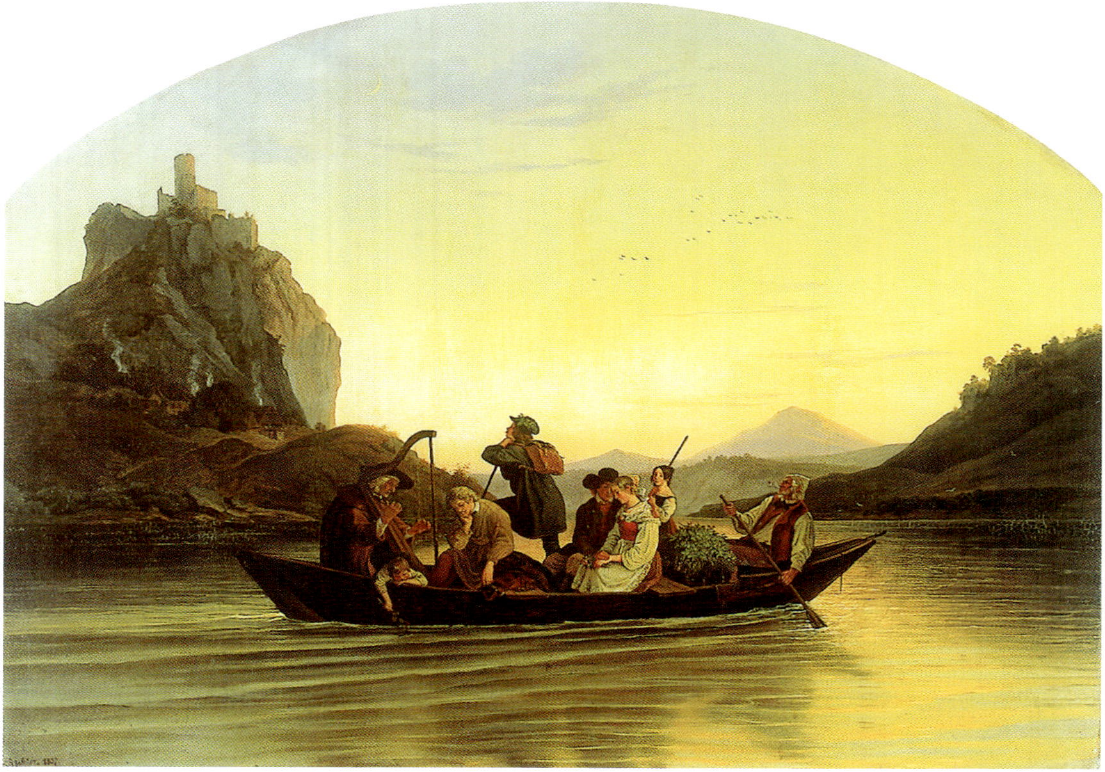

672. **Adrian Ludwig Richter,** 1803-1884, Romanticism, German,
Crossing the Elbe at Aussig, 1837.
Oil on canvas, 116.5 x 156.5 cm.
Gemäldegalerie Neue Meister, Dresden.

673. **J.M.W. Turner,** 1775-1851, Romanticism, English,
*The Burning of the Houses of Lords and Commons,
16 October, 1834*, c. 1835.
Oil on canvas, 91 x 122 cm. Museum of Art, Philadelphia.

674. **J.M.W. Turner,** 1775-1851, Romanticism, English, *The
Fighting "Temeraire"*, 1839. Oil on canvas, 91 x 122 cm.
National Gallery, London.

*It was a standing order of the Royal Navy that everything salvable
and reusable from a ship should be taken off her before she was
moved from her customary anchorage for destruction. As a result,
when the "Temeraire" was towed upriver in 1838, all her masts
had already been removed; had Turner been able to see the
man-of-war under tow, he would only have witnessed the hull
being transported. By replacing all her masts and sails, the painter
was therefore restoring the ship to her original glory, as she had*

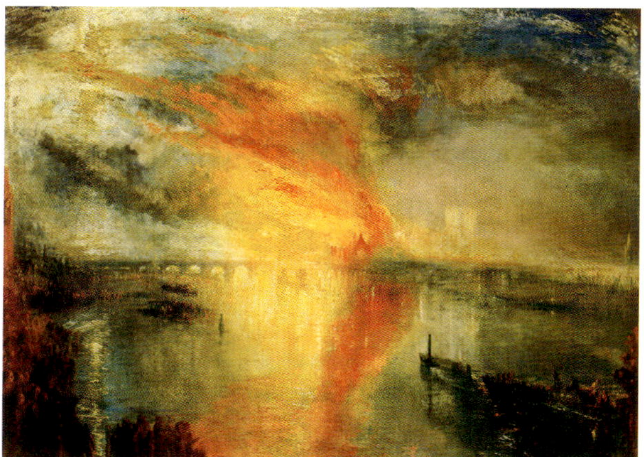

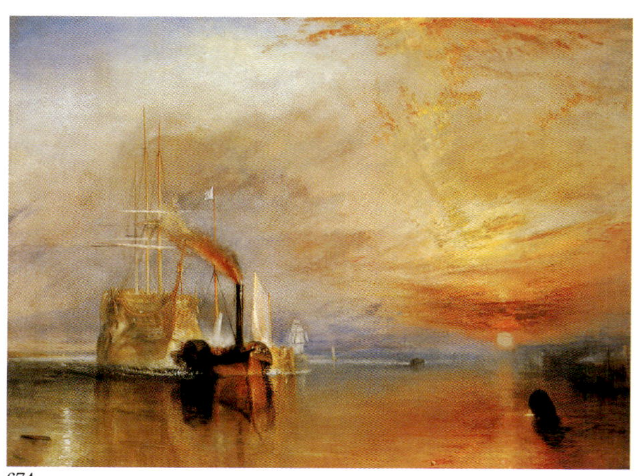

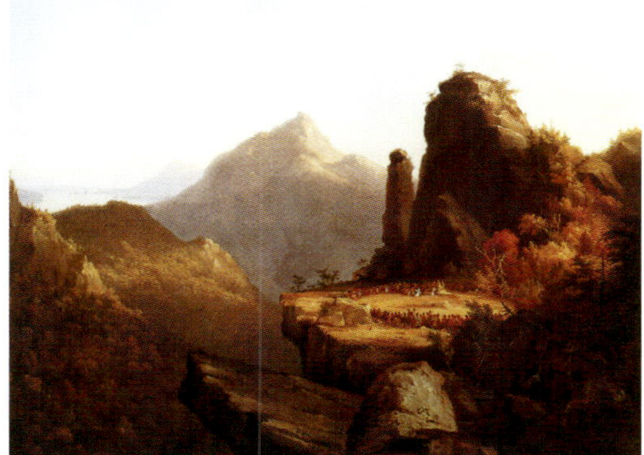

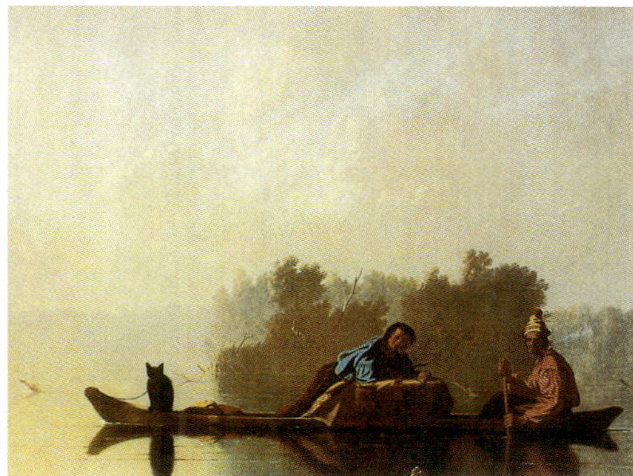

appeared in her heyday some thirty years earlier. And by representing her in such comparatively light tones, he made her look unearthly, like a ghost ship. Naturally that ethereal delicacy is greatly intensified by the contrasting dark tones of the tug. Moreover, to make the "Temeraire" look as majestic as possible – as though she has now risen above the earthly fray – Turner also raised her very high in the water. Consequently, she appears to glide above the Thames, rather than in it, a lofty sight indeed. When this painting was displayed at the Royal Academy in 1839 Turner was criticised for transposing the foremast and funnel of the tug: instead of locating the stack midway between the paddles and thus immediately above the engine, he positioned it at the very prow of the vessel, with the foremast taking its place above the engine. Yet it is easy to see why he effected this transposition: by situating the funnel at the very prow of the tug, he stood it in the vanguard of all the wind-powered shipping in the picture. Clearly he did so in order to symbolise the 'prophetic idea of smoke, soot, iron and steam, coming to the fore in all naval matters', as one of his more astute contemporaries commented. Turner has most appropriately matched his time of day to dramatic meaning; just as the "Temeraire" approaches its end, so the day nears its end, with a moonrise reminding us of the proximity of night. In the case of the doomed vessel, that night will be an extremely long one, indeed.

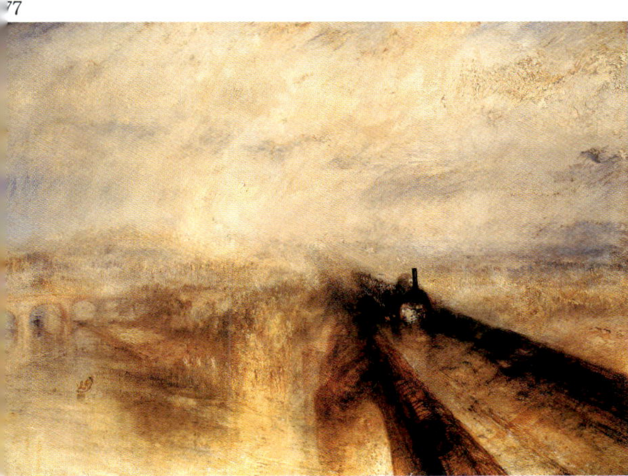

675. **Thomas Cole,** 1801-1848, Hudson River School, American,
The Last of the Mohicans, 1848. Oil on canvas, 64.5 x 89 cm.
Wadsworth Atheneum, Hartford.

Cole is considered the most remarkable painter of the Hudson River School. The painters of the group essentially worked along the Catskill Mountains of New York and the White Mountains of New Hampshire where few Europeans had never gone.

676. **George Caleb Bingham,** 1811-1879, Realism, American,
Fur Traders Descending the Missouri, 1845.
Oil on canvas, 73.7 x 92.7 cm.
The Metropolitan Museum of Art, New York.

Bingham started as a portrait painter. But this work, one of his later works, is a masterpiece of genre painting.

677. **J.M.W. Turner,** 1775-1851, Romanticism, English,
Rain, Steam and Speed, before 1844.
Oil on canvas, 91 x 121.8 cm. National Gallery, London.

Turner here celebrated both the coming of steam locomotion on land, and British technological triumph over water. When this painting was first exhibited at the Royal Academy in 1844 the anonymous critic of Fraser's Magazine warned its readers to hasten to see the work lest the locomotive "should dash out of the picture, and be away up Charing Cross through the wall opposite". The warning seems prudent, given the suggested velocity of the engine. Today that implied movement derives only from the pronounced perspective of the train, railway line and bridge emerging from a distant haze of rain. However, when the paint was still fresh, the sense of speed was augmented by three puffs of steam emanating from the locomotive, whiffs that had already been "left behind by the engine". Sadly, time has rendered them far less visible. Turner joked about speed here, for in front of the train is a hare which has been startled by the approaching machine and is possibly outpacing it. Because of the pictorial proximity of the animal to a ploughman at work in a field beyond the bridge, it seems certain that the artist intended the conjunction of fast hare and slow plough to remind his audience of a popular song 'Speed the Plough', with which he was familiar. In addition to the 'Speed' of the title and the 'Rain' falling across the entire picture, we can also perceive the 'Steam', for Turner has removed the front of the locomotive in order to reveal the inner workings of its boiler. Nothing else would explain the brilliant fiery mass at the front of the engine, for it is too formless to be an outside light. Turner may well have derived this image from explanatory cut-away diagrams of the type that were frequently to be seen in the Victorian popular press. By means of it we are witnessing yet another realisation of his desire to make visible the underlying "causes" of things.

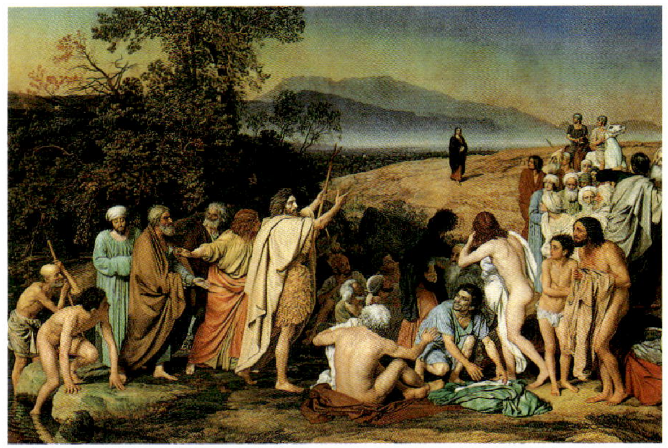

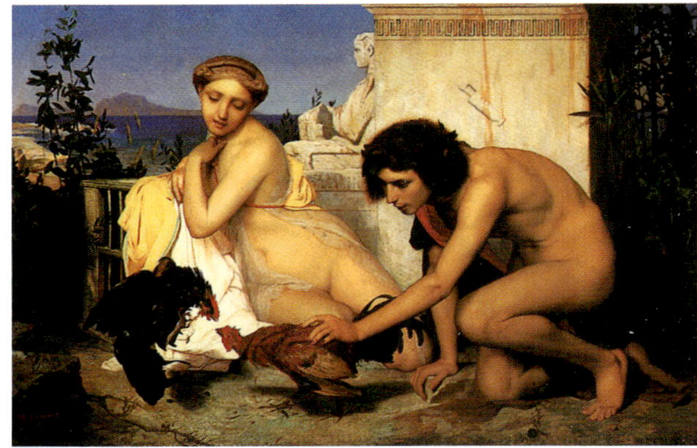

678. **Alexander Ivanov,** 1806-1858, Neoclassicism, Russian,
Christ's First Appearance to the People, 1837-1857.
Oil on canvas, 540 x 750 cm.
The State Tretyakov Gallery, Moscow.

*A contemporary of Briullov, Alexander Ivanov was indisputably
the most influential religious painter of his day. After making his
mark with pictures such as* Apollo, Hyacinth and Zephyr *and* The
Appearance of Christ to Mary Magdalene *(1836), he embarked on*
The Appearance of Christ to the People, *a huge canvas that was
to occupy much of his energy for the next twenty years, from 1837
to the year before he died. Nevertheless, despite all those years of
effort, Ivanov was never happy with the painting and never
regarded it as finished. Indeed, it has an undeniably laboured
quality, and many of his preparatory studies – landscapes, nature
studies, nudes and portraits, including a head of John the Baptist
that is masterpiece in its own right – have a vitality that is absent
from the painting itself.*

679. **Jean-Léon Gérôme,** 1824-1904, Academism, French,
The Cock Fight, 1846. Oil on canvas, 143 x 204 cm.
Musée d'Orsay, Paris.

680. **Thomas Couture,** 1815-1879, Neoclassicism, French,
The Romans of the Decadence, 1847.
Oil on canvas, 466 x 775 cm. Musée d'Orsay, Paris.

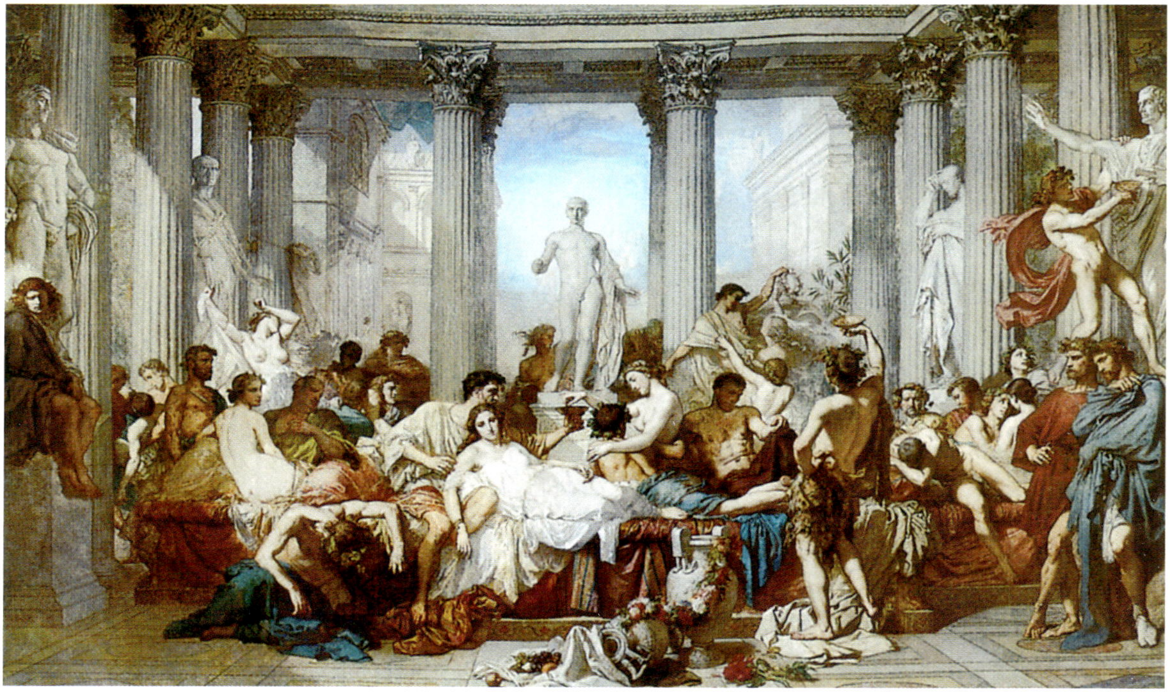

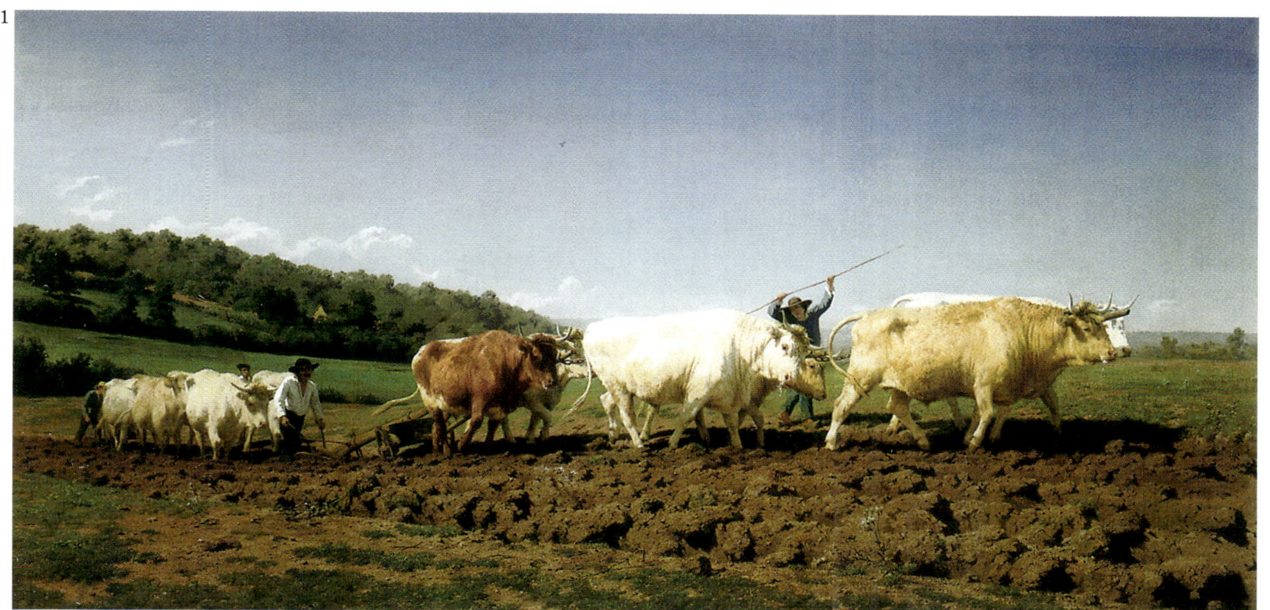

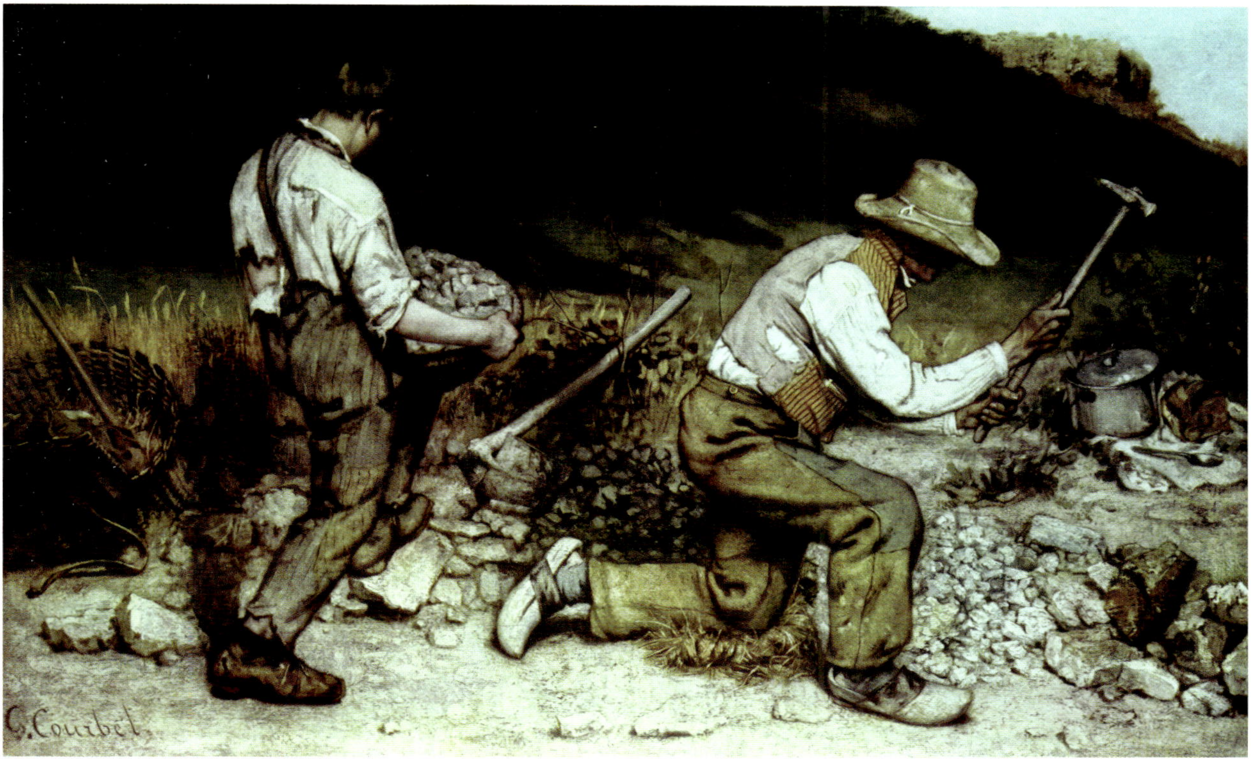

681. **Rosa Bonheur,** 1822-1899, Realism, French,
Ploughing in the Nivernais, 1848-1849.
Oil on canvas, 134 x 260 cm.
Musée d'Orsay, Paris

682. **Gustave Courbet,** 1819-1877, Realism, School of Barbizon, French,
The Stone Breakers, 1849.
Oil on canvas, 165 x 257 cm. Formerly Gemäldegalerie in Dresden.
Believed to have been destroyed in World War II.

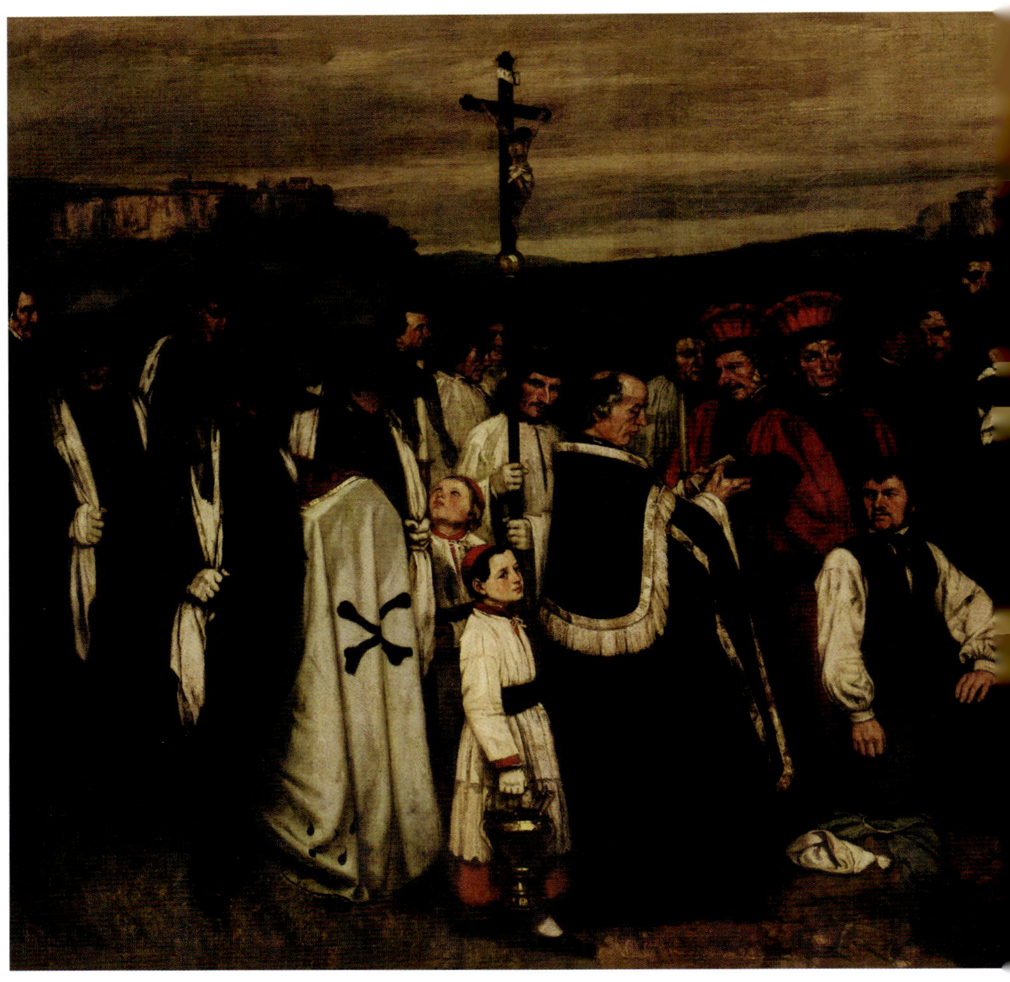

683. **Gustave Courbet,** 1819-1877, Realism,
School of Barbizon, French, *A Burial at Ornans,* 1850.
Oil on canvas, 311.5 x 668 cm. Musée d'Orsay, Paris.

The artist's effort to paint realistic scenes is exemplified in this
unsentimental scene of a burial in the village of his birth.

Realism is especially effective in that the figures in the work are
life-sized. Courbet asked each inhabitant of Ornans to pose in
his workshop for this painting. The variety of expressions
reflects grief, yet a certain individuality is given to each. Several
of the women look away, too sad to watch the final tribute to
one they rather obviously loved. The processional cross seems

GUSTAVE COURBET
(1819 ORNANS – 1877 LA TOUR DE PEILZ)

Ornans, Courbet's birthplace, is near the beautiful valley of the
Doubs River, and it was here as a boy, and later as a man, that
he absorbed the love of landscape.

He was by nature a revolutionary, a man born to oppose
existing order and to assert his independence; he had that quality
of bluster and brutality which makes the revolutionary count in art
as well as in politics. In both directions his spirit of revolt
manifested itself.

He went to Paris to study art, yet he did not attach himself to
the studio of any of the prominent masters. Already in his
country home he had had a little instruction in painting, and
preferred to study the masterpieces of the Louvre. At first his
pictures were not sufficiently distinctive to arouse any
opposition, and were admitted to the Salon. Then followed the
Funeral at Ornans, which the critics violently assailed: "A
masquerade funeral, six metres long, in which there is more to
laugh at than to weep over."

Indeed, the real offence of Courbet's pictures was that they
represented live flesh and blood. They depicted men and women
as they really are and realistically doing the business in which

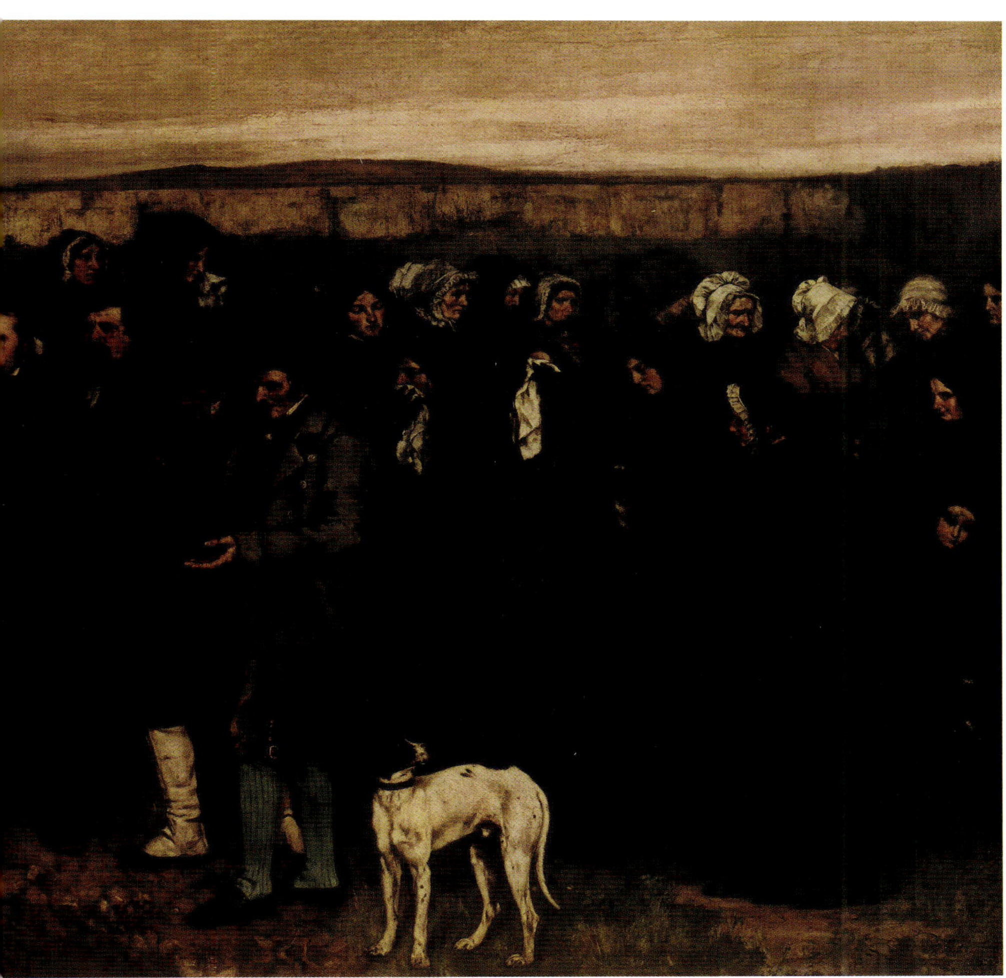

*to align with the crucified Jesus on the distant hillside as if
making the past tragedy present among the sorrowful
townspeople. The bleak landscape reflects the sadness of the
mourners. The main cause of scandal for this painting was the
burial scene showing ordinary country life elevated to high
historical painting level, because of its large size. Courbet*
*considers the little gentries as important and dignified as
historical heroes. The critics hissed. After this work was rejected
by the Jury at the Salon, Courbet created a place called
"Pavillon du Réalisme" where he presented an exhibition of
forty works. The catalogue for this exhibition included a
manifesto of Realism.*

they are engaged. His figures were not men and women deprived
of personality and idealised into a type, posed in positions that
will decorate the canvas. He advocated painting things as they
are, and proclaimed that *la vérité vraie* must be the aim of the
artist. So at the Universal Exposition of 1855 he withdrew his
pictures from the exhibition grounds and set them in a wooden
booth, just outside the entrance. Over the booth he posted a sign
with large lettering. It read, simply: "Courbet – Realist."

Like every revolutionary, he was an extremist. He ignored the
fact that to every artist the truth of nature appears under a
different guise according to his way of seeing and experiencing.
Instead, he adhered to the notion that art is only a copying of
nature and not a matter also of selection and arrangement.

In his contempt for prettiness Courbet often chose subjects
which may fairly be called ugly. But that he also had a sense of
beauty may be seen in his landscapes. That sense, mingled with
his capacity for deep emotion, appears in his marines – these
last being his most impressive work. Moreover, in all his works,
whether attractive or not to the observer, he proved himself a
powerful painter, painting in a broad, free manner, with a fine
feeling for colour, and with a firmness of pigment that made all
his representations very real and stirring.

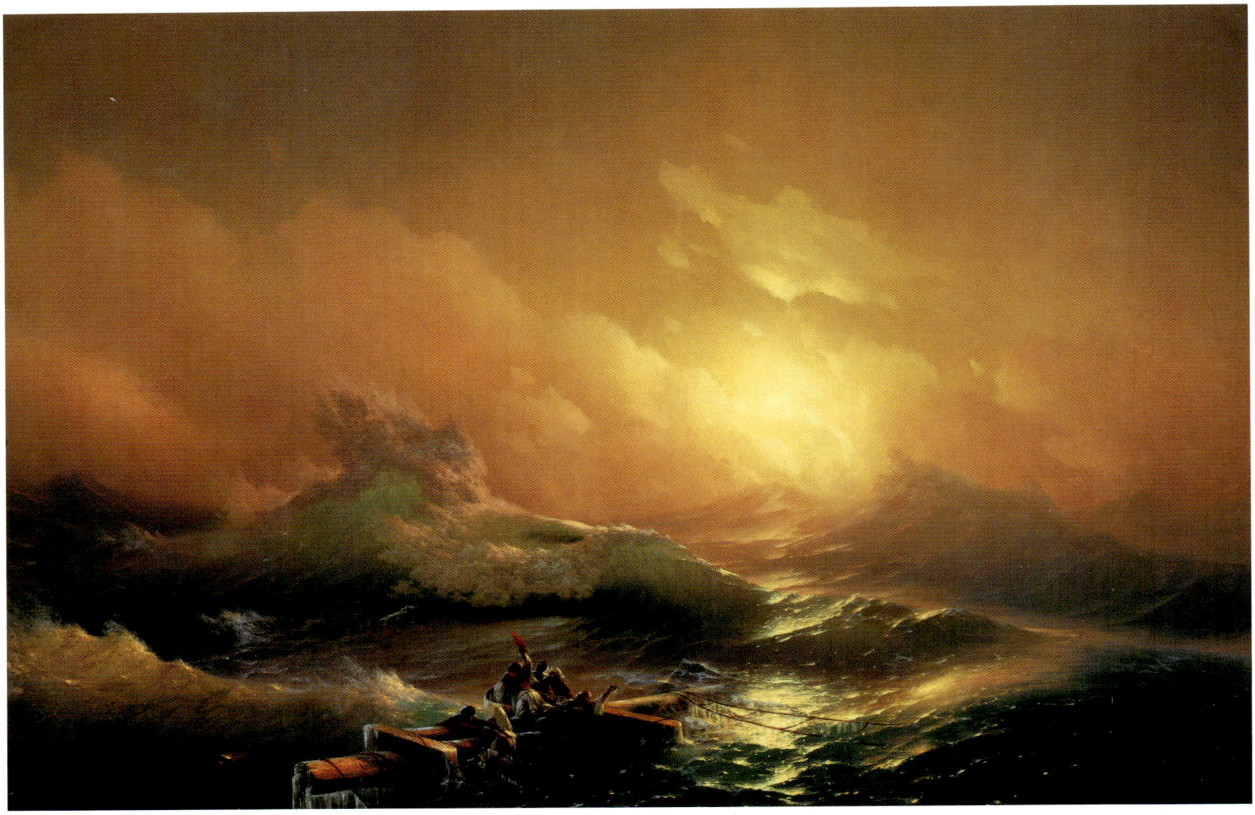

684. **Ivan Aivazovsky,** 1817-1900, Romanticism, Russian,
The Ninth Wave, 1850. Oil on canvas, 221 x 332 cm.
The State Russian Museum, St Petersburg.

One of Aivazovsky's most famous works, The Ninth Wave, *owes its title to the superstition among Russian sailors that in any sequence of waves, the ninth is the most violent. Like many of his paintings, it bears the imprint of Romanticism: the sea and sky convey the power and grandeur of nature, while in the foreground,* the survivors of a shipwreck embody human hopes and fears. *Although the sea is the dominant theme in the majority of the 6,000 paintings that Aivazovsky produced, he also painted views of the coast and countryside, both in Russia (especially in the Ukraine and Crimea) and during travels abroad.*

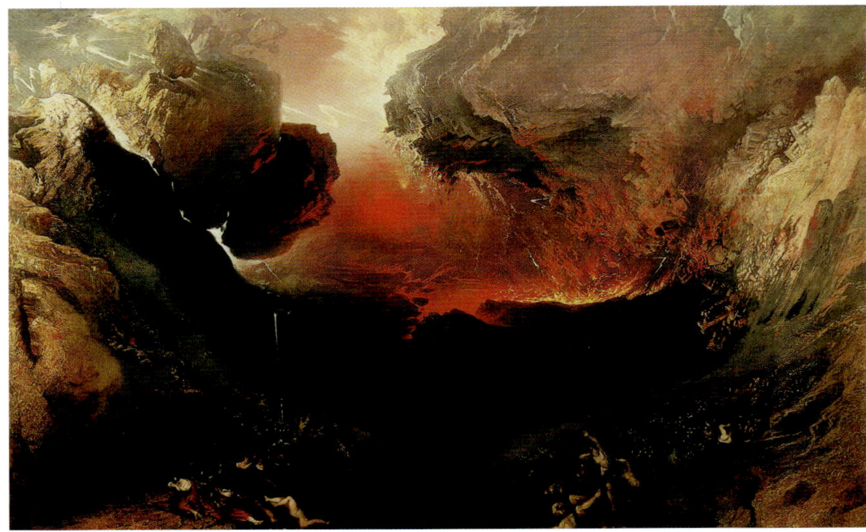

685. **John Martin,** 1789-1854,
Romanticism, English,
The Great Day of His Wrath, 1851.
Oil on canvas, 196 x 303 cm.
Tate Gallery, London.

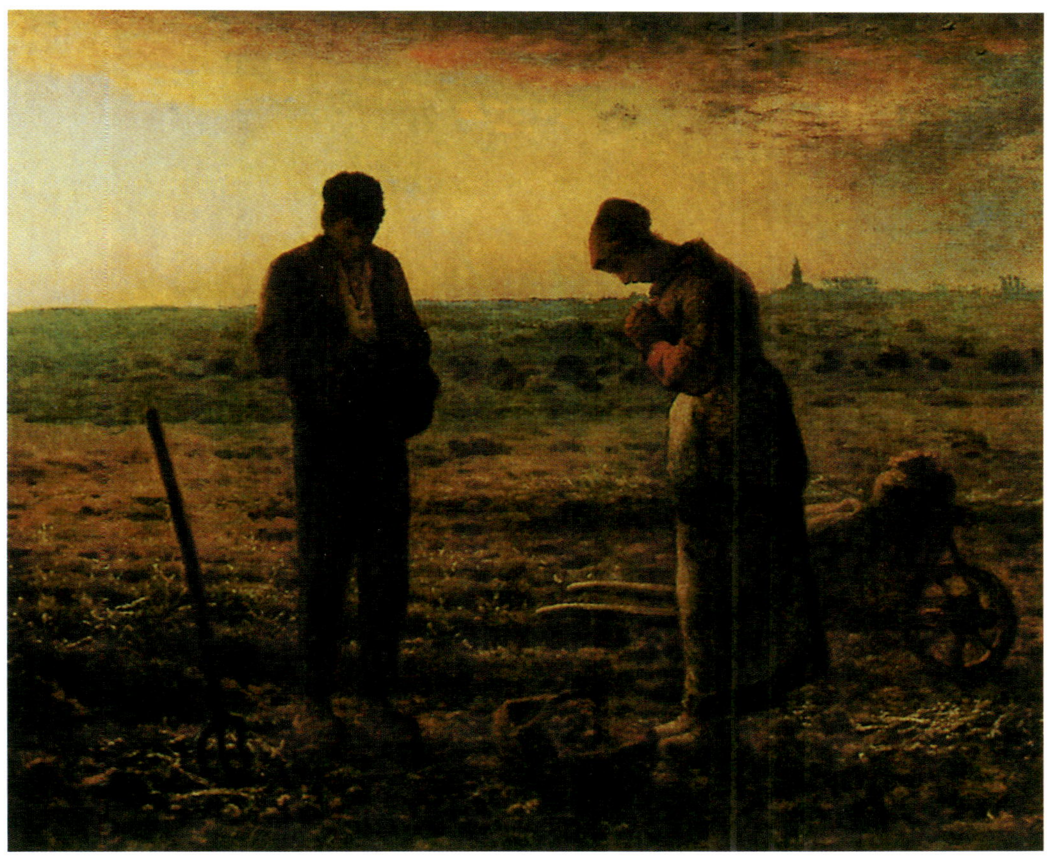

JEAN–FRANÇOIS MILLET
(1814 GRUCHY – 1875 BARBIZON)

Millet was the son of a small farmer, which explains the fact that when he painted rural life, it was not as if he were a city gentleman visiting the country, but as if he belonged to that class.

His early life was very close to nature. He grew up with the air of the hills and of the sea in his nostrils, both conducive to sturdiness of character and to the development of imagination, if a boy chances to have any. He knew nothing of art or artists, but he had the desire to represent what he saw, and in the periods between work on the poor farm he would copy the engravings from the family Bible, or take a piece of charcoal and draw upon a white wall.

An uncle, who was a priest, had taught him as a boy, so that in his manhood he read Shakespeare and Virgil in the original texts. Therefore, although he was of the peasant life, he was greater than it, and brought to the interpretation of its most intimate facts a breadth of view and depth of sympathy which made his pictures much more than studies of peasants. The determination of the farmer in *The Sower* suggests he is not a man to be reckoned with. After the sowing is complete, one could imagine him leading thousands of peasants to Paris; perhaps it is the empowerment of peasants by the skilled hands of artists like Millet that led to this painting's confiscation prior to the revolution.

Millet, with no direct thought of being poetical (or political), sought only to portray the truth as he saw and felt it. He has represented dull, homely facts with such an insight into the relation they bear on the lives of the people engaged in them, that he has created an atmosphere of imagination around the facts.

686. Jean-François Millet, 1814-1875, Realism, School of Barbizon, French, *The Angelus,* c. 1858. Oil on canvas, 55.5 x 66 cm. Musée d'Orsay, Paris.

There is a religious, or at least a sincerely sentimental, tone to Millet's view of labourers ploughing, sowing, or harvesting. This painting, the most popular of his views of that simple life, shows a couple pausing from their toil to pray. The title informs the viewer that the couple is praying the prayer known as the Angelus (Latin for "angel"), the traditional Catholic prayer to the Virgin Mary that is said at six o'clock in the morning, noon and again at six o'clock in the evening. The word refers to the archangel Gabriel, who invited the Virgin during the Annunciation to be the mother of Jesus (Luke 1: 26). An earlier work by Millet, The Sower, is nearly as popular. It likewise shows a slice of the simple but dignified life of farming. Millet brought a dignity to the images of peasants, whereas artists such as Bruegel the Elder often made them appear as standard personifications of human destiny.

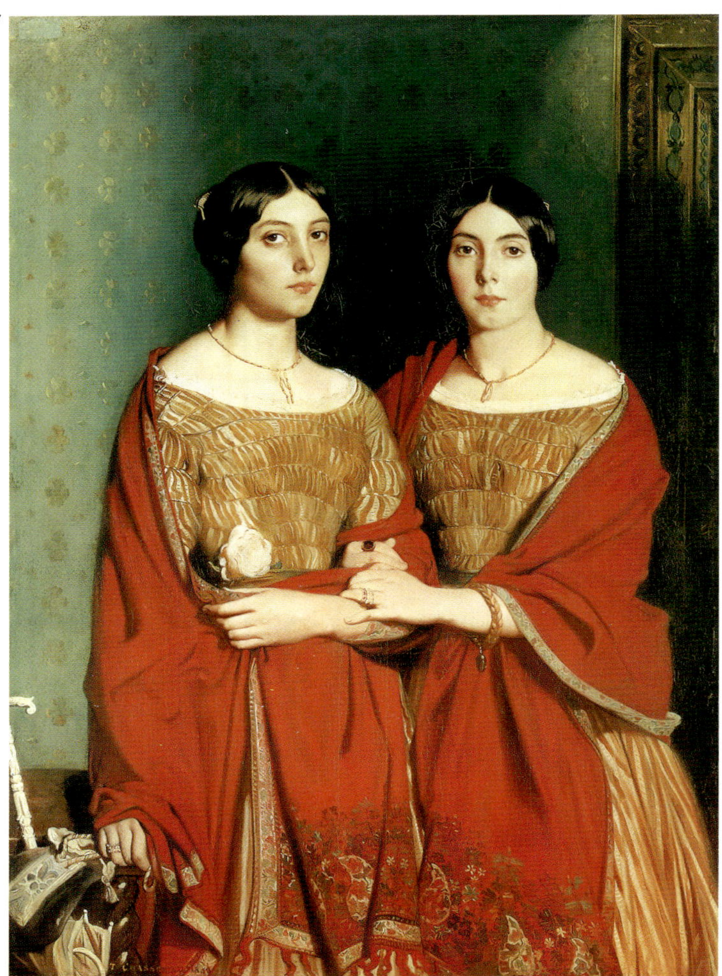

687. **Théodore Chassériau,** 1819-1856, Neoclassicism, French,
The Two Sisters, 1843. Oil on canvas, 180 x 135 cm.
Musée du Louvre, Paris.

*Chassériau was one of Ingres' students. This influence of the
master is discernable through the fine use of colours and elegant
dresses and shawls.*

688. **Jean-Auguste-Dominique Ingres,** 1780-1867, Neoclassicism,
French, *Mrs Moitessier,* 1856. Oil on canvas, 120 x 92 cm.
National Gallery, London.

*It took twelve years for Ingres to achieve this portrait. The mirror
reflects the profile of the sitter. This association of face and
profile in the same painting will inspire Picasso.*

689. **Pavel Fedotov,** 1815-1852, Realism, Russian,
The Major's Courtship, 1848. Oil on canvas, 58.3 x 75.3 cm.
The State Tretyakov Gallery, Moscow.

*By the middle of the nineteenth century, Russian writers and
painters were also beginning to focus attention on other
sectors of society that had, until then, scarcely figured in art.
Landowners, civil servants, the military and the clergy all became*
possible subjects for artistic comment. As a reaction against the
repressive and bureaucratic regime of Nicholas I, the behaviour
of the ruling class was frequently depicted in a satirical light. One
of the most astute social commentators was Pavel Fedotov.
Fedotov's contemporaries would have immediately recognised
the social status of the dramatis personae in his best-known
picture – The Major's Courtship, painted in 1848. Marriageable
young ladies, like the one whose hand the languid major is
seeking, could be seen promenading on Saint Petersburg's
Nevsky Prospekt and in the city's parks. All the figures, down to
the servants in the background, are portrayed with an unerring
eye for detail. Fedotov's art pillories social evils (in this case the
way women were treated as marketable chattels), mostly with
humour though occasionally with bitterness. In 1844, at the age
of twenty-nine, Fedotov abandoned a military career in favour of
painting. Eight years later he died in a mental institution, his
mental state unbalanced by poverty and frustration.*

690. **Adolf Friedrich Erdmann von Menzel,** 1815-1905, Realism,
German, *The Flute Concert of Frederick II at Sanssouci,* c. 1851.
Oil on canvas, 142 x 205 cm.
Alte Nationalgalerie, Berlin.

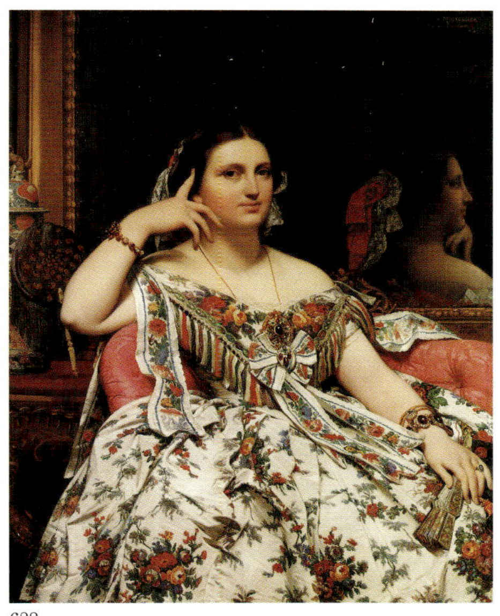

688

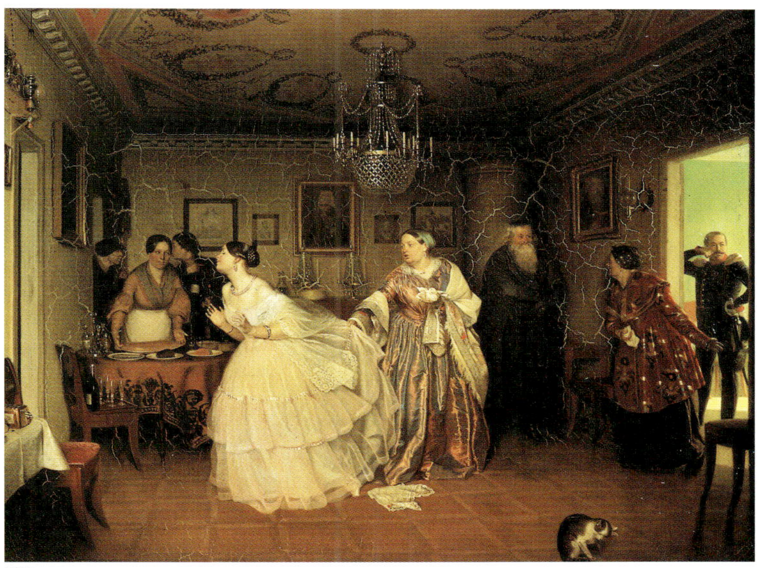

689

690

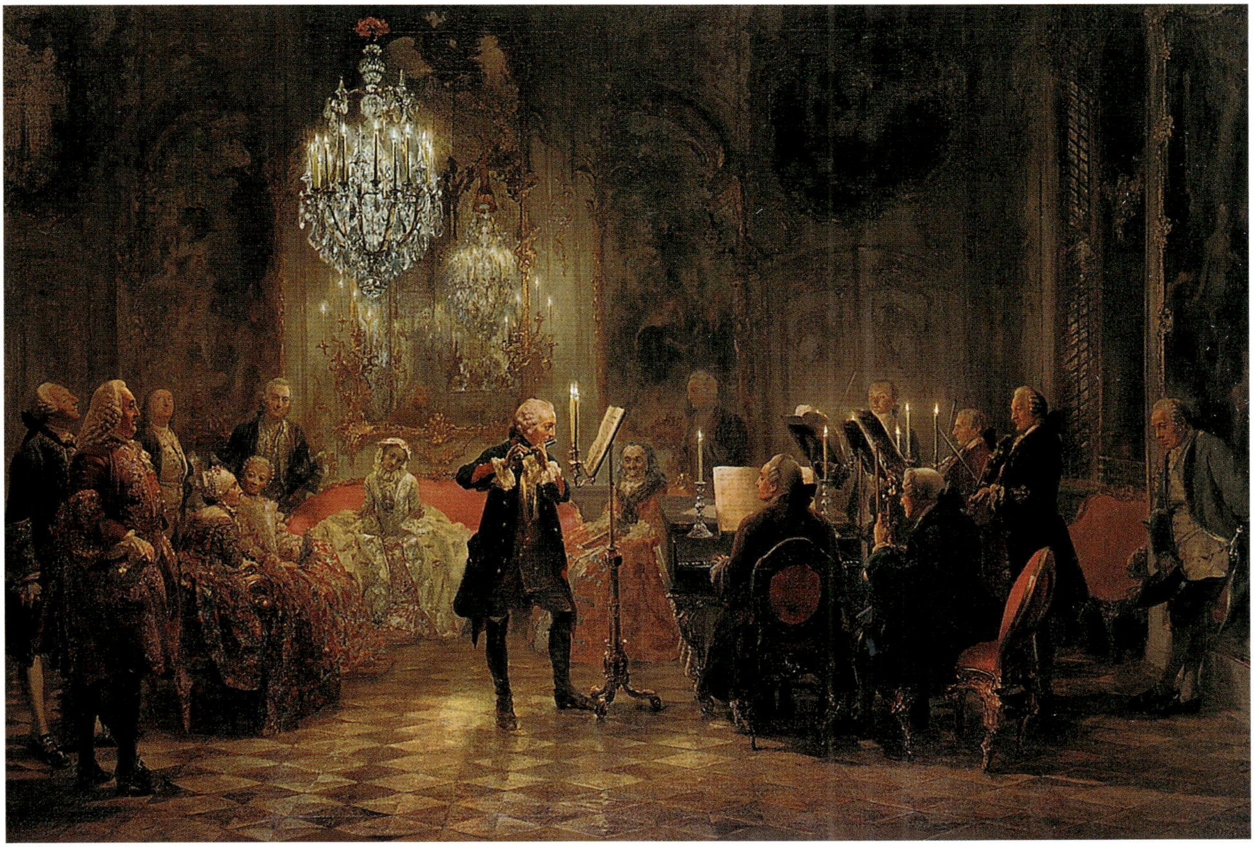

691

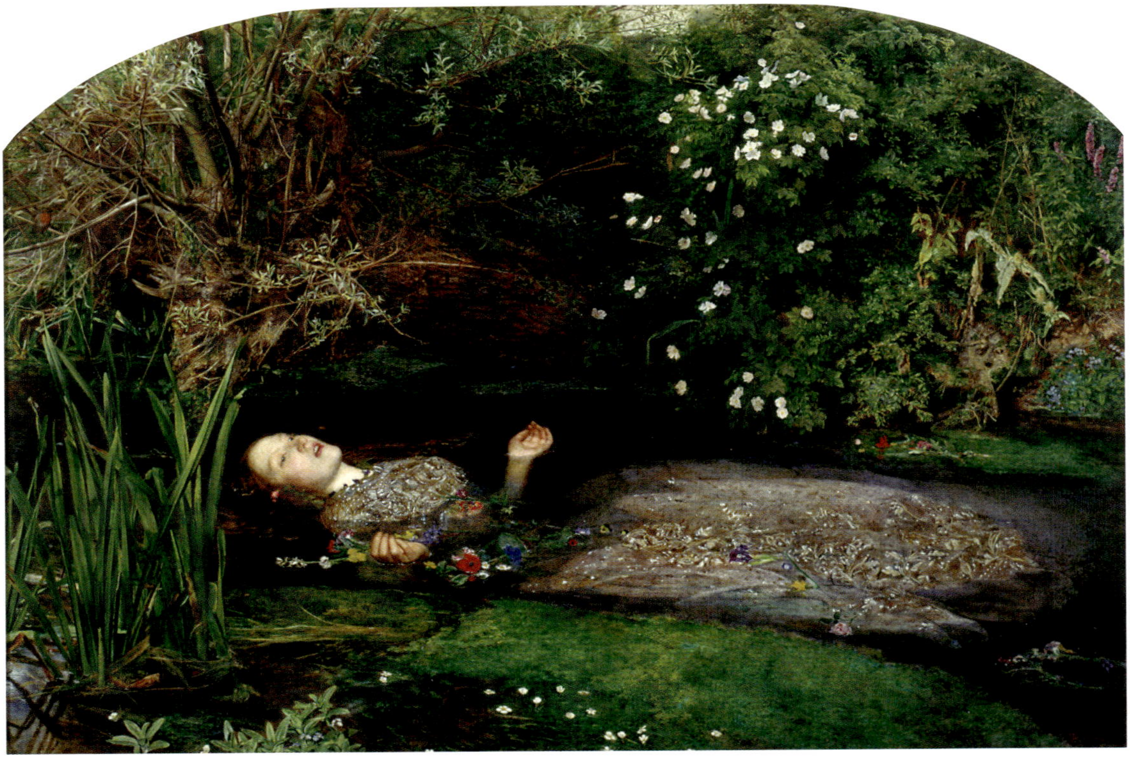

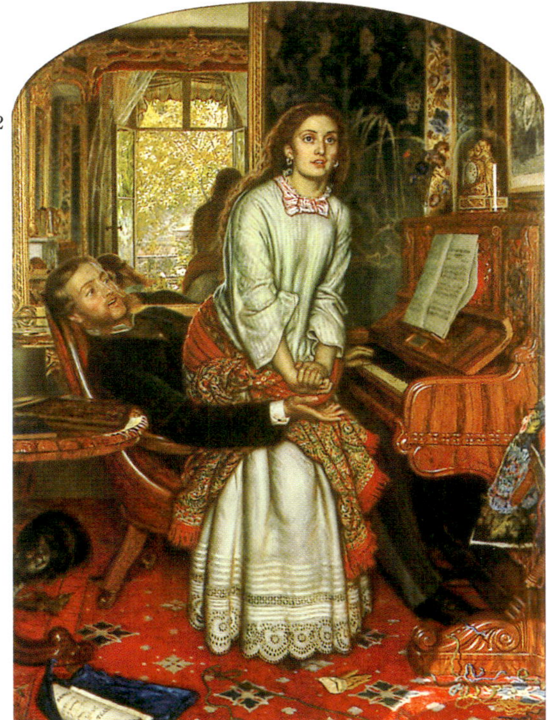

692

692. **William Holman Hunt,** 1827-1910, Pre-Raphaelite, British, *The Awakening Conscience,* 1853. Oil on canvas, 76 x 55 cm. Tate Gallery, London.

The Pre-Raphaelite Brotherhood involved several British artists but existed for only five years between 1880 and 1900. However, Hunt as a charter member continued his life-long commitment to their cause. He continued to be judgmental about what the Brotherhood considered immoral sexual activity. In this work, inspired by Charles Dickens' David Copperfield, the artist shows a man and a woman, who might be his mistress. The man plays the piano and sings a song intended to seduce her, but the sheet music, apparently hers rather than his choice, is for "Oft in the Stilly Night," a song about a girl recalling her childhood innocence. The woman is about to stand up perhaps as she remembers the words to the song that awakens her conscience. Like the song sheet on the piano, the music sheets in the lower left corner are also about lost innocence. It is an adaptation of a poem by Tennyson (1809-1892), familiar in the popular culture at the time. The mirror on the far wall reveals that the woman is looking out, apparently towards the future, where there are white roses symbolising the purity to which the kept woman can return. The cat, like the man, is playing with its prey. But the bird (like the woman) seems to have a chance to escape.

691. **John Everett Millais,** 1829-1896, Pre-Raphaelite, British,
Ophelia, 1851. Oil on canvas, 76 x 112 cm.
Tate Gallery, London.

The beautiful Ophelia from Shakespeare's Hamlet *floats in the stream with eyes heavenward and hands open in resignation to her tragic state of insanity. Her gesture is like that of the prayerful posture Catholic clergy give from their altar of sacrifice. Flower petals have delicately fallen onto her as if nature was welcoming her into its ongoing cycle of life and death. They also recall Hamlet's words, "sweets to the sweet: farewell!" By blending into its rustic textures and liquid flow, her gown anticipates the woman's union with nature: "Let her i' the earth, and from her fair and unpolluted flesh may violets spring."*

693. **Ford Madox Brown,** 1821-1893, Pre-Raphaelite, English,
The Last of England, 1852-1855.
Oil on canvas, 82 x 74 cm.
Birmingham Museum and Art Gallery, Birmingham.

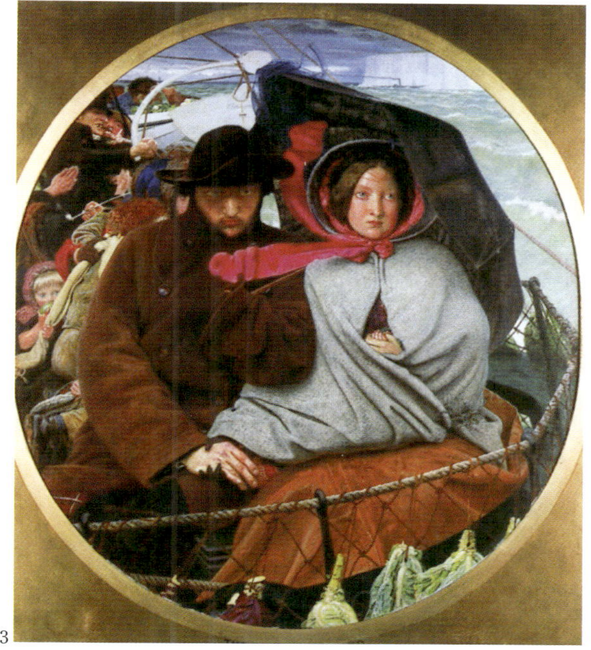

693

694

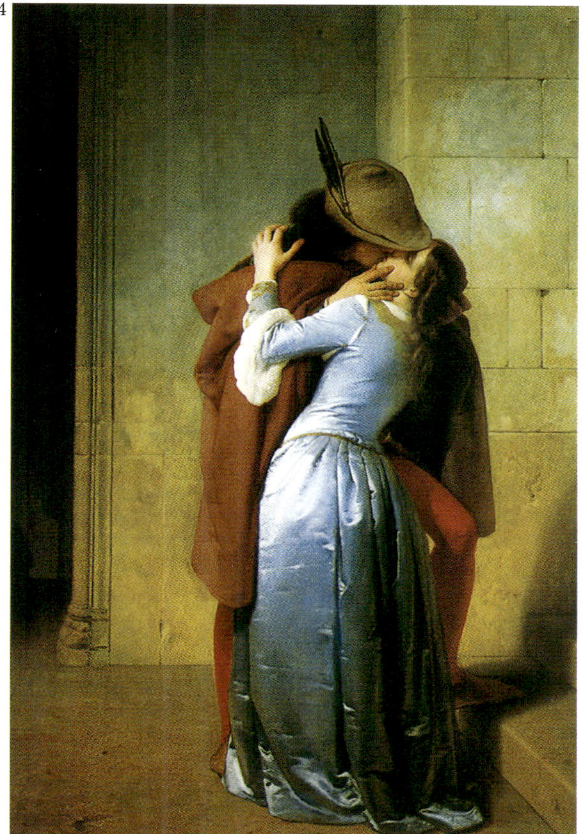

694. **Francesco Hayez,** 1791-1882, Romanticism, Italian,
The Kiss, 1859. Oil on canvas, 112 x 88 cm.
Pinacoteca di Brera, Milan.

Emblematic of Italian Romanticism, this painting also works as a political allegory of the union between Italy and France.

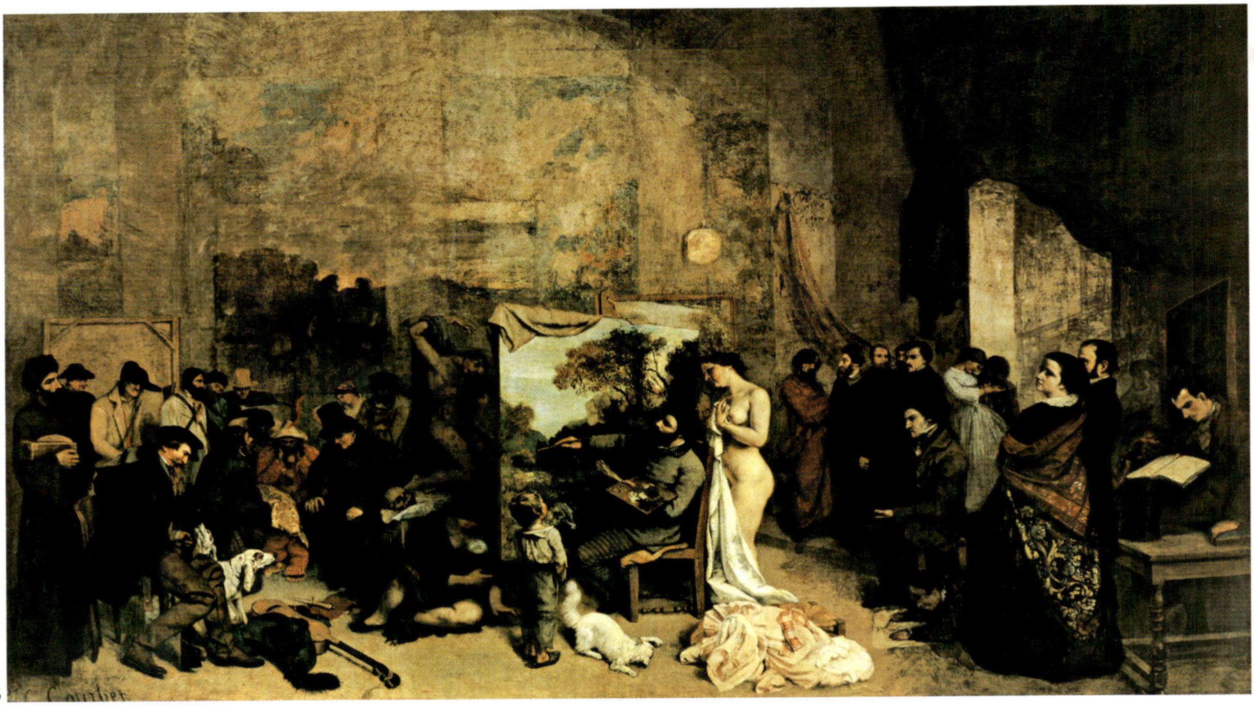

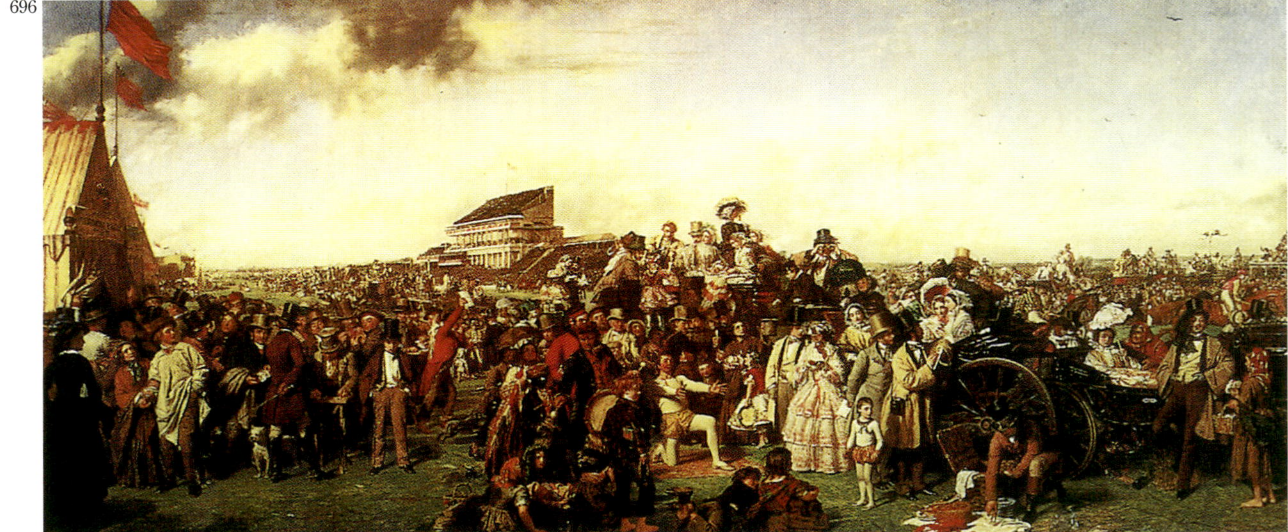

695.

695. **Gustave Courbet,** 1819-1877, Realism, School of Barbizon, French, *The Artist's Studio,* 1855.
Oil on canvas, 361 x 598 cm. Musée d'Orsay, Paris.

Courbet noted: "Painting is an essentially concrete art and can only consist of the representation of real and existing objects." When he was asked to include angels in a painting for a church, he answered: "Show me an angel and I will paint one." Courbet represented Baudelaire and the painter Prod'hon on the right side of the painting.

696. **William Powell Frith,** 1819-1909, Victorian Art, English, *Derby Day,* 1856-1858.
Oil on canvas, 101 x 223 cm.
Tate Gallery, London.

Extremely popular during his lifetime, Frith's art, like Victorian art in general, was re-evaluated after World War II. This work presents a satirical panorama of modern Victorian life. It was first exhibited at the Royal Academy in 1858.

696.

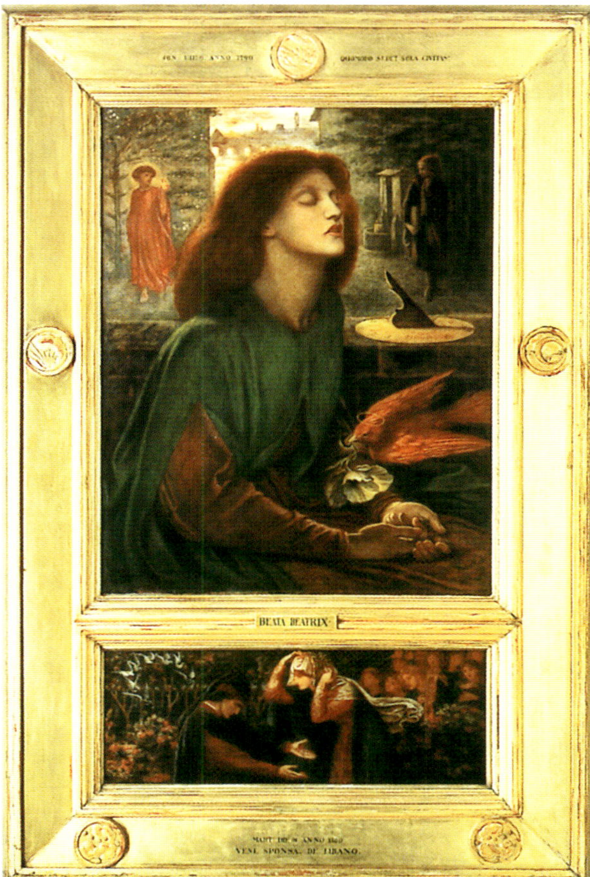

697. Dante Gabriel Rossetti, 1828-1882, Pre-Raphaelite, British, *Beata Beatrix,* c. 1864-1870.
Oil on canvas, 86.4 x 66 cm. Tate Gallery, London.

Rossetti was one of the founders of the Pre-Raphaelite movement that reacted against Victorian artists and wanted to get back to the simplicity of painting before Raphael. This painting, inspired by the Vita Nuova *by Dante, presents the characteristics of Pre-Raphaelite techniques such as the large spots of light and the meticulous attention paid to the symbolic details.*

DANTE GABRIEL ROSSETTI
(1828 LONDON – 1882 BIRCHINGTON)

Rossetti's father, an Italian patriot who had sought refuge in London where he became professor of Italian at King's College, was a distinguished Dante scholar. Dante Gabriel was poet as well as painter.

Rossetti was extraordinarily precocious, and very early he became acquainted with Scott and Shakespeare, but the chief influence of his childhood was the worship of Dante; he knew the poems by heart. He could not find the help he wanted in the systematic methods of the Royal Academy, and he was impatient to paint the pictures that thronged his brain. Consequently he never acquired a complete command of drawing. Perhaps he was not encouraged to try for such mastery, because of his fondness for subjects from Dante and his instinctive feeling that they must be represented with the almost childlike simplicity of feeling.

At the age of twenty-one Rossetti founded, together with Hunt, John Millais, three young sculptors, and Rossetti's younger brother, a society with the title of the Pre-Raphaelite Brotherhood, who were in the habit of affixing to their signatures the letters, P. R. B. The object of the Brotherhood was revolt against existing views and conditions of art; in its original intention not unlike the revolt of Courbet; a plea for Realism. He was ridiculing the dry formalism of the Classicists.

Additionally, while he persevered in painting, he was continually experimenting in poetry. In 1850 he met Miss Elizabeth Siddal, who was introduced to him as a model. She satisfied at once his conception of a perfectly balanced soul and body, of soul beauty shining through the beauty of form, which was his ideal of women. She also became his ideal of Beatrice, and as such he painted her many times. He loved her, but for some reason marriage was postponed for ten years, and then after scarcely two years of marriage she died. But the memory of her abided with him, and almost all his subsequent painting was a representation, in one character or another, of her.

He spent his last year as an invalid recluse, and died in 1882.

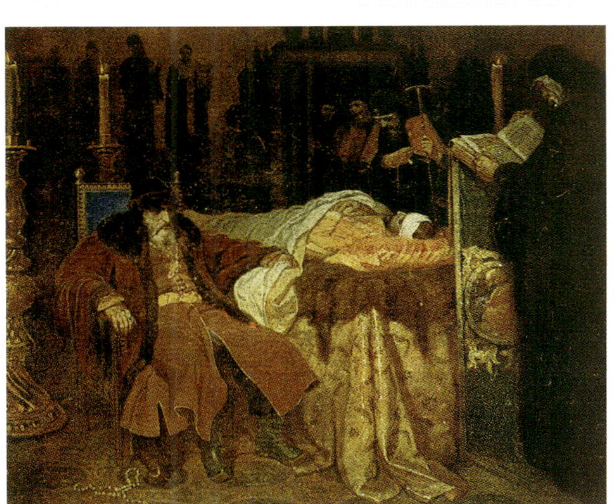

698. Wjatscheslaw Grigorjewitsch Schwarz, 1838-1869, Realism, Russian, *Ivan the Terrible Meditating at the Deathbed of his Son Ivan,* 1861.
Oil on canvas, 71 x 89 cm.
The State Tretyakov Gallery, Moscow.

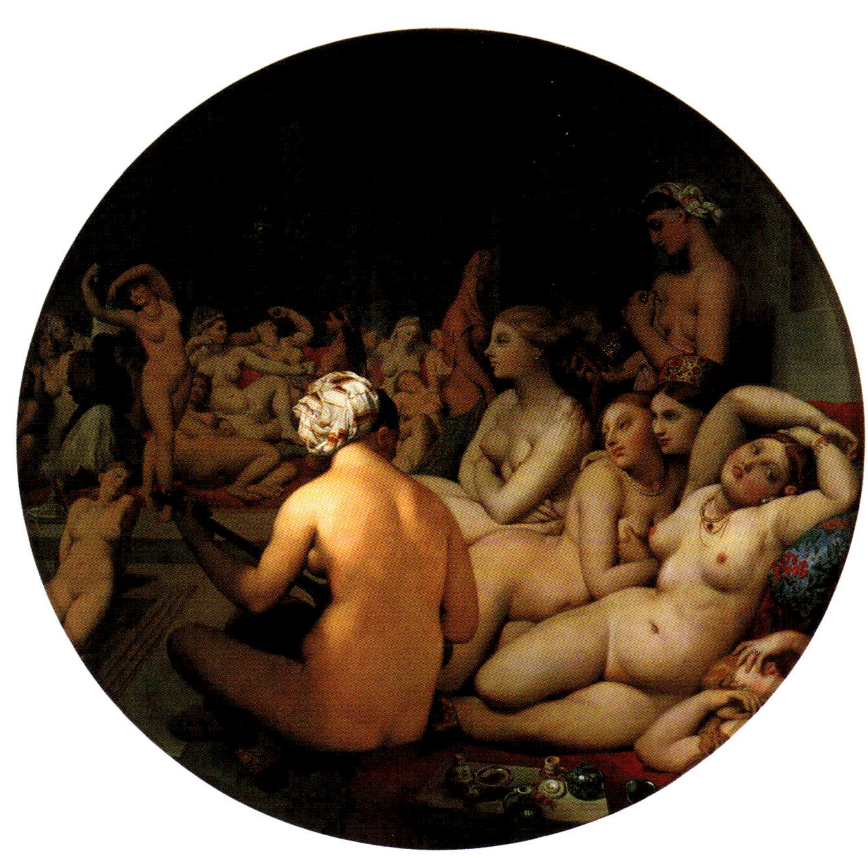

699. **Jean-Auguste-Dominique Ingres,**
1780-1867, Neoclassicism, French,
The Turkish Bath, 1862.
Oil on canvas, Tondo,
diameter: 108 cm.
Musée du Louvre, Paris.

700. **Alexandre Cabanel,** 1825-1905,
Academism, French,
The Birth of Venus, c. 1863.
Oil on canvas, 130 x 225 cm.
Musée d'Orsay, Paris.

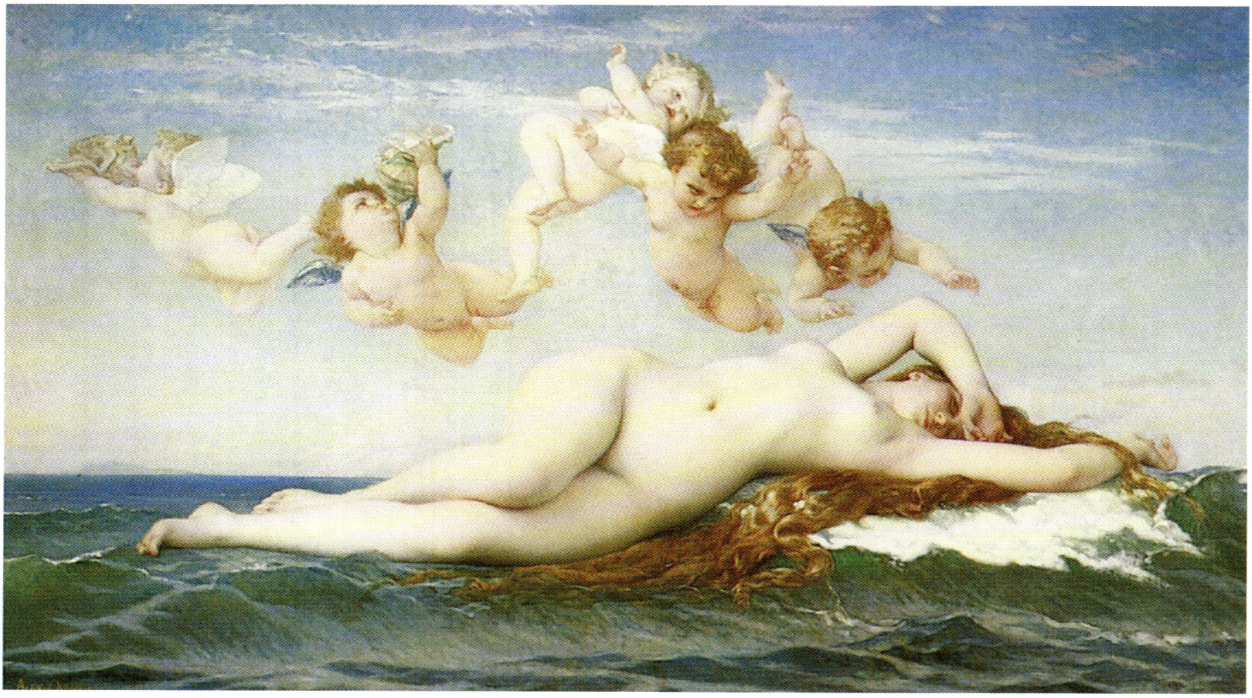

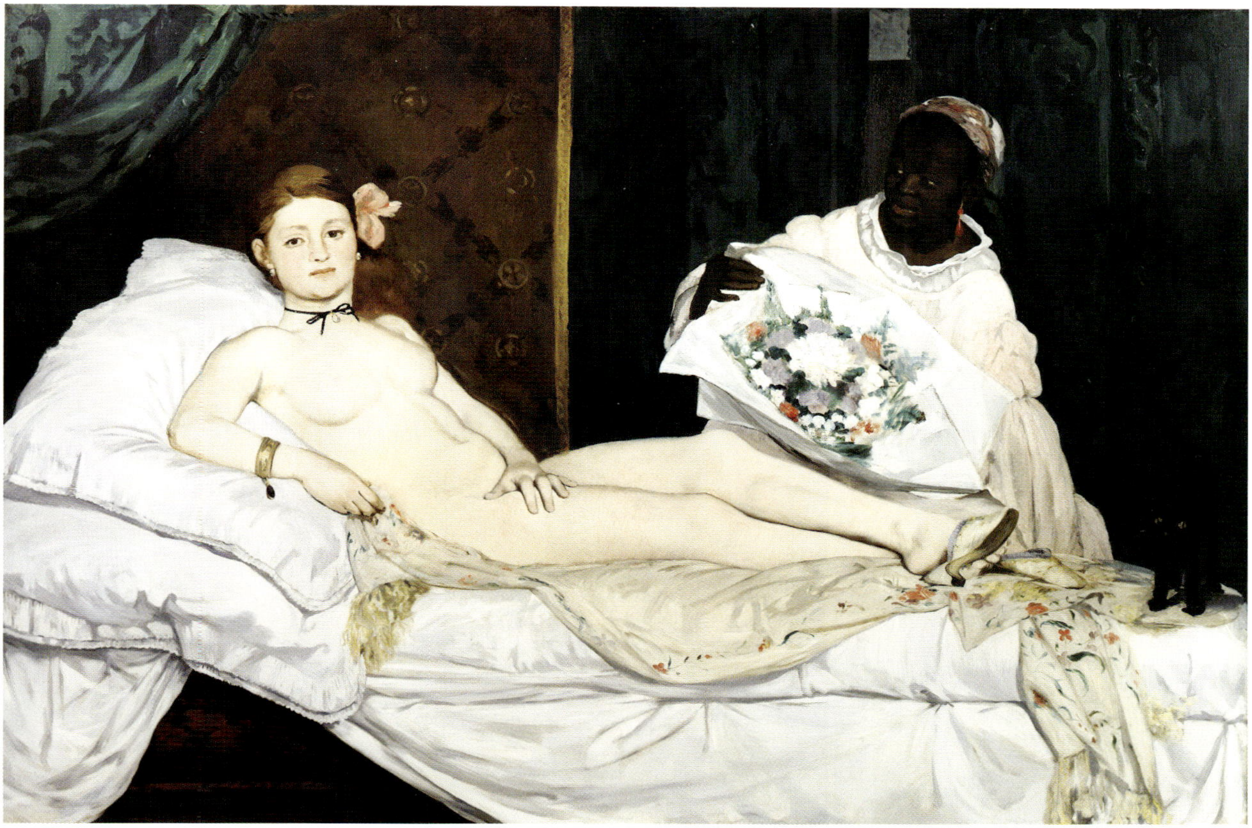

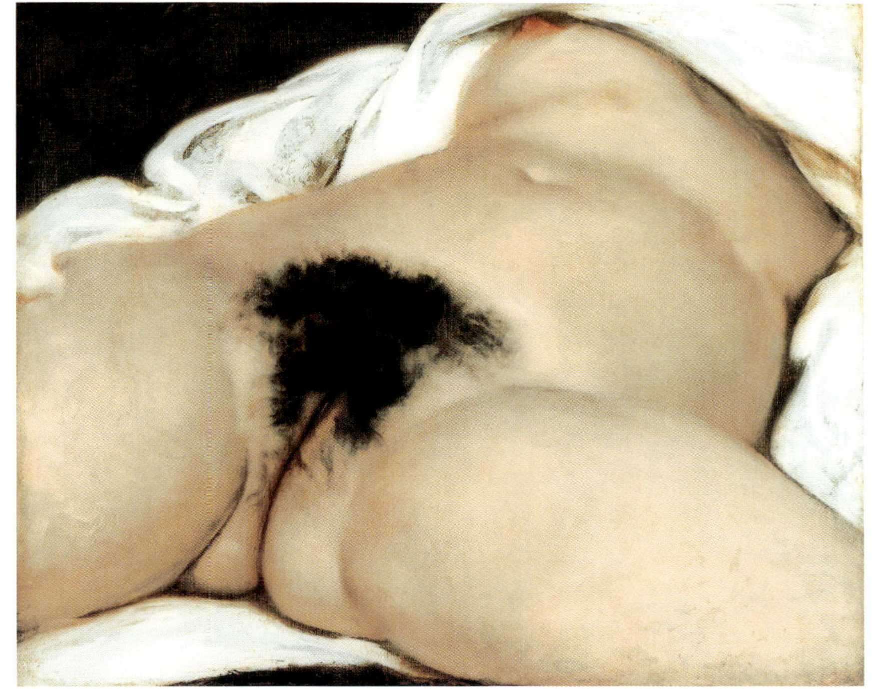

701. **Edouard Manet,** 1832-1883,
Impressionism, French,
Olympia, 1863.
Oil on canvas, 130 x 190 cm.
Musée d'Orsay, Paris.

702. **Gustave Courbet**, 1819-1877,
French (bio. p. 362-363),
The Origin of the World, 1866.
Oil on canvas, 46 x 55 cm.
Musée d'Orsay, Paris.

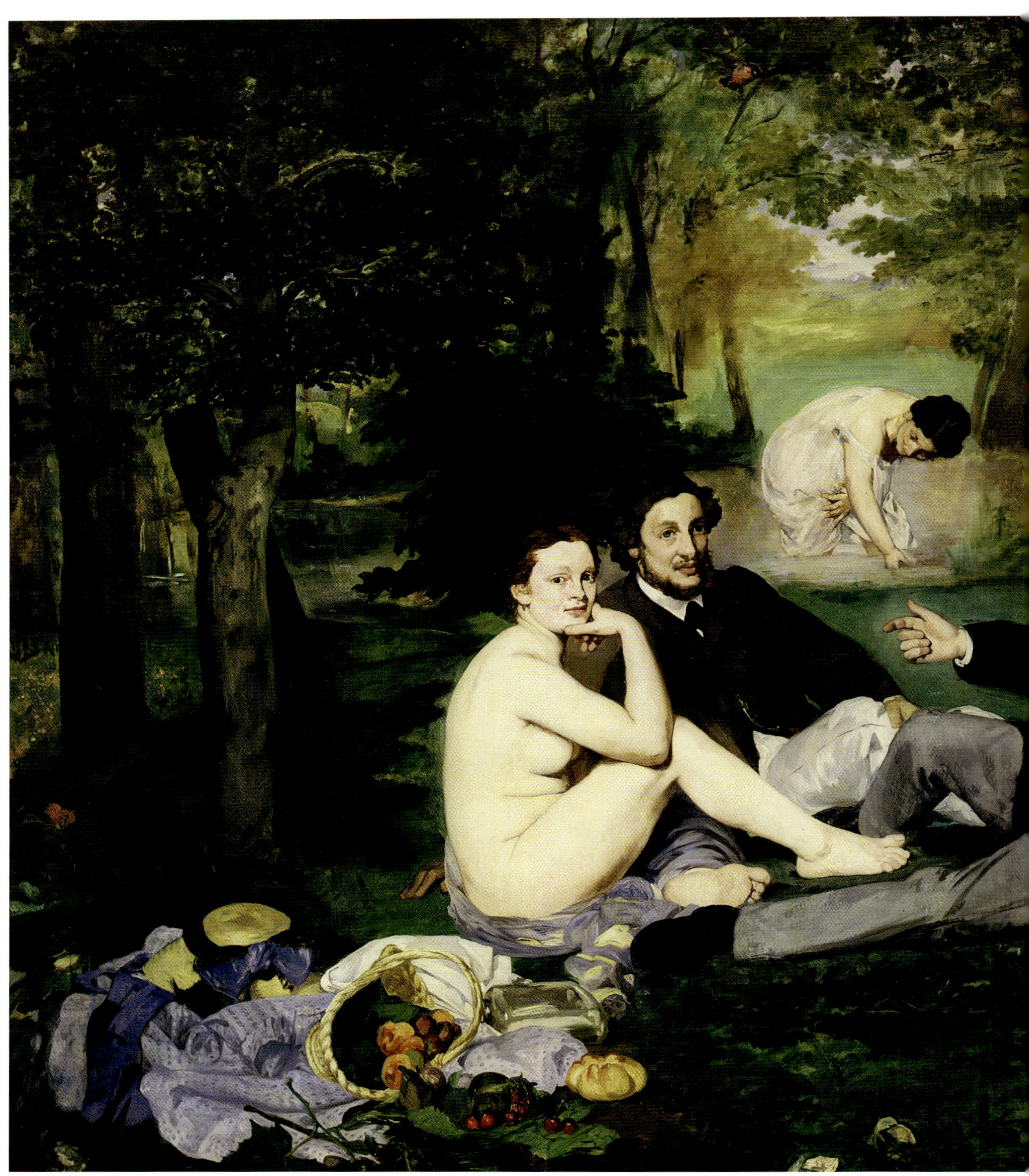

EDOUARD MANET
(1832 PARIS – 1883)

Manet is one of the most famous artists from the second half of the nineteenth century linked to the impressionists, although he was not really one of them. He had great influence on French painting partly because of the choice he made for his subjects from everyday life, the use of pure colours, and his fast and free technique. He made, in his own work, the transition between Courbet's Realism and the work of the impressionists.

Born a high bourgeois, he chose to become a painter after failing the entry to the Marine School. He studied with Thomas Couture, an Academic painter, but it was thanks to the numerous travels he made around Europe from 1852 that he started to find out what would become his own style.

His first paintings were mostly portraits and genre scenes, inspired by his love for Spanish masters like Velázquez and Goya. In 1863 he presented his masterpiece *Luncheon on the Grass* at the Salon des Refusés. His work started a fight between the defenders of Academic art and the young "refusés" artists. Manet became the leader of this new generation of artists.

From 1864, the official Salon accepted his paintings, still provoking loud protests over works such as *Olympia* (fig. 701) in 1865. In 1866, the writer Zolá wrote an article defending Manet's work. At that time, Manet was friends with all the future great impressionist masters: Edgar Degas, Claude Monet, Auguste Renoir, Alfred Sisley, Camille Pissarro and Paul Cézanne, and he influenced their work, even though he cannot strictly be counted as one of them. In 1874 indeed, he refused to present his paintings in the First Impressionist Exhibition. His last appearance in the official Salon was in 1882 with *A Bar at the Folies-Bergère* (fig. 736), one of his most famous works. Suffering from gangrene during the year 1883, he painted flower still-lifes until he became too weak to work. He died leaving behind a great number of drawings and paintings.

703. **Edouard Manet,** 1832-1883, Impressionism, French,
Luncheon on the Grass, 1863.
Oil on canvas, 208 x 264 cm. Musée d'Orsay, Paris.

In 1863, Manet shocked viewers at the Salon des Refusés with his large painting Le Déjeuner sur l'herbe (Luncheon in the Grass) *in which he includes both naked women and dressed male students. He at first had in mind to present a work like Titian's* Pastoral Symphony *(1508). In his previous paintings naked women typically did not look directly at the viewer. In this painting, the expression of the lady is natural, relaxed, and without embarrassment. Manet said that light was the chief actor in the work. The basket of fruit on the blue dress in the foreground takes as much importance as the characters and shows Manet's skills at depicting still-lifes. Reproductions and parodies of the unforgettable work in many media have been presented over the past 150 years. But two decades after this painting was created, Manet no longer needed to shock in order to win attention. See his masterpiece,* A Bar at the Folies-Bergère, *fig. 736. Louise Gardner comments, "Manet raises the veils of allusion and reverie and bluntly confronts the public with reality, demonstrating, incidentally, the incompatibility of myth and realism."*

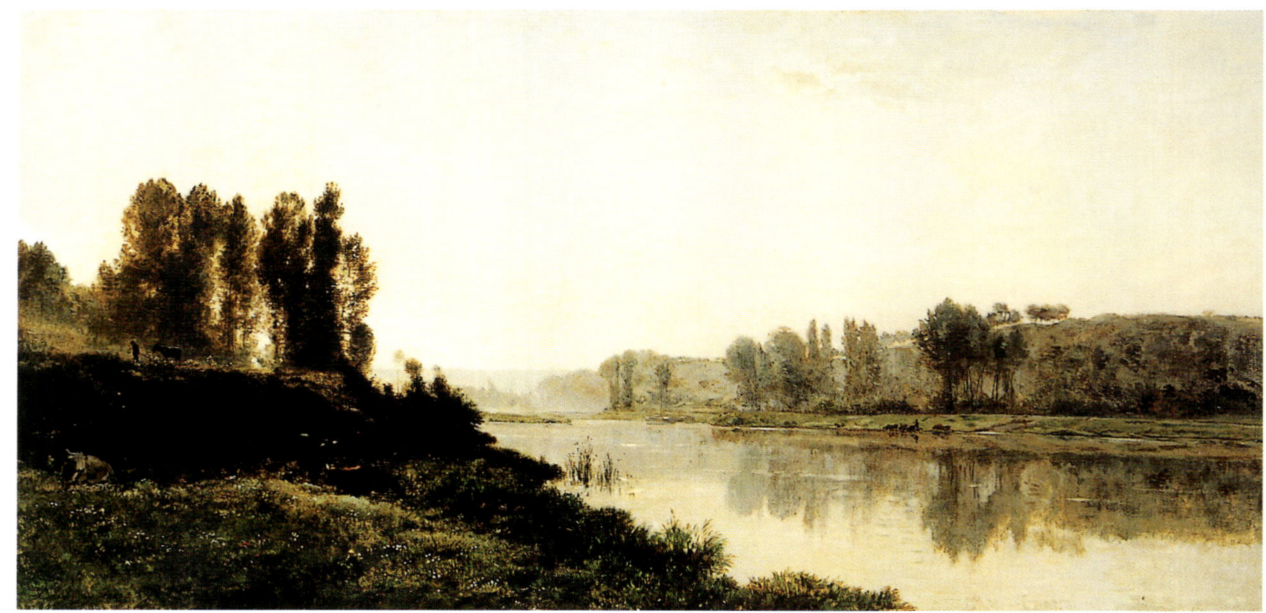

704. Charles-François Daubigny, 1817-1878, Realism, School of Barbizon, French, *On the Banks of Oise*, c. 1860-1865. Oil on canvas, 32.5 x 60 cm. Private collection.

705. Johan Barthold Jongkind, 1819-1891, Impressionism, Dutch, *The Maas at Maassluis*, 1866. Oil on canvas, 33 x 47 cm. Musée des Beaux-Arts, Le Havre.

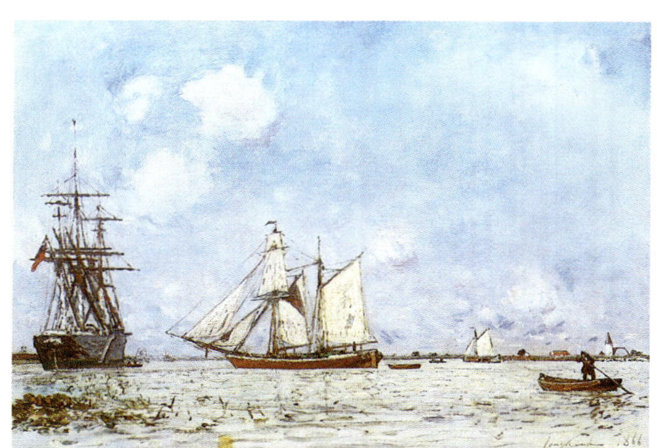

JEAN–BAPTISTE CAMILLE COROT
(1796 – 1875 PARIS)

Corot's parents were court dressmakers in the days of the first Napoleon. Living in comfortable circumstances, their son never wanted for money. His father had apprenticed him to a linen-draper, but after eight years consented to his son's desire to become a painter.

When Corot paid his first visit to Italy, he was so attracted by the moving life on the streets of Rome and Naples that he transferred it to his sketch-book. Because his subjects would not remain still long enough to be treated methodically, he learned to draw, with a few strokes, the general effect of a moving picture and with such success that after a time he could rapidly suggest the appearance of even so intricate a scene as a ballet. This acquired skill became very useful, as when he sought to represent the tremble of foliage in the morning or evening air. It taught him also, by degrees, the value of generalisation, that is, of not representing details so much as of discovering the salient qualities of objects, and of uniting them into a whole that suggested rather than definitively described.

The first inspiration of his work was Italy and the Italian landscape; next the landscape of France began to appeal to his imagination. In his little house in Ville d'Avray, near Paris, he spent his time filling his soul with visions of nature, which, when he returned to Paris, were transferred to canvas. Corot interpreted his moods concerning nature, rather than strictly depicting nature itself. He was not a great descriptive, epic poet, alive to the mighty forces that underlie the vastness of his subject, but a sweet, lyric singer of a few choice moments.

708. Camille Pissarro, 1830-1903, Impressionism, French, *The Marne at Chennevières*, 1864. Oil on canvas, 91.5 x 145.5 cm. National Gallery of Scotland, Edinburgh.

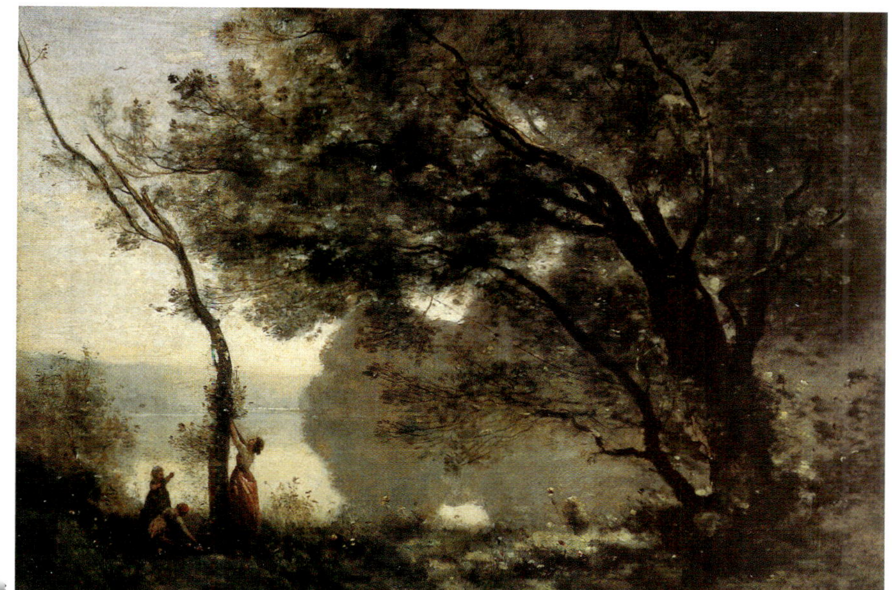

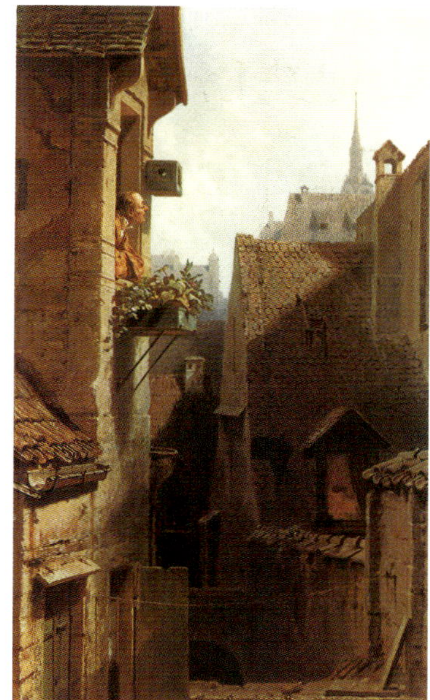

707

706. **Jean-Baptiste Camille Corot**, 1796-1875, Realism, School of
Barbizon, French, *Souvenir of Mortefontaine*, c. 1864.
Oil on canvas, 65 x 89 cm.
Musée du Louvre, Paris.

707. **Carl Spitzweg**, 1808-1885, Romanticism, German,
A Hypochondriac, c. 1865.
Oil on canvas, 53 x 31 cm.
Schack-Galerie, Munich.

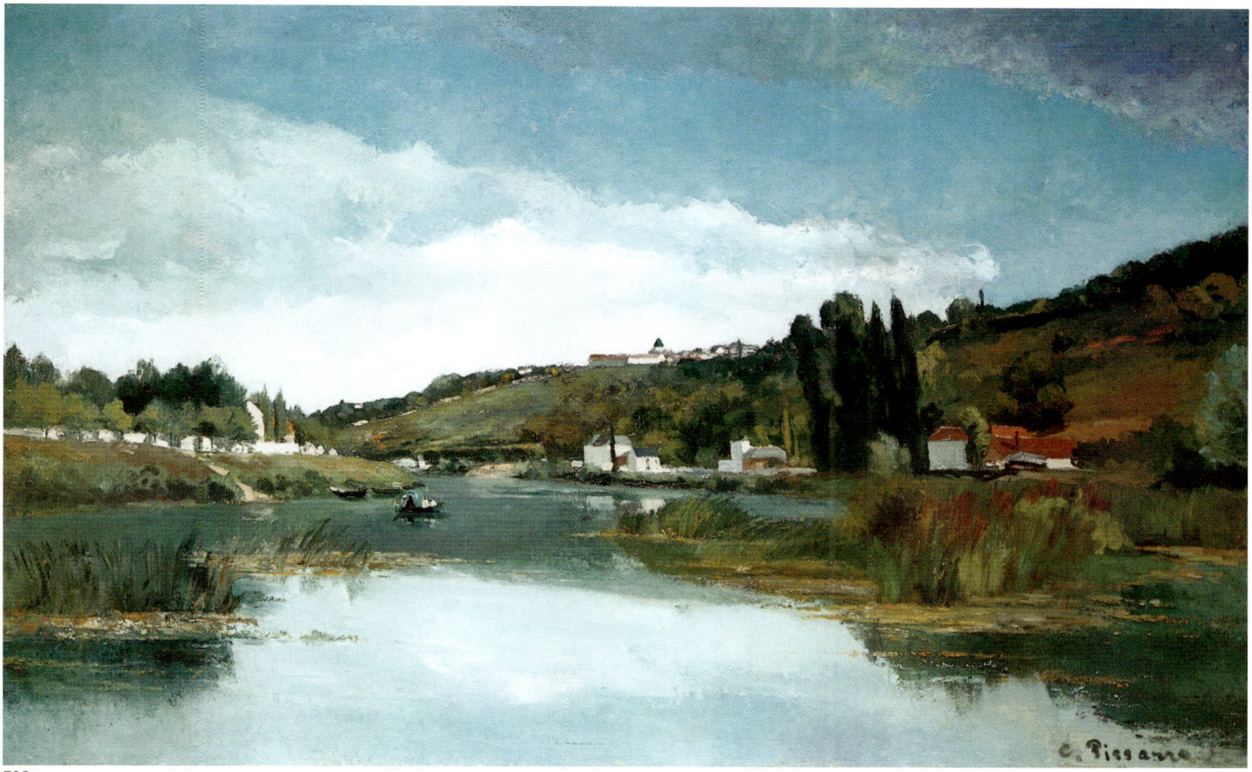

708

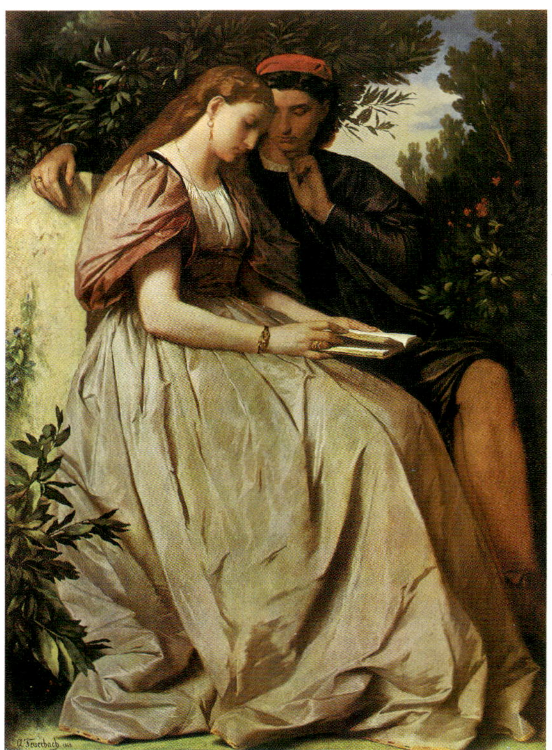

709. **Anselm Feuerbach,** 1829-1880, Neoclassicism, German,
Paolo and Francesca, 1864.
Oil on canvas, 136.5 x 99.5 cm. Shack-Galerie, Munich.

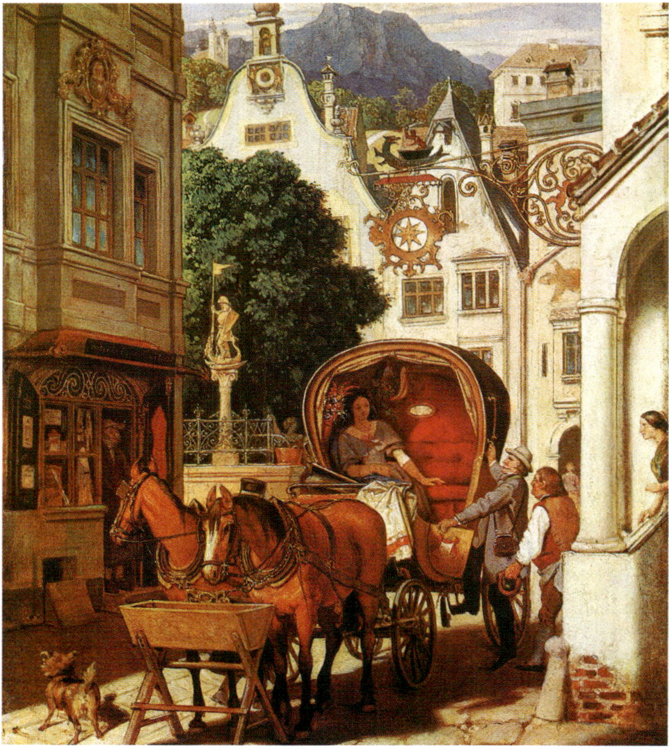

710. **Moritz von Schwind,** 1804-1871, Romanticism, Austrian,
Honeymoon, 1867.
Oil on wood, 52 x 41 cm. Schack-Galerie, Munich.

713. **Claude Monet,** 1840-1926, Impressionism, French,
Women in the Garden, 1867.
Oil on canvas, 255 x 205 cm. Musée d'Orsay, Paris.

711. **Peter Cornelius,** 1783-1867,
Realism, School of Barbizon, German,
The Recognition of Joseph by his Brothers, 1866.
Fresco, 236 x 290 cm. Alte Nationalgalerie, Berlin.

712. **Frédéric Bazille,** 1841-1870, Impressionism, French,
Family Reunion, 1867. Oil on canvas, 152 x 230 cm.
Musée d'Orsay, Paris.

712

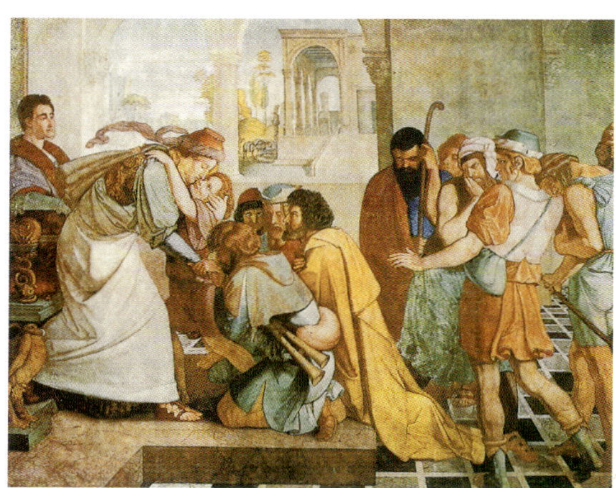

711

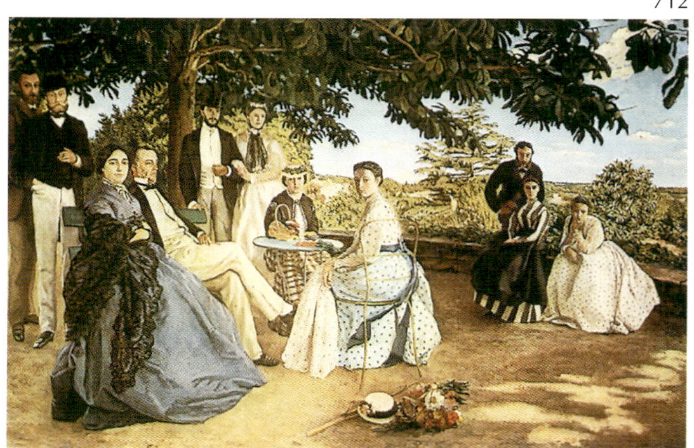

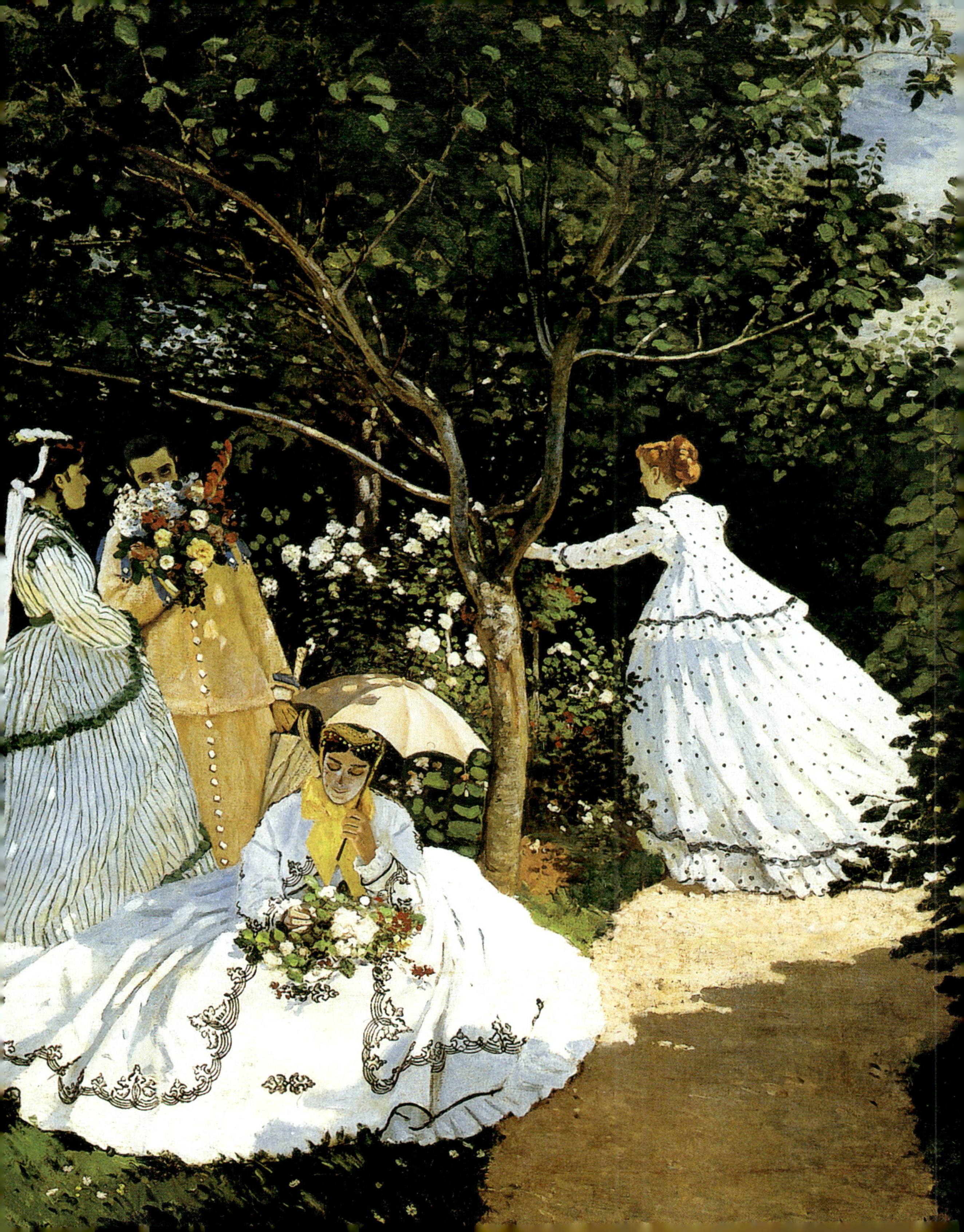

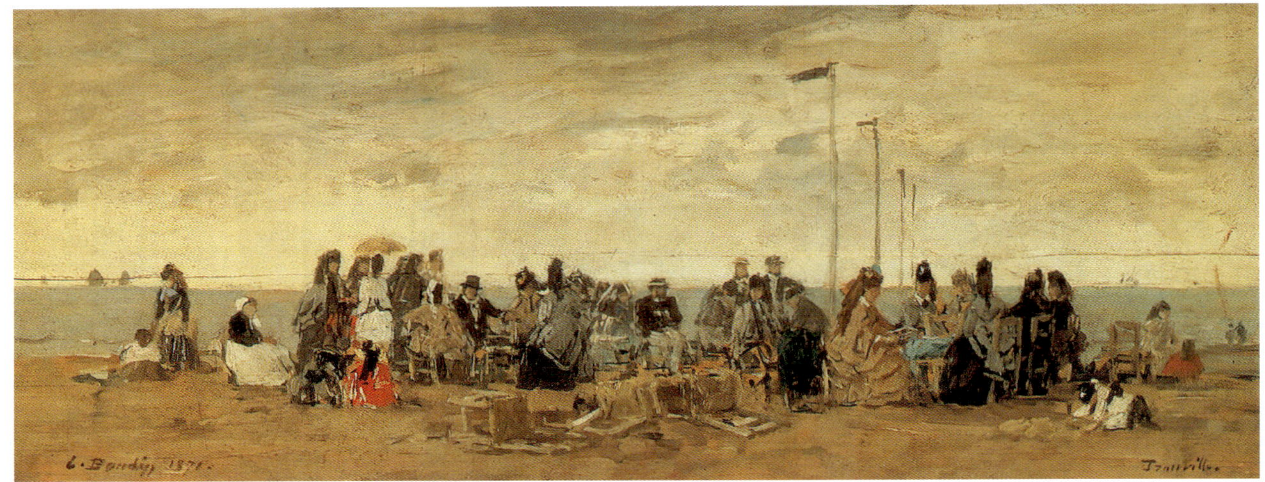

714. **Eugène Boudin,** 1824-1898, Impressionism, French,
The Beach at Trouville, 1871.
Oil on canvas, 19 x 46 cm.
The Pushkin Museum of Fine Arts, Moscow.

HONORÉ DAUMIER
(1808 MARSEILLE – 1879 VALMONDOIS)

Apprenticed to Alexandre Lenoir, Daumier shared
his master's admiration for the antiquities and for
Titian and Rubens. He developed very young a
great aptitude at drawing caricature scathing upon
the foibles of the bourgeoisie, the corruption of
law and the incompetence of the government. As
a painter he was one of the pioneers of Naturalism.
He depicted a wide range of themes such as street
scenes, and literary or mythological scenes, using
various techniques. His brushstrokes are either
thick or fluid and he left a fair number of paintings
unachieved. He did not meet with success until a
year before his death in 1878, when Durand-Ruel
collected his work for exhibition at his gallery.

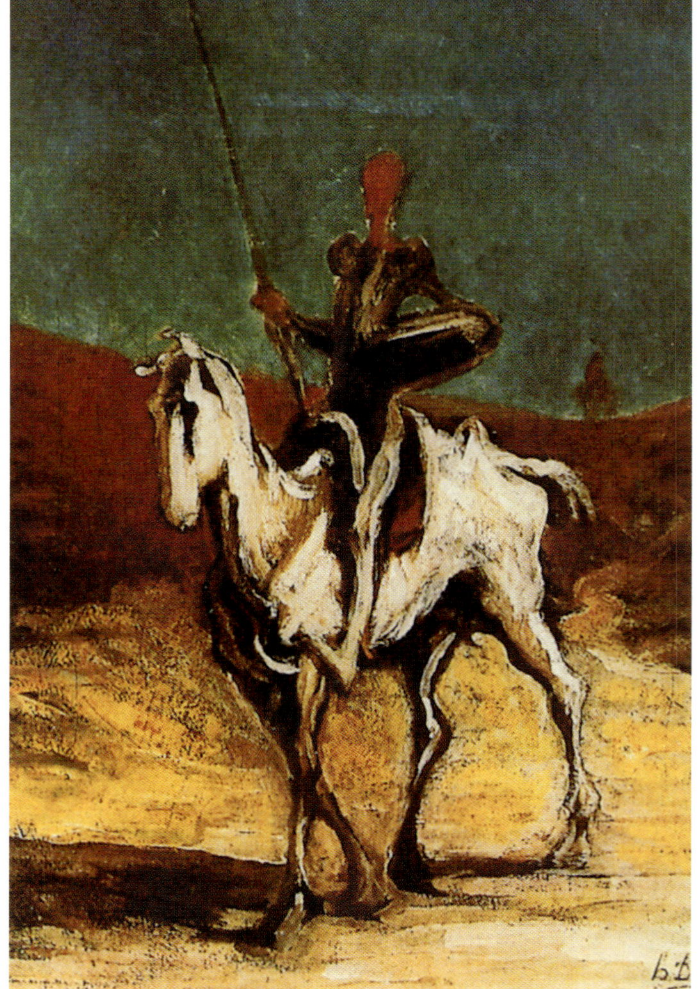

715. **Honoré Daumier,** 1808-1879, Realism, French,
Don Quixote, c. 1868.
Oil on canvas, 52 x 32 cm.
Neue Pinakothek, Munich.

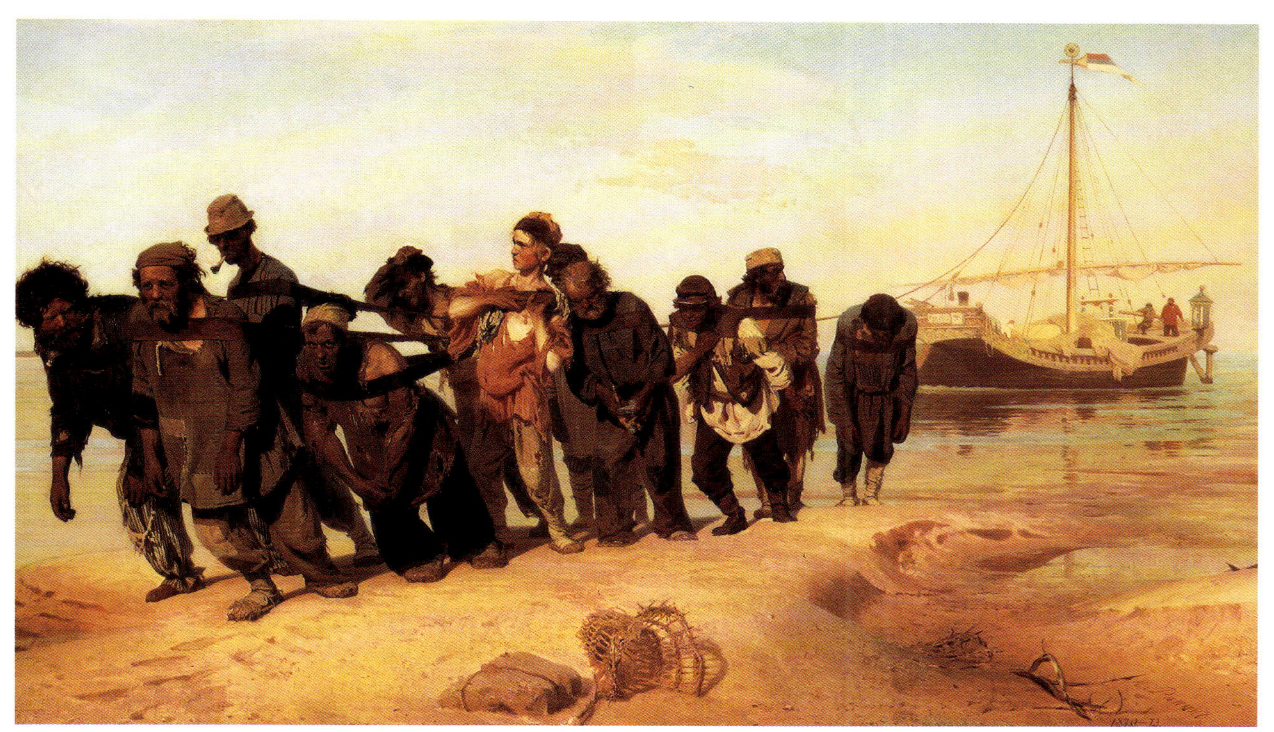

716

ILYA REPIN
(1844 CHUGUYEV – 1930 KUOKKALA)

Ilya Repin was the most gifted of the group known in Russia as "The Itinerants". When only twelve years old, he joined Ivan Bounakov's studio to learn the icon-painter's craft. Religious representations always remained of great importance for him. From 1864 to 1873 Repin studied at the Academy of the Arts in Saint Petersburg under Kramskoï.

Repin also studied in Paris for two years, where he was strongly influenced by outdoor painting, without becoming an Impressionist, a style that he judged too distant from reality. Taken with French pictorial culture, he worked to understand its role in the evolution of contemporary art. Most of Repin's powerful work deals with the social dilemmas of Russian life in the nineteenth century. He established his reputation in 1873 with the celebrated picture *Barge Haulers on the Volga*, symbol of the oppressed Russian people pulling their chains. This struggle against the autocracy inspired many works. He also painted Russia's official history in such works as *Ivan the Terrible Meditating at the Deathbed of his Son Ivan*. Seen as one of the masters of realist painting, he devoted himself to portraying the lives of his contemporaries: the most renowned Russian writers, artists, and intellectuals; peasants at work; the faithful in procession; and revolutionaries on the barricades. He understood the pains of the people perfectly, as well as the needs and the joys of ordinary lives. Kramskoï said on this subject: "Repin has a gift for showing the peasant as he is. I know many painters who show the *moujik*, and they do it well, but none can do so with as much talent as Repin."

Repin's works, which depart from the academic constraints of their predecessors, are both delicate and powerful. He achieved a superior mastery of skill, and found new accents to transcribe the many-coloured and brilliant vibrations he sensed in the ordinary world around him.

716. **Ilya Repin,** 1844-1930,
Realism, Russian,
Barge Haulers on the Volga, 1872-1873.
Oil on canvas, 131.5 x 281 cm.
The State Russian Museum,
St Petersburg.

Repin's reputation was founded on his Barge Haulers, the artist's thoughts on life in the Russian countryside after the reforms of the 1860s, and on the lot of peasants who had to leave the land to take on seasonal work. However, this early canvas, in spite of the fact that it was based on preparatory work in open air, still shows a certain contradiction between the artist's desire to remain true to life and his rationalistic approach to the composition of the picture which consequently acquired a somewhat spectacular quality. In the Chuguyev and Moscow years, the peasant theme at first, a simple expression of the artist's social orientation, became an integral part of his realism.

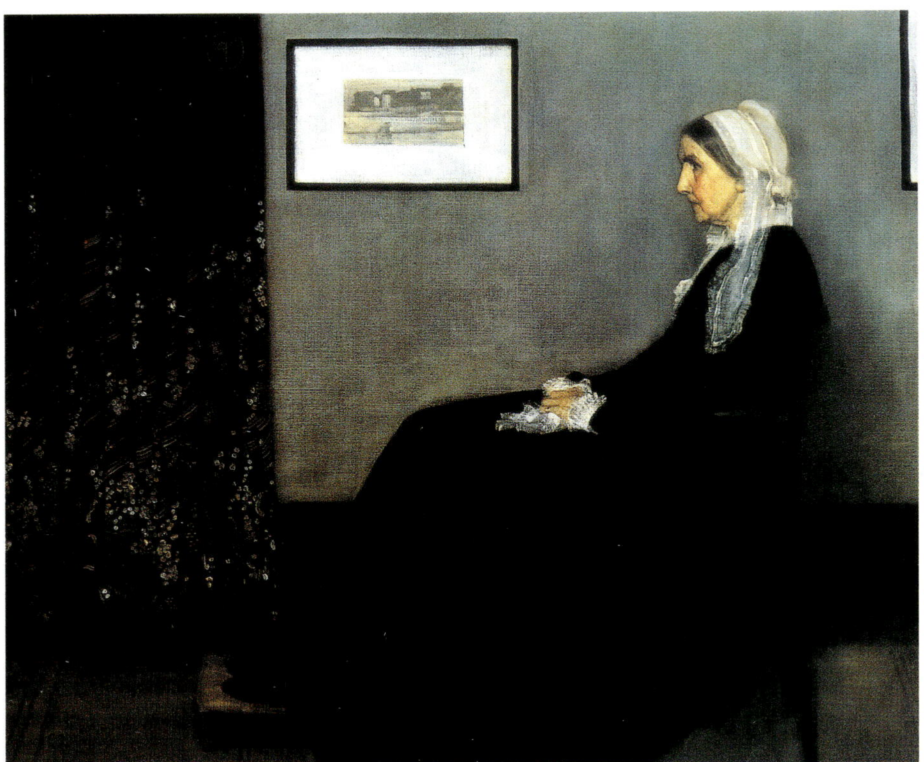

JAMES ABBOTT MCNEILL WHISTLER
(1834 LOWELL – 1903 LONDON)

Whistler suddenly shot to fame like a meteor at a crucial moment in the history of art, a field in which he was a pioneer. Like the impressionists, with whom he sided, he wanted to impose his own ideas. Whistler's work can be divided into four periods. The first may be called a period of research in which he was influenced by the Realism of Gustave Courbet and by Japanese art.

Whistler then discovered his own originality in the Nocturnes and the Cremorne Gardens series, thereby coming into conflict with the academics who wanted a work of art to tell a story. When he painted the portrait of his mother, Whistler entitled it *Arrangement in Grey and Black*, and this is symbolic of his aesthetic theories. When painting the Cremorne Pleasure Gardens it was not to depict identifiable figures but to capture an atmosphere. He loved the mists that hovered over the banks of the Thames, the pale light, and the factory chimneys which at night turned into magical minarets. Night redrew landscapes, effacing the details. This was the period in which he became an adventurer in art; his work, which verged on abstraction, shocked his contemporaries.

The third period is dominated by the full-length portraits that brought him his fame. He was able to imbue this traditional genre with his profound originality. By extracting the poetic substance from individuals he created portraits described as "mediums" by his contemporaries, and which were the inspiration for Oscar Wilde's *The Picture of Dorian Gray*.

Towards the end of his life, the artist began painting landscapes and portraits in the classical tradition, strongly influenced by Velázquez. Whistler proved to be extremely rigorous in ensuring his paintings coincided with his theories. He never hesitated in crossing swords with the most famous art theoreticians of his day. His personality, his outbursts, and his elegance were a perfect focus for curiosity and admiration. He was a close friend of Stéphane Mallarmé, and admired by Marcel Proust, who rendered homage to him in *A La Recherche du Temps Perdu*. He was also a provocative dandy, a prickly socialite, a demanding artist, and a daring innovator.

717. James Abbot McNeill Whistler, 1834-1903, Post-impressionism, American, *Arrangement in Grey and Black Nr.1* or *Portrait of the Artist's Mother*, 1871.
Oil on canvas, 144.3 x 162.5 cm.
Musée d'Orsay, Paris.

Whistler's most famous work is widely, but incorrectly called Whistler's Mother. The artist insisted that the focus in the painting should be the work's arrangement of shapes and the colours. The severity of the masses is assuaged by the two gathering points of intimate expression: the hands and the face. The prevailing gravity, deliberately chosen, and the accent of tenderness contribute largely to the emotion aroused in the spectator's imagination. The expression of the face is the centre and climax of a corresponding expression that pervades the whole canvas, the result of the balance of the full and empty spaces and the colour scheme of black and grey. Whistler reduced his content to its more essential expressive forms, placing his subjects in full length before neutral backgrounds, not unlike works by John Singer Sargent.

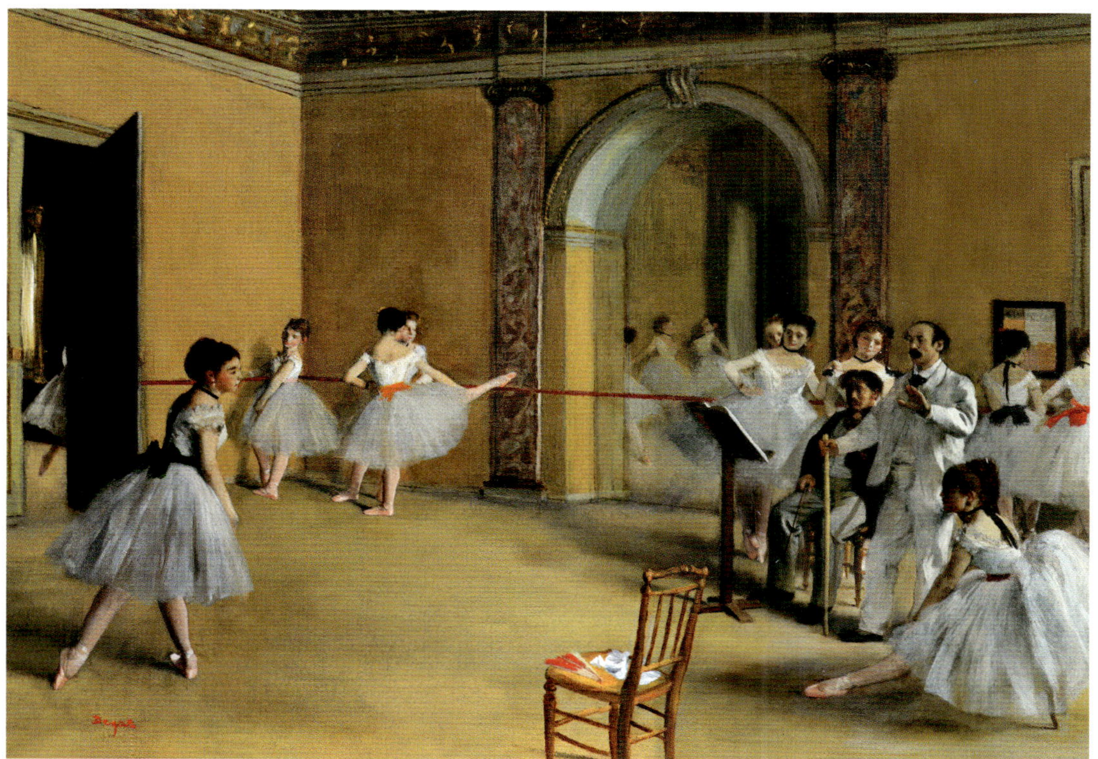

718. **Hilaire Germain Edgar Degas,**
1834-1917, Impressionism, French,
Dance Foyer at the Opera, 1872.
Oil on canvas, 32 x 46 cm.
Musée d'Orsay, Paris.

HILAIRE GERMAIN EDGAR DEGAS
(1834 – 1917 PARIS)

Degas was closest to Renoir in the impressionist's circle, for both favoured the animated Parisian life of their day as a motif in their paintings. Degas did not attend Gleyre's studio; most likely he first met the future impressionists at the Café Guerbois.

He started his apprenticeship in 1853 at the studio of Louis-Ernest Barrias and, beginning in 1854, studied under Louis Lamothe, who revered Ingres above all others, and transmitted his adoration for this master to Edgar Degas. Starting in 1854 Degas travelled frequently to Italy: first to Naples, where he made the acquaintance of his numerous cousins, and then to Rome and Florence, where he copied tirelessly from the Old Masters.

During the 1860s and 1870s he became a painter of racecourses, horses and jockeys. His fabulous painter's memory retained the particularities of movement of horses wherever he saw them. After his first rather complex compositions depicting racecourses, Degas learned the art of translating the nobility and elegance of horses, their nervous movements, and the formal beauty of their musculature.

Around the middle of the 1860s Degas made yet another discovery. In 1866 he painted his first composition with ballet as a subject, *Mademoiselle Fiocre dans le ballet de la Source* (*Mademoiselle Fiocre* in the Ballet 'The Spring') (New York, Brooklyn Museum). Degas had always been a devotee of the theatre, but from now on it would become more and more the focus of his art. Degas' first painting devoted solely to the ballet was *Le Foyer de la danse à l'Opéra de la rue Le Peletier* (The Dancing Anteroom at the Opera on Rue Le Peletier) (Paris, Musée d'Orsay). In a carefully constructed composition, with groups of figures balancing one another to the left and the right, each ballet dancer is involved in her own activity, each one moving in a separate manner from the others. Extended observation and an immense number of sketches were essential to executing such a task. This is why Degas moved from the theatre on to the rehearsal halls, where the dancers practised and took their lessons. The ballet would remain his passion until the end of his days.

CLAUDE MONET
(1840 PARIS – 1926 GIVERNY)

For Claude Monet the designation 'impressionist' always remained a source of pride. In spite of all the things critics have written about his work, Monet continued to be a true impressionist to the end of his very long life. He was so by deep conviction, and for his Impressionism he may have sacrificed many other opportunities that his enormous talent held out to him. Monet did not paint classical compositions with figures, and he did not become a portraitist, although his professional training included those skills. He chose a single genre for himself, landscape painting, and in that he achieved a degree of perfection none of his contemporaries managed to attain.

Yet the little boy began by drawing caricatures. Boudin advised Monet to stop doing caricatures and to take up landscapes instead. The sea, the sky, animals, people, and trees are beautiful in the exact state in which nature created them – surrounded by air and light. Indeed, it was Boudin who passed on to Monet his conviction of the importance of working in the open air, which Monet would in turn transmit to his impressionist friends. Monet did not want to enrol at the Ecole des Beaux-Arts. He chose to attend a private school, L'Académie Suisse, established by an ex-model on the Quai d'Orfèvres near the Pont Saint-Michel. One could draw and paint from a live model there for a modest fee. This was where Monet met the future impressionist Camille Pissarro.

Later in Gleyre's studio, Monet met Auguste Renoir, Alfred Sisley, and Frédéric Bazille. Monet considered it very important that Boudin be introduced to his new friends. He also told his friends of another painter he had found in Normandy. This was the remarkable Dutchman Jongkind. His landscapes were saturated with colour, and their sincerity, at times even their naïveté, was combined with subtle observation of the Normandy shore's variable nature. At this time Monet's landscapes were not yet characterised by great richness of colour. Rather, they recalled the tonalities of paintings by the Barbizon artists, and Boudin's seascapes. He composed a range of colour based on yellow-brown or blue-grey.

At the Third Impressionist Exhibition in 1877 Monet presented a series of paintings for the first time: seven views of the Saint-Lazare train station. He selected them from among twelve he had painted at the station. This motif in Monet's work is in line not only with Manet's *Chemin de fer* (*The Railway*) and with his own landscapes featuring trains and stations at Argenteuil, but also with a trend that surfaced after the railways first began to appear.

In 1883, Monet had bought a house in the village of Giverny, near the little town of Vernon. At Giverny, series painting became one of his chief working procedures. Meadows became his permanent workplace. When a journalist, who had come from Vétheuil to interview Monet, asked him where his studio was, the painter answered, "My studio! I've never had a studio, and I can't see why one would lock oneself up in a room. To draw, yes – to paint, no". Then, broadly gesturing towards the Seine, the hills, and the silhouette of the little town, he declared, "There's my real studio."

Monet began to go to London in the last decade of the nineteenth century. He began all his London paintings working directly from nature, but completed many of them afterwards, at Giverny. The series formed an indivisible whole, and the painter had to work on all his canvases at one time.

A friend of Monet's, the writer Octave Mirbeau, wrote that he had accomplished a miracle. With the help of colours he had succeeded in recreating on the canvas something almost impossible to capture: he was reproducing sunlight, enriching it with an infinite number of reflections.

Alone among the impressionists, Claude Monet took an almost scientific study of the possibilities of colour to its limits; it is unlikely that one could have gone any further in that direction.

719. **Claude Monet,** 1840-1926,
Impressionism, French,
Impression: Sunrise, 1873.
Oil on canvas, 48 x 63 cm.
Musée Marmottan, Paris.

While surely not one of Monet's masterpieces, this work is one of the most important because of its influence on the evolution of art. Ironically, the critic, Louis Leroy, of the exhibition in which this work was first shown, referred to the group of artists in the show as "impressionists". However, in context, the critic was referring to what he thought was the sloppy and "unfinished" work of the group; he wanted the term to be derogatory. As the title indicates, this is not a realistic depiction of nature but "the impression" the artist had of it. Monet gets away from the academic rules, rejects the preliminary drawing and uses a loose brushstroke that suggests rather than delineates, and that represents the variations of light upon each element of the scene. The sun is the only warm touch in the painting, its light reflecting itself in the blue-grey sky and water, and it brings the composition to life.

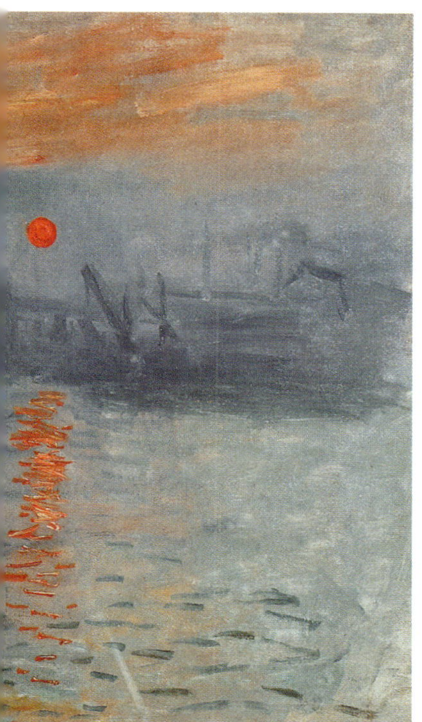

ALFRED SISLEY
(1839 PARIS – 1899 MORET–SUR–LOING)

Alfred Sisley was born in Paris on 30 October 1839 to English parents. He spent five years in England from 1857 to 1861, and in the country of Shakespeare he felt himself to be English for the first time. He studied English literature, but was even more interested in England's great master painters. It was most likely in this way – through exposure to the free brushwork of Turner, and Constable's landscapes, which resembled preparatory studies – that Sisley sensed he had a vocation for the genre.

In October 1862 fate brought him to Charles Gleyre's free studio, where Claude Monet, Auguste Renoir, and Frédéric Bazille had come to study. It was Sisley who had encouraged his friends to give up their apprenticeship at Gleyre's studio and go out to paint from nature. He was outraged, far more so than his friends, at Gleyre's arrogant attitude towards landscapes.

From the beginning, landscape for Sisley was not just an essential pictorial genre; it was the one and only genre in which he was to work his entire life. After leaving Gleyre, Sisley often painted together with Monet, Renoir, and Bazille in the environs of Paris.

From 1870 the first characteristics of the style that later became Impressionism began to appear in Sisley's painting. From this point forward the colour scheme in Sisley's paintings becomes distinctly lighter. This new technique creates an impression of vibrating water, of brightly coloured shimmering on its surface, and of a crisp clarity in the atmosphere. Light, in Sisley's paintings, was born.

Over the course of the four years he lived in Louveciennes, Sisley painted numerous landscapes of the banks of the Seine. He discovered Argenteuil and the little town of Villeneuve-la-Garenne, which in his work would remain the very image of silence and tranquillity; a world that civilisation and industry had not yet disfigured. He was not, in contrast to Pissarro, searching for prosaic accuracy. His landscapes were always coloured by his emotional attitude towards them. As with Monet, Sisley's bridges are set in the countryside in a completely natural way. A serene blue sky is reflected in the barely stirring surface of the river. In harmony with this, some small, light-coloured houses and the coolness of the greenery create the impression of sunlight.

After the First Impressionism Exhibition Sisley spent several months in England. On his return, Sisley moved from Louveciennes to Marly-le Roi. Around this period Sisley truly became a painter of water. It cast a spell over him, forcing him to scrutinise its changing surface and to study its nuances of colour, as Monet did with meadows at Giverny.

720. **Winslow Homer,** 1836-1910, Realism, American, *Breezing Up (A Fair Wind),* 1873-1876. Oil on canvas, 61 x 97 cm. The National Gallery of Art, Washington D.C.

721. **Alfred Sisley,** 1839-1899, Impressionism, French, *Flood at Port-Marly,* 1876. Oil on canvas, 60 x 81 cm. Musée d'Orsay, Paris.

Sisley's landscapes devoted to the Port-Marly flood are a crowning achievement. The painter played with space and perspective, in the end finding the only possible solution: the pink house is frozen in a world where the sky merges with the earth, where the reflection barely ripples, and the clouds glide slowly by. Sisley was the only impressionist whose landscapes do not limit themselves to nature's changing beauty but extend to other realms, sometimes of dreams, sometimes of philosophical reflection.

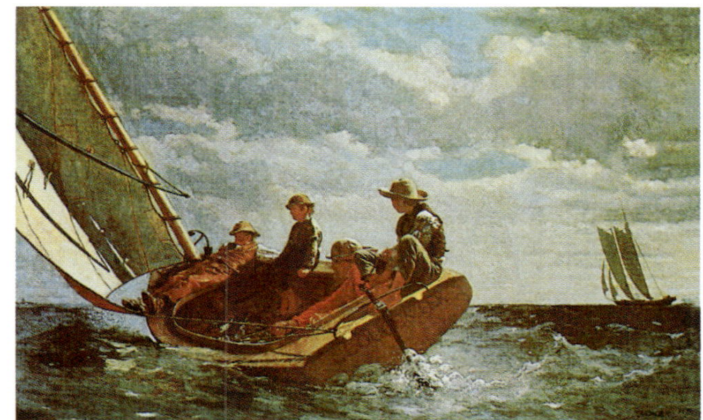

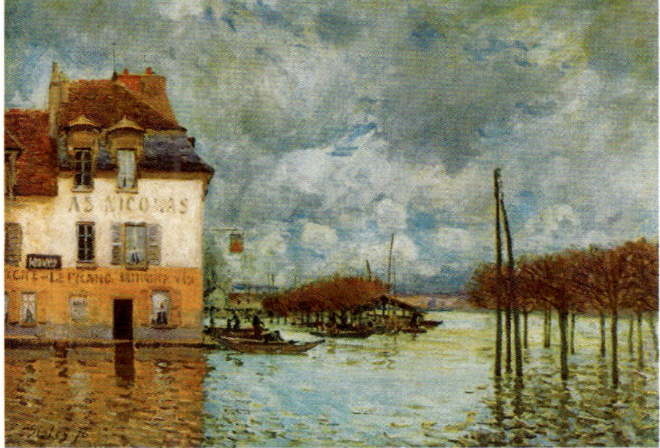

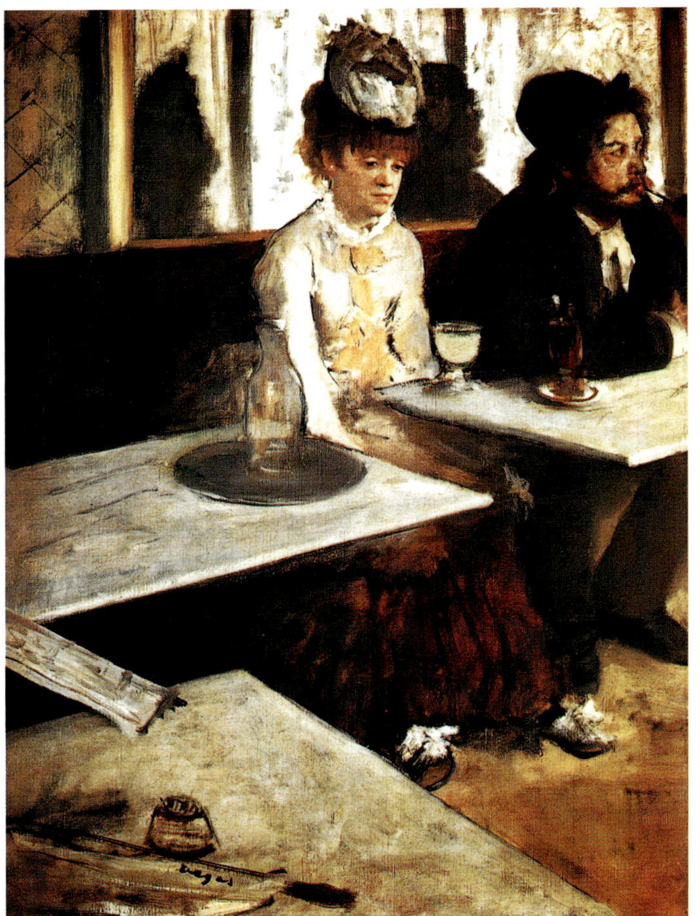

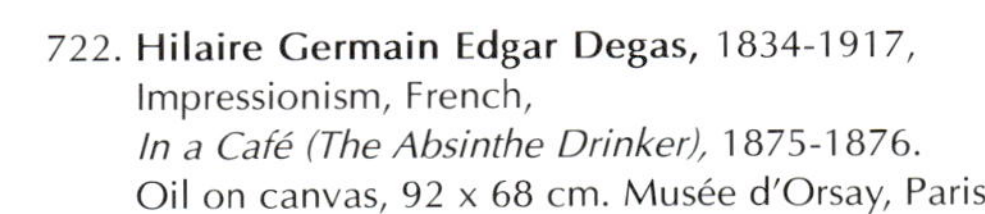

722. Hilaire Germain Edgar Degas, 1834-1917,
Impressionism, French,
In a Café (The Absinthe Drinker), 1875-1876.
Oil on canvas, 92 x 68 cm. Musée d'Orsay, Paris.

In 1876 Degas painted Dans *or* L'Absinthe un Café *(In the Café/Absinthe). At that time most artists had already abandoned the Café Guerbois and reunited at La Nouvelle Athènes in the Place Pigalle. Degas had lived in this neighborhood for a large portion of his life: in Rue Blanche, Rue Fontaine, and Rue Saint-Georges. He could now be seen regularly in the evenings, on the terrace of La Nouvelle Athènes, with Edouard Manet, Emile Zolá, and various impressionists and critics. For his new painting he asked his friend the engraver Marcellin Desboutin, just back from Florence, and the pretty actress Ellen Andrée to pose for him. Ellen Andrée would later pose at the same location, on the terrace of La Nouvelle Athènes, for Edouard Manet's* La Prune (The Plum), *and also for Renoir's* Le Déjeuner sur les Canotiers (The Rower's Lunch) *on the island of Croissy.*

Degas depicted her as a prostitute of the Parisian streets with a lost look, sitting absolutely still before a glass of absinthe, absorbed in thought. At her side, a pipe clenched between his teeth and hat pushed back onto his neck, one of the café regulars is seated. He seems to be looking into the distance, not aware of the woman seated just beside him. Squeezed into a corner behind little empty tables, they are almost touching one other, but each is in their own world. Again, Degas succeeded in setting down on the canvas something almost impossible to capture: the bitter solitude of a human being in the merriest, liveliest city in the world. Here, as well, there is nearly an absence of colour. Only some delicate pinkish and bluish accents work to enhance the range of greys. This attracted attention, and astonished many in the bright, colour-filled world of the impressionists. Degas was indeed a "strange artist". In many respects his positions were identical with those of the impressionists but, at the same time, so many things set him apart from his painting allies.

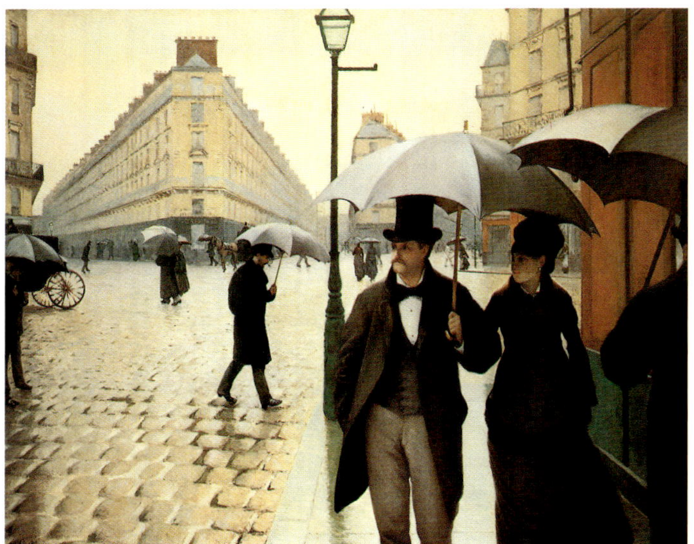

723. Gustave Caillebotte, 1848-1894, Impressionism,
French, *Paris Street, Rainy Day,* 1877.
Oil on canvas, 212.2 x 276.2 cm.
The Art Institute of Chicago, Chicago.

The five hundred or more paintings of Caillebotte were not given much attention during his lifetime. For years, he was considered primarily a generous patron of impressionists, but not as a painter in his own right. Later, his style was seen to be more realistic than those of his friends Degas, Monet and Renoir. In 1874, he helped to organise the First Impressionist Exhibition. However, he did not include his own work – he would show in later impressionist exhibitions. In this typical work he captures the feeling of a new Parisian boulevard in an area of the Batignolles quarter on a rainy day. The realism with which Caillebotte depicts the scene is later praised by the writer Emile Zola: "Paris Street, Rainy Day displays strollers and, in particular, a man and a woman in the foreground, of a beautiful realism. When his talent will have softened a little, Caillebotte will certainly be the most audacious of the group."

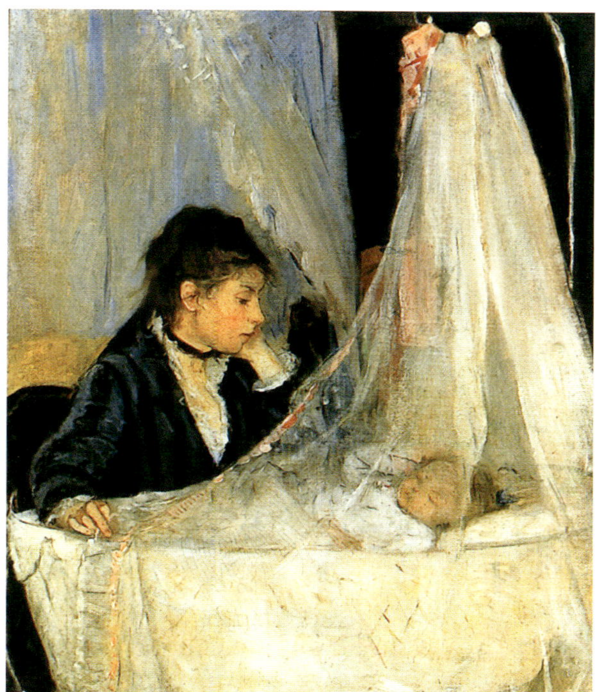

724

724. **Berthe Morisot,** 1841-1895, Impressionism, French,
The Cradle, 1872.
Oil on canvas, 56 x 46 cm. Musée d'Orsay, Paris.

725. **Thomas Eakins,** 1844-1916, Realism, American,
The Gross Clinic, 1875.
Oil on canvas, 244 x 198 cm. Jefferson University, Philadelphia.

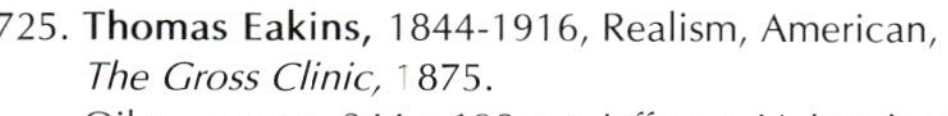

As a pioneer in multiple-exposure photography with a single camera, Eakins knew how to capture and freeze a dramatic moment. His collaboration with pioneering photographer Edward Muybridge (1830-1904) in studying human action impressed academics in France, influenced Degas, and prepared the way for motion pictures. He was also a mathematician and taught human anatomy. However, Eakins became a leader with Winslow Homer of the emerging American School of realism. His paintings reflected his scientific knowledge of both photography and surgery. He witnessed, and later captured on canvas, operations performed by the renowned doctors Gross and Agnew. A later painting is titled The Agnew Clinic. *(1889). In business suits and with total objectivity, the surgeons focus on the patient as Dr Gross gives the lecture. On the left, a woman presumed to be an assisting nurse seems to need to rest. The viewer is made to feel closer and more intimate to the operation than even the note-taking observers in the gallery. Presenting surgery realistically was upsetting for Eakins' contemporaries who considered his works to be "anatomy lessons" rather than fine art to be viewed. Some art historians contrast this work with the unnatural formality of Rembrandt's* The Anatomy Lesson of Dr Tulp *(fig. 441).*

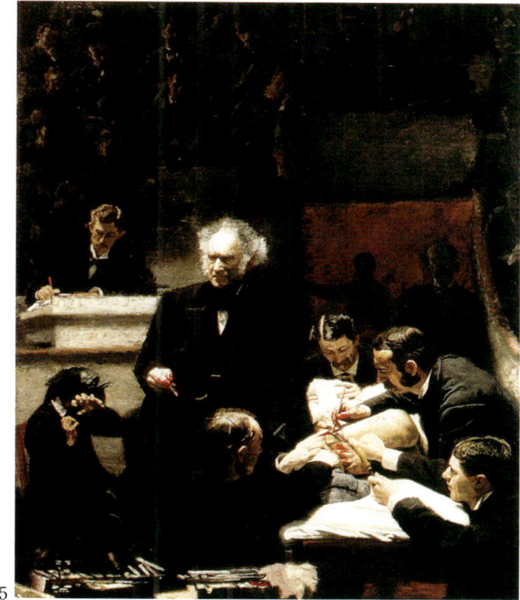

725

BERTHE MORISOT
(1841 BOURGES – 1895 PARIS)

Amongst the women painters in modern history, Berthe Morisot achieved a distinction equalled only by that of Mary Cassatt. Her gifts did not at once receive public recognition, but in recent years they have won more and more appreciation. She was an interesting person. Degas once said of her that she painted pictures as she made bonnets – a suggestion of the femininely instinctive and impulsive action of her talent. One source of her strength, however, was the thoroughness of her training. Her father, an official at Bourges, saw that his daughter's tastes were genuine, and made it easy for her to develop her faculties. She and her sister Edma were sent for instruction to Paris. Edma Morisot abandoned painting when she married, but Berthe continued to work with the brush, exhibiting at the Salon. It was while she was making copies from old masters in the Louvre that she first came to know Edouard Manet. Later, Berthe became intimate with the great impressionist, modifying her style in the light of his example and developing the broad, vivid qualities for which her works are loved today. In 1874 she married Eugene Manet. Degas, Renoir, Pissarro, and Monet frequented her house. She continued to paint, signing her pictures with the name by which she is still remembered in artistic annals. Her rank as an artist was obscured by her position as a woman of the world.

She was not, it is true, a creative artist. It may even be said that she would not have made the progress that is shown in her best works, would not have given them their special character, if Manet had not been there to help her to form her style. Yet upon the groundwork that she owed to her contact with Manet she superimposed qualities of her own. There is a delicate fragrance about her art, a certain feminine subtlety and charm, through which she proved herself an individualised painter.

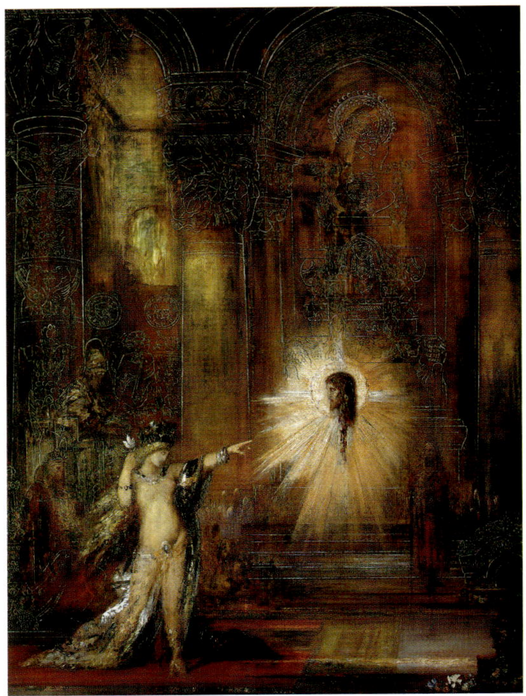

726. **Gustave Moreau,** 1826-1898, Symbolism, French,
Apparition (Salome), 1876-1898.
Oil on canvas, 142 x 103 cm. Musée Gustave Moreau, Paris.

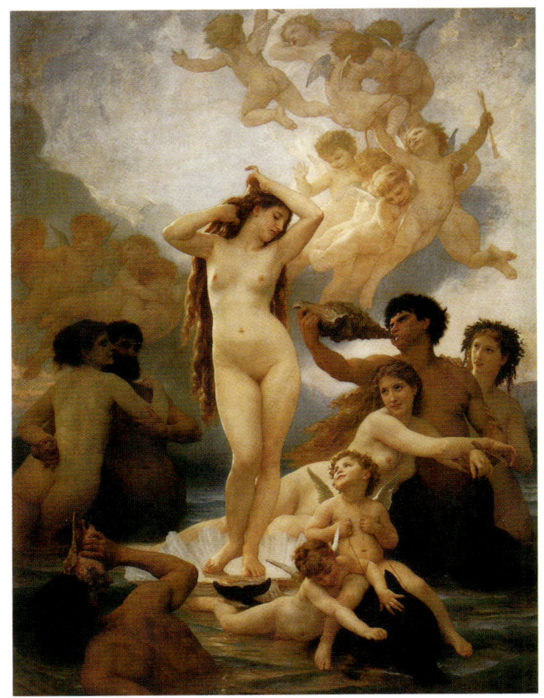

727. **William Bouguereau,** 1825-1905, Academism, French,
The Birth of Venus, 1879.
Oil on canvas, 303 x 216 cm. Musée d'Orsay, Paris.

ARNOLD BÖCKLIN
(1827 BASLE – 1901 SAN DOMENICO)

The son of a Swiss merchant, Böcklin was born in Basle, "one of the most prosaic towns in Europe". At nineteen he entered the art school at Düsseldorf, but was advised by his master to proceed to Brussels and Paris and, later, to Rome where he copied the Old Masters. In this way he learned the art of painting, which, in Germany, had been neglected for some time. There the subject of the painting was held to be of more importance than the method of representing it. Though he returned for a time to Germany and after 1886, lived in Zurich until his death, the country which affected Böcklin's life most deeply, where he lived during the period in which his particular genius unfolded, was Italy. It was from the Roman Campagna, sad and grand, where the Anio plunges down in cataracts, that he drew the inspiration for his landscapes.

He was, in fact, a Greek in his healthy love of nature and his instinct for giving visible expression to her voices; a modern in his feeling for the moods of nature; and in his union of the two, unique. Moreover, he was a great colourist. "At the very time," writes Muther, "when Richard Wagner lured the colours of sound from music, with a glow of light such as no master had kindled before, Böcklin's symphonies of colour streamed forth like a crashing orchestra. Many of his pictures have such an ensnaring brilliancy that the eye is never weary of feasting upon their floating splendour. Indeed, later generations have honoured him as one of the greatest colour-poets of the century."

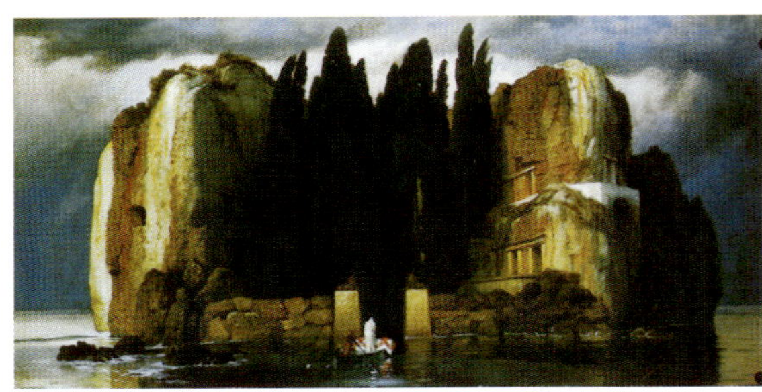

728. **Arnold Böcklin,** 1827-1901, Symbolism, Swiss,
Island of the Dead, 1880.
Oil on wood, 73.7 x 121.9 cm.
The Metropolitan Museum of Art, New York.

Together with Hodler, Böcklin is the most important Swiss painter of the nineteenth century. This painting is the first of five versions on the same theme. His increasing success led him to paint several versions of a subject to respond to subsequent commissions. The composition projects an effect of solemn grandeur and tranquil isolation, reinforced by the contrast between the monumental permanence of the island and the frailty and insignificance of the boat. The isolated boat approaches the in hospitable island, symbolising the immensity of nature's elements.

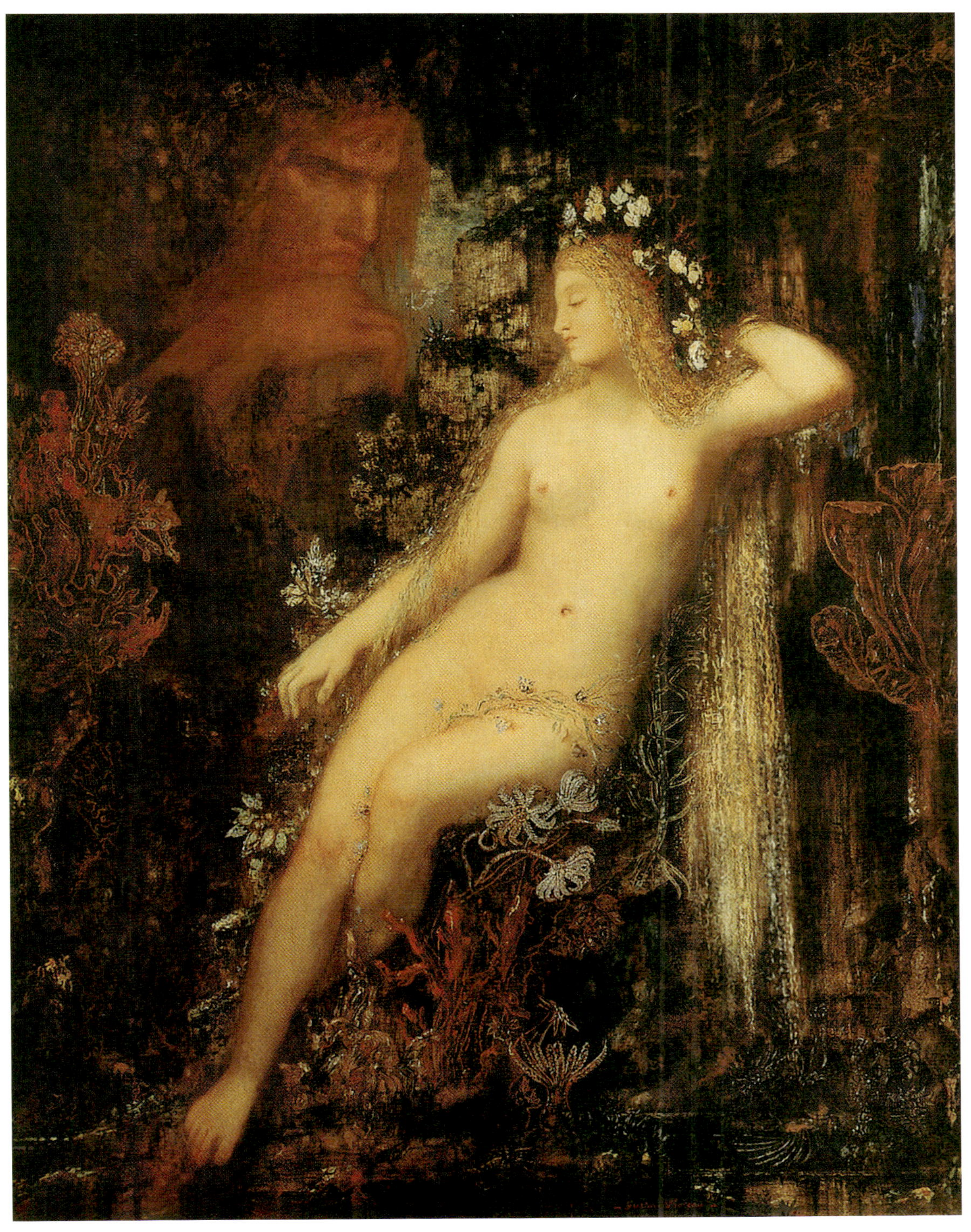

729. **Gustave Moreau,** 1826-1898, Symbolism, French, *Galatea,* 1880.
Oil on panel, 85 x 67 cm. Musée d'Orsay, Paris.

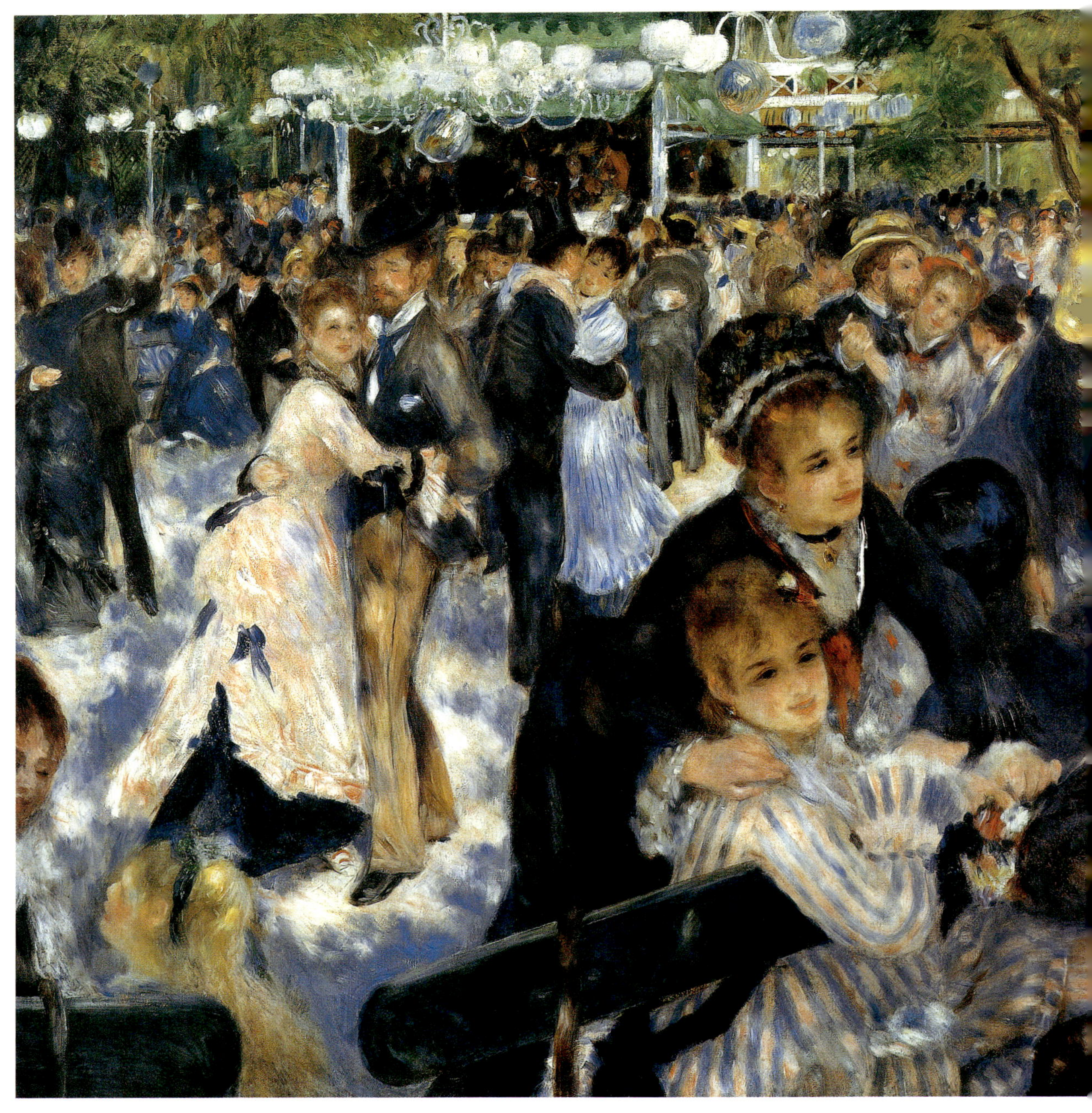

730. **Pierre-Auguste Renoir,** 1841-1919, Impressionism, French, *The Moulin de la Galette,* 1876. Oil on canvas, 131 x 175 cm. Musée d'Orsay, Paris.

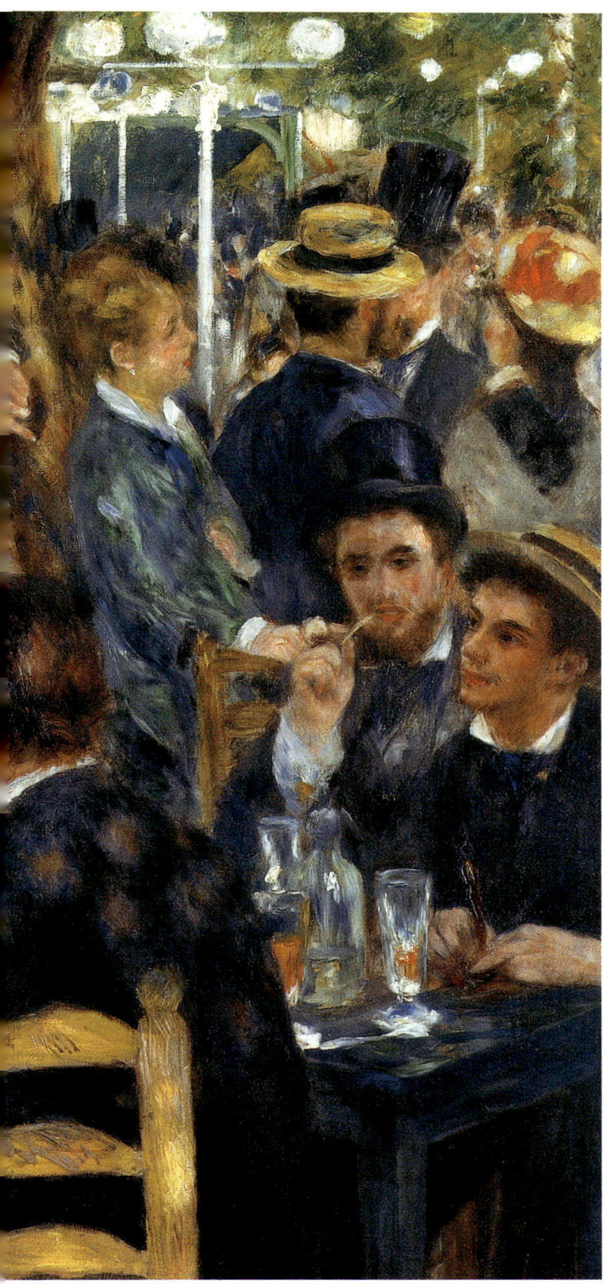

PIERRE–AUGUSTE RENOIR
(1841 LIMOGES – 1919 CAGNES–SUR–MER)

Pierre-Auguste Renoir was born in Limoges on 25 February 1841. In 1854, the boy's parents took him from school and found a place for him in the Lévy brothers' workshop, where he was to learn to paint porcelain. Renoir's younger brother Edmond had this to say this about the move: "From what he drew in charcoal on the walls, they concluded that he had the ability for an artist's profession. That was how our parents came to put him to learn the trade of porcelain painter." One of the Lévys' workers, Emile Laporte, painted in oils in his spare time. He suggested Renoir makes use of his canvases and paints. This offer resulted in the appearance of the first painting by the future impressionist. In 1862 Renoir passed the examinations and entered the Ecole des Beaux-Arts and, simultaneously, one of the independent studios, where instruction was given by Charles Gleyre, a professor at the Ecole des Beaux-Arts. The second, perhaps even the first, great event of this period in Renoir's life was his meeting, in Gleyre's studio, with those who were to become his best friends for the rest of his days and who shared his ideas about art. Much later, when he was already a mature artist, Renoir had the opportunity to see works by Rembrandt in Holland, Velázquez, Goya and El Greco in Spain, and Raphael in Italy. However, Renoir lived and breathed ideas of a new kind of art. He always found his inspirations in the Louvre. "For me, in the Gleyre era, the Louvre was Delacroix," he confessed to Jean.

For Renoir, the First Impressionist Exhibition was the moment his vision of art and the artist was affirmed. This period in Renoir's life was marked by one further significant event. In 1873 he moved to Montmartre, to the house at 35 Rue Saint-Georges, where he lived until 1884. Renoir remained loyal to Montmartre for the rest of his life. Here he found his "plein-air" subjects, his models and even his family. It was in the 1870s that Renoir acquired the friends who would stay with him for the remainder of his days. One of them was the art-dealer Paul Durand-Ruel, who began to buy his paintings in 1872. In summer, Renoir continued to paint a great deal outdoors together with Monet. He would travel out to Argenteuil, where Monet rented a house for his family. Edouard Manet sometimes worked with them too.

In 1877, at the Third Impressionist Exhibition, Renoir presented a panorama of over twenty paintings. They included landscapes created in Paris, on the Seine, outside the city and in Claude Monet's garden; studies of women's heads and bouquets of flowers; portraits of Sisley, the actress Jeanne Samary, the writer Alphonse Daudet and the politician Spuller; and also *The Swing* and *The Ball at the Moulin de la Galette*.

Finally, in the 1880s Renoir hit a "winning streak". He was commissioned by rich financiers, the owner of the Grands Magasins du Louvre and Senator Goujon. His paintings were exhibited in London and Brussels, as well as at the Seventh International Exhibition held at Georges Petit's in Paris in 1886. In a letter to Durand-Ruel, then in New York, Renoir wrote: "The Petit exhibition has opened and is not doing badly, so they say. After all, it's so hard to judge about yourself. I think I have managed to take a step forward towards public respect. A small step, but even that is something."

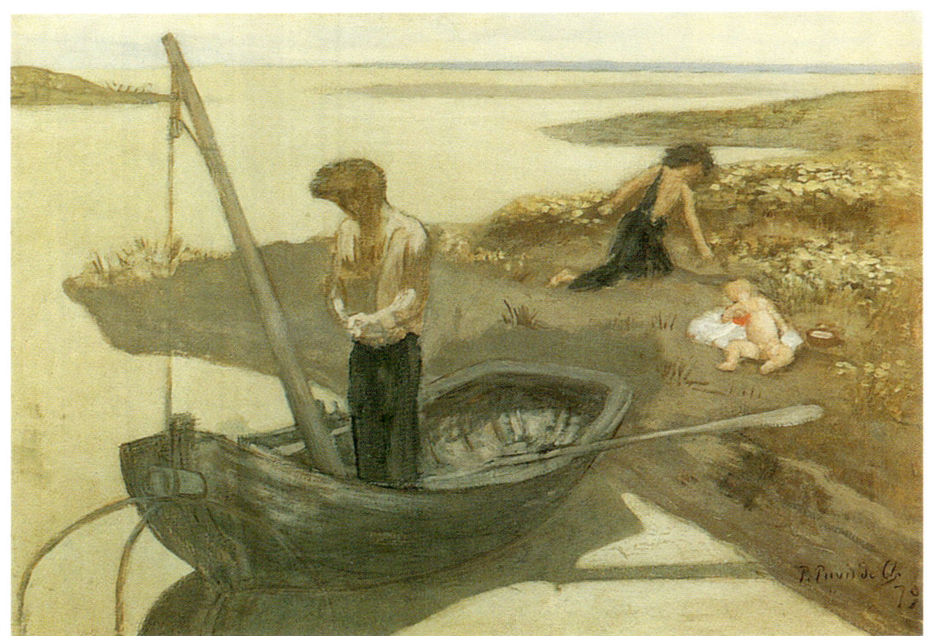

731

PIERRE–CÉCILE PUVIS DE CHAVANNES
(1824 LYON – 1898 PARIS)

Puvis de Chavannes came from an aristocratic family. His father was an engineer of bridges and roads in Lyon and, after receiving a classical and mathematical education, Puvis de Chavannes proceeded to the Polytechnic in Paris to adopt his father's profession. It was not until he was thirty-five that some vacant panels in his brother's new house drew his attention to mural decoration. He made an enlarged copy of one of his drawings and sent it to the Salon. Its acceptance encouraged him to go on in the same vein and that was the beginning of his public career as a mural painter.

Puvis' skill for colour is manifested particularly in the landscape parts. He selected for the sky a tone of blue that has more light in it than the greens of the earth, and varied the tones of the latter by almost imperceptible gradations of light and less light tones. In this management of values and knowledge of forms and construction, he is the equal of the best landscape painters. While his landscapes give an impression of space and seem filled with air that surrounds the figures, they also give the impression of being flat to the wall until by a process of severely logical experiments he was able to depict not form, but its essence and abstract suggestion. The result is that his decorations do not impress upon us the idea of paint; they seem rather to have grown upon the wall like a delicate efflorescence.

731. **Pierre-Cécile Puvis de Chavannes,** 1824-1898, Symbolism, French,
The Poor Fisherman, 1881.
Oil on canvas, 155.5 x 192.5 cm.
Musée d'Orsay, Paris.

732. **Georges Seurat,** 1859-1891, Neo-impressionism, French,
Sunday Afternoon on 'La Grande Jatte', 1884-1886.
Oil on canvas, 207.5 x 308 cm. The Art Institute of Chicago, Chicago.

After two years of work on this painting and after thirty-eight preliminary oils and twenty-three sketches, the thirty-year old artist amazed the art world by showing his masterpiece at the last Impressionist Exhibition (1886). Different classes of people (see the trio in the lower left corner) mix to enjoy the island on the River Seine. Between the capuchin monkey, a favourite pet of the upper class at the time, and the mutt of the reclined worker, a pampered toy dog leaps into play. In the work a peaceful moment in time is frozen for the leaping dog, the skipping girl, the rowing crews, smoke from a pipe and a cigar, smoke blowing in opposite directions from two different boats, and for six butterflies in flight. Yet, the viewer can notice by the shadows that the sun progresses from midday at the top of the lawn, to evening in the foreground. Moreover, shorter subjects cast long shadows and vice versa. The tall trombonist casts nearly no shadow. There seems to be no object from which the shadow is cast to the left of the lady with the red umbrella. The entire work is done using pointillism or divisionism, whereby a desired colour is broken down into its colour elements. Then tiny dots of those elemental colours were applied to the surface so that when seen at the right distance the dots are virtually "mixed by the eye". Perfecting this technique and this work are Seurat's major contributions to neo-Impressionism.

733. **Pierre-Auguste Renoir,** 1841-1919, Impressionism, French,
Luncheon of the Boating Party, c. 1880.
Oil on canvas, 129.5 x 172.7 cm.
The Phillips Collection, Washington, D. C.

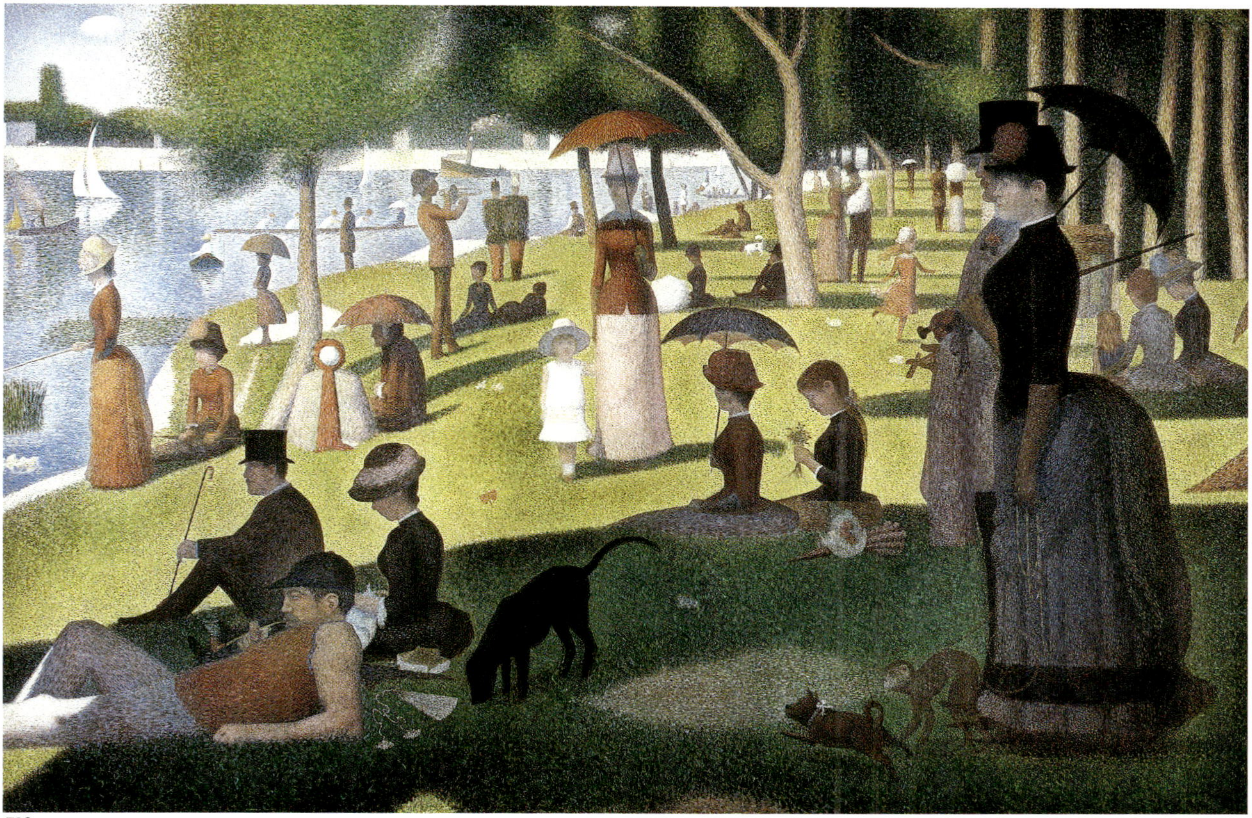

732

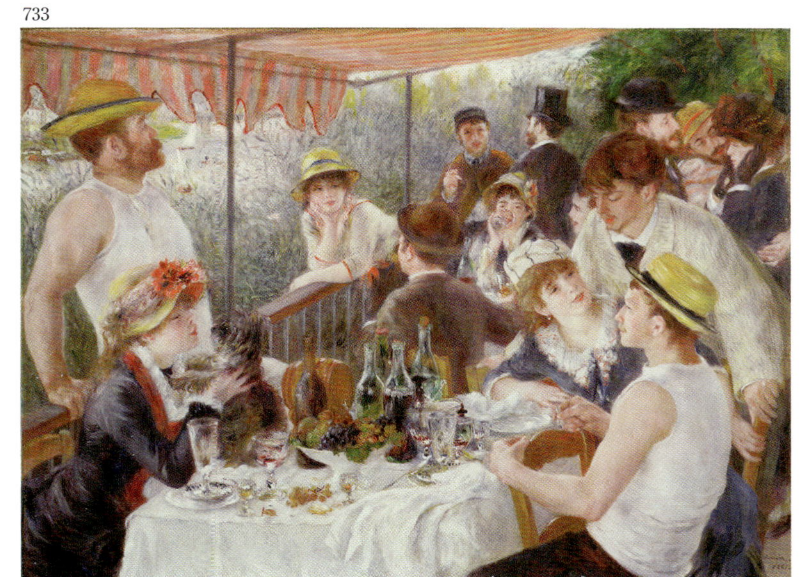

733

GEORGES SEURAT
(1859 PARIS – 1891 PARIS)

Georges Seurat studied at the Ecole des Beaux-Arts between 1878 and 1879. At that time, scientist-writers such as Chevreul, Rood or Sutter wrote treatises about colour and optical perception. Those theories largely influenced Neo-impressionism of which Seurat is one of the pioneers with Paul Signac, Henri-Edmond Cross, Maximilien Luce, and Pissarro. Neo-impressionist painters were interested in colours and their interplay, and would make extensive use of complementary colours in their paintings. But, whereas impressionism was more instinctive, Seurat is well-known for his technique of pointillism and divisionism – the controlled, precise juxtaposition of different coloured painted dots on the canvas. His thoughts and techniques were most respected by Cubists and Neo-constructivists who would follow him.

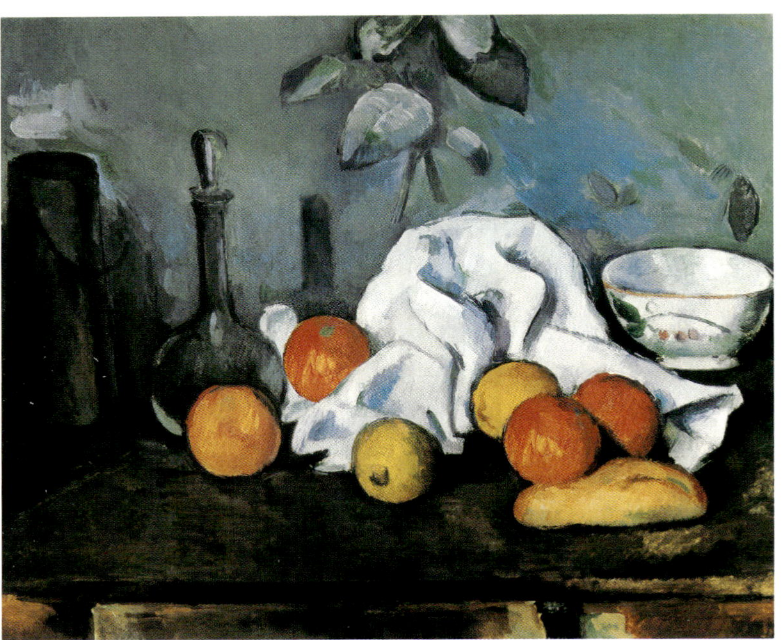

734. Paul Cézanne, 1839-1906,
Post-impressionism, French, *Fruit*, 1879-1880.
Oil on canvas, 45 x 55.3 cm.
The State Hermitage Museum, St Petersburg.

Cézanne painted two groups of still-lifes composed of the same objects: a milk jug, a decanter, a painted bowl, and fruit. The first group is dated, by Venturi, to the years 1873-1877 in Pontoise or Paris. The Hermitage canvas belongs to the second group featuring the same objects but with leaf-patterned wallpaper in the background. Venturi dates this group to 1879-1882. Around 1880, two tendencies were happily combined in Cézanne's work – an inclination to massive, baroque forms and a striving for orderly constructivism. The artist was then evolving his favourite colour range of warm oranges and cool grey-blues, and his brushstroke was becoming extremely flexible, capable of conveying a sense of heavy density or almost weightless transparency.

HENRI FANTIN–LATOUR
(1836 GRENOBLE – 1904 BURÉ)

For Henri Fantin-Latour, still-life painting was almost a curse. He was continually beset by collectors who wanted nothing else from his otherwise immense artistic talent. Consequently, he is known almost exclusively for his delicate still-lifes in which he excelled, although his extraordinary figure depictions and portrait groups also should have stood test of time.

Many of the best examples of Fantin-Latour's floral paintings and still-lifes can be found in English galleries and museums. When viewed close up, they reveal details and objects which lend a starkly realistic impression. They combine drawing with intricate brushwork and lovely harmonies of colour. In this way his still-lifes, like his portraits, have a truthful quality and great pictorial depth.

735. Henri Fantin-Latour, 1836-1904, Realism, French,
Flowers in an Earthenware Vase, 1883.
Oil on canvas, 22.5 x 29 cm.
The State Hermitage Museum, St Petersburg.

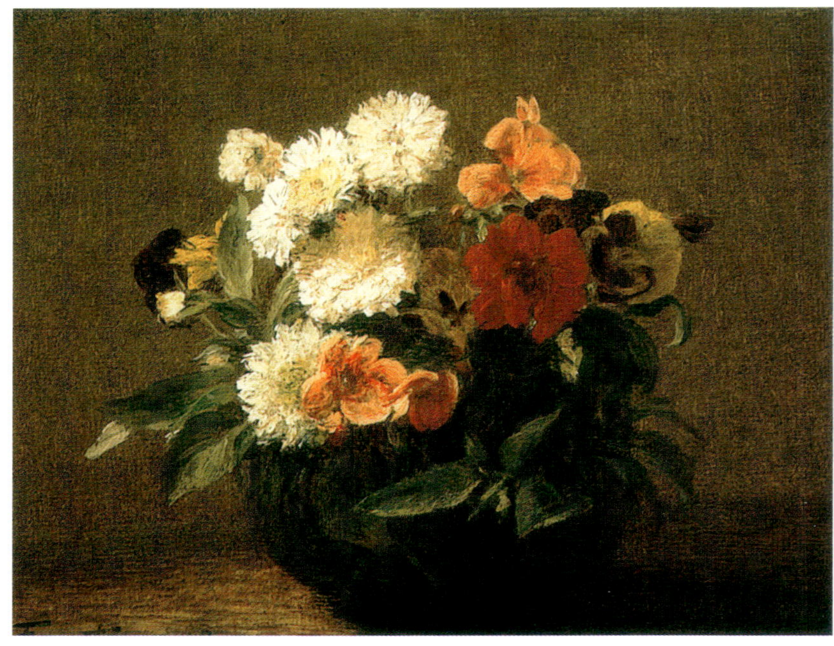

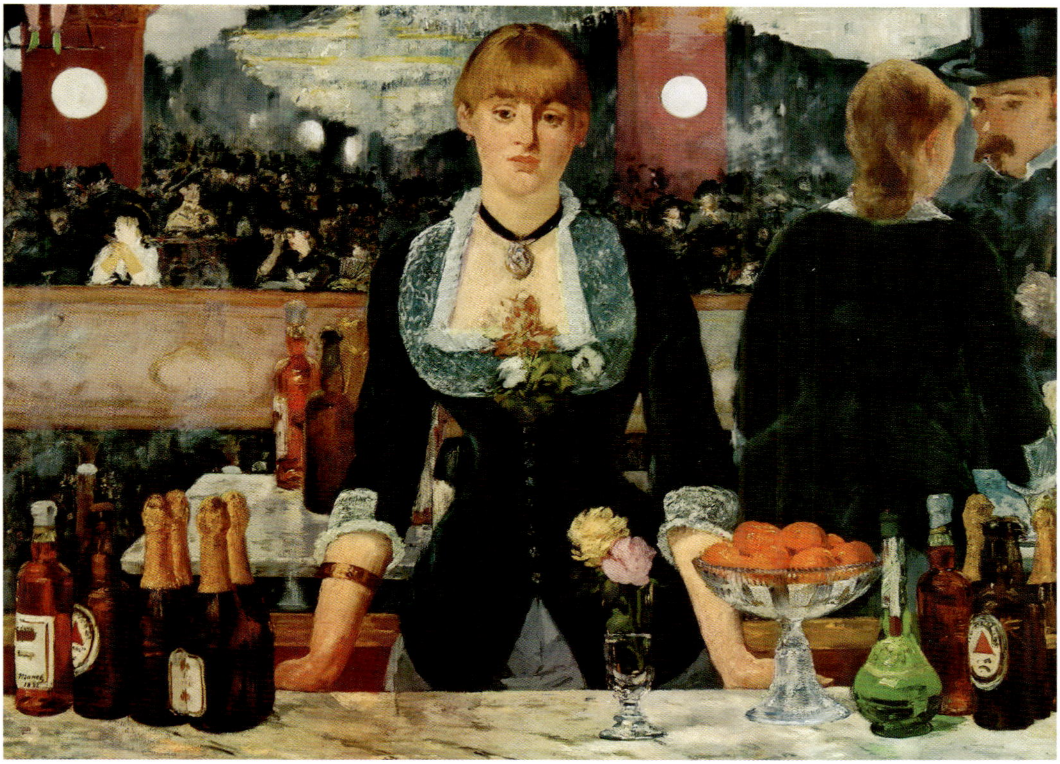

736. **Édouard Manet,** 1832-1883, Impressionism, French,
   A Bar at the Folies-Bergère, 1882.
   Oil on canvas, 96 x 130 cm.
   Courtauld Institute of Art, London.

*Manet was in the inner circle of impressionists with his friends
Monet and Renoir. While he did not set out to present
symbolism, he observed and shared his impressions of what he
saw. The artist loved to frequent this location, popular with
other artists. He incorporated electric lights that were becoming
popular in such public places. The overhead lights seemed to
eliminate shadows, as a symbol of modernity and urban life.
The geometric centre of the work is the barmaid's bodice,
drawing attention to how her right and left sides are nearly
identical and centred in the work, showing her resigned
conformity to her work.*

*However, to her left there at first seems to be a mirrored
reflection. However, the mirror is not reflecting the present
moment as the women's posture and the alignment do not
square properly with the "reflection". Her reflective moment is
frozen, as is the movement of the acrobatic entertainer on a
trapeze in the upper left corner. The strong horizontal line of the
balcony from the left does not align properly with the right side,
again showing that the reflection breaks the barrier between
present and another time, as well as between classes of people.*

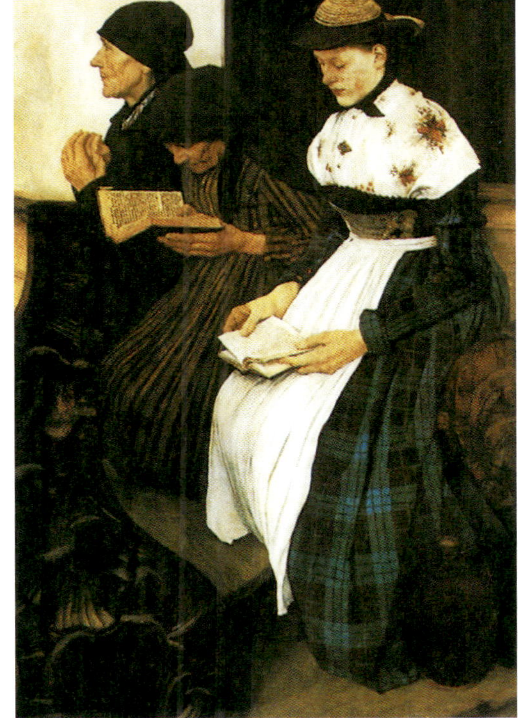

737. **Wilhelm Leibl,** 1844-1900, Realism, German,
   Three Women In Church, 1882.
   Oil on panel, 113 x 77 cm. Kunsthalle, Hamburg.

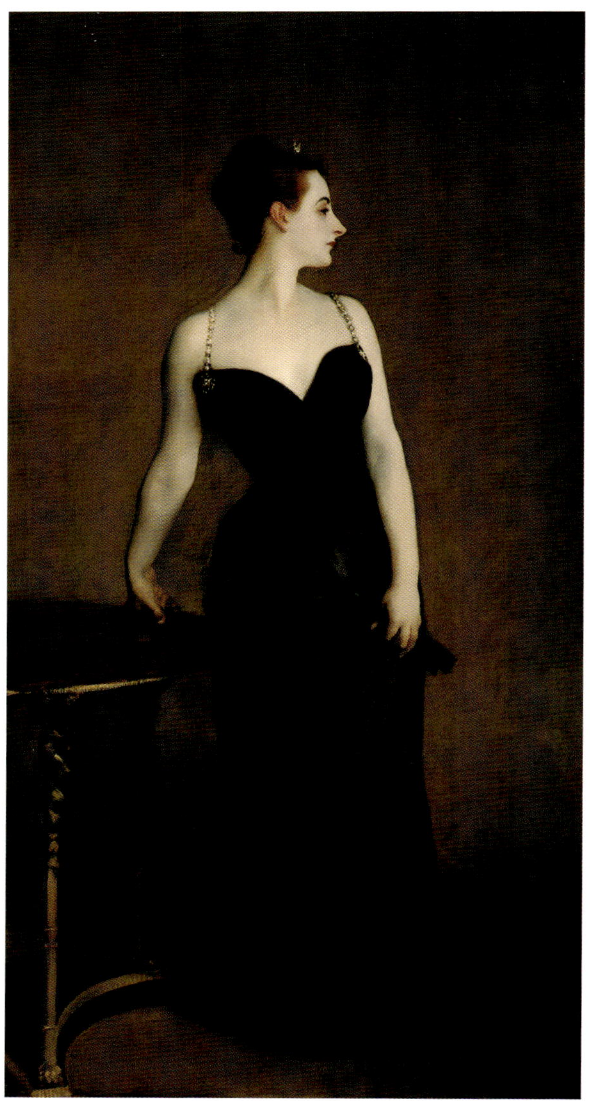

738. John Singer Sargent, 1856-1925, Post-impressionism, American, *Madame X (Madame Pierre Gautreau),* 1883-1884. Oil on canvas, 208.6 x 109.9 cm. The Metropolitan Museum of Art, New York.

The American painter John Singer Sargent visited the States on short trips during the thirty years he lived in Paris, as he retained his American parents' loyalty to their native land. The stereotypically American love of glamour more than class is seen here as the portrait captures a pose rather than a candid moment. He sees appearance more than character. Madame Gautreau is presented in what was a risqué gown, shockingly low-cut for the times. For this and his other unorthodox portraits, he was criticised for being improper. Historian German Bazin referred to him as "a painter of superficial fashionable portraits in a facile and dazzling technique that went far to disguise their empty ideality".

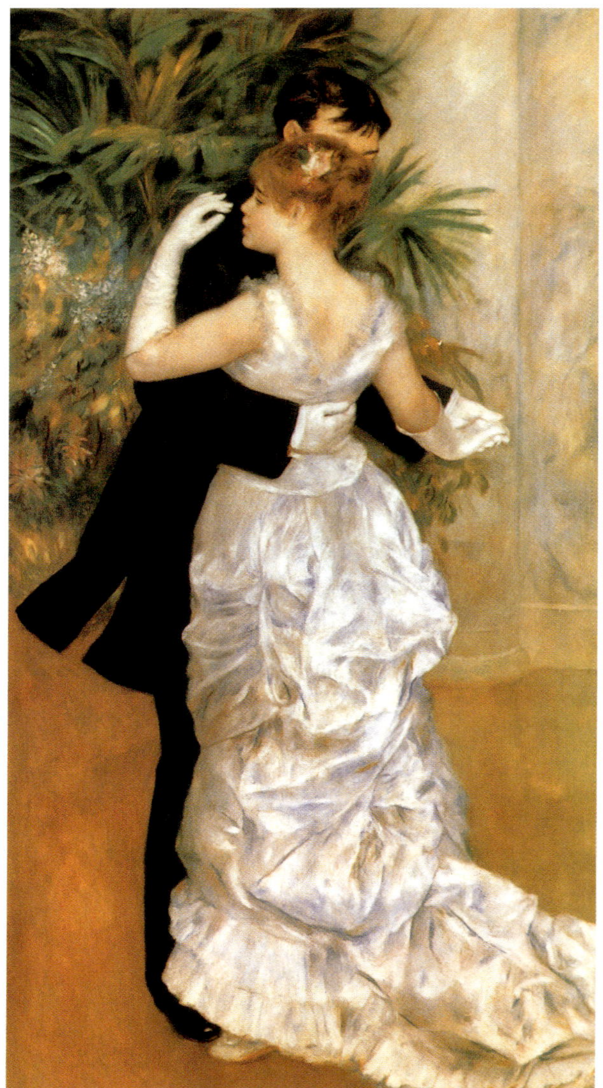

739. Pierre-Auguste Renoir, 1841-1919, Impressionism, French, *Dance in the City,* 1883. Oil on canvas, 180 x 90 cm. Musée d'Orsay, Paris.

In 1883 Renoir's friend and dealer Paul Durand-Ruel commissioned three decorative panels on the theme of dance from him. He displayed two of them that same year at Renoir's first one-man exhibition which was held in his gallery (Dance in the City was entitled Dance in Paris), and the third, Dance in Winter, in Brussels in 1886. Renoir's models, as always, were people close to him. The man's face cannot be seen, but it was probably the artist's friend Paul Lhote who posed for this figure. His partner is the main, and in point of fact the only, concrete figure in the work: a proud head on a long neck, powerful shoulders, and an enchanting profile with a short nose. Her name was Marie-Clementine. She had been a dressmaker in Montmartre before becoming an acrobat. Then, after injuring her leg, she began posing for artists. Later, she made a name for herself as the painter Susanne Valadon and became the mother of the Montmartre landscape painter Maurice Utrillo.

JOHN SINGER SARGENT
(1856 FLORENCE – 1925 LONDON)

Sargent was born in Florence, in 1856, the son of cultivated parents. When Sargent entered the school of Carolus-Duran he attained much more than the average pupils. His father was a retired Massachusetts gentleman, having practised medicine in Philadelphia. Sargent's home life was penetrated with refinement, and outside it were the beautiful influences of Florence, combining the charms of sky and hills with the wonders of art in the galleries and the opportunities of an intellectual and artistic society. Accordingly, when Sargent arrived in Paris, he was not only a skilful draughtsman and painter as a result of his study of the Italian masters, but he also had a refined and cultivated taste, which perhaps had an even greater influence upon his career. Later in Spain, it was chiefly upon the lessons learned from Velázquez that he found his own brilliant method.

Sargent belongs to America, but is claimed by others as a citizen of the world, or a cosmopolitan. Sargent, with the exception of a few months at distant intervals, spent his life abroad. The artistic influences which affected him were those of Europe. Yet his Americanism may be detected in his extraordinary facility to absorb impressions, in the individuality he evolved, and in the subtlety and reserve of his methods – qualities that are characteristic of the best American art.

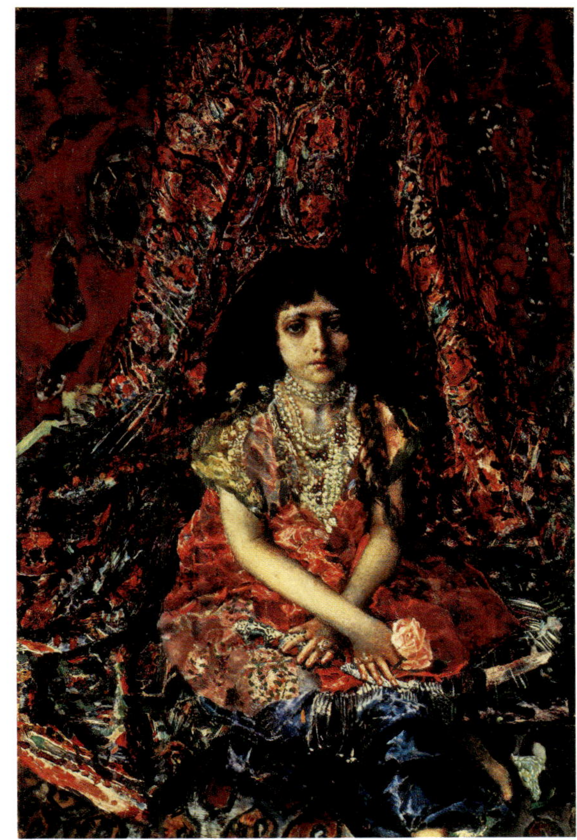

740. **Mikhail Vrubel,** 1856-1910, Symbolism, Russian,
Young Girl against a Persian Carpet, 1886.
Oil on canvas, 104 x 68 cm. Museum of Russian Art, Kiev.

MIKHAIL VRUBEL
(1856 OMSK – 1910 ST PETERSBURG)

One of the first symbolist painters in Russia, and one of the most intriguing, was Mikhaïl Vrubel. Many of his paintings have a surreal, dreamlike quality. Some of the most remarkable, such as *The Bogatyr* (1898), *Pan* (1899), and *The Swan Princess* (1900), are of mythological figures. And many of them feature either the elaborate patterns characteristic of Art Nouveau or mosaic-like patches of colour akin to those found in the paintings of Gustav Klimt.

In 1890 Vrubel was commissioned to illustrate a special edition of the works of Mikhaïl Lermontov, to mark the fiftieth anniversary of the poet's death.

In terms of style, Vrubel's portraits, like Nesterov's, vary enormously in the 1890s. They range from the sober and conventional, for example, the portrait of *Konstantin Artsybushev* that he painted in 1897, to highly decorative works such as *Girl Against a Persian Carpet,* which is both a sensitive portrait of a child and an inspired exploration of pattern and colour.

Tormented by mental illness, Vrubel spent most of the last nine years of his life in hospital, where he continued to work until, in 1906, he lost his sight.

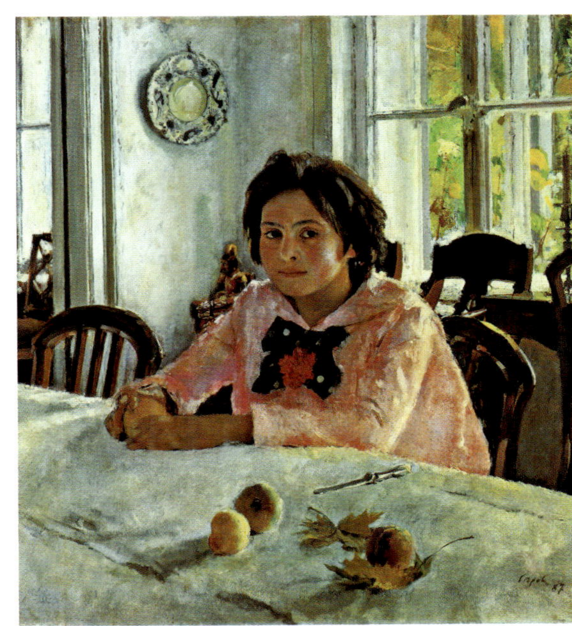

741. **Valentin Serov,** 1865-1911, World of Art Group, Russian,
Girl with Peaches (Portrait of Vera Mamontowa), 1887.
Oil on canvas, 91 x 85 cm. The State Tretyakov Gallery, Moscow.

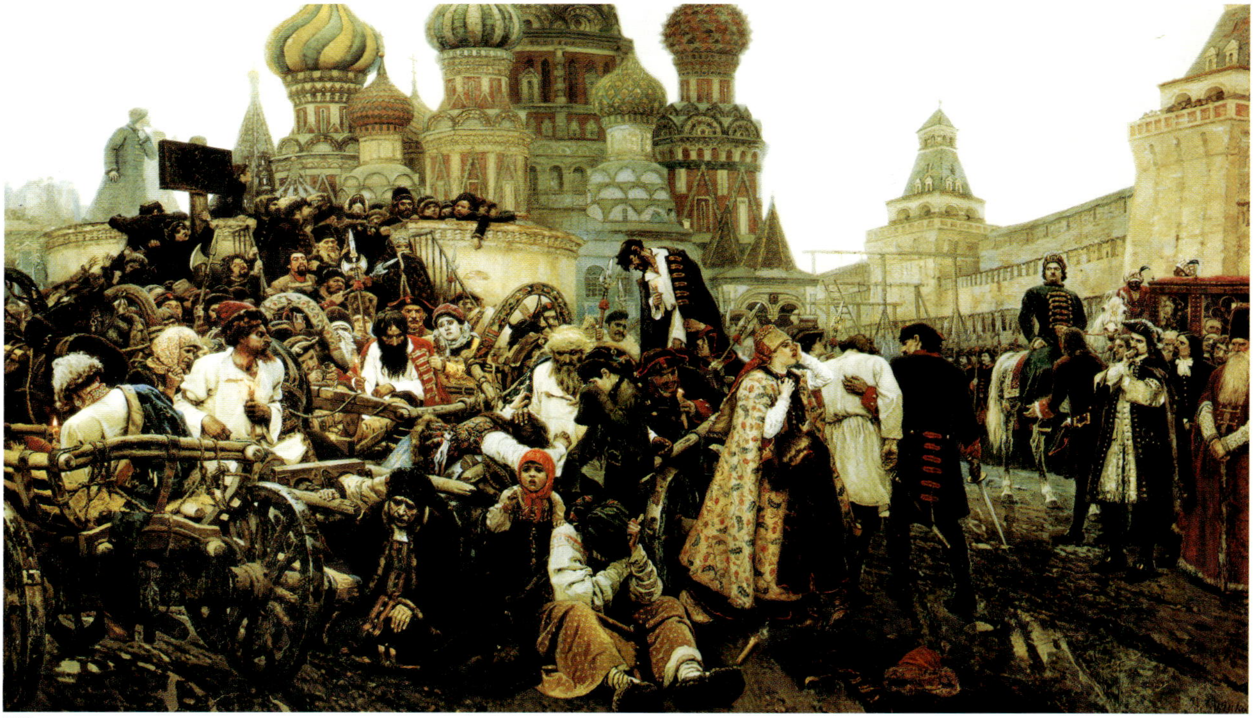

742

743. **Wasily Surikov,** 1848-1916, Realism, Russian,
Boyarina Morozova, 1887. Oil on canvas, 304 x 587.5 cm.
The State Tretyakov Gallery, Moscow.

743

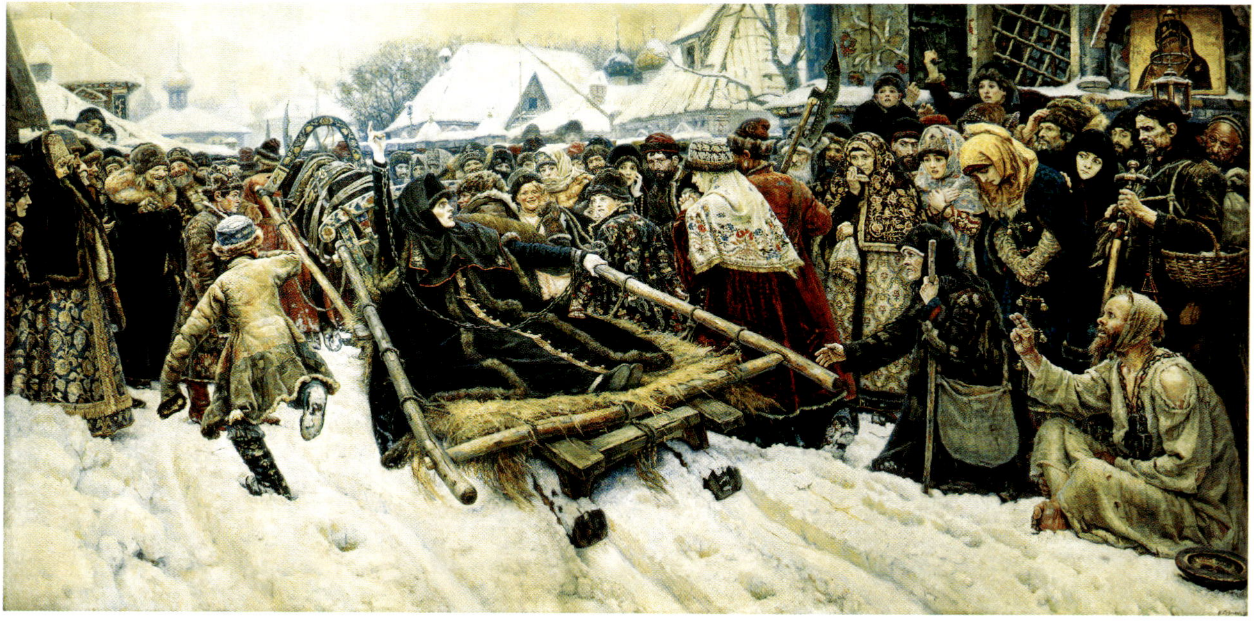

742. Wasily Surikov, 1848-1916, Realism, Russian,
The Morning of the Execution of the Streltsy, 1878-1881.
Oil on canvas, 218 x 379 cm.
The State Tretyakov Gallery, Moscow.

Interesting in this context are the comments on the Streltsy made by Surikov's biographer, which the artist read and approved without changing a word: "The picture turned out powerful, frightening, and above all, truly historical. Looking at it you feel how harrowing the situation is for all concerned. You feel an agonising pity for these hundreds of people condemned to death, but you understand Peter too, as he sits there with clenched teeth, gripping the reins in his fist, and boldly looks into the faces of men he considers sworn enemies of his great cause. As in history itself, you can side with either party, depending on your sympathies and antipathies, but you know that in the final analysis nobody is right in history and nobody wrong, there is only the horror of collisions such as this, that are never resolved but with the shedding of a sea of blood." In three pictures he painted in the 1880s, The Morning of the Execution of the Streltsy, Menshikov at Beriozov, *and* The Boyarynia Morozove Surikov*, depicts seventeenth- and early eighteenth-century history as a tragic chapter of strife in the life of the Russian people.*

744. Ilya Repin, 1844-1930, Realism, Russian,
Ivan the Terrible and His Son Ivan on 15 November 1581, 1885.
Oil on canvas, 199.5 x 224 cm.
The State Tretyakov Gallery, Moscow.

The artist started work on this painting only when the execution of the members of the People's Will Revolutionary Group – those responsible for the assassination of Tsar Alexander II in 1881 – was still fresh in his mind. "A trail of blood ran through that year," Repin later recalled. "Terrible scenes were in everybody's mind… It was natural to look for a way out of this painful and tragic situation in history. I began on an impulse and the picture progressed in fits and starts. My emotions were overburdened with the horrors of contemporary life."

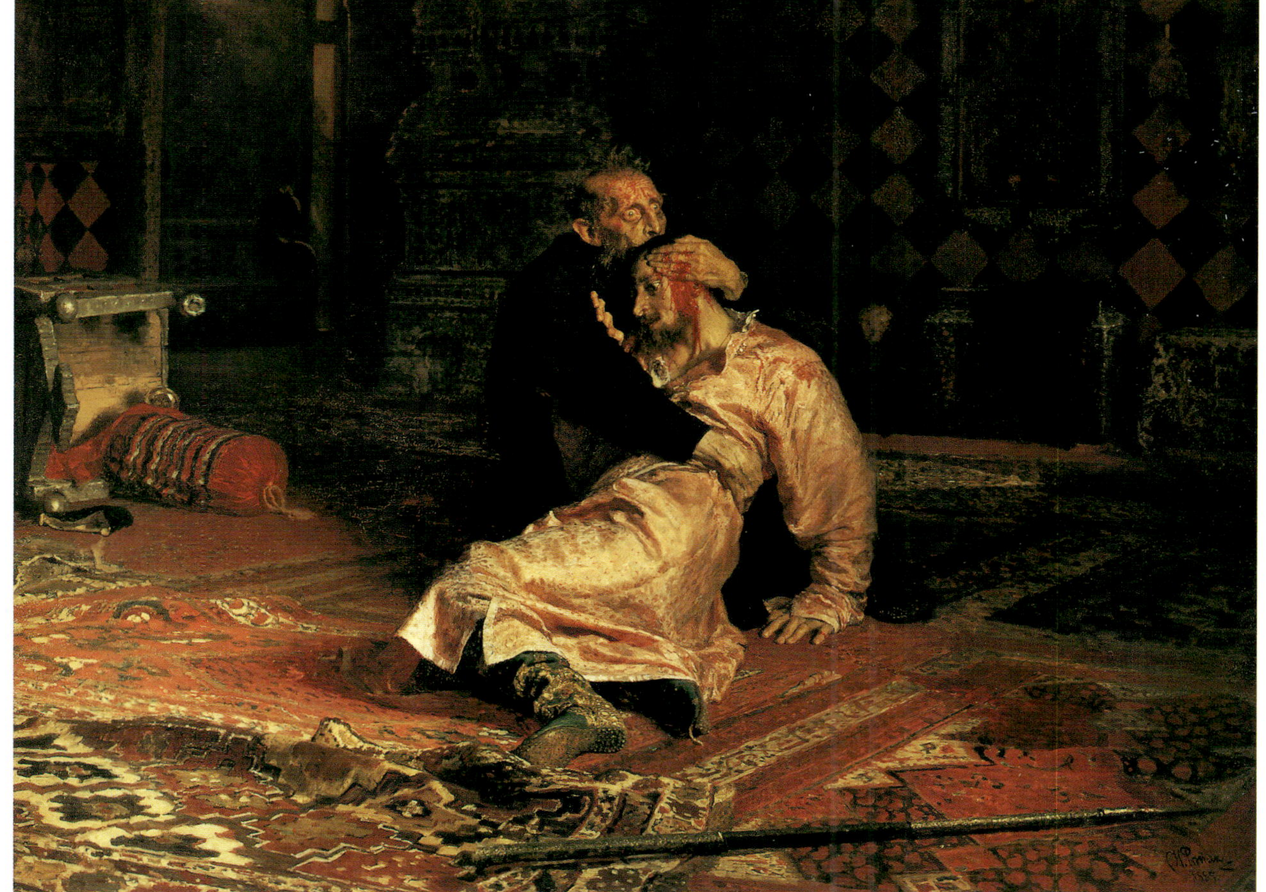

744

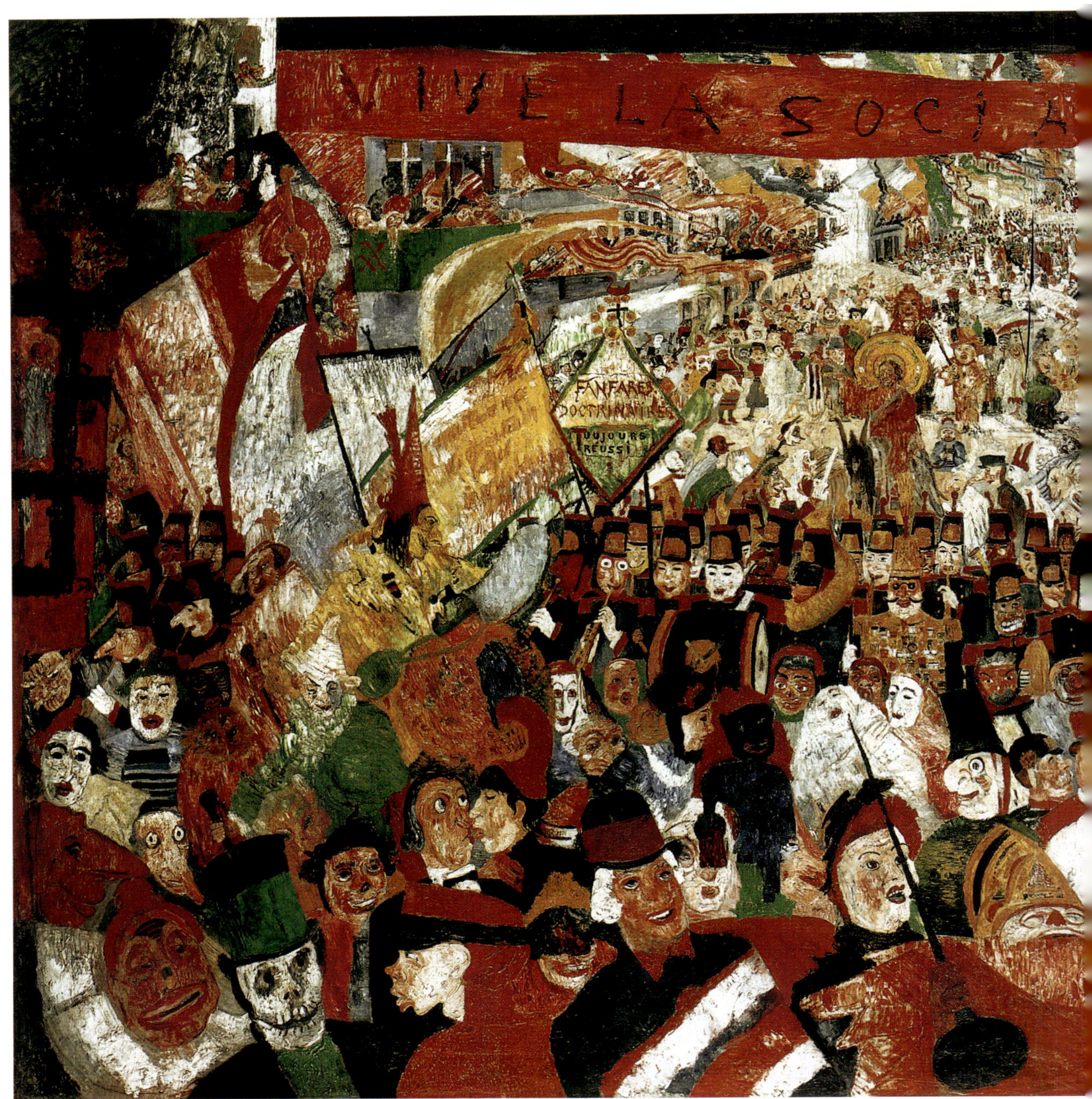

VIVE LA SOCIA
FANFARES
DOCTRINAIRES
TOUJOURS
REUSSI

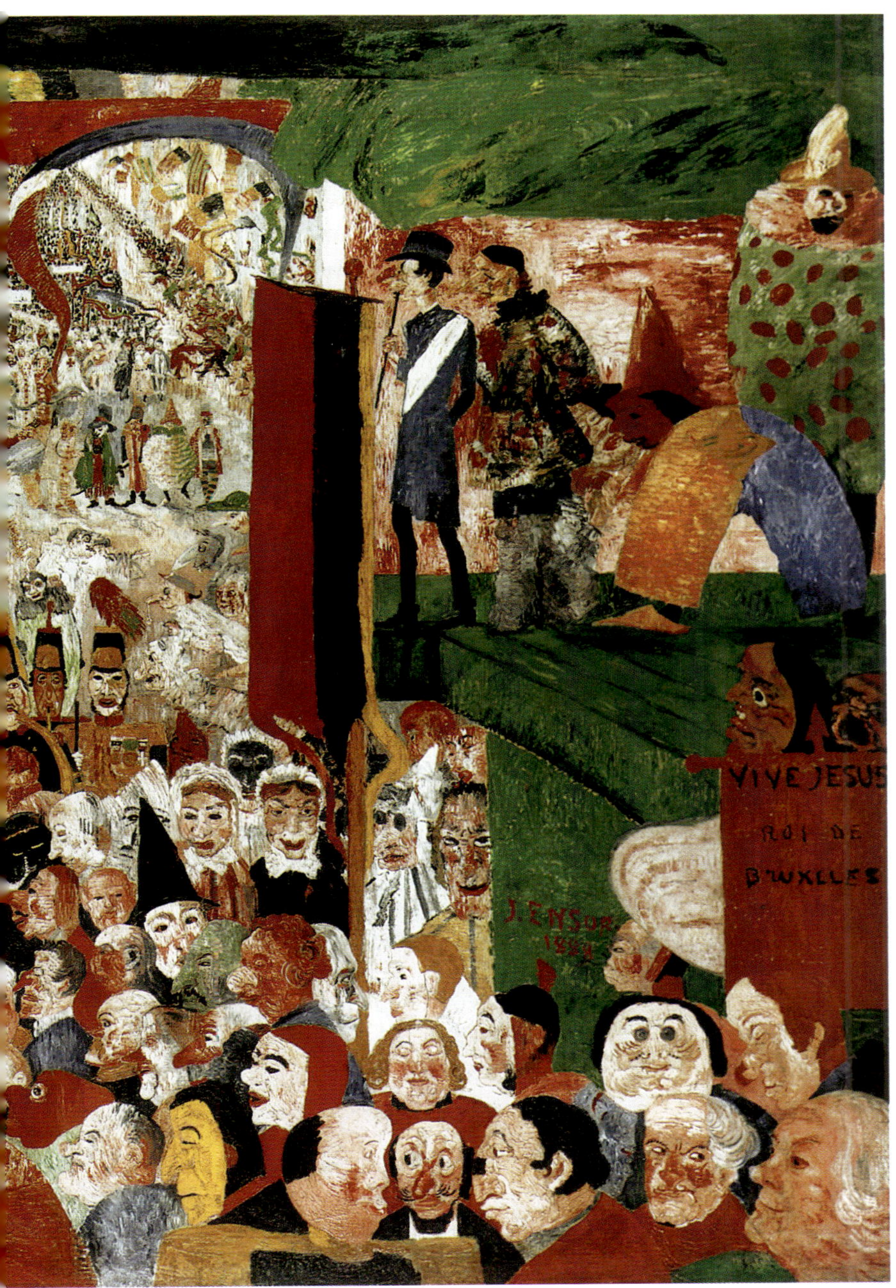

745. **James Ensor,** 1860-1949,
Symbolism/Expressionism, Belgian,
Entry of Christ into Brussels,
1887-1888.
Oil on canvas, 256 x 378 cm.
J. Paul Getty Museum, Los Angeles.

Jesus (slightly up and left from the midpoint of the work) is only one of dozens of interesting figures in this contemporary setting. It seems only a few faces are of masks, while most are of the faces of the 'evil-self' within each person. Commentators usually refer to the scene as a contemporary 'Second Coming' or 'Last Judgment', but it might in fact be more of a Palm Sunday event. These three possibilities are symbolically and theologically related, but in any event, the artist is expressing his identification (before his own artistic success) with Jesus who also was persecuted by his critics. For the Palm Sunday interpretation, consider the carnival, or Mardi Gras, reception such as by the marching band in the centre of the work and the "Viva Jesus" sign on the right.

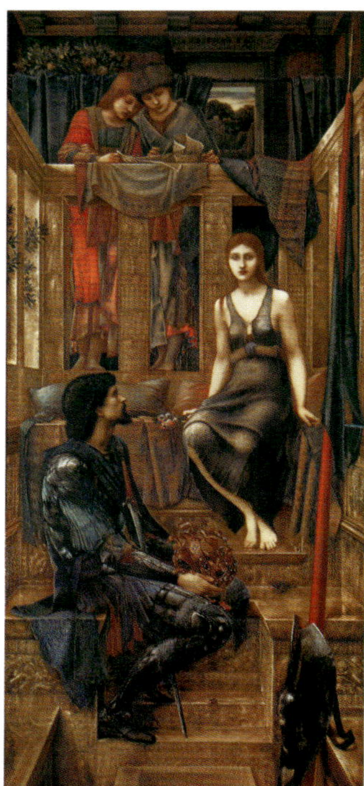

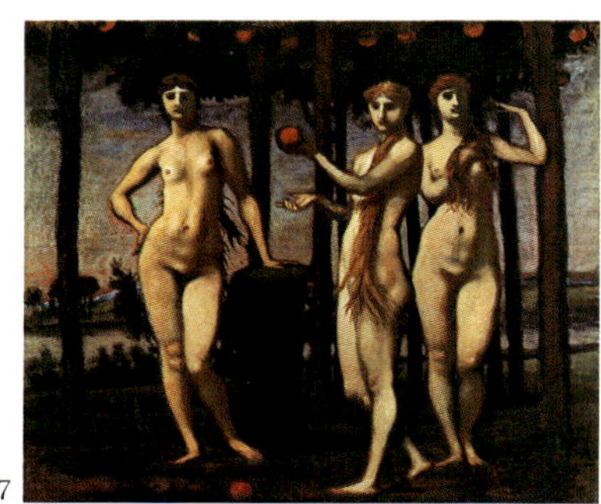
747

EDWARD COLEY BURNE–JONES
(1833 BIRMINGHAM – 1898 LONDON)

Burne-Jones' oeuvre can be understood as an attempt to create in paint a world of perfect beauty, as far removed from the Birmingham of his youth as possible. At that time Birmingham was a byword for the dire effects of unregulated capitalism – a booming, industrial conglomeration of unimaginable ugliness and squalor.

The two great French symbolist painters, Gustave Moreau and Pierre Puvis de Chavannes, immediately recognised Burne-Jones as an artistic fellow traveller. But, it is very unlikely that Burne-Jones would have accepted or even, perhaps, have understood the label of 'symbolist'. Yet he seems to have been one of the most representative figures of the symbolist movement and of that pervasive mood termed "fin-de-siecle".

Burne-Jones is usually labelled as a Pre-Raphaelite. In fact he was never a member of the Brotherhood formed in 1848. Burne-Jones' brand of Pre-Raphaelitism derives not from Hunt and Millais but from Dante Gabriel Rossetti.

Burne-Jones' work in the late 1850s is, moreover, closely based on Rossetti's style. His feminine ideal is also taken from that of Rossetti, with abundant hair, prominent chins, columnar necks and androgynous bodies hidden by copious medieval gowns. The prominent chins remain a striking feature of both artists' depictions of women. From the 1860s their ideal types diverge. As Rossetti's women balloon into ever more fleshy opulence, Burne-Jones' women become more virginal and ethereal to the point where, in some of the last pictures, the women look anorexic.

In the early 1870s Burne-Jones painted several mythical or legendary pictures in which he seems to have been trying to exorcise the traumas of his celebrated affair with Mary Zambaco.

No living British painter between Constable and Bacon enjoyed the kind of international acclaim that Burne-Jones was accorded in the early 1890s. This great reputation began to slip in the latter half of the decade, however, and it plummeted after 1900 with the triumph of Modernism.

With hindsight we can see this flatness and the turning away from narrative as characteristic of early Modernism and the first hesitant steps towards Abstraction. It is not as odd at it seems that Kandinsky cited Rossetti and Burne-Jones as forerunners of Abstraction in his book, "Concerning the Spiritual in Art".

746. Edward Coley Burne-Jones, 1833-1898,
Pre-Raphaelite, British,
King Cophetua and the Beggar-Maid, 1884.
Oil on canvas, 293 x 136 cm.
Tate Gallery, London.

When Burne-Jones' mural-sized canvas of King Cophetua and the Beggar-maid *was exhibited in the shadow of the newly constructed Eiffel Tower at the Paris Exposition Universelle in 1889, it caused a sensation scarcely less extraordinary than the tower itself. Burne-Jones was awarded not only a gold medal at the exhibition but also the cross of the Légion d'Honneur. Burne-Jones did not want King Cophetua's armour to look like that of any particular period, so he studied armour until he felt that he understood the principles of armour-making well enough to design his own. The result is quite extraordinary – a strange, organic, proto-art nouveau, body hugging armour that looks as though it was made of plastic or leather rather than of metal. Burne-Jones also agonised over the elegant designer rags worn by the beggar-maid, wanting them to look "sufficiently beggarly" but at the same time perfectly beautiful. In a letter of 1883, he wrote that he hoped that this had been achieved so that "she shall look as if she deserved to have it made of cloth of gold and set with pearls. I hope the king kept the old one and looked at it now and then". The beggar-maid stares forward fixedly. Her stance and her absence of facial expression convey a vague sense of unease and dread. This princess of hearts, a simple girl destined to be the wife of a king, could be bulimic. Her bruised eyes and her unhealthy pallor are the fin-de-siècle equivalent of "heroin chic".*

747. Hans von Marées, 1837-1887, Symbolism, German,
The Hesperides, central panel of *The Hesperides triptych,*
1885-1887. Oil and tempera on wooden panel, 341 x 482 cm.
Neue Pinakothek, Munich.

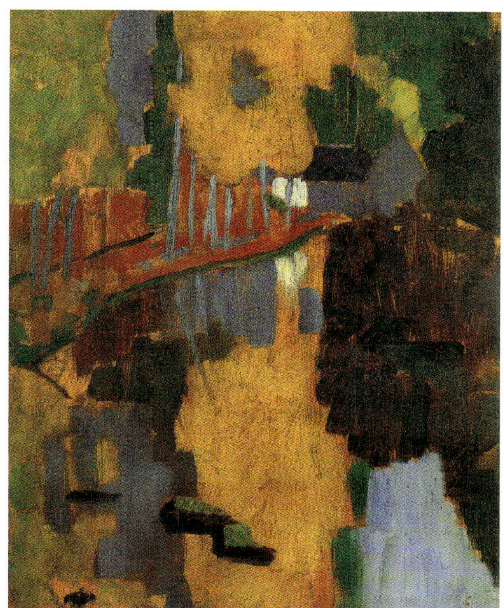

748. **Paul Sérusier,** 1864-1927, Nabism, French, *Talisman,* 1888.
Oil on wood, 27 x 21 cm. Musée d'Orsay, Paris.

Sérusier met Gauguin in Pont-Aven and painted a simplified landscape under his guidance. It became the Talisman. *This painting became the foundation element of the Nabis group (meaning 'prophet' in Hebrew).*

750. **Odilon Redon,** 1840-1916, Symbolism, French, *Lady with Wildflowers,* 1890-1900. Pastel and charcoal on paper, 52 x 37.5 cm. The State Hermitage Museum, St Petersburg.

ODILON REDON
(1840 BORDEAUX – 1916 PARIS)

Redon started drawing as a young child, and at the age of ten he was awarded a drawing prize at school. At age fifteen, he began to study drawing but, upon the insistence of his father, switched to architecture. Any career in architecture ended when he failed to pass the entrance exams at the Ecole des Beaux-Arts in Paris but eventually he studied there under Jean-Léon Gerôme. Back home in his native Bordeaux, he took up sculpture, and Rodolphe Bresdin instructed him in etching and lithography. However, joining the army in 1870 to serve in the Franco-Prussian War interrupted his artistic career. At the end of the war he moved to Paris, working almost exclusively in charcoal and lithography. It would not be until 1878 before his work gained any recognition with *Guardian Spirit of the Waters,* and he published his first album of lithographs titled *Dans le Rêve* in 1879. In the 1890s, he began to use pastel and oils, which dominated his works for the rest of his life. In 1899, he exhibited with the Nabis at Durand-Ruel's. In 1903 he was awarded the Legion of Honour. His popularity increased when a catalogue of etchings and lithographs was published by André Mellerio in 1913 and that same year, he was given the largest single representation at the New York Armory Show.

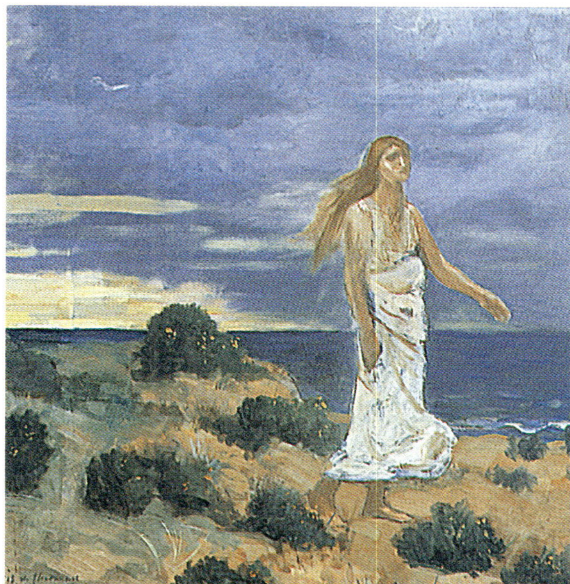

749. **Pierre-Cécile Puvis de Chavannes,** 1824-1898, Symbolism, French, *Woman on the Beach,* 1887. Oil on paper pasted on canvas, 75.3 x 74.5 cm. The State Hermitage Museum, St Petersburg.

750

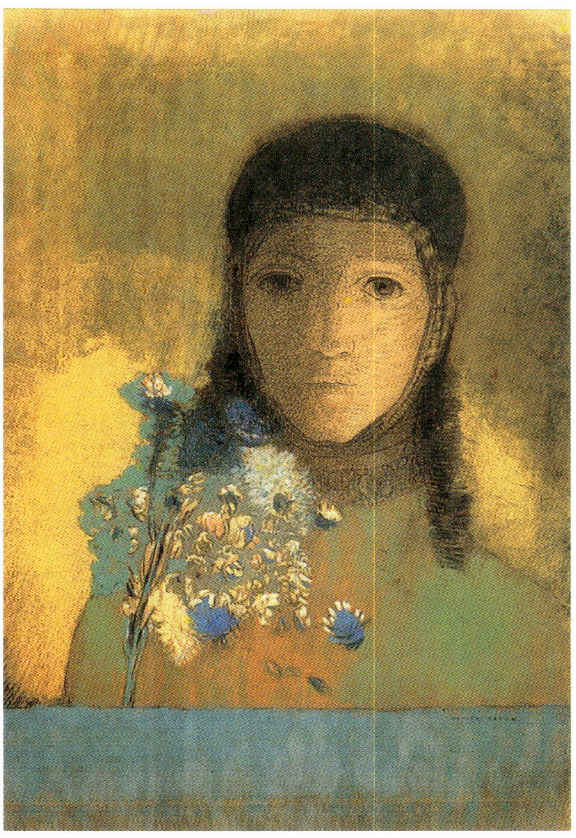

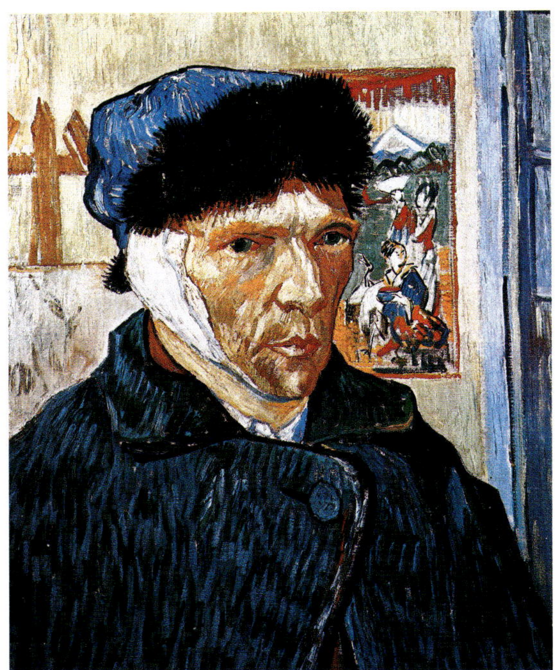

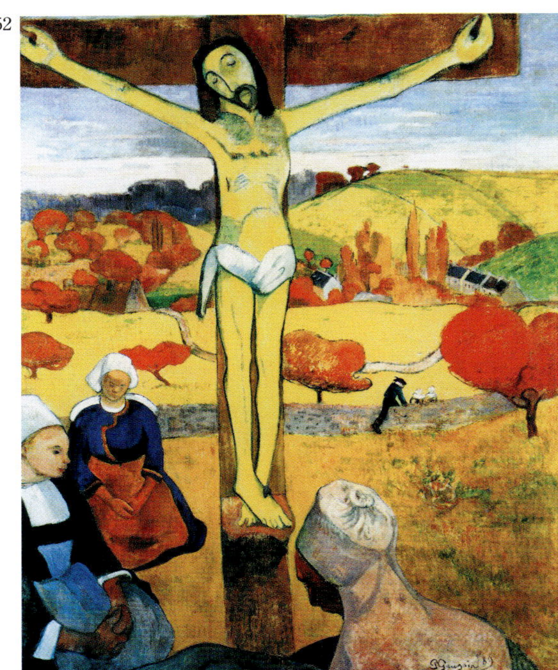

752

751. Vincent van Gogh, 1853-1890, Post-impressionism, Dutch,
Self-portrait with Bandaged Ear, 1889.
Oil on canvas, 60 x 49 cm.
Courtauld Institute of Art, London.

Notice the right ear has bandages in this portrait, whereas Van Gogh injured his left ear, therefore the portrait must have been made in front of a mirror. In a letter preceding this self-portrait (dating from January 1889, as he came out of hospital), Van Gogh wrote to Théo: "I have bought a good mirror on purpose, to work on my own portraits as I am lacking a model, because, if I manage to depict the colours of my own head, challenging enough in itself, I would be able to portrait other men and women."

752. Paul Gauguin, 1848-1903, Post-impressionism, French,
The Yellow Christ, 1889.
Oil on canvas, 92 x 73 cm. Albright-Knox Art Gallery, Buffalo.

Colours are the means of Gauguin's expression. He used them pure, in flat layers on the canvas and nuanced in function of perspective. In this sense he is considered a precursor of the Fauves.

The Yellow Christ's *background shows a landscape from Brittany. Gauguin settled in Brittany, in Pont-Aven, between 1886 and 1890. In this virgin land, empty of any modern element, the artist discovered the churches and their primitive statues. In* The Yellow Christ *he took his inspiration from a wooden Christ, found in a chapel, and he also refers to medieval and Byzantine iconography. This work also betrays a Japanese aspect. At the end of the nineteenth century, Japanese artists began to exhibit in Paris. The eccentric setting and the figures, shown from the back, cut the importance given to the costumes (the women surrounding Christ wear traditional costumes from Brittany). The technique of large, flat brush strokes, and the flattened perspective are different aspects that echo Japanese artworks that, Utamaro Hokusaï would have brought to France.*

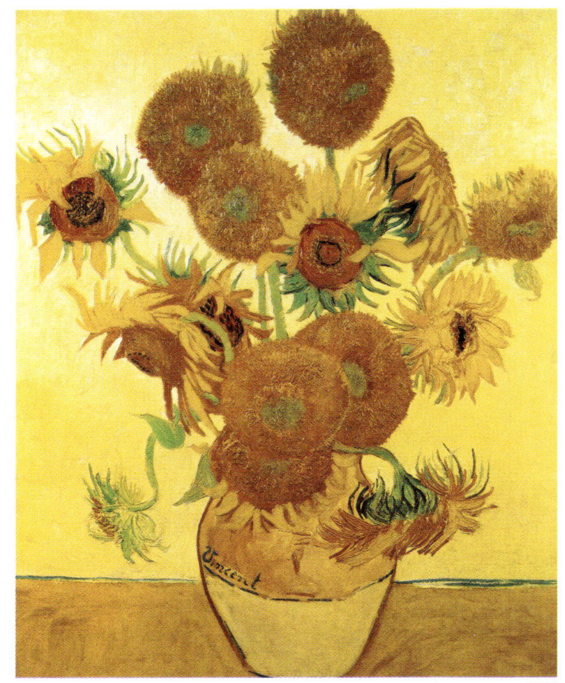

753

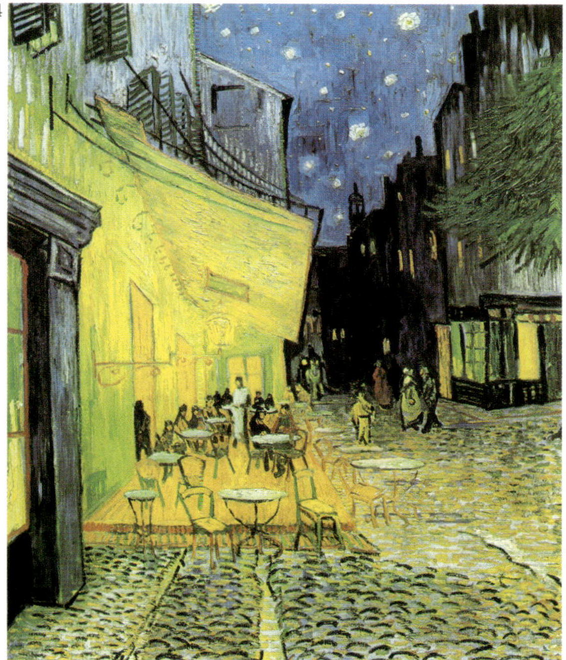

754. **Vincent van Gogh,** 1853-1890, Post-impressionism,
Dutch, *Café Terrasse by Night,* 1888.
Oil on canvas, 81 x 65 cm.
Rijksmuseum Kröller-Müller, Otterlo.

In a letter from Van Gogh to his brother Théo, on 8
September, 1888: "Finally, for the pleasure of the
landlord, of the postman I have depicted, of the visitors,
night prowlers and for my own pleasure, I have stayed up
three nights in a row, sleeping during the day. It often
seemed to me that the night is livelier and richer in colour
than the day."

755. **Vincent van Gogh,** 1853-1890, Post-impressionism,
Dutch, *Starry Night Over the Rhone,* 1888.
Oil on canvas, 72.5 x 92 cm. Musée d'Orsay, Paris.

Fascinated by the colours of the sky at night, Van Gogh,
soon after, painted another version of Starry Night Over the
Rhone *while in an asylum at Saint-Rémy in 1889. This*
popular painting can now be found in the Museum of
Modern Art in New York.

753. **Vincent van Gogh,** 1853-1890, Post-impressionism,
Dutch, *Sunflowers,* 1888. Oil on canvas, 92.1 x 73 cm.
National Gallery, London.

Four works depicting sunflowers were painted by Van Gogh
but he considered only two of them good enough to sign.
This is his first try of "light-colour on light-colour". Through
the variations of brush strokes and the thickness of the paint,
Van Gogh brings the limited nuances of colours to life. The
hatching of the background contrasts with the flat surface of
the vase. The colours are crushed on the flowers, for a
vibrant aspect.

VINCENT VAN GOGH
(1853 ZUNDERT – 1890 AUVERS-SUR-OISE)

Vincent van Gogh's life and work are so intertwined that it is
hardly possible to observe one without thinking of the other. Van
Gogh has indeed become the incarnation of the suffering,
misunderstood martyr of modern art, the emblem of the artist as
an outsider. An article, published in 1890, gave details about
Van Gogh's illness. The author of the article saw the painter as "a
terrible and demented genius, often sublime, sometimes
grotesque, always at the brink of the pathological."

Very little is known about Vincent's childhood. At the age of
eleven he had to leave "the human nest", as he called it himself, for
various boarding schools. The first portrait shows us Van Gogh as an
earnest nineteen year old. At that time he had already been at work
for three years in The Hague and, later, in London in the gallery
Goupil & Co. In 1874 his love for Ursula Loyer ended in disaster and
a year later he was transferred to Paris, against his will. After a
particularly heated argument during Christmas holidays in 1881, his
father, a pastor, ordered Vincent to leave. With this final break, he
abandoned his family name and signed his canvases simply
"Vincent". He left for Paris and never returned to Holland. In Paris he
came to know Paul Gauguin, whose paintings he greatly admired.

The self-portrait was the main subject of Vincent's work from
1886-1888. In February 1888 Vincent left Paris for Arles and tried
to persuade Gauguin to join him. The months of waiting for
Gauguin were the most productive time in Van Gogh's life. He
wanted to show his friend as many pictures as possible and
decorate the Yellow House. But Gauguin did not share his views
on art and finally returned to Paris.

On 7 January, 1889, fourteen days after his famous self-mutilation,
Vincent left the hospital where he was convalescing. Although he
hoped to recover from and to forget his madness, but he actually
came back twice more in the same year. During his last stay in
hospital, Vincent painted landscapes in which he recreated the
world of his childhood.

It is said that Vincent Van Gogh shot himself in the side in a
field but decided to return to the inn and went to bed. The
landlord informed Dr Gachet and his brother Theo, who
described the last moments of his life which ended on 29 July,
1890: "I wanted to die. While I was sitting next to him promising
that we would try to heal him. [...], he answered, 'La tristesse
durera toujours (The sadness will last forever).'"

755

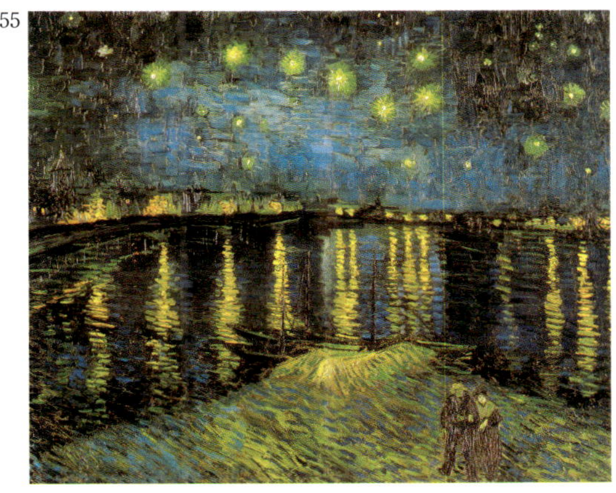

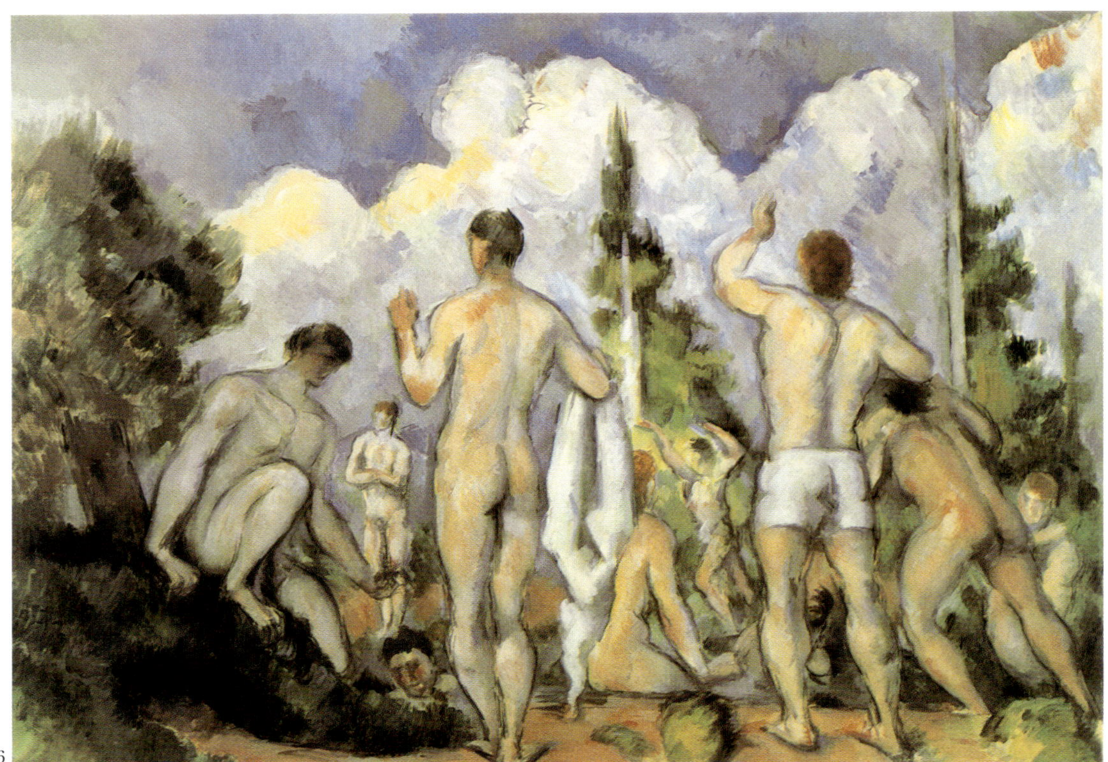

756

PAUL CÉZANNE
(1839 – 1906 AIX–EN–PROVENCE)

Since his death 200 years ago, Cézanne has become the most famous painter of the nineteenth century. He was born in Aix-en-Provence in 1839 and the happiest period of his life was his early youth in Provence, in company with Emile Zolá, another Italian. Following Zolá's example, Cézanne went to Paris in his twenty-first year.

During the Franco-Prussian war he deserted the military, dividing his time between open-air painting and the studio. He said to Vollard, an art dealer, "I'm only a painter. Parisian wit gives me a pain. Painting nudes on the banks of the Arc [a river near Aix] is all I could ask for." Encouraged by Renoir, one of the first to appreciate him, he exhibited with the impressionists in 1874 and in 1877. He was received with derision, which deeply hurt him.

Cézanne's ambition, in his own words, was "to make out of Impressionism something as solid and durable as the paintings of the museums." His aim was to achieve the monumental in a modern language of glowing, vibrating tones. Cézanne wanted to retain the natural colour of an object and to harmonise it with the various influences of light and shade trying to destroy it; to work out a scale of tones expressing the mass and character of the form.

Cézanne loved to paint fruit because it afforded him obedient models and he was a slow worker. He did not intend to simply copy an apple. He kept the dominant colour and the character of the fruit, but heightened the emotional appeal of the form by a scheme of rich and concordant tones. In his paintings of still-life

he is a master. His fruit and vegetable compositions are truly dramatic; they have the weight, the nobility, the style of immortal forms. No other painter ever brought to a red apple a conviction so heated, sympathy so genuinely spiritual, or an observation so protracted. No other painter of equal ability ever reserved for still-life his strongest impulses. Cézanne restored to painting the pre-eminence of knowledge, the most essential quality to all creative effort.

The death of his father in 1886 made him a rich man, but he made no change in his abstemious mode of living. Soon afterwards, Cézanne retired permanently to his estate in Provence. He was probably the loneliest of painters of his day. At times a curious melancholy attacked him, a black hopelessness. He grew more savage and exacting, destroying canvases, throwing them out of his studio into the trees, abandoning them in the fields, and giving them to his son to cut into puzzles, or to the people of Aix.

At the beginning of the century, when Vollard arrived in Provence with intentions of buying on speculation all the Cézannes he could get hold of, the peasantry, hearing that a fool from Paris was actually handing out money for old linen, produced from barns a considerable number of still-lifes and landscapes. The old master of Aix was overcome with joy, but recognition came too late. In 1906 he died from a fever contracted while painting in a downpour of rain.

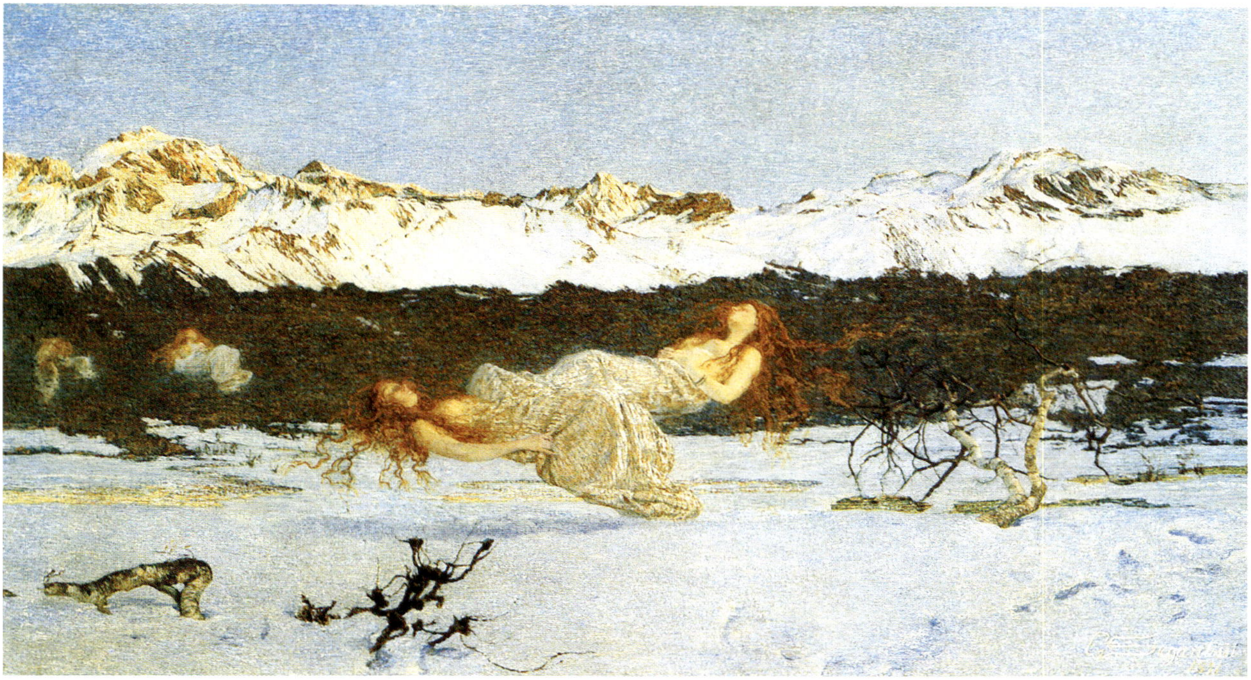

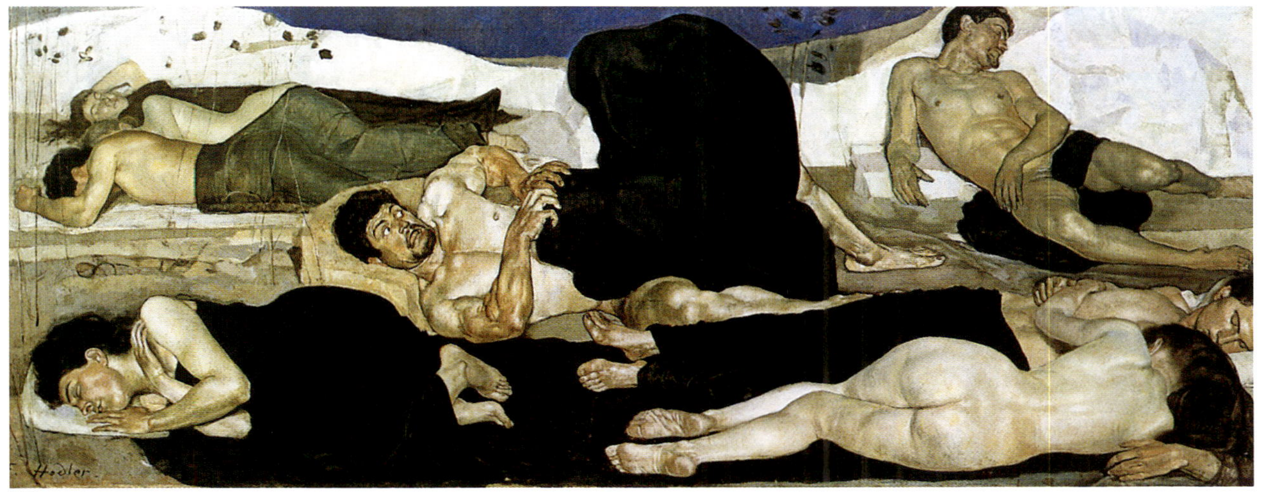

757. **Giovanni Segantini,** 1858-1899, Symbolism, Italian,
The Punishment of Lust, also known as *The Punishment of Luxury,* 1891.
Oil on canvas, 235 x 129.2 cm.
Walker Art Gallery, Liverpool.

756. **Paul Cézanne,** 1839-1906, Post-impressionism, French,
Bathers, 1890-1392.
Oil on canvas, 60 x 82 cm.
Musée d'Orsay, Paris.

758. **Ferdinand Hodler,** 1853-1918, Art Nouveau, Swiss,
Night, 1889-1890.
Oil on canvas, 116 x 229 cm.
Kunstmuseum, Berne.

758

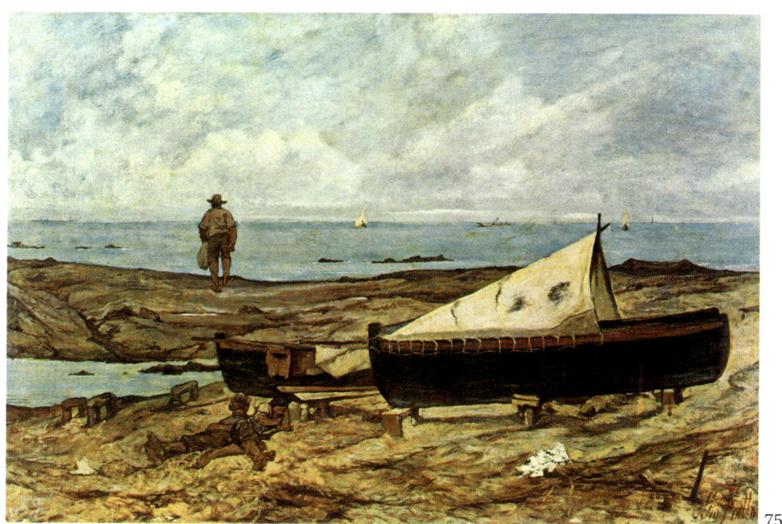

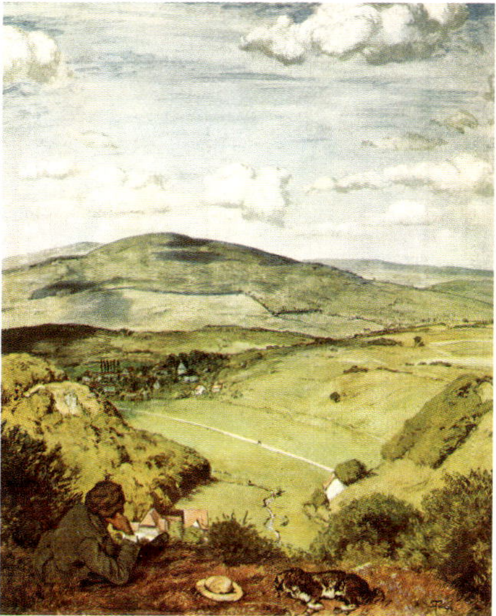

759

7●

ISAAC LEVITAN
(1860 KIBARTAI – 1900 MOSCOW)

One of the greatest and best-known landscape painters among the Itinerants, Isaak Levitan had the advantage of studying under both Savrasov and Polenov. Although his art is perhaps less epic than Shishkin's, his style and subject matter are more varied – perhaps surprisingly, since he died at a comparatively early age.

Levitan, like Shishkin, was a supreme master of the use of colour, composition, light and shade. The seasons of the year, the different times of day, and the infinite variety of nature figure in Levitan's canvases. But, unlike Shishkin, who had a preference for summer landscapes, Levitan preferred the fresh colours of spring and the muted cadences of autumn. When he painted summer scenes, such as *Secluded Monastery*, he preferred to work in the evening, when the light was softer, or even at dusk.

Levitan joined the Society of Itinerant Exhibitions. He was a contemporary of Nesterov, Korovin, Stepaniv, Bakcheev and Arkhipov. He was friends with Ostroukhov and Serov.

Summing up Levitan's mature work, Chekhov (who was a friend) said, "Nobody before him achieved such astonishing simplicity and clarity of purpose… and I don't know whether anyone after him will ever achieve the same."

759. **Giovanni Fattori,** 1825-1908,
Realist, Italian, *On the Beach,* 1890.
Oil on canvas, 69 x 100 cm.
Museo Civico Giovanni Fattori, Livorno.

760. **Hans Thoma,** 1839-1924, Symbolism,
German, *Landscape,* 1890.
Oil on canvas, 113 x 88.8 cm.
Neue Pinakothek, Munich.

762. **Frederic Remington,** 1861-1909, Realism,
American, *The Rock of the Signature,* 1891.
Oil on canvas. Private collection.

763. **Frederic Remington,** 1861-1909, Realism,
American, *The Fall of the Cowboy,* 1895.
Oil on canvas, 63.5 x 89 cm.
Amon Carter Museum, Fort Worth.

761

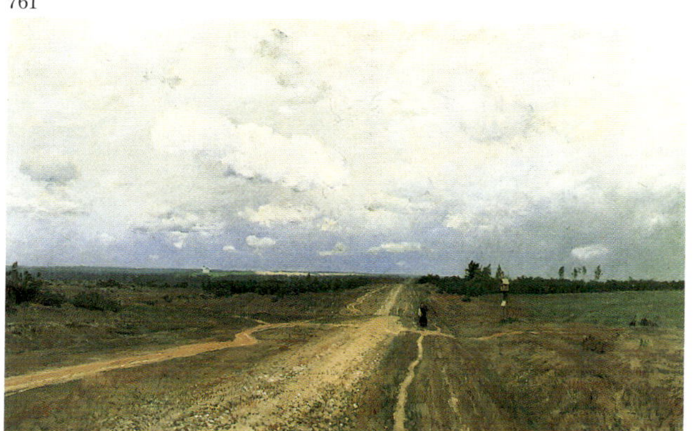

761. **Isaac Levitan,** 1860-1900, Realism, Russian,
The Vladimirka Road, 1892.
Oil on canvas, 79 x 123 cm. The State Tretyakov Gallery, Moscow.

Levitan's paintings are in effect a hymn to nature. Autumn Day: Solniki *and* Summer Evening: Fence *both express the vastness and emptiness of the Russian landscape. The Vladimirka Road is a typical Russian plain that stretches out on the canvas and disappears in the distance. The sky is heavy, grey and cloudy, like a lid that weighs on the entire tract of land crossed by a road alongside of which run paths made by many feet. If the painting is marked by a certain feeling of sadness, an impression of solemnity also emanates from this empty space. The silhouette placed in the painting accentuates even further the feeling of solitude. On the subject of the road, Levitan said (remarks later recounted by the painter Kouvchinnikova), "It's the Vladimirka road, the Vladimirka along which convoys of countless unhappy souls with chained feet formerly made their way toward the prisons of Siberia."*

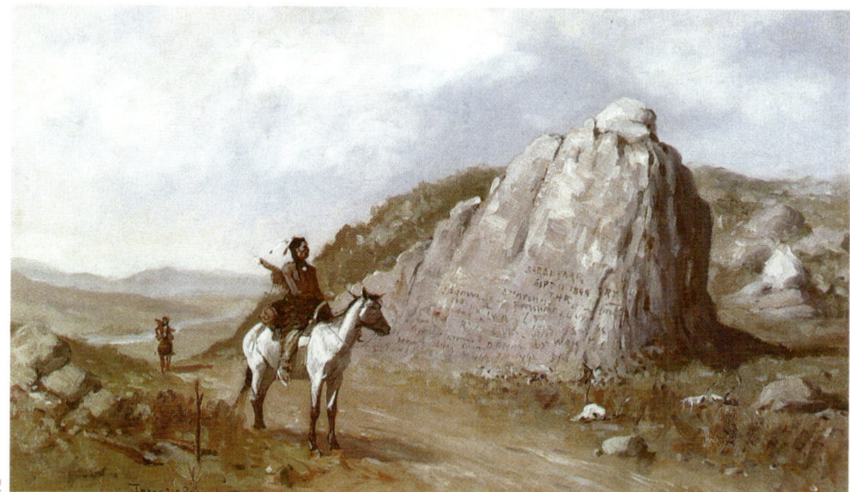

762

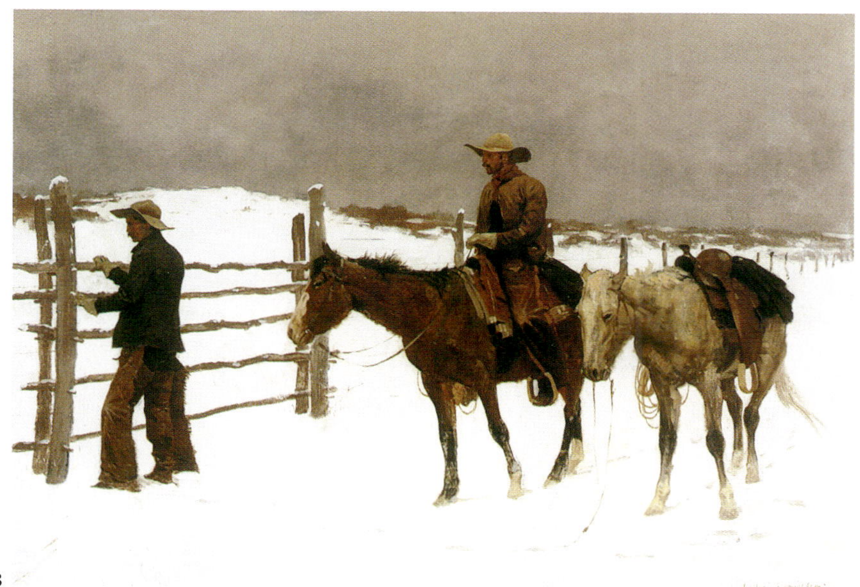

763

FREDERIC REMINGTON
(1861 CANTON – 1909 RIDGEFIELD)

It is impossible to reflect upon Frederic Remington's art without thinking of the merely human elements. Remington became interested in the American Indian, probably because he became interested in the active, exciting life of the American Great Plains. The Indian appealed to him not in any histrionic way, not as a figure stepped out from the pages of *Hiawatha*, but just as a human subject. Remington hit upon this truth when he travelled west. What he found there was majesty that he did not make, solely, an affair of Indians in war paint and feathers.

Remington knew how the light of the moon or of the stars is diffused, how softly and magically it envelops the landscape. There is a sort of artistic honesty in his nocturnal studies. He never set out to be romantic or melodramatic, just to develop his affinity and closeness to nature. The beauty of the painter's motive, too, has communicated itself in his technique. His grey-green tones fading into velvety depths take on transparency, and in his handling of form he uses a touch as firm as need be. The determining influence in his career was that of the creative impulse, urging him to deal in the translation of visible things into pictorial terms.

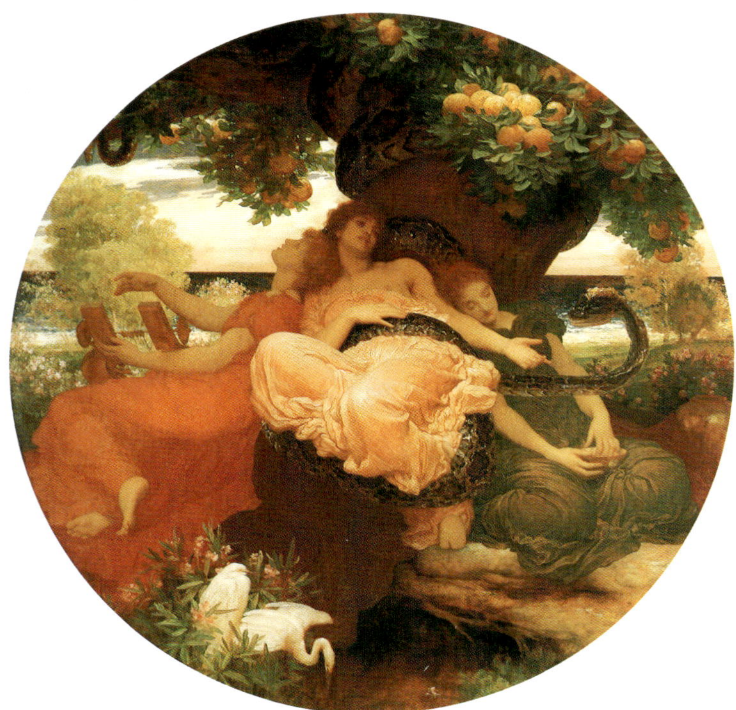

764. **Frederic Leighton,** 1830-1896, Neoclassicism, English,
Garden of the Hesperides, 1892.
Oil on panel, Tondo, diameter: 169 cm.
Lady Lever Art Gallery, Port Sunlight.

*Victorian painter Leighton illustrates the classical academic art of the
end of the nineteenth century.*

PAUL GAUGUIN
(1848 PARIS – 1903 ATUONA,
MARQUESAS ISLANDS)

Paul Gauguin was first a sailor, then a
successful stockbroker in Paris. In 1874 he
began to paint at weekends as a Sunday
painter. Nine years later, after a stock-market
crash, he felt confident of his ability to earn
a living for his family by painting and he
resigned his position and took up the
painter's brush full time. Following the lead
of Cézanne, Gauguin painted still-lifes from
the very beginning of his artistic career. He
even owned a still-life by Cézanne, which is
shown in Gauguin's painting *Portrait of
Marie Lagadu.* The year 1891 was crucial for
Gauguin. In that year he left France for Tahiti,
where he stayed till 1893. This stay in Tahiti
determined his future life and career, for in
1895, after a sojourn in France, he returned
there for good.

In Tahiti, Gauguin discovered primitive
art, with its flat forms and violent colours,
belonging to an untamed nature. With
absolute sincerity, he transferred them onto
his canvas. His paintings from then on
reflected this style: a radical simplification of
drawing; brilliant, pure, bright colours; an
ornamental type composition; and a deliberate
flatness of planes. Gauguin termed this style
"synthetic symbolism".

765

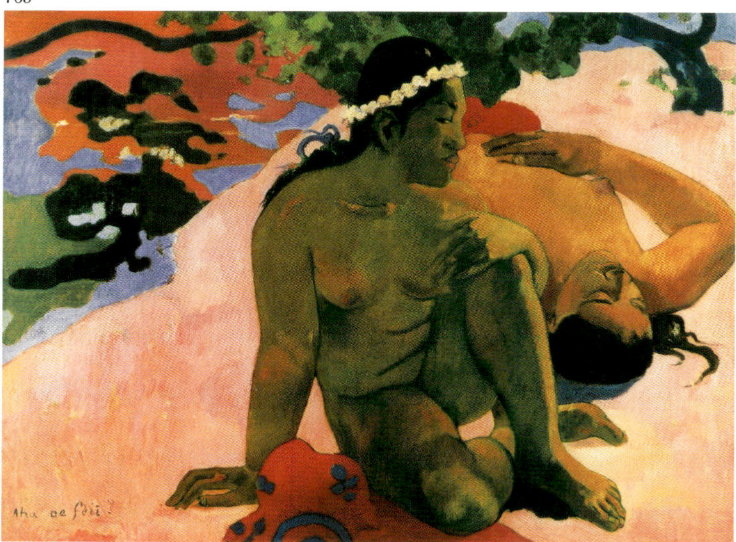

765. **Paul Gauguin,** 1848-1903, Post-impressionism,
French, *Aha Oe Feii? What! Are You Jealous?,* 1892.
Oil on canvas, 66 x 89 cm.
The Pushkin Museum of Fine Arts, Moskow.

*This picture, painted during Gauguin's first
Tahitian period, is one of the earliest examples of
his synthetic style as applied to the treatment of
Tahitian landscape and figures. The women are
depicted on a shore, but the sand and the water
are rendered schematically, being reduced to a
single screen-like surface enlivened by areas of
saturated colour.*

*Gauguin witnessed this scene in Tahiti and later
described it in Noa Noa: "On the shore, two sisters
are lying after bathing, in the graceful poses of
resting animals; they speak of yesterday's love and
tomorrow's conquests. The recollection causes
them to quarrel: What! Are you jealous?"*

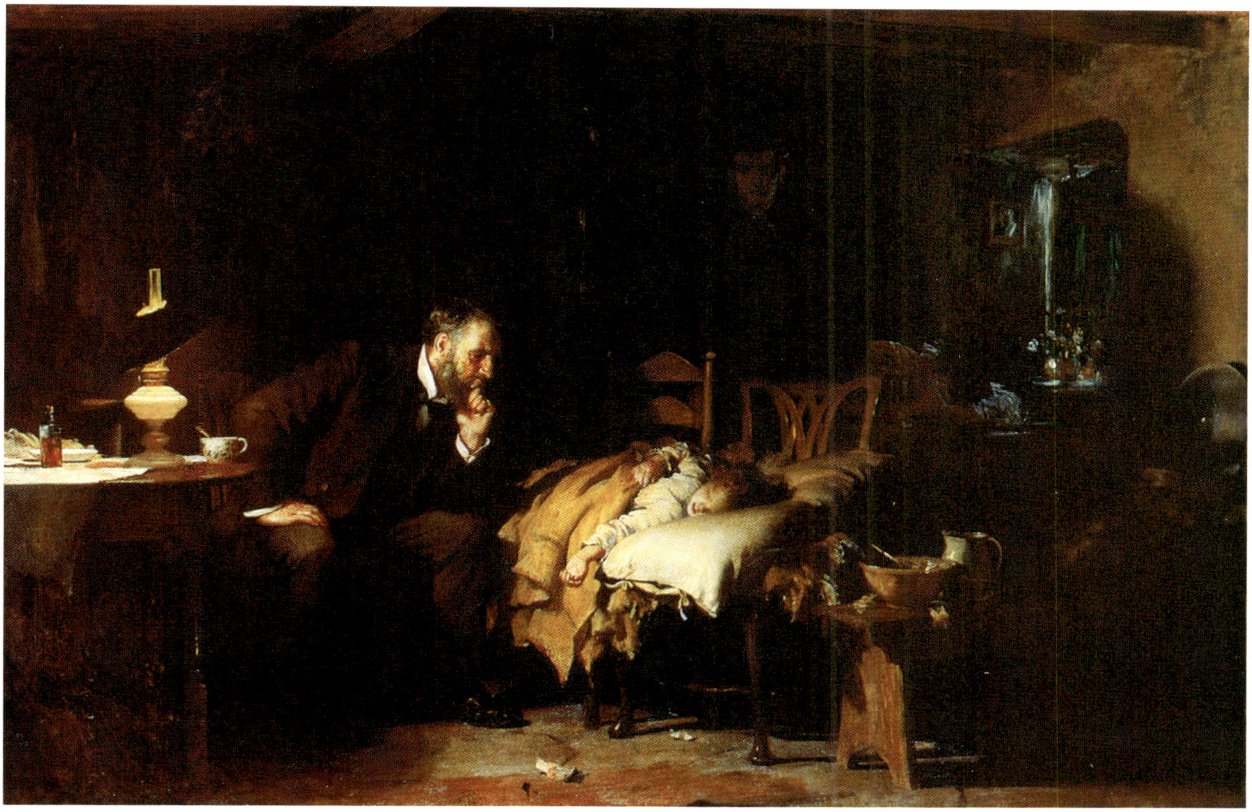

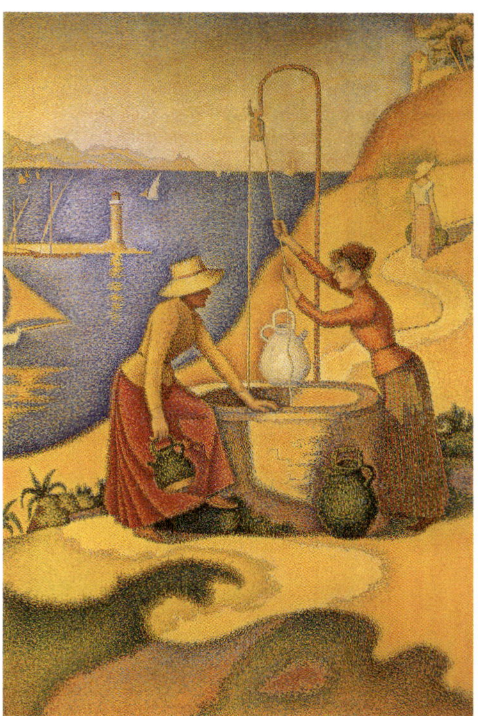

766

766. **Luke Fildes,** 1843-1927, Realism, British, *The Doctor*, 1891.
Oil on canvas, 166.4 x 242 cm.
Tate Gallery, London.

This painting was the star attraction when Sir Henry Tate, the British sugar tycoon (inventor of the sugar cube) and art collector, opened the Tate Gallery.

767. **Paul Signac,** 1863-1935,
Neo-impressionism, French,
Women at the Well, 1892.
Oil on canvas, 210 x 146 cm.
Musée d'Orsay, Paris.

768. **Nicolae Grigorescu,** 1838-1907,
Realism, Romanian,
Cheerful Young Peasant, 1894.
Oil on canvas, 134 x 65 cm.
National Museum of Romania,
Bucarest.

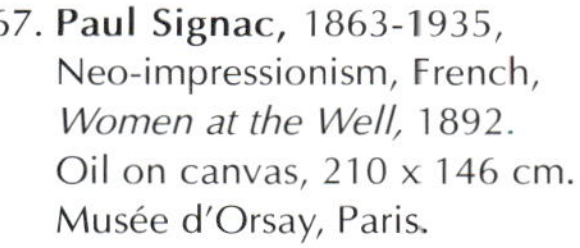

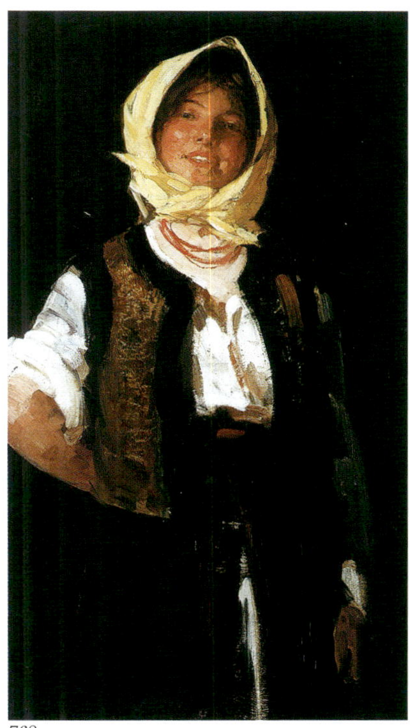

767

768

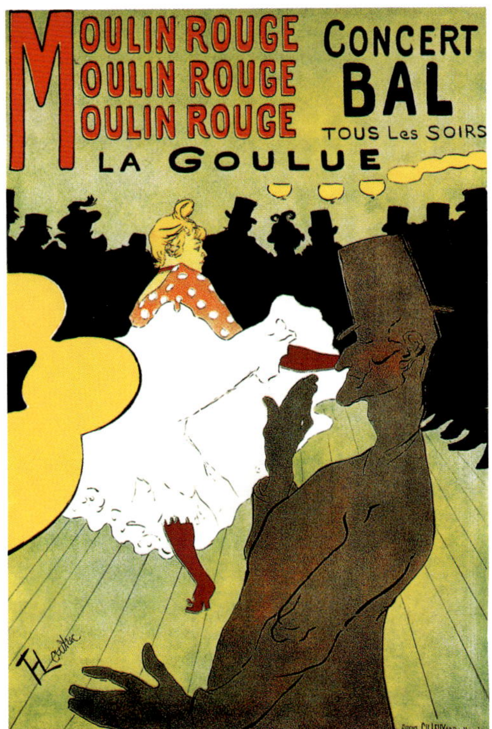

769

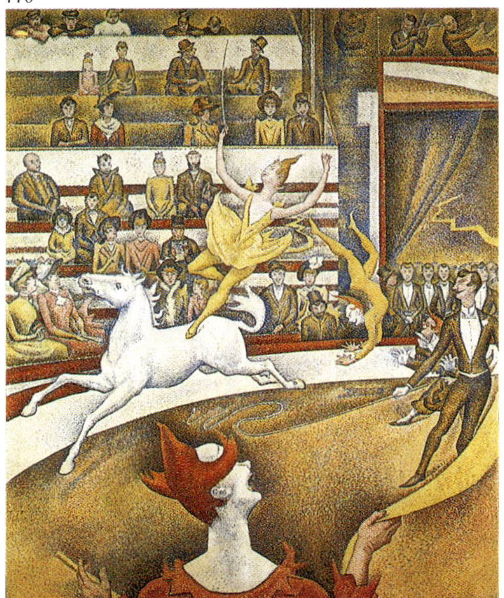

770

HENRI DE TOULOUSE–LAUTREC
(1864 ALBI – 1901 CHÂTEAU DE MALROMÉ)

Lautrec studied with two of the most admired academic painters of the day, Léon Bonnat and Fernand Cormon. Lautrec's time in the studios of Bonnat and Cormon had the advantage of introducing him to the nude as a subject. At that time life-drawing of the nude was the basis of all academic art training in nineteenth-century Paris.

While still a student, Lautrec began to explore Parisian nightlife, which was to provide him with his greatest inspiration, and eventually undermined his health.

Lautrec was an artist able to stamp his vision of the age in which he lived upon the imagination of future generations. Just as we see the English court of Charles I through the eyes of Van Dyck and the Paris of Louis-Philippe through the eyes of Daumier, so we see the Paris of the 1890s and its most colourful personalities, through the eyes of Lautrec. The first great personality of Parisian nightlife whom Lautrec encountered – and a man who was to play an important role in helping Lautrec develop his artistic vision – was the cabaret singer Aristide Bruant. Bruant stood out as an heroic figure in what was the golden age of Parisian cabaret.

Among the many other performers inspiring Lautrec in the 1890s were the dancers La Goulue and Valentin-le-Desossé (who both appear in the famous *Moulin Rouge* poster), and Jane Avril and Loïe Fuller, the singers Yvette Guilbert, May Belfort and Marcelle Lender, and the actress Réjane.

Lautrec was, along with Degas, one of the great poets of the brothel. Degas explored the theme in the late 1870s in a series of monotype prints that are among his most remarkable and personal works. He depicts the somewhat ungainly posturing of the prostitutes and their clients with human warmth and a satirical humour that brings these prints closer to the art of Lautrec than anything else by Degas.

However, the truthfulness with which Lautrec portrayed those aspects of life that most of his more respectable contemporaries preferred to sweep under the carpet naturally caused offence. The German critic Gensel probably spoke for many when he wrote: "There can of course be no talk of admiration for someone who is the master of the representation of all that is base and perverse. The only explanation as to how such filth – there can be no milder term for it – as *Elles* can be publicly exhibited without an outcry of indignations being heard is that one half of the general public does not understand the meaning of this cycle at all, and the other is ashamed of admitting that it does understand it."

771

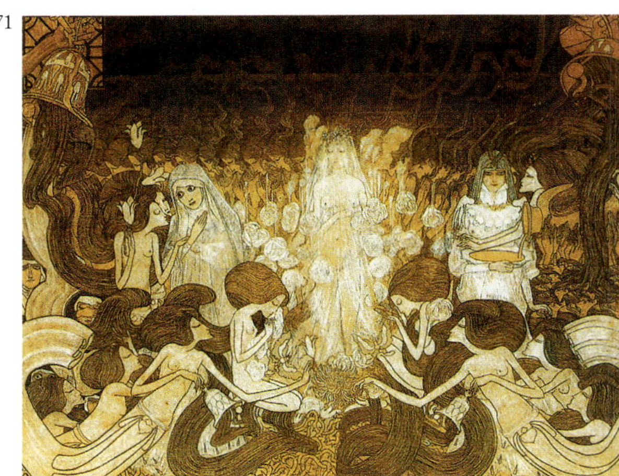

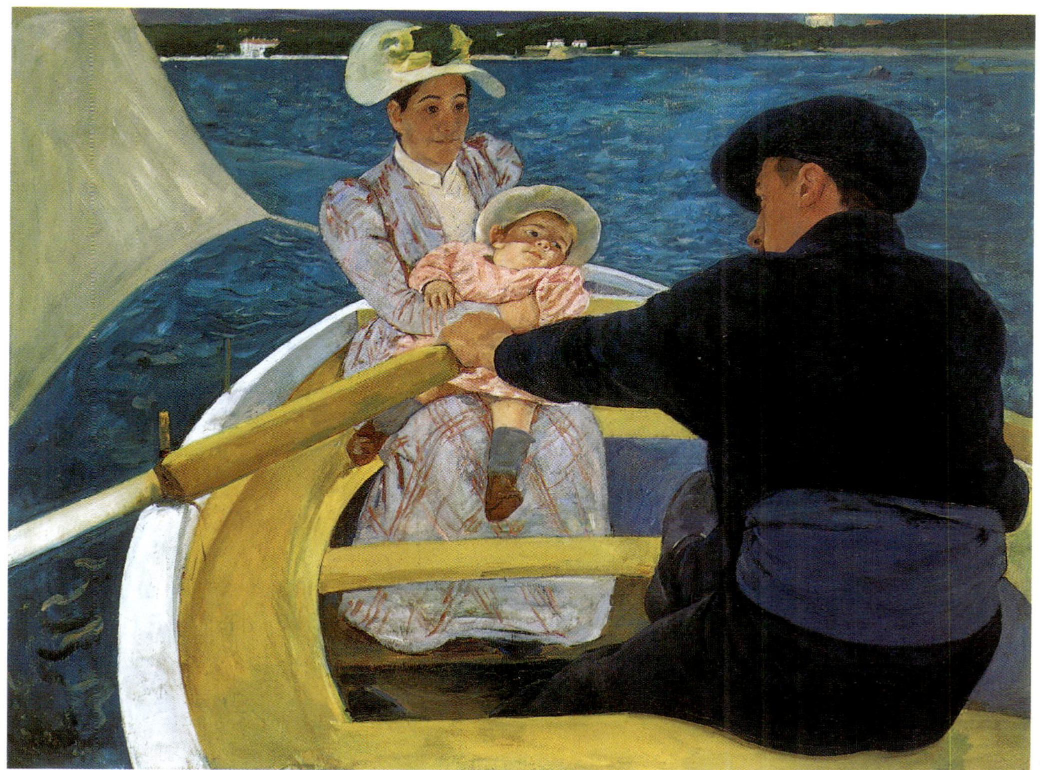

772

772. **Mary Cassatt,** 1844-1926, Impressionism,
American, *The Boating Party*, 1893-1894.
Oil on canvas, 90 x 117.3 cm.
The National Gallery of Art, Washington D.C.

769. **Henri de Toulouse-Lautrec,** 1864-1901,
Post-impressionism, French,
La Goulue, Dance at the Moulin Rouge, 1891.
Colour Lithograph, 191 x 117 cm. Private collection.

770. **Georges Seurat,** 1859-1891, Neo-impressionism,
French, *The Circus,* 1891.
Oil on canvas, 185.5 x 152.5 cm.
Musée d'Orsay, Paris.

*Even though this work remains unfinished, it stands as
one of the greatest examples of the divisionist touch
of the artist. Seurat also depicted the frame of the
painting in the same technique.*

771. **Jan Toorop,** 1858-1928, Symbolism, Dutch,
The Three Brides, 1893.
Oil on canvas, 78 x 97.8 cm.
Rijksmuseum Kröller-Müller, Otterlo.

*Leading artist of the Symbolist movement, Toorop
developed a style with curvilinear figures that
prefigured the Art Nouveau.*

MARY STEVENSON CASSATT
(1844 PITTSBURGH – 1926 CHÂTEAU DE BEAUFRESNE)

Mary was born in Pittsburgh. Her father was a banker of liberal
educational ideas and the entire family appears to have been sympathetic
to French culture. Mary was no more than five or six years old when she
first saw Paris, and she was still in her teens when she decided to become
a painter. She went to Italy, on to Antwerp, then to Rome, and finally
returned to Paris where in 1874, she permanently settled.

In 1872, Cassatt sent her first work to the Salon, others followed in
the succeeding years until 1875, when a portrait of her sister was
rejected. She divined that the jury had not been satisfied with the
background, so she re-painted it several times until, in the next Salon,
the same portrait was accepted. At this moment Degas asked her to
exhibit with him and his friends, the Impressionist Group, then rising
into view, and she accepted with joy. She admired Manet, Courbet and
Degas, and hated conventional art.

Cassatt's biographer stressed the intellectuality and sentiment
apparent in her work, as well as the emotion and distinction with which
she has painted her favourite models: babies and their mothers. He then
speaks of her predominant interest in draughtsmanship and her gift for
linear pattern, a gift greatly strengthened by her study of Japanese art
and her emulation of its style in the colour prints she made. While her
style may partake of the style of others, her draughtsmanship, her
composition, her light, and her colour are, indeed, her own. There are
qualities of tenderness in her work which could have been put there,
perhaps, only by a woman. The qualities which make her work of
lasting value are those put there by an outstanding painter.

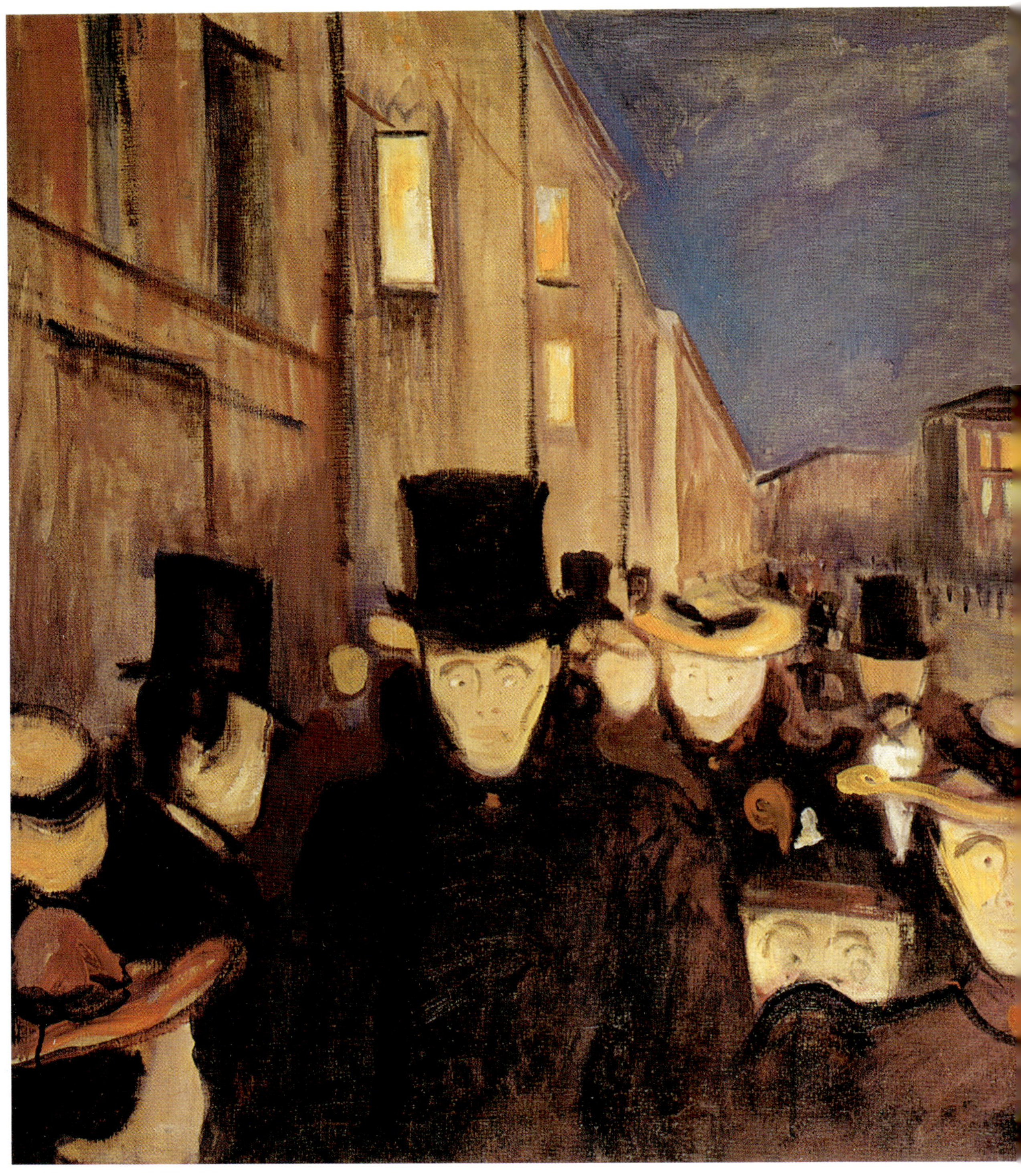

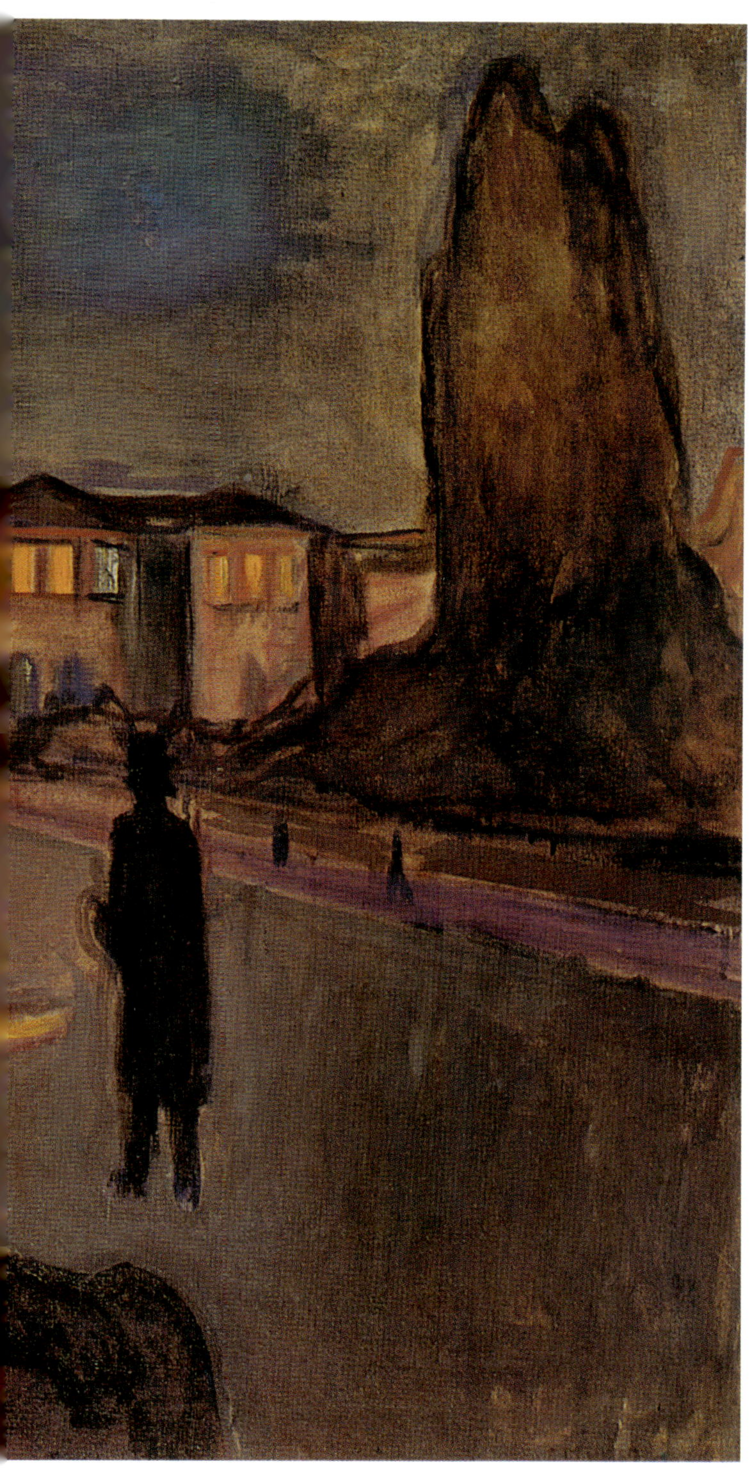

EDVARD MUNCH
(1863 LØTEN – 1944 EKELY, OSLO)

Edvard Munch, born in 1863, was Norway's most popular artist. His brooding and anguished paintings, based on personal grief and obsessions, were instrumental in the development of Expressionism. During his childhood, the death of his parents, his brother and sister, and the mental illness of another sister, were of great influence on his convulsed and tortuous art. In his works, Munch turned again and again to the memory of illness, death and grief.

During his career, Munch changed his idiom many times. At first, influenced by Impressionism and Post-impressionism, he turned to a highly personal style and content, increasingly concerned with images of illness and death. In the 1892s, his style developed a 'Synthetist' idiom as seen in *The Scream* (fig. 778) which is regarded as an icon and the portrayal of modern humanity's spiritual and existential anguish. He painted different versions of it. During the 1890s Munch favoured a shallow pictorial space, and used it in his frequently frontal pictures. His work often included the symbolic portrayal of such themes as misery, sickness, and death. and the poses of his figures in many of his portraits were chosen in order to capture their state of mind and psychological condition. It also lends a monumental, static quality to the paintings. In 1892, the Union of Berlin Artists invited Munch to exhibit at its November exhibition. His paintings invoked bitter controversy at the show, and after one week the exhibition closed. In the 1930s and 1940s, the Nazis labelled his work "degenerate art", and removed his works from German museums. This deeply hurt the anti-fascist Munch, who had come to feel Germany was his second homeland. In 1908 Munch's anxiety became acute and he was hospitalised. He returned to Norway in 1909 and died in Ekely, near Oslo in 1944.

773. **Edvard Munch**, 1863-1944,
Symbolism/Expressionism, Norwegian,
Spring Evening on Karl Johan Street, 1892.
Oil on canvas, 84.5 x 121 cm.
Private collection, Bergen.

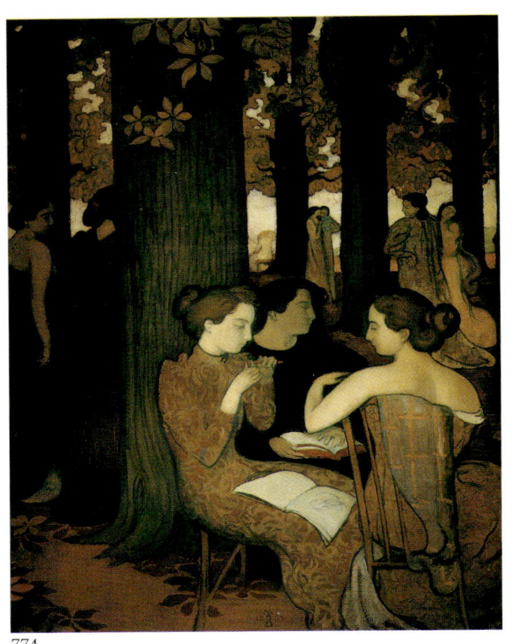

774

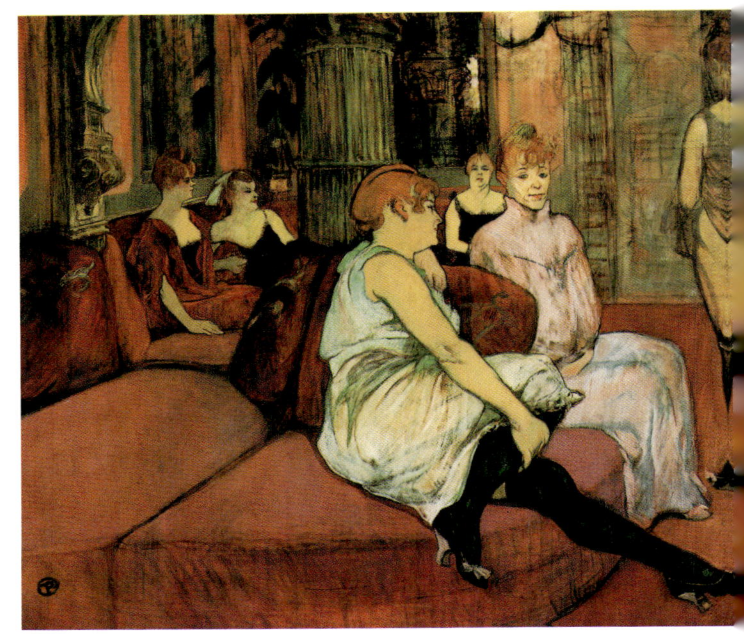

775

776

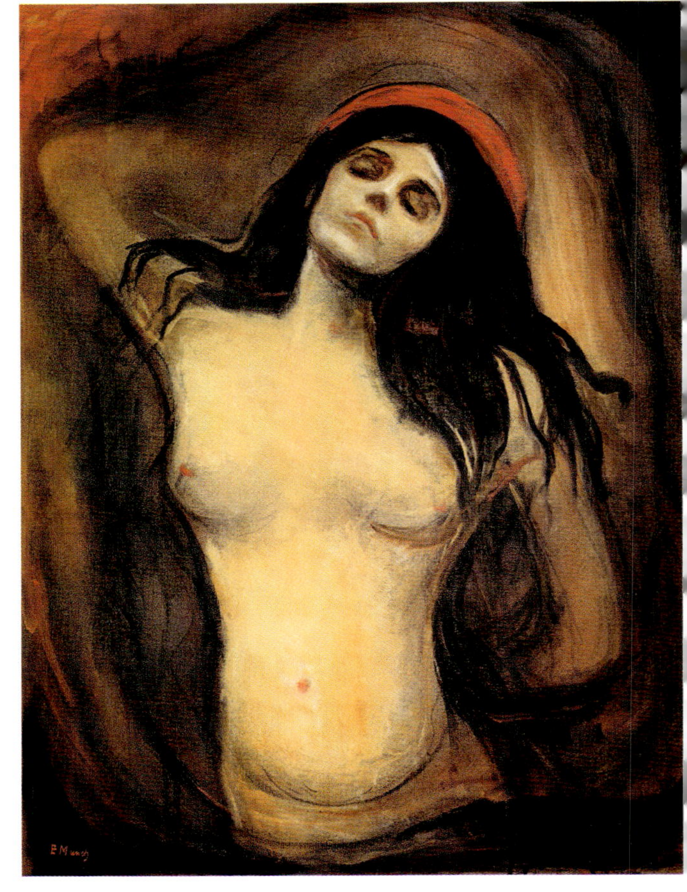

777

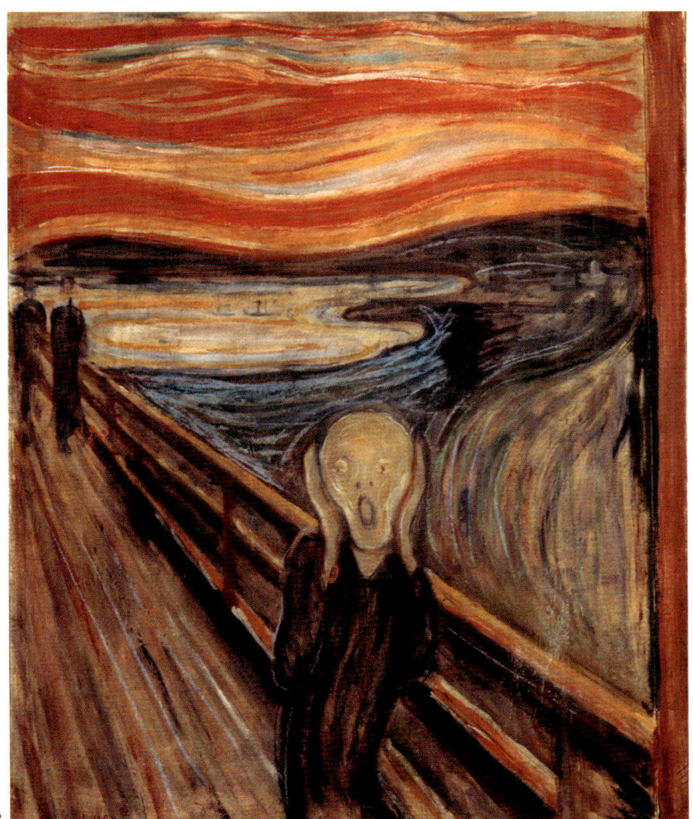

778

774. Maurice Denis, 1870-1943, Nabis/Symbolism, French,
The Muses, 1893.
Oil on canvas, 171.5 x 137.5 cm. Musée d'Orsay, Paris.

Member of the Nabis, Maurice Denis published his first definition of Neo-traditionalism in 1890: "Remember that a picture – before being a war horse or a nude woman or an anecdote – is essentially a flat surface covered with colours assembled in a certain order."
Paul Sérusier and a group of young painters launched the Nabis movement in 1888. Under the influence of Gauguin, the painters only kept the essential subject through a symbol, replacing the representation of reality by the interpretation of an idea. Maurice Denis, the group's theorist, developed a technique exalting pure colour, and simplifying the outline in order to bring out the subject's features. This was a reaction against the allegiance of Impressionism and its depiction of nature.

775. Henri de Toulouse-Lautrec, 1864-1901, Post-Impressionism, French, *At the Salon Rue des Moulins,* 1894.
Black chalk and oil on canvas, 115.5 x 132.5 cm.
Musée Toulouse-Lautrec, Albi.

In Toulouse-Lautrec's ambitious and monumental painting of a brothel At the Salon in the Rue des Moulins of 1894, the atmosphere is solemn and joyless. The colloquial term 'filles de joie' seems singularly inappropriate. The prostitutes loll in attitudes of boredom on plushly upholstered divans under the watchful eye of the severe-looking madame. On the right, we glimpse the half-seen figure of a prostitute lifting her skirts to display what she has to sell to prospective clients.

776. Franz von Stuck, 1863-1928, Symbolism/Expressionism, German, *The Sin,* 1893.
Oil on canvas, 94.5 x 59.5 cm. Neue Pinakothek, Munich.

777. Edvard Munch, 1863-1944, Symbolism/Expressionism, Norwegian, *Madonna,* 1894.
Oil on canvas, 90 x 68.5 cm. Nasjonalmuseet, Oslo.

778. Edvard Munch, 1863-1944, Symbolism/Expressionism, Norwegian, *The Scream,* 1910.
Tempera on board, 83.5 x 66 cm.
Nasjonalmuseet, Oslo (another version of this painting was stolen from the Munch-Museet, Oslo, on the 22nd August 2004).

The name of Edvard Munch conjures up, for most people, one irresistibly memorable picture: The Scream, a shriek of stomach-churning terror uttered by a cringing figure with a skull-like face outlined against a fiery, blood-red sunset. This iconic image has come to epitomise the angst embodied in the Expressionism of the late nineteenth century. Yet its creator, a gentle soul given to introspection and self-analysis, lived to see his eightieth birthday and witnessed the world-wide critical acceptance of the Expressionist movement which he had been largely instrumental in initiating.

417

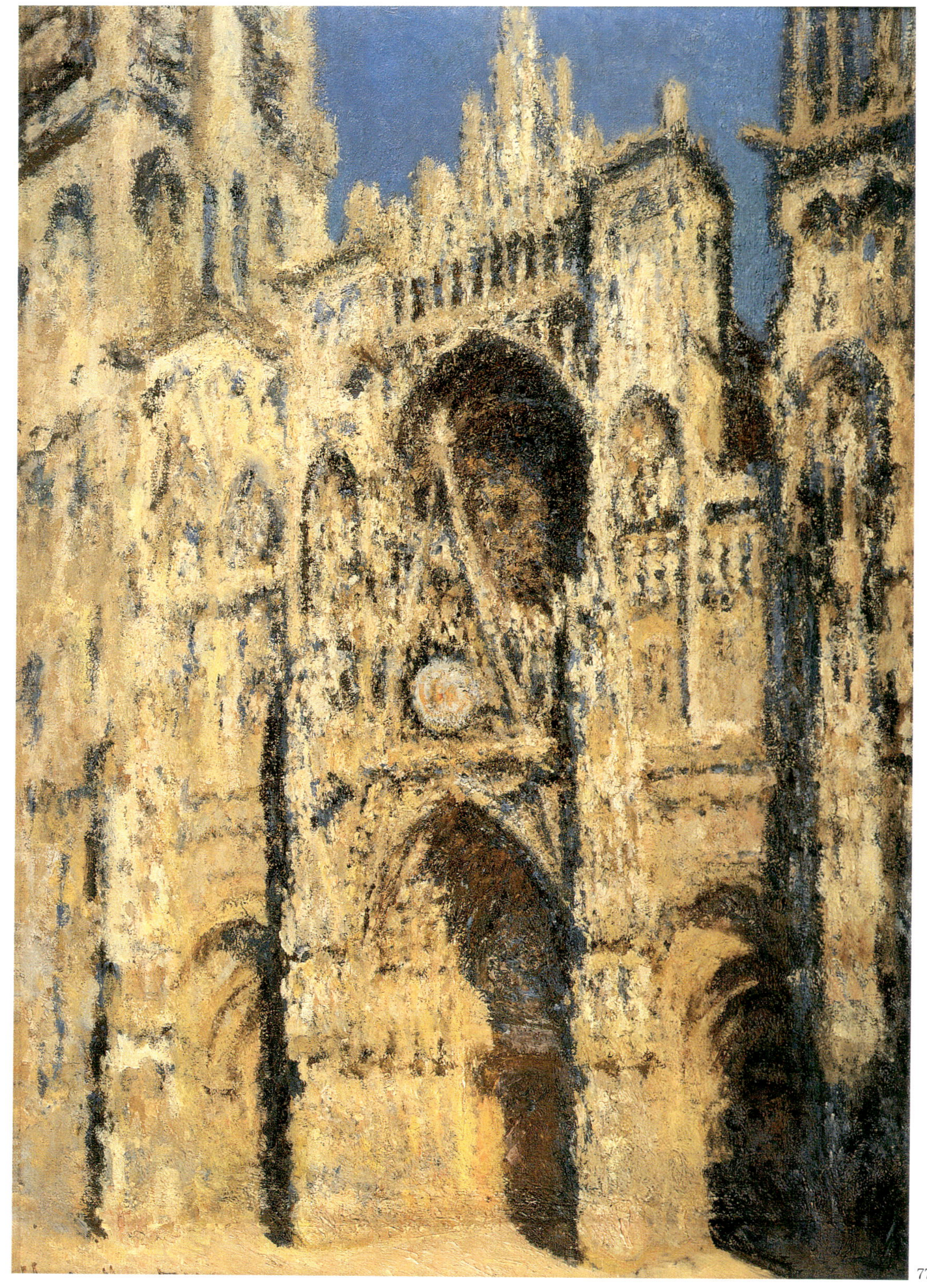

779

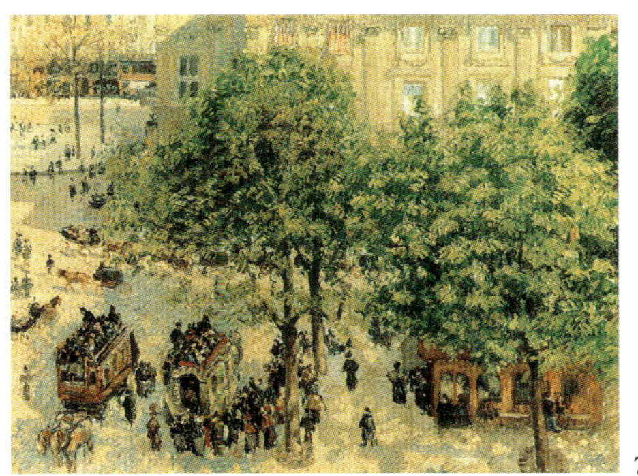

780

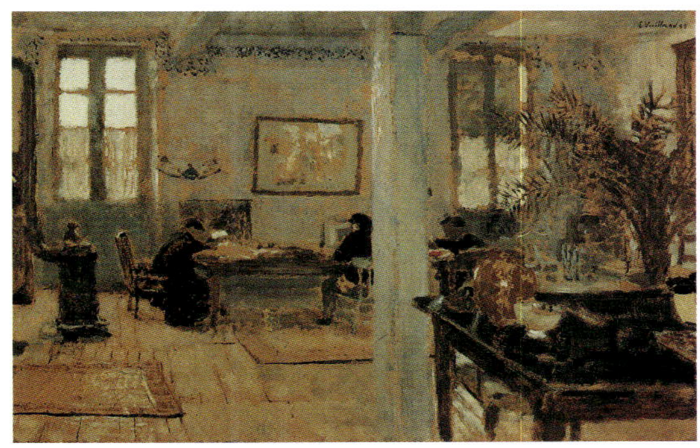

781

780. **Camille Pissarro,** 1830-1903, Impressionism, French,
Place du théâtre français in Paris, 1898.
Oil on canvas, 65.5 x 81.5 cm.
The State Hermitage Museum, St Petersburg.

781. **Edouard Vuillard**, 1868-1940, Nabis, French,
In a Room, 1899.
Oil on cardboard, 52 x 79 cm.
The State Hermitage Museum, St Petersburg.

779. **Claude Monet,** 1840-1926, Impressionism, French,
*Rouen Cathedral, Portal of Saint-Romain's
Tower (Full Sun),* 1894.
Oil on canvas, 107 x 73 cm. Musée d'Orsay, Paris.

Monet liked to use one and the same motif repeatedly. Thus between 1892 and 1895 he produced the famous series of twenty paintings devoted to Rouen Cathedral. The most remarkable work in that series dates from 1894. Monet arrived at Rouen in February 1892 and boarded in a house opposite Rouen Cathedral. From this viewpoint, at close range, the main paintings in the Cathedral series were executed. The view from the window determined the design of all the pictures in the series; the facade of the cathedral occupies almost the entire canvas, the soaring towers cut off by the top edge of the picture.

In his desire to capture all the wealth and variety of lighting effects on the cathedral's surface the artist passed quickly from one canvas to another as the lighting changed with the movement of the sun. The Cathedral series can be regarded as the culmination of the impressionist method in Monet's work. The entire set was first displayed in the year of its completion, 1895; later it was often exhibited both in France and abroad. At present the canvases making up the Rouen Cathedral series are in different museums of the world, the Musée d'Orsay in Paris boasting five of them.

EDOUARD VUILLARD
(1868 CUISEAUX – 1940 LA BAULE)

As a ten-year-old at the Lycée Condorcet, Vuillard made friends with Roussel, who persuaded the young Edouard to enter the *Ecole des Beaux-Arts*. At home and in the small dressmaker's studio which Vuillard's mother ran after her husband's death, the future artist was surrounded from an early age by the unusual patterns and combinations of colours presented by jumbled off-cuts of fabric. Moreover, Vuillard's father, mother, and brother were all fabric designers. Like all in the Nabis group, Vuillard was very well-read. He was fond of Baudelaire, Giraudoux and Valéty, and adored Mallarmé. The Nabis' desire to paint "icons" took an unexpected turn in Vuillard's small paintings of 1890-1891. They were put together from a few small areas of colour that are completely flat and very bright. Their boldness anticipates Fauvism. Immediately afterwards Vuillard returned to calmer colours and abandoned absolute flatness without, however, resorting to the modelling devices used by the Old Masters. His painting became an ornamental pattern with a very complex rhythm. Impressions of Japanese woodcuts or old French *mille-fleurs* suggest themselves as possible inspirations. But the most probable source of Vuillard's inspiration was contemporary cheap fabrics.

Vuillard endows the painting with an inner significance. The artist did not have to resort to an unusual or exotic theme to achieve a rich decorative effect. His subject-matter was always at hand: mainly the lives of his nearest and dearest. By the end of his life, Vuillard's paintings became somehow drier, more "natural", and quite often fell into repetition, especially in his society portraits.

782

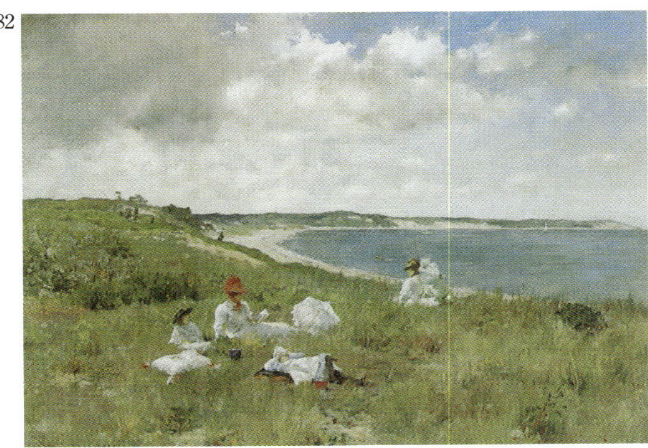

782. **William Merritt Chase,** 1849-1916, Impressionism,
American, *Leisure,* 1894.
Oil on canvas, 64.8 x 90.2 cm.
Amon Carter Museum, Fort Worth.

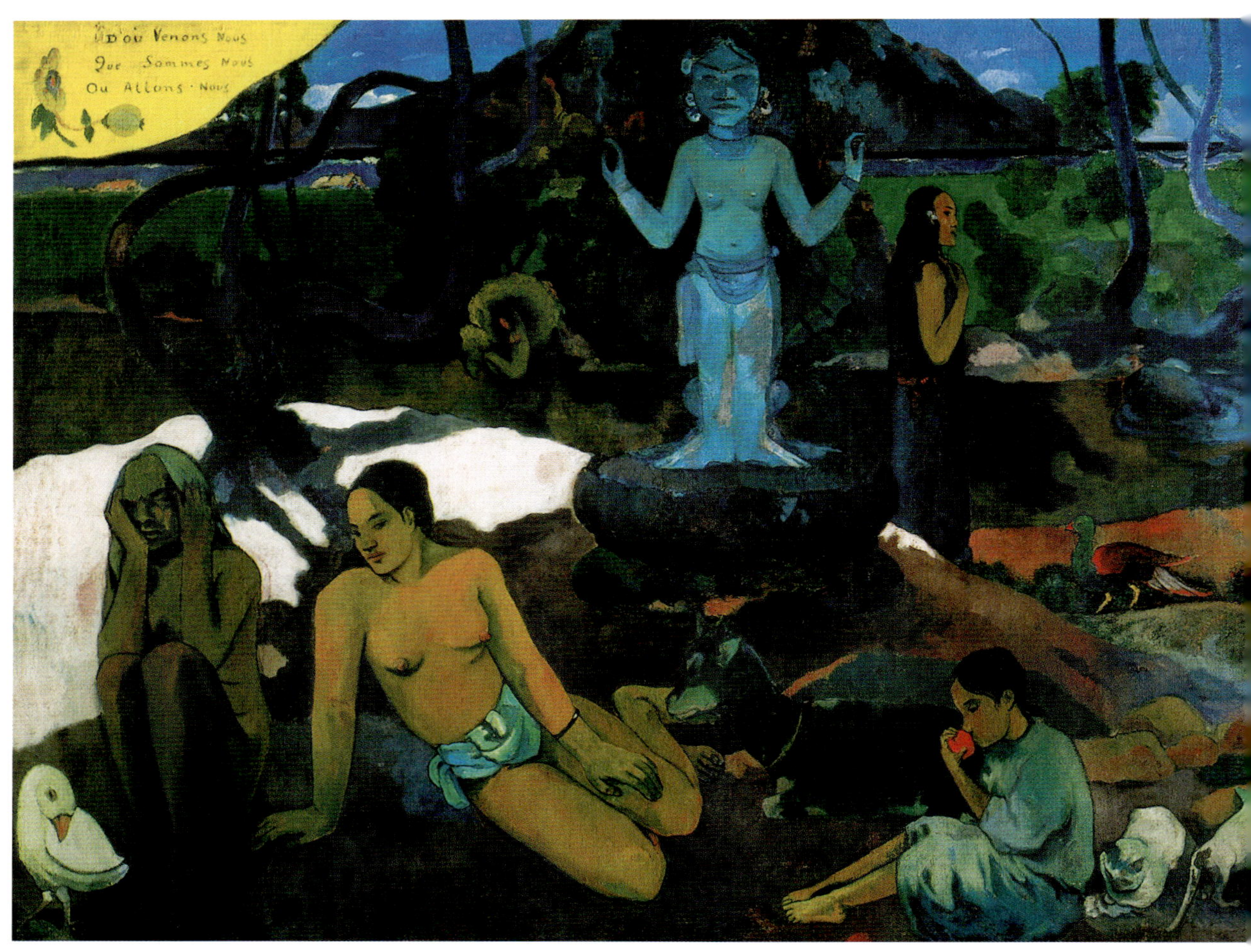

783. **Paul Gauguin,** 1848-1903, Post-impressionism, French, *Where Do We Come From? Who Are We? Where Are We Going?*, 1897. Oil on canvas, 139.1 x 374.6 cm. Museum of Fine Arts, Boston.

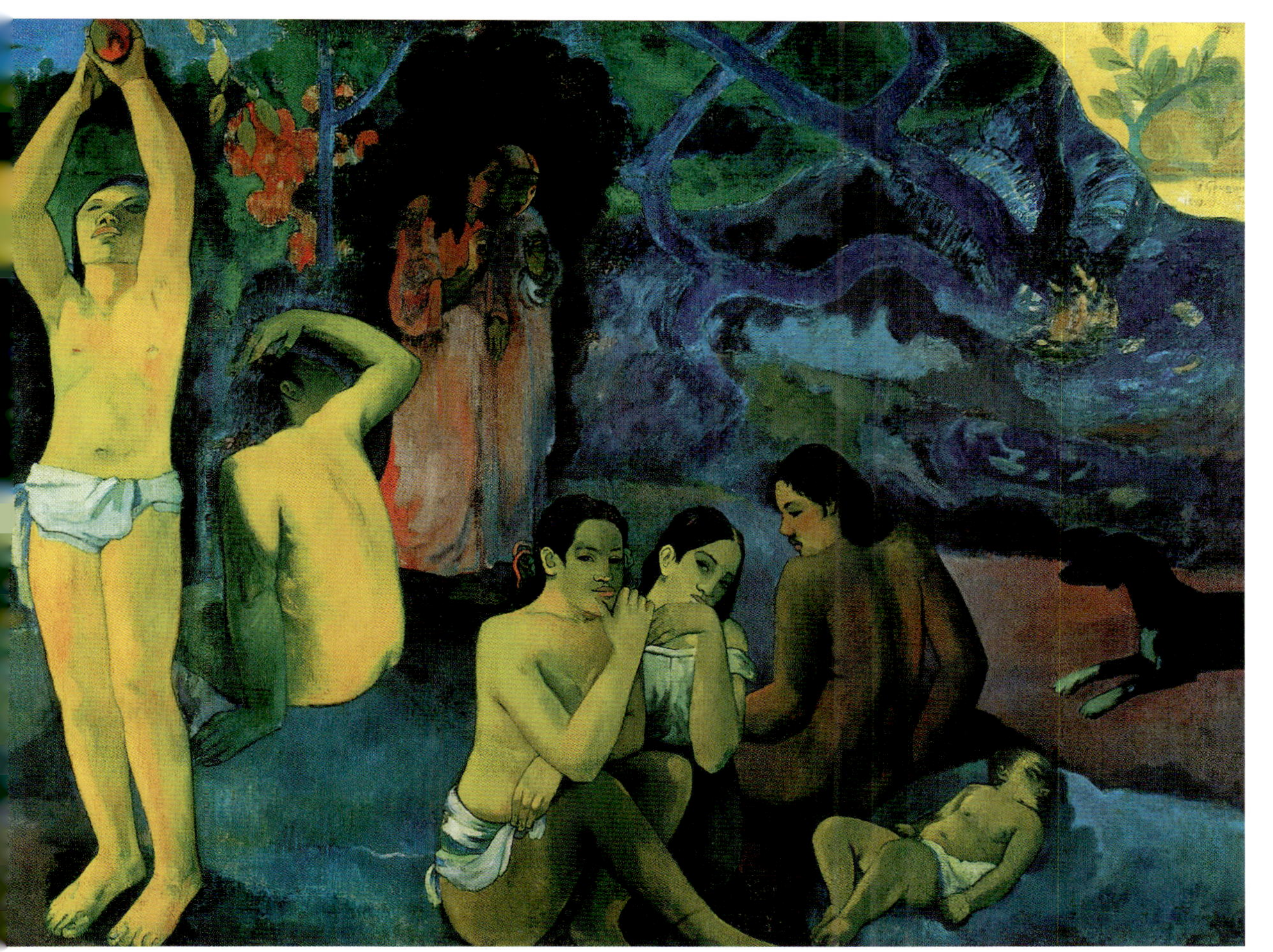

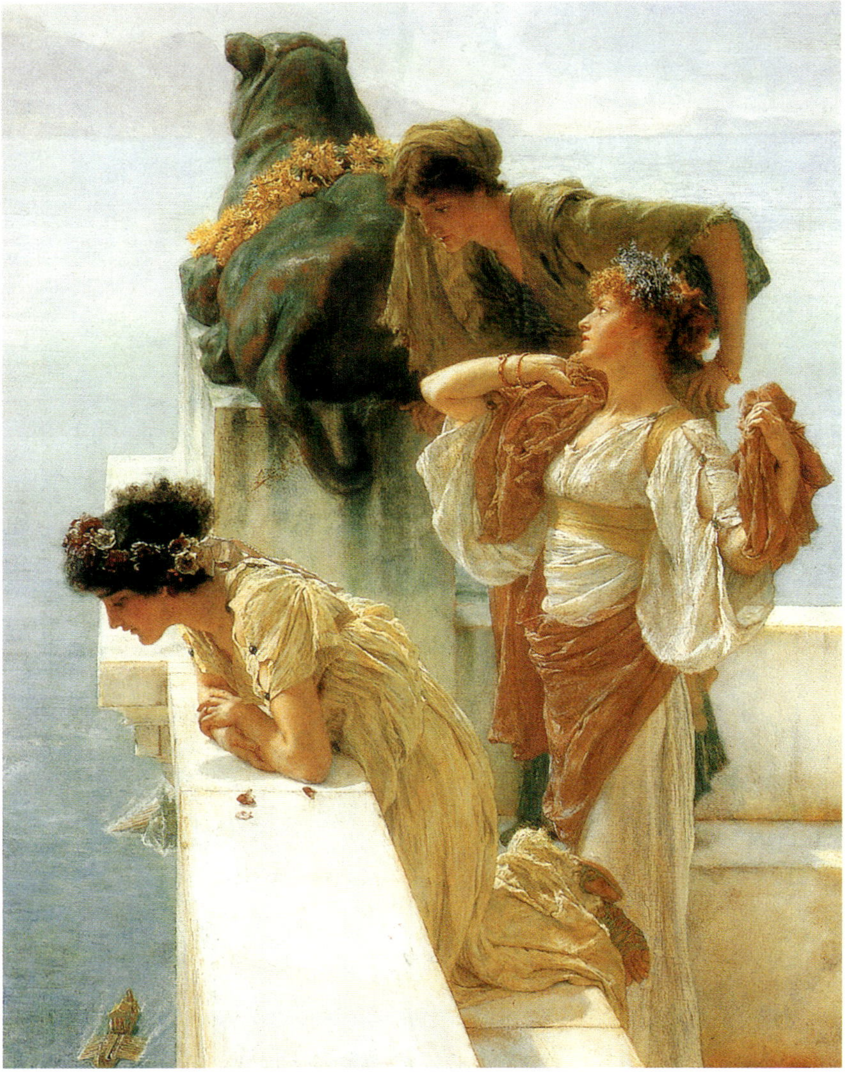

784. Lawrence Alma-Tadema,
1836-1912, Neoclassicism, English,
A Coign of Vantage, 1895.
Oil on canvas, 64.2 x 45 cm.
Private collection.

785. Fernand Khnopff, 1858-1921,
Symbolism, Belgian,
The Caresses, 1896.
Oil on canvas, 50 x 151 cm.
Musées Royaux des Beaux Arts,
Brussels.

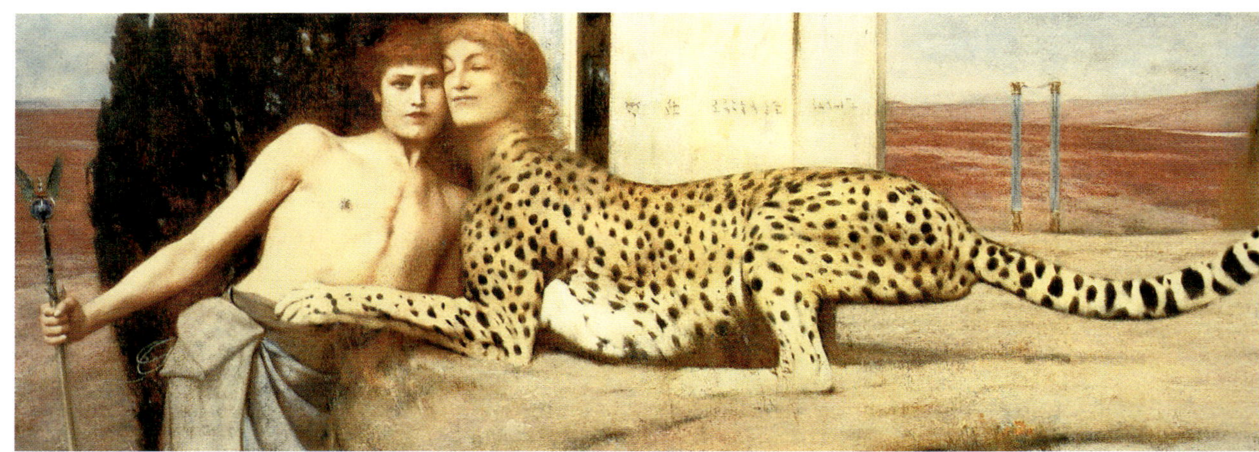

GUSTAV KLIMT
(1862 BAUMGARTEN – 1918 VIENNA)

"I am not interested in myself as a subject for painting, but in others, particularly women…"

Beautiful, sensuous and above all erotic, Gustav Klimt's paintings speak of a world of opulence and leisure, which seems aeons away from the harsh, post-modern environment we live in now. The subjects he treats – allegories, portraits, landscapes and erotic figures – contain virtually no reference to external events, but strive rather to create a world where beauty, above everything else, is dominant. His use of colour and pattern was profoundly influenced by the art of Japan, ancient Egypt, and Byzantium.

Ravenne, the flat, two-dimensional perspective of his paintings, and the frequently stylised quality of his images form an oeuvre imbued with a profound sensuality and one where the figure of woman, above all, reigns supreme.

Klimt's very first works brought him success at an unusually young age. Gustav, born in 1862, obtained a state grant to study at *Kunstgewerbeschule* (the Vienna School of Arts and Crafts) at the age of fourteen. His talents as a draughtsman and painter were quickly noticed, and in 1879 he formed the *Künstlercompagnie* (Artists' Company) with his brother Ernst and another student, Franz Matsch.

The latter part of the nineteenth century was a period of great architectural activity in Vienna. In 1857, the Emperor Franz Joseph had ordered the destruction of the fortifications that had surrounded the medieval city centre. The Ringstrasse was the result, a budding new district with magnificent buildings and beautiful parks, all paid for by public expenses. Therefore the young Klimt and his partners had ample opportunities to show off their talents, and they received early commissions to contribute to the decorations for the pageant organised to celebrate the silver wedding anniversary of the Emperor Franz Joseph and the Empress Elisabeth.

In 1894, Matsch moved out of their communal studio, and in 1897 Klimt, together with his closest friends, resigned from the *Künstlerhausgenossenschaft* (the Cooperative Society of Austrian Artists) to form a new movement known as the Secession, of which he was immediately elected president. The Secession was a great success, holding both a first and second exhibition in 1898. The movement made enough money to commission its very own building, designed for it by the architect Joseph Maria Olbrich. Above the entrance was its motto: "To each age its art, to art its freedom."

From around 1897 onward, Klimt spent almost every summer on the Attersee with the Flöge family. These were periods of peace and tranquillity in which he produced the landscape paintings constituting almost a quarter of his entire oeuvre. Klimt made sketches for virtually everything he did. Sometimes there were over a hundred drawings for one painting, each showing a different detail – a piece of clothing or jewellery, or a simple gesture.

Just how exceptional Gustav Klimt was is perhaps reflected in the fact that he had no predecessors and no real followers. He admired Rodin and Whistler without slavishly copying them, and was admired in turn by the younger Viennese painters Egon Schiele and Oskar Kokoschka, both of whom were greatly influenced by Klimt.

786. **Gustav Klimt**, 1862-1918, Art Nouveau, Austrian,
Nuda Veritas, 1399.
Oil on canvas, 252 x 55 cm.
Österreichische Nationalbibliothek, Vienna.

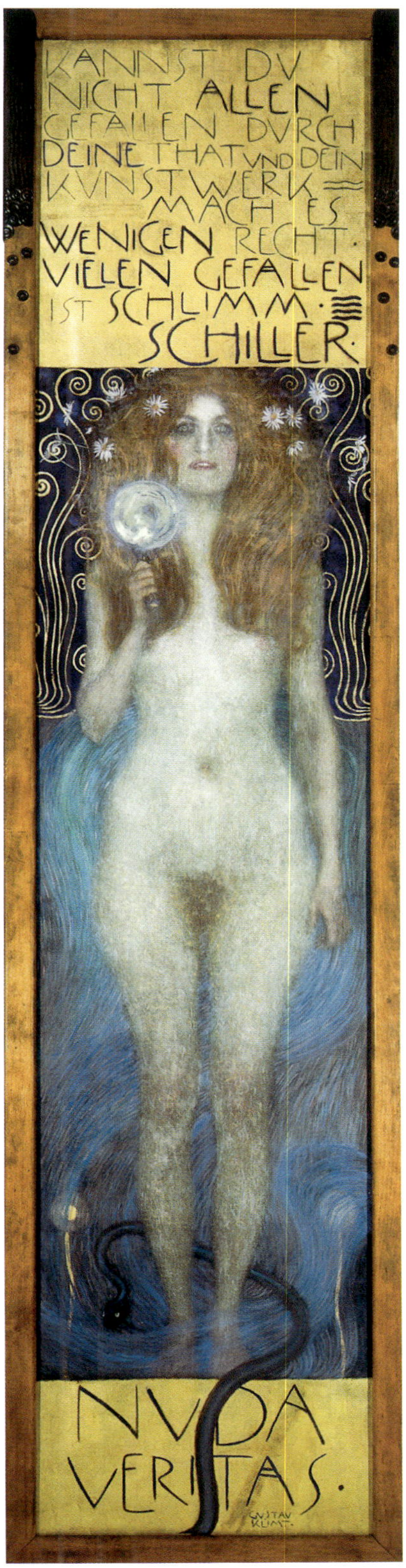

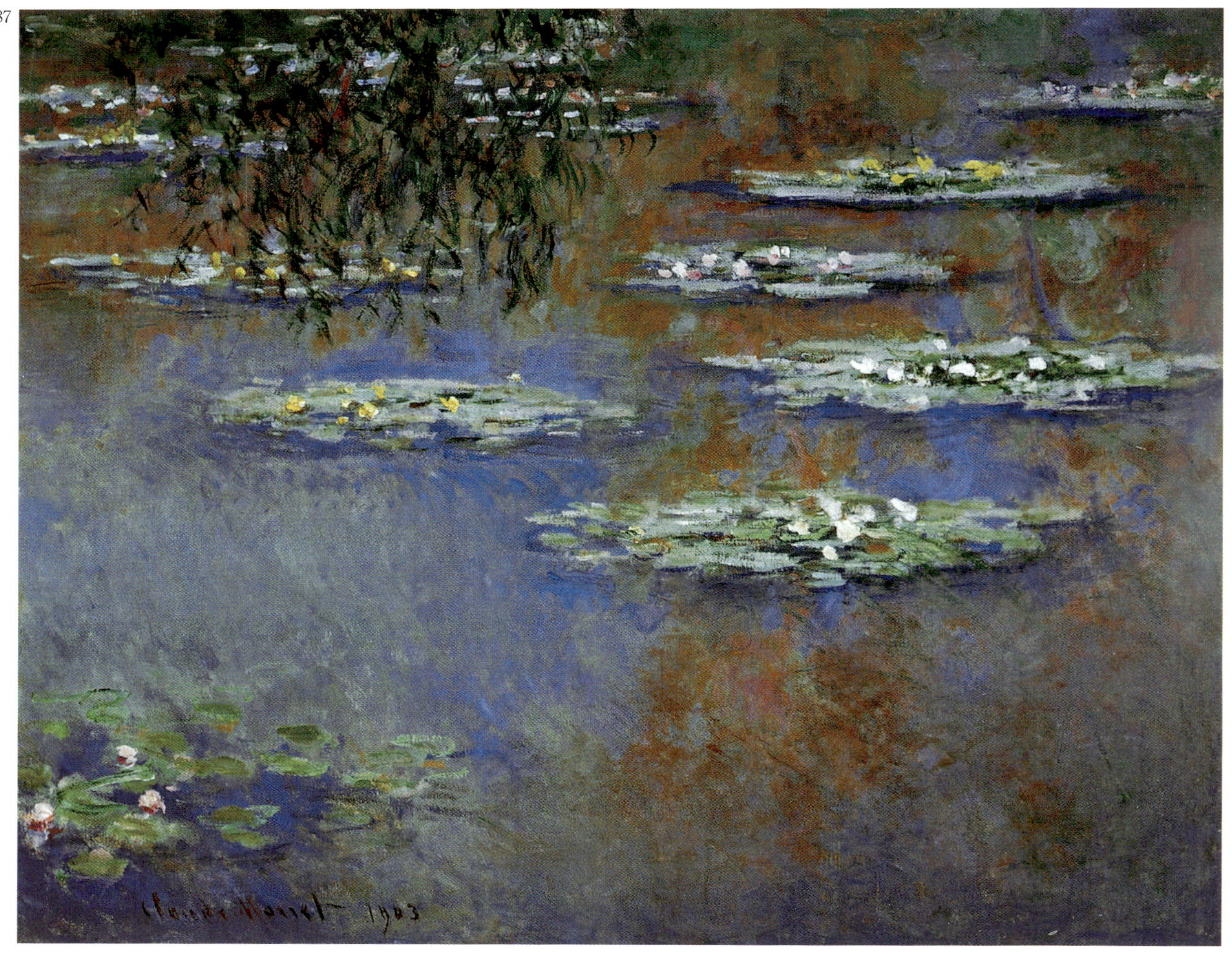

787. **Claude Monet,** 1840-1926, Impressionism, French,
Waterlilies, 1903.
Oil on canvas, 81.5 x 101.5 cm.
Art Institute, Dayton.

788. **Gustav Klimt**, 1862-1918, Art Nouveau, Austrian,
Portrait of Emilie Flöge, 1902.
Oil on canvas, 181 x 84 cm.
Historisches Museum, Vienna.

789. **Paula Modersohn-Becker**, 1876-1907, Expressionism, German,
Trumpeting Girl in a Birch Wood, 1903.
Oil on canvas. Paula Modersohn-Becker Museum, Bremen.

790. **Théo van Rysselberghe**, 1862-1926, Neo-Impressionism,
Belgian, *The Woman in White*, 1904.
Oil on canvas.
Musée d'Art Moderne et d'Art Contemporain, Liège.

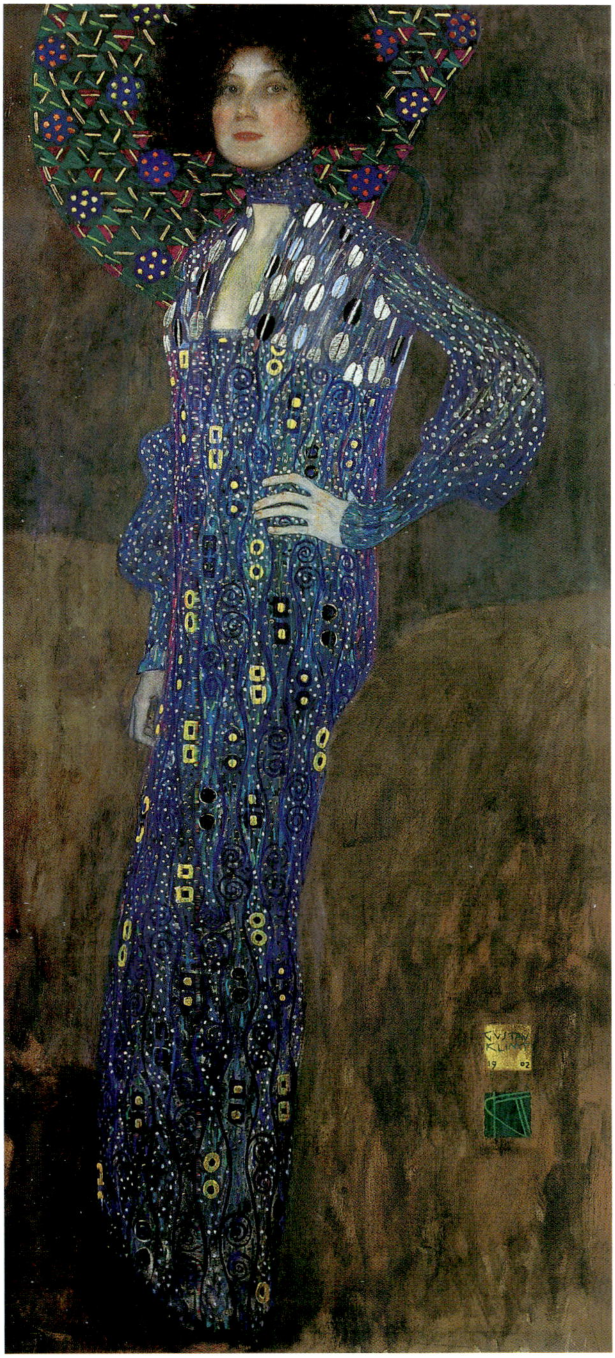

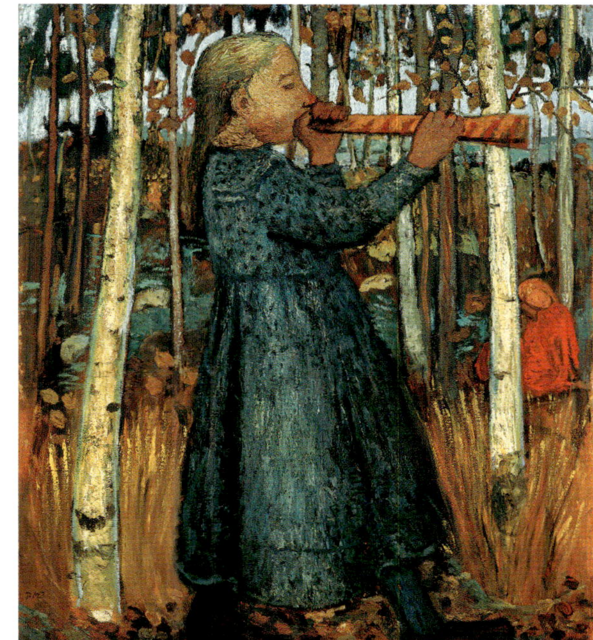

789

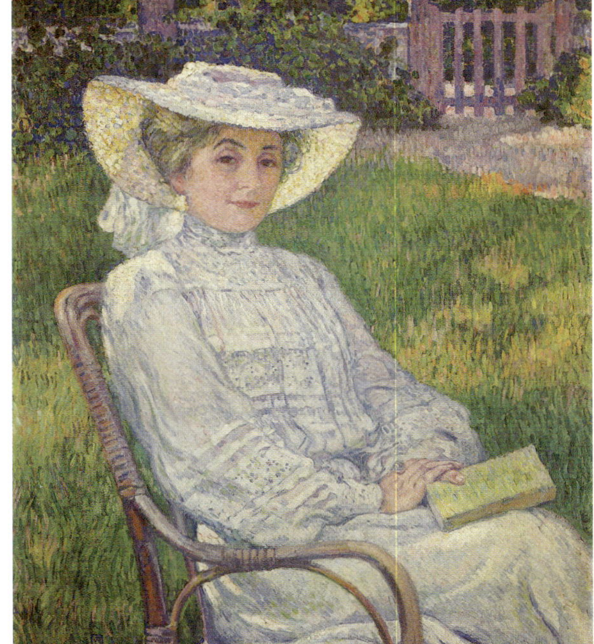

788

790

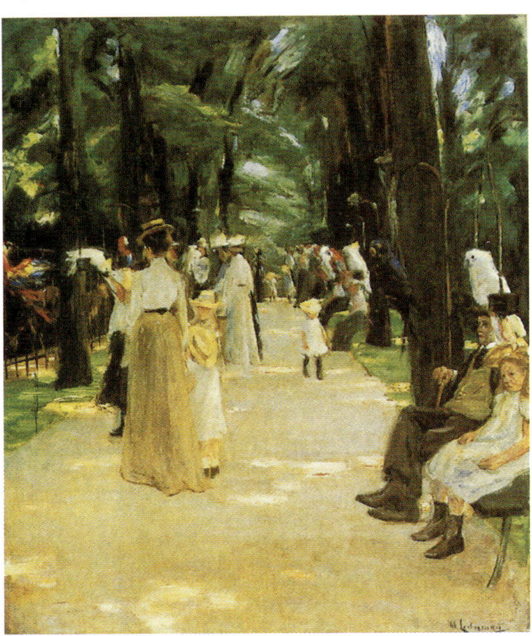

791. **Max Liebermann**, 1847-1935, Impressionism, German,
Papageienallee, 1902.
Oil on canvas, 88.1 x 72.5 cm. Kunsthalle, Bremen.

792. **Maurice Denis,** 1870-1943, Symbolism, French,
Homage to Cézanne, 1900.
Oil on canvas, 180 x 240 cm. Musée d'Orsay, Paris.

In 1901, Denis exhibited a large canvas called Homage to Cézanne *at the Salon de la Société Nationale des Beaux-Arts, which could be regarded as a manifesto of the new art. It was a full-length group portrait of himself, Redon, Sérusier, Bonnard, Roussel, Vuillard and Vollard standing round a still-life by the then little-known artist. The Nabis were enthusiastic admirers of Cézanne, and Denis was among his first advocates and expounders, although his own art owes little to Cézanne. He was much closer to Gauguin, not only when he was first impressed by his Talisman, but also years later. Incidentally, the Cézanne still-life on the easel in the Homage belonged to Gauguin, a fact appreciated only by those "in the know".*

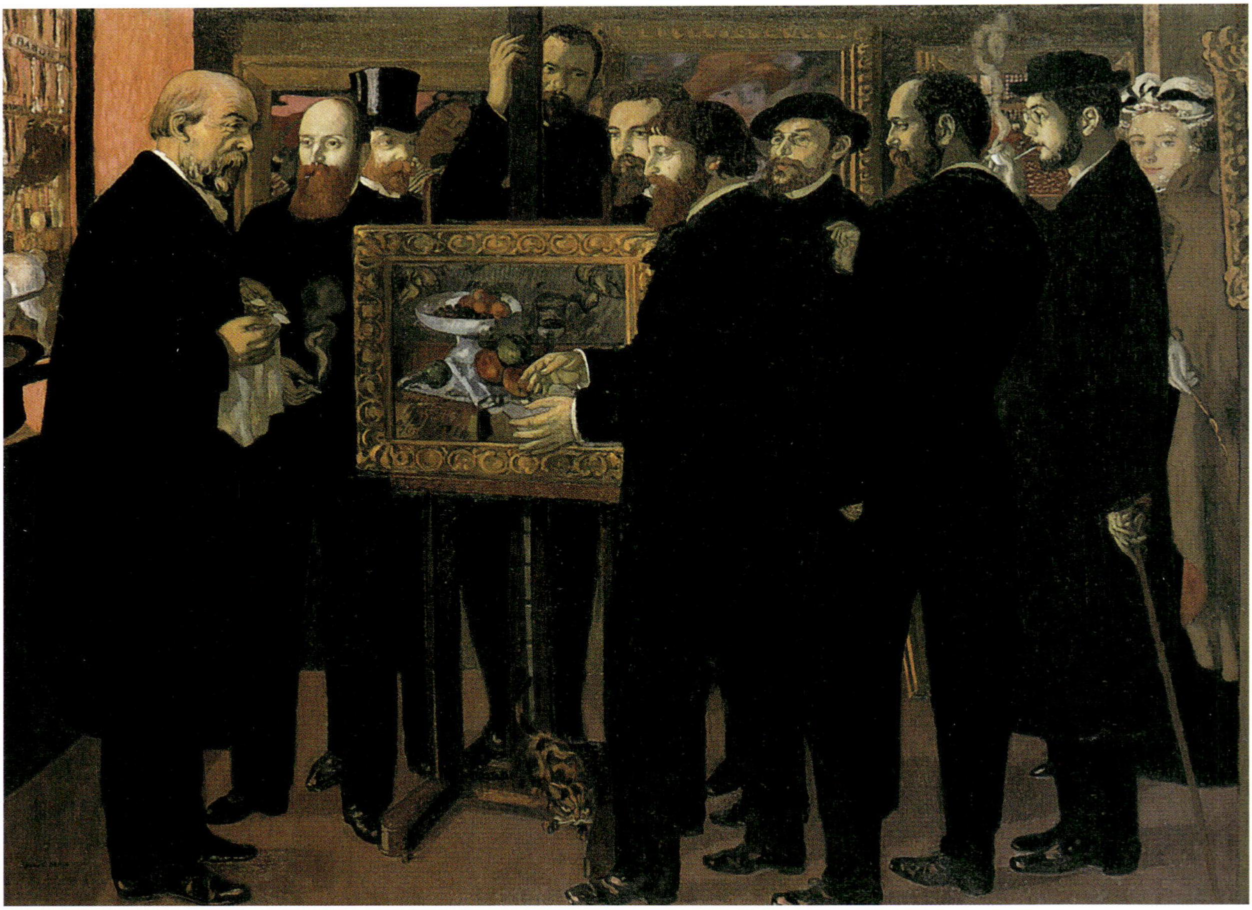

FÉLIX VALLOTTON
(1865 LAUSANNE – 1925 PARIS)

The "foreign Nabi" stood out among the members of the Nabis group, not so much because of his non-French extraction but because of his manner of painting, which was quite unlike that of his fellow artists. For this reason some critics have regarded his affiliation with the Nabis as purely formal.

Vallotton displayed his talent to the full at the very outset of his career. As a boy of sixteen, he amazed his teachers in Lausanne with a study of an old man's head, executed with a sure hand. Soon afterwards he moved to Paris.

As far back as 1885, when Vallotton first showed his works at the Salon des Artistes Français, he drew the attention of art critics. However, both at that time and for years to come, progressive artists who advocated the supremacy of pictorial effect and the unrestrained use of colours looked on his manner as something retrograde. Signac, who could not bear smoothness and "blew up" his surfaces with divided strokes, regarded Vallotton's brushwork as the complete antithesis of his own style and, indeed, of everything that derived from Impressionism. But the young Swiss, who had arrived in Paris when the Impressionists were still striving for recognition, did not know them, or at least had no wish to do so. That was not because he was wholly "indoctrinated" by Jules Lefebvre, Bouguereau and Boulanger at the Académie Julian; in fact, he preferred going to the Louvre and making copies of Antonello da Messina, Leonardo da Vinci and Albrecht Dürer.

Vallotton's art is indispensable for any student of life in that period: the accuracy of his details never needs to be questioned; the design, mood and, with rare exception, bitter astringency of his work set him apart from his contemporaries. His deliberate objectivity and emphatically dispassionate observation, expressed in meticulous draughtsmanship and inexpressive texture, link him not only with the Naturalism of the nineteenth century, but also with the tendencies of the twentieth. It is natural, therefore, that public interest in his work has tended to grow whenever there was a turn towards the concrete, material aspect in the arts.

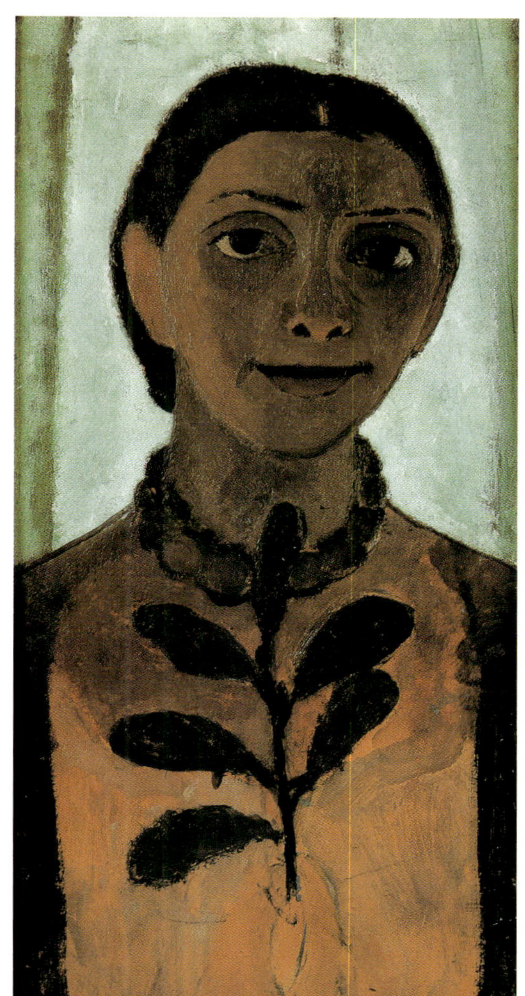

793

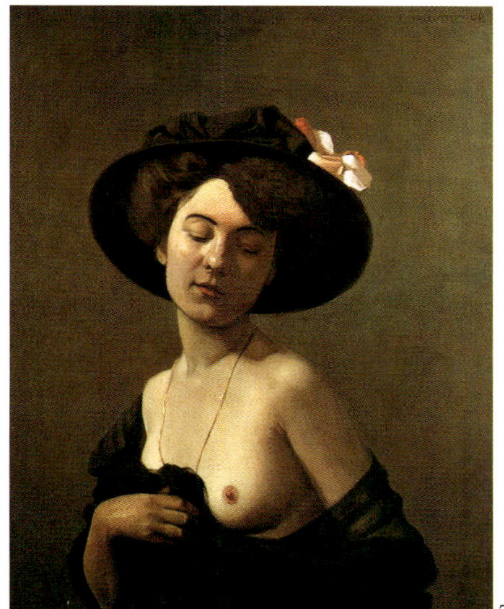

794

793. **Paula Modersohn-Becker**, 1876-1907, Expressionism, German, *Self-Portrait with Amber Necklace*, 1906. Oil on wood, 61.5 x 30.5 cm. Museum Folkwang, Essen.

794. **Félix Vallotton**, 1865-1925, Nabism, Swiss, *Woman with Black Hat*, 1908. Oil on canvas, 81.3 x 65 cm. The State Hermitage Museum, St Petersburg.

Vallotton's Woman with Black Hat *(Woman Wearing a Hat) is undoubtedly a parody, combining the almost uncombinable: the striking turn of the half-clothed figure and a plain, dull face topped with an elaborate flowery hat. The painter's eye seems dispassionate, yet something personal comes across in his attitude toward the woman. Annette Vaillant recollected that Vallotton's Calvinist exterior concealed a strange Ingres-like sensuality. But the intimate effect of the portrait is extinguished by mockery which is noticeable even in the range of colours he uses. His palette is limited here and clearly imitates that of Salon journeyman painters.*

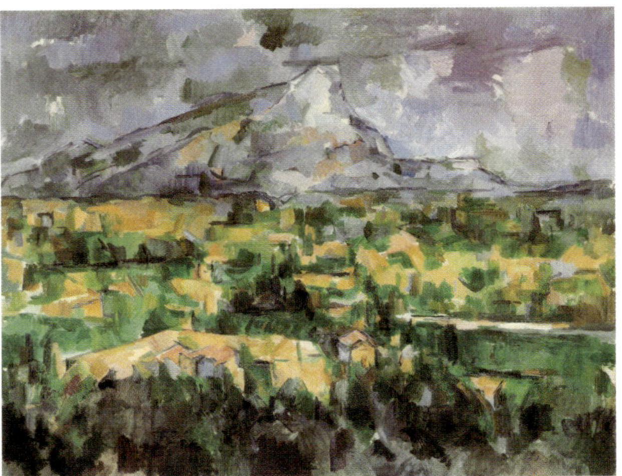

795. **Paul Cézanne,** 1839-1906, Post-Impressionism, French,
Mont Sainte-Victoire, View from Lauves, 1904.
Oil on canvas, 70 x 92 cm. Museum of Art, Philadelphia.

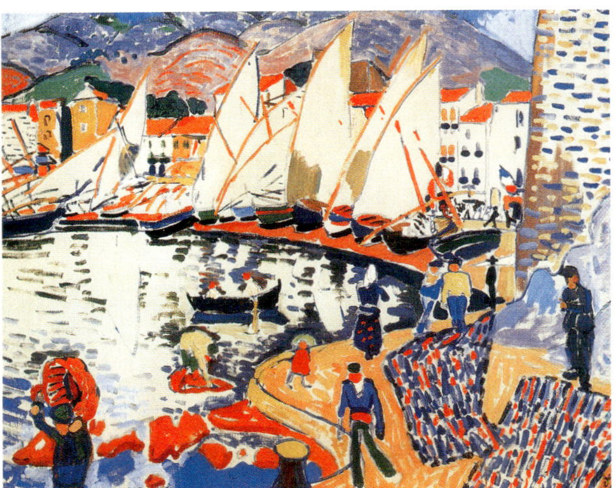

796. **André Derain**, 1880-1954, Fauvism, French,
Fishing Boats, 1905. Oil on canvas, 82 x 101 cm.
Pushkin State Museum of Fine Arts, Moscow.

797. **Maurice de Vlaminck**, 1876-1958, Fauvism, French,
View of the Seine, 1905-1906. Oil on canvas, 54.5 x 65.5 cm.
The State Hermitage Museum, St Petersburg.

View of the Seine depicts the river bank near the Chatou Bridge (a spot where Vlaminck often worked before moving to Bougival), and is reminiscent of August Renoir's Oarsmen at Chatou *(1879, National Gallery, Washington), which Renoir painted at the same place during the Impressionist period. Renoir's red boat, cutting diagonally across the surface of the water, possesses a resonance which seems impossible for the age of Impressionism. Vlaminck's painting, constructed on the parallel, almost horizontal lines of the boats and bank, looks quieter and there are no figures in the foreground adding life. Yet, to use Vlaminck's mode of expression, colour makes his painting a "fanfare" in contrast to Renoir's "piano music!" His red comma of a boat burns in the centre against a river of shimmering blue, red, ochre and white vertical strokes; touches of red on the shore repeat the main melody and red reflections on the white sails echo it again diminuendo. The drawing of objects here is very generalised; the outlines of the trees and the houses are highly abstracted and the sail is inaccurately portrayed, though Vlaminck as an experienced waterman no doubt knew what sails really look like. Vlaminck subordinates everything to the power of colour in his desire to recreate on canvas his vital energy and joie de vivre. In his enthusiasm to capture his momentary responses, Vlaminck often squeezed paint directly from the tube without stopping to mix it. The resulting effect is so powerful that even after many decades the pictures evoke the same feelings of impatience and trepidation which gripped the artist himself. The brush moves freely, temperamentally, laying rich patches of ochre on poplar crowns, and daubing heavy streaks of cobalt blue and white into the sky. Within this apparently irregular patchwork of colour is a pre-dominance of red – and it is not by chance that it is enhanced by the only green patch – and the white of the sail standing out sharply against the saturated colour scheme. There are smudged horizontal lines clearly visible under the first layer of paint – the result of Vlaminck either scraping the paint off with a palette knife, or, perhaps, as he said, wiping the freshly painted picture on the grass in his haste to begin another on the same canvas.*

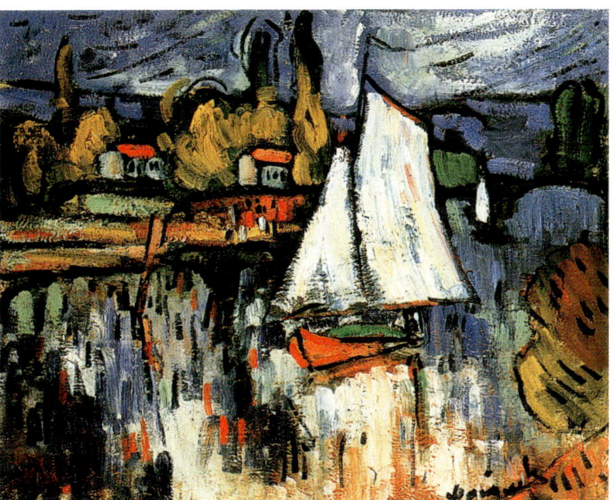

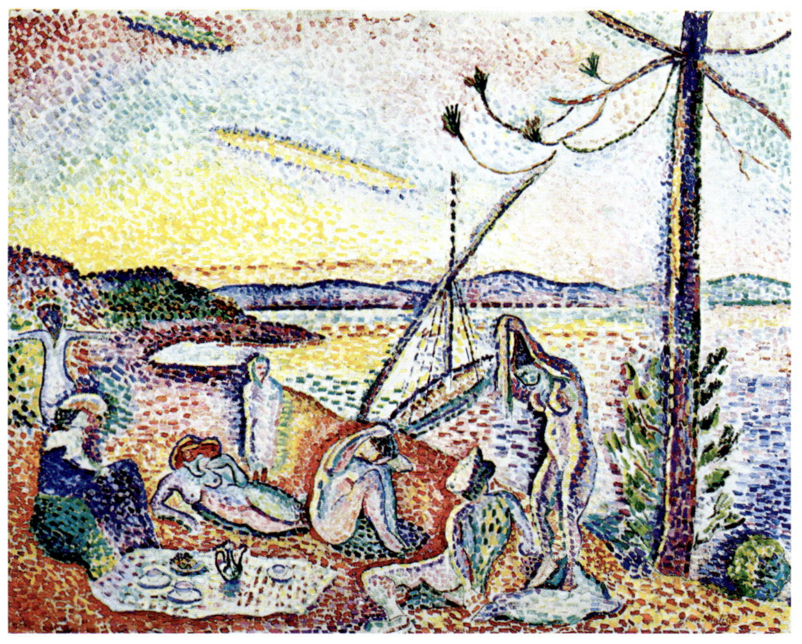

798. **Henri Matisse**, 1869-1954, Fauvism, French,
Luxe, calme et volupté, 1904-1905.
Oil on canvas, 98.5 x 118.5 cm.
Musée national d'art moderne,
Centre Georges-Pompidou, Paris.

Matisse painted his first Fauve paintings in southern France. As a pupil of Gustave Moreau at the School of Fine Arts, Matisse met Dufy and Rouault in the master's workshop.

Harmony comes out of this picture. Matisse is looking for ideal beauty, and here he depicts the Mediterranean Eden of Saint-Tropez. He carries on a tradition commenced by Poussin and Puvis de Chavanne with characters expressing happiness and an out-of-time scenery. The painting betrays a neo-impressionist technique, through the little brush strokes, inspired by Signac.

799. **Ferdinand Hodler**, 1853-1918, Art Nouveau, Swiss,
Day, 1904-1906.
Oil on canvas, 163 x 358 cm.
Kunsthaus, Zurich.

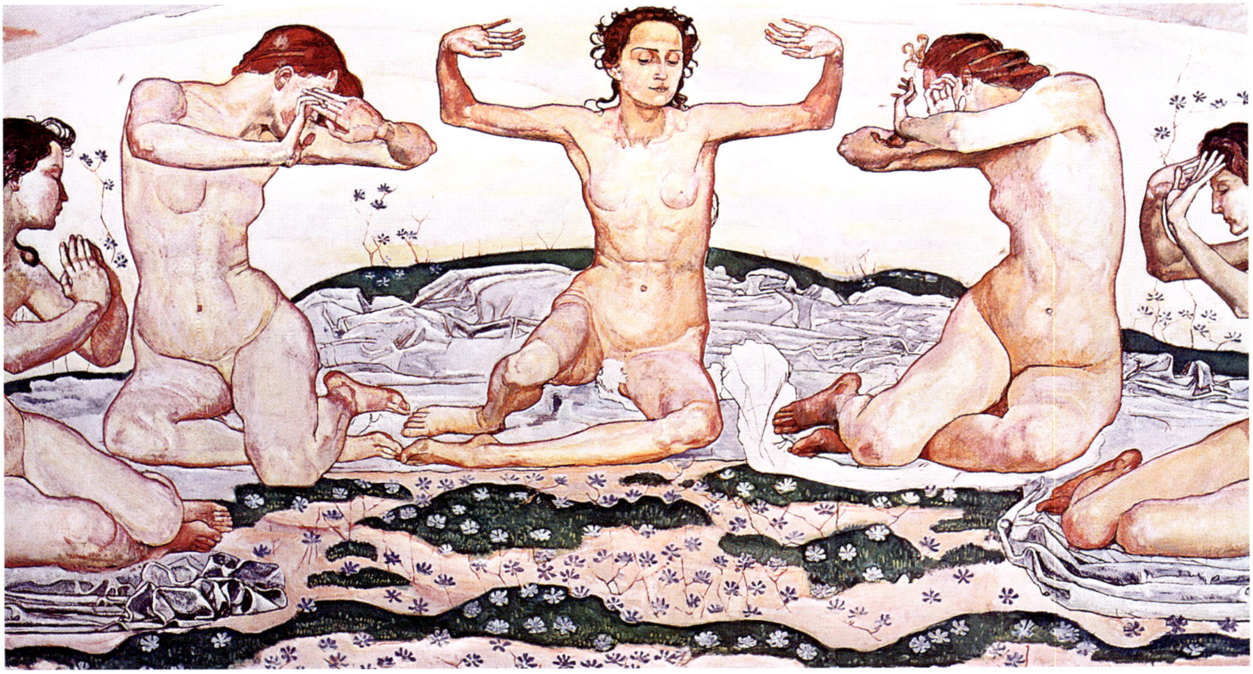

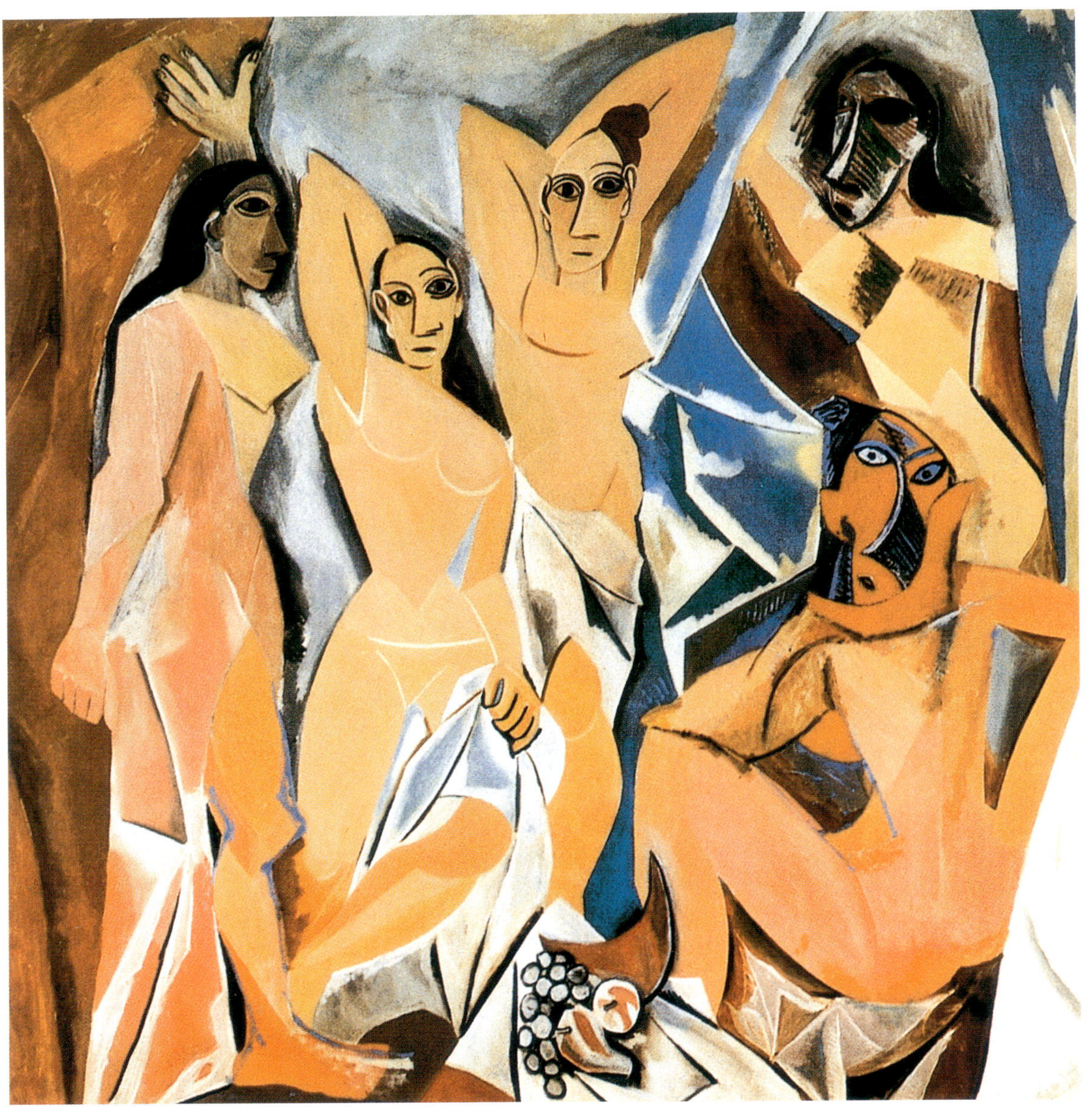

800. **Pablo Picasso**, 1881-1973, Cubism, Spanish,
Les Demoiselles d'Avignon, 1906-1907.
Oil on canvas, 243.9 x 233.7 cm.
The Museum of Modern Art, New York.

Thirty years before painting his masterpiece Guernica, *Picasso showed his early interest in Cubism. In 1907, after being impressed with the almond-shaped eyes and elongated egg-shaped faces of African masks, he returned to a recent work and repainted the faces of its five figures. The blend of the mask shapes with his desire to reduce visual realities to abstract forms and to simultaneously show multiple points-of-view resulted in the breakthrough work that moved the artist from his African period to his most dominant period in pure Cubism. The challenge of evolving this new art form would possess the artist for several years of his long life. The landscapes of Cézanne, and works such as his*

Boy in a Red Vest *(1893-1895), were influences on how Picasso presented the jagged planes of the work so as to give the figures continual motion. The "Avignon" referred to in the title refers to a street in Barcelona's commercial sex district.*

The painting betrays the influence of the Bathers by Cézanne. The faces of the women (especially the two on the right) are also clearly inspired by African art. The exhibition of "art nègre" given in Paris in 1906 had a great impact on the artist. Initially, Picasso had depicted men (sailors and students) in his first drawings. He later excluded them so that it is the spectator who becomes the intruder in the scene.

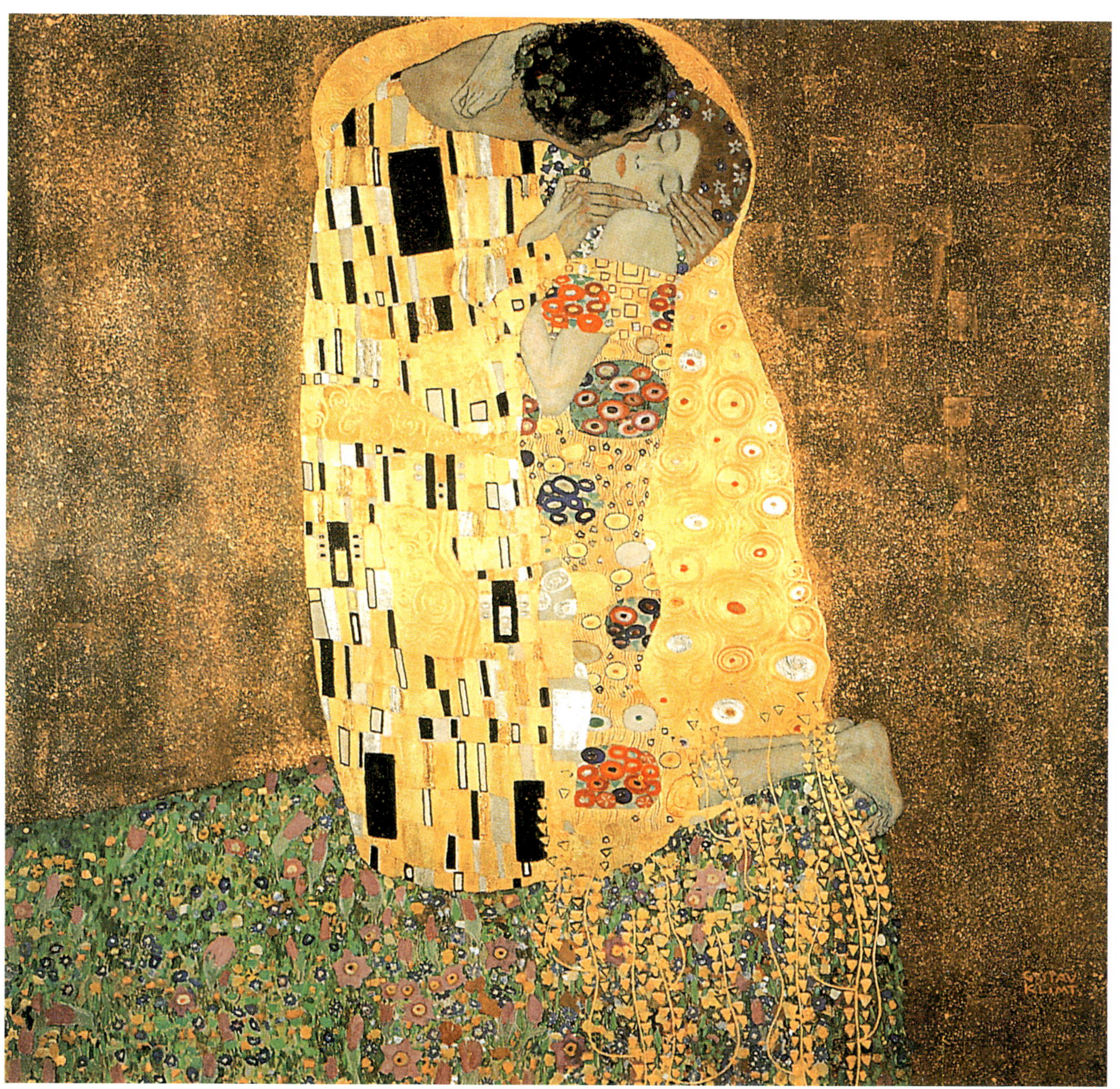

801. **Gustav Klimt**, 1862-1918, Art Nouveau, Austrian,
The Kiss, 1907-1908. Oil on canvas, 180 x 180 cm.
Österreichische Galerie, Vienna.

Klimt's The Kiss *of 1908, which has become his best-known picture, was preceded by two other famous versions of the subject by Rodin and Munch. All three show a pre-occupation with Eros and the troubled sexual relations between man and woman that was characteristic of the turn of the century's Western culture. Klimt's Kiss is less pessimistic and less misogynistic than Munch's puddle of melted human flesh and less pretentious than Rodin's heroically nude pair of marble lovers.*

Of the three though, Klimt's image is the most explicitly sexual with its use of symbolic and erotically charged ornament. The embracing lovers whose combined forms suggest that the moment of climactic ecstasy has just passed. Despite Klimt's not so oblique treatment of a sexual theme, The Kiss *with its sumptuously decorative qualities must have looked reassuringly beautiful beside the harshly expressionistic works of Schiele and Gerstl that were shown with it in the 1908 Kunstschau. For once, Klimt's work was received with enthusiasm, and it was bought directly from the exhibition by the Austrian state.*

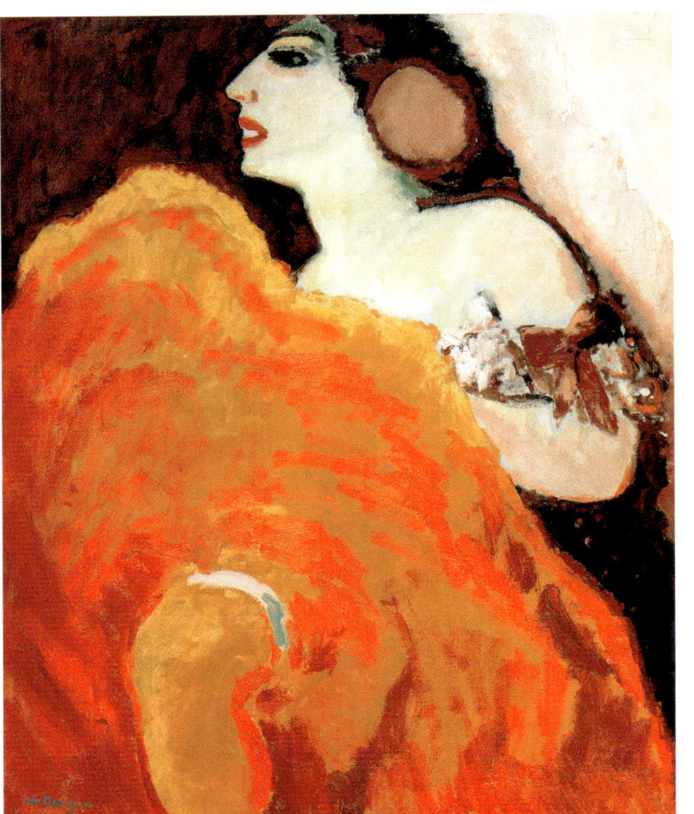

802. **Kees van Dongen**, 1877-1968, Fauvism, Dutch,
The Red Dancer, 1907.
Oil on canvas, 99.7 x 81 cm.
The State Hermitage Museum, St Petersburg.

The Red Dancer was bought in 1909 by the publisher Nikolai Riabushinsky at the Golden Fleece Salon in Moscow. A sea of orange-red flames floods half the canvas which is sharply divided along one diagonal. Laid broadly and coarsely on the ochrous foundation are dabs of colour in varying shapes and sizes tracing the motion of the twirling skirt. One small feature – a tiny particle of pure green on the white garter – is testimony to Van Dongen's far from indifferent attitude to the science of colour. Yet this is a merely subtle nuance just like the green shadow on the face. The blazing red has no need for support for it is borne in the freedom of the painterly texture and the intensity of pure colour applied straight from the tube. Colour decides everything here; it determines the work's design, motion, and space. The wavy contours of the skirt contrast with the abstracted, simplified outlines of the face, neck and shoulder. The line in a graphical sense is replaced by a fading of colour from the figure to the background, which creates an impression of depth, breaching the flatness of the canvas. By the character of the image and the painterly manner, The Red Dancer is closest of all to a portrait of the Dutch male soprano Modjesco performing a woman's role (Museum of Modern Art, New York) in which a critic in 1908 saw a new manner.

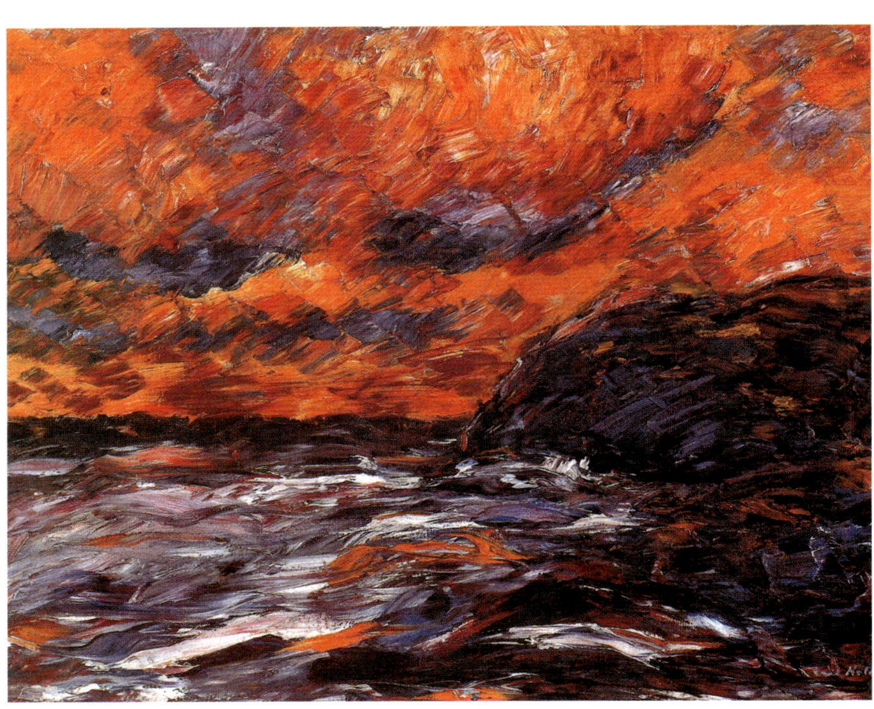

803. **Emil Nolde**, 1867-1956,
Expressionism, German,
Autumn Sea XI, 1910.
Oil on canvas, 73 x 88 cm.
Kunsthaus Zurich, Zurich.

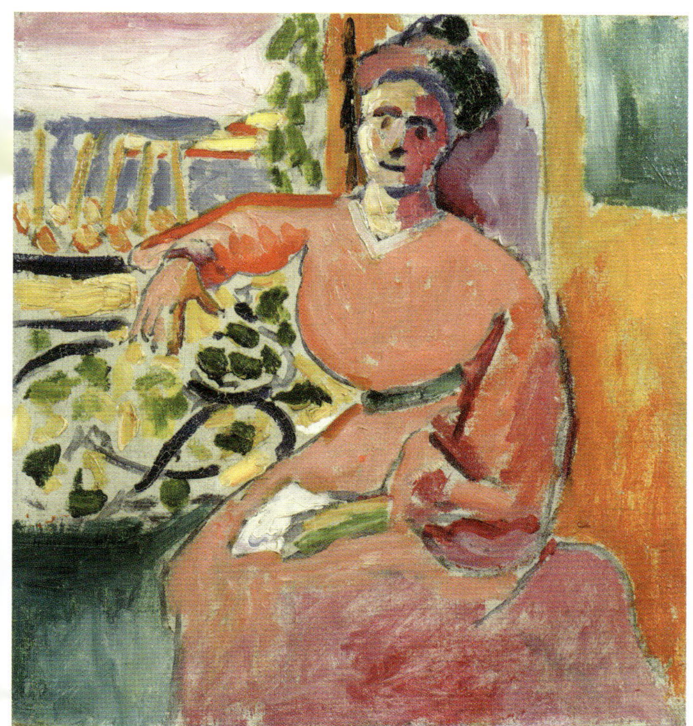

804. **Henri Matisse**, 1869-1954, French, Fauvism,
A Woman Sitting before the Window, 1905.
Oil on canvas, 32 x 30 cm. Private collection.

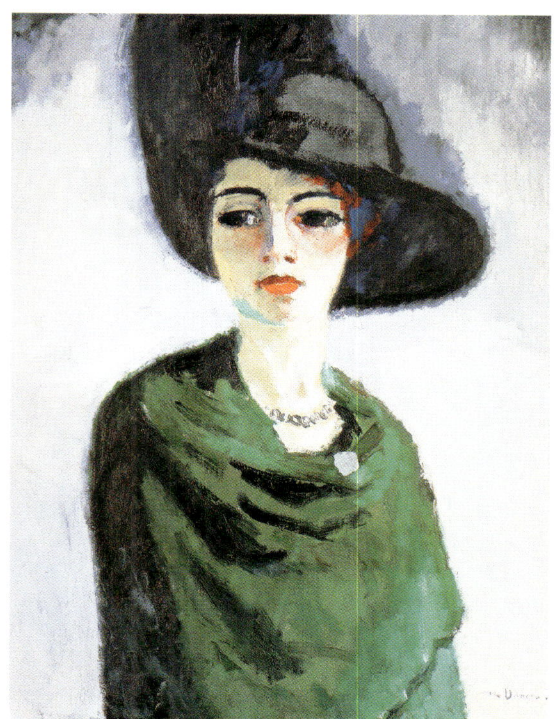

805. **Kees van Dongen**, 1877-1968, Fauvism, Dutch,
Woman in a Black Hat, 1908.
Oil on canvas, 100 x 81.5 cm.
The State Hermitage Museum, St Petersburg.

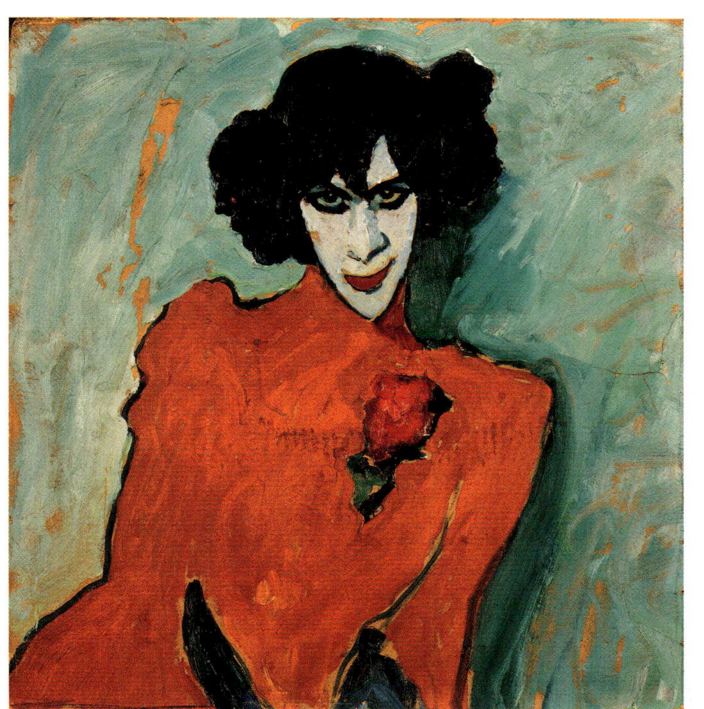

806. **Alexei von Jawlensky**, 1864-1941, Expressionism,
Russian, *Portrait of the Dancer Alexander Sakharov*, 1909.
Oil on canvas.
Städtische Galerie im Lenbachhaus, Munich.

*Russian dancer Alexander Sakharov was captured in an
extraordinary portrait by his friend Alexei von Jawlensky.
The dancer visited the painter one evening before a
performance, already made up and in costume, which
created a particularly androgynous effect. Quickly and
spontaneously – reportedly in less than half an hour –
Jawlensky produced this free, vigorous and highly
memorable image.*

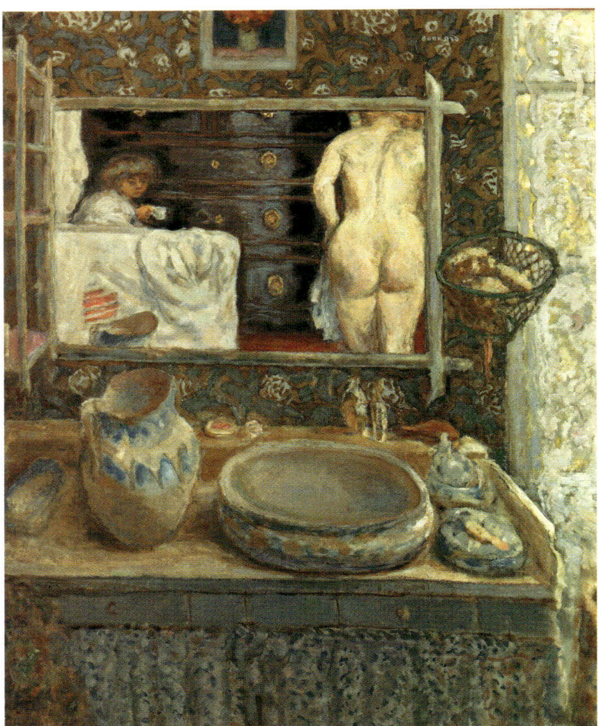

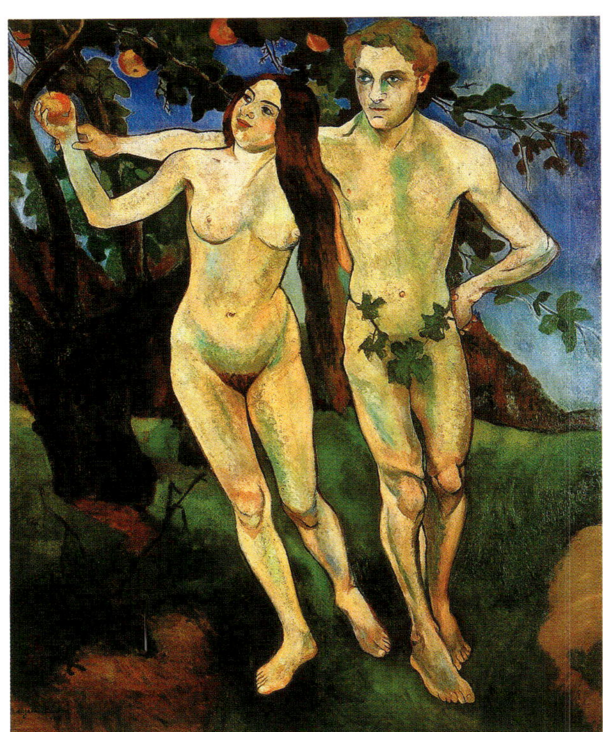

807. **Pierre Bonnard**, 1867-1947, Nabis, French,
The Bathroom Mirror, 1908.
Oil on canvas, 125 x 110 cm.
Pushkin State Museum of Fine Arts, Moscow.

*This painting is one of the most wide-ranging of Bonnard's
works in terms of genre as well as one of the most captivating for
its visual harmony. A painting as complex as this required not
only daring, but also the considerable experience accumulated
over twenty years of work. Bonnard's earliest still-lifes, including
student pieces dating back to 1888, were far removed from the
solution of complex issues of genre and space.*

*The juxtaposition of two women, one naked, the other
clothed, has about it an element of irony, which was highly
characteristic of Bonnard. A somewhat unusual feature of this
painting is the inclusion of the mirror. A detail of this kind
occurred quite often in the work of the Old Masters, most
frequently as an element in vanitas compositions, which
through the idiom of juxtaposed objects, spoke of the transitory
nature of life and of human vanity. Sometimes a mirror was
depicted in combination with a statuette of a half-naked
woman which symbolised Art. However, this kind of object
symbolism had lost its original meaning as early as the
eighteenth century. In their still-lifes, Bonnard's immediate
predecessors, the Impressionists, hardly ever used a mirror as a
compositional element.*

The basic structural elements of The Bathroom Mirror *had
formed long before 1908. For example, in 1894 the artist
painted* The Cup of Coffee *which depicts a girl at a little table
holding a coffee-cup. The following year, in response to a
commission for the decoration of a bathroom and boudoir,
Bonnard produced a series of grisaille and red-chalk nudes in
which we can detect the influence of Degas.*

808. **Suzanne Valadon**, 1865-1938, Post-Impressionist, French,
Adam and Eve, 1909. Oil on canvas, 162 x 131 cm.
Musée national d'art moderne, Centre Georges-Pompidou, Paris.

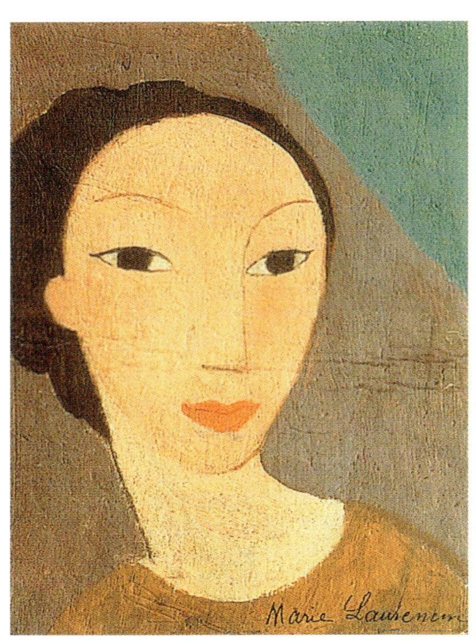

809. **Marie Laurencin**, 1883-1956, French, *Head of a Woman*.
Oil on canvas pasted on cardboard, 35 x 27 cm.
Pushkin State Museum of Fine Arts, Moscow.

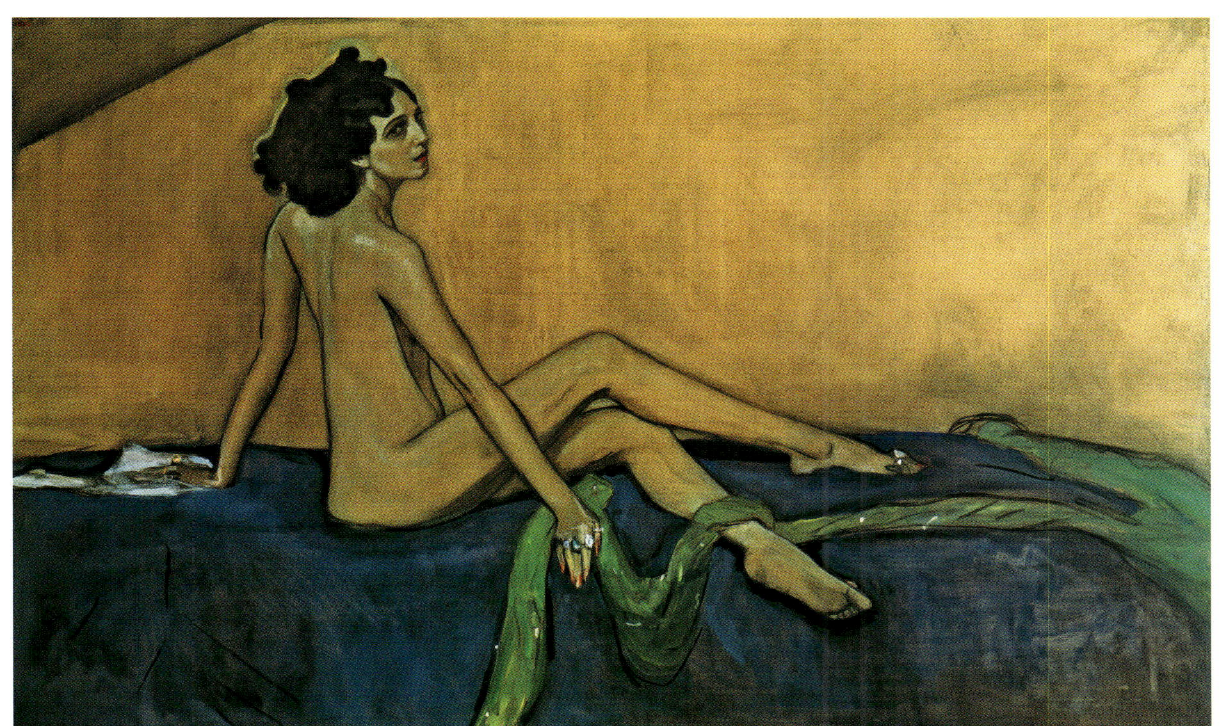

810. **Valentin Serov,** 1865-1911, World of Art group,
Russian, *Portrait of Ida Rubinstein,* 1910.
Tempera and charcoal on paper, 147 x 233 cm.
The State Russian Museum, St Petersburg.

*Portrait of Ida Rubinstein can be said to conform to the
new style in every way. The famous ballerina posed for
Serov in the nude, and this obliged the artist to forestall
any associations of the future portrait with reality. Serov
did not portray Ida Rubinstein: he created an image out
of the boundless possibilities presented by the model.
In doing so he sought to combine the abstract with the
real, something typical of the Art Nouveau, as such,
and also typical of almost all of Serov's portraits. The
curving lines of the contours are traced directly onto
the canvas. Only three hues are present in the colour
scheme – blue, green, and brown – without any gradations
or combinations. Each colour is isolated and local. The
spatial environment is not designed, be it by colour or
compositional arrangement or perspective. She seems
not to be seated, but sprawled, pressed to the canvas,
which, for all her beguiling and extravagant features,
creates and impression of weakness and vulnerability.
Serov regarded Ida Rubinstein with admiration, although
he did not stress the characteristic aspect of her image at
the expense of the ideal. In a number of other portraits,
however, his treatment of the models borders on the
grotesque. This tendency attained its peak in the very
last years of his life and, above all, in the* Portrait of Olga
Orlova *(1911).*

VALENTIN SEROV
(1865 ST PETERSBURG – 1911 MOSCOW)

Among the "young peredvizhniki" who joined the World of Art
group, the most brilliant portraitist was Valentin Serov. Like many of
his contemporaries, he delighted in painting out of doors, and some
of his most appealing portraits – such as *Girl with Peaches, Girl in
Sunlight,* and *In Summer* – owe their naturalness to their setting or
to the interplay of sunlight and shadows. Indeed, Serov regarded
them as "studies" rather than portraits, giving them descriptive titles
that omitted the sitter's name. The subject of *Girl with Peaches* –
painted when Serov was only twenty-two – was in fact Mamontov's
daughter Vera. The model for *In Summer* was Serov's wife.

When only six years old, Serov began to display signs of artistic
talent. At nine years old, Repin acted as his teacher and mentor,
giving him lessons in his studio in Paris, then let Serov work with
him in Moscow, almost like an apprentice. Eventually Repin sent
him to study with Pavel Chistiakov – the teacher of many of the
World of Art painters, including Nesterov and Vrubel. Chistiakov
was to become a close friend. Because Serov's career spanned
such a long period, his style and subject matter vary considerably,
ranging from voluptuous society portraits (the later ones notable for
their grand style and sumptuous dresses) to sensitive studies of
children. Utterly different from any of these is the famous nude
study of the dancer Ida Rubinstein, in tempera and charcoal on
canvas, which he painted towards the end of his life. Although
Serov's early style has much in common with the French
Impressionists, he did not become acquainted with their work until
after he had painted pictures such as *Girl with Peaches.*

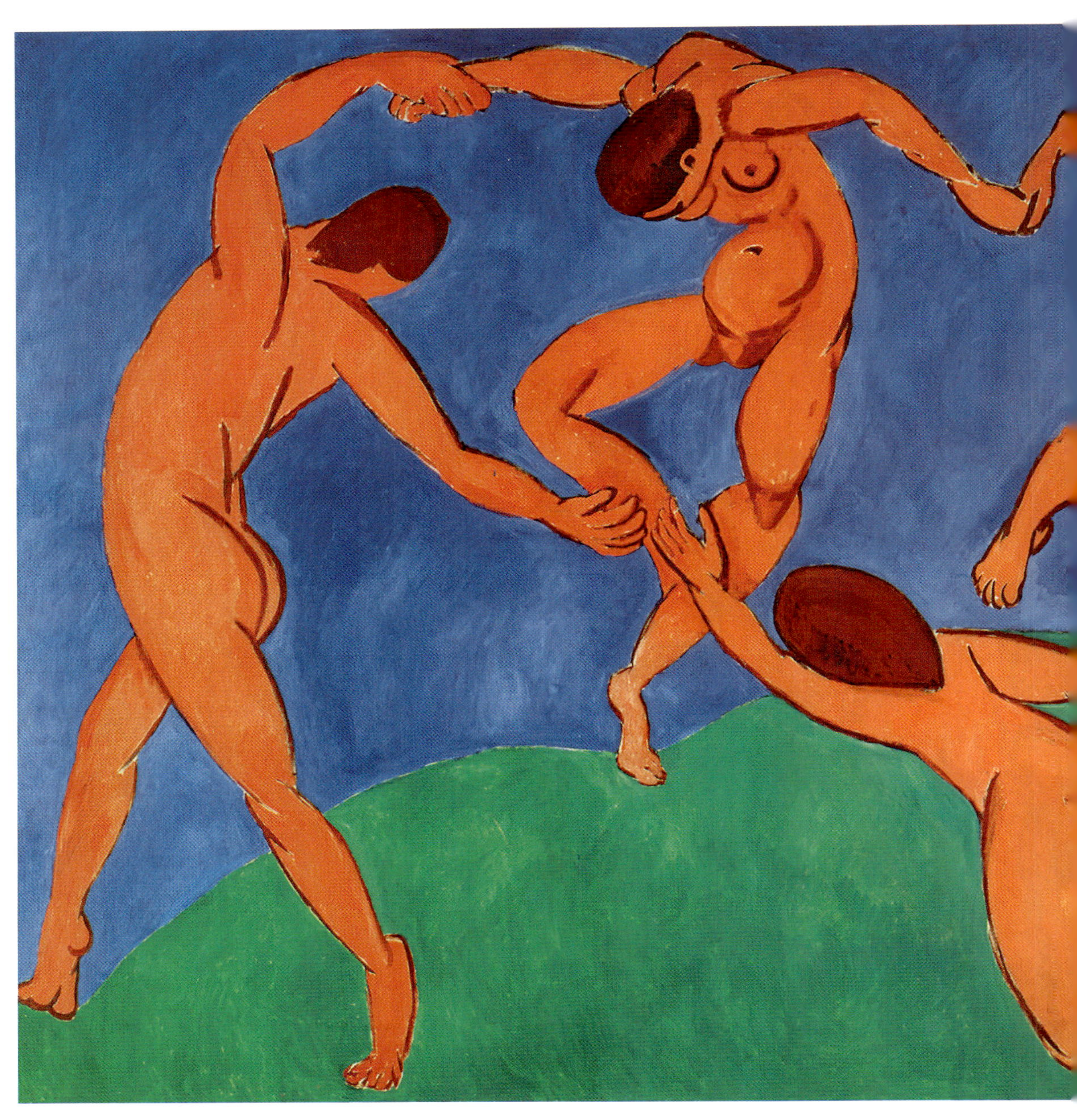

811. **Henri Matisse,** 1869-1954, Fauvism, French, *The Dance*, 1909-1910. Oil on canvas, 260 x 391 cm.

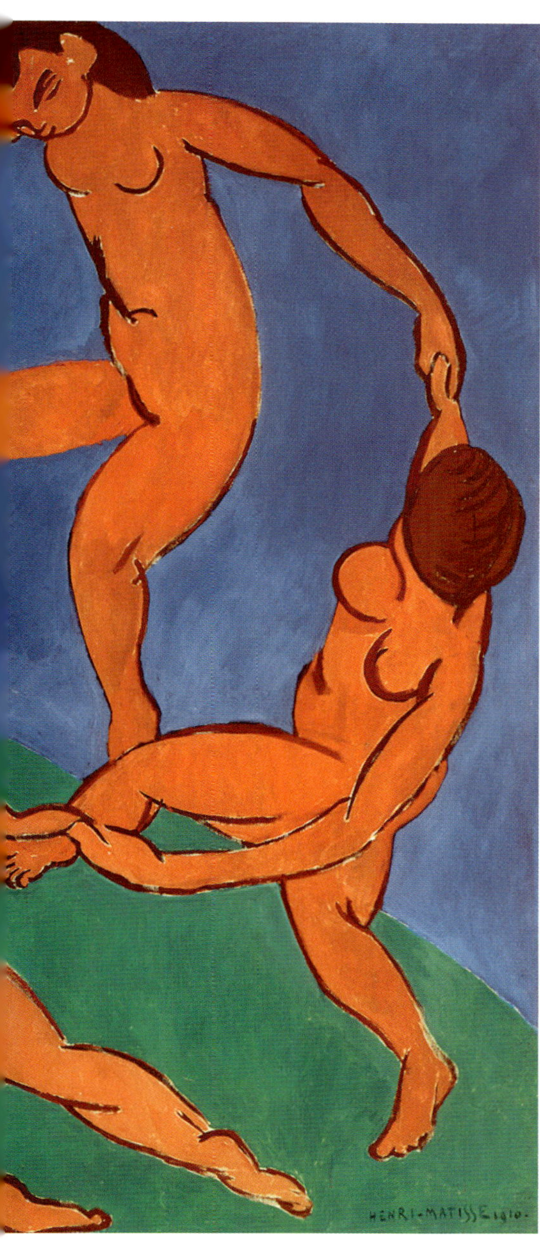

The State Hermitage Museum, St Petersburg.

HENRI MATISSE
(1869 LE CATEAU-CAMBRÉSIS – 1954 NICE)

"Fauvism is when there is a red," said Henri Matisse concisely putting into words the most straightforward notion held of Fauvism. Matisse has in fact become Fauvism's leader over the years as a result of his contemporaries and researchers persistently perpetuating such an idea. Consequently Matisse's œuvre has been scoured through in a search for the ultimate Fauvist painting. Matisse never pretended or aspired to such a role, and on the question of what Fauvism represents in theory and in practice, he never came to a final conclusion.

Matisse started to take lessons at the Académie Julian in 1891, working as a law tutor to help pay his way. In 1892 he abandoned Bouguereau's totally uninspiring lessons and transferred to Gustave Moreau's classes at the Ecole des Beaux-Arts. During the evenings Matisse also attended classes in applied art and there he made friends with Albert Marquet, who soon also became a pupil of Moreau. It was at these classes that a group of artists came together and formed friendships that would endure all the trials and tribulations of their respective lives. This group consisted of the "Three M's" – Matisse, Marquet and Manguin – as well as Georges Rouault, Charles Camoin and Louis Valtat. Working in Léon Bonnat's studio, which was just across the corridor, was another future member, Othon Friesz. And he would later be joined by Raoul Dufy. In 1901 Matisse and his friends started to exhibit their work at the Salon des Indépendants and in Berthe Weill's gallery. In 1903 they were involved in the founding of the Salon d'Automne, where two years later Vauxcelles would see their work and dub them "les fauves". The Salon d'Automne scandal over *Woman with a Hat* in 1905 brought Matisse fame and glory at a time when the preceding generation of artists were only just beginning to receive theirs. Matisse, as a natural inheritor of the French tradition, showed himself more than respectful of his elders. Renoir, whom he often met whilst in the south in 1917-1918, always remained a teacher figure for him. The paintings Matisse produced between 1897 and 1901 demonstrate the mastery of his predecessors' techniques, from the Impressionists through to Cézanne. Matisse began this process around the time of Gustave Moreau's death. Unlike Derain and Vlaminck he was never troubled by the "museum issue" since he learnt to appreciate exhibits and their influence under Moreau's guidance. Fauvism shaped all Matisse's creative work and he himself defined it so well as: "The courage to find the purity of means".

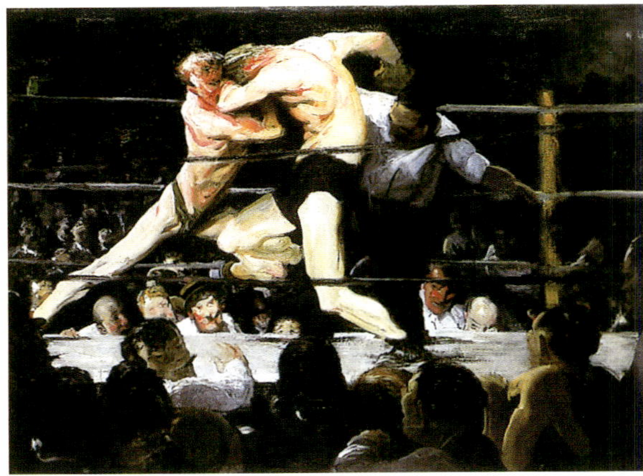

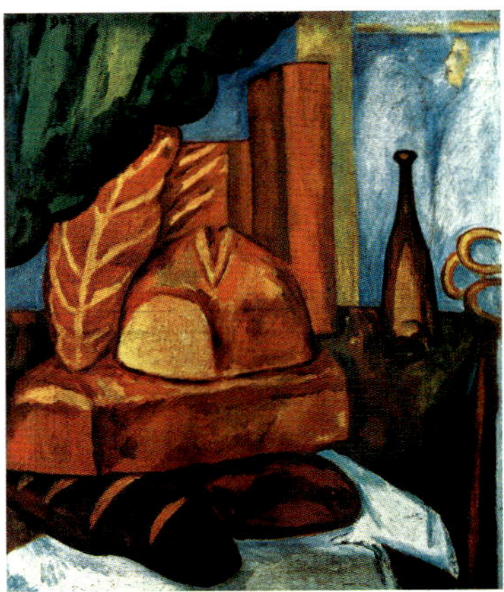

812. **Mikhail Larionov**, 1881-1964, Rayonnism, Russian,
Bread, c. 1910.
Oil on canvas, 102 x 84 cm. Private collection, Paris.

A pyramid of round and oblong loaves of bread takes up the entire surface of this monumental painting. The poet Maximilien Volochine, after having visited the Knave of Diamonds exhibition in late 1910, noted, "Larionov is the most naïve and most spontaneous of our 'Knaves'. His painting Bread *is nothing more than bread: good bread, well baked, that would have been the pride of any bakery had it been on its tinplate sign". While drawing inspiration from signs, Larionov was not content to simply imitate. His approach to the subject is a study in contrariness: weighty and serious for the sign painter, ironic and full of good humour here.*

814. **Vladimir Tatlin**, 1885-1953, Constructivism, Russian,
The Sailor, 1911-1912.
Tempera on canvas, 71.5 x 71.5 cm.
The State Russian Museum, St Petersburg.

Tatlin is the founder of Constructivism. In 1917, after the October revolution, he was commissioned to design the monument to the Third International, a huge spiral tower in iron and glass. Thirty-one years later, the Soviet government declared him an "enemy of the people".

813. **George Wesley Bellows**, 1882-1925,
Ashcan School, American, *Stag at Sharkey's*, 1909.
Oil on canvas, 92 x 122.6 cm.
Cleveland Museum of Art, Cleveland.

George Wesley Bellows is thought of as a member of the Ashcan School of Realism, although he was not one of its charter members. The observation by Bellows of the everyday life of ordinary people, without commentating on the broader socialist unrest of the time, is captured in his masterpiece, which alone qualifies him for the realism movement.

The viewer is placed near ringside at an all male "stag" event. He is slightly elevated above ring, above the heads of the spectators, where Bellows still manages to capture the rawness and the noise of the crowd and the fight taking place.

The atmosphere of the event, which is clearly not just a spontaneous moment, is caught by the artist. The top rope of the ring is adjusted conveniently so as not to obscure the view of the central subject.

815. **Henri Matisse**, 1869-1954, French, Fauvism,
Conversation, 1908-1912.
Oil on canvas, 177 x 217 cm.
The State Hermitage Museum, St Petersburg.

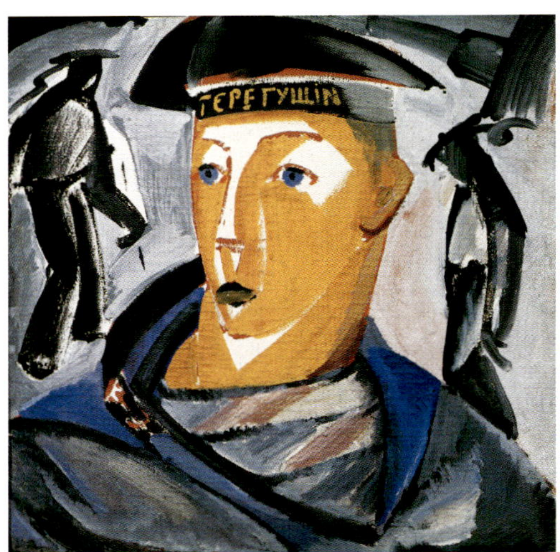

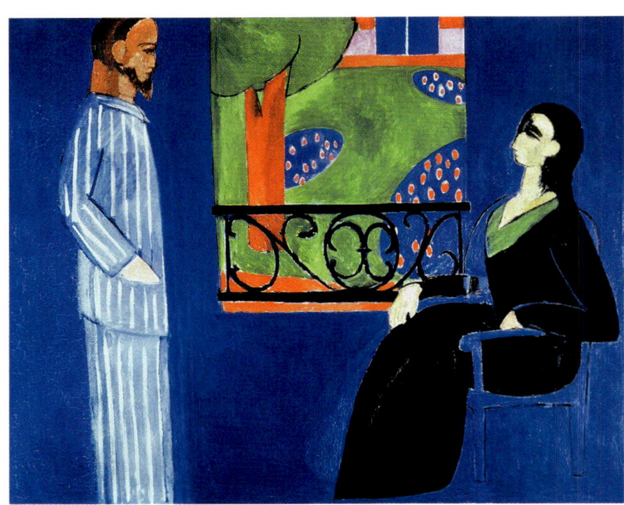

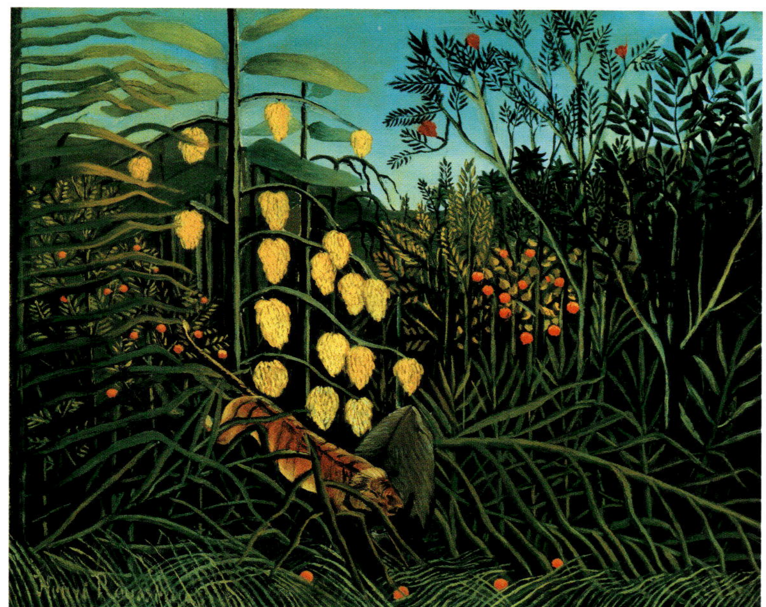

816

816. Henri Rousseau (Le Douanier Rousseau), 1844-1910,
Naïve Art, French, *Tiger Attacking a Bull*, 1908-1909.
Oil on canvas, 46 x 55 cm.
The State Hermitage Museum, St Petersburg.

817. Albert Marquet, 1875-1947, Fauvism, French,
Harbour at Honfleur, c. 1910.
Oil on canvas, 65 x 81 cm.
Pushkin State Museum of Fine Arts, Moscow.

818. André Lhote, 1885-1962, Cubism, French,
Landscape with Houses, after 1911.
Oil on canvas, 65 x 50 cm.
Pushkin State Museum of Fine Arts, Moscow.

LE DOUANIER ROUSSEAU
(HENRI ROUSSEAU)
(1844 LAVAL – 1910 PARIS)

Henri Rousseau served as a customs officer at the Gate of Vanves in Paris. In his free time he painted, sometimes on commission for his neighbours and sometimes in exchange for food. Year after year from 1886 to 1910 he brought his work to the Salon des Indépendants for display. (In 1884 the Salon des Indépendants was launched. It had no selection committee and was set up specifically to put on show the works of those artists who painted for a living but were yet unable or unwilling to meet the requirements of the official salons.) Year after year his work was exhibited despite its total lack of professional worth. Nevertheless he was proud to be numbered among the city's artists, and thoroughly enjoyed the right they all had to see their works shown to the public like the more accepted artists in the better salons.

Rousseau was among the first in his generation to perceive the dawn of a new era in art in which it was possible to grasp the notion of freedom – the freedom to be an artist irrespective of a specific style of painting or the possession professional qualifications. Discussion and appreciation of Rousseau's works inevitably led to discussion and (sometimes) appreciation of the works of others in a similar vein. Accordingly, some perhaps not so talented but undoubtedly original artists were noticed and even encouraged to come forward. A chain of "discoveries" ensued. "Primitive" and "naïve" art was suddenly all around. Professional artists were also becoming heavily involved.

817

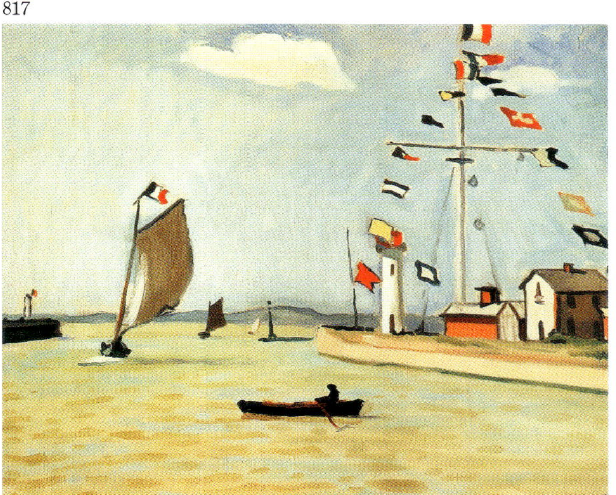

818

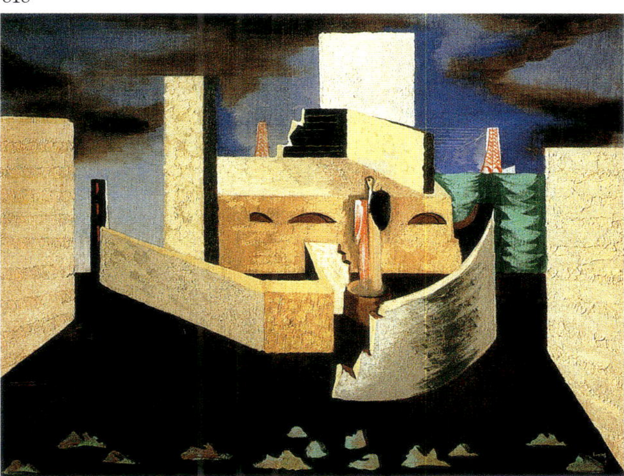

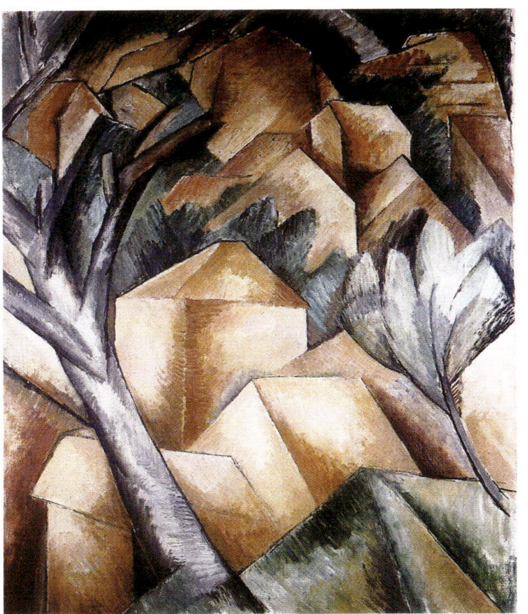

819. **Georges Braque**, 1882-1963, Cubism, French,
Houses at L'Estaque, 1908.
Oil on canvas, 73 x 60 cm.
Kunstmuseum, Berne.

GEORGES BRAQUE
(1882 ARGENTEUIL-SUR-SEINE – 1963 PARIS)

The French painter Georges Braque, born at Argenteuil, near Paris, was one of the major painters of the twentieth century. Together with Picasso he was the founder of Cubism. In addition to the pioneering work in Analytical Cubism that he shared with Picasso, he may also be credited with the development of a thoroughly original and exciting version of Cubism intertwined with Fauve colour effects. The association of Braque and Picasso was so mutual and their association so intense that in many instances only experts can distinguish Braque's paintings of 1910-1912 from those of Picasso. The paintings of this period are all executed in muted greens, greys, ochre, and browns. The objects are fragmented, as though seen from multiple viewpoints. Eventually, Picasso and Braque went separate ways.

Braque served in World War I, and was seriously injured in 1916. He devoted the rest of his career to the exploration of Cubism. Active until the end of his life, Braque produced an oeuvre that includes sculpture, graphics, book illustration, and decorative art. He certainly was the most consistent of the original Cubist painters and one of the half-dozen greatest painters of the century.

820. **Fernand Léger**, 1881-1955, Cubism/ Purism, French,
Nudes in the Forest, 1909-1910,
Oil on canvas, 120 x 170.2 cm. Rijksmuseum Kröller-Müller, Otterlo.

According to Léger, these figures are "a battle of volumes" overlapping and with syncopated rhythm. Unified by the cold light they are "at the antipodes of Impressionism". To a certain extent, this work is an anticipation of Italian Futurism.

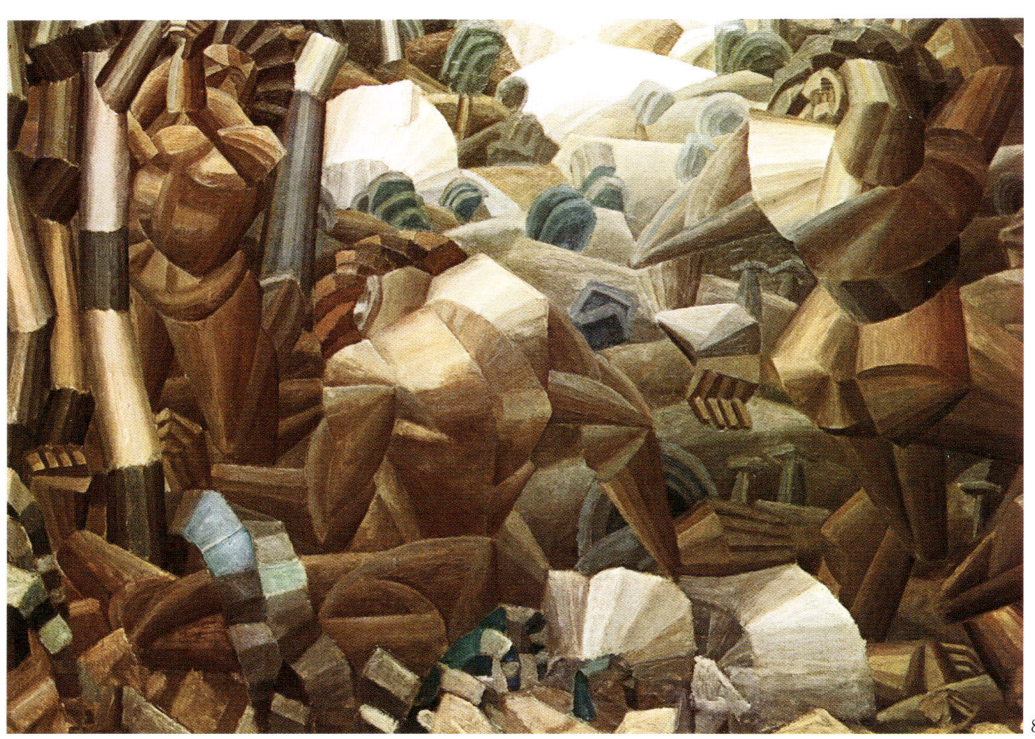

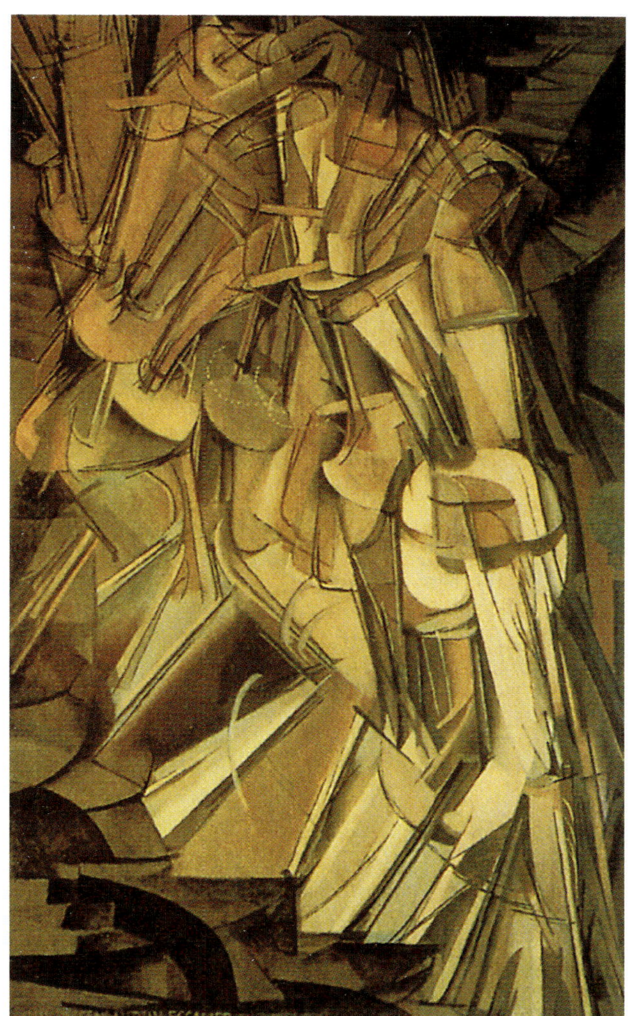

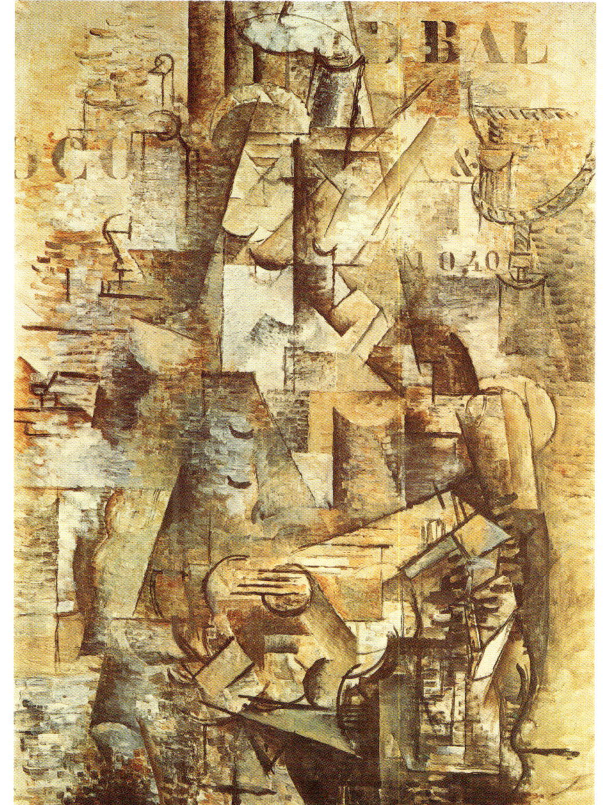

822

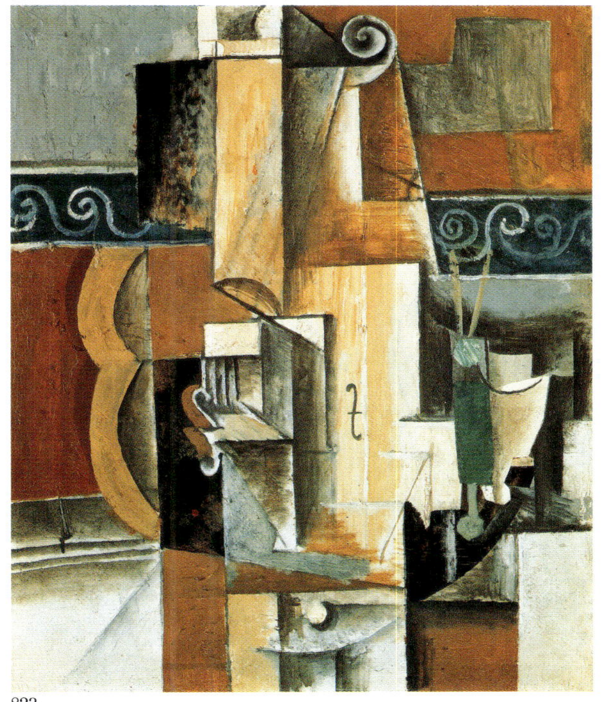

823

821. **Marcel Duchamp**, 1887-1968, Dada, French,
Nude Descending a Staircase (N°. 2), 1912.
Oil on canvas, 146.8 x 89.2 cm.
Philadelphia Museum of Art, Philadelphia.

822. **Georges Braque**, 1882-1963, Cubism, French,
Le Portugais (Der Emigrant), 1913.
Oil and charcoal on canvas, 130 x 73 cm.
Kunstmuseum, Basel.

823. **Pablo Picasso**, 1881-1973, Cubism, Spanish,
Violin and Guitar, c. 1912.
Oil on canvas, 65.5 x 54.3 cm.
The State Hermitage Museum, St Petersburg.

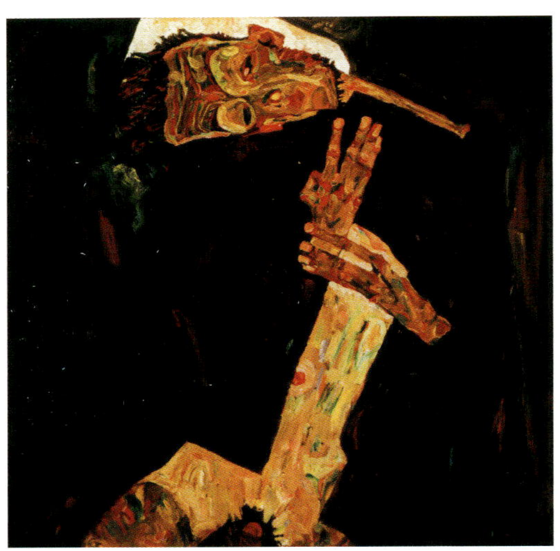

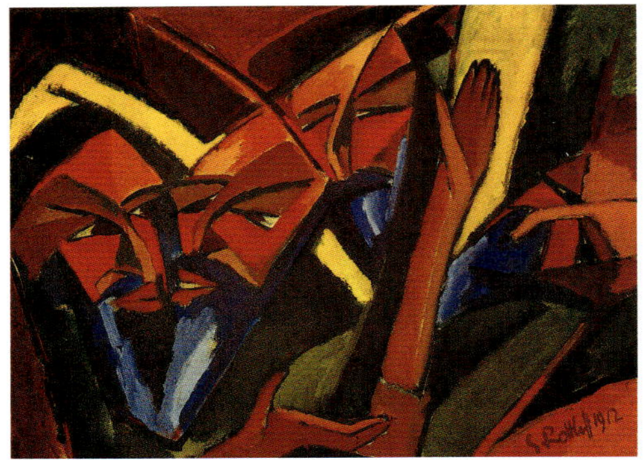

825. **Karl Schmidt-Rottluff**, 1884-1976,
Expressionism, German, *Pharisees*, 1912.
Oil on canvas, 75.9 x 102.9 cm.
The Museum of Modern Art, New York.

824. **Egon Schiele**, 1890-1918,
Expressionism, Austrian,
The Poet (Self-Portrait), 1911.
Oil on canvas, 80.1 x 79.7 cm.
Private collection.

*This is generally considered to be one of
Schiele's early masterpieces and a fine
example of Expressionist portraiture. The
title reminds us of Schiele's notion that all
artistic forms are inter-related. Here he
states that the artist is a condemned
creature who, by virtue of his true vision
of the world, sees more and is, therefore,
condemned to suffer more. An unusual
feature of this painting is that the genitalia
appear to be almost hermaphrodite-like,
with feminine detail being pierced rather
violently by a red-tipped phallic image.*

*This, too, suggests that all artists are as
one, whether female or male. It also hints
at sexual ambiguities and cross-gender
issues which were both fashionable and
still slightly outrageous at this time. The
notion of the hermaphrodite, however,
also leads to the idea that Schiele is both
a creator of art and a mother of all
creation. He is outside the common
sexual and social taboos of society and
thus aligned to his fellow artists, but he
also contains within himself an almost
mythical force and a super-sexual ability
to create and procreate.*

EGON SCHIELE
(1890 TULLN – 1918 VIENNA)

Egon Schiele's work is so distinctive that it resists categorisation. Admitted to the
Vienna Academy of Fine Arts at just sixteen, he was an extraordinarily precocious
artist, whose consummate skill in the manipulation of line, above all, lent a taut
expressivity to all his work. Profoundly convinced of his own significance as an
artist, Schiele achieved more in his abruptly curtailed youth than many other
artists achieved in a full lifetime. His roots were in the *Jugendstil* of the Viennese
Secession movement. Like a whole generation, he came under the overwhelming
influence of Vienna's most charismatic and celebrated artist, Gustav Klimt. In turn,
Klimt recognised Schiele's outstanding talent and supported the young artist, who
within just a couple of years, was already breaking away from his mentor's
decorative sensuality.

Beginning with an intense period of creativity around 1910, Schiele embarked
on an unflinching exposé of the human form – not the least his own – so
penetrating that it is clear he was examining an anatomy more psychological,
spiritual and emotional than physical.

He painted many townscapes, landscapes, formal portraits and allegorical
subjects, but it was his extremely candid works on paper, which are sometimes
overtly erotic, together with his penchant for using under-age models that made
Schiele vulnerable to censorious morality. In 1912, he was imprisoned on suspicion
of a series of offences including kidnapping, rape and public immorality. The most
serious charges (all but that of public immorality) were dropped, but Schiele spent
around three despairing weeks in prison.

Expressionist circles in Germany gave a lukewarm reception to Schiele's work.
His compatriot, Kokoschka, fared much better there. While he admired the Munich
artists of *Der Blaue Reiter*, for example, they rebuffed him. Later, during the First
World War, his work became better known and in 1916 he was featured in an
issue of the left-wing, Berlin-based Expressionist magazine *Die Aktion*. Schiele was
an acquired taste. From an early stage he was regarded as a genius. This won him
the support of a small group of long-suffering collectors and admirers but, nonetheless,
for several years of his life his finances were precarious. He was often in debt and
sometimes he was forced to use cheap materials, painting on brown wrapping
paper or cardboard instead of artists' paper or canvas. It was only in 1918 that he
enjoyed his first substantial public success in Vienna. Tragically, a short time later,
he and his wife Edith were struck down by the massive influenza epidemic of 1918
that had just killed Klimt and millions of other victims, and they died within days
of one another. Schiele was just twenty-eight years old.

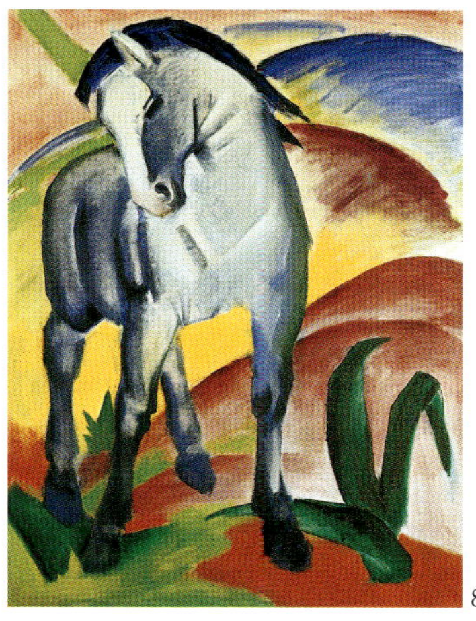

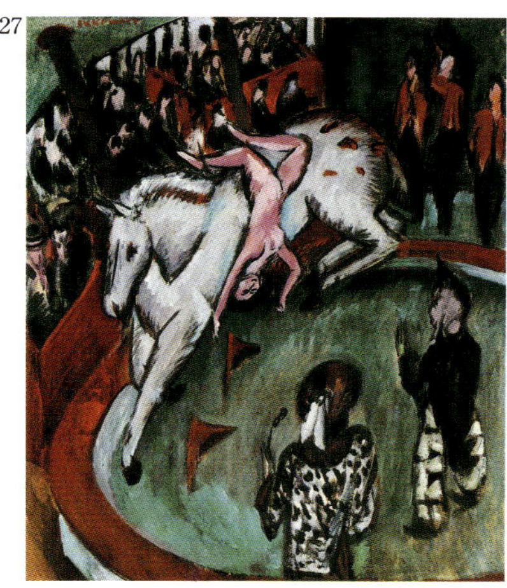

826.

827. **Franz Marc**, 1880-1916, Expressionism, German, *Blue Horse I*, 1911. Oil on canvas, 112.5 x 84.5 cm. Städtische Galerie im Lenbachhaus, Munich.

827. **Ernst Ludwig Kirchner**, 1880-1938, Expressionism, German, *Circus Rider*, 1912. Oil on canvas, 120 x 100 cm. Staatsgalerie moderner Kunst, Munich.

828. **Franz Marc**, 1880-1916, Expressionism, German, *Red Deers II*, 1912. Oil on canvas, 70 x 100 cm. Franz Marc Museum, Kochel am See.

In Red Deers II *of 1912, the painter's concern is no longer primarily with the naturalistic rendition of the deer and their movements. Marc's vision has become much more subjective. The natural subject itself is now more distilled. Incidental details are eliminated in favour of a synthesis of essential elements. In contrast to the naturalistic earth tones of the earlier painting, this work is now a finely tuned composition in colour.*

A common misconception about Expressionism is that it simply involved artists spewing forth onto the canvas or page emotional gestures or instinctive impulses. These kinds of outpourings can be found within Expressionism of course. However, works like Marc's Red Deers II *was a product of several years of intensive experimentation, theorisation, and reflection on the symbolic properties of colours and their effects in juxtaposition.*

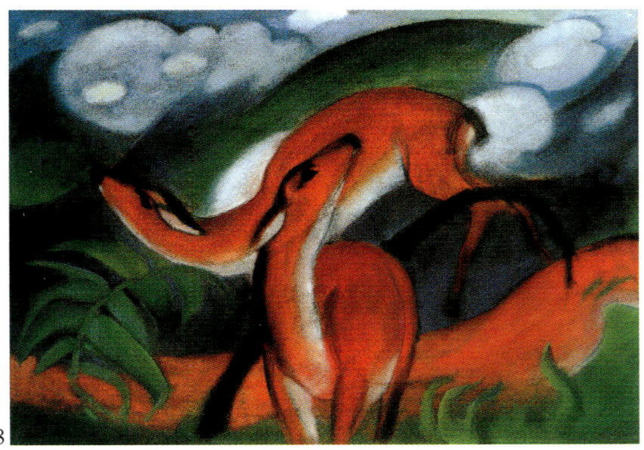

828.

FRANZ MARC
(1880 MUNICH – 1916 VERDUN)

During his lifetime Franz Marc was widely regarded as one of the most promising German painters of his generation. His death in the First World War was mourned as a bitter loss for the art world. It was also a deep personal loss for his surviving friends, Klee and Kandinsky – his other close friend from the *Der Blaue Reiter* circle, Macke, had died before him on the battlefield. As a young student, Marc had intended to study philosophy and theology. Then, in 1900, he decided to become a painter instead, and registered at the Munich Art academy.

Marc's early work was relatively naturalistic, but it showed evidence of his admiration for Van Gogh and Gauguin, whose works he had seen at first hand in Paris. He painted and made some prints and small sculptures. Most of his subjects came from nature. They were landscapes, a few nudes and, increasingly, the animals that would become so central and distinctive in his work. By around 1908 he was starting to intensify his exploration of the movement, behaviour and character of animals. He would spend hours observing and sketching cows and horses in the Bavarian pastures, and watching deer in the wild.

As he matured as an artist, in keeping with Expressionism's tendency to deal in universals – fundamental ethical issues and philosophies – Marc's intellectual concerns were with a future age of "the spiritual" and with the redemptive function of art in the modern society that he and his friends found so shallow and materialistic. Seeking a deeper experience of the ineffable, Marc verbalised it once to his friend Kandinsky: "I want to try to think the thoughts that dance behind a black curtain".

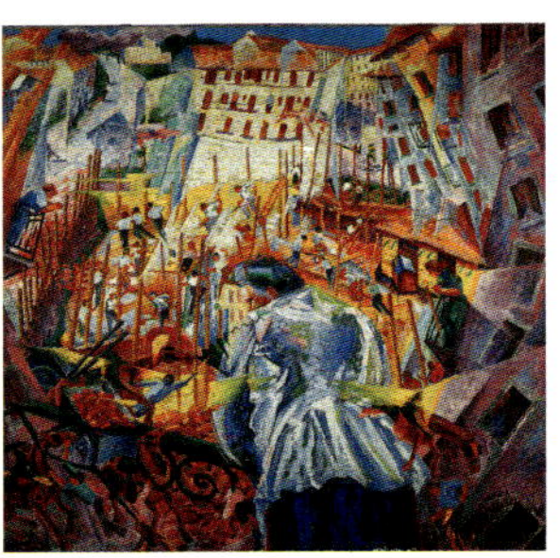

829. Umberto Boccioni,
1882-1916, Futurism, Italian,
The Street Penetrates the House, 1911.
Oil on canvas, 100 x 100 cm.
Sprengel Museum, Hanover.

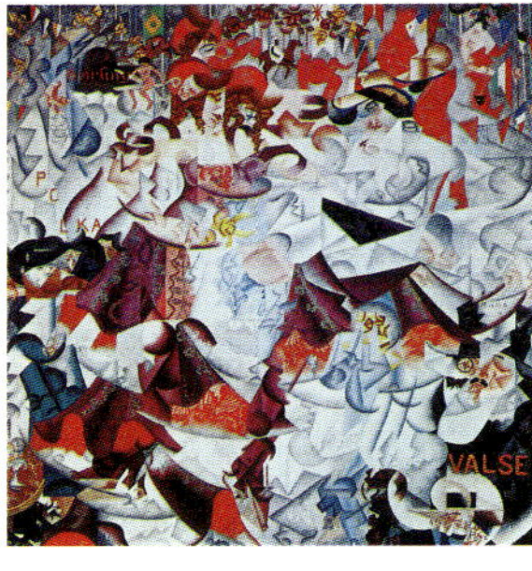

830. Gino Severini, 1883-1966,
Futurism, Italian,
Dynamic Hieroglyphic of the Bal Tabarin, 1912.
Oil on canvas with sequins,
161.6 x 156.2 cm.
The Museum of Modern Art,
New York.

831. **Wassily Kandinsky**, 1866-1944, Lyrical Abstraction/
Der Blaue Reiter, Russian, *Composition VII*, 1913.
Oil on canvas, 200 x 300 cm.
The State Tretyakov Gallery, Moscow.

This work appeared about the same time as his main writing, On the Spiritual in Art, *albeit the Russian artist had written that book two years before. Shortly before that, he was the founding influence on The Blue Rider group (Der Blaue Reiter). While he had not yet given up representational painting entirely at the time of this series, there is no objective content in it. It is only after he left Russia in 1922 that intentional geometric shapes appear in his work, as in* Accented Corners *(1823). Like Gauguin, he wanted to have a spiritual reservoir from which to draw and not to be merely a channel for the beauty of nature.*

Distinct from his "Improvisations", more spontaneous works, Kandinsky's "Compositions" are more elaborate. Also the influence of music upon Kandinsky's work was major. The artist drew a parallel between the use of colours and musical composition, with the same interactions between harmonies and dissonances.

831

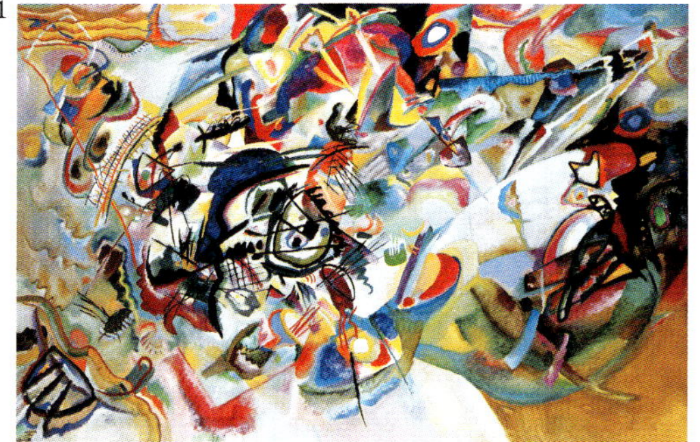

WASSILY KANDINSKY
(1866 MOSCOW – 1944 NEUILLY-SUR-SEINE)

Kandinsky's art does not reflect and is not burdened by the fate of other Russian avant-garde masters. He left Russia well before the semi-official Soviet aesthetic turned its back on modernist art.

He had been to Paris and Italy, even giving Impressionism its due in his earliest works. However, it was only in Germany that he aspired to study. It is obvious that in his preference for Munich over Paris, Kandinsky had been thinking more about schools than about artistic milieu. The qualities of salon Impressionism, a hint of the dry rhythms of modernism (*Jugendstil*), a heavy "demiurgic stroke" reminiscent of Cézanne, the occasionally significant echoes of Symbolism and much more can be found in the artist's early works. Kandinsky began working in Murnau in August, 1908. The intensity with which he worked during this period is stunning. In his early Murnau landscapes it is not hard to recognise a Fauvist boiling of colours and an abruptness in their juxtapositioning, the dramatic tension of Expressionism, which was gathering strength at that time, and the insistent texture of Cézanne.

Kandinsky was leaving behind the earthly gravitational field of objects for the weightlessness of the abstract world, where the principal coordinates of being up and down, space and weight are lost. According to the myths of the twentieth century, by leaving reality behind, Kandinsky renounced illusion and, therefore, drew closer to a higher reality. In 1911, Kandinsky participated in the foundation of the group *Der Blaue Reiter* (Blue Rider). Kandinsky had already acquired a name in his Russian homeland. His *On the Spiritual in Art* (1912) was known from lectures and other accounts. When, with the "Improvisations" and "Compositions" of 1915-1920, Kandinsky made his final break with the object world, he preserved until the early 1930s the feeling of dynamic, even organic, life in his paintings. In the summer of 1922, Kandinsky began teaching at the Weimar Bauhaus. It was then, in the first Bauhaus years, that he began working on his "Worlds", works in which he quite directly contrasted the grandeur of the great and the small. Kandinsky's fame grew with that of the Bauhaus.

Kandinsky determined the essence of what was happening to him in the context of his environment. On the one hand, the presence of surrealistic overtones in his art is unquestionable. Those splendid carnivals of the subconscious, those "landscapes of the soul," realised in his simultaneously menacing and festive paintings from the 1910s, had already been in partial contact with the poetics of Surrealism.

In Russia he had come to know himself as an artist: Russian motifs and sensations nourished his brush for a long time. In Germany he had become a professional and a great master; a transnational master. In France, where he was already welcomed as a world celebrity, he completed brilliantly and a bit dryly what he had begun in Russia and Germany.

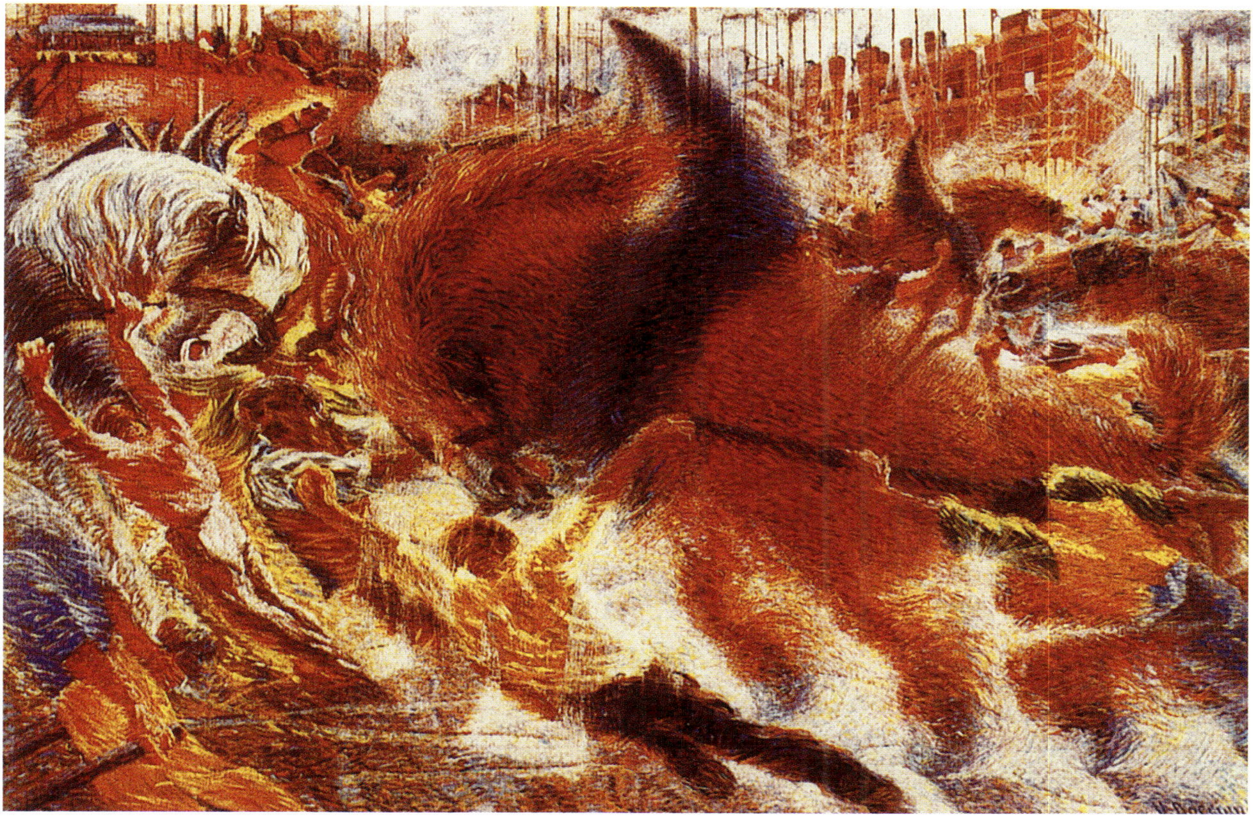

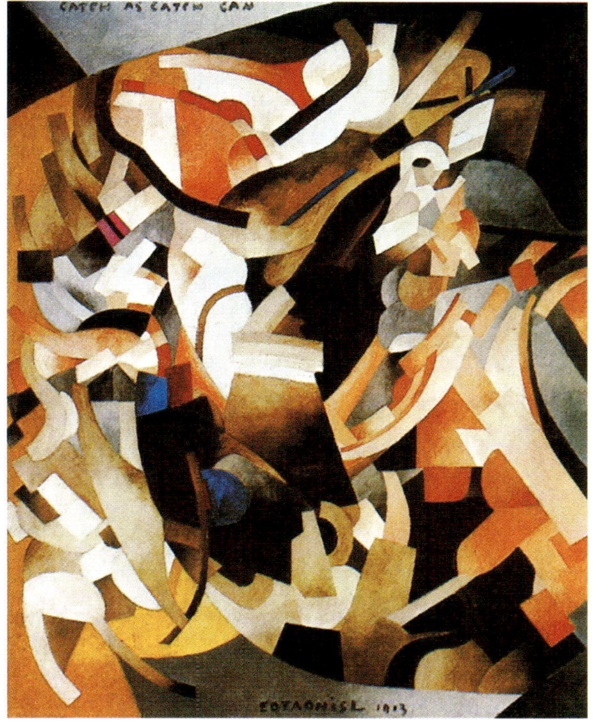

832. **Umberto Boccioni**, 1882-1916, Futurism, Italian,
The City Rises, 1910.
Oil on canvas, 199.3 x 301 cm.
The Museum of Modern Art, New York.

833. **Francis Picabia**, 1879-1953, Dada/ Orphism, French,
Catch as Catch Can, 1913.
Oil on canvas, 100.6 x 81.6 cm.
Philadelphia Museum of Art, Philadelphia.

After meeting Marcel Duchamp, Picabia became a master of Orphism and represented space and movement through fragmented colours.

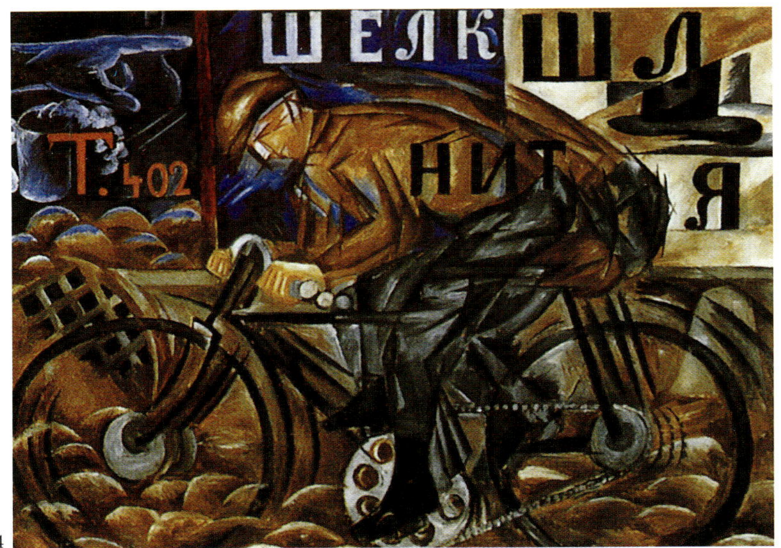

834

834. Natalia Goncharova, 1881-1962, Rayonism, Russian-French, *The Cyclist*, 1913. Oil on canvas, 78 x 105 cm. The State Russian Museum, St Petersburg.

835. Giacomo Balla, 1871-1958, Futurism, Italian, *Dynamism of a Dog on a Leash*, 1912. Oil on canvas, 89.9 x 109.9 cm. Albright-Knox Art Gallery, Buffalo.

Like other followers of the poet Filippo Tomasso Marinetti at the start of the twentieth century, Balla wanted to give birth to an art praising modern society (Futurism). He was fascinated with expressing movement and energy. The viewer may notice here the animation given to the dog's feet, tail and leash. He and other early Modernists, including Duchamp were also influenced by "chronophotography" that dated back to 1886. He was interested especially in recent advances, such as the motion studies of Etienne-Jules Marey that was then passed on to Frank Gilbreth, a student of Frederick Winslow Taylor, and his campaign to use chronophotography to improve industrial productivity.

835

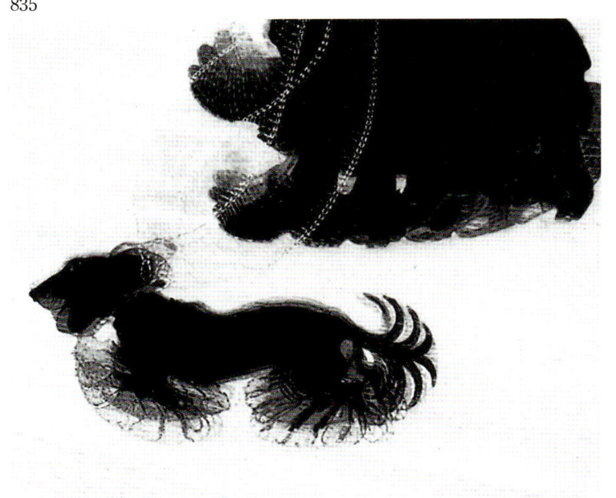

GIACOMO BALLA
(1871 TURIN – 1958 ROME)

As a child, Giacomo Balla studied music before focusing on painting. Following his studies of academic art in Turin he settled in Rome. In 1912, alongside Fillipo Tomasso Marinetti, Balla was one of the originators of Futurism. He contributed to both the political and ideological bases of the movement, which was particularly involved in the depiction of light and movement. Simultaneously, he attempted to capture the modern age of sound and energy in paintings such as *Automobile and Noise* (1912).

Dynamism of a Dog on a Leash appeared in the same year as Duchamp's *Nude Descending the Staircase* (1912) and revealed his interest for the representation of movement and speed. In the 1930s, his art had moved towards abstraction and eventually returned to academic realism.

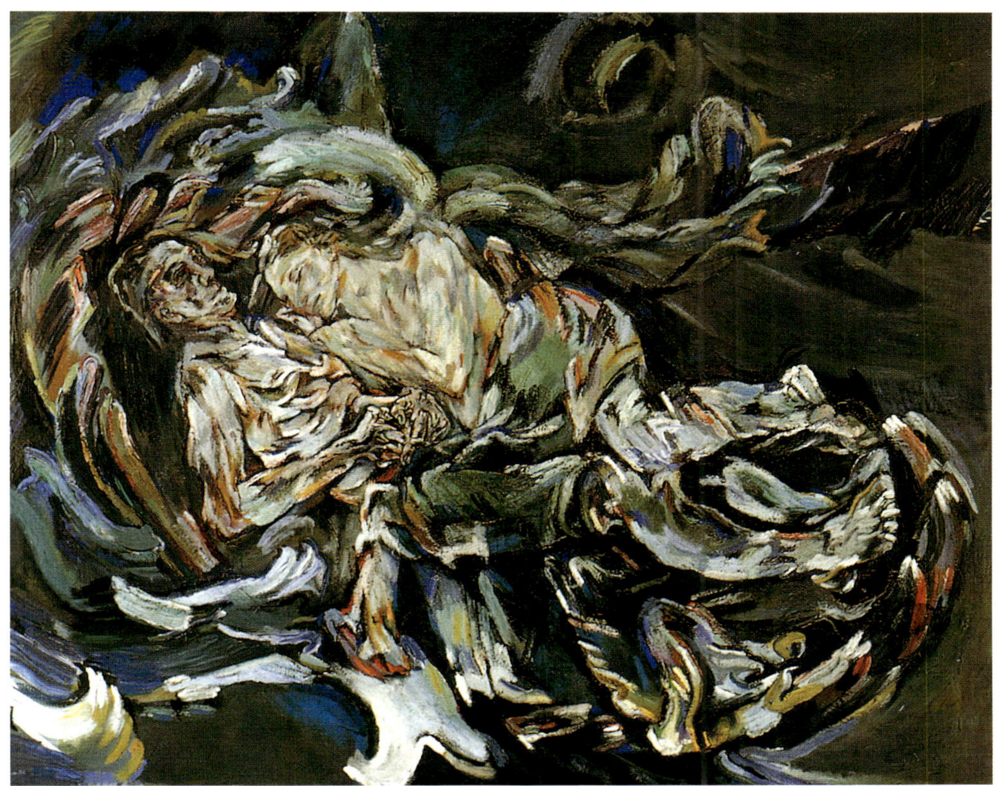

OSKAR KOKOSCHKA
(1886 PÖCHLARN – 1980 MONTREUX)

Oskar Kokoschka painted some of the major works of Expressionism and set a new standard for modern portraiture. Towards the end of his long life, his work was described as "eternal Expressionism". Yet there has long been a strong tendency among critics and curators to regard his earliest work, particularly from the "Vienna years" of 1909-1914, as his best. Certainly Kokoschka created some of his most stunningly original visual and literary work during this period. However, he continued to explore the means for powerful expression in painting throughout his life.

Kokoschka was also a significant writer and active in cultural politics – as an outspoken opponent of the Nazi oppression – in his later career.

Kokoschka was born in Lower Austria and emerged from a milieu still under the thrall of Klimt and Viennese Secessionism. He made his name while still a student at the 1908 Kunstschau in Vienna with works he produced under the aegis of the stylish Wiener Werkstätte. The already radical and unsettling qualities of his work were recognised early. He was dubbed *Oberwildling* or "Chief Savage". Kokoschka did not train as a painter. He studied other techniques at the Kunstgewerbeschule (School of Applied Arts). Yet he had barely graduated when he began his intensive engagement with the portrait genre. Loos recognised the young artist's raw, precocious talent and encouraged him, particularly in his portraiture. It is therefore fitting that one of Kokoschka's first great portraits was of his mentor, painted in 1909.

836. **Oskar Kokoschka**, 1886-1980,
Expressionism, Austrian,
The Tempest (The Bride of the Winds), 1914.
Oil on canvas, 71 x 86 cm.
Kunstmuseum, Basle.

The painting for which Kokoschka is perhaps best known emerged from a passionate love affair he had, which has also become legendary. Die Windsbraut (The Tempest) is a large painting, worked over many times. Its evocative title, which literally means "Bride of the Winds," came from the poet Georg Trakl – Kokoschka had originally envisaged the couple as the Wagnerian lovers Tristan and Isolde. At an early stage the painting was dominated by the red tones suggestive of burning passion. In its final state, however, it is a testimony to the artist's own experience of love and longing crystallised in cold, dreamlike hues of greens, blues, greys and pale pinks. No victim of false modesty, Kokoschka described it as "my strongest and greatest work, the masterpiece of all Expressionist endeavours". The figures, elevated above earthly reality and tossed on the storms of love even as they embrace, are Kokoschka and the woman who possessed his work and his thoughts for many years, his lover Alma Mahler.

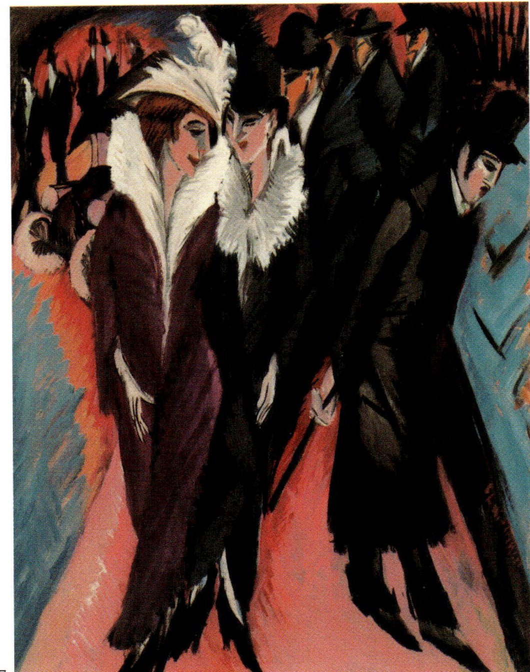

837

ERNST LUDWIG KIRCHNER
(1880 ASCHAFFENBURG – 1938 FRAUENKIRCH)

The self-appointed "leader" of the artists' group *Die Brücke* (Bridge), founded in Dresden in 1905, Ernst Ludwig Kirchner was a key figure in the early development of German Expressionism. His first works show the influence of Impressionism, Post-impressionism and *Jugendstil*, but by about 1909, Kirchner was painting in a distinctive, expressive manner with bold, loose brushwork, vibrant and non-naturalistic colours and heightened gestures. He worked in the studio from sketches made very rapidly from life, often from moving figures, from scenes of life out in the city or from the *Die Brücke* group's trips to the countryside. A little later he began making roughly-hewn sculptures from single blocks of wood. Around the time of his move to Berlin, in 1912, Kirchner's style in both painting and his prolific graphic works became more angular, characterised by jagged lines, slender, attenuated forms and often, a greater sense of nervousness. These features can be seen to most powerful effect in his Berlin street scenes. With the outbreak of the First World War, Kirchner became physically weak and prone to anxiety. Conscripted, he was deeply traumatised by his brief experience of military training during the First World War. From 1917 until his death by suicide in 1938, he lived a reclusive, though artistically productive life in the tranquillity of the Swiss Alps, near Davos.

EMIL NOLDE
(1867 SCHLESWIG-HOLSTEIN – 1956 SEEBÜLL)

Emil Nolde was born Emil Hansen. His attachment to the land of the northern German countryside, and especially to the sea, was given philosophical meaning and a kind of portentousness through the filter of the *völkisch* ideas he gleaned from writers such as Julius Langbehn. Nolde often spoke of the struggle for what he called "*das Heimische*" (roughly translated, the "native regional") in art. However, he also knew and loved his northern region from first-hand experience. His paintings of the sea and landscapes of Schleswig-Holstein therefore emerged from close familiarity as well as the vividness of Nolde's imagination.

As an artist, Nolde saw himself as an outsider. Yet his highly coloured, original and richly imaginative work appealed to the much younger *Die Brücke* artists when they saw it. They responded with enthusiasm and revered, in particular, Nolde's "storms of colour". They asked him to become a member of *Die Brücke*, and Nolde exhibited with them in 1906 and 1907. Schmidt-Rottluff came to the Baltic island of Alsen, where Nolde and his wife Ada had made a home, to paint for a few months, but such collaborative projects and group activities did not come naturally to Nolde. From his own copious writings, the image of the artist that emerges, indeed that these texts construct, is that of a lone visionary.

Some of Nolde's most spectacular paintings are seascapes. The sea, especially at times and seasons on the cusp of change – sunset, sunrise, autumn – was an enduring, yet endlessly changing subject. Nolde painted it, without the need for anecdotal detail, in a vast range of moods and weather effects. It has been argued that only Turner before him had ever painted such dramatic and sensitive evocations of the sea. Nolde created a series of thirteen autumn seascapes in 1910 alone. This series continued the following year.

837. **Ernst Ludwig Kirchner**, 1880-1938, Expressionism, German,
       Street, Berlin, 1913.
       Oil on canvas, 120.6 x 91.1 cm.
       The Museum of Modern Art, New York.

       *Part of the Die Brucke group, Kirchner's search for simplified
       form of expression was strongly influenced by the hectic life
       in Berlin. His work was considered by the Nazis as
       "degenerate art". Distressed and overcome by anxiety, he shot
       himself in 1938.*

838. **Emil Nolde**, 1867-1956, Expressionism, German,
       Young Men from Papua, 1913-1914.
       Oil on canvas, 70 x 103.5 cm.
       Staatliche Museen, Berlin.

839. **Karl Schmidt-Rottluff**, 1884-1976, Expressionism, German,
       Summer, 1913.
       Oil on canvas, 88 x 104 cm.
       Sprengel Museum, Hanover.

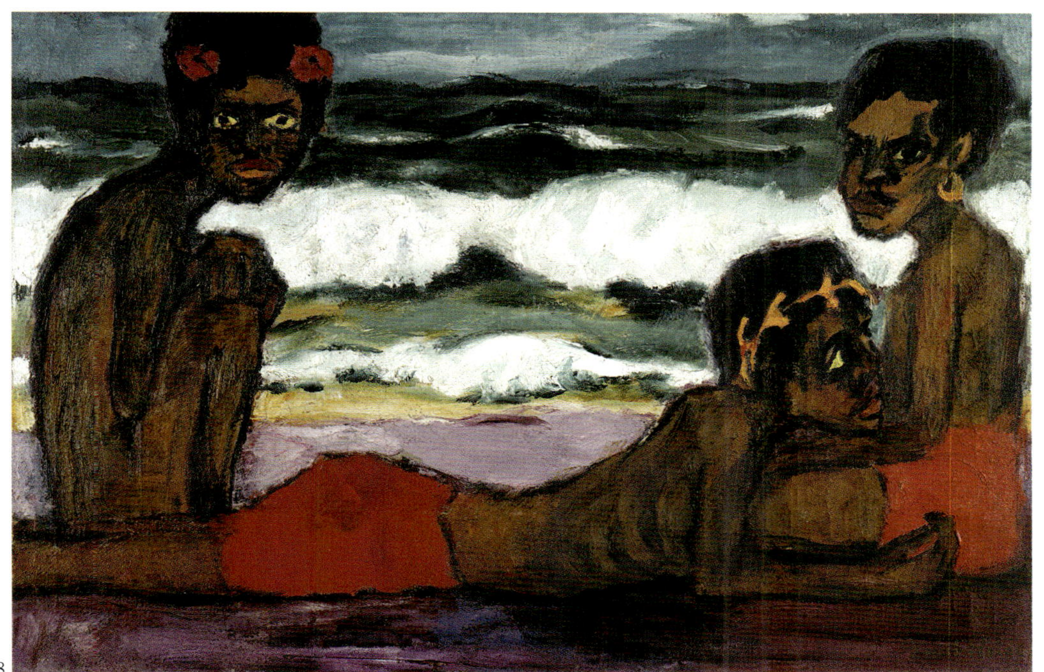

838

839

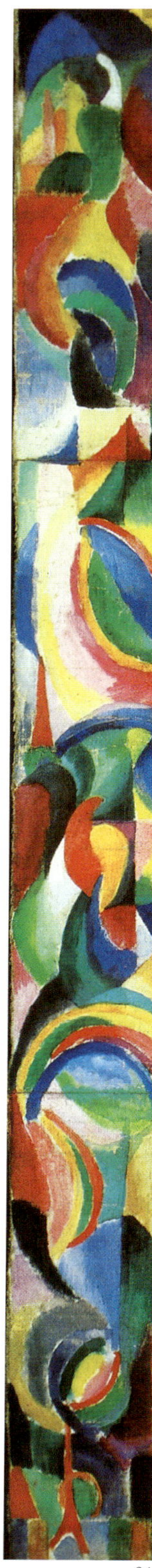

840

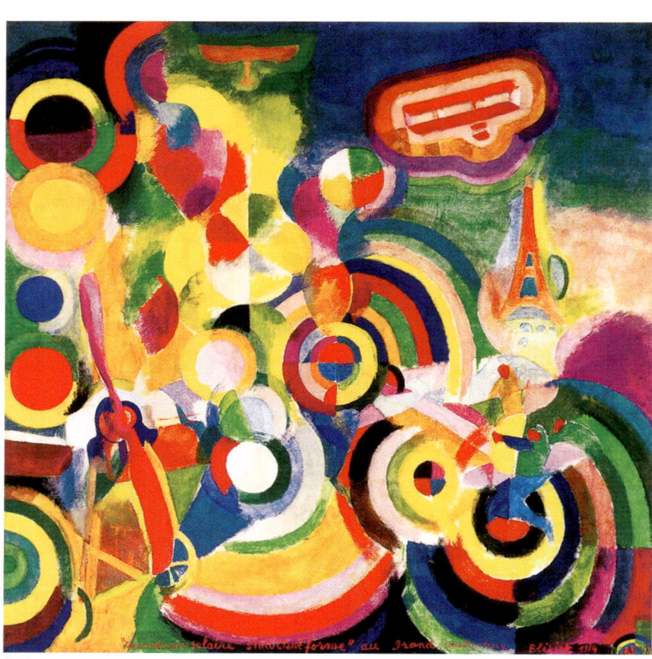

841

840. **Sonia Delaunay-Terk**, 1895-1979,
Orphism, Russian,
*Prose du Transsibérien et de la Petite
Jehanne de France (Prose of the
Trans-Siberian and of the Little
Jehanne of France)*, 1913.
Oil on canvas, 193.5 x 18.5 cm.
Musée national d'art moderne,
Centre Georges-Pompidou, Paris.

841. **Robert Delaunay**, 1885-1941,
Orphism, French, *Hommage à Blériot
(Homage to Blériot)*, 1914.
Oil on canvas, 250.5 x 251.5 cm.
Kunstsammlung, Basle.

*This painting celebrates the first time
that Louis Blériot crossed the Channel
in 1909. This is a preliminary sketch
for a bigger collage displayed in the
Kunstmuseum in Basle.*

842. **David Bomberg**, 1890-1957,
Abstraction, British,
The Mud Bath, 1914.
Oil on canvas, 152.4 x 226.9 cm.
Tate Gallery, London.

*Little known and appreciated, Bomberg's
reputation is now excellent, thanks to a
major exhibition at the Tate Gallery
in 1988. One of the major artists of
London avant-garde, he elaborated
a visual language between Cubism and
Futurism, approaching Abstraction, and
expressing his perception of the modern
urban environment.*

842

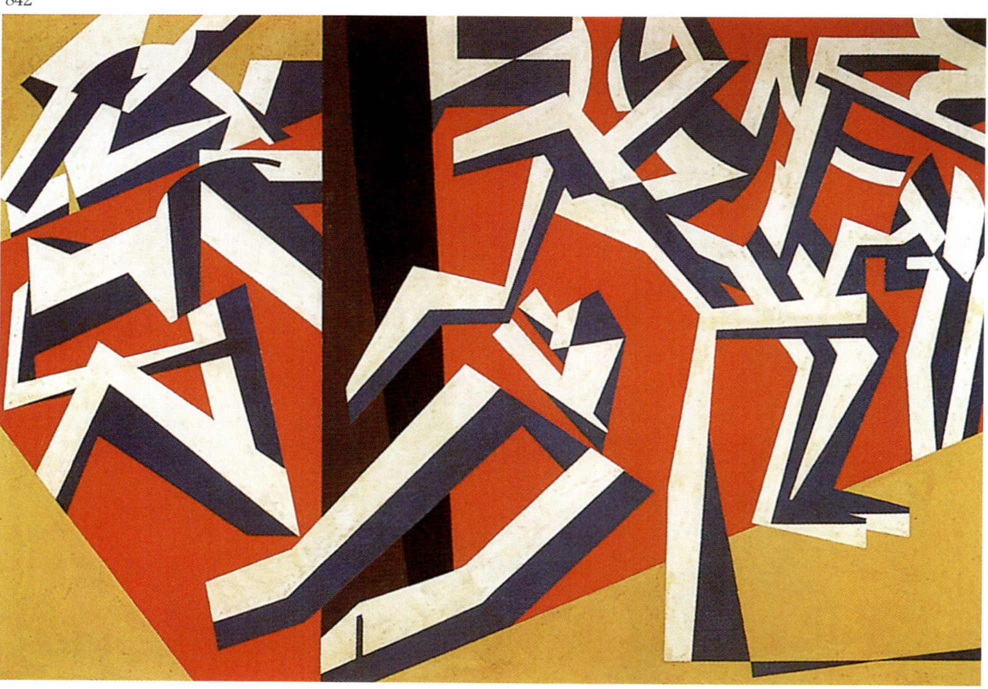

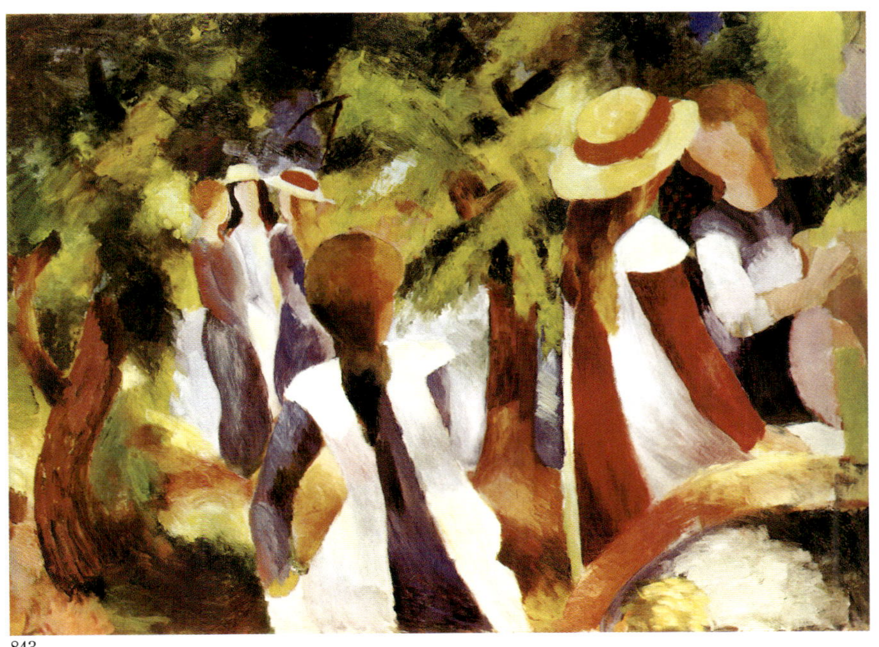

843

843. **August Macke**, 1887-1914,
Expressionism, German,
Girls Under Trees, 1914.
Oil on canvas, 119.5 x 159 cm.
Staatsgalerie moderner Kunst,
Munich.

844. **Roger de La Fresnaye**, 1885-1925,
Cubism, French,
The Conquest of the Air, 1913.
Oil on canvas, 235.9 x 195.6 cm.
The Museum of Modern Art,
New York.

845. **Marsden Hartley**, 1877-1943,
Semi-Abstraction, American,
Portrait of a German Officer, 1914.
Oil on canvas, 173.4 x 105.1 cm.
The Metropolitan Museum of Art,
New York.

844

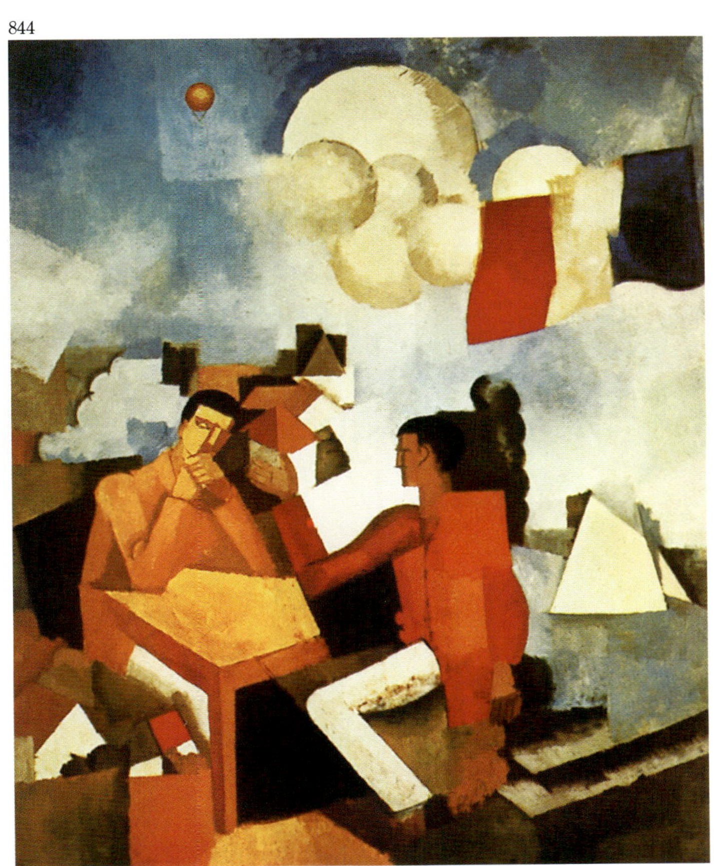

845

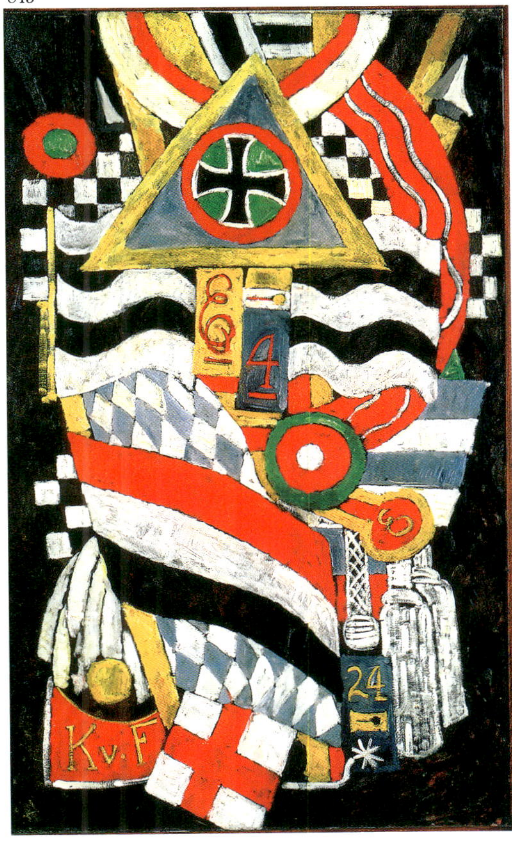

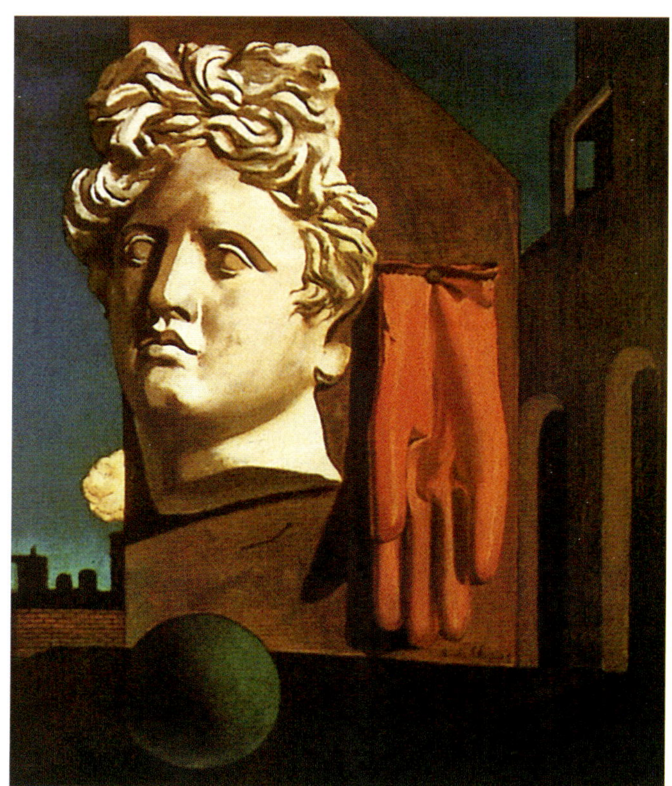

846. **Giorgio de Chirico**, 1888-1978, Surrealism, Italian,
The Song of Love, 1914.
Oil on canvas, 73 x 59.1 cm.
The Museum of Modern Art, New York.

*The artist was one of the signers of the Dada manifesto of
1920. He was born in Greece of Italian parents in 1888.
Not yet twenty years old, he studied mystical romanticism in
Munich, then lived in Milan, Florence and, finally, Paris,
where he met Picasso and Apollinaire. Here, in* The Song of
Love, *we see cold, distant and surrealistic elements that seem
unrelated to each other or to the title. The artist eventually
gave up the metaphysical style, but not before playing a
decisive role in modern art. Describing his landscapes, the
artist said: "Sometimes the horizon is defined by a wall
behind which rises the noise of a disappearing train."*

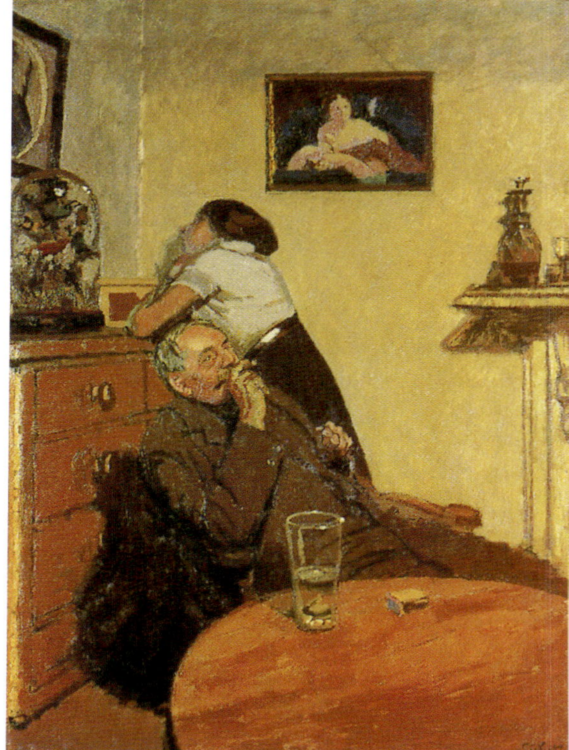

847. **Walter Richard Sickert**, 1860-1942, Impressionism, British,
Ennui, 1914.
Oil on canvas, 152.4 x 112.4 cm.
Tate Gallery, London.

*Born in Germany of a Danish-German father and an Anglo-Irish
mother, his family came to England where he became one of the
most important British artists of his time. The author Virginia Woolf
imagined a whole story behind these figures, referring to the man as
a pub landlord "looking out of his shrewd little pig's eyes at the
intolerable wastes of desolation in front of him".*

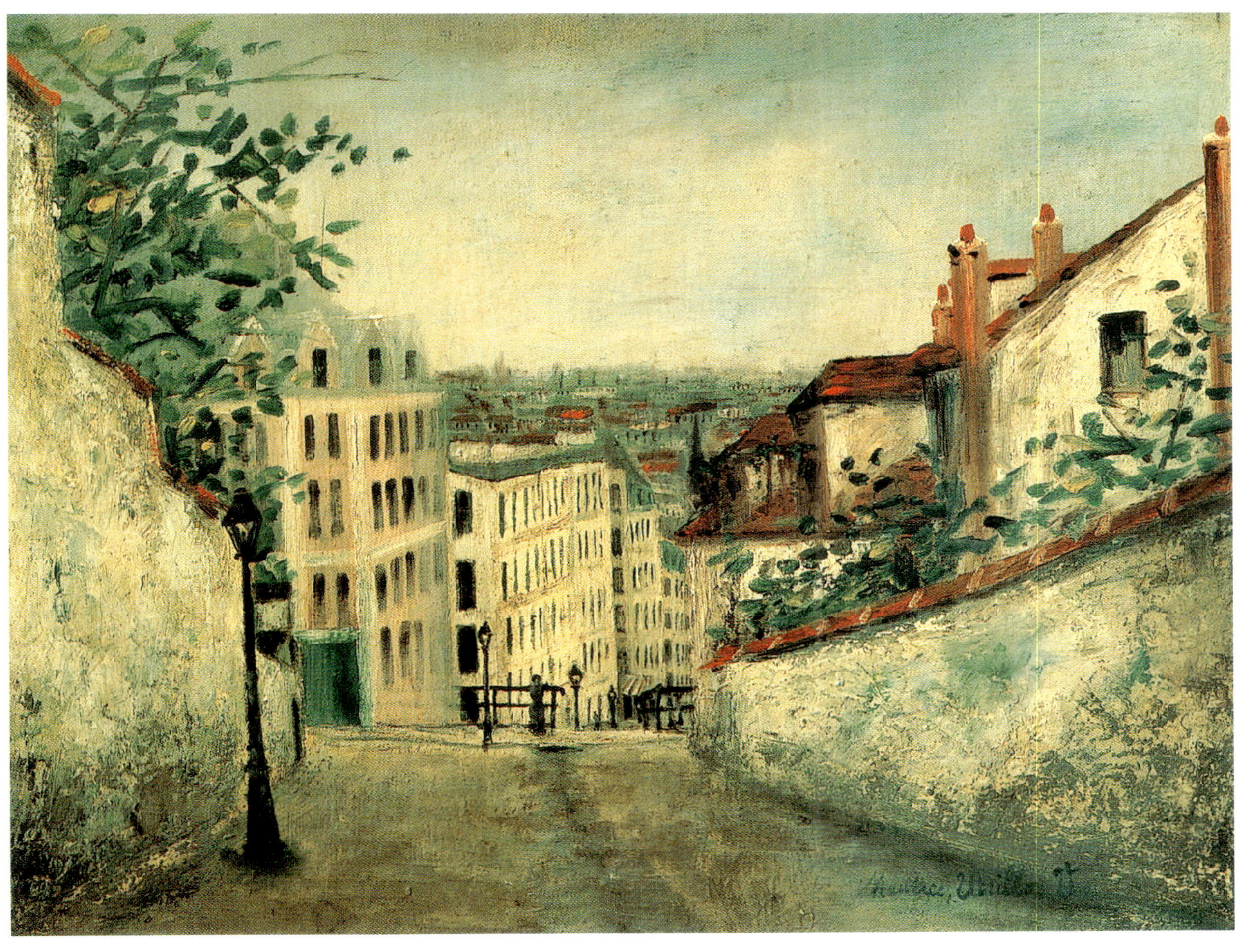

848. **Maurice Utrillo**, 1883-1955, Post-Impressionist, French,
La Rue du Mont-Cenis, 1914-1915.
Oil on canvas, 48 x 63 cm.
Pushkin State Museum of Fine Arts, Moscow.

Born to unwed painter Suzanne Valadon, Utrillo is characterised by a dark and thick manner. Although his Parisian street scenes were grouped with the Impressionists, Utrillo is an autodidact and his style can hardly be categorised. Original in his rendering of space and perspective, he mainly depicted views of Montmartre in Paris.

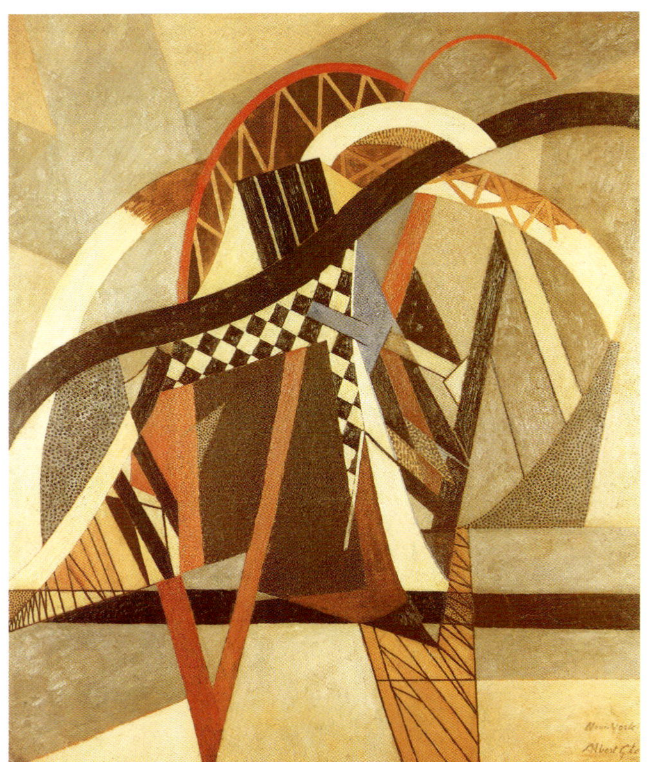

849. **Albert Gleizes**, 1881-1953, Cubism, French,
Brooklyn Bridge, 1915.
Oil on canvas. Private collection.

850. **Francis Picabia**, 1879-1953, Dada/Orphism, French,
Very Rare Picture on Earth, 1915.
Oil and metallic paint on board, and silver and gold leaf on
wood, 125.7 x 97.8 cm.
Peggy Guggenheim Collection, Venice.

MARCEL DUCHAMP
(1887 BLAINVILLE – 1968 NEUILLY SUR SEINE)

Marcel Duchamp came from an artistic family. He lived in Paris, in Montparnasse and studied at the Julian Academy. He and his brother, Raymond, often organised meetings with such artists as Fernand Léger, Francis Picabia, and Robert Delaunay. Eventually, they called themselves the Putteaux group. Duchamp was attracted by Futurism but mainly was influenced by Cubism. His work, either his experiments to Cubism or to Dadaism and Surrealism, definitely change the observer's vision of art. Actually, he seemed to simply find, sign, and display everyday objects, proclaiming them *object d'art*. One such object was a porcelain urinal, which he signed R. Mutt and titled *Fountain* (1917). He mounted a bicycle wheel upside-down on a kitchen stool as one of his "ready-made" artefacts. Duchamp lived also in the United States. His most famous work is *Nude Descending a Staircase #2* (1912) – the centre of attention in the Armory Show of 1913, which was called the most significant exhibition in American art history. This is testimony to the influence of Duchamp's work, and the mark he has left on the art world. As an artist he was in revolt against the established art system and coveted his artistic freedom. In his absurd objects the observer can see his sense of humour and his personal philosophy.

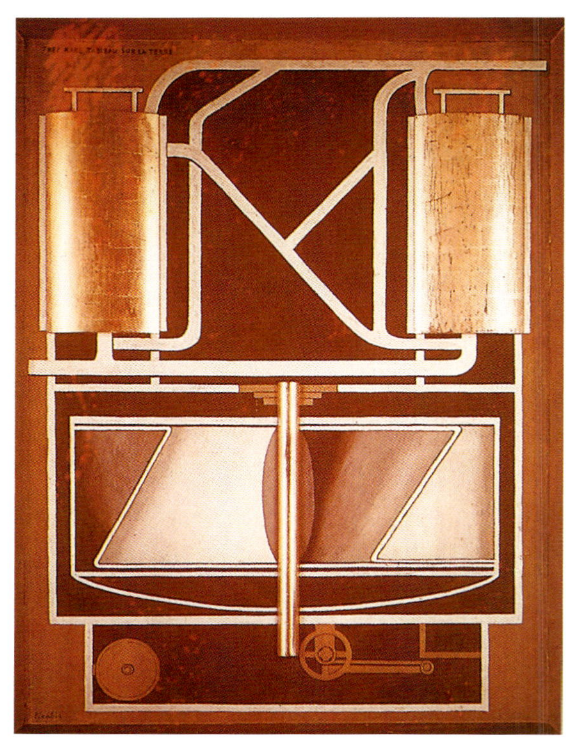

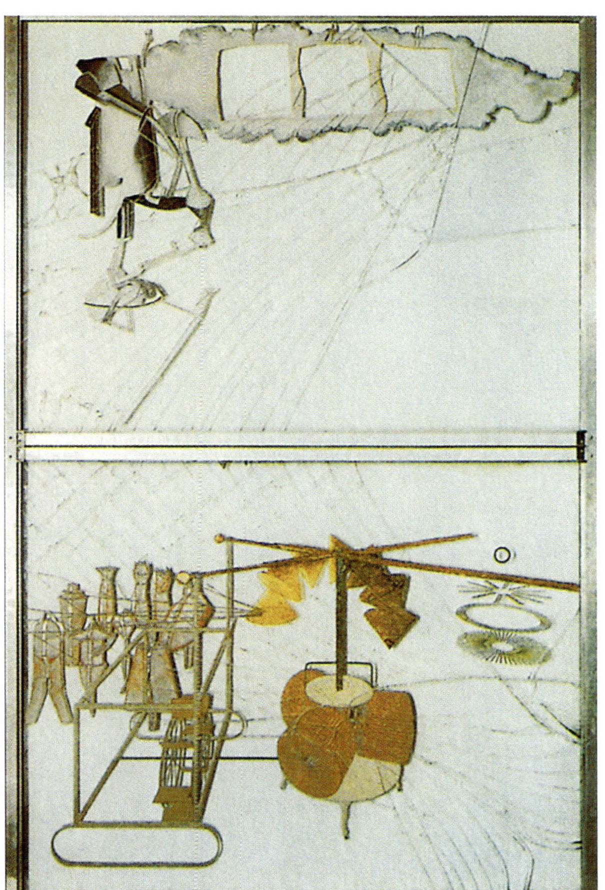

KASIMIR MALEVITCH
(1878 KIEV – 1935 LENINGRAD)

Pioneer of geometric abstract art and one of the most important members of the Russian Avant-garde, Malevitch experimented with various modernist styles. In reaction to the influence of Cubism and Futurism on artists in Russia, Malevitch in his art reduced the world of nature to basic elements and colours, such as in his *Red Square* (1915). He introduced his abstract, non-objective geometric patterns in a style and artistic movement he called Suprematism. One of the important names of the twentieth century, he however turned back to Primitivism once Russia's communist leaders forced him to do so.

851. **Marcel Duchamp**, 1887-1968, Dada, French,
The Bride Stripped Bare by her Bachelors, 1915-1923.
Oil, varnish, lead foil, lead wire, and dust on two glass panels, 277.5 x 176 cm.
Museum of Art, Philadelphia.

852. **Kasimir Malevitch**, 1878-1935, Abstraction/
Suprematism, Russian,
Suprematist Composition: White on White, 1918.
Oil on canvas, 79.4 x 79.4 cm.
The Museum of Modern Art, New York.

The Russian artist's most famous work is also his most minimalist. However, three years before he did present a black canvas simply with a white border. The work involves only a few components, breaking each down to a basic quality. The irony of the title is misleading. This is a work of nearly identical entities: the colours are nearly white; the shapes are nearly square; and the areas are nearly on the same plane, albeit at slightly different angles. This may be the logo work of Suprematism, the early twentieth-century movement in Russia interested in reducing painting to geometry, the science that was considered the "supreme" reality. It might then, in effect, be stating that oneness is an illusion.

853. Amedeo Modigliani, 1884-1920,
Expressionism, Italian,
Reclining Nude, 1917.
Oil on canvas, 60 x 92 cm.
Collection Gianni Mattioli.

Reminiscent of Goya's Naked
Maja *(1800), this painting bears
many of the hallmarks of
Modigliani's nude work during
the years 1917-1919. It is an
overtly sexual picture: the model
lies on her back, propped up on a
cushion, one breast in profile,
arms behind her head; the torso is
elongated, the pelvis twisted
towards the viewer. The legs are
cut off around the thigh so that
all the emphasis is on the sexual
elements of the woman's body.
The hair and lips are depicted
in some detail and the eyes,
although black and blank, look
made-up, giving a modern look
to the woman's face. The
blankness of the eyes effectively
depersonalises her so that, although
she looks at us provocatively,
sexually, there is no expression
of her individual personality in
the gaze. Modigliani's affinity
with sculpture is clear here,
inviting us to examine the sheer
physicality and mass of the body
through the medium of paint.*

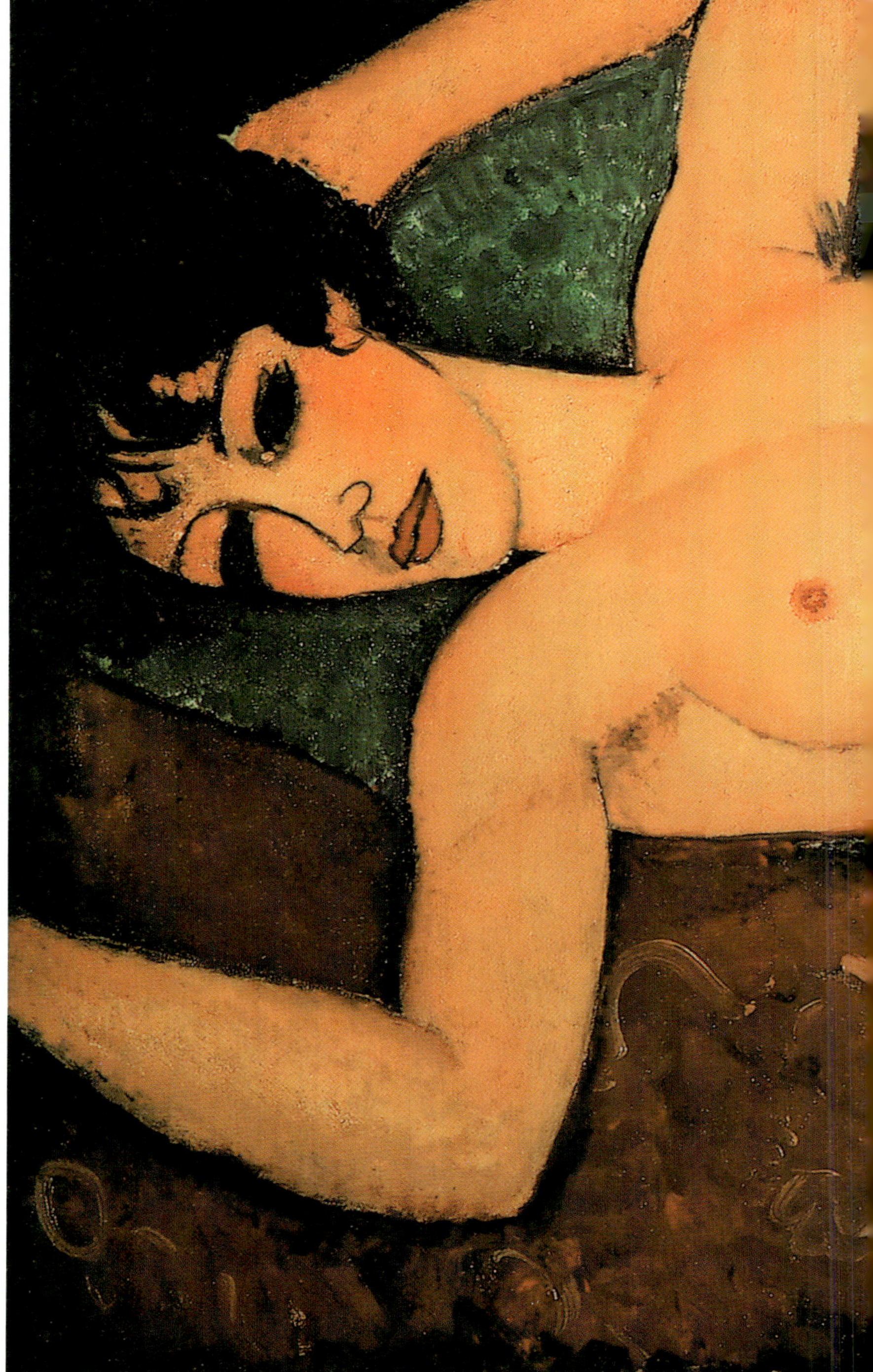

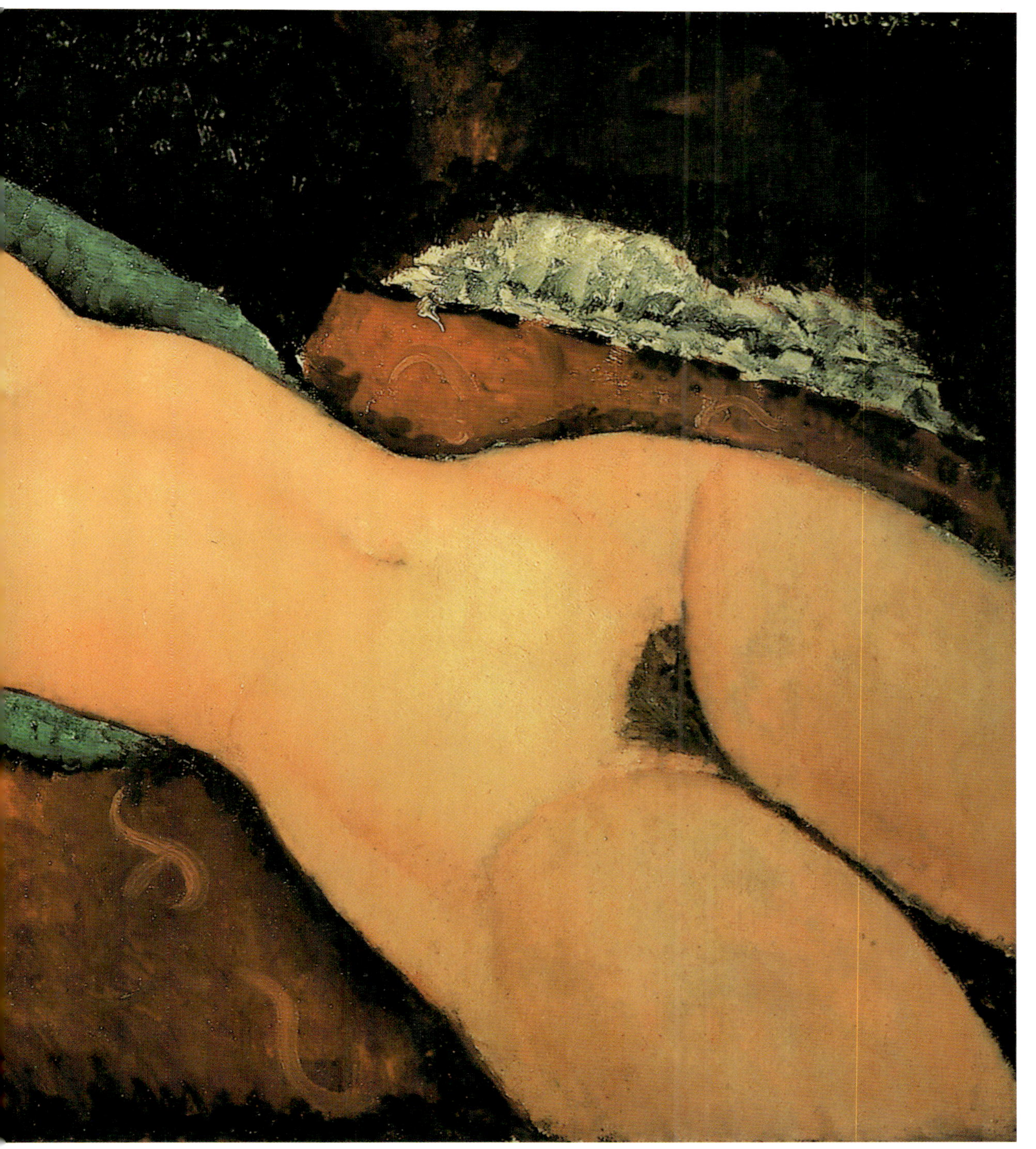

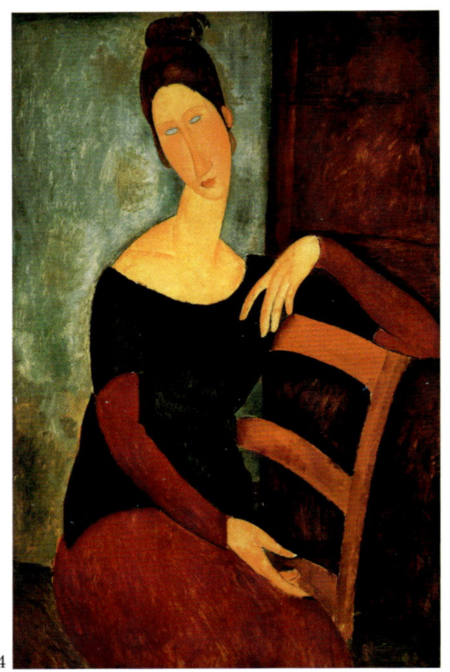

854

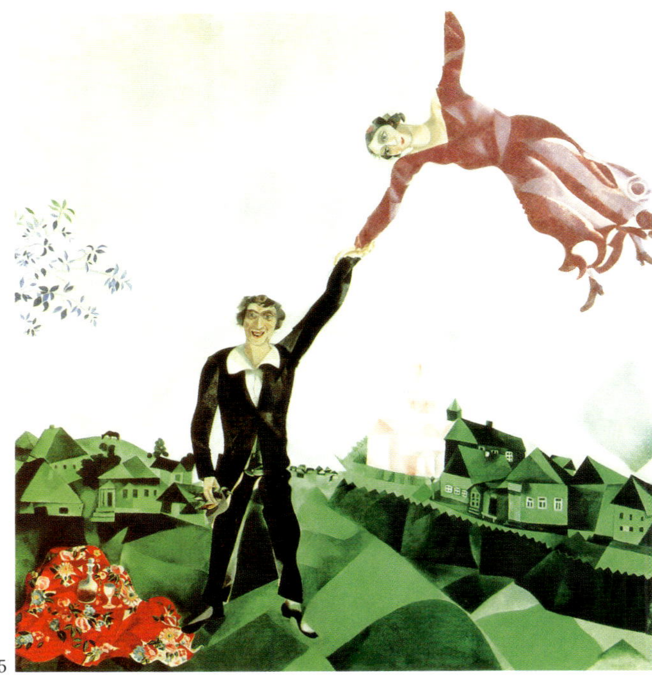

855

AMEDEO MODIGLIANI
(1884 LIVORNO – 1920 PARIS)

Amedeo Modigliani was born in Italy in 1884 and died in Paris at the age of thirty-five. From an early age he was interested in nude studies and in the classical notion of ideal beauty. In 1900-1901 he visited Naples, Capri, Amalfi, and Rome, returning by way of Florence and Venice, and studied first-hand many Renaissance masterpieces. He was impressed by trecento (thirteenth century) artists, including Simone Martini (c. 1284-1344), whose elongated and serpentine figures, rendered with a delicacy of composition and colour, and suffused with tender sadness, were a precursor to the sinuous line and luminosity evident in the work of Sandro Botticelli (c. 1445-1510).

Modigliani's debt to the art of the past was transformed by the influence of ancient art (ancient Greek Cycladic figures essentially), the art of other cultures (African for example) and Cubism. Their balanced circles and curves, despite having a voluptuousness, are carefully patterned rather than naturalistic. Their curves are precursors of the swinging lines and geometric approach that Modigliani later used in such nudes as *Reclining Nude*. Modigliani's drawings of caryatids allowed him to explore the decorative potential of poses that may not have been possible to create in sculpture. Modigliani was also familiar with the work of Francisco de Goya y Lucientes (1746-1828) and Edouard Manet (1832-1883), who had caused controversy by painting real, individual women as nudes, breaking the artistic conventions of setting nudes in mythological, allegorical, or historical scenes.

MARC CHAGALL
(1887 VITEBSK – 1985 SAINT-PAUL-DE-VENCE)

Marc Chagall was born into a strict Jewish family for whom the ban on representations of the human figure had the weight of dogma. A failure in the entrance examination for the Stieglitz School did not stop Chagall from later joining that famous school founded by the Imperial Society for the Encouragement of the Arts and directed by Nicholas Roerich. Chagall moved to Paris in 1910. The city was his "second Vitebsk". At first, isolated in the little room on the Impasse du Maine at La Ruche, Chagall soon found numerous compatriots also attracted by the prestige of Paris: Lipchitz, Zadkine, Archipenko and Soutine, all of whom were to maintain the "smell" of his native land. From his very arrival Chagall wanted to "discover everything". And to his dazzled eyes painting did indeed reveal itself. Even the most attentive and partial observer is at times unable to distinguish the "Parisian" Chagall from the "Vitebskian". The artist was not full of contradictions, nor was he a split personality, but he always remained different; he looked around and within himself and at the surrounding world, and he used his present thoughts and recollections. He had an utterly poetical mode of thought that enabled him to pursue such a complex course. Chagall was endowed with a sort of stylistic immunity: he enriched himself without destroying anything of his own inner structure. Admiring the works of others he studied them ingenuously, ridding himself of his youthful awkwardness, yet never losing his authenticity for a moment.

At times Chagall seemed to look at the world through magic crystal – overloaded with artistic experimentation – of the Ecole de Paris. Naturally, it totally and uneclectically reflected the painterly discoveries of Cézanne, the delicate inspiration of Modigliani, and the complex surface rhythms recalling the experiments of the early Cubists (See-*Portrait at the Easel*, 1914).

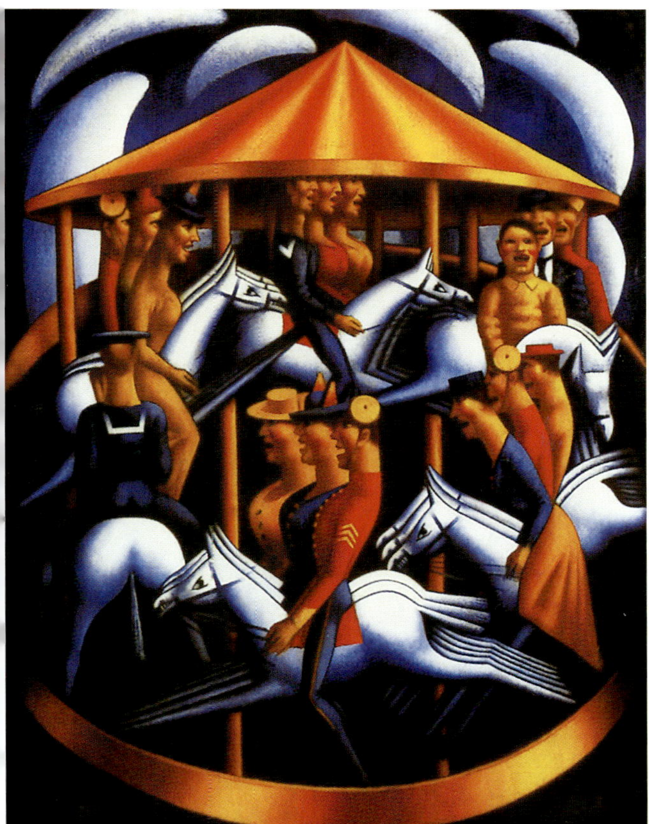

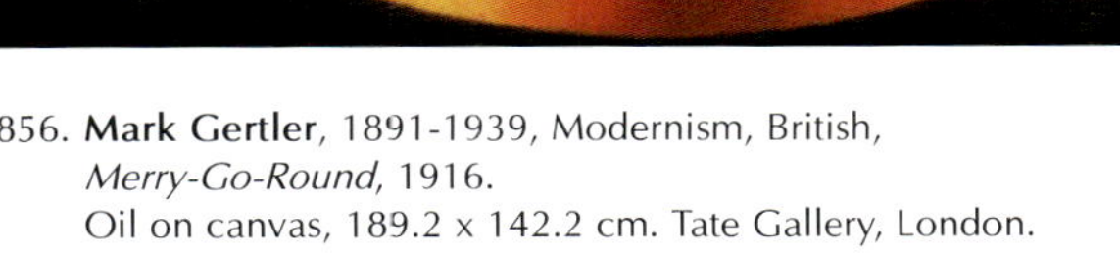

857

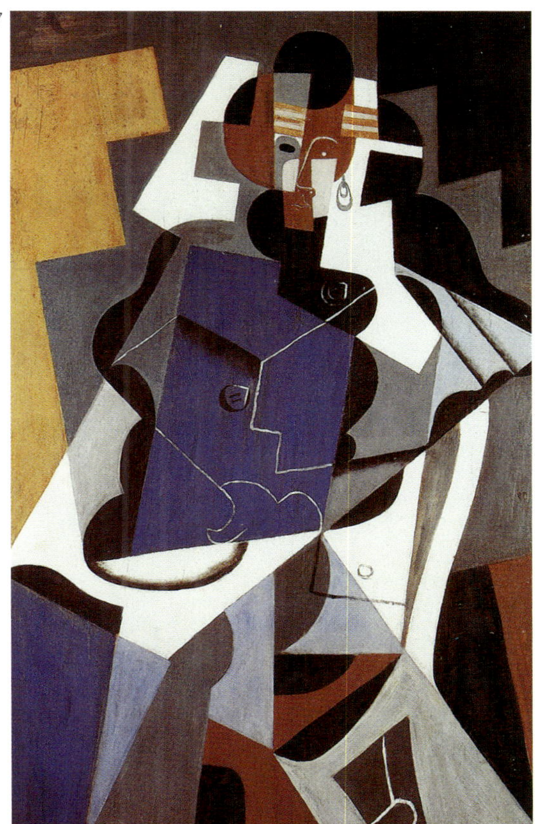

856. **Mark Gertler**, 1891-1939, Modernism, British,
Merry-Go-Round, 1916.
Oil on canvas, 189.2 x 142.2 cm. Tate Gallery, London.

Gertler, a conscientious objector to military service, painted this work at the height of the First World War. The fairground ride becomes here a metaphor of a military machine.

The failure of an exhibition in London at the Lefevre Gallery in 1939 caused him acute distress and, overcome by mental anxiety, he committed suicide.

854. **Amedeo Modigliani**, 1884-1920, Expressionism, Italian,
Portrait of Jeanne Hébuterne, 1918.
Oil on canvas, 100.3 x 65.4 cm.
Norton Simon Art Foundation, Pasadena.

There are many different portraits of Jeanne, and they differ enormously in terms of style and mood. Typically, however, she is depicted with extreme elongation of the neck and arms. Here she is shown during her pregnancy, languidly posed upon a chair. The graceful, elegant curves of her arms and neck are almost Baroque in style, and the warm palette of colours suggest, that this may have been painted in the south of France. However, there is little in the portrait to tell us much about Jeanne's character. Her blue eyes are blank and she sits with rather passive elegance, a subject for a painting rather than a person in her own right.

857. **Juan Gris**, 1887-1927, Cubism, Spanish,
Figure of Woman, 1917.
Oil on canvas, 116 x 73 cm. Private collection.

855. **Marc Chagall**, 1887-1985, Surrealism, Russian,
The Promenade, 1917.
Oil on canvas, 170 x 163.5 cm.
The State Russian Museum, St Petersburg.

The famous Promenade (1917) is a large canvas, almost square (rare for Chagall), in which two basic colours – green and violet-pink – are boldly combined. Old Vitebsk, emerald-green, magical, is barely recognisable in the refined build up of Cubist syncopated volumes in which Bella, wearing a lilac dress, hovers in the air, holding her husband by the hand so as not to fly away into the heavens. The artist himself smiles like a genial, happy clown who has created both his own happiness and this radiant world. And, as always, the mysterious and imposing painting of the sky, melting in the summer haze and signifying the cosmic elements, peacefully co-exists with purely earthly symbols, the carafe and glass on the red shawl which seems to burn against the green grass. The cosmic quality in Chagall's work grows out of everyday life. For a time the artist seems to forget about dramatic "ends" and "beginnings". Birth becomes only a reason for serene happiness. He completely stops recalling death. Clocks do not beat out fatal time but stop it and do not hurry. The artist is, as before, in a state of unceasing flight.

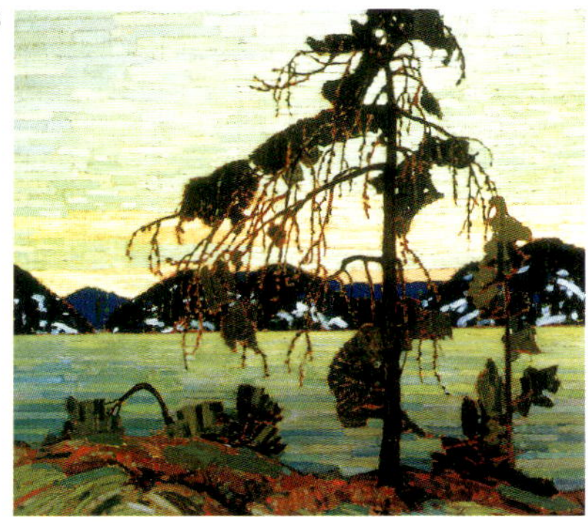

858

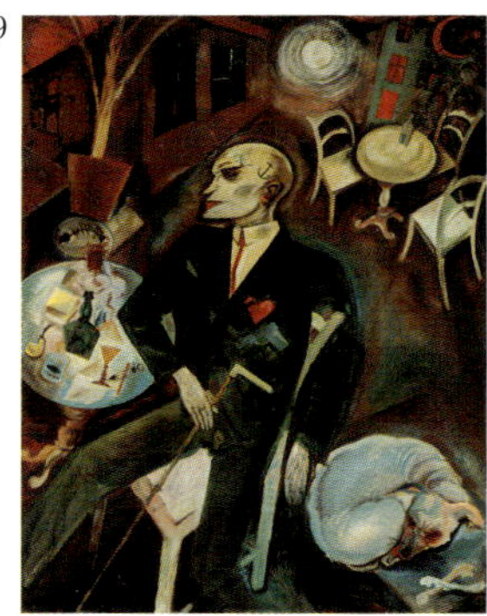

859

858. **Tom Thomson**, 1877-1917, Group of Seven (landscape painter), Canadian,
Jack Pine, 1917.
Oil on canvas, 127.9 x 139.8 cm.
National Gallery of Canada, Ottawa.

Tom Thomson is one of the principal founders of the Canadian school of painting. His life ended tragically when he was drowned in Algonquin Park. Probably because of the mystery that surrounds his death, Thomson has become a legend in Canada.

859. **George Grosz**, 1893-1959, Expressionism, German,
Lovesick, 1916. Oil on canvas, 100 x 78 cm.
Kunstsammlung Nordrhein-Westfalen, Dusseldorf.
Art © George Grosz / Licensed by VAGA, New York, NY.

In a period of reprise from army service which he so hated, in a canvas reeking of Gothic melodrama, Grosz painted a gaunt and deathly pale figure. Loosely based on his ill-nourished wartime self, Grosz called it Liebeskranker (Lovesick). *The palette is that of cold, moon lit, gangrenous, black-and-blue night, and congealed blood. The figure is one of Grosz's alter-ego types – an adventurer dandy. His bearing and silver-handled cane mark him as an aristocratic rogue. The anchor tattoo on his skull and gold earring show him as a rootless, pirate figure of the high seas. The crossbones before the dog curled up on the ground are the pirate pendent to the figure's white skull. At the centre of the composition is the pistol and blood-red heart beating at his breast. Morbidly, they suggest a crime of passion – committed (murder?), or yet being contemplated (suicide?). The accessories for intoxication litter the table – drink and drugs. Grosz was a heavy and enthusiastic drinker.*

The exaggeratedly steep, angular perspective and lack of horizon is typical of many Expressionist visualisations of urban space. Equally striking here, is the way that Grosz elides the distinction between outside and inside, exterior and interior space. In this nocturne, Grosz collapses the objects and ambience of a café interior into the architecture of the street, so that a disorientation – the visual equivalent of the subject queasy intoxication by love and liquor – ensues. We cannot know if the glowing white orb is the moon, a night-club spot or the beam of a search-light. Are we looking in or out of the walls and windows?

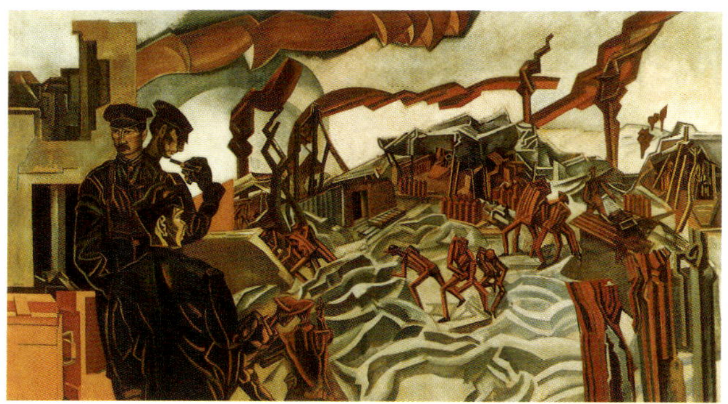

GEORGE GROSZ
(1893 – 1959 BERLIN)

George Grosz, who spent much of his childhood in a small town in the German province of Pomerania, was fascinated by big cities. Those that gripped his imagination most were the biggest and most frenetic – above all, Berlin and New York. He made Berlin his home until the rise of Nazism made Germany unbearable, but he dreamt of America, his youthful imagination fired by stories of cowboys and gold-diggers. Grosz's early work, made during the First World War, is his most "Expressionist". His drawings and paintings of alienated individuals, rioting masses, furtive criminals, prostitutes and (very real) brutal mass violence are staged in the streets, tenements and back alleys of Berlin. He also absorbed some of the Italian Futurists' dynamic, energy-laden compositional devices so well suited to conveying the more spectacular effects of modernity – electric lighting, mass transport and the surging movement of urban crowds.

Described by a Dadaist colleague, Hans Richter, as a "savage boxer, fighter and hater," Grosz became a key figure in the Berlin Dada movement. His pugnacious nature, his fearlessly irreverent sense for the absurd, and dark humour were fuel for Dada's political momentum as well as its anti-art stance. These aspects of Grosz, which infuse much of his work, made him resistant to many of the more literary, romantic and utopian aspects of Expressionism.

However, what Grosz undeniably shares with Expressionist contemporaries is a fascinating sensitivity to the intoxicating life-pulse and dynamism of the city. In 1933, to escape Nazi persecution, he emigrated with his wife to America. In 1959 he finally returned to Berlin, only to die barely a month later after a high-spirited night out on the town.

860. **Wyndham Lewis**, 1882-1957, Camden Town Group, British.
A Battery Shelled, 1919.
Oil on canvas, 152.5 x 317.5 cm.
Imperial War Museum, London.

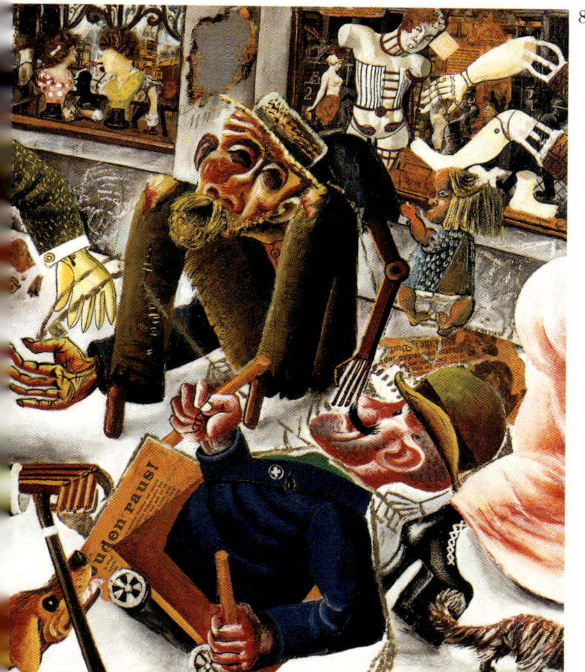

861. **Otto Dix**, 1891-1969, Expressionism, German,
Prager Street, 1920.
Oil and collage on canvas, 100 x 80 cm.
Galerie der Stadt, Stuttgart.

862. **George Grosz**, 1893-1959, Expressionism, German,
Metropolis, 1916-1917. Oil on canvas, 100 x 102 cm.
Thyssen-Bornemisza collection, Lugano.
Art © George Grosz / Licensed by VAGA, New York, NY.

863. **Ernst Ludwig Kirchner**, 1880-1938, Expressionism, German,
Animals Returning Home, 1919.
Oil on canvas, 120 x 167 cm.
Collection SWK, Berne.

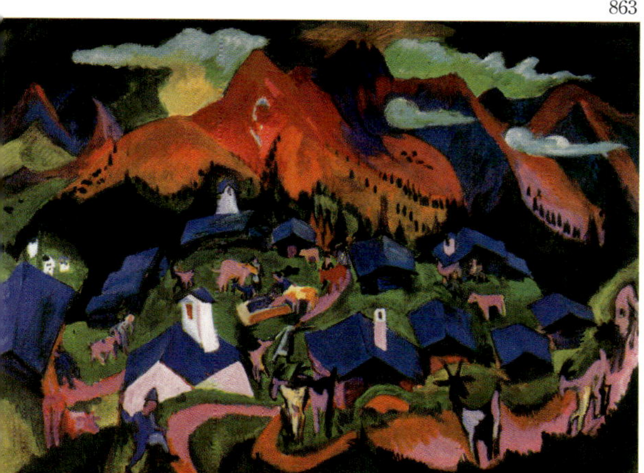

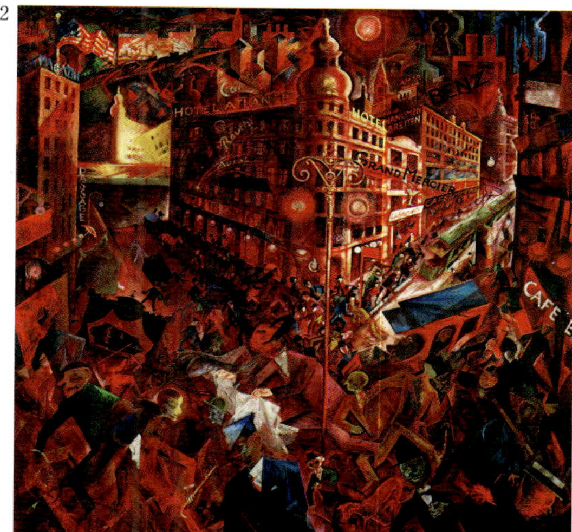

OTTO DIX
(1891 UNTERMHAUS – 1969 SINGEN)

Dix was born near Gera but gained his first experience and training in art in the venerable Baroque city of Dresden. He would return there in 1927 to take up a position as professor at the Academy. However, Dix's first important work was produced in the midst of the violence of the First World War.

Slightly younger than the original Expressionists, he had a long and prolific career in which his work went through significant changes. Loosely, these changes followed the key developments in the German avant-garde, from Expressionism to Dada and then, from about 1923, the so-called *Neue Sachlichkeit* (New Objectivity). However, Dix's work was so varied that it cannot easily be reduced to simple formulae. Although he was one of Germany's foremost modern artists, underlying much of his best work, especially from the mid-1920s on, was a close engagement with the Old German Masters – Cranach, Dürer and Baldung Grien.

When the war was over, Dix became involved in Expressionist and socialist circles such as the Berlin-based *Novembergruppe* and another group in Dresden, which also included the precociously gifted Felixmüller. Dix described himself many times as a "realist". In his speech and behaviour he was blunt and had little time for idealistic dreams of revolution. *Prager Street* was one of Dix's most innovative and memorable responses to the aftermath of war. As with his group of crippled war veterans playing cards of the same year, Dix used the blunt juxtaposition of artificial materials, fragments of everyday objects and oil paint to reconstruct a chaotic reality of broken bodies and alienated modernity.

By the time Dix became a professor at the Dresden Academy, he was working with methods and materials more commonly associated with the Old Masters of the sixteenth century. His *Großstadt* (Metropolis) triptych of 1928 was prepared with infinite care and intended as a modern masterpiece. By this time, Dix had eschewed Expressionism. Nonetheless, the tableaux of sex in the city, based on the glitter and the squalor of Berlin, with its pungent juxtaposition of Eros and death, continues the themes that had preoccupied Dix almost from the start.

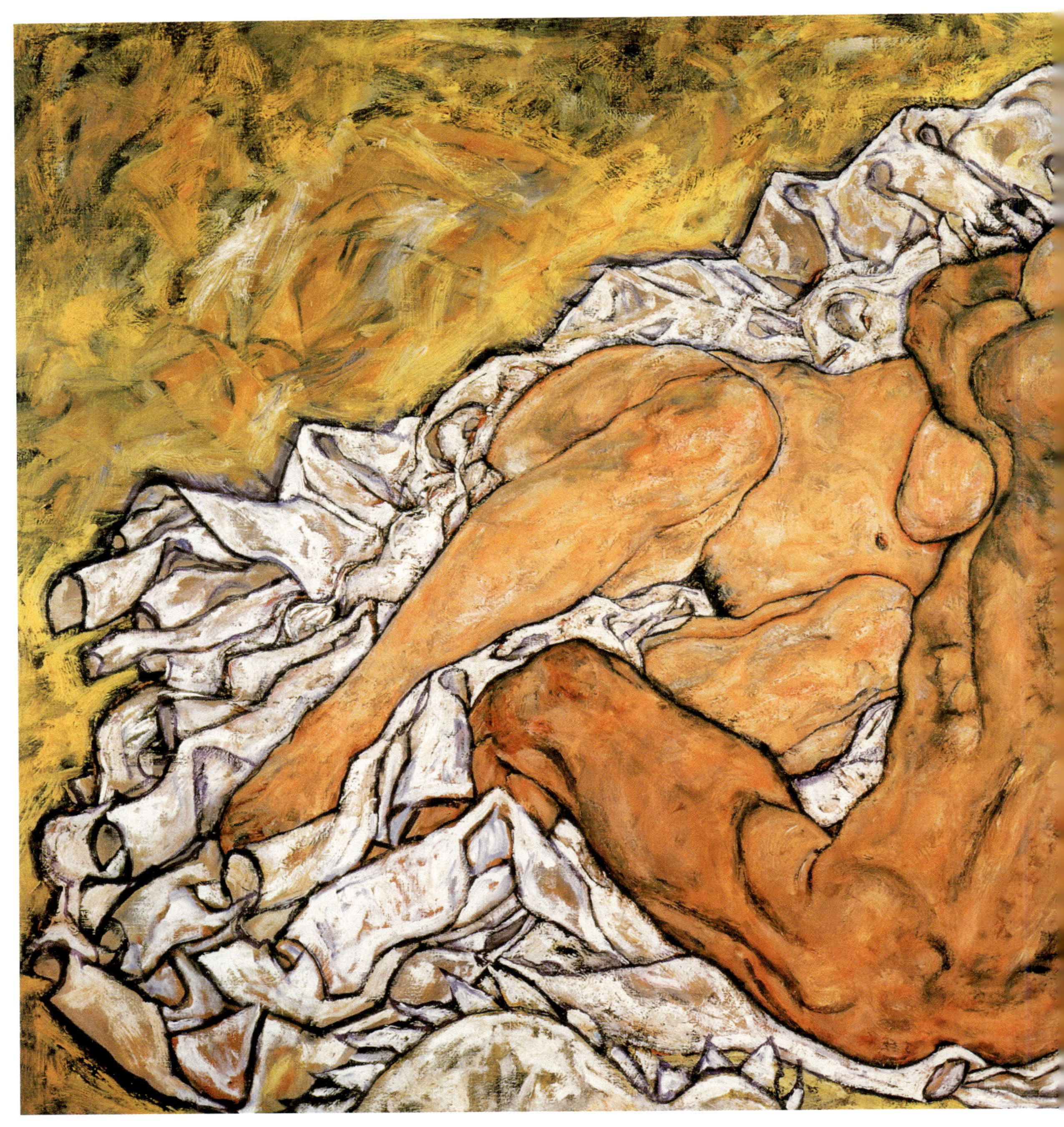

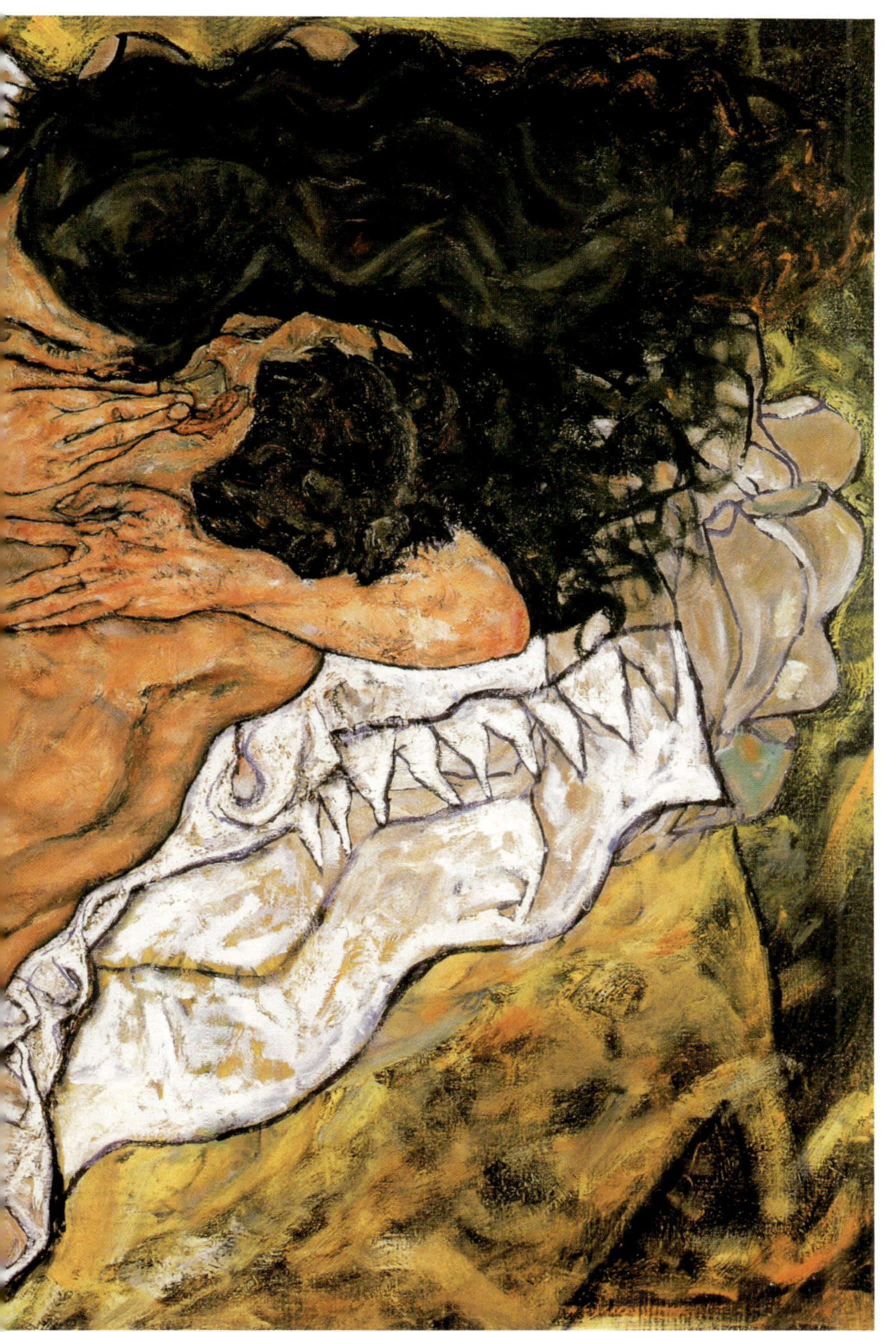

864. **Egon Schiele**, 1890-1918,
Expressionism, Austrian,
Embrace (Lovers II), 1917.
Oil on canvas, 100 x 70 cm.
Österreichische Galerie, Vienna.

This is one of Schiele's best known works and a culmination of his new, semi-classical style. The couple lie together affectionately grasping each other and the artist kisses his wife on the ear. At last, he is able to celebrate a union of two people as one harmonious whole. The lines are smooth; the hair of both heads is joined without distinction; the feet disappear into a single conjoined line. The male and female forms seem to hold each other equally and no one is watching or aware of being watched. The sheet is still crumpled but this is now a modest device to cover the female's genitalia, rather than to expose the brutal animal truth. This is not a pornographic painting but a real image of love. It is as if Schiele is no longer hypnotically enthralled by a juvenile idea of sex and is now focused on actually learning to enjoy his relationship with his wife, Edith. They are two contented people within marriage and, unlike in former works, they are not actually having sex but are locked in a mutually loving embrace.

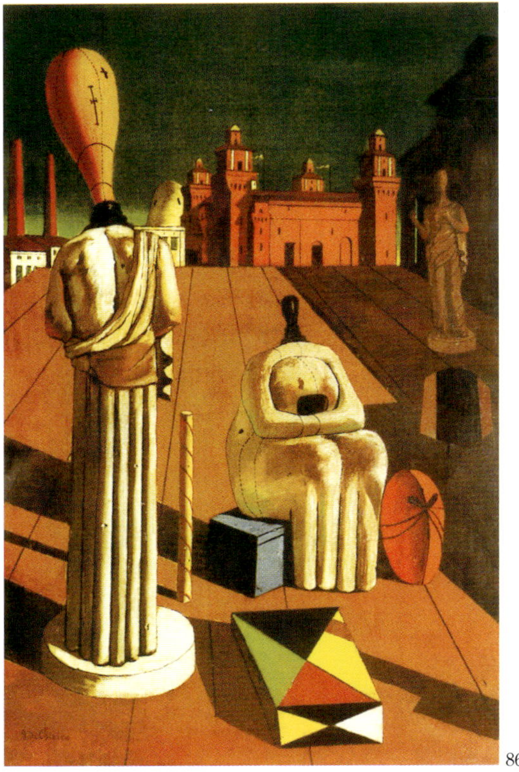

865

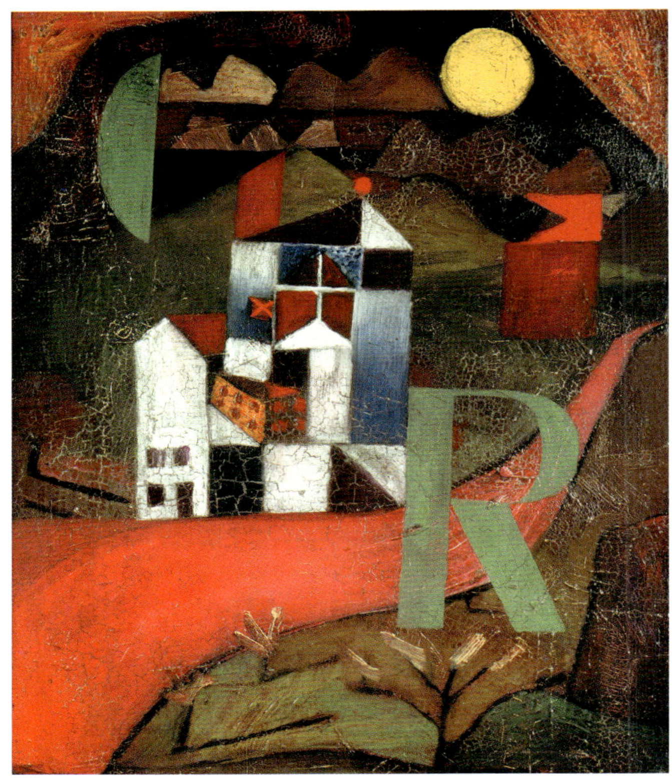

866

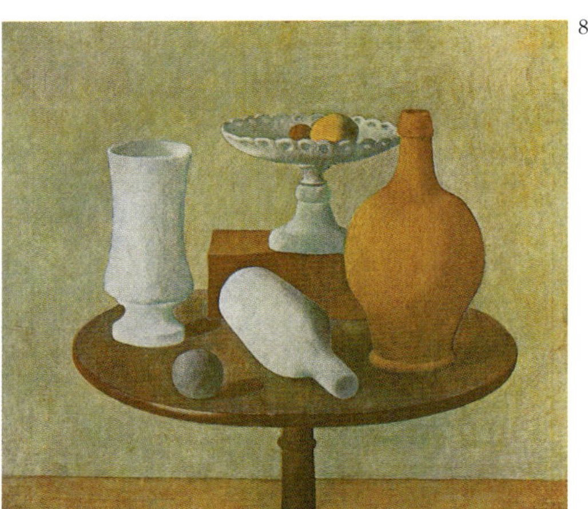

867

865. **Giorgio de Chirico**, 1888-1978, Surrealism, Italian,
The Disquieting Muses, 1916.
Oil on canvas. Private collection, Milan.

866. **Paul Klee**, 1879-1940, Expressionism, German-Swiss,
Villa R, 1919. Oil on panel, 26 x 22 cm.
Öffentliche Kunstsammlung, Basle.

867. **Giorgio Morandi**, 1890-1964, Metaphysical painting, Italian,
Still-Life, 1920. Oil on canvas, 60.5 x 66.5 cm.
Private collection, Milan.

PAUL KLEE
(1879 MÜNCHENBUCHSEE – 1940 MURALTO)

Paul Klee was born in 1879, in Münchenbuchsee, Switzerland, and grew up within a family of musicians. Instead of following his musical roots he chose to study art at the Munich Academy. However, his childhood love of music always remained important in his life and work.

In 1911, Klee met Alexej Jawlensky, Wassily Kandinsky, August Macke, Franz Marc, and other avant-garde figures and participated in important shows of avant-garde art, including the second Blaue Reiter exhibition at Galerie Hans Goltz, Munich, in 1912.

Primitive art, Surrealism and Cubism, all seem blended into his small-scale, delicate paintings of fantasy and satire. Klee's art was also distinguished by an extraordinary diversity and technical innovation, with one of his most effective techniques being oil transfer. This involved the artist drawing with a sharp point on the reverse of a sheet coated in oil paint and laid down over another sheet. Markings and smudges of pigment appeared as a side-effect of the process but it meant Klee achieved, for many of his works, the effect of a "ghostly" impression. Klee was a teacher at the Bauhaus, Germany's most advanced art school, from 1920 to 1931 and immensely productive. Finally, the seizure of power by the National Socialists drove him and his wife to leave Germany for his native Switzerland. Klee's later works, in which simplified, archaic forms dominate, show a preoccupation with mortality. Klee died in 1940, after a long period of illness.

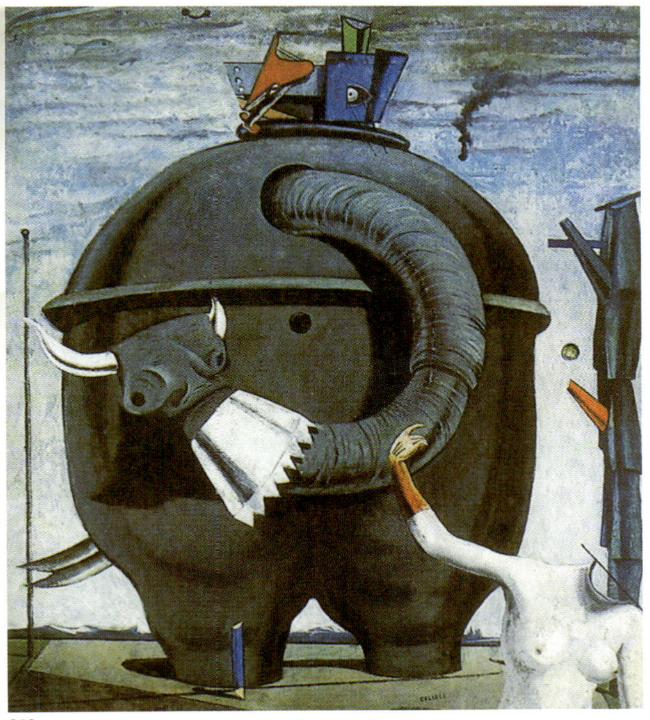

868

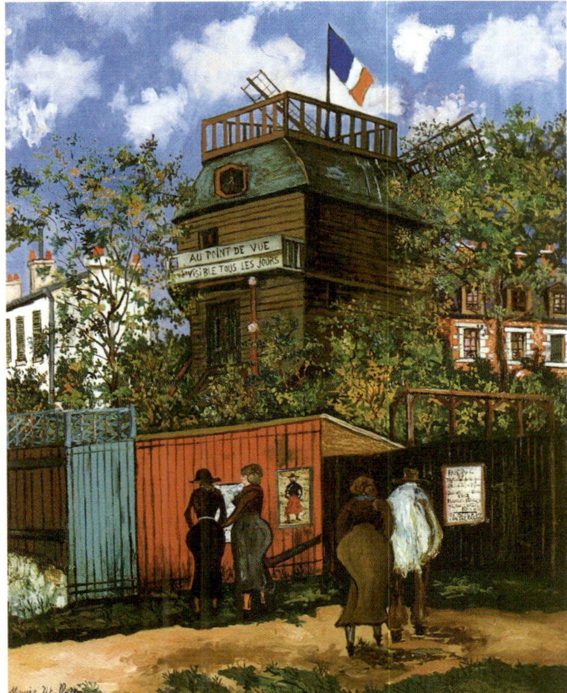

869

870

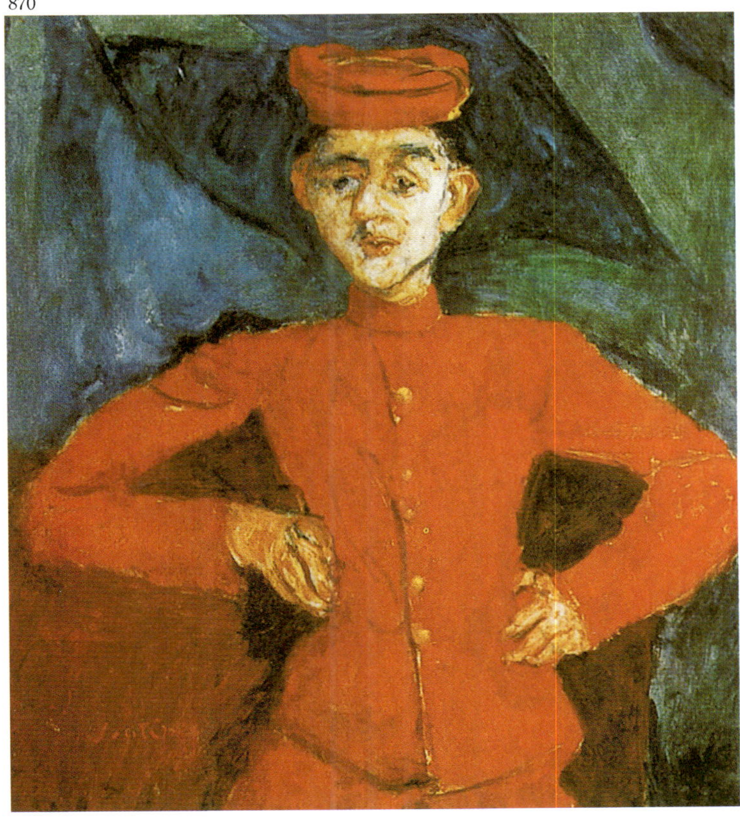

868. **Max Ernst**, 1891-1976, Surrealism, French,
German-born, *Celebes*, 1921.
Oil on canvas, 125.4 x 107.9 cm.
Tate Gallery, London.

*Ernst, leader of the Dada movement in Cologne,
took his inspiration of a Sudanese corn-bin for
the subject of this painting. The work's title
comes from a childish German rhyme that
begins: 'The elephant from Celebes has sticky,
yellow bottom grease...' This painting still
testifies to the influence of De Chirico (the figure
crowning the two-legged monster) as well as
announcing Surrealism.*

869. **Maurice Utrillo**, 1883-1955,
Post-Impressionist, French,
Le Moulin de la Galette, 1922.
Oil on canvas, 106 x 81 cm.
Musée d'Art Moderne et Contemporain, Liège.

870. **Chaïm Soutine**, 1893-1943, Expressionism,
Lithuanian-born, settled in France,
Maxim's Hunter, 1925.
Oil on canvas, 81.9 x 74.9 cm.
Private collection.

*Soutine is mostly influenced by Modigliani in his
portraits. But he remained unsuccessful until he was
discovered by the great American collector, Dr
Albert C. Barnes, in 1923. He then painted a series
of portraits, distinctive through the use of colours:
white for the bakers, white and red for the hunters
(the attributed title to this work is* The Hunter*).*

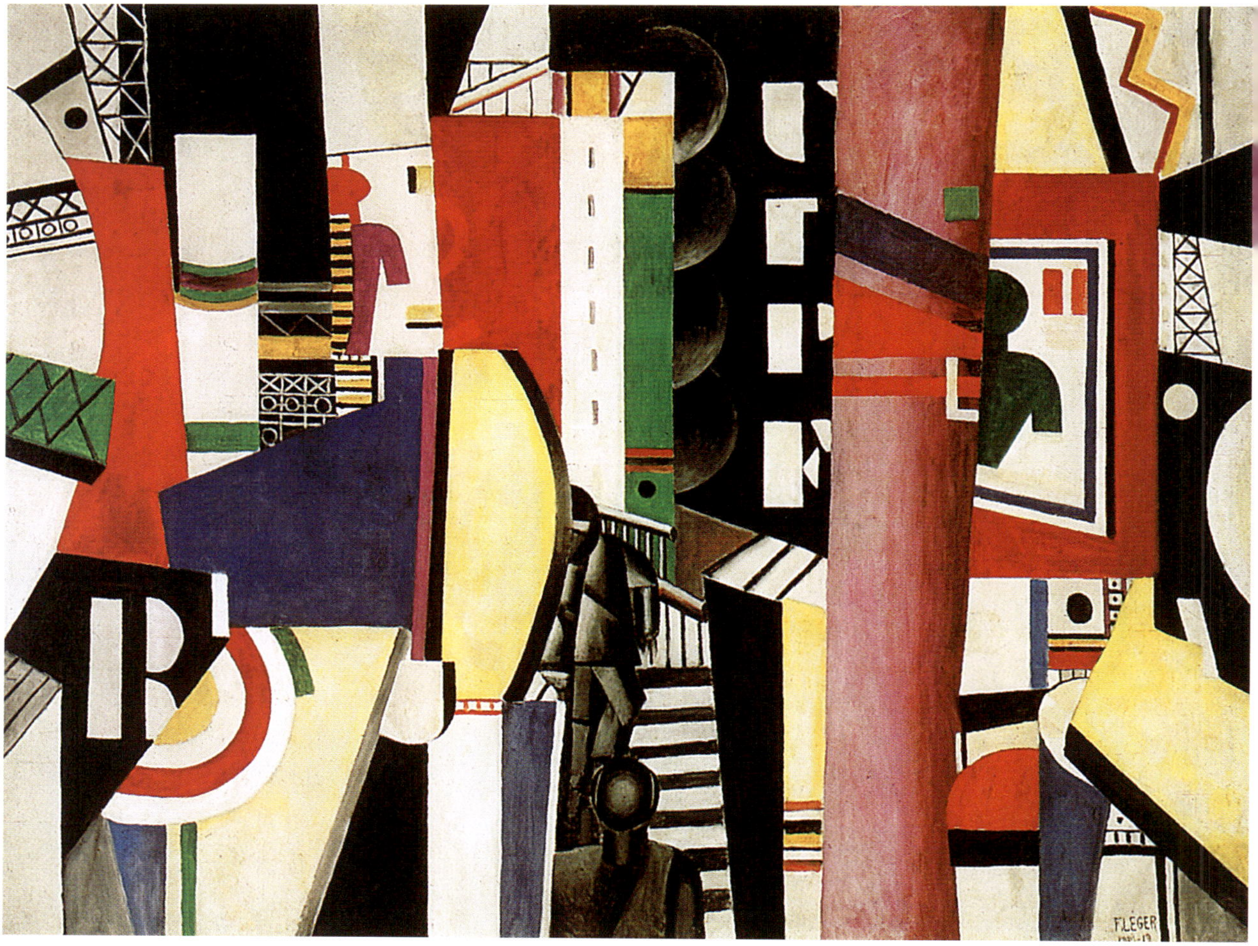

871. **Fernand Léger**, 1881-1955, Cubism/ Purism, French, *The City*, 1919.
Oil on canvas, 230.5 x 297.7 cm.
Philadelphia Museum of Art, Philadelphia.

In this work the French futurist Léger expresses his optimistic trust in the young twentieth century's machine age. He sees conformity as a solution for individuals losing themselves in an idealised Communist system to which he subscribed. In his future city there is a colourful harmony between clean machines and clear communications, all blended without confusion within a variety of popular expressions as seen in the busy metropolis of the future. Ironically, two robotic, faceless comrades on a staircase walk through the maze of hard-edged realities of the city seen as a colourful but ultimately confusing montage. While this is a mid-life expression for the artist, he would eventually favour only three primary colours and show even more simple designs.

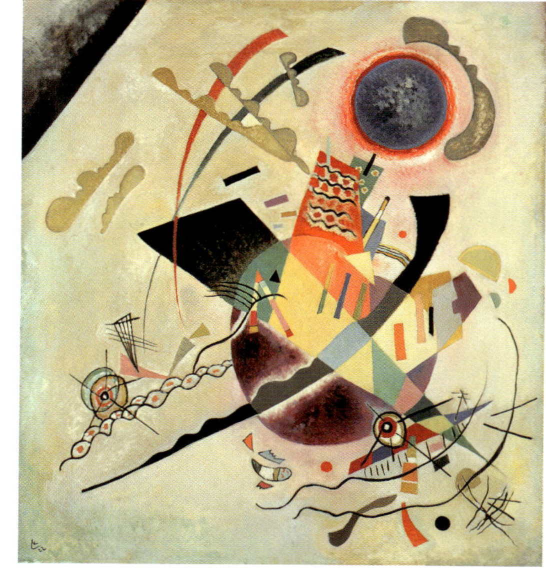

872. **Wassily Kandinsky**, 1866-1944, Lyrical Abstraction/ Der Blaue Reiter, Russian, *Blue Circle*, 1922.
Oil on canvas, 110 x 100 cm.
Guggenheim Museum, New York.

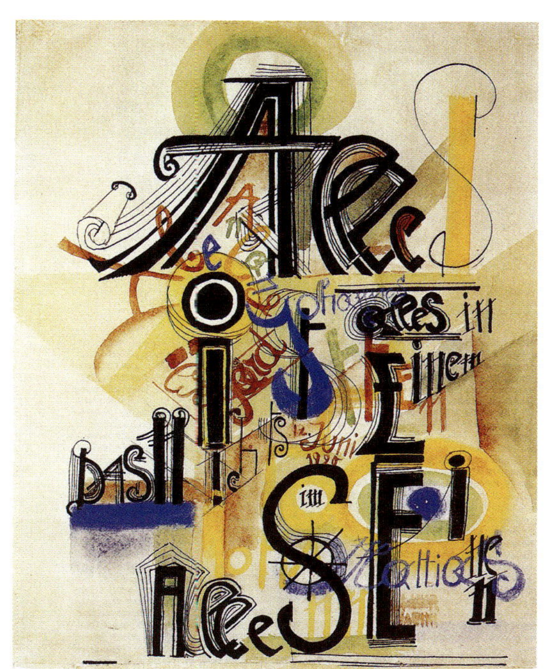

873. **Johannes Itten**, 1888-1967, Bauhaus, Swiss,
All in One, 1922.
Ink and watercolour on paper, 29 x 33 cm.
Private collection.

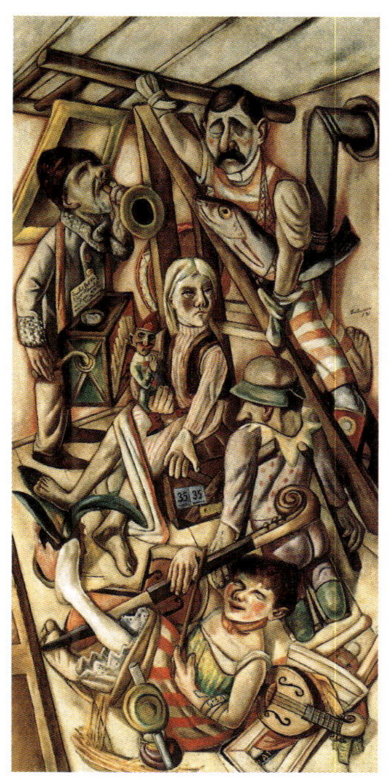

874. **Max Beckmann**, 1884-1950, Expressionism, German,
The Dream, 1921. Oil on canvas, 182 x 91 cm.
Saint Louis Art Museum, St Louis.

*Painted in 1921, Der Traum, (The Dream) contains many
iconographic and compositional elements that were already
or would become established in Beckmann's distinctive
work: figures crowded into an ambiguous interior, musical
instruments and devices, the jester's collar, ambivalent physical
postures and gestures, fragments of signage, and the fish.
The zig-zag composition draws on the steep, subjective
pictorial space and angularity of forms found in Gothic art.*

MAX BECKMANN
(1884 LEIPZIG – 1950 NEW YORK)

As a student in the centre of Germany's Enlightenment,
Weimar, Beckmann read avidly the works of Schopenhauer
and became interested in Kant, Hegel and Nietzsche. Having
graduated in 1903, he painted his early canvases in Paris. He
was particularly impressed by Cézanne. Beckmann's own early
work was in a broadly impressionist mode and could sometimes
be quite traditional in its composition and treatment of historical
or monumental subjects. Beckmann retained through his life an
instinctive feel for the art of the past, gravitating towards images
and epochs in which he saw powerful and simple expression.
As his own distinctive style developed, this took the form
especially of a creative engagement with the art of the Middle
Ages and the Northern Renaissance. Beckmann remained aloof
from Expressionism's core groupings and the impassioned
programmes they issued. In many ways he was never a true
"Expressionist". However, his work between the war years,
especially the mid-1920s, constitutes a major contribution to
avant-garde German art and to the development, and the
decline, of Expressionism.

Beckmann made few public statements about his work,
preferring to confine his expression to painting. Precisely because
of the scarcity of testimony from the artist, his rare statements, in
the form of a *"schöpferische Konfession"* or *"creative credo"*,
written in 1918 and published in 1920 by the writer Kasimir
Edschmid, has become a central document: "I believe that I
particularly love painting so much because it forces one to be
objective. There is nothing I hate more than sentimentality. The
stronger and more intensive my determination to grasp the
unutterable things of the world grows, the deeper and more
powerful the emotion about our existence burns in me, the tighter
I keep my mouth shut, the colder my will becomes, to capture this
monster of vitality and to confine it, to beat it down and to strangle
it with crystal-clear, sharp lines and planes. I do not weep, tears are
despicable to me and signs of slavery. I always think of the thing."

875. **Otto Dix**, 1891-1969, Expressionism, German,
Portrait of the Journalist Sylvia von Harden, 1926.
Mixed medium on wood, 121 x 89 cm.
Musée national d'art moderne,
Centre Georges-Pompidou, Paris.

In the 1920s, it was Dix's reputation as a portraitist that secured him the most success and financial gain. His razor-sharp painting of this ultramodern woman, with a whiff of decay about her, is exemplary of his best works in the unflinching style of so-called Neue Sachlichkeit (New Objectivity).

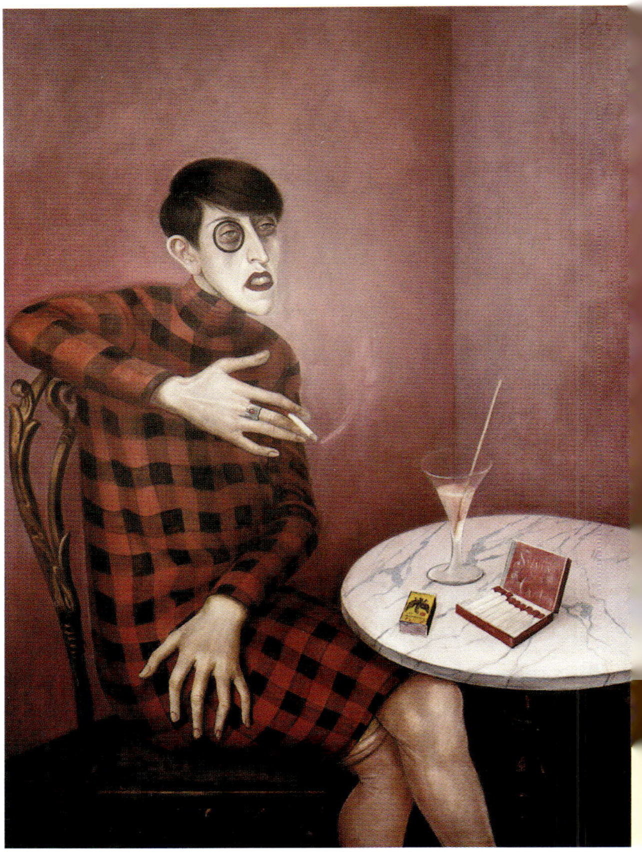

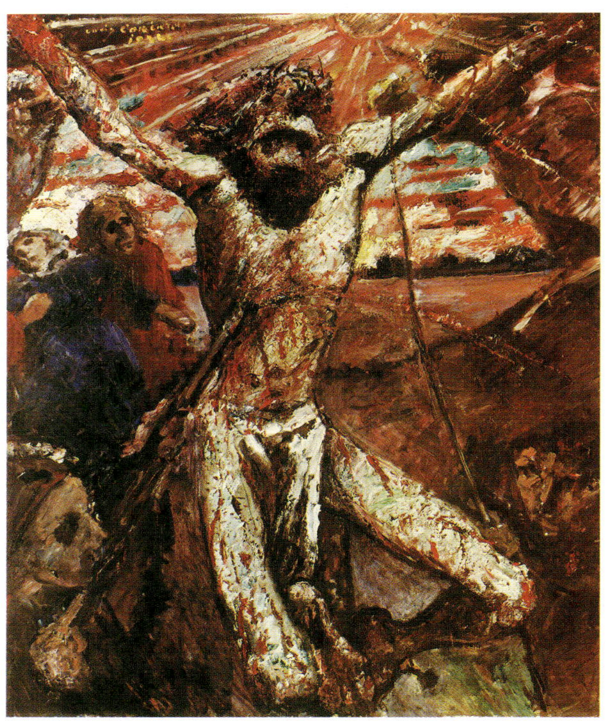

876. **Lovis Corinth**, 1858-1925, Expressionism, German,
The Red Christ, 1922.
Oil on canvas, 129 x 108 cm.
Neue Pinakothek, Munich.

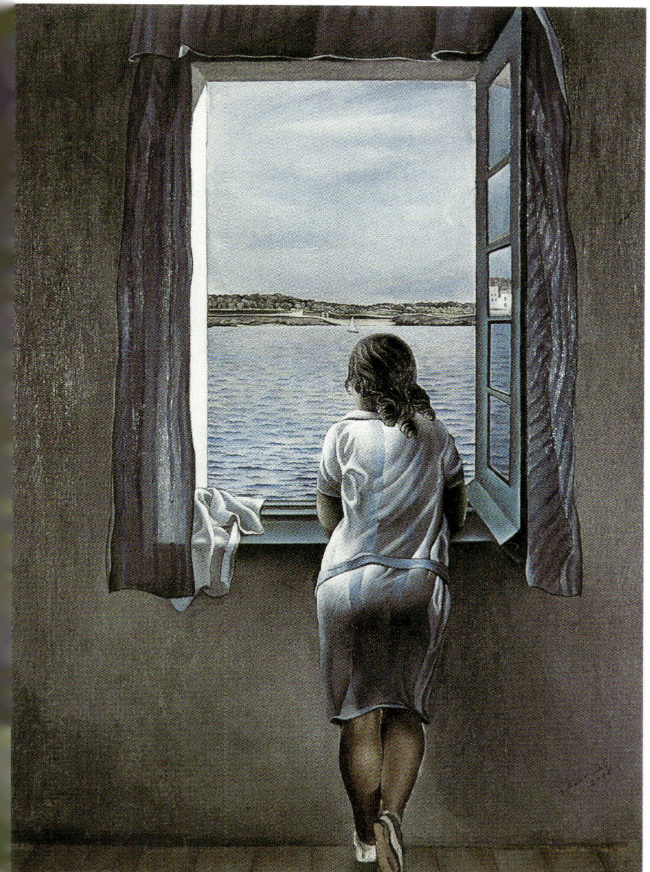

877

877. **Salvador Dalí**, 1904-1989, Surrealism, Spanish,
Woman at the Window, 1925.
Oil on canvas, 103 x 75 cm.
Museo Nacional Centro de Arte Reina Sofia, Madrid.

878. **Oskar Schlemmer**, 1888-1943, Bauhaus, German,
Concentric Group, 1925.
Oil on canvas, 98 x 62 cm.
Staatsgalerie, Stuttgart.

878

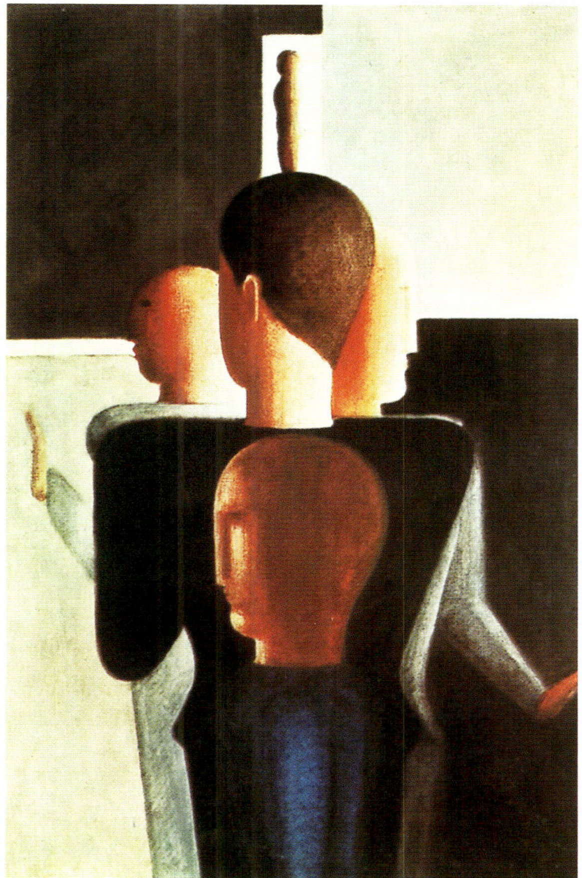

SALVADOR DALÍ
(1904 – 1989 FIGUERAS)

Painter, designer, creator of bizarre objects, author and film maker, Dalí became the most famous of the Surrealists.

Buñuel, Lorca, Picasso and Breton all had a great influence on his career. Dalí's film, *An Andalusian Dog*, produced with Buñuel, marked his official entry into the tightly-knit group of Parisian Surrealists, where he met Gala, the woman who became his lifelong companion and his source of inspiration. But his relationship soon deteriorated until his final rift with André Breton in 1939. Nevertheless Dalí's art remained surrealist in its philosophy and expression and a prime example of his freshness, humour and exploration of the subconscious mind. Throughout his life, Dalí was a genius at self-promotion, creating and maintaining his reputation as a mythical figure.

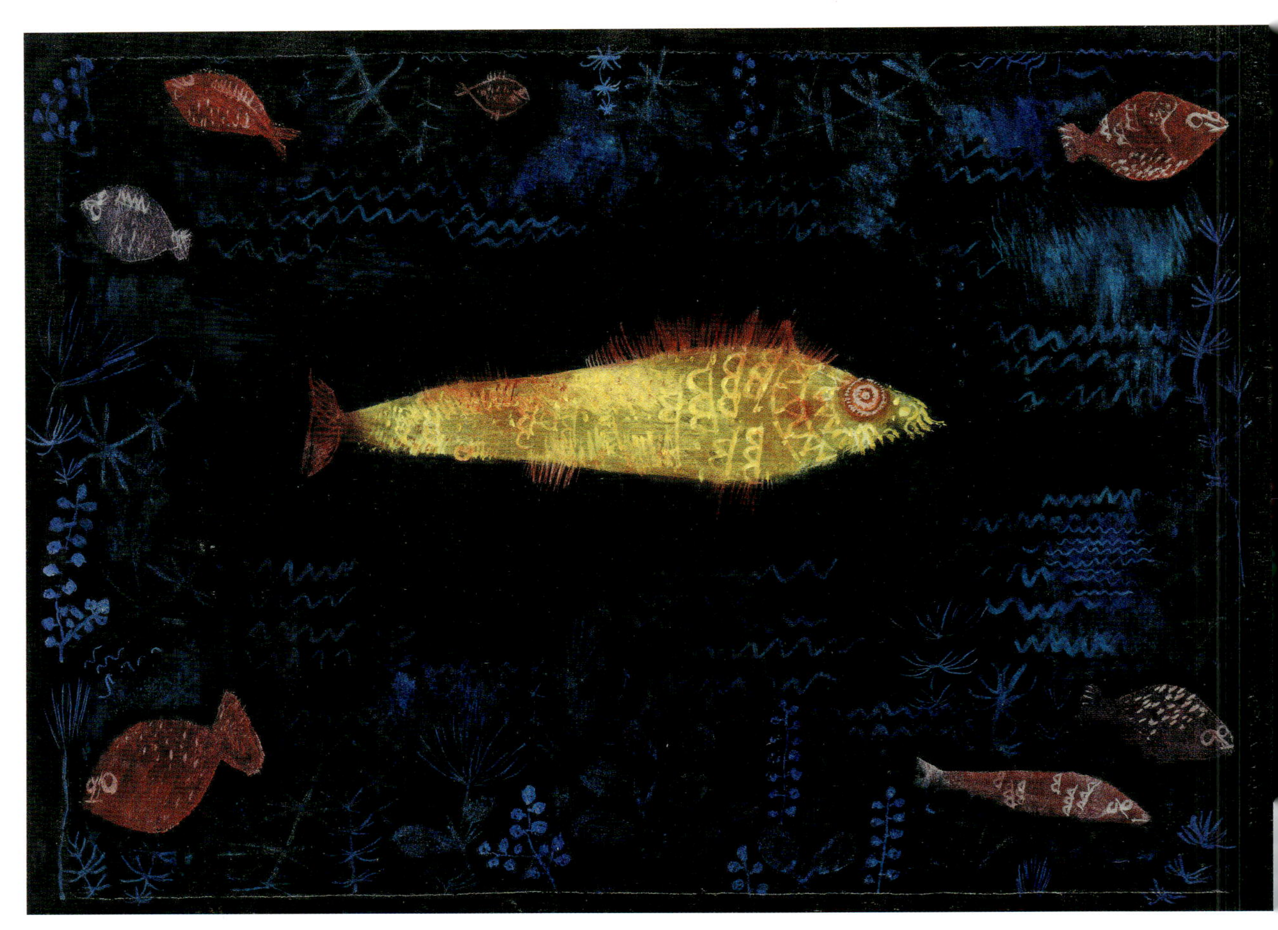

879. **Paul Klee**, 1879-1940, Expressionism, German-Swiss, *The Goldfish*, 1925.
Oil and watercolour on paper, mounted on cardboard, 50 x 69 cm.
Kunsthalle, Hamburg.

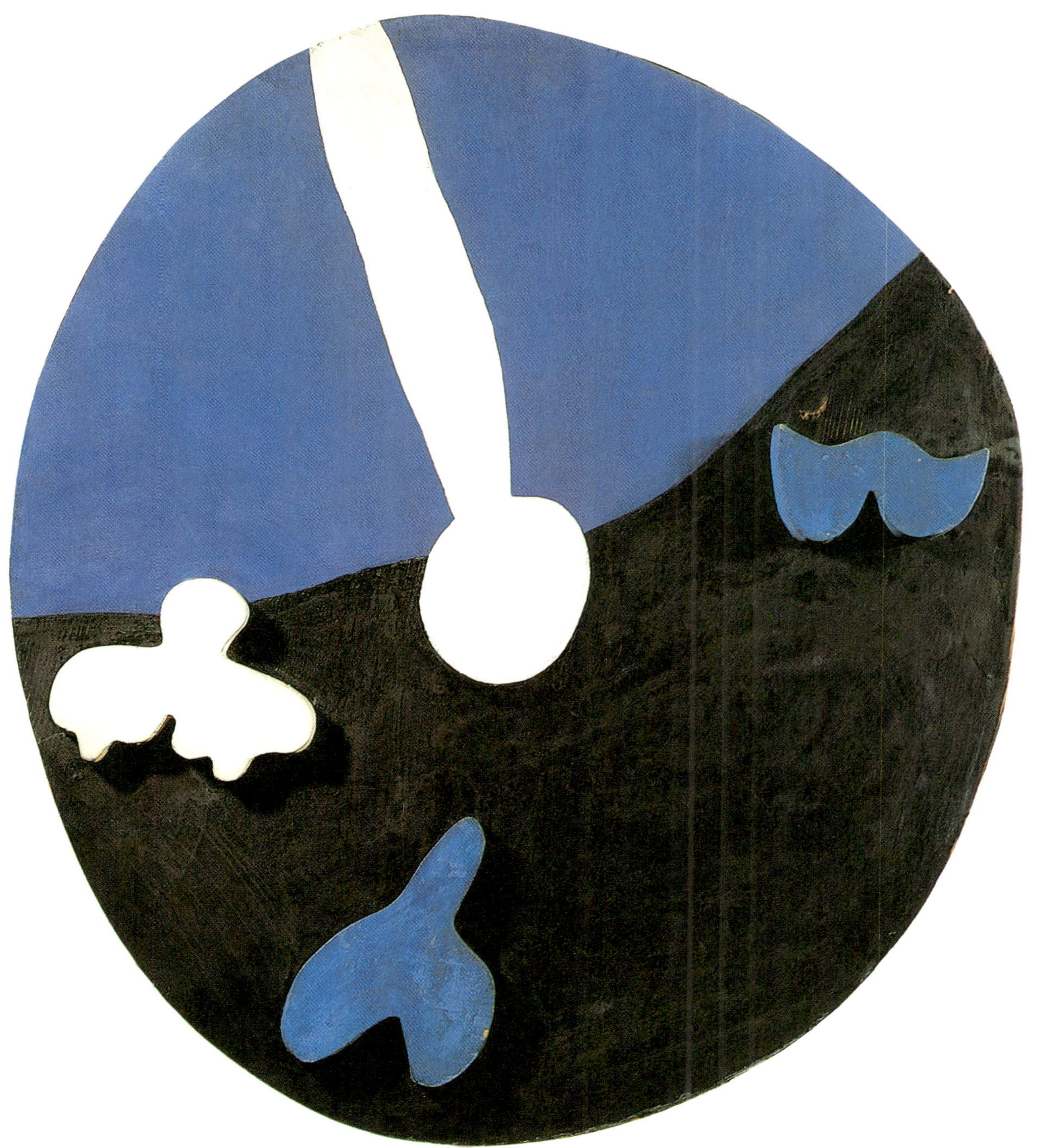

880. **Hans Arp**, 1886-1966, Dada, French, *Clock*, 1924.
Painted Wood. Private collection.

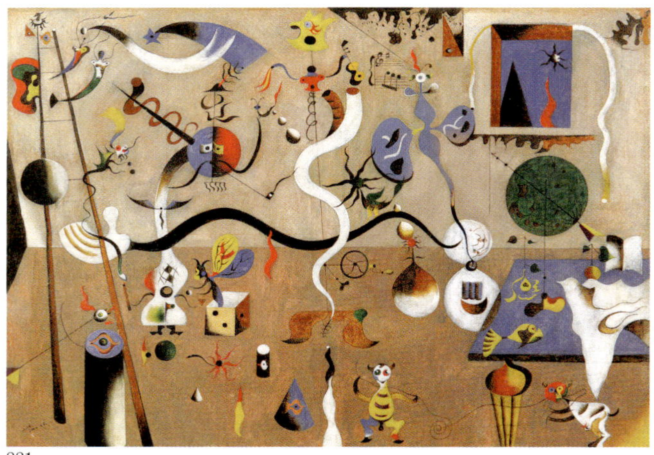

881

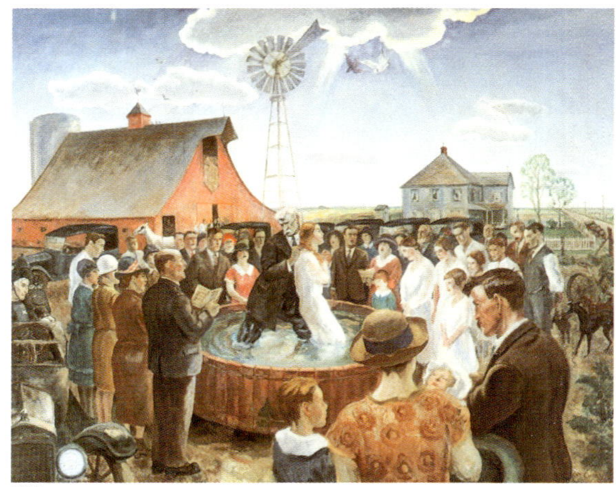

882

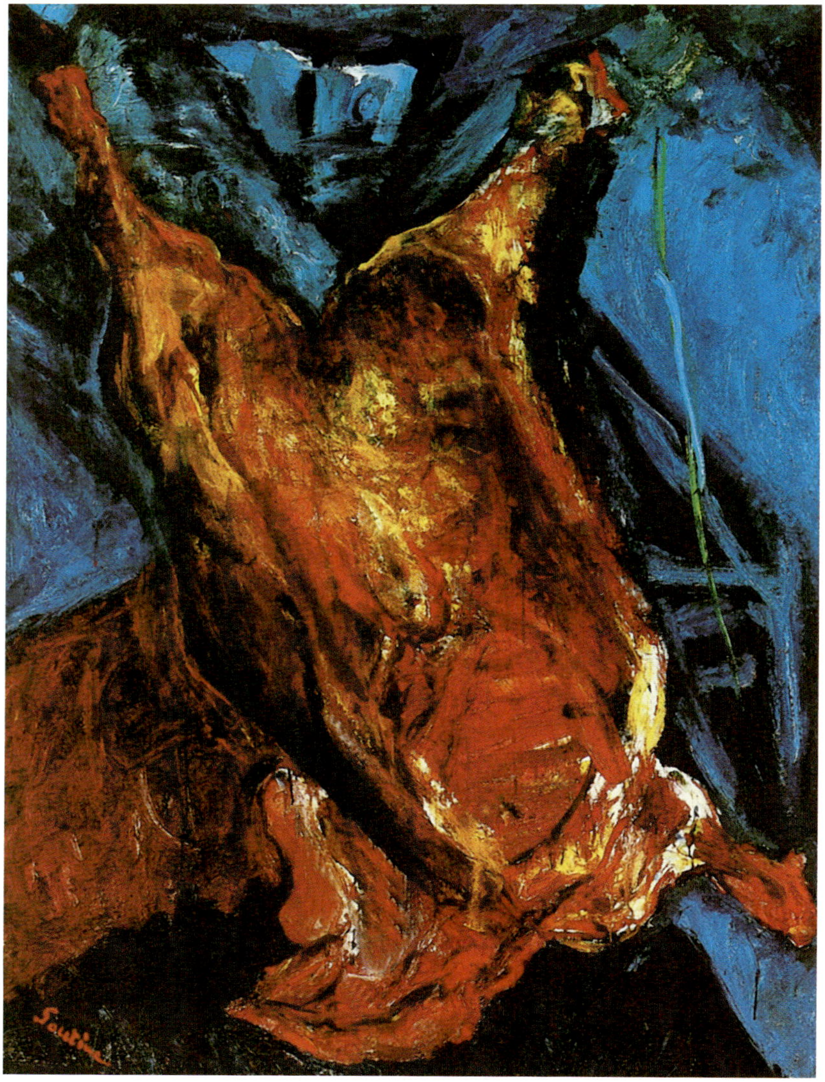

883

881. **Joan Miró**, 1893-1983,
Surrealism, Spanish,
Harlequin's Carnival, 1924-1925.
Oil on canvas, 66 x 93 cm.
Albright-Knox Art Gallery, Buffalo.

André Breton stated: "Miró was probably the most Surrealistic of us all." In 1975, a foundation, close to Barcelona, was dedicated to his work.

882. **John Steuart Curry**, 1897-1946,
Regionalism, American,
Baptism in Kansas, 1928.
Oil on canvas. Whitney Museum of
American Art, New York.

883. **Chaïm Soutine**, 1893-1943,
Expressionism, Lithuanian-born, settled
in France, *Slaughtered Ox*, c. 1925.
Oil on canvas, 140.3 x 107.6 cm.
Albright-Knox Art Gallery, Buffalo.

884. **Joan Miró**, 1893-1983, Surrealism, Spanish,
Dutch Interior I, 1928.
Oil on canvas, 91.8 x 73 cm.
The Museum of Modern Art, New York.

After travels to Belgium and Holland, Miró embarked on a
fascinating series of paintings that he called Dutch Interiors –
distinctively Miróesque reinterpretations of the Dutch masters,
guided by museum postcards he brought home. Pencil studies
show how he transformed the realistic paintings into fantastical
cartoons of their underlying structures, while the final paintings
reflect his characteristic transformation of a shaded world
into large, flat shapes of bright, bold colour. The counterpoint
between realism and fantasy continues throughout the career of
Joan Miró – it is the genius of his art, which makes it both
accessible and mysterious.

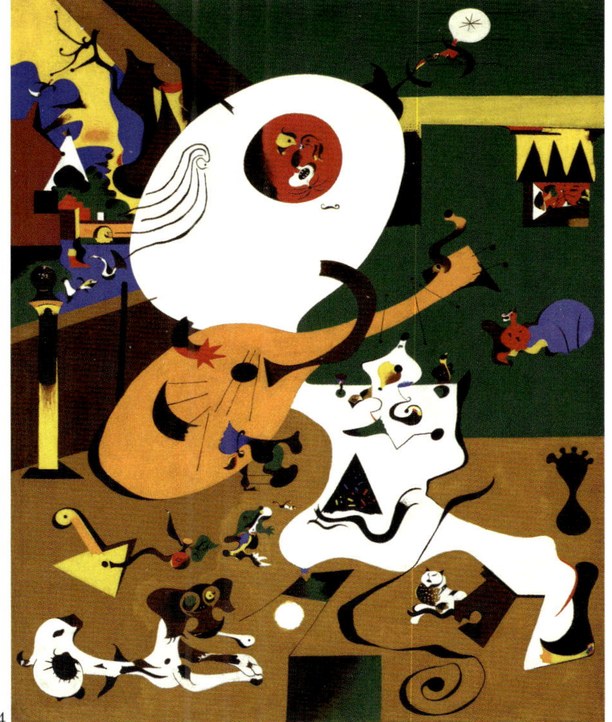

884

JOAN MIRÓ
(1893 BARCELONA – 1983 PALMA DE MALLORCA)

Joan Miró was born in a room with stars pain-ted on the ceiling. He grew up in the city of Barcelona, where rugged independence and creativity go hand in hand. In 1907, he enrolled in art classes at La Escuela de la Lonja, an academic and professionally oriented school of applied arts where a young man named Picasso had impressed the teachers ten years earlier. Then he entered Galí's private classes. Unlike the Lonja School, it offered a setting where Miró's distinctive ways of seeing were rewarded. At Gali's academy, Miró met some of the men who would become not only fellow artists but intimate friends. He and Enric Cristòfol Ricart soon rented a studio together near the Barcelona Cathedral. Later identified as a Surrealist, Miró never really espoused any school or established style of art. "It was clear in his mind," as one critic has put it, "that he had to go beyond all categories and invent an idiom that would express his origins and be authentically his own." Over the course of his career, he even worked hard not to follow his own traditions. Clearly Miró had studied Cubism's broken forms and had learned to admire the strident colours of the Fauves. But he had an eye of his own, and his paintings combined twisted perspectives, heavy brushwork, and surprises in colour. He was finding ways to merge the stylish two-dimensionality of the times with inspirations taken from Catalan folk art and Romanesque church frescos. Joan Miró began to recognise that, like Picasso, if he was going to become an artist in earnest, he needed to move to Paris. For a while he rented a studio at 45 rue Blomet, next door to the painter André Masson. Masson was just the first link in an entire community of artists with which Miró found a home, just as they were beginning to coalesce in the movement of art and sensibility they called "Surrealism". It was a movement of thought that at once extolled the individual and the imagination and at the same time flaunted tradition, rationality, and even common sense. Influenced by the practitioners of surrealism, Miró never really joined their ranks. The joyful freedom espoused by the Dadaists was more to his liking than the manifestos and dogma of the Surrealists. His naïve originality drew the attention and admiration of them all, however, and he was soon the favoured illustrator for the magazine *La Révolution Surréaliste*.

In his last years, Joan Miró spoke to his grandson of his lifelong love of Catalonian folk art – the natural forms, the independent spirit, the naiveté that is both beautiful and surprising. "Folk art never fails to move me," he said. "It is free of deception and artifice. It goes straight to the heart of things." In speaking of the art from the countryside that had nourished him, Joan Miró found the best words to describe himself. With his honesty, spontaneity, and childlike enthusiasm for shape, texture, and colour, he created a universe of artworks sure to delight, puzzle, and reward.

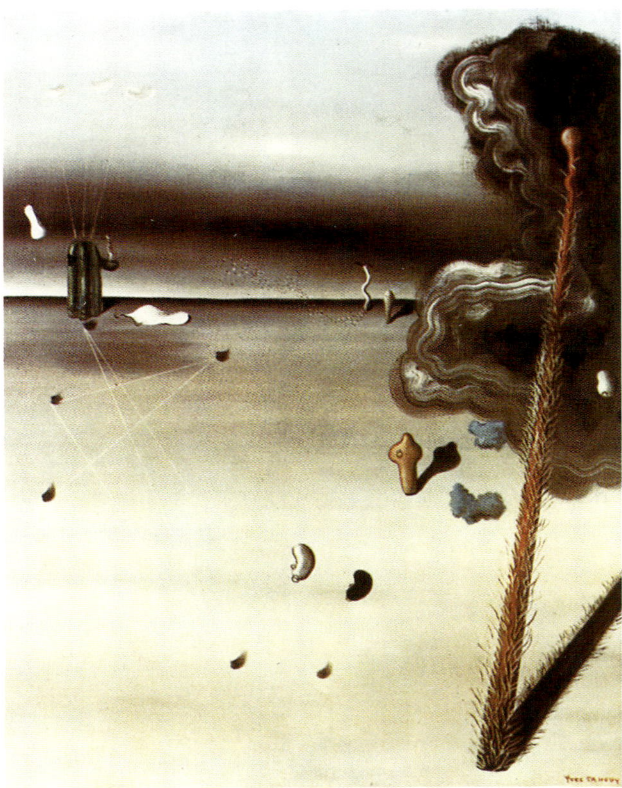

885. **Yves Tanguy**, 1900-1955, Surrealism, French-born, American,
Mama, Papa is Wounded!, 1927.
Oil on canvas, 92.1 x 73 cm.
The Museum of Modern Art, New York.

886. **Georgia O'Keeffe**, 1887-1986, Modernism, American,
Jack-in-the-Pulpit n° V, 1930.
Oil on canvas, 122 x 76.2 cm.
The National Gallery of Art, Washington, D.C.

*In Madison High School the school's art teacher gave
Georgia her first insight into the mysteries and detail of the
Jack-In-The-Pulpit flower. In her autobiography, O'Keeffe says:
"I had seen many Jacks before, but this was the first time I
remember examining a flower… I was a little annoyed at being
interested because I did not like the teacher… But maybe she
started me looking at things – looking very carefully at details."*

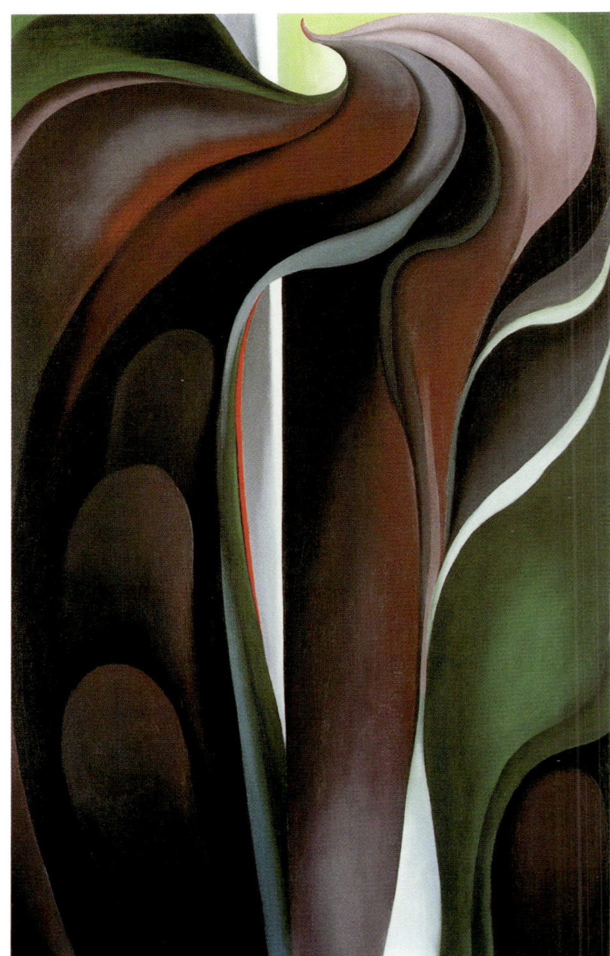

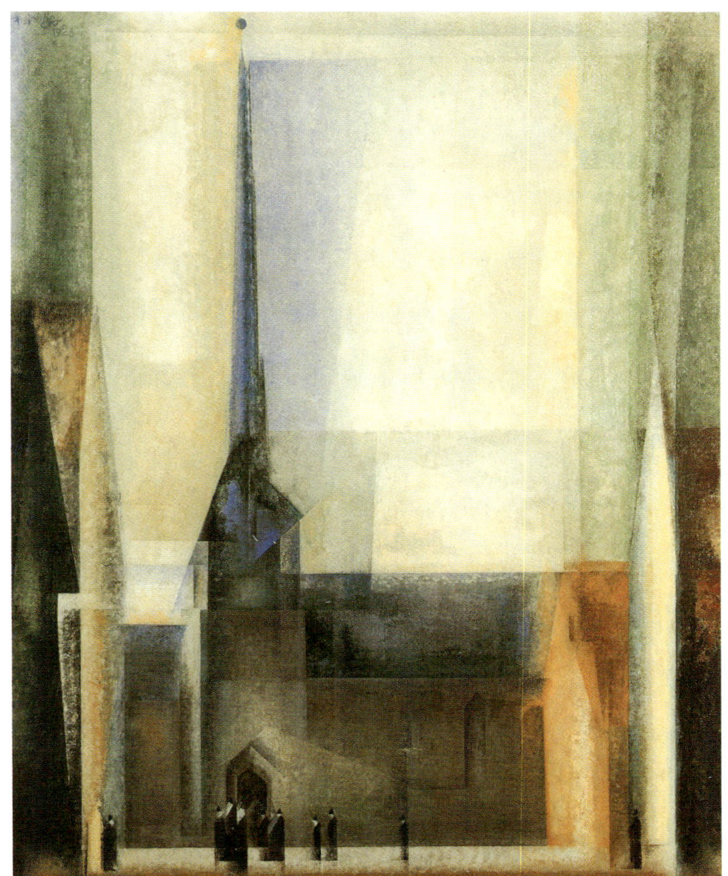

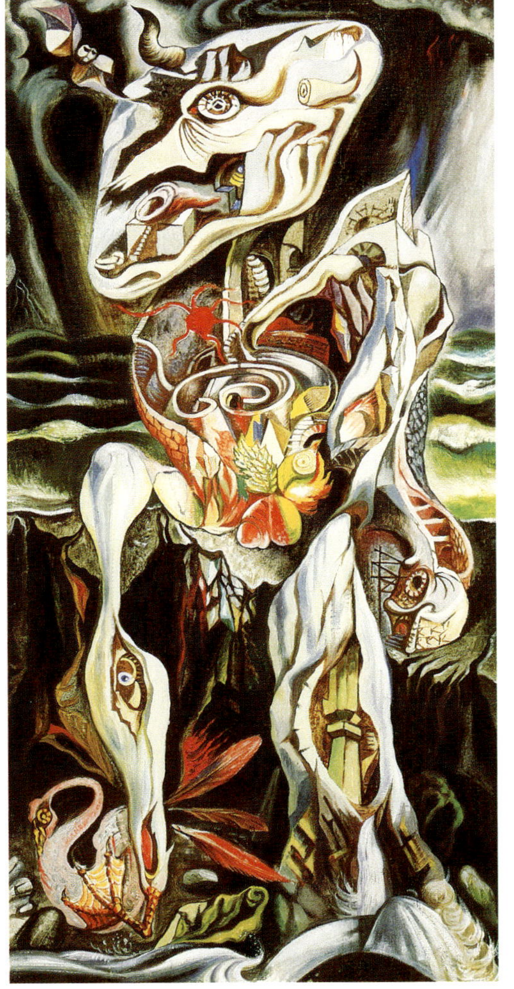

887. **André Masson**, ´896-1987, Surrealism, French,
The Labyrinth, 1930.
Oil on canvas, 120 x 61 cm.
Musée national d'art moderne,
Centre Georges-Pompidou, Paris.

888. **Lyonel Feininger**, 1871-1956, Cubism, American,
Gelmeroda IX, 1926.
Oil on canvas, 108 x 80 cm.
Museum Folkwang, Essen.

The Bauhaus school, founded in 1919, influenced painting as well as architecture, directing it to be closer to Cubism than to the radically abstract. Feininger taught at the Bauhaus right from the beginning, although he was an American citizen. He expressed the challenge in romantic and colourful works that show the Cubist respect for basic shapes, yet find a decorative rendering. He brought to the German school warmth that some found otherwise especially lacking in the pragmatism of Bauhaus architecture. Klee and Kandinsky joined Feininger in teaching, probably more to influence the school than to be influenced by it.

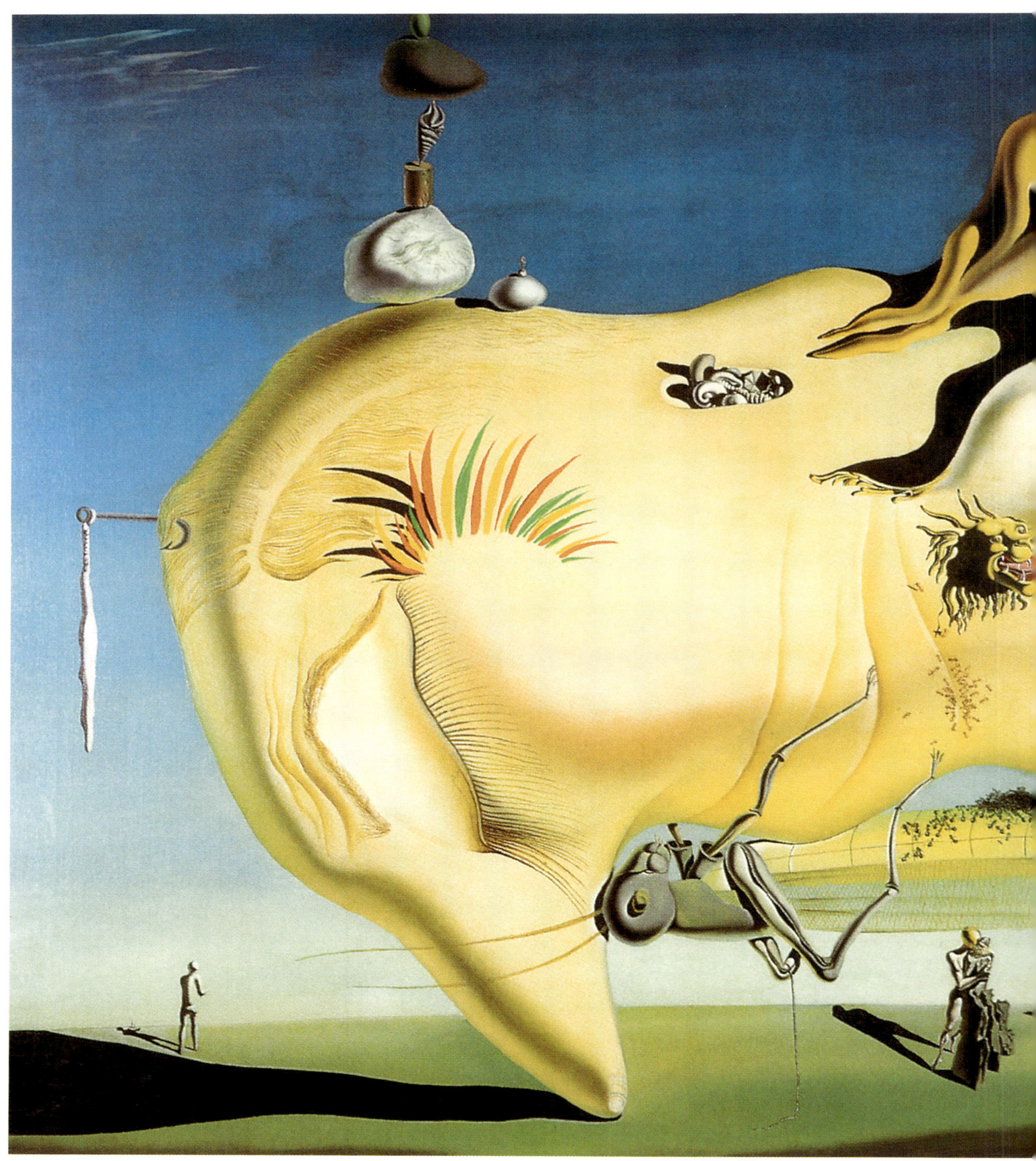

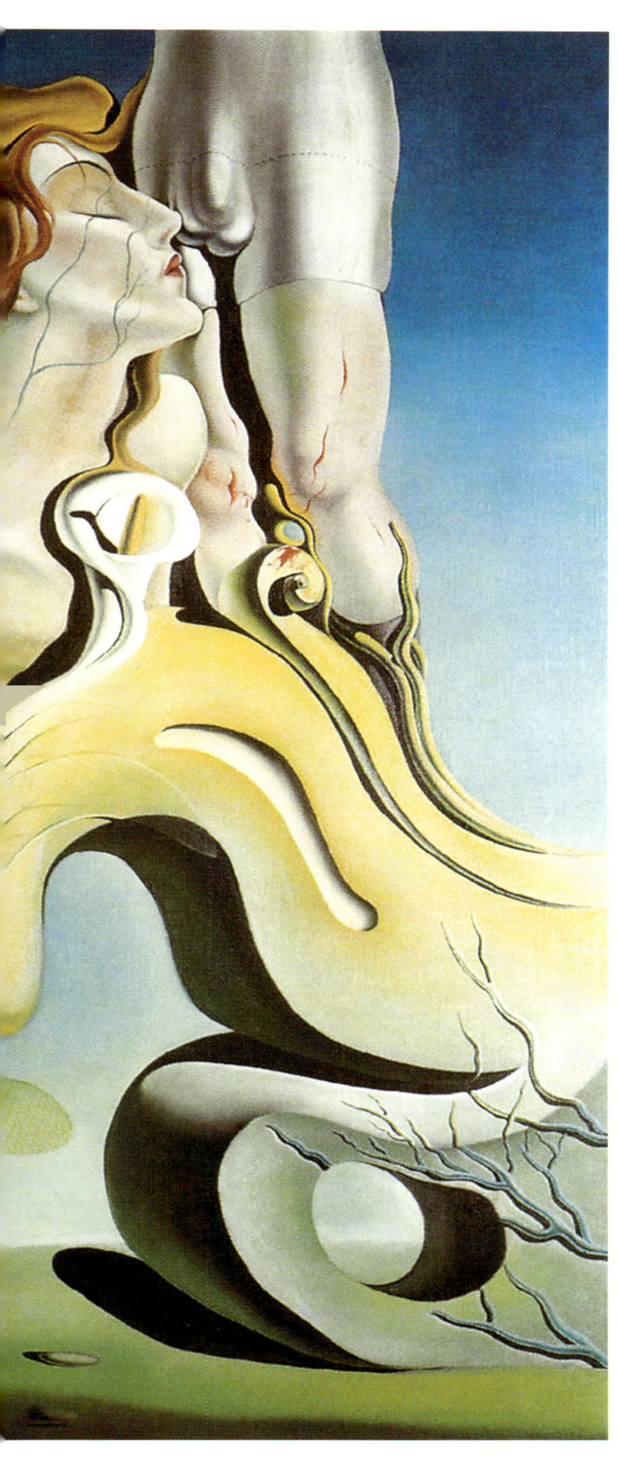

889. **Salvador Dalí**, 1904-1989, Surrealism, Spanish,
The Great Masturbator, 1929.
Oil on canvas, 110 x 150 cm.
Museo Nacional Centro de Arte Reina Sofia, Madrid.

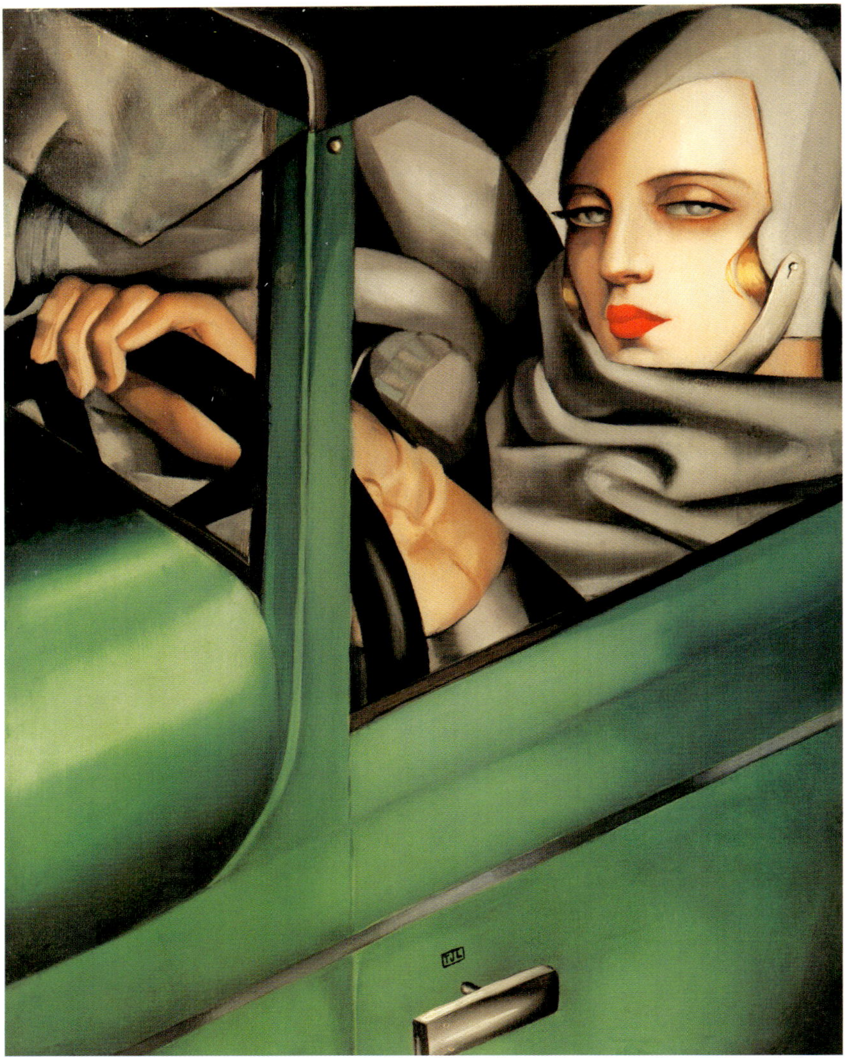

890. **Tamara de Lempicka**, 1898-1980,
Art Deco, Polish-Russian, *Self-portrait
(Tamara in the Green Bugatti)*, 1929.
Oil on wood, 35 x 27 cm.
Private collection.

*Over the past quarter century this has
become a very famous and widely
reproduced picture. It is not a portrait
in the sense of being a likeness of an
individual woman. It is unlikely that
anyone would have recognised de
Lempicka in the street from this
highly stylised image. It is more a
portrait of an era and in particular of
a type of woman who came to the
fore in that era.*

*By the drastic means of slaughtering
a generation of young men the First
World War probably did more for the
advancement and emancipation of
women than any event in history. In the
"Roaring Twenties" the ultimate symbol
of female emancipation for those who
could afford it was an automobile. De
Lempicka's own account of how she
picked up the beautiful Rafaela in the
Bois de Boulogne and drove her back
to her studio is an example of how
useful the motor car could be as an aid
to sexual independence.*

891. **Kasimir Malevitch**, 1878-1935,
Abstraction/ Suprematism, Russian,
Two Peasants in the Field, 1928-1932.
Oil on canvas, 53.5 x 70 cm.
The State Russian Museum,
St Petersburg.

892. **Lyonel Feininger**, 1871-1956,
Cubism, American, *Sailing Boats*,
1929. Oil on canvas, 43 x 72 cm.
The Institute of Art, Detroit.

890

891

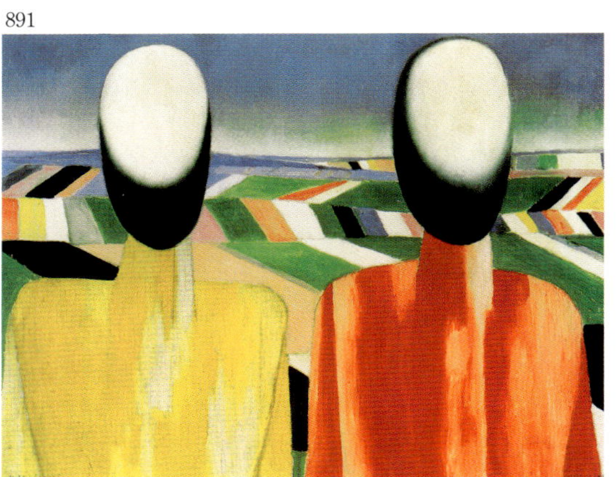

892

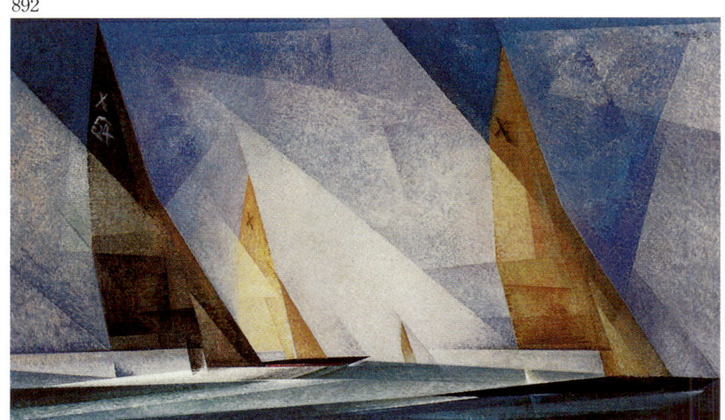

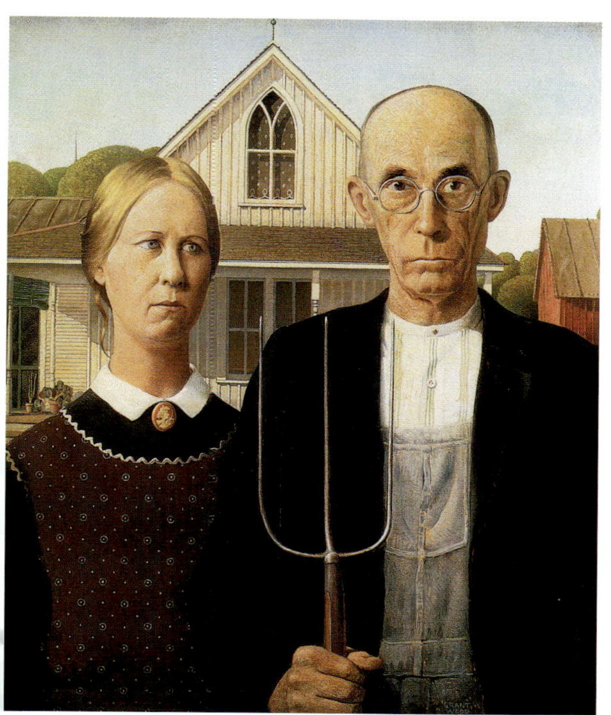

893. **Grant Wood**, 1891-1942, Regionalism, American,
American Gothic, 1930. Oil on beaverboard, 78 x 65.3 cm.
The Art Institute of Chicago, Chicago.
Art © Estate of Grant Wood / Licensed by VAGA, New York, NY.

Although the American artist Wood was from the mid-western state of Iowa, his studio was in the eastern state of Connecticut. When this, by far his most famous work, was first seen by the residents of Iowa, some of them were offended, thinking the work was ridiculing their simple ways and the typically plain appearance of authentic country folk. Wood explained that the elongated faces (mirrored in the cameo and pitchfork) modelled by his sister and his dentist, were shaped to carry out the vertical theme of the American Gothic farmhouse in a realistic style. The Wood work became and remains one of the most popular of all paintings by an American.

894. **René Magritte**, 1898-1967, Surrealism, Belgian,
The Menacing Assassin, 1927.
Oil on canvas, 150.4 x 195.2 cm.
The Museum of Modern Art, New York.

Magritte was probably one of the most powerful Surrealist painters whose disturbing combinations of the erotic, strange, extraordinary and ordinary always surprise. Here this scene combines eroticism and sadism in the surrealist provocative tradition of representing positive aspects of horror scenes.

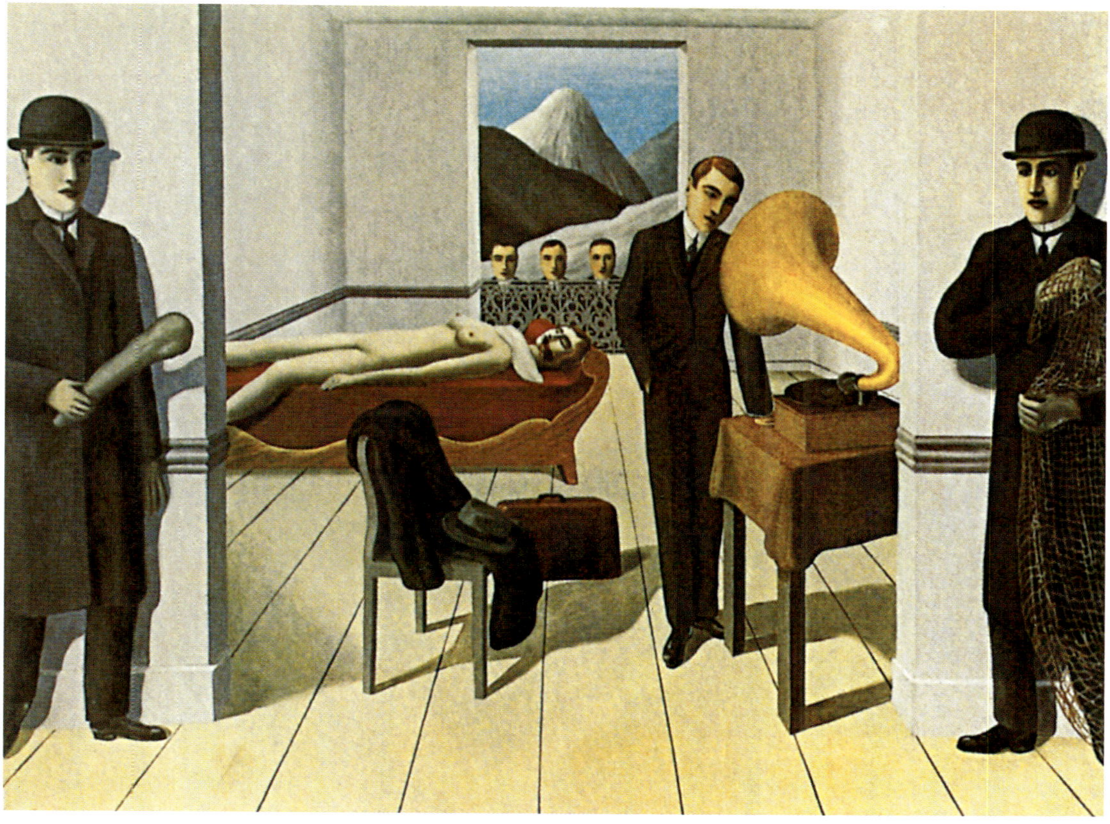

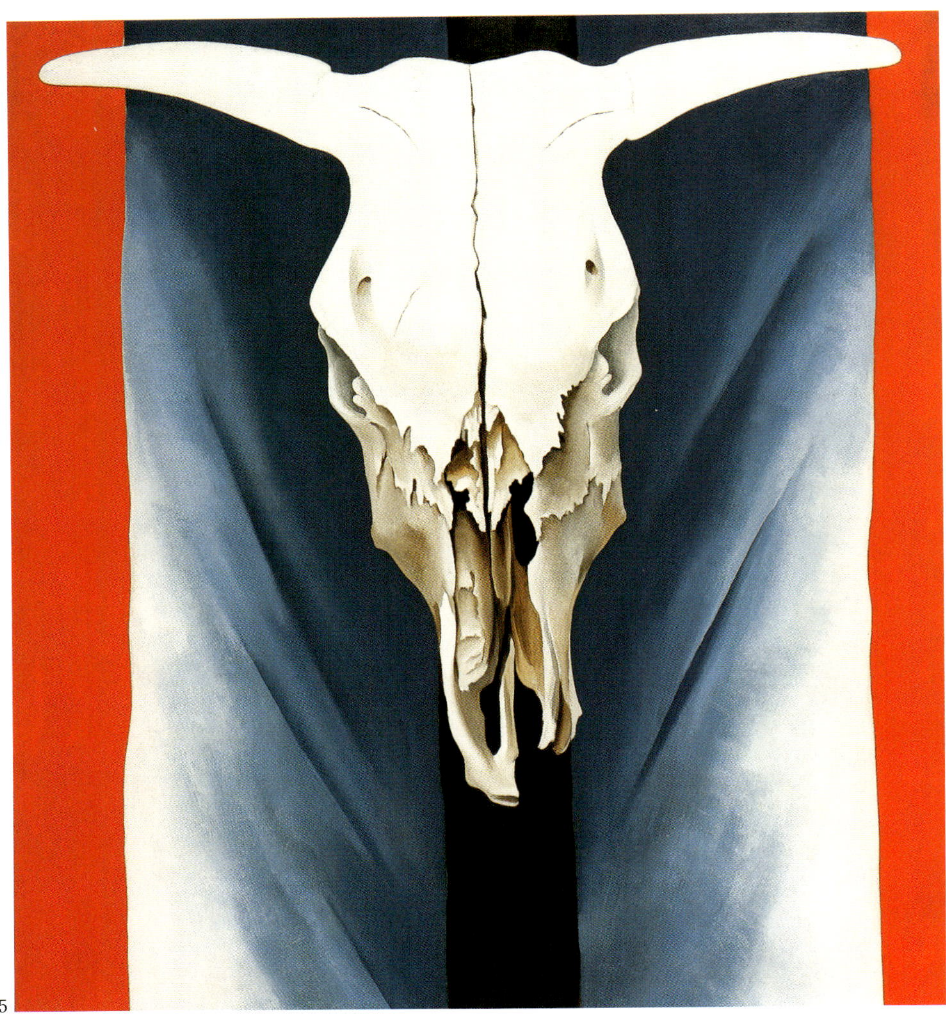

895

GEORGIA O'KEEFFE
(1887 SUN PRAIRIE, WISCONSIN – 1986 SANTA FE)

In 1905 Georgia travelled to Chicago to study painting at the Art Institute of Chicago. In 1907 she enrolled at the Art Students' League in New York City, where she studied with William Merritt Chase. During her time in New York she became familiar with the 291 Gallery owned by her future husband, photographer Alfred Stieglitz. In 1912, she and her sisters studied at university with Alon Bement, who employed a somewhat revolutionary method in art instruction originally conceived by Arthur Wesley Dow. In Bement's class, the students did not mechanically copy nature, but instead were taught the principles of design using geometric shapes. They worked at exercises that included dividing a square, working within a circle and placing a rectangle around a drawing, then organising the composition by rearranging, adding or eliminating elements. It sounded dull and to most students it was. But Georgia found that these studies gave art its structure and helped her understand the basics of abstraction.

During the 1920s O'Keeffe also produced a huge number of landscapes and botanical studies during annual trips to Lake George. With Stieglitz's connections in the arts community of New York – from 1923 he organised an O'Keeffe exhibition annually – O'Keeffe's work received a great deal of attention and commanded high prices. She, however, resented the sexual connotations people attached to her paintings, especially during the 1920s when Freudian theories became a form of what today might be termed "pop psychology". The legacy she left behind is a unique vision that translates the complexity of nature into simple shapes for us to explore and make our own discoveries. She taught us there is poetry in nature and beauty in geometry. Georgia O'Keeffe's long lifetime of work shows us new ways to see the world, from her eyes to ours.

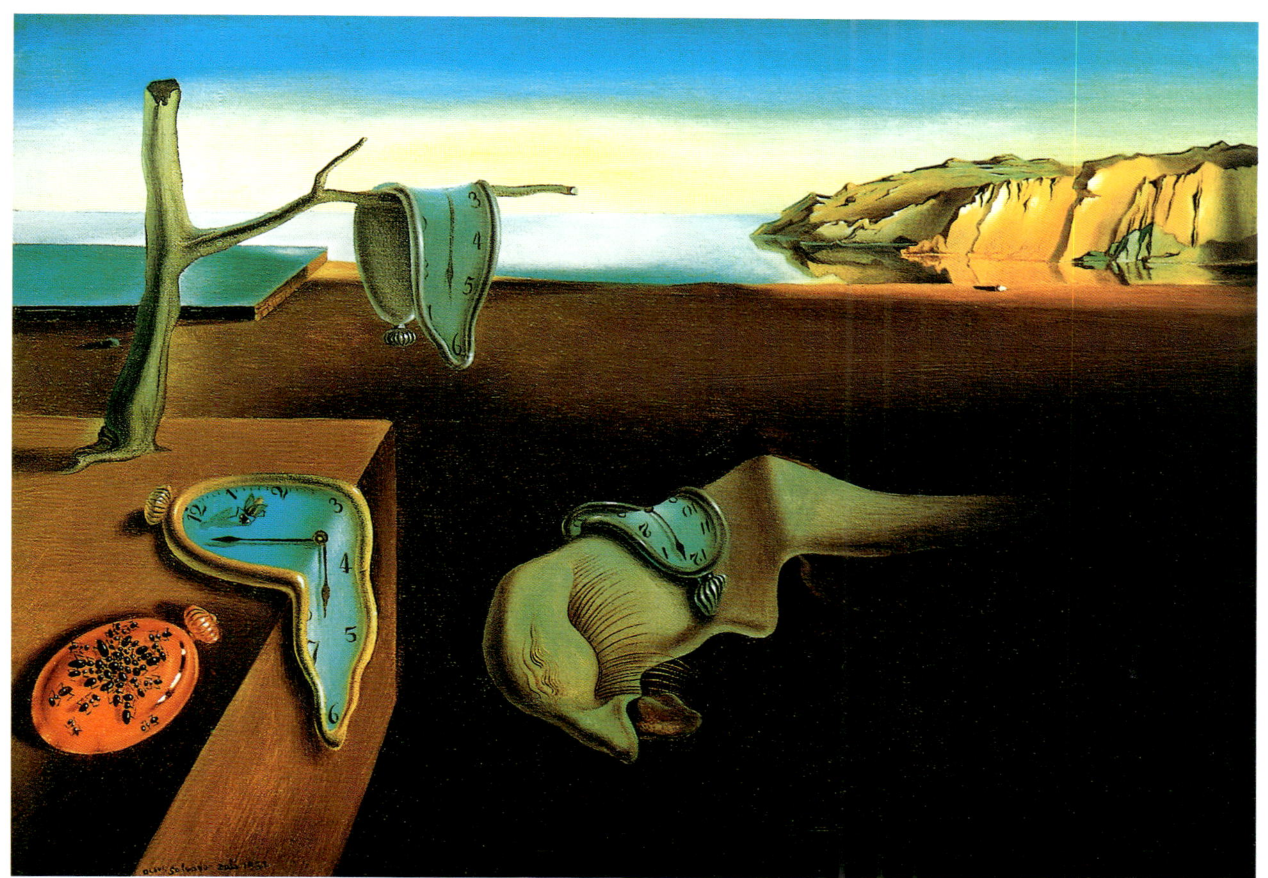

895. **Georgia O'Keeffe**, 1887-1986, Modernism, American,
Red, White and Blue, 1931.
Oil on canvas, 101.3 x 91.1 cm.
The Metropolitan Museum of Art, New York.

With her Red, White and Blue, Georgia O'Keeffe wanted to call people's attention to the country she loved by adding the red stripes on either side. But while the brilliant red, white and blue background is distracting, the eye is still drawn to the lacelike edges of the fragments where the bone has worn away. There is a lifelike facet to the tiny staring "eye holes" giving the skull a macabre quality.

896. **Salvador Dalí**, 1904-1989, Surrealism, Spanish,
The Persistence of Memory, 1931.
Oil on canvas, 24.1 x 33 cm.
The Museum of Modern Art, New York.

Dalí discusses the genesis of the painting in his autobiography. He writes, "Having concluded our dinner with a very strong Camembert and after the others had gone, I remained sitting quietly at the table for a long time considering the philosophical problem of 'Super-Softs' that the cheese had brought to my attention. I stood up, went into my atelier and turned on the light to take one last look at the picture I was presently working on, as was my habit. This picture depicts the landscape at Port Lligat; the cliffs lie in a transparent, melancholy dusk light and an olive-tree with severed branches devoid of leaves stands in the foreground. I knew that the atmosphere which I had been able to create with this landscape was the background for an idea that would serve to create a surprising picture but I didn't know in the slightest what it would be. I was just about to turn off the light when I suddenly 'saw' the answer. I saw two melting watches, one hanging pathetically over the branch of the olive-tree. Although my headache had become so strong that I was suffering, I readied my palette impatiently and got down to work."

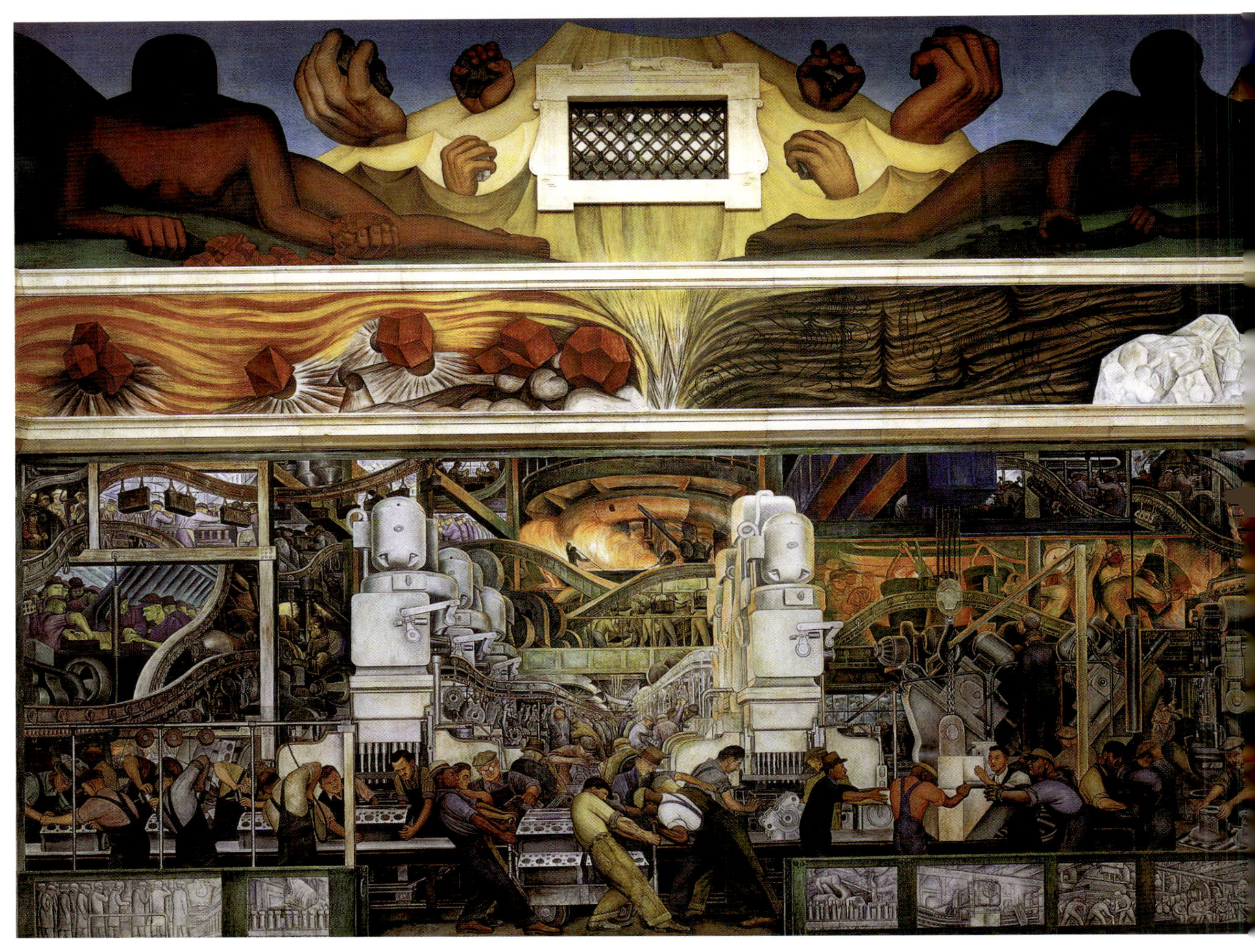

897. **Diego Rivera**, 1886-1957, Social Realism, Mexican, *Detroit Industry,* north wall, 1932.
Fresco. Detroit Institute of Art, Detroit.

After getting around the Impressionists and Divisionists, Rivera is attracted by Synthetic Cubism such as the one practised by Juan Gris. During a journey in Italy in 1920-1921, he discovered the frescos by Giotto and adopted the technique of monumental decoration with a borrowing of pre-columbian elements. Rivera was commissioned by Edsel Ford, president of the Arts Commission as well as of Ford Motor Company, and Dr William Valentiner, director of the DIA, to create two murals for the museum in its Garden Court.

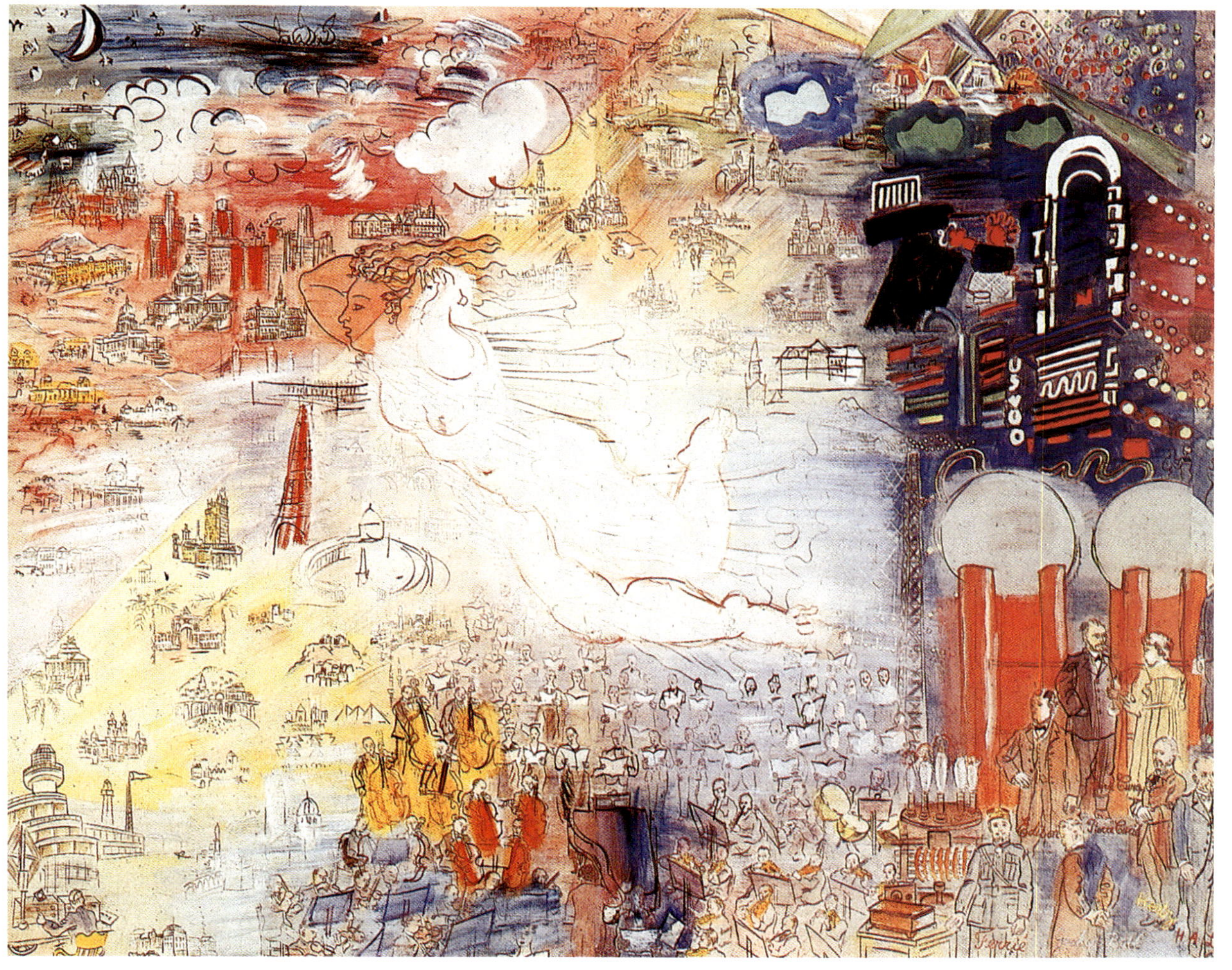

898. **Raoul Dufy**, 1877-1953, Fauvism, French, *The Spirit of Electricity*, 1937.
Oil on wood, 10 x 60 cm (panel).
Musée d'Art Moderne de la ville de Paris, Paris.

RAOUL DUFY
(1877 LE HAVRE – 1953 FORCALQUIER)

Raoul Dufy was born in Le Havre, France, in 1877. He attended the evening classes at the school of Fine Arts where he developed his innate gift for drawing. At the beginning of his career he was significantly influenced by the Fauve movement and his colourful works with bold contours reflect this approach. After a brief phase with Cubism, he enjoyed painting flowers, fashionable tennis courts, views of the French Riviera and elegant parties. In 1938, Dufy created one of the largest frescos in the world, *La Fée Electricité*.

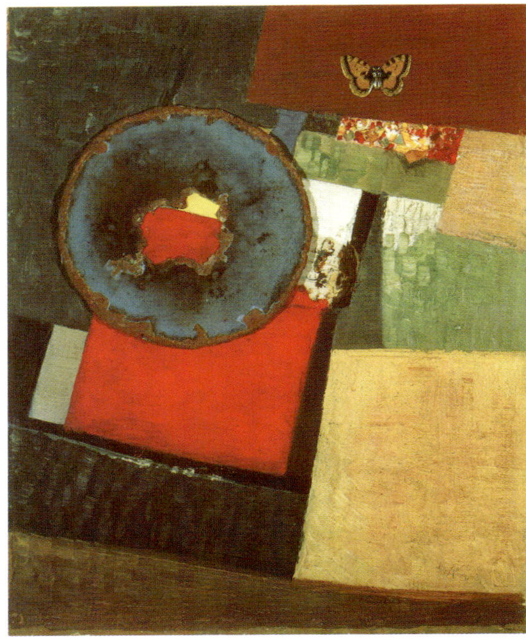

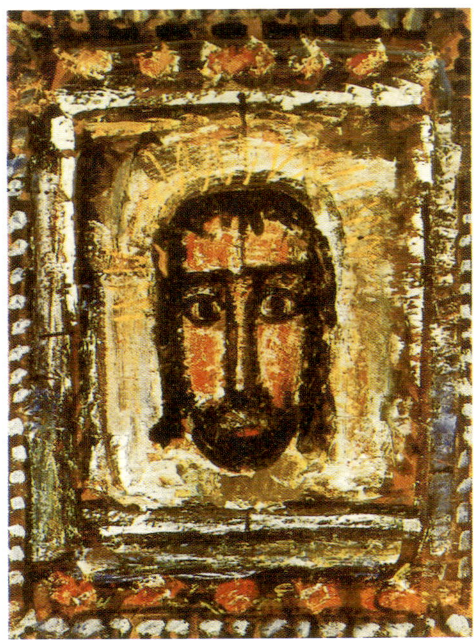

899. **Kurt Schwitters**, 1887-1949, Dada, German, *Maraak, Variation I*, 1930. Oil and assemblage on cardboard, 46 x 37 cm. Peggy Guggenheim Collection, Venice.

900. **Georges Rouault**, 1871-1958, Expressionism, French, *The Holy Face (Christ)*, 1933. Oil and gouache on paper mounted on canvas, 91 x 65 cm. Musée national d'art moderne, Centre Georges-Pompidou, Paris.

901. **René Magritte**, 1898-1967, Surrealism, Belgian, *Red Model*, 1935. Oil on canvas mounted on cardboard, 56 x 46 cm. Musée national d'art moderne, Centre Georges-Pompidou, Paris.

902. **Paul Klee**, 1879-1940, Expressionism/Blaue Reiter, German-Swiss, *New Harmony*, 1936. Oil on canvas, 92.7 x 66 cm. Guggenheim Museum, New York.

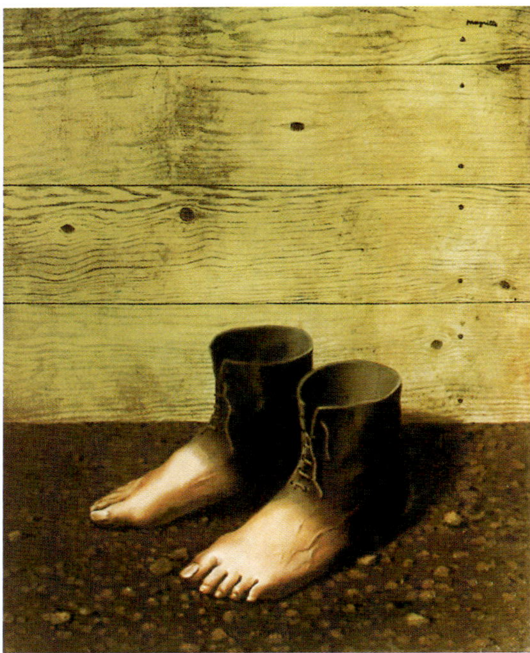

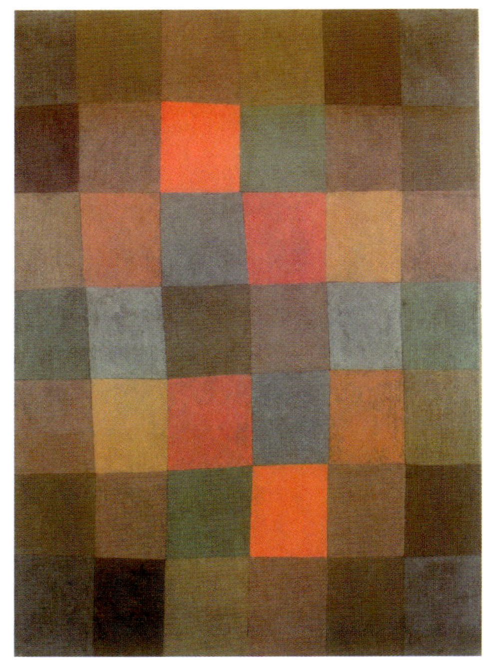

903. **Stanley Spencer**, 1891-1959, Late Pre-Raphaelite, British,
St Francis and the Birds, 1935.
Oil on canvas, 66 x 58.4 cm. Tate Gallery, London.

*St Francis of Assisi, the founder of the Franciscans (here shown
as an old man), is popularly known for his ability to talk to
birds, and pray with them. Stanley Spencer intended to exhibit
this work in his ideal gallery, called 'Church House', but it was
never built.*

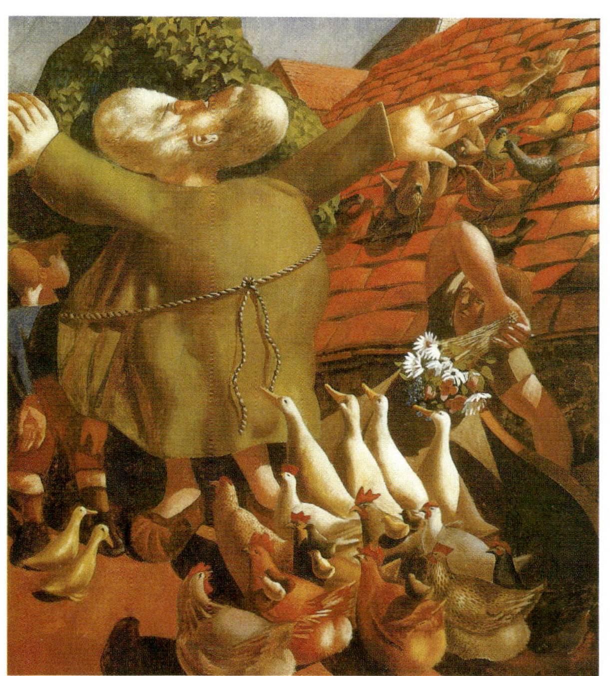

THOMAS HART BENTON
(1889 NEOSHO, MISSOURI – 1975 KANSAS CITY)

Thomas Hart Benton refused to follow a political career, as
his father and grandfather had done, and studied, instead,
at the Art Institute School of Chicago. After studying in Paris,
where he was interested in Impressionism and Pointillism,
he rejected European influences and became a regionalist.
His work idealised the traditional American rural world.
Leader of "The American Scene," he was the teacher of the
brothers Charles and Jackson Pollock at the Art Students'
League, and friend of the latter throughout life. He is
known almost entirely for his murals, especially those at the
New School for Social Research of New York.

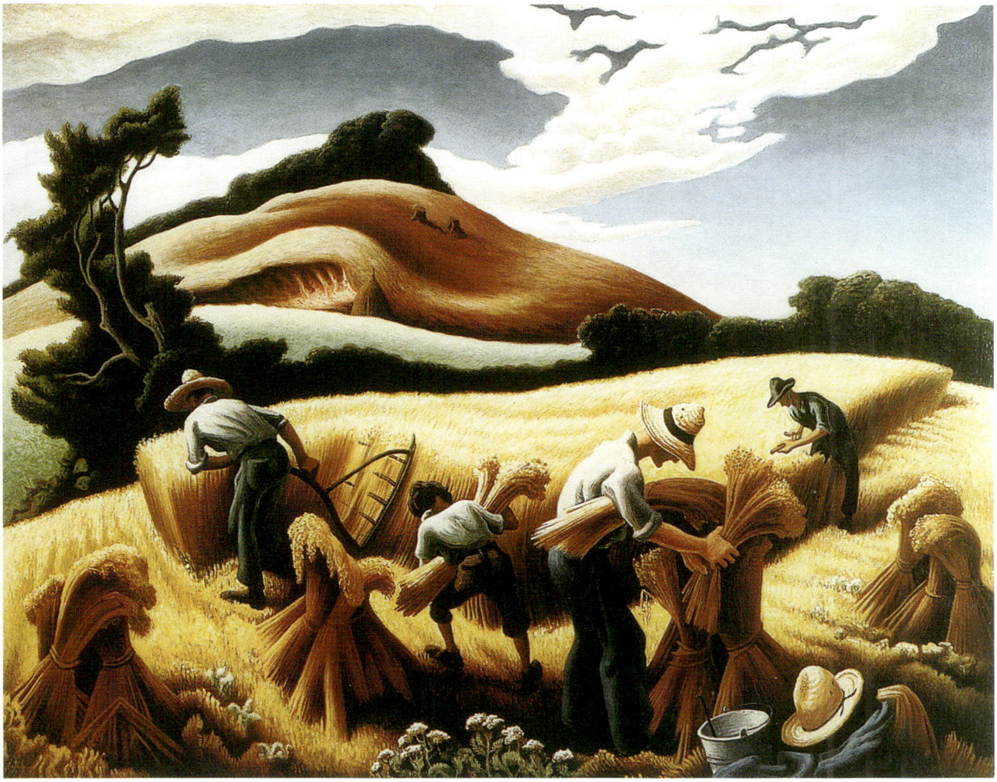

904. **Thomas Hart Benton**,
1889-1975,
Regionalism, American,
Cradling Wheat, 1938.
Tempera and oil on
wood, 78.7 x 96.5 cm.
Saint Louis Art Musem,
St Louis.
Art © Thomas Hart
Benton / Licensed by
VAGA, New York, NY.

905. **Pablo Picasso**, 1881-1973, Cubism, Spanish,
Guernica, 1937. Oil on canvas, 349.3 x 776.5 cm.
Museo Nacional Centro de Arte Reina Sofía, Madrid.

The bloody historical event that moved Picasso to create this masterpiece in one month took place shortly before its first exhibition at the International Exhibition in Paris in 1937. The images and feelings of the three-hour bombing and destruction of the Basque capital of Guernica by Nazi planes were still fresh in the public consciousness. Today, at least one almanac lists the first showing of the work as a highlight of that year, but ironically doesn't mention the event that killed 1,654 people and inspired the artist (Time Almanac, 2002). The brutally stark monochrome work was controversial both as a reactive political statement and as art. Initially, Picasso had put touches of colours in his work. The black and white must have been inspired by photographs taken of the war (particularly those of Robert Capa). It was a major expression of the cubist movement to disregard the distinction between the profile and the full face view of it subjects. The viewer sees the subject from different angles at the same time.

While the work is secular, it is often compared to religious triptychs in composition as well as in the intensity of its thematic presentation. The vertical line between the left panel and the central might run between the bull and house, cutting through the horse's right rear leg. The right panel cuts vertically through the thigh area of the pleading women in the lower right. The geometric centre of the work runs vertically between symbols of hope (the single flower that has survived beneath the broken sword) and the corner of the building from which the horrified, lamp-carrying victim emerges. The tragedy of the small town is extended to all of Spain by including the bull, a symbol of the nation's obsession with bullfighting at that time, but here the bull has its tail raised in anger. It would seem to show defiance, in contrast to the anguished horse that is dismembered like the fallen victim below it. However, Picasso said the horse "represents the people," while the bull is "the brutality and darkness" of fascism. While the head in the lower left seems to still have some life, the child in the anguished

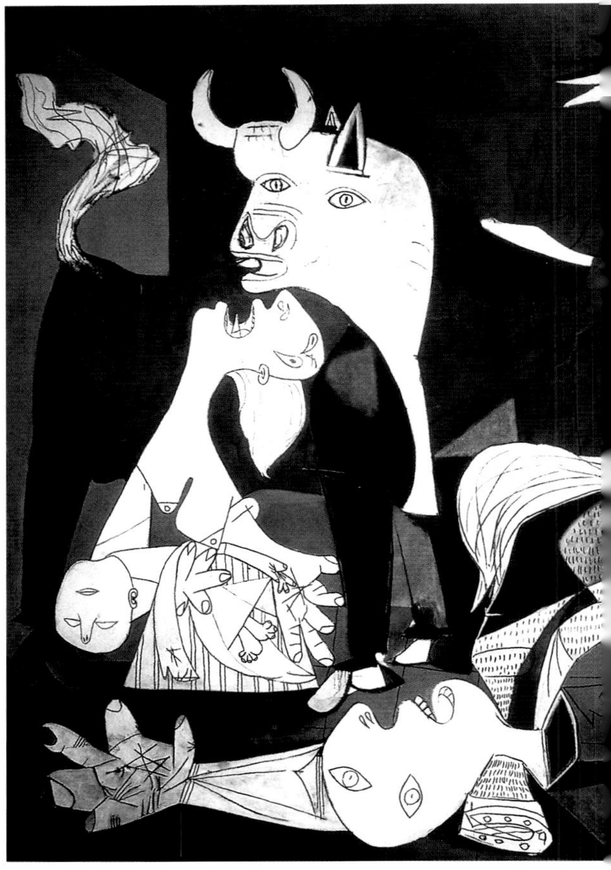

mother's arms appears lifeless. The top central symbol is like an eye with a light bulb as its pupil. It is also like a sun that seems

PABLO RUIZ PICASSO
(1881 MÁLAGA – 1973 MOUGINS)

Picasso was born a Spaniard and, so they say, began to draw before he could speak. As an infant he was instinctively attracted to artist's tools. In early childhood he could spend hours in happy concentration drawing spirals with a sense and meaning known only to himself. At other times, shunning children's games, he traced his first pictures in the sand. This early self-expression held out promise of a rare gift.

Málaga must be mentioned, for it was there, on 25 October 1881, that Pablo Ruiz Picasso was born and it was there that he spent the first ten years of his life. Picasso's father was a painter and professor at the School of Fine Arts and Crafts. Picasso learnt from him the basics of formal academic art training. Then he studied at the Academy of Arts in Madrid but never finished his degree. Picasso, who was not yet eighteen, had reached the point of his greatest rebelliousness; he repudiated academia's anemic aesthetics along with realism's pedestrian prose and, quite naturally, joined those who called

themselves modernists, the non-conformist artists and writers, those whom Sabartés called "the élite of Catalan thought" and who were grouped around the artists' café Els Quatre Gats. During 1899 and 1900 the only subjects Picasso deemed worthy of painting were those which reflected the "final truth"; the transience of human life and the inevitability of death. His early works, ranged under the name of "Blue Period" (1901-1904), consist in blue-tinted paintings influenced by a trip through Spain and the death of his friend, Casagemas. Even though Picasso himself repeatedly insisted on the inner, subjective nature of the Blue Period, its genesis and, especially, the monochromatic blue were for many years explained as merely the results of various aesthetic influences. Between 1905 and 1907, Picasso entered a new phase, called "Rose Period" characterised by a more cheerful style with orange and pink colours. In Gosol, in the summer of 1906 the nude female form assumed an extraordinary importance for

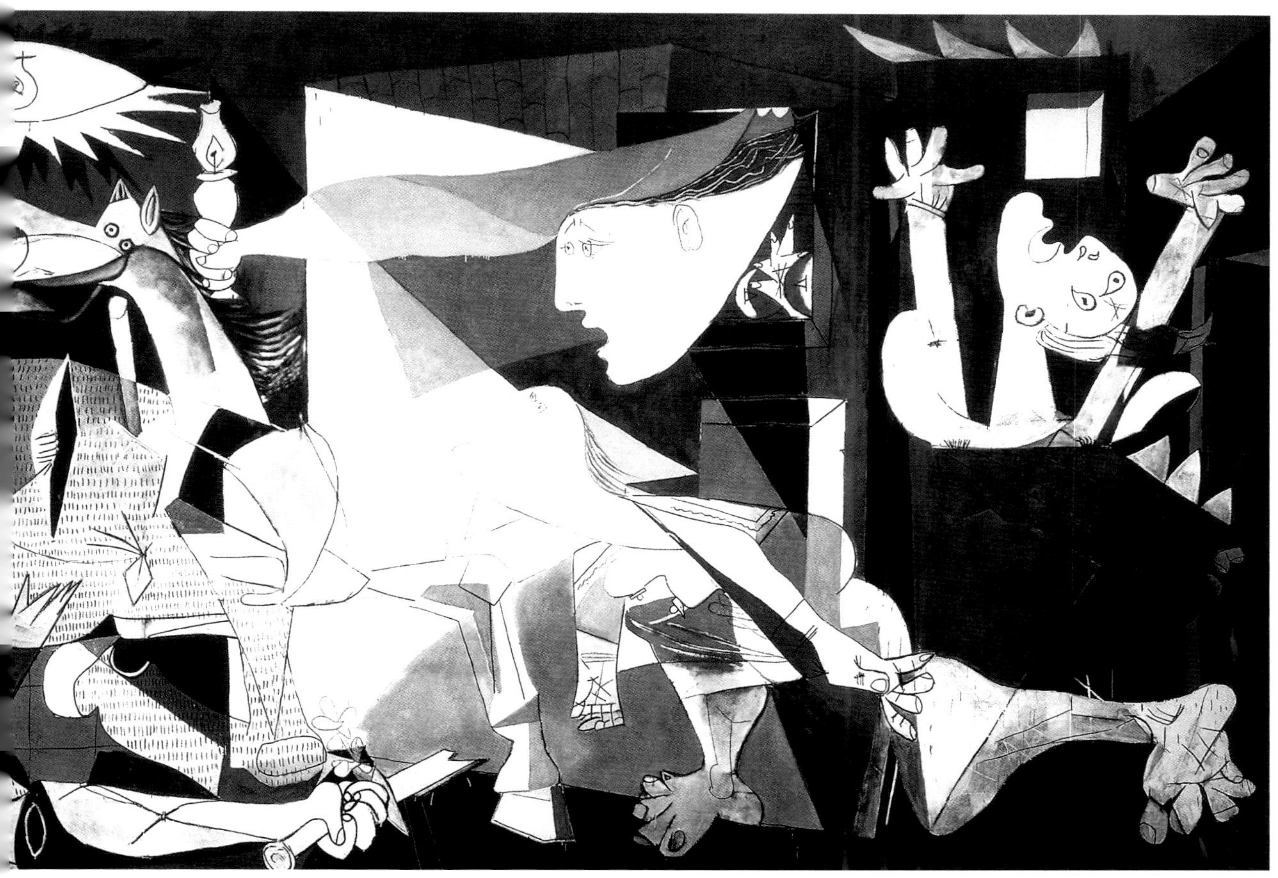

Picasso; he equated a depersonalised, aboriginal, simple nakedness with the concept of "woman". The importance that female nudes were to assume as subjects for Picasso in the next few months (in the winter and spring of 1907) came when he developed the composition of the large painting, *Les Demoiselles d'Avignon*.

Just as African art is usually considered the factor leading to the development of Picasso's classic aesthetics in 1907, the lessons of Cézanne are perceived as the cornerstone of this new progression. This relates, first of all, to a spatial conception of the canvas as a composed entity, subjected to a certain constructive system. Georges Braque, with whom Picasso became friends in the autumn of 1908 and together with whom he led Cubism during the six years of its apogee, was amazed by the similarity of Picasso's pictorial experiments to his own. He explained that: "Cubism's main direction was the materialisation of space." After his Cubist period, in the 1920s, Picasso returned to a more figurative style and got closer to the surrealist movement. He represented distorted and monstrous bodies but in a very personal style. After the bombing of Guernica during 1937, Picasso made one of his most famous works which starkly symbolises the horrors of that war and, indeed, all wars. In the 1960s, his art changed again and Picasso began looking at the art of great masters and based his paintings on ones by Velázquez, Poussin, Goya, Manet, Courbet and Delacroix. Picasso's final works were a mixture of style, becoming more colourful, expressive and optimistic. Picasso died in 1973, in his villa in Mougins. The Russian Symbolist Georgy Chulkov wrote: "Picasso's death is tragic. Yet how blind and naïve are those who believe in imitating Picasso and learning from him. Learning what? For these forms have no corresponding emotions outside of Hell. But to be in Hell means to anticipate death. The Cubists are hardly privy to such unlimited knowledge".

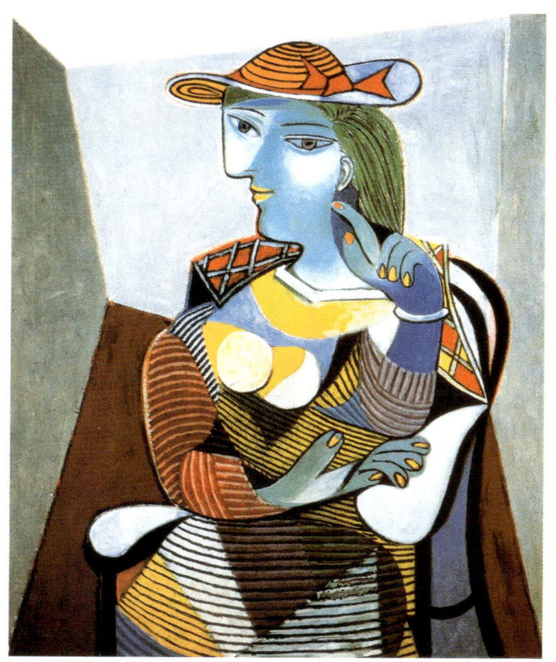

906

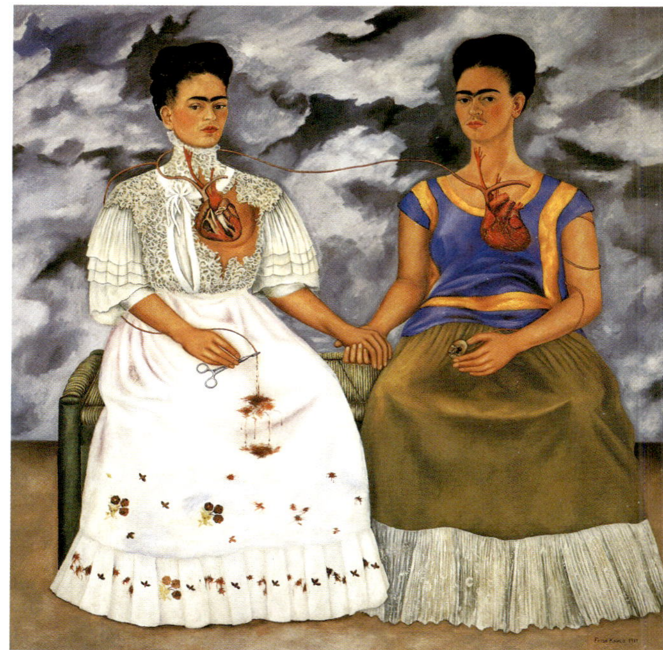

907

906. **Pablo Picasso**, 1881-1973, Cubism, Spanish,
Portrait of Marie-Thérèse Walter, 1937.
Oil on canvas, 100 x 81 cm.
Musée Picasso, Paris.

907. **Frida Kahlo**, 1907-1954, Surrealism, Mexican,
The Two Fridas, 1939.
Oil on canvas, 170.2 x 170.2 cm.
Museo de Arte Moderno, Mexico City.

The 1.8 square metre Two Fridas *would become Frida Kahlo's signature masterpiece. A mirror had long played a central role in her paintings, at first from necessity due to her bed-ridden state. Later, the mirror became a reflection of reality that could be manipulated and translated into a fantasy vision of her very personal verité. In* The Two Fridas, *the mirror duality becomes a schizophrenic visualisation of Frida's personal dilemma, the European woman (Frida) in white with lace and appliqués befitting a chaste Catholic girl, and the Tehuana woman of darker skin and colourful costume – the earthy peasant persona encouraged by Diego Rivera. Both hearts are exposed and a vine-like blood vessel connects a small amulet that is a miniature portrait of Diego as a child. The two hearts are the "Fridas". The European "Frida's" heart is ripped and savaged while she grips the end of the shared artery with a surgical clamp. But blood still drips from its end onto her snow white dress.*

908. **Paul Delvaux**, 1897-1994, Surrealism, Belgian,
Entry into the City, 1940.
Oil on canvas, 170 x 190 cm.
Musée Delvaux, Saint Idesbald.

909. **Paul Nash**, 1889-1946, Surrealism, British,
Totes Meer (Dead Sea), 1940-1941.
Oil on canvas, 101.6 x 152.4 cm.
Tate Gallery, London.

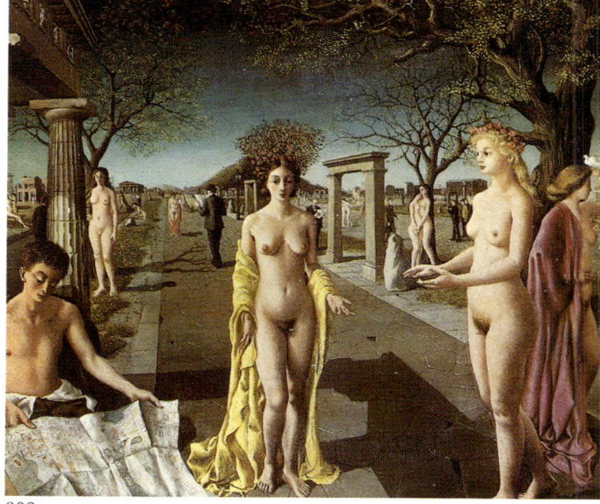

908

909

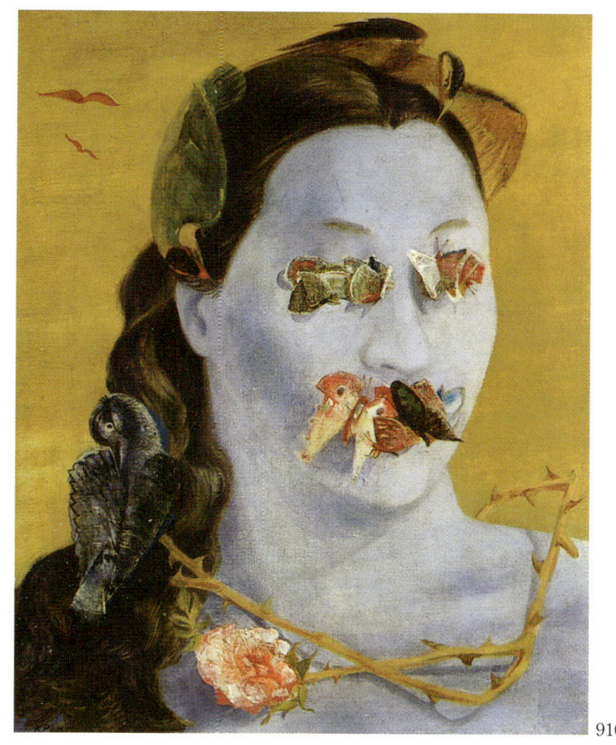

910

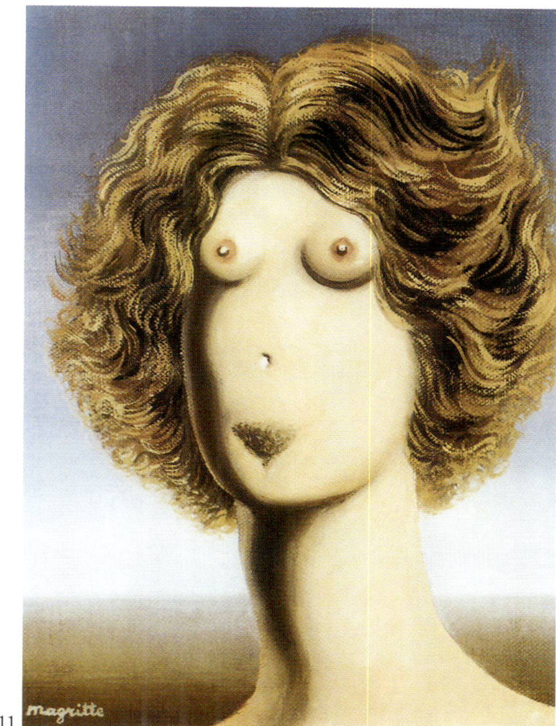

911

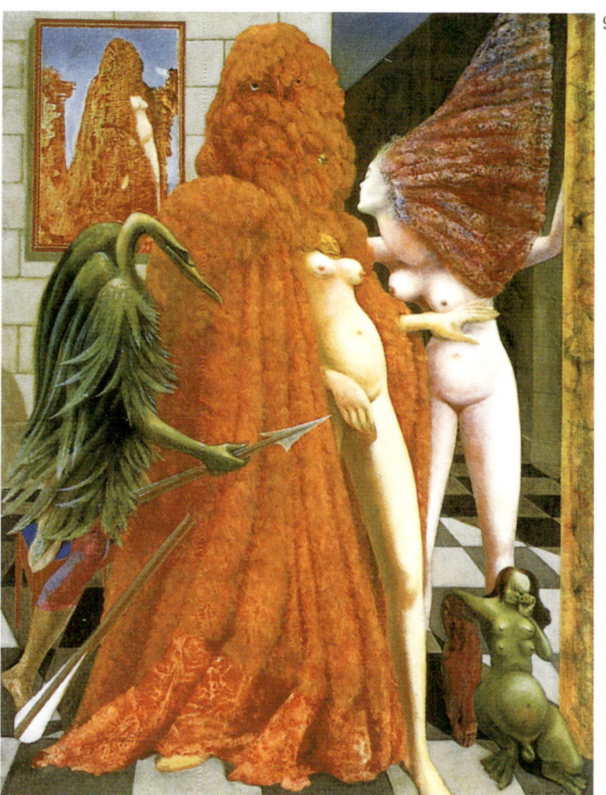

912

913

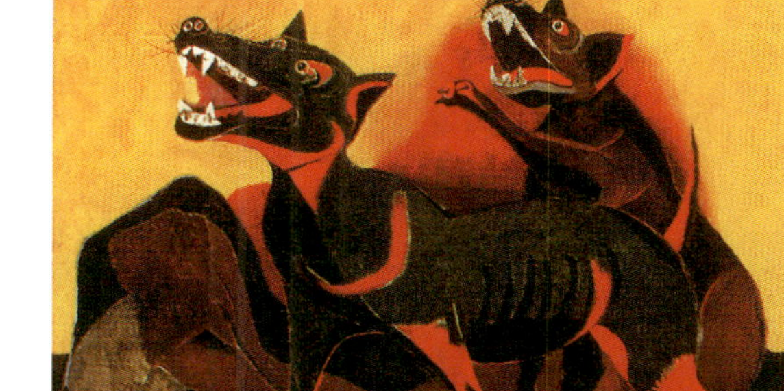

910. **Roland Penrose**, 1900-1984, Surrealism, British,
Winged Domino, 1938. Oil on canvas, 60 x 46 cm.
Penrose Collection, Chiddingly.

911. **René Magritte**, *The Rape*, 1934.
Oil on canvas, 73 x 54 cm. The Menil Collection, Houston.

912. **Max Ernst**, 1891-1976, Surrealism, French, German-born,
Attirement of the Bride, 1940. Oil on canvas, 129.6 x 96.3 cm.
Peggy Guggenheim Collection, Venice.

913. **Rufino Tamayo**, 1899-1991, Mexican, *Animals*, 1941.
Oil on canvas, 76.5 x 101.6 cm.
The Museum of Modern Art, New York.

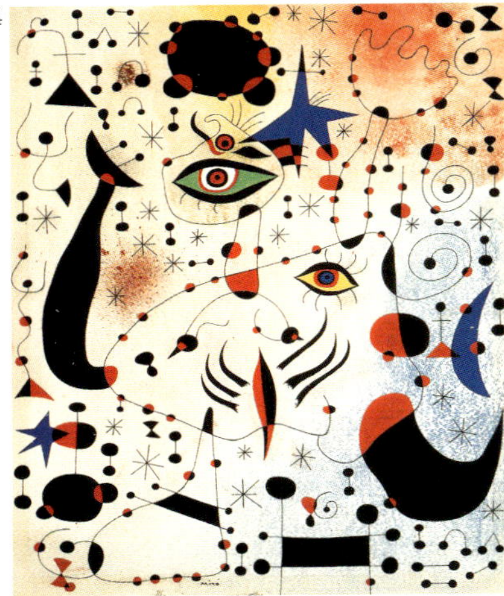

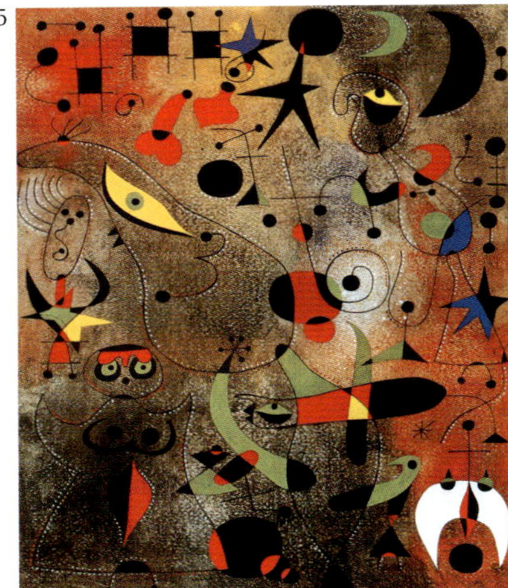

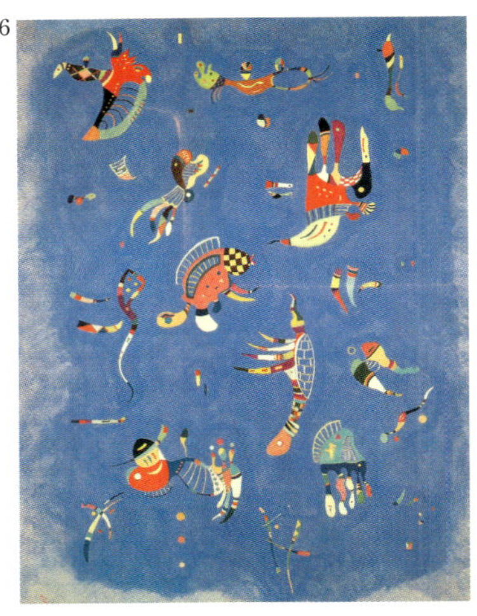

914. **Joan Miró**, 1893-1983, Surrealism, Spanish,
Ciphers and Constellations in Love with a Woman, 1941.
Gouache and oil wash on paper, 46 x 38 cm.
The Art Institute of Chicago, Chicago.

915. **Joan Miró**, 1893-1983, Surrealism, Spanish,
Constellation: Awakening in the Early Morning, 1941.
Gouache and oil wash on paper, 46 x 38 cm.
Kimbell Art Museum, Fort Worth.

Miró had begun the paintings collectively called "Constellations" while staying in the Normandy countryside, in Varengeville-sur-Mer, a tiny village near Dieppe where he lived from August 1939 to May 1940. He was so caught up with his work that he did not understand how that location put him into the path of the escalating war. He was busy creating the techniques and sensibility that would carry through a tight series of twenty-three paintings.

He began by moistening his paper, scratching its surface and stirring up texture as background to the firmament he was creating. Familiar imagery floated onto the page – eyes, stars, birds, faces, ribs – but also simple geometric shapes – triangles, circles, crescents, swashes. Some shapes are flat black, others primary colours, but all interconnect within the frame, so that the totality is as much the interest of the painting as its component parts.

916. **Wassily Kandinsky**, 1866-1944, Lyrical Abstraction/ Der Blaue Reiter, Russian, *Blue Heaven*, 1940.
Oil on canvas, 100 x 73 cm.
Musée national d'art moderne, Centre Georges-Pompidou, Paris.

917. **Stuart Davis**, 1894-1964, Cubism, American,
Swing Landscape, 1938. Oil on canvas, 217 x 440 cm.
Indiana University Art Museum, Bloomington.
Art © Stuart Davis Estate / Licensed by VAGA, New York, NY.

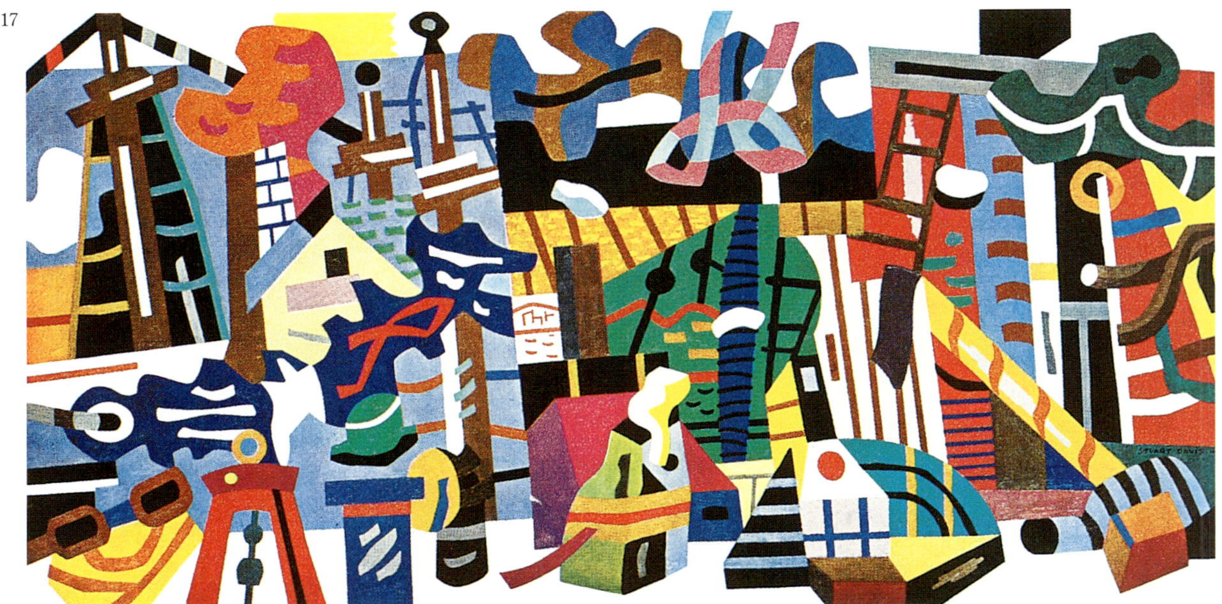

917

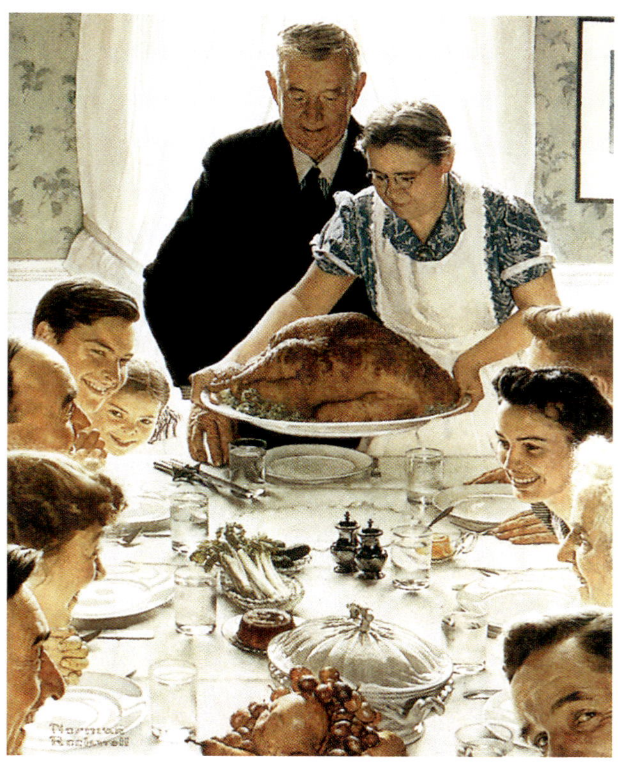

918. **Norman Rockwell**, 1894-1978, Realism, American,
Freedom from Want, 1943.
Oil on canvas, 117.3 x 91 cm.
Norman Rockwell Art Collection Trust, Stockbridge,
Massachusetts.

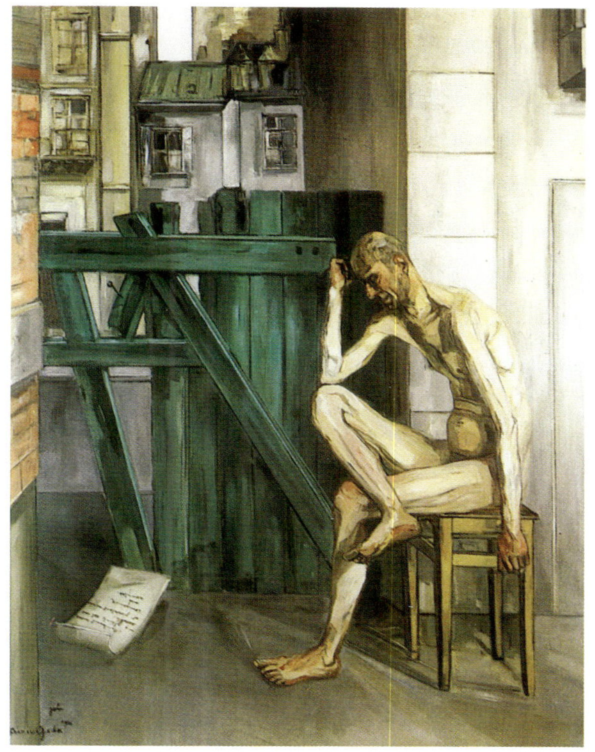

919. **Francis Gruber**, 1912-1948, Miserabilism, French,
Job, 1944.
Oil on canvas, 162 x 130 cm.
Tate Gallery, London.

*This painting was exhibited at the Salon d'Automne in 1944
which was called "Salon of the Liberation" because of the
German occupation of Paris. This painting symbolises
oppressed people, suffering like Job, and is an allegory of the
survival of hope under the Occupation. Because of this and
other works, Gruber is considered the father of the Miserabiliste
variety of French painting.*

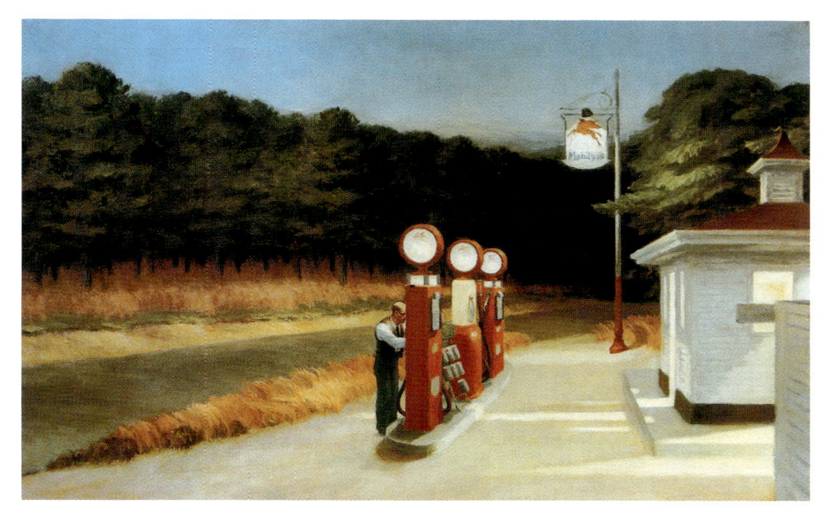

920. **Edward Hopper**, 1882-1967, Realism,
American,
Gas, 1940.
Oil on canvas, 66.7 x 102.2 cm.
The Museum of Modern Art, New York.

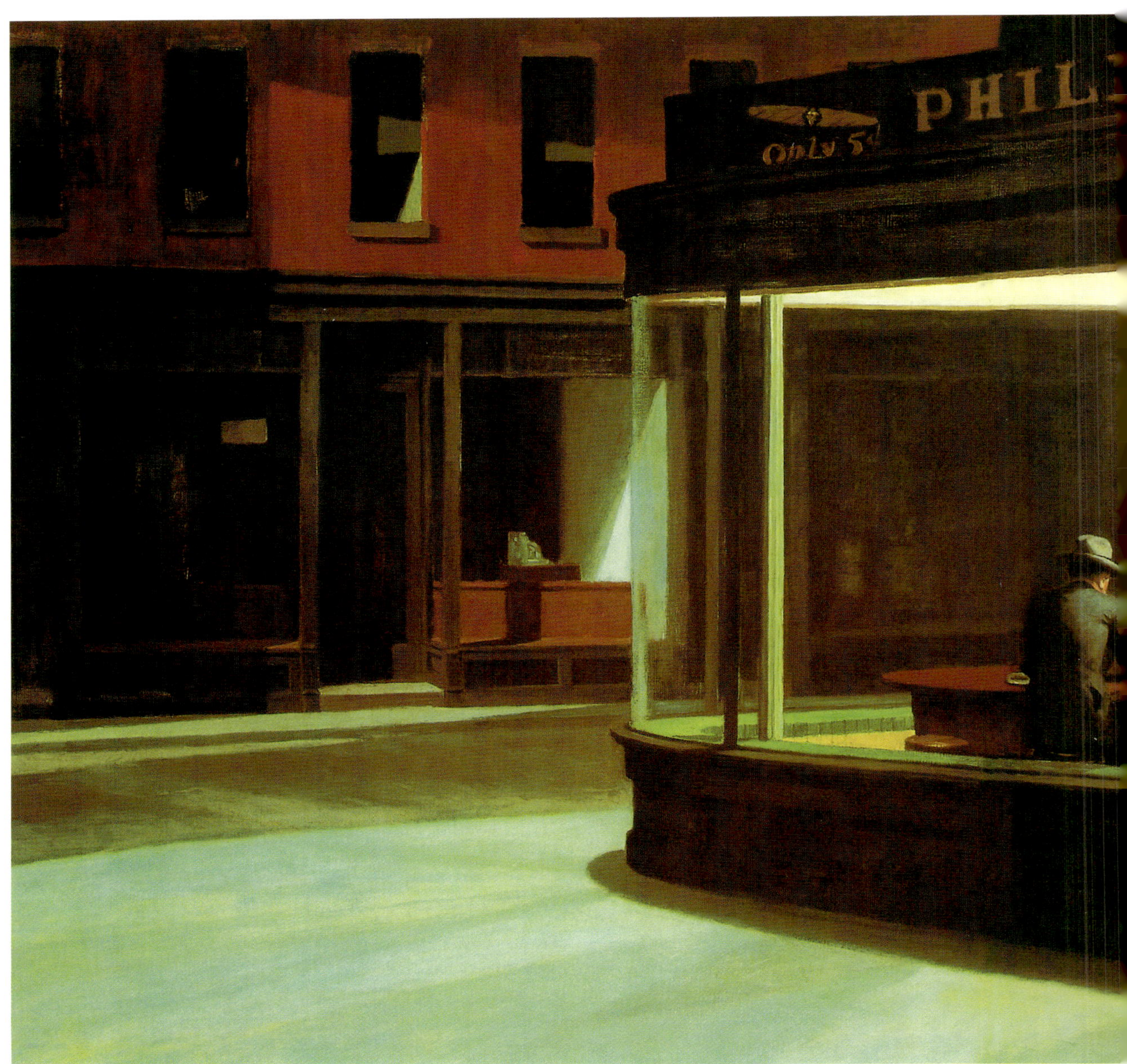

PHIL
Only 5¢

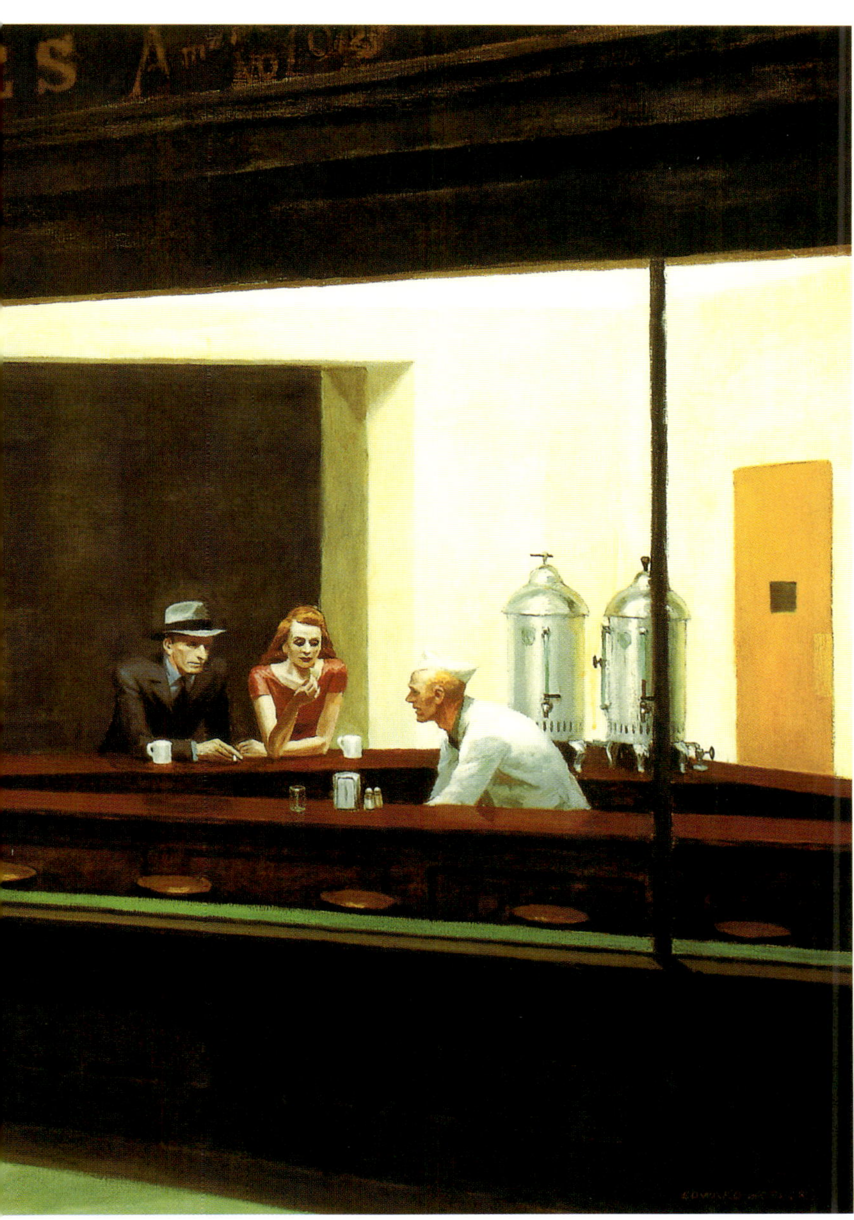

921. **Edward Hopper**, 1882-1967,
Realism, American,
Nighthawks, 1942.
Oil on canvas, 84.1 x 152.4 cm.
The Art Institute of Chicago,
Chicago.

Hopper's teacher, Robert Henri (1865-1929), was of the Ashcan School, a realism movement in America shortly before World War I. The influence is seen in the artist's frequent choice of ordinary cityscapes (called American vernacular architecture) and street subjects (ex. Early Sunday Morning, *1930). However, the artist's treatment of light and shadow, seen dramatically demonstrated in* Nighthawks, *is distinctively and immediately recognisable as his own. In this quiet view of two people at a late night coffee shop, there is a cold distance between the couple, symbolised by the separation of their cups and expressionless faces. The waiter is in an unusual posture on a lower plane apparently so as not to distract from the main subjects. An isolated customer is not relating to either the couple or the waiter; he even has his back to the viewer, albeit he is geometrically at the centre. The lighting distracts the viewer from him. The viewer is even more distant from the interior, left outside of its warmer and more secure world. Referring to American cinema in the setting, the light, and the characters' attitudes, Hopper reflects the Great Depression of America in the 1930s. The loneliness and melancholy mood and dramatic lighting is typical of Hopper's work, in sharp contrast to the optimistic jingoism of either the Ashcan School or later the contemporary American illustrator Norman Rockwell, for example. Yet, there is a universal appeal for Hopper's work, or at least an immediate familiarity with the bleakness he frequently expressed.*

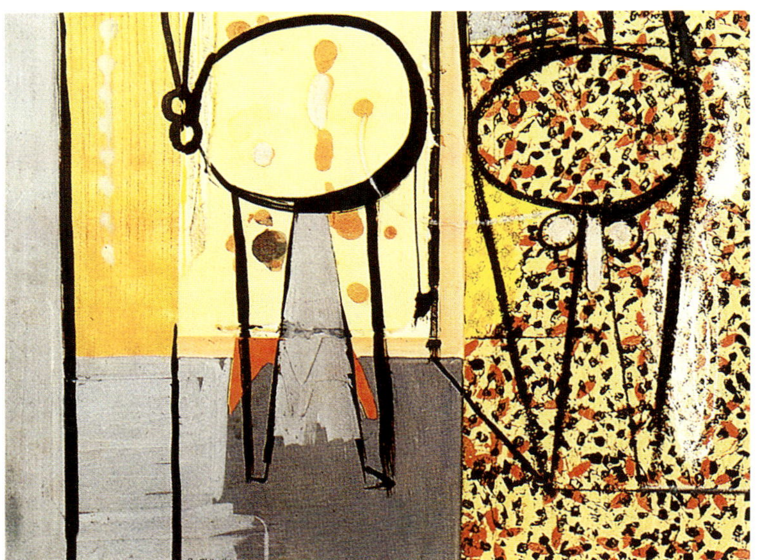

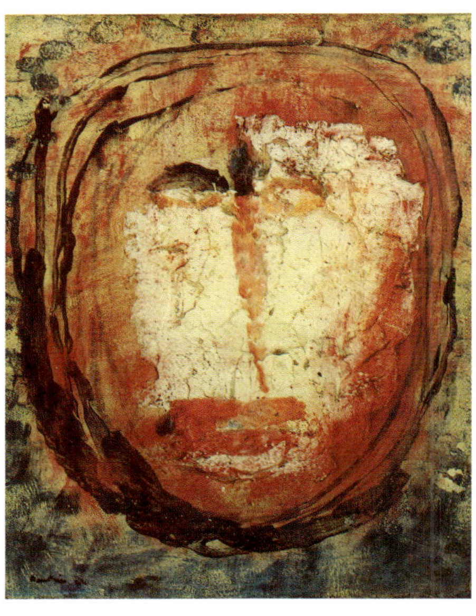

922. **Robert Motherwell**, 1915-1991, Abstract Expressionism,
American, *Pancho Villa, Dead and Alive*, 1943.
Gouache and oil, collage on cardboard, 71.1 x 91.1 cm.
The Museum of Modern Art, New York.
Art © Robert Motherwell / Licensed by VAGA, New York, NY.

923. **Jean Fautrier**, 1898-1964, Art Informel,
French, *Hostage Head n° 2*, 1943.
Private collection. Paris.

924. **Jean Dubuffet**, 1901-1985, Art Brut (Raw Art), French,
Jazz Band (Dirty Style Blues), 1944.
Oil on canvas, 97 x 130 cm.
Musée national d'art moderne, Centre Georges-Pompidou, Paris.

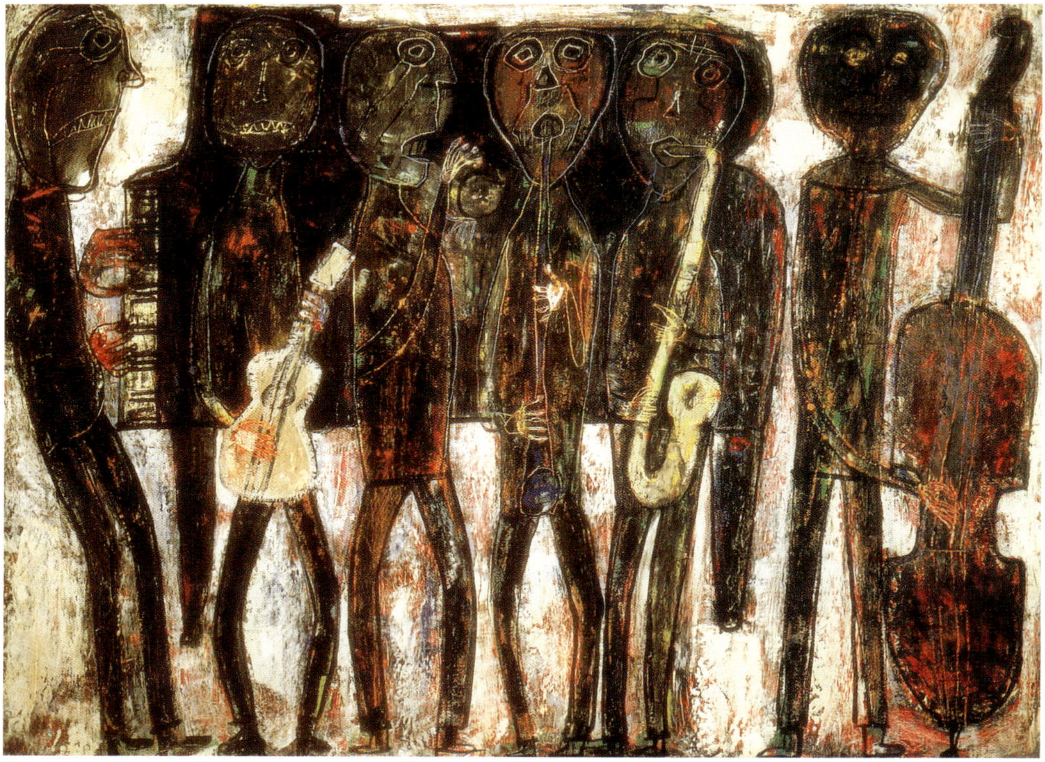

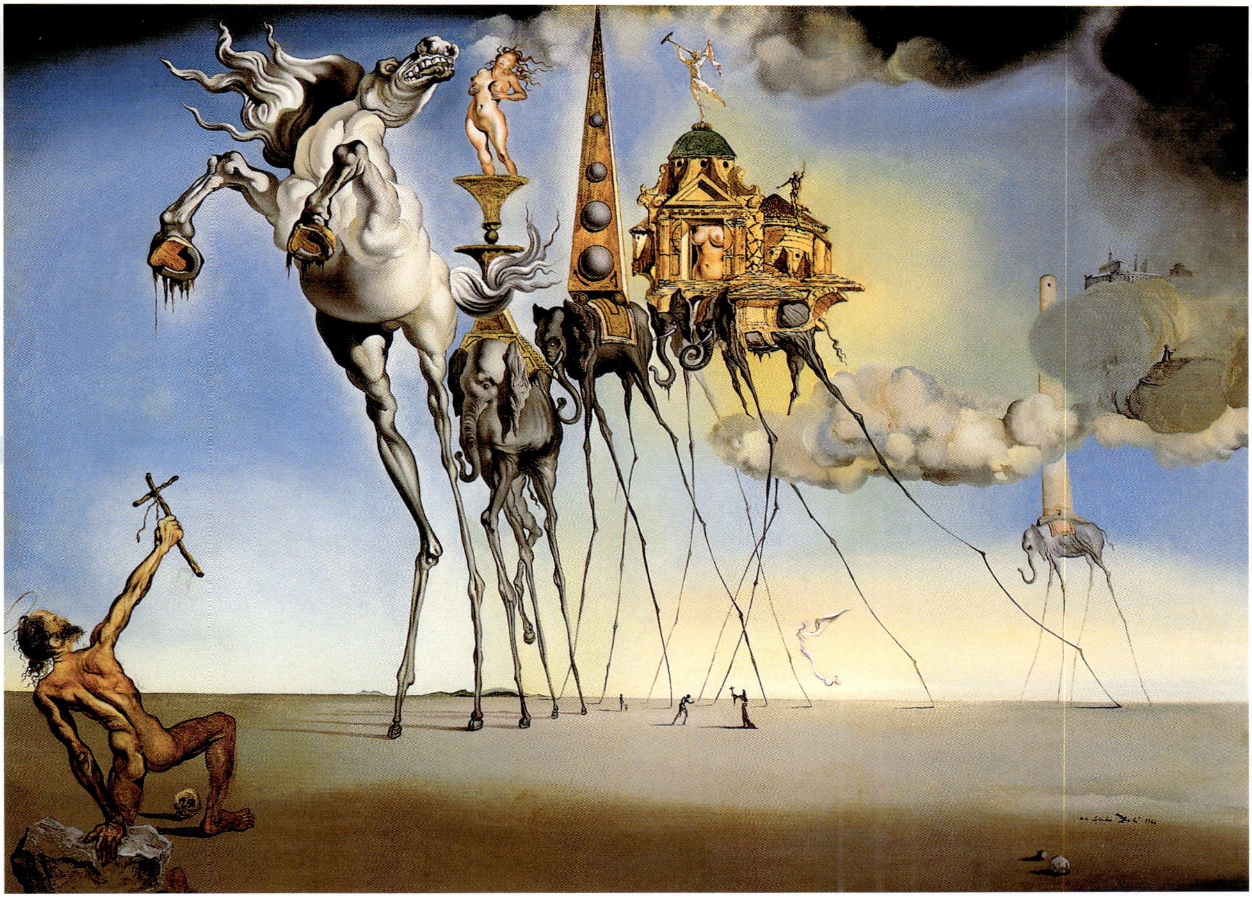

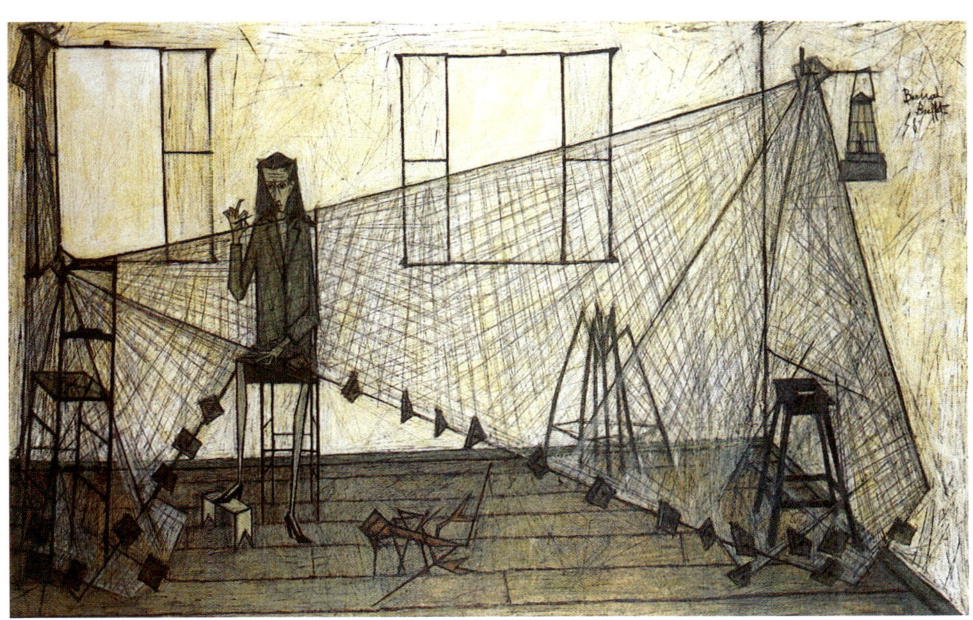

925. **Salvador Dalí**,
1904-1989, Surrealism,
Spanish,
*The Temptation of St
Anthony*, 1946.
Oil on canvas,
89.5 x 119.5 cm.
Musées Royaux des
Beaux-Arts de Belgique,
Brussels.

926. **Bernard Buffet**,
1928-1999, French,
La Ravaudeuse de Filet,
1948.
Oil on canvas,
200 x 308 cm.
Private collection. Paris.

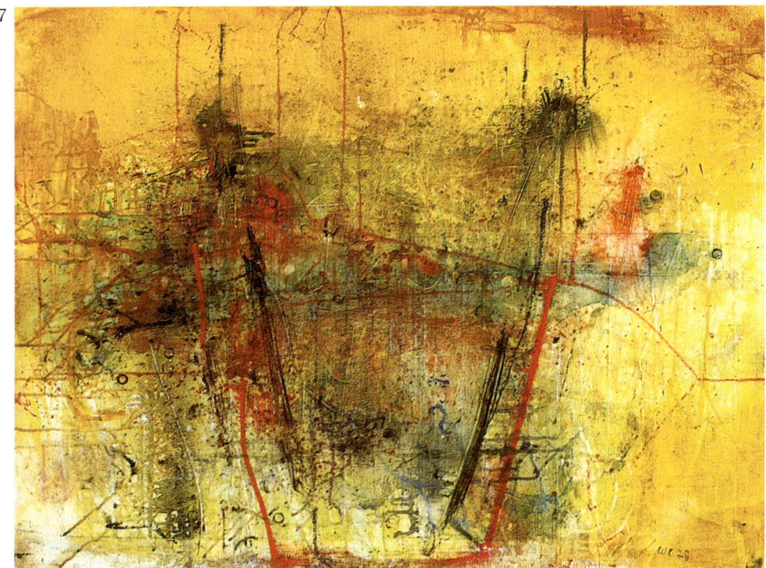

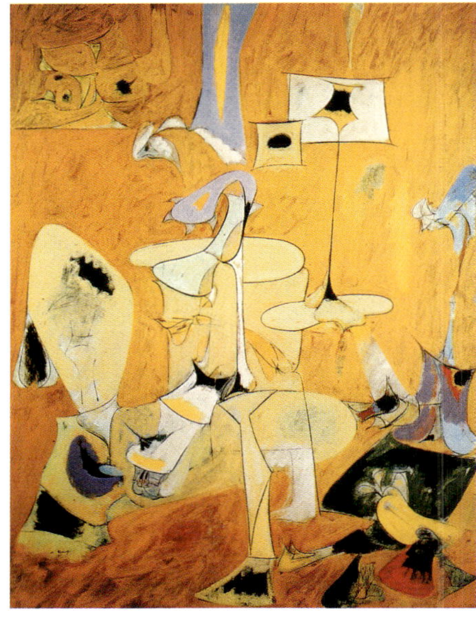

927. **Wols (Alfred Otto Wolfgang Schulze)**, 1913-1951,
Art Informel, German-born,
active in France,
Yellow Composition, 1947.
Oil on canvas, 73 x 92 cm.
Neue Nationalgalerie, Berlin.

928. **Arshile Gorky**, 1904-1948,
Abstract Expressionism, American,
The Engagement II, 1947.
Oil on canvas, 71.1 x 90.1 cm.
Whitney Museum of American Art,
New York.

929. **Andrew Wyeth**, 1917-2009,
Realism, American,
Christina's World, 1948.
Tempera on gessoed panel,
81.9 x 121.3 cm.
The Museum of Modern Art,
New York.

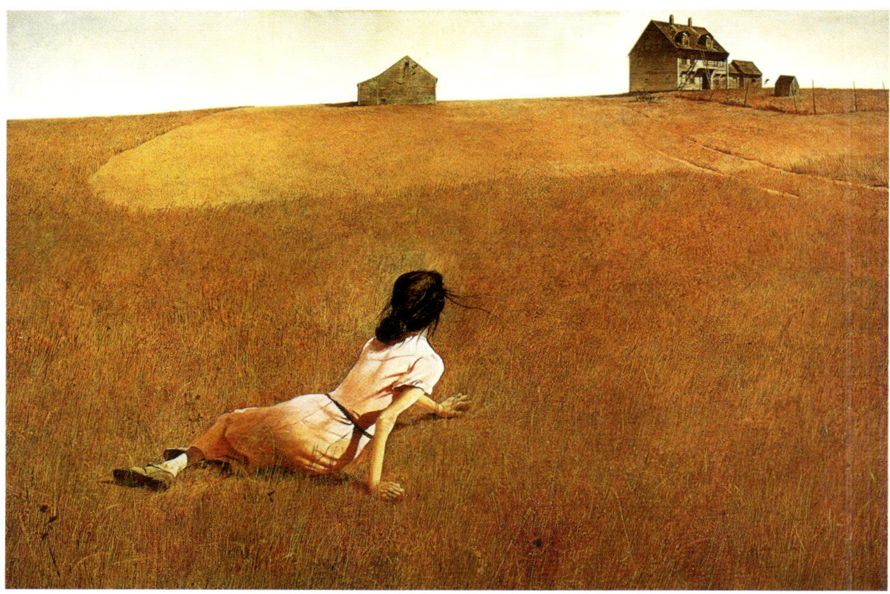

929

ANDREW WYETH
(CHADDS FORD, PENNSYLVANIA, 1917 – 2009)

Andrew Wyeth, the youngest of five children, sprang from an unusually artistic family. His father, Newell Convers Wyeth (1882-1945), a distinguished illustrator, gave him a rigorous artistic training. Two of Andrew's siblings were noted artists as well as his own son James. Early in his career, Andrew was noted for his impressionistic watercolours. His mature style was characterised by realistic interpretations, overt beauty and an almost photographic exactitude. For over fifty years his landscapes and interiors were consistently realistic and succeeded to convey a strong emotional current. His later works often contained symbolic elements, such as his most famous work, *Christina's World* (1948) which depicts his wife Betsy Merle James. Wyeth's most important subjects were his neighbours and their farms, his wife and her family. Consequently, he is referred to as the 'painter of the people'. According to Webster's *American Biographies* (1984), he is one of the best-known American painters of the 20th century.

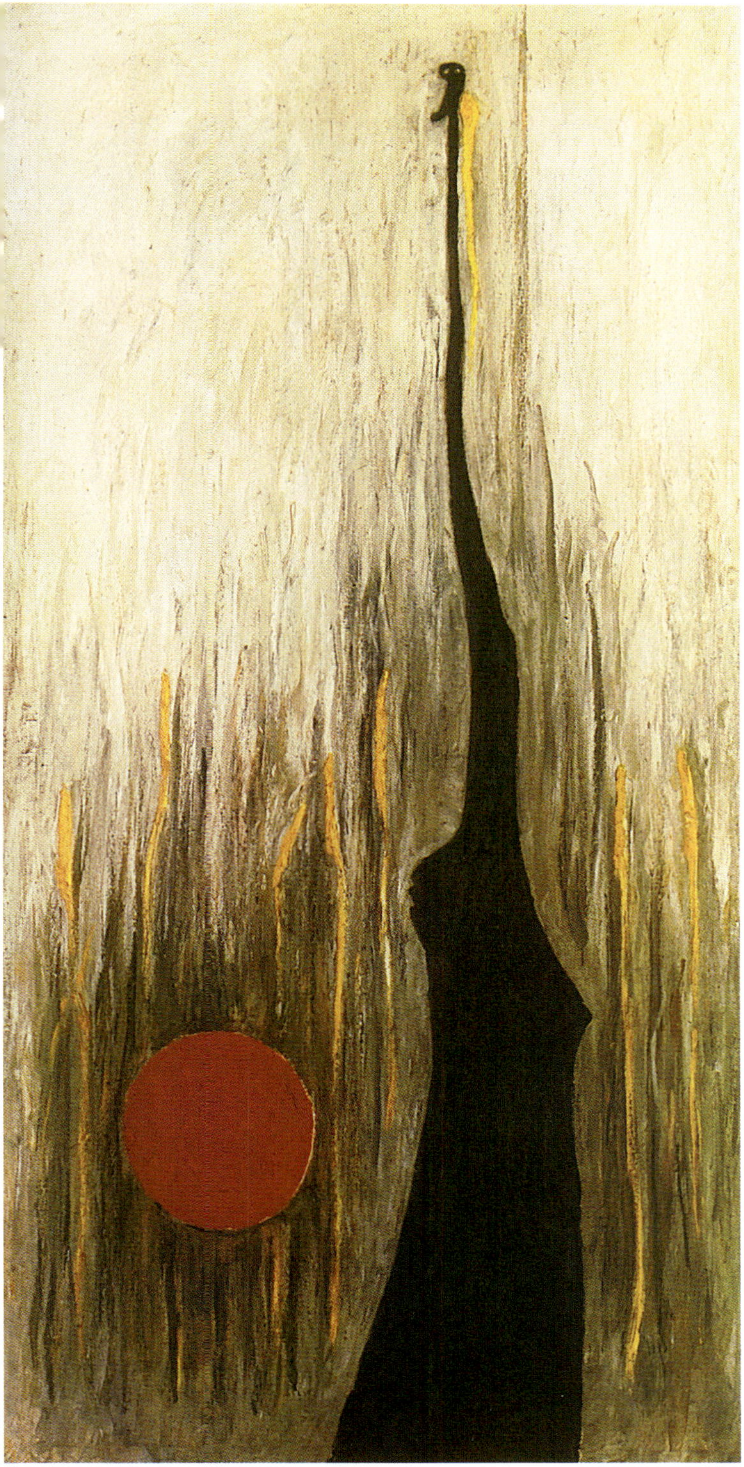

930. **Clyfford Still**, 1904-1980, Abstract Expressionism, American,
Jamais, 1944. Oil on canvas, 165.2 x 82 cm.
Guggenheim Museum, New York.

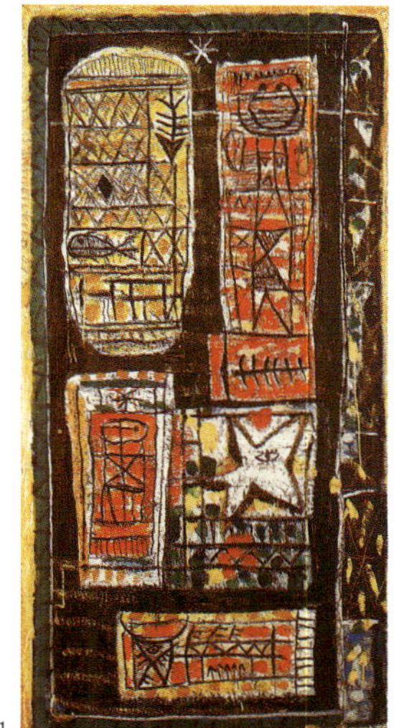

931. **Roger Bissière**, 1886-1964, Non-figuration,
French, *Great Composition*, 1947.
Oil on paper mounted on canvas, 41 x 27 cm.
Private collection.

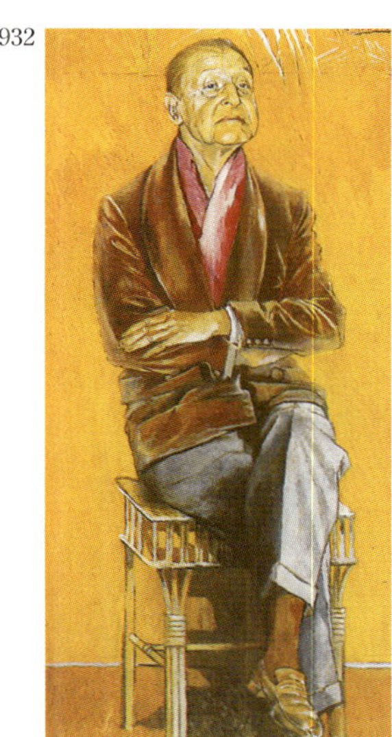

932. **Graham Sutherland**, 1903-1980,
Semi-abstraction, British,
Somerset Maugham, 1949.
Oil on canvas, 137.2 x 63.5 cm.
Tate Gallery, London.

*From 1940 to 1945 Sutherland worked as an
official war artist. Then from 1947 through the
mid-1960s he moved to the south of France
where he painted a number of new motifs.
During this period, Sutherland painted his first
portrait commission,* Somerset Maugham, *which
proved to be such a success that he received
numerous commissions.*

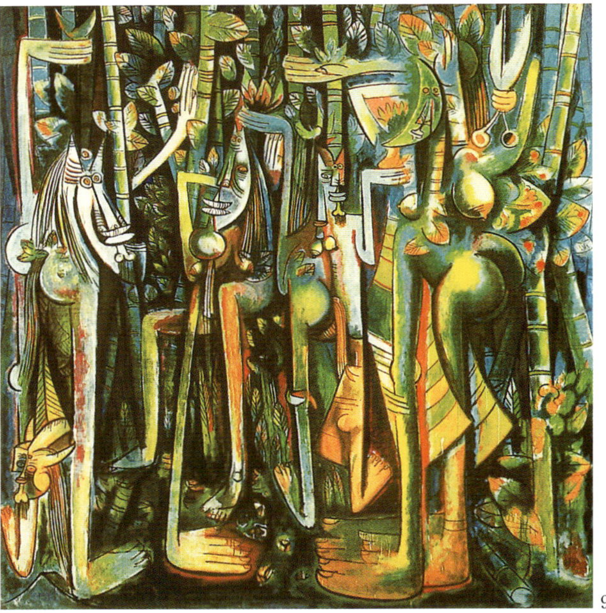

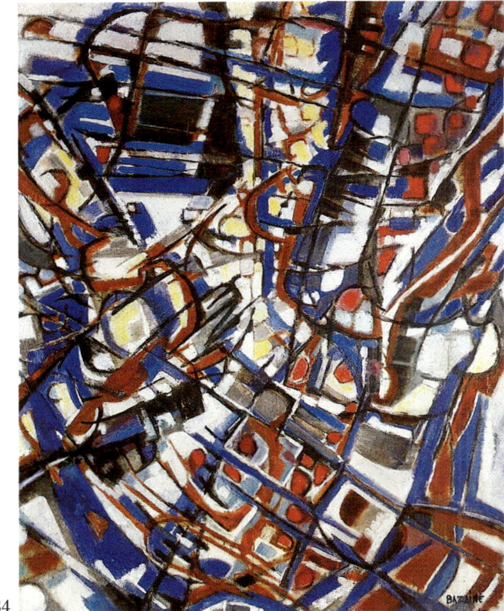

933

934

933. **Wifredo Lam**, 1902-1982, Surrealism, Cuban,
The Jungle, 1943.
Gouache on paper mounted on canvas, 239.4 x 229.9 cm.
The Museum of Modern Art, New York.

934. **Jean René Bazaine**, 1904-2001, Non-figuration, French, *The Diver*, 1949.
Oil on canvas, 114 x 115 cm.
Ludwig Museum, Cologne.

935. **Jackson Pollock**, 1912-1956, Abstract Expressionism, American,
The She-Wolf, 1943.
Oil, gouache and plaster on canvas, 106.4 x 170.2 cm.
The Museum of Modern Art, New York.

Pollock's nickname was "Jack the Dripper". She-Wolf is an earlier painting of Pollock's, brimming over with archetypal Jungian imagery. This painting shows the beginnings of his 'drip and pour' technique.

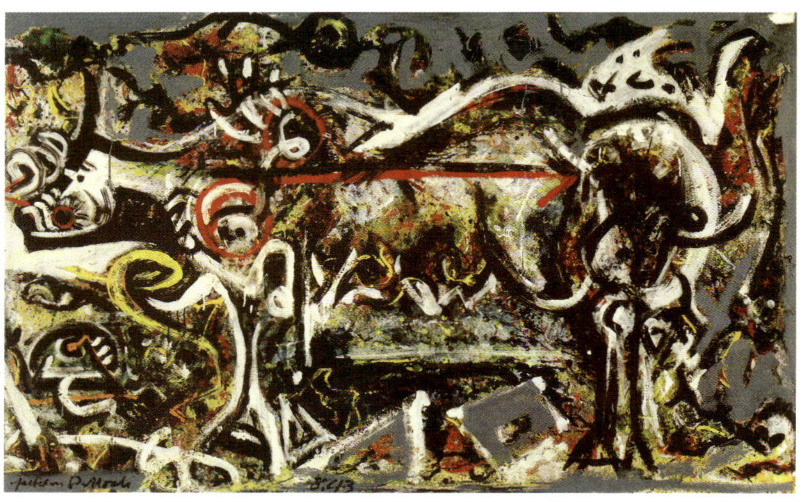

JACKSON POLLOCK
(1912 CODY, WYOMING – 1956 EAST HAMPTON, NEW YORK)

Born in 1912, in a small town in Wyoming, Jackson Pollock embodied the American dream as the country found itself confronted with the realities of a modern era replacing the fading nineteenth century. Pollock left home in search of fame and fortune in New York City. Thanks to the Federal Art Project he quickly won acclaim, and after the Second World War became the biggest art celebrity in America. For De Kooning, Pollock was the "icebreaker". For Max Ernst and Masson, Pollock was a fellow member of the European Surrealist movement. And for Motherwell, Pollock was a legitimate candidate for the status of the Master of the American School. During the many upheavals in his life in New York in the 1950s and 60s, Pollock lost his bearings – success had simply come too fast and too easily. It was during this period that he turned to alcohol and disintegrated his marriage to Lee Krasner. His life ended like that of 50s film icon James Dean behind the wheel of his Oldsmobile, after a night of drinking.

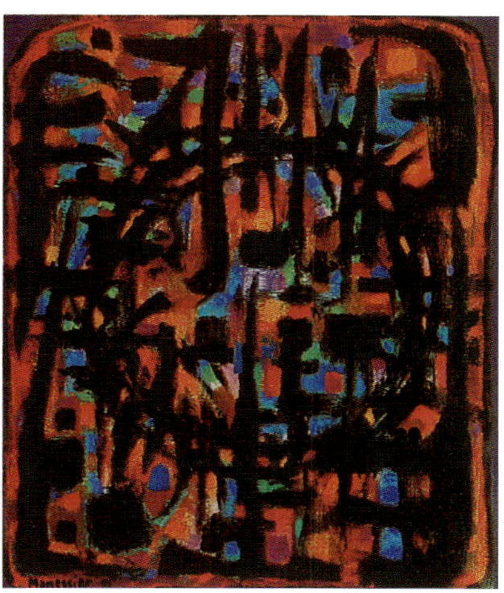 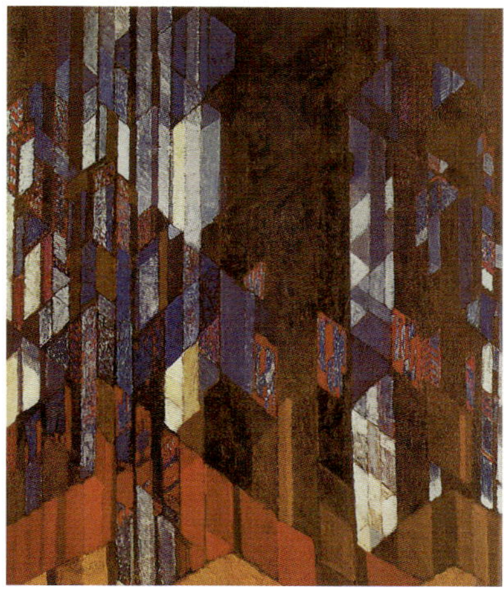 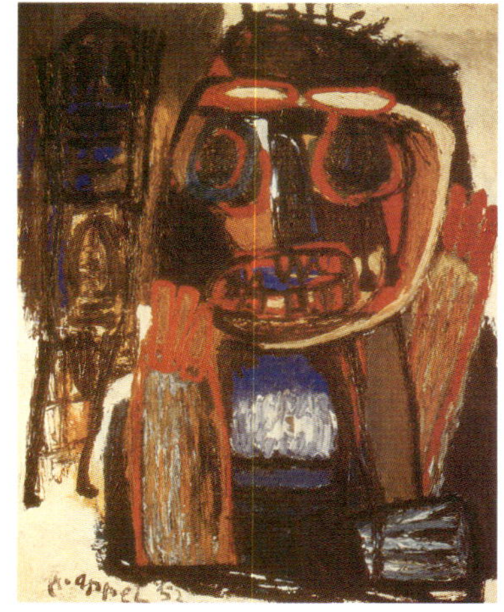

936. **Alfred Manessier**, 1911-1993,
Non-Figuration, French,
Crown of Thorns, 1951.
Oil on paper mounted on canvas,
38.8 x 49.8 cm.
Museum Folkwang, Essen.

937. **Frantisek Kupka**, 1871-1957,
Abstraction, Czech,
Cathedral, 1951.
Oil on canvas, 180 x 150 cm.
Private collection.

938. **Karel Appel**, 1921-, COBRA, Dutch,
Phantom with Mask, 1952.
Oil on canvas, 116 x 89 cm.
Private collection.

Karel Appel was the founder of COBRA. This movement is characterised by an energetic manner in the execution of the paintings, and spontaneous expression.

939. **Jackson Pollock**, 1912-1956, Abstract Expressionism, American,
Number 1, 1950 (Lavender Mist), 1950.
Oil, enamel and aluminium on canvas, 221 x 299.7 cm.
The National Gallery of Art, Washington, D.C.

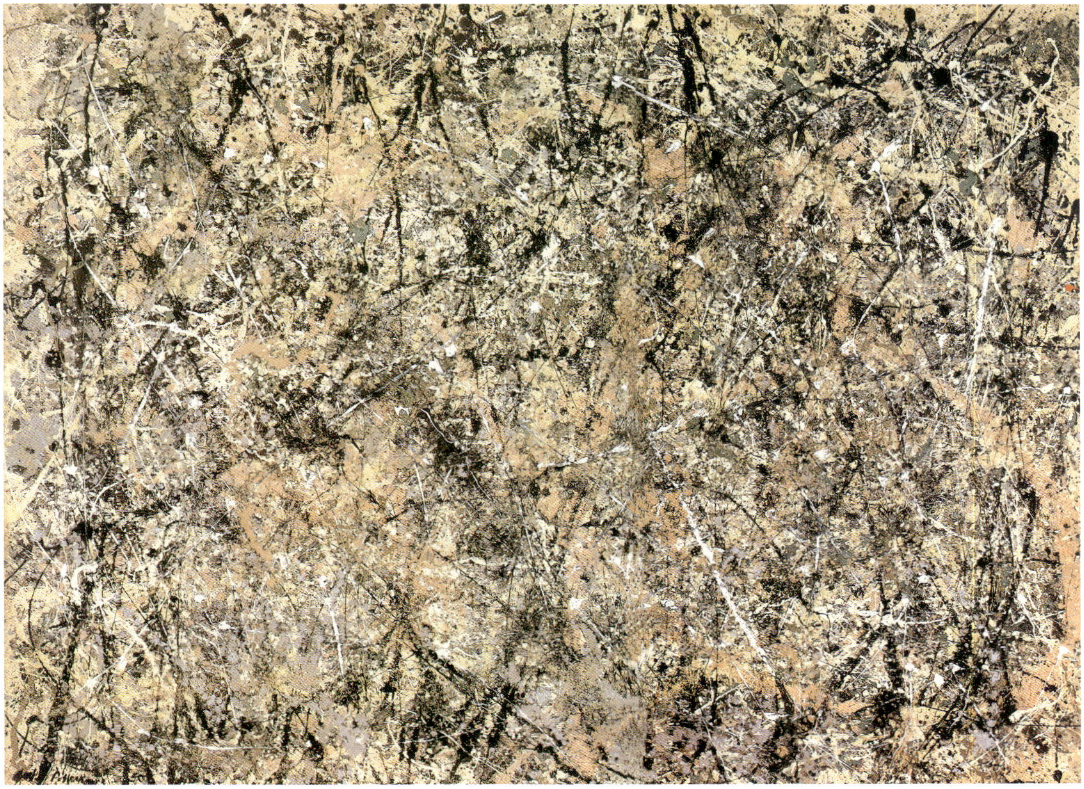

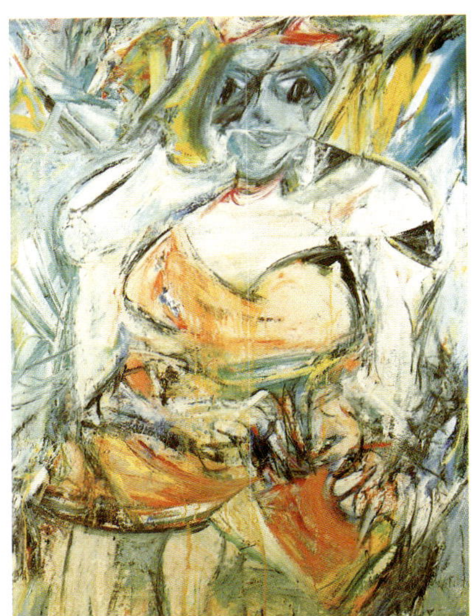

940. **Willem De Kooning**, 1904-1997,
Abstract Expressionism, American,
Dutch-born, *Woman II*, 1952. Oil on
canvas, 149.9 x 109.3 cm.
The Museum of Modern Art, New York.

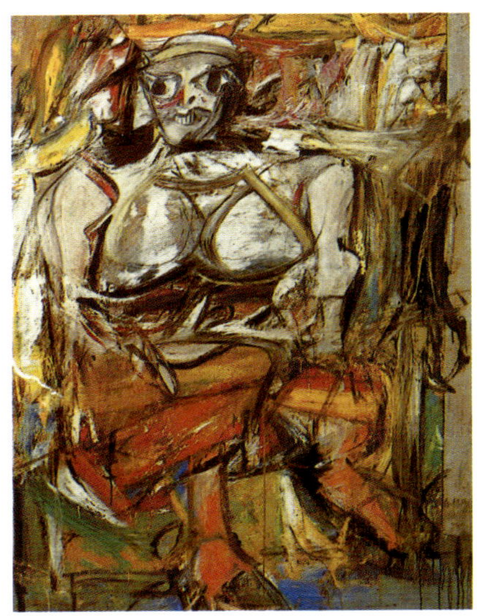

941. **Maria Helena Vieira da Silva**, 1908-1992,
Non-figuration, Portuguese, *Summer*.
Oil on canvas, 81 x 99 cm.
Musée Fabre, Montpellier.

*Central figure of the Ecole de Paris after the
Second World War, Vieira da Silva's paintings
are extremely elaborate and the use of a
complex game of colours is characteristic of
her work.*

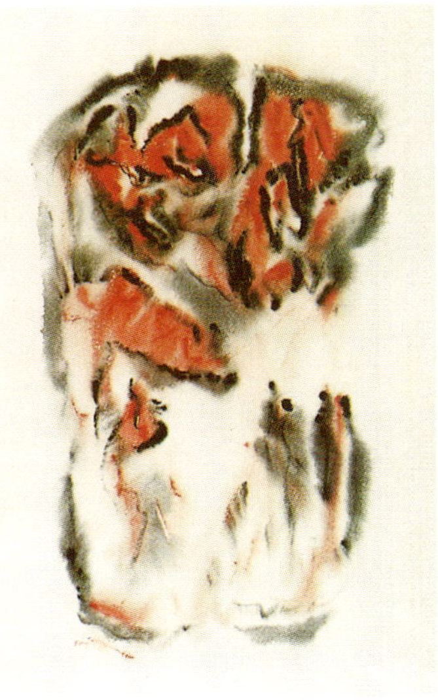

942. **Henri Michaux**, 1899-1984,
Art Informel, French,
Untitled, 1948.
Watercolour on paper,
50 x 31.5 cm.
Musée national d'art moderne,
Centre Georges-Pompidou, Paris.

WILLEM DE KOONING
(1904 ROTTERDAM – 1997 EAST HAMPTON,
LONG ISLAND)

Willem De Kooning lived in the Netherlands before going to
Belgium and then to the USA where he began to work as a
house painter. His studies at the Rotterdam Academy of Fine
Art gave him a strong knowledge of painting especially in
abstract art. His work done under the auspices of the WPA
Federal Art Project shows the great influence that Picasso and
Cubism had on him. Under the influence of Gorky, one of his
closest friends, he introduced male reproductions but his
paintings are almost all centred on the female figure. De
Kooning alternated between representative and abstract
painting. He is considered, nowadays, as one of the leaders
of abstract expressionism with Pollock, Rothko and Clyfford
Still. Action painting characterises his work.

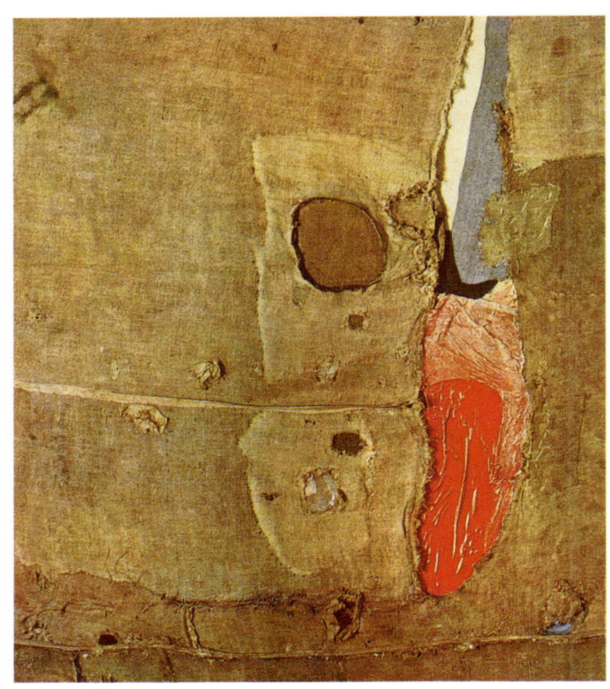

943. **Alberto Burri**, 1915-1995, Arte Povera, Italian,
Sack 5P, 1953.
Mixed media and collage, 150 x 130 cm.
Fondazione Palazzo Albizzini, Città di Castello.

*Burri was a doctor in the Italian army. He was captured and his
works reflect the horrors of war. The use of sacking characterises his
works of the 1950s. His use of red paint is reminiscent of blood.*

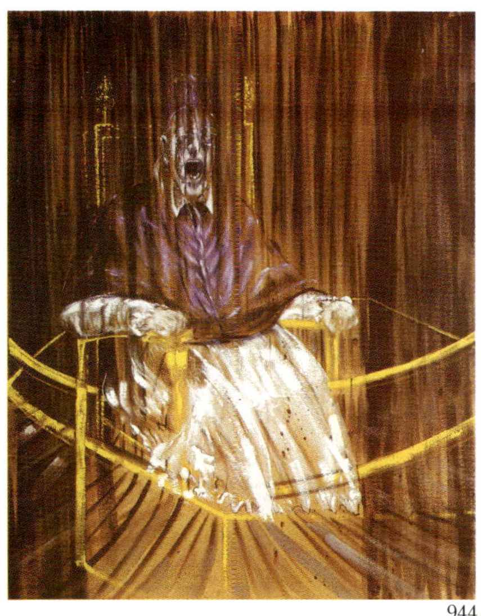

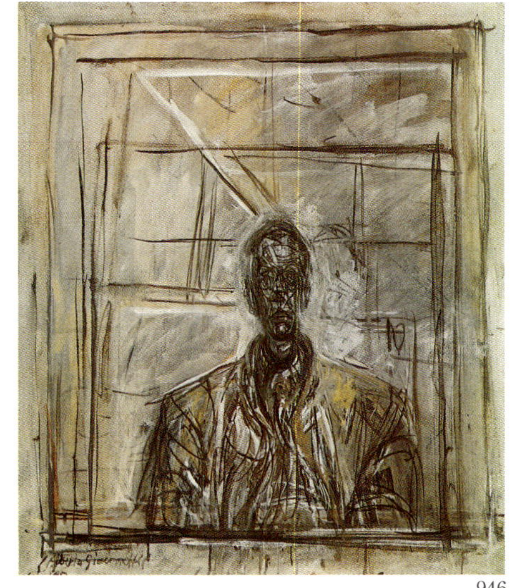

944

945

946

944. **Francis Bacon**, 1909-1992, New Figuration, British, *Study after Velázquez's Portrait of Pope Innocent X*, 1953. Oil on canvas, 153 x 118 cm. Des Moines Art Center, Des Moines.

945. **Mark Tobey**, 1890-1976, Tachism, American, *Edge of August*, 1955, Casein on panel, 121.9 x 71.1 cm. The Museum of Modern Art, New York.

946. **Alberto Giacometti**, 1901-1966, Surrealism, Swiss, *Head of a Man*, 1951. Oil on canvas, 73.3 x 60.3 cm. Private collection.

Both a painter and a sculptor, Giacometti concentrated essentially on the representation of human figures. His drawings and paintings often inspired him in the special representation of his sculptural works.

947. **Helen Frankenthaler**, 1928-, Abstract Expressionism, American, *Mountains and Sea*, 1952. Oil on canvas. The National Gallery of Art, Washington, D.C.

Frankenthaler is one of the important figures of post-war American painting. She was married to Robert Motherwell.

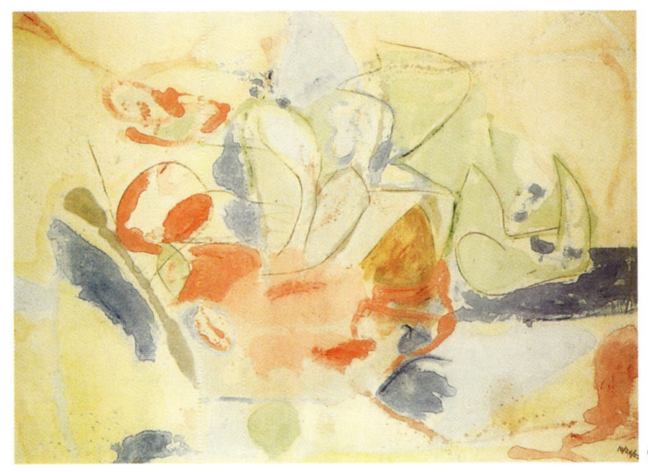

947

FRANCIS BACON
(1909 DUBLIN – 1992 MADRID)

The British painter of Irish birth, Francis Bacon, is probably one of England's most controversial and disturbing artists. Marked by Picasso and later by the Surrealists, his work was expressionist in style. Bacon nevertheless remained an independent artist. Obsessed by pictures of diseases of the mouth, Bacon set out to capture expression without total abstraction and specifically tried to represent corrupt and disgusting humanity, intolerable pain or panic, seen in the faces of the damned in the painting of Michelangelo's *The Last Judgment* (1536-1541) and particularly in Edvard Munch's *The Scream* (1893). In works such as *Three Studies for Figures at the Base of a Crucifixion* which portrayed carcass like figures on crosses, he expressed the satirical, horrifying and hallucinatory. Bacon deliberately subverted artistic conventions in painting a series of variations on figural themes such as the famous portrait by Velázquez *Pope Innocent* X into a shockingly grotesque screaming mask.

948. Mark Rothko, 1903-1970, Abstract
Expressionism, Russian-born, American,
Number 10, 1950. Oil on canvas, 229.6 x 145.1 cm.
The Museum of Modern Art, New York.

*Colour field painting in America in the late 1940s
was partly an identity-seeking reaction to the
action painting of Pollock in particular and
Abstract Expressionism in general. Large works
showing soft edged areas of colour washes
dominated his output. In this typical Rothko work,
shades of uplifting blue separated by a central and
dominating earthy and pedestrian brown might
reflect what ultimately proved to be the artist's
melancholy and pessimism about life itself. He
committed suicide.*

949. Willi Baumeister, 1889-1955, Abstraction, German, *Martaruru with
Red Overhead*, 1955.
Oil on board, 100 x 81 cm. Private collection.

*Baumeister belonged to those painters that the Nazis declared
"degenerate" and he had to leave his position as a professor of the Städel
School in Frankfurt.*

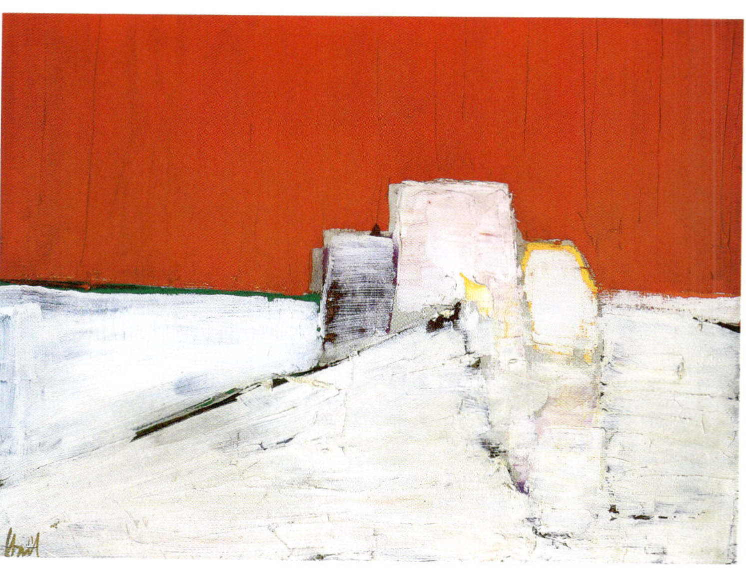

950. Nicolas de Staël, 1914-1955, Abstraction,
Russian-French, *The Beach at Agrigento*, 1954.
Oil on canvas, 81 x 99.8 cm.
Private collection.

*In the 1950s Nicolas de Staël travelled frequently
in southern France and depicted more and more
elementary landscapes in vivid colours.*

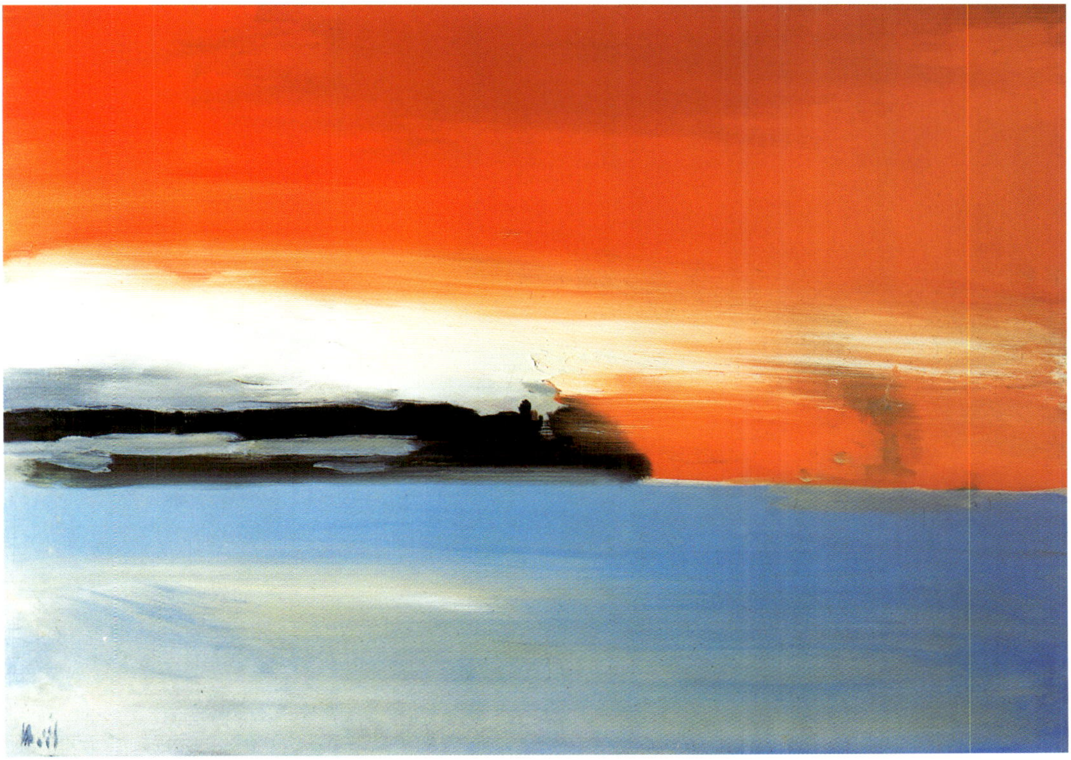

951. **Nicolas de Staël**, 1914-1955, Abstraction, Russian-French,
Seaside Railway Line in the Setting Sun, 1955.
Oil on canvas, 70 x 100 cm.
Private collection.

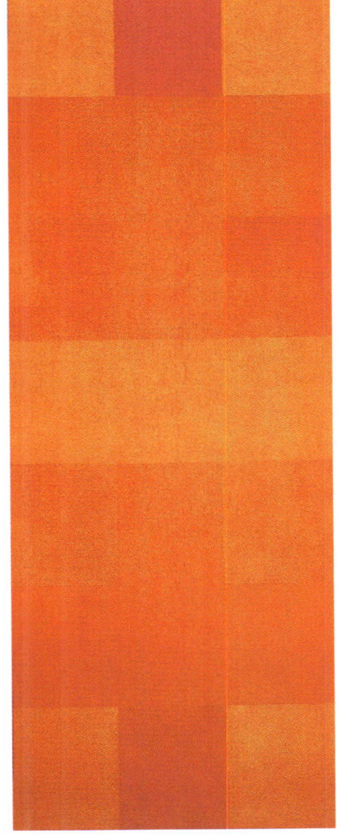

952. **Ad Reinhardt**, 1913-1967, Abstract Expressionism, American,
Abstract Painting, Red, 1952.
Oil on canvas, 274.4 x 102 cm.
The Museum of Modern Art, New York.

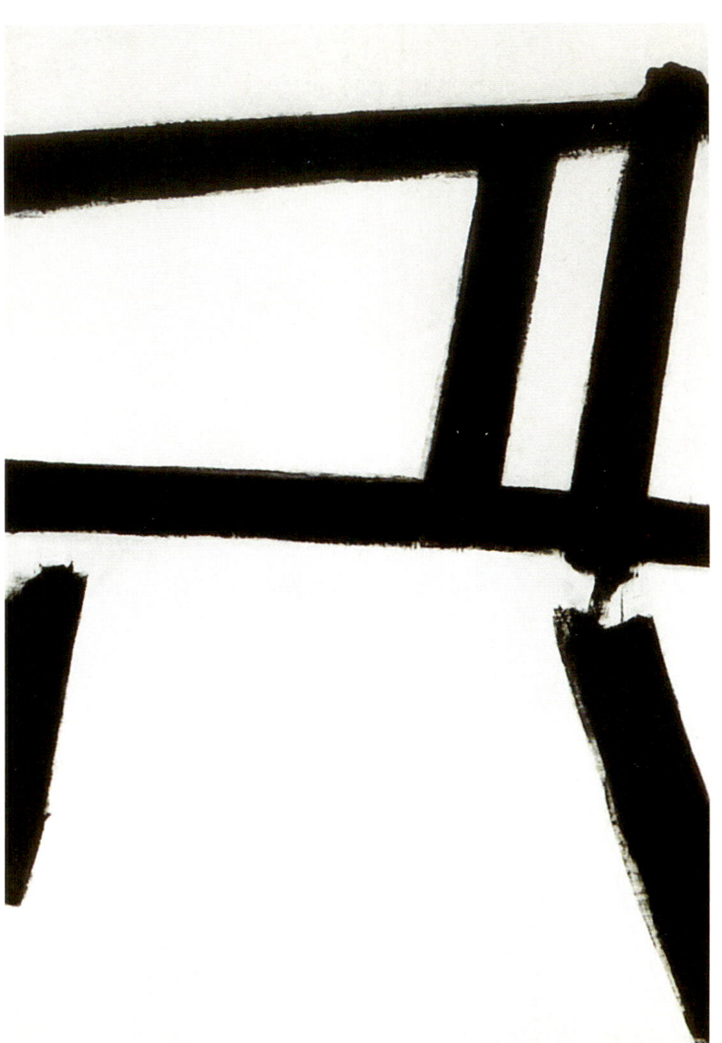

953. **Franz Kline**, 1910-1962, Abstract Expressionism, American, *White Forms*, 1955.
Oil on canvas, 188.9 x 127.6 cm.
The Museum of Modern Art, New York.

954. **Alberto Magnelli**, 1888-1971, Abstraction, Italian, *Dialogue*, 1956.
Oil on canvas, 130 x 162 cm.
Galleria Nazionale d'Arte Moderna, Rome.

955. **Robert Rauschenberg**, 1925-, Abstract Expressionism, American,
Monogram, 1955-1959. Angora goat, tyre, paint, collage and metal on canvas, 129 x 186 x 185 cm.
Moderna Museet, Stockholm.
Art © Robert Rauschenberg / Licensed by VAGA, New York, NY.

This is one of Rauschenberg's first and most famous "combines" and it consists of an unlikely set of materials: a stuffed angora goat, a tyre, a police barrier, the heel of a shoe, a tennis ball, and paint. The idea of combining and of noticing combinations of objects and images has remained at the core of Rauschenberg's work.

Rauschenberg is one of the founders of EAT (Experiments in Art and Technology) because he believed he saw in the combination of art and the development of new technologies a new way of expression.

954

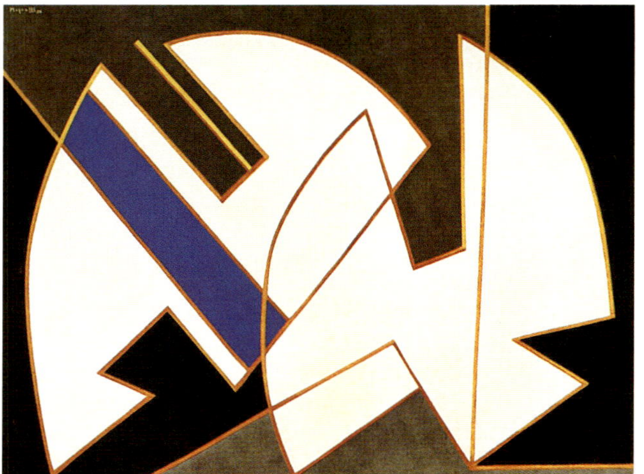

955

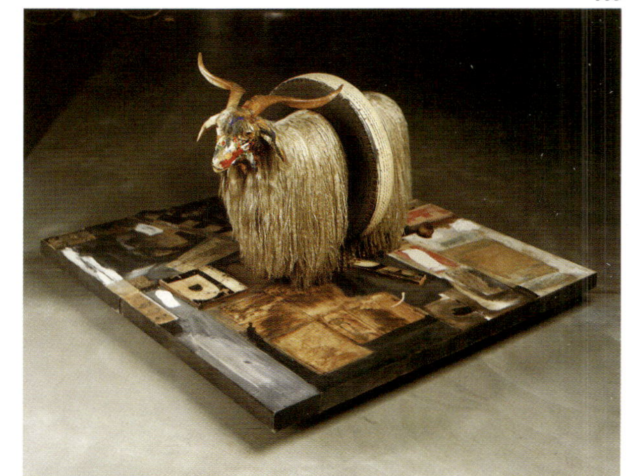

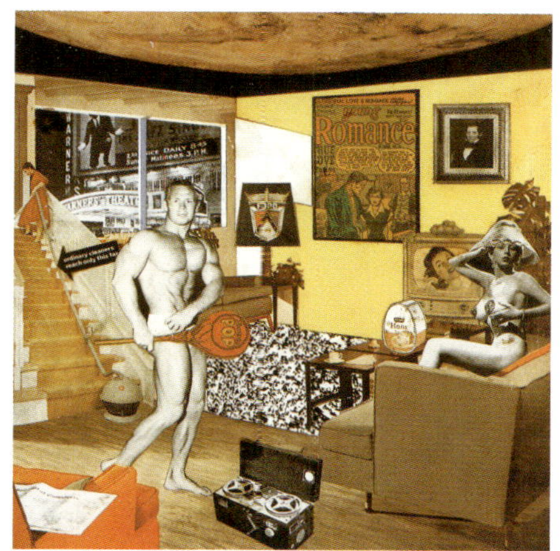

956

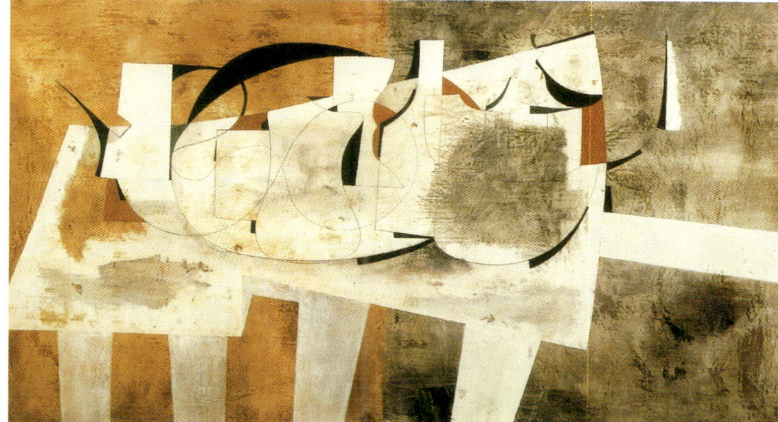

957

958

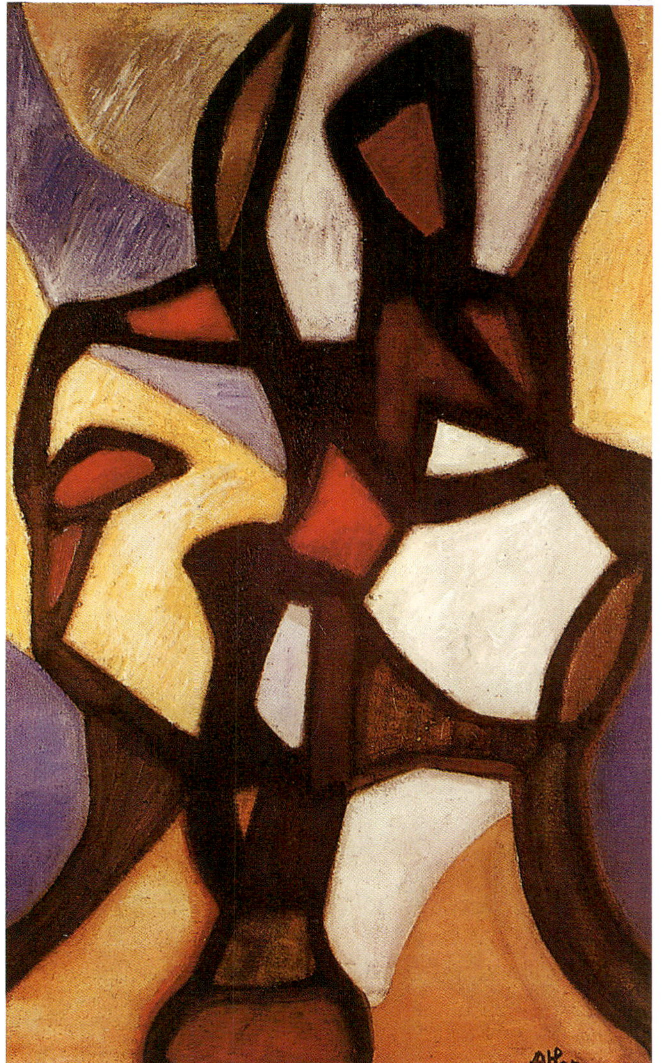

956. **Richard Hamilton**, 1922-, Pop Art, British,
Just what is it that makes today's homes so different, so appealing?, 1956.
Collage on paper, 26 x 25 cm.
Kunsthalle, Tübingen.

This small collage was a design for the monochrome poster advertising the very first Pop/Mass-Culture Art exhibition ever to be held, namely the 'This is Tomorrow' show mounted at the Whitechapel Art Gallery in London in 1956 by the Independent Group, of which Hamilton was a member. The design demonstrates exactly why its creator is deemed so important to the tradition of Pop/Mass-Culture Art, for it is almost a lexicon of all the themes that would soon be touched upon by both Hamilton and others. Thus the Young Romance comic strip image hanging on the wall points towards things to come from Roy Lichtenstein; the nude on the right coupled with the adjacent tin of ham, bowl of fruit and television set suggests future images by Tom Wesselmann; the word-bearing pointer on the stairs would be paralleled in works by Andy Warhol, just as that selfsame artist would devote a major part of his art to "superstars," as seen here in the form of Al Jolson in The Jazz Singer *of 1929; the word "POP" carried on a paddle by the semi-nude male points the way to the future employment of words by Ed Ruscha, Robert Indiana, Allan D'Arcangelo and by Hamilton himself; and the corporate logo appearing on the lampshade anticipates the work of Ashley Bickerton by several decades.*

957. **Ben Nicholson,** 1894-1982, Abstraction, English,
August 1956 (Valley of Orcia), 1956.
Oil and crayon on cardboard, 122 x 214 cm.
Tate Gallery, London.

958. **Jean-Michel Atlan**, 1913-1960, Abstraction, French,
La Kahena, 1958.
Oil on canvas, 146 x 89 cm.
Musée national d'art moderne,
Centre Georges-Pompidou, Paris.

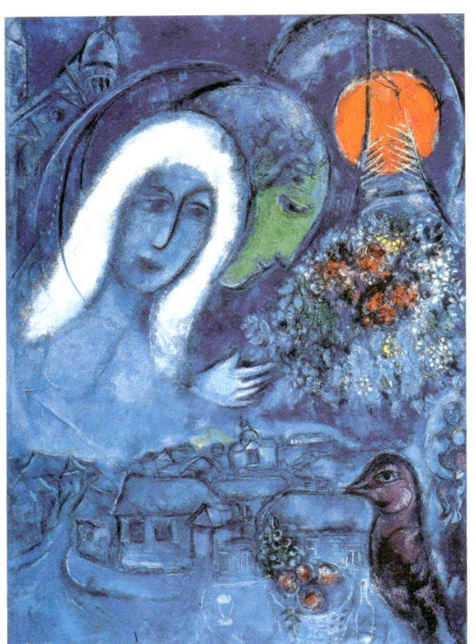

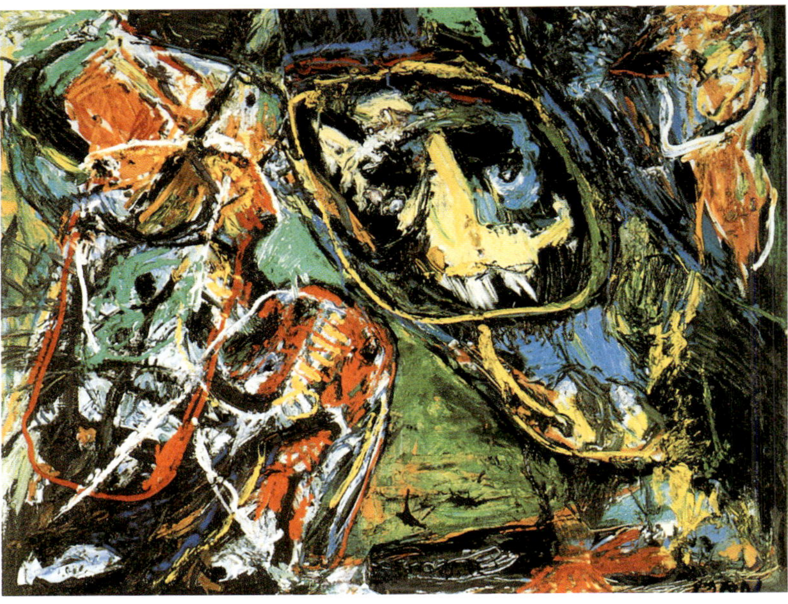

959. **Marc Chagall**, 1887-1985, Surrealism,
Russian, *Champ de Mars*, 1954-1955.
Oil on canvas, 149.5 x 105 cm.
Folkwang Museum, Essen.

960. **Asger Jorn**, 1914-1973, COBRA, Danish, *Loss of the Mean,* 1958.
Oil on canvas, 141 x 146 cm.
Stedelijk Museum voor Actuele Kunst, Gent.

961. **Hundertwasser (Friedenrich Stowasser)**, 1928-2000, Austrian,
Grass for Those who Cry.
Mixed technique, 65 x 92 cm. Private collection.

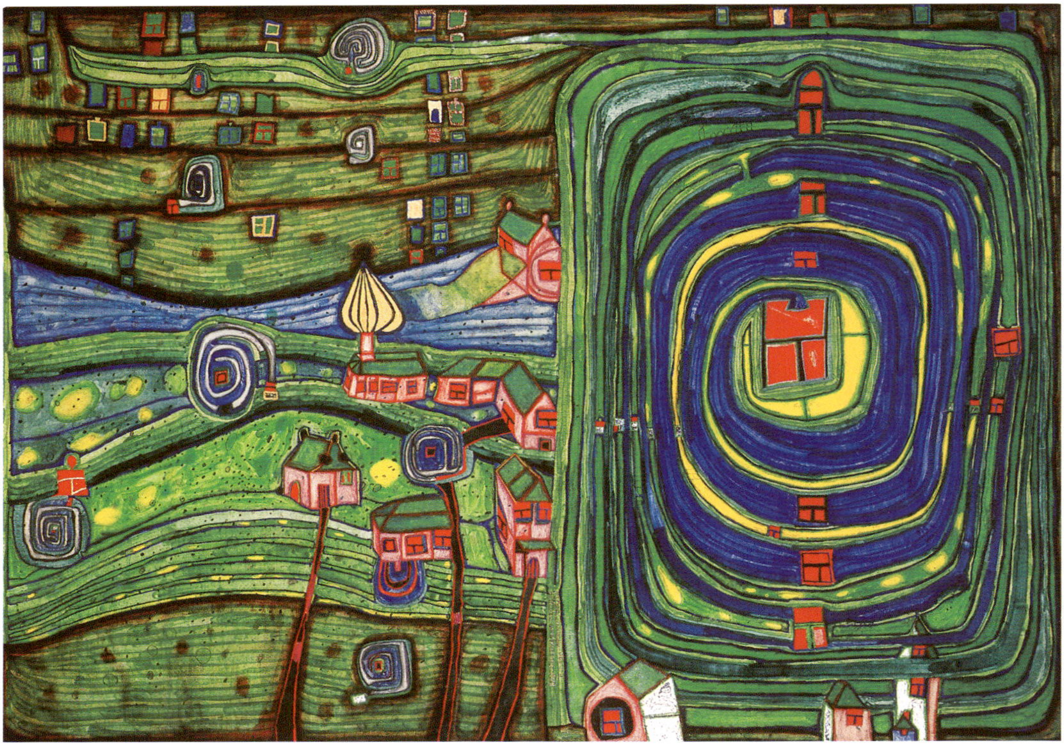

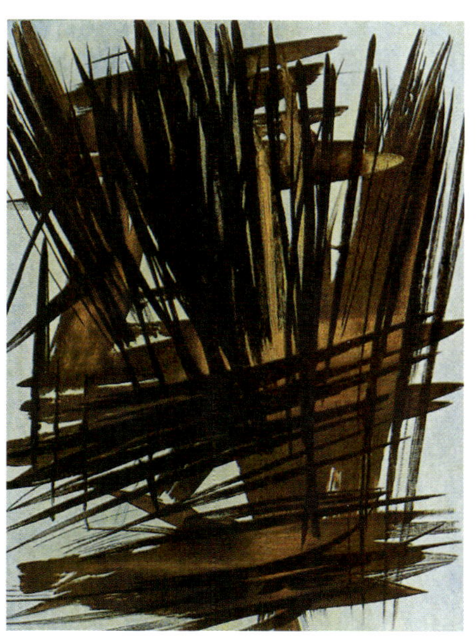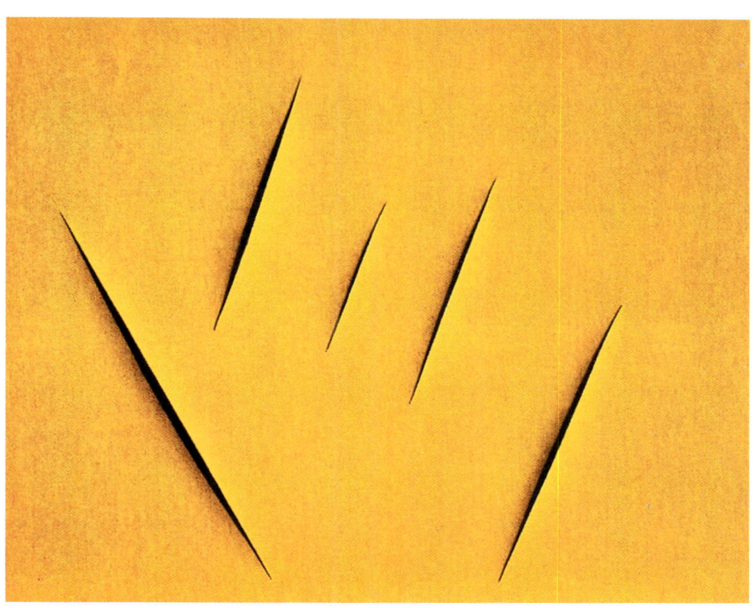

962. **Hans Hartung**, 1904-1989, Abstraction, German,
T., 1956. Oil on canvas, 180 x 137 cm.
Collection Anne-Eva Bergman, Antibes.

963. **Lucio Fontana**, 1899-1968, Abstraction, Italian,
Concetto Spaziale – Attese (T 104), 1959.
Oil (vinylique) on canvas, incisions, 125 x 100.5 cm.
Galleria d'Arte del Naviglio, Milan.

964. **Pierre Soulages**, 1919-, Abstraction, French,
Painting, 1956.
Oil on canvas, 195 x 130 cm.
Musée national d'art moderne, Centre Georges-Pompidou, Paris.

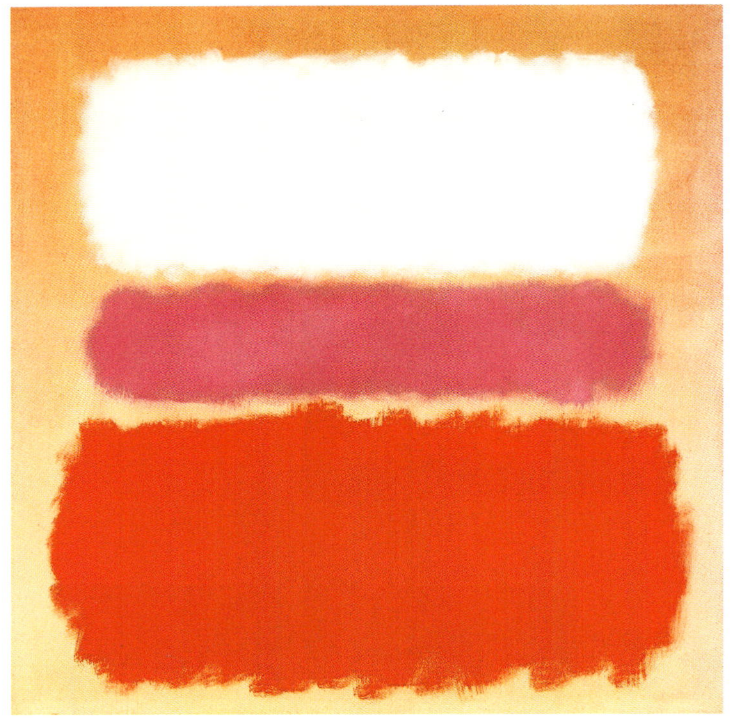
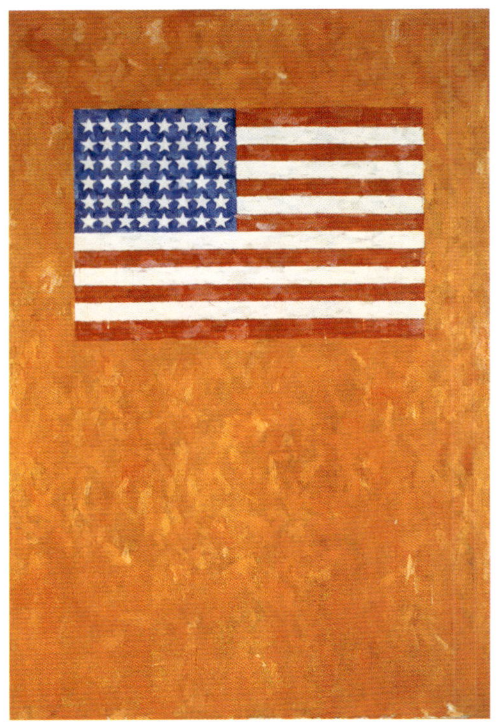

965

966

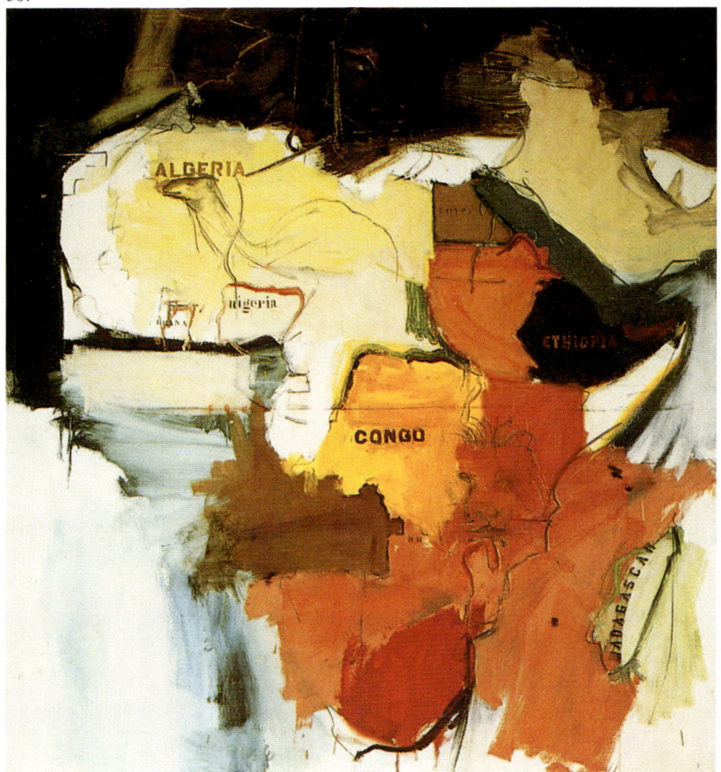

967

965. **Mark Rothko**, 1903-1970, Abstract
Expressionism, Russian-born, American,
Untitled, 1957. Oil on canvas, 143 x 138 cm.
Private collection.

966. **Jasper Johns**, 1930-, Pop Art, American,
Flag on Orange Field, 1957.
Oil on canvas, 167.6 x 124.5 cm.
Ludwig Museum, Cologne.
Art © Jasper Johns / Licensed by VAGA,
New York, NY.

967. **Larry Rivers**, 1923-2002, Pop Art, American,
Africa I, 1961-1962.
Oil on canvas, 185.4 x 165.1 cm.
Private collection.
Art © Estate of Larry Rivers / Licensed by VAGA,
New York, NY.

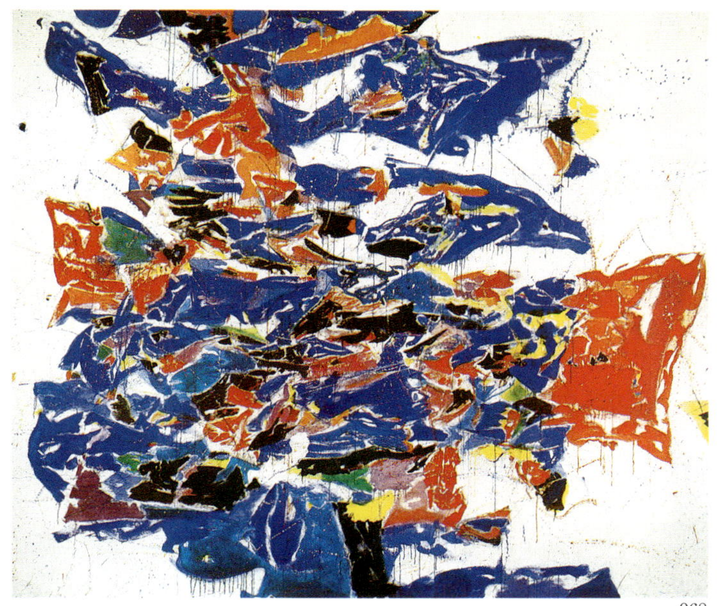

968

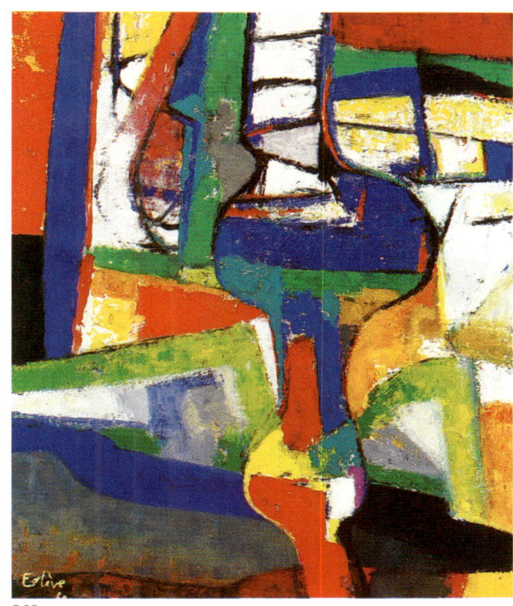

969

970

968. **Sam Francis**, 1923-1994, Abstract
Expressionism, American,
Around the World, 1958.
Oil on canvas, 274.3 x 321.3 cm.
Private collection.

969. **Maurice Estève**, 1904-2001,
Non-Figuration, French,
Fressiline, 1960.
Oil on canvas, 46 x 38 cm.
Henie-Onstad Art Center, Hovikodden.

970. **Yves Klein**, 1923-1962, New Realism,
French, *Untitled, Blue Monochrome
(IKB 82)*, 1959. Dry pigment in synthetic
resin on canvas, mounted on board,
92.1 x 71.8 cm.
Guggenheim Museum, New York.

*Klein began to exhibit his monochromes
in the mid-1950s. Klein patented "The
International Klein Bleu" in 1960, a deep
blue colour that is kept intact when being
mixed with a synthetic resin.*

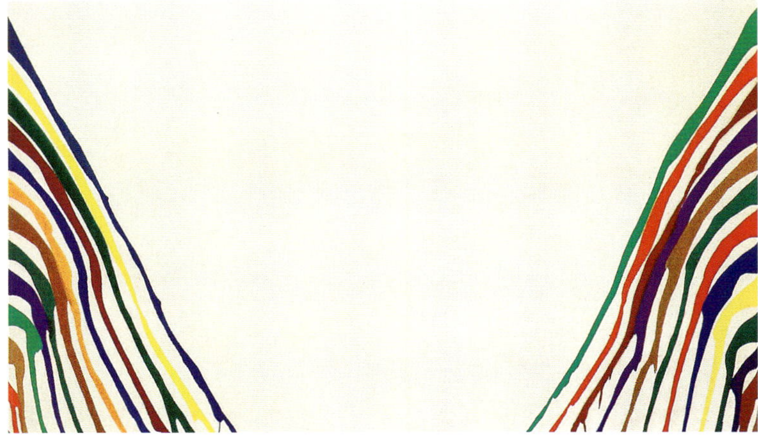

971. **Morris Louis**, 1912-1962, Abstract Expressionism, American,
K S I, 1959. Acrylic on canvas, 264 x 438 cm.
Museum Folkwang, Essen.

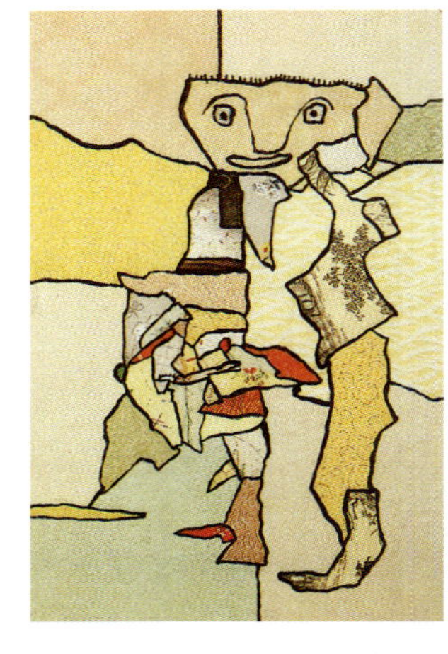

972. **Gaston Chaissac**, 1910-1964, Art Brut (Raw Art), French,
Untitled: Character, 1961-1962. Wall-paper collage, ink and
gouache on paper mounted on canvas, 95 x 65.5 cm.
Musée national d'art moderne, Centre Georges-Pompidou, Paris.

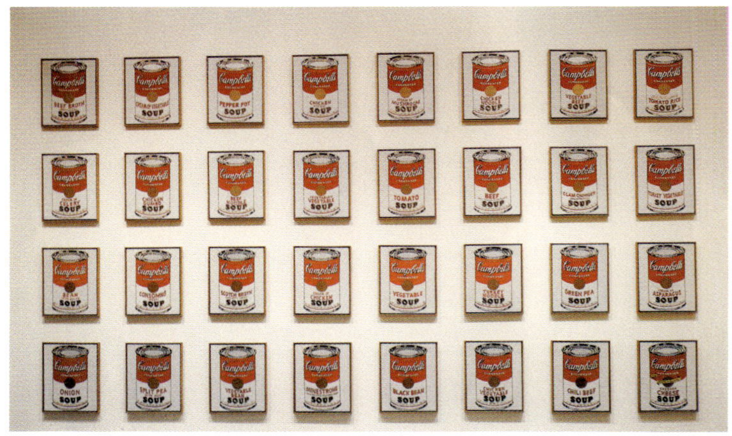

973

973. **Andy Warhol**, 1928-1987, Pop Art, American,
32 Soup Cans, 1961-1962.
Oil on canvas, each 50.8 x 40.6 cm.
The Museum of Modern Art, New York.

This is the seminal work in Warhol's oeuvre. It was developed from an idea sold to the painter for fifty dollars by Muriel Latow in December 1961, although the visual realisation of the concept was entirely Warhol's own. The group of canvases formed the artist's first one-man exhibition, held at Irving Blum's Ferus Gallery in Los Angeles in July 1962, where the works were displayed in a single line around the gallery walls, rather than in four rows of eight canvases, as here. The original display maximised the repetition of the imagery by being so spatially extended, given that it filled the gallery. Then, too, any art exhibition necessarily creates a finite world of its own. The show must, therefore, have ultimately projected the fearsome notion that the entire visible universe was filled with Campbell's soup.

This work was equally the first of Warhol's largescale iconic projections. The painter developed the notion of taking an image familiar to millions and presenting it frontally, without painterly qualities, and with a flat surround (as though it were some kind of holy icon) from the Flags paintings of Jasper Johns which were well known to him. In the Flags, Johns treated the holiest of American icons, the national flag, known as the Stars and Stripes, as the starting point for a series of implied painterly and cultural questionings. However, Warhol went much further than Johns in the degree of objectivity with which he projected his icons, for by now an alliance between quasi-abstract expressionist paint-handling and popular cultural imagery in the manner of Johns no longer interested him. Instead, he isolated each of the thirty-two varieties of Campbell's soup so as to emphasise the sterile appearances of mechanically produced objects, and the different varieties of soup as stated on the labels force us to look hard at the images in order to perceive those slight variations, thus making us aware of how we look (or should look) at a work of art. In their subject matter these images both fly in the face of traditional notions of 'art' and, simultaneously, enforce the recognition that no objects are inaccessible to artistic treatment simply because they are familiar or banal.

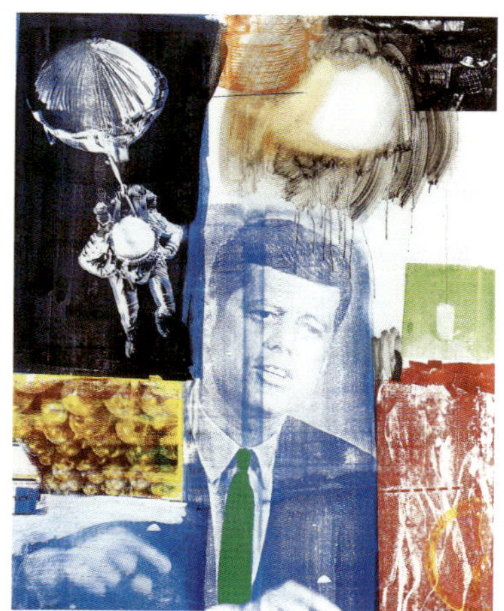

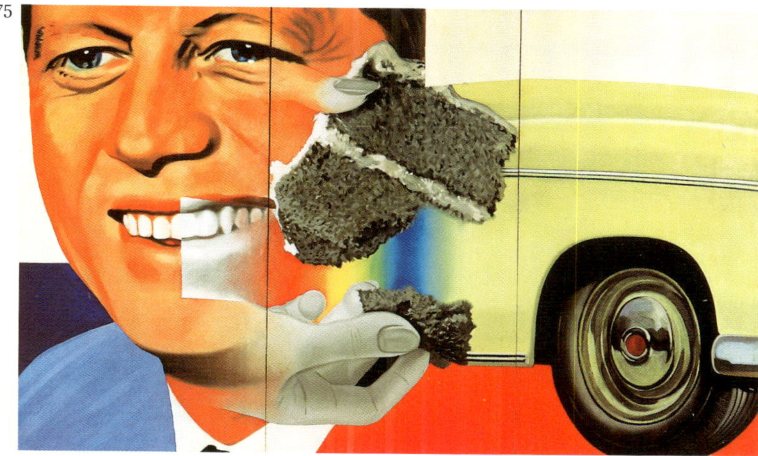

974. **Robert Rauschenberg**, 1925-2008, Abstract Expressionism,
American, *Retroactive I*, 1964.
Oil and silkscreen on canvas, 213 x 152.4 cm.
Wadsworth Atheneum, Hartford.
Art © Robert Rauschenberg / Licensed by VAGA, New York, NY.

Among its various meanings the word "retroactive" denotes the extension of things to the past. By the time this work was created John F. Kennedy was dead, and so a portrait that brings him back to life is necessarily 'retroactive'. By repeating the dead president's hand-gesture, Rauschenberg stressed the man's decisiveness. Clearly the astronaut alludes to the fact that Kennedy had been largely responsible for expediting the American space programme, as the artist was well aware. The nude woman seen walking in multiple positions at the lower-right might equally serve to remind us that the human drive towards the exploration of space has its roots in very primal aspirations indeed: biologically, our species first crawled out of the swamp, then we stood upright and learned to walk, and as a result sooner or later we might conquer the stars.

This is another of the crowded pictures Rauschenberg created not long after discovering the visual immediacy afforded by photo-silkscreen. The apparently arbitrary organisation of the blocks of imagery strongly parallels the randomness of life itself, and certainly the density of imagery parallels the overload we receive daily through the media. Rauschenberg exploits to the full the graininess that results from using silkscreen on a fairly open-weave canvas, as well as the drips that flow from extremely thinned paint. These differing ways of mark-making add to the vivid sense of spontaneity throughout.

976. **Andy Warhol**, 1928-1987, Pop Art, American,
Triple Elvis, 1962.
Aluminium paint and silkscreen ink on canvas,
208.3 x 180.3 cm.
Virginia Museum of Fine Arts, Richmond.

975. **James Rosenquist**, 1933-, Pop Art, American,
President Elect, 1960-1961.
Oil on masonite, 228 x 366 cm.
Musée national d'art moderne, Centre Georges-Pompidou, Paris.
Art © James Rosenquist / Licensed by VAGA, New York, NY.

John F. Kennedy was elected President of the United States on 8 November 1960, and this painting was begun very soon afterwards. It was one of two pictures created in 1960-1961 that proved to be Rosenquist's breakthrough works in artistic terms. The other painting is entitled 47, 48, 50, 61 and it shows three men's ties above the dates 1947, 1948 and 1950, thereby implicitly commenting upon fashion and history. The present painting seems no less meaningful, given the happy visage of one of America's most famous, youthful and handsome presidents, from whose head emerges two perfect female hands holding some pieces of appetising cake placed in front of a shining car. With merely a hint of irony – for everything is just a little too faultless – Rosenquist alludes to the perfect consumer society as projected by its ever-optimistic politicians.

The work was developed from a three-part collage Rosenquist had made using an old magazine photo of Kennedy and ads for cake and a 1949 Chevrolet. The study reveals more of the vehicle than seen here, and includes two figures standing behind the car, looking at it admiringly.

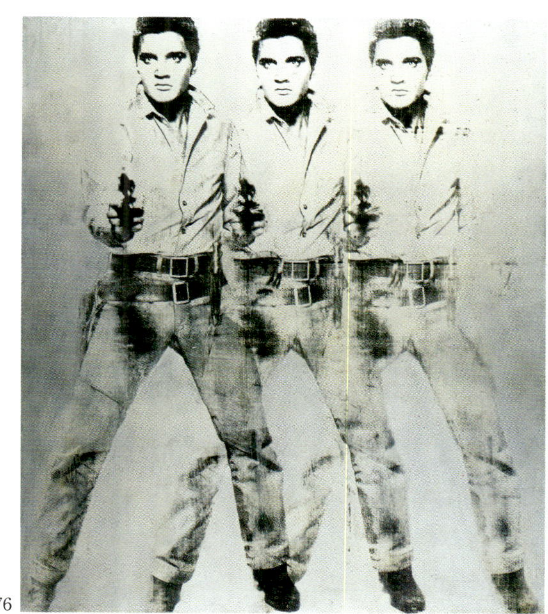

976

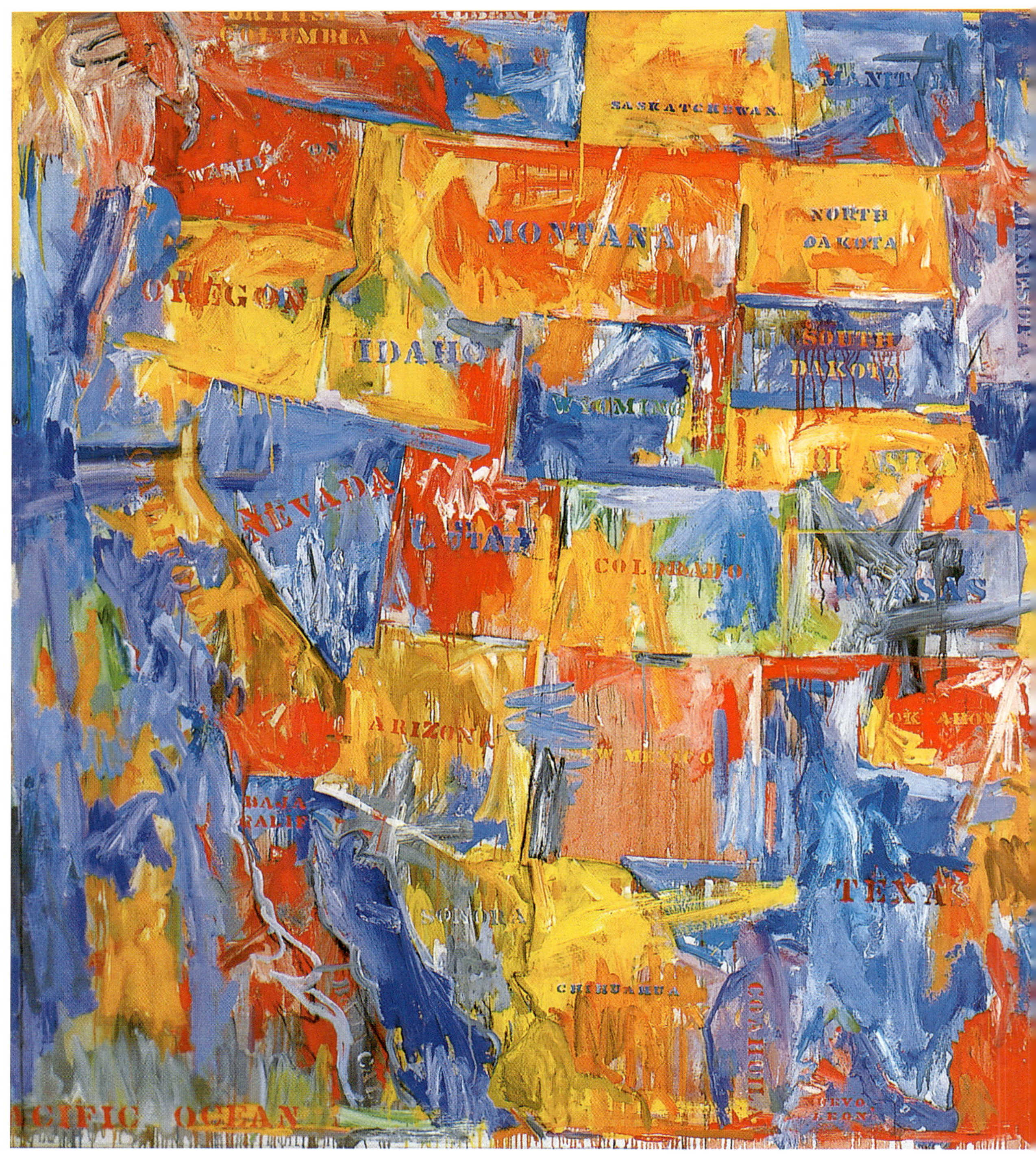
BRITISH COLUMBIA
ALBERTA
SASKATCHEWAN
MANITOBA
WASHINGTON
MONTANA
NORTH DAKOTA
MINNESOTA
OREGON
IDAHO
SOUTH DAKOTA
WYOMING
NEBRASKA
NEVADA
UTAH
COLORADO
KANSAS
ARIZONA
NEW MEXICO
OKLAHOMA
BAJA CALIFORNIA
SONORA
TEXAS
CHIHUAHUA
COAHUILA
NUEVO LEON
PACIFIC OCEAN

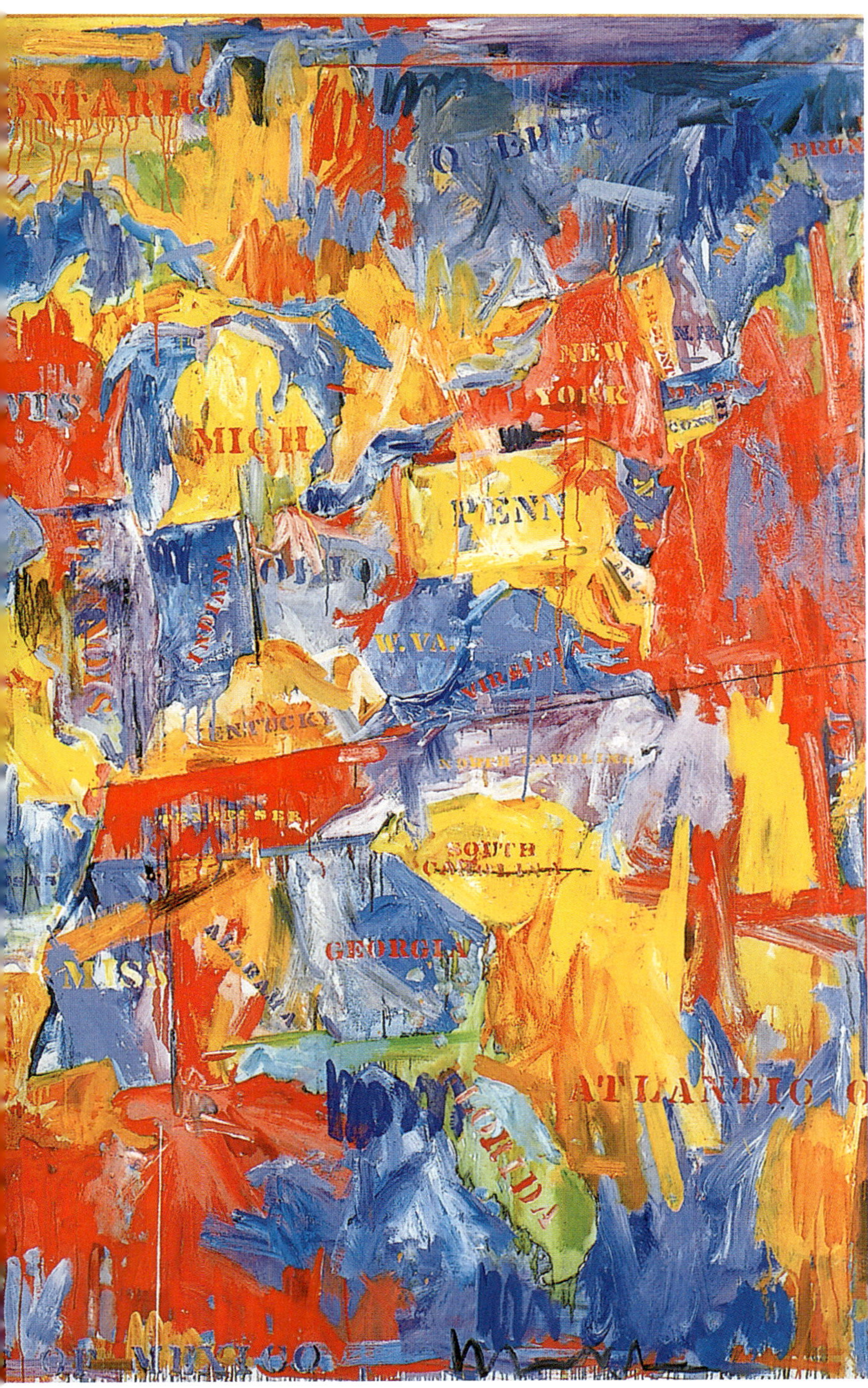

977. **Jasper Johns**, 1930-, Pop Art, American, *Map*, 1961.
Oil on canvas, 198.2 x 307.7 cm.
The Museum of Modern Art, New York.
Art © Jasper Johns / Licensed by VAGA, New York, NY.

In his Flags, Targets and Numbers series of paintings, Johns employed encaustic paint in order to build up the surfaces patiently, and thus prevent any excess emotionalism entering the images. For the Maps paintings, however, he moved in the opposite direction and used oil paint for its dynamism, a gesturality normally associated with Abstract Expressionism. This enacted a clever paradox, for the flurried surfaces go against the grain of most true maps, which are almost always pictorially flattened, diagrammatic affairs, totally devoid of any expression whatsoever.

Naturally, the emphatic marks used by Johns often blur or totally obliterate the boundaries of individual states, thereby possibly commenting upon the increasing political irrelevance of such divisions within an America that had grown enormously in political coherence and wealth since the Second World War. At a time of growing transcontinental air and road travel, national television coverage, the countrywide distribution of mass-produced goods, and nationwide advertising campaigns for those products, such a breakdown or disregard of local boundaries seems highly relevant.

Johns' use of stencilled lettering invokes exactly the same associations of mass-production it had when employed after 1911 by Picasso and Braque, for it is very "low culture" indeed, being primarily found on the sides of packing crates and the like where identifications need to be effected quickly and without any refinement. As employed by Johns, the use of such a uniform type of lettering says much about the blurring of local individuality, the increasing homogeneity of national identity, and the growth of consumerism everywhere.

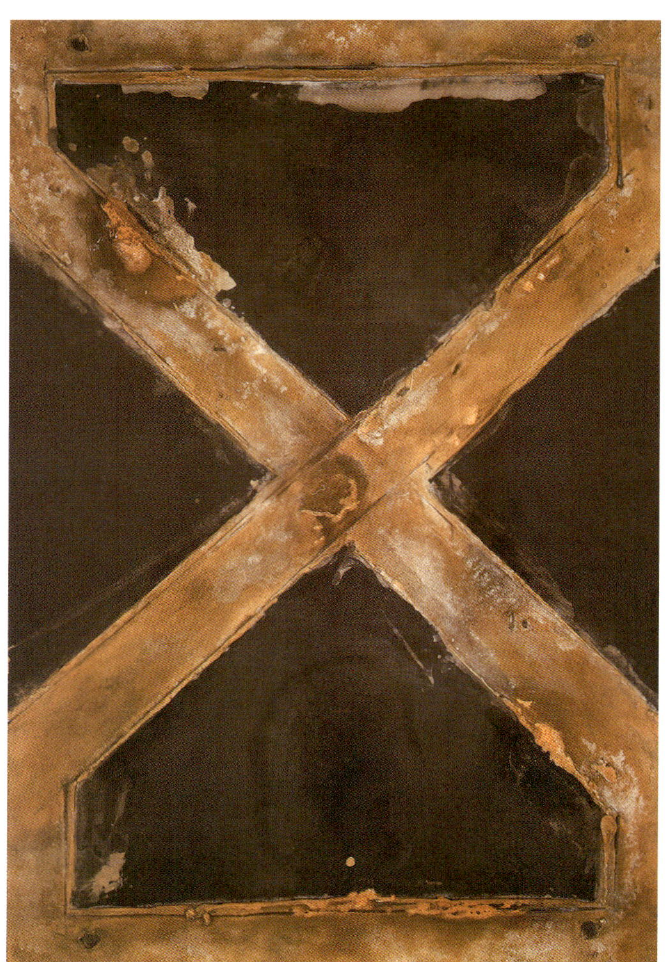

978

979

978. **Antoni Tàpies**, 1923-, Dau al Set Group, Spanish,
Grand Square, 1962.
Mixed medium on canvas, 195 x 130 cm.
Museo de Arte Abstracto Español, Cuenca.

979. **Roy Lichtenstein**, 1923-1997, Pop Art, American,
Great Painting n° 6, 1965.
Oil and Magna on canvas, 233 x 328 cm.
Kunstsammlung Nordrhein Westfalen, Düsseldorf.

980. **Francis Bacon**, 1909-1992, Expressionism, British,
Three Studies for a Crucifixion, 1962.
Oil with sand on canvas, 198.1 x 144.8 cm.
Guggenheim Museum, New York.

980

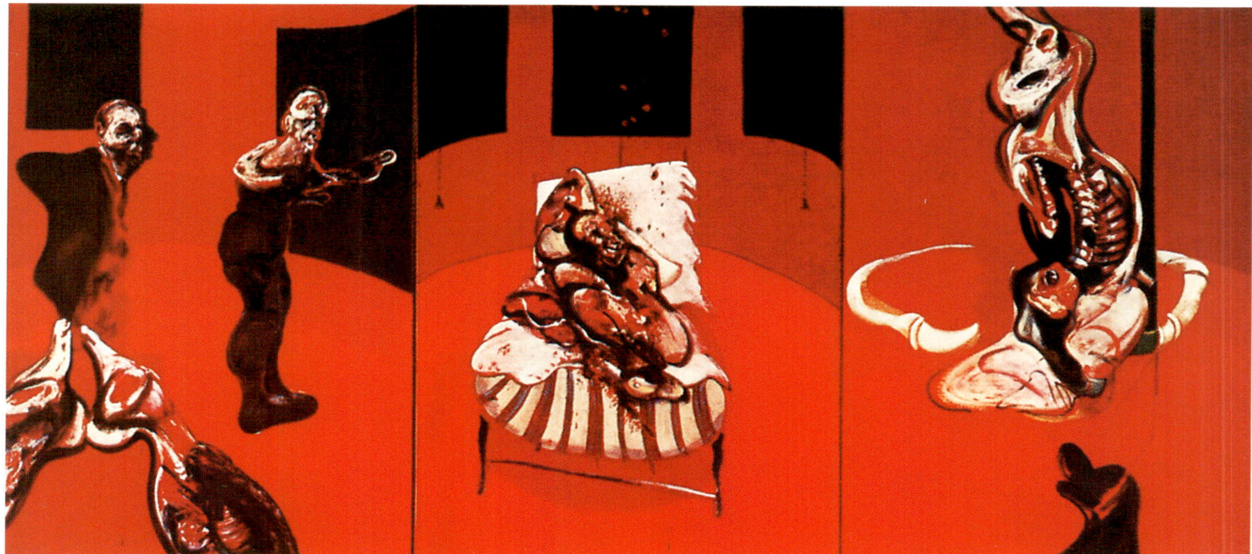

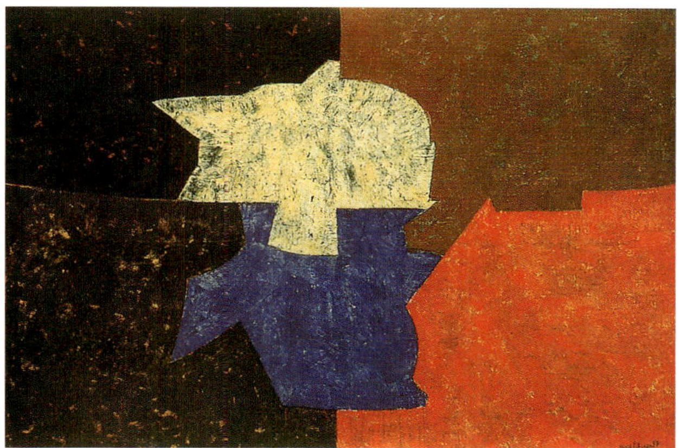

981. **Serge Poliakoff**, 1906-1969, Abstraction, Russian-born, active in Paris,
   Abstract Composition, 1969.
   Oil on canvas, 89 x 130 cm. Archives Serge Poliakov, Paris.

982. **Frank Stella**, 1936-, Minimal Art, American, *Nunca Pasa Nada*, 1964.
   Metallic polymer on canvas, 279.4 x 558.8 cm. Private collection.

983. **Robert Motherwell**, 1915-1991, Abstract Expressionism, American,
   Elegy to the Spanish Republic, 1969.
   Acrylic on canvas, 237.5 x 300 cm. Private collection.
   Art © Robert Motherwell / Licensed by VAGA, New York, NY.

984. **Ellsworth Kelly**, 1923-, Minimal Art, American,
   Red Blue Green, 1963. Oil on canvas, 213.4 x 345.4 cm.
   Museum of Contemporary Art, San Diego.

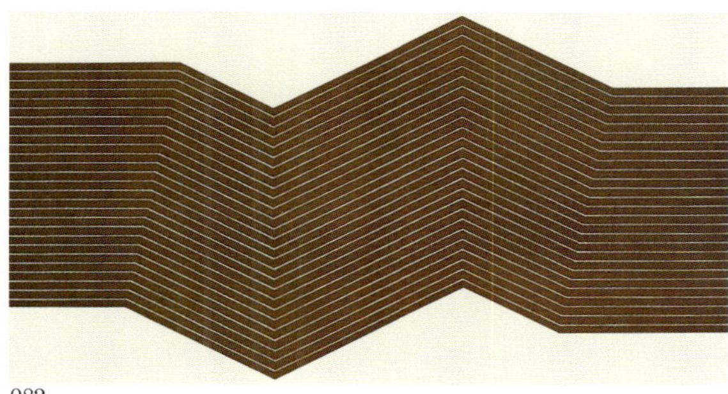
982

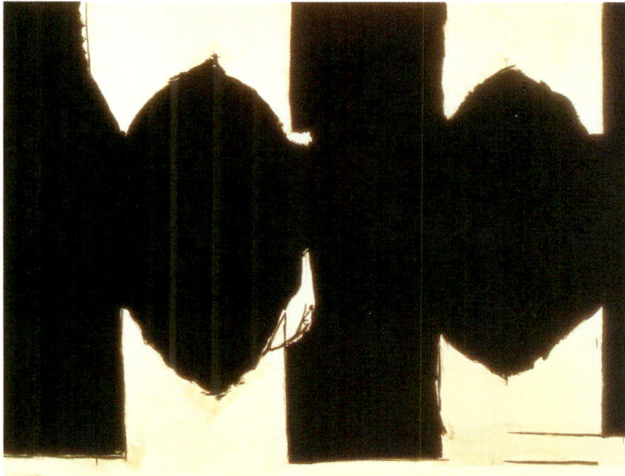
983

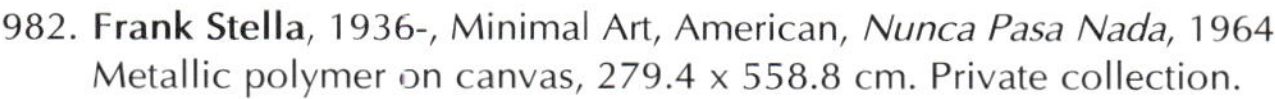
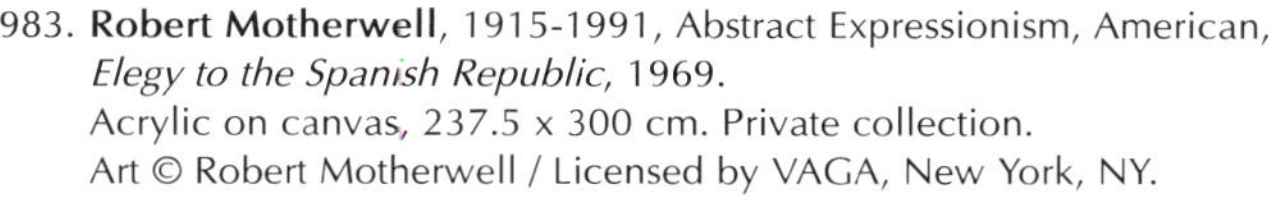
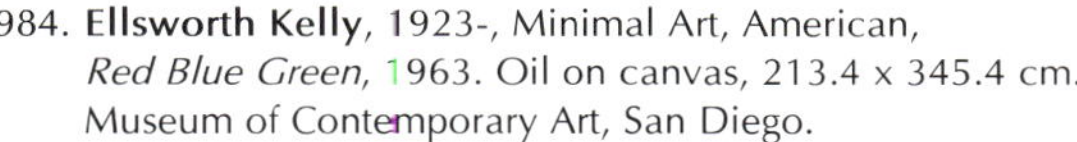
984

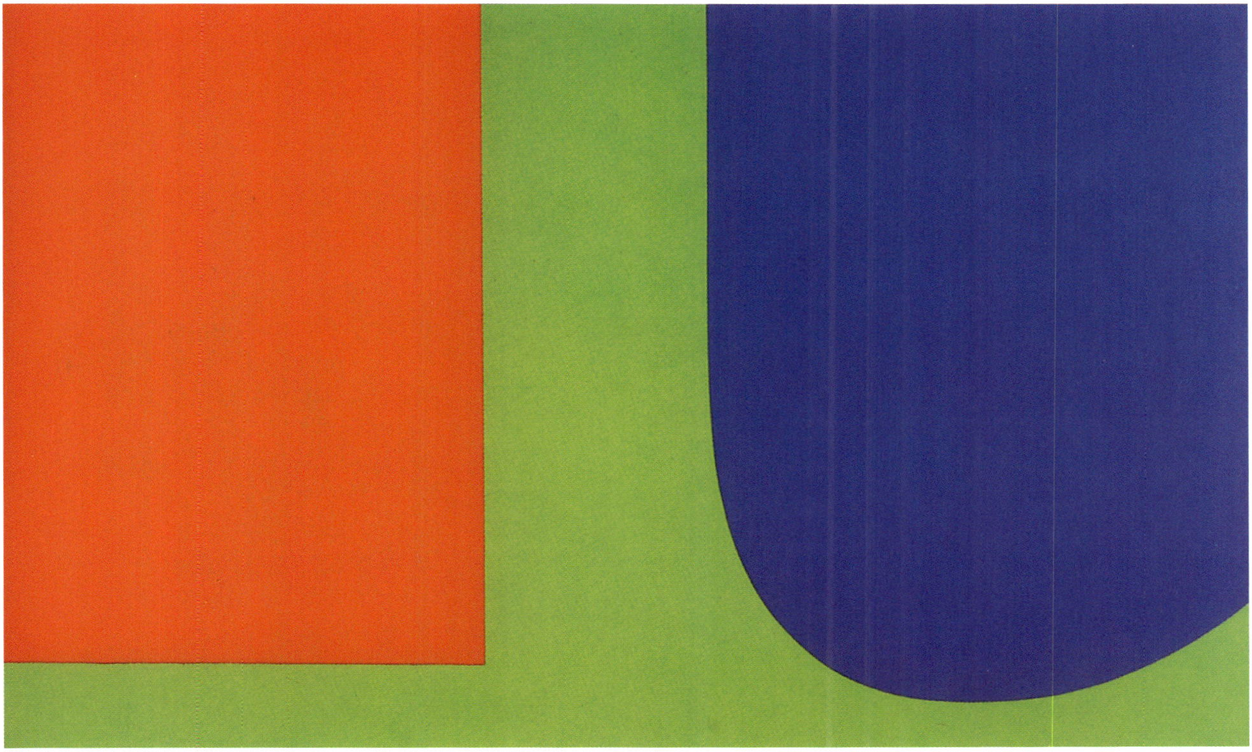

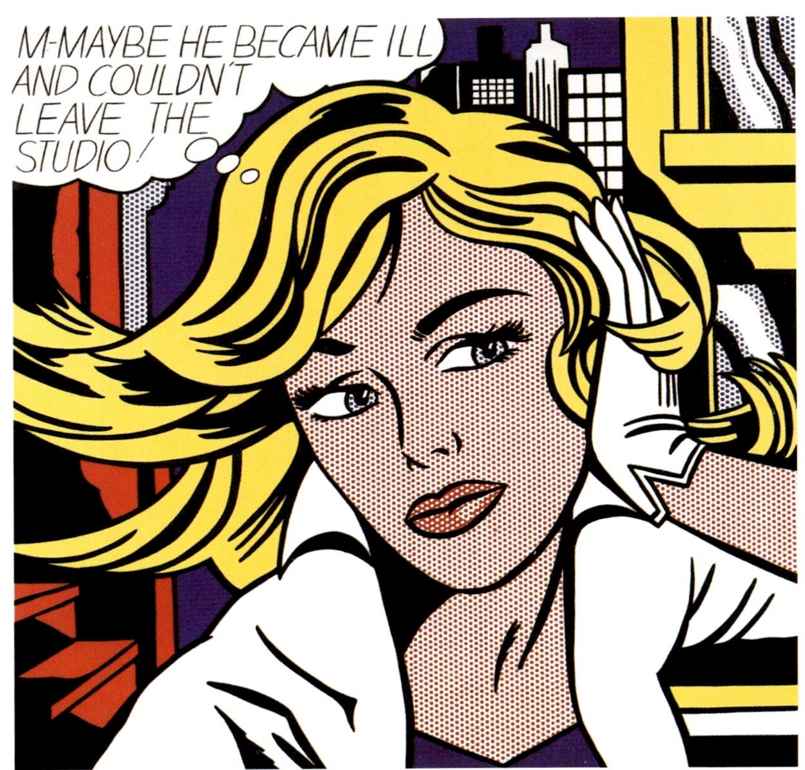

985. **Roy Lichtenstein**, 1923-1997, Pop Art,
American, *M-Maybe*, 1965.
Oil on canvas, 152 x 152 cm.
Wallraf-Richartz Museum, Cologne.

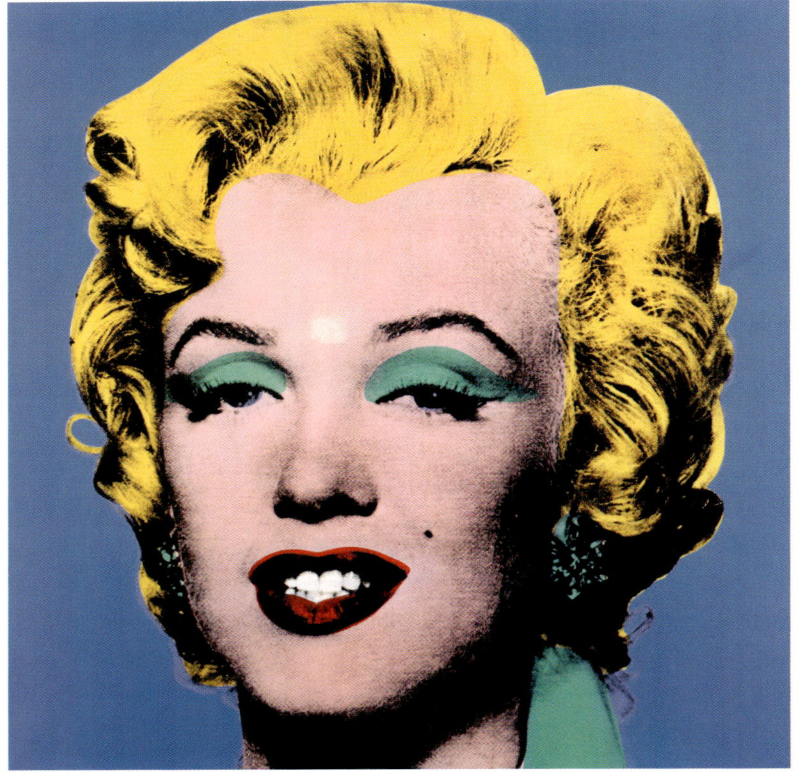

986. **Andy Warhol**, 1928-1987, Pop Art,
American, *Shot Blue Marilyn*, 1964.
Silkscreen and acrylic on canvas,
101.6 x 101.6 cm.
The Brant Foundation, Greenwich.

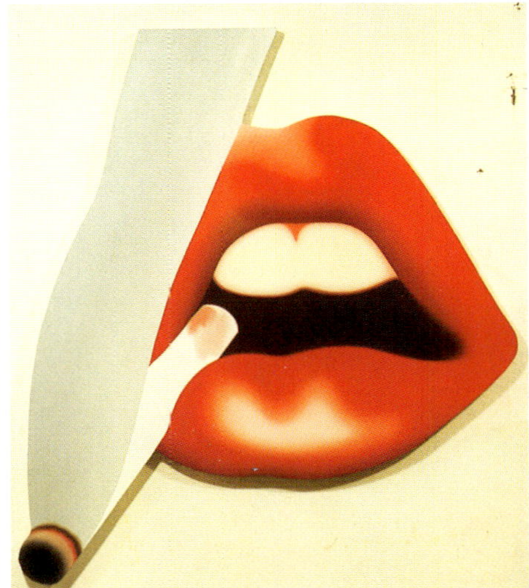

987. **Tom Wesselmann**, 1931-2004, Pop Art, American,
Mouth #18 (Smoker #4), 1968.
Oil on canvas, 224.8 x 198.1 cm.
Courtesy Sidney Janis Gallery, New York.
Art © Estate of Tom Wesselmann / Licensed by VAGA,
New York, NY.

988. **David Hockney**, 1937-, Pop Art, British,
A Bigger Splash, 1967.
Acrylic on canvas, 242.5 x 243.9 cm. Tate Gallery, London.

This is justifiably Hockney's most popular picture, not least of all because the scene depicted typifies the hedonistic lifestyle towards which so many people aspire within contemporary mass-culture. By the time Hockney painted the canvas he had already created two pictures of splashes in swimming pools, one of which he named The Little Splash. *That explains the title of the present work.*

All is heat and light in the garden of the American Dream. The fairly strident yellow, pink and puce colours of, respectively, the diving board, the patio, and the wall stand at the opposite end of the spectrum to the cool blues of water and sky, thereby generating an immense torridity. That intensity is increased by the climactic white at the heart of the image and by the warm colour of the large, empty surround to the painted area. Hockney created this to reinforce our awareness that we are looking at a fictive space within the enclosure, rather than an actual one. He had already been using this device for some time when he created A Bigger Splash, *as can be seen in the* Portrait of Nick Wilder *of 1966.*

On the patio stands a chair, of the type we often associate with Hollywood movie directors. Its presence suggests that the swimmer, who has presumably just vacated it, is a person of some importance. It is not difficult to imagine the sound of the splash breaking the apparent silence. Because we do not see the swimmer, the vacancy of the scene remains intact.

As in the Portrait of Nick Wilder, *the influence of Vermeer is apparent, with many lines running parallel to the edges of the image. These create a sense of pictorial rigidity against which the diagonal of the diving board and the free forms of the splash contrast greatly. The unseen swimmer has surely been physically liberated and refreshed by his dive, as, presumably, we all would be in such torrid surroundings.*

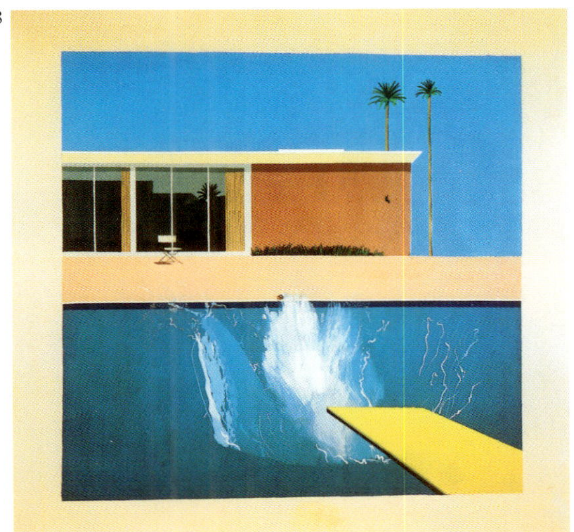

989. **Josef Albers**, 1888-1976, Abstraction, German,
Study for Homage to the Square: Departing in Yellow, 1964.
Oil on board, 78 x 78 cm.
Tate Gallery, London.

Albers, in a very analytical way, preferred to work on an idea by developing it during a series of paintings, keeping the overview in mind as he developed each work in that series. The Study for Homage to the Square: Departing in Yellow series explored the possibilities of the geometric form with a variety of colours, giving optical illusion close to pop art (although Albers is rather related to abstract art). While he used standard commercial paints, he developed a complex theory of colour. He distilled the base colours by adding greys and whites, and the resulting colours combined into layers that draw the viewer forward and back within the work. The size of the squares interplays with the juxtaposed colours, with no two works in the series identical.

989

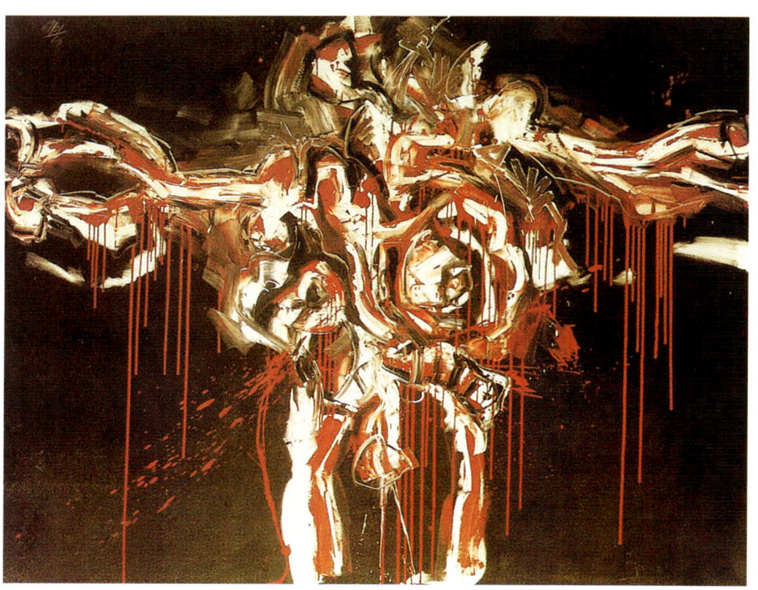

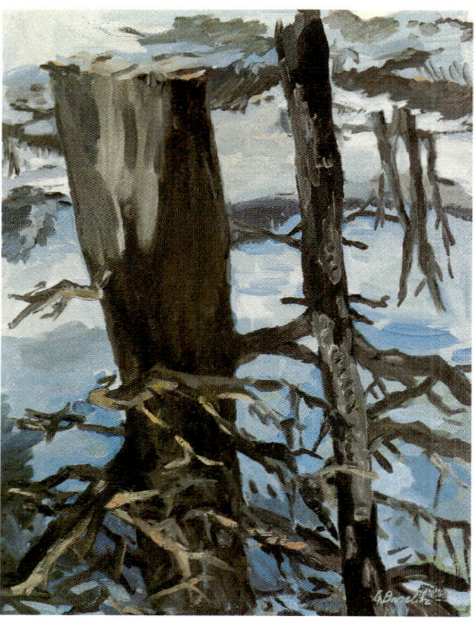

990. **Antonio Saura**, 1930-1998, Art Informel, Spanish,
The Great Crucifixion, 1963. Oil on canvas, 195 x 245 cm.
Boijmans Museum, Rotterdam.

991. **Georg Baselitz**, 1938-, Neo-Expressionism,
German, *The Wood on its Head*, 1969.
Oil on canvas, 250 x 190 cm.
Museum Ludwig, Cologne.

992. **Bram van Velde**, 1895-1981, Abstraction, Dutch,
Untitled: Composition, 1966.
Oil on canvas, 130 x 195 cm.
Musée national d'art moderne, Centre Georges-Pompidou, Paris.

993. **Frank Stella**, 1936-, Minimal Art, American,
Kastura, 1979.
Oil and epoxy on aluminium and wire mesh
with metal tubing, 292.1 x 233.7 cm.
The Museum of Modern Art, New York.

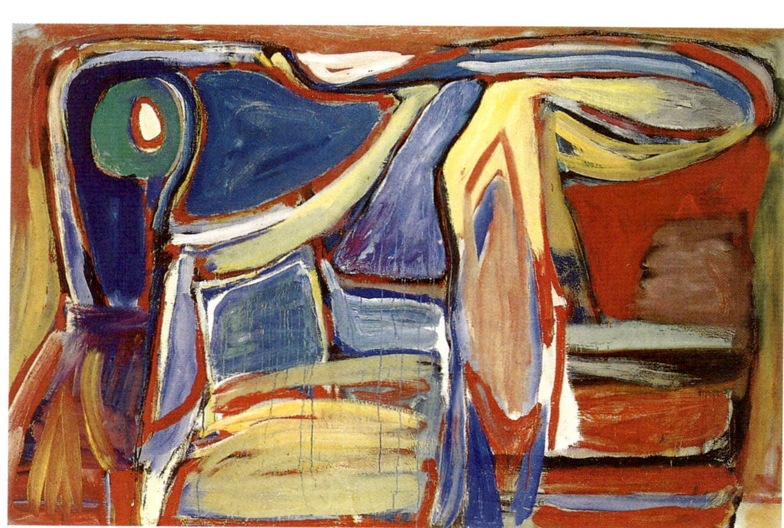

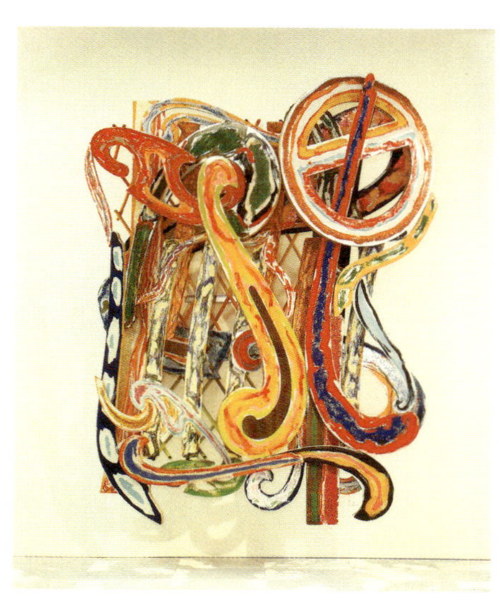

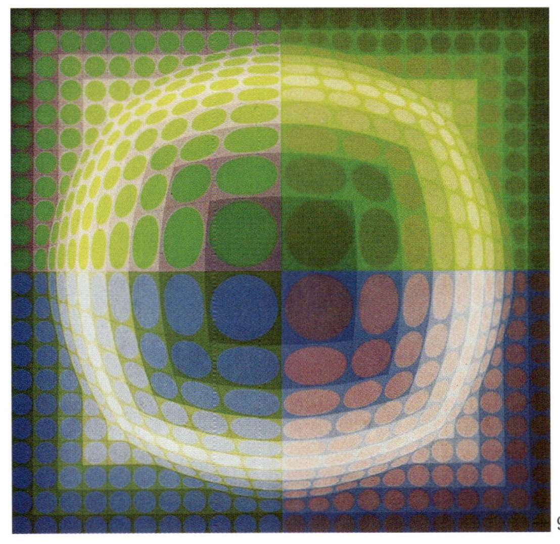

995

994. **Victor Vasarely**, 1908-1997, Op Art, French,
Pal-Ket, 1973-1974.
Acrylic on canvas, 151.2 x 150.8 cm.
Museo de Bellas Artes, Bilbao.

995. **Bridget Riley**, 1931-, Op Art, British,
Cataract 3, 1967.
PVA emulsion on canvas, 221.9 x 222.9 cm.
British Council, London.

996. **Barnett Newman**, 1905-1970, Minimal Art,
American, *Who's Afraid of Red, Yellow, and Blue III*,
1967-1968.
Oil on canvas, 274 x 603 cm.
Stedelijk Museum, Amsterdam.

BRIDGET RILEY
(1931 LONDON)

The English painter Bridget Riley is one of the foremost artists of the late-twentieth century Op Art. After studying at Goldsmiths College and later at the Royal College of Art with Peter Blake and Frank Auerbach, she began exploring the interplay of shape, light and lines. She worked on large canvases with interlocking bands, undulating curves or repeated squares and triangles, and mastered the subtle variations in size, shape or placement of serialised units in an all-over pattern. Her interest in optical effects came partly from her study of Seurat's pointillism. Riley's work has earned attention since the early 1950s when she worked in black and white and used geometric patterns to create the illusion of movement. Her first solo show was in 1962, and her international reputation was established in 1968 when she won the International Prize for Painting, the highest honour at the 1968 Venice Biennale.

996

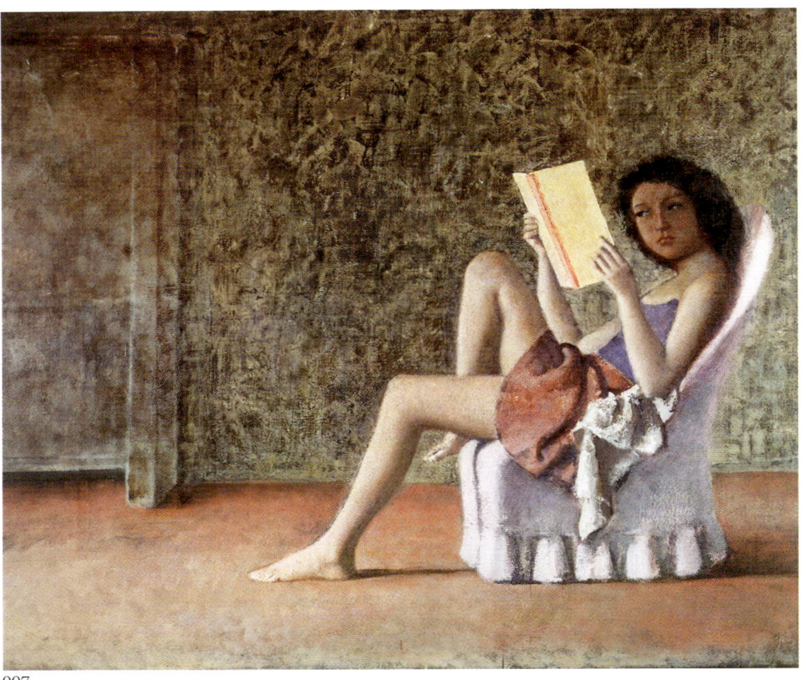

997

1000. **Andy Warhol**, 1928-1987, Pop Art,
American, *Last Supper*, 1986.
Polymer on canvas, 101 x 101 cm.
The Andy Warhol Museum, Pittsburgh.

997. **Balthasar Balthus**, 1908-2001, French.
Katia Reading, 1968-1976.
Casein and tempera on canvas.
Private collection, New York.

999. **Corneliu Baba**, 1906-1997, Realism,
Romanian, *The Mad King*, 1981.
Oil on canvas, 49 x 33 cm.
Artist's collection.

998

999

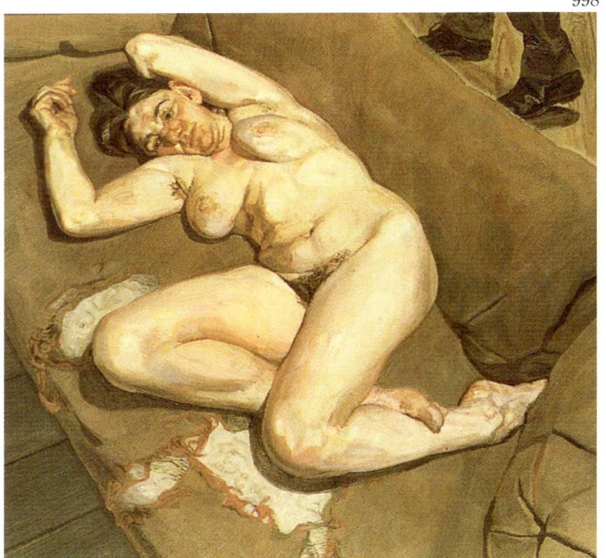

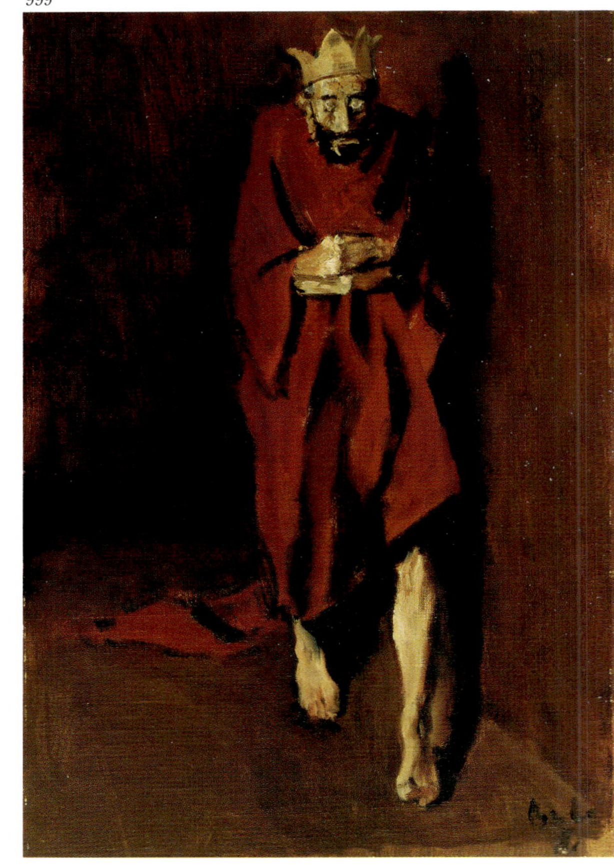

998. **Lucian Freud**, 1922-2011, New Realism, British,
Naked Portrait with Reflection, 1980.
Oil on canvas, 225.2 x 225.2 cm.
Private collection.

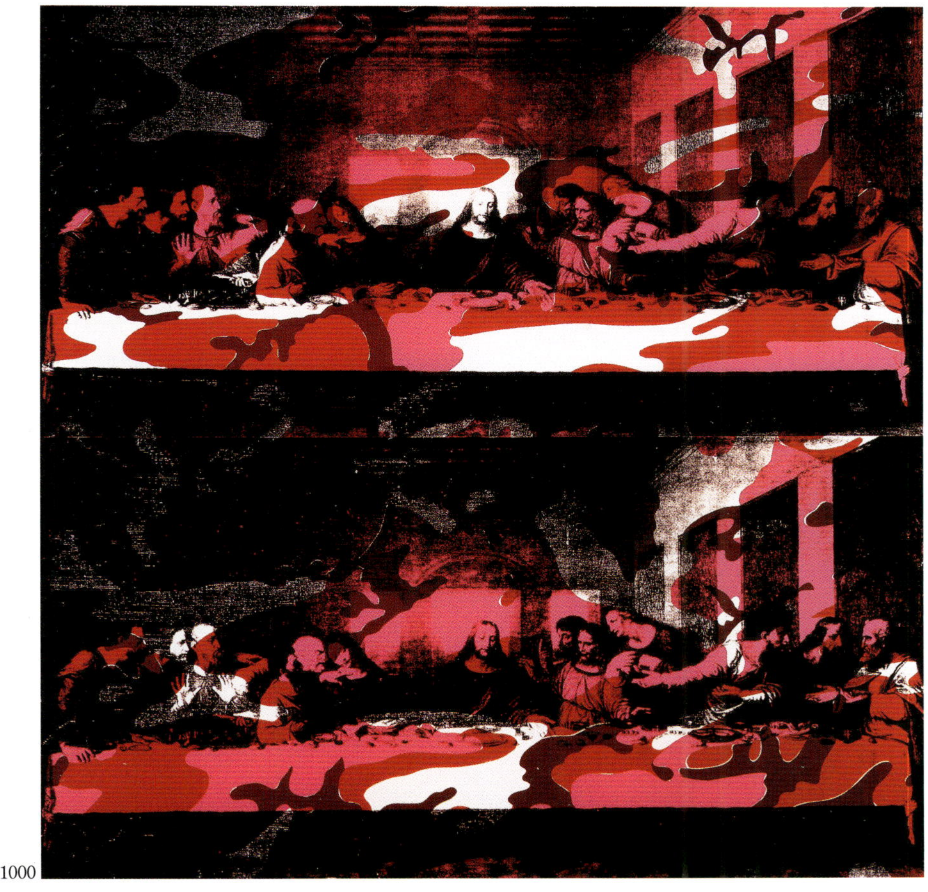

1000

ANDY WARHOL
(1928 PITTSBURGH – 1987 NEW YORK)

Andy Warhol was an artist who undoubtedly put his finger on the pulse of modern culture. Through pioneering a variety of techniques, but principally by means of the visual isolation of imagery, its repetition and enforced similarity to printed images, and the use of garish colour to denote the visual garishness that is often encountered in mass culture, he threw much direct or indirect light upon modern anomie or world-weariness, nihilism, materialism, political manipulation, economic exploitation, conspicuous consumption, media hero-worship, and the creation of artificially-induced needs and aspirations. Moreover, in his best paintings and prints he was a very fine creator of images, with a superb colour sense and a brilliant feel for the visual rhythm of a picture which resulted from his intense awareness of the pictorial potentialities inherent in forms. Initially, his images might appear rather simple. Yet, because of that very simplicity, they not only enjoy a high degree of immediate visual impact, but also possess the rare power of projecting huge implications through the mental associations they set in motion. For example, the visual repetition that Warhol employed within a great many of his images was intended, associatively, to parallel the vast repetition of images that are employed in a mass-culture in order to sell goods and services. This includes vehicles of communication such as movies and TV programmes. By incorporating into his images the very techniques of mass production that are central to a modern industrial society, Warhol directly mirrored larger cultural uses and abuses, while emphasising, to the point of absurdity, the complete detachment from emotional commitment that he saw everywhere around him. Moreover, in addition to employing imagery derived from popular culture in order to offer a critique of contemporary society, Warhol also carried forward the assaults on art and bourgeois values that the Dadaists had earlier pioneered; by manipulating images and the public persona of the artist, he was able to throw back in our faces the contradictions and superficialities of contemporary art and culture. Ultimately, it is the trenchancy of his cultural critique, as well as the vivaciousness with which he imbued it, that will surely lend his works their continuing relevance long after the particular objects he represented – such as Campbell's Soup cans and Coca-Cola bottles – have perhaps become technologically outmoded, or the outstanding people he depicted, such as Marilyn Monroe, Elvis Presley, and Mao Zedong, have come to be regarded merely as the superstars of yesterday.

CHRONOLOGY

	3 000 000 BCE-400 000 BCE	400 000 BCE-3000 BCE
	Prehistory	
IBERIAN PENINSULA	800 000 BCE: First Neanderthal men (Spain)	15 500-13 500 BCE: Rock paintings in the Altamira cave
ITALY		
FRANCE	1 800 000 BCE: First tools used (pebbles) 400 000 BCE: Fire harnessing	25 000-23 000 BCE: Venus of Lespugue 21 000 BCE: Venus of Brassempouy 18 000-15 000 BCE: Rock paintings of Lascaux 4000 BCE: Beginnings of the megalithic civilisation
BRITISH ISLES		
CENTRAL EUROPE (GERMANY INCLUDED)		23 000 BCE: Venus of Willendorf
FLANDERS (BELGIUM, NETHERLANDS)		
GREECE		3200-2700 BCE: The Cyclades civilisation
AFRICA	3 000 000 BCE: First men's appearance in Eastern and Southern Africa	4000 BCE: Sahara desert's dryness, migrations towards Western Africa 3300 BCE: First handwritings' appearance in Egypt
AMERICAS		
RUSSIA		

<table>
<tr><th colspan="3">Antiquity</th></tr>
<tr><th></th><th>3000 BCE-0</th><th>0-476 CE</th></tr>
<tr>
<td>IBERIAN PENINSULA</td>
<td>1000 BCE: Beginnings of the Iron Age
2nd-1st centuries BCE: Roman conquest</td>
<td></td>
</tr>
<tr>
<td>ITALY</td>
<td>800 BCE: Beginnings of the Etruscan civilisation in Tuscany
753 BCE: Foundation of Rome
3rd-2nd centuries BCE: Punic wars
44 BCE: Julius Caesar's murder
31 BCE: Actium battle. Birth of the Roman Empire</td>
<td>64: Great fire of Rome and first Christians persecutions led by Nero
79: Vesuvius eruption, destruction of Pompei and Herculanum
293: Diocletian installs the Triumvirate, dividing the Empire's government between Eastern and Western
410: The sack of Rome by the Visigoths
476: Fall of the Western Roman Empire</td>
</tr>
<tr>
<td>FRANCE</td>
<td>600 BCE: Founding of Marseille, first mention of Gaul
58-51 BCE: Gallic wars. Vercingetorix's defeat</td>
<td>406: Beginnings of the great invasions in Gaul, because of the Rhine's frost</td>
</tr>
<tr>
<td>BRITISH ISLES</td>
<td></td>
<td></td>
</tr>
<tr>
<td>CENTRAL EUROPE (GERMANY INCLUDED)</td>
<td>2nd millennium BCE: Appearance of the Germanic peoples</td>
<td>9: Teutoburg battle, victory of the Germanic tribes over the Romans</td>
</tr>
<tr>
<td>FLANDERS (BELGIUM, NETHERLANDS)</td>
<td></td>
<td></td>
</tr>
<tr>
<td>GREECE</td>
<td>2700-1200 BCE: Minoan civilisation in Crete
800 BCE: Increasing of the trade with the Near East, then with Italy
800-510 BCE: Archaic period
750 BCE: Beginnings of the Greek colonisation towards the West
561 BCE: Pisistratus becomes a tyrant of Athens. Autocracy in all the Greek cities
510-323 BCE: Classical Greece
508 BCE: Cleisthenes installs democracy in Athens
490-479 BCE: Greco-Persian wars
323-146 BCE: Hellenistic Greece</td>
<td>1st century CE: Beginnings of Christianity
330: Founding of Constantinople</td>
</tr>
<tr>
<td colspan="3" align="center">146 BCE-330 CE: Roman Period</td>
</tr>
<tr>
<td>AFRICA</td>
<td>3100-343 BCE: Pharaonic Egypt
814 BCE: The Phoenicians found Carthage
332 BCE: Alexander the Great enters in Egypt
331 BCE: Founding of Alexandria
146 BCE: Destruction of Carthage by the Romans
30 BCE: Egypt goes under the Roman rule</td>
<td>2nd-3rd centuries: Christianity expands through North Africa
429: Arrival of the Vandals in Africa</td>
</tr>
<tr>
<td>AMERICAS</td>
<td></td>
<td></td>
</tr>
<tr>
<td>RUSSIA</td>
<td></td>
<td></td>
</tr>
</table>

<table>
<thead>
<tr><th colspan="3" align="center">Middle Ages</th></tr>
<tr><th></th><th align="center">476-1200</th><th align="center">1200-1299</th></tr>
</thead>
<tbody>
<tr>
<td>IBERIAN PENINSULA</td>
<td>542: Great bubonic plague
596: Toledo becomes the capital of the Visigothic kingdom
711: Beginnings of the Muslim conquest
756: Abd al-Rahman founds the Umayyad Emirate in Cordoba</td>
<td>1200: Introduction of the Arabic numerals in Europe
1212: The combined armies of Aragon and Castile defeat the Almohads at the Battle of Las Navas de Tolosa
1238: The Moors set their last refuge in Grenada</td>
</tr>
<tr>
<td>ITALY</td>
<td>756: Pepin the Short delivers Rome besieged by the Lombards
962-973: Otton the first is crowned in Rome, first emperor of the Holy Roman Germanic Empire</td>
<td>c. 1200: The compass arrives in Europe for purpose of navigation
c. 1200: Paper arrives in Europe
1204: Sack of Constantinople by the Crusaders
1209: Foundation of Franciscan and Domenican monastic orders preaching against heresy and praising poverty and charity
1215: Lateran Council
1271: Marco Polo reaches China
1276: First paper mill set in Italy</td>
</tr>
<tr>
<td>FRANCE</td>
<td>481: Clovis becomes king of the Franks
496: Clovis becomes a convert to Christianity
511-751: Merovingian dynasty
732: Charles Martel defeats the Muslim army in Poitiers
751-987: Carolingian dynasty
800: Charlemagne is crowned emperor
987: Hughes Capet, first king of the Capetian dynasty
987-1328: Capetian dynasty
1066: Conquest of England by William, duke of Normandy
1095: First crusade

1180-1223: King Philip Augustus II of France. Building of the Louvre</td>
<td>1226-1270: King St Louis of France (Louis IX), last crusade
1233: Pope Gregory IX starts the Papal Inquisition. Extirpation of the Cathars in southern France</td>
</tr>
<tr>
<td>BRITISH ISLES</td>
<td></td>
<td>1215: King John forced to sign the Magna Carta</td>
</tr>
<tr>
<td>CENTRAL EUROPE (INCLUDING GERMANY)</td>
<td>843: Treaty of Verdun, division of the Carolingian empire into three kingdoms
919-936: Henry I the Fowler, king of Germany
962: Creation of the Holy Roman Empire
1122: Concordat of Worms
1138-1152: Conrad III of Germany. Hohenstaufen dynasty</td>
<td>1260: Albert the Great writes a major book on botanical studies</td>
</tr>
<tr>
<td>FLANDERS (BELGIUM, NETHERLANDS)</td>
<td></td>
<td>1214: Philip Augustus of France wins the Battle of Bouvines. Starts along period of French control</td>
</tr>
<tr>
<td>GREECE</td>
<td>1054: Definitive schism between the Orthodox Church and the Roman Catholic Church
1185: Storming of Salonica by the Normans</td>
<td></td>
</tr>
<tr>
<td>AFRICA</td>
<td>634: Omar I unifies Arabia and starts the first Muslim conquest (Hijra)
7th century: North Africa conquest by Arabs
800: Introduction of the Arabic numerals</td>
<td></td>
</tr>
<tr>
<td>AMERICAS</td>
<td></td>
<td></td>
</tr>
<tr>
<td>RUSSIA</td>
<td>862: Arrival of the Viking King Rourik, founder of the first Russian dynasty
989: The emperor Vladimir converts Russians to christianity
1157-1327: Vladimir-Suzdal principality</td>
<td>1207: The Mongols spread xylography in Eastern Europe
1223: Invasion of Russia by Mongols
1242: Alexander Nevsky begins to unify Russia</td>
</tr>
</tbody>
</table>

<table>
<tr><th colspan="3" style="text-align:center">Middle Ages</th></tr>
<tr><th></th><th style="text-align:center">1300-1349</th><th style="text-align:center">1350-1399</th></tr>
<tr><td>IBERIAN PENINSULA</td><td>1309: First portulan (navigation map)</td><td>1385: Victory of Juan I of Portugal over the Castilians</td></tr>
<tr><td></td><td colspan="2" style="text-align:center">1232-1492: The Nasrid dynasty rules Granada</td></tr>
<tr><td rowspan="2">ITALY</td><td>1308: Dante writes the Divine Comedy. Flourishing of vernacular literature
1348: The plague (known as the Black Death) arrives in Europe</td><td>1378: Two popes are elected, one in Italy, one in France. Beginning of the Great Schism</td></tr>
<tr><td colspan="2" style="text-align:center">1349-1353: Boccaccio writes the Decameron</td></tr>
<tr><td rowspan="2">FRANCE</td><td>1320-1330: Endemic wars and development of sea trade</td><td>1378: Two popes are elected, one in Italy, one in France. Beginning of the Great Schism</td></tr>
<tr><td colspan="2" style="text-align:center">1309-1423: Avignon becomes residence of the Pope Clement V
1328-1589: House of Valois
1337-1453: England and France start the Hundred Years' War</td></tr>
<tr><td rowspan="2">BRITISH ISLES</td><td>1346: Canon powder arrives in Europe and used for the first time at the battle of Crecy</td><td>1382: John Wycliffe finishes translating the latin Bible into English</td></tr>
<tr><td colspan="2" style="text-align:center">1337-1453: England and France start the Hundred Years' War</td></tr>
<tr><td>CENTRAL EUROPE (INCLUDING GERMANY)</td><td>1310: Experiments on reflection and refraction of light</td><td>1356: Emperor Charles IV issues the Golden Bull. Prague center of learning and culture</td></tr>
<tr><td>FLANDERS (BELGIUM, NETHERLANDS)</td><td></td><td>1369: Marriage of Philip the Bold, Duke of Burgundy, to Margaret of Flanders, beginning of Burgundian rule in the Low Countries</td></tr>
<tr><td>GREECE</td><td colspan="2" style="text-align:center">14th century: Beginnings of the Ottoman Empire</td></tr>
<tr><td>AFRICA</td><td></td><td></td></tr>
<tr><td>AMERICAS</td><td></td><td></td></tr>
<tr><td>RUSSIA</td><td></td><td></td></tr>
</table>

<table>
<tr><th colspan="3" style="text-align:center">Renaissance</th></tr>
<tr><th></th><th>1400-1449</th><th>1450-1499</th></tr>
<tr>
<td>IBERIAN PENINSULA</td>
<td>Early 15th c.: Galions, particularly used by Spanish to carry precious materials from the Americas

15th c. – 16th c.: Navigation with caravels</td>
<td>1456: The Portuguese discover the Cape Verde
1469: Reign of the Catholic Monarchs (Ferdinand of Aragon and Isabella of Castille)
1478: Sixtus IV issues the Bull establishing the Spanish Inquisition
1492: Moors driven out of Spain. End of 800 years of Islamic presence in Spain. Columbus reaches the New World
1498: Vasco de Gama arrives in India
1500: Pedro Alvares Cabral discovers Brazil</td>
</tr>
<tr>
<td>ITALY</td>
<td>1407: Bank of St George established in Genoa as the first public bank
1413: Brunelleschi invents the pictorial perspective</td>
<td>1453: Turkish conquest of Constantinople
1498: Vasco de Gama discovers the sea route to India</td>
</tr>
<tr>
<td>FRANCE</td>
<td>1429: Saint Joan of Arc leads the French to victory against the English
1431: Joan of Arc is burned alive in Rouen

 1328-1589: Valois dynasty </td>
<td></td>
</tr>
<tr>
<td>BRITISH ISLES</td>
<td></td>
<td>1455: War of the Roses
1485-1509: Reign of Henri VII Tudor, King of England</td>
</tr>
<tr>
<td>CENTRAL EUROPE (INCLUDING GERMANY)</td>
<td>1445: Invention of the moveable type (first printer)</td>
<td>1456: Gutenberg produces the first printed Bible
1493: Maximilien I establishes the Habsburg family as a major international power
Late 15th c.: Invention of the art of etching (with Daniel Hopfer)</td>
</tr>
<tr>
<td>FLANDERS (BELGIUM, NETHERLANDS)</td>
<td></td>
<td></td>
</tr>
<tr>
<td>GREECE</td>
<td></td>
<td></td>
</tr>
<tr>
<td>AFRICA</td>
<td colspan="2"> Mid 15th c.: Beginning of the slave trade by the Europeans </td>
</tr>
<tr>
<td>AMERICAS</td>
<td></td>
<td>1492: Columbus reaches the New World</td>
</tr>
<tr>
<td>RUSSIA</td>
<td></td>
<td>1480: Ivan III Vasilevich frees Russia from Mongol domination</td>
</tr>
</table>

<table>
<tr><td colspan="3" align="center">Renaissance</td></tr>
<tr><td></td><td align="center">1500-1549</td><td align="center">1550-1599</td></tr>
<tr>
<td>IBERIAN PENINSULA</td>
<td>1500: First Portuguese explorers disembark in Brazil
1506: Hernán Cortés, conquistador, arrives in the New World
1513: Pacific Ocean discovered by Vasco Nuñez de Balboa
1520: Magellan sails across the Pacific Ocean
1521: Hernán Cortés defeat the Aztecs. A 300 year colonial period starts
1543: First scientific study of human anatomy (Andreas Vesalius)
1549: Francis Xavier establishes the first Christian mission in Japan</td>
<td>1571: Battle of Lepanto, Ottomans defeated by the Venetian and the Spanish

1588: Spanish Armada defeated by England.
End of Spanish commercial supremacy</td>
</tr>
<tr><td></td><td colspan="2" align="center">1516-1555: Charles V, Holy Roman Emperor</td></tr>
<tr>
<td>ITALY</td>
<td colspan="2" align="center">1494-1559: Italian wars
1527: Sack of Rome by the troops of Charles V
1530: End of the Florence Republic (1500-1530). Under the reign of Cosimo de' Medici, Tuscany acquires the title of Grand Duchy
1545-1563: Council of Trent. Counter-Reformation</td>
</tr>
<tr>
<td>FRANCE</td>
<td>1515-1547: Francis I, King of France
1515: Battle of Marignan, victory of Francis I against the Swiss</td>
<td>1552: Ambroise Paré performs the first blood vessel ligature
1592-1598: Wars of Religion
1572: St Bartholomew's Day massacre: massive killings of Protestants in France during the night of the St Bartholomew
1598: Edict of Nantes proclaimed by French King Henry IV.
End of the Wars of Religion</td>
</tr>
<tr><td></td><td colspan="2" align="center">1328-1589: Valois dynasty
1494-1559: Italian wars
1589-1792: House of Bourbon</td></tr>
<tr>
<td>BRITISH ISLES</td>
<td>1485-1509: Reign of Henri VII Tudor, King of England
1533: Henry VIII is excommunicated by the Catholic Church</td>
<td>1553-1558: Reign of Marie Tudor, Queen of England. Return to Catholicism
1558-1603: Elizabeth I, Queen of England. Protestantism established in the Church of England</td>
</tr>
<tr>
<td>CENTRAL EUROPE (INCLUDING GERMANY)</td>
<td>1508-1519: Reign of Maximilan I, emperor of the Holy Roman Empire. Spreads the Habsburgs' reign to Burgundy, the Netherlands, Franche-Comté, Hungary and Bohemia
1517: Martin Luther posts his 95 theses: Protestant Revolt and beginning of the Reformation
1519-1555: Reign of Charles V, emperor of the Holy Roman Empire
1529: Turkish invasions, Siege of Vienna
1543: Copernican Revolution with the theory of heliocentrism</td>
<td>1560: Spreading of Calvinism</td>
</tr>
<tr>
<td>FLANDERS (BELGIUM; NETHERLANDS)</td>
<td>1508-1519: Reign of Maximilan I, emperor of the Holy Roman Empire. Spreads the Habsburgs' reign to Burgundy, the Netherlands, Franche-Comté, Hungary and Bohemia</td>
<td>1568: General revolt in the Netherlands
1581: Creation of the Dutch Republic (Independence of the Northern provinces from Spain)</td>
</tr>
<tr><td></td><td colspan="2" align="center">1519-1555: Reign of Charles V, emperor of the Holy Roman Empire</td></tr>
<tr>
<td>GREECE</td>
<td></td>
<td></td>
</tr>
<tr>
<td>AFRICA</td>
<td></td>
<td></td>
</tr>
<tr>
<td>AMERICAS</td>
<td>1500: First Portuguese explorers disembark in Brazil
1506: Hernán Cortés, conquistador, arrives in the New World
1521: The conquistador Hernán Cortés defeats the Aztecs
1531-1534: Pizarro conquers the Inca Empire</td>
<td>1588: Spanish Armada defeated by England.
End of Spanish commercial Supremacy</td>
</tr>
<tr>
<td>RUSSIA</td>
<td colspan="2" align="center">1533-1584: Ivan IV of Russia (Ivan the Terrible) first ruler of Russia to assume the title of tsar</td>
</tr>
</table>

<table>
<tr><th colspan="3" style="text-align:center">Baroque</th></tr>
<tr><th></th><th>1600-1649</th><th>1650-1699</th></tr>
<tr><td>IBERIAN PENINSULA</td><td>1598-1621: Philip III rules Spain, Naples, Sicily, Southern Netherlands and Portugal
1621: Victories against the French and Dutch
1648: Defeat of Spain against France, peace of Westphalia, concession of the Flanders' territories</td><td></td></tr>
<tr><td>ITALY</td><td>1610: Galileo Galilei first uses the telescope
1616: Galileo forbidden by the Church to further scientific work
1644: Evangelista Torricelli invents the barometer</td><td></td></tr>
<tr><td>FRANCE</td><td>1610-1643: Louis XIII, King of France
1618-1648: The Thirty Years War
1648: Defeat of Spain against France, peace of Westphalia, concession of the Flanders' territories</td><td>1661-1715: Louis XIV, King of France. Castle of Versailles transformed
1685: Revocation of the Edict of Nantes (Protestantism declared illegal in France)</td></tr>
<tr><td>BRITISH ISLES</td><td>1600: Founding of the British East India Company
1640-1660: English Revolution. Led by Oliver Cromwell (1599-1658)</td><td>1666: Great fire in London
1687: Isaac Newton's theories of the law motion and principle of gravity
1698: Invention of the steam engine by Thomas Savery</td></tr>
<tr><td>CENTRAL EUROPE (INCLUDING GERMANY)</td><td>1619-1637: Reign of Ferdinand II, emperor of Holy Roman Empire</td><td></td></tr>
<tr><td>FLANDERS (BELGIUM; NETHERLANDS)</td><td>1608: Hans Lippershey invents the telescope
1625: Dutch settle in Manhattan and establish New York</td><td>1672-1678: Intruding of Louis XIV's army in the Netherlands</td></tr>
<tr><td>GREECE</td><td></td><td></td></tr>
<tr><td>AFRICA</td><td></td><td></td></tr>
<tr><td>AMERICAS</td><td>1607-1675: British colonisation of North America
1624: Dutch settle in and around Manhattan</td><td>1681: King Charles II of England grants a land charter to William Penn for the area that now includes Pennsylvania</td></tr>
<tr><td>RUSSIA</td><td></td><td></td></tr>
</table>

<table>
<tr><td colspan="3" align="center">Baroque</td></tr>
<tr><td></td><td align="center">1700-1749</td><td align="center">1750-1799</td></tr>
<tr><td>IBERIAN PENINSULA</td><td>1701-1714: War of the Spanish Succession and Treaty of Utrecht</td><td></td></tr>
<tr><td>ITALY</td><td>1709 and 1748: Discovery of the ruins of Herculaneum and Pompeii</td><td></td></tr>
<tr><td>FRANCE</td><td></td><td>1756-1763: Seven Years War
1763: Treaty of Paris. France ceded Canada and all its territory east of the Mississippi River to England
1770: Nicolas-Joseph Cugnot built the first automobile
1783: First flight in hot air balloon
1789: Lavoisier publishes studies of chemistry
1789: Beginning of the French Revolution
1793-1994: Reign of Terror led by Robespierre
1792-1804: First Republic established
1793: Louis XVI executed. Opening of the Musée du Louvre
1798-1799: Expedition of Bonaparte in Egypt</td></tr>
<tr><td>BRITISH ISLES</td><td>1707: Acts of Union merges the Kingdom of England and the Kingdom of Scotland in the "United Kingdom."</td><td>1768-1779: James Cook explores the Pacific
1768: The Royal Academy is founded, with the painter Joshua Reynolds
1780-1810: First Industrial Revolution in England
1788: Colonisation of Australia by the United Kingdom</td></tr>
<tr><td>CENTRAL EUROPE (INCLUDING GERMANY)</td><td>1738: Vienna Treaty. End of the war of Polish Succession
1741: Beginning of the Austrian War of Succession</td><td>1796: Aloys Senefelder invents lithography</td></tr>
<tr><td>FLANDERS (BELGIUM; NETHERLANDS)</td><td></td><td>1794: Southern Netherlands conquered by the French</td></tr>
<tr><td>GREECE</td><td></td><td></td></tr>
<tr><td>AFRICA</td><td></td><td>1794: in France, the Convention forbids slavery</td></tr>
<tr><td>AMERICAS</td><td>Early 18th c.: Benjamin Franklin invents the bifocal lens and performs studies on electricity</td><td>1763: Treaty of Paris. France cedes Canada and all its territory east of the Mississippi River to England
1775: American War of Independence
1776: Official founding of the United States, declaration of Independence from Great Britain
1789: Election of George Washington</td></tr>
<tr><td>RUSSIA</td><td>1703: Foundation of St Petersburg
1721-1725: Reign of Peter I of Russia, first emperor of the Russian Empire</td><td>1762-1796: Catherine II, Empress of Russia</td></tr>
</table>

Modern Times

	1800-1810	1811-1820	1821-1830	1831-1840	1841-1850
IBERIAN PENINSULA	1810-1826: The Spanish colonies of America, except for Cuba and Puerto Rico, conquered their independence				
ITALY					
FRANCE	1802: Treaty of Amiens (end of the wars with France) 1804: Napoleon I crowned emperor	1814: Abdication of Napoleon defeated by the armies of Britain, Russia and Austria. Louis XVIII ascends the throne	1822: Champollion deciphers hieroglyphs	1839: Nicéphore Niepce and Louis Daguerre invent the daguerreotype (early process of photography)	1848: Napoleon III is sacr\[...\] Emperor of the 2ⁿᵈ Empire
BRITISH ISLES		1811-1820: Regency period. Flowering of the arts and literature 1815: George Stephenson invents the railroad locomotive		1834: A furnace destroys most of Wesminster Palace 1837-1901: Reign of Victoria I, Queen of the United King\[...\] Great Britain and Ireland	
CENTRAL EUROPE (INCLUDING GERMANY)	1806: Dissolution of the Holy Roman Empire				
FLANDERS (BELGIUM; NETHERLANDS)		1815: Defeat of the French army against Prussia and England at Waterloo		1831: Belgian independence from the Netherlands	
GREECE			1821: Beginning of the Greek Independence War 1830: Creation of the first Greek independent state		
AFRICA	1802: Slavery is reestablished by Napoleon			1833: Slavery is abolished in the British colonies 1880-1881: First Boer War	1848: Slavery is abolished second time in the french \[...\]
AMERICAS	1803: Louisiana sold to the United States by Napoleon	1812: War with Great Britain	1823: Monroe Doctrine	1834: Thomas Davenport makes the first electric motor commercially successful	1848: James W. Marshall \[...\] gold in California
	1810-1826: The Spanish colonies of America, except for Cuba and Puerto Rico, conquered their independence				
RUSSIA	1801: Assassination of Tsar Paul I. Alexander I is brought to power	1812: Napoleon invades Russia	1825-1855: Nicolas I, Tsar of Russia, enforces military discipline, censorship and traditions of the Orthodox Church		

Modern Times

1851-1860	1861-1870	1871-1880	1881-1890	1891-1900
	1861: Italian Kingdom is proclaimed. Victor-Emmanuel II is crowned			
1856: Crimean War, United [King]dom and France declare war [on Rus]sia	1869: Charles Cros invents a process for colour photography (based on three colours)	1871: Repression of the Commune in Paris	1885: First use of vaccine for rabies invented by Louis Pasteur	1895: August and Louis Lumière invent the first motion-picture projector
				1898: Marie Curie discovers radium
	1870: French defeated by Prussian. Fall of Second Empire	1871-1914: Expansion of French Colonial Empire (Indochina and Africa)		
			1875-1940: Third Republic	
1856: Crimean War, United [King]dom and France declare war [on Rus]sia	1867: Publication of the first volume of *Das Kapital* by Karl Marx			
[1859: P]ublication of Darwin's *Origin of Species*				
1837-1901: Victoria, Queen of Great Britain. India under control of the British Empire (1857-1947)				
	1867: Bismarck becomes Chancellor of the North German Confederation	1871: Proclamation of the German Empire 1877: Heinrich Hertz discovers electromagnetic radiation, first radio emission	1890-1900: Discovery of psychoanalysis by Sigmund Freud in Vienna	
		1888-1918: Reign of William II, German Emperor and King of Prussia		
			1884-1885: Partition of Africa between the colonial powers during the Berlin Conference	1899-1902: Second Boer War
[1860:] Election of Abraham Lincoln	1862: Emancipation Proclamation (end of slavery) 1861-1865: American Civil War 1868: Christopher Latham Sholes develops the typing machine	1876: Alexandre Graham Bell invents the telephone 1879: First incandescent lamp (Thomas Alva Edison and Joseph Wilson Swan)	1890: Halifax first city to be totally lit up with electricity	1897: *New York Journal* publishes the first comic strip 1898: Spanish-American War
1848-1896: Gold rushes toward West America				
1856: Crimean War, United [King]dom and France declare war [on Ru]ssia	1860s: Russian populist movement (the narodniki) 1861: Emancipation of the serfs			
1855-1881: Tsar Alexander II of Russia				

Modern Times

	1900-1910	1911-1920	1921-1930	1931-1940
IBERIAN PENINSULA		1914-1918: First World War		1931: Attempted coup by Franco 1936-1939: Spanish Civil War 1939-1945: Second World War
ITALY		1914-1918: First World War 1915: Vittorio Emanuel III declares war on Austria-Hungary	1922-1943: Mussolini leads Italy, creation of a fascist state 1922: Benito Mussolini's march on Rome. Creation of the U.S.S.R, Joseph Stalin becomes General Secretary of the Communist Party 1929: Lateran Treaties, creation of the State of Vatican	1939-1945: Second World War
FRANCE	1907: Louis Lumière develops a process for colour photography 1908: First cartoon shown (invention of cellulos)	1914-1918: First World War 1919: Treaty of Versailles (Official end of World War I)		1939-1945: Second World War
BRITISH ISLES	1903: Women's right to vote	1914-1918: First World War	1925: John Baird invents the television	1939-1945: Second World War
CENTRAL EUROPE (INCLUDING GERMANY)		1912-1913: Balkan Wars 1914: Assassination of the archiduke François-Ferdinand and his wife the duchess of Hohenberg at Sarajevo 1914-1918: First World War 1915: Einstein works out the theory of relativity 1916: Freud. *Introduction to psychoanalysis*	1925-1926: Heisenberg and Schrödinger theories of quantum mechanics 1919-1933: Weimar Republic	1933-1945: Hitler, Chancellor of Germany
	1888-1918: Reign of William II, German Emperor and King of Prussia			
FLANDERS (BELGIUM; NETHERLANDS)		1914-1918: First World War		1939-1945: Second World War
GREECE		1912-1913: Balkan Wars		
AFRICA		1914-1918: Germany loses its colonies		
AMERICAS	1900: First flight of a biplane by Wilbur and Orville Wright 1910: Dunwoody and Pickard invent the crystal detector (used for receiving radio broadcasts)	1914: Henry Ford mechanises mass-production 1914: Inauguration of the Panama Canal 1917: USA enters the First World War		1939-1945: Second World War
RUSSIA	1904-1905: Russo-Japanese War. Rivalry for dominance in Korea and Manchuria	1914-1918: First World War 1917: Russian Revolutions. Abdication of Tzar Nicolas II	1922-1953: Stalin General Secretary of the Communist Party of the Soviet	1939-1945: Second World War

Modern Times

1941-1950	1951-1960	1961-1970	1971-1980	1981-1990	1991-2000
			1975: Death of Franco. Restoration of the Spanish monarchy		
Execution of Mussolini. fascist state					
1960: Conflicts and Decolonisation. Algeria (1945-1947), ...ina (1946-1954), Africa (1956-1960), Maghreb (1954-1962)	1958: Fifth Republic	1969: First trial flight of the Concorde between France and Great Britain			
India gains its independence the British Empire	1953: James Watson and Francis Crick discover the structure of DNA		1973: First babies born through in-vitro fertilisation		
	1955: First radio telescope by Jodrell Bank				
		1947-1991: Cold War			
1945: Second World War		1961: Erection of the Berlin Wall		1989: Fall of the Berlin Wall	
1949: Civil War				1981: Greece enters the EU	
South Africa apartheid	1951: Independence of Libya 1956: Independence of Morocco and Tunisia 1960: Almost all French colonies take their independence	1962: Algerian Independence	1974-1975: end of the Portuguese colonies		1994: Genocide in Rwanda 1994: Nelson Mandela is elected in South Africa
Attack of Pearl Harbour by ...panese First nuclear fission bomb First computer at the ...ersity of Pennsylvania Atomic bombing of ...hima	1950-1953: The Korean War 1951: First nuclear reactor 1960: Theodore Maiman invents the laser 1960: First satellite for telecommunication created by NASA	1969: Neil Armstrong and Edwin 'Buzz' Aldrin walk on the moon	1972-1976: Vietnam War 1973: Oil Crisis. Military Coup in Chile	1981: First space shuttle launched by the United States	
Yalta Conference	1953: Khrushchev, leader of Soviet Union, starts De-Stalinisation 1957: Sputnik, first satellite launched	1961: First cosmonaut Yuri Gagarin orbits the Earth		1989: Collapse of communism	

LEGEND

PREHISTORY

- Paleolithic
- Neolithic
- Ancient Egypt
- Ancient Greece

ANTIQUITY

- Ancient Egypt
- Ancient Greece
- Ancient Rome

MIDDLE AGES

- Byzantine
- Gothic
- Romanesque

RENAISSANCE

- Byzantine
- Renaissance
- High Renaissance
- Mannerism

BAROQUE

- Baroque
- Neoclassicism
- Rococo
- Romanticism

MODERN ERA

- Arts & Crafts
- Naïve Art
- Art Nouveau
- Pre-Raphaelite Brotherhood
- Barbizon School
- Hudson River School
- Impressionism
- Naturalism
- Neoclassicism
- Post-Impressionism
- Realism
- Romanticism
- Symbolism
- Abstract Art
- American Scene
- Art Deco
- Art Informel
- Minimal Art
- Arte Povera
- Ashcan School

- Bauhaus
- Camden Town group
- COBRA
- Constructivism
- Cubism
- Dadaism
- Expressionism
- Abstract Expressionism
- Fauvism
- Figuration Libre
- Futurism
- Nouveau Réalisme
- Pop Art
- Rayonism
- Regionalism
- Social Realism
- Surrealism

GLOSSARY

Abstract Art:
International, 20th century. Artists: Kandinsky, Kupka, Pollock, De Kooning.
Artistic style ushered by Kandinsky in 1910. Involves the renunciation of naturalistic representations, creates art without references to figurative reality. The term is also used to describe different movements of Abstraction, such as geometric Abstraction, Abstract Expressionism and Lyrical Abstraction.

Academic Art (or art pompier):
France, middle of the 19th century. Artists: Bouguereau, Cabanel.
Official style influenced by the standards of the French Académie des Beaux-Arts (in particular by History painting).

Acrylic (paint):
International, 20th century.
Acrylic-based quick-setting synthetic paint. Acrylic paints can be diluted with water, but become water-resistant when dry.

Action painting:
USA, born after the 2nd World War. Artist: Pollock.
Generally associated with abstract Expressionism. Way of projecting paint spontaneously on a surface. Term describes the process of creating more than the finished work of art.

Art Deco:
International, beginning of the 1920s. Artist: Lempicka.
Painting influenced by sculpture, Synthetic Cubism and Futurism. It touches different realms of art such as painting, sculpture, architecture and design.

Art Informel (informal art):
Europe, 1950s. Artist: Tapiés.
Involves the rejection of formal preoccupations with composition, employing the reasoning of abstract expressionism.

Art nouveau:
International, late 19th century and beginning of the 20th. Artist: Klimt.
Painting characterised by decorative motifs, with shapes inspired by vegetation, sinuous curves, simple compositions, and a denial of volume. Style influencing painting, sculpture, architecture and design.

Arte povera:
Italy, late 1960s. Artist: Burri.
Politically engaged art rejecting the consumer society and using ephemeral (or "poor") materials, both organic and industrial.

Ashcan School:
USA, early 20th century. Artist: Bellows.
School characterised by the representation of urban subjects, centred on the neighbourhood and everyday life.

Atticism:
France, middle of the 17th century. Artists: Le Sueur, La Hyre, Bourdon.
Movement advocating a return to the simplicity of classicism, in response to the works of Vouet, and to the appealing aesthetics of Vignon's works.

Barbizon school:
France, 1830-1860. Artists: T. Rousseau, Corot, Courbet, Millet.
Landscape or rural scene painters who gathered near the Fontainebleau forest, inspired by romanticism and contributed to realism.

Baroque:
Europe, 17th and first half of the 18th century. Artists: Caravaggio, Carracci, Tiepolo, Rubens, Murillo, Vouet.
In opposition to intellectualism and the coldness of mannerism, Baroque has a more immediate iconography. Characterised by dramatic light effects, dynamic movements, contrasting forms and optical illusions.

Byzantine art:
Europe, from the 5th to 15th century.
Style derived from early Christian iconography, and characterised by a frontal representation, a hieratic expression and the extreme stylisation of the figures. The icon is the Byzantine work par excellence.

Camden Town Group:
England, 1911-1913. Artist: Lewis.
Group of 16 Post-Impressionnist artists, inspired by Sickert and working in Sickert's Studio in Camden Town, a working-class neighbourhood in London. The group focused mainly on the description of urban realistic scenes and sometimes on landscapes.

Camera obscura:
Dark box or room with a hole or a lens in one of its walls. The light rays that pass through the opening form on the opposite wall (a glass plate or sheet of paper) an image of objects located on the outside, which can then be reproduced or traced. Vermeer and Canaletto, among others, used it to draw.

Casein (painting):
Paint pigments linked by a precipitate of milk. Generally applied to rough surfaces such as cardboard, wood or plaster.

Chiaroscuro:
Europe, from the 16th to the 18th century. Artists: Rembrandt, de La Tour, Caravaggio.
This technique existed before Caravaggio but was established by him. Based on strong contrasts of light and shadow, suggesting three-dimensional volumes and giving a great theatricality to the subjects.

Classicism:
Europe, 17th century. Artists: Carracci, Poussin, Le Lorrain.
Style aiming for an ideal of beauty inspired by the Greco-Roman Antiquity. Carracci developed it in Italy, while it was imported to France by Poussin and Le Lorrain. Emphasises the perfection of the drawing and the superiority of historic painting.

CoBrA (coined from Copenhagen, Brussels and Amsterdam):
France, 1948. Artists: Jorn, Appel.
Avant-garde movement formed by Expressionist artists, defending a semi-abstract painting, and the return to natural, primitive and instinctive values.

Constructivism:
Russia, c. 1920, founded by Tatlin.
Movement praising an industrial art, based on dynamic rhythms, and aspiring to an intimate union between painting, sculpture and architecture. Works are mainly geometric and non-figurative.

Cubism:
France, 1907-1914, born with Picasso and Braque.
Designates works representing fractionated then reassembled subjects. Representation of the object under multiple angles of perspective, simultaneously, in order to reduce the representation of nature to geometric elements.

Dadaism:
International, 1916-1924, lead by Duchamp and Picabia.
Movement created in reaction to bourgeois values and to the First World War. Focuses on the absurd while ignoring the rules of aesthetic. Found expression through the so-called 'readymade' objects.

Divisionism:
See Neo-Impressionism.

Expressionism:
Germanic countries, early 20th century. Artists: Kirchner, Dix, Kokoschka.
Works of a great expressivity, characterised by thick outlines, strong colours, anatomic and spatial distortions. Associated with the *Der Blaue Reiter* and *Die Brücke* groups.

Fauvism:
France, 1905-1907. Artists: Matisse, Derain, Vlaminck.
Movement which emerged out of Pointillism and was influenced by Gauguin. First real artistic revolt against Impressionism and the academic rules of painting. Resorts to bright colours treated as tint area. Movement that initiated the accession of Modernism.

Fresco:
Painting technique on fresh plaster needing a preliminary drawing on the wall (Sinopia), applying a layer of fresh plaster, then paint made of mineral pigments mixed with water and lemon.

Futurism:
Italy, early 20th century. Artists: Balla, Boccioni.
Movement praising the industrial era, glorifying the war and, in this respect, close to fascism. Characterised by the expression of dynamism and the repetition of forms in order to suggest movement.

Gothic:
Europe, from 13th to early 16th century. Artists: Monaco, Francke.
Style characterised by an organisation of space and more dynamic representations. An international gothic style of great ornamental wealth emerged in Burgundy, Bohemia, and Italy (14th-15th century).

Hudson River School:
USA, 1825-1870. Artist: Cole.
Group of American landscape painters inspired by the beauty of the American desert and its peculiar light effects.

Impressionism:
France, late 19th century. Artists: Monet, Renoir, Manet, Degas (the 'heart' of the group).
A way of painting that attempts to capture the subjective impressions caused by the effects of light and colour in a scene. Outdoor-painted landscapes are the most common topics.

Magna (paint):
Range of acrylic paint, based on acrylic resin and elaborated in the 20th century, often used by Roy Lichtenstein.

Mannerism:
Europe, 1525-1600. Artists: Pontormo, Tintoretto.
Elegant and refined style, dominated by secular subjects, complex compositions, long muscular and stylised bodies, captured in complex poses, and having an abundance of precious details.

Minimalism:
USA, late 1960s. Artists: Newman, Stella.
Based on a reduction of historic content and expressive in a minimum degree. Geometric and tall, simplified forms.

Nabis:
France, late 19th to early 20th centuries. Artists: Bonnard, Vuillard.
Post-Impressionist avant-garde movement galvanised by Sérusier. Characterised by a tinted are painting, using the colours directly from the tube, with a very-often esoteric meaning.

Naïve Art:
France, late 19th century. Artist: Le Douanier Rousseau.
Style characterised by paintings of primitive appearance, with improbable perspective and childish patterns, painted in very cheerful colours.

Naturalism:
Europe, 1880-1900.
Extension of realism, Naturalism praises an even more realistic approach of nature.

Nazarene:
Germanic countries, early 19th century. Artist: Overbeck.
Artistic movement born in Vienna, whose goal was to reanimate the honesty and the spirituality of Christian Art.

Neoclassicism:
Europe, 1750-1830. Artists: David, Mengs, Ingres.
Movement inspired by the theories of J. J. Winckelmann about Ancient Greek art, praising its simplicity and moral values. An art of balance and elegance, far from the earlier representations of passion.

Neo-impressionism:
France, late 19th century. Artists: Seurat, Signac.
Movement included in Post-impressionism and based on a painting style, pointillism, in which secondary and intermediate colours are generated by the optical mix of juxtaposed primary colour dots.

Neo-expressionism:
International, 1970s. Artist: Baselitz.
Vehement painting, realised with aggressive colours.

Neorealism:
Europe, 1960s, co-founded by Klein and the art critic Pierre Restany.
Artistic movement denouncing the commercial objects of mass production.

Non-figurative:
France, from 1930 to the end of the 20th century. Artists: Bazaine, Manessier, da Silva, Estève.
Art finding its inspiration in nature without trying to imitate it.

Oil Painting:
Appeared in the 15th century. Easel painting, consisting of powdered pigments mixed with a new binder: oil. The Van Eyck brothers were the first artists to popularise and develop the technique.

Op Art:
International, 1960s. Artists: Riley, Vasarely.
Abstract geometric art confronting itself with geometric illusions.

Orphism:
France, 1912. Artist: Delaunay.
Visionary and lyrical paintings.

Outsider Art (or Art Brut):
France, c. 1950, term coined by Jean Dubuffet.
Refers to forms of art created outside conventional art movements, born of a solitary process and fed by pure and authentic creative impulses.

Perspective:
Mathematical system used to create the illusion of space and distance on a plain surface. The first scientific study on perspective was done by Alberti, in his treatise *De Pictura* (1435).

Pop Art:
England, USA, 1950s. Artists: Warhol, Hamilton, Johns.
Movement characterised by the integration of mass popular culture into technique, style and imagery, opposing a culture said to be elitist.

Post-impressionism:
France, late 19th century. Artists: Seurat, Cézanne, Van Gogh, Gauguin, Utrillo, Valadon, Toulouse-Lautrec.

Young artists and movements reacting in different ways against Impressionism, which was imposed as the 'official' style at the end of the century.

Pre-Raphaelite (brotherhood):
England, middle of the 19th century. Artists: Millais, Rossetti, Hunt.
Group of artists who believed that the classical compositions of Raphael had corrupted the academic teaching of art. They developed a naturalist style through paintings inspired by medieval or religious subjects.

Primitivism:
Europe, late 19th century. Artists: Gauguin, Picasso, Nolde.
Style inspired by the tribal art of Africa, Oceania and North America, which was considered to be 'less developed'.

Purism:
France, 1920s. Artist: Léger.
Purism departed from Cubism and sought to determine the ideas and sentiments naturally associated with forms and colours. It sought the purification of art in line with the idea of functional modernity.

Rayonism:
Russia, early 20th century, founded by Larionov.
One of the first forms of abstract expression in painting. Depicts volume intersecting rays of colour.

Realism:
France, middle of the 19th century. Artist: Courbet.
The rendering of everyday characters, subjects and events in a manner close to reality, in contrast to classical, idealised forms. It inspired Corot, Millet and the Barbizon School of painters.

Regionalism:
USA, 1930s. Artists: Curry, Benton, Wood.
Style encompassing anti-modernist artists with humble aspirations, depicting rural scenes of the Mid-West.

Renaissance:
Europe, c.1400-1520. Artists: Botticelli, da Vinci, Dürer.
Period of great creative and intellectual activity, breaking away from the restrictions of Byzantine Art. Study of anatomy and perspective through an appreciation and understanding of the natural world.

Rococo:
Europe, 1700-1770. Artists: Watteau, Boucher, Fragonard.
An exuberant style which began in France, characterised by great displays of ornamentation; tumultuous compositions; light, delicate colours; and curving forms.

Romantism:
Europe, 1750-1850. Artists: Friedrich, Delacroix.
Anti-classical aesthetics bearing emotional content, often depicting melancholic and poetic landscapes or exotic aspects.

Semi-abstraction:
International, 20th century. Artists: Hartley, Sutherland.
Art directed toward abstraction.

Screen printing:
Print-making technique based on stencilling on a porous fabric. Adopted by American graphic artists in the 1930s, it was popularised by Pop Artists in the 1960s.

Social Realism:
America, 1930s. Artist: Rivera.
Naturalistic realism depicting working class activities and contemporary socio-political issues.

Surrealism:
Europe, from 1923 to the middle of the 20th century. Artists: Ernst, Dali, Magritte.
Artistic exploration of dreams, the intimate, and the imagery of the subconscious mind. Use of the technique of psychic automatism.

Symbolism:
Europe, late 19th century. Artists: Moreau, Redon.
Movement taking inspiration in poetry, mythology, legends or in the Bible, characterised by flattened forms, undulating lines, and search of aesthetic harmony.

Tachisme:
Europe, 1950s. Artist: Tobey.
One of the styles deriving from informal art.

Tempera:
Painting technique in which the pigment is diluted in water. The binding material is often fig milk, eggs, or flaxoil. In constant use during the Renaissance, it was overtaken by oil painting in the 15th century.

Trompe l'oeil:
Painting technique that renders images the viewer cannot distinguish from three-dimensional reality (often architectural or scenic details). Frequent in roof paintings such as works by Mantegna.

Index by Artist

Note: Images are noted by figure number, rather than page number.